ARTS AND CULTURE
AN INTRODUCTION TO THE HUMANITIES

Volume II

ARTS AND CULTURE
AN INTRODUCTION TO THE HUMANITIES
Revised First Edition

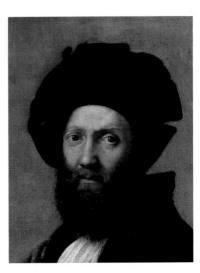

JANETTA REBOLD BENTON
PACE UNIVERSITY, NY

ROBERT DIYANNI
THE COLLEGE BOARD

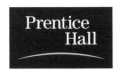
Prentice
Hall

Upper Saddle River, New Jersey 07458

Library of Congress Cataloging-in-Publication Data

Benton, Janetta Rebold
    Arts and culture: an introduction to the humanities/ Janetta
Rebold Benton, Robert DiYanni. -- Combined ed.
      p.   cm.
    Includes bibliographical references and index.
    ISBN 0-13-863192-1
    1. Arts--History. I. DiYanni, Robert. II. Title.
NX440.B46 1998
700--dc21   97-17901
                        CIP

For our children:
Alexander, Ethan, Meredith, and Leland;
Karen and Michael.

Editorial Director: Charlyce Jones Owen
Publisher: Bud Therien
Director of Manufacturing and Production: Barbara Kittle
Production editor: Joe Scordato
Editor-in-chief of development: Susanna Lesan
Marketing manager: Chris Ruel
Creative director: Leslie Osher
Interior design: Joseph Rattan Design
Manufacturing manager: Nick Sklitsis
Manufacturing buyer: Sherry Lewis
Editorial assistant: Wendy Yurash
Cover art: Raphael (Raffaello Santi) (1483–1520). Count
Baldassare Castiglione, poet. Oil on canvas (transposed to
canvas) (1514). 82 cm. × 67cm.—Inv. 611. © Erich
Lessing/Art Resource, NY. Louvre, Paris France.

This book was set in 10/12 Janson and was printed and bound
by RR Donnelley & Sons, Inc. The cover was printed by The
Lehigh Press, Inc.

© 2002 by Pearson Education, Inc.
Upper Saddle River, NJ 07458

Printed in the United States of America
10 9 8 7 6 4 3

ISBN 0-13-097500-1

Pearson Education Ltd.
Pearson Education Australia Pty. Ltd.
Pearson Education Singapore, Pte. Ltd.
Pearson Education North Asia Ltd.
Pearson Education Canada, Ltd.
Pearson Educación de Mexico, S.A. de C.V.
Pearson Education–Tokyo, Japan
Pearson Education Malaysia, Pte. Ltd.
Pearson Education, Upper Saddle River, New Jersey

Contents Overview

Contents

CHAPTER 18

The *Belle Époque* 300

CHAPTER 19

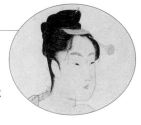

Chinese and Japanese Civilizations 338

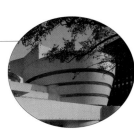

Preface

Arts and Culture provides an introduction to the world's major civilizations—to their artistic achievements, their history, and their cultures. Through an integrated approach to the humanities, *Arts and Culture* offers an opportunity to view works of art, listen to music, and read literature, in historical and cultural contexts.

The most accomplished works of painting, sculpture, and architecture, of music, literature, and philosophy are studied for what they reveal about human life. They open doors to the past, especially to the values and belief systems from which those artworks sprang. They also tell us about human attitudes and feelings, about ideas and ideals that continue to have value today.

Works of art from different cultures reveal common human experiences of birth and death, love and loss, pleasure and pain, hope and frustration, elation and despair. Study of the humanities—history, literature, philosophy, religion, and the arts—also reveals what others value and believe, inviting each of us to consider our personal, social, and cultural values in relation to those of others.

In studying the humanities, our attention is focused on works of art in the broadest sense, works that reflect and embody the central values and beliefs of particular cultures and specific historical moments. The following questions deserve consideration:

1. *What kind of artwork is it? To what artistic category does it belong? What is its type?* These questions lead to considerations of genre. A painting, for example, might be a portrait or a landscape, a religious icon or an abstract design. A musical work might be a song or a symphony, a chamber instrumental work, such as a string quartet, or a religious cantata.

2. *Why was the artwork made? What was its function, purpose, or use? Who was responsible for producing it? Who paid for or commissioned it?* These questions lead to considerations of context. Many works of art were commissioned by religious institutions and wealthy patrons. Many paintings and sculptures were commissioned by the Church and were intended to be both didactic and decorative. Many eighteenth and nineteenth century string quartets and piano trios were written for performance at the home of the patrons who paid composers to write them.

3. *What does the work express or convey? What does it reveal about its creator? What does it reveal about its historical and social context?* These questions lead to considerations of meaning. Some paintings and sculptures are intended to record actual events or to encourage (or discourage) particular types of behaviour. A lyric poem written in ancient China or India may express feelings of sadness or longing, elation at seeing the beloved, grief over the death of a friend. Such poetic lyrics, whatever their age, language and country of origin, reveal not only the writer's feelings, but also cultural attitudes and social values.

4. *How was the artwork made or constructed?* This question leads to considerations of technique. Paintings made during the Middle Ages in Europe were likely to be done in egg tempera on a wooden panel. A painting from Renaissance Europe may be a fresco painted on the interior wall of a church or other building. A painting may also have been done in oil on canvas for framing and hanging in a private home. Or to take an example on a much larger scale, an Islamic mosque, a Catholic cathedral, a Greek or Japanese temple—all are constructed according to specified plans, their interior spaces designed to serve particular religious purposes.

Architectural structures such as these were also made of many types of materials and built using the technologies and tools available at the time of their construction. Developments in technology continually liberated the artistic imagination of painters, sculptors, architects, and composers, who were able to create, for example, new musical tones with the extension of the sonic range of instruments and with the invention of instruments such as the piano.

5. *What are the parts or elements of a work of art? How are these parts related to create a unified artwork?* These questions lead to considerations of formal analysis, understanding the ways the artwork coheres as a whole. Painters, sculptors, and architects work with line, form, color, composition, texture, and other aesthetic elements. In the same way, a Gregorian chant, like a Blues song or a German *Lied* or artsong, reveals a particular structural pattern or organizational design. So does an Elizabethan sonnet, a Japanese haiku, an Arabic qasida, and a Greek epic. Analysis of the form of artworks leads to an appreciation of their artistic integrity and their meaning.

6. *What social, cultural, and moral values does the work express, reflect, or embody?* Works of art bear the social, moral, and cultural values of their creators. They also reflect the times and circumstances of their creation—even when the individual artist, composer, or writer worked against the cultural ethos of the times. We study

works of art to understand the human values they embody for artworks give us insight into human experience. Unlike scientific works or creations—whether formulas, such as Newton's formula for gravitational attraction or Einstein's E=mc²—which are predictive and practical, works of art produce a creative discovery or enlightenment in viewers and readers. They appeal to the human capacity for feeling and thought through the imagination. In contrast to science, which seeks to explain what exists, art seeks to create something new—but something that bears a distinct relationship to what exists.

Balancing the social, cultural, and historical realities that works of art reflect are their uniquely personal visions of experience. Works of art are experiments in living. Through them readers and viewers can experience other imaginative perspectives, share other visions of human life. Works of art provide an imaginative extension of life's possibilities for those who remain open to their unique forms of creative expression.

MAKING CONNECTIONS

A study of the humanities involves more than an examination of the artistic monuments of civilizations past and present. More importantly, it involves a consideration of how forms of human achievement in many times and places echo and reinforce, alter and modify each other. An important aspect of humanities study involves seeing connections among the arts of a given culture and discovering relationships between the arts of different cultures.

Three forms of connection are of particular importance: (1) *interdisciplinary connections* among artworks of an individual culture; (2) *cross currents* among artworks of different cultures; (3) *transhistorical links* between past and present, then and now.

These forms of connection invite readers and viewers to locate relationships among various humanities disciplines and to identify links between and among the achievements of diverse cultures. Discovering such connections can be intellectually stimulating and emotionally stirring since the forms of human experience reflected and embodied in the works of art of many cultures resonate with common human concerns. These artworks address and answer social questions about who we are, philosophical questions about why we exist at all, and religious questions concerning what awaits us after death. These and numerous other perennial questions and the varying perspectives taken on them have been central to every culture, and find expression in their arts. Consider the following examples.

Interdisciplinary CONNECTIONS

One type of interdisciplinary connection appears in the ways the music and architecture of Renaissance Florence were influenced by mathematical proportion and ancient notions of "harmony." Mathematics played a crucial role in all the arts of the Renaissance. Architects were guided in the design of their buildings by mathematical ratios and proportions; composers likewise wrote music that reflected mathematical ratios in both its melody and harmony.

Other kinds of interdisciplinary connections are evident in the collaboration of artists, choreographers, and composers in creating producing and ballets, such as those performed by the Ballets Russes in the early twentieth century. Still other interdisciplinary connections appear in literature and music in the poems of Johan Wolfgang von Goethe that Franz Schubert set to music.

Cultural CROSS CURRENTS

Cultural cross currents reflect the ways artistic ideals, literary movements, and historical events influence the arts of other cultures. Turkish military music, for example, found its way into the symphonies and piano compositions of Viennese composers, such as Mozart and Beethoven. Japanese woodblock prints influenced the art of the Impressionist painter Claude Monet and the Post-Impressionist painter Vincent van Gogh. And the dynamic cybernetic sculpture of contemporary artist Wen-Ying Tsai weds western technology with ancient Chinese aesthetic principles.

Transhistorical Connections—THEN & NOW

Arts and Culture also considers connections between the past and present. A series of THEN & NOW boxes offers discussions of a wide range of subjects that form various types of historical bridges. Discussions range from such subjects as cities, ghettos, and legal codes to movies and monuments, revealing parallels and links between the old and the new in art and architecture, literature and music, philosophy and film.

BALANCING THE WORK AND ITS WORLD

Study of the humanities provides a balance between appreciating masterful individual works of art in themselves and understanding their social and historical contexts. *Arts and Culture* highlights the individual artistic qualities of numerous works—paintings, sculptures, architectural monuments, buildings, and other visual images, such as photographs; poems, plays, novels, and essays; songs, symphonies, and other musical compositions; philosophical and religious systems of belief—always in light of the cultural worlds in which they were created. Each work's significance is discussed in conjunction with the social attitudes and cultural values it embodies, without losing sight of its individual expression and artistic achievement.

This balancing act appears throughout the book, though it sometimes leans more in one direction than the other. In discussing ancient Chinese and Japanese sculpture and architecture, for example, explanations of the Buddhist religious ideals they reflect are accompanied by considerations of their artistic forms. In discussing Renaissance literature the focus sometimes shifts between the artistic individuality of the works examined—as with Shakespeare's *Hamlet*—and particular cultural values the works embody.

The cultural traditions included in *Arts and Culture* reflect a broad rather than a narrow understanding of the term "culture," a humanistic approach to culture rather than an anthropological or sociological study. The idea of culture presented in this book reflects the complex of distinctive attainments, beliefs, and traditions of a civilization. This sense of culture is embodied in works of art and in historical forces that reveal the social, intellectual and artistic aspects of the civilizations that produced them.

Two important questions underlie the choice of works included in *Arts and Culture*: (1) What makes a work a masterpiece of its type? (2) What qualities of a work of art enable it to be appreciated over time? These questions imply that some works of art are better, more perfect embodiments of their genre, or type, than others. The implication is also that masterpieces are worthy of more attention, more studied effort, more reflective consideration than other "lesser" works.

One of the most interesting of all questions in the humanities concerns the way in which particular works become cultural icons, enabling them to represent the cultures out of which they arose. How does the Parthenon represent Greek cultural and artistic ideals? How did Beethoven's Symphony No. 5 come to stand for the very idea of a symphony? Why does the Eiffel Tower symbolize France?

Certain works richly embody the spirit of a particular culture and yet can simultaneously transcend that culture to reflect broader universal values. It is a stunning paradox that those works that do come to speak beyond the confines of the times and places that produced them are often rooted in the local and the particular. The short stories in James Joyce's book *Dubliners*, for example, describe the lives of middle-class Irish people as they lived in early twentieth-century Dublin. Yet Joyce's stories speak to people beyond Dublin, and even beyond Europe, across time and cultures to a set of shared human concerns.

Arts and Culture includes a wide-ranging representation of the world's civilizations. In addition to Western culture, the civilizations of Africa, China, India, Japan, Latin America, and Mesoamerica are examined, along with a special chapter devoted exclusively to Russian civilization. Significant attention is accorded the contributions of women, from the eleventh-century writings of the Japanese Murasaki Shikibu, the twelfth-century music of Germany's Hildegard of Bingen, and the fourteenth-century writings of the Italian Christine de Pizan, to the Rococo art of the French Marie-Louise-Elisabeth Vigée-Le Brun, the Romantic music of Clara Schumann, and the numerous women writers, painters, architects, sculptors, and photographers of the nineteenth and twentieth centuries, European and American.

The final chapter of *Arts and Culture* brings together a broad spectrum of styles, voices, and perspectives, which, though focusing on contemporary multicultural America, reflects trends and influences from around the globe. A number of current issues in the arts are raised, including what constitutes worthwhile contemporary art, which works will endure, and how technology has globalized the arts today. The numerous and varied contributions of artists and writers include works by Native-American painters such as Lisa Fifield and Jaune Quick-to-See Smith, Latina/Latino writers such as Sandra Cisneros and Oscar Hijuelos, and Australian Aborigine artists.

Throughout the book as a whole, the authors have tried to present the arts and cultures of the world to suggest their richness, variety, and humanity. Readers of *Arts and Culture* can find in these pages the background necessary to understand not only the artistic achievements of many civilizations but also the representation of human experience in all its complexity. In a time of rapid social change when the world's cultures are becoming increasingly globalized, it has become necessary to understand the values of human beings around the world. The common humanity we share has been recorded, inscribed, and celebrated in arts and achievements of all cultures. Our survival and our happiness as human beings about to enter a new millennium warrants nothing less than understanding our human heritage as revealed in the art and cultural achievements that *Arts and Culture* brings together.

A complete package of supplementary material accompanies *Arts and Culture*.

– Student Study Guide—designed to make students' lives easier. It is carefully coordinated with the text and is thoughtfully presented to help students work their way through unfamiliar material.

– Music Compact Disk—a collection of music that contains important works discussed in the text.

– Instructors' Manual—provides chapter summaries, further topics for discussion, other activities, and a test bank. These are all carefully organized to make preparation, classroom instruction, and student testing smoother and more effective.

– Faculty Slide Set—for qualified adoptions an accompanying set of slides is available free to instructors. Contact your local Prentice Hall representative for information on ordering this supplement.

– Prentice Hall Custom Test—this computerized text item file allows you to create your own personalized exams using your own computer. Available for DOS, Windows, and Macintosh.

And finally a comprehensive website (http://www.prenhall.com/benton) has been developed to integrate many of the study guide features with many of the existing links to the arts currently found on the Internet.

Art and Humanities on the World Wide Web is a comprehensive website designed to augment *Arts and Culture*. The website is designed for professors and students teaching and studying the humanities. By utilizing the technology of "hypertext," the web allows users access to a vast array of historical, cultural, and general interest sites organized around and correlated to chapters and content found in the text.

NEW—Prentice Hall Humanities CD-ROM presents fourteen segments that bring to life basic terms and ideas from two-dimensional and three-dimensional visual art, architecture, music, theatre, dance and literature. These two- to seven-minute video and audio presentations, connected by narrative, demonstrate how paintings and drawings achieve deep space, how sculpture is carved and modeled, how modern dance and ballet turn motion into art, how a theatre director works, and how a theatre building is used in production. In addition, a tour of an orchestra demonstrates the basic musical instrument groups, a series of vignettes brings various musical forms to life, and the concept of rhythm in dance and music is explored. A tour of the Parthenon illustrates classical architecture, Romanesque and Gothic styles emerge in examinations of medieval churches, and Frank Lloyd Wright's Taliesin West highlights modern style.

ACKNOWLEDGMENTS

Arts and Culture represents the cooperative efforts of many people. The book originated with a suggestion ten years ago by Tony English, then of Macmillan Publishing. Work on the project began with Tony and his Macmillan colleagues and continued with Prentice Hall when Macmillan was acquired by Simon & Schuster in 1993.

At Prentice Hall we have had the good fortune to work with Bud Therien, Publisher, who oversaw the book's development in every respect, and Clare Payton, Development Editor, whose guidance and critical eye shaped the book. Important contributions were made by Bud and Clare and by their colleagues Susanna Lesan, Editor-in-Chief of Development; Charlyce Jones Owen, Editorial Director; Sheryl Adams, Marketing Manager; Leslie Osher, Creative Director; Joe Scordato, Production Liaison; and Gianna Caradonna, Editorial Assistant. These and other Prentice Hall staff, including the President of the Humanities and Social Sciences division, Phil Miller, offered wise counsel and made numerous helpful suggestions. The intelligence and enthusiasm Phil and his colleagues brought to their work have helped make *Arts and Culture* the book it is.

We have been fortunate as well that Calmann & King Ltd effectively handled the book's production. We have enjoyed working with Robert Shore, Editor, who not only supervised the production of *Arts and Culture*, but who also assumed responsibility for the development of Vol. I midway through the process. Dr. Shore's multiple talents ensured the book's completion on schedule, to the delight of publisher and authors alike.

Also deserving of particular mention are Sylvia Moore for her contribution to the introductory materials and Jenny Moss for her hard work on the timelines and glossary.

We owe a special debt of gratitude to Henry Sayre, without whom we simply could not have completed *Arts and Culture* on schedule. Professor Sayre helped us shape the drafts of our chapters, melding our styles and recommending organizational changes that have resulted, we believe, in an integrated and compelling overview of the humanities. His engaging contributions to the historical narrative that informs the book have been of inestimable value to the project.

From readers of various drafts of *Arts and Culture* we received thoughtful criticism along with helpful suggestions for improvement. We would like to thank the following reviewers for their insight and advice: Martha G. Anderson, Alfred University; William Cloonan, Florida State University; Roger Crum, University of Dayton; Jane Anderson Jones, Manatee Community College; Kimberley Jones, Seminole Community College; Elizabeth Jordan, University of California, San Diego; Leslie Lambert, Sante Fe Community College; Virginia Pond, Catonsville Community College; Alan Pope, Albuquerque TV-I Community College; Sylvia White, Florida Community College at Jacksonville; and Judith B. Wise, Clark State Community College.

We would also like to thank each other for offering mutual support, encouragement, advice, and help throughout a long and sometimes arduous process of writing, revising, and editing. Our families, too deserve our thanks, for without their patience and understanding we could not have completed our work with equanimity and good humor. In particular, the encouragement and loving support of our spouses, Elliot Benton and Mary DiYanni, enabled us to do our work on *Arts and Culture* with a minimum of anxiety and a maximum of pleasure.

Introduction

Arts and Culture is an introduction to the humanities and the arts, from the earliest times to the present day. The goal of the book is to familiarize readers with a fundamental body of art, history, and ideas that are a basis for understanding both Western and non-Western cultures. In demonstrating the interrelationships, obvious or subtle, between the creators of art and the historical and social forces at work in a given culture at any particular time, the text seeks to foster an understanding of the creative process and the uses of the arts.

One challenge for the reader lies in appreciating the sheer array of human creativity on display across a wide spectrum of arts and cultures. Though *Arts and Culture* focuses on Western civilization, from its ancient roots to the present, it does not limit itself to the West. Rather, Western European culture is presented within a multicultural global framework, represented by chapters on non-European cultures and cross-cultural features within the Western chapters.

An additional challenge for the reader is to become familiar with the vocabularies and concepts of the arts and humanities. An understanding of a wide range of artistic terms and concepts is necessary to appreciate artistic achievements. It is also essential for being able to discuss the arts knowledgeably and for the expansion of personal taste.

The Humanities and the Arts

The humanities are those areas of thought and creation whose subject is human experience. They include history, philosophy, religion, and the arts. Broadly speaking, the arts are artificial objects or experiences created by human beings. Although the term "artificial" often has a negative connotation, when used to mean "phony" or "fake," it is used here in its original sense, meaning "not from nature," that is, something made by humans. The word "art" comes from the same root. The role of the human creator, therefore, is central to any study of the arts since, ultimately, the arts and humanities are a record of human experience and concerns. The arts convey information—a lyric poem can describe a summer's day, for example—yet this is not their primary function. More importantly, the arts give form to what is imagined, express human subjective beliefs and emotions, create beauty, celebrate sensual pleasure, and entertain their audiences.

The arts include visual art and architecture, drama, music, and literature, and photography and film. Seeing the arts within their historical and social context

is necessary for understanding their development. For example, the figure of the biblical giant-killer, David, was popular during the Renaissance in the Italian city-state of Florence. Michelangelo's *David* was commissioned by the Florentine city officials (fig. 0.1; see also fig. 13.32). Florence had recently fought off an attempt at annexation by the much larger city-state of Milan. Thus, the biblical David slaying the giant, Goliath, became a symbol of Florentine cleverness and courage in defense of independence. It is a theme particular to its time and place, yet one that has been used throughout history to express the success of the "little" person against powerful exploiters.

Enlightenment and Revolution

We study what survives, which is not necessarily all that once existed. Not all arts survive the passage of time. Art can be divided into the durable and the ephemeral, or short-lived. Surviving objects tend to be large (the

Figure 0.1 Michelangelo, *David* (detail), 1501–04, marble, height 13'5" (4.09 m), Galleria dell'Accademia, Florence.

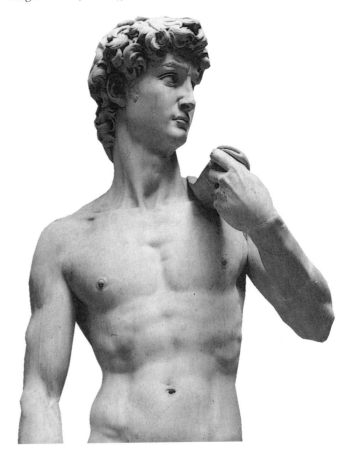

Pyramids) or hidden (the contents of tombs). Until human beings created the means of capturing moving images and sounds, the ephemeral arts such as music and dance could be described but not reexperienced. Therefore, some of the oldest arts—music and dance of the ancient world, for example—are lost. With the development of writing, humans began the long process of liberating themselves from the tyranny of time. They began to communicate across space and time, leaving a record of their lives. In our own century, we have seen our recording abilities explode from sound recording and silent movies at the turn of the century into the digitized world of the CD-ROM and the Internet today. The result has been an unprecedented expansion in the humanities.

The Role of the Artist

The functions of the artist and the artwork have varied widely during the past five thousand years. To understand these functions it may be necessary to set aside some modern assumptions about art and artists. In our time, the artist is seen as an independent worker, dedicated to the expression of a unique subjective experience. Often the artist's role is that of the outsider, a critical or rebellious figure. He or she is a specialist who has usually undergone advanced training in a university department of art or theater, or a school with a particular focus, such as a music conservatory. In our societies, works of art are presented in specialized settings: theaters, concert halls, performance spaces, galleries, and museums. There is usually a sharp division between the artist and her or his audience of non-artists. We also associate works of art with money: art auctions in which paintings sell for millions of dollars, ticket sales to the ballet, or fundraising for the local symphony.

In other societies and in parts of our own society, now and in the past, the arts are closer to the lives of ordinary people. For the majority of their history, artists have expressed the dominant beliefs of a culture, rather than rebelling against them. In place of our emphasis on the development of a personal or original style, artists were trained to conform to the conventions of their art form. Nor have artists always been specialists; in some societies and periods, all members of a society participated in art. The modern Western economic mode, which treats art as a commodity for sale, is not universal. In societies such as that of the Navajo, the concept of selling or creating a salable version of a sand painting would be completely incomprehensible. Selling Navajo sand paintings created as part of a ritual would profane a sacred experience.

Artists' identities are rarely known before the Renaissance, with the exception of the period of Classical Greece, when artists were highly regarded for their individual talents and styles. Among artists who were known, there were fewer women than men. In the twentieth century, many female artists in all the disciplines have been recognized. Their absence in prior centuries does not indicate lack of talent, but reflects lack of opportunity. The necessary social, educational, and economic conditions to create art rarely existed for women in the past.

Artists of color have also been recognized in the West only recently. The reasons for this absence range from the simple—there were few Asians in America and Europe prior to the middle of the nineteenth century—to the complexities surrounding the African diaspora. The art of indigenous peoples, while far older than that of the West, did not share the same expressive methods or aims as Western art. Until recently, such art was ignored or dismissed in Western society by the dominant cultural gatekeepers.

Art and Ritual

Throughout much of the history of the Western humanities, the arts have had a public function as religious or social ritual in which beauty and representation were secondary. The ritual function of art survives in the liturgical music, dance, and art of all cultures. Socially, the arts often serve to reinforce, demonstrate, or celebrate the dominant values of a society. In our own time, the arts may reflect the preferences of a large group of people—popular music and action movies, for example—or a small but influential elite—the audience for opera, or avant-garde theater, for instance.

Critical Thinking and Evaluation of the Arts

Because of their manifold functions, the arts are understood through the use of different human faculties. We know them by our senses. We can apply our intellects to analyze and describe what we see and experience. We also respond to the arts subjectively, through nonrational means such as intuition, subjective interpretation, and emotional response. Our understanding of the arts depends in part on our knowledge of the historical and social context surrounding a work. For instance, for whom was a particular work intended—a private or a public audience? What was or is its setting—public, private, accessible, or hidden? How is the work related to the economic workings of its time: for example, was it commissioned by a ruler, a religious organization, a group of guildspeople, a corporation? Was it created by nuns or monks, by peasants, or by specially trained craftspersons? Each of these considerations expands our understanding of a given work, even when we cannot know all the answers.

The branch of philosophy devoted to thinking about the arts is called "aesthetics." Aesthetic knowledge is both intuitive and intellectual; that is, we can grasp a work of art on an emotional level while at the same time analyzing it. There is no single, unquestionable body of aesthetic knowledge, although philosophers have tried to create universal systems. Each culture has its own aesthetic preferences. In addition, different disciplines and different styles within a culture reflect different aesthetic values. Today, for example, rap music coexists with country, jazz, classical, and other types of music.

Each of us is, at one time or another, a critic of the arts. For example, deciding what movie to attend, what book to read, or what recording to purchase are all critical acts, based on personal taste and judgment. Criticism in the arts takes this natural human trait and refines it.

FORM AND CONTENT DISTINCTIONS

When discussing works of art, it is useful to distinguish between the form of the artwork and its content. The form of a work of art is its structural or organizing principle—the shape of its content. A work's content is what it is about—its subject matter. At its most basic, formal analysis provides a description of the apparent properties of an artwork. Artists use these properties to engineer our perception and response. In music, for example, a formal analysis would discuss the melody, the harmony, and the structure. In visual art, comparable elements would be line, color, and composition. The goal of formal analysis is to understand how an artwork's form expresses its content.

Contextual approaches to the arts seek to situate artworks within the circumstances of their creation. Historians of the arts conduct research aimed at recreating the context of a given work. Armed with this information, the historian interprets the work in light of that context. Knowing, for example, that *Guernica* (fig. 0.2; see also fig. 21.20), Pablo Picasso's anti-war painting, depicts an aerial bombing of a small village of unarmed civilians in the Spanish Civil War, drives its brutal images of pain and death home to viewers. Picasso chose black, white, and grey for this painting because he learned of the attack through the black and white photojournalism of the newspapers. Knowing the reason for this choice, which may otherwise have seemed arbitrary to modern viewers of the work, adds to the meaning of the image. Picasso's choice of black and white also intensifies the horrors he depicts.

Figure 0.2 Pablo Picasso, *Guernica*, 1937, oil on canvas, 11'5$\frac{1}{2}$" × 25'5$\frac{1}{2}$" (3.49 × 7.75 m), Centro de Arte Reina Sofia, Madrid.

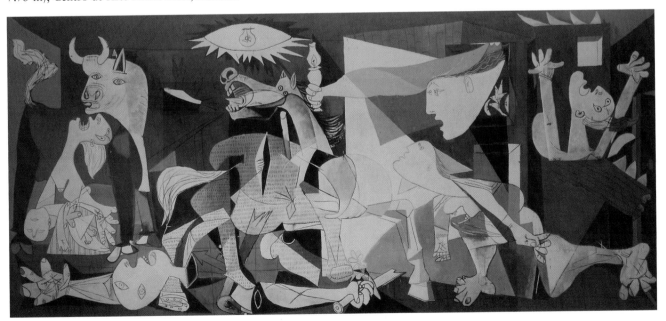

Starter Kit

This Starter Kit provides you with a brief reference guide to key terms and concepts for studying the humanities. The following section will give you a basis for analyzing, understanding, and describing art forms.

Commonalities. We refer to the different branches of humanities—art and architecture, music, literature, philosophy, history—as the **disciplines.** The humanistic disciplines and the arts have many key terms in common. However, each discipline has defining characteristics, a distinct vocabulary, and its own conventions, so that the same word may mean different things in different disciplines.

Every work of art has two core components: form and content. **Form** refers to the arrangement, pattern, or structure of a work, how a work is presented to our senses. **Content** is what a work is about, its meaning or substance. The form might be an Impressionist painting; the content might be the beauty of nature in a particular place. To comprehend how the form expresses the content is one of the keys to understanding a work of art, music or literature.

The term **artist** is used for the producer of artworks in any discipline. All artworks have a **composition,** the arrangement of its constituent parts. **Technique** refers to the process or method that produced the art. The **medium** is the physical material that makes up the work, such as oil paint on canvas. **Crafts** refers to the technical skill of the artist, which is apparent in the execution of the work.

Style. We use the term **style** to mean several different things. Most simply, style refers to the manner in which something is done. Many elements form a style. Artists working at the same time and place are often trained in the same style. In a text, historical styles are usually capitalized, as in *Classical Greek* art, referring to the arts of that particular time and place, which shared distinct characteristics. If used with lowercase letters, such as *classical* style, the term refers to works which, although not from Classical Greece, are similar in character to Classical Greek art, or to Roman art, which was largely derived from Greek forms.

Conventions are accepted practices, such as the use of a frontal eye in a profile face, found in the art of the ancient Egyptians, or the use of the sonnet form by Shakespeare and his contemporaries.

Functions and Genres. In general, the functions of the arts can be divided into religious and secular art. **Religious** or liturgical art, music, or drama is used as part of the ritual of a given religion. Art that is not religious art is termed **secular** art. Secular art is primarily used for entertainment purposes, but among other functions has been its use in the service of political or propaganda ends, as films were used in Nazi Germany.

Each discipline has subsets, called **genres.** In music, for example, we have the symphony, a large, complex work for orchestra, in contrast to a quartet, written for only four instruments. In literature we might contrast the novel, with its extended narrative and complexities of character, with the compression of a short story. From the seventeenth to the nineteenth centuries, certain subjects were assigned higher or lower rank by the academies that controlled the arts in most European countries. Portrait painting, for example, was considered lower than history painting. That practice has been abandoned; today the genres are usually accorded equal respect and valued for their distinctive qualities.

THE VISUAL ARTS

The visual arts are first experienced by sight, yet they often evoke other senses such as touch or smell. Because human beings are such visual creatures, our world is saturated with visual art, in advertising, on objects from CD covers to billboards, on TV and the Internet. The visual arts occur in many varieties of two-dimensional and three-dimensional forms, from painting, printmaking, and photography, to sculpture and architecture.

As is the case with other arts, the origins of the visual arts are now lost. However, their development represents a milestone in human civilization. Drawing, the representation of three-dimensional forms (real or imagined) on a two-dimensional surface, is an inherent human ability, and failure to draw by a certain stage in a child's growth is a sign of serious trouble. Attaining the ability to draw is an important cognitive development in both babies and human history. The creation and manipulation of images was and is a first step toward mastery of the physical world itself.

The visual arts serve a variety of purposes, using different methods. **Representation** is an ancient function of visual art, in which a likeness of an object or life form is produced. There are many different conventions of representation, which have to be learned by artist and viewer alike. One important convention is **perspective,** which gives the illusion of depth and distance. Systems of perspective were perfected by artists and theorists of the Renaissance period. In **abstract** art, the artist may extract some element from the actual appearance of an object and use it for its expressive or symbolic properties. For example, an artist may use red and orange tones on a canvas to suggest a brilliant poppy. **Nonobjective** art is entirely free from representation; a nonobjective sculpture may be a group of geometric shapes welded

Visual Arts

Line: A mark on a surface. Lines may be continuous or broken. They are used to create patterns and textures, to imply three dimensions, and to direct visual movement.

Shape: An area with identifiable boundaries. Shapes may be **organic,** based on natural forms and thus rounded or irregular, or they may be **geometric,** based on measured forms.

Mass: The solid parts of a three-dimensional object. An area of space devoid of mass is called **negative space;** while **positive space** is an area occupied by mass.

Form: The shape and structure of something. In discussions of art, form refers to visual aspects such as line, shape, color, texture, and composition.

Color: The sensation produced by various wavelengths of light. Also called **hue.** Red, blue, and yellow are the **primary colors,** which cannot be made from mixing other colors. **Secondary colors** (orange, green, and purple) are hues produced by mixing two primary colors.

Value: The lightness or darkness of an area of color, or as measured between black and white. The lighter, the higher in value it is; the darker, the lower in value.

Texture: The appearance or feel of a surface, basically smooth or rough. Texture may be actual, as the surface of a polished steel sculpture, or implied, as in a painting of human flesh or the fur of an animal.

Composition: The arrangement of the formal components of a work, most frequently used to describe the organization of elements in a drawing or painting.

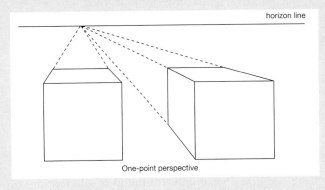

One-point perspective

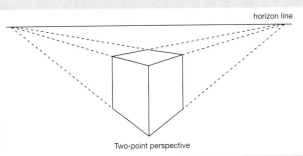

Two-point perspective

Perspective: A system of rendering three-dimensional space on a two-dimensional surface. In **single-point** perspective objects are portrayed with all lines from the picture plane (p) leading toward a single **vanishing point** on the horizon line. In **two-point** perspective there are two or more vanishing points. **Atmospheric** or **aerial** perspective uses properties of light and air, in which objects become less distinct and cooler in color as they recede into distance.

together. Abstract and nonobjective art, arising in the twentieth century, are more concerned with the elements on the **picture plane** (the paper or canvas) rather than depth of **pictorial space.** Visual art also often has a purely decorative or ornamental purpose, used to create visual pleasure or to add visual interest to a functional item, as in wallpaper, fabric, or furniture design.

Formal Analysis. To analyze a work of visual art formally, its visual elements are considered without reference to the content, whereas moving to more sophisticated levels involves the content as well. At its simplest, the content is what is represented, the subject matter, whether a person, an orange, or a flag. However, the image may not stop with the representation; there may be a symbolic element. It is useful to distinguish between signs and symbols. **Signs** convey visual information economically by means of images or words. **Symbols** are images that have resonance, or additional meaning. Works of visual art may use both signs and symbols.

Artists use symbolic systems, part of the visual language of their time. Like all languages, these must be learned. Sometimes artists create their own symbols.

The **iconography** of a work of art, that is, the meaning assigned to the symbols, is often religious in nature. For example, different representations of Jesus derive from incidents in his life. To understand the deeper levels of the work, it is necessary to understand the language of the iconography. The use of personal iconography by an artist is a relatively recent development of the past few centuries.

The following analysis of *The Scream* by Edvard Munch (fig. 0.3) will serve as an example of this process. Viewed formally, the major visual elements used by Munch in this painting are line and color. There are two kinds of lines: the geometric lines that form the sharply receding bridge contrast with the swirling organic lines of the main figure and the landscape, sea, and sky. There is little or no modelling or shading. The colors contrast bright red and yellow with rich blue, offset by neutral

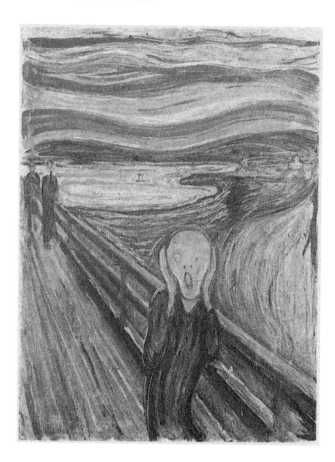

Figure 0.3 Edvard Munch, *The Scream*, 1893, tempera and casein on cardboard, 36 × 29" (91.3 × 73.7 cm), Nasjonalgalleriet, Oslo.

tones. *The Scream* is a painting executed on cardboard with rapid, loose brushstrokes. The composition is dynamic; the artist has used exaggerated diagonals to suggest a dramatic perspective for the bridge. The figure at the front is the focal point. The craft is secondary to the expressive purpose of the work.

It should be obvious that in *The Scream* more is going on than the preceding analysis indicates. Three people are on a bridge at sunset. Two are walking away; one stands transfixed with his hands over his ears. The expression on his face functions as a sign to convey shock or horror. To understand the significance of his expression, we turn to the historical context and the artist's life. Munch, a Norwegian artist who worked in the late nineteenth and early twentieth centuries, was one of the artists who rejected conventions and created personal symbolic systems, based largely on his experience. *The Scream* is usually interpreted as representing a screaming person. This is not correct. As we know from the artist's diary, the work refers to the "scream of nature." The image captured is a powerful evocation of a sensitive man overwhelmed by nature's power, which his companions cannot sense. The swirling lines suggest the impact of screaming nature on this person. The blood-red sky

resonates as a symbol of savage nature oblivious to the puny humans below.

Components of the Visual Arts. The basic elements used to construct a work of visual art are line, shape, mass—a shape in three dimensions—color and value, real or implied texture, and composition, the arrangement of all the elements. While many drawings are executed in black mediums, such as pencil and charcoal, on a white ground, color is a vital ingredient of art, especially important in conveying information as well as emotion to the viewer. Color affects us both physically and psychologically and has significance to us both in our personal lives and in our cultural traditions.

There can be no color without light. In the seventeenth century, Sir Isaac Newton observed that sunlight passing through a glass prism broke up, or **refracted** the light into rainbow colors. Our perception of color depends upon reflected light rays of various wavelengths. Theorists have arranged colors on a **color wheel** (fig. 0.4) that is well-known to students of painting and even young schoolchildren. On it are the **primary colors**—red, yellow, and blue—and **secondary colors**—orange, green, and purple. Some wheels show **tertiary colors** such as yellow-green and red-purple. The primary colors cannot be created by mixing other colors, but secondary and tertiary colors are made, respectively, by mixing two primaries, or primaries and secondaries, together. **Complementary** colors are those opposite each other on the wheel, so that red is opposite from green, orange from blue, and yellow from purple. Many artists have studied and worked with the **optical effects** of color, especially the French Impressionist Claude Monet and

Figure 0.4 Color wheel.

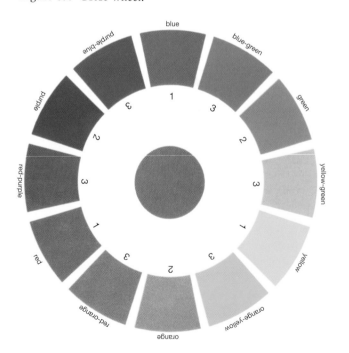

Architecture

Architect: One who designs and supervises the construction of buildings. Ideally, the architect is part builder with a sound knowledge of engineering principles, materials, structural systems, and other such practical necessities, as well as part artist who works with form, space, scale, light, and other aesthetic properties.

Scale: The relative size of one thing compared to another. The relationship of a building to another element, often the height of a human being.

Site: The location of an object or building. Care must be taken to choose a solid, attractive, and appropriate building site.

Structural System: The engineering principles used to create a structure. Two basic kinds of structural system are the **shell** system, where one or more building materials such as stone or brick provide both support and covering, and the **skeleton and skin** system, as in modern skyscrapers with steel skeletons and glass skin.

Column: a supporting pillar consisting of a base, a cylindrical shaft, and a decorative capital at the top. Three Classical orders, established in ancient Greece, are the **Doric, Ionic,** or **Corinthian**, identified by the capital.

Post and Lintel: A basic structural system dating from ancient times that uses paired vertical elements (posts) to support a horizontal element (lintel).

Arch, dome, and vault: An arch consists of a series of wedged-shaped stones, called **voussoirs,** locked in place by a keystone at the top center. In principle, an arch rotated 180 degrees creates a **dome.** A series of arches forms a **barrel** or **tunnel vault.** When two such vaults are constructed so that they intersect at right angles, a **cross** or **groin vault** is created. Roman and Romanesque masons used semi-circular arches, whereas Gothic masons built with pointed arches to create vaults that were reinforced with **ribs,** permitting large openings in the walls. The true arch, dome, and vault are dynamic systems—the lateral thrust that they exert must be buttressed externally to prevent collapse.

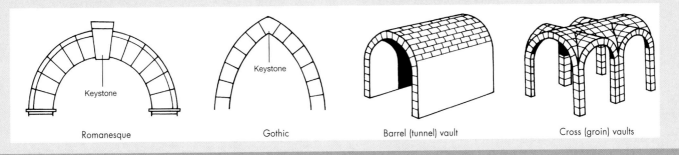

Romanesque   Gothic   Barrel (tunnel) vault   Cross (groin) vaults

the Post-Impressionist Georges Seurat.

Architecture. Architecture is a branch of the visual arts that combines practical function and artistic expression. The function served by a building usually determines its form. In addition to the purely useful purpose of providing shelter, architecture answers prevailing social needs. The use of architects to design and erect public and religious structures has given rise to many innovative forms throughout history. Architecture reflects the society in which it is built as it controls the actions of those who use it. Structural systems depend upon the available building materials, technological advancements, the intended function of the building, and aesthetics of the culture. The relationship between a building and its **site,** or location, is integral to architecture. The Greek Parthenon (fig. 0.5), for example, crowns a hill overlooking Athens. The elevated location indicates its importance, and the pathway one must ascend to reach the Parthenon is part of the experience.

Figure 0.5 Ictinus and Callicrates, Parthenon, Acropolis, Athens, 448–432 B.C.

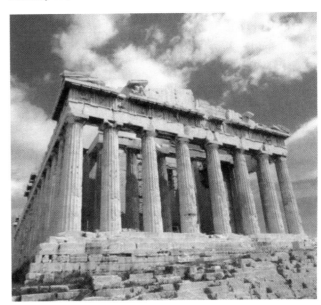

LITERATURE

Speech, Writing, and Literature.   Literature differs from the visual arts since it is not built from physical elements, such as paint and stone; nor is it composed of sound as is music, but from words, the basic elements of language. Paint and sound have no intrinsic meaning; words do. Speech depends on meaningful units of sound—words, which are the building blocks of communication in language. Literature presupposes language, with its multitudes of meaning (content), its **grammar** (rules for construction), and its **syntax,** the arrangement of words.

Language, essentially communicative, has many functions. We use language to make emotional contact with others: for example, a parent using baby talk to a child too young to understand the meaning of words. Through language we convey information to each other, as in the classroom, where a dialogue between teacher and student is part of the educational process. All literature is language, but not all language is literature. Distinguishing between literature and other forms of language is sometimes difficult, but refinement in language and careful structuring or ordering typically characterizes literature.

Literature, in the broadest sense, is widely apparent in everyday life. Popular songs, magazine essays, greeting card verse, hymns and prayers are all forms of literature. One meaning of the word *literature*, in fact, is what is written. Generally, however, the term "literature" is reserved for those works that exhibit "the best that has been thought and said," works that represent a culture's highest literary achievements.

Literacy and Literature.

The Development of Literature   Literature predates literacy. Ancient literature was **oral**—spoken—rather than written. To make it easier to remember and recite, much of this was in the form of song or poetry. The invention of writing enabled people to communicate across space and time. It was with this invention that recorded history was born. The earliest writings of the ancient world are businesslike records of laws, prayers, and commerce—informative but not expressive. When mechanical methods of printing were developed, literacy spread. Today, universal literacy is a goal in all civilized countries.

The Functions of Literature   Literature serves a variety of social functions. One of its most ancient functions is as **religious literature,** the prayers and mythology of a given culture. The myths of the Greeks and Romans have exerted a powerful influence on Western culture; their origins lie deep in the history of Egypt and Mesopotamia. **Epic literature,** such as the Greek poet Homer's *The Iliad* and *The Odyssey*, or the sagas from Norway and Iceland, combine history and imagination.

Immense bodies of literature such as these were passed down by oral tradition. Literature distinct from liturgical or epic forms was invented by the ancient Greeks. Their literary forms included history, philosophy, drama, and poetry. Novels and short stories were a later development. The novel in its modern form was named for tales popular in Italy in the late thirteenth century, though the novel is generally identified with prose narratives that developed in the eighteenth century in Europe.

Since literature is a communicative act, it is important to consider the audience and setting. Silent reading is a recent development, alien to the oral roots of literature. Most literature through the ages was meant to be recited, sung, or read aloud in groups ranging from general public gatherings to the intimate setting of the private home. Authors today may give readings from their work in libraries, bookstores, and educational institutions.

Forms of Literature.   Literature can be divided into fiction and nonfiction, poetry and prose.

Poetry is distinguished by its concentrated and precise language, "the best words in the best order," as one poet defined it. **Diction** is the poet's selection of words, and **syntax** the ordering of those words in sentences. Other poetic elements include images—details that evoke sense perception—along with metaphor and other forms of comparison With its roots in song, poetry of many eras and places exhibits rhyme and other types of sound play as well as rhythm and meter, the measured pattern of accent in poetic lines. Drama, plays intended for performance, are somtimes written in verse, rhymed or unrhymed, as, for example, in **blank verse**.

Prose   Language that is not poetry is **prose.** Not all prose is literature; some, such as journalism or technical writing, is purely descriptive or informative, as some visual art is purely representational. Literature can be fiction or nonfiction, or a combination of both. Fiction is a work of the imagination. Fictional forms can be long and complex, as in a novel or play, or short and concise, as in a novella or short story. Nonfiction, which deals with actual events or persons, includes expressions of opinion, such as political essays. Functions of nonfiction include explanation, persuasion, commentary, exposition, or any blend of these. Sometimes philosophic essays and works of history are included in the category of literature.

Fiction and drama, and much nonfiction as well, create their effects through elements such as the plot, or story line, characters, description of the setting, dialogue between the characters, and exposition, or explanation. The latter is presented in the voice of a narrator, who may represent the author using the third-person perspective, or may instead be a character expressing a first-person point of view.

Literature

Fiction: Literature that is imaginative, rather than descriptive of actual events. Typical fictional forms are the short story and the novel, which has greater length and complexity.

Nonfiction: An account of actual events and people. Forms of nonfiction include essays, biography and autobiography, and journalistic writing, as for newspapers and magazines.

Narrative: The telling of a story; a structured account of events.

Narrator: The storyteller from whose **point of view** the story is told. The point of view can be **first-person** or **third-person,** and may shift within the work. The narrator can be **omniscient,** knowing everything, or limited to what she or he can know personally or be told by others.

Plot: The plan or story line. To plot a story is to conceive and arrange the action of the characters and the sequence of events. Plots typically involve **rising action,** events that complicate the plot and move it forward to a **climax,** the moment of greatest intensity. This is followed by the **denouement,** the resolution of the plot.

Characters: The people in a literary work. The leading character is known as the **protagonist,** a word stemming from ancient Greek drama in which the protagonist was opposed by an **antagonist.**

Dialogue: Conversation between two or more characters. Drama is mainly rendered through dialogue; it is used in fiction to a lesser extent.

Setting: Where the events take place; includes location, time, and situation. In theatrical productions, a **set** is the scenery, sometimes very elaborate, constructed for a stage performance. In films the set is the sound stage or the enclosure where a scene is filmed.

Exposition: Explanatory material, which, especially in drama, often lays out the current situation as it arises from the past.

In common with visual art and music, literature has **themes,** or overarching ideas that are expressed by all the elements working together. The structure of a work of literature is analogous to the composition of a symphony or a painting. Writers use symbolism, much as visual artists do. A successful work of literature will likely establish a mood, hold the reader's interest through a variety of incidents or ideas with evident focus, yet possess an overall sense of unity.

Autobiography, as a separate literary and historical endeavor, began with the *Confessions* of St. Augustine (A.D. 354–430), in which he told the story of his life and the progress of his religious convictions. Autobiography is history written from a subjective point of view. The memoir, so popular in recent years, is descended from this first, spiritual autobiography.

Biography is a branch of both literature and history. The author's role is complicated because a biographer must check the facts of the subject's life, usually by interviewing both the subject and many other people. Deciding the major theme of a person's life, the relationship between that person and his or her time, and considering what is true as well as what is germane are the biographer's responsibility. Different biographers may offer quite different interpretations of a subject's life.

History is a powerful force that shapes the humanities as a whole. The writing of history varies across cultures, and as cultures change, history itself is continuously under revision. The leaders of some societies would never allow the publication of versions of history that vary from their orthodox beliefs, no matter what the facts might be. Because history is an interpretative discipline, several versions of events may coexist, with scholars arguing and defending the merits of each. This is particularly true in our multicultural and pluralist era.

MUSIC

We are surrounded by sounds at all times. The art that derives from our sense of hearing is music, order given to sounds by human intent. A temporal art, one that exists in time, music is the least material of the arts, its basic elements being sound and silence. Silence in music is analogous to a painter's, sculptor's, or architect's use of negative space: unoccupied but important, so that the intervals between the notes are necessary parts of a musical piece. Music permeates our daily lives—in the movies, on radio and television, in elevators and stores. The success of the Sony Walkman reflects our human desire to surround ourselves with music.

Until the development of sound recording, music was one of the **ephemeral** arts, like dance and live theater, which exist only for the duration of their performances. Until the late Middle Ages, music in the West was not written down, or **notated**. It was taught by ear, passed on from one generation to the next.

Social and Ritual Roles. Music has many different functions. It has been and remains a major element in

M·usic

Acoustics: The qualities of sound, often used to describe the relationship between sound and architecture, as in a concert hall.

Vibrations: Trembling or oscillating motions that produce sound. When singers or stringed instruments produce a wavering sound, causing a fluctuation in pitch, it is termed **vibrato.**

Pitch: The sound produced by vibrations. The speed of vibrations controls the pitch: slow vibrations produce low pitches; fast vibrations produce high pitches.

Tempo: The speed at which music is played or sung. This is shown on sheet music, usually in Italian terms, by **tempo marks** that indicate the desired speed. A device called a **metronome** can indicate tempo with precision.

Timbre: The characteristic sound or tonal quality of an instrument or voice. Also termed **color,** it can refer to the combination produced by more than one instrument's timbres, as **orchestral color.**

Tone: A sound of specific pitch and quality, the basic building material of music. Its properties are pitch, timbre, duration, and intensity.

Note: The written symbol for a tone, shown as **whole notes, half notes,** etc. These indicate the time a note is held, with a corresponding **rest** sign. **Notation** is the use of a set of symbols to record music in written form.

Melody: The succession of notes or pitches played or sung. Music with a single melodic line is called **monophony,** while music with more than one melodic line is **polyphony.**

Texture: In music, this refers to the number of different melodic lines; the greater the number, the thicker the texture.

Harmony: The combination of notes sung or played at one time, or **chords;** applies to homophonic music. **Consonance** refers to the sound of notes that are agreeable together; **dissonance** to the sound of notes that are discordant.

religious ritual. It is also used frequently in collective labor; the regular rhythm that characterizes work songs keeps the pace steady and makes the work more fun. For example, aerobics classes and workout tapes depend on music to motivate exercisers and help them keep the pace. On the other hand, parents use lullabies to lull their babies to sleep.

Since the late Middle Ages, Western music has developed many conventional types. These genres vary with the audience, the instruments, and the musical structures. **Liturgical** music was designed for churches, used sacred texts, and took advantage of church acoustics. The soaring vaults of Gothic cathedrals were perfect for the music of the Middle Ages. Music known as **chant** or **plainsong** is simply the human voice singing a religious text without instrumental accompaniment. When the voice is unaccompanied, it is known as **a cappella.** When the sound is made by specialized devices, called **instruments,** the music is termed **instrumental.**

Secular, that is nonreligious, music brought about other forms. **Chamber music,** instrumental music that was originally played in palaces for royalty and nobility, calls for more intimate spaces, a small ensemble of players, and small audiences. **Orchestral music** is the most public and complex form, involving a full orchestra and a concert hall, where the acoustics, or quality of sound, is very important. **Popular music,** often shortened to **pop,** appeals to a wide audience. It includes rock, folk, country, rap, and other types of music. **Jazz** is an improvisational form that arose in the United States from blues and ragtime. **Musical theater,** as the name

implies, is a combination of drama and music. Its songs often enter the pop repertoire as **show tunes. Opera,** a narrative in which both dialogue and exposition is sung, combines music with literature and drama.

Instruments. Musical instruments, which vary widely across cultures, can nevertheless be grouped in families. Probably most ancient are the **percussion** instruments, which make noise as they are struck. Drums, blocks, cymbals, and tambourines are percussion instruments. **Stringed** instruments, deriving from the hunting bow, have strings stretched between two points; sounds are produced when they are plucked, strummed, bowed, or struck. **Woodwinds** are hollow instruments that were originally made of wood, such as the flute, recorder, and panpipes. **Reed** instruments, such as the oboe, are woodwinds that use a mouthpiece created from a compressed reed. **Brasses** are metal horns like the tuba, trumpet, and cornet. In addition to their musical function, brasses were long used by the military to communicate over distances in battle or in camp. Using a prearranged trumpet call, the commander could sound "retreat" or "charge."

Musical Qualities and Structure. Musical structure ranges from a simple tune or rhythm to the intricacy of a symphony or an opera. The tone, or sound of a specific quality, is the basis of all music, using varieties of high or low pitches and timbres with varying intensity and tempos. Music appeals to our emotions through tempo, musical color or timbre, and harmonic structure. We associate different emotions with different timbres. The harp, for example, evokes gentleness or calm, whereas brasses evoke more stirring emotions.

Musical structure can be simple, such as Ravel's *Bolero*, which uses the repetition of a single melody with increased tempo and volume to build to a climax. Increases in tempo generate excitement, literally increasing the listener's heart rate and breathing speed. These qualities were used to good advantage in Blake Edwards's film *10*. Composers of movie music manipulate our emotions expertly, heightening the appeal of the action.

The comparatively uncomplicated pop songs we sing are based on melodies, a succession of notes, with accompanying words. We are also familiar with the 32-bar structure of most pop and rock music, in which **verses** alternate with repeated **choruses**. To appreciate and enjoy more complex music, some understanding of structure is important. The simple song "Row, Row, Row Your Boat," familiar to many of us from childhood, is a **round** or **canon;** the same melody is sung by each voice, but voices enter one after the other, creating overlapping notes, or **chords.** More elaborate forms stemming from such simple structures are found in **classical** music, beginning with European music of the eighteenth and nineteenth centuries.

Harmonic structure is a complex topic. Western music is written in **keys,** a system of notes based on one central note, such as the key of C Major. The different keys have their own emotional connotations. A **minor key** is often associated with sadness, a **major key** seems happier or more forceful. Notes that seem to fit together are consonant, while clashing notes are dissonant. Generally, consonance seems peaceful or happy to most people, while dissonance may be unsettling.

Listening to Music. Music is a temporal art, designed to be listened to from beginning to end without interruption. We use music as a background so much it is sometimes difficult to learn to really listen to it. If you are listening to recorded music, reduce your distractions by turning off the television or lowering the lights. At a performance, concentrate on the performers or look at a particular spot while you absorb the music. Read program notes carefully to find out all you can about the piece and the composer. Analyze your reactions to the music, keeping in mind all you have learned about the forms, the instruments, and the musical structure.

HISTORY AND PHILOSOPHY

History, the recording and explanation of events, and philosophy, the search for truth, have both influenced the arts. These subjects have themselves evolved as humanistic disciplines. **Aesthetics,** the branch of philosophy concerned with the functions, practice, and appreciation of the arts, along with their role in society, is an important part of this book and of cultural studies in general.

History. Unlike expressive literature, or fiction, history is an inquiry into and report upon real events and people. Its origins lie in the epic literature of the ancients with its creation myths. Such literature contains much that we now consider historical: stories of wars, reigns, natural disasters. However, until the Greek historian Herodotus, traveling in the Mediterranean lands of the sixth century B.C., turned his questioning and skeptical eye on the received beliefs and tales of peoples he met, history was inseparable from religious faith and folk memory. Historians have since developed methods of inquiry, questioning the likelihood of stories and delving into the motives of their informants. They learned to consider nonhistorical accounts and records as checks on the official versions of events. They began, in Byzantium, to consider the psychological motives of the people they chronicled. The artistry of their presentation became a part of the discipline.

Religion and Philosophy. Religion has played a crucial role in the development of the arts, which provide images, sounds, and words for use in worship, prayers, and religious stories. **Theology,** the theory of religious belief, prescribes religious practices, moral beliefs, and rules for social behavior. The dominant religion in a culture often controls the art, either directly by training artists and commissioning art, or indirectly. The medieval Catholic belief in the efficacy of **relics** to heal or give aid, for example, led to the practice of pilgrimage, and from that to the creation of great cathedrals. As religious orders acquired holy relics, they housed them in shrines within the churches. Problems arose when the many pilgrims who came to be healed and blessed disrupted services. Romanesque architects then developed the **ambulatory,** or walkway, that allowed pilgrims to see the relics without interrupting worshipers at a service, thereby altering religious architecture. Different religions hold different aesthetic beliefs. Nudity was acceptable in the temple statues of Classical Greece and Hindu India. Islam prohibits any figurative images in places of worship, and some Native Americans believe a permanent house of worship is itself inappropriate.

In Western culture, philosophy and religion are intertwined. Like religion, philosophy is concerned with the basic truths and principles of the universe. Both are also concerned with human perception and understanding of these truths, and with the development of moral and ethical principles for living. However, their means differ. Philosophy is based on logic; religion on faith. Like so many other humanistic inventions and advances, philosophy, along with its specialized branch of aesthetics, originated in ancient Greece.

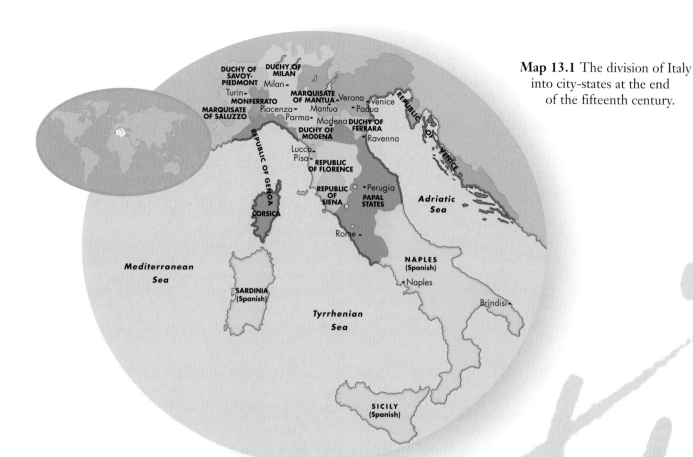

Map 13.1 The division of Italy into city-states at the end of the fifteenth century.

THE RENAISSANCE AND MANNERISM IN ITALY

CHAPTER 13

↞ *The Early Renaissance*

↞ *The High Renaissance*

↞ *Mannerism*

Sandro Botticelli, *Birth of Venus*, 1484–86, Galleria degli Uffizi, Florence.

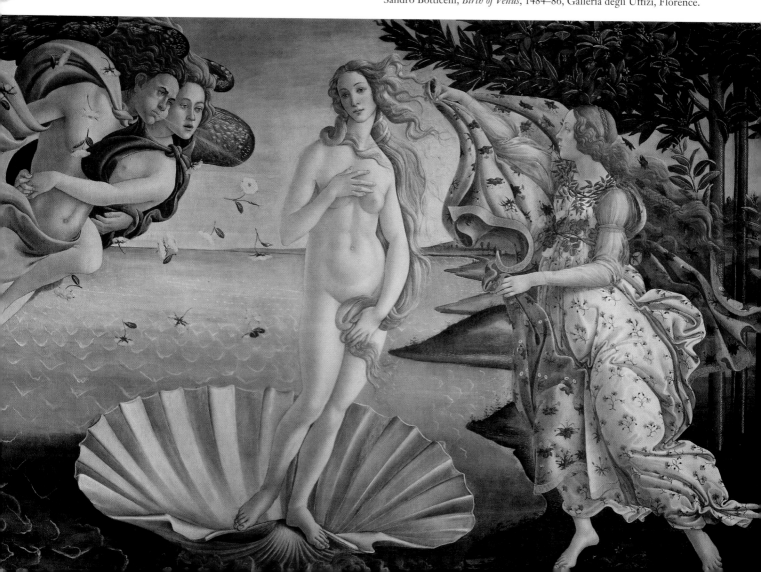

THE EARLY RENAISSANCE

In the middle of the fourteenth century, from around 1348 to 1351, Europe was ravaged by bubonic plague. Called the "Black Death," it was propagated by fleas, carried on the air by coughing and sneezing, and it killed somewhere between one-third and one-half of the population of Western Europe. In small, closed societies, such as monasteries, the infection of one person meant the death of all. The plague first incited fear, then undermined belief systems, and finally spawned widespread social unrest and turmoil. In the midst of this confusion, old ideas were challenged, and new ideas began to take hold, ideas that would lead to the sense of renewal and rebirth that we have come to call the **Renaissance.**

The term "Renaissance" is a French word literally meaning "rebirth," first employed in the nineteenth century to describe the period extending from the early fifteenth century to the middle of the next. The Italians of the time themselves believed that this period marked a radical break from the past and a reinvention in the present of the civilization and ideals of classical Greece and Rome. Today, we are aware that Italian Renaissance culture actually drew heavily on its medieval past, especially its Christian heritage; but as it followed so closely upon the plague's devastation, it is hardly surprising that Italian artists and intellectuals and their patrons believed that they had embarked on a path that would restore Italy to its place at the center of civilization, with a prestige it had not enjoyed since the fall of Rome.

This new culture would not have been possible unless the economic conditions necessary to support it were already in place. During the thirteenth and fourteenth centuries, as a result of the ongoing struggle between the popes and the European emperors, a number of city-states had grown powerful in Italy—the kingdom of Naples in the south, the Church states around Rome, and in the north, the duchy of Milan, and the republics of Venice and Florence. The last three were important trading centers, with close ties to the north. Located on the main road connecting Rome with the north, Florence had become the center of trade, and European banking had been established with credit operations available to support and spur on an increase in trade (Fig. 13.1).

Florence itself was ruled by its guilds, or *arti.* The seven major guilds, which were controlled by bankers, lawyers, and exporters, originally ran the civic government, but by the middle of the fourteenth century all the guilds, even the lesser guilds of middle-ranking tradesmen, had achieved some measure of political voice, and the city prided itself on its "representative" government and its status as a republic. Still, the major long-standing division between those who favored the Holy Roman Emperor (the old nobility, called the Ghibellines) and those who favored the popes (the new entrepreneurs, called the Guelphs) continued relatively unabated in Florence. Such civil strife, sometimes marked by street battles, had one inevitable result. By the fifteenth century, what the city needed most if its security were to be maintained was a leader with enough political skill, power, and wealth to stop the feuding once and for all.

THE MEDICI'S FLORENCE

It was a single family, the Medici, who led Florence to its unrivaled position as the cultural center of Renaissance Europe in the fifteenth century. The family had begun to

Figure 13.1 A map of Florence in 1490.

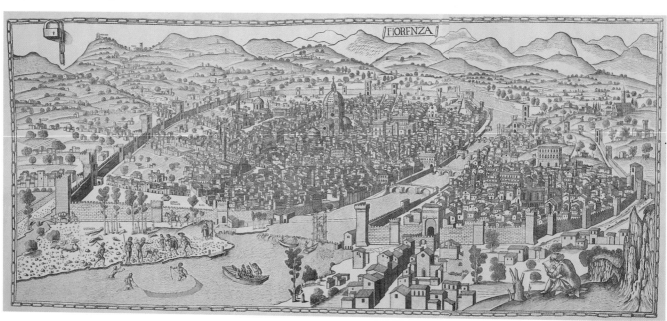

accumulate its fortune by lending money to other Florentines out of income derived from its two wool workshops. GIOVANNI DI BICCI DE' MEDICI [geo-VAHN-nee deh MED-uh-chee] (1360–1429) multiplied this fortune by setting up branch banks in major Italian cities and creating close financial allegiances with the papacy in Rome, allegiances that tended to switch the balance of power, making secular concerns more important than religious ones to the Vatican.

Cosimo de' Medici. It was his son, COSIMO [CAH-zee-moh] (1389–1464), however, who led the family to a position of unquestioned preeminence, not only in Florence but, as branches of the Medici banks opened elsewhere, in Europe as a whole. Though never the official leader of the city, Cosimo ruled, with what amounted to absolute power, from behind the scenes. By 1458, Pope Pius II described him as "master of the country … Political questions are settled at his house. The man he chooses holds office … He it is who decides peace and war and controls the laws … He is King in everything but name."

Cosimo's power was based substantially on calculated acts of discretion and benevolence. "Do not appear to give advice," his father had counseled him, "but put your views forward discreetly in conversation … never display any pride should you receive a lot of votes … Avoid litigation and political controversy and keep out of the public eye." At the same time, Cosimo knew that if he gave a significant portion of his wealth to the city, the city would give its loyalty in return. So give Cosimo did. He built the first public library since ancient times and stocked it with ancient manuscripts and books, chiefly of Greek and Roman origin, with a special eye toward the works of Plato and Aristotle. Though it is difficult to estimate how much money he actually spent on his library collection in today's currency, $25 million would not be far from the truth. At some point, virtually every major Italian artist, architect, writer, philosopher, or scholar of the day was in his employ.

In many ways, Cosimo simply solidified what was already fact—Florence had been recognized as a cultural center since the middle of the fourteenth century. Giotto's naturalistic fresco paintings signaled the beginning of the end of the highly stylized and conventional portrayals of medieval art. A prominent member of Florence's *Arti Maggiori*, or seven "major guilds," Giotto painted the Bardi and Peruzzi chapels of Santa Croce in Florence between 1315 and 1330 and was appointed city architect and master of works for the building of Florence Cathedral in 1334 (see Chapter 12). His design of the cathedral's **campanile**, or bell tower, with its clear and logical structural relationships, harks back to classical principles of design. It was also in Florence, in 1274, that Dante first met his lifelong muse, Beatrice, when he was but nine years old. Dante would later reject the city as a pothole of "self-made men and fast-got gain" when he was exiled in 1302. In the *Inferno* section of his epic poem, *The Divine Comedy*, Dante depicts Florence's burgeoning mercantile culture in some of his most bitter passages. Boccaccio's great collection of stories, *The Decameron*, begins in a chapel of Florence's Santa Maria Novella, where one Tuesday morning after Mass in about 1348, his "seven ladies young and fair" and three men leave a city ravaged by plague to seek beauty and tranquillity in the surrounding countryside, to "hear the birds sing, and see the green hills, and the plains, and the fields covered with grain and undulating, like the sea."

Already, in these examples, we can see many of the characteristics of Renaissance art and culture: in the growing naturalism of the arts in the renewed interest in

Timeline 13.1 The Florentine Renaissance: Works commissioned by the Medici.

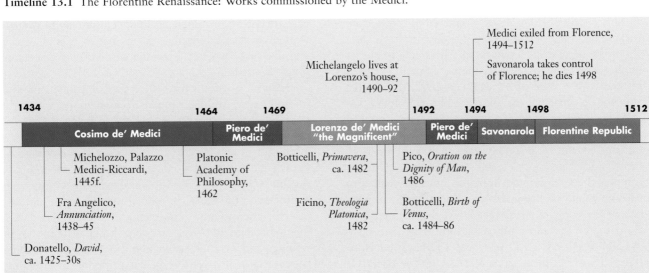

classical values (Giotto's admiration for classical principles of reason and logic), and in the rise of humanism
(Dante's negative view of Florence's rampant individualism in those "self-made men," which his still medieval
sensibility abhorred). The growing wealth of the city
itself, together with the peace brought by Cosimo's leadership, created an atmosphere in which the arts could
not only prosper but be enjoyed and appreciated, and
this in turn contributed to the increasing sophistication
of its citizenry. As early as 1402–03, the first historian
of Florence, LEONARDO BRUNI [BREW-nee]
(1374–1444), a translator of Plato, Aristotle, and
Plutarch, and later a Chancellor of the Republic, praised
Florence for its similarity to classical Athens; and with
the ascendancy of the Medici, the citizenry truly
believed that they had embarked on a new Golden Age.

Lorenzo the Magnificent. The city's dream of
achieving the status of the Golden Age of Athens was
fully realized, many felt, by LORENZO [LOR-enn-
zoh] (1449–1492), Cosimo's grandson, who assumed his
place as head of the Medici at the age of twenty in 1469,
inaugurating twenty-three years of great influence.
Lorenzo's father, PIERO [pea-AIR-oh] (1416–1469),
cursed with ill health, had ruled for only five years after
Cosimo before his own death, but he had raised Lorenzo
in Cosimo's image, and Lorenzo quickly established
himself as a force to be reckoned with. "Lorenzo the
Magnificent," he was called (Fig. 13.2) and indeed, he
lived with a sense of grandeur and magnificence. He was
one of the leading poets of his day, as well as an accomplished musician, playing the lute and composing
numerous dances. He surrounded himself with scholars,
built palaces and parks, sponsored festivals and pageants,
all the while dipping deeply into the city's coffers, which
he controlled, as well as his own. Surprisingly, he commissioned little in the way of painting, preferring instead
to spend money on such things as gemstones and ancient
vases, which he believed to be better investments than
painting. Many of the precious stones in his collection,
for example, were valued at over a thousand florins (the
coin of the day), while a painting by Botticelli might be
bought for as little as a hundred florins. Spend Lorenzo
did, and by the time of his death in 1492, the Medici
bank was in financial trouble and Florence itself was
verging on bankruptcy.

Although the Medici ruled Florence with minor
interruptions until 1737, they never again held the same
power and authority as Cosimo and Lorenzo. Outside
Florence, the most important patron of the Renaissance
in Rome would be Lorenzo's son, Pope Leo X. In generations to come, several female Medici descendants
would marry the most powerful figures in Europe—
CATHERINE DE' MEDICI (1519–1589) was queen to
Henry II of France, and MARIA DE' MEDICI
(1573–1642) was Henry IV of France's Queen Consort.

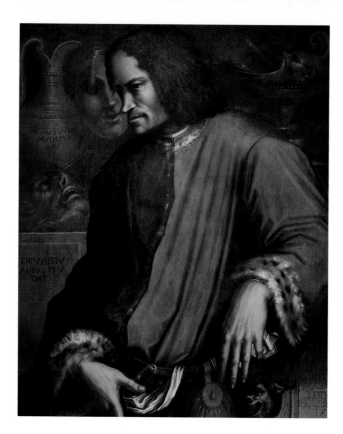

Figure 13.2 Giorgio Vasari, *Posthumous Portrait of
Lorenzo the Magnificent*, oil on canvas, Galleria degli Uffizi,
Florence. The impressive presence of Lorenzo, as well as his
broken nose, are recorded in this painting by Vasari, author
of the *Lives of the Most Eminent Painters, Sculptors, and
Architects*.

THE HUMANIST SPIRIT

Cosimo, Piero, and Lorenzo de' Medici were all
humanists—that is, those who believed in the worth
and dignity of the individual and who, in seeking to discover what was best about humanity, turned their attention to the culture of classical antiquity. In the literature,
history, rhetoric, and philosophy of ancient Greece and
Rome, they discovered what the Latin scholar and poet
PETRARCH [PEH-trark] (1304–1372) had called a
century before a "golden wisdom." Cosimo and Lorenzo
worked to make Florence the humanist capital of the
world, a place where the golden wisdom of the ancients
might flourish once again.

Petrarch is often called the father of humanism, and
in many ways he determined its high moral tone. He
believed that learning was the key to living a virtuous
life, and that life should be an eternal quest for truth.
Each individual's leading a virtuous life in the pursuit of
knowledge and truth would provide a basis for improv-
ing humanity's lot. He wholeheartedly encouraged an
appreciation of beauty, in nature and in human endeav-
or, which he thought to be a manifestation of the divine.
The personal letter became one of his favorite modes of
writing, and he took to writing letters to the ancients
themselves as if they were personal friends, even family.
He called the poet Virgil his brother and Cicero his

Cross Currents

MONTEZUMA'S TENOCHTITLAN

While Florence stood as the center of the Early Renaissance world, in the other hemisphere stood a city of equal importance and grandeur, one that the Europeans did not know existed until Hernán Cortés invaded Mexico in 1519. It was called Tenochtitlan, and it was the capital of Montezuma's Aztec empire.

The Aztecs, who founded the city, believed that they had been ordered by their god Huitzilopochtli to wander until they saw an eagle perched upon a prickly pear, or *tenochtli*. They finally encountered such a vision in 1325 on an island in the marches of Lake Texcoco in the Valley of Mexico. There they built their city, connecting it to the mainland by four causeways. By the end of the fifteenth century, it was a metropolis inhabited by 150,000 to 200,000 people and ruled by a priest and emperor, Montezuma.

The *Codex Mendoza* (fig. 13.3) is the fullest account that we have of early sixteenth-century Aztec life. It consists of seventy-two annotated pictorial pages together with sixty-three more pages of related Spanish commentary. It was compiled under the supervision of Spanish friars and at the request of the Spanish crown in about 1541 to aid in their colonial expansion.

As depicted by Aztec scribes, the city is represented by the eagle on the cactus, the shield and arrows symbolizing war, and the waterways dividing the city into equal quadrants. At the heart of the city was the Great Pyramid, imaged by the scribes in the temple at the top. Here, the Aztecs worshiped both Huitzilopochtli, god of the sun and of warfare, and Tlaloc, god of rain and fertility, and here they engaged in ritual human sacrifice to both gods by cutting out the still-beating hearts of their victims, then decapitating them.

As the cultural center of the Aztec civilization, Tenochtitlan was magnificent, grander in fact than anything in Europe at the time. In the words of one of Cortés's soldiers: "When we saw … that straight and level causeway going towards Tenochtitlan, we were amazed … Some of our soldiers even asked whether the things that we saw were not a dream."

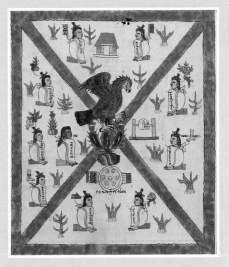

Figure 13.3 *The Founding of Tenochtitlan*, page from the *Codex Mendoza*, Aztec, sixteenth century, ink and color on paper, $8\frac{7}{16} \times 12\frac{3}{8}''$ (21.5 × 31.5 cm), The Bodleian Library, Oxford. The skull rack just to the right of center is one of the very few images in the Codex that openly acknowledges the practice of human sacrifice in Aztec life.

father. In the writings of the ancients, Petrarch felt he could sense their uniquely human (noble and ignoble) qualities. Thus, for Petrarch, reading the ancients was like having conversations with them.

Moreover, there were many ancient texts to read. In the middle of the fourteenth century, Petrarch's friend, the writer Boccaccio, had been one of the first men to study Greek since the classical age itself. During the next fifty years, humanist scholars combed monastery libraries for long-ignored ancient Greek texts and translated them into Latin and Italian. By 1400, the works of Homer, Aeschylus, Sophocles, Euripides, Aristophanes, Herodotus, Thucydides, and all of Plato's dialogues were available. In addition, after the fall of Constantinople in 1453, Greek scholars flooded into Italy seeking refuge. Greek learning spread further with the rapid rise of printing in Italy following Johann Gutenberg's invention of printing with movable type and the publication of a Bible in 1455. Between 1456 and 1500, more books were published than had been copied by manuscript scribes in the previous thousand years. Many of these were in vernacular (or native) Italian, such as the works of Dante and Boccaccio. This contributed to the growing literacy of the middle class, and by the start of the sixteenth century, any educated person could expect to own the complete works of Plato.

THE PLATONIC ACADEMY OF PHILOSOPHY

The center of humanist study during the Renaissance was the Platonic Academy of Philosophy in Florence, founded by Cosimo de' Medici in 1462, and supported with special enthusiasm by Lorenzo the Magnificent. The academy sponsored **Neoplatonism**, or a "new Platonism," which sought to revive Platonic ideals in contemporary culture.

Marsilio Ficino. At the head of the academy was MARSILIO FICINO [fi-CHEE-noh] (1433–1499), who translated into Latin both Plato and Plotinus [Ploh-TINE-us] and wrote the *Theologia Platonica* (1482). Ficino's Neoplatonism was a conscious rereading of Plato (see Chapter 4), particularly his dualistic vision of the psyche (roughly equivalent to the soul or spirit) trapped in the body, but Ficino thought we could glimpse the higher world of Forms or Ideas through study and learning, and so he looked to the Roman philosopher Plotinus (A.D. 205–270), who was a follower of Plato. Plotinus argued that the material and spiritual worlds could be united through ecstatic, or mystical, vision. Following Plotinus, Ficino conceived of beauty in the things of this world as God's means of making himself manifest to humankind. The contemplation and study of beauty in nature—and in all things—was a form of worship, a manifestation of divine or spiritual love, and Plato's ideas about love were, in fact, central to Ficino's philosophy. Like erotic love, spiritual love is inspired by physical beauty, but spiritual love moves beyond the physical to an intellectual plane and, eventually, to such an elevated spiritual level that it results in the soul's union with God. Thus, in Neoplatonic terms, Lorenzo's fondness for gems was a type of spiritual love, as was Petrarch's love for Laura, celebrated in his sonnets, and so was the painter Botticelli's love of the human form (both discussed later in this chapter). If in real things one could discover the divine, then the determination of Renaissance artists to represent the world in ever more naturalistic terms becomes clear. It could be said that realism becomes, in Neoplatonic terms, a form of idealism. In fact, Ficino saw "Platonic love," the love of beauty, as a kind of spiritual bond upon which the strongest kind of community could be constructed. In this way, Neoplatonism even had political implications. The Neoplatonists envisioned Florence as a city whose citizenry was spiritually bound together in a common love of the beautiful.

Pico della Mirandola. Another great Neoplatonic philosopher at the academy was PICO DELLA MIRANDOLA [PEA-coh DELL-ah mee-RAN-doh-lah] (1463–1494), whose religious devotion, intense scholarship, and boundless optimism attracted many followers to the humanist movement. His famous *Oration on the Dignity of Man* (1486) encapsulates one of the central impulses of the Renaissance: humankind serving as a link between the lower orders of nature, including animals, and the higher spiritual orders, of which angels are a part. For Pico, human beings possess free will and are able to make of themselves what they wish. Though linked with the lower order of matter, they are capable of rising to the higher realm of spirit and ultimately being united with God. Each person's destiny is thus a matter of individual choice.

In the *Oration*, Pico presents God speaking to Adam, telling him that "in conformity with thy free judgment in whose hands I have placed thee, thou art confined by no bonds, and constrained by no limits." God also tells Adam directly that he is "the molder and maker" of himself, who "canst grow downward into the lower natures which are brutes" or "upward from the mind's reason into the higher natures which are divine." This central tenet of humanist philosophy is often misunderstood to

mean that an emphasis on the individual results in or implies a rejection of God. Although Pico, and humanists in general, place the responsibility for human action squarely on humans and not on the Almighty, he also believed that the human mind—with its ability to reason and imagine—could conceive of and move toward the divine. It follows that individual genius, which was allowed to flower in Renaissance Italy as never before in Western culture, is the worldly manifestation of divine truth.

SCULPTURE

One of the ways that Renaissance culture cultivated the notion of individual genius was by encouraging competitions among artists for prestigious public and religious commissions. As early as 1401, the Florentine humanist historian Leonardo Bruni sponsored a competition to determine who would make the doors of Florence Cathedral's octagonal **baptistery**, the small structure separated from the main church where baptisms are performed. Seven sculptors were asked to submit depictions of the sacrifice of Isaac.

Lorenzo Ghiberti. The winner of the competition was the young sculptor LORENZO GHIBERTI [ghee-BAIR-tee] (1378–1455), and his reaction typifies the heightened sense of self-worth that Renaissance artists felt about their artistic abilities and accomplishments: "To me was conceded the palm of victory by all the experts … To me the honor was conceded universally and with no exception. To all it seemed that I had at that time surpassed the others." He had, admittedly, defeated the much more established sculptor Filippo Brunelleschi in the competition—and perhaps it was losing the competition to the younger Ghiberti, at least in some small part, that caused Brunelleschi to turn away from sculpture to become the preeminent architect of his day (see p. 22)—but Ghiberti's pride nevertheless borders on the excessive. Still, we sense in that pride the drive and spirit that would come to define Renaissance individualism.

The subject matter of the baptistery doors was a series of New Testament stories, each told in one of twenty-eight gilded bronze reliefs, which in all took Ghiberti over twenty years to complete. Trained as a painter, Ghiberti pursued concerns of spatial illusion and visual harmony inherited from fourteenth-century painters such as Giotto. Like the reliefs on the ancient Roman Ara Pacis (see Chapter 5), the figures in Ghiberti's *Nativity with the Annunciation to the Shepherds* (fig. 13.4) are set on an empty background that looks more like air than a flat wall—there is, in other words, a sense of physical space behind them. Unlike medieval art, in which the size of figures was determined by their importance, here size reflects position in space: the foreground figures are larger and in higher relief than those in the background.

In addition, the figures themselves not only get progressively larger as they emerge from the depths of the composition, but are arranged in such a way that they connect one to the next, creating a sense of linear movement from back to front. The angel flies forward through the air in a remarkable example of sculptural **foreshortening**, proclaiming the birth of Jesus to the shepherds.

So well were these doors received that as soon as they were completed Ghiberti was immediately commissioned to make a second set for the east side of the baptistery. The eastern doors, depicting ten stories from the Old Testament, were completed in 1452 and are by far the more famous of the two sets. Impressed by their beauty, Michelangelo called them the "Gates of Paradise," and the name stuck. The *Gates of Paradise*, mounted on the east, face the cathedral facade, occupying the most prominent position on the baptistery.

The panels are fewer in number and larger in size; scenes are set in simple square formats, and this time the whole square is gilded rather than just the raised areas. Each panel actually includes several scenes. The first, for instance, *The Creation* (fig. 13.5), portrays five scenes from Genesis. At the top God creates the heavens and earth. At the bottom left, Adam is created from the earth,

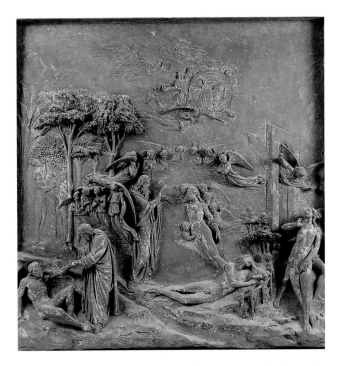

Figure 13.5 Lorenzo Ghiberti, *The Creation of Adam and Eve*, 1425–52, gilt bronze, $31\frac{1}{4} \times 31\frac{1}{4}$" (79.4 × 79.4 cm), relief panel from the *Gates of Paradise*, east doors, Baptistery, Florence, now in the Museo dell'Opera del Duomo, Florence. Because of their beauty, Michelangelo referred to these doors as the "Gates of Paradise."

Figure 13.4 Lorenzo Ghiberti, *Nativity with the Annunciation to the Shepherds*, 1403–24, gilt bronze, $20\frac{1}{2} \times 17\frac{3}{4}$" (52.1 × 45.1 cm), relief panel from the north doors, Baptistery, Florence. The angel announces the birth of Jesus to the shepherds, while Joseph sleeps. Inclusion of the ox and the ass derives from a biblical passage (Isaiah 1:3), "the ox knoweth his owner, and the ass his master's crib."

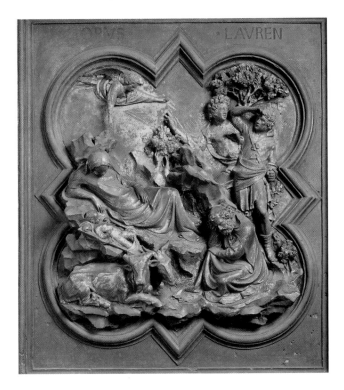

pressing himself up firmly with an extraordinarily muscular right hand. The central scene depicts Eve being created from Adam's rib. To the left, and behind, Adam and Eve are tempted by Satan in the guise of a serpent. And to the right, Adam and Eve are expelled from the Garden of Eden. This is a simultaneous presentation of events that took place sequentially, a technique called **continuous narration**.

Although medieval artists had depicted events on a single plane, now Renaissance artists allowed the viewer to follow a story through the space of the landscape. The events depicted are organized spatially rather than narratively from left to right. Ghiberti later wrote of the *Gates of Paradise*: "I strove to imitate nature as closely as I could, and with all the perspective I could produce ... The scenes are in the lowest relief and the figures are seen in the planes; those that are near appear large, those in the distance small, as they do in reality ... Executed with the greatest study and perseverance, of all my work it is the most remarkable I have done and it was finished with skill, correct proportions, and understanding."

Donatello. Ghiberti's insistence on correct perspective, proper proportions, and the most accurate representation of nature was shared by DONATELLO [don-ah-TELL-oh] (1386–1466), who by 1405 was working in

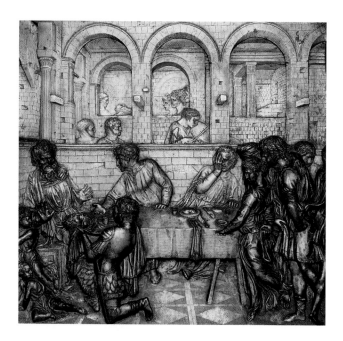

Figure 13.6   Donatello, *Feast of Herod*, ca. 1423–27, gilt bronze, 23½ × 23½″ (59.7 × 59.7 cm), relief panel from baptismal font, baptistery of cathedral, Siena. Donatello's harsh drama contrasts with Ghiberti's fluid charm.

Ghiberti's studio, assisting him on the first set of doors for the baptistery. In 1425, Donatello made the *Feast of Herod* (fig. 13.6), a gilded bronze relief for the font in the baptistery of Siena Cathedral. It is a triumph in the creation of perspectival space. Although perspective had been employed by the ancient Romans in their murals, the general principles of Renaissance **perspective** are believed to have been developed by Filippo Brunelleschi, whom Ghiberti had defeated in the original competition for the Florentine baptistery doors. These principles were later codified by the architect Leon Battista Alberti in his *De pictura* (*On Painting*), published in 1435. In the simplest terms, perspective allows the picture plane (or surface of the picture) to function as a window through which a specific scene is presented to the viewer.

Alberti begins his description of perspective by instructing his reader to draw a rectangle with a figure in the foreground (fig. 13. 7). A horizon line is then drawn at the height of the figure's head. One third of the height of the figure is measured and the foreground is marked off into units of this dimension. A **vanishing point**—the spot where all orthogonals, or receding lines perpendicular to the picture plane, will appear to converge—is drawn at or near the center of the horizon line, and the orthogonals are then drawn from the foreground units to the vanishing point. To make the horizontal division in the pavement, Alberti advised creating a "small space" beside the drawing. A line is drawn perpendicular to the foreground line, and where this vertical line intersects the orthogonals, horizontals are drawn. Accuracy may be checked with a diagonal line.

The effectiveness of linear perspective in organizing the composition and in creating the illusion of physical space cannot be overestimated. The actual physical space of Donatello's *Feast of Herod* is very shallow, as it is in all

Figure 13.7   Diagram of Alberti's method of drawing in one-point linear perspective. An illusion of three dimensions on a two-dimensional surface can be created by use of his system. Alberti's method used a single vanishing point for lines perpendicular to the canvas, and additional points on either side at which oblique lines seemed to converge (*a* height of person, *b* base line, *c* vanishing point, *d* orthogonals, *e* "small space", *f* distance point, *g* vertical intersection, *h* transversals).

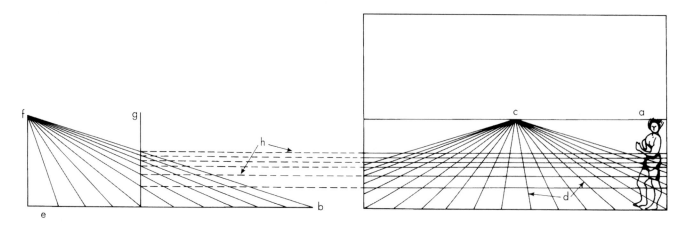

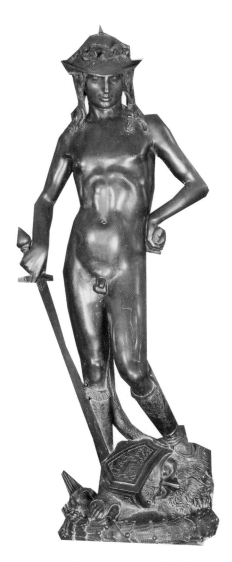

Figure 13.8 Donatello, *David*, ca. 1425–30s, bronze, height 5'2¼" (1.58 m), Museo Nazionale del Bargello, Florence. The Early Renaissance interest in antiquity and the accurate portrayal of the nude are evidenced in Donatello's work.

Donatello went on to a very different subject, one of special popularity in the Early Renaissance, the shepherd boy David (fig. 13.8) who slew the giant, Goliath, with a stone from his slingshot. For the Florentines, David was a symbol of liberty—he triumphed over Goliath the way tiny Florence triumphed over her mightier enemies. In Christian terms, David symbolized Christ triumphing over Satan, an interpretation that reinforced Florence's sense of its own essential goodness.

In Donatello's *David* (ca. 1425–30s), the stone is still in David's sling, although Goliath's head lies beneath David's foot. By depicting David both before and after the conflict, Donatello provides a condensed version of the story. With the first life-size nude created since Roman antiquity, Donatello rejects the idealized forms

Figure 13.9 Donatello, *Mary Magdalene*, 1453–55, wood, painted and gilded, height 6'2" (1.88 m), Museo dell'Opera del Duomo, Florence. Not only beauty, but also its absence can be used to create emotionally moving art, as in this portrayal of the repentant sinner.

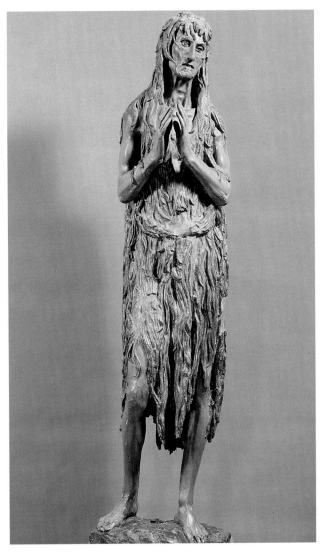

reliefs, but perspective creates the illusion of a very deep space, with two courtyards extending back behind the foreground action. In each courtyard the people are progressively smaller. The floor pattern, drawn in linear perspective, enhances the illusion of recession. Donatello's emphasis on the mathematical discipline of his design and his rigorous application of the laws of perspective are balanced in works such as this one by the dramatic and emotional content of the scene. Indeed, the *Feast of Herod* possesses a dramatic force never before seen in Italian sculpture. The composition is split down the middle so that there are two competing centers of attention, an unusual device. John the Baptist's head is brought on a platter to Herod on the left and Salome dances seductively on the right. This split adds to the emotional impact and tension of the composition.

of antique sculpture and portrays his hero as an adolescent male wearing a rather refined hat and boots. (In the Bible, incidentally, David casts off his armor as too cumbersome for battle.) In addition, David adopts the antique *contrapposto* posture, in which the weight of the body rests on one leg, elevating the hip and the opposite shoulder, putting the spine into an "S" curve. Donatello had been to Rome in 1400 and went again in 1431; it may be assumed that he studied antique sculpture on these visits. Although he adopted individual antique motifs, he combined them in un-antique ways. David's posture and nudity may be derived from the ancients, but the body contours are so natural that the story arose that the limbs had been cast from a living model.

Throughout Donatello's career, no matter the subject, scale, or sculptural medium used, he maintained his interest in dramatically powerful imagery. Between 1453 and 1455, he carved one of his most mesmerizing works: the polychromed wooden figure of *Mary Magdalene* (fig. 13.9), which stands over six feet high. Traditionally known for her physical beauty, Mary Magdalene was the repentant prostitute at Jesus's side, anointing his feet, attending to his burial, guarding his tomb, and discovering his resurrection. Donatello depicts her after years of living in the desert, rejecting the life of the body in anticipation of the immortal life of the soul. Her body now gaunt, her arms and legs withered, she prays. While Ghiberti had taught Donatello to create drama in sculpture (see fig. 13.5), Ghiberti never attempted to challenge his viewer. His work remains delicate, almost sentimental, and appealing. Donatello's figure, by comparison, is intentionally unnerving, even repulsive. Viewers respond to Mary Magdalene with compassion and pity, or they admire her sacrifice, but they are not allowed to respond—at least not in a traditional manner—to the beauty of her appearance.

The beauty Donatello presents is of another kind. Traditionally, we define the aesthetic sense as the appreciation of beauty. Surprisingly, many people find Donatello's *Mary Magdalene* to be one of the most aesthetically pleasing of his works. In a very Neoplatonic manner, it triggers a higher level of thought and awareness in the viewer, who experiences this intellectual and imaginative stimulus—this higher order of thought—as a form of beauty in its own right. Mary Magdalene may be physically repulsive, but she is spiritually beautiful. This Neoplatonic emphasis on where we locate beauty—in the mind, not the body—typifies the way in which the Renaissance imagination becomes increasingly self-aware. It also frees the Renaissance artist to give up the idealized representations of the Middle Ages and depict the world in more and more realistic detail, since an image of even the most everyday thing might stimulate the imagination to the contemplation of the spiritual.

ARCHITECTURE

As Renaissance artists and thinkers turned their attention more and more to the power of the individual human mind, the powers of reason and logic (which Pico pronounced held us above the beasts) attracted them more than the mind's emotional world. Renaissance architecture in particular reflects a renewed interest in ancient Roman models, with their mathematically determined proportions and emphasis on clarity and logic of construction.

Filippo Brunelleschi.   The greatest architect of the Early Renaissance in Italy was FILIPPO BRUNELLESCHI [brew-nuh-LESS-key] (1377–1446), who had lost to Ghiberti in the competition to design the doors of the Florence baptistery. Brunelleschi proved to be an excellent architect, and his triumph is the enormous dome he designed for Florence Cathedral (fig. 13.10). Measuring 138½ feet wide and 367 feet high, it was the largest dome to have been built since the Pantheon in A.D. 125 (see Chapter 5). Although influenced by antique architecture, the octagonal dome of Florence Cathedral does not look like the hemispherical dome of the ancient Roman Pantheon. Using the basic structural principles perfected in the pointed arches of Gothic cathedrals, Brunelleschi produced a dome with less outward thrust than a hemispherical one. This was necessary because his predecessor, Arnolfo di Cambio, had designed the base of the dome to be of an extraordinary width. Brunelleschi needed to be inventive, and he flanked his octagonal dome with three half-domes that serve to buttress it.

Brunelleschi used different building materials for different parts of the dome: for the bottom, stone; for the upper portion, brick. Use of heavier material at the bottom produced a self-buttressing system, an idea that was not Brunelleschi's own but had actually been used in the Roman Pantheon. Brunelleschi's innovation was to build his dome with an inner and an outer shell—a dome within a dome that was much lighter than the solid concrete dome of the Pantheon. The octagonal dome is reinforced by eight major ribs, visible on the exterior, plus three minor ribs between every two major ribs (fig. 13.11). Finally, Brunelleschi designed an open structure to crown the roof, called a **lantern**. The metal lantern's weight stabilized the whole, its downward pressure keeping the ribs from spreading apart at the top.

Leon Battista Alberti.   The other great architect of the day, LEON BATTISTA ALBERTI [al-BEAR-tee] (1404–1472), shared Brunelleschi's love of the antique. He considered Brunelleschi the prime exponent of the new intellectual style that we have come to think of as the "Renaissance style." Born into one of the great families of Florence, Alberti was educated as a humanist, studied at the University of Bologna, and earned a doctorate in canon law. Celebrated as an architect and as an author, he was the first to detail the principles of linear perspective so important to Renaissance artists in his treatise *De pictura* (*On Painting*), written in 1434–35. His ten books on architecture, *De re aedificatoria*, completed about 1450, were inspired by the late first-century B.C. Roman writer Vitruvius, who had himself written an encyclopedic ten-volume survey of classical architecture.

Alberti worked to create a beauty in architecture that was derived from harmony among all parts, using mathematics to determine the proportions of his buildings. A prime example is the church of Sant' Andrea in Mantua (fig. 13.12), designed in 1470 and built after his death. Hampered by an older building on the site, Alberti had to adapt his ideal design of the church to the pre-existing surroundings. His solution exemplifies Renaissance theory; for the facade he combined the triangular **pediment** of a classical temple with arches characteristic of ancient Roman triumphal arches—one large central arch flanked by two smaller arches. The facade balances horizontals and verticals, with the height of the facade equaling the width. Four colossal Corinthian pilasters paired with small pilasters visually unite the stories of the facade. Large and small pilasters of the same

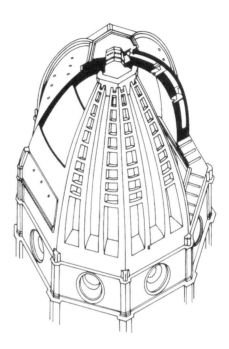

Figure 13.11 Line drawing of Brunelleschi's dome for Florence Cathedral indicating the double-shell construction.

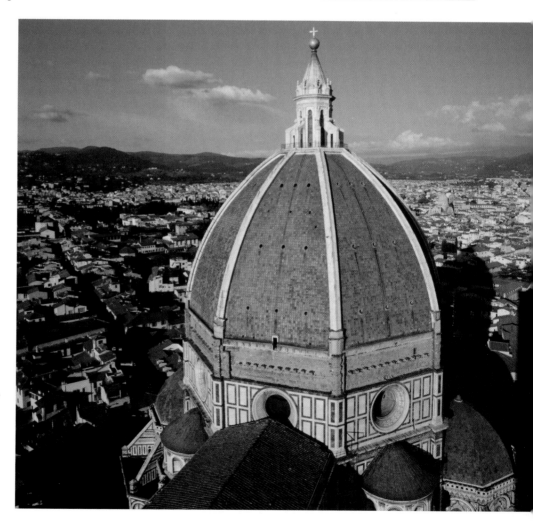

Figure 13.10 Filippo Brunelleschi, Florence Cathedral, dome, 1420–36; lantern completed 1471. Brunelleschi managed to erect this enormous double-shell pointed dome without the use of temporary scaffolding. It is the major landmark of Florence.

dimensions appear in the nave, linking the exterior and interior in a harmonious whole.

Michelozzo di Bartolommeo. In fifteenth-century Florence wealthy families customarily hired architects to build huge fortress-like palaces for them, emblems of their power. One such Florentine palace, the Palazzo Medici-Riccardi (fig. 13.13), was designed by the architect MICHELOZZO DI BARTOLOMMEO [MEE-kel-LOTZ-oh] (1396–1472). The Palazzo Medici-Riccardi was begun in 1445 and probably completed by 1452. Although built for Cosimo de' Medici, the palazzo was acquired in the seventeenth century by the Riccardi family. Standing on a corner of the Via Larga, the widest street in Florence, it was an imposing residence, dignified yet grand, that heralded its resident—the city's most powerful person—literally and metaphorically at the center of the city's cultural and political life.

Michelozzo created an austere three-story stone building. The stonework, beginning with a ground level of rusticated stone (the same rough-hewn masonry used in fortifications), becomes increasingly smoother from bottom story to top. What are now its ground-level windows were originally arches that opened into the street

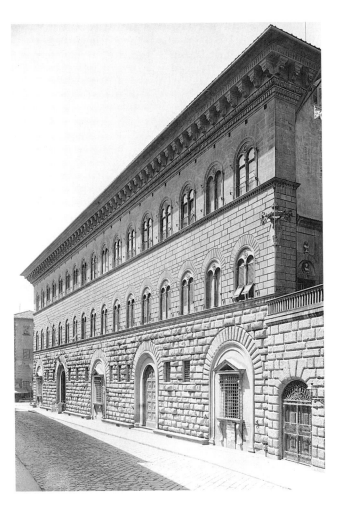

Figure 13.13   Michelozzo di Bartolommeo, Palazzo Medici-Riccardi, Florence, exterior, begun 1445; probably completed by 1452; ground-floor windows by Michelangelo, ca. 1517. Typical of Early Renaissance palazzi, the facades of this massive city residence, built for Cosimo de' Medici the Elder, are neatly divided into three stories with evenly-spaced windows.

Figure 13.12   Leon Battista Alberti, Sant' Andrea, Mantua, facade, designed 1470. An ideal demonstration of the Early Renaissance devotion to the antique, the design of this facade combines the form of an ancient temple with that of an ancient triumphal arch.

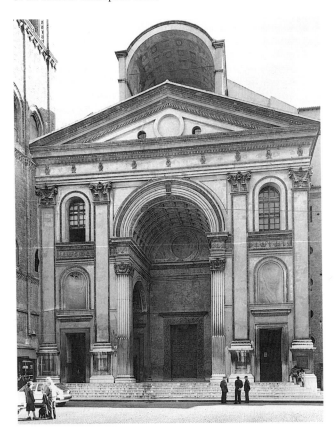

creating a *loggia*, or covered gallery. (The arches were filled and the windows added in the sixteenth century by Michelangelo.) The first story provided offices and storage rooms for the Medici business, and the family's living quarters were on the second level. Typically for the Renaissance, the division of the stories is neat and clear, and the divisions are formed by classical moldings. Michelozzo differentiated the levels visually by successively diminishing the height of each, though they all remain over twenty feet high.

The Early Renaissance interest in orderliness is seen also in the even spacing of the windows. The form of window used—two arched openings within an overriding arch—was already popular in the Middle Ages. At the top of the palazzo, a heavy projecting cornice fulfills both aesthetic and architectural roles. The cornice serves visually to frame and conclude the architectural composition.

With a flair for practicality, Michelozzo created a cornice that sent the rainwater wide of the wall. On the corners of the second story is the Medici coat-of-arms with its seven balls.

The rooms of the Palazzo Medici-Riccardi are arranged around a central, colonnaded courtyard, a typical Florentine system in which the palace is turned in on itself, ostensibly for protection but also for privacy and quiet. While the plain exterior reflected the owner's (Cosimo's) own public posture as a careful, even conservative man, the inside, especially the second floor, or *piano nobile* (the grand and "noble" family rooms of the palace), displayed ostentatious grandeur.

PAINTING

In their emphasis on proper spatial relationships and proportions, architects of the Early Renaissance made an important contribution to the development of the arts at the time. They perfected the art of perspective, the principles of which had been little used since ancient Roman times. In his own day Alberti was known as much for his treatise *On Painting*, which codified the laws of perspective for painters, as for his architectural accomplishments. As was noted in the discussion of Donatello's *Feast of Herod* (fig. 13.6), the system provides the means to achieve a highly naturalistic and convincing depiction of deep space on a two-dimensional surface. Linear perspective was one tool, among many others, that helped artists to satisfy their desire to create ever more naturalistic images.

Masaccio.   Of all the Early Renaissance painters, it was MASACCIO [mah-SAH-chee-oh] (1401–1429) who, in the short span of his life, carried the naturalistic impulse in painting furthest. In the 1436 Italian edition of *On Painting*, Alberti named Masaccio, along with Brunelleschi, Donatello, and Ghiberti, as a leading artist of the day.

Masaccio's extraordinary inventiveness is particularly evident in the wall frescoes painted for the Brancacci Chapel in Santa Maria del Carmine, Florence, which he completed in 1428. As Giorgio Vasari later wrote in his important 1550 book on the outstanding artists of the Italian Renaissance, *Lives of the Most Eminent Painters, Sculptors, and Architects*: "All the most celebrated sculptors and painters since Masaccio's day have become excellent and illustrious by studying their art in this chapel." In one such fresco, *The Tribute Money* (fig. 13.14), Masaccio utilizes continuous narration, as Ghiberti did later in the *Gates of Paradise*, to depict the scene from the Bible in which Jesus orders his disciples to "render unto Caesar that which is Caesar's, and unto God the things that are God's." In the center, Jesus, in

Figure 13.14   Masaccio, *The Tribute Money*, finished 1428, fresco, 8′1″ × 19′7″ (2.3 × 6.0 m), Brancacci Chapel, Santa Maria del Carmine, Florence. A narrative based on Matthew 17:24–27 is related in a three-part perfectly balanced composition, seemingly illuminated by light coming from the chapel windows. Perspective converges to a point behind Jesus's head, thereby directing the viewer's eyes to Jesus.

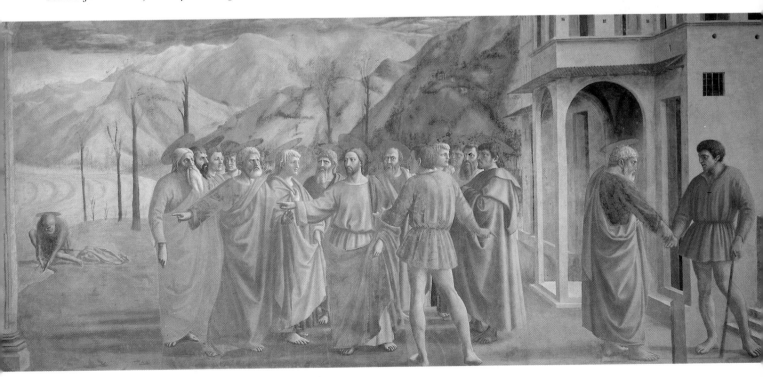

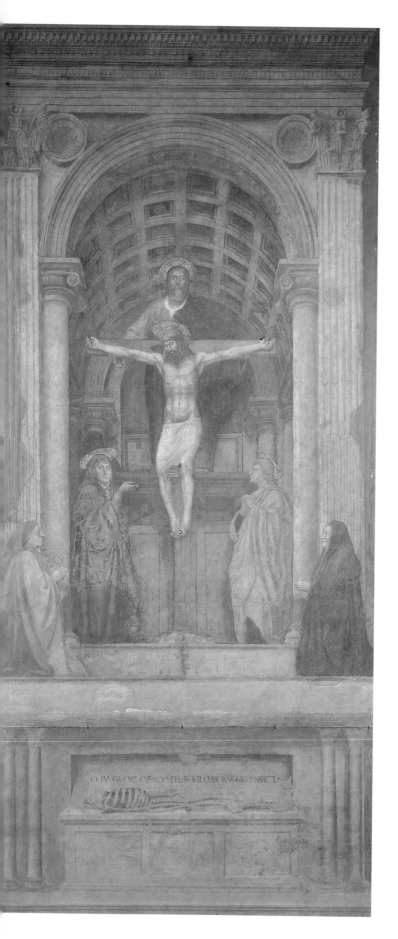

response to the arrival of a Roman tax collector, tells his disciple Peter to look for money in the mouth of a fish. On the left, having removed his cloak, Peter takes the money from the fish. On the right, he gives the money to the tax collector.

Masaccio's figures are harmoniously arranged, the main figure-group placed to the left of center balancing the visually "heavier" group on the far right. As a result, the placement of the figures in the painting seems natural, as if the painter had found the people thus. The entire space is carefully composed by the one-point perspective of the architecture, the vanishing point of which coincides with Jesus's face. The depth of the whole scene is further unified by means of **atmospheric (aerial) perspective**; that is, objects further away from the viewer's eyes appear less distinct, often bluer or cooler in color, and the contrast between light and dark is reduced.

The individual figures seem to stand in real space. The tax collector, in the short tunic, has turned his back to us, standing in a *contrapposto* pose, balanced, relaxed, and natural. When Vasari later wrote that "Masaccio made his figures stand upon their feet," he was praising the naturalism of such poses. The tax collector also echoes our own relationship to the space. We all, viewers and figures alike, look at Jesus. All the faces are individualized, not idealized, and reflect Masaccio's models, real people of the peasant class of Florence. They are also **modeled** far more carefully than in earlier painting—that is, Masaccio's use of light and shadow creates an illusion of three-dimensional, almost sculptural, figures moving in space. They are lit from the right in imitation of reality, since the windows in the Brancacci Chapel are on the right of the fresco.

The bottom part of Masaccio's fresco of the *Trinity with the Virgin, St. John the Evangelist, and Donors* (fig. 13.15), in Santa Maria Novella in Florence, done as early as 1427–28, is painted to look like a real stone funerary monument. The Renaissance interest in lifelike portraiture can be seen in the life-size depictions of the Lenzi family, who commissioned the work. Unlike the anonymous, marginal figures of donors seen in medieval paintings, the members of the Lenzi family have a real presence in the scene. So successful was Masaccio in his use of perspective that the chapel appears to recede into the wall. The architectural setting is drawn in linear perspective, with the vanishing point just below the bottom of the cross, five feet from the floor, which is approximately eye level for the adult viewer. Situated deeper in the space and therefore

Figure 13.15   Masaccio, *Trinity with the Virgin, St. John the Evangelist, and Donors*, probably 1427 or 1428, fresco, 21′ × 10′5″ (6.5 × 3.2 m), Santa Maria Novella, Florence. The architectural setting demonstrates the Early Renaissance interest in the antique and in spatial illusion, while the naturalistic portrayal of the life-size donors indicates the new concern for the individual.

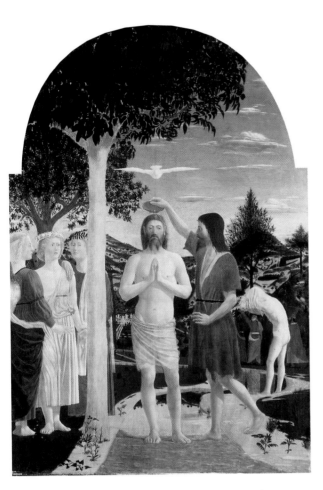

Figure 13.16 Piero della Francesca, *Baptism of Jesus*, 1450s, oil on panel, 5′6″ × 3′9¾″ (1.68 × 1.16 m), National Gallery, London. Piero's sculpturesque figures, seemingly members of a monumental geometricized race, convey a sense of complete calm.

drawn smaller than the Lenzis, Mary and John the Evangelist act as intercessors pleading with Jesus on behalf of humankind. The only figure to defy natural logic is God; for his feet are on the back wall yet he holds the cross in the foreground.

Piero della Francesca. The new perspectival space defined in Masaccio's painting is realized to an even greater degree in the paintings of PIERO DELLA FRANCESCA [pea-AIR-oh del-uh fran-CHES-kah] (ca. 1406/12–1492). Piero believed that perspective in painting was based firmly on geometry, and he put his ideas on mathematical theory and perspective into writing in his *On Painting in Perspective* and his *On the Five Regular Bodies*. According to Piero, mathematics was the key to understanding not only painting, but nature, humankind, and God—the purest manifestation of truth on earth.

Less naturalistic than Masaccio's figures—perhaps because of Piero's insistence on submitting everything, including human anatomy, to the dictates of geometry—

his people are smooth and sturdy rather than graceful. In the *Baptism of Jesus* (fig. 13.16), St. John the Baptist pours baptismal water on Jesus, while three substantial angels stand on the left and a man, next to be baptized, undresses on the right. With their oval heads and cylindrical necks, they convey a stately, noble, and authoritative air, yet they have an austere rigidity. Immobile and without facial expressions, the figures display a sculptural quality enhanced by the pale stony colors that Piero employs.

Piero's geometric precision pervades the entire composition of the *Baptism*. Figures appear in three different sizes, and trees appear in four different sizes, all on four different planes and all created to give the illusion of depth. An excellent observer of nature, Piero not only creates a naturalistic landscape with convincing spatial distance, but he also accurately records the different types of flora found in a cultivated Tuscan landscape. In a highly self-conscious move, he draws attention to the meaning of representation by having the landscape reflected in the water behind Jesus's feet. "What does it mean to reflect the world, to *re-present* the landscape in painting?" Piero might have asked himself. In Neoplatonic terms, it might mean that nature reflects God's truth, and that the act of painting nature can be a reflection of God's truth.

Piero was also deeply interested in portraiture, which is hardly surprising considering the increasingly humanist nature of society, the popularity of humanistic ideas, and the increase in Florentine wealth. His double depiction of Battista Sforza and Federico da Montefeltro (figs. 13.17 and 13.18) shows wife and husband holding their heads motionless, high above the landscape behind them. They are noble, elevated, grand. The profile presentation was especially popular at this time; Roman coins had shown profiles of important figures. Not only does a profile insist on geometry in the composition—the sitter is at a ninety-degree angle to the viewer—but it can reveal the sitter's most distinctive features.

Piero began the portraits in 1472, the year that Countess Battista Sforza died, suggesting that her portrait was made from her death mask. She is shown in the fashion of the times, with her plucked and shaved forehead, her elaborate hairstyle, and sparkling jewels. Count Federico da Montefeltro was ruler of Urbino, which had begun to compete with Florence as an intellectual center. The Count was a gentleman, scholar, bibliophile, and warrior, whose court included humanists, philosophers, poets, and artists. Piero dedicated his book on perspective to him. A profile view was chosen, not only because of fashion but also because the Count had lost his right eye and the bridge of his nose to a sword in a tournament. It is nonetheles with unsparing realism that Piero presents him "warts and all." We can assume that the Countess and Count looked exactly like this, and that Piero faithfully recorded all the peaks and crevices of their facial terrain.

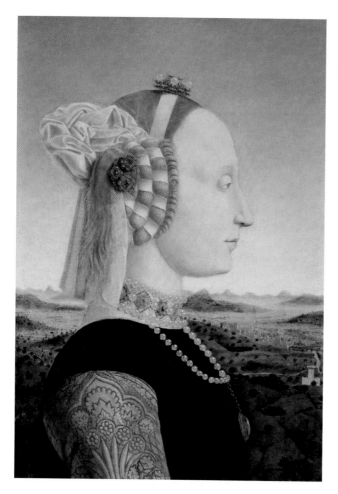

Figure 13.17   Piero della Francesca, *Battista Sforza*, 1472–73, oil on panel, 18½″ × 13″ (47 × 33 cm), Galleria degli Uffizi, Florence. The profile portrait was favored in the Early Renaissance; later the three-quarter view became popular.

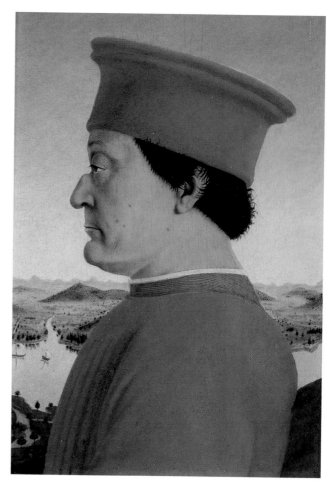

Figure 13.18   Piero della Francesca, *Federico da Montefeltro*, 1472–73, oil on panel, 18½ × 13″ (47 × 33 cm), Galleria degli Uffizi, Florence. In this pair of portraits, wife and husband are recorded with unsparing realism. An accident in combat accounts for the Count's curious profile.

The growing naturalism evident in the work of Masaccio and Piero della Francesca was not, however, the only direction followed by painters in the fifteenth century. In the work of Fra Angelico and Botticelli, many of the artistic conventions of the Middle Ages are perpetuated. For all the emphasis on the individual, on nature, and on lifelike representation, the fifteenth century remained, in its never-ending quest for manifestations of the divine, an idealist age.

Fra Angelico.   Born Guido di Pietro, FRA ANGELICO [FRAH an-JELL-ee-coh] (ca. 1400–1455) was given the name by which we know him now (it means "Angelic Brother") by his brother Dominican monks. The most popular painter in Florence in the first half of the fifteenth century, Fra Angelico was well aware of Masaccio's innovations before the end of his own career, yet he chose not to pursue realistic painting in the way that Masaccio did.

Consider, for instance, his depiction of the *Annunciation* (fig. 13.19), painted between 1438 and 1445 in the monastery of San Marco in Florence, part of a vast project in which Fra Angelico painted the walls of the ground-floor cloister, the small refectory, and the corridors, landings, and cells of the upstairs dormitory with the help of assistants. For all his conservatism, the *Annunciation* was remarkably contemporary. The scene is accurately set within the architecture of San Marco, newly finished by the architect Michelozzo; thus the Annunciation is shown to take place in a specific and contemporary building. The immediacy and conviction of the event were enhanced for the monks who saw the Angel Gabriel and the Virgin Mary in their own monastery.

It would be difficult to create gentler, more graceful gestures than those of Mary and Gabriel in this scene. Both cross their arms in a sign of respect; they refer to Jesus's cross and prefigure his crucifixion. In the garden to the left are accurate depictions of real plants, but Fra

Angelico, in a more medieval fashion, has placed them perfectly, evenly spaced across the ground so that each maintains its separate identity. While the architecture of the space is rendered with typical Early Renaissance respect for the laws of perspective (clearly, the artist learned well from Brunelleschi and Alberti), Fra Angelico has placed his figures in the architectural setting without regard to proper relative scale. If Mary and Gabriel were to stand, they would take over the space like giants, a prospect entirely at odds with their grace. Fra Angelico has followed a convention from medieval painting: his figures possess an emotional importance that transcends the confinement of physical space. By making them larger than life, Fra Angelico affirms, like his medieval forebears, their spiritual essence.

Sandro Botticelli. The spirituality so evident in Fra Angelico's work was also of particular interest to SAN-DRO BOTTICELLI [bott-tee-CHEL-lee] (1445–1510), who received his artistic training as an assistant to

Fra Filippo Lippi, a Renaissance painter who had worked with Fra Angelico.

His *Primavera* (fig. 13.20), painted about 1482, is a complex allegory of spring taken from the Latin writers Horace and Lucretius. It embodies the growing interest in classical literature and pagan mythology of the Neoplatonists of the Florentine Academy. Botticelli was himself a member of this Neoplatonist circle, which also included Lorenzo de' Medici. The *Primavera* was commissioned by Lorenzo di Pierfrancesco de' Medici, a cousin of Lorenzo's, for a chamber next to his bedroom.

Botticelli seems to have been totally unconcerned with the representation of deep space; his orange grove behind functions more like a stage backdrop than an actual landscape. However, Botticelli is, above all, a master of line, and the emphasis of his work is on surface pattern. Neither solid nor three-dimensional, his figures are clearly outlined, and they seem to flow along the rhythmic lines of a dance or procession. The painting moves

Figure 13.19 Fra Angelico, *Annunciation*, 1438–45, fresco, 7'6" × 10'5" (2.29 × 3.18 m), monastery of San Marco, Florence. Fra Angelico cleverly painted the Annunciation as if it were taking place within the actual architecture of the monastery of San Marco.

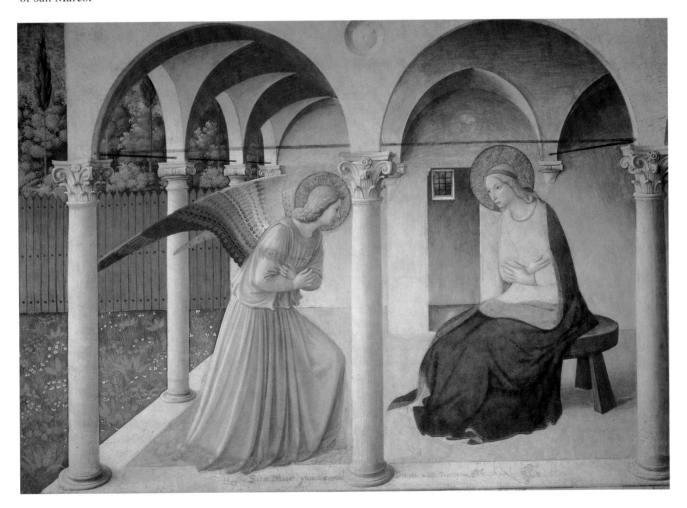

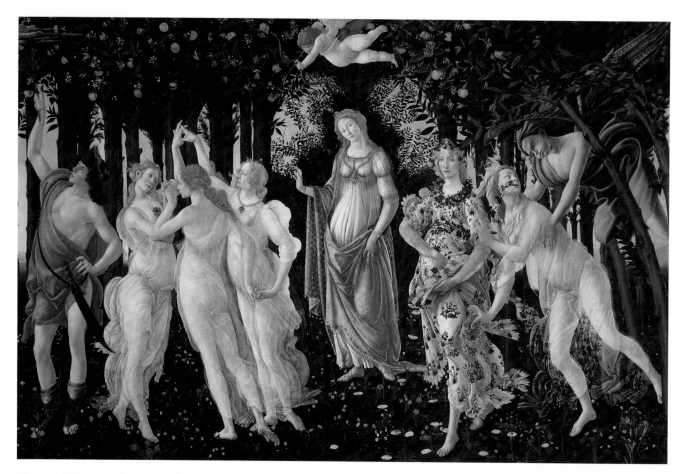

Figure 13.20   Sandro Botticelli, *Primavera*, ca. 1482 (?), tempera on panel, 6'8" × 10'4" (2.03 × 3.15 m), Galleria degli Uffizi, Florence. Neoplatonic theory is given visual form in this allegory, perhaps a depiction of the Floralia, an ancient Roman celebration of spring. It was made for a cousin of Lorenzo de' Medici, ruler of Florence.

from right to left, its figures connected by lines of sight and by a sort of spiral or braid of hands and arms that continually reach to the left, as if blown on the breath of Zephyrus, god of the west wind, shown with his cheeks puffed out on the far right. He seems to want to capture Chloris, the spring nymph, who has a leafy vine coming from her mouth. Beside her is Flora, the goddess of flowers, who is strewing their path with petals. In the middle stands Venus, goddess of love, shown pregnant as a symbol of her fruitfulness in spring. With her, the movement of the scene almost comes to a halt, but she gestures toward the three Graces, as Cupid, above her, shoots an arrow in their direction. The three Graces themselves, daughters of Zeus and the personifications of beauty and charm, twirl and whirl us around, but they too seem to spin to the left where finally Mercury, messenger of the gods, holds up his caduceus, or staff, as if to halt the entire procession as he pushes away the remnants of a vaporous cloud. If Masaccio's figures "stand upon their feet," as Vasari put it, Botticelli's seem to stand upon the air, floating just above ground on the gentle breezes of his painted worlds.

But what are viewers to make of such a complex image? In Neoplatonic terms, Venus, the pagan goddess of beauty, is here the embodiment of Heavenly Love. In allegorical terms, she is a type, or figure, for Mary, who would bear the son of God as a sign of God's love for humankind. Her right hand is bent upward in what scholars have come to recognize as a gesture of welcome, as she invites the viewer to enter her garden. "Primavera," the Italian word for spring, can also be translated as "first truth"; in the birth of nature in spring, we are also witnesses to the birth of truth.

The entire composition, but especially the three Graces, recalls a dance for three people composed by Lorenzo the Magnificent in the 1460s and underscores the close connection of the painter to his patron and to the Neoplatonic circle of the Medici court. Called simply "Venus," Lorenzo's dance is based on the movement of two figures around a third one: "First they do a slow sidestep, and then together they move with two pairs of forward steps, beginning with the left foot; then the middle dancer turns round and across with two reprises, one on the left foot sideways and the other on the right foot, also across; and during the time that the middle dancer is carrying out these reprises the other two go forward with two triplet steps and then give half a turn on the right foot in such a way as to face each other." Thus in the painting Venus, who is, incidentally, dressed in Renaissance costume, oversees a dance that might have taken place in the Medici palace. The music to accompany the dance may have been written by a composer such as Guillaume Dufay. Dufay was hired by Lorenzo to write music for lyrics written in 1467 that might have been one of the "carnival songs" written by Lorenzo himself:

> Fair is youth and free of sorrow,
> Yet how soon its joys we bury!
> Let who would be, now be merry:
> Sure is no one of tomorrow.

The *Primavera* takes its place in this idealized world, a world made possible, practically speaking, by the Medici's wealth and, philosophically speaking, by the Medici's constant support of humanist and Neoplatonic thought.

In Botticelli's *Birth of Venus* (fig. 13.21), of ca. 1484–86, also painted for Lorenzo di Pierfrancesco de' Medici, the birth of Venus is equivalent to the birth of the human soul, as yet uncorrupted by the matter of the world. In Neoplatonic terms, the soul is free to choose for itself whether to follow a path toward sin and degradation or to attempt to regain, through the use of reason, a spiritual perfection manifested in the beauty of creation and felt in the love of God. To love beauty is to love not the material world of sensual things, but rather the world's abstract and spiritual essence. In the *Birth of Venus*, beauty (or the spiritual truth of the soul) is caught between the cold winds of passion, on the left, and the comforting robes of reason, offered by the figure on the right.

Shortly after Florence reached full flower as a cultural center, the city's domination of Italian culture ended. In 1494, a Dominican friar, Girolamo Savonarola, who had lived in the same San Marco convent that Fra Angelico had painted, took control of the city. Savonarola preached to as many as ten thousand people at the cathedral, proclaiming that Florence had condemned itself to perdition. Its painters—artists such as Botticelli—"make the Virgin look like a harlot." The city was populated by prostitutes who were mere "pieces of meat with eyes." "Repent, O Florence," he admonished, "while there is still time." Should Florence reject "the white garments of purification," he threatened that plague, war, and

Figure 13.21   Sandro Botticelli, *Birth of Venus*, ca. 1484–86, tempera on canvas, 6′7″ × 9′2″ (2.01 × 2.79 m), Galleria degli Uffizi, Florence. Botticelli painted this important revival of the nude based upon antique prototypes.

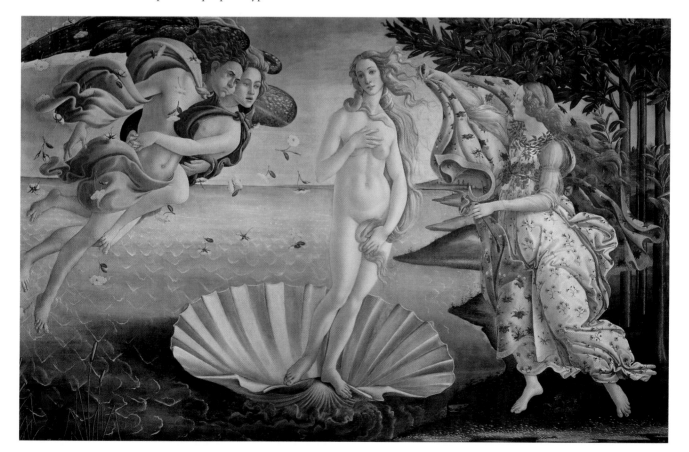

invaders "armed with gigantic razors" would soon follow. A "Bonfire of the Vanities" was built in the Piazza della Signoria, the main square of the city, and on it books, clothing, wigs, make-up, mirrors, false beards, board games, and paintings were burned.

EARLY RENAISSANCE MUSIC

March 15, 1436 was a day of dedication for the completed Florence Cathedral, now crowned by Brunelleschi's extraordinary dome. A procession wound its way through the city's streets and entered the cathedral, led by Pope Eugene IV followed by no fewer than seven cardinals, thirty-six bishops, and untold numbers of church officials, civic leaders, artists, scholars, and musicians. The papal choir included one of the greatest figures in Renaissance music, the composer Guillaume Dufay. The choir performed a motet called "Il Duomo" composed by Dufay especially for the occasion. As one eyewitness recalled, "The whole space of the temple was filled with such choruses of harmony, and such a concert of diverse instruments, that it seemed (not without reason) as though the symphonies and songs of the angels and of divine paradise had been sent forth from Heaven to whisper in our ears an unbelievable celestial sweetness."

Guillaume Dufay.   More than any other composer, GUILLAUME DUFAY [dew-FAY] (1400–1474) shaped the musical language of the Early Renaissance. Born in northern France, Dufay served first as a music teacher for the French court of Burgundy, then as a court composer in Italy, working at various times in Bologna, Florence, and Rome. A musical celebrity, he was often solicited to compose music for solemn occasions, such as the dedication of "Il Duomo."

Dufay wrote music in all the popular genres of his time: masses for liturgies, Latin motets, or compositions for multiple voices, for ceremonies, and French and Italian *chansons*, or songs, for the pleasure of his patrons and friends. In each genre, Dufay provided melodies and rhythms more easily identifiable to the listener than those of earlier composers.

Motets.   Dufay wrote many **motets**: one-movement compositions that set a sacred text to polyphonic choral music, usually with no instrumental accompaniment. Dufay's motet *Alma Redemptoris Mater*, composed in about 1430, fuses medieval **polyphony**—that is, the simultaneous singing of several voices each independent of the others—with a newer Early Renaissance form. Earlier composers typically put the **plainchant** melody, or main melody, in the lowest voice, but Dufay puts the main melody in the highest or uppermost voice, where it can be better heard. He also avoids the rhythmic distortion of medieval composition. The three voices of Dufay's *Alma Redemptoris Mater*—bass, tenor, and soprano—maintain rhythmic independence (also a late medieval characteristic) until the third and last section of the motet. Then Dufay blocks them together in chords to emphasize the text's closing words, which ask Mary to be merciful to sinners; the chords, arranged in graceful harmonies, soothe the listener's ears more than those of the traditional medieval motet. In this last part Dufay adds an additional voice by giving the sopranos two different parts to sing. In doing so, he moves toward the four-part texture of soprano, alto, tenor, and bass that was to become the norm for later Renaissance vocal music.

Word painting.   Dufay's emphasis on the words of his motet for Mary is an early example of what the Renaissance would come to call **word painting**, in which the meaning of words is underscored and emphasized through the music that accompanies them. One sixteenth-century musical theorist, for instance, made the following suggestion to composers: "When one of the words expresses weeping, pain, heartbreak, sighs, tears, and other similar things, let the harmony be full of sadness." A composer might also employ a descending melodic line (going from high to low), or a bass line, to express anguish; conversely, an ascending line (going from low to high), utilizing soprano voices, might express joy and hope. This increasing sense of the drama of language, comparable to the Renaissance artists' attention to the drama of the stories they chose to depict—Donatello's *Mary Magdalene* (see fig. 13.9), for example—led Renaissance composers to use music to enrich the feelings their music expressed, and to support the meaning of a song's text, whether sacred or secular. Though little music had survived from ancient Greece, humanist philosophers like Ficino understood that Aristotle had considered music the highest form of art, and that the rhythms of Greek music imitated the rhythms of Greek poetry, for which it served as a setting. Thus, word painting as the intimate relation of sound and sense has classical roots.

As in the Middle Ages, musicians like Dufay were employed by the churches, towns, and courts. However, unlike music in the Middle Ages, which served mostly religious ends, music in the Renaissance became increasingly secularized. Musicians in the Renaissance still depended upon such patronage, but commissions came from wealthy burghers and aristocrats such as the Medici family, as well as from the Church, which nonetheless remained the staunchest of musical patrons. The secular works commissioned by the nobility were to accompany formal occasions such as coronations, weddings, processions, and even political events. However, before long secular music also found its way into sacred settings. Dufay, for instance, introduced the popular French folksong *"L'Homme armé"* ("The Man in Armor") into a mass, and other composers soon followed suit, creating an entire musical genre known as *chanson masses*, or "song masses."

Connections

MATHEMATICAL PROPORTIONS: BRUNELLESCHI AND DUFAY

Mathematics played an important part in all the arts of the Renaissance. Architects designed buildings guided by mathematical ratios and proportions. Painters employed the mathematical proportions governed by linear perspective. Composers wrote music that reflected mathematical ratios between the notes of a melody and in the intervals between notes sounded together in harmony. Poets structured their poems according to mathematical proportions.

One especially striking set of relationships exists between the proportions of the dome built by Filippo Brunelleschi for Florence Cathedral and "Il Duomo," the motet for four voices that Guillaume Dufay wrote for its dedication in 1436. Its formal title is *Nuper Rosarum Flores* (*Flowers of Roses*), the word *flores* referring to Florence itself. The mathematical ratios in Dufay's motet are evident in its rhythm rather than its melody. The slower-moving lower voices of the two tenors proceed in strict rhythmic progressions that reflect the ratio of 6:4:2:3. The initial ratio of 6:4 is reducible to 3:2; thus, it is a mirror reverse ratio of 3:2:2:3, which appears in the number of beats in each of the work's four sections: 6, 4, 4, and 6. In addition, Dufay's motet contains a total of 168 measures, proportionally divided into four harmonious parts of 56, 56, 28, and 28 measures each. The last two parts contain exactly half the number of measures of the first two, creating a mathematically harmonious and intellectually pleasing structure.

Brunelleschi's dome's proportions exhibit mathematical ratios that are 6:4:2:3, just as in Dufay's motet. This is the ratio of the internal dimensions to the external ones. And motet and dome both have a doubling. Dufay's motet employs a doubling of the tenor voices, which sing the lower melody five notes apart. Brunelleschi's dome is a double shell, having an internal and an external structure.

In these and numerous other instances of Renaissance architecture and music, as well as perspectivist painting, sculptural proportions, and poetry, mathematics lies at the heart of the harmonious nature of the works. This concern with geometric symmetry and mathematical proportions illustrates one more way in which the arts of the Renaissance were a legacy of the golden age of Greece.

Musical accomplishment was one of the marks of an educated person in the Renaissance, and most people associated with the nobility both played an instrument and sang. Moreover, many uneducated people were accomplished musicians; in fact, the music of the uneducated masses—their songs and dances—was most influenced by the secular music of the age. Music was an integral part of an evening's entertainment. While it was common for professionals to provide this entertainment, increasingly individuals at a party might entertain the group. Dance, too, became the focus of social gatherings, and much of the instrumental music of the day was composed to accompany dances.

One final factor that led to the growth and popularity of music during the Renaissance was the rise of music printing. Although by 1455 Gutenberg had perfected the art of printing from movable type, the first collection of music printed in this way, *One Hundred Songs*, was not published until 1501 in Venice by Ottaviano de' Petrucci. Half a century later, printed music was widely available for use by scholars and amateurs alike. With the greater availability of printed scores, Renaissance composers quickly became more familiar with each other's works and increasingly began to influence one another. Amateurs were able to buy and study the same music, and soon songs and dances in particular achieved the kind of widespread popularity that today might put a song into the "Top Ten."

LITERATURE

Petrarch. The first great figure of Italian Renaissance letters as well as the first important representative of Italian Renaissance humanism was Petrarch, a scholar and prolific writer, whose work simultaneously reflects the philosophy of Greek antiquity and the new ideas of the Renaissance. Born Francesco Petrarca in Arezzo and taken, at the age of eight, to Avignon, where the papal courts had moved in 1309, Petrarch studied law in Bologna and Montpellier, then returned in 1326 to Avignon. Petrarch once said of himself, "I am a pilgrim everywhere," for he also traveled widely in France and Italy, hunting down classical manuscripts.

Unlike his Florentine predecessor, Dante Alighieri, whose *Divine Comedy* (see Chapter 12) summed up the sensibility of late medieval culture, Petrarch positioned himself at the beginning of a new literary and artistic era, one that placed greater emphasis on human achievement. Without rejecting the importance of spirituality and religious faith, Petrarch celebrated human accomplishment as the crowning glory of God's creation but gave human beings praise for their achievements as well. With an emphasis on humanity, Petrarch inaugurated a series of intellectual and literary experiments better suited to his psychological interests and humanist aesthetic.

Petrarch's work is poised between two powerful and inextricably intertwined impulses. One is the religious and moral impulse felt by early medieval thinkers such as

St. Augustine; the other is the humanist dedication to the disciplined study of ancient writers, coupled with a striving for artistic excellence.

Petrarch was especially affected by the elegance and beauty of early Latin literature. He disliked, however, the Latin of the Middle Ages, seeing in it a barbarous falling off from the heights of eloquence exemplified by ancient Roman writers such as Virgil, Horace, Ovid, Seneca, and Cicero. Petrarch strove to revive classical literature rather than absorb its elements into contemporary Italian civilization. He considered classical culture a model to be emulated and an ideal against which to measure the achievements of other civilizations. For Petrarch, ancient culture was not merely a source of scientific information, philosophical knowledge, or rhetorical rules; it was also a spiritual and intellectual resource for enriching the human experience. Petrarch would help first Italy, and then Europe, recollect its noble classical past. And although Petrarch did not invent humanism, he breathed life into it and worked tirelessly as its advocate.

Soon after his return to Avignon in 1326, Petrarch fell in love with a woman whose identity is unknown, but whom he called Laura in his *Canzoniere (Songbook)*. This is a collection of 366 poems in various forms—sonnets, ballads, sestinas, madrigals, and *canzoni* (songs)—which Petrarch wrote and reworked over a period of more than forty years. The poems, many of which are about love, are notable for their stylistic elegance and their formal perfection. Those about Laura are the most beautiful and the most famous. These poems fanned the flames of a passion for Petrarch that would last throughout the Renaissance and beyond, which spawned a profusion of verses written in imitation of him, borrowing situations, psychological descriptions, imagery and other forms of figurative language, and particularly the sonnet form Petrarch devised.

The Petrarchan Sonnet. Thematically, Petrarch's sonnets introduced what was to become one of the predominant subjects of Renaissance lyric poetry: the expression of a speaker's love for a woman and his experience of the joy and pain of love's complex and shifting emotional states. Laura's beauty and behavior cause the poet/speaker to sway between hope and despair, pleasure and pain, joy and anguish. Throughout the sequence of poems, Laura remains unattainable. Like so many figures in Renaissance painting, she is at once a real person and an ideal form, a contradiction expressed in the sometimes ambivalent feelings the poet/speaker has about her.

As an extended sequence, Petrarch's sonnets inspired poets throughout Europe to write their own sonnet sequences. The most famous examples in English are Philip Sidney's *Astrophel and Stella* (1591), Edmund Spenser's *Amoretti* (1595), and William Shakespeare's 154 sonnets. Petrarch's sonnet structure established itself as one of the two dominant sonnet patterns used by poets.

The Petrarchan (sometimes called the Italian) sonnet is organized in two parts: an octave of eight lines and a sestet of six. The octave typically identifies a problem or situation, and the sestet proposes a solution; or the octave introduces a scene, and the sestet comments on or complicates it. The rhyme scheme of the Petrarchan sonnet reinforces its logical structure, with different rhymes occurring in octave and sestet. The octave rhymes *abba abba* (or *abab abab*), and the sestet rhymes *cde cde* (or *cde ced; cde dce;* or *cd, cd, cd*).

The following sonnet was the most popular poem in the European Renaissance; it depicts the lover's ambivalence in a series of paradoxes or apparent contradictions.

> I find no peace and all my war is done,
> I fear and hope, I burn and freeze like ice;
> I fly above the wind yet can I not arise,
> And nought I have and all the world I sesan.°
> That loseth nor locketh holdeth me in prison   *5*
> And holdeth me not, yet can I escape nowise;
> Nor letteth me live nor die at my devise,
> And yet of death it giveth me occasion.
> Without eyes, I see, and without tongue I plain,°
> I desire to perish, and yet I ask health,   *10*
> I love an other, and thus I hate my self,
> I feed me in sorrow and laugh in all my pain,
> Likewise displeaseth me both death and life,
> And my delight is cause of this strife.

⁴ *sesan:* seize.   ⁹ *plain:* complain.

THE HIGH RENAISSANCE

FRA SAVONAROLA AND THE FLORENTINES

When Fra Savonarola warned the Florentines that if they did not mend their ways invaders "armed with gigantic razors" would soon descend upon them, his promise was not as far-fetched as it might have seemed. Just to the north, in the Po valley, as early as 1487 Leonardo da Vinci had designed an instrument of destruction for the Duke of Milan. Leonardo's scythed chariot was designed to cut down armies, and his "armored car" (fig. 13. 22), when powered by eight men inside, could "take the place of elephants" in battle. Leonardo promised, "There is no host of armed men so great that they would not be broken by them." However, before Leonardo went to Milan, he made his reputation as a painter.

PAINTING

Leonardo da Vinci. Born in Vinci, about twenty miles west of Florence, LEONARDO DA VINCI [lay-o-NAR-doh dah VIN-chee] (1452–1519) was the illegitimate son of a peasant named Caterina and Ser Piero, a Florentine lawyer or notary with a house in Vinci.

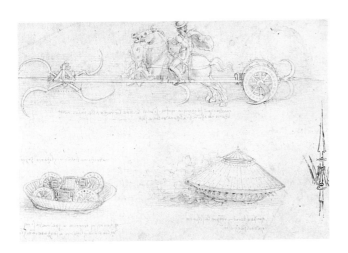

Figure 13.22 Leonardo da Vinci, *A Scythed Chariot, Armored Car, and Pike*, ca. 1487, pen and ink and wash, $6\frac{3}{4} \times 9\frac{3}{4}"$ (17.1 × 24.8 cm), British Museum, London. Leonardo's interest in defensive devices is indicative of the frequent wars in Italy.

Leonardo later joined his father in Florence, and in 1469 he entered the workshop of Andrea del Verrocchio, whose other apprentices included Sandro Botticelli. Giorgio Vasari wrote of Leonardo's "beauty as a person," describing him as "divinely endowed" and "so pleasing in conversation that he won all hearts." But he was, Vasari noted, unstable in temperament, often abandoning projects, constantly searching and restless.

Leonardo was sent to Milan by Lorenzo the Magnificent in 1481 or 1482 as an ambassador, charged with presenting an ornate lyre to the Duke, Ludovico Sforza, as a gesture of peace. Leonardo chose to remain in Milan. In Florence, Leonardo had been known as a painter and sculptor, but he was, he explained to the Duke, primarily a designer of military and naval weaponry and only secondarily an architect, painter, drainage engineer, and sculptor capable of creating a giant bronze horse that Ludovico planned as a memorial to his father. He was, in short, the epitome of what we have come to call the "Renaissance" or "universal man," a person not merely capable but talented in an extraordinarily wide range of endeavors.

Although Leonardo was, by any standard, a Renaissance man, he did not share the Florentine taste for classical humanist scholarship, avoiding philosophy and literature. Rather, he was a student of nature amply evidenced in his *Madonna of the Rocks* (fig. 13.23), begun in 1483, soon after his arrival in Milan. The flowers and plants are minute observations from nature. The geology—cliffs, mountains, and a grotto filled with stalactites and stalagmites—comes out of his lifelong fascination with the effects of wind and water on the environment. Hurricanes and deluges particularly intrigued him, as did the eddies and currents of moving water. The *Madonna of the Rocks* makes evident his preoccupation

with the interrelated effects of perspective, light, color, and optics. The naturalistic lighting and atmospheric perspective developed earlier by Masaccio are taken to new heights. In fact, in his *Notebooks* Leonardo would refine the art of modeling the figure in light and dark developed by Masaccio and codify rules for atmospheric perspective (here, the haze that envelops objects in the distance diminishes the clarity of form and color).

Chiaroscuro is the term used to describe Leonardo's modeling technique. In Italian, *chiaro* means "clear" or "light," and *oscuro* means "obscure," or "dark." Chiaroscuro describes the subtle shift from light to dark across a rounded surface. In Leonardo's hands, the technique was used to achieve an extraordinary sense of sculptural dimensionality as well as a powerful emotion-

Figure 13.23 Leonardo da Vinci, *Madonna of the Rocks*, begun 1483, oil on panel, transferred to canvas, $6'6\frac{1}{2}" \times 4'$ (2.0 × 1.2 m), Musée du Louvre, Paris. Leonardo, artist and scientist, created a grotto setting with stalactites, stalagmites, and identifiable foliage, an unusual environment for these religious figures.

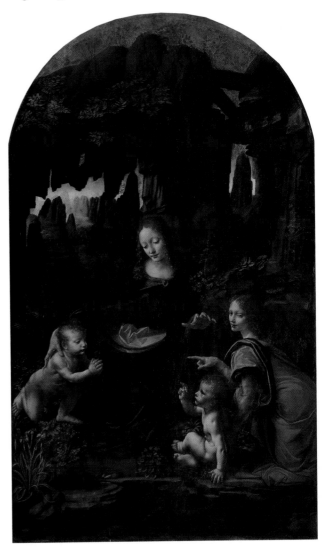

al impact. In the *Madonna of the Rocks*, the child Jesus blesses his cousin John (the infant John the Baptist) who represents the congregation of Christians, literally protected by Mary's cloak but figuratively taken under her all-loving wing. Compositionally, Leonardo has taken a traditional triangular grouping and extended it into three dimensions, making a pyramid. Each figure seems to possess real psychological depth, from the tranquillity and calm of Mary to the seriousness of purpose etched in the infant John's brow. Leonardo's ability to render subtle aspects of human expression, remarkable in itself and the result of a careful study of human nature, is increased by his use not only of chiaroscuro and atmospheric perspective but also of **sfumato** (in Italian, "smoky"). *Sfumato* is the intentional suppression of the outline of a figure in a hazy, almost smoky atmosphere. Leonardo's figures do not so much emerge from the darkness of the grotto, as they are immersed in it, surrounded by it, even protected by it, as if the grotto were the womb of the earth itself and Mary the site's resident mother goddess.

Leonardo's greatest achievement in Milan, however, was *The Last Supper* (fig. 13.24), a huge mural located in the refectory of Santa Maria delle Grazie, before which resident monks would themselves take their supper. Painted between 1495 and 1498, it is a painting of supreme physical delicacy. Leonardo, always experimenting, created a new fresco technique, painting on dry plaster with a combination of oil and tempera in order to lengthen the drying time and achieve more naturalistic effects. Even before he finished, moisture crept behind the paint, causing it to flake off the wall. Subjected to years of dirt and smoke, to say nothing of previously botched restoration efforts and bombing in World War II, the deterioration continued virtually unabated until 1977, when a painstaking restoration process began.

The composition of *The Last Supper* clarifies the painting's meaning. The largest of the three windows on the back wall is directly behind Jesus, thereby emphasizing him. The curved pediment, which arches above his head, serves as a halo. He is perfectly centered in the mural, and all perspective lines converge toward a vanishing point directly behind his head, thereby directing the viewer's eyes to him. The twelve apostles are arranged six on each side, divided into four groups of three figures. The result is a composition that is almost perfectly balanced symmetrically around the central figure of Jesus, whose arms are extended diagonally to the right and left in such a way that he himself forms an equilateral triangle. The arrangement of the five segments is theatrical—action comes from the wings but Jesus remains calm in the center.

Leonardo chose the most psychologically powerful moment in the story: Jesus has just announced that one of his apostles will betray him, and they respond in unison, "exceedingly sorrowful, and [begin] every one of them to say unto him, Lord is it I?" (Matt. 21:22). Judas, his betrayer, sits between John and Peter directly to the left of Jesus, his face lost in shadow as he leans away,

---

Figure 13.24   Leonardo da Vinci, *The Last Supper*, 1495–98, tempera and oil on plaster, 15′2″ × 28′10″ (4.60 × 8.80 m), refectory, Santa Maria delle Grazie, Milan. The mural's poor condition is due to the experimental media in which Leonardo painted. Nevertheless, his ability to merge form and content, using perspective to simultaneously create an illusion of a cubic space and focus the viewer's attention on Jesus, can still be appreciated.

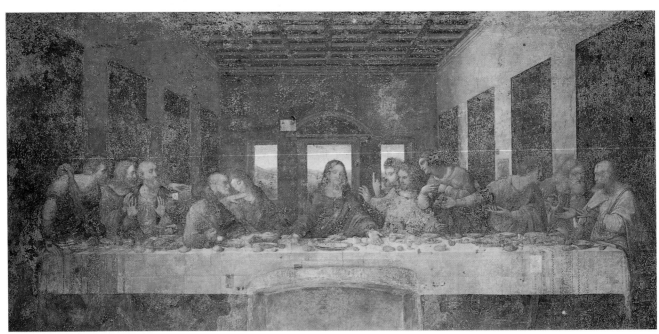

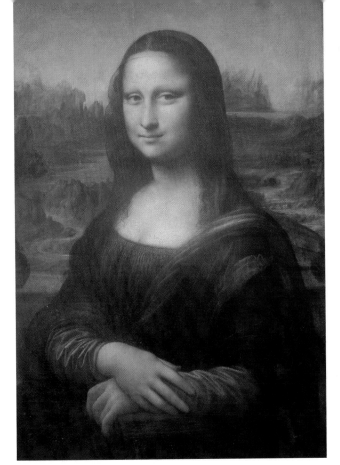

Figure 13.25   Leonardo da Vinci, *Mona Lisa*, ca. 1503, oil on panel, 2′6¼″ × 1′9″ (76.8 × 53.3 cm), Musée du Louvre, Paris. Probably the most famous painting in the world, Mona Lisa's mysterious smile continues to intrigue viewers today.

clutching a money bag in his right hand. We know from preparatory sketches that Leonardo wanted to depict a different emotion on each of the apostles' faces. The most difficult thing to paint, Leonardo said, was "the intention of Man's soul." It could only be shown by pose, facial expression, and surrounding events and figures. Judas and Jesus, apparently, gave him the most difficulty. Vasari tells the story:

> The prior [of Santa Maria delle Grazie] was in a great hurry to see the picture done. He could not understand why Leonardo would sometimes remain before his work half a day together, absorbed in thought … [Leonardo] made it clear that men of genius are sometimes producing most when they seem least to labor, for their minds are then occupied in the shaping of those conceptions to which they afterward give form. He told the duke [Sforza, under whose protection the monastery was] that two heads were yet to be done: that of the Savior, the likeness of which he could not hope to find on earth and … the other, of Judas … As a last resort he could always use the head of that troublesome and impertinent prior.

Leonardo solved his problem with Judas by grouping him with Peter and John. "I say," Leonardo explained in his *Notebooks*, "that in narratives it is necessary to mix closely together direct contraries, because they provide a

great contrast with each other, and so much more if they are adjacent, that is to say the ugly to the beautiful."

Sometime in 1503, after Leonardo had been forced to return to Florence, he painted the famous *Mona Lisa* (fig. 13.25), a portrait of Lisa di Antonio Maria Gherardini, the twenty-four-year-old wife of a Florentine official, Francesco del Gioconda—hence the painting is sometimes called *La Gioconda*. Compared to Piero della Francesca's rigid portrait of Battista Sforza (see fig. 13.17), Mona Lisa appears relaxed and natural. While Piero presented his sitter in a bust-length profile, Leonardo shows a half-length three-quarter view. With this pose, Leonardo established a type, which has the hands showing—for Leonardo, emotion could be read in the disposition of a figure's hands—and the figure itself set against a landscape. Probably no other painting in history has so successfully conveyed psychological depth and mystery to generation after generation of viewers. It is as if Leonardo has captured in Mona Lisa's face the extraordinary range of Nature's moods depicted in the landscape behind her.

Just before October 1503, Leonardo was commissioned by Florence's new republican government to paint a mural celebrating the Florentine past for the new Council Chamber in the Palazzo Vecchio. He chose the Battle of Anghiari, a great Florentine military victory. By 1505 he had "commenced coloring." Leonardo never finished the *Battle of Anghiari*, though he did a portion, the "Fight for the Standard," which unfortunately has not survived. However, a chalk and pen rendering of this section, done by the Flemish painter Peter Paul Rubens, does (fig. 13.26).

Figure 13.26   Peter Paul Rubens, copy of Leonardo's *Battle of Anghiari*, ca. 1603, chalk worked over with pen and bodycolor, 17¾ × 25″ (45.2 × 63.5 cm), Musée du Louvre, Paris. There is some evidence that Leonardo's *Battle of Anghiari* was, like his *Last Supper*, painted in an experimental technique. He may well have abandoned the project due to technical problems.

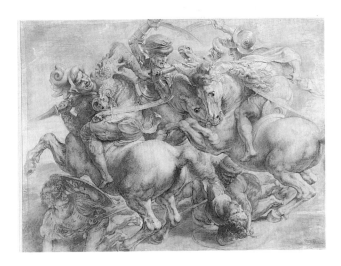

In 1504, while Leonardo was busy preparing the mural and doing sketches, another Florentine artist was working in the Council Chamber—Michelangelo, twenty-three years his junior and fresh from the success of his monumental *David* (see fig. 13.32). He was painting the *Battle of Cascina* (now also known only in a copy of a portion of this composition). It was an unofficial competition to see who was the greatest painter—as exciting a competition as the one Ghiberti and Brunelleschi had engaged in a century earlier. By the end of the summer, a young artist named Raphael, only twenty-one years of age, had arrived in Florence to watch the artists work. With these three masters in Florence—two established masters and one promisingly talented student—the "High" Renaissance was in full swing.

THE REINVENTION OF ROME

It was not in Florence, however, but in a reborn Rome that the Italian high Renaissance came to fruition. By the middle of the fifteenth century, after the papacy had moved to Avignon in 1309, Rome lay in a sorry state of disrepair. When Pope Nicholas V returned the papacy to Rome in 1447, all that changed. Pope Nicholas V had close ties to the Florentine humanist tradition, and accompanying him upon his return to Rome was none other than Leon Battista Alberti. Alberti roamed though the ancient ruins of the city, creating as he went his massive survey of classical architecture, *De re aedificatoria*. With Alberti as his chief consultant, Nicholas began rebuilding Rome's ancient churches and initiated plans to remake the Vatican as a new sacred city. Nicholas also began assembling a massive classical library, paying humanist scholars to translate ancient Greek texts into Latin and Italian.

Pope Sixtus IV. The Vatican library would become one of the chief preoccupations of Pope Sixtus IV (reigned 1471–83). With his appointment of Platina as its head, the Vatican library established rules for usage, a permanent location, and an effective, permanent administration. It became a true "Vatican," or "public," library. Platina's appointment is celebrated in a fresco painted by Melozzo da Forlì for the library (fig. 13.27). The Latin couplets below the scene, written by Platina himself, outline Sixtus's campaign to restore the city of Rome, rebuilding churches, streets, walls, bridges, and aqueducts, but praise Sixtus IV most of all for the creation of the library. By 1508, the Vatican Library was said to be the "image" of Plato's Academy. Athens had been reborn in Rome.

As the city was rebuilt and archaeological discoveries made, its reinvented role was as the classical center of learning and art. Sixtus immediately established a museum in 1474 to house the recently uncovered Etruscan bronze statue of the she-wolf that had nourished Romulus and Remus, the mythical twin founders of the city (see Chapter 5). Other discoveries followed: *Spinario*, a Hellenistic bronze of a youth pulling a thorn from his

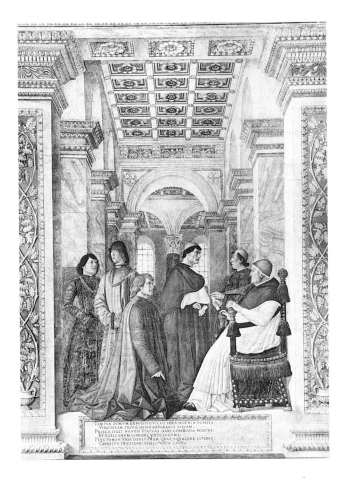

Figure 13.27 Melozzo da Forlì, *Sixtus IV Appoints Platina Head of the Vatican Library*, 1480–81, fresco, 13′1″ × 10′4″ (3.99 × 3.15 m), Pinacoteca Vaticana, Rome. Platina kneels before Pope Sixtus IV while the Pope's nephews stand behind. In the middle is Cardinal Giuliano della Rovere, later Pope Julius II.

foot; *Hercules*, the life-size bronze discovered in the ruined temple of Hercules in the Forum Boarium; and two antique marble river gods that came from the ruins of the Constantinian baths.

The New Vatican. Executing Pope Nicholas's plans for a new Vatican palace, Sixtus IV commissioned the Sistine Chapel, which he named after himself, and inaugurated plans for its decoration. Perugino and Botticelli, among others, painted frescoes for the Chapel's walls, which were completed in 1482. But it was not until Sixtus's nephew, Pope Julius II (reigned 1503–13), took control of the Vatican that Pope Sixtus's plans would finally be realized. Classical sculpture was placed in the sloping gardens: the *Apollo Belvedere*, which had been discovered during excavations, and the *Laocoön* (see Chapter 4), discovered buried in the ruins of some Roman baths.

Famous composers were hired to write new hymns. Josquin des Près would serve in the small sixteen- to

Timeline 13.2 The New Rome: works commissioned by the Popes.

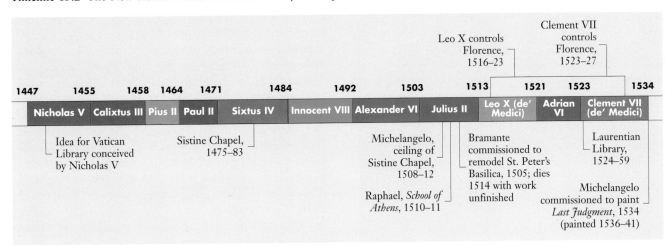

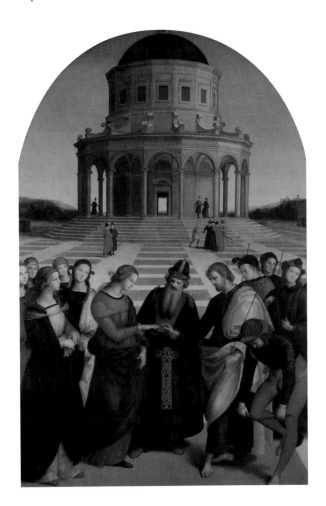

Figure 13.28 Raphael, *Marriage of the Virgin*, 1504, oil on panel, 5′7″ × 3′10½″ (1.70 × 1.18 m), Brera Gallery, Milan. Raphael's carefully composed scene includes figures in the foreground, middleground, and background. The lines of perspective lead to a central plan building (the type favored by Bramante), while the marriage is shown taking place in the foreground, dividing the composition.

twenty-four-member *Sistina Cappella*, or Sistine Choir, from 1476 to 1484. Soon the rough rhythms of medieval poetry were supplanted by the softer, finer meter of the Horatian odes. To add to the pomp of the liturgical processions, Julius established a large chorus to perform exclusively in St. Peter's, the *Cappella Giulia*, or Julian Choir, which remains active to this day. And, most important of all, Julius invited Raphael and Michelangelo to work in Rome.

PAINTING AND SCULPTURE

Raphael. When RAPHAEL [RAFF-ay-el], born Raffaello Santi of Urbino (1483–1520), was invited to Rome by Julius II in 1508, he was not yet twenty-five years old, but his renown as a painter was already well established. He had grown up surrounded by culture and beauty. He studied painting under his father, Giovanni Santi, a painter for the dukes of Urbino. In Perugia he studied with Perugino, who in 1482 had painted *Christ Delivering the Keys of the Kingdom to St. Peter* for Sixtus IV in the Sistine Chapel.

One of Raphael's first major works is directly indebted to Perugino's *Christ Delivering the Keys*. It is the *Marriage of the Virgin* (fig. 13.28), signed and dated in 1504, the year he came to Florence. As in Perugino's work, the composition is divided into a foreground with large figures, a middleground of open space with smaller figures, and a background with a temple and tiny figures. In the foreground, Mary and Joseph wed. The story says that Joseph, although older than the many other suitors, was selected because, among all the symbolic rods presented her, his alone flowered. Beside him a disgruntled suitor snaps his own rod in half over his knee. The absence of facial expression is a stylistic habit derived from Perugino, which Raphael would soon discard under the influence of Leonardo and Michelangelo. Everything in Raphael's painting is

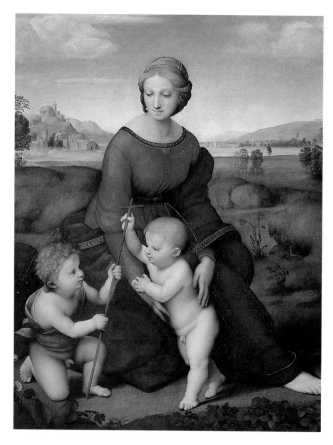

Figure 13.29   Raphael, *Madonna of the Meadows*, 1505, oil on panel, $44\frac{1}{2}'' \times 34\frac{1}{4}''$ (113 × 87 cm), Kunsthistorisches Museum, Vienna. Often considered the epitome of High Renaissance painters, Raphael was celebrated for his ability to arrange several figures into compact units. Mary, Jesus, and John the Baptist form a pyramid, a favorite Renaissance compositional device.

measured and rendered in careful perspective, as is emphasized in the pattern of rectangles that cross the square. In fact, so powerful is the perspective grid that the viewer's eyes are led away from the marriage in the foreground to the temple behind, and the viewer is left to wonder why, given the deliberateness of this grid.

Raphael became particularly famous for his many paintings of the Madonna and Child. His *Madonna of the Meadows (Belevédere)* (fig. 13.29), painted in 1505, displays the type of Madonna he repeated and perfected—pale, sweet, and serious. She is meditative, thinking ahead to Christ's passion, prefigured by the cross offered by the infant St. John, who in turn is identified by the camel-hair garment he would wear as an adult. Mary shows maternal tenderness in the gentle but firm hold she has taken of Jesus, as if to ward off what she knows will one day occur. In most Early Renaissance depictions of this subject, the Madonna is usually elevated on a throne. Raphael's Madonna has descended to our earthly level; she even sits upon the ground—in this pose she is referred to as the "Madonna of Humility." The differences between the

sacred and the secular are minimized—even the figures' halos have become thin gold bands.

A master of composition, Raphael contrasts the curved and rounded shapes of his figures with their triangular and pyramidal positions in space. The rounded lines create a sense of serenity, smoothness, and grace. The triangular format recalls that of Leonardo's *Madonna of the Rocks* (fig. 13.23), but the difference between the dark grotto setting of Leonardo's painting and Raphael's pastoral countryside is instructive. Raphael's composition is simpler, possessing far less contrast between light and dark. His figures are more tightly grouped: Jesus and John almost touch in Raphael's painting; in Leonardo's a great deal of space lies between them. Leonardo's children have serious facial expressions, lending them the emotional complexity of adults; Raphael's are far more playful.

Soon after Raphael arrived in Rome in 1508, Julius II commissioned him to paint several rooms in the Vatican Palace, including the Stanza della Segnatura, the room where papal documents were signed. The subjects, determined by Julius II, were to express Neoplatonic ideas in the four areas of learning:

Law and Justice: represented by the *Cardinal Virtues*
The Arts: represented by *Mount Parnassus*
Theology: represented by the *Dispute over the Sacrament* (which is the revelation of Divine Truth)
Philosophy: represented by the *School of Athens*

Each of these works is extremely complex. The *School of Athens* (fig. 13.30), in fact, could be said to embody, in its entirety, the Renaissance humanist's quest for classical learning and truth.

In the center of this bilaterally symmetrical composition are the ancient Greek philosophers, Plato and Aristotle. The figure of Plato, which might be a portrait of Leonardo da Vinci, holds Plato's *Timaeus* and points upward, indicating the realm of his ideal Forms. Aristotle holds his book *Ethics* and points toward earth, indicating his emphasis on material reality. The scene includes representations of Diogenes, sprawling on the steps in front of the philosophers; Pythagoras, calculating on a slate at the lower left; Ptolemy, holding a globe at the right; and Euclid in front of him, inscribing a slate with a compass. Raphael has painted his own portrait, the second figure from the right, looking at us. Pope Julius had made Raphael "prefect of antiquities," in charge of the papal excavation and preservation of antiques. Perhaps because of this, the setting is based on the ancient Roman baths and has the classical statues of Apollo (god of sunlight, rationality, and poetry) and Minerva (goddess of wisdom).

Michelangelo.   In his *Lives of the Most Eminent Painters, Sculptors, and Architects*, Vasari describes how the architect Bramante let Raphael in to see Michelangelo's frescoes on the ceiling of the Sistine Chapel shortly after

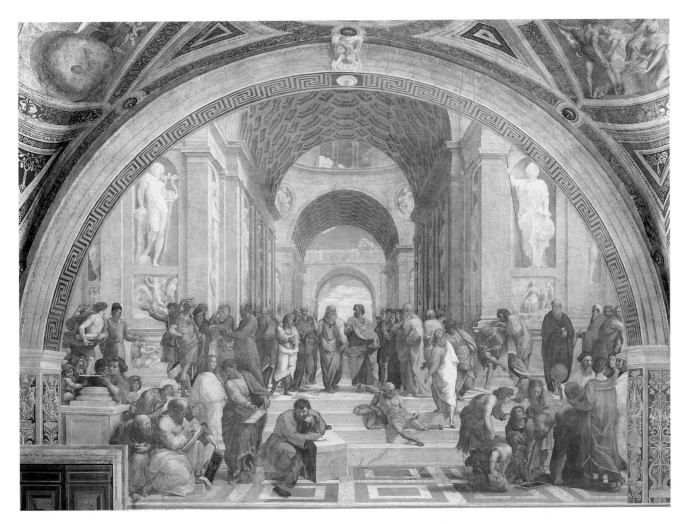

Figure 13.30 Raphael, *School of Athens*, 1510–11, fresco, 19 × 27′ (5.79 × 8.24 m), Stanza della Segnatura, Vatican, Rome. Raphael painted several rooms in the Vatican for Pope Julius II, a great patron of the arts. Statues of Apollo and Minerva flank Plato and Aristotle, shown surrounded by scientists and philosophers of antiquity, some of whom have been given the facial features of Raphael's contemporaries.

Raphael's arrival in Rome, saying, "He profited so greatly by what he had seen in the work of Michelangelo that his manner was inexpressibly enlarged and received henceforth an obvious increase in majesty." In fact, Raphael gave Michelangelo a central place in the *School of Athens*: he is the solitary, brooding figure in the foreground leaning on a block of marble while sketching.

It was as a sculptor that MICHELANGELO BUONARROTI [my-kuhl-AN-gel-oh] (1475–1564) first achieved fame. When he signed the ceiling of the Sistine Chapel in 1511, he obstinately inscribed "Michelangelo, Sculptor." Born near Florence, he lived as a child in the Palazzo Medici, which served not only as Lorenzo the Magnificent's home but also as an art school, and there he studied sculpture under Giovanni Bertoldo, once a student of Donatello. In Lorenzo's palace, bursting with Neoplatonic and humanist ideas, Michelangelo was nurtured on the virtues of antique classical sculpture. Nevertheless, his skill as a draftsman was notable from the first. According to Vasari, he "copied drawings of the old masters so perfectly that his copies could not be distinguished from the originals, since he smoked and tinted the paper to give it the appearance of age. He was often able to keep the originals and return his copies in their stead." His skill at painting was also not to be dismissed. As a boy, in Florence, he studied fresco painting under Domenico del Ghirlandaio and routinely copied the frescoes by Giotto in Santa Croce and those by Masaccio in Santa Maria del Carmine. He was, like so many Renaissance artists, skilled in many areas—painting, architecture, poetry—but always in his own mind he was a sculptor.

His approach to sculpture was based on the belief that the figure is imprisoned within the block in the same way that the soul is trapped within the body. In fact, to release the figure from the marble was a matter of subtraction, as the sculptor chiseled away the shell of stone that hid the figure within. Michelangelo's approach to his craft was, in short, profoundly Neoplatonic; sculpture, from his point of view, both revealed and liberated the human ideal, as the first stanza of the following poem by him suggests:

> Even the best of artists can conceive no idea
> That a single block of marble will not contain
> In its excess, and such a goal is achieved
> Only by the hand that obeys the intellect.
>
> The evil which I flee and the good I promise myself   5
> Hides in you, my fair, proud, and divine lady;
> And working against my very life,
> My skill is contrary to my purpose.
>
> My ill cannot be blamed upon your beauty,
> Your harshness, bad fortune, or your disdain,   10
> Nor upon my destiny or my fate,
>
> If in your heart you bear both death and mercy
> At the same time, and if my lowly talent
> Ardently burning, can draw forth only death.

Unlike Leonardo, who believed that beauty was found in nature, Michelangelo believed that beauty was found in the imagination, and it is the power of the

Figure 13.31   Michelangelo, *Pietà*, 1498/99–1500, marble, height 5′8½″ (1.70 m), St. Peter's, Vatican, Rome. "Pietà" refers to the depiction of Mary mourning over Jesus lying across her lap. Although the subject was developed in Gothic Germany, the most famous *Pietà* is surely Michelangelo's version.

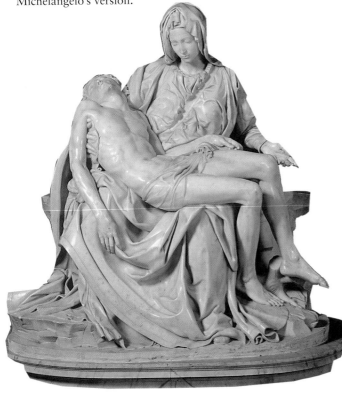

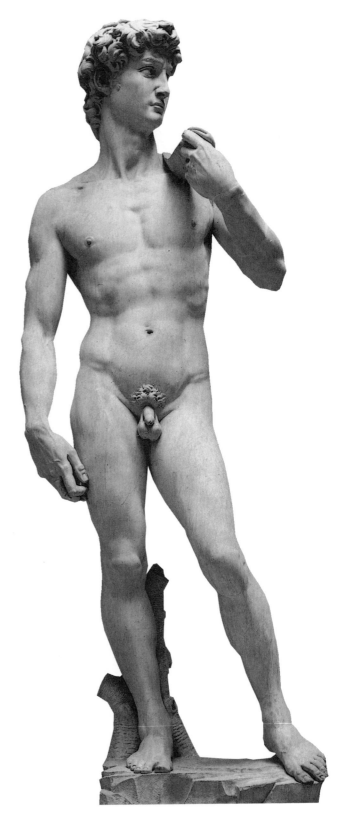

Figure 13.32   Michelangelo, *David*, 1501–04, marble, height 13′5″ (4.09 m), Galleria dell'Accademia, Florence. A magnificent marble man, akin to the heroic nudes of antiquity and undated by costume, David becomes a universal symbol of the individual facing unseen conflict.

human imagination that his sculptures constantly evoke. One of his earliest and most celebrated sculptures is a *Pietà* (fig. 13.31), which literally means "pity." The term refers to depictions of the Virgin Mary mourning over the dead Jesus in her lap. Commissioned by a French cardinal as a tomb monument in Old St. Peter's in the Vatican, his *Pietà* would be, Michelangelo bragged, "the most beautiful work in marble that exists today in Rome." In order to heighten the viewer's feelings of pity and sorrow, Michelangelo has made the figure of Jesus disproportionately small in comparison to the monumental figure of Mary. Mary is, furthermore, a young woman here, despite the fact that Jesus died as a grown man of thirty-three. The implication is that Mary thinks back to when Jesus was not dead in her lap but an infant cradled there, adding to the poignancy.

Just before being called to Rome by Pope Julius II, Michelangelo carved what is perhaps his most famous sculpture, the enormous *David* (fig. 13.32), made between 1501 and 1504. Intended as a decoration for Florence Cathedral, its huge scale—it is over 13 feet tall—comes from the fact that it was intended to stand 40 feet above the ground on a buttress. It was carved from block of marble that had been quarried forty years earlier, a block so cracked that earlier sculptors, including Leonardo, when offered the opportunity to work on the stone, refused. Michelangelo saw in the block a

potential others had been blind to. Once it had been carved, the city fathers designated it a "masterpiece," too good to be placed on top of the cathedral; instead it was placed in front of the Palazzo Vecchio in the Piazza della Signoria. There, in the square where political meetings took place, it would symbolize not only freedom of speech, but the Republic of Florence itself, free from foreigners, papal domination, and Medici rule. (The Medici had been exiled in 1494.)

The *David*'s pose is taken from antiquity, with the weight on one leg in the *contrapposto*, or counterpoise, position. The sculptor's virtuosity is most evidenced in David's tightly muscled form, his tendons and veins recorded. A sense of enormous pent-up energy emerges, of latent power about to explode, and the question seems to be less *if* he will move than *when*. Above all, physical potentiality is mirrored in his confident, focused expression. The Greek respect for the athlete is rekindled in Renaissance terms—this is a mind in control of its body, a body poised to do precisely what it is told.

Michelangelo was called to Rome in 1505 to create the monumental tomb of Pope Julius II. The project was halted by Julius himself soon after Michelangelo's arrival when the Pope decided that finishing the painting of the Sistine Chapel, a project initiated by his predecessor Sixtus IV, should take priority. Michelangelo is reputed

Figure 13.33 Michelangelo, *Creation of Adam*, 1511–12, fresco, 9′2″ × 18′8″ (2.79 × 5.69 m), detail of Sistine Chapel ceiling, Vatican, Rome. Adam's enormous latent power will be released in the next instant when swift-moving God, with Eve already under his arm, brings him to life.

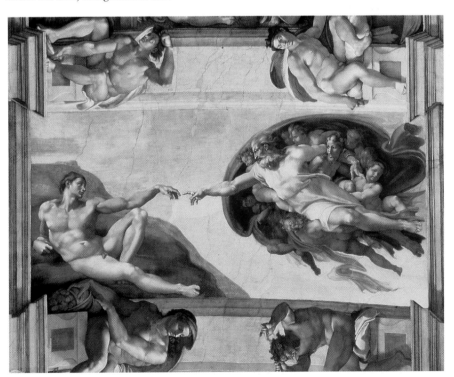

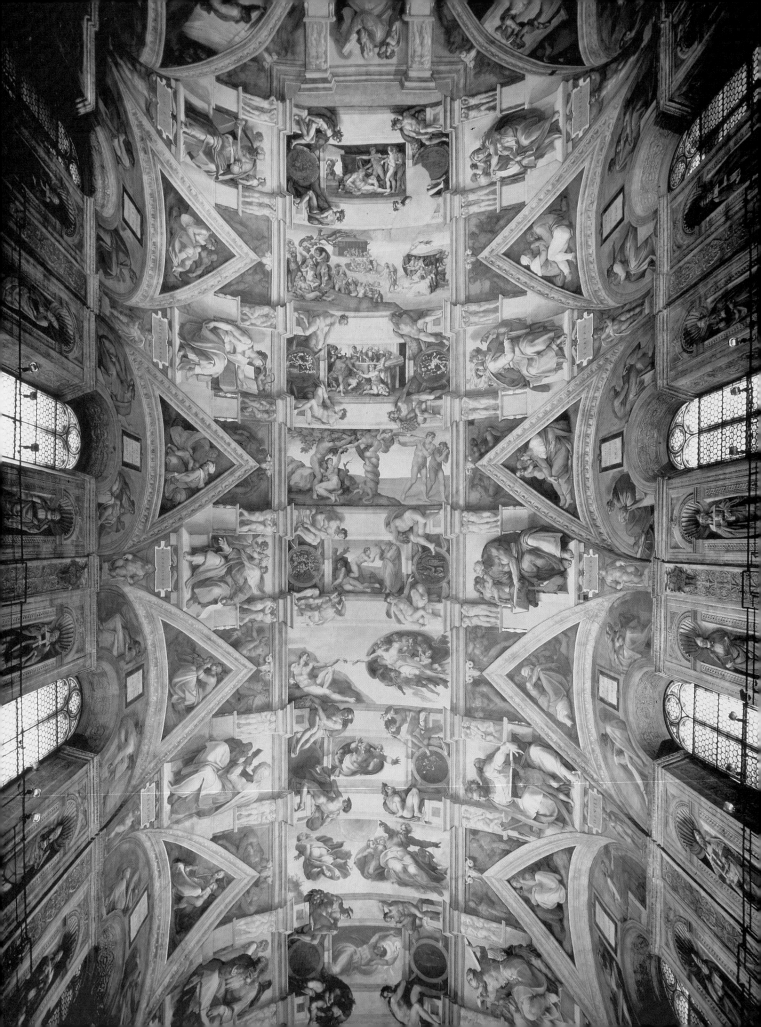

to have said, "Painting is for women, sculpture for men." He apparently even tried to flee but was called back, and, reluctantly, began to paint.

Michelangelo had not worked with fresco since his youth. The ceiling, which covered more than 5800 square feet, was nearly seventy feet high. The curve and height of the vault posed complex perspective problems. He would have to work long hours on his back, paint dripping on him.

The center of the ceiling (fig. 13.34) shows the story of the Creation—nine scenes from Genesis. Four further scenes from the Old Testament appear in the corner triangles, called *vele* ("sails" in Italian). In addition, Old Testament prophets and ancient pagan sibyls (female prophets) inhabit the other triangular spandrels (spaces between the curved arches), along with Jesus's ancestors, and assorted medallions, *putti* (cherubs), and male nudes. There are over three hundred figures in all, many of which have no known meaning. Michelangelo claimed that Julius II let him paint what he pleased, but the complexity of the program suggests that he had advisers. Neoplatonist numerology, symbolism, and philosophy inform much of the composition, although scholars continue to argue over meanings. The notion of prefiguration appears—that is, stories in the Old Testament anticipate those in the New Testament. Pagan stories and motifs are also evident.

In the scene of the *Creation of Adam* (fig. 13.33), God, noble and powerful, flies in swiftly, bringing Eve with him under his arm. Compare this scene with Ghiberti's depiction in the *Gates of Paradise* (see fig. 13.5). Michelangelo's dynamic God contrasts with a listless Adam, whose figure Michelangelo derived from an ancient Roman coin. Momentarily, God will give Adam his soul and bring him fully to life, for their fingers are about to touch. Note how the shape of God's billowing drapery is very close to the shape of the human brain, as if all of creation is an idea in the mind of God. In the end, however, it is touch—the touch of the painter and sculptor as well as the touch of God—that brings the figure to life. Consider, too, the masculine musculature of the figures; even the female figures on the Sistine ceiling are based on male models. Michelangelo's figures are heroic and powerful, yet they have a grace and beauty worthy of Raphael.

While painting the ceiling, Michelangelo endured great physical hardship. Vasari claimed that the work impaired his vision so that, for several months afterward, he was unable to read unless he lay on his back and looked upward. When he finished work on the ceiling he

was but thirty-seven years of age. With the death of Julius II in 1513, Michelangelo went to work once again for the Medicis, this time for Lorenzo the Magnificent's son, the new pope, Leo X.

THE NEW ST. PETER'S BASILICA

In 1506, Pope Julius II made the daring decision to tear down the old St. Peter's Basilica, which had stood at the Vatican since the time of Constantine in the early fourth century. He would replace it, he thought, with a new church more befitting the dignity and prestige of the papacy, and to this end he appointed as architect a man dedicated to the revival of Greek and Roman architectural ideals.

Donato Bramante. DONATO BRAMANTE [bra-MAHN-tay] (1444–1514) had a reputation based largely on a building called the Tempietto, or "little temple" (fig. 13.35) constructed from 1502, on the site where St. Peter was believed to have been crucified. Commissioned by Ferdinand and Isabella of Spain (patrons of the explorer Christopher Columbus), the Tempietto is an adaptation

Figure 13.35 Donato Bramante, Tempietto, San Pietro in Montorio, Rome, 1502–after 1511. Small in size but of great importance, the Tempietto demonstrates the reuse of ancient pagan architecture for Renaissance Christian purposes.

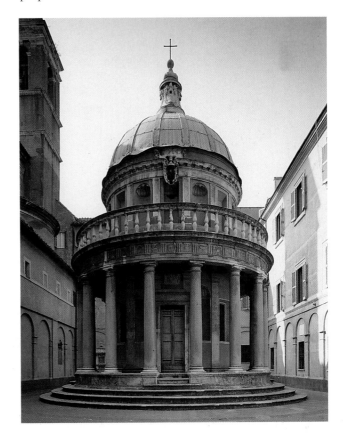

Figure 13.34 Michelangelo, Sistine Chapel, overview of ceiling, 1508–12, fresco, 44 × 128′ (13.4 × 39.0 m), Vatican, Rome. Although Michelangelo considered himself a sculptor, he was compelled to paint the Sistine ceiling by Pope Julius II.

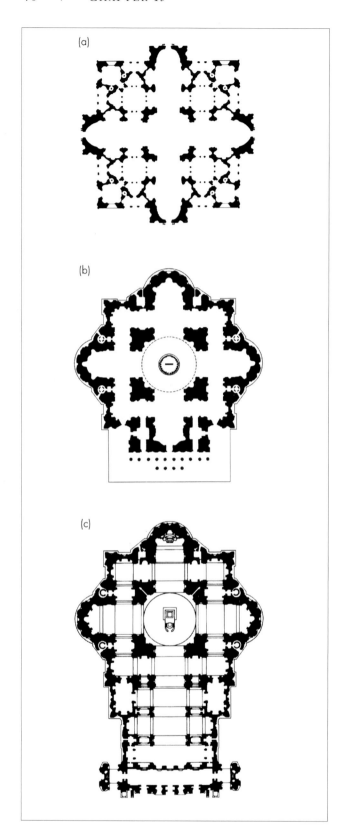

Figure 13.36 Floor plans for St. Peter's, Rome, by a) Bramante, b) Michelangelo, and c) Carlo Maderno. Although Bramante and Michelangelo intended Greek-cross plans, the long nave of the Latin-cross plan was added by Maderno to accommodate the crowds of people.

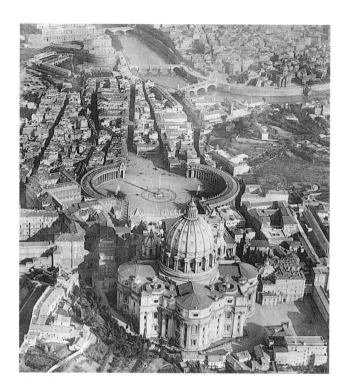

Figure 13.37 View of St. Peter's, Rome. St. Peter's underwent so many changes that only a hint of the simplicity and beauty of Bramante and Michelangelo's original Greek-cross plan remains.

of a classical temple of the Doric order (see Chapter 3), including a complete entablature.

The building itself is set on a stepped base and surrounded by a **peristyle**, or continuous row of columns. The first story is topped by a **balustrade**, or carved railing, inside which is a **drum**, or circular wall, upon which Bramante set a hemispheric dome. The plan, with its deeply recessed spaces, creates a dramatic play of light and dark despite the relatively small scale of the building itself.

Bramante's plan for St. Peter's Basilica (fig. 13.36) is, essentially, a grander version of the Tempietto, over 450 feet in diameter instead of fifteen. Instead of basing his plan on the traditional Latin cross (three short arms and one long one), Bramante chose to utilize a Greek cross (four arms of equal length). The result is symmetrical and harmonious, symbolizing the perfection of God, topped by an enormous dome modeled after the Pantheon's.

Michelangelo's St. Peter's. With the death of Julius II in 1513 and Bramante's own death in 1514, the entire project was put on hold, and several other architects, including Raphael, attempted to revise Bramante's plan. Finally, in 1546, Michelangelo was appointed architect. He described Bramante's original design, saying it was "clear and straightforward … Indeed," he wrote, "every architect who has departed from Bramante's plan …

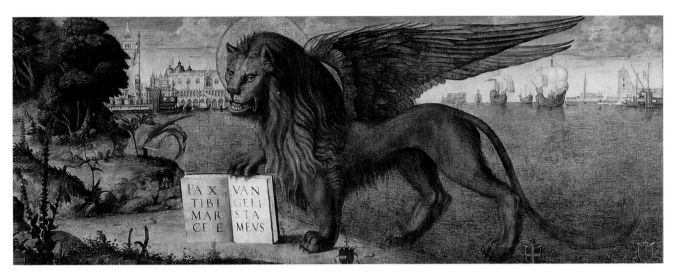

Figure 13.38 Vittore Carpaccio, *Lion of St. Mark*, 1516, oil on canvas, 4′6¾″ × 12′1″ (1.40 × 3.70 m), Ducal Palace, Venice. The winged lion was a symbol of the Evangelist Mark and of Venice. This painting documents the early sixteenth-century appearance of the city, with its campanile, Ducal palace, and the domes of St. Mark's Cathedral.

has departed from the right way." Nevertheless, Michelangelo modified the original (fig. 13.36). Instead of an interior of interlocking Greek crosses, which gave the effect of a giant snowflake, Michelangelo simplified the scheme. It was, in part, a matter of engineering. Available masonry was not strong enough to carry the weight of so great a dome. Thus the four main piers supporting the dome in the center of the church had to be massively enlarged, in turn causing him to simplify the remaining interior space. Moreover, he intended a double-columned portico across the front.

Michelangelo did not live to see the completion of his plan. The dome was finished in 1590 (fig. 13.37), with a somewhat higher and slimmer profile than Michelangelo had intended, in part because of engineering requirements. And then, in 1606, Pope Paul V appointed the architect Carlo Maderno to restore the church to a Latin-cross plan (fig. 13.36).

VENICE

Throughout the fifteenth century and into the sixteenth, Venice was one of the most powerful city-states in all of Europe, exercising control over the entire Adriatic and much of the Eastern Mediterranean. Petrarch described the city in glowing terms: "Most august city of Venice, today the only abode of liberty, peace, and justice, the one refuge of the good and haven for those who, battered on all sides by the storms of tyranny and war, seek to live in tranquillity: city rich in gold but richer in fame, mighty in resources but mightier in virtue, built on solid marble but based on the more solid foundations of civic concord, surrounded by salty waters but more secure through her saltier councils." This is the city celebrated

in Vittore Carpaccio's famous *Lion of St. Mark* (fig. 13.38), painted in 1516 for a government office in the city's Ducal Palace. The lion is the symbol of the city's patron saint, Mark the Evangelist, whom God was said to have visited on the Evangelist's arrival at the Venice lagoon, thereby designating Venice as the saint's final resting-place. Greeting St. Mark, God's angel is said to have announced, "Peace Unto You, Mark, My Evangelist," the Latin words inscribed on the tablet held in the lion's paws. The lion stands with its front paws on land and its hind paws in the water, signifying Venice's dominion over land and sea. Behind the lion, to the left, is the Ducal Palace itself, the seat of government and law and the source of the city's order and harmony. The Byzantine domes of St. Mark's Cathedral rise behind it, the basis of the city's moral fabric, and the giant campanile (bell tower) that dominates St. Mark's Square stands on the far left housing the five bells of St. Mark's, one of which chimed to announce the beginning and end of each working day. Behind the lion to the right is a fleet of Venetian merchant ships, the source of the city's wealth and prosperity.

Venetian Oil Painting. Venice was unique not only because of its enduring peace and prosperity. Surrounded by water and built over a lagoon, its humidity made fresco painting, so popular elsewhere in Europe, a virtual impossibility. From 1475 on, after the introduction of oil painting, a technique first developed in the Netherlands, attempts at fresco painting in the city's public buildings gradually ceased. The use of oil on canvas led, in fact, to a new kind of painting as well. Applying colors in glazes—that is, layers of transparent color—created by mixing a little pigment with lot of linseed oil—painters were able to create a light in painting that seemed to emanate from the depths of the painting itself. Often, a small amount of yellow pigment would be added to the final protective layer of glaze, creating what has been called the "golden glow" of Venetian painting. Furthermore, the texture of the canvas itself was exploited. Stroked over a woven surface, the brush deposits more paint on the top of the weave and less in the crevices. This textured surface in turn "catches" actual light, lending, especially to a glazed surface, an almost shimmering vibrancy.

Giorgione and Titian. The two most celebrated Venetian painters of the early sixteenth century were GIORGIONE [GEORGE-jee-oh-nay] (ca. 1477–1510) and Tiziano Vecelli, known as TITIAN [TISH-un] (ca. 1488–1576). When Giorgione died of the plague in 1510, he had completed only a handful of canvases, but he had been working side by side with Titian, whom he had hired as an assistant in 1507. Scholars have long debated just who is responsible for painting the *Fête champêtre* (fig. 13.39), or *Country Festival*, completed the year of Giorgione's death: Some say it was Giorgione, others argue for Titian. The confusion simply underscores how completely each of these two artists defined the new Venetian style of painting.

The content of the *Fête champêtre* is ambiguous. Why does the woman to the left pour water into the well? Why does one man appear to be a refined gentleman, the other a rustic peasant? The lute was an instrument played at court, the flute by shepherds—why are they seen together? Perhaps it is an allegory of sacred and profane love, an allegory of poetry, or a treatise on the secularization of contemporary culture.

However, the painting is clearly a play of opposites, as in the play of light and dark across its surface. The

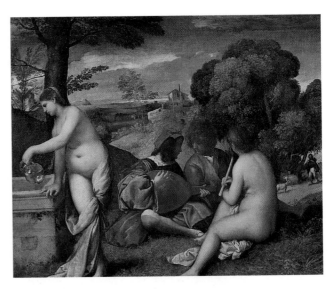

Figure 13.39 Giorgione and/or Titian, *Fête champêtre*, ca. 1510–11, oil on canvas, 3′1¼″ × 4′6⅜″ (1.10 × 1.38 m), Musée du Louvre, Paris. Botticelli's slender Early Renaissance figure type "matured" in the work of later, High Renaissance painters to a full-bodied ideal of feminine beauty, as exemplified in this painting.

effects of light achieved here are quite the opposite of those of the other Renaissance master of light, Leonardo, whom Giorgione met in late 1499. Leonardo tended to emphasize darkness, as a function of both perspectival and emotional depth; Giorgione and Titian emphasized light. In fact, such Venetian paintings are literally built up from light to dark. The effect here is of a palpable sense of sunlight striking the landscape through a series of dark broken clouds with the intensity of a spotlight. Such atmospheric pyrotechnics would have a profound impact on Baroque painters such as Peter Paul

Timeline 13.3 The Renaissance and Mannerism in Italy.

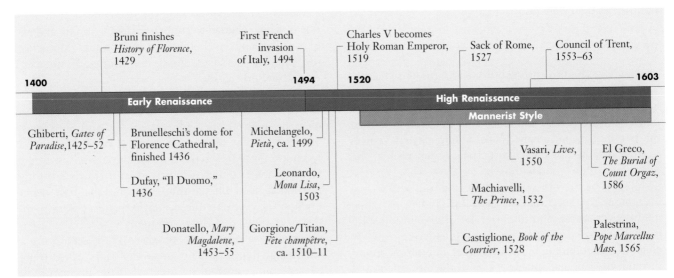

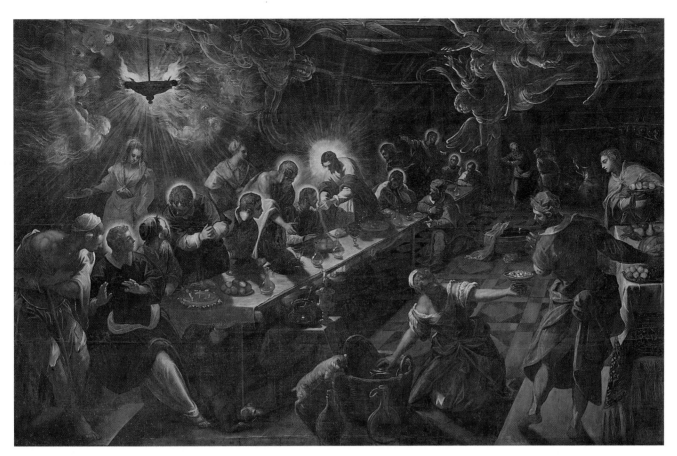

Figure 13.40   Tintoretto, *The Last Supper*, 1592–94, oil on canvas, 12′ × 18′8″ (3.66 × 5.69 m), San Giorgio Maggiore, Venice. In striking contrast to the compositional clarity of Leonardo da Vinci's High Renaissance depiction (see fig. 13.24), the viewer may have some difficulty in locating Jesus in Tintoretto's Mannerist version of this subject, for the perspective leads away from, rather than toward, Jesus.

Rubens (see Chapter 15) and on nineteenth-century painters such as J.M.W. Turner (see Chapter 17), who actually came to Venice to paint.

Tintoretto.   TINTORETTO [tin-toe-RET-toe] (1518–1594), named "little dyer" after his father's trade, took the techniques of Giorgione and Titian, whom he had served as an apprentice, and heightened and exaggerated them. Tintoretto posted a sign in his studio declaring his intent to combine Titian's color with Michelangelo's drawing ability. His version of *The Last Supper* (fig. 13.40) can be usefully compared to Leonardo's (see fig. 13.24). Gone is the sense of balance achieved in the earlier work by virtue of its central perspective, with its vanishing point directly behind Jesus in the center. By comparison, Tintoretto's painting seems to be tilted askew. Its perspective is still accurate, but the vanishing point has been moved off-center, toward the upper right. Jesus remains at the center of the painting, but it is light, not geometry, that draws our attention to him. In fact, he competes with the serving woman in the foreground for our attention, and with the cat who seems intent on getting at the fish she is serving. As in the *Fête champêtre*, the painting seems to collapse the distinction between religious and secular imagery. Here, the Last Supper is part and parcel of real life.

MUSIC

The reinvention of Rome would require the reinvention of music—a new St. Peter's needed a new Mass to fill its vast space with sound.

Josquin des Près.   The most important composer of the new Rome naturally took on the job: JOSQUIN DES PRÈS [JOZ-skanh de-PRAY] (1440–1521), from Flanders. Josquin is the composer we most closely associate with the High Renaissance. It was he who led the Sistine Choir as Michelangelo painted the ceiling and Raphael worked in the papal suites. Like Dufay, Josquin spent many years in Italy, serving the Sforza family in Milan, the Estes at their court in Ferrara, and finally several Roman popes, including Sixtus IV (for whom he directed the Sistine Choir), Julius II, and Leo X. So highly regarded was Josquin in his own time that the French King Louis XII and the Austrian Queen Margaret made bids for his services. His contemporaries extolled him as "the Father of Musicians" and "the best of composers." An enchanted Martin Luther remarked that Josquin was "the master of the notes; they must do as he wills."

Josquin composed approximately two hundred works—motets, Masses, and *chansons* (songs). His many motets and *chansons* attest to his interest in exploring new trends in setting words to music. His motet "Ave Maria … virgo serena" ("Hail, Mary … Serene Virgin") (1502) exemplifies his style. The opening employs imitative counterpoint with the melody for the words "Ave Maria" first heard in the soprano, then repeated in succession by the alto, the tenor, and the bass, while the original parts continue, as in a round.

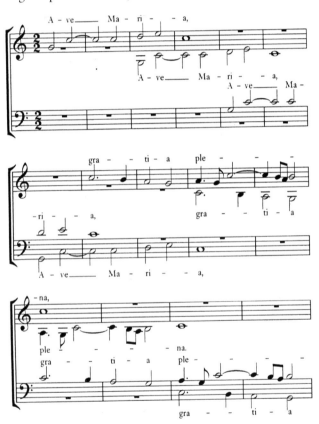

On the words "gratia plena" ("full of grace") Josquin introduces a new, second melody, again in the soprano, and which is again passed from one voice to the next. Josquin overlaps the voices in both melodies, allowing the altos to enter, for example, before the sopranos have sung the complete melody. This overlapping of voices enriches the music's texture, giving it body and providing it with a continuous and fluid motion. Josquin also allows two voices, and sometimes three or four, to sing the same melody simultaneously—a duet between the two lower voice parts (tenor and bass), for instance, will imitate a duet between alto and soprano. The motet concludes serenely with emphatic slow chords on the words "O

mater Dei, memento mei" ("O mother of God, remember me"). Just before this ending, Josquin introduces a significant silence that sounds at first like an ending. He uses this silence to focus the listener's attention on the true ending, which comes immediately after. The dignified serenity and graceful restraint of Josquin's "Ave Maria … virgo serena" can be compared with the quiet beauty and restrained elegance of Raphael's madonnas.

Palestrina. The music of the Italian GIOVANNI PIERLUIGI DA PALESTRINA [pal-uh-STREE-nah] (1525–1594) came to dominate the Church throughout most of the sixteenth century. As the Church came under attack from the north for its excessive spending and ornate lavishness, it responded by simplifying the Mass and the music designed to accompany it. Although it considered banning polyphony altogether, thinking it too elaborate to be easily understood by lay people, in the end the Church endorsed the controlled and precise style of Palestrina.

Palestrina held a number of important Church positions. He was organist and choirmaster of the large chorus that performed exclusively in St. Peter's, the *Cappella Giulia* (Julian Choir), and he was music director for the Vatican. His music evokes the Gregorian roots of traditional Church music and relies directly upon the emotional appeal of the listener's potential union with God. He wrote nearly a thousand compositions, including over a hundred Masses. Among the most beautiful of all Palestrina's works is his *Pope Marcellus Mass*, written in honor of the pope and set for an **a cappella**—or unaccompanied—choir in six voice parts: soprano, alto, two tenors, and two basses. It contains music for the Kyrie, Gloria, Credo, Sanctus, Benedictus, and Agnus Dei, as did the Gregorian Mass before it, and Palestrina utilizes the traditional Gregorian melodies connected with each of these parts of the Mass. Still, it is clearly Renaissance in its style, utilizing an orderly and clear imitative polyphony that allows the listener to follow each of the voices in the Mass as they weave in and out of one another with precision. The words that Michelangelo used to praise Bramante's architectural plan for St. Peter's might be used to define Palestrina's music as well—they are both equally "clear and straightforward."

LITERATURE

Baldassare Castiglione. BALDASSARE CASTIGLIONE [KAS-till-YOH-nay] (1478–1529) spent his life serving as an important and influential courtier and diplomat. He grew up in the company of nobility, counted the princes of Mantua among his friends, and studied at the university in Milan. He served as a courtier to the Italian ducal courts, first at the court of Francesco Gonzaga, the ruler of Mantua in the early sixteenth century, and then at the court of Urbino, established by

Federico da Montefeltro (fig. 13.18), the father of Guidobaldo da Montefeltro, in whose service Castiglione prospered. Later unrest caused him to return to service in Duke Francesco's court. After then serving as ambassador to Rome for a number of years, Castiglione was appointed by Pope Clement VII as papal ambassador to Spain, where he lived out the remaining years of his life.

While at Urbino, Castiglione wrote the *Book of the Courtier*, which memorializes, celebrates, and idealizes life at court, especially Urbino, where Castiglione was impressed not only with the nobility of the Montefeltro dukes but also with the Duchess of Montefeltro, Elisabetta, who often appears in the book. It is cast in the form of a series of four dialogues spread out over four evenings at the court of Urbino. The central topic is the manners, education, and behavior of the ideal courtier, whose virtues Castiglione extols throughout the book. Most important for the courtier is the range and substance of his accomplishment. He must be a man of courage who has experience in war; he must be learned in the classics and in classical languages; he must be able to serve his prince with generosity. Castiglione's ideal courtier had to be physically and emotionally strong, able to perform feats requiring agility, skill, courage, and daring. His physical prowess was measured by his grace as a dancer and elegance as a singer and musician. He was also expected to be an engaging and witty conversationalist, a good companion, an elegant writer, even a bit of a poet. In short, Castiglione's courtier was the ideal Renaissance gentleman—of sound mind, body, and character, and learned in the ideas of Renaissance humanism. Leonardo da Vinci exemplified this ideal during the Renaissance; people such as Thomas Jefferson have been cited as "Renaissance men" since. In addition to the ideal courtier's range of accomplishments, Castiglione applauds *sprezzatura*, the ability to make difficult tasks look easy, in the manner of a great athlete or musician.

Castiglione's blending of the soldier and the scholar, his merging of the ideals of medieval chivalry with those of Renaissance humanism, made his *Book of the Courtier* popular both in its own time and afterward. Its emphasis on good breeding and elegant manners suggests that, as in the codes of chivalry, polish was as important as prowess. Elegant speech, graceful demeanor, and consummate skill were all expected of the courtier. Castiglione himself was no exception and embodied the ideals his book celebrated. Raphael's portrait of him (fig. 13.41) displays many of the qualities Castiglione extols, from the nobility of the graceful head to the intelligence of the shining eyes, complemented by the elegant refinement of the attire.

Niccolò Machiavelli. A contemporary of Castiglione, NICCOLÒ MACHIAVELLI [mak-ee-ah-VEL-ee] (1469–1527) is often paired with him since he also wrote a guidebook on behavior—*The Prince*, a manual for princes and rulers.

Like Castiglione, Machiavelli was well educated in the Renaissance humanist tradition. Like Castiglione's courtier, Machiavelli's prince is a type or model of an ideal. The difference between the two writers' "ideals," however, is dramatic: Castiglione supported the tenets of Renaissance humanism, but Machiavelli challenged them by introducing a radically different set of standards, standards that inform, among other things, Mannerist art.

Young Machiavelli was employed as a clerk and secretary to the Florentine magistrates responsible for war and internal affairs. From 1498 to 1512, he also served as an ambassador to, among others, the Holy Roman Emperor Maximilian, the King of France, and Pope Julius II. During his lifetime, the Italian city-states were almost continually at war either with one another or with outside countries such as France and Spain. Machiavelli himself suffered from the changing fortunes of various ruling families. Notably, when the Medici

Figure 13.41 Raphael, *Baldassare Castiglione*, ca. 1515, oil on panel, transferred to canvas, $32\frac{1}{4} \times 26\frac{1}{2}''$ (81.9 × 67.3 cm), Musée du Louvre, Paris. Castiglione wrote about the qualities of the ideal courtier; it is not surprising that Raphael, a refined gentleman, was a personal friend of his. Perhaps some of the calm restraint recommended by Castiglione is seen in Raphael's portrait with its restricted range of color.

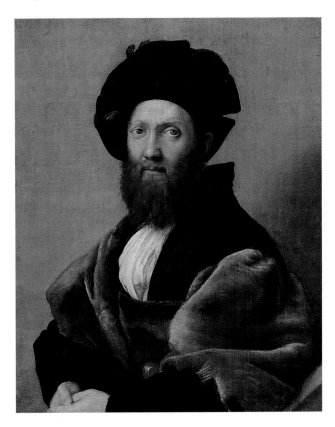

came to power in Florence, he was accused of conspiracy, tortured, then imprisoned. Later, when the Medici government collapsed, he was accused of being a Medici sympathizer. At the time some claimed that he wrote *The Prince* for the Medici as a guide to tyrannical rule.

The Prince was written in 1513 and published in 1532 after Machiavelli's death. It quickly acquired fame or, as some would have it, notoriety. Based on a series of premises about human nature—none favorable—*The Prince* asserts that people are basically selfish, deceitful, greedy, and gullible. Accordingly, Machiavelli advises princes to rule in ways that play upon these fundamental human characteristics. A prince, therefore, can be, indeed should be, hypocritical, cruel, and deceitful when necessary. He should keep faith with no one but himself, and employ ruthlessness and cunning to maintain his power over the people. For, as Machiavelli writes, "it is far better to be feared than loved," though as he also notes, "the prince must nonetheless make himself feared in such a way that, if he is not loved, he will at least avoid being hated."

The view of human beings that forms the foundation of Machiavelli's arguments in *The Prince* reflects political expediency, based upon Machiavelli's observation of Florentine politics and the politics of other city-states and countries he visited as a Florentine ambassador. Having witnessed the instability of power in Italy, particularly the surrender of parts of Italy to France and Spain, Machiavelli wrote that a ruler must be strong enough to keep himself in power, for only with the strength of absolute power could he rule effectively.

After the Bible, Machiavelli's *The Prince* was the most widely read book of its time. The questions it raises about the relationship between politics and morality, the starkly realistic depiction of power it presents, and the authority, immediacy, and directness with which it is written, ensured its success. Whatever one may think of its vision of human nature or of the advice it offers rulers, it is hard to deny the force of its arguments, the power of its language, and the strength of its convictions. In addition, *The Prince* influenced the creation of a stable state in the section of Italy known as the Romagna, where Cesare Borgia, the illegitimate son of Pope Alexander VI (Rodrigo Borgia), put its ideas into practice.

Mannerism

A stylistic trend began to develop in Italian art as early as 1520 that we have come to call **Mannerism**. The rise of Mannerism coincides with a period of political and religious unrest. Florence had endured a return to Medici rule that, in the eyes of many Florentines, made a mockery of the family name, and certainly of the republic. First the vicious Giuliano de' Medici ruled the city, and then the syphilitic Lorenzo, Duke of Urbino and a grandson of Lorenzo the Magnificent, who was hardly a Florentine at all. France invaded Italy, and the sack of Rome in 1527 by the troops of the Holy Roman Emperor Charles V, together with the six months of murder and destruction that followed it, undermined the confidence of Renaissance humanists. The Protestant Reformation divided Christendom as a whole, and a century of religious wars was under way.

If Mannerism reflects an age of anxiety and crisis, it is nevertheless a result of the High Renaissance's cult of the individual genius. All of its chief practitioners—Rosso Fiorentino, Pontormo, Parmigianino, Bronzino, and Giulio Romano—were inspired by Leonardo, Raphael, and Michelangelo, the great masters of the generation before them. What they admired most in the great masters' work was its technical virtuosity, a virtuosity synonymous in their minds with genius itself.

PAINTING

Each Mannerist artist cultivated a distinct personal *maniera* (or "in the manner of"). Although there is no definitive Mannerist style, Mannerism is marked by its rejection of many of the principles of the High Renaissance. While High Renaissance painting is characterized by clear presentations of subject matter, balanced compositions, normal or "natural" body proportions, scientific spatial constructions, and a preference for primary colors, Mannerist painting is notable for its intentional obscurity of subject matter, unbalanced compositions, bodies with distorted proportions and contorted poses, strained, inappropriate, or even monstrous facial expressions, confusing spatial constructions, and a preference for secondary and acidic colors.

Michelangelo.   In both the bleakness of its mood and its freewheeling play with human anatomy, Michelangelo's *The Last Judgment* reflects the Mannerist style. Although his plan for St. Peter's, done in 1546, embodies the ideals of the High Renaissance, much of his other late work leaves those ideals far behind. A new spirit entered his art in *The Last Judgment* (fig. 13.42), commissioned for the altar wall of the Sistine Chapel in 1534 by a dying Pope Clement VII (a bastard grandson of Lorenzo the Magnificent). Painted between 1536 and 1541, it lacks the optimism and sense of beauty that define Michelangelo's work on the ceiling. His figures, no longer beautifully proportioned, now look twisted

Figure 13.42   Michelangelo, *The Last Judgment*, 1536–41, fresco, 48′ × 44′ (14.63 × 13.41 m), Sistine Chapel, Vatican, Rome. Michelangelo's optimism and the idealized beauty of the ceiling of this chapel are now replaced with a pessimistic view and anatomical anomalies.

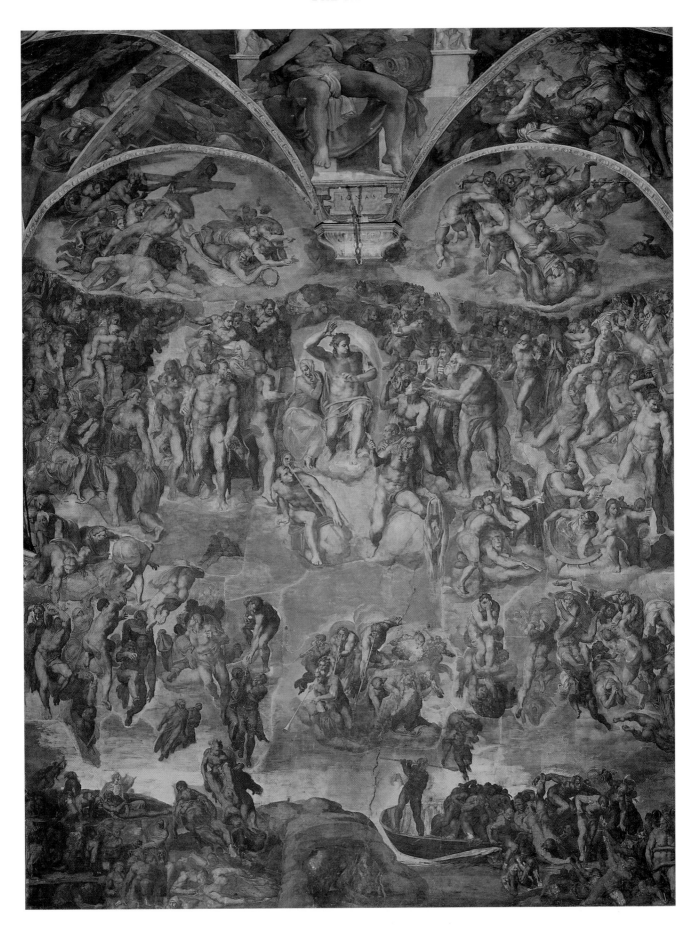

the chasm of hell that opens at the bottom of the painting, where a monstrous Charon (the ferryman of the dead) guides his boat across the River Styx, driving the damned before him into perpetual torment. The graves on the left and hell on the right are the bases of the painting's pyramidal structure. Not coincidentally, these are at eye-level.

Parmigianino. Among the most characteristic painters of the Mannerist style is PARMIGIANINO [par-mee-jah-NEE-noh] (1503–1540) of Parma. His *Madonna with the Long Neck* (fig. 13.43), painted in 1534–40 shows figures that, by contrast with the classical proportions admired in the Renaissance, have unreal features: they are elongated and affected, yet graceful and refined, beyond both the rules of realism and nature's capabilities. Mary is very large, with an almost balloon-like inflation through the hips and thighs. The curving contours of her right hand emphasize her gesture and not the physical structure of her hand.

The composition is unbalanced; the figures crowd the left side. The column in the background is a symbol of the torture of Jesus (he was bound to a column and flagellated), but it is proportionally too large. The whole space is odd and unclear, and the viewer looks up to the main figures but down on the prophet in the bottom right.

Bronzino. Another representative of the Mannerist style is BRONZINO [bron-ZEE-noh] (1503–1572), court painter to Cosimo de' Medici, or Cosimo I, ruler of Florence from 1537 to 1574 (not the original Cosimo but a related descendant). Bronzino's painting of the *Allegory with Venus and Cupid* (fig. 13.44), ca. 1546, demonstrates the intentional ambiguity of Mannerist iconography. The two main figures, Venus and Cupid, are unquestionably erotic. On the right, Folly throws roses. In the upper right, Father Time uncovers the follies of love—or perhaps he tries to hide them. In the background on the right, Deceit coils with the body of a snake with the left and right hands reversed, while the masks suggest falseness. Figures in the left background could be Hatred and Inconstancy. Typical of Mannerist art are the complexity and obscurity of the allegory, which has been interpreted in various ways by historians.

The absence of a single center of focus is also characteristic of Mannerism—the figures seem to compete with each other for the viewer's attention. Spatial contradictions abound—a floor plan of this space and its inhabitants cannot be drawn, for neither linear nor aerial perspective is used. The figures choke the space. Relative scale is inconsistent. In colors that are acidic and metallic, they assume tense poses, elegant but affected, agitated, and exaggerated—certainly difficult for anyone to actually mimic—and their uneasy expressions cause them to appear psychologically as well as physically distorted.

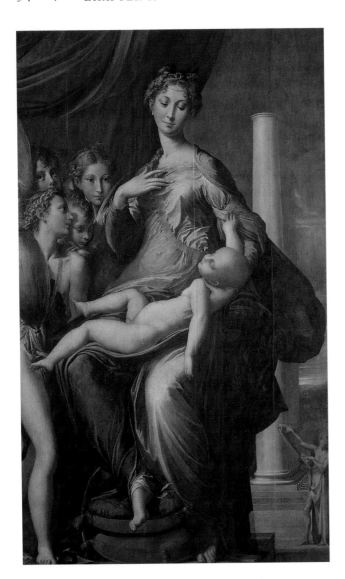

Figure 13.43 Parmigianino, *Madonna with the Long Neck*, 1534–40, oil on panel, 7′1″ × 4′4″ (2.16 × 1.32 m), Galleria degli Uffizi, Florence. Comparison with Raphael's High Renaissance *Madonna of the Meadows* (see fig. 13.29) makes obvious the Mannerist preference for distorted figures and spatial ambiguity.

and grotesque, with heads too small for their giant, lumbering bodies. The figures from Genesis that inhabit his ceiling have now aged, their flesh corrupted and their souls lost.

However, this style befits Michelangelo's subject. The dead are dragged from their graves and pulled upward to be judged by Jesus. Mary, at his side, cringes at the vision. At his feet, to his right, is St. Bartholomew. Legend states that Bartholomew was martyred by being skinned alive, and he holds his grotesquely distorted skin in his hand. But the face is a grim self-portrait of Michelangelo, and such grimness extends to the whole painting. The hands of Bartholomew's flayed skin seem to reach downward, to

El Greco. One of the most interesting practitioners of the Mannerist style was not Italian. Known as EL GRECO [el GRECK-oh] (1541–1614), or "the Greek," Domenikos Theotokopoulos was born on the island of Crete. He studied in Venice from about 1566, where he was deeply influenced by Titian, and then for seven years in Rome. In 1577, he emigrated to Spain, first to Madrid and then to Toledo.

The most important of his major commissions is the masterpiece, *The Burial of Count Orgaz* (fig. 13.45) of 1586. Legend held that at the Count's burial in 1323, Saints Augustine and Stephen appeared and lowered him into his grave even as his soul was seen ascending to heaven. In the painting, the burial and the ascension occur in two separate realms, neither of which fits spatially with the other, and both of which are packed with figures. Below, El Greco has painted the local, contemporary aristocracy he knew in attendance at the funeral, not the aristocracy of the Count's day. In fact, El Greco's eight-year-old son stands at the lower left next to St. Stephen, and above him, looking out at the viewer from the back row, is quite possibly El Greco himself.

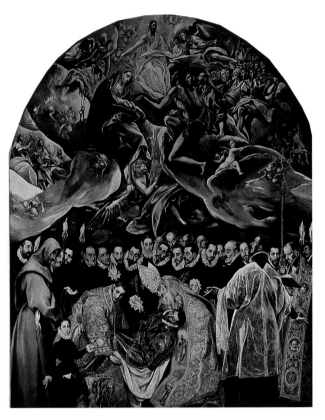

Figure 13.45 El Greco, *The Burial of Count Orgaz*, 1586, oil on canvas, 16′ × 11′10″ (4.88 × 3.61 m), Church of San Tomé, Toledo, Spain. Although El Greco's distorted figures were once attributed to astigmatism, they are now recognized as part of the Mannerist preference for elongated bodily proportions.

Figure 13.44 Agnolo Bronzino, *Allegory with Venus and Cupid*, ca. 1546, oil on panel, 4′9½″ × 3′9¼″ (1.46 × 1.16 m), National Gallery, London. Typically Mannerist are the intentionally complex iconography (including an oddly erotic encounter between Venus and Cupid) and the pictorial space choked with figures.

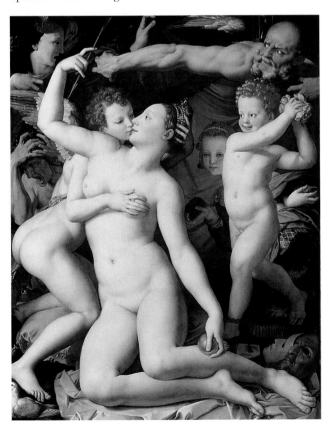

The top half of the scene is as spatially ambiguous as any example of Mannerist painting. A crowd of saints enters from a deep space at the top right. A chorus of angels playing instruments occupies a sort of middle space on the left. In the foreground, St. John and the Virgin Mary greet the angel who arrives with the soul of the Count. The soul is shown about the size of a baby, as if to emphasize its innocence. They plead the Count's case with Jesus, who is peculiarly small and seated far enough in the distance almost to occupy the vanishing point to the heavens. The most notable aspect of El Greco's style is exemplified by Jesus's right arm, which stretches far forward into the space above Mary's head. The elongated hands and arms are the most "mannered" feature of El Greco's art, and yet it is difficult to label his work "Mannerist." His aim is to move his audience by conveying a sense of the spiritual, almost mystical power of deeply religious faith and conviction. In this, his painting anticipates that of the Baroque age, and captures something of the power of the great Spanish mystics of his own day, Teresa of Avila and Ignatius Loyola, both of whom would be made saints in Rome in 1622.

SCULPTURE

The Mannerist style spread outside Italy and by the mid-sixteenth century, Mannerism was the dominant style in France, largely as a result of the influence of Italian artists working there, the result of the sack of Rome in 1527 and the consequent dispersal of artists. One such Italian artist was Benvenuto Cellini whose sculpture and writings reflected the full flowering of the style.

Benvenuto Cellini. BENVENUTO CELLINI [che-LEE-nee] (1500–1571) was a Florentine who worked in France for the King, Francis I (reigned 1515–47). For him, Cellini made an extraordinary gold and enamel *Saltcellar* (fig. 13.46), between 1539 and 1543. It was functional, yet wonderfully elegant and thoroughly fantastic. Salt is represented by the male figure Neptune, because salt comes from the sea (the salt is actually in a little boat), and pepper is represented by the female figure Earth, because pepper comes from the earth (the pepper is actually in a little triumphal arch). On the base are complex allegorical figures of the four seasons and four parts of the day, meant to evoke both festive seasonal celebrations and the daily meal schedule. The figures are typically elongated, with small heads and boneless limbs. Their postures are a virtual impossibility to maintain—either they are both about to fall backward or they have been captured midway through the process of sitting up.

The Autobiography of Benvenuto Cellini. Among the most widely read of Renaissance works, Cellini's *Autobiography* is notable for the way in which it portrays the Italian Mannerist sculptor and goldsmith. Like Montaigne's *Essays*, which were published a

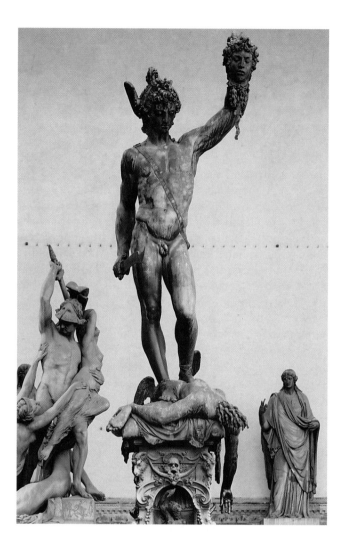

Figure 13.47   Benvenuto Cellini, *Perseus*, 1545–54, bronze, height 18′ (5.4 m), Loggia dei Lanzi, Florence. Even the depiction of the decapitation of the ancient mythological gorgan Medusa, blood gushing, attains elegance in the Mannerist style.

Figure 13.46   Benvenuto Cellini, *Saltcellar of Francis I*, 1539–43, gold with enamel, $10\frac{1}{4} \times 13\frac{1}{8}''$ (26 × 33.3 cm), Kunsthistorisches Museum, Vienna. An example of extreme elegance and opulence, this table ornament contained salt and pepper.

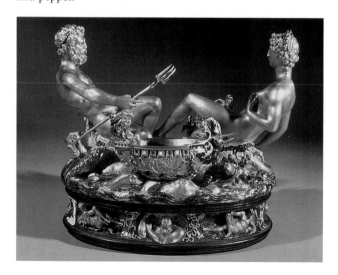

generation later, Cellini's *Autobiography* records far more than external facts about his life.

An example of Cellini's Mannerist extravagance can be discerned in his response to his later patron, the Duke of Florence, Cosimo de' Medici, who had just commissioned a new sculpture, *Perseus* (fig. 13.47). When he questioned Cellini's ability to complete the sculpture in bronze, the artist responded vigorously, exhibiting supreme confidence. He emphasizes his strength of character, portraying himself as heroic, brave, violent, passionate, promiscuous, and entirely committed to his art.

Cellini's *Autobiography* can be considered a work in the Mannerist mode because of its extravagance and its exaggeration. Like the elongated figures in Parmigianino's paintings, Cellini's exaggerated portrayal of himself and others typifies the Mannerist tendency. Unlike Parmigianino's delicacy and grace, however, Cellini is all drama and vigor. Cellini's *Autobiography*, in the end, is akin to his *Perseus*. His sculpture extends the Mannerist style to its very limits—the decorous classical ideal of his Renaissance predecessors is gone.

ARCHITECTURE

Mannerist architecture reuses the vocabulary of antique architecture in unusual ways. Very different from the revival of the antique seen in Bramante's Tempietto (see fig. 13.35), Mannerist architects responded in extremely unorthodox ways. The vestibule of the Laurentian Library in Florence (fig. 13.48) is one such example, built as the Medici family library above the monastery of the church of San Lorenzo. Begun by Michelangelo in 1524, the staircase was designed between 1558 and 1559, and the room completed by GIORGIO VASARI [va-SAH-ree] (1511–1574) and AMMANATI [ah-mahn-AH-tee] (1511–1592). One of the most peculiar rooms ever built, the foyer has among its oddities a two-story ceiling and a form that is higher than it is long or wide. The niches (wall recesses) are smaller at the bottom than at the top, and the same inversion of the norm is true of the pilasters that flank the niches. The columns are set into the wall, not in front of it, reversing the usual column and wall relationship. Scroll brackets, usually supporting elements, are rendered nonfunctional by their placement. The impression is one of walls pushing in, crushing the visitor. Finally, and strangest of all, the staircase has three separate flights at the bottom but only one into the doorway at the top— a guaranteed traffic problem. This intriguing and uncomfortable room, in which everything is contrary to the classical rules of architecture, may be regarded as an ingenious Mannerist interpretation of the antique vocabulary.

Figure 13.48   Michelangelo, Vasari, and Ammanati, vestibule of Laurentian Library, begun 1524, staircase completed 1559, monastery of San Lorenzo, Florence. The antique architectural vocabulary has been used to create a space in which the visitor is unlikely to feel comfortable. The stairs, which seem to flow downward, fill most of the floor space, and, because three flights lead to a single doorway at the top, a traffic jam is likely.

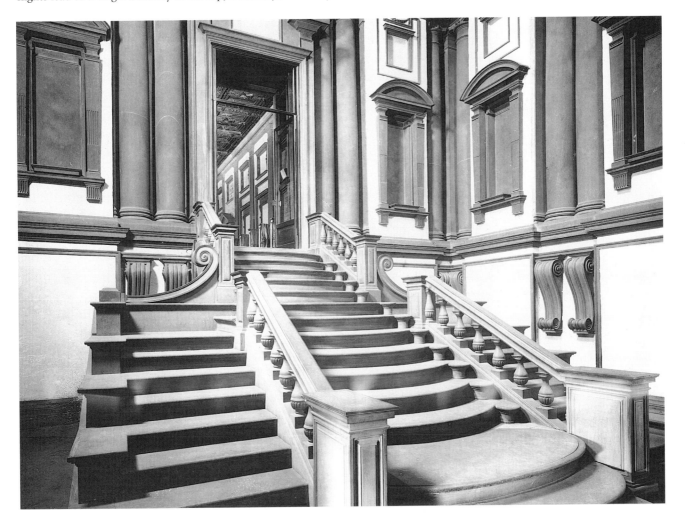

Then & Now

THE VENICE GHETTO

One of the most horrifying events in twentieth-century history is the Holocaust, the anti-Semitism movement in Hitler's Germany that led to the murder of approximately seven million Jews. One of the reasons Hitler could so easily identify the Jewish population in Europe was that the vast majority of Jews lived in official or unofficial ghettos in the major European capitals. The earliest known segregation of Jews into their own distinct neighborhoods occurred in Spain and Portugal in the fourteenth century, but a large ghetto was established in Frankfurt in 1460. Ghettos in Venice appeared early in the sixteenth century.

A Jewish presence in Venice dates to the early fourteenth century, and by 1381 the city had authorized Jews to live in the city, practice usury—the lending of money with interest—and sell secondhand clothes and objects, which led to the profession of pawn-broking. In 1397, all Jews were expelled, ostensibly because of irregularities that had been discovered in the monetary practices of Jewish bankers and merchants. They were permitted to visit the city for no more than fifteen consecutive days and forced to wear an emblem identifying their religion. But this order became more and more laxly enforced, and the Venetian Jewish community flourished until 1496, when they were once again banished, and this time only permitted to stay in Venice for two weeks a year.

In 1508, Julius II formed an alliance with the rest of Italy and Europe against Venice, and when his army approached the city in the spring of 1509, the large Jewish community that lived on the mainland at the lagoon's edge fled to Venice proper. Many Jewish leaders offered much-needed financial support, and the city found itself in a quandary about where they should be allowed to live. The issue was hotly debated for seven years. Franciscan sermons routinely warned that God would punish the city if Jews were admitted. Finally, on March 29, 1516, a substantial majority of the Senate approved a proposal to move the Jews *en masse* to an islet linked to the rest of the city by two points of access that could be closed at night. In this way, Venice could make use of the skills—and money—of the Jewish community and still segregate them.

The island to which they were banished was the site of a new foundry. The Venetian word for the smelting process is *gettare*, and the new foundry built on the island was named *getto nuovo*. Soon the island itself was called Ghetto Nuovo, and the word "ghetto" entered the language, and came to be used throughout Europe to describe the areas in cities where Jewish communities were to be found.

READINGS

❧

❧ PETRARCH
Sonnet 159

The following poem is just one of the many in which Petrarch celebrated his beloved Laura. Consider how the poet refers to Neoplatonic and humanist ideas. Petrarch was master of the extended metaphor; here it comprises the entire sonnet.

From what part of the Heavens, from what Idea
did Nature take the model to derive
that lovely face of charm by which she chose
to show down here her power up above?

What fountain nymph, what woodland goddess ever   5
let such fine hair of gold flow in the breeze?
How did a heart collect so many virtues
the sum of which is guilty of my death?

Who seeks for divine beauty seeks in vain,
if he has not yet looked upon those eyes   10
and seen how tenderly she makes them move;

he does not know how love can heal and kill,
who does not know the sweetness of her sighs,
the sweetness of her speech, how sweet her smile.

❧ VITTORIA DA COLONNA
I Live on This Depraved and Lonely Cliff

Vittoria da Colonna (1490–1547), one of the most celebrated women of the Italian Renaissance, was a member of the nobility and a friend to prominent artists and writers. She is generally recognized as the inspiration for a number of Michelangelo's poems. In all her own poems, exclusively written in sonnet form, Vittoria da Colonna describes her relationship with and love for her husband. The following poem contains Neoplatonic light imagery, popular in Renaissance lyric poetry.

I live on this depraved and lonely cliff
like a sad bird abhorring a green tree
or plashing water; I move forcefully
away from those I love, and I am stiff
even before myself, so that my thoughts   5
may rise and fly to him: sun I adore
and worship. Though their wings could hurry more,
they race only to him; the forest rots
until the instant when they reach that place.
Then deep in ecstasy, though brief, they feel   10
a joy beyond all earthly joy. I reel,
and yet if they could recreate his face
as my mind, craving and consuming, would,
then here perhaps I'd own the perfect good.

BALDASSARE CASTIGLIONE
from the *Book of the Courtier*

The Book of the Courtier *was not published until 1528, but it is one of the most representative books of the Italian High Renaissance. It is also one of the most highly regarded. The English scholar Roger Ascham (1515–1568) claimed that, when diligently read, Castiglione's book was more instructive than a three-year sojourn in Italy. Among other things, it offered practical advice to the Renaissance gentleman on how to get ahead. However, it was in some respects a bit naive, as Machiavelli's* The Prince *would show.*

"Then, as for the physical appearance of the courtier, I would say that all that is necessary is that he should be neither too small nor too big, since either of these two conditions causes a certain contemptuous wonder and men built in this way are stared at as if they were monsters. However, if one is forced to choose between the two evils, then it is better to be on the small side than unduly large; for men who are so huge are often found to be rather thick-headed, and moreover, they are also unsuited for sport and recreation, which I think most important for the courtier. So I wish our courtier to be well built, with finely proportioned members, and I would have him demonstrate strength and lightness and suppleness and be good at all the physical exercises befitting a warrior. Here, I believe, his first duty is to know how to handle expertly every kind of weapon, either on foot or mounted, to understand all their finer points, and to be especially well informed about all those weapons commonly used among gentlemen. For apart from their use in war, when perhaps the finer points may be neglected, often differences arise between one gentleman and another and lead to duels, and very often the weapons used are those that come immediately to hand. So, for safety's sake, it is important to know about them. And I am not one of those who assert that all skill is forgotten in a fight; because anyone who loses his skill at such a time shows that he has allowed his fear to rob him of his courage and his wits.

"I also believe that it is of the highest importance to know how to wrestle, since this often accompanies combat on foot. Next, both for his own sake and for his friends, the courtier should understand about seeking restitution and the conduct of disputes, and he should be skilled in seizing the advantage, and in all this he must show both courage and prudence. Nor should he be too anxious for these engagements, save when his honour demands it; for, as well as the considerable danger that an uncertain outcome brings with it, whoever rushes into these things precipitately and without urgent cause deserves to be gravely censured, even if he is successful. However, when a man has committed himself so far that he cannot withdraw without reproach then both in the preliminaries and in the duel itself he should be very deliberate. He should always show readiness and courage; and he should not behave like those who are always quibbling and arguing over points of honour, and when they have the choice of weapons, select those which can neither cut nor prick, arm themselves as if they had to face a cannonade, and, thinking it enough if they are not defeated, retreat all the time and keep on the defensive, giving proof of utter cowardice, and in this way making themselves the sport of children, like those two men from Ancona who fought at Perugia a little while ago, and made everyone who saw them burst out laughing."

"And who were they?" asked Gaspare Pallavicino.

"Two cousins," answered Cesare.

"And in their fighting, more like two dear brothers," said the Count. Then he continued:

"Weapons are also often used in various sports during peace-time, and gentlemen often perform in public spectacles before the people and before ladies and great lords. So I wish our courtier to be an accomplished and versatile horseman and, as well as having a knowledge of horses and all the matters to do with riding, he should put every effort and diligence into surpassing the rest just a little in everything, so that he may always be recognized as superior. And as we read of Alcibiades, that he surpassed all those peoples among whom he lived, and each time in regard to what they claimed to be best at, so this courtier of ours should outstrip all others, and in regard to the things they know well. Thus it is the peculiar excellence of the Italians to ride well with the rein, to handle spirited horses very skilfully, and to tilt and joust; so in all this the courtier should compare with the best of them. In tourneys, in holding his ground, in forcing his way forward, he should compare with the best of the French; in volleying, in running bulls, in casting spears and darts, he should be outstanding among the Spaniards. But, above all, he should accompany his every act with a certain grace and fine judgement if he wishes to earn that universal regard which everyone covets." …

"If I remember rightly, my dear Count, it seems to me that you have repeated several times this evening that the courtier has to imbue with grace his movements, his gestures, his way of doing things and in short, his every action. And it appears to me that you require this in everything as the seasoning without which all other attributes and good qualities would be almost worthless. Now I admit that everyone should easily be persuaded of this, seeing that, by the very meaning of the word, it can be said that a man who behaves with grace finds it with others. You have said that this is very often a natural, God-given gift, and that even if it is not quite perfect it can be greatly enhanced by application and effort. It seems to me that those who are born as fortunate and as rich in such treasures as some we know have little need of any further instruction, since the gracious favour they have received from heaven raises them, almost despite themselves, higher than they might have desired, and makes everyone both like and admire them. I do not argue about this, since it is not in our power to acquire it of ourselves. But regarding those who receive from Nature only so much as to make it possible for them to acquire grace through enterprise, application and effort, I should like to know by what art, teaching and method they can gain this grace, both in sport and recreation which you believe are so important, and in everything else they say or do. Now since by praising this quality so highly you have, I believe, aroused in all of us a strong desire to obtain it, because of the task given you by signora Emilia, you are also obliged to satisfy us by teaching the way to do so." …

"Therefore anyone who wants to be a good pupil must not only do things well but must also make a constant effort to imitate and, if possible, exactly reproduce his master. And when he feels he has made some progress it is very profitable for him to observe different kinds of courtiers and, ruled by the good judgement that must always be his guide, take various qualities now from one man and now from another. Just as in the summer fields the bees wing their way among the plants from one flower to the next, so the courtier must acquire this grace from those who appear to possess it and take from each one the quality that seems most commendable. And he should certainly not act like a friend of ours, whom you all know, who thought that he greatly resembled King Ferdinand the Younger of Aragon, but had not tried to imitate him except in the way he raised his head and twisted a corner of his mouth, a habit which the King had acquired through illness. There are many like this, who think they are marvellous if they can simply resemble a great man in some one thing; and often they seize on the only defect he has. However, having already thought a great deal about how this grace is acquired, and leaving aside those who are endowed with it by their stars, I have discovered a universal rule which seems to apply more than any other in all human actions or words: namely, to steer away from affectation at all costs, as if it were a rough and dangerous reef, and (to use perhaps a novel word for it) to practise in all things a certain nonchalance which conceals all artistry and makes whatever one says or does seem uncontrived and effortless. I am sure that grace springs especially from this, since everyone knows how difficult it is to accomplish some unusual feat perfectly, and so facility in such things excites the greatest wonder; whereas, in contrast, to labour at what one is doing and, as we say, to make bones over it, shows an extreme lack of grace and causes everything, whatever its worth, to be discounted. So we can truthfully say that true art is what does not seem to be art; and the most important thing is to conceal it, because if it is revealed this discredits a man completely and ruins his reputation. I remember once having read of certain outstanding orators of the ancient world who, among the other things they did, tried hard to make everyone believe that they were ignorant of letters; and, dissembling their knowledge, they made their speeches appear to have been composed very simply and according to the promptings of Nature and truth rather than effort and artifice. For if the people had known of their skills, they would have been frightened of being deceived. So you see that to reveal intense application and skill robs everything of grace. Who is there among you who doesn't laugh when our Pierpaolo dances in that way of his, with those little jumps and with his legs stretched on tiptoe, keeping his head motionless as if he were made of wood, and all so laboured that he seems to be counting every step? Who is so blind that he doesn't see in this the clumsiness of affectation? And in contrast we see in many of the men and women who are with us now, that graceful and nonchalant spontaneity (as it is often called) because of which they seem to be paying little, if any, attention to the way they speak or laugh or hold themselves, so that those who are watching them imagine that they couldn't and wouldn't ever know how to make a mistake."

Then, without waiting, Bernardo Bibbiena said:

"Well, it seems that our Roberto has now found someone who will praise his style of dancing, which you all despise. For if the excellence we are discussing consists in being nonchalant, and displaying indifference, and thinking of anything except what one is actually doing, then when it comes to dancing Roberto is without equal, because to demonstrate that he isn't thinking what he is doing he lets his clothes fall from his back and his slippers from his feet, and he dances away without bothering to pick them up."

The Count went on: "Since you wish me to continue with the discussion, I shall now say something about our faults. Do you not realize that what you are calling nonchalance in Roberto is in fact affectation, since he evidently goes to great pains to show that he is not thinking about what he is doing? He is really taking too much thought, and by passing the bounds of moderation his nonchalance is affected and inappropriate, and it has exactly the opposite effect of what is intended, namely the concealment of art. So although nonchalance is praiseworthy as such, when it leads to someone letting the clothes fall off his back it degenerates as easily into affectation as does a meticulous regard for one's personal appearance (also praiseworthy as such), when it means holding one's head rigid for fear of spoiling one's coiffure, or carrying a mirror in the fold of one's cap and a comb in one's sleeve, and walking through the streets always followed by a page with a brush and sponge. For this kind of self-regard and nonchalance goes too much to extremes, which is always a fault and the opposite of the pure and agreeable simplicity which appeals to everyone. Notice how ungraceful a rider is when he forces himself to sit bolt upright in the saddle, as is said, in the Venetian way, in comparison with another who sits on his horse as free and relaxed as if he were on the ground. How much more agreeable and admired is a warrior when he is modest, saying little and boasting hardly ever, than one who is forever singing his own praises and threatening all and sundry with his swearing and bragging! And this is simply the affectation of wanting to appear a bold fellow. The same applies whatever one's profession; indeed, it holds good for every single thing we do or say."

At this, the Magnifico Giuliano remarked: "It certainly holds true in music, in which it is very wrong to have two perfect consonances one after the other; for our sense of hearing abhors this, whereas it often likes a second or a seventh, which in itself is a harsh and unbearable discord. This is because to continue in perfect consonances produces satiety and offers a harmony which is too affected; but this disappears when imperfect consonances are introduced to establish the contrast which keeps the listener in a state of expectancy, waiting for and enjoying the perfect consonances more eagerly and delighting in the discord of the second or seventh, as in a display of nonchalance."

"So you see," answered the Count, "that affectation is as dangerous in music as in other things. Moreover, it is said to have been proverbial among certain great painters of the ancient world that excessive diligence is harmful; and Protogenes is said to have been censured by Apelles for not knowing when to take his hands from the board."

Then Cesare added: "It seems to me that our Fra Serafino shares this same fault of not being able to take his hands from the board, at least not before all the food has been taken away as well."[1]

---

[1] The pun, untranslatable into English, relies on the use of the same word *tavola* for both table and board or panel.

The Count laughed and continued: "What Apelles meant was that when painting Protogenes did not know when he had done enough; in other words, he was blaming him for finishing his work too thoroughly. So this quality which is the opposite of affectation and which we are now calling nonchalance, apart from being the real source of grace, brings with it another advantage; for whatever action it accompanies, no matter how trivial it is, it not only reveals the skill of the person doing it but also very often causes it to be considered far greater than it really is. This is because it makes the onlookers believe that a man who performs well with so much facility must possess even greater skill than he does, and that if he took great pains and effort he would perform even better. To give other examples, consider a man using weapons, and about to throw a dart or handle a sword or some other weapon. If, without thinking about it, he casually takes up a position at the ready, so naturally that it seems as if his whole body assumes the right posture without any strain, then even if he does nothing more he demonstrates that he is in complete command of what he is doing. Similarly in dancing, a single step, a single unforced and graceful movement of the body, at once demonstrates the skill of the dancer. When a musician is singing and utters a single word ending in a group of notes with a sweet cadence, and with such ease that it seems effortless, that touch alone proves that he is capable of far more than he is doing. Then again, in painting, a single line which is not laboured, a single brush stroke made with ease, in such a way that it seems that the hand is completing the line by itself without any effort or guidance, clearly reveals the excellence of the artist, about whose competence everyone will then make his own judgement. The same happens in almost every other thing. Our courtier, therefore, will be judged to be perfect and will show grace in everything, and especially in his speech, if he shuns affectation. However, affectation is a vice of which only too many people are guilty, and sometimes our Lombards more than others, who, if they have been away from home for a year, on their return immediately start speaking Roman or Spanish or French, and God knows what. And all this springs from the over-anxiety to show how much they know; so that they put care and effort into acquiring a detestable vice. Certainly it would require a great deal of effort on my part if in these discussions of ours I wished to use those old Tuscan words which the Tuscans of today have discarded; and what's more I'm sure you would all laugh at me."

At this, Federico remarked: "It is true that in talking among ourselves as we are doing now it would perhaps be wrong to use those old Tuscan words; because, as you say, they would prove tedious both for the speaker and his listeners, and many of us would have difficulty in understanding them. But for myself I believe that it would be wrong not to make use of them in writing, because they impart considerable grace and authority to what is written, and they produce a style which is more dignified and sonorous than can be achieved with modern words."

To this, the Count replied: "I can hardly think how grace and authority may be conferred by words which should be eschewed not only (as you yourself admit) in the kind of conversation we are enjoying at the moment but also in any conceivable circumstance. For if any man of good judge-ment had to make a speech on a serious subject before the very senate of Florence, which is the capital of Tuscany, or had to discuss important business in private with a high-ranking Florentine, or even amusing things with a close friend, or romantic affairs with ladies or gentlemen, or had to join in the jesting and joking at feasts, games or anywhere else, whatever the time, place or subject, I am certain that he would go out of his way to avoid using those old Tuscan words. And if he did use them, as well as making a fool of himself he would give no little annoyance to anyone listening. So it seems to me very curious to accept as good in writing those very words which are shunned as wrong in all kinds of conversation, and to insist that what is never appropriate in speech should be highly appropriate when it comes to writing. For it is my belief that writing is nothing other than a kind of speech which remains in being after it has been uttered, the representation, as it were, or rather the very life of our words. And so in speech, which ceases to exist as soon as it is uttered, some things are perhaps tolerable which are not so in writing; because writing preserves the words and submits them to the judgement of the reader, who has the time to give them his considered attention. Therefore it is right that greater pains should be taken to make what is written more polished and correct; not, however, that the written words should be different from those which are spoken, but they should be chosen from the most beautiful of those employed in speech. If we were to allow in writing what is not allowed in speech, in my opinion there would be one very unfortunate result: namely, more liberties could be taken in an area demanding the strictest discipline, and all the endeavour that goes into writing would be harmful instead of beneficial. So surely the rule is that what is proper in writing is also proper in speaking; and the finest speech resembles the finest writing. Moreover, I believe that it is more important to make one's meaning clear in writing than in speaking; because unlike someone listening, the reader is not always present when the author is writing. However, I would praise any man who, as well as shunning the use of many old Tuscan words, also makes certain, whether he is writing or speaking, that he employs words in current usage in Tuscany or elsewhere in Italy which possess a certain grace when they are pronounced. It seems to me that anyone who follows some other practice runs the risk of that affectation which attracts so much censure and about which we were talking a moment ago."

Then Federico said: "I cannot deny, Count, that writing is a kind of speech. I would say, however, that if the spoken word is at all obscure what is said will fail to penetrate the mind of the listener and, since it will not be understood, will be useless. And this is not the case with writing, for if the words used by the writer carry with them a certain, I will not say difficulty but veiled subtlety, and so are not as familiar as those commonly used in speech, they give what is written greater authority and cause the reader to be more attentive and aware, and so reflect more deeply and enjoy the skill and message of the author; and by judiciously exerting himself a little he experiences the pleasure that is to be had from accomplishing difficult tasks. If the reader is so ignorant that he cannot overcome these difficulties, that is not the fault of the writer and his language should not, on this account, be judged to lack beauty. Therefore in writing I believe that it is right to use Tuscan words, and only those employed by the ancient Tuscans, because that is a convincing proof, tested by time, that they are sound and effective in conveying what they mean. Furthermore, they possess the grace and dignity which great age imparts not only to words but also to buildings, statues, pictures and to everything that is able to endure. And often simply by such splendour and dignity they beautify one's diction, through whose force and eloquence everything, no matter how mean, can be so embellished that it deserves the highest praise. But this matter of contemporary usage, on which you put so much stress, seems to me highly dangerous and very often wrong. If some solecism or other is adopted by many ignorant people, this, in my opinion, hardly means that it should be accepted as a rule and followed by others. What is more, current practice varies a great deal, and there's not a city in Italy where the mode of speech is not different from everywhere else. However, since you have not felt obliged to declare which of them is the best, a man might just as well take up Bergamasque as Florentine and, according to you, this would be perfectly correct. It seems to me, therefore, that if one wants to avoid all misgivings and be absolutely certain, one has to decide to imitate someone who by common consent is accepted as sound, and to employ him continuously as a guide and protection against hostile critics. And this model (I mean in the vernacular) should be none other, I think, than Petrarch or Boccaccio; and whoever strays from these two has to grope his way, like a man walking through the darkness without a light, and will frequently take the wrong path. But nowadays we are so headstrong that we are contemptuous of doing what the best men did in the ancient world, namely, of practising imitation. But unless we do I believe it is impossible to write well. It seems to me that there is convincing proof of this in Virgil who, although his inspired judgement and genius were such that he made it impossible for anyone afterwards to hope to imitate him successfully, yet himself wished to imitate Homer."

✦ **NICCOLÒ MACHIAVELLI**
from *The Prince*

Fundamentally, Machiavelli's The Prince *is a book about power, especially how power is seized and administered. The political arena is a jungle in which the strongest prevail, a relentlessly competitive world in which maintaining moral standards and ethical behavior is merely naive. For the prince who wants to retain his power, the end justifies the means. To gain and hold power, Machiavelli notes, the prince requires the cunning of the fox and the strength of the lion. The heart of Machiavelli's advice appears in the chapters extolling the "virtues" of a prince; an excerpt follows.*

XV. The things for which men, and especially princes, are praised or blamed

It now remains for us to see how a prince must govern his conduct towards his subjects or his friends. I know that this has often been written about before, and so I hope it will not be thought presumptuous for me to do so, as, especially in discussing this subject, I draw up an original set of rules. But since my intention is to say something that will prove of practical use to the inquirer, I have thought it proper to represent things as they are in real truth, rather than as they are imagined. Many have dreamed up republics and principalities which have never in truth been known to exist; the gulf between how one should live and how one does live is so wide that a man who neglects what is actually done for what should be done learns the way to self-destruction rather than self-preservation. The fact is that a man who wants to act virtuously in every way necessarily comes to grief among so many who are not virtuous. Therefore if a prince wants to maintain his rule he must learn how not to be virtuous, and to make use of this or not according to need.

So leaving aside imaginary things, and referring only to those which truly exist, I say that whenever men are discussed (and especially princes, who are more exposed to view), they are noted for various qualities which earn them either praise or condemnation. Some, for example, are held to be generous, and others miserly (I use the Tuscan word rather than the word avaricious: we call a man who is mean with what he possesses, miserly, and a man who wants to plunder others, avaricious).[1] Some are held to be benefactors, others are called grasping; some cruel, some compassionate; one man faithless, another faithful; one man effeminate and cowardly, another fierce and courageous; one man courteous, another proud; one man lascivious, another pure; one guileless, another crafty; one stubborn, another flexible; one grave, another frivolous; one religious, another sceptical; and so forth. I know everyone will agree that it would be most laudable if a prince possessed all the qualities deemed to be good among those I have enumerated. But, because of conditions in the world, princes cannot have those qualities, or observe them completely. So a prince has of necessity to be so prudent that he knows how to escape the evil reputation attached to those vices which could lose him his state, and how to avoid those vices which are not so dangerous, if he possibly can; but, if he cannot, he need not worry so much about the latter. And then, he must not flinch from being blamed for vices which are necessary for safeguarding the state. This is because, taking everything into account, he will find that some of the things that appear to be virtues will, if he practises them, ruin him, and some of the things that appear to be vices will bring him security and prosperity.

XVI. Generosity and parsimony

So, starting with the first of the qualities I enumerated above, I say it would be splendid if one had a reputation for generosity; nonetheless if you do in fact earn a reputation for generosity you will come to grief. This is because if your generosity is good and sincere it may pass unnoticed and it will not save you from being reproached for its opposite. If you want to acquire a reputation for generosity, therefore, you have to be ostentatiously lavish; and a prince acting in that fashion will soon squander all his resources, only to be forced in the end, if he wants to maintain his reputation, to lay excessive burdens on the people, to impose extortionate taxes, and to do everything else he can to raise money. This

---

[1] The two words Machiavelli uses are *misero* and *avaro*.

will start to make his subjects hate him, and, since he will have impoverished himself, he will be generally despised. As a result, because of this generosity of his, having injured many and rewarded few, he will be vulnerable to the first minor setback, and the first real danger he encounters will bring him to grief. When he realizes this and tries to retrace his path he will immediately be reputed a miser.

So as a prince cannot practise the virtue of generosity in such a way that he is noted for it, except to his cost, he should if he is prudent not mind being called a miser. In time he will be recognized as being essentially a generous man, seeing that because of his parsimony his existing revenues are enough for him, he can defend himself against an aggressor, and he can embark on enterprises without burdening the people. So he proves himself generous to all those from whom he takes nothing, and they are innumerable, and miserly towards all those to whom he gives nothing, and they are few. In our own times great things have been accomplished only by those who have been held miserly, and the others have met disaster. Pope Julius II made use of a reputation for generosity to win the papacy but subsequently he made no effort to maintain this reputation, because he wanted to be able to finance his wars. The present king of France has been able to wage so many wars without taxing his subjects excessively only because his long-standing parsimony enabled him to meet the additional expenses involved. Were the present king of Spain renowned for his generosity he would not have started and successfully concluded so many enterprises.

So a prince must think little of it, if he incurs the name of miser, so as not to rob his subjects, to be able to defend himself, not to become poor and despicable, not to be forced to grow rapacious. Miserliness is one of those vices which sustain his rule. Someone may object: Caesar came to power by virtue of his generosity, and many others, because they practised and were known for their generosity, have risen to the very highest positions. My answer to this is as follows. Either you are already a prince, or you are on the way to becoming one. In the first case, your generosity will be to your cost; in the second, it is certainly necessary to have a reputation for generosity. Caesar was one of those who wanted to establish his own rule over Rome; but if, after he had established it, he had remained alive and not moderated his expenditure he would have fallen from power.

Again, someone may retort: there have been many princes who have won great successes with their armies, and who have had the reputation of being extremely generous. My reply to this is: the prince gives away what is his own or his subjects', or else what belongs to others. In the first case he should be frugal; in the second, he should indulge his generosity to the full. The prince who campaigns with his armies, who lives by pillaging, sacking, and extortion, disposes of what belongs to aliens; and he must be open-handed, otherwise the soldiers would refuse to follow him. And you can be more liberal with what does not belong to you or your subjects, as Caesar, Cyrus, and Alexander were. Giving away what belongs to strangers in no way affects your standing at home; rather it increases it. You hurt yourself only when you give away what is your own. There is nothing so self-defeating as generosity: in the act of practising it, you lose the ability to do so, and you become either poor and despised or, seeking to escape poverty, rapacious and hated. A prince must try to avoid, above all else, being despised and hated; and generosity results in your being both. Therefore it is wiser to incur the reputation of being a miser, which invites ignominy but not hatred, than to be forced by seeking a name for generosity to incur a reputation for rapacity, which brings you hatred as well as ignominy.

XVII. Cruelty and compassion; and whether it is better to be loved than feared, or the reverse

Taking others of the qualities I enumerated above, I say that a prince must want to have a reputation for compassion rather than for cruelty: nonetheless, he must be careful that he does not make bad use of compassion. Cesare Borgia was accounted cruel; nevertheless, this cruelty of his reformed the Romagna, brought it unity, and restored order and obedience. On reflection, it will be seen that there was more compassion in Cesare than in the Florentine people, who, to escape being called cruel, allowed Pistoia to be devastated.[2] So a prince must not worry if he incurs reproach for his cruelty so long as he keeps his subjects united and loyal. By making an example or two he will prove more compassionate than those who, being too compassionate, allow disorders which lead to murder and rapine. These nearly always harm the whole community, whereas executions ordered by a prince only affect individuals. A new prince, of all rulers, finds it impossible to avoid a reputation for cruelty, because of the abundant dangers inherent in a newly won state. Vergil, through the mouth of Dido, says:

> *Res dura, et regni novitas me talia cogunt*
> *Moliri, et late fines custode tueri.*[3]

Nonetheless, a prince must be slow to take action, and must watch that he does not come to be afraid of his own shadow; his behaviour must be tempered by humanity and prudence so that over-confidence does not make him rash or excessive distrust make him unbearable.

From this arises the following question: whether it is better to be loved than feared, or the reverse. The answer is that one would like to be both the one and the other; but because it is difficult to combine them, it is far better to be feared than loved if you cannot be both. One can make this generalization about men: they are ungrateful, fickle, liars, and deceivers, they shun danger and are greedy for profit; while you treat them well, they are yours. They would shed their blood for you, risk their property, their lives, their children, so long, as I said above, as danger is remote; but when you are in danger they turn against you. Any prince who has come to depend entirely on promises and has taken no other precautions ensures his own ruin; friendship which

---

[2] Pistoia was a subject-city of Florence, which forcibly restored order there when conflict broke out between two rival factions in 1501–02. Machiavelli was concerned with this business at first hand.

[3] "Harsh necessity, and the newness of my kingdom, force me to do such things and to guard my frontiers everywhere." *Aeneid* i, 563.

is bought with money and not with greatness and nobility of mind is paid for, but it does not last and it yields nothing. Men worry less about doing an injury to one who makes himself loved than to one who makes himself feared. The bond of love is one which men, wretched creatures that they are, break when it is to their advantage to do so; but fear is strengthened by a dread of punishment which is always effective.

The prince must nonetheless make himself feared in such a way that, if he is not loved, at least he escapes being hated. For fear is quite compatible with an absence of hatred; and the prince can always avoid hatred if he abstains from the property of his subjects and citizens and from their women. If, even so, it proves necessary to execute someone, this is to be done only when there is proper justification and manifest reason for it. But above all a prince must abstain from the property of others; because men sooner forget the death of their father than the loss of their patrimony. It is always possible to find pretexts for confiscating someone's property; and a prince who starts to live by rapine always finds pretexts for seizing what belongs to others. On the other hand, pretexts for executing someone are harder to find and they are less easily sustained.

However, when a prince is campaigning with his soldiers and is in command of a large army then he need not worry about having a reputation for cruelty; because, without such a reputation, no army was ever kept united and disciplined. Among the admirable achievements of Hannibal is included this: that although he led a huge army, made up of countless different races, on foreign campaigns, there was never any dissension, either among the troops themselves or against their leader, whether things were going well or badly. For this, his inhuman cruelty was wholly responsible. It was this, along with his countless other qualities, which made him feared and respected by his soldiers. If it had not been for his cruelty, his other qualities would not have been enough. The historians, having given little thought to this, on the one hand admire what Hannibal achieved, and on the other condemn what made his achievements possible.

That his other qualities would not have been enough by themselves can be proved by looking at Scipio, a man unique in his own time and through all recorded history. His armies mutinied against him in Spain, and the only reason for this was his excessive leniency, which allowed his soldiers more licence than was good for military discipline. Fabius Maximus reproached him for this in the Senate and called him a corrupter of the Roman legions. Again, when the Locri were plundered by one of Scipio's officers, he neither gave them satisfaction nor punished his officer's insubordination; and this was all because of his having too lenient a nature. By way of excuse for him some senators argued that many men were better at not making mistakes themselves than at correcting them in others. But in time Scipio's lenient nature would have spoilt his fame and glory had he continued to indulge it during his command; when he lived under orders from the Senate, however, this fatal characteristic of his was not only concealed but even brought him glory.

So, on this question of being loved or feared, I conclude that since some men love as they please but fear when the prince pleases, a wise prince should rely on what he con-

trols, not on what he cannot control. He must only endeavour, as I said, to escape being hated.

XVIII. How princes should honour their word

Everyone realizes how praiseworthy it is for a prince to honour his word and to be straightforward rather than crafty in his dealings; nonetheless contemporary experience shows that princes who have achieved great things have been those who have given their word lightly, who have known how to trick men with their cunning, and who, in the end, have overcome those abiding by honest principles.

You must understand, therefore, that there are two ways of fighting: by law or by force. The first way is natural to men, and the second to beasts. But as the first way often proves inadequate one must needs have recourse to the second. So a prince must understand how to make a nice use of the beast and the man. The ancient writers taught princes about this by an allegory, when they described how Achilles and many other princes of the ancient world were sent to be brought up by Chiron, the centaur, so that he might train them his way. All the allegory means, in making the teacher half beast and half man, is that a prince must know how to act according to the nature of both, and that he cannot survive otherwise.

So, as a prince is forced to know how to act like a beast, he must learn from the fox and the lion; because the lion is defenceless against traps and a fox is defenceless against wolves. Therefore one must be a fox in order to recognize traps, and a lion to frighten off wolves. Those who simply act like lions are stupid. So it follows that a prudent ruler cannot, and must not honour his word when it places him at a disadvantage and when the reasons for which he made his promise no longer exist. If all men were good, this precept would not be good; but because men are wretched creatures who would not keep their word to you, you need not keep your word to them. And no prince ever lacked good excuses to colour his bad faith. One could give innumerable modern instances of this, showing how many pacts and promises have been made null and void by the bad faith of princes: those who have known best how to imitate the fox have come off best. But one must know how to colour one's actions and to be a great liar and deceiver. Men are so simple, and so much creatures of circumstance, that the deceiver will always find someone ready to be deceived.

There is one fresh example I do not want to omit. Alexander VI never did anything, or thought of anything, other than deceiving men; and he always found victims for his deceptions. There never was a man capable of such convincing asseverations, or so ready to swear to the truth of something, who would honour his word less. Nonetheless his deceptions always had the result he intended, because he was a past master in the art.

A prince, therefore, need not necessarily have all the good qualities I mentioned above, but he should certainly appear to have them. I would even go so far as to say that if he has these qualities and always behaves accordingly he will find them harmful; if he only appears to have them they will render him service. He should appear to be compassionate, faithful to his word, kind, guileless, and devout.

And indeed he should be so. But his disposition should be such that, if he needs to be the opposite, he knows how. You must realize this: that a prince, and especially a new prince, cannot observe all those things which give men a reputation for virtue, because in order to maintain his state he is often forced to act in defiance of good faith, of charity, of kindness, of religion. And so he should have a flexible disposition, varying as fortune and circumstances dictate. As I said above, he should not deviate from what is good, if that is possible, but he should know how to do evil, if that is necessary.

A prince, then, must be very careful not to say a word which does not seem inspired by the five qualities I mentioned earlier. To those seeing and hearing him, he should appear a man of compassion, a man of good faith, a man of integrity, a kind and a religious man. And there is nothing so important as to seem to have this last quality. Men in general judge by their eyes rather than by their hands; because everyone is in a position to watch, few are in a position to come in close touch with you. Everyone sees what you appear to be, few experience what you really are. And those few dare not gainsay the many who are backed by the majesty of the state. In the actions of all men, and especially of princes, where there is no court of appeal, one judges by the result. So let a prince set about the task of conquering and maintaining his state: his methods will always be judged honourable and will be universally praised. The common people are always impressed by appearances and results. In this context, there are only common people, and there is no room for the few when the many are supported by the state. A certain contemporary ruler, whom it is better not to name, never preaches anything except peace and good faith;[+] and he is an enemy of both one and the other, and if he had ever honoured either of them he would have lost either his standing or his state many times over.

✦ BENVENUTO CELLINI
from *The Autobiography*

Cellini displays self-pride and self-confidence in the following lively description of his problems in casting his sculpture, Perseus, *boasting how he overcame enormous obstacles and performed near-superhuman feats, all in heightened drama. Cellini casts himself as the hero, of course, and the plot begins with an exposition on the difficult technical requirements, proceeding to a dramatic climax when Cellini frantically tries to undo the near-disastrous work his assistant has done. It concludes in a quiet denouement, as everyone celebrates the completion; even here, Cellini continues his unabashed self-promotion.*

Having succeeded so well with the cast of the Medusa, I had great hope of bringing my Perseus through; for I had laid the wax on, and felt confident that it would come out in bronze as perfectly as the Medusa. The waxen model produced so fine an effect, that when the Duke saw it and was struck with its beauty—whether somebody had persuaded him it could not be carried out with the same finish in metal, or whether he thought so for himself—he came to visit me more frequently than usual, and on one occasion said:

"Benvenuto, this figure cannot succeed in bronze: the laws of art do not admit of it." These words of his Excellency stung me so sharply that I answered: "My lord, I know how very little confidence you have in me; and I believe the reason of this is that your most illustrious Excellency lends too ready an ear to my calumniators, or else indeed that you do not understand my art." He hardly let me close the sentence when he broke in: "I profess myself a connoisseur, and understand it very well indeed." I replied: "Yes, like a prince, not like an artist; for if your Excellency understood my trade as well as you imagine, you would trust me on the proofs I have already given. These are, first, the colossal bronze bust of your Excellency, which is now in Elba; secondly, the restoration of the Ganymede in marble, which offered so many difficulties and cost me so much trouble, that I would rather have made the whole statue new from the beginning; thirdly, the Medusa, cast by me in bronze, here now before your Excellency's eyes, the execution of which was a greater triumph of strength and skill than any of my predecessors in this fiendish art have yet achieved. Look you, my lord! I constructed that furnace anew on principles quite different from those of other founders; in addition to many technical improvements and ingenious devices, I supplied it with two issues for the metal, because this difficult and twisted figure could not otherwise have come out perfect. It is only owing to my intelligent insight into means and appliances that the statue turned out as it did; a triumph judged impossible by all the practitioners of this art."

With all the forces of my body and my purse, employing what little money still remained to me, I set to work. First I provided myself with several loads of pinewood from the forests of Serristori, in the neighbourhood of Montelupo. While these were on their way, I clothed my Perseus with the clay which I had prepared many months beforehand, in order that it might be duly seasoned. After making its clay tunic (for that is the term used in this art) and properly arming it and fencing it with iron girders, I began to draw the wax out by means of a slow fire. This melted and issued through numerous air-vents I had made; for the more there are of these, the better will the mould fill. When I had finished drawing off the wax, I constructed a funnel-shaped furnace all round the model of my Perseus. It was built of bricks, so interlaced, the one above the other, that numerous apertures were left for the fire to exhale at. Then I began to lay on wood by degrees, and kept it burning two whole days and nights. At length, when all the wax was gone, and the mould was well baked, I set to work at digging the pit in which to sink it. This I performed with scrupulous regard to all the rules of art. When I had finished that part of my work, I raised the mould by windlasses and stout ropes to a perpendicular position, and suspending it with the greatest care one cubit above the level of the furnace, so that it hung exactly above the middle of the pit, I next lowered it gently down into the very bottom of the furnace, and had it firmly placed with every possible precaution for its safety. When this delicate operation was accomplished, I began to bank it up with the earth I had excavated; and, ever as the earth grew higher, I introduced its proper air-vents, which were little tubes of earthenware, such as folk use for drains and such-like purposes. At length, I felt sure that it was admirably fixed, and that the filling-in of the pit and the

---

[+] Ferdinand of Aragon.

placing of the air-vents had been properly performed. I also could see that my workpeople understood my method, which differed very considerably from that of all the other masters in the trade. Feeling confident, then, that I could rely upon them, I next turned to my furnace, which I had filled with numerous pigs of copper and other bronze stuff. The pieces were piled according to the laws of art, that is to say, so resting one upon the other that the flames could play freely through them, in order that the metal might heat and liquefy the sooner. At last I called out heartily to set the furnace going. The logs of pine were heaped in, and, what with the unctuous resin of the wood and the good draught I had given, my furnace worked so well that I was obliged to rush from side to side to keep it going. The labour was more than I could stand; yet I forced myself to strain every nerve and muscle. To increase my anxieties, the workshop took fire, and we were afraid lest the roof should fall upon our heads; while, from the garden, such a storm of wind and rain kept blowing in, that it perceptibly cooled the furnace.

Battling thus with all these untoward circumstances for several hours, and exerting myself beyond even the measure of my powerful constitution, I could at last bear up no longer, and a sudden fever, of the utmost possible intensity, attacked me. I felt absolutely obliged to go and fling myself upon my bed. Sorely against my will having to drag myself away from the spot, I turned to my assistants, about ten or more in all, what with master-founders, hand-workers, country-fellows, and my own special journeymen, among whom was Bernardino Mannellini of Mugello, my apprentice through several years. To him in particular I spoke: "Look, my dear Bernardino, that you observe the rules which I have taught you; do your best with all despatch, for the metal will soon be fused. You cannot go wrong; these honest men will get the channels ready; you will easily be able to drive back the two plugs with this pair of iron crooks; and I am sure that my mould will fill miraculously. I feel more ill than I ever did in all my life, and verily believe that it will kill me before a few hours are over." Thus, with despair at heart, I left them, and betook myself to bed.

No sooner had I got to bed, than I ordered my serving-maids to carry food and wine for all the men into the workshop; at the same time I cried: "I shall not be alive to-morrow." They tried to encourage me, arguing that my illness would pass over, since it came from excessive fatigue. In this way I spent two hours battling with the fever, which steadily increased, and calling out continually: "I feel that I am dying." My housekeeper, who was named Mona Fiore da Castel del Rio, a very notable manager and no less warm-hearted, kept chiding me for my discouragement; but, on the other hand, she paid me every kind attention which was possible. However, the sight of my physical pain and moral dejection so affected her, that, in spite of that brave heart of hers, she could not refrain from shedding tears; and yet, so far as she was able, she took good care I should not see them. While I was thus terribly afflicted, I beheld the figure of a man enter my chamber, twisted in his body into the form of a capital S. He raised a lamentable, doleful voice, like one who announces their last hour to men condemned to die upon the scaffold, and spoke these words: "O Benvenuto! your statue is spoiled, and there is no hope whatever of saving it." No sooner had I heard the shriek of that wretch than

I gave a howl which might have been heard from the sphere of flame. Jumping from my bed, I seized my clothes and began to dress. The maids, and my lad, and every one who came around to help me, got kicks or blows of the fist, while I kept crying out in lamentation: "Ah! traitors! enviers! This is an act of treason, done by malice prepense! But I swear by God that I will sift it to the bottom, and before I die will leave such witness to the world of what I can do as shall make a score of mortals marvel."

When I had got my clothes on, I strode with soul bent on mischief toward the workshop; there I beheld the men, whom I had left erewhile in such high spirits, standing stupefied and downcast. I began at once and spoke: "Up with you! Attend to me! Since you have not been able or willing to obey the directions I gave you, obey me now that I am with you to conduct my work in person. Let no one contradict me, for in cases like this we need the aid of hand and hearing, not of advice." When I had uttered these words, a certain Maestro Alessandro Lastricati broke silence and said: "Look you, Benvenuto, you are going to attempt an enterprise which the laws of art do not sanction, and which cannot succeed." I turned upon him with such fury and so full of mischief, that he and all the rest of them exclaimed with one voice: "On then! Give orders! We will obey your least commands, so long as life is left in us." I believe they spoke thus feelingly because they thought I must fall shortly dead upon the ground. I went immediately to inspect the furnace, and found that the metal was all curdled; an accident which we express by "being caked." I told two of the hands to cross the road, and fetch from the house of the butcher Capretta a load of young oak-wood, which had lain dry for above a year; this wood had been previously offered me by Madame Ginevra, wife of the said Capretta. So soon as the first armfuls arrived, I began to fill the grate beneath the furnace. Now oak-wood of that kind heats more powerfully than any other sort of tree; and for this reason, where a slow fire is wanted, as in the case of gun-foundry, alder or pine is preferred. Accordingly, when the logs took fire, oh! how the cake began to stir beneath that awful heat, to glow and sparkle in a blaze! At the same time I kept stirring up the channels, and sent men upon the roof to stop the conflagration, which had gathered force from the increased combustion in the furnace; also I caused boards, carpets, and other hangings to be set up against the garden, in order to protect us from the violence of the rain.

When I had thus provided against these several disasters, I roared out first to one man and then to another: "Bring this thing here! Take that thing there!" At this crisis, when the whole gang saw the cake was on the point of melting, they did my bidding, each fellow working with the strength of three. I then ordered half a pig of pewter to be brought, which weighed about sixty pounds, and flung it into the middle of the cake inside the furnace. By this means, and by piling on wood and stirring now with pokers and now with iron rods, the curdled mass rapidly began to liquefy. Then, knowing I had brought the dead to life again, against the firm opinion of those ignoramuses, I felt such vigour fill my veins, that all those pains of fever, all those fears of death, were quite forgotten.

All of a sudden an explosion took place attended by a tremendous flash of flame, as though a thunderbolt had formed and been discharged amongst us. Unwonted and appalling terror astonished every one, and me more even than the rest. When the din was over and the dazzling light extinguished, we began to look each other in the face. Then I discovered that the cap of the furnace had blown up, and the bronze was bubbling over from its source beneath. So I had the mouths of my mould immediately opened, and at the same time drove in the two plugs which kept back the molten metal. But I noticed that it did not flow as rapidly as usual, the reason being probably that the fierce heat of the fire we kindled had consumed its base alloy. Accordingly I sent for all my pewter platters, porringers, and dishes, to the number of some two hundred pieces, and had a portion of them cast, one by one, into the channels, the rest into the furnace. This expedient succeeded, and every one could now perceive that my bronze was in most perfect liquefaction and my mould was filling; whereupon they all with heartiness and happy cheer assisted and obeyed my bidding, while I now here, now there, gave orders, helped with my own hands, and cried aloud: "O God! Thou that by Thy immeasurable power didst rise from the dead, and in Thy glory didst ascend to heaven!" ... even thus in a moment my mould was filled; and seeing my work finished, I fell upon my knees, and with all my heart gave thanks to God.

After all was over, I turned to a plate of salad on a bench there, and ate with hearty appetite, and drank together with the whole crew. Afterwards I retired to bed, healthy and happy, for it was now two hours before morning, and slept as sweetly as though I had never felt a touch of illness. My good housekeeper, without my giving any orders, had prepared a fat capon for my repast. So that, when I rose, about the hour for breaking fast, she presented herself with a smiling countenance, and said: "Oh! is that the man who felt that he was dying? Upon my word, I think the blows and kicks you dealt us last night, when you were so enraged, and had that demon in your body as it seemed, must have frightened away your mortal fever! The fever feared that it might catch it too, as we did!" All my poor household relieved in like measure from anxiety and overwhelming labour, went at once to buy earthen vessels in order to replace the pewter I had cast away. Then we dined together joyfully; nay, I cannot remember a day in my whole life when I dined with greater gladness or a better appetite.

After I had let my statue cool for two whole days, I began to uncover it by slow degrees. The first thing I found was that the head of Medusa had come out most admirably, thanks to the air-vents; for, as I had told the Duke, it is the nature of fire to ascend. Upon advancing farther, I discovered that the other head, that, namely, of Perseus, had succeeded no less admirably; and this astonished me far more, because it is at a considerably lower level than that of the Medusa. Now the mouths of the mould were placed above the head of Perseus and behind his shoulders; and I found that all the bronze my furnace contained had been exhausted in the head of this figure. It was a miracle to observe that not one fragment remained in the orifice of the channel, and that nothing was wanting to the statue. In my great astonishment I seemed to see in this the hand of God arranging and controlling all.

I went on uncovering the statue with success, and ascertained that everything had come out in perfect order, until I reached the foot of the right leg on which the statue rests. There the heel itself was formed, and going farther, I found the foot apparently complete. This gave me great joy on the one side, but was half unwelcome to me on the other, merely because I had told the Duke that it could not come out. However, when I reached the end, it appeared that the toes and a little piece above them were unfinished, so that about half the foot was wanting. Although I knew that this would add a trifle to my labour, I was very well pleased because I could now prove to the Duke how well I understood my business. It is true that far more of the foot than I expected had been perfectly formed; the reason of this was that from causes I have recently described, the bronze was hotter than our rules of art prescribe; also that I had been obliged to supplement the alloy with my pewter cups and platters, which no one else, I think, had ever done before.

Having now ascertained how successfully my work had been accomplished, I lost no time in hurrying to Pisa, where I found the Duke. He gave me a most gracious reception, as did also the Duchess; and although the major-domo had informed them of the whole proceedings, their Excellencies deemed my performance far more stupendous and astonishing when they heard the tale from my own mouth. When I arrived at the foot of Perseus, and said it had not come out perfect just as I previously warned his Excellency, I saw an expression of wonder pass over his face, while he related to the Duchess how I had predicted this beforehand. Observing the princes to be so well disposed towards me, I begged leave from the Duke to go to Rome. He granted it in most obliging terms, and bade me return as soon as possible to complete his Perseus; giving me letters of recommendation meanwhile to his ambassador, Averardo Serristori.

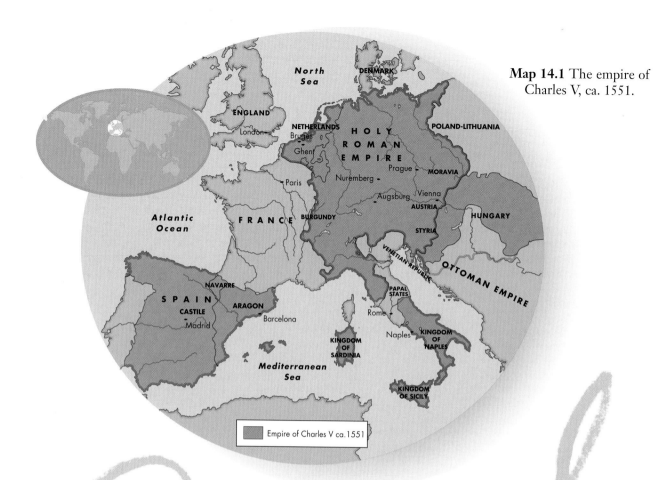

Map 14.1 The empire of Charles V, ca. 1551.

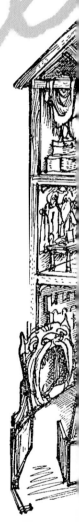

THE
RENAISSANCE
IN THE NORTH

The Globe Playhouse, London, 1599—1613.

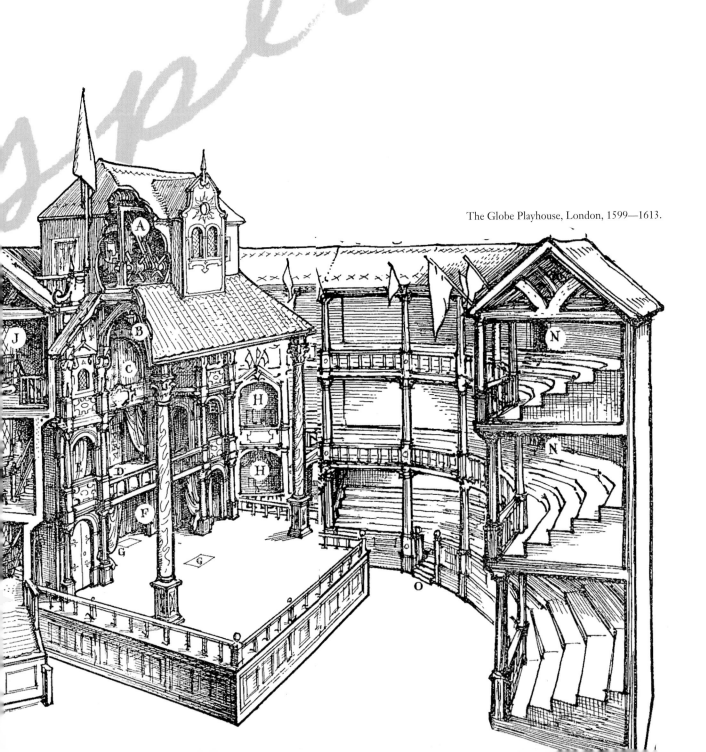

THE EARLY RENAISSANCE IN NORTHERN EUROPE

The traditions of the Renaissance emerged in the north of Europe and in England more slowly than in Italy. The Renaissance was, after all, a "rebirth" of classical values, including Roman values, and the north, even a thousand years after the fact, still smarted from the knowledge that it had been conquered by Rome, and that its peoples had once served as Roman slaves. Yet trade and commerce inevitably brought Italian ideas northward. There they met with a strong artistic tradition, fostered by the Burgundian dukes and the guild systems that had led to the creation of the great Gothic cathedrals. And as trade grew in the north, particularly the Netherlands, so did wealth, fostering the same conditions of patronage that had led to the Renaissance in Italy—with one important difference. In the north, trade also brought prosperity to an ever more influential merchant class, who soon became the most important patrons of their day.

GHENT AND BRUGES

As in Italy, where the Renaissance developed in the great city-states of Florence, Milan, and Venice, and flourished in the revitalized city of Rome, the Renaissance in northern Europe was also a largely urban phenomenon. But the urban centers of the north—such as Martin Luther's Wittenberg in Germany—were, by comparison with Florence and Milan, small towns. By the early sixteenth century in Germany, for instance, fully seventy per cent of the population still lived in the countryside. The area's largest cities were Cologne and Nuremburg, which doubled in size between 1400 and 1500 to reach populations of between forty and fifty thousand, but the vast majority of cities were much smaller, averaging between two and three thousand inhabitants. It was in such small towns that the literate, educated classes lived. And it was in such towns that new ideas flourished.

In the Low Countries, the areas known today as Belgium and the Netherlands, there were, however, a number of substantial cities by the dawn of the fifteenth century. Cities such as Ghent were commercial centers dedicated to trade, surrounded by agricultural lands and located, for trading purposes, along the rivers and coast. In 1340, Ghent was also the site of a flourishing textile industry producing tapestries, lace, and other fine textiles, which it exported to the world from its own substantial port on the River Scheldt. But by 1400 it had lost its place as the region's commercial center, supplanted by the nearby port of Bruges, which had become the financial capital of all northern Europe. There were many reasons for Bruges's rise, among them Ghent's devastating population loss to the Black Plague. Perhaps the most important reason was that Bruges, not Ghent, became the favorite city of the dukes of Burgundy, especially Philip the Good (1396–1467). Philip dreamed of creating in Flanders a court culture that might compete with that of the French, and early in the fifteenth century he moved his court from Dijon to Bruges. Meanwhile, the Medici founded an important branch of their own bank in the city, and fresh news of developments on the Florentine cultural scene was always at hand.

Philip's grandfather, Philip the Bold, and his brother, Jean, Duke of Berry, were great patrons of art in fourteenth- and early fifteenth-century northern Europe, just as the Medici were in fifteenth-century southern Europe. It was Jean who commissioned the Limbourg Brothers' famous illuminated manuscript of the Book of Hours, the *Très Riches Heures du Duc de Berry*, completed in 1416 (see Chapter 12). Their court was obsessed with chivalry and consumed by chivalrous entertainments—jousts, tournaments, pageants, and processions. They dressed in gold-threaded cloth, ermine, and jewels; they commissioned the finest tapestries; and they surrounded themselves with poets, musicians, scholars, and painters. Unfortunately, by the late fifteenth century, the harbor at Bruges was filled with silt, and the city, dwindling in size, lost importance as a financial capital. Virtually untouched and forgotten for four hundred years, it remains one of the finest examples of an early Renaissance city in Europe, its streets and buildings still very much as they were.

FLEMISH OIL PAINTING

Oil paint had, in fact, been used for centuries, particularly to paint stone and metal, but it was not used on canvas until the early fifteenth century. In the past painters had used egg tempera, as seen in the paintings of the southern Renaissance. With egg tempera (pigments mixed with egg yolk), the artist must work quickly because the mixture on the surface dries rapidly. Illusions of space, texture, and and subtle modeling are thus almost impossible to achieve since the paint cannot be blended very readily and since, once applied, the paint is opaque. Oil paint (pigments mixed with linseed oil) stays wet a long time, so colors can be mixed with other colors right on the painting surface, and the artist can work and rework a small section, blending and shading the colors. Depicting the texture of things—soft skin, fluffy hair, velvet, wood, metal, or plaster—would have been impossible to achieve with egg tempera. Furthermore, oil paint could be applied in very thin layers called **glazes** to create a glow to the objects, much as the Venetian painters did (see Chapter 13).

Robert Campin.   One of the first important uses of the oil painting technique is the *Mérode Altarpiece* (fig. 14.1). It is attributed to the Master of Flémalle, com-

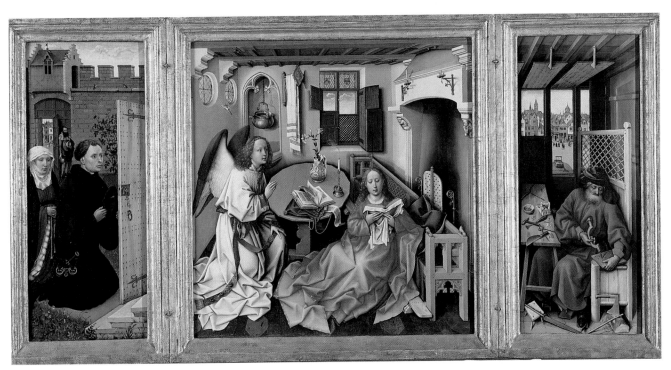

Figure 14.1   Robert Campin (Master of Flémalle), *Mérode Altarpiece*, ca. 1426, oil on panel, center $25\frac{3}{16} \times 24\frac{7}{8}$″ (64.1 × 63.2 cm), each wing $25\frac{3}{8} \times 10\frac{7}{8}$″ (64.5 × 27.6 cm), Metropolitan Museum of Art, New York. Illusions of texture and atmosphere are made possible by painting in oil rather than egg tempera, the medium favored during the Middle Ages. Equally innovative is the depiction of the Annunciation in a middle-class fifteenth-century Flemish home.

monly supposed to be the same person as ROBERT CAMPIN [cam-PEN] (ca. 1375–1444), a member of both the Tournai painters' guild and the city council.

Elements in the altarpiece echo artistic conventions from the Middle Ages: the two figures of Mary and Gabriel are sized according to their importance, not to the reality of the architectural setting. If they were to stand, they would be a full head higher than the door itself. In his treatment of the Annunciation, Campin inaugurates a new matter-of-factness in painting, an attention to the details of reality never before depicted, facilitated by the use of oil paint. Painting around 1426, Campin employed a "mixed" technique in the altarpiece, using egg tempera for the underpainting, then proceeding immediately to paint over it in oil.

The basic format of the altarpiece is that of a **triptych**—a three-paneled painting. The practical advantages of the triptych format are apparent: the wings are hinged and can be closed to protect the painting inside; when they are opened out at an angle, the altarpiece can stand up unaided. The central panel depicts the Annunciation. Shown sitting on the floor, this Mary is referred to as the Madonna of Humility. Yet more noteworthy is the fact that this is the earliest known case in which the Annunciation was depicted as taking place not in a church or holy realm but in a home. This traditional religious subject has been combined with an accurate recording of observed daily life.

In the left panel, the patron, Ingelbrecht of Mechlin, and his wife look through an open doorway, the jamb of which is just visible in the central panel. Their rich garments, together with their patronage of the altarpiece itself, are indicative of the prosperity of the early fifteenth-century Flemish merchant class. The coats-of-arms in the windows of the central panel are thought to be those of the families depicted. Ingelbrecht and his wife are looking into the house, witnessing the miraculous event. Not only does this device establish an ingenious spatial relationship uniting the two panels in a continuum of space, but it collapses historical time as well, uniting past and present, thus underscoring the significance of the Annunciation to the everyday life of the Northern Renaissance Christian.

Using tiny details, the artist documents visual facts about each of the many objects portrayed. Every part of the painted surface is covered with something that catches and holds the viewer's eye. Moreover, this interest in microscopic details is infused with religious symbolism. For example, the lions that serve as decorative finials on the bench are symbols of watchfulness as well as of Jesus and his resurrection; the dog finials are symbols of fidelity and domesticity. The candle refers to the light brought into the world by Jesus. The lily, a symbol of purity, is the flower of the Virgin (Madonna lily). Perhaps the most interesting of these symbolic details is a tiny figure coming in through the window on supernatural rays of golden light, heading directly for Mary's abdomen. This miniature man is a prefiguration of Jesus—in the next instant the Incarnation will take place. Jesus carries a tiny cross, foreshadowing his crucifixion. Together, the motifs would seem to be an amalgamation of the alpha and the omega, the beginning and the end, as Jesus was to call himself.

That seemingly ordinary household items could be subject to religious interpretation was based on the belief that all visible objects were infused with God, and thus virtually every object could carry **iconographic** (or symbolic) implications. Although the symbolism is often elusive today, ambiguity was not the artist's intent. Perhaps the most curious example of symbolism is that employed in the right panel. Here, Mary's husband Joseph works in his carpentry shop. The painting superbly documents a fifteenth-century Flemish carpenter's shop complete with his tools. Through the window a typical Flemish town, perhaps Tournai itself, is seen. Joseph is shown, most remarkably, making mousetraps. This presumably symbolizes what St. Augustine said, that Jesus's Incarnation was God's trap for catching the devil. The Lord's cross was a mousetrap for the devil, and his death was the bait by which the devil would be caught.

Jan van Eyck. In the 1420s, the painter JAN VAN EYCK [van IKE] (ca. 1390–1441) served Philip the Good, not only as a painter but also as a diplomat, accepting assignments to Spain and Portugal. In Portugal, he painted portraits of Philip's future bride, Princess Isabella, so that Philip, back in Flanders, could see what she looked like. He became a renowned painter, sought after not only by the Burgundian court but by visiting notables from abroad, especially by Italians. By the middle of the next century, Giorgio Vasari was referring to him in his *Lives* as the "inventor of oil painting."

Van Eyck is considered, too, the founder of the Flemish school, a painterly tradition in which artists, like Van Eyck and Robert Campin, recorded the real world in minute detail as a way toward truth. Jan van Eyck completed his own altarpiece in 1432, just a few years after the *Mérode Altarpiece* was finished. The *Ghent Altarpiece* is a much more ambitious work in which he was probably aided by his brother Hubert.

In the St. Bavon cathedral in Ghent, this enormous **polyptych**—or work consisting of more than three panels—has twenty-six panels. Closed, it depicts the Annunciation (fig. 14.2), which takes place across four panels cleverly treated as one room. The frame appears to be part of the architecture; it casts a shadow into the room. In the center of the lower tier are painted sculptures of John the Baptist and John the Evangelist, the

former identified by his camel hair garment and the lamb he is holding, the latter by a chalice with snakes. These figures appear to be set in actual architectural niches. Van Eyck has painted light falling from the right as it would have done in nature, creating a sense of verisimilitude.

St. Bavon was dedicated to John the Baptist, the patron saint of the city of Ghent. The Lamb of God John holds is his identifying attribute and also links him to the wool industry, the source of the city's prosperity. The altarpiece's patrons, depicted in the outside panels of the lower tier, did in fact gain their wealth from wool. A deed dated May 13, 1535 establishes Joos Vijd, on the left, and his wife Elizabeth Borluut, on the right, as founders of the chapel in St. Bavon where the altarpiece stood. On the outer frame, below the donors, is found this inscription: "Hubert van Eyck, the most famous painter ever known, started this work of art at the request of Joos Vijd; his brother Jan, who was the second in art, finished

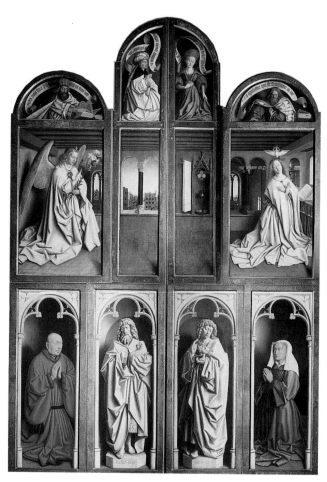

Figure 14.2 Jan and Hubert van Eyck, *Ghent Altarpiece* (closed), ca. 1425–32, oil on panel, 11'5¾" × 7'6¾" (3.4 × 2.3 m), St. Bavon, Ghent. Although Gabriel and Mary are too large to stand up, the space is ingeniously depicted as if continuous through all four panels behind the frame—which itself appears to cast shadows into the room.

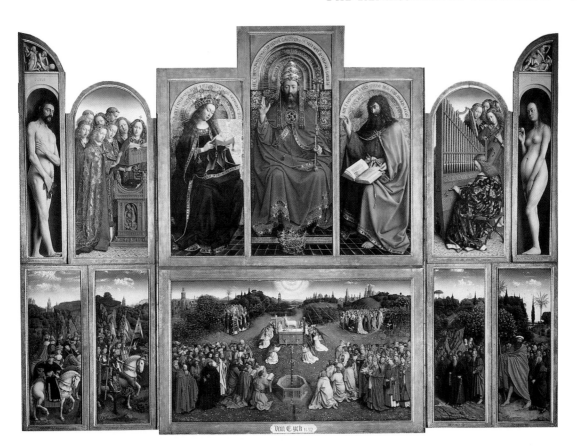

Figure 14.3 Jan and Hubert van Eyck, *Ghent Altarpiece* (open), ca. 1425–32, oil on panel, 11′5¾″ × 15′1½″ (3.4 × 4.6 m), St. Bavon, Ghent. Because of the lower center scene in which the multitudes are shown venerating the Lamb of God (Agnus Dei), this monumental polyptych is sometimes referred to as the *Mystic Lamb*.

the monumental commission. With this verse the donor consigns the work to your charge on May 6, 1432." Little is known about Hubert van Eyck, despite the inscription. It is generally believed that Hubert sculpted the original elaborate framework for the piece, a structure long lost, and that Jan went on, as "second in art," to paint it. Still, it is significant that the artists are mentioned on the work itself, indicating a shift from the anonymity of the medieval guild system to recognition of individual artists.

Inside, the altarpiece focuses on the salvation and redemption of humankind (fig. 14.3). The glowing colors of the interior, dominated by red, blue, and green, contrast dramatically with the somber colors of the exterior panels. The central panel on the lower level takes up the theme introduced by John the Baptist, depicting the *Adoration of the Lamb*; the entire altarpiece is sometimes referred to as the *Mystic Lamb*. The Apocalyptic Lamb is sacrificed, its blood spurting into the chalice, which symbolizes Jesus's sacrifice. In the foreground is the Fountain of Life, its twelve jets of water symbolizing the Mass from which grace unceasingly flows.

In an urge for inclusiveness, the crowds of people shown paying homage to the Lamb include Old Testament prophets and patriarchs, classical poets and philosophers, New Testament apostles, and people of all classes, times, and places. Various body types and facial expressions individualize the figures with their blemishes and deformities included.

Realism is further heightened by Van Eyck's use of atmospheric perspective (see Chapter 13). The colors and the edges of objects in the background are not as intense or as sharp as those in the foreground. The distant hills merge with the sky, which is no longer golden but tinged with an appropriate lighter blue near the horizon. Consider how different this is from the *Mérode Altarpiece* in which the artist gave each object equal attention, whether in the foreground or background.

Unlike the lower panels, the upper panels do not form a unified composition. In the center is either God or Jesus, lavishly adorned in a deep scarlet mantle and gemstones that appear, by virtue of Van Eyck's careful glazing, to catch the light. This figure seems to incorporate all aspects of the Trinity within himself—the Father, Son, and Holy Ghost. Inscribed on the throne behind his head is the inscription: "This is God, the Almighty by reason of His divine majesty [the Father]; the Highest

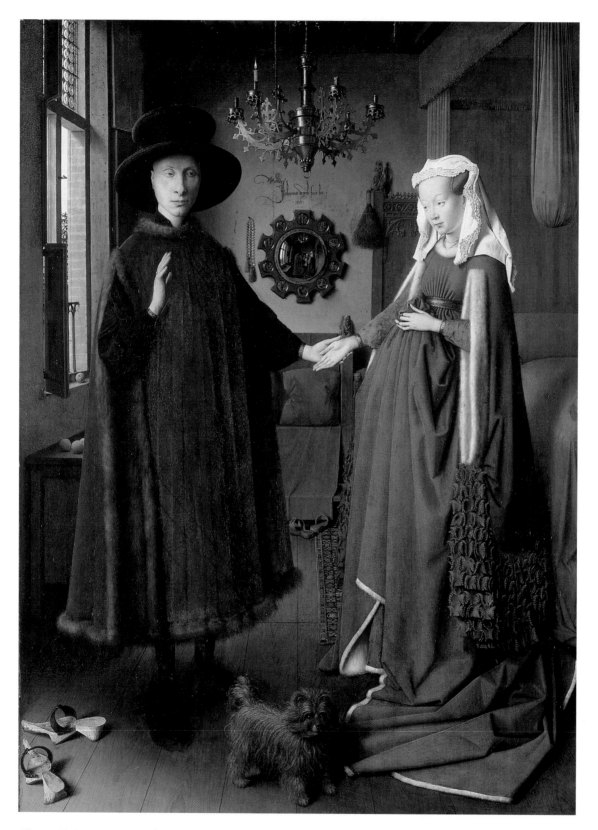

Figure 14.4   Jan van Eyck, *Giovanni Arnolfini and His Wife Giovanna Cenami*, signed
and dated 1434, oil on panel, $32\frac{1}{4} \times 23\frac{1}{2}''$ (83.8 × 57.2 cm), National Gallery, London.
The growing interest in portraiture is evidenced here. Cenami's protruding abdomen was a
fashion of the times (note Eve's comparable contour in the *Ghent Altarpiece*) rather than
an impetus for the exchanging of wedding vows.

and Best, by reason of his goodness [the Son]; the Most Liberal Giver by reason of his boundless generosity [the Holy Ghost, who bestows grace on the elect]." The outermost figures are Adam and Eve, the earliest large-scale nudes in northern European panel painting. Highly naturalistic, they were obviously painted from models; every eyelash is recorded. Adam is shown with his mouth slightly open, as if speaking. Eve's physique, with the protruding abdomen, is the preferred body type of the day rather than an indication of pregnancy. They are drawn as if seen from below. The bottom of Adam's foot is visible as he steps on the frame, because the viewer must look up at these figures.

Because of the enormous ambition involved and the extraordinary realism portrayed, the *Ghent Altarpiece* is one of the most famous paintings of the Renaissance. It came to symbolize the aspirations of an entire age, from the hope of salvation embodied in its commission to the appreciation of the genius of Van Eyck's extraordinary achievement.

Van Eyck's assertion that painting is an act of an individual's particular vision is carried further in his commissioned portrait of *Giovanni Arnolfini and His Wife Giovanna Cenami*, often called *The Arnolfini Wedding* (fig. 14.4). On the back wall, above the mirror, are the words "*Johannes de Eyck fuit hic. 1434*" ("Jan van Eyck was here, 1434"). We see reflections in the mirror: the backs of Arnolfini and Cenami and, beyond them, two other figures, standing in the same place as the viewer. The man in the red turban is perhaps the artist himself, suggesting that he was, in fact, present.

Giovanni Arnolfini was an Italian merchant working in Bruges as an agent for the Medici, both as a banker and a businessman involved in trade. His wife's protruding abdomen again does not suggest pregnancy but a fashionable physique, probably achieved by a small padded sack over the abdomen and emphasized by the cut of the garment and posture of its wearer.

Though it has long been assumed that the couple are shown in a bridal chamber, exchanging marriage vows before two witnesses, persuasive arguments have recently been made to suggest instead that we are witness here not to a marriage but to an engagement, and that the room is not a bedroom but the main room of Arnolfini's house. The moment is not unlike that described by Shakespeare in *Henry V*, when the English king proposes to Katherine, the French princess: "Give me your answer; i' faith, do; and so clap hands and a bargain: how say you lady?" Such a touching of the hands was the common sign of a mutual agreement to wed. As for the room itself, it has been pointed out that canopy beds were "furniture of estate," important status symbols commonly displayed in the principal room of the house as a sign of the owner's prestige and influence.

The painting is replete with common objects that seem to hold iconographic significance, in "disguised"

symbolism. Thus St. Margaret, patron saint of childbirth, adorns the bedpost. The couple's shoes are off to signify that they stand on holy ground. Ten scenes in the mirror frame represent the passion of Jesus, and the single candle in the chandelier is thought to represent the all-seeing God. The dog is a symbol of fidelity, especially appropriate in this subject, although dogs were popular everywhere in northern Europe, and the Duke of Berry was said to have 1500. He also notes that wax candles were extraordinarily expensive (the price of tallow was four times that of meat), requiring households to use them sparingly, if at all. Everything that Van Eyck has included in the painting can be justified by reference to everyday reality. However, the power of these objects' potential symbolism is enhanced rather than diminished by such realism. In everyday reality, Northern Renaissance artists found signs of God's presence on earth.

The painting remains a stunning representation of the prosperity of the rising merchant class in fifteenth-century Bruges. With its dazzling play of rich colors, the lavish textures of its textiles, and the beauty of its ornament and finery, it records a prosperity that would not last long.

Hieronymus Bosch. Very different from Jan van Eyck's efforts to portray the real world are those of HIERONYMUS BOSCH [BOSH] (1450 or 1453–1516). He grew up and worked in 's-Hertogenbosch [s-HER-toe-gen-bos] in southern Holland (now called Den Bosch). This town was off the main roads, isolated from the progressive ideas that informed the Burgundian court. It was middle-class and commercial and situated within an area of religious, political, social, and economic unrest. In Bosch's world, people believed in witches. Astrology was taught at the universities, and visions were accepted as fact. Although a member of a Catholic fraternity until his death in 1516, Bosch was openly critical of certain regional religious practices.

As an artist, Bosch displays an extraordinary imagination and a highly personal style. He is best known for his blatantly bizarre and menacing creatures, part-human, part-animal. It wasn't only subject matter that distinguished Bosch from his contemporaries. He painted ***alla prima*** [AH-la PREE-ma]—without any preliminary drawing. His style is based upon delicate draftsmanship; the effect is fragile, fluid, transparent. Where other Flemish painters stressed the solid dimensionality of each object, Bosch chose not to. While his contemporaries tricked the viewer's eyes with their skill in representing texture, Bosch shows no concern for this kind of illusionism. In an era when other artists created atmospheric environments filled with natural light, Bosch disregarded light and shadow. Bosch's interest was in his subject matter and in his moralistic and satirical presentation of it.

Bosch's *Hay Wain* (fig. 14.5), a triptych painted ca. 1495–1500, illustrates the Flemish proverb, "The world is a hay wagon and each seeks to grab what he can." The hay wagon is a symbol of earthly goods and worldly pleasures, and the painting is a powerful sermon on the evils of greed. As in all his paintings, Bosch fills this one with a multitude of telling vignettes. In the center panel people of all classes, rich and poor, even members of the religious hierarchy (the pope has been identified as Alexander VI), fight each other for the hay. Some are crushed under the wheels. A quack physician fills his purse. Nuns, supervised by a gluttonous monk, push hay into a bag. On top of the hay is a group of lovers. Here a man plays a lute, while the demon on the right plays his nose like a flute, and dances to his own tune. A couple kiss in the bushes. Only the angel on the left notices Jesus above. On the left panel is a scene from the Creation, focusing, however, on sin. Rebel angels are thrown out of heaven; the sky is full of monsters. On the right panel is hell—to which the wagon, pulled by devils, is rolling. People are tortured; buildings are destroyed.

Bosch's most famous painting, the *Garden of Earthly Delights* (fig. 14.6), probably painted between 1505 and 1510, is the most iconographically complex of all his paintings. A triptych like the *Hay Wain*, it is likewise a sermon on folly and its punishment in hell. Again, the Creation is shown on the left panel, and hell on the right. But here the pleasures of the flesh, portrayed on the central panel, are the focus of punishment.

The central panel is populated by innumerable tiny humans, bizarre animals, and fantastic plants. The huge fruits portrayed are those that are especially soft, fragile, and short-lived, such as cherries, strawberries, and blackberries—rotting fruit is a recurrent image. The implication is that pleasure, too, is fragile and short-lived. In this environment, carefree people cavort amorously. Gluttonous lovers sit inside a berry, luring others in. Other lovers are surrounded by a transparent capsule, unaware that their actions are seen by all.

The left panel shows the creation of Eve, her presentation to Adam, the Tree of Knowledge, and the beginning of sin with the Fall. Cruel beasts abound—sin already lurks in Eden. The right panel shows a terrifying vision of hell. At the top, cities burn. A pair of ears is separated by a knife, but held together by an arrow. There is a convent, roofed by a horse's skull and populated by demons. A knight is devoured by dogs. Musical instruments alluding to lust become instruments of torture in Bosch's hell. At the time lust was called the "music of the flesh," and the bagpipe referred specifically to the male sexual organ. A bird-creature consumes

Figure 14.5 Hieronymus Bosch, *Hay Wain*, ca. 1495–1500 (?), oil on panel, center $4'7\frac{1}{8}'' \times 3'3\frac{3}{8}''$ (1.40 × 1.00 m), each wing $4'9\frac{7}{8}'' \times 2'2''$ (147 × 66 cm), Museo del Prado, Madrid. Another version of this painting is in the Escorial, near Madrid—scholars debate which is the original. People of all types try to grab the hay which, according to proverb, represents material possessions.

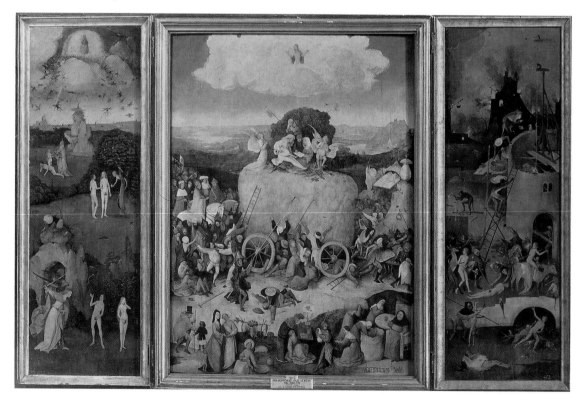

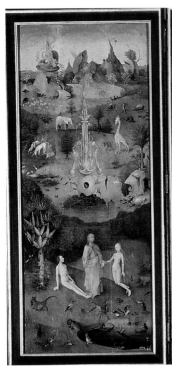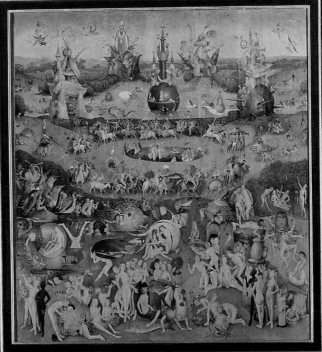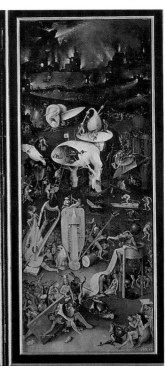

Figure 14.6 Hieronymus Bosch, *Garden of Earthly Delights*, ca. 1505–10, oil on panel, center 7′2½″ × 6′4¾″ (2.20 × 1.95 m), each wing 7′2½″ × 3′2″ (2.20 × 0.97 m), Museo del Prado, Madrid. Bosch's predilection for the bizarre, his juxtapositions of seemingly unrelated objects, and the irregular scale foreshadow Salvador Dalí and twentieth-century Surrealism (see Chapter 21).

and excretes the damned. A miser vomits gold coins into a sewer. Every type of sin receives appropriate punishment in hell. Is the face looking out at us from behind the egg actually a self-portrait, as has been claimed? If so, then Bosch has placed himself in hell!

Although much of Bosch's meaning is lost to us today, some aspects remain quite clear. When he portrayed a mother superior pig giving a small, naked (i.e. dying) man an unwelcome embrace, Bosch was publicly yet cryptically criticizing current Church practices. He was alluding to the way wills that benefited monasteries were often made under the duress of imminent death. Members of the clergy during Bosch's time were often corrupt, living in licentious luxury even as they preached austerity and abstinence to others.

The German artist Albrecht Dürer later said of Bosch's paintings that nothing like them was ever "seen before nor thought of by any other man." This may be true in purely visual terms; yet soon his critical vision of the Church would become that of the majority, part of a general call for reform. Many artists, writers, and intellectuals were beginning to attack the Church on every front. Those such as Bosch's eventually led the papacy in Rome, under popes Julius II and Leo X, to reinvent Rome as a center of classical learning, unsurpassed artistic accomplishment, and holy endeavors.

THE HIGH RENAISSANCE IN NORTHERN EUROPE

THE HABSBURG PATRONAGE

A measure of the centrality of Bosch's themes to the culture of the new century is the fact that he would become the favorite northern painter of Philip II of Spain, the richest and greatest collector of art in the last half of the sixteenth century. Not only did Philip own the *Garden of Earthly Delights*, but he owned over thirty other paintings attributed to Bosch. The painter's work struck a chord with the elegant, highly educated, and refined prince, who saw in Bosch the very reflection of his times.

Philip II was the nephew of both Charles V, Emperor of the Holy Roman Empire, and Mary of Hungary, the Emperor's sister. The Habsburg [HAPS-burg] Charles V controlled Spain, the Low Countries, the German empire, Hungary, Spanish America, and parts of Italy. Though not a strong supporter of the arts, Charles discovered the paintings of the southern Renaissance painter Titian in 1532 and became, together with Mary, the artist's chief patron. Titian's portrait from 1548 of *Charles V on Horseback* (fig. 14.7) shows the Emperor with

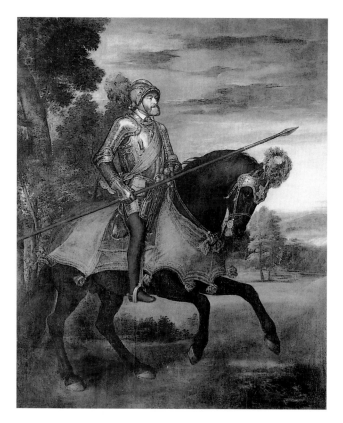

Figure 14.7   Titian, *Charles V on Horseback*, 1548, oil on canvas, 10′11″ × 9′2″ (3.33 × 2.79 m), Museo del Prado, Madrid. The portrait is notable for its clear representation of the famous Habsburg chin, a hereditary trait shared by all family members.

the thrusting chin that was an inherited Habsburg trait. Mary of Hungary also served as governor of the Netherlands from 1531 to 1556, and in that time developed a passionate taste for fifteenth-century Flemish painting, acquiring, among others, Van Eyck's portrait *Giovanni Arnolfini and His Wife Giovanna Cenami* (see fig. 14.4). She also cultivated the Habsburg habit of collecting the best Flemish work together with the best from Italy.

Financed by gold and silver from the Americas, Philip added to the great collections of his uncle and aunt. Like Charles V and Mary before him, he favored Titian, granting him an annual stipend and allowing him to paint whatever he chose. When Titian died in 1576, Philip had amassed dozens of his paintings. From Flanders Philip collected works by Campin and Bosch. By the time Philip was done, he had brought more than 1500 paintings of indisputable quality to Spain.

ICONOCLASM

While the Habsburgs in Spain during the sixteenth century acquired art and endorsed individual artistic expression, there was a growing iconoclasm further north.

Iconoclasm [eye-KON-o-KLAZ-em] is the systematic destruction of religious icons because of their accepted religious connotations. As anti-Catholic religious reform movements spread throughout northern Europe in the sixteenth century, an iconoclastic fever spread with them. The Old Testament prohibition against images that led to idolatry was widely cited as justification for this destruction. The extraordinary visualization of religious beliefs that had flourished under the patronage of popes Julius II and Leo X at the Vatican in Rome became for many the very symbol of the papacy's corruption. In Switzerland, John Calvin wrote: "Therefore it remains that only those things are to be sculpted or painted which the eyes are capable of seeing: let not God's majesty, which is far above the perception of the eyes, be debased through unseemly representations." Such sentiments led Church supporters to dismantle the *Ghent Altarpiece* in 1566 and hide it in the tower of St. Bavon, safe from the hands of those who wished to destroy it—"filthy swines," said one eyewitness. In Zurich, the religious leader Ulrich Zwingli [ZWING-glee] even prohibited the use of music in worship.

The most systematic iconoclasm occurred in England, beginning with King Henry VIII's (fig. 14.8) ordering of

Figure 14.8   Hans Holbein the Younger, *Henry VIII*, ca. 1540, oil on panel, 2′9½″ × 2′5½″ (82.6 × 75 cm), Galleria Nazionale d'Arte Antica, Rome. The English monarch is shown in wedding dress—an attire he donned six times. As we can see, at the age of forty-nine he was already, as he was described in his later years, a "man-mountain."

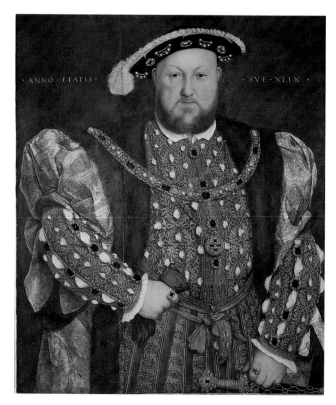

Timeline 14.1 Religious Reformation during the Renaissance.

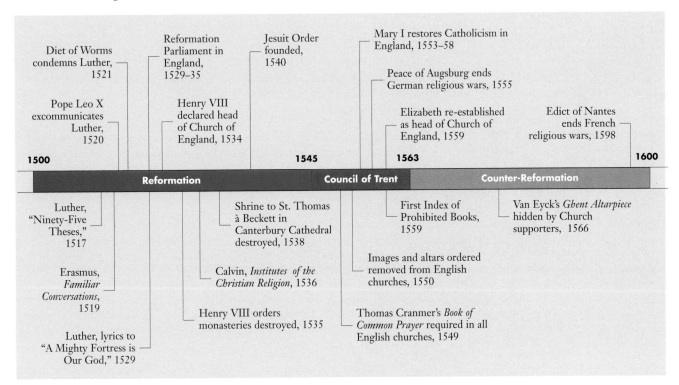

the destruction of the monasteries in 1535. Henry's motives were as much political as they were religious. When he wanted to divorce his first wife, Catherine of Aragon, and marry Anne Boleyn, from whom he hoped for a male heir, as a Catholic he could not do so. After six years of negotiations with Pope Clement VII in Rome, Henry drafted legislation that eliminated papal authority in England. Thus the Church of England was born—the Anglican Church—and it granted his divorce. (An heir was born, though Henry was disappointed, since the child was a girl—the future Queen Elizabeth I.)

Henry first attacked the monasteries, the ruins of many of which still stand: Glastonbury, the mythological burial place of King Arthur, and Tintern Abbey, which later inspired a poem by William Wordsworth. When Shakespeare wrote of "these bare ruin'd choirs where late the sweet birds sang," he was referring to such ruins. Thomas Cromwell, Henry's minister, ordered the destruction of the objects of idolatry, particularly "feigned images ... abused with pilgrimages or offerings." Soon, the shrine to St. Thomas à Beckett in Canterbury Cathedral was torn down and his sainthood recanted.

The widespread destruction of religious images would never have occurred without the acquiescence of the English people themselves. Iconoclasm was, in fact, the logical offspring of sentiments expressed early in the sixteenth century by Erasmus, considered by many the most learned man of his day. In Erasmus's words: "How many dedicate candles to the Virgin and Mother of God, even

in mid-day when it serves no purpose? How few dedicate themselves equally to a life of chastity, modesty, and love to spiritual things?"

ERASMUS AND NORTHERN HUMANISM

Like his contemporary Hieronymus Bosch, the northern humanist scholar DESIDERIUS ERASMUS [ee-RAZ-mus] (1466–1536), born in Rotterdam, the Netherlands, saw the religious world of late fifteenth- and early sixteenth-century Europe through a highly critical lens, but he was no iconoclast. In fact, in A Pilgrimage for Religion's Sake, he marveled at the shrine to Thomas à Beckett in Canterbury Cathedral: "Ye Gods! What a show was there of silken vestments, what a power of golden candlesticks ... Treasures beyond all calculation [were] displayed. The most worthless thing there was gold, every part glowed, sparkled and flashed with rare and large gems, some of which were bigger than a goose egg."

Erasmus blended a scholarly study of classical civilization with a strong Christian faith. Combining an acute critical intelligence with deeply held spiritual convictions, Erasmus brought together the thought of Plato with that of St. Paul, and the philosophy of Aristotle with that of St. Augustine. He never pursued learning for its own sake, but, in his own words, "for one object, that we may know Christ and honor Him." He was educated by the Brethren of the Common Life, an order of devout laymen who modeled their lives on that of Jesus Christ.

Then & Now

ICONOCLASM AND THE ATTACK ON THE ARTS

The iconoclastic practices of sixteenth-century European Protestants were focused on the destruction of "idolatrous" images of God. From the Protestant point of view, such images diminished God by making him appear like humankind. This logic quickly extended to all images within churches, which could distract the worshiper from the true contemplation of salvation. It was not a question of artistic merit; they were viewed solely for their sacrilegious content.

Since 1985, artists in the United States have also been attacked for creating art that is considered obscene or blasphemous, specifically those works that, to some people, challenge the very idea of Christianity and the values they associate with a Christian lifestyle. Recent attacks have had a political flavor because the art and artists in question—Robert Mapplethorpe and Andreas Serrano, for example—were funded in part by the National Endowment for the Arts. The attackers argue that the government, supported by taxpayers' money, should not fund work that offends or upsets those who pay for it.

Senator Alphonse D'Amato, a Republican from New York, tore a photograph of one of Serrano's works into pieces on the floor of the US Senate on May 18, 1989. "This so-called piece of art is a deplorable, despicable display of vulgarity," he exclaimed. On July 26, 1989, Senator Jesse Helms, a Republican from North Carolina, introduced an amendment to legislation funding the National Endowment that would prohibit the use of appropriated funds to, among other things, "promote, disseminate, or produce ... obscene or indecent materials, including but not limited to depictions of sadomasochism, homo-eroticism, the exploitation of children, or individuals engaged in sex acts; or ... material which denigrates the objects or beliefs of the adherents of a particular religion or non-religion."

Supporters of artists' rights of self-expression found the last word of that statement particularly alarming, since if the amendment were to be passed, the government could prohibit funding of any material that denigrated *anyone's* belief about *anything*. It seemed to many like government-supported censorship.

The amendment failed, and thus began a legislative battle that continues to this day. Should the government take on the role of artistic patron? If not, who will? Many of the country's great dance companies, symphony orchestras, theater companies, artists, and writers depend on government funds to complete their projects.

Thus, the link between Renaissance iconoclasm and today's debates over funding of the arts is clear. How our current society settles the debate remains in question.

He joined an Augustinian monastery in 1487 and was ordained a priest in 1492. Erasmus traveled widely, studying and teaching in most of the cultural centers in Europe, including England. At Oxford, he became friends with Sir Thomas More; at Cambridge, he was Professor of Divinity and of Greek.

Erasmus wrote his *Familiar Conversations* (1519) to attack abuses occurring within the Catholic Church. Erasmus's readers found the satire of Church figures from local priests to the pope savagely funny and scathingly accurate. Forty editions of the book were published in Erasmus's lifetime, and John Milton, more than a hundred years later, remarked that everyone was still reading it at Cambridge. His *Conversations*, moreover, was so antagonistic to the clergy that Charles V, the Holy Roman Emperor, issued an edict to the effect that any teacher using the work in the classroom would be liable to immediate execution.

Erasmus had never intended to set himself up as a counter-authority to the Catholic Church. His goal was to purify the Church from within by ridiculing its abuses and thereby stimulating a desire for internal reform. In this respect, Erasmus differed from other reformers, who were advocating separation from the Church.

MARTIN LUTHER AND THE REFORMATION

If one individual could be said to dominate the history of sixteenth-century Europe, that person would be MARTIN LUTHER [LOO-ther] (1483–1546). Like Erasmus, Luther (fig. 14.9) was an Augustinian monk and a humanist scholar, and, again like Erasmus, he was no iconoclast, although he was well aware that his teachings sparked the iconoclastic frenzy. He was an avid lover of the arts, especially music. He wrote hymns for his new Protestant church services. Many are still sung, especially "A Mighty Fortress Is Our God." Two centuries later, Johann Sebastian Bach used Luther's chorales, embellishing them in his cantatas.

Luther was a Professor of Philosophy and Biblical Studies at Wittenberg [VIT-en-burg] University. When Shakespeare's Hamlet expresses his desire "to return to school in Wittenberg," he is referring to Luther and Luther's ideas taught at the school. At Wittenberg Latin was the language of instruction, and the method of teaching was a detailed study of the classics with particular attention to Aristotle's logic. The learning process depended on "disputations," or debates. Faculty and students attended weekly disputations, which were judged on success according to the rules of logic.

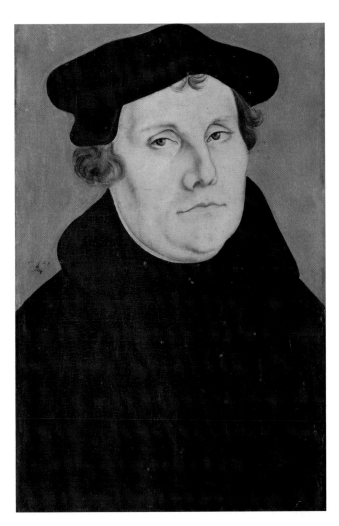

Figure 14.9 Lucas Cranach, *Portrait of Martin Luther*, ca. 1526, oil on panel, 15 × 9″ (38.1 × 22.9 cm), Uffizi Gallery, Florence. Cranach was a staunch supporter of Luther, whose criticism of church practices, such as indulgences, began the Protestant Reformation.

The faculty of Wittenberg University came largely from an Augustinian monastery in the city, where Luther was a monk. Luther specialized in the language and grammar of the Bible. After 1516, he studied in particular the Greek New Testament translated by Erasmus. The task of making his own translation into German led him to rethink the question of salvation. Salvation, he now believed, was not delivered through achievement but through faith. According to Luther, the gospel repudiates "the wicked idea of the entire kingdom of the pope … [with its idea that] a Christian man must be uncertain about the grace of God toward him. If this opinion stands, then Christ is completely useless … Therefore the papacy is a veritable torture chamber of consciousness and the very kingdom of the devil."

Such language would obviously offend Rome, but the incident that drew Luther to the attention of Pope Leo X was the publication, on October 31, 1517, of his "Ninety-Five Theses." These were written in the form of a traditional disputation. Attacking the practice of papal indulgences, Luther was inspired by the example of the Dominican monk Tetzel [TET-sel]. Accepting payment for indulgences, which theoretically remitted penalties to be suffered in the afterlife (including release from purgatory) and paved the sinner's way to heaven, had long been practiced by the clergy. The Dominican Tetzel was, in effect, a traveling indulgence salesman. "As soon as the coin into the box rings," Tetzel would remind his audience, "a soul from purgatory to heaven springs." Frederick the Wise had banned Tetzel from Wittenberg, but the city's populace simply went out to meet him in the countryside. The people informed Luther, who also served as their pastor, that they no longer needed to confess or attend Mass because they had purchased lifetime indulgences from the Dominican monk. Luther was outraged, and the "Ninety-Five Theses" soon followed.

Luther's ideas were given greater impact by the advent of printing—Luther considered the printing press a gift from God. In 1500, there were over two hundred printing presses in Europe; soon there were seven in Wittenberg alone, pumping out the writings of the "heretic" Martin Luther as fast as they could. Over 750,000 copies of Luther's German translation of the Bible were in circulation by the time of his death in 1546.

In Rome, Luther was viewed as an Augustinian monk who had made an attack on the Dominican pope Leo X, and a rebuttal was quickly drafted by the papal theologian Prierias entitled *Dialogue Against the Arrogant Theses of Martin Luther Concerning the Power of the Pope*. It was not Luther's questioning of the practice of indulgences that so troubled Rome as much as the fact that his theses argued against papal supremacy and papal practices. Why, for instance, couldn't the pope pardon repentant sinners by an act of love rather than a tribute of money? And why didn't Leo, a Medici, finance the rebuilding of St. Peter's and Michelangelo's painting of the Sistine Chapel with his own money? On August 7, 1518, Luther was given sixty days to appear in Rome to answer the charge of heresy.

Luther avoided going to Rome through the machinations of his protector Frederick III (the Wise), ruler of German Saxony. If Frederick had any doubts about Luther, Erasmus dispelled them. Frederick asked the elder humanist what he thought about the dispute arising out of the publication of the theses, and Erasmus replied: "He has committed a great sin—he has hit the monks in their belly, and the Pope in his crown!"

Luther concluded that to get back to central Christian truths, everything non-essential in religious practice would need to be stripped away. For Luther these non-essentials included scholastic philosophy and Church ritual, along with its hierarchy, sacraments, organizational structure, and even its prayers and services. Believers could be "justified by faith alone," a faith centered on Scripture.

Even so, Luther was also extraordinarily community-minded. No one, he believed, should have to beg in Wittenberg. Every city should take care of its poor. Disappointed in the unwillingness of the people of Wittenberg to contribute to the community chest (established by him in late 1520 to provide social welfare), Luther scolded his ministry for being "unthankful beasts," and, declaring his unwillingness to be "the shepherd of such pigs," actually quit preaching until the situation was remedied. He argued, "Christ and all saints are one spiritual body, just as the inhabitants of a city are one community and a body, each citizen being a member of the other and of the entire city." Thus in religious practices were the grounds laid for social democracy and equality, attitudes that would, in the next century, lead to social revolution throughout Europe and the Americas.

JOHN CALVIN AND THE *INSTITUTES OF THE CHRISTIAN RELIGION*

While Luther was reforming the Church in Germany, another more radical Protestant leader was active in Geneva in Switzerland, John Calvin. JOHN CALVIN [KAL-vin] (1509–1564) was a French humanist who underwent a religious conversion of great intensity. His reformist religious views were not well received in France, and he fled to Switzerland, where he first published his *Institutes of the Christian Religion* in Basel and later set up a theocratic state in Geneva—that is, a state ruled by a religious figure or group.

Calvin's reforms, like Luther's, involved stripping away what he considered external and distracting to true Christian piety. He rejected images of saints and limited the use of music to psalms. Many other activities were prohibited in Calvin's Geneva, including feasting and dancing; wearing rouge, jewelry, and lace, and dressing immodestly; swearing, gambling, and playing cards; reading immoral books and engaging in sexual activity outside of marriage. People caught breaking the rules were warned the first time, fined the second, and severely punished after that. Some were banished, others executed.

Like Luther, Calvin recognized the Bible as the supreme source of knowledge and the only recourse for religious living. His *Institutes* drew out the principles embedded in biblical teaching. They include the following:

(1) human beings are born in total depravity as a result of Adam's fall, whereby they inherit original sin;

(2) the will of God is absolute and all-powerful;

(3) faith is superior to good works, since humans lack the capacity to choose to do works that are truly good in God's eyes;

(4) salvation comes through God's freely given grace rather than through any acts of the people;

(5) God divinely predestines some to eternal salvation—the Elect—and others to eternal perdition—the Damned; and since no one knows with absolute certainty whether he or she is one of the Elect, all must live as if they were, obeying God's commands.

Timeline 14.2 Science and ideas of the Northern Renaissance.

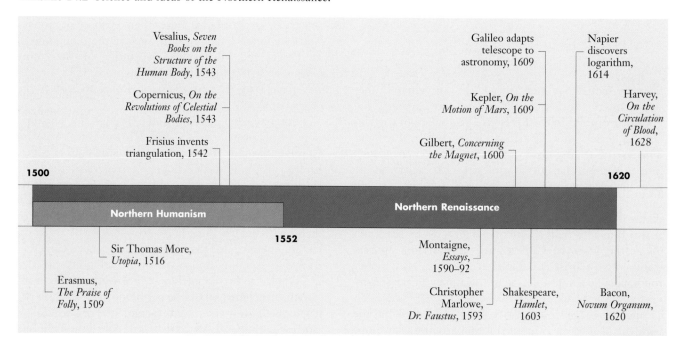

Cross Currents

DÜRER DESCRIBES MEXICAN TREASURES

When Hernán Cortés landed in Mexico in 1519, he did so as the representative of King Charles V of Spain, the Habsburg ruler who actually lived in Vienna. He sent Charles a series of letters recounting his conquests there, and with them a collection of treasures. When the latter arrived in Brussels, Albrecht Dürer was among the many who came to see them.

Among the collection was the famous Dresden Codex, a folding-screen manuscript made of bark paper dating to as early as the thirteenth century. It recounts agricultural rituals, establishes the Mayan calendar, and, in the richness of its drawings of costumes and gods, is by far the most detailed description of Mayan life that we have today. Only its having been sent back to Europe saved it from the total destruction of all "pagan" and "idolatrous" manuscripts ordered by Diego de Landa, Charles V's first appointee as bishop of Yucatán.

But Dürer was most impressed by the extraordinary gold- and metalwork sent from the "New World": "I saw the things brought to the King from the New Golden Land," Dürer wrote, "a sun entirely of gold, a whole fathom wide; likewise, a moon, made entirely of silver, and just as big; also, a variety of other curiosities from weapons, to armor, and missiles ... These things were all so precious that they were valued at a hundred thousand gilders. But I have never seen in all my days anything that caused my heart to rejoice so as these things have. For I saw among them amazing art objects, and I marveled over the subtle ingenuity of the men in distant lands who made them." This Aztec goldwork was, however, soon melted down by Charles for currency, the fate of almost all such metalwork sent back to Europe from Mexico.

Calvin identified the Elect by their unambiguous profession of faith, their upright life, and their pious participation in the sacraments, whose number, like Luther, Calvin reduced.

From Geneva Calvinism spread into France, the Netherlands, England, Scotland, and North America, and it had a marked impact on the social, political, and intellectual life of these countries. It can be traced in the rise of the Puritans, in Milton's *Paradise Lost* and the works of seventeenth-century American Puritan writers Edward Taylor and Cotton Mather, and in nineteenth-century works such as Nathaniel Hawthorne's *The Scarlet Letter* and Herman Melville's *Moby Dick*.

THE AGE OF DISCOVERY

Ever since Marco Polo had returned to his native Venice from China in the thirteenth century, the world map had been undergoing almost continual revision. Most of the geographic details of the real world Europeans learned in the two centuries after 1450, in their world explorations. Though this exploration was fueled by both missionary and economic zeal—the twin forces of God and gold—it also spawned an awareness of peoples and cultures hitherto unknown.

Renaissance Explorers. In 1488, the Portuguese explorer Bartolomeu Dias [DEE-es] was blown far south off the West African coast by an enormous storm, and heading northeast afterward he found that he had rounded what would come to be called the Cape of Good Hope. The fact that Africa was surrounded by water was confirmed. In 1497, the Portuguese explorer Vasco da Gama [VAS-koe de GAM-uh] followed Dias's route and reached India ten months and fourteen days after setting out from Lisbon. Meanwhile, Christopher Columbus had made landfall on a small island in the Bahamas in 1492, and in 1500 the Portuguese Pedro Cabral [ka-BRAHL] had pushed west from the bulge of Africa and landed in what is now Brazil. Magellan had successfully sailed around the tip of South America, across the Pacific to the Philippines, across the Indian Ocean and around Africa, thus circumnavigating the globe and demonstrating that the world was indeed round. On September 8, 1522, Ferdinand Magellan's crew with only eighteen survivors arrived back in Cadiz, Spain, three years after setting out.

However, an age of discovery is also an age of doubt, doubt that what we know about the world is necessarily true. Thus not only the realm of geography underwent revision in the sixteenth century. The Reformation, as we have seen, was a period of intense religious inquiry and questioning and a radical assertion of the individual conscience against the authority of an institutionalized orthodoxy. In asserting that authority resided in the independent heart of each Christian, Luther echoed the humanist trend away from a concern with religion and toward a concern with humanity. Luther's emphasis on individual conscience, on private judgment, and the individual act of faith put the Reformation firmly in the context of a larger cultural transformation that would lead eventually to developments in the secularization of society and the rise of scientific investigation. Scientific study became a secularized activity.

Nicolas Copernicus. It was in the spirit of geographical "discovery" of the world that the Polish astronomer NICOLAS COPERNICUS [koh-PUR-nikus] (1473–1543) published *On the Revolutions of Celestial Bodies* in the year of his death. Building on the work of the Ancient Greek geographer and astronomer Ptolemy, whose writings had been rediscovered and translated in 1410, Copernicus argued that earth and the other planets orbit the sun, rather than the sun and planets revolving around earth. Theologians, Protestant and Catholic alike, refused to believe this—that the earth was not at the center of the universe. Copernicus's book was placed on the Index of Prohibited Books in 1616. But Copernicus's work could not be suppressed. Though the sun *appeared* to move across the sky, it was the earth that was moving in relation to a stationary sun. The appearance of things was not necessarily or empirically true. Other scientists drew a lesson from this.

The New Scientists. In England, FRANCIS BACON (1562–1626) would further the cause by advocating a new "scientific method" in which careful and objective observation of the appearances of things needed to be made in scrupulously controlled experiments. All scientific hypotheses needed to be tested and proved; there was no room in science for blind "faith."

Copernicus's new vision of the universe was just one among many important discoveries. In the same year that he published *On the Revolutions of Celestial Bodies*, ANDREAS VESALIUS [vi-SAY-lee-es] (1514–1564) published his *Seven Books on the Structure of the Human Body*, which illustrated the musculature and anatomy of the human body in unprecedented detail. In England, Sir William Harvey soon discovered the existence of

Map 14.2 The Reformation in Europe, ca. 1560.

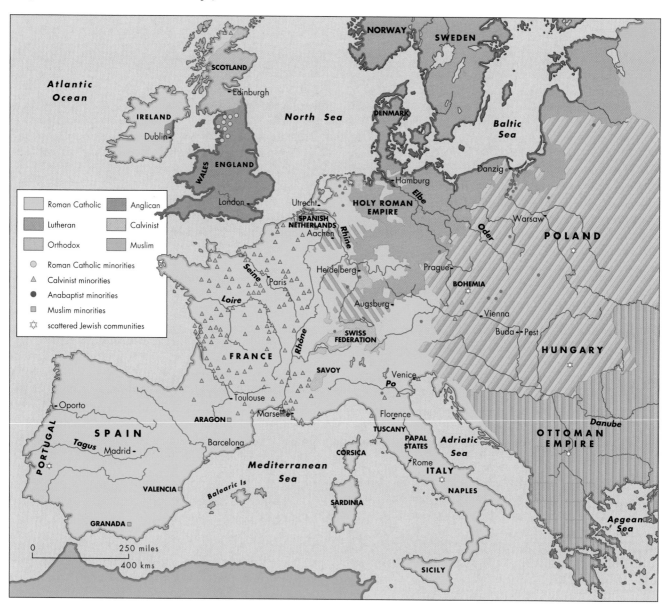

capillaries in the human circulation system, solving the mystery of how blood returned to the heart from the arteries. The English mathematician John Napier [NAY-pee-er] discovered the logarithm, freeing mathematicians forever from long and arduous calculations. Even map-making itself was dramatically improved when, in 1542, GEMMA FRISIUS [FREE-zi-yus] discovered new principles for increasing accuracy in surveying, using the technique of triangulation.

PAINTING AND PRINTMAKING

Albrecht Dürer. If any artist in the north can be said to embody the ideals of the Renaissance and the spirit of discovery that had begun to define it, it is ALBRECHT DÜRER [DYOU-ruhr] (1471–1528), painter, printer, draftsman, theoretician, writer, humanist, and publisher—the very image of the multi-talented Renaissance individual. His lifetime artistic output was enormous, with more than a hundred paintings and over a thousand drawings and prints.

Dürer was born in Nuremberg [NOOR-em-burg]; his mother was a German, his father a Hungarian goldsmith. Like his Italian counterpart Leonardo da Vinci, and subscribing to the general Renaissance interest in the real world, Dürer was fascinated with nature and studied it intensely. An example is his meticulous 1502 watercolor rendering of a rabbit (fig. 14.10). Throughout his career, Dürer made various studies of animals, birds, and plants, all sketched or painted "from life." However, the rabbit

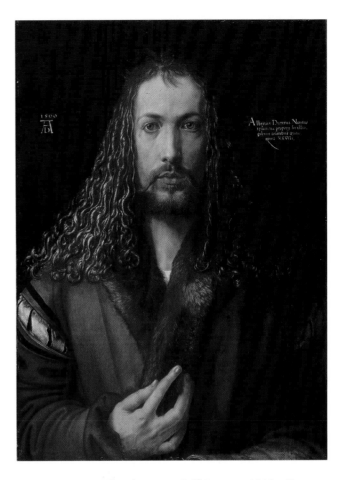

Figure 14.11   Albrecht Dürer, *Self-Portrait*, 1500, oil on panel, 26¼ × 19¼″ (66.3 × 49 cm), Alte Pinakothek, Munich. Dürer, carrying the Renaissance interest in the self further than most, completed several self-portraits throughout his life. Here, hardly subtle, Dürer depicts himself in Christ-like mode.

Figure 14.10   Albrecht Dürer, *Rabbit*, 1502, watercolor, 10″ × 9″ (25.1 × 22.9 cm), Albertina, Vienna. Indicative of the Renaissance interest in nature, Dürer drew this rabbit from life. But rather than working out-of-doors, as would later artists, he worked in his Nuremberg studio.

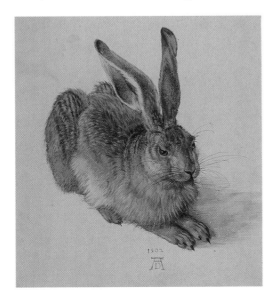

was a stuffed one that Dürer painted in his Nuremberg studio.

The artist produced a significant number of self-portraits. In some, such as the *Self-Portrait* of 1500 (fig. 14.11), he recorded himself in a most self-congratulatory way, suggesting not only a Renaissance emphasis on the individual imagination but also on his sense of his own genius. "Art," he wrote, "derives from God; it is God who has created all art; it is not easy to paint artistically. Therefore, those without aptitude should not attempt it, for it is an inspiration from above." Dürer believed that he was endowed with a God-given gift, a humanistic and individualistic view that he shared with Michelangelo.

This *Self-Portrait* displays the fine finish and meticulous execution of the Flemish oil technique. Dürer shows himself against a black background, in a full-frontal stare. The effect is rigid, commanding, and deliberately Christ-like. Also, it looks amazingly real; it was reported that a dog barked and wagged its tail at one of his self-

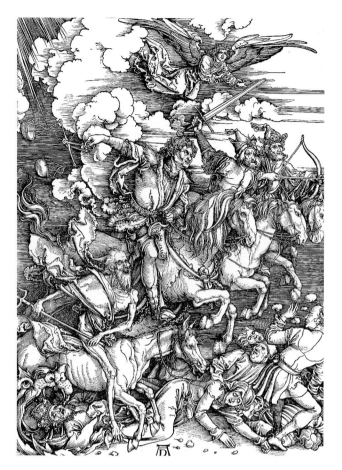

Figure 14.12 Albrecht Dürer, *Four Horsemen of the Apocalypse*, 1497–98, woodcut, $15\frac{1}{2} \times 11\frac{1}{8}''$ (39.4 × 28.3 cm), Metropolitan Museum of Art, New York. Dürer's genius elevated graphic art (printmaking) to a fine art. When making a woodcut, the artist draws a reverse image on a block of wood, then cuts away the wood from the drawing. The remaining raised areas of the wooden block are inked, the paper is pressed onto the block, and an image of the raised area is made.

portraits. He emphasizes the long fingers of his hand—the hand with which he created this image, through which his God-inspired gift is made manifest. From the turn of the century on, Dürer signed and dated much of his work, using the initials "AD," as seen on the upper left. The painting is inscribed, "Thus I, Albrecht Dürer from Nuremberg, painted myself with indelible colors at the age of 28 years."

Despite his genius at painting, much of Dürer's fame derives from his skill as a printer. In woodcuts and engravings, the precision and detail of his work, the richness of its effects and their variety, raised the standard of printing from a pedestrian craft of illustration to a fine art in its own right. Working without color and on the small scale of a piece of paper, Dürer was able to achieve an extraordinary sense of monumentality. Among the several series of prints Dürer produced on specific sub-

jects is that of the *Apocalypse*, published in 1498. This consisted of fifteen woodcuts with the text printed on the back of each sheet of paper. Reissued several times, it had great influence on Dürer's contemporaries and did much to spread his fame. From the *Apocalypse* series comes the gruesome *Four Horsemen of the Apocalypse* (fig. 14.12). Death, War, Pestilence, and Famine are shown to ride rampant over the earth, specifically over the burghers, artisans, merchants, and other citizens of Nuremberg. This is a woodcut, in which the negative, or white (nonprinted), areas of the final print are cut into the block and the black areas are left uncut, thereby raised in relief. Ink is rolled over the surface, paper is placed on the inked surface, and the image transferred to the paper simply by applying pressure to the back of the paper. Dürer's enormous skill becomes readily apparent when one considers how carefully such a complex image, with its dynamic and dramatic sweeping movements and forceful expressiveness, must be cut. Working in a refined technique with the highest level of technical dexterity, the artist executed the details on a seemingly microscopic scale.

Figure 14.13 Albrecht Dürer, *Adam and Eve*, 1504, engraving, $9\frac{7}{8} \times 7\frac{5}{8}''$ (25.1 × 19.4 cm), Philadelphia Museum of Art, Philadelphia. In an engraving, the recessed areas are printed. The artist cuts the lines into a metal plate, the recessed lines take the ink, paper is applied to the inked plate, and the ink transferred to the paper by the pressure of a printing press.

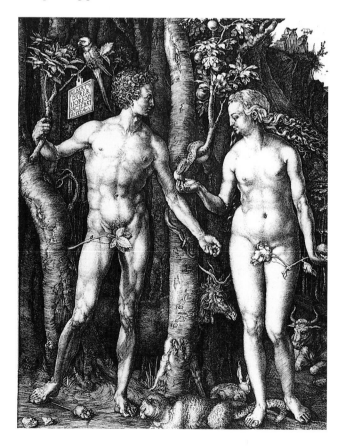

Adam and Eve (fig. 14.13) is an engraving, signed and dated on the plaque on the tree branch, "Albrecht Dürer of Nuremberg made this in 1504." Unlike a woodcut, an engraving is printed from a design inscribed in the surface of a metal plate. Using a sharp **burin** or steel gouging tool, the design is cut into the surface of the plate. Ink is forced into these recesses and the surface of the plate is wiped clean. Damp paper is then placed on the inked plate. The pressure exerted by a printing press is required to force the paper into the recesses to pick up the ink. For both engravings and woodcuts, the image that is printed is the reverse of the original, so artists had to draw "backwards."

After studying art in Italy, Dürer became increasingly interested in the human figure, and the subject of Adam and Eve was essentially an excuse to depict ideal male and female nudes. Dürer used mathematical proportions and drew from a male model and from Italian works and interpretations of antiquity. He created an Adam similar to the Hellenistic Greek *Apollo Belvedere*, which had been recently discovered, and an Eve like the *Venus de Milo*.

Dürer believed that a person's physical shape was influenced by one of the four temperaments, a notion derived from classical philosophy. The animals in the detailed background of *Adam and Eve* symbolize these temperaments: the cat is choleric (angry, irate); the rabbit sanguine (confident, optimistic); the elk melancholic (depressed); and the ox phlegmatic (impassive).

In 1515 Dürer was made court painter to Emperor Maximilian I—an important position and a great honor. Now among the rich and famous, Dürer had a shop of people working for him. In later years he worked more and more on theories of measurement and proportion. Like Leonardo da Vinci, Dürer relied on Vitruvius's scheme of human proportions, and in 1525 he published *The Teaching of Measurements with Rule and Compass (Manual of Measurements)* and later *Four Books on Human Proportions*. Concerned with practical application, Dürer designed devices to aid the artist in doing perspective drawings. In all, his interests in antiquity, the natural world, anatomy, and perspective were analogous to those of his Italian contemporaries.

Although Dürer did paint and print religious subjects, including a Nativity, a Crucifixion, and a Lamentation, most were executed early in his career. In 1519, Dürer became a devout follower of Martin Luther, siding with the Protestants against the established Church. Perhaps because of his strong religious beliefs, however, his most sympathetic rendering of Jesus could be said to be his own self-portrait of 1500 (see fig. 14.11). As the Reformation gained momentum, and as iconoclasm took hold, painters in the north turned more and more to secular subjects. In fact, Dürer was most renowned and appreciated for his more secular work, which is hardly surprising given the climate of the times.

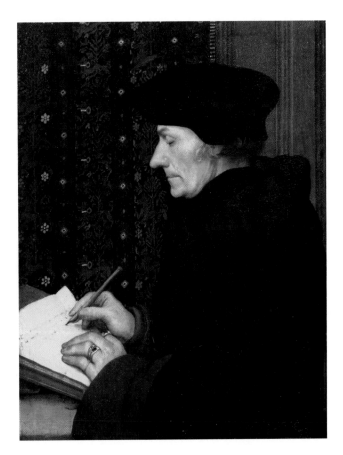

Figure 14.14   Hans Holbein the Younger, *Erasmus of Rotterdam*, ca. 1523, oil on panel, $16\frac{1}{2} \times 12\frac{1}{2}''$ (42 × 31.4 cm), Musée du Louvre, Paris. Holbein's portrait of the Dutch humanist Erasmus, shown as he records his ideas, conveys his intellectual authority.

Hans Holbein the Younger.   The art of HANS HOLBEIN THE YOUNGER [HOLE-bine] (1497/98–1543), reflects this increasing secularity. Holbein's fame grew from his great skill at portraiture, and he painted many important figures. Born in Augsburg into a family of artists, he worked in the shop of his father, Hans Holbein the Elder, and he also studied in Basel, in Switzerland, where in 1519 he set up shop. Around 1523, Holbein painted *Erasmus of Rotterdam* (fig. 14.14), a portrait of the famous Dutch humanist who had settled in Basel in 1521. Holbein revered Erasmus, became his close friend, and portrayed him several times. Erasmus is shown almost half-length, in profile, calm and noble. Using the carefully crafted Flemish oil technique, Holbein created a perfectly balanced arrangement of light and dark tones, a decoratively patterned surface, and a delicate modeling.

Erasmus provided Holbein with letters of introduction to the English court, where he was to become famous. In 1536 Holbein became court painter to Henry VIII, making portraits of the king and his family. In his depiction of Henry VIII (see fig. 14.8) the King wears wedding dress, fairly typical attire in view of his six marriages. One of Holbein's jobs as Henry's court painter was to paint portraits of his prospective brides. Holbein's working method was to begin with a chalk sketch, the face drawn in careful detail, the body and costume loosely indicated. Later, the portrait was painted in his studio, the face reproduced almost exactly with color added, and the garment made very elaborate and detailed. The sitter could send to Holbein's studio any garment she or he wished to be shown wearing. No one was expected to pose motionless while waiting for Holbein carefully to craft every puff and pleat.

More than mere likenesses, these portraits display exquisite line and sensitive modeling with little concern for spatial illusion. Holbein may have varied the format of his portraits, but he always made the figure look dignified and emotionally composed; thus he was very popular.

Pieter Bruegel the Elder. In contrast to Holbein's work at court, PIETER BRUEGEL THE ELDER [BROY-gul] (ca. 1525–1569) portrayed the peasantry and the countryside. Little is known about his life. When he was born remains uncertain; where, perhaps in Flanders. He was well educated, but he chose not to portray the upper class. He went to Rome to study humanism, classicism, and the new trends, but the trip seems to have had little impact on his art. In 1563 he married his teacher's daughter and moved from Antwerp to Brussels where he was to remain until 1569. His two sons became painters.

Bruegel earned considerable income by imitating the paintings of Hieronymus Bosch, which were extremely popular by the middle of the sixteenth century. But his best paintings depict the peasants and inhabitants of small towns and record the daily life of ordinary people, a type of work that has come to be known as **genre painting**. Typical of his paintings is the *Harvesters* (fig.

Figure 14.15 Pieter Bruegel the Elder, *Harvesters*, 1565, oil on panel, $3'10\frac{1}{2}'' \times 5'3\frac{1}{4}''$ (1.18 × 1.61 m), Metropolitan Museum of Art, New York. A genuine interest in landscape as a subject, rather than as mere background, first appears in Bruegel's series of paintings depicting the seasons and their corresponding labors.

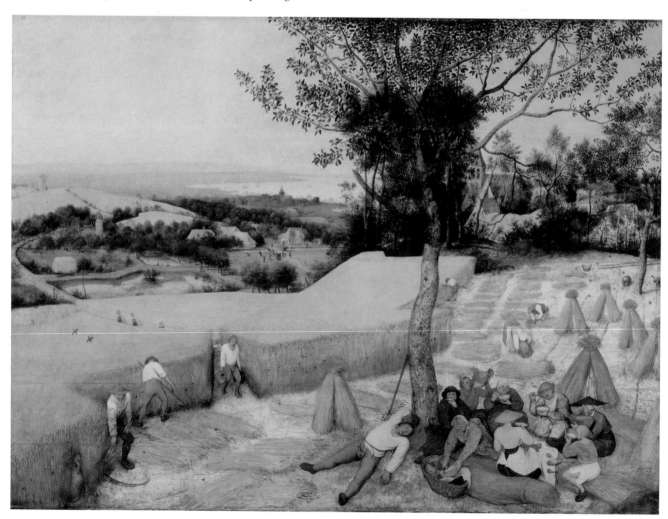

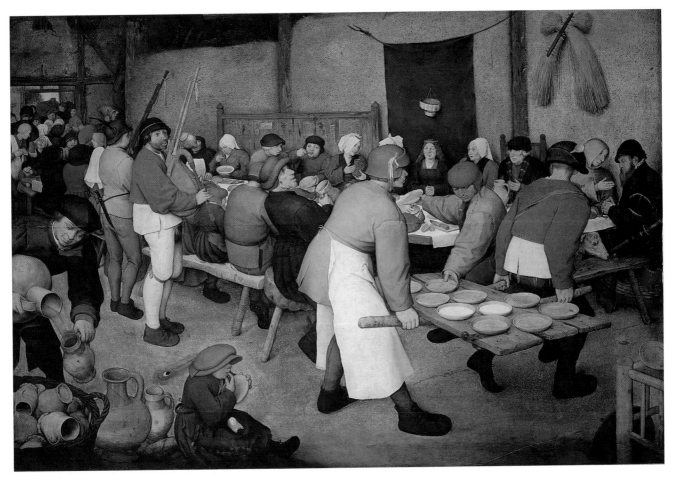

Figure 14.16 Pieter Bruegel the Elder, *Peasant Wedding*, ca. 1566–67, oil on panel, 3′8⅞″ × 5′4″ (1.10 × 1.60 m), Kunsthistorisches Museum, Vienna. Unlike his contemporaries, Bruegel was concerned not so much with the individual as with the type and, in particular, with the peasant class.

14.15) of 1565. Bruegel was commissioned to paint a series of scenes of the months of the year with, presumably, one painting representing every two months; the *Harvesters* represents August and September. Bruegel gave the landscape itself prominence; it no longer served merely as a setting for a portrait or religious event. Theoretically, the wheat is being harvested; in fact, most of the people in the scene are not working but sleeping, eating, or playing. Interested in basic human behavior, Bruegel signed his drawings "*Nart het leven*"—"Made from life."

The Limbourg brothers (see Chapter 12) had completed a series on the months of the year in their Book of Hours in 1416. What is new in Bruegel's paintings is the way in which the landscape is shown. The figures, rather than being placed in front of a landscape background, are now fully integrated into the setting. The colors convey the feeling of a warm summer afternoon—rich yellows and tans in the foreground, cool greens in the background.

Another famous painting of peasant life is Bruegel's *Peasant Wedding* (fig. 14.16), of ca. 1566–67. In this record of country wedding practices, the bride sits before a dark hanging cloth smiling shyly, hands clasped. Two men carrying bowls of rice pudding on wooden planks create the foreground. The bagpiper looks on at this dessert which, because rice was not a local product, was considered a speciality.

Although the composition of the *Peasant Wedding* appears informal, it is in fact carefully constructed. The foreground is reinforced by the figures in the lower left, including a child licking his fingers. The arrangement in space is diagonal; the diagonal line of the table continues with the plank on which the dessert is served. Rather than modeling his figures with highlights and shadows, Bruegel used flat areas of color and simplified forms to create a decorative, patterned quality. His strong, stocky figures convey the robustness and earthy liveliness of the peasants.

ARCHITECTURE

During the Renaissance, a significant number of castles were built in northern Europe. As the economic situation

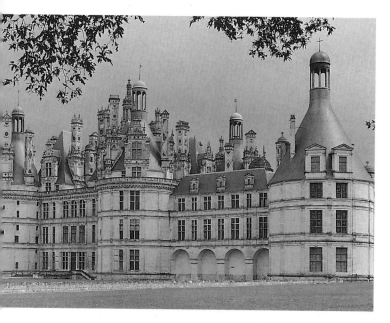

Figure 14.17 Domenico da Cortona (?), Château of Chambord, Loire Valley, begun in 1519, north facade. Ascend the monumental double-spiral staircase to the roof—where a little town has been constructed atop this extraordinary castle.

improved and the merchant class rose in importance, secular patronage of the arts grew, along with the interest in personal luxury and the display of wealth as a means of gaining and maintaining power and prestige. Castles were an effective means of showing one's importance. The most splendid of these were the **châteaux** (castles) of France. A concentration of Renaissance castles is found in the Loire [LWAR] valley, which was an especially agreeable area because of its fine climate and abundant game.

Château of Chambord.

Perhaps the most extraordinary of the French Renaissance châteaux is that of Chambord [sham-BORE] (fig. 14.17), begun in 1519 for the king, Francis I. The original architect is believed to have been an Italian, DOMENICO DA CORTONA [dah kor-TOE-nuh] (d. 1549). The largest of all Renaissance châteaux, Chambord has 440 rooms, 365 chimneys (one for every day of the year), fourteen big staircases, and seventy smaller staircases. The plan of Chambord is that of a medieval castle with a central keep, four corner towers, a surrounding wall, and, originally, a moat. Yet Chambord was built not for defense but for display.

The château at Chambord has two extraordinary features, one of which is outside, the other inside. Outside, on the flat roof, is a tiny town with winding streets, squares, and turrets. To walk on the roof is to wander within an intricate, overgrown sculpture, a sort of fairyland in the sky. Inside, the main attraction is the central double-spiral staircase. The spiral in itself was not novel,

but no one had attempted a double one before. It is built within a circle 30 feet in diameter and 80 feet high, going up to the roof. The two spiral staircases intertwine, but do not meet—two people on opposite staircases can see each other across the central well, but they cannot touch.

Hardwick Hall.

Although in terms of novelty English architecture lagged behind that of Italy and France, England's fortified castles with massive walls and small windows gradually gave way to airy homes with huge glass windows. These were built for the newly enfranchised nobility created by Henry VIII, when he granted monastery and Church lands to his supporters. When the monasteries fell, the new English aristocracy started to build enormous country houses. Hardwick Hall (fig. 14.18), built in 1591–96 and probably the work of the leading English architect ROBERT SMYTHSON [SMITH-son] (ca. 1535–1614), is one example. It was built for the extremely able and determined Elizabeth of Shrewsbury, also known as Bess of Hardwick, who amassed a fortune not only from her four marriages but as a businesswoman in her own right. Along with Queen Elizabeth I, she represents the growing power of women throughout Europe. Her initials are seen silhouetted several times along the roof line—a Renaissance assertion of the self.

The plan of Hardwick Hall is symmetrical and compact, built with a central great hall and square corner towers. The layout is innovatively arranged to separate rooms used for public functions from those kept for private activities. The floors were divided according to function and the more ceremonial the use of a room, the higher it was located in the house. Thus the great hall and the areas used by servants were on the ground floor;

Figure 14.18 Robert Smythson (?), Hardwick Hall, Derbyshire, 1591–96, facade. The importance of large windows as a sign of wealth is made clear by the comment, "Hardwick Hall, more glass than wall."

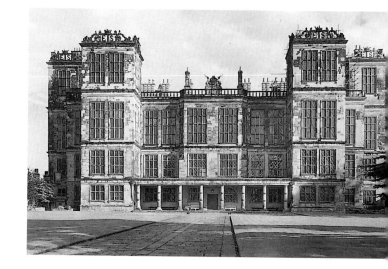

the private family apartments on the next floor; and the state rooms at the top of the house. This is the opposite plan of the southern Renaissance homes for families such as the Medici. Those residences had state and ceremonial rooms below and private quarters above (see Chapter 13). Hardwick Hall includes an invention of the English Renaissance, a **long gallery**—an unusually long room in which to take exercise when the weather is bad.

Hardwick Hall's massiveness and symmetry are characteristic of Elizabethan architecture. Its symmetry unifies the four facades and the building's extensive use of glass. Hardwick Hall was noted in particular for the great size of its windows, made memorable by the line coined at the time, "Hardwick Hall, more glass than wall," and indicating the importance and luxury of such large panes of glass. Note, too, that the size of the windows increases as the floors ascend, corresponding to the social uses of the floors.

SECULAR MUSIC

In keeping with the new emphasis on humankind during the Renaissance, **secular music** (music not associated with religious meanings or ceremonies) became increasingly popular. Giorgione and Titian's *Fête champêtre* (see fig. 13.39) documents this popularity in its depiction of people playing instruments. Unlike sacred vocal music, which typically set to music Latin or Greek texts, such as those used for the Mass, secular vocal music was composed for texts written in the vernacular, or common language spoken in a particular country or region. Although secular vocal compositions, such as madrigals, were written in many European languages including Italian, French, Spanish, German, Dutch, and English, there were two main schools of madrigal writng—English in the north and Italian in the south.

English Madrigals.

The **madrigal** is a vocal piece composed for a small group of singers, usually with no accompaniment. Like sacred motets (religious texts set to a polyphonic composition), madrigals were composed in polyphonic style, with multiple voice parts. (For an explanation of polyphony, see Chapter 13.) Unlike motets, however, which were typically performed by a small choir singing the same text in polyphony, madrigals were often performed by a few singers, each of whom sang a different vocal part. The madrigal was particularly appealing to an educated audience and was thus a popular court entertainment. Castiglione's circle found the madrigal an enjoyable form of entertainment.

Typically settings of short lyric poems, madrigals were often about love and frivolity. Their language and musical settings were often witty. The madrigalist's challenge was to set the poem's text to music perfectly. Madrigalists often tried to outdo each other in finding musical expression for the passions described in the text. They were especially inventive in setting words associated with weeping, sighing, trembling, and dying.

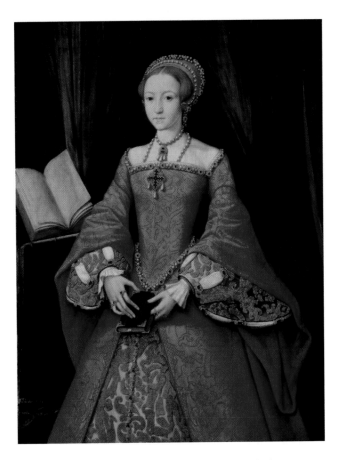

Figure 14.19   Levina Bening Teerling (?), *Elizabeth I as a Princess*, ca. 1559, oil on oak panel, 42³⁄₄ × 32¹⁄₄" (108.5 × 81.8 cm), The Royal Collection © Her Majesty Queen Elizabeth II, Windsor Castle, Windsor, England. The book is indicative of Elizabeth's love of learning and support of the arts.

Thomas Weelkes.

A composer best known for his madrigals, THOMAS WEELKES [WILKS] (1575–1623) was the organist at Chichester Cathedral. His madrigal "As Vesta Was Descending" was included in an early sixteenth-century collection of madrigals, *The Triumph of Oriana*, composed in honor of Queen Elizabeth I (fig. 14.19). Written for six voices—two sopranos, alto, two tenors, and bass—Weelkes's madrigal was a setting of the following poem:

As Vesta was from Latmos hill descending,
She spied a maiden Queen the same ascending,
Attended only by all the shepherds swain,
To whom Diana's darlings came running down amain:

First two by two, then three by three together,
Leaving their goddess all alone, hasted thither,
And mingling with the shepherds of her train,
With mirthful tunes her presence entertain.

Then sang the shepherds and nymphs of Diana,
Long live fair Oriana.

Weelkes takes advantage of the opportunities the poem affords for word painting. On the words "descending" and "ascending," for example, he uses descending and ascending musical lines respectively. He also expresses musically the text's description of the attendants running "two by two, then three by three together, / Leaving their goddess all alone," by having first two singers then three, and finally all six join in before dropping back to a solo singer. Weelkes also uses fast notes for the words "running down amain," and he writes lively and upbeat music for the line "With mirthful tunes her presence entertain." Finally, for the word "long" in the last line, Weelkes provides singers with their longest held note. (For further explanation of word painting, see Chapter 13.)

Thomas Morley.   Another well-known composer of madrigals was THOMAS MORLEY (1557–1603). Morley actually favored another form of vocal music: the **ballett**, a dancelike song for a variety of solo voices. The ballett differs from the madrigal in being composed mostly in **homophonic texture**, in which a single melody, not several, is employed with harmonic support. He also uses the same music for each stanza of the poem, with the nonsense syllables *fa-la* sung as a refrain. The playfulness of the music complements the playfulness of the words, which, as with much Elizabethan poetry, reveal a true love of the English language.

Morley's madrigal, "Now Is the Month of Maying," scored for five voices, describes the carefree flirting and courtship games common in the English countryside in spring. Morley's melody has a distinct and readily discernible rhythm and the easy tunefulness of a folk dance. It is structured in two parts, each of which is repeated and each of which concludes with the *fa-la* refrain. Here is the text:

> Now is the month of maying,
> When merry lads are playing, *fa la*,
> Each with his bonny lass
> Upon the greeny grass. *Fa la*.
>
> The spring, clad all in gladness,
> Doth laugh at winter's sadness, *fa la*,
> And to the bagpipe's sound
> The nymphs tread out their ground. *Fa la*.
>
> Fie then! why sit we musing,
> Youth's sweet delight refusing? *Fa la*,
> Say, dainty nymphs, and speak,
> Shall we play barley break? *Fa la*.

The lyrics to both Weelkes's and Morley's madrigals depict delicate nymphs and good-natured shepherds, lighthearted diversions that appealed to the privileged classes.

LITERATURE

Michel de Montaigne.   The fame of MICHEL DE MONTAIGNE [mahn-TAYN] (1533–1592) rests on his *Essays*, a stunning example of Renaissance individualism grounded in humanism. Montaigne was one of the most learned individuals of his time, with a deep knowledge of the writers of Roman antiquity. His *Essays*, however, are distinguished less by depth of knowledge of the past than by a profound knowledge of the self.

Michel de Montaigne was born in Bordeaux, southern France. Well educated, Montaigne studied law, spent time at court, and became a member of the Bordeaux parliament, serving as an arbitrator between the warring Protestant and Catholic royal factions. When he was thirty-eight, Montaigne decided to retire to his castle, where he had a library, and devoted himself to the quiet pastimes of reflection and writing. Nevertheless, he came out of retirement to serve two terms as mayor of Bordeaux (1581–85).

Reflecting his respect for antiquity, Montaigne's early essays (in French, *essais*) contain numerous quotations from his reading. In his second book of essays, however, Montaigne relied less on the authority of the past and more on expressing his views in his own voice. In his third and last book of essays, Montaigne used quotations sparingly in presenting a vigorous self-portrait.

Montaigne said that he wrote about himself because he knew himself better than he knew anything else. In "Of Experience," he wrote that "no man ever treated of a subject that he knew and understood better than I do this … and in this I am the most learned man alive." Montaigne notes, however, that like everything else in the world, he exists in a perpetual state of flux. "I must adapt my history to the moment," he wrote, for "I may presently change, not only by chance, but also by intention." And thus his books of essays represent "a record of diverse and changeable events, of undecided, and … contradictory ideas."

Montaigne asks many questions in his essays, though without providing clear and singular answers. "Perhaps" and "I think" are among his most frequently used expressions, and "*Que sais-je?*" ("What do I know?") is his most recurring question. The very name he coined for the genre he created, *essai*, means trial or attempt, which suggests a process rather than a finished product, openness rather than conclusiveness, the journey itself and not the destination. It is one of the wonderful paradoxes of reading Montaigne that, as much as his essays reveal him, they also reveal readers to themselves. Montaigne's emphasis on questions rather than answers, coupled with a celebration of the individual, makes his work distinctly part of the Renaissance.

In his essay "Of Smells," Montaigne explores his own personal sense of smell and then poses some larger meanings for this sense. At one point he concludes that odors can affect the human mind and spirit, an idea that has gained currency today: "The doctors might, I believe, derive more use from odors than they do; for I have often noticed that they make a change in me and writer in the English language. His fame and popularity rest on his thirty-seven plays and 154 sonnets. What accounts for Shakespeare's popularity is his revelation of human character, especially his exploration of complex states of mind and feeling, and his explosive and exuberant language, particularly the richness and variety of his metaphors. His manipulation of language and his revelation of character are particularly evident in his **soliloquies**, those meditative reflections spoken aloud. From *Hamlet* (fig. 14.20) alone, we glean the following famous sayings:

- ❧ In my mind's eye;
- ❧ I must be cruel only to be kind;
- ❧ Brevity is the soul of wit;
- ❧ To be or not to be, that is the question;
- ❧ Neither a borrower nor a lender be;
- ❧ Something's rotten in the state of Denmark;
- ❧ What a piece of work is a man.

Shakespeare was born in Stratford-upon-Avon in April 1564. He attended the local school, but did not go on to Oxford or Cambridge. Instead, in 1582, at the age of eighteen, he married Anne Hathaway, who bore him three children in as many years. At that time Shakespeare began writing and acting in plays. Although many tributes have been paid to Shakespeare, one stands above the rest: his contemporary Ben Jonson's judgment that "he is not for an age, but for all time."

Shakespeare's sonnets display dramatic power and narrative drive as well as melodic lyricism. Their range of emotional experience is wide, including melancholy, despair, hope, shame, guilt, fear, jealousy, and exhilaration. Written during the 1590s, they were not published until 1609—though two of them were printed in a 1599 collection, *The Passionate Pilgrim*, apparently without Shakespeare's authorization. Like John Donne's poems, Shakespeare's sonnets circulated in manuscript before publication and, according to contemporary testimony, were much admired.

Shakespeare's soliloquies further reveal the human spirit. In a soliloquy from *Macbeth*, Shakespeare uses obsessive, bitter language to characterize Macbeth's tragedy. The following soliloquy from Act V, Scene i occurs when Macbeth discovers that though he is now king, his wife, Lady Macbeth, is dead:

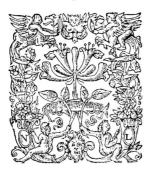

Figure 14.20 Title-page, *Hamlet* (1603), The Huntington Library, California. This is the title-page of the first quarto edition of the play that was printed.

work upon my spirits according to their properties; which makes me approve of the idea that the use of incense and perfumes in churches, so ancient and widespread in all nations and religions, was intended to delight us and arouse and purify our senses to make us more fit for contemplation."

"Of Smells" exemplifies a kind of writing that did not exist before Montaigne invented it. Montaigne varied the kinds of essay he wrote without predetermining their form. Both writer and reader share in the mental exploration, making it seem natural, familiar, unstudied. The modern novelist and essayist Virginia Woolf put it this way: "This talking of oneself, following one's own vagaries, giving the whole map, weight, colour, and circumference of the soul in its confusion, its variety, its imperfection—this art belonged to one man only: to Montaigne."

William Shakespeare. WILLIAM SHAKESPEARE [SHAYK-speer] (1564–1616) is perhaps the greatest

Tomorrow, and tomorrow, and tomorrow
Creeps in this petty pace from day to day,   *20*
To the last syllable of recorded time;
And all our yesterdays have lighted fools
The way to dusty death. Out, Out, brief candle!
Life's but a walking shadow, a poor player
That struts and frets his hour upon the stage   *25*
And then is heard no more. It is a tale
Told by an idiot, full of sound and fury
Signifying nothing.

Written in **blank verse**—verse in unrhymed **iambic pentameter** (each line has ten syllables with alternating stresses)—the soliloquy portrays Macbeth's despair over the apparent meaninglessness of life. Shakespeare emphasizes life's brevity and fragility implied by the snuffed candle, and he compares life to a shadow, an insubstantial and dark reflection of reality. The soliloquy's final metaphor suggests Macbeth's feeling that life has no more meaning than that of a confused and incoherent story.

Shakespeare's plays have captured the imagination of the world and assured his position as the greatest playwright of all time. The political astuteness of plays such as *Julius Caesar* and *Antony and Cleopatra* are comple-

mented by the playful romanticism of comedies such as *As You Like It* and *Much Ado About Nothing*, and the more tempered romantic qualities of Shakespeare's final plays, of which *The Tempest* is the most glorious example.

The drama of Shakespeare's time, the Elizabethan Age (1558–1603), shares some features with Greek drama, though the Elizabethan dramatists extended the possibilities of both comedy and tragedy. The Elizabethan dramatists, including Shakespeare's contemporary Christopher Marlowe, wrote domestic tragedies, tragedies of character, and revenge tragedies, of which *Hamlet* is the most famous and the greatest example. The Elizabethan dramatists also wrote comedies of manners and comedies of humors, which extended the range of

Figure 14.21   Globe Playhouse, London, 1599–1613. This imaginative reconstruction by C. Walter Hodges depicts the open-air theater where *Hamlet* and other plays by Shakespeare were first performed.

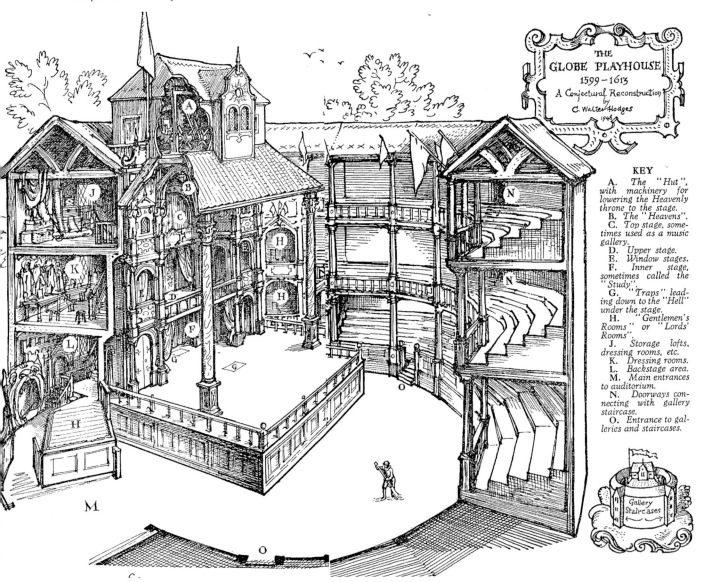

Connections

SHAKESPEARE AND MUSIC

Shakespeare employs music in his plays for various purposes. He uses music to suggest a change in locale and time, indicating that the action of a play has shifted scene. Music signals the entrance or exit of an important character; trumpet flourishes announce the arrival or departure of royalty. Trumpets also sound a battle charge.

Music and Character Revelation

Perhaps the most important function of music in Shakespeare's plays is to reveal character. Shakespeare's characters disclose their states of mind through the songs they sing. In *Hamlet*, the young Ophelia reveals her unstable mental state through singing about love, loss, and death. In *Othello*, Desdemona, Othello's wife, conveys an ominous foreboding about her imminent death in the "Willow Song."

Musical Imagery

Shakespeare's plays are also rife with musical images. Some of these are simple passing references, such as those in *Romeo and Juliet*. When Romeo and Juliet part, Juliet cries out in disappointment, "the lark sings so out of tune, / Straining harsh discords and unpleasing sharps." Often, however, Shakespeare developed elaborate patterns of musical imagery. A striking example occurs when Hamlet speaks to his boyhood friends Rosencrantz and Guildenstern, who are about to betray him. In complaining about their deceit, Hamlet likens himself to a recorder, or flute, playing in the background:

> HAMLET Why, look you now, how unworthy a thing you make of me! You would play upon me, you would seem to know my stops, you would pluck out the heart of my mystery, you would sound me from my lowest note to the top of my compass; and there is much music, excellent voice, in this little organ, yet cannot you make it speak. 'Sblood, do you think I am easier to be played on than a pipe? Call me what instrument you will, though you can fret me, you cannot play upon me.

Act III, Scene ii, ll. 349–57

Dramatically, Shakespeare has the ever-alert Hamlet hear the musicians, then ask Guildenstern if he will play upon him as a musician plays upon a recorder. When Guildenstern responds that he doesn't know how to play the instrument, Hamlet presses him by comparing playing the recorder to the act of trying to find out what someone is really thinking, which is what Guildenstern has been doing all along. In this elaborated metaphor, everything Hamlet says proves to be literally true.

Composers and Instruments

Instruments used for Shakespearean music include brass, woodwind, strings, and percussion (fig. 14.22). Trumpets were the most frequently used brass instrument; wooden flutes and recorders of various sizes were the most common woodwind instruments. Stringed instruments included the violin, harp, lyre, and lute, among others. Percussion was almost always supplied by a tabor or drum, which often was accompanied by a fife, the smallest of the flutes.

Shakespeare did not compose the music that accompanied his plays. In Shakespeare's lifetime, his contemporaries, such as Thomas Morley, set his words to music, including "O Mistress Mine" from *Twelfth Night*, which Morley may have written at Shakespeare's request. Other music used to accompany songs included traditional arrangements that antedated the plays, as with the "Willow Song," sung by Desdemona in *Othello*, and the gravedigger's song "In Youth When I Did Love" from *Hamlet*.

Figure 14.22 Anon., *Le Concert champêtre: la musique* (*The Musicians of a Country Concert*), Italian School, sixteenth century. Musée de l'Hotel l'Allemant, Bourges, Giraudon/Art Resource, New York. Here is a depiction of a typical chamber music ensemble, consisting of a harpsichord, lute, recorder, and bass viol.

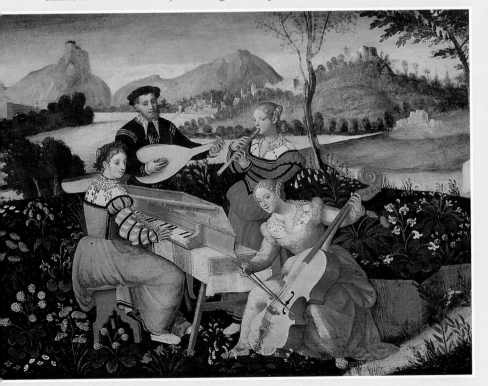

earlier romantic and satiric comedies. In both Greek and Elizabethan theater, props were few, scenery was simple, and the dialogue alone indicated changes of locale and time.

An Elizabethan playhouse such as the Globe (fig. 14.21), where many of Shakespeare's plays were staged, had a much smaller seating capacity than the large Greek amphitheaters, which could seat thousands. The Globe could accommodate about 2300 people, including roughly eight hundred groundlings who, exposed to the weather, stood around the stage. The stage itself projected from an inside wall into their midst. More prosperous spectators sat in one of the three stories that nearly encircled the stage. The vastly reduced size and seating capacity of the Elizabethan theater and the projection of its stage made for a greater intimacy between actors and audience. Though actors still had to project their voices and exaggerate their gestures, they could be heard and seen without the aid of large megaphonic masks and elevated shoes, as in the ancient Greek theater. Elizabethan actors could modulate their voices and vary their pitch, stress, and intonation in ways unsuited to the Greek stage. They could also make wider and more subtle use of facial expression and gesture.

In addition to greater intimacy, the Elizabethan stage also offered more versatility than its Greek counterpart. Although the Greek *skene* building could be used for scenes occurring above the ground, such as a god descending from above by means of a crane (*deus ex machina*), the Greek stage was really a single-level acting area. Not so the Elizabethan stage, which contained a second-level balcony, utilized in *Othello* and in *Romeo and Juliet*, for instance. Shakespeare's stage also had doors at the back for entrances and exits, a curtained alcove useful for scenes of intrigue, and a stage-floor trapdoor, from which the ghost ascends in *Hamlet*.

READINGS
❖

← **DESIDERIUS ERASMUS**
from *The Praise of Folly*

Erasmus's The Praise of Folly *(1509) is the most important satirical work of the Renaissance. Erasmus casts a wide net, catching all manner of vanities, arrogance, selfishness, pomposity, and other human failings. He criticizes clerics, scholars, teachers, theologians, and scientists. In the following passage, Erasmus, speaking in the voice of Folly, zeroes in on the clerics, then moves on to princes and courtiers, using sharply piercing wit.*

Next to them in bliss come those who are popularly called "men of religion" and "monks." Both names are completely false since most of them avoid religion as much as they can, and wherever you go you can't help running into these men who've "withdrawn" from the world. I simply can't imagine what would be more wretched than their condition, unless I helped them out in all sorts of ways. For everyone loathes them so much that simply for one of them to show his face is considered bad luck; yet they flatter themselves gloriously. First, they think it a main point of piety to be ignorant of good letters, preferably not to be able to read at all. Then when like donkeys in church they bray out their psalms (memorized indeed, but not understood) they can imagine they are ravishing the ears of the saints with infinite delight. A good many of them make an excellent living out of their beggars' rags, bellowing for bread from door to door, and shoving into inns, carriages, and boats to the great prejudice of other beggars. And thus these delightful fellows represent themselves to us as apostles—by virtue of their filth, stupidity, grossness, and impudence, forsooth!

What can be funnier than their habit of doing everything by the book, as if following mathematical rules that it would be a sin to break? So many knots are required in the shoelace, a cloak can have only so many colors and must be of a certain material, the girdle must also be of a certain material and so many straws wide, the cowl can be cut only one way and capable of holding only so many pecks, the hair must be trimmed to the length of so many fingers, sleep is permitted for only so many hours. This rigid equality, imposed on people so very different in body and mind, is most unequal in its effects, as who can help seeing? And yet by these tricks they succeed in feeling superior not only to ordinary laymen but to one another—so that these men dedicated to apostolic charity will make frightful scenes over a habit worn with the wrong girdle or a bit too dark in color. Some you can find so severely religious that they use only rough Cilician cloth for their outer robe, though the undergarment is of fine Milesian wool; a variation of this trick is to wear linen on the outside, wool inside. Still others reject mere contact with money as if it were a most contagious poison, though they are less scrupulous about wine-bibbing or intimate relations with women.

Finally, they all try as hard as possible not to agree with each other in their way of life; they are far less interested in resembling Christ than in differing among themselves. Thus they take special delight in their various names, some calling themselves "Cordeliers" but then subdividing their order into "Coletans," "Friars Minor," "Minims," and "Bullists." Again we have the "Benedictines" and the "Bernardines," the "Brigetines" and the "Augustinians," the "Williamites" and the "Jacobites"—as if it was their last concern to be known as Christians.

The greater number of them insist so vehemently on their own ceremonies and petty traditions that they think a single heaven will hardly be adequate reward for such outstanding merit—never imagining that Christ, despising all these observances, will judge by his own standard, which is that of charity. One monk will point to his paunch, distended by eating every variety of fish; another will pour forth psalms by the bushel. Another will number up his myriads of fasts, and account for his bursting belly by the fact that he eats only one meal at midday. Another points to his huge pile of ceremonies performed, so many they couldn't be laden on seven naval transports. Another brags that for sixty years he has never touched money except with fingers protected by two pairs of gloves. Still another wears a cowl so dirty and slimy that no sailor would let it touch his body. Another boasts that for more than half a century he has led the life of a sponge, always fixed to the same spot; his neighbor claims credit for a voice hoarsened by constant singing; another for a lethargy contracted during years of solitude; and still another for a tongue atrophied during years of silence. But Christ, interrupting their boasts (which otherwise would never end), will ask, "Where did this new race of Jews come from? I recognize no law but my own, and about it I hear nothing whatever. Long ago, speaking openly and using no intricate parables, I promised that my father's kingdom would be granted, not to cowls, prayers, or fasts, but to works of faith and charity. Nor do I recognize those who make too much of their own merits and want to seem more sanctified than me; let them go live in the heavens of Abraxa or, if they want, get a new heaven built for them outside mine by the men whose foolish traditions they have preferred before my commandments." When they hear these words, and see sailors and coachmen preferred before them, with what expressions do you suppose they will stare at each other? But meanwhile they cherish their own comfortable illusions, not without help from me.

Even though they have no political power, nobody dares to scorn the monks, least of all the mendicants, because they hold the keys of everyone's secret life under the seal of the confessional, as they call it. Revealing such secrets they consider very wrong, unless when they're drunk, and want to please the company with spicy stories; then they sketch the outlines of the tale, but allusively, leaving out all the names. But if anyone stirs up these hornets, then they defend themselves in public sermons, alluding indirectly and subtly to their enemy, so that only a complete dummy will fail to get the point. And there'll be no end to their yapping till you stop their mouths with a bone.

Tell me, now, what comic actor or street-corner charlatan would you rather watch in action than these fellows making their sermons? Though they can't avoid ridiculous blunders, they try to imitate everything the old rhetoricians have handed down on the art of discourse. Good lord, how they gesticulate, how they change pitch, how they crow and strut and fling themselves wildly about, putting on special expressions from time to time, and getting everything mixed up in their outcries. And this art of oratory they hand down as a secret tradition from brother to brother: gradually, they limp painfully through the first part, break out in a wild clamor even though they're in the dullest part of their subject, and then fall silent so abruptly you'd think they were out of breath. Finally, they've learned from the rhetoricians that it's a good idea to indulge a little humor now and then, so they try to mix a few jokes in with their talk; "Lord help us all," how gracefully they do it, and how *à propos*—you'd say it was a clear case of "an ass with a lyre." From time to time, they give a little satirical nip, too, but they take care to tickle rather than wound. And in fact they never flatter more than when they pretend to be "speaking most sharply." In short, the whole performance is such that you'd swear the preachers must have studied with street-corner charlatans, who are better performers, indeed, but follow the same procedures so closely that it's obvious one group must have learned its rhetorical tricks from the other.

And yet these preachers find that, thanks to my assistance, their audiences imagine that they're hearing a modern Demosthenes or a Cicero. Shopkeepers and women are the hearers they like best, and they try hardest to please them, because the former if stroked the right way may be coaxed into untying their moneybags, and the ladies, among many other reasons for liking the clergy, know they can always find there an understanding ear in which to pour out their grievances against their husbands.

You see now, I guess, how much men of the cloth owe to me, since with their petty little ceremonies, their trifling formulas, and loud mouths, they can wield a practical tyranny over the laity, and pass themselves off as actual Saint Pauls or Saint Anthonys. But I'm happy to be rid of these shoddy play-actors, who are as good at taking my gifts without showing gratitude as they are at putting up a show of piety for the public. For now I'd like to say something about princes and courtiers who, like the free and liberal-minded men they are, seek my favors quite openly and unabashedly. These noblemen, if they have just half an ounce of good heart, must surely lead the most wretched lives in the world, and the most to be avoided. For what man would ever dream of trying to seize royal power by perjury or parricide if he reflected what a heavy burden falls on the shoulders of anyone who assumes the part of a true prince? If he wants to guide the ship of state, he must think continually of the public welfare, not his own; indeed, he can consider nothing but the public good. He must not depart by a finger's breadth from the laws he has designed and promulgated; he must see to the integrity of all his officers and magistrates. His own life is exposed to public scrutiny; thus, if his manners are virtuous, he can be a star to steer by, and of the utmost benefit in all human affairs—or if, on the contrary, he is like a deadly comet, he can bring total destruction in his wake. Other men's vices are not so obvious, nor are they so far-reaching in their effects. A prince stands on such an eminence that if something turns him ever so slightly from the path of honesty, a moral pestilence spreads through thousands of his subjects. Then because a ruler's position brings with it many things to distract him from virtue, such as pleasure, leisure, flattery, and luxury, he must be vigilant and keen to avoid disgracing his office. Finally, passing over all the plots, jealousies, and other perils that threaten, he is subject to the judgment of that one true King who will exact retribution for his least failing, and the more strictly, the greater has been his authority. If a prince would reflect on these and similar matters—and he would if he were wise—I doubt if he would enjoy either his evening dinner or a good night's sleep.

But now, thanks to my bounty, princes dismiss all these problems and send them to Jericho; they look out for their own sweet selves and won't even admit anyone to their presence who can't keep the conversation light, and far away from disagreeable subjects. They suppose they're performing all the duties of a prince if they ride regularly to hounds, keep a stable full of fine horses, sell government offices for their own profit, and think every day of a new way to squeeze money out of the citizens and funnel it into the royal treasury. But these tricks are always performed under cover of precedent, so that even if the proceedings are iniquitous, they can at least make a pretence of equity; and they're always accompanied by a few words of flattery, to keep on the good side of public opinion.

Picture to yourself a man, like quite a few existing nowadays, who is ignorant of the law, almost an open enemy of the public good, concerned only with his own private advantage, a hater of liberty, learning, and truth, thinking of nothing less than the welfare of his country, but judging everything by his own pleasures, his own profit. Now hang a golden chain on his neck to symbolize the linkage of all the virtues, and set on his head a crown studded with gems to remind him that he should excel everyone else in heroic qualities. Put a scepter in his hand to symbolize justice and a heart free from corruption, and give him a purple robe to show his outstanding devotion to the welfare of his country. If a prince were to compare these symbols with his actual behavior, I think he might be ashamed of his trappings, and fear lest some satiric commentator might turn all his fine apparel into a ridiculous joke.

Courtiers are another story. Though generally they're the most meeching, slavish, stupid, abject creatures conceivable, they fancy themselves the most distinguished of men. In one respect, they take the prize for modesty, because they content themselves with the gold, gems, purple robes, and other insignia of virtue while relinquishing to others all concern for the virtues themselves. One thing makes them perfectly happy if they can address the king as "Sire," if they can speak three words of greeting to him, and then fill out the rest of their speech with formulas like "Serene Majesty," "Your Lordship," and "Your Imperial Highness." The rest of their talent is just barefaced flattery. And these are the proper skills of a noble courtier. But if you look more closely at their way of life, you'll find they are nothing but Phacacians, or Penelope's suitors—you know the rest of the poem, which Echo can give you better than I. They sleep till noon, when some miserable, mercenary little priest comes to their bedside and runs through mass for them almost before they're awake. Next to breakfast, which is hardly finished before it's lunchtime. Then on to dicing, draughts, betting, comedians, fools, drabs, games, and dirty stories, with a goodie to nibble on every so often between these activities. Dinner time now, followed by drinks, more than one, you can be sure. And in this way, without a moment's boredom, hours, days, months, years, and ages glide away. I myself get thoroughly sick of them, and take off, when I see them "putting on the dog," their ladies preening themselves on their long trains as if that made them superior beings, the men elbowing one another out of the way so they can be seen standing next to the prince, or when they string heavy gold chains around their necks, as if trying to show off their muscles at the same time as their money.

For a long time now, this courtly manner of life has been eagerly imitated by the loftiest Popes, Cardinals, and Bishops, some of whom have even surpassed their originals. But does anyone think what the priest's linen vestment means by its snow-white color, that it is the sign of a spotless life? Or what is the meaning of that two-horned mitre, with each point rising to a tight knot, if not to indicate absolute knowledge of the Old and New Testaments? Or why his hands are covered with gloves, if not to keep them clean of all contact with human affairs, and free to administer the sacraments? Why does he carry a crozier, if not to

take vigilant care of the flock entrusted to him? Why the cross carried before him if not to signify victory over all human appetites? If any one of the clergy were to reflect on these and many other similar matters, I ask you, wouldn't he live a pretty sorry and wretched life? But now they're perfectly content, as long as they've stuffed themselves. As for watching over the flock, they either let Christ take care of that chore or put it off on curates and the "Brethren," as they call them. They never even think of the meaning of their title "Bishop," which means "overseer," and implies work, caring, taking pains. Yet when it comes to raking in the revenues, they're sharp-sighted enough; no "careless oversight" there.

Likewise the Cardinals, if they reflected that they are successors to the Apostles, and that the same things are required of them as of their predecessors, might consider that they are not masters but administrators of spiritual gifts, for which an exact accounting will have to be rendered. They might even philosophize for a moment over their vestments, and ask themselves a few questions. For example: what is the meaning of this white outer garment, if not supreme, spotless innocence of life? Why the purple beneath, if not to show an ardent love of God? And again, that capacious cloak spreading out to envelop not only the Most Reverend Father but his mule as well—and sufficient to cover even a camel—does it not signify universal charity, extending to every person everywhere, in the form of teaching, exhorting, correcting, admonishing, pacifying quarrels, resisting wicked princes, and freely expending for the benefit of the Christian community not only his money but his blood? And why do they need money at all if they stand in the place of the Apostles, who were all poor men? If they thought over these matters, as I say, they wouldn't be so ambitious for the post, might even resign it—or at least live lives as strenuous and devoted as those of the original Apostles.

And the Popes themselves, vicars of Christ, if they tried to imitate his life—his poverty, his toil, his teaching, his suffering on the cross, his contempt of life—if they ever thought of the name "Pope," which means Father, or their title "Your Holiness," what soul on earth would be more downcast? Who would purchase that position at the expense of all his belongings, or would defend it, once bought, with sword, poison, and violence of every sort? Think how many comforts would be lost to them if they ever admitted a gleam of reason! Reason, did I say? Rather, just a grain of the salt Christ spoke of. Off they would go, all those riches, honors, powers, triumphs, appointments, dispensations, special levies and indulgences; away with the troops of horses, mules, flunkies, and all the pleasures that go with them! (You'll note what a marketplace, what a harvest, what an ocean of pleasures I've crammed into a few words.) Instead of which, wisdom would bring wakeful nights, long fasts, tears, prayers, sermons, hours of study, sighs, and a thousand other griefs of that sort. And let's not forget the other circumstances, all those scribes, copyists, notaries, advocates, prosecutors, and secretaries, all those mule-drivers, stable hands, money-changers, pimps, and—I almost added something gentler, but I'm afraid it would grate on certain ears. In short, this whole gang of people which battens on the Holy See—sorry, I meant to say, "which distinguishes it"—would be reduced to want. What a crime! abominable and inhuman; and to make it worse, the highest princes of the church and true lights of the world would be reduced to taking up scrip and staff.

But as things stand now, whatever work may be called for in the church is passed along to Peter and Paul, who have ample free time; if there's any splendor or pleasure being given out, that our church leaders are willing to take on. And so it happens that, thanks to my efforts, no class of men live more comfortably or with less trouble. They think they've amply fulfilled Christ's commandments if they play the part of bishop with mystical and almost theatrical pomp, with formulas of Your Beatitude, Your Reverence, and Your Holiness, salted with some blessings and anathemas. Performing miracles is, for them, old-fashioned and obsolete, not at all in tune with modern times; teaching the people is hard work, prayer is boring, tears are weak and womanish, poverty is degrading, and meekness is disgraceful, quite unworthy of one who barely admits even the greatest kings to kiss his feet. Death is a most unattractive prospect, and the idea of dying on a cross is quite out of the question.

All that's left to them in the way of weapons are those good words and fair speeches described by Paul (and of those things they are sufficiently generous)—along with interdicts, suspensions, warnings many times repeated, anathemas, fearful images, and that horrifying thunderbolt with which, by a mere nod of the head, they dispatch the souls of mortal men to the depths of Tartarus. It's a weapon that the most holy fathers in God and vicars of Christ on earth launch at no one more fiercely than at those who, instigated by the Devil, try to whittle away the patrimony of Peter to a mere morsel. This patrimony, though the Evangelist says, "We have left all and followed you," is understood to include farmlands, taxes, tithes, and judicial privileges. Ablaze with Christian zeal, they fight with fire and sword to defend these belongings, at no small expense of Christian blood—and all the time they declare that this is the apostolic way to defend the church, the bride of Christ, by putting to flight her enemies, as they call them. As if, indeed, there were any enemies of the church more pernicious than impious popes, who by their silence allow Christ to be forgotten, lock him up behind their money-making laws, contaminate his teachings with their interpretations, and murder him with their atrocious manner of life.

MARTIN LUTHER

Ninety-Five Theses; or, Disputation on the Power and Efficacy of Indulgences

The following are the ninety-five theses Martin Luther nailed to the door of Castle Church at Wittenberg in 1517. They were essentially an invitation to debate and quickly became a rallying point for criticism of Church practices. The indulgences Luther was attacking were pardons from sin given out by Church officials in exchange for monetary donations.

The central concern of the ninety-five theses is with penance, which for Luther was a permanent inner attitude. He believed that indulgences misled the faithful into believing they could be absolved of their sins simply through their outward purchase. Luther, however, held that sincere repentance was necessary for the forgiveness of sin

and the remission of punishment. Luther begins his ninety-five theses with references to these more general issues of sin and repentance. The first mention of "indulgence" comes in the twenty-first thesis.

Out of love and zeal for truth and the desire to bring it to light, the following theses will be publicly discussed at Wittenberg under the chairmanship of the reverend father Martin Lutther,[1] Master of Arts and Sacred Theology and regularly appointed Lecturer on these subjects at that place. He requests that those who cannot be present to debate orally with us will do so by letter.[2]

In the Name of Our Lord Jesus Christ. Amen.

1. When our Lord and Master Jesus Christ said, "Repent" [Matt. 4:17],[3] he willed the entire life of believers to be one of repentance.

2. This word cannot be understood as referring to the sacrament of penance, that is, confession and satisfaction, as administered by the clergy.

3. Yet it does not mean solely inner repentance; such inner repentance is worthless unless it produces various outward mortifications of the flesh.

4. The penalty of sin[4] remains as long as the hatred of self, that is, true inner repentance, until our entrance into the kingdom of heaven.

5. The pope neither desires nor is able to remit any penalties except those imposed by his own authority or that of the canons.[5]

6. The pope cannot remit any guilt, except by declaring and showing that it has been remitted by God; or, to be sure, by remitting guilt in cases reserved to his judgment. If his right to grant remission in these cases were disregarded, the guilt would certainly remain unforgiven.

7. God remits guilt to no one unless at the same time he humbles him in all things and makes him submissive to his vicar, the priest.

8. The penitential canons are imposed only on the living, and, according to the canons themselves, nothing should be imposed on the dying.

9. Therefore the Holy Spirit through the pope is kind to us insofar as the pope in his decrees always makes exception of the article of death and of necessity.[6]

---

[1] Luther spelled his name Lutther in this preamble.

[2] There was actually no debate, for no one responded to the invitation. The contents of the ninety-five theses were soon widely disseminated by word of mouth and by the printers, and in effect a vigorous debate took place that lasted for a number of years.

[3] The Latin form, *poenitentiam agite*, and the German, *tut Busse*, may be rendered in two ways, "repent," and "do penance."

[4] Catholic theology distinguishes between the "guilt" and the "penalty" of sin.

[5] The canons, or decrees of the church, have the force of law. Those referred to here and in Theses 8 and 85 are the so-called penitential canons.

[6] Commenting on this thesis in the *Explanations of the Ninety-five Theses*, Luther distinguishes between temporal and eternal necessity "Necessity knows no law." "Death is the necessity of necessities."

10. Those priests act ignorantly and wickedly who, in the case of the dying, reserve canonical penalties for purgatory.

11. Those tares of changing the canonical penalty to the penalty of purgatory were evidently sown while the bishops slept [Matt. 13:25].

12. In former times canonical penalties were imposed, not after, but before absolution, as tests of true contrition.

13. The dying are freed by death from all penalties, are already dead as far as the canon laws are concerned, and have a right to be released from them.

14. Imperfect piety or love on the part of the dying person necessarily brings with it great fear; and the smaller the love, the greater the fear.

15. This fear or horror is sufficient in itself, to say nothing of other things, to constitute the penalty of purgatory, since it is very near the horror of despair.

16. Hell, purgatory, and heaven seem to differ the same as despair, fear, and assurance of salvation.

17. It seems as though for the souls in purgatory fear should necessarily decrease and love increase.

18. Furthermore, it does not seem proved, either by reason or Scripture, that souls in purgatory are outside the state of merit, that is, unable to grow in love.

19. Nor does it seem proved that souls in purgatory, at least not all of them, are certain and assured of their own salvation, even if we ourselves may be entirely certain of it.

20. Therefore the pope, when he uses the words "plenary remission of all penalties," does not actually mean "all penalties," but only those imposed by himself.

21. Thus those indulgence preachers are in error who say that a man is absolved from every penalty and saved by papal indulgences.

22. As a matter of fact, the pope remits to souls in purgatory no penalty which, according to canon law, they should have paid in this life.

23. If remission of all penalties whatsoever could be granted to anyone at all, certainly it would be granted only to the most perfect, that is, to very few.

24. For this reason most people are necessarily deceived by that indiscriminate and high-sounding promise of release from penalty.

25. That power which the pope has in general over purgatory corresponds to the power which any bishop or curate has in a particular way in his own diocese or parish.

26. The pope does very well when he grants remission to souls in purgatory, not by the power of the keys, which he does not have,[7] but by way of intercession for them.

27. They preach only human doctrines who say that as

soon as the money clinks into the money chest, the soul flies out of purgatory.

28. It is certain that when money clinks in the money chest, greed and avarice can be increased; but when the church intercedes, the result is in the hands of God alone.

29. Who knows whether all souls in purgatory wish to be redeemed, since we have exceptions in St. Severinus and St. Paschal,[8] as related in a legend.

30. No one is sure of the integrity of his own contrition, much less of having received plenary remission.

31. The man who actually buys indulgences is as rare as he who is really penitent; indeed, he is exceedingly rare.

32. Those who believe that they can be certain of their salvation because they have indulgence letters will be eternally damned, together with their teachers.

33. Men must especially be on their guard against those who say that the pope's pardons are that inestimable gift of God by which man is reconciled to him.

34. For the graces of indulgences are concerned only with the penalties of sacramental satisfaction[9] established by man.

35. They who teach that contrition is not necessary on the part of those who intend to buy souls out of purgatory or to buy confessional privileges[10] preach unchristian doctrine.

36. Any truly repentant Christian has a right to full remission of penalty and guilt,[11] even without indulgence letters.

37. Any true Christian, whether living or dead, participates in all the blessings of Christ and the church; and this is granted him by God, even without indulgence letters.

38. Nevertheless, papal remission and blessing are by no means to be disregarded, for they are, as I have said [Thesis 6], the proclamation of the divine remission.

39. It is very difficult, even for the most learned theologians, at one and the same time to commend to the people the bounty of indulgences and the need of true contrition.

---

[7] This is not a denial of the power of the keys that is, the power to forgive and to retain sin, but merely an assertion that the power of the keys does not extend to purgatory.

[8] Luther refers to this legend again in the *Explanations of the Ninety-five Theses*. The legend is to the effect that these saints, Pope Severinus (638–640) and Pope Paschal I (817–824), preferred to remain longer in purgatory that they might have greater glory in heaven.

[9] Satisfaction is that act of the penitent, in connection with the sacrament of penance, by means of which he pays the temporal penalty for his sins. If at death he is in arrears in paying his temporal penalty for venial sins, he pays the penalty in purgatory. Indulgences are concerned with this satisfaction of the sacrament of penance—they permit a partial or complete (plenary) remission of temporal punishment. According to Roman Catholic theology, the buyer of an indulgence still has to confess his sins, be absolved from them, and be truly penitent.

[10] These are privileges entitling the holder of indulgence letters to choose his own confessor and relieving him, the holder, of certain satisfactions.

[11] To justify the placing of absolution before satisfaction, contrary to the practice of the early church, theologians distinguished between the guilt and the penalty of sin.

40. A Christian who is truly contrite seeks and loves to pay penalties for his sins; the bounty of indulgences, however, relaxes penalties and causes men to hate them—at least it furnishes occasion for hating them.

41. Papal indulgences must be preached with caution, lest people erroneously think that they are preferable to other good works of love.

42. Christians are to be taught that the pope does not intend that the buying of indulgences should in any way be compared with works of mercy.

43. Christians are to be taught that he who gives to the poor or lends to the needy does a better deed than he who buys indulgences.

44. Because love grows by works of love, man thereby becomes better. Man does not, however, become better by means of indulgences but is merely freed from penalties.

45. Christians are to be taught that he who sees a needy man and passes him by, yet gives his money for indulgences, does not buy papal indulgences but God's wrath.

46. Christians are to be taught that, unless they have more than they need, they must reserve enough for their family needs and by no means squander it on indulgences.

47. Christians are to be taught that the buying of indulgences is a matter of free choice, not commanded.

48. Christians are to be taught that the pope, in granting indulgences, needs and thus desires their devout prayer more than their money.

49. Christians are to be taught that papal indulgences are useful only if they do not put their trust in them, but very harmful if they lose their fear of God because of them.

50. Christians are to be taught that if the pope knew the exactions of the indulgence preachers, he would rather that the basilica of St. Peter were burned to ashes than built up with the skin, flesh, and bones of his sheep.

51. Christians are to be taught that the pope would and should wish to give of his own money, even though he had to sell the basilica of St. Peter, to many of those from whom certain hawkers of indulgences cajole money.

52. It is vain to trust in salvation by indulgence letters, even though the indulgence commissary, or even the pope, were to offer his soul as security.

53. They are enemies of Christ and the pope who forbid altogether the preaching of the Word of God in some churches in order that indulgences may be preached in others.

54. Injury is done the Word of God when, in the same sermon, an equal or larger amount of time is devoted to indulgences than to the Word.

55. It is certainly the pope's sentiment that if indulgences, which are a very insignificant thing, are celebrated with one bell, one procession, and one ceremony, then the gospel, which is the very greatest thing, should be preached with a hundred bells, a hundred processions, a hundred ceremonies.

56. The treasures of the church,[12] out of which the pope distributes indulgences, are not sufficiently discussed or known among the people of Christ.

57. That indulgences are not temporal treasures is certainly clear, for many [indulgence] preachers do not distribute them freely but only gather them.

58. Nor are they the merits of Christ and the saints, for, even without the pope, the latter always work grace for the inner man, and the cross, death, and hell for the outer man.

59. St. Laurence said that the poor of the church were the treasures of the church, but he spoke according to the usage of the word in his own time.

60. Without want of consideration we say that the keys of the church[13] given by the merits of Christ are that treasure;

61. For it is clear that the pope's power is of itself sufficient for the remission of penalities and cases reserved by himself.

62. The true treasure of the church is the most holy gospel of the glory and grace of God.

63. But this treasure is naturally most odious for it makes the first to be last [Matt. 20:16].

64. On the other hand the treasure of indulgences is naturally most acceptable for it makes the last to be first.

65. Therefore the treasures of the gospel are nets with which one formerly fished for men of wealth.

66. The treasures of indulgences are nets with which one now fishes for the wealth of men.

67. The indulgences which the demagogues acclaim as the greatest graces are actually understood to be such only insofar as they promote gain.

68. They are nevertheless in truth the most insignificant graces when compared with the grace of God and the piety of the cross.

69. Bishops and curates are bound to admit the commissaries of papal indulgences with all reverence.

70. But they are much more bound to strain their eyes and ears lest these men preach their own dreams instead of what the pope has commissioned.

71. Let him who speaks against the truth concerning papal indulgences be anathema and accursed;

72. But let him who guards against the lust and license of the indulgence preachers be blessed;

73. Just as the pope justly thunders against those who by any means whatsoever contrive harm to the sale of indulgences.

74. But much more does he intend to thunder against those who use indulgences as a pretext to contrive harm to holy love and truth.

---

[12] The treasury of merits is a reserve fund of good works accumulated by Christ and the saints upon which the pope could draw when he remitted satisfaction in indulgences.

[13] The office of the keys: the preaching of the gospel, the celebrating of the sacraments, the remitting of sins to the penitent, and the excommunicating of impenitent sinners.

75. To consider papal indulgences so great that they could absolve a man even if he had done the impossible and had violated the mother of God is madness.

76. We say on the contrary that papal indulgences cannot remove the very least of venial sins as far as guilt is concerned.

77. To say that even St. Peter, if he were now pope, could not grant greater graces is blasphemy against St. Peter and the pope.

78. We say on the contrary that even the present pope, or any pope whatsoever, has greater graces at his disposal, that is, the gospel, spiritual powers, gifts of healing, etc., as it is written in I Cor. 12 [:28].

79. To say that the cross emblazoned with the papal coat of arms, and set up by the indulgence preachers, is equal in worth to the cross of Christ is blasphemy.

80. The bishops, curates, and theologians who permit such talk to be spread among the people will have to answer for this.

81. This unbridled preaching of indulgences makes it difficult even for learned men to rescue the reverence which is due the pope from slander or from the shrewd questions of the laity,

82. Such as: "Why does not the pope empty purgatory for the sake of holy love and the dire need of the souls that are there if he redeems an infinite number of souls for the sake of miserable money with which to build a church? The former reasons would be most just; the latter is most trivial."

83. Again, "Why are funeral and anniversary masses for the dead continued and why does he not return or permit the withdrawal of the endowments founded for them, since it is wrong to pray for the redeemed?"

84. Again, "What is this new piety of God and the pope that for a consideration of money they permit a man who is impious and their enemy to buy out of purgatory the pious soul of a friend of God and do not rather, because of the need of that pious and beloved soul, free it for pure love's sake?"

85. Again, "Why are the penitential canons, long since abrogated and dead in actual fact and through disuse, now satisfied by the granting of indulgences as though they were still alive and in force?"

86. Again, "Why does not the pope, whose wealth is today greater than the wealth of the richest Crassus,[14] build this one basilica of St. Peter with his own money rather than with the money of poor believers?"

87. Again, "What does the pope remit or grant to those who by perfect contrition already have a right to full remission and blessings?"[15]

88. Again, "What greater blessing could come to the church than if the pope were to bestow these remissions and blessings on every believer a hundred times a day, as he now does but once?"[16]

89. "Since the pope seeks the salvation of souls rather than money by his indulgences, why does he suspend the indulgences and pardons previously granted when they have equal efficacy?"[17]

90. To repress these very sharp arguments of the laity by force alone, and not to resolve them by giving reasons, is to expose the church and the pope to the ridicule of their enemies and to make Christians unhappy.

91. If, therefore, indulgences were preached according to the spirit and intention of the pope, all these doubts would be readily resolved. Indeed, they would not exist.

92. Away then with all those prophets who say to the people of Christ, "Peace, peace," and there is no peace! [Jer. 6:14].

93. Blessed be all those prophets who say to the people of Christ, "Cross, cross," and there is no cross!

94. Christians should be exhorted to be diligent in following Christ, their head, through penalties, death, and hell;

95. And thus be confident of entering into heaven through many tribulations rather than through the false security of peace [Acts 14:22].

✦ **LOUISE LABÉ**

Sonnet 18 "Kiss Me Again, Rekiss Me, Kiss Me More"

French poet Louise Labé [LAH-bay] (1525–1566), a renowned equestrian and archer, is reputed to have fought on horseback in battles with the Spanish and to have participated in jousting tournaments. In her poetry, however, she concentrated on love. The following sonnet echoes a love poem by the ancient Roman poet Catullus, who asks his Lesbia to kiss him numerous times. The poem, with its witty and imaginative playfulness, is quite suggestively erotic.

Kiss me again, rekiss me, kiss me more,
give me your most consuming, tasty one,
give me your sensual kiss, a savory one,
I'll give you back four burning at the core.
Are you up in arms? Well, I'll give you ten   *5*
erotic kisses for your appetite
and we will mingle kisses and excite
our bodies with an easy joy again.
Then we will live a double life, and each
of us will be alone and yet will blend   *10*
our love. Love, please allow a little madness:
I'm always hurt and live with temperate speech,
veiling these days in which I find no gladness
if I can't leave myself and find my friend.

---

[14] Marcus Licinius Crassus (115–53 B.C.), also called Dives ("the Rich"), was noted for his wealth and luxury by the classical Romans. Crassus means "the Fat."

[15] See Theses 36 and 37.

[16] The indulgence letter entitled its possessor to receive absolution once during his lifetime and once at the approach of death.

[17] During the time when the jubilee indulgences were preached, other indulgences were suspended.

QUEEN ELIZABETH I
Speech to the English Troops at Tilbury

The reign of Queen Elizabeth I of England (1558–1603) represents one of the most glorious periods of English history and includes the early career of Shakespeare. Elizabeth was an accomplished woman of letters and used public occasions to demonstrate her knowledge of Greek and Latin, which she learned as part of her humanistic education.

Queen Elizabeth also translated many important literary works from their original language, including the Bible (the Psalms), and works from Plutarch, Seneca, and Petrarch. In addition, she wrote poetry and prose. The following speech was given to her troops as they were poised to do battle with the Spanish. In it, she exhibits great mastery of the classical tenets of rhetoric as well as an ability to rally her men to defend England.

My loving people,

We have been persuaded by some that are careful of our safety, to take heed how we commit our selves to armed multitudes, for fear of treachery; but I assure you I do not desire to live to distrust my faithful and loving people. Let tyrants fear, I have always so behaved myself that, under God, I have placed my chiefest strength and safeguard in the loyal hearts and good-will of my subjects; and therefore I am come amongst you, as you see, at this time, not for my recreation and disport, but being resolved, in the midst and heat of the battle, to live or die amongst you all; to lay down for my God, and for my kingdom, and my people, my honour and my blood, even in the dust. I know I have the body but of a weak and feeble woman; but I have the heart and stomach of a king, and of a king of England too, and think foul scorn that Parma or Spain, or any prince of Europe, should dare to invade the borders of my realm; to which rather than any dishonour shall grow by me, I myself will take up arms, I myself will be your general, judge, and rewarder of every one of your virtues in the field. I know already, for your forwardness you have deserved rewards and crowns; and We do assure you in the word of a prince, they shall be duly paid you. In the mean time, my lieutenant general shall be in my stead, than whom never prince commanded a more noble or worthy subject; not doubting but by your obedience to my general, by your concord in the camp, and your valour in the field, we shall shortly have a famous victory over those enemies of my God, of my kingdom, and of my people.

MICHEL DE MONTAIGNE
Of Cannibals

In his essay "Of Cannibals," Montaigne defends, surprisingly, cannibal culture—"that other world" in which men capture, kill, cook, and eat their enemies. This world, considered by Montaigne's contemporaries to be wholly uncivilized, Montaigne finds "civilized" in comparison to sixteenth-century Europe. He proves his point by comparing cannibalism to the Renaissance methods of punishment—being drawn and quartered—or literally pulled apart alive—for instance. To Montaigne, "there is more barbarity in eating a man alive than in eating him dead; and in tearing by tortures and the rack a body still full of feeling, in roasting him bit by bit … than in roasting and eating him after he is dead."

One of Montaigne's main concerns is the "human disease" of war, and he contrasts the methods and motivations of war in the two cultures. Throughout his essay, Montaigne characterizes the cannibals as honest, courageous, and intelligent, while presenting the Europeans as cowardly and cruel. As he notes, "the worth and value of a man is in his heart and his will." In its use of difference to shed light on the moral and cultural attitudes of his countrymen, "Of Cannibals" can be compared with Jonathan Swift's Gulliver's Travels *(Chapter 16). Like Swift, Montaigne utilizes humor, irony, and surprise to prod his readers to examine their cultural values.*

When King Pyrrhus passed over into Italy, after he had reconnoitered the formation of the army that the Romans were sending to meet him, he said: "I do not know what barbarians these are" (for so the Greeks called all foreign nations), "but the formation of this army that I see is not at all barbarous." The Greeks said as much of the army that Flamininus brought into their country, and so did Philip, seeing from a knoll the order and distribution of the Roman camp, in his kingdom, under Publius Sulpicius Galba. Thus we should beware of clinging to vulgar opinions, and judge things by reason's way, not by popular say.

I had with me for a long time a man who had lived for ten or twelve years in that other world which has been discovered in our century, in the place where Villegaignon landed, and which he called Antarctic France.[1] This discovery of a boundless country seems worthy of consideration. I don't know if I can guarantee that some other such discovery will not be made in the future, so many personages greater than ourselves having been mistaken about this one. I am afraid we have eyes bigger than our stomachs, and more curiosity than capacity. We embrace everything, but we clasp only wind.

Plato brings in Solon, telling how he had learned from the priests of the city of Saïs in Egypt that in days of old, before the Flood, there was a great island named Atlantis, right at the mouth of the Strait of Gibraltar, which contained more land than Africa and Asia put together, and that the kings of that country, who not only possessed that island but had stretched out so far on the mainland that they held the breadth of Africa as far as Egypt, and the length of Europe as far as Tuscany, undertook to step over into Asia and subjugate all the nations that border on the Mediterranean, as far as the Black Sea; and for this purpose crossed the Spains, Gaul, Italy, as far as Greece, where the Athenians checked them; but that some time after, both the Athenians and themselves and their island were swallowed up by the Flood.

It is quite likely that that extreme devastation of waters made amazing changes in the habitations of the earth, as people maintain that the sea cut off Sicily from Italy—

> *'Tis said an earthquake once asunder tore*
> *These lands with dreadful havoc, which before*
> *Formed but one land, one coast*
>
> VIRGIL

—Cyprus from Syria, the island of Euboea from the mainland of Boeotia; and elsewhere joined lands that were divided, filling the channels between them with sand and mud:

---

[1] In Brazil, in 1557.

A sterile marsh, long fit for rowing, now
Feeds neighbor towns, and feels the heavy prow.

HORACE

But there is no great likelihood that that island was the new world which we have just discovered; for it almost touched Spain, and it would be an incredible result of a flood to have forced it away as far as it is, more than twelve hundred leagues; besides, the travels of the moderns have already almost revealed that it is not an island, but a mainland connected with the East Indies on one side, and elsewhere with the lands under the two poles; or, if it is separated from them, it is by so narrow a strait and interval that it does not deserve to be called an island on that account.

It seems that there are movements, some natural, others feverish, in these great bodies, just as in our own. When I consider the inroads that my river, the Dordogne, is making in my lifetime into the right bank in its descent, and that in twenty years it has gained so much ground and stolen away the foundations of several buildings, I clearly see that this is an extraordinary disturbance; for if it had always gone at this rate, or was to do so in the future, the face of the world would be turned topsy-turvy. But rivers are subject to changes: now they overflow in one direction, now in another, now they keep to their course. I am not speaking of the sudden inundations whose causes are manifest. In Médoc, along the seashore, my brother, the sieur d'Arsac, can see an estate of his buried under the sands that the sea spews forth; the tops of some buildings are still visible; his farms and domains have changed into very thin pasturage. The inhabitants say that for some time the sea has been pushing toward them so hard that they have lost four leagues of land. These sands are its harbingers; and we see great dunes of moving sand that march half a league ahead of it and keep conquering land.

The other testimony of antiquity with which some would connect this discovery is in Aristotle, at least if that little book *Of Unheard-of Wonders* is by him. He there relates that certain Carthaginians, after setting out upon the Atlantic Ocean from the Strait of Gibraltar and sailing a long time, at last discovered a great fertile island, all clothed in woods and watered by great deep rivers, far remote from any mainland; and that they, and others since, attracted by the goodness and fertility of the soil, went there with their wives and children, and began to settle there. The lords of Carthage, seeing that their country was gradually becoming depopulated, expressly forbade anyone to go there any more, on pain of death, and drove out these new inhabitants, fearing, it is said, that in course of time they might come to multiply so greatly as to supplant their former masters and ruin their state. This story of Aristotle does not fit our new lands any better than the other.

This man I had was a simple, crude fellow[2]—a character fit to bear true witness; for clever people observe more things and more curiously, but they interpret them; and to lend weight and conviction to their interpretation, they cannot help altering history a little. They never show you things as they are, but bend and disguise them according to

the way they have seen them; and to give credence to their judgment and attract you to it, they are prone to add something to their matter, to stretch it out and amplify it. We need a man either very honest, or so simple that he has not the stuff to build up false inventions and give them plausibility; and wedded to no theory. Such was my man; and besides this, he at various times brought sailors and merchants, whom he had known on that trip, to see me. So I content myself with his information, without inquiring what the cosmographers say about it.

We ought to have topographers who would give us an exact account of the places where they have been. But because they have over us the advantage of having seen Palestine, they want to enjoy the privilege of telling us news about all the rest of the world. I would like everyone to write what he knows, and as much as he knows, not only in this, but in all other subjects; for a man may have some special knowledge and experience of the nature of a river or a fountain, who in other matters knows only what everybody knows. However, to circulate this little scrap of knowledge, he will undertake to write the whole of physics. From this vice spring many great abuses.

Now, to return to my subject, I think there is nothing barbarous and savage in that nation, from what I have been told, except that each man calls barbarism whatever is not his own practice; for indeed it seems we have no other test of truth and reason than the example and pattern of the opinions and customs of the country we live in. *There* is always the perfect religion, the perfect government, the perfect and accomplished manners in all things. Those people are wild, just as we call wild the fruits that Nature has produced by herself and in her normal course; whereas really it is those that we have changed artificially and led astray from the common order, that we should rather call wild. The former retain alive and vigorous their genuine, their most useful and natural, virtues and properties, which we have debased in the latter in adapting them to gratify our corrupted taste. And yet for all that, the savor and delicacy of some uncultivated fruits of those countries is quite as excellent, even to our taste, as that of our own. It is not reasonable that art should win the place of honor over our great and powerful mother Nature. We have so overloaded the beauty and richness of her works by our inventions that we have quite smothered her. Yet wherever her purity shines forth, she wonderfully puts to shame our vain and frivolous attempts:

Ivy comes readier without our care;
In lonely caves the arbutus grows more fair;
No art with artless bird song can compare.

PROPERTIUS

All our efforts cannot even succeed in reproducing the nest of the tiniest little bird, its contexture, its beauty and convenience; or even the web of the puny spider. All things, says Plato, are produced by nature, by fortune, or by art; the greatest and most beautiful by one or the other of the first two, the least and most imperfect by the last.

These nations, then, seem to me barbarous in this sense, that they have been fashioned very little by the human mind, and are still very close to their original naturalness. The laws of nature still rule them, very little corrupted by

---

[2] The traveler Montaigne spoke of at the beginning of the chapter.

ours; and they are in such a state of purity that I am some-times vexed that they were unknown earlier, in the days when there were men able to judge them better than we. I am sorry that Lycurgus and Plato did not know of them; for it seems to me that what we actually see in these nations sur-passes not only all the pictures in which poets have idealized the golden age and all their inventions in imagining a happy state of man, but also the conceptions and the very desire of philosophy. They could not imagine a naturalness so pure and simple as we see by experience; nor could they believe that our society could be maintained with so little artifice and human solder. This is a nation, I should say to Plato, in which there is no sort of traffic, no knowledge of letters, no science of numbers, no name for a magistrate or for politi-cal superiority, no custom of servitude, no riches or pover-ty, no contracts, no successions, no partitions, no occupa-tions but leisure ones, no care for any but common kinship, no clothes, no agriculture, no metal, no use of wine or wheat. The very words that signify lying, treachery, dissim-ulation, avarice, envy, belittling, pardon—unheard of. How far from this perfection would he find the republic that he imagined: *Men fresh sprung from the gods* [Seneca].

These manners nature first ordained.

VIRGIL

For the rest, they live in a country with a very pleasant and temperate climate, so that according to my witnesses it is rare to see a sick man there; and they have assured me that they never saw one palsied, bleary-eyed, toothless, or bent with age. They are settled along the sea and shut in on the land side by great high mountains, with a stretch about a hundred leagues wide in between. They have a great abun-dance of fish and flesh which bear no resemblance to ours, and they eat them with no other artifice than cooking. The first man who rode a horse there, though he had had deal-ings with them on several other trips, so horrified them in this posture that they shot him dead with arrows before they could recognize him.

Their buildings are very long, with a capacity of two or three hundred souls; they are covered with the bark of great trees, the strips reaching to the ground at one end and sup-porting and leaning on one another at the top, in the man-ner of some of our barns, whose covering hangs down to the ground and acts as a side. They have wood so hard that they cut with it and make of it their swords and grills to cook their food. Their beds are of a cotton weave, hung from the roof like those in our ships, each man having his own; for the wives sleep apart from their husbands.

They get up with the sun, and eat immediately upon ris-ing, to last them through the day; for they take no other meal than that one. Like some other Eastern peoples of whom Suidas tells us, who drank apart from meals, they do not drink then; but they drink several times a day, and to capacity. Their drink is made of some root, and is of the color of our claret wines. They drink it only lukewarm. This beverage keeps only two or three days; it has a slightly sharp taste, is not at all heady, is good for the stomach, and has a laxative effect upon those who are not used to it; it is a very pleasant drink for anyone who is accustomed to it. In place of bread they use a certain white substance like preserved coriander. I have tried it; it tastes sweet and a little flat.

The whole day is spent in dancing. The younger men go to hunt animals with bows. Some of the women busy them-selves meanwhile with warming their drink, which is their chief duty. Some one of the old men, in the morning before they begin to eat, preaches to the whole barnful in common, walking from one end to the other, and repeating one single sentence several times until he has completed the circuit (for the buildings are fully a hundred paces long). He recom-mends to them only two things: valor against the enemy and love for their wives. And they never fail to point out this obligation, as their refrain, that it is their wives who keep their drink warm and seasoned.

There may be seen in several places, including my own house, specimens of their beds, of their ropes, of their wooden swords and the bracelets with which they cover their wrists in combats, and of the big canes, open at one end, by whose sound they keep time in their dances. They are close shaven all over, and shave themselves much more cleanly than we, with nothing but a wooden or stone razor. They believe that souls are immortal, and that those who have deserved well of the gods are lodged in that part of heaven where the sun rises, and the damned in the west.

They have some sort of priests and prophets, but they rarely appear before the people, having their home in the mountains. On their arrival there is a great feast and solemn assembly of several villages—each barn, as I have described it, makes up a village, and they are about one French league from each other. The prophet speaks to them in public, exhorting them to virtue and their duty; but their whole ethical science contains only these two articles: resoluteness in war and affection for their wives. He prophesies to them things to come and the results they are to expect from their undertakings, and urges them to war or holds them back from it; but this is on the condition that when he fails to prophesy correctly, and if things turn out otherwise than he has predicted, he is cut into a thousand pieces if they catch him, and condemned as a false prophet. For this reason, the prophet who has once been mistaken is never seen again.

Divination is a gift of God; that is why its abuse should be punished as imposture. Among the Scythians, when the soothsayers failed to hit the mark, they were laid, chained hand and foot, on carts full of heather and drawn by oxen, on which they were burned. Those who handle matters sub-ject to the control of human capacity are excusable if they do the best they can. But these others, who come and trick us with assurances of an extraordinary faculty that is beyond our ken, should they not be punished for not making good their promise, and for the temerity of their imposture?

They have their wars with the nations beyond the moun-tains, further inland, to which they go quite naked, with no other arms than bows or wooden swords ending in a sharp point, in the manner of the tongues of our boar spears. It is astonishing what firmness they show in their combats, which never end but in slaughter and bloodshed; for as to routs and terror, they know nothing of either.

Each man brings back as his trophy the head of the enemy he has killed, and sets it up at the entrance to his dwelling. After they have treated their prisoners well for a long time with all the hospitality they can think of, each man who has a prisoner calls a great assembly of his acquaintances. He ties a rope to one of the prisoner's arms, by the end of which he holds him, a few steps away, for fear of being hurt, and gives his dearest friend the other arm to hold in the same way; and these two, in the presence of the whole assembly, kill him with their swords. This done, they roast him and eat him in common and send some pieces to their absent friends. This is not, as people think, for nourishment, as of old the Scythians used to do, it is to betoken an extreme revenge. And the proof of this came when they saw the Portuguese, who had joined forces with their adversaries, inflict a different kind of death on them when they took them prisoner, which was to bury them up to the waist, shoot the rest of their body full of arrows, and afterward hang them. They thought that these people from the other world, being men who had sown the knowledge of many vices among their neighbors and were much greater masters than themselves in every sort of wickedness, did not adopt this sort of vengeance without some reason, and that it must be more painful than their own; so they began to give up their old method and to follow this one.

I am not sorry that we notice the barbarous horror of such acts, but I am heartily sorry that, judging their faults rightly, we should be so blind to our own. I think there is more barbarity in eating a man alive than in eating him dead; and in tearing by tortures and the rack a body still full of feeling, in roasting a man bit by bit, in having him bitten and mangled by dogs and swine (as we have not only read but seen within fresh memory, not among ancient enemies, but among neighbors and fellow citizens, and what is worse, on the pretext of piety and religion), than in roasting and eating him after he is dead.

Indeed, Chrysippus and Zeno, heads of the Stoic sect, thought there was nothing wrong in using our carcasses for any purpose in case of need, and getting nourishment from them; just as our ancestors, when besieged by Caesar in tile city of Alésia, resolved to relieve their famine by eating old men, women, and other people useless for fighting.

The Gascons once, 'tis said, their life renewed
By eating of such food.

JUVENAL

And physicians do not fear to use human flesh in all sorts of ways for our health, applying it either inwardly or outwardly. But there never was any opinion so disordered as to excuse treachery, disloyalty, tyranny, and cruelty, which are our ordinary vices.

So we may well call these people barbarians, in respect to the rules of reason, but not in respect to ourselves, who surpass them in every kind of barbarity.

Their warfare is wholly noble and generous, and as excusable and beautiful as is human disease can be; its only basis among them is their rivalry in valor. They are not fighting for the conquest of new lands, for they still enjoy that natural abundance that provides them, without toil and trouble with all necessary things in such profusion that they have no wish to enlarge their boundaries. They are still in that happy state of desiring only as much as their natural needs demand; anything beyond that is superfluous to them.

They generally call those of the same age, brothers; those who are younger, children; and the old men are fathers to all the others. These leave to their heirs in common the full possession of their property, without division or any other

title at all than just the one that Nature gives to her creatures in bringing them into the world.

If their neighbors cross the mountains to attack them and win a victory, the gain of the victory is glory, and the advantage of having proved the master in valor and virtue; for apart from this they have no use for the goods of the vanquished, and they return to their own country, where they lack neither anything necessary nor that great thing, the knowledge of how to enjoy their condition happily and be content with it. These men of ours do the same in their turn. They demand of their prisoners no other ransom than that they confess and acknowledge their defeat. But there is not one in a whole century who does not choose to die rather than to relax a single bit, by word or look, from the grandeur of an invincible courage; not one who would not rather be killed and eaten than so much as ask not to be. They treat them very freely, so that life may be all the dearer to them, and usually entertain them with threats of their coming death, of the torments they will have to suffer, the preparations that are being made for that purpose, the cutting up of their limbs, and the feast that will be made at their expense. All this is done for the sole purpose of extorting from their lips some weak or base word, or making them want to flee, so as to gain the advantage of having terrified them and broken down their firmness. For indeed, if you take it the right way, it is in this point alone that true victory lies:

It is no victory
Unless the vanquished foe admits your mastery.

CLAUDIAN

The Hungarians, very bellicose fighters, did not in olden times pursue their advantage beyond putting the enemy at their mercy. For having wrung a confession from him to this effect, they let him go unharmed and unransomed, except, at most, for exacting his promise never again to take up arms against them.

We win enough advantages over our enemies that are borrowed advantages, not really our own. It is the quality of a porter, not of valor, to have sturdier arms and legs; agility is a dead and corporeal quality; it is a stroke of luck to make our enemy stumble, or dazzle his eyes by the sunlight; it is a trick of art and technique, which may be found in a worthless coward, to be an able fencer. The worth and value of a man is in his heart and his will; there lies his real honor. Valor is the strength, not of legs and arms, but of heart and soul; it consists not in the worth of our horse or our weapons, but in our own. He who falls obstinate in his courage, *if he has fallen, he fights on his knees* [Seneca]. He who relaxes none of his assurance, no matter how great the danger of imminent death; who, giving up his soul, still looks firmly and scornfully at his enemy—he is beaten not by us, but by fortune; he is killed, not conquered.

The most valiant are sometimes the most unfortunate. Thus there are triumphant defeats that rival victories. Nor did those four sister victories, the fairest that the sun ever set eyes on—Salamis, Plataea, Mycale, and Sicily—ever dare match all their combined glory against the glory of the annihilation of King Leonidas and his men at the pass of Thermopylae.

Who ever hastened with more glorious and ambitious desire to win a battle than Captain Ischolas to lose one?

Who ever secured his safety more ingeniously and painstakingly than he did his destruction? He was charged to defend a certain pass in the Peloponnesus against the Arcadians. Finding himself wholly incapable of doing this, in view of the nature of the place and the inequality of the forces, he made up his mind that all who confronted the enemy would necessarily have to remain on the field. On the other hand, deeming it unworthy both of his own virtue and magnanimity and of the Lacedaemonian name to fail in his charge, he took a middle course between these two extremes, in this way. The youngest and fittest of his band he preserved for the defense and service of their country, and sent them home; and with those whose loss was less important, he determined to hold this pass, and by their death to make the enemy buy their entry as dearly as he could. And so it turned out. For he was presently surrounded on all sides by the Arcadians, and after slaughtering a large number of them, he and his men were all put to the sword. Is there a trophy dedicated to victors that would not be more due to these vanquished? The role of true victory is in fighting, not in coming off safely; and the honor of valor consists in combating, not in beating.

To return to our story. These prisoners are so far from giving in, in spite of all that is done to them, that on the contrary, during the two or three months that they are kept, they wear a gay expression; they urge their captors to hurry and put them to the test; they defy them, insult them, reproach them with their cowardice and the number of battles they have lost to the prisoners' own people.

I have a song composed by a prisoner which contains this challenge, that they should all come boldly and gather to dine off him, for they will be eating at the same time their own fathers and grandfathers, who have served to feed and nourish his body. "These muscles," he says, "this flesh and these veins are your own, poor fools that you are. You do not recognize that the substance of your ancestors' limbs is still contained in them. Savor them well; you will find in them the taste of your own flesh." An idea that certainly does not smack of barbarity. Those that paint these people dying, and who show the execution, portray the prisoner spitting in the face of his slayers and scowling at them. Indeed, to the last gasp they never stop braving and defying their enemies by word and look. Truly here are real savages by our standards; for either they must be thoroughly so, or we must be; there is an amazing distance between their character and ours.

The men there have several wives, and the higher their reputation for valor the more wives they have. It is a remarkably beautiful thing about their marriages that the same jealousy our wives have to keep us from the affection and kindness of other women, theirs have to win this for them. Being more concerned for their husbands' honor than for anything else, they strive and scheme to have as many companions as they can, since that is a sign of their husbands' valor.

Our wives will cry "Miracle!" but it is no miracle. It is a properly matrimonial virtue, but one of the highest order. In the Bible, Leah, Rachel, Sarah, and Jacob's wives gave their beautiful handmaids to their husbands; and Livia seconded the appetites of Augustus, to her own disadvantage; and Stratonice, the wife of King Deiotarus, not only lent her husband for his use a very beautiful young chambermaid in her service, but carefully brought up her children, and backed them up to succeed to their father's estates.

And lest it be thought that all this is done through a simple and servile bondage to usage and through the pressure of the authority of their ancient customs, without reasoning or judgment, and because their minds are so stupid that they cannot take any other course, I must cite some examples of their capacity. Besides the warlike song I have just quoted, I have another, a love song, which begins in this vein: "Adder, stay; stay, adder, that from the pattern of your coloring my sister may draw the fashion and the workmanship of a rich girdle that I may give to my love; so may your beauty and your pattern be forever preferred to all other serpents." This first couplet is the refrain of the song. Now I am familiar enough with poetry to be a judge of this: not only is there nothing barbarous in this fancy, but it is altogether Anacreontic. Their language, moreover, is a soft language, with an agreeable sound, somewhat like Greek in its endings.

Three of these men, ignorant of the price they will pay some day, in loss of repose and happiness, for gaining knowledge of the corruptions of this side of the ocean; ignorant also of the fact that of this intercourse will come their ruin (which I suppose is already well advanced: poor wretches, to let themselves be tricked by the desire for new things, and to have left the serenity of their own sky to come and see ours!)—three of these men were at Rouen, at the time the late King Charles IX was there. The king talked to them for a long time; they were shown our ways, our splendor, the aspect of a fine city. After that, someone asked their opinion, and wanted to know what they had found most amazing. They mentioned three things, of which I have forgotten the third, and I am very sorry for it; but I still remember two of them. They said that in the first place they thought it very strange that so many grown men, bearded, strong, and armed, who were around the king (it is likely that they were talking about the Swiss of his guard) should submit to obey a child, and that one of them was not chosen to command instead. Second (they have a way in their language of speaking of men as halves of one another), they had noticed that there were among us men full and gorged with all sorts of good things, and that their other halves were beggars at their doors, emaciated with hunger and poverty; and they thought it strange that these needy halves could endure such an injustice, and did not take the others by the throat, or set fire to their houses.

I had a very long talk with one of them; but I had an interpreter who followed my meaning so badly, and who was so hindered by his stupidity in taking in my ideas, that I could get hardly any satisfaction from the man. When I asked him what profit he gained from his superior position among his people (for he was a captain, and our sailors called him king), he told me that it was to march foremost in war. How many men followed him? He pointed to a piece of ground, to signify as many as such a space could hold; it might have been four or five thousand men. Did all his authority expire with the war? He said that this much remained, that when he visited the villages dependent on him, they made paths for him through the underbrush by which he might pass quite comfortably.

All this is not too bad—but what's the use? They don't wear breeches.

WILLIAM SHAKESPEARE
Hamlet

Shakespeare's plays appealed to an audience ranging from the illiterate to the educated: bawdy jokes exist alongside sublime poetry; subtly introspective moments coexist with passionate outbursts. His language is among the richest and most resourceful ever set on paper, and Hamlet *testifies to its exuberance and vitality. Written in a mixture of prose and verse, it employs a language rich in metaphor and puns, plays on words with double meanings. The play's characters have become reference points for standards of action and inaction, for proverbial wisdom and witty comment. For the beauty of its language, the complexity of its characters, and the rich unpredictability of its plot,* Hamlet *remains Shakespeare's most ambitious play and his best known.*

Hamlet is a revenge tragedy, a genre popular in Shakespeare's time, but one with roots in Greek and Roman drama. A revenge tragedy involves a central character avenging the death of a murdered relative. The play's emphasis is on mystery and manners, wit and logic, the sacred and the secular, which make it an apt emblem of Renaissance culture.*

Edited by Alice Griffin°

CHARACTERS

CLAUDIUS, *King of Denmark*
HAMLET, *Son to the former, and nephew to the present King*
POLONIUS, *Lord Chamberlain*
HORATIO, *Friend to Hamlet*
LAERTES, *Son to Polonius*
VALTEMAND
CORNELIUS
ROSENCRANTZ } *Courtiers*
GUILDENSTERN
OSRIC
A GENTLEMAN
A PRIEST
MARCELLUS } *Officers*
BARNARDO
FRANCISCO, *a Soldier*
REYNALDO, *Servant to Polonius*
PLAYERS
TWO CLOWNS, *gravediggers*
FORTINBRAS, *Prince of Norway*
A NORWEGIAN CAPTAIN
ENGLISH AMBASSADORS
GERTRUDE, *Queen of Denmark, mother to Hamlet*
OPHELIA, *Daughter to Polonius*
GHOST OF HAMLET'S FATHER
LORDS, LADIES, OFFICERS, SOLDIERS, SAILORS, MESSENGERS, ATTENDANTS

Scene: Elsinore

Professor Griffin's text for *Hamlet* was the Second Quarto (edition) published in 1604, with modifications based on the First Folio, published in 1623. Stage directions in those editions are printed here without brackets; added stage directions are printed within brackets. We have edited Griffin's notes for this text.

Act 1

Scene 1. [A platform on the battlements of the castle]

Enter Barnardo and Francisco, two Sentinels

BARNARDO　Who's there?　　　　　　　　　　　1
FRANCISCO　Nay, answer me. Stand and unfold°
　　yourself.
BARNARDO　Long live the king.
FRANCISCO　Barnardo?
BARNARDO　He.　　　　　　　　　　　　　　5
FRANCISCO　You come most carefully upon your hour.
BARNARDO　'Tis now struck twelve, get thee to bed
　　Francisco.
FRANCISCO　For this relief much thanks, 'tis bitter cold,
　　And I am sick at heart.
BARNARDO　Have you had quiet guard?　　　　10
FRANCISCO　　　　　　　　　　　Not a mouse
　　stirring.
BARNARDO　Well, good night:
　　If you do meet Horatio and Marcellus,
　　The rivals° of my watch, bid them make haste.

Enter Horatio and Marcellus.

FRANCISCO　I think I hear them. Stand ho, who is
　　there?
HORATIO　Friends to this ground.
MARCELLUS　　　　　　　　　And liegemen° to the
　　Dane.°　　　　　　　　　　　　　　　15
FRANCISCO　Give you good night.
MARCELLUS　　　　　　　　　O, farewell honest
　　soldier,
　　Who hath relieved you?
FRANCISCO　　　　　　　　Barnardo hath my place;
　　Give you good night.　　　　　*Exit Francisco*
MARCELLUS　　　　　　　　Holla, Barnardo!
BARNARDO　　　　　　　　　　　　Say,
　　What, is Horatio there?
HORATIO　　　　　　　A piece of him.
BARNARDO　Welcome Horatio, welcome good
　　Marcellus.　　　　　　　　　　　　20
HORATIO　What, has this thing appeared again
　　tonight?
BARNARDO　I have seen nothing.
MARCELLUS　Horatio says 'tis but our fantasy,°
　　And will not let belief take hold of him,
　　Touching this dreaded sight twice seen of us,　25
　　Therefore I have entreated him along
　　With us to watch the minutes of this night,
　　That if again this apparition come,
　　He may approve° our eyes and speak to it.
HORATIO　Tush, tush, 'twill not appear.
BARNARDO　　　　　　　　　　　　Sit down
　　awhile,　　　　　　　　　　　　　　30
　　And let us once again assail your ears,

---

² *unfold:* reveal.　¹³ *rivals:* partners.　¹⁵ *liegemen:* subjects. *Dane:* King of Denmark.　²³ *fantasy:* imagination.　²⁹ *approve:* prove reliable.

That are so fortified against our story,
What we have two nights seen.
HORATIO   Well, sit we down,
And let us hear Barnardo speak of this.   *35*
BARNARDO   Last night of all,
When yon same star that's westward from the
pole°
Had made his course t'illume that part of heaven
Where now it burns, Marcellus and myself,
The bell then beating one—

Enter Ghost.

MARCELLUS   Peace, break thee off, look where it
comes again.   *40*
BARNARDO   In the same figure like the king that's dead.
MARCELLUS   Thou art a scholar, speak to it Horatio.
BARNARDO   Looks a' not like the king? mark it
Horatio.
HORATIO   Most like, it harrows me with fear and
wonder.
BARNARDO   It would be spoke to.
MARCELLUS   Question it Horatio.   *45*
HORATIO   What art thou that usurp'st° this time of
night,
Together with that fair and warlike form,
In which the majesty of buried Denmark°
Did sometimes° march? by heaven I charge thee
speak.
MARCELLUS   It is offended.
BARNARDO   See, it stalks away.   *50*
HORATIO   Stay, speak, speak, I charge thee speak.
                                        Exit Ghost.
MARCELLUS   'Tis gone and will not answer.
BARNARDO   How now Horatio, you tremble and look
pale,
Is not this something more than fantasy?
What think you on't?   *55*
HORATIO   Before my God I might not this believe,
Without the sensible and true avouch°
Of mine own eyes.
MARCELLUS   Is it not like the king?
HORATIO   As thou art to thyself.
Such was the very armour he had on,   *60*
When he the ambitious Norway° combated:
So frowned he once, when in an angry parle°
He smote the sledded Polacks° on the ice.
'Tis strange.
MARCELLUS   Thus twice before, and jump° at this
dead hour,   *65*
With martial stalk hath he gone by our watch.
HORATIO   In what particular thought to work, I know
not,
But in the gross and scope° of mine opinion,
This bodes some strange eruption to our state.

MARCELLUS   Good now sit down, and tell me he that
knows,   *70*
Why this same strict and most observant watch
So nightly toils the subject° of the land,
And why such daily cast of brazen cannon
And foreign mart,° for implements of war,
Why such impress° of shipwrights, whose sore°
task   *75*
Does not divide the Sunday from the week,
What might be toward° that this sweaty haste
Doth make the night joint-labourer with the day,
Who is't that can inform me?
HORATIO   That can I.
At least the whisper goes so; our last king,   *80*
Whose image even but now appeared to us,
Was as you know by Fortinbras of Norway,
Thereto pricked on by a most emulate° pride,
Dared to the combat; in which our valiant Hamlet
(For so this side of our known world esteemed
him)   *85*
Did slay this Fortinbras, who by a sealed
compact,°
Well ratified by law and heraldy,°
Did forfeit (with his life) all those his lands
Which he stood seized° of, to the conqueror:
Against the which a moiety competent°   *90*
Was gagèd° by our King, which had returned
To the inheritance of Fortinbras,
Had he been vanquisher; as by the same co-mart,°
And carriage of the article designed,°
His fell to Hamlet; now sir, young Fortinbras,   *95*
Of unimprovèd mettle° hot and full,
Hath in the skirts° of Norway here and there
Sharked up° a list of lawless resolutes°
For food and diet to some enterprise
That hath a stomach° in't, which is no other,   *100*
As it doth well appear unto our state,
But to recover of us by strong hand
And terms compulsatory, those foresaid lands
So by his father lost; and this I take it,
Is the main motive of our preparations,   *105*
The source of this our watch, and the chief head°
Of this post-haste and romage° in the land.
BARNARDO   I think it be no other, but e'en so;
Well may it sort° that this portentous figure
Comes armèd through our watch so like the king   *110*
That was and is the question of these wars.
HORATIO   A mote it is to trouble the mind's eye:
In the most high and palmy° state of Rome,
A little ere the mightiest Julius fell,
The graves stood tenantless, and the sheeted dead *115*

---

³⁶ *pole:* North Star. ⁴⁶ *usurp'st:* wrongfully occupy (both the time and the shape of the dead king). ⁴⁸ *buried Denmark:* the buried King of Denmark. ⁴⁹ *sometimes:* formerly. ⁵⁷ *Sensible … avouch:* assurance of the truth of the senses. ⁶¹ *Norway:* King of Norway. ⁶² *parle:* parley, verbal battle. ⁶³ *sledded Polacks:* Poles on sleds. ⁶⁵ *jump:* just. ⁶⁸ *gross and scope:* general view.

⁷²*toils the subject:* makes the subjects toil. ⁷⁴ *mart:* trade. ⁷⁵ *impress:* conscription. *sore:* difficult. ⁷⁷ *toward:* forthcoming. ⁸³ *emulate:* rivaling. ⁸⁶ *compact:* treaty. ⁸⁷ *law and heraldy:* heraldic law regulating combats. ⁸⁹ *seized:* possessed. ⁹⁰ *moiety competent:* equal amount. ⁹¹ *gagèd:* pledged. ⁹³*co-mart:* joint bargain. ⁹⁴ *carriage … designed:* intent of the treaty drawn up. ⁹⁶ *unimprovèd mettle:* untested (1) metal (2) spirit. ⁹⁷ *skirts:* outskirts. ⁹⁸ *Sharked up:* gathered up indiscriminately (as a shark preys). *lawless resolutes:* determined outlaws. ¹⁰⁰ *stomach:* show of courage. ¹⁰⁶ *head:* fountainhead. ¹⁰⁷ *romage:* bustle (rummage). ¹⁰⁹ *sort:* turn out. ¹¹³ *palmy:* triumphant.

Did squeak and gibber in the Roman streets,
As stars with trains of fire,° and dews of blood,
Disasters° in the sun; and the moist star,°
Upon whose influence Neptune's empire stands,
Was sick almost to doomsday with eclipse.   120
And even the like precurse° of feared events,
As harbingers preceding still° the fates
And prologue to the omen° coming on,
Have heaven and earth together demonstrated
Unto our climatures° and countrymen.   125

Enter Ghost.

But soft, behold, lo where it comes again.
I'll cross° it though it blast me: *Spreads his arms.*
                                       stay illusion,
If thou hast any sound or use of voice,
Speak to me.
If there be any good thing to be done   130
That may to thee do ease, and grace° to me,
Speak to me.
If thou art privy° to thy country's fate
Which happily° foreknowing may avoid,
O speak: 135
Or if thou hast uphoarded in thy life
Extorted treasure in the womb of earth,
For which they say you spirits oft walk in death,

                                        The cock crows.

Speak of it, stay and speak. Stop it Marcellus.
MARCELLUS   Shall I strike at it with my partisan?°   140
HORATIO   Do, if it will not stand
BARNARDO   'Tis here.
HORATIO   'Tis here.
MARCELLUS   'Tis gone.   *Exit Ghost.*
We do it wrong being so majestical,
To offer it the show of violence,
For it is as the air, invulnerable,   145
And our vain blows malicious mockery.°
BARNARDO   It was about to speak when the cock crew.°
HORATIO   And then it started like a guilty thing,
Upon a fearful summons; I have heard,
The cock that is the trumpet to the morn,   150
Doth with his lofty and shrill-sounding throat
Awake the god of day, and at his warning
Whether in sea or fire, in earth or air,°
Th'extravagant and erring° spirit hies°
To his confine, and of the truth herein   155
This present object made probation.°
MARCELLUS   It faded on the crowing of the cock.
Some say that ever 'gainst° that season comes

Wherein our Saviour's birth is celebrated
This bird of dawning singeth all night long,   160
And then they say no spirit dare stir abroad,
The nights are wholesome,° then no planets
strike,°
No fairy takes,° nor witch hath power to charm,
So hallowed, and so gracious is that time.
HORATIO   So have I heard and do in part believe it.   165
But look, the morn in russet° mantle clad
Walks o'er the dew of yon high eastward hill:
Break we our watch up and by my advice
Let us impart what we have seen tonight
Unto young Hamlet, for upon my life   170
This spirit dumb to us, will speak to him:
Do you consent we shall acquaint him with it,
As needful in our loves,° fitting our duty?
MARCELLUS   Let's do't I pray, and I this morning know
Where we shall find him most convenient.
Exeunt.°   175

Scene 2. [A room of state in the castle]

*Flourish.° Enter Claudius King of Denmark, Gertrude the
Queen, [members of the] Council: as Polonius; and his son Laertes,
Hamlet, [Valtemand and Cornelius] cum aliis.°*

KING   Though yet of Hamlet our dear brother's death
The memory be green, and that it us befitted
To bear our hearts in grief, and our whole kingdom
To be contracted in one brow of woe,
Yet so far hath discretion fought with nature,°   5
That we° with wisest sorrow think on him
Together with remembrance of ourselves:°
Therefore our sometime° sister,° now our queen,
Th'imperial jointress° to this warlike state,
Have we as 'twere with a defeated joy,   10
With an auspicious, and a dropping eye,°
With mirth in funeral, and with dirge in marriage,
In equal scale weighing delight and dole,
Taken to wife: nor have we herein barred
Your better wisdoms,° which have freely gone   15
With this affair along—for all, our thanks.
Now follows that you know, young Fortinbras,
Holding a weak supposal of our worth,°
Or thinking by our late dear brother's death
Our state to be disjoint and out of frame,°   20
Colleaguèd° with this dream of his advantage,°
He hath not failed to pester us with message
Importing the surrender of those lands
Lost by his father, with all bands° of law,
To our most valiant brother—so much for him: 25

---

¹¹⁷ *stars . . . fire:* meteors. ¹¹⁸ *Disasters:* unfavorable portents.
moist star: moon. ¹²¹ *precurse:* portent. ¹²² *still:* always.
¹²³ *omen:* disaster. ¹²⁵ *climatures:* regions. ¹²⁷ *cross:* (1) cross its
path (2) spread my arms to make a cross of my body (to ward
against evil). ¹³¹ *grace:* (1) honor (2) blessedness. ¹³³ *art privy:*
know secretly of. ¹³⁴ *happily:* perhaps. ¹⁴⁰ *partisan:* spear.
¹⁴⁶ *malicious mockery:* mockery because they only imitate harm.
¹⁴⁷ *cock crew:* (traditional signal for ghosts to return to their confines). ¹⁵³ *sea . . . air:* the four elements (inhabited by spirits,
each indigenous to a particular element). ¹⁵⁴ *extravagant and
erring:* going beyond its bounds (vagrant) and wandering. *hies:*
hastens. ¹⁵⁶ *made probation:* gave proof. ¹⁵⁸ *'gainst:* just before.

¹⁶² *wholesome:* healthy (night air was considered unhealthy).
strike: exert evil influence ¹⁶³ *takes:* bewitches. ¹⁶⁶ *russet:* reddish. ¹⁷³ *needful . . . loves:* urged by our friendship. stage
direction: *Exeunt:* all exit. stage direction: *Flourish:* fanfare of
trumpets. *cum aliis:* with others. ⁵ *nature:* natural impulse (of
grief). ⁶ *we:* royal plural. The King speaks not only for himself,
but for his entire government. ⁷ *remembrance of ourselves:*
reminder of our duties. ⁸ *sometime:* former. *sister:* sister-in-law.
⁹ *jointress:* widow who inherits the estate. ¹¹ *auspicious . . . eye:*
one eye happy, the other tearful. ¹⁴⁻¹⁵ *barred . . . wisdoms:* failed
to seek and abide by your good advice. ¹⁸ *weak . . . worth:* low
opinion of my ability in office. ²⁰ *out of frame:* tottering.
²¹ *Colleaguèd:* supported. *advantage:* superiority. ²⁴ *bands:* bonds.

Now for ourself, and for this time of meeting,
Thus much the business is. We have here writ
To Norway, uncle of young Fortinbras—
Who impotent and bed-rid scarcely hears
Of this his nephew's purpose—to suppress   30
His further gait° herein, in that the levies,
The lists, and full proportions are all made
Out of his subject:° and we here dispatch
You good Cornelius, and you Valtemand,
For bearers of this greeting to old Norway,   35
Giving to you no further personal power
To business with the king, more than the scope
Of these delated° articles allow:
Farewell, and let your haste commend your duty.°

CORNELIUS, VALTEMAND   In that, and all things, will
we show our duty.   40

KING   We doubt it nothing, heartily farewell.

Exeunt Valtemand and Cornelius.

And now Laertes what's the news with you?
You told us of some suit, what is't Laertes?
You cannot speak of reason to the Dane
And lose your voice;° what wouldst thou beg
Laertes,   45
That shall not be my offer, not thy asking?°
The head is not more native° to the heart,
The hand more instrumental to the mouth,
Than is the throne of Denmark to thy father.
What wouldst thou have Laertes?

LAERTES   My dread lord,   50
Your leave and favour° to return to France,
From whence, though willingly I came to
Denmark,
To show my duty in your coronation,
Yet now I must confess, that duty done,
My thoughts and wishes bend again toward France,   55
And bow them to your gracious leave and pardon.°

KING   Have you your father's leave? What says
Polonius?

POLONIUS   He hath my lord wrung from me my slow
leave
By laboursome petition, and at last
Upon his will I sealed my hard consent.°   60
I do beseech you give him leave to go.

KING   Take thy fair hour Laertes, time be thine,
And thy best graces spend it at thy will.
But now my cousin° Hamlet, and my son—

HAMLET   [*Aside.*] A little more than kin,° and less than
kind.°   65

KING   How is it that the clouds still hang on you?

HAMLET   Not so my lord, I am too much in the sun.°

QUEEN   Good Hamlet cast thy nighted colour° off
And let thine eye look like a friend on Denmark,°
Do not for ever with thy vailèd° lids   70
Seek for thy noble father in the dust,
Thou know'st 'tis common, all that lives must die,
Passing through nature to eternity.

HAMLET   Ay madam, it is common.°

QUEEN   If it be,
Why seems it so particular with thee?   75

HAMLET   Seems, madam? nay it is, I know not
"seems."
'Tis not alone my inky cloak good mother,
Nor customary suits of solemn black,
Nor windy suspiration of forced breath,
No, nor the fruitful river in the eye,°   80
Nor the dejected haviour° of the visage,
Together with all forms, moods, shapes of grief,
That can denote me truly: these indeed seem,
For they are actions that a man might play,°
But I have that within which passes show,   85
These but the trappings and the suits of woe.°

KING   'Tis sweet and commendable in your nature
Hamlet,
To give these mourning duties to your father:
But you must know your father lost a father,
That father lost, lost his, and the survivor bound   90
In filial obligation for some term
To do obsequious sorrow:° but to persever
In obstinate condolement,° is a course
Of impious stubbornness, 'tis unmanly grief,
It shows a will most incorrect to heaven,   95
A heart unfortified, a mind impatient,
An understanding simple and unschooled:
For what we know must be, and is as common
As any the most vulgar thing to sense,°
Why should we in our peevish opposition   100
Take it to heart? Fie, 'tis a fault to heaven,
A fault against the dead, a fault to nature,
To reason most absurd, whose common theme
Is death of fathers, and who still° hath cried
From the first corse,° till he that died today,   105
"This must be so." We pray you throw to earth
This unprevailing° woe, and think of us
As of a father, for let the world take note
You are the most immediate° to our throne,
And with no less nobility of love   110

⁳¹*gait:* progress.   ³¹⁻³³*levies . . . subject:* Taxes, conscriptions, and
supplies are all obtained from his subjects.   ³⁸*delated:* accusing.
³⁹*haste . . . duty:* prompt departure signify your respect.   ⁴⁵*lose
your voice:* speak in vain.   ⁴⁶*offer . . . asking:* grant even before
requested.   ⁴⁷*native:* related.   ⁵¹*leave and favour:* kind permission.   ⁵⁶*pardon:* allowance.   ⁶⁰*Upon . . . consent:* (1) At his
request, I gave my grudging consent. (2) On the soft sealing
wax of his (legal) will, I stamped my approval.   ⁶⁴*cousin:* kinsman (used for relatives outside the immediate family).   ⁶⁵*more
than kin:* too much of a kinsman, being both uncle and stepfa-
ther. *less than kind:* (1) unkind because of being a kin (proverbial) and taking the throne from the former king's son (2)
unnatural (as it was considered incest to marry the wife of one's
dead brother).

⁶⁷*in the sun:* (1) in presence of the king (often associated
metaphorically with the sun) (2) proverbial: "out of heaven's
blessing into the warm sun" (3) of a "son."
⁶⁸*nighted colour:* black.   ⁶⁹*Denmark:* the King of Denmark.
⁷⁰*common:* (1) general (2) vulgar.   ⁸⁰⁻⁸¹*windy
. . . eye:* (hyperbole used to describe exaggerated sighs and tears).
⁸¹*haviour:* behavior.   ⁸⁴*play:* act.   ⁸⁶*trappings . . . woe:* outward,
superficial costumes of mourning.   ⁹²*do obsequious sorrow:*
express sorrow befitting obsequies or funerals.   ⁹³*condolement:*
grief.   ⁹⁹*As any . . . sense:* as the most ordinary thing the senses
can perceive.   ¹⁰⁴*still:* always.   ¹⁰⁵*corse:* corpse (of Abel, also,
ironically, the first fratricide).   ¹⁰⁷*unprevailing:* useless.   ¹⁰⁹*most
immediate:* next in succession (though Danish kings were elect-
ed by the council, an Elizabethan audience might feel that
Hamlet, not Claudius, should be king).

Than that which dearest father bears his son,
Do I impart toward you. For your intent
In going back to school in Wittenberg,
It is most retrograde° to our desire,
And we beseech you, bend you° to remain   115
Here in the cheer and comfort of our eye,
Our chiefest courtier, cousin, and our son.

QUEEN   Let not thy mother lose her prayers Hamlet,
I pray thee stay with us, go not to Wittenberg.

HAMLET   I shall in all my best obey you madam.   120

KING   Why 'tis a loving and a fair reply,
Be as ourself in Denmark. Madam come,
This gentle and unforced accord of Hamlet
Sits smiling to my heart, in grace whereof,
No jocund health that Denmark drinks today,   125
But the great cannon to the clouds shall tell,
And the king's rouse° the heaven shall bruit° again,
Re-speaking earthly thunder; come away.

Flourish, Exeunt all but Hamlet.

HAMLET   O that this too too sullied° flesh would melt,
Thaw and resolve itself into a dew,   130
Or that the Everlasting had not fixed
His canon° 'gainst self-slaughter. O God, God,
How weary, stale, flat, and unprofitable
Seems to me all the uses of this world!
Fie on't, ah fie, 'tis an unweeded garden   135
That grows to seed, things rank° and gross in
nature
Possess it merely.° That it should come to this,
But two months dead, nay not so much, not two,
So excellent a king, that was to this
Hyperion° to a satyr,° so loving to my mother,   140
That he might not beteem° the winds of heaven
Visit her face too roughly—heaven and earth,
Must I remember? why, she would hang on him
As if increase of appetite had grown
By what it fed on,° and yet within a month—   145
Let me not think on't: Frailty, thy name is
woman—
A little month or ere those shoes were old
With which she followed my poor father's body
Like Niobe° all tears, why she, even she—
O God, a beast that wants° discourse of reason   150
Would have mourned longer—married with my
uncle,
My father's brother, but no more like my father
Than I to Hercules: within a month,
Ere yet the salt of most unrighteous° tears
Had left the flushing° in her gallèd° eyes,   155

She married. O most wicked speed, to post°
With such dexterity to incestuous° sheets:
It is not, nor it cannot come to good,
But break my heart, for I must hold my tongue.

Enter Horatio, Marcellus and Barnardo.

HORATIO   Hail to your lordship.

HAMLET   I am glad to see you
well;   160
Horatio, or I do forget my self.

HORATIO   The same my lord, and your poor servant
ever.

HAMLET   Sir my good friend, I'll change° that name
with you:
And what make you from Wittenberg, Horatio?
Marcellus.   165

MARCELLUS   My good lord.

HAMLET   I am very glad to see you: good even, sir.
But what in faith make you from Wittenberg?

HORATIO   A truant disposition, good my lord.

HAMLET   I would not hear your enemy say so,   170
Nor shall you do mine ear that violence
To make it truster of your own report
Against yourself. I know you are no truant,
But what is your affair in Elsinore?
We'll teach you to drink deep ere you depart.   175

HORATIO   My Lord, I came to see your father's funeral.

HAMLET   I prithee do not mock me, fellow student,
I think it was to see my mother's wedding.

HORATIO   Indeed my lord it followed hard upon.

HAMLET   Thrift, thrift, Horatio, the funeral baked
meats°   180
Did coldly° furnish forth the marriage tables.
Would I had met my dearest° foe in heaven
Or ever I had seen that day Horatio.
My father, methinks I see my father.

HORATIO   Where my lord?

HAMLET   In my mind's eye Horatio.   185

HORATIO   I saw him once, a' was a goodly° king.

HAMLET   A' was a man, take him for all in all,
I shall not look upon his like again.

HORATIO   My lord, I think I saw him yesternight.

HAMLET   Saw? Who?   190

HORATIO   My lord, the king your father.

HAMLET   The king my
father?

HORATIO   Season your admiration° for a while
With an attent ear till I may deliver
Upon the witness of these gentlemen
This marvel to you.

HAMLET   For God's love let me hear!   195

HORATIO   Two nights together had these gentlemen,
Marcellus and Barnardo, on their watch
In the dead waste and middle of the night,
Been thus encountered. A figure like your father

---

¹¹⁴ *retrograde:* movement (of planets) in a reverse direction.
¹¹⁵ *beseech … you:* hope you will be inclined. ¹²⁷ *rouse:* toast that empties the wine cup. *bruit:* sound. ¹²⁹ *sullied:* tainted.
¹³² *canon:* divine edict. ¹³⁶ *rank:* (1) luxuriant, excessive (2) bad-smelling. ¹³⁷ *merely:* entirely. ¹⁴⁰ *Hyperion:* god of the sun. *satyr:* part-goat, part-man woodland deity (noted for lust). ¹⁴¹ *beteem:* allow. ¹⁴⁴⁻¹⁴⁵ *As if … on:* as if the more she fed, the more her appetite increased. ¹⁴⁹ *Niobe:* (who boasted of her children before Leto and was punished by their destruction; Zeus changed the weeping mother to a stone dropping continual tears). ¹⁵⁰ *wants:* lacks. ¹⁵⁴ *unrighteous:* (because untrue). ¹⁵⁵ *flushing:* redness. *gallèd:* rubbed sore.

¹⁵⁶ *post:* rush. ¹⁵⁷ *incestuous:* (the church forbade marriage to one's brother's widow). ¹⁶³ *change:* exchange (and be called your friend). ¹⁸⁰ *funeral baked meats:* food prepared for the funeral. ¹⁸¹ *coldly:* when cold. ¹⁸² *dearest:* direst. ¹⁸⁶ *goodly:* handsome. ¹⁹² *Season your admiration:* control your wonder.

Armed at point exactly, cap-a-pe,°   *200*
Appears before them, and with solemn march,
Goes slow and stately by them; thrice he walked
By their oppressed° and fear-surprisèd eyes
Within his truncheon's° length, whilst they distilled°
Almost to jelly with the act of fear,   *205*
Stand dumb and speak not to him; this to me
In dreadful secrecy° impart they did,
And I with them the third night kept the watch,
Where as they had delivered, both in time,
Form of the thing, each word made true and good,   *210*
The apparition comes: I knew your father,
These hands are not more like.

HAMLET   But where was this?

MARCELLUS   My lord upon the platform where we watch.

HAMLET   Did you not speak to it?

HORATIO   My lord I did,
But answer made it none, yet once methought   *215*
It lifted up it° head, and did address
Itself to motion° like as it would speak:
But even then the morning cock crew loud,
And at the sound it shrunk in haste away
And vanished from our sight.

HAMLET   'Tis very strange.   *220*

HORATIO   As I do live my honoured lord 'tis true,
And we did think it writ down in our duty
To let you know of it.

HAMLET   Indeed indeed sirs, but this troubles me.
Hold you the watch tonight?

ALL   We do my lord.   *225*

HAMLET   Armed say you?

ALL   Armed my lord.

HAMLET   From top to toe?

ALL   My lord from head to foot.

HAMLET   Then saw you not his face.

HORATIO   O yes my lord, he wore his beaver° up.   *230*

HAMLET   What, looked he frowningly?

HORATIO   A countenance more in sorrow than in anger.

HAMLET   Pale, or red?

HORATIO   Nay, very pale.

HAMLET   And fixed his eyes upon you?

HORATIO   Most constantly.

HAMLET   I would I had been there.   *235*

HORATIO   It would have much amazed you.

HAMLET   Very like, very like, stayed it long?

HORATIO   While one with moderate haste might tell° a hundred.

MARCELLUS, BARNARDO   Longer, longer.

HORATIO   Not when I saw't.

HAMLET   His beard was grizzled,° no?   *240*

HORATIO   It was as I have seen it in his life,
A sable silvered.°

HAMLET   I will watch tonight;
Perchance 'twill walk again.

HORATIO   I warr'nt it will.

HAMLET   If it assume my noble father's person,
I'll speak to it though hell itself should gape   *245*
And bid me hold my peace;° I pray you all
If you have hitherto concealed this sight
Let it be tenable° in your silence still,
And whatsoever else shall hap tonight,
Give it an understanding but no tongue.   *250*
I will requite your loves, so fare you well:
Upon the platform 'twixt eleven and twelve
I'll visit you.

ALL   Our duty to your honour.

HAMLET   Your loves, as mine to you:° farewell.

                                       Exeunt.

My father's spirit (in arms) all is not well,   *255*
I doubt° some foul play, would the night were come;
Till then sit still my soul, foul deeds will rise,
Though all the earth o'erwhelm them, to men's eyes.

                                       Exit.

Scene 3. [Polonius's chambers]

Enter Laertes and Ophelia his sister.

LAERTES   My necessaries are embarked, farewell,
And sister, as the winds give benefit
And convoy° is assistant, do not sleep
But let me hear from you.

OPHELIA   Do you doubt that?

LAERTES   For Hamlet, and the trifling of his favour,   *5*
Hold it a fashion, and a toy in blood,°
A violet in the youth of primy nature,°
Forward,° not permanent, sweet, not lasting,
The perfume and suppliance of° a minute,
No more.

OPHELIA   No more but so?

LAERTES   Think it no more.   *10*
For nature crescent° does not grow alone
In thews and bulk,° but as this temple waxes°
The inward service of the mind and soul
Grows wide withal.° Perhaps he loves you now,
And now no soil nor cautel° doth besmirch   *15*
The virtue of his will:° but you must fear,
His greatness weighed,° his will is not his own,
For he himself is subject to his birth:
He may not as unvalued persons° do,
Carve° for himself, for on his choice depends   *20*

---

²⁰⁰ *at point . . . cap-a-pe:* in every detail, head to foot. ²⁰³ *oppressed:* overcome by horror. ²⁰⁴ *truncheon:* staff (of office). *distilled:* dissolved. ²⁰⁷ *in dreadful secrecy:* as a dread secret. ²¹⁶ *it:* its. ²¹⁶⁻²¹⁷ *address . . . motion:* start to move. ²³⁰ *beaver:* visor. ²³⁸ *tell:* count. ²⁴⁰ *grizzled:* grey.

²⁴² *A sable silvered:* black flecked with grey. ²⁴⁵⁻²⁴⁶ *though hell . . . peace:* despite the risk of hell (for speaking to a demon) warning me to be silent. ²⁴⁸ *tenable:* held, kept. ²⁵⁴ *Your loves . . . you:* offer your friendship (rather than duty) in exchange for mine. ²⁵⁶ *doubt:* fear. ³ *convoy:* conveyance. ⁶ *toy in blood:* whim of the passions. ⁷ *youth of primy nature:* early spring. ⁸ *Forward:* premature. ⁹ *suppliance of:* supplying diversion for. ¹¹ *nature crescent:* man as he grows. ¹² *thews and bulk:* sinews and body. *temple waxes:* body grows (1 Cor. 6:19). ¹⁴ *withal:* at the same time. ¹⁵ *cautel:* deceit. ¹⁶ *will:* desire. ¹⁷ *weighed:* considered. ¹⁹ *unvalued persons:* common people. ²⁰ *Carve:* choose (as does the one who carves the food).

The sanctity and health of this whole state,
And therefore must his choice be circumscribed
Unto the voice and yielding° of that body
Whereof he is the head. Then if he says he loves you,
It fits your wisdom so far to believe it 25
As he in his particular act and place
May give his saying deed,° which is no further
Than the main voice of Denmark goes withal.
Then weigh what loss your honour may sustain
If with too credent° ear you list° his songs, 30
Or lose your heart, or your chaste treasure open
To his unmast'red importunity.°
Fear it Ophelia, fear it my dear sister,
And keep you in the rear of your affection,
Out of the shot and danger of desire. 35
The chariest° maid is prodigal enough
If she unmask her beauty to the moon.
Virtue itself 'scapes not calumnious strokes.
The canker galls the infants° of the spring
Too oft before their buttons° be disclosed, 40
And in the morn and liquid dew of youth
Contagious blastments° are most imminent.
Be wary then, best safety lies in fear,
Youth to itself rebels,° though none else near.

OPHELIA   I shall the effect° of this good lesson keep 45
As watchman to my heart: but good my brother,
Do not as some ungracious° pastors do,
Show me the steep and thorny way to heaven,
Whiles like a puffed and reckless libertine
Himself the primrose path of dalliance treads, 50
And recks not his own rede.°

Enter Polonius.

LAERTES   O fear me not,°
I stay too long, but here my father comes:
A double blessing is a double grace,
Occasion smiles upon a second leave.°
POLONIUS   Yet here Laertes? aboard, aboard for shame, 55
The wind sits in the shoulder of your sail,
And you are stayed for: there, my blessing with thee,
And these few precepts in thy memory
Look thou character.° Give thy thoughts no tongue,
Nor any unproportioned thought his act: 60
Be thou familiar, but by no means vulgar:°
Those friends thou hast, and their adoption tried,°
Grapple them unto thy soul with hoops of steel,

But do not dull° thy palm with entertainment
Of each new-hatched unfledged° comrade. Beware 65
Of entrance to a quarrel, but being in,
Bear't that th'opposèd may beware of thee.
Give every man thy ear, but few thy voice:
Take each man's censure,° but reserve thy judgment.
Costly thy habit° as thy purse can buy, 70
But not expressed in fancy;° rich, not gaudy,
For the apparel oft proclaims the man,
And they in France of the best rank and station,
Are of a most select and generous chief° in that:
Neither a borrower nor a lender be, 75
For loan oft loses both itself and friend,
And borrowing dulls the edge of husbandry;°
This above all, to thine own self be true
And it must follow as the night the day,
Thou canst not then be false to any man. 80
Farewell, my blessing season° this in thee.
LAERTES   Most humbly do I take my leave my lord.
POLONIUS   The time invites you, go, your servants tend.°
LAERTES   Farewell Ophelia, and remember well
What I have said to you.
OPHELIA   'Tis in my memory locked, 85
And you yourself shall keep the key of it.
LAERTES   Farewell.   *Exit Laertes.*
POLONIUS   What is't Ophelia he hath said to you?
OPHELIA   So please you, something touching the Lord Hamlet.
POLONIUS   Marry,° well bethought: 90
'Tis told me he hath very oft of late
Given private time to you, and you yourself
Have of your audience been most free and bounteous.
If it be so, as so 'tis put on me,
And that in way of caution, I must tell you, 95
You do not understand yourself so clearly
As it behooves my daughter, and your honour.
What is between you? give me up the truth.
OPHELIA   He hath my lord of late made many tenders°
Of his affection to me. 100
POLONIUS   Affection, puh, you speak like a green girl
Unsifted° in such perilous circumstance.
Do you believe his tenders as you call them?
OPHELIA   I do not know my lord what I should think.
POLONIUS   Marry, I will teach you; think yourself a baby 105
That you have ta'en these tenders° for true pay
Which are not sterling.° Tender yourself more dearly,°

---

²³ *voice and yielding:* approving vote. ²⁶⁻²⁷ *in his … deed:* limited by personal responsibilities and rank, may perform what he promises. ³⁰ *credent:* credulous. *list:* listen to. ³¹⁻³² *your chaste … importunity:* lose your virginity to his uncontrolled persistence. ³⁶ *chariest:* most cautious. ³⁹ *canker … infants:* cankerworm or caterpillar harms the young plants. ⁴⁰ *buttons:* buds. ⁴² *blastments:* blights. ⁴⁴ *to itself rebels:* lusts by nature. ⁴⁵ *effect:* moral. ⁴⁷ *ungracious:* lacking God's grace. ⁵¹ *recks … rede:* does not follow his own advice. *fear me not:* Don't worry about me. ⁵⁴ *Occasion … leave:* opportunity favors a second leave-taking. ⁵⁹ *character:* write, impress, imprint. ⁶¹ *vulgar:* indiscriminately friendly. ⁶² *adoption tried:* loyalty proved.

⁶⁴ *dull:* get calluses on. ⁶⁵ *new-hatched, unfledged:* new and untested. ⁶⁹ *censure:* opinion. ⁷⁰ *habit:* clothing. ⁷¹ *expressed in fancy:* so fantastic as to be ridiculous. ⁷⁴ *select … chief:* judicious and noble eminence. ⁷⁷ *husbandry:* thrift. ⁸¹ *season:* bring to maturity. ⁸³ *tend:* attend, wait. ⁹⁰ *Marry:* (a mild oath, from "By the Virgin Mary"). ⁹⁹ *tenders:* offers (see lines 106–109). ¹⁰² *Unsifted:* untested. ¹⁰⁶ *tenders:* offers (of money). ¹⁰⁷ *sterling:* genuine (currency). *Tender … dearly:* hold yourself at a higher value.

Or (not to crack the wind of the poor phrase,
Running it thus°) you'll tender me a fool.°
OPHELIA   My lord he hath importuned me with love   110
In honourable fashion.
POLONIUS   Ay, fashion you may call it, go to, go to.
OPHELIA   And hath given countenance° to his speech,
my lord,
With almost all the holy vows of heaven.
POLONIUS   Ay, springes° to catch woodcocks.° I do
know   115
When the blood burns, how prodigal the soul
Lends the tongue vows: these blazes daughter,
Giving more light than heat, extinct in both,
Even in their promise, as it is a-making,°
You must not take for fire. From this time   120
Be something scanter of your maiden presence,
Set your entreatments at a higher rate
Than a command to parle;° for Lord Hamlet,
Believe so much in him that he is young,
And with a larger tether may he walk   125
Than may be given you: in few° Ophelia,
Do not believe his vows, for they are brokers°
Not of that dye which their investments° show,
But mere implorators° of unholy suits,
Breathing° like sanctified and pious bonds,°   130
The better to beguile. This is for all,
I would not in plain terms from this time forth
Have you so slander any moment leisure
As to give words or talk with the Lord Hamlet.
Look to't I charge you, come your ways.°   135
OPHELIA   I shall obey, my lord.   [*Exeunt.*]

Scene 4. [The platform on the battlements]

Enter Hamlet, Horatio and Marcellus.

HAMLET   The air bites shrewdly,° it is very cold.
HORATIO   It is a nipping and an eager° air.
HAMLET   What hour now?
HORATIO   I think it lacks of twelve.
MARCELLUS. No, it is struck.
HORATIO   Indeed? I heard it not: it then draws near the
season,°   5
Wherein the spirit held his wont to walk.

A flourish of trumpets, and two pieces [of ordnance] go off.

What does this mean my lord?
HAMLET   The king doth wake° tonight and takes his
rouse,°

Keeps wassail° and the swagg'ring up-spring° reels:
And as he drains his draughts of Rhenish° down,   10
The kettle-drum and trumpet thus bray out
The triumph of his pledge.°
HORATIO   Is it a custom?
HAMLET   Ay marry is't,
But to my mind, though I am native here
And to the manner born,° it is a custom   15
More honoured in the breach than the observance.°
This heavy-headed revel east and west
Makes us traduced and taxed of° other nations:
They clepe° us drunkards, and with swinish phrase
Soil our addition,° and indeed it takes   20
From our achievements, though performed at
height,°
The pith and marrow of our attribute.°
So oft it chances in particular men,
That for some vicious mole of nature° in them,
As in their birth, wherein they are not guilty   25
(Since nature cannot choose his origin),
By the o'ergrowth of some complexion,°
Oft breaking down the pales° and forts of reason,
Or by some habit, that too much o'er-leavens°
The form of plausive° manners—that these men,   30
Carrying I say the stamp of one defect,
Being nature's livery,° or fortune's star,°
His virtues else be they as pure as grace,
As infinite as man may undergo,
Shall in the general censure° take corruption   35
From that particular fault: the dram of evil
Doth all the noble substance of a doubt,
To his own scandal.°

Enter Ghost.

HORATIO   Look my lord, it comes.
HAMLET   Angels and ministers of grace defend us:
Be thou a spirit of health, or goblin damned,°   40
Bring with thee airs from heaven, or blasts from
hell,
Be thy intents wicked, or charitable,
Thou com'st in such a questionable° shape,
That I will speak to thee. I'll call thee Hamlet,
King, father, royal Dane. O answer me,   45
Let me not burst in ignorance, but tell
Why thy canonized° bones hearsèd° in death

108–109 *crack … thus:* make the phrase lose its breath.   109 *tender …
fool:* (1) make me look foolish (2) present me with a baby.
113 *countenance:* confirmation.   115 *springes:* snares. *woodcocks:*
snipelike birds (believed to be stupid and therefore easily
trapped).   118–119 *extinct … a-making:* losing both appearance,
because of brevity, and substance, because of broken promises.
122–123 *Set … parle:* Don't rush to negotiate a surrender as soon as
the besieger asks for a discussion of terms.   126 *few:* short.
127 *brokers:* (1) business agents (2) procurers.   128 *investments:* (1)
business ventures (2) clothing.   129 *implorators:* solicitors.
130 *Breathing:* speaking softly. *bonds:* pledges.   135 *come your ways:*
come along.   1 *shrewdly:* piercingly.   2 *eager:* sharp.   5 *season:*
time, period.   8 *wake:* stay awake. *rouse:* drinks that empty the
cup.

9 *Keeps wassail:* holds drinking bouts. *up-spring:* a vigorous
German dance.   10 *Rhenish:* Rhine wine.   12 *triumph … pledge:*
victory of emptying the cup with one draught.   15 *to … born:*
accustomed to the practice since birth.   16 *More … observance:*
better to break than to observe.   18 *traduced and taxed of:*
defamed and taken to task by.   19 *clepe:* call.   19–20 *with swinish …
addition:* blemish our reputation by comparing us to swine.   21 *at
height:* to the maximum.   22 *attribute:* reputation.   24 *mole of
nature:* natural blemish.   27 *o'ergrowth … complexion:* overbal-
ance of one of the body's four humors or fluids believed to
determine temperament.   28 *pales:* defensive enclosures.   29 *too
much o'er-leavens:* excessively modifies (like too much leaven in
bread).   30 *plausive:* pleasing.   32 *nature's livery:* marked by
nature. *fortune's star:* destined by chance.   35 *general censure:*
public opinion.   36–38 *the dram … scandal:* the minute quantity of
evil casts doubt upon his noble nature, to his shame.   40 *spirit …
damned:* true ghost or demon from hell.   43 *questionable:* ques-
tion-raising.   47 *canonized:* buried in accordance with church
edict. *hearsèd:* entombed.

Have burst their cerements°? why the sepulchre,
Wherein we saw thee quietly interred
Hath oped his ponderous and marble jaws, 50
To cast thee up again? What may this mean
That thou, dead corse, again in complete steel
Revisits thus the glimpses of the moon,
Making night hideous, and we fools of nature°
So horridly to shake our disposition 55
With thoughts beyond the reaches of our souls,
Say why is this? wherefore? what should we do?

Ghost beckons Hamlet.

HORATIO   It beckons you to go away with it,
As if it some impartment did desire°
To you alone.

MARCELLUS   Look with what courteous action 60
It waves you to a more removèd ground,
But do not go with it.

HORATIO   No, by no means.

HAMLET   It will not speak, then I will follow it.

HORATIO   Do not my lord.

HAMLET   Why what should be the fear?
I do not set my life at a pin's fee,° 65
And for my soul, what can it do to that
Being a thing immortal as itself;
It waves me forth again, I'll follow it.

HORATIO   What if it tempt you toward the flood my lord,
Or to the dreadful summit of the cliff 70
That beetles o'er° his base into the sea,
And there assume some other horrible form
Which might deprive your sovereignty of reason,°
And draw you into madness? think of it,
The very place puts toys of desperation,° 75
Without more motive, into every brain
That looks so many fathoms to the sea
And hears it roar beneath.

HAMLET   It waves me still:
Go on, I'll follow thee.

MARCELLUS   You shall not go my lord.

HAMLET   Hold off your hands. 80

HORATIO   Be ruled, you shall not go.

HAMLET   My fate cries out,
And makes each petty artire° in this body
As hardy as the Nemean lion's° nerve;°
Still am I called, unhand me gentlemen,
By heaven I'll make a ghost of him that lets° me: 85
I say away; go on, I'll follow thee.

Exeunt Ghost and Hamlet.

HORATIO   He waxes desperate° with imagination.

MARCELLUS   Let's follow, 'tis not fit thus to obey him.

HORATIO   Have after—to what issue will this come?

MARCELLUS   Something is rotten in the state of
Denmark. 90

HORATIO   Heaven will direct it.

MARCELLUS   Nay, let's follow him.

Exeunt.

Scene 5. [Another part of the platform]

Enter Ghost and Hamlet.

HAMLET   Whither wilt thou lead me? Speak, I'll go no
further.

GHOST   Mark me.

HAMLET   I will.

GHOST   My hour is almost come
When I to sulphurous and tormenting flames
Must render up myself.

HAMLET   Alas poor ghost.

GHOST   Pity me not, but lend thy serious hearing 5
To what I shall unfold.

HAMLET   Speak, I am bound° to hear.

GHOST   So art thou to revenge, when thou shalt hear.

HAMLET   What?

GHOST   I am thy father's spirit,
Doomed for a certain term to walk the night, 10
And for the day confined to fast in fires,
Till the foul crimes done in my days of nature°
Are burnt and purged away: but that I am forbid
To tell the secrets of my prison-house,
I could a tale unfold whose lightest word 15
Would harrow up thy soul, freeze thy young blood,
Make thy two eyes like stars start from their spheres,°
Thy knotted and combinèd locks to part,
And each particular hair to stand an° end,
Like quills upon the fretful porpentine:° 20
But this eternal blazon° must not be
To ears of flesh and blood; list, list, O list:
If though didst ever thy dear father love—

HAMLET   O God!

GHOST   Revenge his foul and most unnatural murder. 25

HAMLET   Murder?

GHOST   Murder most foul, as in the best it is,
But this most foul, strange and unnatural.

HAMLET   Haste me to know't, that I with wings as swift
As meditation or the thoughts of love, 30
May sweep to my revenge.

GHOST   I find thee apt,°
And duller shouldst thou be than the fat° weed
That rots itself in ease on Lethe wharf,°
Wouldst thou not stir in this; now Hamlet hear,
'Tis given out, that sleeping in my orchard,° 35
A serpent stung me, so the whole ear of Denmark

---

⁴⁸*cerements:* waxed cloth wrappings.   ⁵⁴*fools of nature:* mocked by our natural limitations when faced with the supernatural.   ⁵⁹*some ... desire:* desired to impart something.   ⁶⁵*fee:* value.   ⁷¹*beetles o'er:* overhangs.   ⁷³*deprive ... reason:* dethrone your reason from its sovereignty.   ⁷⁵*toys of desperation:* desperate whims.   ⁸²*artire:* ligament.   ⁸³*Nemean lion:* (killed by Hercules as one of his twelve labors). *nerve:* sinew.   ⁸⁵*lets:* prevents.   ⁸⁷*waxes desperate:* grows frantic.

⁶*bound:* obliged by duty.   ¹²*crimes ... nature:* sins committed during my life on earth.   ¹⁷*spheres:* (1) orbits (according to Ptolemy, each planet was confined to a sphere revolving around the earth) (2) sockets.   ¹⁹*an:* on.   ²⁰*fretful porpentine:* angry porcupine.   ²¹*eternal blazon:* revelation about eternity.   ³¹*apt:* ready.   ³²*fat:* slimy.   ³³*Lethe wharf:* the banks of Lethe (river in Hades from which spirits drank to forget their past lives).   ³⁵*orchard:* garden.

Is by a forgèd process° of my death
Rankly abused:° but know thou noble youth,
The serpent that did sting thy father's life
Now wears his crown.
HAMLET   O my prophetic soul!   40
    My uncle?
GHOST   Ay, that incestuous, that adulterate° beast,
    With witchcraft of his wit, with traitorous gifts,
    O wicked wit and gifts, that have the power
    So to seduce; won to his shameful lust   45
    The will of my most seeming-virtuous queen;
    O Hamlet, what a falling-off was there,
    From me whose love was of that dignity
    That it went hand in hand, even with the vow
    I made to her in marriage, and to decline   50
    Upon° a wretch whose natural gifts were poor
    To° those of mine;
    But virtue, as it never will be moved,
    Though lewdness court it in a shape of heaven,°
    So lust, though to a radiant angle linked,   55
    Will sate itself in a celestial bed
    And prey on garbage.
    But soft, methinks I scent the morning air,
    Brief let me be; sleeping within my orchard,
    My custom always of the afternoon,   60
    Upon my secure° hour thy uncle stole
    With juice of cursèd hebona° in a vial,
    And in the porches of my ears did pour
    The leperous° distilment, whose effect
    Holds such an enmity with blood of man,   65
    That swift as quicksilver it courses through
    The natural gates and alleys of the body,
    And with a sudden vigour it doth posset°
    And curd, like eager° droppings into milk,
    The thin and wholesome° blood; so did it mine,   70
    And a most instant tetter° barked about°
    Most lazar°-like with vile and loathsome crust
    All my smooth body.
    Thus was I sleeping by a brother's hand,
    Of life, of crown, of queen at once dispatched,   75
    Cut off even in the blossoms of my sin,
    Unhouseled, disappointed, unaneled,°
    No reck'ning° made, but sent to my account°
    With all my imperfections on my head;
    O horrible, O horrible, most horrible!   80
    If thou hast nature in thee bear it not,
    Let not the royal bed of Denmark be
    A couch for luxury° and damnèd incest.
    But howsoever thou pursues this act,
    Taint not thy mind, nor let thy soul contrive   85
    Against thy mother aught;° leave her to heaven,

And to those thorns that in her bosom lodge
To prick and sting her. Fare thee well at once,
The glow-worm shows the matin° to be near
And 'gins to pale this uneffectual fire:°   90
Adieu, adieu, adieu, remember me.   *Exit.*
HAMLET   O all you host of heaven! O earth! what else?
    And shall I couple° hell? O fie! Hold, hold my
    heart,
    And you my sinews, grow not instant old,
    But bear me stiffly up; remember thee?   95
    Ay thou poor ghost, whiles memory holds a seat
    In this distracted globe.° Remember thee?
    Yea, from the table° of my memory
    I'll wipe away all trivial fond° records,
    All saws of books,° all forms, all pressures° past   100
    That youth and observation copied there,
    And thy commandment all alone shall live
    Within the book and volume of my brain,
    Unmixed with baser matter, yes by heaven:
    O most pernicious woman!   105
    O villain, villain, smiling damnèd villain!
    My tables,° meet° it is I set it down
    That one may smile, and smile, and be a villain,
    At least I am sure it may be so in Denmark.
    So uncle, there you are: now to my word,°   110
    It is 'Adieu, adieu, remember me.'
    I have sworn't.

    Enter Horatio and Marcellus.

HORATIO   My lord, my lord!
MARCELLUS   Lord Hamlet!
HORATIO   Heaven
    secure° him.
HAMLET   So be it.
MARCELLUS   Illo, ho, ho, my lord!   115
HAMLET   Hillo, ho, ho, boy, come° bird, come.
MARCELLUS   How is't my noble lord?
HORATIO   What news my
    lord?
HAMLET   O, wonderful!
HORATIO   Good my lord, tell it.
HAMLET   No, you will reveal it.
HORATIO   Not I my lord, by heaven.
MARCELLUS   Nor I my lord.   120
HAMLET   How say you then, would heart of man once
    think it?
    But you'll be secret?
BOTH   Ay, by heaven, my lord.
HAMLET   There's ne'er a villain dwelling in all
    Denmark
    But he's an arrant° knave.
HORATIO   There needs no ghost my lord, come from
    the grave   125

---

³⁷ *process:* account. ³⁸ *abused:* deceived. ⁴² *adulterate:* adulterous.
⁵⁰⁻⁵¹ *decline Upon:* descend to. ⁵² *To:* compared to. ⁵⁴ *shape of heaven:* angelic appearance. ⁶¹ *secure:* unsuspecting. ⁶² *hebona:* poisonous sap of the ebony or henbane. ⁶⁴ *leperous:* leprosy-causing. ⁶⁸ *posset:* curdle. ⁶⁹ *eager:* sour. ⁷⁰ *wholesome:* healthy.
⁷¹ *tetter:* skin eruption. *barked about:* covered (like bark on a tree).
⁷² *lazar:* leper. ⁷⁷ *Unhouseled … unaneled:* without final sacrament, unprepared (without confession) and lacking extreme unction (anointing). ⁷⁸ *reck'ning:* (1) accounting (2) payment of my bill (3) confession and absolution. *account:* judgment. ⁸³ *luxury:* lust. ⁸⁶ *aught:* anything.

⁸⁹ *matin:* dawn. ⁹⁰ *'gins … fire:* his light becomes ineffective, made pale by day. ⁹³ *couple:* engage in a contest against. ⁹⁷ *distracted globe:* (his head). ⁹⁸ *table:* tablet, "table-book." ⁹⁹ *fond:* foolish. ¹⁰⁰ *saws of books:* maxims (sayings) copied from books. *forms, pressures:* ideas, impressions.
¹⁰⁷ *tables:* See note for line 98. *meet:* fitting. ¹¹⁰ *word:* motto (to guide my actions). ¹¹³ *secure:* protect. ¹¹⁶ *Hillo … come:* falconer's cry with which Hamlet replies to their calls. ¹²⁴ *arrant:* thoroughgoing.

To tell us this.
HAMLET   Why right, you are in the right,
    And so without more circumstance° at all
    I hold it fit that we shake hands and part,
    You, as your business and desire shall point you,
    For every man hath business and desire   130
    Such as it is, and for my own poor part,
    Look you, I will go pray.
HORATIO   These are but wild and whirling words my
    lord.
HAMLET   I am sorry they offend you, heartily,
    Yes faith, heartily.
HORATIO   There's no offence my lord.   135
HAMLET   Yes by Saint Patrick, but there is Horatio,
    And much offence too: touching this vision here,
    It is an honest° ghost, that let me tell you:
    For your desire to know what is between us,
    O'ermaster't as you may. And now good friends,   140
    As you are friends, scholars, and soldiers,
    Give me one poor request.
HORATIO   What is't, my lord? we will.
HAMLET   Never make known what you have seen
    tonight.
BOTH   My lord we will not.
HAMLET   Nay, but swear't.
HORATIO   In faith   145
    My lord, not I.
MARCELLUS   Nor I my lord, in faith.
HAMLET   Upon my sword.
MARCELLUS   We have sworn my lord already.
HAMLET   Indeed, upon my sword,° indeed.
GHOST   Swear.   *Ghost cries under the stage.*
HAMLET   Ha, ha, boy, say'st thou so, art thou there,
    truepenny°?   150
    Come on, you hear this fellow in the cellarage,
    Consent to swear.
HORATIO   Propose the oath my lord.
HAMLET   Never to speak of this that you have seen.
    Swear by my sword.
GHOST   [*Beneath.*] Swear.   155
HAMLET   Hic et ubique?° then we'll shift our ground:
    Come hither gentlemen,
    And lay your hands again upon my sword,
    Swear by my sword
    Never to speak of this that you have heard.   160
GHOST   [*Beneath.*] Swear by his sword.
HAMLET   Well said old mole, canst work i'th' earth so
    fast?
    A worthy pioner°—once more remove,° good
    friends.
HORATIO   O day and night, but this is wondrous
    strange.
HAMLET   And therefore as a stranger give it welcome. 165
    There are more things in heaven and earth
    Horatio,
    Than are dreamt of in your philosophy.

But come,
    Here as before, never so help you mercy,
    How strange or odd some'er I bear myself,   170
    (As I perchance hereafter shall think meet
    To put an antic disposition on°)
    That you at such times seeing me, never shall
    With arms encumbered° thus, or this head-shake,
    Or by pronouncing of some doubtful phrase,   175
    As "Well, well, we know," or "We could and if we
    would,"
    Or "If we list° to speak," or "There be and if they
    might,"
    Or such ambiguous giving out, to note
    That you know aught of me; this do swear,
    So grace and mercy at your need help you.   180
GHOST   [*Beneath.*] Swear.   [*They swear.*]
HAMLET   Rest, rest, perturbed spirit: so gentlemen,
    With all my love I do commend me to you,°
    And what so poor a man as Hamlet is,
    May do t'express his love and friending to you   185
    God willing shall not lack: let us go in together,
    And still° your fingers on your lips I pray.
    The time is out of joint: O cursèd spite,
    That ever I was born to set it right.
    Nay come, let's go together.   *Exeunt.* 190

Act 2

Scene 1. [Polonius's chambers]

Enter old POLONIUS *with his man Reynaldo.*

POLONIUS   Give him this money, and these notes
    Reynaldo.
REYNALDO   I will my lord.
POLONIUS   You shall do marvellous° wisely, good
    Reynaldo,
    Before you visit him, to make inquire
    Of his behaviour.
REYNALDO   My lord, I did intend it.   5
POLONIUS   Marry, well said, very well said; look you
    sir,
    Inquire me first what Danskers° are in Paris,
    And how, and who, what means, and where they
    keep,°
    What company, at what expense, and finding
    By this encompassment° and drift of question   10
    That they do know my son, come you more
    nearer
    Than your particular demands° will touch it,
    Take you as 'twere some distant knowledge of him,
    As thus, "I know his father, and his friends,
    And in part him"—do you mark this, Reynaldo?   15
REYNALDO   Ay, very well my lord.

---

¹²⁷ *circumstance:* ceremony.   ¹³⁸ *honest:* true (not a devil in disguise).   ¹⁴⁸ *sword:* (the cross-shaped hilt).   ¹⁵⁰ *truepenny:* old pal.
¹⁵⁶ *Hic et ubique:* here and everywhere.   ¹⁶³ *pioner:* digger (army
trencher). *remove:* move elsewhere.

¹⁷² *put … on:* assume a mad or grotesque behavior.   ¹⁷⁴ *encumbered:* folded.   ¹⁷⁷ *list:* please.   ¹⁸³ *commend … you:* put myself in
your hands.   ¹⁸⁷ *still:* always.   ³ *marvellous:* wonderfully.
⁷ *danskers:* Danes.   ⁸ *keep:* lodge.   ¹⁰ *encompassment:* roundabout
way.   ¹² *particular demands:* specific questions.

POLONIUS "And in part him, but," you may say, "not well,
    But if't be he I mean, he's very wild,
    Addicted so and so;" and there put on him
    What forgeries° you please, marry none so rank°   20
    As may dishonour him, take heed of that,
    But sir, such wanton, wild, and usual slips,
    As are companions noted and most known
    To youth and liberty.
REYNALDO   As gaming my lord.
POLONIUS   Ay, or drinking, fencing, swearing,   25
    Quarrelling, drabbing°—you may go so far.
REYNALDO   My lord, that would dishonour him.
POLONIUS   Faith no, as you may season it in the charge.°
    You must not put another scandal on him,
    That he is open to incontinency,°   30
    That's not my meaning, but breathe his faults so quaintly°
    That they may seem the taints of° liberty,
    The flash and outbreak of a fiery mind,
    A savageness in unreclaimèd blood,°
    Of general assault.°
REYNALDO   But my good lord—   35
POLONIUS   Wherefore° should you do this?
REYNALDO   Ay my lord,
    I would know that.
POLONIUS   Marry sir, here's my drift,
    And I believe it is a fetch of warrant:°
    You laying these slight sullies on my son,
    As 'twere a thing a little soiled i'th' working,°   40
    Mark you, your party in converse, him you would sound,
    Having ever seen° in the prenominate crimes°
    The youth you breathe of guilty, be assured
    He closes with you in this consequence,°
    "Good sir," or so, or "friend," or "gentleman,"   45
    According to the phrase, or the addition°
    Of man and country.
REYNALDO   Very good my lord.
POLONIUS   And then sir, does a'° this, a' does, what was I about to say?
    By the mass I was about to say something,
    Where did I leave?
REYNALDO   At "closes in the consequence,"   50
    At "friend, or so, and gentleman."
POLONIUS   At "closes in the consequence," ay marry,
    He closes thus, "I know the gentleman,
    I saw him yesterday, or th'other day,
    Or then, or then, with such or such, and as you say,   55

There was a' gaming, there o'ertook in's rouse,°
There falling out at tennis," or perchance
"I saw him enter such a house of sale,"
Videlicet,° a brothel, or so forth. See you now,
Your bait of falsehood takes this carp of truth,   60
And thus do we of wisdom, and of reach,°
With windlasses,° and with assays of bias,°
By indirections find directions out:
So by my former lecture and advice
Shall you my son; you have me, have you not?   65
REYNALDO   My lord I have.
POLONIUS   God bye ye, fare ye well.
REYNALDO   Good my lord.
POLONIUS   Observe his inclination in yourself.°
REYNALDO   I shall my lord.
POLONIUS   And let him ply° his music.
REYNALDO   Well my lord.   70
POLONIUS   Farewell.

Exit Reynaldo.

Enter Ophelia.

               How now Ophelia, what's the matter?
OPHELIA   O my lord, my lord, I have been so affrighted.
POLONIUS   With what, i'th'name of God?
OPHELIA   My lord, as I was sewing in my closet,°
    Lord Hamlet with his doublet all unbraced,°   75
    No hat upon his head, his stockings fouled,
    Ungart'red, and down-gyvèd° to his ankle,
    Pale as his shirt, his knees knocking each other,
    And with a look so piteous in purport°
    As if he had been loosèd out of hell   80
    To speak of horrors, he comes before me.
POLONIUS   Mad for thy love?
OPHELIA   My lord I do not know,
    But truly I do fear it.
POLONIUS   What said he?
OPHELIA   He took me by the wrist, and held me hard,
    Then goes he to the length of all his arm,°   85
    And with his other hand thus o'er his brow,
    He falls to such perusal of my face
    As° a' would draw it; long stayed he so,
    At last, a little shaking of mine arm,
    And thrice his head thus waving up and down,   90
    He raised a sigh so piteous and profound
    As it did seem to shatter all his bulk,°
    And end his being; that done, he lets me go,
    And with his head over his shoulder turned
    He seemed to find his way without his eyes,   95
    For out adoors he went without their helps,
    And to the last bended their light on me.
POLONIUS   Come, go with me, I will go seek the king,

---

[20] *forgeries:* inventions. *rank:* excessive. [26] *drabbing:* whoring. [28] *season … charge:* temper the charge as you make it. [30] *incontinency:* uncontrolled lechery. [31] *quaintly:* delicately. [32] *taints of:* blemishes due to. [34] *unreclaimèd blood:* unbridled passion. [35] *general assault:* attacking all (young men). [36] *Wherefore:* why. [38] *fetch of warrant:* trick guaranteed to succeed. [40] *working:* handling. [42] *Having ever seen:* if he has ever seen. *prenominate crimes:* aforenamed sins. [44] *closes … consequence:* comes to terms with you as follows. [46] *addition:* title, form of address. [48] *'a:* he.

[56] *o'ertook in's rouse:* overcome by drunkenness. [59] *Videlicet:* namely. [61] *reach:* far-reaching knowledge. [62] *windlasses:* roundabout approaches. *assays of bias:* indirect attempts. [68] *in yourself:* personally. [70] *ply:* practice. [74] *closet:* private room. [75] *doublet all unbraced:* jacket all unfastened. [77] *down-gyvèd:* down around his ankles (like prisoners' fetters or gyves). [79] *purport:* expression. [85] *goes … arm:* holds me at arm's length. [88] *As:* as if. [92] *bulk:* body.

This is the very ecstasy° of love,
Whose violent property fordoes itself,° 100
And leads the will to desperate undertakings
As oft as any passion under heaven
That does afflict our natures: I am sorry.
What, have you given him any hard words of late?

OPHELIA   No my good lord, but as you did command 105
I did repel his letters, and denied
His access to me.

POLONIUS   That hath made him mad.
I am sorry that with better heed and judgment
I had not quoted° him. I feared he did but trifle
And meant to wrack° thee, but beshrew my
jealousy:° 110
By heaven it is as proper to our age
To cast beyond ourselves in our opinions,°
As it is common for the younger sort
To lack discretion; come, go we to the king,
This must be known, which being kept close,
might move 115
More grief to hide, than hate to utter love.°

[Exeunt.]

Scene 2. [A room in the Castle]

*Flourish. Enter King and Queen, Rosencrantz and Guildenstern,
cum aliis.*

KING   Welcome dear Rosencrantz and Guildenstern.
Moreover° that we much did long to see you,
The need we have to use you did provoke
Our hasty sending. Something have you heard
Of Hamlet's transformation—so call it. 5
Sith° nor th'exterior nor the inward man
Resembles that it was. What it should be,
More than his father's death, that thus hath put
him
So much from th'understanding of himself,
I cannot dream of: I entreat you both, 10
That being of so young days° brought up with
him,
And sith so neighboured to his youth and haviour,
That you vouchsafe your rest° here in our court
Some little time, so by your companies
To draw him on to pleasures, and to gather 15
So much as from occasion you may glean,
Whether aught to us unknown afflicts him thus,
That opened° lies within our remedy.

QUEEN   Good gentlemen, he hath much talked of you,
And sure I am, two men there are not living 20
To whom he more adheres. If it will please you
To show us so much gentry° and good will,
As to expend your time with us awhile,
For the supply and profit of our hope,

Your visitation shall receive such thanks 25
As fits a king's remembrance.

ROSENCRANTZ   Both your majesties
Might by the sovereign power you have of us,
Put your dread pleasures more into command
Than to entreaty.

GUILDENSTERN   But we both obey,
And here give up ourselves in the full bent,° 30
To lay our service freely at your feet
To be commanded.

KING   Thanks Rosencrantz, and gentle Guildenstern.

QUEEN   Thanks Guildenstern, and gentle
Rosencrantz.
And I beseech you instantly to visit 35
My too much changèd son. Go some of you
And bring these gentlemen where Hamlet is.

GUILDENSTERN   Heavens make our presence and our
practices°
Pleasant and helpful to him.

QUEEN.   Ay, amen.

Exeunt Rosencrantz and Guildenstern.

Enter Polonius.

POLONIUS   Th'ambassadors from Norway my good
lord, 40
Are joyfully returned.

KING   Thou still° hast been the father of good news.

POLONIUS   Have I, my lord? Assure you, my good
liege,
I hold my duty as I hold my soul,
Both to my God and to my gracious king; 45
And I do think, or else this brain of mine
Hunts not the trail of policy° so sure
As it hath used to do, that I have found
The very cause of Hamlet's lunacy.

KING   O speak of that, that do I long to hear. 50

POLONIUS   Give first admittance to th' ambassadors,
My news shall be the fruit° to that great feast.

KING   Thyself do grace to them, and bring them in.
[Exit Polonius.]
He tells me my dear Gertrude, he hath found
The head and source of all your son's distemper. 55

QUEEN   I doubt° it is no other but the main,
His father's death and our o'erhasty marriage.

KING   Well, we shall sift him.

Enter Polonius, Valtemand, and Cornelius.

                Welcome, my good
friends.
Say Valtemand, what from our brother Norway?

VALTEMAND   Most fair return of greetings and desires; 60
Upon our first,° he sent out to suppress
His nephew's levies, which to him appeared
To be a preparation 'gainst the Polack,
But better looked into, he truly found

---

⁹⁹ *ecstasy*: madness.   ¹⁰⁰ *Whose … itself*: that, by its violent nature,
destroys the lover.   ¹⁰⁹ *quoted*: observed.   ¹¹⁰ *wrack*: ruin. *beshrew
my jealousy*: curse my suspicion.   ¹¹¹⁻¹¹² *proper … opinions*: natural for old people to read more into something than is actually
there.   ¹¹⁵⁻¹¹⁶ *being kept … love*: if kept secret, might cause more
grief than if we risked the king's displeasure.   ² *Moreover*: in
addition to the fact.   ⁶ *Sith*: since.   ¹¹ *of … days*: from your early
days.   ¹³ *vouchsafe your rest*: agree to stay.   ¹⁸ *Opened*: discovered.
²² *gentry*: courtesy.

---

³⁰ *in the full bent*: to the utmost (in archery, bending the bow).
³⁸ *practices*: (1) actions (2) plots.   ⁴² *still*: always.   ⁴⁷ *policy*: politics (2) plots.   ⁵² *fruit*: dessert.   ⁵⁶ *doubt*: suspect.   ⁶¹ *first*: first
presentation.

It was against your highness, whereat grieved 65
That so his sickness, age, and impotence
Was falsely borne in hand,° sends out arrests
On Fortinbras, which he in brief obeys,
Receives rebuke from Norway, and in fine,°
Makes vow before his uncle never more 70
To give th'assay° of arms against your majesty:
Whereon old Norway, overcome with joy,
Gives him threescore thousand crowns in annual
fee,
And his commission to employ those soldiers
So levied (as before) against the Polack, 75
With an entreaty herein further shown,
That it might please you to give quiet pass°
Through your dominions for this enterprise,
On such regards of safety and allowance
As therein are set down.   [Giving a paper.]
KING   It likes° us well, 80
And at our more considered time,° we'll read,
Answer, and think upon this business:
Meantime, we thank you for your well-took labour,
Go to your rest, at night we'll feast together.
Most welcome home.   Exeunt Ambassadors.
POLONIUS   This business is well ended. 85
My liege and madam, to expostulate°
What majesty should be, what duty is,
Why day is day, night night, and time is time.
Were nothing but to waste night, day, and time.
Therefore since brevity is the soul of wit,° 90
And tediousness the limbs and outward
flourishes,°
I will be brief. Your noble son is mad:
Mad call I it, for to define true madness,
What is't but to be nothing else but mad?
But let that go.
QUEEN   More matter, with less art. 95
POLONIUS   Madam, I swear I use no art at all:
That he is mad 'tis true: 'tis true, 'tis pity,
And pity 'tis 'tis true: a foolish figure,°
But farewell it, for I will use no art.
Mad let us grant him then, and now remains 100
That we find out the cause of this effect,
Or rather say, the cause of this defect,
For this effect defective comes by cause:
Thus it remains, and the remainder thus.
Perpend.° 105
I have a daughter, have while she is mine,
Who in her duty and obedience, mark,
Hath given me this, now gather and surmise.
[Reads.] "To the celestial, and my soul's idol, the
most beautified° Ophelia,"— 110
That's an ill phrase, a vile phrase, "beautified" is a
vile phrase, but you shall hear. Thus: [Reads.]
"In her excellent white bosom, these," &c.—

QUEEN   Came this from Hamlet to her?
POLONIUS   Good madam stay awhile, I will be
faithful.   [Reads.] 115
       "Doubt thou the stars are fire,
              Doubt that the sun doth move,°
       Doubt° truth to be a liar,
              But never doubt I love.
O dear Ophelia, I am ill at these numbers, I have 120
not art to reckon° my groans, but that I love thee
best, O most best, believe it. Adieu.
       Thine evermore, most dear lady, whilst
              this machine° is to° him, Hamlet."
This in obedience hath my daughter shown me, 125
And more above hath his solicitings,
As they fell out by time, by means, and place,
All given to mine ear.
KING   But how hath she
Received his love?
POLONIUS   What do you think of me?
KING   As of a man faithful and honourable. 130
POLONIUS   I would fain prove so. But what might you
think
When I had seen this hot love on the wing,
As I perceived it (I must tell you that)
Before my daughter told me, what might you,
Or my dear majesty your queen here think, 135
If I had played the desk or table-book,°
Or given my heart a winking° mute and dumb,
Or looked upon this love with idle° sight,
What might you think? No, I went round to work,
And my young mistress this I did bespeak, 140
"Lord Hamlet is a prince out of thy star,°
This must not be:" and then I prescripts° gave her
That she should lock herself from his resort,°
Admit no messengers, receive no tokens:
Which done, she took the fruits of my advice, 145
And he repellèd, a short tale to make,
Fell into a sadness, then into a fast,
Thence to a watch,° thence into a weakness,
Thence to a lightness,° and by this declension,
Into the madness wherein now he raves, 150
And all we mourn for.
KING   Do you think 'tis this?
QUEEN   It may be very like.
POLONIUS   Hath there been such a time, I would fain
know that,
That I have positively said "'Tis so,"
When it proved otherwise?
KING   Not that I know. 155
POLONIUS   Take this, from this, if this be otherwise;

[Points to his head and shoulder.]

If circumstances lead me, I will find

---

⁶⁷ borne in hand: deceived.   ⁶⁹ fine: finishing.   ⁷¹ assay: test.
⁷⁷ pass: passage.   ⁸⁰ likes: pleases.   ⁸¹ at … time: when time is
available for consideration.   ⁸⁶ expostulate: discuss.   ⁹⁰ wit:
understanding.   ⁹¹ tediousness … flourishes: embellishments and
flourishes cause tedium.   ⁹⁸ figure: rhetorical figure.
¹⁰⁵ Perpend: consider.   ¹¹⁰ beautified: beautiful.

¹¹⁷ move: (as it was believed to do, around the earth).   ¹¹⁸ Doubt:
suspect.   ¹²¹ reckon: express in meter.   ¹²⁴ machine: body. to:
attached to.   ¹³⁶ played … book: kept it concealed as in a desk or
personal notebook.   ¹³⁷ given … winking: had my heart shut its
eyes to the matter.   ¹³⁸ idle: unseeing.   ¹⁴¹ out … star: out of
your sphere (above you in station).   ¹⁴² prescripts: orders.
¹⁴³ resort: company.   ¹⁴⁸ watch: sleeplessness.   ¹⁴⁹ lightness: light-
headedness.

Where truth is hid, though it were hid indeed
Within the center.
KING   How may we try° it further?
POLONIUS   You know sometimes he walks four hours
    together
    Here in the lobby.   160
QUEEN   So he does indeed.
POLONIUS   At such a time, I'll loose° my daughter to
    him.
    Be you and I behind an arras° then,
    Mark the encounter: if he love her not,   165
    And be not from his reason fall'n thereon,
    Let me be no assistant for a state,°
    But keep a farm and carters.
KING   We will try it.

Enter HAMLET *reading on a book.*

QUEEN   But look where sadly the poor wretch comes
    reading.
POLONIUS   Away, I do beseech you both away,
    I'll board him presently,° O give me leave.   170

Exeunt King and Queen.

    How does my good Lord Hamlet?
HAMLET   Well, God-a-mercy.
POLONIUS   Do you know me, my lord?
HAMLET   Excellent well, you are a fishmonger.°
POLONIUS   Not I my lord.   175
HAMLET   Then I would you were so honest a man.
POLONIUS   Honest, my lord?
HAMLET   Ay sir, to be honest as this world goes, is to
    be one man picked out of ten thousand.
POLONIUS   That's very true, my lord.   180
HAMLET   For if the sun breed maggots° in a dead dog,
    being a good
    kissing carrion°—have you a daughter?
POLONIUS   I have my lord.
HAMLET   Let her not walk i'th'sun:° conception° is a
    blessing, but as your daughter may conceive, friend
    look to't.   185
POLONIUS   [*Aside.*] How say you by that? Still harping on
    my daughter, yet he knew me not at first, a' said I was
    a fishmonger. A' is far gone, far gone, and truly in my
    youth, I suffered much extremity for love, very near
    this. I'll speak to him again. What do you read my
    lord?   190
HAMLET   Words, words, words.
POLONIUS   What is the matter my lord?
HAMLET   Between who?
POLONIUS   I mean the matter° that you read, my lord.
HAMLET   Slanders sir; for the satirical rogue says here,

that old men have grey beards, that their faces are 195
are wrinkled, their eyes purging thick amber and
plum-tree gum,° and that they have a plentiful lack of
wit, together with most weak hams. All which sir,
though I most powerfully and potently believe, yet I
hold it not honesty° to have it thus set down, for   200
yourself sir shall grow old as I am: if like a crab you
could go backward.
POLONIUS   [*Aside.*] Though this be madness, yet there
    is method in't.
    Will you walk out of the air° my lord?   205
HAMLET   Into my grave.
POLONIUS   [*Aside.*] Indeed that's out of the air; how
    pregnant° sometimes his replies are, a happiness° that
    often madness hits on, which reason and sanity could
    not so prosperously° be delivered of. I will leave   210
    him and suddenly contrive the means of meeting
    between him and my daughter. My honourable lord,
    I will most humbly take leave of you.
HAMLET   You cannot sir take from me anything that I
    will more willingly part withal: except my life,   215
    except my life, except my life.
POLONIUS   Fare you well my lord.
HAMLET   These tedious old fools.

Enter Rosencrantz and Guildenstern.

POLONIUS   You go to seek the Lord Hamlet, there he is.
ROSENCRANTZ   [*To Polonius.*] God save you sir.   220
    [*Exit Polonius.*]
GUILDENSTERN   My honoured lord.
ROSENCRANTZ   My most dear lord.
HAMLET   My excellent good friends, how dost thou
    Guildenstern?
    Ah Rosencrantz, good lads, how do you both?
ROSENCRANTZ. As the indifferent° children of the earth. 225
GUILDENSTERN   Happy, in that we are not over-happy:
    On Fortune's cap we are not the very button.°
HAMLET   Nor the soles of her shoe?
ROSENCRANTZ   Neither my lord.
HAMLET   Then you live about her waist, or in the   230
    middle of her favours?
GUILDENSTERN   Faith, her privates° we.
HAMLET   In the secret parts of Fortune? O most true,
    she is a strumpet.° What news?
ROSENCRANTZ   None my lord, but that the world's
    grown honest.   235
HAMLET   Then is doomsday near: but your news is
    not true. Let me question more in particular: what
    have you my good friends, deserved at the hands of
    Fortune, that she sends you to prison hither?
GUILDENSTERN   Prison, my lord?   240
HAMLET   Denmark's a prison.
ROSENCRANTZ   Then is the world one.
HAMLET   A goodly one, in which there are many

---

159 *try:* test.   162 *loose:* (1) release (2) turn loose.   163 *arras:* hanging
tapestry.   166 *assistant … state:* state official.   170 *board him*
presently: approach him immediately.   174 *fishmonger:* (1) fish
dealer (2) pimp.   181 *breed maggots* (in the belief that the rays of
the sun caused maggots to breed in dead flesh).   182 *kissing car-*
rion: piece of flesh for kissing.   184 *Let … sun:* (1) (proverbial:
"out of God's blessing, into the warm sun") (2) because the sun
is a breeder (3) don't let her go near me (with a pun on "sun"
and "son"). *conception:* (1) understanding (2) pregnancy.
194 *matter:* (1) content (Polonius's meaning) (2) cause of a quarrel (Hamlet's interpretation).

197–198 *purging … gum:* exuding a viscous yellowish discharge.
200 *honesty:* decency.   205 *out … air:* (in the belief that fresh air was
bad for the sick).   208 *pregnant:* full of meaning. *happiness:* apt-
ness.   210 *prosperously:* successfully.   225 *indifferent:* ordinary.
227 *on Fortune's … button:* we are not at the height of our fortunes.
232 *privates:* (1) intimate friends (2) private parts.   234 *strumpet:*
inconstant woman, giving favor to many.

confines, wards,° and dungeons; Denmark being one o'th'worst.

ROSENCRANTZ   We think not so my lord. 245

HAMLET   Why then 'tis none to you; for there is nothing either good or bad, but thinking makes it so: to me it is a prison.

ROSENCRANTZ   Why then your ambition makes it one: 'tis too narrow for your mind.

HAMLET. O God, I could be bounded in a nutshell, and count myself a king of infinite space; were it not 250 that I have bad dreams.

GUILDENSTERN   Which dreams indeed are ambition: for the very substance of the ambitious, is merely the shadow of a dream.

HAMLET   A dream itself is but a shadow. 255

ROSENCRANTZ   Truly, and I hold ambition of so airy and light a quality, that it is but a shadow's shadow.

HAMLET   Then are our beggars bodies, and our monarchs and outstretched heroes the beggars' shadows:° shall we to th' court? for by my fay,° I cannot reason. 260

BOTH   We'll wait upon° you.

HAMLET   No such matter. I will not sort° you with the rest of my servants: for to speak to you like an honest man, I am most dreadfully attended. But in the beaten way of friendship, what make you at Elsinore? 265

ROSENCRANTZ   To visit you my lord, no other occasion.

HAMLET   Beggar that I am, I am even poor in thanks, but I thank you, and sure dear friends, my thanks are too dear a halfpenny:° were you not sent for? is it your own inclining? is it a free° visitation? come, 270 come, deal justly with me, come, come, nay speak.

GUILDENSTERN   What should we say my lord?

HAMLET   Anything but to th'purpose: you were sent for, and there is a kind of confession in your looks, which your modesties have not craft enough to colour: I 275 know the good king and queen have sent for you.

ROSENCRANTZ   To what end my lord?

HAMLET   That you must teach me: but let me conjure° you, by the rights of our fellowship, by the consonancy of our youth,° by the obligation of our ever-preserved love, 280 and by what more dear a better proposer can charge you withal,° be even and direct with me whether you were sent for or no.

ROSENCRANTZ   [Aside to Guildenstern.] What say you?

HAMLET   Nay then, I have an eye of° you: If you 285 love me, hold not off.

GUILDENSTERN   My lord, we were sent for.

HAMLET. I will tell you why, so shall my anticipation prevent° your discovery,° and your secrecy to the king and queen moult no feather.° I have of late, 290 but wherefore I know not, lost all my mirth, forgone

all custom of exercises: and indeed it goes so heavily with my disposition, that this goodly frame the earth, seems to me a sterile promontory, this most excellent canopy the air, look you, this brave° o'erhanging 295 firmament, this majestical roof fretted° with golden fire,° why it appeareth nothing to me but a foul and pestilent congregation of vapours.° What a piece of work is a man! How noble in reason, how infinite in faculties,° in form and moving, how 300 express° and admirable in action, how like an angel in apprehension, how like a god: the beauty of the world; the paragon of animals; and yet to me, what is this quintessence of dust? Man delights not me, no, nor woman neither, though by your smiling, you 305 seem to say so.

ROSENCRANTZ   My lord, there was no such stuff in my thoughts.

HAMLET   Why did ye laugh then, when I said "man delights not me"? 310

ROSENCRANTZ   To think, my lord, if you delight not in man, what lenten entertainment° the players shall receive from you: we coted° them on the way, and hither are they coming to offer you service.

HAMLET   He that plays the king shall be welcome, 315 his majesty shall have tribute of me, the adventurous knight° shall use his foil and target,° the lover shall not sigh gratis,° the humorous man° shall end his part in peace,° the clown shall make those laugh whose lungs are tickle o'th'sere,° and the lady 320 shall say her mind freely: or the blank verse shall halt° for't. What players are they?

ROSENCRANTZ   Even those you were wont to take such delight in, the tragedians of the city.

HAMLET   How chances it they travel? Their 325 residence° both in reputation and profit was better both ways.

ROSENCRANTZ. I think their inhibition comes by the means of the late innovation.°

HAMLET   Do they hold the same estimation they did 330 when I was in the city; are they so followed?

ROSENCRANTZ   No indeed are they not.

HAMLET   How comes it? Do they grow rusty?

ROSENCRANTZ   Nay, their endeavour keeps in the wonted pace; but there is sir an aery° of children, like 335 eyases,° that cry out on the top of question,° and are

---

243 *wards*: cells. 258–259 *Then are … shadows*: then beggars are the true substance and ambitious kings and heroes the elongated shadows of beggars' bodies (for only a real substance can cast a shadow). 260 *fay*: faith. 261 *wait upon*: attend. 262 *sort*: class. 268–269 *too dear a halfpenny*: worth not even a halfpenny (as I have no influence). 270 *free*: voluntary. 278 *conjure*: appeal to. 279–280 *consonancy … youth*: agreement in our ages. 282 *withal*: with. 285 *of*: on. 289 *prevent*: forestall. *discovery*: disclosure. 290 *moult no feather*: change in no way.

295 *brave*: splendid. 296 *fretted*: ornamented with fretwork. 297 *golden fire*: stars. 298 *pestilent … vapours*: (clouds were believed to carry contagion). 300 *faculties*: physical powers. 301 *express*: well framed. 312 *lenten entertainment*: meager treatment. 313 *coted*: passed. 316–317 *adventurous knight*: knight errant (a popular stage character). 317 *foil and target*: sword blunted for stage fighting, and small shield. 318 *gratis*: (without applause). *humorous man*: eccentric character with a dominant trait, caused by an excess of one of the four humors, or bodily fluids. 319 *in peace*: without interruption. 320 *tickle o'th'sere*: attuned to respond to laughter, as the finely adjusted gunlock responds to the touch of the trigger (fr. hunting). 322 *halt*: limp (if she adds her own opinions and spoils the meter). 326 *residence*: i.e., in a city theatre. 328–329 *inhibition … innovation*: i.e., they were forced out of town by a more popular theatrical fashion. The following speeches allude to the "War of the Theatres" (1601–1602) between the child and adult acting companies. 335 *aery*: nest. 336 *eyases*: young hawks. 336 *that cry … question*: whose shrill voices can be heard above all others.

most tyrannically° clapped for't: these are now the fashion, and so berattle° the common stages° (so they call them) that many wearing rapiers° are afraid of goose-quills,° and dare scarce come thither. 340

HAMLET   What, are they children? Who maintains 'em? How are they escoted°? Will they pursue the quality no longer than they can sing°? Will they not say afterwards if they should grow themselves to common players (as it is most like, if their means 345 are not better) their writers do them wrong, to make them exclaim against their own succession°?

ROSENCRANTZ   Faith, there has been much to-do on both sides: and the nation holds it no sin to tarre° them to controversy. There was for a while, no 350 money bid for argument,° unless the poet and the player went to cuffs in the question.°

HAMLET   Is't possible?

GUILDENSTERN   O there has been much throwing about of brains.

HAMLET   Do the boys carry it away°? 355

ROSENCRANTZ   Ay, that they do my lord, Hercules and his load too.°

HAMLET   It is not very strange, for my uncle is king of Denmark, and those that would make mows° at him while my father lived, give twenty, forty, fifty, a hundred ducats apiece for his picture in little.° 360 'Sblood,° there is something in this more than natural, if philosophy° could find it out.

A flourish for the Players.

GUILDENSTERN   There are the players.

HAMLET   Gentlemen, you are welcome to Elsinore: your hands, come then, th'appurtenance° of welcome 365 is fashion and ceremony; let me comply with you in this garb,° lest my extent° to the players, which I tell you must show fairly outwards, should more appear like entertainment than yours.° You are welcome: but my uncle-father, and aunt-mother, are deceived. 370

GUILDENSTERN   In what my dear lord?

HAMLET   I am but mad north-north-west; when the wind is southerly, I know a hawk from a handsaw.°

Enter Polonius.

POLONIUS   Well be with you, gentlemen.

HAMLET   Hark you Guildenstern, and you too, at 375

each ear a hearer: that great baby you see there is not yet out of his swaddling clouts.°

ROSENCRANTZ   Happily° he is the second time come to them, for they say an old man is twice a child.

HAMLET.   I will prophesy, he comes to tell me of the 380 players, mark it.—You say right sir, a Monday morning, 'twas then indeed.

POLONIUS   My lord, I have news to tell you.

HAMLET   My lord, I have news to tell you. When Roscius° was an actor in Rome— 385

POLONIUS   The actors are come hither, my lord.

HAMLET   Buz, buz.°

POLONIUS   Upon my honour.

HAMLET   Then came each actor on his ass—

POLONIUS   The best actors in the world, either for 390 tragedy, comedy, history, pastoral, pastoral-comical, historical-pastoral, tragical-historical, tragical-comical-historical-pastoral, scene individable,° or poem unlimited.° Seneca cannot be too heavy, nor Plautus° too light for the law of writ, and the 395 liberty:° these are the only men.

HAMLET   O Jephthah,° judge of Israel, what a treasure hadst thou.

POLONIUS   What a treasure had he, my lord?

HAMLET   Why
"One fair daughter and no more, 400
The which he lovèd passing° well."

POLONIUS   [*Aside.*] Still on my daughter.

HAMLET   Am I not i'th' right, old Jephthah?

POLONIUS   If you call me Jephthah my lord, I have a daughter that I love passing well. 405

HAMLET   Nay, that follows not.

POLONIUS   What follows then, my lord?

HAMLET   Why
"As by lot, God wot,"
and then you know 410
"It came to pass, as most like° it was:"
the first row° of the pious chanson will show you more, for look where my abridgement° comes.

Enter four or five Players.

You are welcome masters, welcome all. I am glad to see thee well: welcome, good friends. O my old 415 friend, why thy face is valanced° since I saw thee last, com'st thou to beard me in Denmark? What, my young lady° and mistress? by'r lady, your ladyship is nearer to heaven than when I saw you last, by the altitude of a chopine.° Pray God your voice, like a 420 piece of uncurrent° gold, be not cracked within the

---

337 *tyrannically:* strongly. 338 *berattle:* berate. *common stages:* public playhouses (the children's companies performed in private theatres). 339 *wearing rapiers:* (worn by gentlemen). 340 *goose-quills:* pens (of satirical dramatists who wrote for the children). 342 *escoted:* supported. 342–343 *pursue ... sing:* continue acting only until their voices change. 347 *succession:* inheritance. 349 *tarre:* provoke. 351 *bid for argument:* paid for the plot of a proposed play. 352 *went ... question:* came to blows on the subject. 355 *carry it away:* carry off the prize. 356 *Hercules ... too:* (Shakespeare's own company at the Globe Theatre, whose sign was Hercules carrying the globe of the world). 358 *mows:* mouths, grimaces. 360 *little:* a miniature. 361 *'Sblood:* by God's blood. 362 *philosophy:* science. 365 *appurtenance:* accessory. 366–367 *comply ... garb:* observe the formalities with you in this style. 367 *extent:* i.e., of welcome. 368–369 *should ... yours:* should appear more hospitable than yours. 373 *I know ... handsaw:* I can tell the difference between two things that are unlike ("hawk" = (1) bird of prey (2) mattock, pickaxe; "handsaw" = (1) hernshaw or heron bird (2) small saw).

377 *swaddling clouts:* strips of cloth binding a newborn baby. 378 *Happily:* perhaps. 385 *Roscius:* famous Roman actor. 387 *Buz, buz:* (contemptuous). 393 *scene individable:* play observing the unities (time, place, action). 394 *poem unlimited:* play ignoring the unities. 394–395 *Seneca, Plautus:* Roman writers of tragedy and comedy, respectively. 395–396 *law ... liberty:* "rules" regarding the unities and those exercising freedom from the unities. 397 *Jephthah:* (who was forced to sacrifice his only daughter because of a rash promise: Judges 11:29–39). 401 *passing:* surpassingly. 411 *like:* likely. 412 *row:* stanza. 413 *abridgement:* (the players who will cut short my song). 416 *valanced:* fringed with a beard. 418 *lady:* boy playing woman's role. 420 *chopine:* thick-soled shoe. 421 *uncurrent:* not legal tender.

ring.° Masters, you are all welcome: we'll e'en to't like French falconers, fly at any thing we see:° we'll have a speech straight. Come give us a taste of your quality: come, a passionate speech.   *425*

I. PLAYER   What speech, my good lord?

HAMLET   I heard thee speak me a speech once, but it was never acted, or if it was, not above once, for the play I remember pleased not the million, 'twas caviary to the general,° but it was (as I received it, and   *430* others, whose judgments in such matters cried in the top of mine°) an excellent play, well digested in the scenes, set down with as much modesty as cunning.° I remember one said there were no sallets° in the lines, to make the matter savoury, nor no matter in the   *435* phrase that might indict the author of° affection, but called it an honest method, as wholesome as sweet, and by very much more handsome than fine:° one speech in't I chiefly loved, 'twas Aeneas' tale to Dido, and thereabout of it especially where he speaks of   *440* Priam's slaughter.° If it live in your memory begin at this line, let me see, let me see:
          "The rugged Pyrrhus,° like th'Hyrcanian beast"°—
'tis not so: it begins with Pyrrhus—
          "The rugged Pyrrhus, he whose sable° arms,   *445*
Black as his purpose, did the night resemble
When he lay couched in th'ominous horse,°
Hath now this dread and black complexion smeared
With heraldy more dismal: head to foot
Now is he total gules,° horridly tricked°   *450*
With blood of fathers, mothers, daughters, sons,
Baked and impasted° with the parching° streets,
That lend a tyrannous and damnèd light
To their lord's murder. Roasted in wrath and fire,
And thus o'er-sizèd° with coagulate gore,   *455*
With eyes like carbuncles,° the hellish Pyrrhus
Old grandsire Priam seeks;"
So proceed you.

POLONIUS   'Fore God, my lord, well spoken, with good accent and good discretion.°   *460*

I. PLAYER.   "Anon he finds him,
Striking too short at Greeks, his antique° sword,
Rebellious to his arm, lies where it falls,
Repugnant to command;° unequal matched,
Pyrrhus at Priam drives, in rage strikes wide,   *465*
But with the whiff and wind of his fell° sword,
Th'unnervèd father falls: then senseless Ilium,°
Seeming to feel this blow, with flaming top

Stoops to his base; and with a hideous crash
Takes prisoner Pyrrhus' ear. For lo, his sword   *470*
Which was declining on the milky head
Of reverend Priam, seemed i'th'air to stick;
So as a painted° tyrant Pyrrhus stood,
And like a neutral to his will and matter,°
Did nothing: *475*
But as we often see, against° some storm,
A silence in the heavens, the rack° stand still,
The bold winds speechless, and the orb° below
As hush as death, anon the dreadful thunder
Doth rend the region, so after Pyrrhus' pause,   *480*
A rousèd vengeance sets him new awork,
And never did the Cyclops'° hammers fall
On Mars's armour, forged for proof eterne,°
With less remorse than Pyrrhus' bleeding sword
Now falls on Priam.   *485*
Out, out, thou strumpet Fortune: all you gods,
In general synod° take away her power,
Break all the spokes and fellies from her wheel,°
And bowl the round nave° down the hill of heaven
As low as to the fiends."°   *490*

POLONIUS   This is too long.

HAMLET   It shall to the barber's with your beard; prithee say on: he's for a jig, or a tale of bawdry, or he sleeps. Say on, come to Hecuba.

I. PLAYER.   "But who, ah woe, had seen the mobled° queen—"   *495*

HAMLET   "The mobled queen"?

POLONIUS   That's good, "mobled queen" is good.

I. PLAYER   "Run barefoot up and down, threat'ning the flames
With bissom rheum,° a clout° upon that head
Where late the diadem stood, and for a robe,   *500*
About her lank and all o'er-teemèd° loins,
A blanket in the alarm of fear caught up—
Who this had seen, with tongue in venom steeped,
'Gainst Fortune's state° would treason have pronounced;
But if the gods themselves did see her then,   *505*
When she saw Pyrrhus make malicious sport
In mincing with his sword her husband's limbs,
The instant burst of clamour that she made,
Unless things mortal move them not at all,
Would have made milch° the burning eyes of heaven,   *510*
And passion in the gods."

POLONIUS   Look whe'r° he has not turned° his colour, and has tears in's eyes, prithee no more.

HAMLET   'Tis well, I'll have thee speak out the rest of this soon. Good my lord, will you see the players   *515* well bestowed;° do you hear, let them be well used,

---

⁴²² *ring:* (1) ring enclosing the design on a gold coin (to crack it within the ring [to steal the gold] made it "uncurrent") (2) sound. ⁴²³ *fly … see:* undertake any difficulty. ⁴²⁹⁻⁴³⁰ *caviary … general:* spoke with caviar, too rich for the general public. ⁴³¹⁻⁴³² *cried … mine:* spoke with more authority than mine. ⁴³³ *modesty as cunning:* moderation as skill. ⁴³⁴ *sallets:* spicy bits. ⁴³⁶ *indict … of:* charge … with. ⁴³⁸ *handsome than fine:* dignified than finely wrought. ⁴⁴¹ *Priam's slaughter:* the murder of the King of Troy (as told in the Aeneid). ⁴⁴³ *Pyrrhus:* son of Achilles. *Hyrcanian beast:* tiger noted for fierceness. ⁴⁴⁵ *sable:* black. ⁴⁴⁷ *horse:* the hollow wooden horse used by the Greeks to enter Troy. ⁴⁵⁰ *gules:* red. *horridly tricked:* horribly decorated. ⁴⁵² *impasted:* coagulated. *parching:* (because the city was on fire). ⁴⁵⁵ *o'er-sized:* covered over. ⁴⁵⁶ *carbuncles:* red gems. ⁴⁶⁰ *discretion:* interpretation. ⁴⁶² *antique:* ancient. ⁴⁶⁴ *Repugnant to command:* refusing to obey its commander. ⁴⁶⁶ *fell:* savage. ⁴⁶⁷ *senseless Ilium:* unfeeling Troy.

⁴⁷³ *painted:* pictured. ⁴⁷⁴ *like … matter:* unmoved by either his purpose or its achievement. ⁴⁷⁶ *against:* before. ⁴⁷⁷ *rack:* clouds. ⁴⁷⁸ *orb:* earth. ⁴⁸² *Cyclops:* workmen of Vulcan, armorer of the gods. ⁴⁸³ *for proof eterne:* to be eternally invincible. ⁴⁸⁷ *synod:* assembly. ⁴⁸⁸ *fellies … wheel:* curved pieces of the rim of the wheel that fortune turns, representing a man's fortunes. ⁴⁸⁹ *nave:* hub. ⁴⁹⁰ *fiends:* i.e., of hell. ⁴⁹⁵ *mobled:* muffled in a scarf. ⁴⁹⁹ *bissom rheum:* blinding tears. *clout:* cloth. ⁵⁰¹ *o'er-teemed:* worn out by excessive childbearing. ⁵⁰⁴ *state:* reign. ⁵¹⁰ *milch:* milky, moist. ⁵¹² *whe'r:* whether. *turned:* changed. ⁵¹⁶ *bestowed:* lodged.

for they are the abstract° and brief chronicles° of the
time; after your death you were better have a bad
epitaph than their ill report while you live.

POLONIUS   My lord, I will use them according to their
   desert.°   520

HAMLET   God's bodkin° man, much better. Use every
   man after° his desert, and who shall 'scape whipping?
   Use them after you own honour and dignity: the less
   they deserve, the more merit is in your bounty. Take
   them in.

POLONIUS   Come sirs.   525

    Exeunt Polonius and Players.

HAMLET   Follow him friends, we'll hear a play tomorrow;
   [*Stops the First Player.*] dost thou hear me, old friend,
   can you play The Murder of Gonzago?

I. PLAYER   Ay my lord.

HAMLET   We'll ha't tomorrow night. You could for a   530
   need° study a speech of some dozen or sixteen lines,
   which I would set down and insert in't, could you not?

I. PLAYER   Ay my lord.

HAMLET   Very well, follow that lord, and look you mock
   him not.

    [*Exit First Player.*]

[*To Rosencrantz and Guildenstern.*] My good friends,
   I'll leave you till night, you are welcome to   535
   Elsinore.

ROSENCRANTZ   Good my lord.

    [*Exeunt Rosencrantz and Guildenstern.*]

HAMLET   Ay so, God bye to you, now I am alone.
   O what a rogue and peasant slave am I.
   Is it not monstrous that this player here,   540
   But in a fiction, in a dream of passion,°
   Could force his soul so to his own conceit°
   That from her working all his visage wanned,°
   Tears in his eyes, distraction in his aspect,
   A broken voice, and his whole function° suiting   545
   With forms° to his conceit; and all for nothing,
   For Hecuba!
   What's Hecuba to him, or he to Hecuba,
   That he should weep for her? what would he do,
   Had he the motive and the cue for passion   550
   That I have? he would drown the stage with tears,
   And cleave the general ear° with horrid speech,
   Make mad the guilty and appal the free,°
   Confound° the ignorant, and amaze indeed
   The very faculties of eyes and ears; yet I,   555
   A dull and muddy-mettled° rascal, peak°
   Like John-a-dreams,° unpregnant of° my cause,
   And can say nothing; no, not for a king,
   Upon whose property and most dear life,
   A damned defeat was made: am I a coward?   560

Who calls me villain, breaks my pate° across,
Plucks off my beard° and blows it in my face,
Tweaks me by the nose, gives me the lie i'th'throat
As deep as to the lungs,° who does me this?
Ha, 'swounds,° I should take it; for it cannot be   565
But I am pigeon-livered,° and lack gall
To make oppression bitter, or ere this
I should ha' fatted all the region kites°
With this slave's offal: bloody, bawdy villain,
Remorseless, treacherous, lecherous, kindless°
villain!   570
O vengeance!
Why what an ass am I, this is most brave,°
That I, the son of a dear father murdered,
Prompted to my revenge by heaven and hell,
Must like a whore unpack my heart with words,   575
And fall a-cursing like a very drab,°
A scullion,° fie upon't, foh.
About, my brains; hum, I have heard,
That guilty creatures sitting at a play,
Have by the very cunning of the scene   580
Been struck so to the soul, that presently°
They have proclaimed their malefactions:
For murder, though it have no tongue, will speak
With most miraculous organ: I'll have these
players
Play something like the murder of my father   585
Before mine uncle, I'll observe his looks,
I'll tent° him to the quick, if a' do blench°
I know my course. The spirit that I have seen
May be a devil, and the devil hath power
T'assume a pleasing shape, yea, and perhaps   590
Out of my weakness, and my melancholy,
As he is very potent with such spirits,
Abuses me to damn me; I'll have grounds
More relative than this: the play's the thing
Wherein I'll catch the conscience of the king.

                                                        Exit.

[Act 3]

Scene 1. [A room in the castle]

*Enter King, Queen, Polonius, Ophelia, Rosencrantz,
Guildenstern, and Lords.*

KING   And can you by no drift of conference°
   Get from him why he puts on this confusion,°
   Grating so harshly all his days of quiet
   With turbulent and dangerous lunacy?

ROSENCRANTZ   He does confess he feels himself
   distracted,   5

---

517 *abstract:* summary (noun). *brief chronicles:* history in brief.
520 *desert:* merit. 521*God's bodkin:* God's little body, the communion wafer (an oath). 522 *after:* according to. 530–531*for a need:* if
necessary. 541 *dream of passion:* portrayal of emotion. 542 *conceit:*
imagination. 543 *wanned:* grew pale. 545 *function:* bearing.
546 *With forms:* in appearance. 552 *general ear:* ears of all in the
audience. 553 *free:* innocent. 554 *Confound:* confuse. 556*muddy-
mettled:* dull-spirited. *peak:* pine, mope. 557 *John-a-dreams:* a
daydreaming fellow. *unpregnant of:* unstirred by.

561 *pate:* head. 562 *Plucks … beard:* (a way of giving insult).
563–564 *gives … lungs:* insults me by calling me a liar of the worst
kind (the lungs being deeper than the throat). 565 *'swounds:*
God's wounds. 566 *pigeon-livered:* meek and uncouraged.
568 *region kites:* vultures of the upper air. 570 *kindless:* unnatural.
572 *brave:* fine. 576 *drab:* whore. 577 *scullion:* kitchen wench.
816 *presently:* immediately. 587 *tent:* probe. *blench:* flinch. 1 *drift
of conference:* turn of conversation. 2 *puts … confusion:* seems so
distracted ("puts on" indicates the king's private suspicion that
Hamlet is playing mad).

But from what cause, a' will by no means speak.

GUILDENSTERN   Nor do we find him forward to be
    sounded,°
    But with a crafty madness keeps aloof
    When we would bring him on to some confession
    Of his true state.

QUEEN   Did he receive you well?   10

ROSENCRANTZ   Most like a gentleman.

GUILDENSTERN   But with much forcing of his
    disposition.°

ROSENCRANTZ   Niggard of question,° but of our
    demands
    Most free in his reply.

QUEEN   Did you assay° him
    To any pastime?   15

ROSENCRANTZ   Madam, it so fell out that certain
    players
    We o'er-raught° on the way: of these we told him,
    And there did seem in him a kind of joy
    To hear of it: they are here about the court,
    And as I think, they have already order   20
    This night to play before him.

POLONIUS   'Tis most true,
    And he beseeched me to entreat your majesties
    To hear and see the matter.°

KING   With all my heart, and it doth much content me
    To hear him so inclined.   25
    Good gentlemen, give him a further edge,°
    And drive his purpose into these delights.

ROSENCRANTZ   We shall my lord.
          Exeunt Rosencrantz and Guildenstern.

KING   Sweet Gertrude,
    leave us too,
    For we have closely° sent for Hamlet hither,
    That he, as 'twere by accident, may here   30
    Affront° Ophelia;
    Her father and myself, lawful espials,°
    Will so bestow° ourselves, that seeing unseen,
    We may of their encounter frankly° judge,
    And gather by him as he is behaved,   35
    If't be th'affliction of his love or no
    That thus he suffers for.

QUEEN   I shall obey you.
    And for your part Ophelia, I do wish
    That your good beauties be the happy cause
    Of Hamlet's wildness, so shall I hope your virtues   40
    Will bring him to his wonted° way again,
    To both your honours.

OPHELIA   Madam, I wish it may.
          [*Exit Queen.*]

POLONIUS   Ophelia, walk you here—Gracious,° so
    please you,
    We will bestow ourselves—read on this book,°

That show of such an exercise° may colour°   45
    Your loneliness; we are oft to blame in this,
    'Tis too much proved,° that with devotion's visage
    And pious action, we do sugar o'er
    The devil himself.

KING   [*Aside.*] O 'tis too true,°
    How smart a lash that speech doth give my
    conscience.   50
    The harlot's cheek, beautied with plast'ring art,
    Is not more ugly to° the thing that helps it,
    Than is my deed to my most painted word:°
    O heavy burden!

POLONIUS. I hear him coming, let's withdraw my lord.
    Exeunt.   55

    Enter Hamlet.

HAMLET   To be, or not to be, that is the question,
    Whether 'tis nobler in the mind° to suffer
    The slings and arrows of outrageous fortune,
    Or to take arms against a sea of troubles,
    And by opposing, end them: to die, to sleep,   60
    No more; and by a sleep, to say we end
    The heart-ache, and the thousand natural shocks
    That flesh is heir to; 'tis a consummation
    Devoutly to be wished. To die, to sleep,
    To sleep, perchance to dream, ay there's the rub,°   65
    For in that sleep of death what dreams may come
    When we have shuffled off this mortal coil°
    Must give us pause—there's the respect°
    That makes calamity of so long life:°
    For who would bear the whips and scorns of time,   70
    Th'oppressor's wrong, the proud man's
    contumely,°
    The pangs of disprized love, the law's delay,°
    The insolence of office,° and the spurns
    That patient merit of th'unworthy takes,
    When he himself might his quietus° make   75
    With a bare bodkin;° who would fardels° bear,
    To grunt and sweat under a weary life,
    But that the dread of something after death,
    The undiscovered° country, from whose bourn°
    No traveller returns, puzzles the will,   80
    And makes us rather bear those ills we have,
    Than fly to others that we know not of.
    Thus conscience does make cowards of us all,
    And thus the native hue° of resolution
    Is sicklied o'er with the pale cast of thought,   85
    And enterprises of great pitch° and moment,°

---

7 *forward … sounded:* disposed to be sounded out. 12 *forcing … disposition:* forcing himself to be so. 13 *Niggard of question:* unwilling to talk. 14 *assay:* tempt. 17 *o'er-raught:* overtook. 23 *matter:* i.e., of the play. 26 *give … edge:* encourage his keen interest. 29 *closely:* secretly. 31 *Affront:* meet face to face with. 32 *espials:* spies. 33 *bestow:* place. 34 *frankly:* freely. 41 *wonted:* customary. 43 *Gracious:* i.e., Your Grace. 44 *book:* (of prayer).

45 *exercise:* religious exercise. *colour:* make plausible. 47 *'Tis … proved:* it is all too apparent. 49 *'tis too true:* (the king's first indication that he is guilty). 52 *to:* compared to. 51-53 *harlot's cheek … word:* just as the harlot's cheek is even uglier by contrast to the makeup that tries to beautify it, so my deed is uglier by contrast to the hypocritical words under which I hide it. 57 *nobler in the mind:* best, according to "sovereign" reason. 65 *rub:* obstacle. 67 *mortal coil:* (1) turmoil of mortal life (2) coil of flesh encircling the body. 68 *respect:* consideration. 69 *makes calamity of so long life:* makes living long a calamity. 71 *contumely:* contempt. 72 *law's delay:* longevity of lawsuits. 73 *office:* officials. 75 *quietus:* settlement of his debt. 76 *bare bodkin:* mere dagger. *fardels:* burdens. 79 *undiscovered:* unknown, unexplored. *bourn:* boundary. 84 *native hue:* natural complexion. 86 *pitch:* height, excellence. *moment:* importance.

With this regard° their currents turn awry,°
And lose the name of action. Soft you now,
The fair Ophelia—Nymph, in thy orisons°
Be all my sins remembered.

OPHELIA   Good my lord,   90
How does your honour for this many a day°?

HAMLET   I humbly thank you: well, well, well.

OPHELIA   My lord, I have remembrances of yours
That I have longèd long to re-deliver,
I pray you now receive them.

HAMLET   No, not I,   95
I never gave you aught.

OPHELIA   My honoured lord, you know right well you
did,
And with them words of so sweet breath°
composed
As made the things more rich: their perfume lost,
Take these again, for to the noble mind   100
Rich gifts wax° poor when givers prove unkind.
There my lord.

HAMLET   Ha, ha, are you honest°?

OPHELIA   My lord.

HAMLET   Are you fair°?   105

OPHELIA   What means your lordship?

HAMLET   That if you be honest and fair, your honesty
should admit no discourse to your beauty.°

OPHELIA   Could beauty my lord, have better
commerce than with honesty?   110

HAMLET   Ay truly, for the power of beauty will sooner
transform honesty° from what it is to a bawd,° than
the force of honesty can translate beauty into his
likeness. This was sometime° a paradox, but now the
time gives it proof. I did love you once.   115

OPHELIA   Indeed my lord, you made me believe so.

HAMLET   You should not have believed me, for virtue
cannot so inoculate our old stock, but we shall relish
of it.° I loved you not.

OPHELIA   I was the more deceived.   120

HAMLET. Get thee to a nunnery,° why wouldst thou be a
breeder of sinners? I am myself indifferent honest,°
but yet I could accuse me of such things, that it were
better my mother had not borne me: I am very
proud, revengeful, ambitious, with more offences   125
at my beck,° than I have thoughts to put them in,
imagination to give them shape, or time to act them
in: what should such fellows as I do, crawling
between earth and heaven? we are arrant° knaves all,
believe none of us, go thy ways to a nunnery. Where's
your father?   130

OPHELIA   At home my lord.

HAMLET   Let the doors be shut upon him, that he may
play the fool no where but in's own house. Farewell.

OPHELIA   O help him, you sweet heavens.

HAMLET   If thou dost marry, I'll give thee this plague°   135
for thy dowry: be thou as chaste as ice, as pure as
snow, thou shalt not escape calumny; get thee to a
nunnery, go, farewell. Or if thou wilt needs marry,
marry a fool, for wise men know well enough what
monsters° you make of them: to a nunnery go, and
quickly too, farewell.   140

OPHELIA   O heavenly powers, restore him.

HAMLET   I have heard of your paintings too, well
enough. God hath given you one face, and you make
yourselves another: you jig,° you amble, and you
lisp,° you nick-name God's creatures, and make   145
your wantonness your ignorance;° go to, I'll no more
on't, it hath made me mad. I say we will have no moe°
marriage. Those that are married already, all but one
shall live, the rest shall keep as they are: to a nunnery, go.

Exit Hamlet.

OPHELIA   O what a noble mind is here o'erthrown!   150
The courtier's, soldier's, scholar's, eye, tongue, sword,
Th'expectancy and rose° of the fair state,
The glass° of fashion, and the mould of form,°
Th'observed of all observers, quite quite down,
And I of ladies most deject and wretched,   155
That sucked the honey of his music vows,
Now see that noble and most sovereign° reason
Like sweet bells jangled, out of tune and harsh,
That unmatched form and feature° of blown° youth
Blasted with ecstasy.° O woe is me,   160
T'have seen what I have seen, see what I see.

Enter King and Polonius.

KING   Love? his affections° do not that way tend,
Nor what he spake, though it lacked form a little,
Was not like madness. There's something in his soul
O'er which his melancholy sits on brood,   165
And I do doubt,° the hatch and the disclose°
Will be some danger; which for to prevent,
I have in quick determination
Thus set it down: he shall with speed to England,
For the demand of our neglected° tribute: 170
Haply° the seas, and countries different,
With variable° objects, shall expel
This something°-settled matter in his heart,
Whereon his brains still beating puts him thus
From fashion of himself.° What think you on't?   175

POLONIUS   It shall do well. But yet do I believe
The origin and commencement of his grief

---

45 *exercise:* religious exercise. *colour:* make plausible.   89 *orisons:*
prayers (referring to her prayer book).   91 *this … day:* all these
days.   98 *breath:* speech.   101 *wax:* grow.   103 *honest:* (1) chaste (2)
truthful.   105 *fair:* (1) beautiful (2) honorable.   107–108 *admit …
beauty:* (1) not allow communication with your beauty (2) not
allow your beauty to be used as a trap (Hamlet may have over-
heard the Polonius–Claudius plot or spotted their movement
behind the arras).   112 *honesty:* chastity. *bawd:* procurer, pimp.
114 *sometime:* once.   118 *inoculate … it:* change our sinful nature (as
a tree is grafted to improve it) but we will keep our old taste (as
will the fruit of the grafted tree).   121 *nunnery:* (1) cloister (2)
slang for "brothel" (cf. "bawd" above).   122 *indifferent honest:*
reasonably virtuous.   126 *beck:* beckoning.   129 *arrant:* absolute.

---

135 *plague:* curse.   139 *monsters:* horned cuckolds (men whose wives
were unfaithful).   144 *jig:* walk in a mincing way.   145 *lisp:* put on
affected speech.   145–146 *make your … ignorance:* excuse your
caprices as being due to ignorance.   147 *moe:* more.   152 *expectancy and rose:* fair hope.   153 *glass:* mirror. *mould of form:* model of
manners.   157 *sovereign:* (because it should rule).   159 *feature:*
external appearance.   159 *blown:* flowering.   160 *Blasted with ecstasy:* blighted by madness.   162 *affections:* emotions, afflictions.
166 *doubt:* fear.   165–166 *on brood … hatch … disclose:* (metaphor of a
hen sitting on eggs).   170 *neglected:* (being unpaid).   171 *Haply:*
perhaps.   172 *variable:* varied.   173 *something-:* somewhat-.
175 *fashion of himself:* his usual self.

Sprung from neglected° love. How now Ophelia?
You need not tell us what Lord Hamlet said,
We heard it all. My lord, do as you please,   *180*
But if you hold it fit, after the play,
Let his queen-mother all alone entreat him
To show his grief, let her be round° with him,
And I'll be placed (so please you) in the ear
Of° all their conference. If she find° him not,   *185*
To England send him: or confine him where
Your wisdom best shall think.

KING   It shall be so,
Madness in great ones must not unwatched go.

                                                                Exeunt.

Scene 2. [A hall in the castle]

Enter Hamlet and three of the Players.

HAMLET   Speak the speech° I pray you as I pronounced it
to you, trippingly on the tongue, but if you mouth it°
as many of your players do, I had as lief the town-
crier spoke my lines. Nor do not saw the air too
much with your hand thus, but use all gently, for   *5*
in the very torrent, tempest, and as I may say,
whirlwind of your passion, you must acquire and beget°
a temperance that may give it smoothness. O it offends
me to the soul, to hear a robustious° periwig-pated°
fellow tear a passion to tatters, to very rags, to split   *10*
the ears of the groundlings,° who for the most part are
capable of° nothing but inexplicable dumb shows° and
noise: I would have such a fellow whipped for
o'erdoing Termagant:° it out-herods Herod,° pray
you avoid it.

I. PLAYER   I warrant your honour.   *15*

HAMLET   Be not too tame neither, but let your own
discretion be your tutor, suit the action to the word,
the word to the action, with this special observance,
that you o'erstep not the modesty° of nature: for any
thing so o'erdone, is from° the purpose of playing,   *20*
whose end both at the first, and now, was and is, to
hold as 'twere the mirror up to nature, to show virtue
her own feature, scorn° her own image, and the very
age and body of the time his form and pressure.°
Now this overdone, or come tardy off,° though it   *25*
make the unskilful° laugh, cannot but make the
judicious grieve, the censure of the which one,° must
in your allowance° o'erweigh a whole theatre of
others. O there be players that I have seen play, and
heard others praise, and that highly (not to speak it   *30*

profanely) that neither having th'accent of
Christians, nor the gait of Christian, pagan, nor man,
have so strutted and bellowed, that I have thought
some of nature's journeymen° had made men, and
not made them well, they imitated humanity so
abominably.   *35*

I. PLAYER   I hope we have reformed that
indifferently° with us, sir.

HAMLET   O reform it altogether, and let those that play
your clowns speak no more than is set down for
them,° for there be of them that will themselves
laugh, to set on some quantity of barren°   *40*
spectators to laugh too, though in the meantime,
some necessary question° of the play be then to be
considered: that's villainous, and shows a most pitiful
ambition in the fool that uses it. Go make youeready.

                                                Exeunt Players.

Enter Polonius, Rosencrantz, and Guildenstern.

How now my lord, will the king hear this piece of
work?   *45*

POLONIUS   And the queen too, and that presently.

HAMLET   Bid the players make haste.   *Exit Polonius.*
Will you two help to hasten them?

ROSENCRANTZ   Ay my lord.   *Exeunt they two.*

HAMLET   What ho, Horatio!

Enter Horatio.

HORATIO   Here sweet lord, at your service.

HAMLET   Horatio, thou art e'en as just° a man
As e'er my conversation coped withal.°   *50*

HORATIO   O my dear lord.

HAMLET   Nay, do not think I flatter,
For what advancement may I hope from thee,
That no revenue hast but thy good spirits
To feed and clothe thee? Why should the poor be
flattered?
No, let the candied° tongue lick° absurd pomp,   *55*
And crook the pregnant° hinges of the knee
Where thrift may follow fawning.° Dost thou hear,
Since my dear soul was mistress of her choice,
And could of men distinguish her election,°
Sh'hath sealed° thee for herself, for thou hast been   *60*
As one in suff'ring all that suffers nothing,
A man that Fortune's buffets° and rewards
Hast ta'en with equal thanks; and blest are those
Whose blood° and judgment are so well co-mingled,
That they are not a pipe for Fortune's finger   *65*
To sound what stop° she please:° give me that man
That is not passion's slave, and I will wear him
In my heart's core, ay in my heart of heart,

---

178 neglected: unrequited.   *183 round:* direct.   *184–185 in the ear Of:* so as to overhear.   *185 find:* find out.   *1 the speech:* i.e., that Hamlet has inserted.   *2 mouth it:* deliver it slowly and overdramatically.   *7 acquire and beget:* achieve for yourself and instill in other actors.   *9 robustious:* boisterous.   *9 periwig-pated:* wig-wearing.   *11 groundlings:* audience who paid least and stood on the ground floor.   *12 capable of:* able to understand. *dumb shows:* pantomimed synopses of the action to follow (as below).   *14 Termagant:* violent, ranting character in the guild or mystery plays. *out-herods Herod:* outdoes even Herod, King of Judea (who commanded the slaughter of the innocents and who was a ranting tyrant in the mystery plays).   *19 modesty:* moderation.   *20 from:* away from.   *23 scorn:* that which should be scorned.   *24 age ... pressure:* shape of the times in its accurate impression.   *25 come tardy off:* understated, underdone.   *26 unskilful:* unsophisticated.   *27 one:* the judicious.   *28 allowance:* estimation.

34 journeymen: artisans working for others and not yet masters of their trades.   *36 indifferently:* reasonably well.   *38-39 speak no more ... them:* stick to their lines.   *40 barren:* witless.   *42 question:* dialogue.   *49 just:* well balanced.   *50 coped withal:* had to do with.   *55-57 candied ... fawning:* (metaphor of a dog licking and fawning for candy).   *55 candied:* flattering. *lick:* pay court to.   *56-57 crook ... fawning:* obsequiously kneel when personal profit may ensue.   *56 pregnant:* quick in motion.   *59 election:* choice.   *60 sealed:* confirmed.   *62 buffets:* blows.   *64 blood:* passions.   *66 sound ... please:* play whatever tune she likes. *stop:* finger hole in wind instrument for varying the sound.

As I do thee. Something too much of this.
There is a play tonight before the king,   70
One scene of it comes near the circumstance
Which I have told thee of my father's death.
I prithee when thou seest that act afoot,
Even with the very comment° of thy soul
Observe my uncle: if his occulted° guilt   75
Do not itself unkennel° in one speech,
It is a damnèd ghost° that we have seen,
And my imaginations are as foul
As Vulcan's stithy;° give him heedful note,
For I mine eyes will rivet to his face,   80
And after we will both our judgments join
In censure of his seeming.°

HORATIO   Well my lord,
If a' steal aught the whilst this play is playing,
And 'scape detecting, I will pay° the theft.

Sound a flourish.

HAMLET   They are coming to the play. I must be idle,°   85
Get you a place.

*Enter Trumpets and Kettledrums, King, Queen, Polonius,
Ophelia, Rosencrantz, Guildenstern, and other Lords attendant,
with his Guard carrying torches. Danish March.*

KING   How fares° our cousin Hamlet?
HAMLET   Excellent i'faith, of the chameleon's dish: I eat the
    air,° promise-crammed, you cannot feed capons so.°
KING   I have nothing with° this answer Hamlet, these
    words are not mine.°   90
HAMLET   No, nor mine now. [*To Polonius.*] My lord,
    you played once i'th'university you say?
POLONIUS   That did I my lord, and was accounted a
    good actor.
HAMLET   What did you enact?   95
POLONIUS   I did enact Julius Caesar, I was killed
    i'th'Capitol, Brutus killed me.
HAMLET   It was a brute part of him to kill so capital a
    calf there. Be the players ready?
ROSENCRANTZ   Ay my lord, they stay upon your
    patience.°   100
QUEEN   Come hither my dear Hamlet, sit by me.
HAMLET   No, good mother, here's metal more attractive.°
POLONIUS   [*To the King.*] O ho, do you mark that?
HAMLET   Lady, shall I lie in your lap?
OPHELIA   No my lord.   105
HAMLET   I mean, my head upon your lap?
OPHELIA   Ay my lord.
HAMLET   Do you think I meant country° matters?

OPHELIA   I think nothing my lord.
HAMLET   That's a fair thought to lie between maids'
    legs.   110
OPHELIA   What is, my lord?
HAMLET   Nothing.
OPHELIA   You are merry my lord.
HAMLET   Who, I?
OPHELIA   Ay my lord.   115
HAMLET   O God, your only jig-maker: what should a
    man do but be merry, for look you how cheerfully my
    mother looks, and my father died within's two hours.
OPHELIA   Nay, 'tis twice two months my lord.
HAMLET   So long? Nay then let the devil wear black,   120
    for I'll have a suit of sables;° O heavens, die two
    months ago, and not forgotten yet? Then there's
    hope a great man's memory may outlive his life half a
    year, but by'r lady° a' must build churches then, or
    else shall a' suffer not thinking on,° with the   125
    hobby-horse,° whose epitaph is "For O, for O, the
    hobby-horse is forgot."

*The trumpets sound. The Dumb Show° follows. Enter a King and
a Queen, very lovingly, the Queen embracing him, and he her. She
kneels and makes show of protestation unto him. He takes her up,
and declines his head upon her neck. He lies him down upon a bank
of flowers; she seeing him asleep leaves him: anon comes in another man, takes off his crown, kisses it, pours poison in the sleeper's
ears, and leaves him: the Queen returns, finds the King dead, and
makes passionate action. The poisoner with some three or four
mutes° comes in again, seeming to condole with her. The dead body
is carried away. The poisoner wooes the Queen with gifts: she seems
harsh and unwilling awhile, but in the end accepts his love.*

Exeunt.

OPHELIA   What means this, my lord?
HAMLET   Marry, this is miching mallecho,° it means
    mischief.
OPHELIA   Belike this show imports the argument° of the
    play.

Enter Prologue.

HAMLET   We shall know by this fellow: the players   130
    cannot keep counsel,° they'll tell all.
OPHELIA   Will a' tell us what this show meant?
HAMLET   Ay, or any show that you will show him. Be not
    you ashamed to show, he'll not shame to tell you
    what it means.   135
OPHELIA   You are naught,° you are naught, I'll mark
    the play.
PROLOGUE.   For us and for our tragedy,
    Here stooping to your clemency,
    We beg your hearing patiently.   [*Exit.*]
HAMLET   Is this a prologue, or the posy° of a ring?   140

---

74 *very comment:* acutest observation.   75 *occulted:* hidden.
76 *unkennel:* force from hiding.   77 *damnèd ghost:* devil (not the
ghost of my father).   79 *Vulcan's stithy:* the forge of the black-
smith of the gods.   82 *censure … seeming:* (1) judgment of his
appearance (2) disapproval of his pretending.   84 *pay:* i.e., for.
85 *be idle:* act mad.   87 *fares:* does, but Hamlet takes it to mean
"eats" or "dines."   88 *eat the air:* the chamelion supposedly ate air,
but Hamlet also puns on "heir."   89 *you cannot … so:* (1) even a
capon cannot feed on air and your promises (2) like a capon
stuffed with food before being killed, I am stuffed (fed up) with
your promises.   90 *nothing with:* nothing to do with.   91 *not mine:*
not in answer to my question.   100 *stay … patience:* await your
permission.   102 *metal more attractive:* (1) iron more magnetic (2)
stuff ("mettle") more beautiful.   108 *country:* rustic, sexual (with a
pun on a slang word for the female sexual organ).

---

121 *sables:* (1) rich fur (2) black mourning garb.   124 *by'r lady:* by
Our Lady (the Virgin Mary).   125 *not thinking on:* being forgotten.   126 *hobby-horse:* (1) character in the May games (2) slang for
"prostitute."   stage direction: *Dumb Show:* pantomimed synop-
sis of the action to follow.   stage direction: *mutes:* actors without speaking parts.   128 *miching mallecho:* skulking mischief.
129 *imports the argument:* signifies the plot.   131 *counsel:* a secret.
136 *naught:* naughty, lewd.   140 *posy:* motto (engraved in a ring).

OPHELIA   'Tis brief, my lord.

HAMLET   As woman's love.

Enter Player King and Queen.

PLAYER KING   Full thirty times hath Phoebus' cart° gone round

Neptune's salt wash,° and Tellus' orbèd ground,°

And thirty dozen moons with borrowed sheen   145

About the world have times twelve thirties been,

Since love our hearts, and Hymen° did our hands

Unite commutual,° in most sacred bands.

PLAYER QUEEN   So many journeys may the sun and moon

Make us again count o'er ere love be done,   150

But woe is me, you are so sick of late,

So far from cheer, and from your former state,

That I distrust you:° yet though I distrust,

Discomfort you, my lord, it nothing must.

For women fear too much, even as they love,   155

And women's fear and love hold quantity,°

In neither aught, or in extremity:°

Now what my love is, proof° hath made you know,

And as my love is sized, my fear is so.

Where love is great, the littlest doubts are fear,   160

Where little fears grow great, great love grows there.

PLAYER KING   Faith, I must leave thee love, and shortly too,

My operant° powers their functions leave° to do,

And thou shalt live in this fair world behind,

Honoured, beloved, and haply° one as kind   165

For husband shalt thou—

PLAYER QUEEN   O confound the rest:

Such love must needs be treason in my breast.

In second husband let me be accurst,

None wed the second, but who killed the first.

HAMLET   [*Aside.*] That's wormwood,° wormwood.   170

PLAYER QUEEN   The instances° that second marriage move°

Are base respects of thrift,° but none of love.

A second time I kill my husband dead,

When second husband kisses me in bed.

PLAYER KING   I do believe you think what now you speak,   175

But what we do determine, oft we break:

Purpose is but the slave to memory,

Of violent birth but poor validity:°

Which now like fruit unripe sticks on the tree,

But fall unshaken when they mellow be.   180

Most necessary 'tis that we forget

To pay ourselves what to ourselves is debt:°

What to ourselves in passion we propose,

The passion ending, doth the purpose lose.

The violence of either grief or joy   185

Their own enactures° with themselves destroy:

Where joy most revels, grief doth most lament;

Grief joys, joy grieves, on slender accident.

This world is not for aye,° nor 'tis not strange

That even our loves should with our fortunes change: 190

For 'tis a question left us yet to prove,

Whether love lead fortune, or else fortune love.°

The great man down, you mark his favourite flies,

The poor advanced, makes friends of enemies:

And hitherto doth love on fortune tend,   195

For who not needs, shall never lack a friend,

And who in want a hollow friend doth try,

Directly seasons him° his enemy.

But orderly to end where I begun,

Our wills and fates do so contrary run,   200

That our devices still° are overthrown,

Our thoughts are ours, their ends none of our own.

So think thou wilt no second husband wed,

But die thy thoughts when thy first lord is dead.

PLAYER QUEEN   Nor earth to me give food, nor heaven light,   205

Sport and repose lock from me day and night,

To desperation turn my trust and hope,

An anchor's° cheer in prison be my scope,

Each opposite that blanks° the face of joy,

Meet what I would have well, and it destroy,   210

Both here and hence° pursue me lasting strife,

If once a widow, ever I be wife.

HAMLET   If she should break it now.

PLAYER KING   'Tis deeply sworn: sweet, leave me here awhile,

My spirits grow dull, and fain° I would beguile   215

The tedious day with sleep.   *Sleeps.*

PLAYER QUEEN   Sleep rock thy brain.

And never come mischance between us twain.

          Exit.

HAMLET   Madam, how like you this play?

QUEEN   The lady doth protest too much methinks.

HAMLET   O but she'll keep her word.   220

KING   Have you heard the argument°? Is there no offence in't?

HAMLET   No, no, they do but jest, poison in jest, no offence i'th'world.

KING   What do you call the play?

HAMLET   The Mouse-trap. Marry, how? Tropically:°

this play is the image of a murder done in   225

Vienna: Gonzago is the duke's name, his wife

Baptista, you shall see anon, 'tis a knavish piece of

work, but what of that? Your majesty, and we

---

¹⁴³ *Phoebus' cart:* chariot of the sun.   ¹⁴⁴ *wash:* sea. *Tellus' … ground:* the earth (Tellus was a Roman earth goddess).
¹⁴⁷ *Hymen:* Roman god of marriage.   ¹⁴⁸ *commutual:* mutually.
¹⁵³ *distrust you:* am worried about you.   ¹⁵⁶ *quantity:* proportion.
¹⁵⁷ *In neither … extremity:* their love and fear are either absent or excessive.   ¹⁵⁸ *proof:* experience.   ¹⁶³ *operant:* vital. *leave:* cease.
¹⁶⁵ *haply:* perhaps.   ¹⁷⁰ *wormwood:* bitter (like the herb).
¹⁷¹ *instances:* causes. *move:* motivate.   ¹⁷² *respects of thrift:* consideration of profit.   ¹⁷⁸ *validity:* strength.   ¹⁸¹⁻¹⁸² *Most … debt:* we are easy creditors to ourselves and forget our former promises (debts).

¹⁸⁶ *enactures:* fulfillments.   ¹⁸⁹ *aye:* ever.   ¹⁹² *fortune love:* fortune lead love.   ¹⁹⁸ *seasons him:* causes him to become.   ²⁰¹ *devices still:* plans always.   ²⁰⁸ *anchor's:* hermit's.   ²⁰⁹ *opposite that blanks:* contrary event that pales.   ²¹¹ *here and hence:* in this world and the next.   ²¹⁵ *fain:* gladly.   ²²¹ *argument:* plot.   ²²⁵ *Tropically:* figuratively.

that have free° souls, it touches us not: let the galled
jade winch,° our withers are unwrung.°   230

Enter Lucianus.

This is one Lucianus, nephew to the king.
OPHELIA   You are as good as a chorus,° my lord.
HAMLET   I could interpret between you and your love,
if I could see the puppets dallying.
OPHELIA   You are keen my lord, you are keen.°   235
HAMLET   It would cost you a groaning to take off
mine edge.
OPHELIA   Still better and worse.°
HAMLET   So you mistake° your husbands. Begin,
murderer. Pox,° leave thy damnable faces° and begin.
Come, the croaking raven doth bellow for
revenge.   240
LUCIANUS   Thoughts black, hands apt, drugs fit, and
time agreeing,
Confederate season, else no creature seeing,°
Thou mixture rank, of midnight weeds collected,
With Hecate's° ban° thrice blasted, thrice infected,
Thy natural magic, and dire property,   245
On wholesome° life usurps immediately.
                              Pours the poison in his ears.
HAMLET   A' poisons him i'th'garden for's estate, his
name's Gonzago, the story is extant, and written in
very choice Italian, you shall see anon how the
murderer gets the love of Gonzago's wife.   250
OPHELIA   The king rises.
HAMLET   What, frighted with false fire°?
QUEEN   How fares my lord?
POLONIUS   Give o'er the play.
KING   Give me some light. Away!   255
ALL   Lights, lights, lights!
                  Exeunt all but Hamlet and Horatio.
HAMLET   Why, let the stricken deer go weep,
The hart ungallèd° play,°
For some must watch while some must sleep,
Thus runs the world away.   260
Would not this° sir, and a forest of feathers,° if the
rest of my fortunes turn Turk with° me, with two
Provincial roses° on my razed° shoes, get me a
fellowship° in a cry° of players?
HORATIO   Half a share.°
HAMLET   A whole one, I.   265
For thou dost know, O Damon° dear,

This realm dismantled was
Of Jove° himself, and now reigns here
A very very—pajock.°
HORATIO   You might have rhymed.°   270
HAMLET   O good Horatio, I'll take the ghost's word
for a thousand pound. Didst perceive?
HORATIO   Very well my lord.
HAMLET   Upon the talk of the poisoning?
HORATIO   I did very well note him.   275

Enter Rosencrantz and Guildenstern.

HAMLET   Ah ha, come, some music. Come, the
recorders.°
For if the king like not the comedy,
Why then belike he likes it not, perdy.°
Come, some music.
GUILDENSTERN   Good my lord, vouchsafe me a word
with you.   280
HAMLET   Sir, a whole history.
GUILDENSTERN   The king, sir—
HAMLET   Ay sir, what of him?
GUILDENSTERN   Is in his retirement, marvellous
distempered.
HAMLET   With drink sir?   285
GUILDENSTERN   No my lord, with choler.°
HAMLET   Your wisdom should show itself more richer to
signify this to the doctor: for, for me to put him to
his purgation,° would perhaps plunge him into more
choler.
GUILDENSTERN   Good my lord, put your discourse   290
into some frame,° and start not so wildly from my
affair.
HAMLET   I am tame sir, pronounce.
GUILDENSTERN   The queen your mother, in most
great affliction of spirit, hath sent me to you.
HAMLET   You are welcome.   295
GUILDENSTERN   Nay good my lord, this courtesy is not
of the right breed.° If it shall please you to make me a
wholesome° answer, I will do your mother's
commandment: if not, your pardon° and my return
shall be the end of my business.
HAMLET   Sir I cannot.   300
ROSENCRANTZ   What, my lord?
HAMLET   Make you a wholesome answer: my wit's
diseased. But sir, such answer as I can make, you shall
command, or rather as you say, my mother: therefore
no more, but to the matter. My mother you say.   305
ROSENCRANTZ   Then thus she says, your behaviour
hath struck her into amazement and admiration.°
HAMLET   O wonderful son that can so 'stonish a
mother. But is there no sequel at the heels of this
mother's admiration? Impart.
ROSENCRANTZ   She desires to speak with you in her
closet° ere you go to bed.   310

---

229 *free:* innocent.   229-230 *galled jade winch:* chafed old horse wince
(from its sores).   230 *withers are unwrung:* (1) shoulders are
unchafed (2) consciences are clear.   232 *chorus:* actor who introduced the action.   235 *keen:* (1) sharp (Ophelia's meaning) (2)
sexually excited (Hamlet's interpretation).   237 *better and worse:*
better wit but a worse meaning, with a pun on "better" and "bitter."   238 *mistake:* mis-take. *Pox:* a plague on it.   239 *faces:* exaggerated facial expressions.   242 *Confederate ... seeing:* no one seeing
me except time, my confederate.   244 *Hecate:* goddess of witchcraft. *ban:* evil spell.   246 *wholesome:* healthy.   252 *false fire:* discharge of blanks (not gunpowder).   257-258 *deer ... play:* (the belief
that a wounded deer wept, abandoned by the others).   258 *ungal-
lèd:* unhurt.   261 *this:* i.e., sample (of my theatrical talent). *feathers:* plumes (worn by actors).   262 *turn Turk with:* cruelly turn
against.   263 *Provincial roses:* rosettes named for Provins, France.
razed: slashed, decorated with cutouts.   264 *fellowship:* partner-
ship. *cry:* pack, troupe.   264 *share:* divisions of profits among
members of a theatrical production company.   266 *Damon:* legendary ideal friend to Pythias.

268 *Jove:* (Hamlet's father).   269 *pajock:* peacock (associated with
lechery).   270 *rhymed:* (used "ass" instead of "pajock").
276 *recorders:* soft-toned woodwind instruments, similar to flutes.
278 *perdy:* by God (*par dieu*).   286 *choler:* anger.   288 *purgation:* (1)
purging of excessive bile (2) judicial investigations (3) purgatory.   290 *frame:* order.   297 *breed:* (1) species (2) manners.
298 *wholesome:* reasonable.   299 *pardon:* permission to depart.
307 *admiration:* wonder.   310 *closet:* private room, bedroom.

HAMLET   We shall obey, were she ten times our
    mother. Have you any further trade with us?
ROSENCRANTZ   My lord, you once did love me.
HAMLET   And do still, by these pickers and stealers.°   315
ROSENCRANTZ   Good my lord, what is your cause of
    distemper? You do surely bar the door upon your
    own liberty, if you deny your griefs to your friend.°
HAMLET   Sir, I lack advancement.
ROSENCRANTZ   How can that be, when you have the
    voice° of the king himself for your succession   320
    in Denmark?
HAMLET   Ay sir, but 'while the grass grows'°—the
    proverb is something musty.°

Enter the Players with recorders.

    O the recorders, let me see one. To withdraw°
    with you, why do you go about to recover the wind of
    me,° as if you would drive me into a toil°?   325
GUILDENSTERN   O my lord, if my duty be too bold,
    my love is too unmannerly.°
HAMLET   I do not well understand that. Will you play
    upon this pipe°?   330
GUILDENSTERN   My lord I cannot.
HAMLET   I pray you.
GUILDENSTERN   Believe me. I cannot.
HAMLET   I do beseech you.
GUILDENSTERN   I know no touch of it° my lord.   335
HAMLET   It is as easy as lying; govern these ventages°
    with your fingers and thumb, give it breath with your
    mouth, and it will discourse most eloquent music.
    Look you, these are the stops.
GUILDENSTERN   But these cannot I command to any
    utt'rance of harmony, I have not the skill.   340
HAMLET   Why look you now how unworthy a thing
    you make of me: you would play upon me, you would
    seem to know my stops, you would pluck out the
    heart of my mystery, you would sound me from my
    lowest note to the top of my compass:° and there   345
    is much music, excellent voice in this little organ,°
    yet cannot you make it speak. 'Sblood, do you think I
    am easier to be played on than a pipe? Call me what
    instrument you will, though you can fret° me, you
    cannot play upon me.   350

Enter Polonius.

    God bless you sir.
POLONIUS   My lord, the queen would speak with you,
    and presently.
HAMLET   Do you see yonder cloud that's almost in
    shape of a camel?
POLONIUS   By th'mass and 'tis, like a camel indeed.

HAMLET   Methinks it is like a weasel.   355
POLONIUS   It is backed like a weasel.
HAMLET   Or like a whale?
POLONIUS   Very like a whale.
HAMLET   Then I will come to my mother by and by.°
    [*Aside.*] They fool me to the top of my bent.°   360
    I will come by and by.
POLONIUS   I will say so.   *Exit.*
HAMLET   "By and by" is easily said.
    Leave me, friends.   [*Exeunt all but Hamlet.*]
    'Tis now the very witching time of night.   365
    When churchyards yawn,° and hell itself breathes
    out
    Contagion° to this world: now could I drink hot
    blood,
    And do such bitter business as the day
    Would quake to look on: soft, now to my
    mother—
    O heart, lose not thy nature,° let not ever   370
    The soul of Nero° enter this firm bosom,
    Let me be cruel, not unnatural.
    I will speak daggers to her, but use none:
    My tongue and soul in this be hypocrites,°
    How in my words somever she be shent,°   375
    To give them seals,° never my soul consent.   *Exit.*

Scene 3. [A room in the castle]

Enter King, Rosencrantz, and Guildenstern.

KING   I like him not, nor stands it safe with us
    To let his madness range. Therefore prepare you,
    I your commission will forthwith dispatch,°
    And he to England shall along with you:
    The terms of our estate° may not endure   5
    Hazard so near's° as doth hourly grow
    Out of his brows.°
GUILDENSTERN   We will ourselves provide:°
    Most holy and religious fear it is
    To keep those many many bodies safe
    That live and feed upon your majesty.   10
ROSENCRANTZ   The single and peculiar° life is bound
    With all the strength and armour of the mind
    To keep itself from noyance,° but much more
    That spirit, upon whose weal° depends and rests
    The lives of many; the cess° of majesty   15
    Dies not alone, but like a gulf° doth draw
    What's near it, with it. O 'tis a massy wheel
    Fixed on the summit of the highest mount,
    To whose huge spokes, ten thousand lesser things
    Are mortised° and adjoined, which when it falls,   20
    Each small annexment, petty consequence,

---

³¹⁵*pickers and stealers:* hands (from the prayer, "Keep my hands from picking and stealing"). ³¹⁷⁻³¹⁸*deny … friend:* refuse to let your friend know the cause of your suffering. ³²⁰*voice:* vote. ³²²*while … grows:* (the proverb ends: "the horse starves"). ³²³*something musty:* somewhat too old and trite (to finish). ³²⁴*withdraw:* speak privately. ³²⁵*recover … me:* drive me toward the wind, as with a prey, to avoid its scenting the hunter. ³²⁶*toil:* snare. ³²⁷⁻³²⁸*is too unmannerly:* makes me forget my good manners. ³³⁰*pipe:* recorder. ³³⁵*know … it:* have no skill at fingering it. ³³⁶*ventages:* holes, stops. ³⁴⁵*compass:* range. ³⁴⁶*organ:* musical instrument. ³⁴⁹*fret:* (1) irritate (2) play an instrument that has "frets" or bars to guide the fingering.

³⁵⁹*by and by:* very soon. ³⁶⁰*fool me … bent:* force me to play the fool to my utmost. ³⁶⁶*churchyards yawn:* graves open. ³⁶⁷*Contagion:* (1) evil (2) diseases. ³⁷⁰*nature:* natural affection. ³⁷¹*Nero:* (who killed his mother). ³⁷⁴*My tongue … hypocrites:* I will speak cruelly but intend no harm. ³⁷⁵*shent:* chastised. ³⁷⁶*give them seals:* confirm them with action (as a legal "deed" is confirmed with a "seal"). ³*forthwith dispatch:* immediately have prepared. ⁵*terms … estate:* circumstances of my royal office. ⁶*near's:* near us. ⁷*brows:* effronteries. *provide:* prepare. ¹¹*peculiar:* individual. ¹³*noyance:* harm. ¹⁴*weal:* well-being. ¹⁵*cess:* cessation, death. ¹⁶*gulf:* whirlpool. ²⁰*mortised:* securely fitted.

Attends° the boist'rous ruin. Never alone
Did the king sigh, but with a general groan.
KING   Arm° you I pray you, to this speedy voyage,
    For we will fetters put about this fear   25
    Which now goes too free-footed.
ROSENCRANTZ   We will haste us.

Exeunt [Rosencrantz and Guildenstern.]

Enter Polonius.

POLONIUS   My lord, he's going to his mother's closet:
    Behind the arras I'll convey myself
    To hear the process.° I'll warrant she'll tax him
      home,
    And as you said, and wisely was it said,   30
    'Tis meet° that some more audience than a
      mother,
    Since nature makes them partial, should o'erhear
    The speech of vantage;° fare you well my liege,°
    I'll call upon you ere you go to bed,
    And tell you what I know.
KING   Thanks, dear my lord.

                    Exit [Polonius.] 35
    O my offence is rank, it smells to heaven,
    It hath the primal eldest curse° upon't,
    A brother's murder. Pray can I not,
    Though inclination be as sharp as will:°
    My stronger guilt defeats my strong intent,   40
    And like a man to double business bound,
    I stand in pause where I shall first begin,
    And both neglect; what if this cursèd hand
    Were thicker than itself with brother's blood,
    Is there not rain enough in the sweet heavens   45
    To wash it white as snow? Whereto serves mercy
    But to confront the visage of offence°?
    And what's in prayer but this two-fold force,
    To be forestallèd° ere we come to fall,
    Or pardoned being down? Then I'll look up,   50
    My fault is past. But O what form of prayer
    Can serve my turn? "Forgive me my foul murder":
    That cannot be, since I am still possessed
    Of those effects° for which I did the murder:
    My crown, mine own ambition, and my queen.   55
    May one be pardoned and retain th'offence?
    In the corrupted currents of this world,
    Offence's gilded hand may shove by justice,
    And oft 'tis seen the wicked prize itself
    Buys out the law;° but 'tis not so above,   60
    There is no shuffling,° there the action lies
    In his true nature,° and we ourselves compelled
    Even to the teeth and forehead of our faults°
    To give in evidence. What then? What rests°?

Try what repentance can. What can it not?   65
    Yet what can it, when one can not repent?
    O wretched state? O bosom black as death!
    O limèd soul, that struggling to be free,
    Art more engaged;° help, angels, make assay:°
    Bow stubborn knees, and heart with strings of
      steel,   70
    Be soft as sinews of the new-born babe,
    All may be well.   *[He kneels.]*

Enter Hamlet.

HAMLET   Now might I do it pat,° now a' is a-praying,
    And now I'll do't, *[Draws his sword.]* and so a' goes
      to heaven,
    And so am I revenged: that would be scanned:°   75
    A villain kills my father, and for that,
    I his sole son, do this same villain send
    To heaven.
    Why, this is hire and salary, not revenge.
    A' took my father grossly,° full of bread,°   80
    With all his crimes° broad blown,° as flush° as
      May,
    And how his audit° stands who knows save heaven,
    But in our circumstance and course of thought,
    'Tis heavy° with him: and am I then revenged
    To take him in the purging of his soul,   85
    when he is fit and seasoned° for his passage?
    No.   *[Sheathes his sword.]*
    Up sword, and know thou a more horrid hent,°
    When he is drunk asleep, or in his rage,
    Or in th'incestuous pleasure of his bed,   90
    At game, a-swearing, or about some act
    That has no relish° of salvation in't,
    Then trip him that his heels may kick at heaven,
    And that his soul may be as damned and black
    As hell whereto it goes; my mother stays,   95
    This physic° but prolongs thy sickly days.   *Exit.*
KING   *[Rises.]* My words fly up, my thoughts remain
    below,
    Words without thoughts never to heaven go.   *Exit.*

Scene 4. [The queen's closet]

Enter Queen and Polonius.

POLONIUS   A' will come straight, look you lay home°
    to him,
    Tell him his pranks have been too broad° to bear
    with,
    And that your grace hath screened and stood between
    Much heat° and him. I'll silence me° even here:

---

²² *Attends:* accompanies. ²⁴ *Arm:* prepare. ²⁹ *the process:* what proceeds. ³¹ *meet:* fitting. ³³ *of vantage:* from an advantageous position. *liege:* lord. ³⁷ *primal ... curse:* curse of Cain. ³⁹*inclination ... will:* my desire to pray is as strong as my determination to do so. ⁴⁷ *confront ... offence:* plead in man's behalf against sin (at the Last Judgment). ⁴⁹ *forestalled:* prevented. ⁵⁴ *effects:* results. ⁵⁹⁻⁶⁰*wicked ... law:* fruits of the crime bribe the judge. ⁶¹ *shuffling:* evasion. ⁶¹⁻⁶² *action ... nature:* (1) deed is seen in its true nature (2) legal action is sustained according to the truth. ⁶³ *to the teeth ... faults:* meeting our sins face to face. ⁶⁴ *rests:* remains.

⁶⁸⁻⁶⁹*limèd ... engaged:* like a bird caught in lime (a sticky substance spread on twigs as a snare), the soul in its struggle to clear itself only becomes more entangled. ⁶⁹ *make assay:* I'll make an attempt. ⁷³ *pat:* opportunely. ⁷⁵ *would be scanned:* needs closer examination. ⁸⁰ *grossly:* unpurified (by final rites). *bread:* self-indulgence. ⁸¹ *crimes:* sins. *broad blown:* in full flower. *flush:* lusty. ⁸² *audit:* account. ⁸⁴ *heavy:* grievous. ⁸⁶ *seasoned:* ready (prepared). ⁸⁸ *horrid hent:* horrible opportunity ("hint") for seizure ("hent") by me. ⁹² *relish:* taste. ⁹⁶ *physic:* (1) medicine (2) purgation of your soul by prayer. ¹ *lay home:* thrust home; speak sharply. ² *broad:* unrestrained. ⁴ *heat:* anger. *silence me:* hide in silence.

Pray you be round with him. 5
HAMLET [*Within.*] Mother, mother, mother.
QUEEN I'll war'nt you,
  Fear me not. Withdraw, I hear him coming.
    [*Polonius hides behind the arras.*]

Enter Hamlet.

HAMLET Now mother, what's the matter?
QUEEN Hamlet, thou hast thy father much offended.
HAMLET Mother, you have my father much offended. 10
QUEEN Come, come, you answer with an idle° tongue.
HAMLET Go, go, you question with a wicked tongue.
QUEEN Why, how now Hamlet?
HAMLET What's the matter now?
QUEEN Have you forgot me?
HAMLET No by the rood,° not so,
  You are the queen, your husband's brother's wife, 15
  And would it were not so, you are my mother.
QUEEN Nay, then I'll set those to you that can speak.°
HAMLET Come, come, and sit you down, you shall not budge,
  You go not till I set you up a glass°
  Where you may see the inmost part of you. 20
QUEEN What wilt thou do? Thou wilt not murder me?
  Help, help, ho!
POLONIUS [*Behind the arras.*] What ho! help, help, help!
HAMLET How now, a rat? dead for a ducat,° dead.

Kills Polonius [through the arras.]

POLONIUS O I am slain!
QUEEN. O me, what hast thou done?
HAMLET Nay I know not, 25
  Is it the king?
QUEEN O what a rash and bloody deed is this!
HAMLET A bloody deed, almost as bad, good mother,
  As kill a king, and marry with his brother.
QUEEN As kill a king?
HAMLET Ay lady, it was my word. 30
  [*To Polonius.*] Thou wretched, rash, intruding fool, farewell,
  I took thee for thy better,° take thy fortune,
  Thou find'st to be too busy is some danger.
  [*To the Queen.*] Leave wringing of your hands, peace, sit you down,
  And let me wring your heart, for so I shall 35
  If it be made of penetrable stuff,
  If damnèd custom° have not brazed° it so,
  That it be proof° and bulwark against sense.°
QUEEN What have I done, that thou dar'st wag thy tongue
  In noise so rude against me?

HAMLET Such an act 40
  That blurs the grace and blush of modesty,
  Calls virtue hypocrite, takes off the rose°
  From the fair forehead of an innocent love
  And sets a blister there,° makes marriage vows
  As false as dicers' oaths, O such a deed, 45
  As from the body of contraction° plucks
  The very soul, and sweet religion makes
  A rhapsody° of words; heaven's face does glow,°
  Yea this solidity and compound mass°
  With heated visage, as against the doom,° 50
  Is thought-sick at the act.
QUEEN Ay me, what act,
  That roars so loud, and thunders in the index°?
HAMLET Look here upon this picture, and on this,
  The counterfeit presentment° of two brothers:
  See what a grace was seated on this brow, 55
  Hyperion's° curls, the front° of Jove himself,
  An eye like Mars, to threaten and command,
  A station° like the herald Mercury,
  New-lighted on a heaven-kissing hill,
  A combination and a form indeed, 60
  Where every god did seem to set his seal
  To give the world assurance of a man.
  This was your husband. Look you now what follows.
  Here is your husband, like a mildewed ear,°
  Blasting° his wholesome brother. Have you eyes? 65
  Could you on this fair mountain leave to feed,°
  And batten° on this moor? Ha! Have you eyes?
  You cannot call it love, for at your age
  The hey-day in the blood° is tame, it's humble,
  And waits upon the judgment, and what judgment 70
  Would step from this to this? Sense° sure you have
  Else could you not have motion,° but sure that sense
  Is apoplexed,° for madness would not err,
  Nor sense to ecstasy was ne'er so thralled°
  But it reserved some quantity of choice 75
  To serve in such a difference.° What devil was't
  That thus hath cozened you at hoodman-blind°?
  Eyes without feeling, feeling without sight,
  Ears without hands or eyes, smelling sans all,°
  Or but a sickly part of one true sense 80
  Could not so mope:° O shame, where is thy blush?
  Rebellious hell,
  If thou canst mutine in a matron's bones,
  To flaming youth let virtue be as wax

---

¹¹ *idle:* foolish. ¹⁴ *rood:* cross. ¹⁷ *speak:* i.e., to you as you should be spoken to. ¹⁹ *glass:* looking glass. ²³ *for a ducat:* I wager a ducat (an Italian gold coin). ³² *thy better:* the king. ³⁷ *custom:* habit. *brazed:* brass-plated (brazened). ³⁸ *proof:* armor. *sense:* sensibility.

⁴²*rose:* (symbol of perfection and innocence). ⁴⁴ *blister there:* (whores were punished by being branded on the forehead). ⁴⁶*body of contraction:* marriage contract. ⁴⁸ *rhapsody:* (meaningless) mixture. *glow:* blush. ⁴⁹ *solidity ... mass:* solid earth, compounded of the four elements. ⁵⁰ *against the doom:* expecting Judgment Day. ⁵² *index:* (1) table of contents (2) prologue. ⁵⁴ *counterfeit presentment:* painted likeness. ⁵⁶ *Hyperion:* Greek sun god. *front:* forehead. ⁵⁸ *station:* bearing. ⁶⁴ *ear:* i.e., of grain. ⁶⁵ *Blasting:* blighting. ⁶⁶ *leave to feed:* leave off feeding. ⁶⁷ *batten:* gorge yourself. ⁶⁹*hey-day in the blood:* youthful passion. ⁷¹ *Sense:* perception by the senses. ⁷² *motion:* impulse. ⁷³*apoplexed:* paralyzed. ⁷⁴ *sense ... thralled:* sensibility was never so enslaved by madness. ⁷⁶ *in ... difference:* where the difference was so great. ⁷⁷ *cozened ... blind:* cheated you at blindman's bluff. ⁷⁹ *sans all:* without the other senses. ⁸¹*so mope:* be so dull.

And melt in her own fire. Proclaim no shame   85
When the compulsive° ardour gives the charge,°
Since frost itself as actively doth burn,
And reason panders will.°

QUEEN   O Hamlet, speak no
    more,
Thou turn'st my eyes into my very soul,
And there I see such black and grainèd° spots   90
As will not leave their tinct.°

HAMLET   Nay, but to live
In the rank sweat of an enseamèd° bed,
Stewed in corruption, honeying, and making love
Over the nasty sty.

QUEEN   O speak to me no more,
These words like daggers enter in mine ears,   95
No more, sweet Hamlet.

HAMLET   A murderer and a villain,
A slave that is not twentieth part the tithe°
Of your precedent lord, a vice° of kings,
A cutpurse° of the empire and the rule,
That from a shelf the precious diadem stole   100
And put it in his pocket.

QUEEN   No more.

HAMLET   A king of shreds and patches—

Enter the Ghost in his night-gown.°

Save me and hover o'er me with your wings,
You heavenly guards. What would your gracious
    figure?

QUEEN   Alas, he's mad.   105

HAMLET   Do you not come your tardy son to chide,
That lapsed in time and passion° lets go by
Th'important acting of your dread command?
O say!

GHOST   Do not forget: this visitation   110
Is but to whet thy almost blunted purpose.
But look, amazement on thy mother sits,
O step between her and her fighting soul,
Conceit° in weakest bodies strongest works,
Speak to her Hamlet.

HAMLET   How is it with you lady?   115

QUEEN   Alas, how is't with you,
That you do bend your eye on vacancy,°
And with th'incorporal° air do hold discourse?
Forth at your eyes your spirits° wildly peep,
And as the sleeping soldiers in th'alarm,   120
Your bedded° hairs, like life in excrements,°
Start up and stand an° end. O gentle son,
Upon the heat and flame of thy distemper
sprinkle cool patience. Whereon do you look?

HAMLET   On him, on him, look you how pale he
    glares,   125

His form and cause conjoined, preaching to
    stones,
Would make them capable.° Do not look upon
    me,
Lest with this piteous action you convert
My stern effects,° then what I have to do
Will want° true colour,° tears perchance for
    blood.   130

QUEEN   To whom do you speak this?

HAMLET   Do you see
    nothing there?

QUEEN   Nothing at all, yet all that is I see.

HAMLET   Nor did you nothing hear?

QUEEN   No, nothing but
    ourselves.

HAMLET   Why look you there, look how it steals away,
My father in his habit as he lived,°   135
Look where he goes, even now out at the portal.

                                    Exit [Ghost.]

QUEEN   This is the very coinage of your brain,
This bodiless creation ecstasy
Is very cunning in.°

HAMLET   Ecstasy?
My pulse as yours doth temperately keep time,   140
And makes as healthful music. It is not madness
That I have uttered; bring me to the test
And I the matter will re-word, which madness
Would gambol° from. Mother, for love of grace,
Lay not that flattering unction° to your soul,   145
That not your trespass but my madness speaks,
It will but skin and film the ulcerous place,
Whiles rank corruption mining° all within,
Infects unseen. Confess yourself to heaven,
Repent what's past, avoid what is to come,   150
And do not spread the compost° on the weeds
To make them ranker. Forgive me this my virtue,°
For in the fatness° of these pursy° times
Virtue itself of vice must pardon beg,
Yea curb and woo° for leave to do him° good.   155

QUEEN   O Hamlet, thou hast cleft my heart in twain.

HAMLET   O throw away the worser part of it,
And live the purer with the other half.
Good night, but go not to my uncle's bed,
Assume° a virtue if you have it not.   160
That monster custom, who all sense doth eat
Of habits evil,° is angel yet in this,
That to the use° of actions fair and good,
He likewise gives a frock or livery
That aptly° is put on. Refrain tonight,   165
And that shall lend a kind of easiness
To the next abstinence, the next more easy:

---

⁸⁶*compulsive:* compelling. *gives the charge:* attacks.   ⁸⁸*panders will:* pimps for lust.   ⁹⁰*grained:* dyed in grain, unfading.   ⁹¹*leave their tinct:* lose their color.   ⁹²*enseamèd:* greasy.   ⁹⁷*tithe:* one-tenth part.   ⁹⁸*vice:* buffoon (like the character of Vice in the morality plays).   ⁹⁹*cutpurse:* pickpocket. *stage direction: night-gown:* dressing gown.   ¹⁰⁷*lapsed ... passion:* having let time elapse and passion cool.   ¹¹⁴*Conceit:* imagination.   ¹¹⁷*vacancy:* (she cannot see the ghost).   ¹¹⁸*incorporal:* bodiless.   ¹¹⁹*spirits:* vital forces.   ¹²¹*bedded:* lying flat. *excrements:* outgrowths (of the body).   ¹²²*an:* on.

¹²⁷*capable:* i.e., of feeling pity.   ¹²⁸⁻¹²⁹*convert ... effects:* transform my outward signs of sternness.   ¹³⁰*want:* lack. *colour:* (1) complexion (2) motivation.   ¹³⁵*habit ... lived:* clothing he wore when alive.   ¹³⁸⁻¹³⁹*bodiless ... cunning in:* madness (ecstasy) is very skillful in causing an affected person to hallucinate.   ¹⁴⁴*gambol:* leap.   ¹⁴⁵*unction:* salve.   ¹⁴⁸*mining:* undermining.   ¹⁵¹*compost:* manure.   ¹⁵²*virtue:* sermon on virtue.   ¹⁵³*fatness:* grossness. *pursy:* flabby.   ¹⁵⁵*curb and woo:* bow and plead. *him:* vice.   ¹⁶⁰*Assume:* put on the guise of.   ¹⁶¹⁻¹⁶²*all sense ... evil:* confuses the sense of right and wrong in a habitué.   ¹⁶³*use:* habit.   ¹⁶⁵*aptly:* readily.

For use° almost can change the stamp° of nature,
And either . . . the° devil, or throw him out
With wondrous potency: once more good night,   170
And when you are desirous to be blessed,
I'll blessing beg of you. For this same lord,°
I do repent; but heaven hath pleased it so
To punish me with this, and this with me,
That I must be their scourge and minister.°   175
I will bestow° him and will answer well°
The death I gave him; so again good night.
I must be cruel only to be kind;
This bad begins, and worse remains behind.°
One word more, good lady.

QUEEN   What shall I do?   180

HAMLET   Not this by no means that I bid you do:
Let the bloat° king tempt you again to bed,
Pinch wanton on your cheek, call you his mouse,
And let him for a pair of reechy° kisses,
Or paddling in your neck with his damned fingers, 185
Make you to ravel° all this matter out
That I essentially am not in madness,
But mad in craft. 'Twere good you let him know,
For who that's but a queen, fair, sober, wise,
Would from a paddock, from a bat, a gib,°   190
Such dear concernings hide? who would do so?
No, in despite of sense and secrecy,
Unpeg the basket on the house's top,
Let the birds fly, and like the famous ape,
To try conclusions° in the basket creep,   195
And break your own neck down.°

QUEEN   Be thou assured, if words be made of breath,
And breath of life, I have no life to breathe
What thou hast said to me.

HAMLET   I must to England, you know that.

QUEEN   Alack,   200
I had forgot: 'tis so concluded on.

HAMLET   There's letters sealed, and my two school-
fellows,
Whom I will trust as I will adders fanged,
They bear the mandate, they must sweep my way
And marshal me to knavery:° let it work,   205
For 'tis the sport to have the enginer°
Hoist with his own petar,° and't shall go hard
But I will delve one yard below their mines,
And blow them at the moon: O 'tis most sweet
When in one line two crafts directly meet.°   210

This man shall set me packing,°
I'll lug the guts into the neighbour room;
Mother good night indeed. This counsellor
Is now most still, most secret, and most grave,
Who was in life a foolish prating knave.   215
Come sir, to draw toward an end with you.
Good night mother

                              Exit Hamlet tugging in Polonius.

[Act 4]

Scene 1. [A room in the castle]

Enter King and Queen with Rosencrantz and Guildenstern.

KING   There's matter in these sighs, these profound
heaves,
You must translate, 'tis fit we understand them.
Where is your son?

QUEEN   Bestow this place on us° a little while.

                    Exeunt Rosencrantz and Guildenstern.

Ah mine own lord, what have I seen tonight!   5

KING   What, Gertrude? How does Hamlet?

QUEEN   Mad as the sea and wind when both contend
Which is the mightier, in his lawless fit,
Behind the arras hearing something stir,
Whips out his rapier, cries "A rat, a rat,"   10
And in this brainish apprehension° kills
The unseen good old man.

KING   O heavy deed!
It had been so with us° had we been there:
His liberty is full of threats to all,
To you yourself, to us, to every one.   15
Alas, how shall this bloody deed be answered?
It will be laid to us,° whose providence°
Should have kept short,° restrained, and out of
haunt°
This mad young man; but so much was our love,
We would not understand what was most fit,   20
But like the owner of a foul disease,
To keep it from divulging,° let it feed
Even on the pith of life: where is he gone?

QUEEN   To draw apart the body he hath killed,
O'er whom his very madness, like some ore   25
Among a mineral of metals base,°
Shows itself pure: a' weeps for what is done.

KING   O Gertrude, come away:
The sun no sooner shall the mountains touch,
But we will ship him hence and this vile deed   30
We must with all our majesty and skill
Both countenance° and excuse. Ho Guildenstern!

Enter Rosencrantz and Guildenstern.

Friends both, go join you with some further aid;
Hamlet in madness hath Polonius slain,

---

168 *use:* habit. *stamp:* form. 169 *either . . . the:* (word omitted, for which "tame," "curb," and "quell" have been suggested). 172 *lord:* Polonius. 175 *their . . . minister:* heaven's punishment and agent of retribution. 176 *bestow:* stow away. *answer well:* assume full responsibility for. 179 *bad . . . behind:* is a bad beginning to a worse end to come. 182 *bloat:* bloated with dissipation. 184 *reechy:* filthy. 186 *ravel:* unravel. 190 *paddock, bat, gib:* toad, bat, tomcat ("familiars" or demons in animal shape that attend on witches). 193–196 *Unpeg . . . down:* (the story refers to an ape that climbs to the top of a house and opens a basket of birds; when the birds fly away, the ape crawls into the basket, tries to fly, and breaks his neck. The point is that if she gives away Hamlet's secret, she harms herself). 195 *try conclusions:* experiment. 204–205 *sweep . . . knavery:* (like the marshal who went before a royal procession, clearing the way, so Rosencrantz and Guildenstern clear Hamlet's path to some unknown evil). 206 *enginer:* maker of war engines. 207 *Hoist . . . petar:* blown up by his own bomb. 210 *in one . . . meet:* the digger of the mine and the digger of the countermine meet halfway in their tunnels.

211 *packing:* (1) i.e., my bags (2) rushing away (3) plotting. 4 *Bestow . . . us:* leave us. 11 *brainish apprehension:* insane delusion. 13 *us:* me (royal plural). 17 *laid to us:* blamed on me. *providence:* foresight. 18 *short:* tethered by a short leash. *out of haunt:* away from others. 22 *divulging:* being divulged. 25–26 *ore . . . base:* pure ore (such as gold) in a mine of base metal. 32 *countenance:* defend.

And from his mother's closet hath he dragged him. *35*
Go seek him out, speak fair, and bring the body
Into the chapel; I pray you haste in this.
Exeunt Gent[lemen.]
Come Gertrude, we'll call up our wisest friends,
And let them know both what we mean to do
And what's untimely done: [so haply slander,]   *40*
Whose whisper o'er the world's diameter,
As level° as the cannon to his blank°
Transports his° poisoned shot, may miss our name,
And hit the woundless° air. O come away,
My soul is full of discord and dismay.   *Exeunt. 45*

Scene 2. [Another room in the castle]

Enter Hamlet.

HAMLET   Safely stowed.
Gentlemen within: Hamlet, Lord Hamlet!
But soft, what noise, who calls on Hamlet?
O here they come.

Enter Rosencrantz and Guildenstern.

ROSENCRANTZ   What have you done my lord with the
dead body?
HAMLET   Compounded it with dust whereto 'tis kin.   *5*
ROSENCRANTZ   Tell us where 'tis that we may take it
thence,
And bear it to the chapel.
HAMLET   Do not believe it.
ROSENCRANTZ   Believe what?
HAMLET   That I can keep your counsel° and not mine   *10*
own.° Besides, to be demanded of° a sponge, what
replication° should be made by the son of a king?
ROSENCRANTZ   Take you me for a sponge, my lord?
HAMLET   Ay sir, that soaks up the king's countenance,°
his rewards, his authorities. But such officers do   *15*
the king best service in the end; he keeps them like an
apple in the corner of his jaw, first mouthed to be last
swallowed: when he needs what you have gleaned, it
is but squeezing you, and sponge, you shall be dry
again.
ROSENCRANTZ   I understand you not my lord.   *20*
HAMLET   I am glad of it: a knavish speech sleeps in° a
foolish ear.
ROSENCRANTZ   My lord, you must tell us where the
body is, and go with us to the king.
HAMLET   The body is with the king, but the king° is
not with the body. The king is a thing—   *25*
GUILDENSTERN   A thing my lord?
HAMLET   Of nothing, bring me to him. Hide fox, and
all after.°   *Exeunt.*

[Scene 3. Another room in the castle.]

Enter King and two or three.

KING   I have sent to seek him, and to find the body:
How dangerous is it that this man goes loose,
Yet must not we put the strong law on him,
He's loved of the distracted multitude,°
Who like not in° their judgment, but their eyes,   *5*
And where 'tis so, th'offender's scourge° is
weighed
But never the offence: to bear all° smooth and
even,
This sudden sending him away must seem
Deliberate pause:° diseases desperate grown,
By desperate appliance° are relieved,   *10*
Or not at all.

Enter Rosencrantz and all the rest.

How now, what hath befallen?
ROSENCRANTZ   Where the dead body is bestowed my
lord,
We cannot get from him.
KING   But where is he?
ROSENCRANTZ   Without, my lord, guarded,° to know
your pleasure.
KING   Bring him before us.
ROSENCRANTZ   Ho, bring in the lord.   *15*

Enter Hamlet (guarded) and Guildenstern.

KING   Now Hamlet, where's Polonius?
HAMLET   At supper.
KING   At supper? where?
HAMLET   Not where he eats, but where a' is eaten: a
certain convocation of politic° worms are e'en°   *20*
at him. Your worm is your only emperor for diet, we
fat all creatures else to fat us, and we fat ourselves for
maggots. Your fat king and your lean beggar is but
variable service,° two dishes but to one table, that's
the end.
KING   Alas, alas.   *25*
HAMLET   A man may fish with the worm that hath eat of
a king, and eat of the fish that hath fed of that worm.
KING   What dost thou mean by this?
HAMLET   Nothing but to show you how a king may go a
progress° through the guts of a beggar.   *30*
KING   Where is Polonius?
HAMLET   In heaven, send thither to see. If your
messenger find him not there, seek him i'th'other
place yourself: but if indeed you find him not within
this month, you shall nose him as you go up the stairs
into the lobby.   *35*
KING   [*To Attendants.*] Go seek him there.

---

⁴² *As level*: with a straight aim. *blank*: white bull's-eye at the target's center.   ⁴³ *his*: slander's.   ⁴⁴ *woundless*: invulnerable.   ¹⁰*counsel*: (1) advice (2) secret.   ¹⁰⁻¹¹ *keep … own*: follow your advice and not keep my own secret.   ¹¹ *demanded of*: questioned by.   ¹² *replication*: reply to a charge.   ¹⁴ *countenance*: favor.   ²¹*sleeps in*: means nothing to.   ²⁴ *king … king*: Hamlet's father … Claudius.   ²⁷ *Hide fox … after*: (cry in a children's game, like hide-and-seek).

⁴ *distracted multitude*: confused mob.   ⁵ *in*: according to.   ⁶ *scourge*: punishment.   ⁷ *bear all*: carry out everything.   ⁹ *Deliberate pause*: considered delay.   ¹⁰ *appliance*: remedy.   ¹⁴ *guarded*: (Hamlet is under guard until he boards the ship).   ²⁰ *politic*: (1) statesmanlike (2) crafty. *e'en*: even now.   ²⁴ *variable service*: different types of food.   ²⁹⁻³⁰ *go a progress*: make a splendid royal journey from one part of the country to another.

HAMLET   A' will stay till you come.   [*Exeunt.*]

KING   Hamlet, this deed, for thine especial safety—
          Which we do tender,° as we dearly grieve
          For that which thou hast done—must send thee
          hence   *40*
          With fiery quickness. Therefore prepare thyself,
          The bark is ready, and the wind at help,°
          Th'associates tend,° and every thing is bent
          For England.

HAMLET   For England.

KING   Ay Hamlet.

HAMLET   Good.

KING   So is it if thou knew'st our purposes.   *45*

HAMLET   I see a cherub° that sees them: but come, for
          England. Farewell dear mother.

KING   Thy loving father, Hamlet.

HAMLET   My mother: father and mother is man and
          wife, man and wife is one flesh, and so my mother:
          come, for England.   *Exit. 50*

KING   [*To Rosencrantz and Guildenstern.*]
          Follow him at foot,° tempt him with speed aboard,
          Delay it not, I'll have him hence tonight.
          Away, for every thing is sealed and done
          That else leans on° th'affair, pray you make haste.
                                                          [*Exeunt.*]
          And England,° if my love thou hold'st at aught°—   *55*
          As my great power thereof may give thee sense,
          Since yet thy cicatrice° looks raw and red
          After the Danish sword, and thy free awe
          Pays homage° to us—thou mayst not coldly set°
          Our sovereign process,° which imports at full   *60*
          By letters congruing° to that effect,
          The present° death of Hamlet. Do it England,
          For like the hectic° in my blood he rages,
          And thou must cure me; till I know 'tis done,
          Howe'er my haps,° my joys were ne'er begun. *Exit. 65*

Scene 4. [A plain in Denmark]

Enter Fortinbras with his army over the stage.

FORTINBRAS   Go captain, from me greet the Danish
          king,
          Tell him that by his license, Fortinbras
          Craves the conveyance° of a promised march
          Over his kingdom. You know the rendezvous:
          If that his majesty would aught with us,   *5*
          We shall express our duty in his eye,°
          And let him know so.

CAPTAIN   I will do't, my lord.

FORTINBRAS   Go softly° on.   *Exit.*

Enter Hamlet, Rosencrantz, [Guildenstern,] etc.

HAMLET   Good sir whose powers° are these?

CAPTAIN   They are of Norway sir.   *10*

HAMLET   How purposed sir I pray you?

CAPTAIN   Against some part of Poland.

HAMLET   Who commands them sir?

CAPTAIN   The nephew to old Norway, Fortinbras.

HAMLET   Goes it against the main° of Poland sir,   *15*
          Or for some frontier?

CAPTAIN   Truly to speak, and with no addition,
          We go to gain a little patch of ground
          That hath in it no profit but the name.°
          To pay five ducats, five, I would not farm it;   *20*
          Nor will it yield to Norway or the Pole
          A ranker° rate, should it be sold in fee.°

HAMLET   Why then the Polack never will defend it.

CAPTAIN   Yes, it is already garrisoned.

HAMLET   Two thousand souls, and twenty thousand
          ducats   *25*
          Will not debate the question of° this straw:°
          This is th'imposthume of much wealth and peace,°
          That inward breaks, and shows no cause without
          Why the man dies. I humbly thank you sir.

CAPTAIN   God bye you sir.   [*Exit.*]

ROSENCRANTZ   Will't please you go my
          lord?   *30*

HAMLET. I'll be with you straight, go a little before.

                [Exeunt all but Hamlet.]

          How all occasions do inform against me,
          And spur my dull revenge. What is a man
          If his chief good and market° of his time
          Be but to sleep and feed? a beast, no more: *35*
          Sure he that made us with such large discourse,°
          Looking before and after,° gave us not
          That capability and god-like reason
          To fust° in us unused. Now whether it be
          Bestial oblivion,° or some craven° scruple   *40*
          Of thinking too precisely on th'event°—
          A thought which quartered hath but one part
          wisdom,
          And ever three parts coward—I do not know
          Why yet I live to say "This thing's to do,"
          Sith I have cause, and will, and strength, and
          means   *45*
          To do't; examples gross° as earth exhort me:
          Witness this army of such mass and charge,°
          Led by a delicate and tender° prince,
          Whose spirit with divine ambition puffed,
          Makes mouths° at the invisible event,°   *50*
          Exposing what is mortal, and unsure,
          To all that fortune, death, and danger dare,

---

³⁹ *tender:* cherish. ⁴² *at help:* helpful. ⁴³ *tend:* wait. ⁴⁶ *cherub:* (considered the watchmen of heaven). ⁵¹ *at foot:* at his heels. ⁵⁴ *leans on:* relates to. ⁵⁵ *England:* King of England. *my love … aught:* you place any value on my favor. ⁵⁷ *cicatrice:* scar. ⁵⁸⁻⁵⁹ *free … homage:* awe which you, though free, still show by paying homage. ⁵⁹ *coldly set:* lightly estimate. ⁶⁰ *process:* command. ⁶¹ *congruing:* agreeing. ⁶² *present:* immediate. ⁶³ *hectic:* fever. ⁶⁵ *haps:* fortunes. ³ *conveyance of:* escort for. ⁶ *in his eye:* face to face. ⁸ *softly:* slowly.

⁹ *powers:* troops. ¹⁵ *main:* body. ¹⁹ *name:* glory. ²²*ranker:* higher (as annual interest on the total). *in fee:* outright. ²⁶*debate … of:* settle the dispute over. *straw:* triviality. ²⁷*imposthume … peace:* swelling discontent (inner abscess) resulting from too much wealth and peace. ³⁴*market:* profit. ³⁶*discourse:* power of reasoning. ³⁷*Looking … after:* seeing causes and effects. ³⁹*fust:* grow moldy. ⁴⁰*Bestial oblivion:* forgetfulness, as a beast forgets its parents. *craven:* cowardly. ⁴¹ *event:* outcome. ⁴⁶*gross:* obvious. ⁴⁷*charge:* expense. ⁴⁸*delicate and tender:* gentle and young. ⁵⁰*mouths:* faces. *event:* outcome.

Even for an egg-shell. Rightly to be great,
Is not to stir without great argument,
But greatly to find quarrel in a straw   55
When honour's at the stake.° How stand I then
That have a father killed, a mother stained,
Excitements° of my reason, and my blood,
And let all sleep, while to my shame I see
The imminent death of twenty thousand men,   60
That for a fantasy and trick° of fame
Go to their graves like beds, fight for a plot
Whereon the numbers cannot try the cause,°
Which is not tomb enough and continent°
To hide the slain. O from this time forth,   65
My thoughts be bloody, or be nothing worth. *Exit.*

Scene 5. [A room in the castle]

Enter Queen, Horatio and a Gentleman.

QUEEN   I will not speak with her.
GENTLEMAN   She is importunate, indeed distract,°
     Her mood will needs be° pitied.
QUEEN What would she have?
GENTLEMAN   She speaks much of her father, says she
          hears
     There's tricks i'th'world, and hems,° and beats her
          heart,   5
     Spurns enviously at straws,° speaks things in
          doubt°
     That carry but half sense: her speech is nothing,
     Yet the unshapèd use of it doth move
     The hearers to collection;° they aim° at it,
     And botch° the words up fit to their own thoughts, 10
     Which as her winks, and nods, and gestures yield
          them,
     Indeed would make one think there might be
          thought,
     Though nothing sure, yet much unhappily.
HORATIO   'Twere good she were spoken with, for she
          may strew
     Dangerous conjectures in ill-breeding minds.   15
QUEEN   Let her come in.   *Exit Gentleman.*
     [*Aside.*] To my sick soul, as sin's true nature is,°
     Each toy° seems prologue to some great amiss,°
     So full of artless jealousy° is guilt,
     It spills itself, in fearing to be spilt.   20

Enter Ophelia, distracted.°

OPHELIA   Where is the beauteous majesty of Denmark?
QUEEN   How now Ophelia?
OPHELIA. [*Sings.*] How should I your true love know

                    From another one?
          By his cockle hat and staff,°   25
               And his sandal shoon.°
QUEEN   Alas sweet lady, what imports this song?
OPHELIA   Say you? nay, pray you mark.
     [*Sings.*] He is dead and gone, lady,
               He is dead and gone,   30
          At his head a grass-green turf,
               At his heels a stone.
     O ho.
QUEEN   Nay but Ophelia—
OPHELIA   Pray you mark.
     [*Sings.*] White his shroud as the mountain snow—

Enter King.

QUEEN   Alas, look here my lord.   35
OPHELIA   [*Sings.*] Larded° all with sweet flowers,
     Which bewept to the ground did not go,
     With true-love showers.
KING   How do you, pretty lady?
OPHELIA   Well, God 'ild° you. They say the owl was a 40
     baker's daughter.° Lord, we know what we are,
     butknow not what we may be. God be at your table.°
KING   Conceit° upon her father.
OPHELIA   Pray you let's have no words of this, but
     when they ask you what it means, say you this: 45

     [*Sings.*] Tomorrow is Saint Valentine's day,

          All in the morning betime,°
     And I a maid at your window
          To be your Valentine.
     Then up he rose, and donned his clo'es,   50
          And dupped° the chamber door,
     Let in the maid, that out a maid,
          Never departed more.
KING   Pretty Ophelia.
OPHELIA   Indeed, la, without an oath I'll make an end
     on't.   55
     [*Sings.*] By Gis° and by Saint Charity,
          Alack and fie for shame,
     Young men will do't, if they come to't,
          By Cock° they are to blame.
     Quoth she, Before you tumbled me,   60
          You promised me to wed.
(He answers)
          So would I ha' done, by yonder sun,
          An° thou hadst not come to my bed.
KING   How long hath she been thus?   65
OPHELIA   I hope all will be well. We must be patient, but
     I cannot choose but weep to think they would lay
     him i'th'cold ground. My brother shall know of it,

53–56 *Rightly ... stake*: the truly great do not fight without just cause ("argument"), but it is nobly ("greatly") done to fight even for a trifle if honor is at stake.   58 *Excitements*: incentives.   61 *fantasy and trick*: illusion and trifle.   63 *Whereon ... cause*: too small to accommodate all the troops fighting for it.   64 *continent*: container.   2 *distract*: insane.   3 *will needs be*: needs to be.   5 *hems*: coughs.   6 *Spurns ... straws*: reacts maliciously to trifles. *in doubt*: ambiguous.   9 *collection*: inference. *aim*: guess.   10 *botch*: patch.   17 *as sin's ... is*: as natural for the guilty.   18 *toy*: trifle. *amiss*: disaster.   19 *artless jealousy*: uncontrollable suspicion. stage direction: *distracted*: insane.

25 *cockle hat and staff*: (marks of the pilgrim, the cockle shell symbolizing his journey to the shrine of St. James; the pilgrim was a common metaphor for the lover).   26 *shoon*: shoes.   36 *Larded*: trimmed.   40 *God 'ild*: God yield (reward).   40–41 *owl ... daughter*: (in a medieval legend, a baker's daughter was turned into an owl because she gave Jesus short weight on a loaf of bread).   42 *God ... table*: (a blessing at dinner).   43 *Conceit*: thinking.   47 *betime*: early (because the first woman a man saw on Valentine's Day would be his true love).   51 *dupped*: opened.   56 *Gis*: contraction of "Jesus."   59 *Cock*: (vulgarization of "God" in oaths).   64 *An*: if.

and so I thank you for your good counsel. Come, my
coach: good night ladies, good night. Sweet ladies,
good night, good night.   [*Exit Ophelia.*]   70
KING   Follow her close, give her good watch I pray
you.   [*Exit Horatio.*]
O this is the poison of deep grief, it springs
All from her father's death, and now behold:
O Gertrude, Gertrude,
When sorrows come, they come not single spies,   75
But in battalions: first her father slain,
Next, your son gone, and he most violent author
Of his own just remove, the people muddied,°
Thick and unwholesome in their thoughts and
whispers
For good Polonius' death: and we have done but
greenly°   80
In hugger-mugger° to inter him: poor Ophelia
Divided from herself and her fair judgment,
Without the which we are pictures or mere beasts,
Last, and as much containing° as all these,
Her brother is in secret come from France,   85
Feeds on his wonder,° keeps himself in clouds,°
And wants not buzzers° to infect his ear
With pestilent speeches of his father's death,
Wherein necessity, of matter beggared,
Will nothing stick our person to arraign°   90
In ear and ear:° O my dear Gertrude, this
Like to a murdering-piece° in many places
Gives me superfluous death.   *A noise within.*
QUEEN   Alack, what noise is
this?
KING   Attend! *Enter a Messenger.*
Where are my Switzers°? Let them guard the door. 95
What is the matter?
MESSENGER   Save yourself, my lord.
The ocean, overpeering of his list,°
Eats not the flats° with more impiteous haste
Than young Laertes in a riotous head°
O'erbears your officers: the rabble call him lord, 100
And as the world were now but to begin,
Antiquity forgot, custom not known,
The ratifiers and props of every word,
They cry "Choose we, Laertes shall be king!"
Caps, hands, and tongues applaud it to the clouds, 105
"Laertes shall be king, Laertes king!"
                                A noise within.
QUEEN   How cheerfully on the false trail they cry.
O this is counter,° you false Danish dogs.
KING   The doors are broke.

Enter Laertes with others.

LAERTES   Where is this king? Sirs, stand you all
without.°   110
DANES   No, let's come in.
LAERTES   I pray you give me leave.°
DANES   We will, we will. [*They retire.*]
LAERTES   I thank you, keep the door. O thou vile king,
Give me my father.
QUEEN   Calmly, good Laertes.
LAERTES   That drop of blood that's calm proclaims me
bastard,   115
Cries cuckold° to my father, brands° the harlot
Even here between the chaste unsmirchèd brows
Of my true mother.
KING   What is the cause Laertes,
That thy rebellion looks so giant-like?
Let him go Gertrude, do not fear° our person,   120
There's such divinity° doth hedge a king,
That treason can but peep to° what it would,
Acts little of his° will. Tell me Laertes,
Why thou art this incensed. Let him go Gertrude.
Speak man.   125
LAERTES   Where is my father?
KING   Dead.
QUEEN   But not by him.
KING   Let him demand his fill.
LAERTES   How came he dead? I'll not be juggled with.
To hell allegiance, vows to the blackest devil,
Conscience and grace, to the profoundest pit.   130
I dare damnation: to this point I stand,
That both the worlds I give to negligence,°
Let come what comes, only I'll be revenged
Most throughly for my father.
KING   Who shall stay you?
LAERTES   My will, not all the world's:°   135
And for my means, I'll husband° them so well,
They shall go far with little.
KING   Good Laertes,
If you desire to know the certainty
Of your dear father, is't writ in your revenge
That swoopstake,° you will draw both friend and
foe,   140
Winner and loser?
LAERTES   None but his enemies.
KING   Will you know them
then?
LAERTES   To his good friends thus wide I'll ope my
arms,
And like the kind life-rend'ring pelican,°
Repast them with my blood.
KING   Why now you speak   145
Like a good child, and a true gentleman.
That I am guiltless of your father's death,

---

78 *muddied:* stirred up.   80 *done but greenly:* acted like amateurs.
81 *hugger-mugger:* secret haste.   84 *containing:* i.e., cause for sorrow.   86 *Feeds … wonder:* sustains himself by wondering about
his father's death. *clouds:* gloom, obscurity.   87 *wants not buzzers:*
lacks not whispering gossips.   89–90 *Wherein … arraign:* in which
the tellers, lacking facts, will not hesitate to accuse me.   91 *In
ear and ear:* whispering from one ear to another.   92 *murdering-
piece:* small cannon shooting shrapnel, to inflict numerous
wounds.   95 *Switzers:* Swiss guards.   97 *overpeering … list:* rising
above its usual limits.   98 *flats:* lowlands.   99 *head:* armed force.
108 *counter:* following the scent backward.

---

110 *without:* outside.   111 *leave:* i.e., to enter alone.   116 *cuckold:*
betrayed husband. *brands:* (so harlots were punished).   120 *fear:*
i.e., for.   121 *divinity:* divine protection.   122 *peep to:* strain to see.
123 *his:* treason's.   132 *both … negligence:* I care nothing for this
world or the next.   135 *world's:* i.e., will.   136 *husband:* econo-
mize.   140 *swoopstake:* sweeping in all the stakes in a game, both
of winner and loser.   144 *pelican:* (the mother pelican was
believed to nourish her young with blood pecked from her own
breast).

And am most sensibly° in grief for it,
It shall as level° to your judgment 'pear
As day does to your eye.　　　　　　　　　　　150

[A noise within.]

[Crowd shouts.] Let her come in.
LAERTES　　How now, what noise is that?

Enter Ophelia.

O heat, dry up my brains, tears seven time salt,
Burn out the sense and virtue° of mine eye!
By heaven, thy madness shall be paid with weight,°
Till our scale turn the beam,° O rose of May,　155
Dear maid, kind sister, sweet Ophelia:
O heavens, is't possible a young maid's wits
Should be as mortal as an old man's life?
Nature is fine in love, and where 'tis fine,
It sends some previous instance of itself　　160
After the thing it loves.°
OPHELIA. *[Sings.]* They bore him barefaced on the bier,
　　　　Hey non nonny, nonny, hey nonny:
　　　　And in his grave rained many a tear—
Fare you well my dove.　　　　　　　　　　165
LAERTES　　Hadst thou thy wits, and didst persuade
　　revenge,
　　It could not move thus.
OPHELIA　　You must sing "adown adown," and you call
　　him adown-a. O how the wheel becomes it.° It is the
　　false steward that stole his master's daughter.　170
LAERTES　　This nothing's more than matter.°
OPHELIA　　There's rosemary,° that's for remembrance,
　　pray you love remember: and there is pansies, that's
　　for thoughts.
LAERTES　　A document° in madness, thoughts and
　　remembrance fitted.°　　　　　　　　　　175
OPHELIA　　There's fennel for you, and columbines.° There's
　　rue° for you, and here's some for me, we may call it
　　herb of grace° o'Sundays: O, you must wear your rue
　　with a difference.° There's a daisy,° I would give you
　　some violets,° but they withered all when my father　180
　　died: they say a' made a good end;
　　[Sings.] For bonny sweet Robin is all my joy.
LAERTES　　Thought and affliction, passion, hell itself,
　　She turns to favour and to prettiness.
OPHELIA　　*[Sings.]* And will a' not come again,　　185
　　　　　　And will a' not come again?

No, no, he is dead,
　　Go to thy death-bed,
　　He never will come again.
　　His beard was as white as snow,　　190
　　All flaxen was his poll,°
　　　　He is gone, he is gone,
　　　　And we cast away moan,
　　　　God ha' mercy on his soul.
And of all Christian souls, I pray God. God bye
you.　　　　　　　　　　　　　　　　195

　　　　　　　　　　　　Exit Ophelia.

LAERTES　　Do you see this, O God?
KING　　Laertes, I must commune with your grief,
　　Or you deny me right: go but apart,
　　Make choice of whom your wisest friends you will,
　　And they shall hear and judge 'twixt you and me;　200
　　If by direct or by collateral° hand
　　They find us touched,° we will our kingdom give,
　　Our crown, our life, and all that we call ours
　　To you in satisfaction; but if not,
　　Be you content to lend your patience to us,　　205
　　And we shall jointly labour with your soul
　　To give it due content.
LAERTES　　　　　　　　Let this be so.
　　His means of death, his obscure funeral,
　　No trophy,° sword, nor hatchment° o'er his bones,
　　No noble rite, nor formal ostentation,°　　210
　　Cry° to be heard as 'twere from heaven to earth,
　　That I must call't in question.
KING　　　　　　　　　　So you shall,
　　And where th'offence is, let the great axe fall.
　　I pray you go with me.　　　　　*[Exeunt.]*

Scene 6. [Another room in the castle]

Enter Horatio and others.

HORATIO　　What are they that would speak with me?
GENTLEMAN　　Seafaring men sir, they say they have
　　letters for you.
HORATIO　　Let them come in.　　*[Exit Attendant.]*
　　I do not know from what part of the world
　　I should be greeted, if not from Lord Hamlet.　5

Enter Sailors.

SAILOR　　God bless you sir.
HORATIO　　Let him bless thee too.
SAILOR　　A' shall sir, an't please him. There's a letter for
　　you sir, it came from th'ambassador that was bound
　　for England, if your name be Horatio, as I am let to
　　know it is.　　　　　　　　　　　　10
HORATIO　　*[Reads the letter.]* "Horatio, when thou shalt
　　have overlooked° this, give these fellows some means
　　to the king, they have letters for him. Ere we were
　　two days old at sea, a pirate of very warlike

---

¹⁴⁸ *sensibly:* feelingly.　¹⁴⁹ *level:* plain.　¹⁵³ *sense and virtue:* feeling and power.　¹⁵⁴ *with weight:* with equal weight.　¹⁵⁵ *turn the beam:* outweigh the other side.　¹⁵⁹⁻¹⁶¹ *Nature ... loves:* filial love that is so refined and pure sends some precious token (her wits) after the beloved dead.　¹⁶⁹ *wheel becomes it:* refrain ("adown") suits the subject (Polonius's fall).　¹⁷¹ *more than matter:* more eloquent than sane speech.　¹⁷² *There's rosemary:* (given to Laertes; she may be distributing imaginary or real flowers).　¹⁷⁴ *document:* lesson.　¹⁷⁴⁻¹⁷⁵ *thoughts ... fitted:* thoughts of revenge matched with remembrance of Polonius.　¹⁷⁶ *fennel ... columbines:* (given to the king, symbolizing flattery and ingratitude).　¹⁷⁷ *rue:* (given to the queen, symbolizing sorrow or repentance).　¹⁷⁸ *herb of grace:* (because it symbolizes repentance).　¹⁷⁹ *with a difference:* for a different reason (Ophelia's is for sorrow and the queen's for repentance).　¹⁷⁹ *daisy:* (symbolizing dissembling).　¹⁸⁰ *violets:* (symbolizing faithfulness).

¹⁹¹ *flaxen ... poll:* white was his head.　²⁰¹ *collateral:* indirect.　²⁰² *touched:* tainted with guilt.　²⁰⁹ *trophy:* memorial.　*hatchment:* tablet displaying coat of arms.　²¹⁰ *ostentation:* ceremony.　²¹¹ *Cry:* cry out.　¹² *overlooked:* read over.

appointment° gave us chase. Finding ourselves too 15
slow of sail, we put on a compelled valour, and in the
grapple° I boarded them. On the instant they got
clear of our ship, so I alone became their prisoner.
They have dealt with me like thieves of mercy,° but
they knew what they did. I am to do a good turn 20
for them. Let the king have the letters I have sent,
and repair° thou to me with as much speed as thou
wouldst fly death. I have words to speak in thine ear
will make thee dumb, yet are they much too light for
the bore° of the matter. These good fellows will 25
bring thee where I am. Rosencrantz and
Guildenstern hold their course for England. Of them
I have much to tell thee. Farewell.

    He that thou knowest thine, Hamlet."
Come, I will give you way° for these your letters, 30
And do't the speedier that you may direct me
To him from whom you brought them.   *Exeunt.*

Scene 7. [Another room in the castle]

Enter King and Laertes.

KING   Now must your conscience my acquittance seal,°
    And you must put me in your heart for friend,
    Sith you have heard and with a knowing ear,
    That he which hath your noble father slain
    Pursued my life.
LAERTES   It well appears: but tell me 5
    Why you proceeded not against these feats
    So crimeful and so capital in nature,
    As by your safety, greatness, wisdom, all things else,
    You mainly were stirred up.°
KING   O for two special reasons,
    Which may to you perhaps seem much unsinewed,° 10
    But yet to me they're strong. The queen his mother
    Lives almost by his looks, and for myself,
    My virtue or my plague, be it either which,
    She's so conjunctive° to my life and soul,
    That as the star moves not but in his sphere,° 15
    I could not but by her. The other motive,
    Why to a public count° I might not go,
    Is the great love the general gender° bear him,
    Who dipping all his faults in their affection,
    Would like the spring that turneth wood to stone,° 20
    Convert his gyves to graces,° so that my arrows,
    Too slightly timbered° for so loud a wind,

    Would have reverted to my bow again,
    And not where I had aimed them.
LAERTES   And so have I a noble father lost, 25
    A sister driven into desperate terms,°
    Whose worth, if praises may go back° again,
    Stood challenger on mount of all the age
    For her perfections.° But my revenge will come.
KING   Break not your sleeps for that, you must not think 30
    That we are made of stuff so flat and dull,
    That we can let our beard be shook with danger,
    And think it pastime. You shortly shall hear more,
    I loved your father, and we love ourself,
    And that I hope will teach you to imagine— 35

Enter a Messenger with letters.

    How now. What news?
MESSENGER   Letters my lord, from Hamlet.
    These to your majesty, this to the queen.
KING   From Hamlet? Who brought them?
MESSENGER   Sailors my lord they say, I saw them not:
    They were given me by Claudio, he received them 40
    Of him that brought them.
KING   Laertes you shall hear them:
    Leave us.   *Exit [Messenger]*
    [*Reads*] "High and mighty, you shall know I am set
    naked° on your kingdom. Tomorrow shall I beg leave
    to see your kingly eyes, when I shall, first asking your
    pardon° thereunto, recount the occasion of my 45
    sudden and more strange return.
        Hamlet."
    What should this mean? Are all the rest come back?
    Or is it some abuse,° and no such thing?
LAERTES   Know you the hand?
KING   'Tis Hamlet's character.°
    "Naked," 50
    And in a postscript here he says "alone."
    Can you devise° me?
LAERTES   I am lost in it my lord, but let him come,
    It warms the very sickness in my heart
    That I shall live and tell him to his teeth, 55
    "Thus didest thou."
KING   If it be so Laertes—
    As how should it be so? how otherwise?—
    Will you be ruled by me?
LAERTES   Ay my lord,
    So you will not o'errule me to a peace.
KING   To thine own peace: if he be now returned, 60
    As checking at° his voyage, and that he means
    No more to undertake it, I will work him
    To an exploit, now ripe in my device,°
    Under the which he shall not choose but fall:
    And for his death no wind of blame shall breathe, 65

---

¹⁵ *appointment:* equipment. ¹⁶⁻¹⁷ *in the grapple:* when the pirate ship hooked onto ours.¹⁹ *of mercy:* merciful. ²² *repair:* come. ²⁵ *bore:* size, caliber.³⁰ *way:* access (to the king). ¹ *my acquittance seal:* confirm my acquittal. ⁹ *mainly ... up:* were strongly urged. ¹⁰ *much unsinewed:* very weak. ¹⁴ *conjunctive:* closely allied. ¹⁵ *in his sphere:* (referring to the Ptolemaic belief that each planet, fixed in its own sphere, revolved around the earth). ¹⁷ *count:* accounting. ¹⁸ *general gender:* common people. ²⁰ *the spring ... stone:* (the baths of King's Newnham in Warwickshire were described as being able to turn wood into stone because of their high concentrations of lime). ²¹ *Convert ... graces:* regard his fetters (had he been imprisoned) as honors. ²² *slightly timbered:* light-shafted.

²⁶ *desperate terms:* madness. ²⁷ *go back:* i.e., before her madness. ²⁸⁻²⁹ *challenger ... perfections:* like a challenger on horseback, ready to defend against the world her claim to perfection. ⁴³ *naked:* without resources. ⁴⁵ *pardon:* permission. ⁴⁹ *abuse:* deception. ⁵⁰ *character:* handwriting. ⁵² *devise me:* explain it. ⁶¹ *checking at:* altering the course of (when the falcon forsakes one quarry for another). ⁶³ *ripe in my device:* already planned by me.

But even his mother shall uncharge the practice,°
And call it accident.

LAERTES   My lord, I will be ruled,
The rather if you could devise it so
That I might be the organ.°

KING   It falls right.
You have been talked of since your travel much,   70
And that in Hamlet's hearing, for a quality
Wherein they say you shine: your sum of parts°
Did not together pluck such envy from him
As did that one, and that in my regard
Of the unworthiest siege.°

LAERTES   What part is that my lord?   75

KING   A very riband° in the cap of youth,
Yet needful too, for youth no less becomes°
The light and careless livery° that it wears,
Than settled age his sables° and his weeds°
Importing health and graveness; two months
since,°   80
Here was a gentleman of Normandy—
I have seen myself, and served against the French,
And they can° well on horseback—but this gallant
Had witchcraft in't, he grew unto his seat,
And to such wondrous doing brought his horse,   85
As had he been incorpsed and demi-natured°
With the brave beast. So far he topped my
thought,
That I in forgery of° shapes and tricks
Come short of what he did.

LAERTES   A Norman was't?

KING   A Norman.   90

LAERTES   Upon my life, Lamord.

KING   The very same.

LAERTES   I know him well, he is the brooch° indeed
And gem of all the nation.

KING   He made confession° of you,
And gave you such a masterly report   95
For art and exercise in your defence,
And for your rapier most especial,
That he cried out 'twould be a sight indeed
If one could match you; the scrimers° of their
nation
He swore had neither motion, guard, nor eye,   100
If you opposed them; sir this report of his
Did Hamlet so envenom° with his envy,
That he could nothing do but wish and beg
Your sudden coming o'er to play with him.
Now out of this—

LAERTES   What out of this, my lord?   105

KING   Laertes, was your father dear to you?
Or are you like the painting of a sorrow,
A face without a heart?

LAERTES   Why ask you this?

KING   Not that I think you did not love your father,
But that I know love is begun by time,   110
And that I see in passages of proof,°
Time qualifies° the spark and fire of it:
There lives within the very flame of love
A kind of wick or snuff that will abate it,°
And nothing is at a like goodness still,°   115
For goodness growing to a plurisy,°
Dies in his own too-much. That we would do
We should do when we would: for this "would"°
changes,
And hath abatements and delays as many
As there are tongues, are hands, are accidents,   120
And then this "should"° is like a spendthrift sigh,
That hurts by easing;° but to the quick° of
th'ulcer:
Hamlet comes back, what would you undertake
To show yourself in deed your father's son
More than in words?

LAERTES   To cut his throat i'th'church.   125

KING   No place indeed should murder sanctuarize,°
Revenge should have no bounds: but good
Laertes,
Will you do this, keep close within your chamber:
Hamlet returned shall know you are come home,
We'll put on° those shall praise your excellence,   130
And set a double varnish on the fame
The Frenchman gave you, bring you in fine°
together,
And wager on your heads; he being remiss,°
Most generous, and free from all contriving,
Will not peruse the foils, so that with ease,   135
Or with a little shuffling, you may choose
A sword unbated,° and in a pass of practice°
Requite him for your father.

LAERTES   I will do't,
And for the purpose, I'll anoint my sword.
I bought an unction° of a mountebank°   140
So mortal,° that but dip a knife in it,
Where it draws blood, no cataplasm° so rare,
Collected from all simples° that have virtue°
Under the moon,° can save the thing from death
That is but scratched withal: I'll touch my point   145
With this contagion, that if I gall° him slightly,
It may be death.

KING   Let's further think of this,
Weigh what convenience both of time and means

---

⁶⁶ *uncharge the practice:* acquit the plot (of treachery).   ⁶⁹*organ:* instrument.   ⁷⁵ *your sum of parts:* all your accomplishments.   ⁷⁵*siege:* rank.   ⁷⁶*riband:* decoration.   ⁷⁷*becomes:* befits.   ⁷⁸*livery:* clothing (denoting rank or occupation).   ⁷⁹ *sables:* fur-trimmed gowns. *weeds:* garments.   ⁸⁰ *since:* ago.   ⁸³ *can:* can do.   ⁸⁶*incorpsed … natured:* made into one body, sharing half its nature.   ⁸⁸ *in forgery of:* imagining.   ⁹²*brooch:* ornament.   ⁹⁴*confession:* report.   ⁹⁹*scrimers:* fencers.   ¹⁰²*envenom:* poison.

¹¹¹ *passages of proof:* examples drawn from experience.   ¹¹² *qualifies:* weakens.   ¹¹⁴ *snuff … it:* charred end of the wick that will diminish the flame.   ¹¹⁵ *still:* always.   ¹¹⁶ *plurisy:* excess.   ¹¹⁸ *"would":* will to act.   ¹²¹*"should":* reminder of one's duty.   ¹²¹⁻¹²² *spendthrift … easing:* A sigh which, though giving temporary relief, wastes life, as each sigh draws a drop of blood away from the heart (a common Elizabethan belief).   ¹²² *quick:* most sensitive spot.   ¹²⁶*murder sanctuarize:* give sanctuary to murder.   ¹³⁰ *put on:* incite.   ¹³² *in fine:* finally.   ¹³³ *remiss:* easy-going.   ¹³⁷ *unbated:* not blunted (the edges and points were blunted for fencing). *pass of practice:* (1) match for exercise (2) treacherous thrust.   ¹⁴⁰ *unction:* ointment. *mountebank:* quack doctor, medicine man.   ¹⁴¹ *mortal:* deadly.   ¹⁴² *cataplasm:* poultice.   ¹⁴³ *simples:* herbs. *virtue:* power (of healing).   ¹⁴⁴ *Under the moon:* (when herbs were supposed to be collected to be most effective).   ¹⁴⁶ *gall:* scratch.

May fit us to our shape;° if this should fail,
And that our drift° look through° our bad
performance,   *150*
'Twere better not assayed; therefore this project
Should have a back or second that might hold
If this did blast in proof;° soft, let me see,
We'll make a solemn wager on your cunnings°—
I ha't: *155*
When in your motion you are hot and dry,
As make your bouts more violent to that end,
And that he calls for drink, I'll have prepared him
A chalice for the nonce,° whereon but sipping,
If he by chance escape your venomed stuck,°   *160*
Our purpose may hold there; but stay, what noise?

Enter Queen.

     How, sweet queen?
QUEEN   One woe doth tread upon another's heel,
    So fast they follow; your sister's drowned, Laertes.
LAERTES   Drowned! O where?   *165*
QUEEN   There is a willow grows aslant a brook,
    That shows his hoar° leaves in the glassy stream,
    There with fantastic garlands did she make
    Of crow-flowers,° nettles, daisies, and long
    purples,°
    That liberal° shepherds give a grosser name,   *170*
    But our cold° maids do dead men's fingers call
    them.
    There on the pendent boughs her coronet weeds°
    Clamb'ring to hang, an envious sliver° broke,
    When down her weedy trophies and herself
    Fell in the weeping brook: her clothes spread
    wide,   *175*
    And mermaid-like awhile they bore her up,
    Which time she chanted snatches of old tunes,
    As one incapable of° her own distress,
    Or like a creature native and indued
    Unto° that element: but long it could not be   *180*
    Till that her garments, heavy with their drink,
    Pulled the poor wretch from her melodious lay
    To muddy death.
LAERTES   Alas, then she is drowned?
QUEEN   Drowned, drowned.
LAERTES   Too much of water hast thou, poor Ophelia, *185*
    And therefore I forbid my tears; but yet
    It is our trick, nature her custom holds,
    Let shame say what it will; when these° are gone,
    The woman will be out.° Adieu my lord,
    I have a speech o' fire that fain would blaze, *190*
    But that this folly douts it.°   *Exit.*
KING   Let's follow, Gertrude,

How much I had to do to calm his rage;
Now fear I this will give it start again,
Therefore let's follow.   *Exeunt.*

[Act 5]

Scene 1. [A churchyard]

Enter two Clowns.°

1. CLOWN   Is she to be buried in Christian burial,°
when she wilfully seeks her own salvation?°
2. CLOWN   I tell thee she is, therefore make her grave
straight.° The crowner hath sat on her,° and finds it
Christian burial.
1. CLOWN   How can that be, unless she drowned   *5*
herself in her own defence?°
2. CLOWN   Why, 'tis found so.
1. CLOWN   It must be "se offendendo,"° it cannot be else:
for here lies the point: if I drown myself wittingly, it
argues an act, and an act hath three branches, it is   *10*
to act, to do, and to perform; argal,° she drowned
herself wittingly.
2. CLOWN   Nay, but hear you, goodman delver.
1. CLOWN   Give me leave: here lies the water, good.
Here stands the man, good. If the man go to this
water and drown himself, it is, will he nill he,° he   *15*
goes, mark you that. But if the water come to him,
and drown him, he drowns not himself. Argal, he that
is not guilty of his own death, shortens not his own
life.
2. CLOWN   But is this law?
1. CLOWN   Ay marry is't, crowner's quest° law.   *20*
2. CLOWN   Will you ha' the truth on't? If this had not
been a gentlewoman, she would have been buried out
o'Christian burial.
1. CLOWN   Why there thou say'st, and the more pity that
great folk should have countenance° in this world   *25*
to drown or hang themselves more thantheir even-
Christen.° Come, my spade; there is no ancient
gentlemen but gardeners, ditchers and grave-makers;
they hold up Adam's profession.
2. CLOWN   Was he a gentleman?
1. CLOWN   A' was the first that ever bore arms.°   *30*
2. CLOWN   Why, he had none.
1. CLOWN   What, art a heathen? How dost thou
understand the Scripture? The Scripture says Adam
digged; could he dig without arms? I'll put another
question to thee; if thou answerest me not to the
purpose, confess thyself—   *35*
2. CLOWN   Go to.

---

[149] *shape:* plan. [150] *drift:* aim. *look through:* be exposed by.
[153] *blast in proof:* fail when tested (as a bursting cannon). [154] *cunnings:* skills. [159] *nonce:* occasion. [160] *stuck:* thrust. [167] *hoar:* grey
(on the underside). [169] *crow-flowers:* buttercups. *long purples:*
spikelike early orchid. [170] *liberal:* libertine. [171] *cold:* chaste.
[172] *coronet weeds:* garland of weeds. [173] *envious sliver:* malicious
branch [178] *incapable of:* unable to understand. [179–180] *indued Unto:*
endowed by nature to exist in. [188] *these:* i.e., tears. [189] *woman
… out:* womanly habits will be out of me. [191] *folly douts it:* tears
put it out.

Stage direction: *clowns:* rustics. [1] *Christian burial:* consecrated
ground within a churchyard (where suicides were not allowed
burial). [2] *salvation:* i.e., "damnation." The gravediggers make a
number of such "mistakes," later termed "malapropisms."
[4] *straight:* straightaway, at once. *crowner … her:* coroner has
ruled on her case. [6] *her own defence:* (as self-defense justifies
homicide, so may it justify suicide). [8] *"se offendendo":* (he means
"se defendendo," in self-defense). [11] *argal:* (corruption of "ergo"
= therefore). [15] *will he nill he:* will he or will he not (willy nilly).
[20] *quest:* inquest. [25] *countenance:* privilege. [26–27] *even-Christen:*
fellow Christian. [30] *arms:* (with a pun on "coat of arms").

1. CLOWN   What is he that builds stronger than either the mason, the shipwright, or the carpenter?

2. CLOWN   The gallows-maker, for that frame outlives a thousand tenants.   40

1. CLOWN   I like thy wit well in good faith, the gallows does well, but how does it well? It does well to those that do ill. Now thou dost ill to say the gallows is built stronger than the church. Argal, the gallows may do well to thee.° To't again, come.   45

2. CLOWN   'Who builds stronger than a mason, a shipwright, or a carpenter?'

1. CLOWN   Ay, tell me that, and unyoke.°

2. CLOWN   Marry, now I can tell.

1. CLOWN   To't.   50

2. CLOWN   Mass,° I cannot tell.

1. CLOWN   Cudgel thy brains no more about it, for your dull ass will not mend his pace with beating, and when you are asked this question next, say "a grave-maker:" the houses he makes last till doomsday. Go get thee to Yaughan,° and fetch me a   55 stoup° of liquor.   [*Exit 2. Clown.*]

Enter Hamlet and Horatio afar off.

1. CLOWN   (*Sings.*) In youth when I did love, did love,
    Methought it was very sweet,
To contract oh the time for a° my behove,°
    O methought there a was nothing a meet.°   60

HAMLET   Has this fellow no feeling of his business, that a'sings in grave-making?

HORATIO   Custom hath made it in him a property of easiness.°

HAMLET   'Tis e'en so, the hand of little employment hath the daintier sense.°   65

1. CLOWN   (*Sings.*) But age with his stealing steps
    Hath clawed me in his clutch,
And hath shipped me intil° the land,
    As if I had never been such.   [*Throws up a skull.*]

HAMLET   That skull had a tongue in it, and could   70 sing once: how the knave jowls° it to the ground, as if 'twere Cain's jaw-bone,° that did the first murder. This might be the pate of a politician, which this ass now o'erreaches;° one that would circumvent° God, might it not?

HORATIO   It might my lord.   75

HAMLET   Or of a courtier, which could say "Good morrow sweet lord, how dost thou good lord?" This might be my lord such-a-one, that praised my lord such-a-one's horse, when a'meant to beg it, might it not?

HORATIO   It might my lord.   80

HAMLET   Why e'en so, and now my Lady Worm's, chopless,° and knocked about the mazzard° with a sexton's spade; here's fine revolution an° we had the trick° to see't. Did these bones cost no more the breeding, but to play at loggets° with them? Mine ache to think on't.   85

1. CLOWN   (*Sings.*) A pick-axe and a spade, a spade,
    For and a shrouding sheet,
O a pit of clay for to be made
    For such a guest is meet.°   [*Throws up another skull.*]

HAMLET   There's another: why may not that be the skull of a lawyer? Where be his quiddities° now, his   90 quillets,° his cases, his tenures,° and his tricks? Why does he suffer this rude knave now to knock him about the sconce° with a dirty shovel, and will not tell him of his action of battery? Hum, this fellow might be in's time a great buyer of land, with his   95 statutes,° his recognizances,° his fines,° his double vouchers,° his recoveries:° is this the fine° of his fines, and the recovery° of his recoveries, to have his fine pate full of fine dirt? Will his vouchers vouch him no more of his purchases, and double ones   100 too, than the length and breadth of a pair of indentures?° The very conveyances° of his lands will scarcely lie in this box,° and must th'inheritor° himself have no more, ha?

HORATIO   Not a jot more my lord.

HAMLET   Is not parchment made of sheep-skins?   105

HORATIO   Ay my lord, and of calves'-skins too.

HAMLET   They are sheep and calves which seek out assurance° in that. I will speak to this fellow. Whose grave's this, sirrah?

1. CLOWN   Mine sir:
[*Sings.*] O a pit of clay for to be made   110
For such a guest is meet.

HAMLET   I think it be thine indeed, for thou liest in't.

1. CLOWN   You lie out on't° sir, and therefore 'tis not yours; for my part I do not lie in't, and yet it is mine.

HAMLET   Thous dost lie in't, to be in't and say it is   115 thine: 'tis for the dead, not for the quick,° therefore thou liest.

1. CLOWN   'Tis a quick lie sir, 'twill away again from me to you.

HAMLET   What man dost thou dig it for?

1. CLOWN   For no man sir.

HAMLET   What woman then?   120

1. CLOWN   For none neither.

HAMLET   Who is to be buried in't?

1. CLOWN   One that was a woman sir, but rest her soul she's dead.

---

⁴⁵ *to thee:* i.e., by hanging you. ⁴⁸ *unyoke:* unharness (your wits, after this exertion). ⁵¹ *Mass:* by the mass. ⁵⁵ *Yaughan:* probably a local innkeeper. ⁵⁶ *stoup:* stein, drinking mug. ⁵⁹ *oh, a:* (he grunts as he works). *behove:* benefit. ⁶⁰ *meet:* suitable. ⁶³ *Custom … easiness:* being accustomed to it has made him indifferent. ⁶⁵ *daintier sense:* finer sensibility (being uncalloused). ⁶⁸ *intil:* into. ⁷¹ *jowls:* casts (with obvious pun). ⁷² *Cain's jaw-bone:* the jawbone of an ass with which Cain murdered Abel. ⁷⁴ *o'erreaches:* (1) reaches over (2) gets the better of. *would circumvent:* tried to outwit.

⁸² *chopless:* lacking the lower jaw. *mazzard:* head. ⁸³ *an:* if. ⁸⁴ *trick:* knack. ⁸⁴ *loggets:* game in which small pieces of wood were thrown at fixed stakes. ⁸⁹ *meet:* fitting. ⁹⁰ *quiddities:* subtle definition. ⁹¹ *quillets:* minute distinctions. *tenures:* property holdings. ⁹³ *sconce:* head. ⁹⁶ *statutes:* mortgages. *recognizances:* promissory bonds. ⁹⁶⁻⁹⁷ *fines … recoveries:* legal processes for transferring real estate. ⁹⁷ *vouchers:* persons who vouched for a title to real estate. *fine:* end. ⁹⁸ *recovery:* attainment. ¹⁰¹⁻¹⁰² *length … indentures:* contracts in duplicate, which spread out, would just cover his grave. ¹⁰² *conveyances:* deeds. ¹⁰³ *box:* the grave. *inheritor:* owner. ¹⁰⁸ *assurance:* (1) security (2) transfer of land. ¹¹³ *on:* of. ¹¹⁶ *quick:* living.

HAMLET   How absolute° the knave is, we must speak by
    the card,° or equivocation° will undo us. By the   125
    lord, Horatio, this three years I have took note of it,
    the age is grown so picked,° that the toe of the peasant
    comes so near the heel of the courtier, he galls his
    kibe.° How long hast thou been grave-maker?
1. CLOWN   Of all the days i'th'year I came to't that   130
    day that our last king Hamlet overcame Fortinbras.
HAMLET   How long is that since?
1. CLOWN   Cannot you tell that? Every fool can tell that.
    It was the very day that young Hamlet was born: he
    that is mad and sent into England.   135
HAMLET   Ay marry, why was he sent into England?
1. CLOWN   Why because a' was mad: a' shall recover his
    wits there, or if a' do not, 'tis no great matter there.
HAMLET   Why?
1. CLOWN   'Twill not be seen in him there, there the   140
    men are as mad as he.
HAMLET   How came he mad?
1. CLOWN   Very strangely they say.
HAMLET   How strangely?
1. CLOWN   Faith, e'en with losing his wits.   145
HAMLET   Upon what ground?
1. CLOWN   Why here in Denmark: I have been sexton
    here man and boy thirty years.
HAMLET   How long will a man lie i'th'earth ere he rot?
1. CLOWN   Faith, if a' be not rotten before a' die, as   150
    we have many pocky° corses nowadays that will
    scarce hold the laying in, a' will last you some eight
    year, or nine year. A tanner will last you nine year.
HAMLET   Why he more than another?
1. CLOWN   Why sir, his hide is so tanned with his   155
    trade, that a' will keep out water a great while; and
    your water is a sore° decayer of your whoreson dead
    body. Here's a skull now: this skull hath lain you
    i'th'earth three-and-twenty years.
HAMLET   Whose was it?
1. CLOWN   A whoreson mad fellow's it was, whose do you
    think it was?   160
HAMLET   Nay, I know not.
1. CLOWN   A pestilence on him for a mad rogue, a'
    poured a flagon of Rhenish° on my head once; this
    same skull sir, was sir, Yorick's skull, the king's
    jester.   165
HAMLET   This?
1. CLOWN   E'en that.
HAMLET   Let me see. [Takes the skull.] Alas poor Yorick, I
    knew him Horatio, a fellow of infinite jest, of most
    excellent fancy,° he hath borne me on his back a   170
    thousand times: and now how abhorred in my
    imagination it is: my gorge rises at it. Here hung
    those lips that I have kissed I know not how oft.
    Where be your gibes now? your gambols, your songs,
    your flashes of merriment, that were wont to set   175

the table on a roar?° not one now to mock your own
    grinning? quite chop-fallen?° Now get you to my
    lady's chamber, and tell her, let her paint an inch
    thick, to this favour° she must come. Make her laugh
    at that. Prithee Horatio, tell me one thing.
HORATIO   What's that, my lord?   180
HAMLET   Dost thou think Alexander looked o' this
    fashion i'th'earth?
HORATIO   E'en so.
HAMLET   And smelt so? pah.   [Puts down the skull.]
HORATIO   E'en so my lord.   185
HAMLET   To what base uses we may return, Horatio.
    Why may not imagination trace the noble dust of
    Alexander, til a'find it stopping a bung-hole?°
HORATIO   'Twere to consider too curiously,° to consider
    so.
HAMLET   No faith, not a jot, but to follow him   190
    thither with modesty° enough, and likelihood to lead
    it;as thus: Alexander died, Alexander was buried,
    Alexander returneth to dust, the dust is earth, of
    earth we make loam,° and why of that loam whereto
    he was converted, might they not stop a beer-
    barrel?   195
    Imperious Caesar, dead and turned to clay,
    Might stop a hole to keep the wind away.
    O that that earth which kept the world in awe,
    Should patch a wall t'expel the winter's flaw.°
    But soft, but soft awhile, here comes the king,   200
    The queen, the courtiers.

*Enter King, Queen, Laertes, [Doctor of Divinity], and a coffin,
with Lords attendant.*

                                    Who is this they follow?
    And with such maimèd° rites? This doth betoken
    The corse they follow did with desp'rate hand
    Fordo it° own life; 'twas of some estate.°
    Couch° we awhile, and mark.
    [They retire.]   205
HAMLET   That is Laertes,
    A very noble youth: mark.
LAERTES   What ceremony else?
DOCTOR   Her obsequies have been as far enlarged
    As we have warranty: her death was doubtful,°   210
    And but that great command o'ersways the order,
    She should in ground unsanctified have lodged
    Til the last trumpet: for charitable prayers,
    Shards,° flints and pebbles should be thrown on
    her:
    Yet here she is allowed her virgin crants,°   215
    Her maiden strewments,° and the bringing home
    Of° bell and burial.
LAERTES   Must there no more be done?

---

[124] *absolute:* precise.   [124-125] *by the card:* exactly to the point (card
on which compass points are marked).   [125] *equivocation:* ambiguity. [127] *picked:* fastidious ("picky").   [128] *galls his kibe:* chafes the sore
on the courtier's heel.   [151] *pocky:* rotten (with venereal disease).
[157] *sore:* grievous.   [164] *Rhenish:* Rhine wine.   [170] *fancy:* imagination.

[176] *on a roar:* roaring with laughter.   [177] *chop-fallen:* (a) lacking a
lower jaw (2) dejected, "down in the mouth." [179] *favour:* appearance. [188] *bung-hole:* hole in a cask.   [189] *curiously:* minutely.
[191] *modesty:* moderation.   [193] *loam:* a clay mixture used as plaster.
[199] *flaw:* windy gusts.   [202] *maimèd:* abbreviated.   [204] *Fordo it:*
destroy its. *estate:* social rank.   [205] *Couch:* hide.   [210] *doubtful:* suspicious.   [214] *Shards:* bits of broken pottery.   [215] *crants:* garland.
[216] *strewments:* flowers strewn on the grave.   [216-217] *bringing home
Of:* laying to rest with.

DOCTOR   No more be done:
We should profane the service of the dead,
To sing sage requiem° and such rest to her   220
As to peace-parted souls.
LAERTES   Lay her i'th'earth,
And from her fair and unpolluted flesh
May violets spring: I tell thee churlish priest,
A minist'ring angel shall my sister be,
When thou liest howling.
HAMLET What, the fair Ophelia?   225
QUEEN   [Scattering flowers.] Sweets to the sweet,
farewell.
I hoped thou shouldst have been my Hamlet's wife:
I thought thy bride-bed to have decked, sweet maid,
And not have strewed thy grave.
LAERTES   O treble woe
Fall ten times treble on that cursèd head   230
Whose wicked deed thy most ingenious sense°
Deprived thee of. Hold off the earth awhile,
Till I have caught her once more in mine arms;
                                    Leaps in the grave.
Now pile your dust upon the quick° and dead,
Till of this flat a mountain you have made   235
T'o'ertop old Pelion,° or the skyish head
Of blue Olympus.
HAMLET   [Comes forward.] What is he whose grief
Bears such an emphasis? whose phrase of sorrow
Conjures the wand'ring stars,° and makes them
stand
Like wonder-wounded hearers? This is I,   240
Hamlet the Dane.   Hamlet leaps in after Laertes.
LAERTES   [Grapples with him.] The devil take thy soul.
HAMLET   Thou pray'st not well,
I prithee take thy fingers from my throat,
For though I am not splenitive° and rash,
Yet have I in me something dangerous,   245
Which let thy wiseness fear; hold off thy hand.
KING   Pluck them asunder.
QUEEN   Hamlet, Hamlet!
ALL   Gentlemen!
HORATIO   Good my lord, be quiet.

          [Attendants part them, and they come out of the grave.]

HAMLET   Why, I will fight with him upon this theme
Until my eyelids will no longer wag.   250
QUEEN   O my son, what theme?
HAMLET   I loved Ophelia, forty thousand brothers
Could not with all their quantity of love
Make up my sum. What wilt thou do for her?
KING   O he is mad, Laertes.   255
QUEEN   For love of God, forbear° him.
HAMLET   'Swounds,° show me what thou't do:

Woo't° weep? woo't fight? woo't fast? woo't tear
thyself?
Woo't drink up eisel?° eat a crocodile?°
I'll do't. Dost thou come here to whine?   260
To outface me with leaping in her grave?
Be buried quick with her, and so will I.
And if thou prate of mountains, let them throw
Millions of acres on us, till our ground,
Singeing his pate against the burning zone,°   265
Make Ossa° like a wart. Nay, an thou'lt mouth,
I'll rant as well as thou.
QUEEN   This is mere° madness,
And thus awhile the fit will work on him:
Anon as patient as the female dove
When that her golden couplets° are disclosed,   270
His silence will sit drooping.
HAMLET   Hear you sir,
What is the reason that you use me thus?
I loved you ever; but it is no matter.
Let Hercules himself do what he may,
The cat will mew, and dog will have his day.
                              Exit Hamlet.   275
KING   I pray thee good Horatio, wait upon him.
[Horatio follows.]
[Aside to Laertes.] Strengthen your patience in our
last night's speech,
We'll put the matter to the present push°—
Good Gertrude, set some watch over your son—
This grave shall have a living monument:°   280
An hour of quiet shortly shall we see,
Till then, in patience our proceeding be.
Exeunt.

Scene 2. [A hall in the castle]

Enter Hamlet and Horatio.

HAMLET   So much for this sir, now shall you see the
other;
You do remember all the circumstance.
HORATIO   Remember it my lord!
HAMLET   Sir, in my heart there was a kind of fighting
That would not let me sleep; methought I lay   5
Worse than the mutines in the bilboes.° Rashly—
And praised be rashness for it: let us know,
Our indiscretion sometimes serves us well
When our deep plots do pall,° and that should
learn us
There's a divinity that shapes our ends,   10
Rough-hew them how we will—
HORATIO   That is most
certain.
HAMLET   Up from my cabin,
My sea-gown° scarfed about me, in the dark

---

²²⁰ *sage requiem:* solemn dirge.   ²³¹ *sense:* mind.   ²³⁴ *quick:* live.
²³⁶ *Pelion:* mountain (on which the Titans placed Mt. Ossa, to
scale Mt. Olympus and reach the gods).   ²³⁹ *Conjures ... stars:*
casts a spell over the planets.   ²⁴⁴ *splenitive:* quick-tempered
(anger was thought to originate in the spleen).   ²⁵⁶ *forbear:* be
patient with.   ²⁵⁷ *'Swounds:* corruption of "God's wounds."

²⁵⁸ *Woo't:* wilt thou.   ²⁵⁹ *eisel:* vinegar (thought to reduce anger and
encourage melancholy). *crocodile:* (associated with hypocritical
tears).   ²⁶⁵ *burning zone:* sun's sphere.   ²⁶⁶ *Ossa:* (see above, line
236 n.).   ²⁶⁷ *mere:* absolute.   ²⁷⁰ *golden couplets:* fuzzy yellow twin
fledglings.   ²⁷⁸ *present push:* immediate test.   ²⁸⁰ *living monument:*
(1) lasting tombstone (2) living sacrifice (Hamlet) to memorialize
it.   ⁶ *mutines ... bilboes:* mutineers in shackles.   ⁹ *pall:* fail.   ¹³ *sea-
gown:* short-sleeved knee-length gown worn by seamen.

Groped I to find out them, had my desire,
Fingered° their packet, and in fine° withdrew   15
To mine own room again, making so bold,
My fears forgetting manners, to unseal
Their grand commission; where I found, Horatio—
Ah royal knavery—an exact command,
Larded° with many several sorts of reasons,   20
Importing Denmark's health, and England's too,
With ho, such bugs and goblins in my life,°
That on the supervise,° no leisure bated,°
No, not to stay° the grinding of the axe,
My head should be struck off.

HORATIO   Is't possible?   25

HAMLET   Here's the commission, read it at more leisure.
But wilt thou hear now how I did proceed?

HORATIO   I beseech you.

HAMLET   Being thus be-netted round with villainies,
Ere I could make a prologue to my brains,   30
They had begun the play.° I sat me down,
Devised a new commission, wrote it fair°—
I once did hold it, as our statists° do,
A baseness° to write fair, and laboured much
How to forget that learning, but sir now   35
It did me yeoman's° service: wilt thou know
Th'effect of what I wrote?

HORATIO   Ay, good my lord.

HAMLET   An earnest conjuration° from the king,
As England was his faithful tributary,
As love between them like the palm might
    flourish,   40
As peace should still her wheaten garland wear
And stand a comma° 'tween their amities,
And many such like "as'es"° of great charge,°
That on the view and know of these contents,
Without debatement further, more or less,   45
He should those bearers put to sudden death,
Not shriving° time allowed.

HORATIO   How was this sealed?

HAMLET   Why even in that was heaven ordinant,°
I had my father's signet° in my purse,
Which was the model° of that Danish seal: 50
Folded the writ up in the form of th'other,
Subscribed° it, gave't th'impression,° placed it
    safely,
The changeling° never known: now the next day
Was our sea-fight, and what to this was sequent
Thou knowest already.   55

HORATIO   So Guildenstern and Rosencrantz go to't.

HAMLET   Why man, they did make love to this
    employment,°
They are not near my conscience, their defeat
Does by their own insinuation° grow:
'Tis dangerous when the baser nature comes   60
Between the pass° and fell° incensed points
Of mighty opposites.

HORATIO   Why, what a king is this!

HAMLET   Does it not, think thee, stand me now upon°—
He that hath killed my king, and whored my mother,
Popped in between th'election° and my hopes,   65
Thrown out his angle° for my proper° life,
And with such cozenage°—is't not perfect conscience
To quit° him with this arm? And is't not to be
    damned,
To let this canker of our nature° come
In further evil?   70

HORATIO   It must be shortly known to him from England
What is the issue of the business there.

HAMLET   It will be short, the interim is mine,
And a man's life's no more than to say "One."°
But I am very sorry good Horatio,   75
That to Laertes I forgot myself;
For by the image of my cause, I see
The portraiture of his;° I'll court his favours:
But sure the bravery° of his grief did put me
Into a towering passion.

HORATIO   Peace, who comes here?   80

Enter young Osric.

OSRIC   Your lordship is right welcome back to Denmark.

HAMLET   I humbly thank you sir. [*Aside to Horatio.*]
Dost know this water-fly?

HORATIO   No my good lord.

HAMLET   Thy state is the more gracious,° for 'tis a   85
vice to know him: he hath much land, and fertile: let
a beast be lord of beasts, and his crib shall stand at
the king's mess;° 'tis a chough,° but as I say, spacious
in the possession of dirt.

OSRIC   Sweet lord, if your lordship were at leisure, I   90
should impart a thing to you from his majesty.

HAMLET   I will receive it sir, with all diligence of spirit;
put your bonnet° to his right use, 'tis for the head.

OSRIC   I thank your lordship, it is very hot.

HAMLET   No, believe me, 'tis very cold, the wind is
northerly.

OSRIC   It is indifferent° cold my lord indeed.   95

HAMLET   But yet methinks it is very sultry and hot for
my complexion.°

---

¹⁵*Fingered:* got my fingers on. *in fine:* to finish.   ²⁰ *Larded:*
embellished.   ²² *bugs … life:* imaginary evils attributed to me,
like imaginary goblins ("bugs") meant to frighten children.
²³*supervise:* looking over (the commission). *leisure bated:* delay
excepted.   ²⁴*stay:* await.   ³⁰⁻³¹ *Ere … play:* Before I could outline
the action in my mind, my brains started to play their part.
³²*wrote it fair:* wrote a finished (neat) copy, a "fair copy."   ³³ *statists:*
statesmen.   ³⁴ *baseness:* mark of humble status.   ³⁶ *yeoman's:* (in
the sense of "faithful").   ³⁸ *conjuration:* entreaty (he parodies the
rhetoric of such documents).   ⁴²*comma:* connection.   ⁴³*as'es:* (1)
the "as" clauses in the commission (2) asses. *charge:* (1) weight
(in the clauses) (2) burdens (on the asses).   ⁴⁷*shriving:* confession and absolution.   ⁴⁸ *was heaven ordinant:* it was divinely
ordained.   ⁴⁹*signet:* seal.   ⁵⁰*model:* replica.   ⁵²*Subscribed:* signed.
impression: i.e., of the seal.   ⁵³ *changeling:* substitute (baby imp
left when an infant was spirited away).

---

⁵⁷*did … employment:* asked for it.   ⁵⁹ *insinuation:* intrusion.
⁶¹*pass:* thrust. *fell:* fierce.   ⁶³ *stand … upon:* become incumbent
upon me now.   ⁶⁵ *election:* (the Danish king was so chosen).
⁶⁶*angle:* fishing hook. *proper:* very own.   ⁶⁷ *cozenage:* deception.
⁶⁸*quit:* repay, requite.   ⁶⁹*canker of our nature:* cancer of humanity.   ⁷⁴*to say "One":* to score one hit in fencing.   ⁷⁷⁻⁷⁸ *by the image
… his:* in the depiction of my situation, I see the reflection of
his.   ⁷⁹ *bravery:* ostentation.   ⁸⁵ *gracious:* favorable.   ⁸⁶⁻⁸⁷ *let a
beast … mess:* An ass who owns enough property can eat with the
king.   ⁸⁷ *chough:* chattering bird, jackdaw.   ⁹² *bonnet:* hat.
⁹⁵*indifferent:* reasonably.   ⁹⁷*complexion:* temperament.

OSRIC   Exceedingly, my lord, it is very sultry, as 'twere, I cannot tell how: but my lord, his majesty bade me signify to you that a' has laid a great wager on   100
your head. Sir, this is the matter—

HAMLET   [*Moves him to put on his hat.*] I beseech you remember—

OSRIC   Nay good my lord, for mine ease,° in good faith. Sir, here is newly come to court Laertes, believe me, an absolute gentleman, full of most excellent   105
differences,° of very soft society, and great showing: indeed to speak feelingly of him, he is the card° or calendar of gentry: for you shall find in him the continent of what part a gentleman would see.°

HAMLET   Sir, his definement° suffers no perdition°   110
in you, though I know to divide him inventorially would dozy° th'arithmetic of memory, and yet but yaw neither, in respect of his quick sail,° but in the verity of extolment,° I take him to be a soul of great article,° and his infusion° of such dearth and   115
rareness, as to make true diction of him, his semblable° is his mirror, and who else would trace° him, his umbrage,° nothing more.°

OSRIC   Your lordship speaks most infallibly of him.

HAMLET   The concernancy° sir? why do we wrap   120
the gentleman in our more rawer breath?°

OSRIC   Sir?

HORATIO   Is't not possible to understand in another tongue?° You will do't sir, really.

HAMLET   What imports the nomination° of this gentleman?

OSRIC   Of Laertes?   125

HORATIO   His purse is empty already, all's golden words are spent.

HAMLET   Of him, sir.

OSRIC   I know you are not ignorant—

HAMLET   I would you did sir, yet in faith if you did, it would not much approve me.° Well, sir.   130

OSRIC   You are not ignorant of what excellence Laertes is—

HAMLET   I dare not confess that, lest I should compare with him in excellence, but to know a man well were to know himself.°

OSRIC   I mean sir for his weapon, but in the   135

imputation° laid on him by them in his meed,° he's unfellowed.°

HAMLET   What's his weapon?

OSRIC   Rapier and dagger.

HAMLET   That's two of his weapons—but well.

OSRIC. The king sir, hath wagered with him six Barbary   140
horses, against which he has impawned,° as I take it, six French rapiers and poniards,° with their assigns,° as girdle, hangers,° and so. Three of thecarriages° in faith are very dear to fancy,° very responsive to the hilts, most delicate carriages, and of very liberal conceit.°   145

HAMLET   What call you the carriages?

HORATIO   I knew you must be edified by the margent° ere you had done.

OSRIC   The carriages sir, are the hangers.

HAMLET   The phrase would be more germane to the matter, if we could carry a cannon by our sides: I   150
would it might be hangers till then, but on: six Barbary horses against six French swords, theirassigns, and three liberal-conceited carriages— that's the French bet against the Danish. Why is this all "impawned" as you call it?   155

OSRIC   The king sir, hath laid sir, that in a dozen passes between yourself and him, he shall not exceed you three hits°; he hath laid on twelve for nine, and it would come to immediate trial, if your lordship would vouchsafe the answer.°   160

HAMLET   How if I answer no?

OSRIC   I mean my lord, the opposition of your person in trial.

HAMLET   Sir, I will walk here in the hall; if it please his majesty, it is the breathing time° of day with me; let the foils be brought, the gentleman willing, and   165
the king hold his purpose, I will win for him an I can, if not, I will gain nothing but my shame and the odd hits.

OSRIC   Shall I re-deliver you° e'en so?

HAMLET   To this effect sir, after what flourish your nature will.°

OSRIC   I commend° my duty to your lordship.   170

HAMLET   Yours, yours.   [*Exit Osric.*]
He does well to commend it himself, there are no tongues else for's turn.°

HORATIO   This lapwing° runs away with the shell on his head.

HAMLET   A' did comply° sir, with his dug° before a'   175
sucked it: thus has he—and many more of the same bevy that I know the drossy° age dotes on—only got

---

[103] *for mine ease:* for my own comfort.   [106] *differences:* accomplishments.   [107] *card:* shipman's compass card.   [109] *continent … see:* (continuing the marine metaphor) (1) geographical continent (2) all the qualities a gentleman would look for.   [110–118] *Sir … more:* (Hamlet outdoes Osric in affected speech).   [110] *definement:* description. *perdition:* loss.   [112] *dozy:* dizzy.   [113] *yaw … sail:* (1) moving in an unsteady course (as another boat would do, trying to catch up with Laertes' "quick sail") (2) staggering to one trying to list his accomplishments.   [113–114] *in … extolment:* to praise him truthfully.   [115] *article:* scope. *infusion:* essence.   [116–118] *as to make … more:* to describe him truly I would have to employ his mirror to depict his only equal—himself, and who would follow him is only a shadow.   [117] *semblable:* equal. *trace:* (1) describe (2) follow.   [118] *umbrage:* shadow.   [120] *concernancy:* relevance.   [121] *rawer breath:* crude speech.   [122–123] *Is't not … tongue:* Cannot Osric understand his own way of speaking when used by another?   [124] *nomination:* naming.   [129–130] *if you did … me:* If you found me to be "not ignorant," it would prove little (as you are no judge of ignorance).   [133–134] *to know … himself:* to know a man well, one must first know oneself.

[136] *imputation:* repute. *meed:* worth. *unfellowed:* unequaled.   [141] *impawned:* staked.   [142] *poniards:* daggers. *assigns:* accessories.   [143] *girdle, hangers:* belt, straps attached thereto, from which swords were hung. *carriages:* hangers.   [144] *dear to fancy:* rare in design.   [145] *liberal conceit:* elaborate conception.   [147] *margent:* marginal note.   [156–158] *laid … three hits:* wagered that in twelve bouts Laertes must win three more than Hamlet.   [160] *answer:* acceptance of the challenge (Hamlet interprets as "reply").   [164] *breathing time:* exercise period.   [168] *re-deliver you:* take back your answer.   [169] *after … will:* embellished as you wish.   [170] *commend:* offer (Hamlet interprets as "praise").   [173] *no tongues … turn:* no others who would.   [174] *lapwing:* (reported to be so precocious that it ran as soon as hatched).   [175] *comply:* observe the formalities of courtesy. *dug:* mother's breast.   [177] *drossy:* frivolous.

the tune of the time, and out of an habit of
encounter,° a kind of yeasty collection,° which carries
them through and through the most fond and   *180*
winnowed° opinions; and do but blow them to their
trial, and bubbles are out.°

Enter a Lord.

LORD   My lord, his majesty commended him to you by
young Osric, who brings back to him that you attend
him in the hall. He sends to know if your pleasure *185*
hold to play with Laertes, or that you will take longer
time.

HAMLET   I am constant to my purposes, they follow the
king's pleasure, if his fitness speaks,° mine is ready:
now or whensoever, provided I be so able as now.

LORD   The king, and queen, and all are coming down. *190*

HAMLET   In happy time.

LORD   The queen desires you to use some gentle
entertainment° to Laertes, before you fall to play.

HAMLET   She well instructs me.   *[Exit Lord.]*

HORATIO   You will lose this wager, my lord.   *195*

HAMLET   I do not think so, since we went into France, I
have been in continual practice, I shall win at the
odds; but thou wouldst not think how ill all's here
about my heart: but it is no matter.

HORATIO   Nay good my lord—   *200*

HAMLET   It is but a foolery, but it is such a kind of
gaingiving° as would perhaps trouble a woman.

HORATIO   If your mind dislike any thing, obey it. I will
forestall their repair° hither, and say you are not fit.

HAMLET   Not a whit, we defy augury;° there is a   *205*
special providence in the fall of a sparrow.° If it be
now, 'tis not to come: if it be not to come, it will be
now; if it be not now, yet it will come—the readiness
is all. Since no man has aught of what he leaves, what
is't to leave betimes?° let be.   *210*

*A table prepared. Trumpets, Drums, and officers with cushions. Enter
King, Queen, and all the state, [Osric], foils, daggers, and Laertes.*

KING   Come Hamlet, come and take this hand from me.

[Puts Laertes' hand into Hamlet's.]

HAMLET   Give me your pardon sir, I have done you
wrong,
But pardon't as you are a gentleman. This presence
knows, and you must needs have heard,
How I am punished with a sore distraction.°   *215*
What I have done
That might your nature, honour, and exception°
Roughly awake, I here proclaim was madness: Was't
Hamlet wronged Laertes? never Hamlet.

If Hamlet from himself be ta'en away,   *220*
And when he's not himself, does wrong Laertes,
Then Hamlet does it not, Hamlet denies it:
Who does it then? his madness. If't be so, Hamlet is
of the faction that is wronged,
His madness is poor Hamlet's enemy.   *225*
Sir, in this audience,
Let my disclaiming from a purposed evil,
Free me so far in your most generous thoughts,
That I have shot my arrow o'er the house
And hurt my brother.°   *230*

LAERTES   I am satisfied in nature,
Whose motive in this case should stir me most
To my revenge, but in my terms of honour
I stand aloof, and will no reconcilement,
Till by some elder masters of known honour   *235*
I have a voice and precedent° of peace
To keep my name ungored:° but till that time,
I do receive your offered love, like love,
And will not wrong it.

HAMLET   I embrace it freely, And will
this brother's wager frankly° play.   *240*
Give us the foils: come on.

LAERTES   Come, one for me.

HAMLET   I'll be your foil° Laertes, in mine ignorance
Your skill shall like a star i'th' darkest night
Stick fiery off° indeed.

LAERTES You mock me sir.   *245*

HAMLET   No, by this hand.

KING   Give them the foils young Osric. Cousin° Hamlet,
You know the wager.

HAMLET   Very well my lord.
Your grace has laid the odds o'th' weaker side.   *250*

KING   I do not fear it, I have seen you both,
But since he is bettered,° we have therefore odds.

LAERTES   This is too heavy: let me see another.°

HAMLET   This likes° me well, these foils have all a°
length?

OSRIC   Ay my good lord.   *255*
                                    Prepare to play.

KING   Set me the stoups° of wine upon that table:
If Hamlet give the first or second hit,
Or quit in answer of° the third exchange,
Let all the battlements their ordnance fire.
The king shall drink to Hamlet's better breath,   *260*
And in the cup an union° shall he throw,
Richer than that which four successive kings
In Denmark's crown have worn: give me the cups,
And let the kettle° to the trumpet speak,
The trumpet to the cannoneer without,   *265*

178–179 *habit of encounter:* habitual association (with others as frivolous).. ¹⁷⁹ *yeasty collection:* frothy assortment of phrases.
^{180–181} *fond and winnowed:* trivial and considered. ¹⁸² *blow ... out:* blow on them to test them and they are gone. ¹⁸⁸ *his fitness speaks:* it agrees with his convenience. ^{192–193} *gentle entertainment:* friendly treatment. ²⁰² *gaingiving:* misgiving. ²⁰⁴ *repair:* coming. ²⁰⁵ *augury:* omens. ²⁰⁶ *special ... sparrow:* ("Are not two sparrows sold for a farthing? and one of them shall not fall on the ground without your Father": Matthew 10:29). ²¹⁰ *betimes:* early (before one's time). ²¹⁵ *sore distraction:* grievous madness. ²¹⁷ *exception:* disapproval.

^{229–230} *That I have ... brother:* (that it was accidental). ²³² *voice and precedent:* opinion based on precedent. ²³³ *name ungored:* reputation uninjured. Laertes says that he cannot accept Hamlet's apology formally until he is assured that his acceptance will not harm his honor or damage his reputation. ²⁴⁰ *frankly:* freely.
²⁴² *foil:* (1) the blunted sword with which they fence (2) leaf of metal set under a jewel to make it shine more brilliantly.
²⁴⁴ *Stick fiery off:* show in shining contrast. ²⁴⁷ *Cousin:* kinsman.
²⁵² *bettered:* either (a) judged to be better, or (b) better trained.
²⁵³ *another:* (the unbated and poisoned sword). ²⁵⁴ *likes:* pleases.
all a: all the same. ²⁵⁶ *stoups:* goblets. ²⁵⁸ *quit in answer of:* score a draw in. ²⁶¹ *union:* large pearl. ²⁶⁴ *kettle:* kettledrum.

The cannons to the heavens, the heaven to earth,
"Now the king drinks to Hamlet." Come begin.
And you the judges bear a wary eye.   *Trumpets the*
                                         while.

HAMLET   Come on sir.
LAERTES   Come my lord.   *They play.*
HAMLET   One.
LAERTES   No.
HAMLET   Judgment.
OSRIC   A hit, a very palpable hit.

> *Flourish. Drum, trumpets and shot. A piece° goes off.*

LAERTES   Well, again.   270
KING   Stay, give me drink. Hamlet, this pearl is
    thine.Here's to thy health: give him the cup.
HAMLET   I'll play this bout first, set it by a while.
    Come.   [*They play.*]
    Another hit. What say you?
LAERTES   A touch, a touch, I do confess't.   275
KING   Our son shall win.
QUEEN   He's fat° and scant of
    breath.Here Hamlet, take my napkin,° rub thy
    brows.
                        [*She takes Hamlet's cup.*]
    The queen carouses° to thy fortune, Hamlet.
HAMLET   Good madam.
KING   Gertrude, do not drink.
QUEEN   I will my lord, I pray you pardon me.   280
KING   [*Aside.*] It is the poisoned cup, it is too late.
HAMLET   I dare not drink yet madam: by and by.
QUEEN   Come, let me wipe thy face.
LAERTES   [*To the King.*] My lord, I'll hit him now.
KING   I do not think't.   285
LAERTES   [*Aside.*] And yet 'tis almost 'gainst my
    conscience.
HAMLET   Come for the third Laertes, you do but dally,
    I pray you pass° with your best violence,
    I am afeard you make a wanton of me.°
LAERTES   Say you so? Come on.   290
                                            Play.
OSRIC   Nothing neither way   [*They break off.*]
LAERTES   Have at you now.°   [*Wounds Hamlet.*]

> *In scuffling they change rapiers.*

KING   Part them, they are incensed.
HAMLET   Nay, come again.   [*The Queen falls.*]
OSRIC   Look to the queen there, ho!   295

> [*Hamlet wounds Laertes.*]

HORATIO   They bleed on both side. How is it, my lord?
OSRIC   How is't, Laertes?
LAERTES   Why as a woodcock° to my own springe,°
    Osric,
    I am justly killed with mine own treachery.

HAMLET   How does the queen?   300
KING   She sounds° to see them bleed.
QUEEN   No, no, the drink, the drink, O my dear Hamlet,
    The drink, the drink, I am poisoned.   [*Dies.*]
HAMLET   O villainy! ho! let the door be locked,
    Treachery, seek it out!   305
LAERTES   It is here Hamlet. Hamlet, thou art slain,
    No medicine in the world can do thee good,
    In thee there is not half an hour of life,
    The treacherous instrument is in thy hand,
    Unbated° and envenomed. The foul practice°   310
    Hath turned itself on me, lo, here I lie
    Never to rise again: thy mother's poisoned:
    I can no more: the king, the king's to blame.
HAMLET   The point envenomed too:
    Then venom, to thy work.   315
    Hurts the King.
ALL   Treason! treason!
KING   O yet defend me friends, I am but hurt.°
HAMLET   Here, thou incestuous, murderous, damnèd
    Dane,
    Drink off this potion: is thy union here?
    Follow my mother.   320
    King dies.
LAERTES   He is justly served,
    It is a poison tempered° by himself:
    Exchange forgiveness with me, noble Hamlet,
    Mine and my father's death come not upon thee,°
    Nor thine on me.   325
                                            Dies.
HAMLET   Heaven make thee free° of it, I follow thee
    I am dead, Horatio; wretched queen, adieu.
    You that look pale, and tremble at this chance,
    That are but mutes,° or audience to this act,
    Had I but time, as this fell sergeant° Death   330
    Is strict in his arrest, O I could tell you—
    But let it be; Horatio, I am dead,
    Thou livest, report me and my cause aright
    To the unsatisfied.°
HORATIO   Never believe it;
    I am more an antique Roman° than a Dane: 335
    Here's yet some liquor left.
HAMLET   As thou'rt a man,
    Give me the cup, let go, by heaven I'll ha't.
    O God, Horatio, what a wounded name,
    Things standing thus unknown, shall live behind me.
    If thou didst ever hold me in thy heart,   340
    Absènt thee from felicity awhile,
    And in this harsh world draw thy breath in pain
    To tell my story.   *A march afar off, and shot within.*
                        What warlike noise is this?
OSRIC   Young Fortinbras with conquest come from
    Poland,
    To th'ambassadors of England gives   345

---

stage direction: *piece:* i.e., a cannon.   ²⁷⁶*fat:* sweating (sweat was thought to be melted body fat).   ²⁷⁷*napkin:* handkerchief. ²⁷⁸*carouses:* drinks.   ²⁸⁸*pass:* thrust.   ²⁸⁹*make a wanton of me:* are indulging me like a spoiled child.   ²⁹²*Have … now:* (the bout is over when Laertes attacks Hamlet and catches him off guard). ²⁹⁸*woodcock:* snipe-like bird (believed to be foolish and therefore easily trapped). *springe:* trap.

³⁰¹*sounds:* swoons.   ³¹⁰*Unbated:* not blunted. *practice:* plot. ³¹⁷*but hurt:* only wounded.   ³²²*tempered:* mixed.   ³²⁴*come … thee:* are not to be blamed on you.   ³²⁶*free:* guiltless.   ³²⁹*mutes:* actors without speaking parts.   ³³⁰*fell sergeant:* cruel sheriff's officer.   ³³⁴*unsatisfied:* uninformed.   ³³⁵*antique Roman:* ancient Roman (who considered suicide honorable).

This warlike volley.

HAMLET   O I die Horatio,
The potent poison quite o'er-crows° my spirit,
I cannot live to hear the news from England,
But I do prophesy th'election° lights
On Fortinbras, he has my dying voice,°   350
So tell him, with th'occurrents more and less°
Which have solicited°—the rest is silence.   *Dies.*

HORATIO   Now cracks a noble heart: good night sweet
    prince,
And flights of angels sing thee to thy rest.
Why does the drum come hither?   355

*Enter Fortinbras and English Ambassadors, with drum, colours,
and attendants.*

FORTINBRAS   Where is this sight?
HORATIO   What is it you would see?If aught of woe,
    or wonder, cease your search.
FORTINBRAS   This quarry cries on havoc.° O proud death,
What feast is toward° in thine eternal cell,   360
That thou so many princes at a shot
So bloodily hast struck?
AMBASSADOR   The sight is dismal,
And our affairs from England come too late;
The ears° are senseless that should give us
    hearing,   365
To tell him his commandment is fulfilled,
That Rosencrantz and Guildenstern are dead:
Where should we have our thanks?
HORATIO   Not from his
    mouth,Had it th'ability of life to thank you;
He never gave commandment for their death;   370
But since so jump° upon this bloody question,

You from the Polack wars, and you from England
Are here arrived, give order that these bodies
High on a stage be placèd to the view,
And let me speak to th'yet unknowing world   375
How these things came about; so shall you hear
Of carnal, bloody and unnatural acts,
Of accidental judgments, casual° slaughters,
Of deaths put on° by cunning and forced cause,°
And in this upshot, purposes mistook,   380
Fall'n on th'inventors' heads:° all this can I
Truly deliver.
FORTINBRA   Let us haste to hear it,
And call the noblest to the audience.
For me, with sorrow I embrace my fortune;
I have some rights of memory° in this kingdom,   385
Which now to claim my vantage° doth invite me.
HORATIO   Of that I shall have also cause to speak,
And from his mouth whose voice will draw on more:°
But let this same° be presently performed,
Even while men's minds are wild,° lest more
    mischance   390
On° plots and errors happen.
FORTINBRAS   Let four captains
Bear Hamlet like a soldier to the stage,
For he was likely, had he been put on,°
To have proved most royal; and for his passage,°
The soldiers' music and the rite of war   395
Speak loudly for him:
Take up the bodies, such a sight as this,
Becomes the field, but here shows much amiss.
Go bid the soldiers shoot.

Exeunt marching: after the which a peal of ordnance are shot off.

---

³⁴⁷ *o'er-crows:* overpowers, conquers. ³⁴⁹ *election:* (for king of Denmark). ³⁵⁰ *voice:* vote. ³⁵¹ *occurrents more and less:* events great and small. ³⁵² *solicited:* incited me.³⁵⁹ *quarry ... havoc:* heap of dead bodies proclaims slaughter done here. ³⁶⁰ *toward:* in preparation. ³⁶⁵ *ears:* (of Claudius). ³⁷¹ *jump:* opportunely.

³⁷⁸ *casual:* unpremeditated. ³⁷⁹ *put on:* prompted by. *forced cause:* being forced to act in self-defense. ³⁸⁰⁻³⁸¹ *purposes ... heads:* plots gone wrong and destroying their inventors. ³⁸⁵ *of memory:* remembered. ³⁸⁶ *vantage:* advantageous position. ³⁸⁸ *draw on more:* influence more (votes). ³⁸⁹ *this same:* this telling of the story. ³⁹⁰ *wild:* upset. ³⁹¹ *On:* on top of. ³⁹³ *put on:* i.e., put on the throne. ³⁹⁴ *passage:* i.e., to the next world.

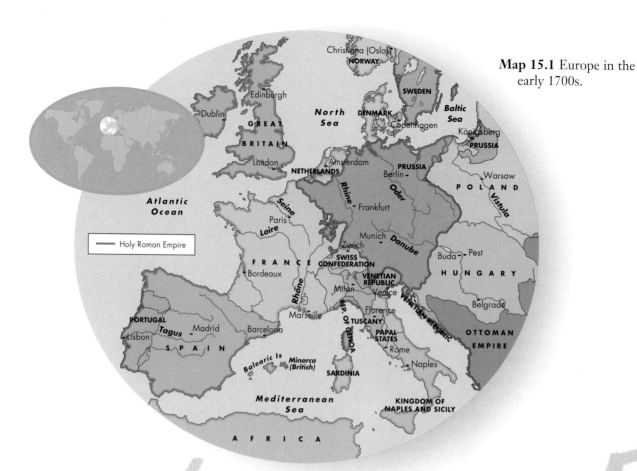

Christiana (Oslo)
NORWAY
SWEDEN
Baltic
Sea
Edinburgh
North
Sea
DENMARK
Copenhagen
Königsberg
PRUSSIA
Dublin
GREAT
BRITAIN
London
NETHERLANDS
Amsterdam
PRUSSIA
Berlin
Warsaw
POLAND
Atlantic
Ocean
Seine
Rhine
Oder
Frankfurt
Vistula
Paris
Loire
Munich
Danube
—— Holy Roman Empire
Zurich
Buda - Pest
FRANCE
Bordeaux
SWISS
CONFEDERATION
VENETIAN
REPUBLIC
Milan
Venice
HUNGARY
Rhône
Rhône
VENETIAN REPUBLIC
Florence
Belgrade
PORTUGAL
Tagus
Madrid
Barcelona
Marseille
REP. OF GENOA
TUSCANY
PAPAL
STATES
Rome
OTTOMAN
EMPIRE
Lisbon
SPAIN
Balearic Is
Minorca
(British)
SARDINIA
Naples
Mediterranean
Sea
KINGDOM OF
NAPLES AND SICILY
AFRICA

Map 15.1 Europe in the early 1700s.

THE BAROQUE AGE

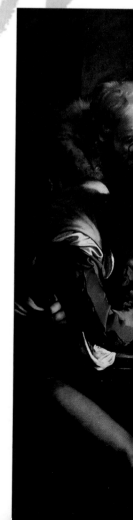

CHAPTER 15

‹ *The Baroque in Italy*

‹ *The Baroque outside Italy*

Caravaggio, Calling of St. Matthew (Detail), ca. 1599—1602, Rome.

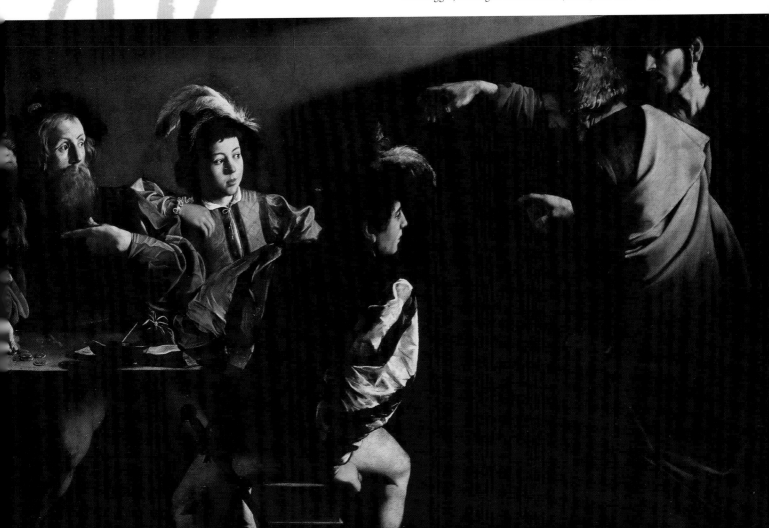

THE BAROQUE IN ITALY

The term **baroque**, from the Portuguese word *barrocco*, originally means a large, irregularly shaped pearl and was initially used as a pejorative, or negative, term. Gradually it came to describe the complex, multi-faceted, international phenomenon—it can hardly be called a style—of the Baroque. The Baroque is defined not so much in formal terms as in attitude and relationship to the audience. Baroque artists intended to involve their audiences emotionally. Formally, the style reflected a heightened realism and sense of motion in its creation of theatrical spaces, its use of classical elements in emotionally charged settings, its figurative sculpture, and in the surprising use of irregular forms in its architecture.

At least as important in defining the Baroque style is understanding the patronage that supported it. During the Counter-Reformation, Church-sponsored art in Rome thrived as it never had before. Though other secular patrons were equally important in the development of Baroque art (particularly Philip IV in Spain and Marie de' Medici and Louis XIV in France), the Church in Rome assumed the role of the center of the Baroque art world.

As pope succeeded pope, each brought with him an entourage of family and friends who expected and received lucrative positions in the government and who vied with each other to give expression to their newfound wealth and position. The popes commissioned palaces and chapels—along with paintings and sculptures to decorate them. Artists flocked to Rome to take advantage of the situation. And since popes tend to be appointed late in life, their period in power was often short. The promise of a new pope, and with him a new family assuming the powers of patronage, was something that artists could, with some confidence, count on.

THE COUNTER-REFORMATION IN ROME

When Martin Luther posted his famous "Ninety-Five Theses" in 1517, Pope Leo X and the Catholic Church in Rome recognized the powerful threat that the Protestant Reformation represented. The Church sought to remake Rome as the cultural center of the Western world. The strategy it developed to defend Rome's prestige and dominion was continued for over a hundred years, culminating in the twenty-one-year pontificate of Urban VIII (1623–44). The Roman popes thus once again became the great patrons of art and architecture they had been in the early sixteenth century.

A theological justification for this patronage came at the Council of Trent, which convened in three sessions from 1545 to 1563 to address the crisis of the Reformation. The Council decided to "counter" the Protestant threat "by means of the stories of the mysteries of our Redemption portrayed by paintings or other representations, [whereby] the people [shall] be instructed and confirmed in the habit of remembering, and continually revolving in mind the articles of faith." The Council further suggested that religious art be directed toward clarity (to increase understanding), realism (to

Timeline 15.1 The Counter-Reformation in Rome.

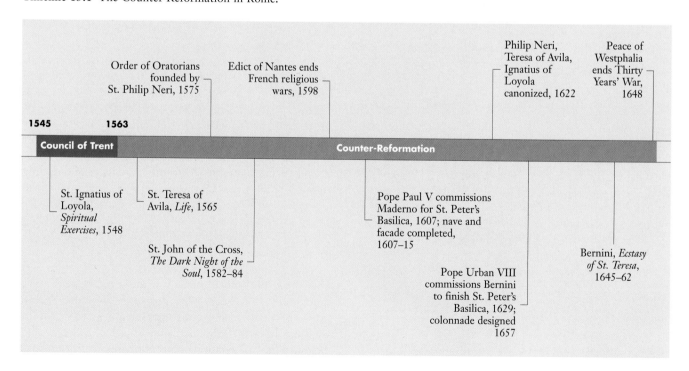

make it more meaningful in every day fashion), and emotion (to arouse piety and religious fervor).

According to the Council's recommendations, art had to be easily understood; complicated allegories were discouraged. Music had to be accessible and lyrics intelligible; complex polyphonic writing was consequently also discouraged. Literature should celebrate religious values and ideals. These recommendations were designed to counter the ultra-refined and highly stylized paintings of the Mannerist period. Mannerist painting tended to be elegant, anti-naturalistic, technically virtuosic, highly decorative, complex in color and structure, and mythological or allegorical in content. Baroque art was to make direct religious statements on important subjects already familiar to the masses of uneducated common people. Still, from the Mannerists Baroque artists inherited a reliance on emotionally charged and dramatic action. The Council of Trent began a renewal of faith and a fresh stirring of spiritual feeling. Religious fervor was encouraged, through the increased psychological depth and broader emotional range of the Church's art and architecture, and through liturgies, rituals, and dogmas.

Out of the Council of Trent emerged two new religious orders, one for laymen, the Oratorians, and the other for clergy, the Jesuits. Both were of central importance to the religious mission.

The Oratorians. The Oratory movement was founded by a lay person, St. Philip Neri. The Oratorians were groups of lay Catholics who met informally for spiritual conversation, study, and prayer. They met not in churches but in prayer halls called **oratories**. They were not a religious order: they took no vows, and members could leave at any time. Music played an essential role in the religious devotions of the Oratorians, especially vocal music. The composer who was most important for them was Palestrina (see Chapter 13), whose *Laude*, or songs of praise, were easy to sing. Later, musical performances became increasingly dramatic. Eventually, they resembled unstaged miniature music dramas and were the forerunners of the oratorios written by George Frederick Handel.

The Jesuits. In 1534 the Jesuit order of Catholic priests was established by St. Ignatius Loyola, and there was nothing informal about the Jesuits' organization or goals. The order was to follow a militaristic discipline. Members followed strict vows of poverty, chastity, and obedience, while pursuing a rigorous education in preparation for their missionary role. Jesuit priests played an important part in the religious life of the age, serving as confessors and spiritual advisers to prominent artists such as Bernini and to political leaders, including Queen Christina of Sweden.

The most influential aspect of Jesuit spirituality derives from the work written by the order's founder, St. Ignatius. His *Spiritual Exercises*, published in 1548, were designed to guide believers through a sequence of spiritual practices to intensify their relationship with God. The *Exercises* attempted to involve each of the senses so that the individual might obtain more than just an intellectual understanding of God. For example, when contemplating sin and hell, the soul is exhorted to consider in order: the sights of hell (flames); the sounds of hell (groans of the damned and shrieks of devils); the smells of hell (the fetid stench of corrupting bodies); the tastes of hell (the suffering of hunger and thirst); and the tactile experience of hell (the intense heat, which scorches the body and boils the blood).

Complementing the work of the Oratorians and the Jesuits were the writings of sixteenth- and seventeenth-century Spanish mystics such as St. John of the Cross, who wrote *The Dark Night of the Soul*, and St. Teresa of Avila, who wrote an autobiography. Both exhibited an uncanny ability to blend the contemplative life with a commitment to a life of action.

Philip Neri, Teresa of Avila, and Ignatius of Loyola were all canonized as Catholic saints in a single ceremony in 1622, during the papacy of Gregory XV. Not long after their canonization, the immense work of honoring these saints in painting, music, sculpture, architecture, and literature began. Their lives and miracles were celebrated; their worldly and spiritual missions were depicted. All this was aimed at strengthening the beliefs of the faithful and admonishing them to emulate the saints as well as honor them.

SCULPTURE AND ARCHITECTURE IN ROME

St. Peter's Basilica. The Church's most visible effort to arouse the piety of the people was the continued work on the new St. Peter's Basilica, work initiated by Pope Julius II in 1502 (see Chapter 13). In 1607, Pope Paul V commissioned CARLO MADERNO [mah-DEHR-no] (1556–1629) as Vatican architect to convert Michelangelo's Greek plan into a traditional Latin-cross plan complete with a new facade. There was a practical reason for this: the long nave of the Latin-cross plan provided space for more people to attend services. The interior space Maderno created was the largest of any church in Europe, actually capable of containing almost any other church within its massive interior. It is difficult to measure such vastness with the human eye and to fully appreciate its size. The experience is meant to evoke emotionally the spiritual vastness of God Himself.

Maderno's facade (fig. 15.1) followed Michelangelo's original conception of using colossal orders to unite the stories, and of topping the entrance by a triangular pediment. In fact, Maderno's composition is more theatrical than Michelangelo intended, with wings gesturing to center stage. Pope Paul V conceived of this as a backdrop to his own public appearances and required Maderno to design a balcony from which he could bless the people below. The architectural crescendo rises from the sides

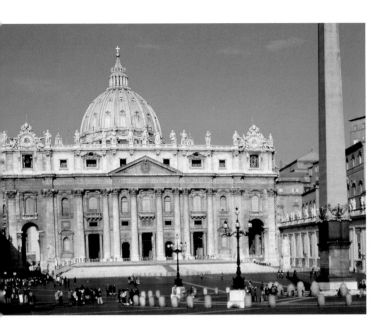

Figure 15.1 Carlo Maderno, facade of St. Peter's, Rome, 1607–15, height 147′ (44.81 m), width 374′ (114 m). The facade is treated like a theatrical performance that builds from the wings: starting from the corners, the pilasters double, then become columns, which then also double, and, finally, the center section seems to push out to meet the visitor.

of the facade toward the central portal: flat corner pilasters become columns, the columns then double, and the center facade projects forward. A dramatic, which is to say Baroque, effect is created.

Gianlorenzo Bernini. The theatricality of Maderno's facade was, to Pope Urban VIII, only a beginning. When Maderno died in 1629, Urban VIII replaced him with GIANLORENZO BERNINI [ber-NEE-nee] (1598–1680), who had collaborated with Maderno for five years. Although Bernini considered himself a classicist, but he fused his classicism with an extraordinary sense of the dramatic and the emotional. His sculpture and architecture in many ways define the chief characteristics of Baroque art.

In 1657, Bernini, now working for another pope, designed and supervised the building of a **colonnade** (fig. 15.2), or row of columns, for the giant open area in front of St. Peter's. Beginning in two straight **porticoes**, or covered walkways, the Doric columns extend down a slight incline from the church facade, then swerve into two enormous curved porticoes that surround and embrace the open space of the square, like "the motherly arms of the church," as Bernini himself put it (fig. 15.3). Forgoing the preferred square and circular forms of the Renaissance, Bernini's colonnade used an ellipse

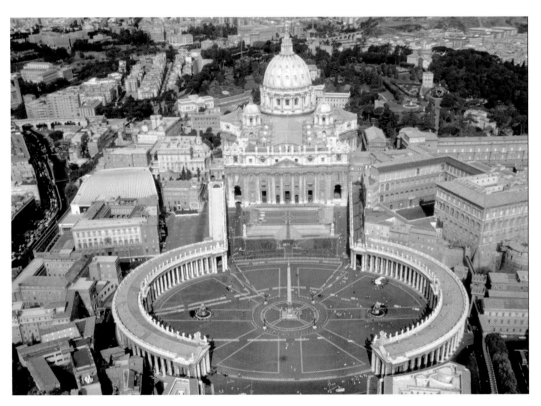

Figure 15.2 St. Peter's, Rome. Facade by Carlo Maderno, dome completed by Giacomo della Porta, and colonnade by Gianlorenzo Bernini. Bernini created an architectural environment for St. Peter's. The visitor passes through elliptical and trapezoidal spaces outlined by colonnaded porticoes before entering the immense basilica.

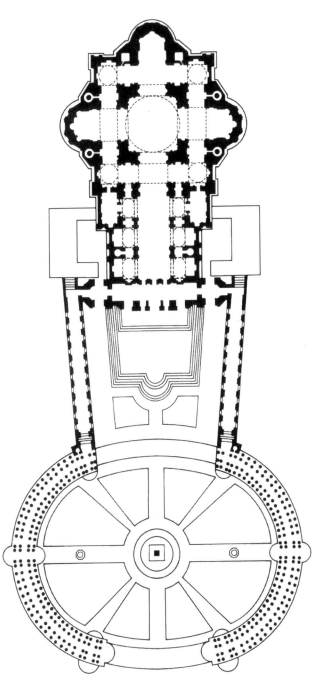

to invention. This opposition between retaining traditional values and discovering new ones will continue to play a greater and greater role in the development of Western art well into the twentieth century.

Bernini was also commissioned to design an enormous cast-bronze **baldacchino** [ball-dah-KEY-noh], or canopy, for the main altar of St. Peter's (fig. 15.4). Nearly one hundred feet high, the work is at once sculpture and architecture, its twisted columns topped with a sphere, representing the universe, and a cross. Hanging down are tasseled bronze panels that imitate hanging cloth, and

Figure 15.4 Gianlorenzo Bernini, Baldacchino, 1624–33. Gilt bronze, height approx. 100′ (30.50 m), St. Peter's Basilica, Vatican, Rome. The bronze used to make the baldacchino was taken from the beams of the pantheon roof (see chapter 5), giving rise to the saying, "What the Barbarians did not do, the Barberini have done."

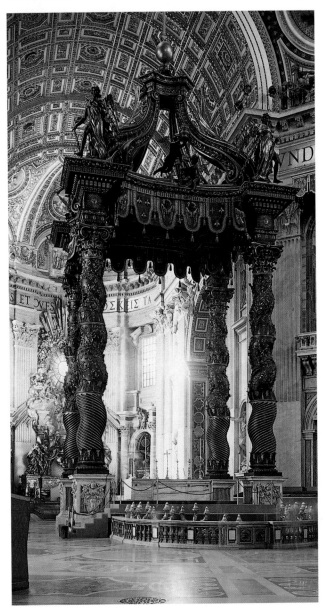

Figure 15.3 Plan of Bernini's colonnade. This plan illustrates the perfect half-moons of the colonnade and the radiating lines in the pavement of the piazza.

and a trapezoid, much more dynamic forms. In the center of the oval stands an **obelisk,** or four-sided shaft topped by a pyramid. From there, lines on the pavement radiate out to the colonnade. Finally, standing over each inner column is a different statue, creating an irregular silhouette along the top of the colonnade.

As Bernini's colonnade makes clear, the virtues of the classical were continually upheld in the Baroque age, but there is in the variety of statues across the top of the columns, for instance, a counter-tendency, a dedication already carved marble sculptures of considerable merit. He spent much time drawing the Vatican collection, including the *Laocoön* and the work of Michelangelo and Raphael. His sculpture of *David* (fig. 15.5), carved in 1623 and characteristic of his style, deserves comparison to Michelangelo's High Renaissance *David* (see Chapter 13). In its realistic depiction of dramatic action, Bernini's work is closer to the ideals of Hellenistic sculpture as embodied in the *Laocoön*. Michelangelo's *David*, by contrast, seems restrained, controlled. Whereas Michelangelo depicts an unspecified moment before David's conflict with Goliath, Bernini captures the split-second before David releases from his sling the stone that kills the giant. Bernini's *David* implies the presence of a second figure to "complete" the action; it is David's pose and facial expression that indicate with precision the direction in which Goliath is to be found. The space surrounding the sculpture becomes charged with tension. So effective is Bernini in activating this space that people

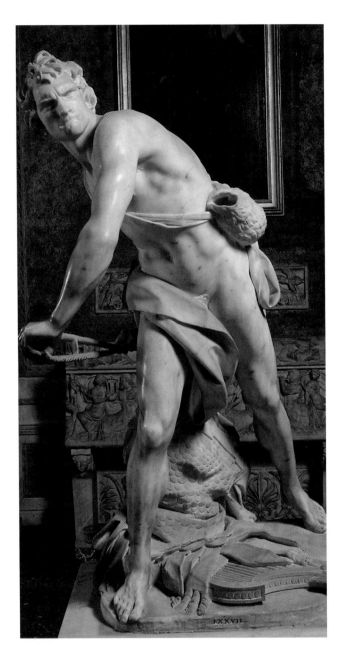

Figure 15.5 Gianlorenzo Bernini, *David*, marble, 1623, height 5′7″ (1.7 m), Galleria Borghese, Rome. Unlike Michelangelo's static *David*, Bernini's is caught at the split-second of the action when its direction is about to reverse—much like the ancient Greek *Discus Thrower*. Bernini effectively indicates the position of the giant Goliath, something that is sensed by viewers, who quickly move out of the implied line of fire.

Figure 15.6 Gianlorenzo Bernini, *Ecstasy of St. Teresa*, 1645–52, overview of Cornaro Chapel, height of figure group 11′6″ (3.51 m), Santa Maria della Vittoria, Rome. This dramatic depiction of Teresa's written description is literally theatrical, for the chapel is arranged like a theater, complete with box seats occupied by marble figures of members of the Cornaro family.

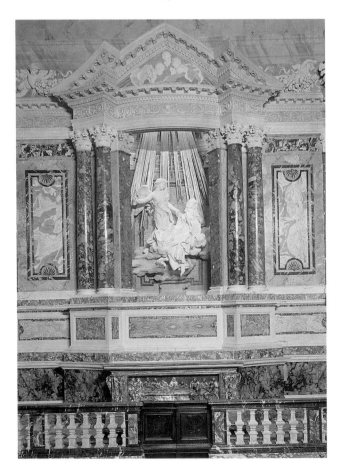

prominently embossed on them are honeybees and suns, and laurel leaves on climbing vines, the emblems of the Barberini, Pope Urban VIII's family. The baldacchino thus is a monument not only to St. Peter, over whose grave it stands, but also to Pope Urban VIII, who commissioned it.

As a child, Bernini had moved from Naples to Rome to study under his father. By the age of eight, he had

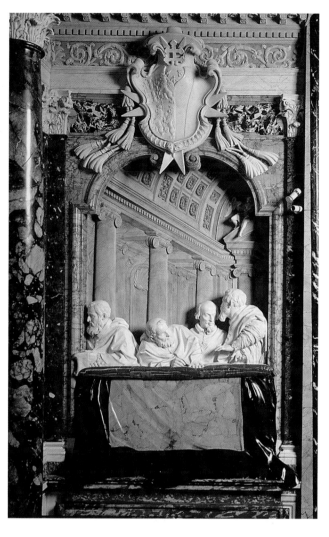

Figure 15.7 Gianlorenzo Bernini, *Cornaro Family in Theater Box*, life-size figures, Cornaro Chapel, Santa Maria della Vittoria, Rome. By placing sculptures depicting his patrons in boxes at the side of the chapel, Bernini converts religious into theatrical space.

who come to view the statue find that they intuitively avoid standing between David and Goliath.

Bernini's sculptural *Ecstasy of St. Teresa* (fig. 15.6) is one of the most important works created to celebrate the lives of the Counter-Reformation saints. Bernini designed it for the Cornaro Chapel of Santa Maria della Victoria in Rome and positioned it in a huge oval niche above the altar, framed by green marble pilasters. Created between 1645 and 1652, the multimedia sculpture depicts the moment in St. Teresa's autobiography when she says an angel pierced her heart with a flaming golden arrow, causing her to swoon in religious ecstasy—simultaneous pleasure and agony. "The pain was so great that I screamed aloud," she wrote, "but at the same time I felt such infinite sweetness that I wished the pain to last forever … It was the sweetest caressing of

the soul by God." Abandoning Renaissance restraint, Bernini captures the raw power of the narrative by portraying the sensual reality of her experience, evoking an emotional response in the viewer.

To the left and right of the depiction of St. Teresa, Bernini created theater boxes containing marble spectators, who, like us, witness the highly charged, theatrical moment (fig. 15.7). These spectators are Bernini's patron, Cardinal Federigo Cornaro, his deceased father, and the six other cardinals in the Cornaro family. While two read from prayer books, others talk among themselves, and one leans out as if to look at us as we enter the chapel. This setting makes Bernini's—and the Baroque's—dramatic intentions clear. It is as if, like the Cornaro family, visitors are witness to Teresa's actual swoon.

Francesco Borromini. A nephew of Carlo Maderno, FRANCESCO BORROMINI [bor-ro-MEE-nee] (1599–1667), joined his uncle in Rome in 1619 and soon was working for Bernini on the baldacchino in St. Peter's, some aspects of which are now attributed to him. So powerfully innovative was his sense of design that Borromini soon became Bernini's chief rival in Rome, reasserting the importance of originality, experimentation, and self-expression that had characterized Mannerist art. Very different in personality from the worldly Bernini, Borromini was a secretive and unstable man whose life ended in suicide.

New chapels had to be designed and constructed to celebrate a noble family's promotion, or else older chapels, those associated with the cardinals (often nephews of the pope), required redecoration. Francesco Borromini is best known for his design of one such little chapel, San Carlo alle Quattro Fontane (fig. 15.8), or St. Charles of the Four Fountains, named for the fountains on the junction of four streets where it is located in Rome. The interior of the church was designed between 1638 and 1641, and the facade between 1665 and 1667. On a tiny and irregular plot, Borromini built a tiny and irregular church. San Carlo could fit easily within Saint Peter's. Deviating from the classical tradition in architecture, the columns are of no known order—instead, Borromini designed a new order of his own. Rather than building with the traditional flat surfaces of ancient architecture, Borromini designed this fantastic facade, seemingly elastic, to curve in and out, the stone appearing to undulate in a serpentine concave–convex motion. So three-dimensional is this facade that it almost becomes sculpture, the light and shade pattern created by its ripples and recesses evoking its own drama in Rome's brilliant sunlight.

Borromini designed San Carlo alle Quattro Fontane with a double facade, a clever solution to a practical problem. The church faces a small intersection; it is not possible to stand back far enough to view the facade in its

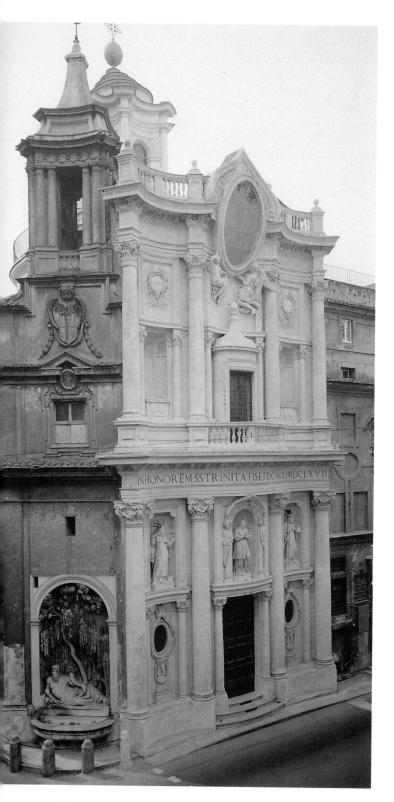

Figure 15.8   Francesco Borromini, San Carlo alle Quattro Fontane, 1638–67, width of facade 34′ (10.36 m). Because this church is located at an intersection of narrow streets, the viewer cannot easily see the entire facade. Borromini therefore created two separate compositions, undulating and sculptural, linked by the entablature of the lower story that forms a balcony for the upper story.

entirety. Borromini's double facade divides the surface into two smaller compositions, yet the entablature of the lower story forms the balcony of the upper story, typical of the Baroque concern for total unity of design.

Borromini's extravagance was immediately popular. The head of the religious order for whom San Carlo alle Quattro Fontane was built wrote with great pride: "Nothing similar can be found anywhere else in the world. This is attested by the foreigners who . . . try to procure copies of the plan. We have been asked for them by Germans, Flemings, Frenchmen, Italians, Spaniards, and even Indians."

PAINTING IN ITALY

As with sculptors and architects, the demand for painters during the Counter-Reformation was enormous. While some were hired to work permanently for a given patron, by far the majority worked in studios in Rome, displaying their works in progress and gladly accepting commissions from all comers. Competition for the best artists was fierce, and as a result they could demand fees that greatly increased their social standing.

Caravaggio.   One of the most important art patrons was Cardinal Scipione Borghese, nephew of Pope Paul. Borghese's villa contained a vast quantity of paintings and frescoes and was set in a large park full of niches and statuary. One of Borghese's favorite painters was CARAVAGGIO [ka-ra-VAH-joh] (1573–1610), whose real name was Michelangelo Merisi but who took his name as a painter from his birthplace, the village of Caravaggio near Milan. Borghese acquired many of the artist's works after his death. Caravaggio was a bohemian artist with a terrible temper who led a short and turbulent life (with a long police record bordering on the criminal). Despite his lifestyle, Caravaggio was a great religious painter whose work established one of the two major directions of painting in the Baroque age.

Caravaggio painted the *Calling of St. Matthew* (fig. 15.9) in about 1599–1602 for the private chapel of the Contarelli family in the Church of San Luigi dei Francesi in Rome. A large oil painting on canvas, it depicts the climactic moment of Matthew's calling. Caravaggio deftly portrays the psychological action and reaction of the moment (as told in the Bible, Matthew 9:9). Jesus points to the tax collector Matthew, who gestures with disbelief toward himself, as if to say, "Who? Me?"

This biblical tale is shown in the everyday environment of a Roman tavern and is enacted by people who could have been Caravaggio's contemporaries (who were indeed probably the models for the work). Although Matthew and his associates are richly attired, the two figures on the right are in rags. Jesus's halo is barely visible. Yet a religious atmosphere is created by Caravaggio's dramatic use of light, known as **tenebrism**—a "dark

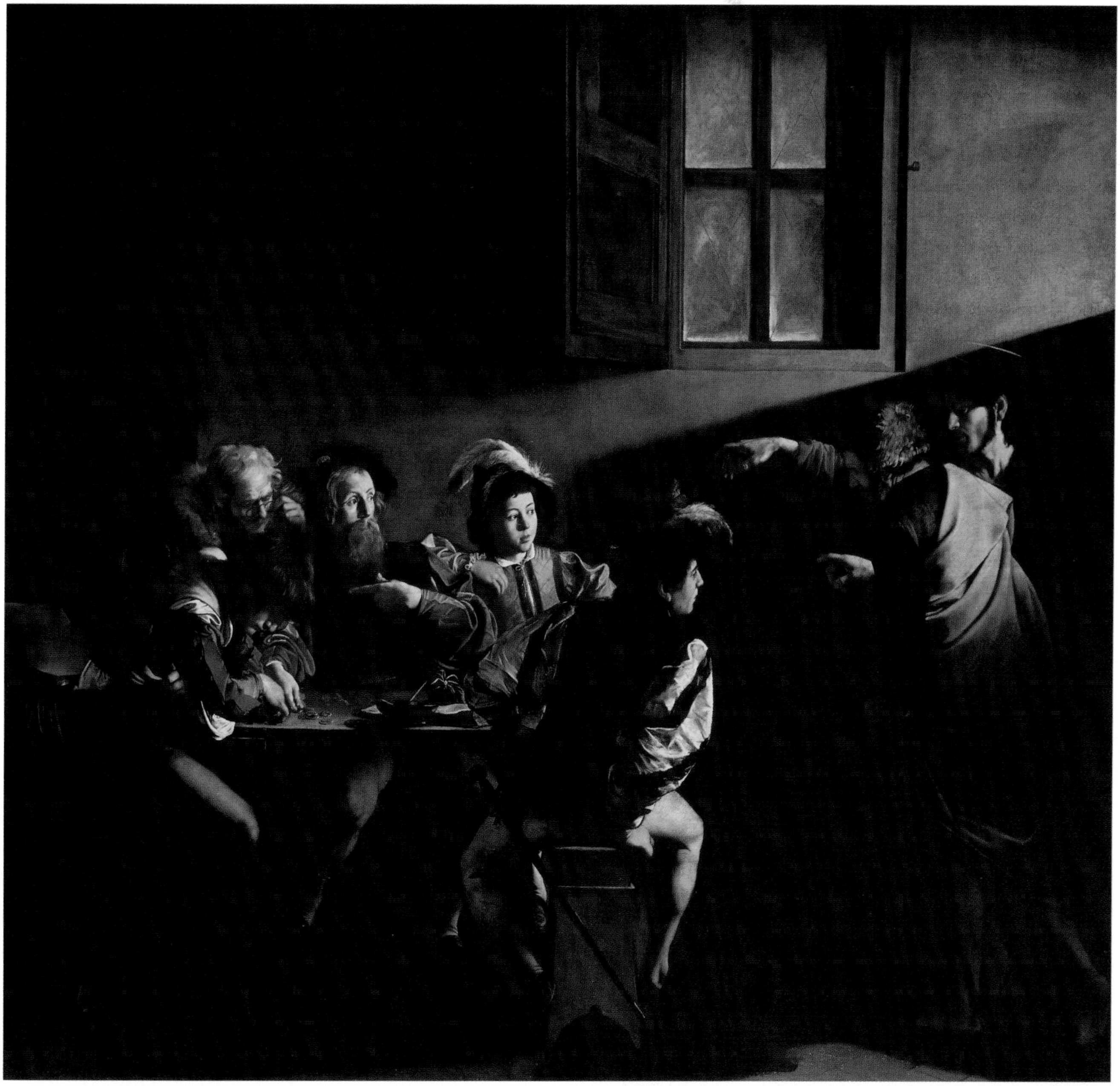

Figure 15.9 Caravaggio, *Calling of St. Matthew*, ca. 1599–1602, oil on canvas, 11′1″ × 11′5″ (3.38 × 3.48 m), Contarelli Chapel, San Luigi dei Francesi, Rome. Although Matthew is seated in a tavern when he receives Jesus's call, Caravaggio uses tenebristic lighting to reveal the religious nature of this event.

manner," in which light and dark contrast strongly, the highlights picking out only what the artist wants the viewer to see. The light comes from above, like a spotlight centering on an actor on stage, but no obvious light source is shown.

Caravaggio also painted the *Entombment* (fig. 15.10), executed in 1603 for a chapel in Santa Maria in Vallicella, Rome, the church of St. Philip Neri's Congregation of the Oratory. Nothing distracts from the painting's emotional impact. The unnatural theatrical light reveals only a hint of the setting; clarity is achieved by Caravaggio's highlighting of select figures and features. The platform on which his figures stand is at the viewers' eye level and seems to extend into the viewers' space, increasing the impact of the scene by drawing them toward it, and making them feel virtual participants in the event. Indeed, the implication is that the viewers stand in the tomb itself, about to receive Jesus's body from the bending foreground figure who looks down on them. The physical labor required to lower the body is almost palpable.

The *Entombment* makes the words of the sermon visible, explicit, almost tangible. Caravaggio portrays Jesus's associates as people much like himself. He refused to raise his subjects to the level of the heroic, as had customarily been done. This aspect of Caravaggio's art was not well received by his contemporaries, who felt he had gone too far in reducing the barriers between heaven and earth.

Artemisia Gentileschi. The emotional and dramatic side of the Baroque is demonstrated also by ARTE-MISIA GENTILESCHI [jen-tee-LESS-kee] (1593–ca. 1653). Born in Rome, her style seems to have been influenced by that of her father, Orazio Gentileschi, a painter in Caravaggio's style. She was herself known as one of several "Caravaggisti," or "night painters," those whose work was identifiable by its use of tenebrism.

Figure 15.10 Caravaggio, *Entombment*, 1603, oil on canvas, 9′10$\frac{1}{8}$″ × 6′7$\frac{15}{16}$″ (3.00 × 2.03 m), Musei Vaticani, Pinacoteca, Rome. The painting's impact is enhanced by bringing the figures close to the picture plane. By locating the stone slab at eye level, Caravaggio suggests the viewer is actually in the tomb, ready to receive Jesus's body.

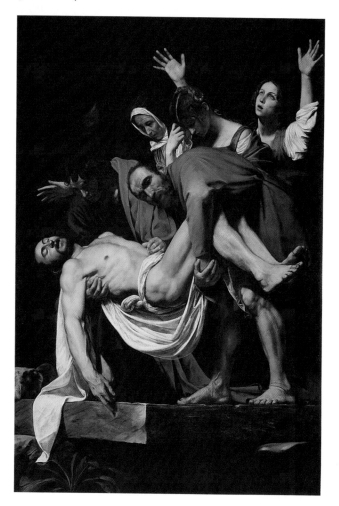

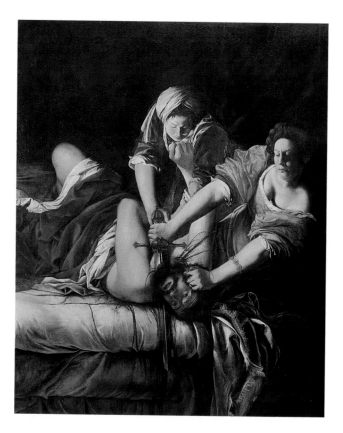

Figure 15.11 Artemisia Gentileschi, *Judith Slaying Holofernes*, ca. 1620, oil on canvas, 6′6$\frac{1}{3}$″ × 5′4″ (1.99 × 1.63 m), Galleria degli Uffizi, Florence. Drama and horror are magnified by the proximity of the figures and by the powerful spotlight focusing attention on the beheading, leaving all else in shadow.

Gentileschi's paintings often depicted the popular biblical subjects of Bathsheba and David and of Judith and Holofernes. Her *Judith Slaying Holofernes* (fig. 15.11), painted ca. 1620, effectively conveys a sense of intrigue and violence. The beautiful Jewish widow Judith saved her people from Nebuchadnezzar's Assyrian army by enticing their leader, Holofernes, into a tent where he drank himself to sleep. She then cut off his head with his own sword. The unnerving drama is enhanced by the dark tenebristic lighting that spotlights the actors as if on stage. The large figures fill the picture and seem to press forward as if about to burst through the picture plane.

Her highly charged and emotional paintings have been linked to her own experience. Gentileschi was sexually assaulted at the age of fifteen by one of her teachers. Later she was tortured in court with a thumb-screw (a device designed to compress the thumb to the point of smashing it) to verify the validity of her accusation.

Annibale Carracci. Many Roman priests did not endorse the Caravaggisti style. They preferred the more "academic" approach to painting established in large part

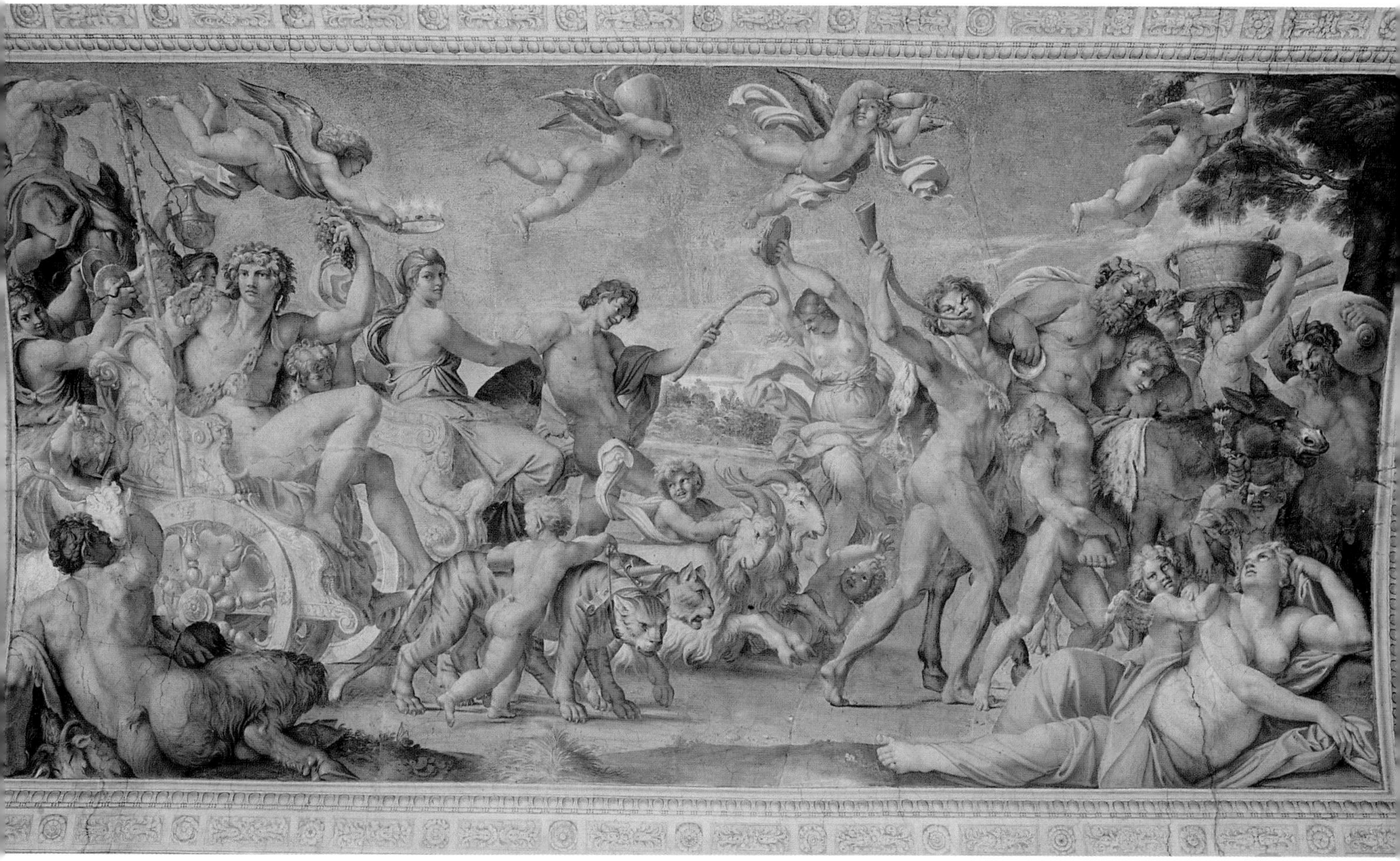

Figure 15.12 Annibale Carracci, *Triumph of Bacchus and Ariadne*, 1597–1600, ceiling fresco, Palazzo Farnese, Rome. The academic classicizing trend of the Baroque exemplified by Annibale Carracci contrasts with the dramatic emotional approach of Caravaggio, Gentileschi, and their followers.

by ANNIBALE CARRACCI [car-RAH-chee] (1560–1609) of Bologna, who came from a family of painters. With his brother Agostino and his cousin Lodovico, Carracci set up a workshop, which led to the establishment of an art academy in Bologna in 1585. The guiding principle of the Carraccis' academy was that art could be taught, and that by examining the works of classical and Renaissance masters, and by long study of anatomy and practice in life drawing, a highly developed and "correct" style could be learned.

Annibale Carracci's greatest work is a large ceiling fresco, painted between 1597 and 1600, in the Palazzo Farnese in Rome, the palace of the powerful Jesuit Cardinal Farnese, himself from Bologna. Turning away from the Mannerist style, Annibale Carracci looked to the High Renaissance, to nature, and to antiquity. Curiously, Carracci painted scenes of love from Ovid's *Metamorphoses* for his very Christian patron. The scenes are painted within an architectural framework and fea-

ture twisting male nudes that recall Michelangelo's Sistine Chapel ceiling. Carracci's framing is intentionally illusionistic, made to appear as if lit from below, the shadows painted in. As on the Sistine Chapel ceiling, the individual scenes are treated as if they were easel paintings applied to the ceiling, without regard for the viewer's position below. The center is occupied by the *Triumph of Bacchus and Ariadne* (fig. 15.12). The happy procession has Baroque exuberance, yet in this classicizing Baroque style the appeal is largely intellec-tual rather than emotional. Action is carefully controlled, and figures do not appear to fly out of the picture. In this, it differs from the illusionistic ceiling frescoes that were popular in Baroque Rome.

Fra Andrea Pozzo. The epitome of the illusionist ceiling fresco was achieved by FRA ANDREA POZZO [POT-zoh] (1642–1709), in his depiction of the *Triumph of St. Ignatius of Loyola* (fig. 15.13), of 1691–94, on the nave ceiling of Sant'Ignazio, Rome. The effect is aston-

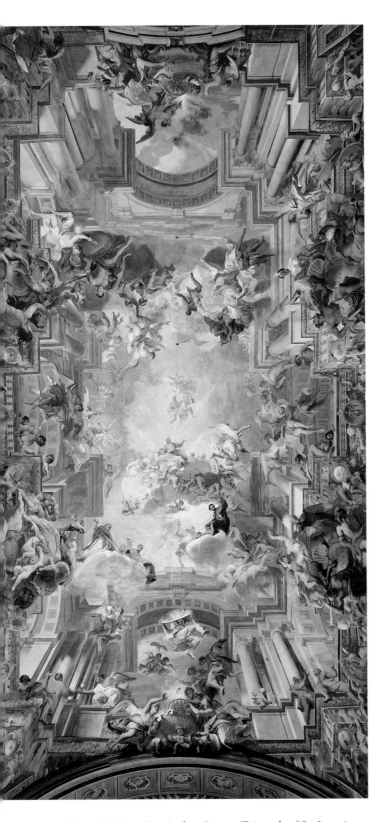

Figure 15.13 Fra Andrea Pozzo, *Triumph of St. Ignatius of Loyola*, 1691–94, ceiling fresco, Sant'Ignazio, Rome. If the viewer stands directly below the center of this quintessentially Baroque illusionistic ceiling painting, it is not possible to see where the actual architecture ends and the painted architecture begins.

ishing; the solid vault of the ceiling has been painted away. It is an extreme example of what the Italians called *quadrattura* and what the French call *trompe-l'oeil* illusionism, used to trick the eye into believing that the architecture of the church, its columns and arches, extends past the actual ceiling. This perspective is calculated to be seen from a specific point on the floor, which is marked. When standing there, it is difficult if not impossible to determine where the real architecture ends and the painted architecture begins. The center of the ceiling appears to be open sky from which saints and angels descend. Some sit on painted architecture or clouds; others fly through space in a dazzling display of Baroque artistic dexterity.

MUSIC IN ITALY

Claudio Monteverdi and Early Opera. It is hardly surprising, given the emphasis on dramatic theatricality so fundamental to Baroque painting, that the Baroque era produced a new musical form, known as **opera**. *Opera* is the Italian word for "a work," and *opera drammatica in musica*, "a dramatic work in music," has been abbreviated to "opera." An opera combines vocal music, instrumental music, and drama; it is essentially a staged work sung to the accompaniment of an orchestra.

The first operas were written and performed before 1600, but the first notable work in the genre, *Orfeo* (*Orpheus*) by CLAUDIO MONTEVERDI [mon-teh-VAIR-dee] (1567–1643), was composed for his patron, the Duke of Mantua, in 1607. It deals with the Greek mythological figure Orpheus, a poet and musician who goes down to Hades, the underworld, to bring back his dead wife, Eurydice.

The opera includes **recitative**, a form of musically heightened speech midway between spoken dialogue and melodic arias. Orpheus's recitative is a monologue in the "agitated style," in which the composer expresses musically the feelings described by the text. Monteverdi created a descending line on the words "*più profondi abissi*" ("deepest abysses") and an ascending line to accompany the words "*a riverder le stelle*" ("to see again the stars").

Antonio Vivaldi and the Concerto Grosso. Invented by ARCANGELO CORELLI [ko-REL-lee] (1653–1713), the **concerto** is a musical form consisting of three parts, or movements, featuring contrast, and written in a fast–slow–fast form. Typically, the first movement of a Baroque concerto is energetic, the second is tranquil, and the third and final movement more vigorous than the first.

One of the most prolific Baroque composers of the concerto was ANTONIO VIVALDI [vee-VAHL-dee] (1674–1741), who wrote 450 concertos, forty operas, and numerous vocal and chamber works. Born in Venice in 1678, Vivaldi, an ordained priest, spent most of his life as music master at a Venetian school for orphaned girls. Many of his works were composed for student recitals.

Vivaldi's most popular work is *The Four Seasons*, a set of four concertos for solo violin and orchestra. Each of Vivaldi's four concertos—Winter, Spring, Summer, and Fall—is accompanied by a sonnet describing the appropriate season. In the original edition, the words were printed above musical passages which depicted in sound the descriptive words. The Spring Concerto, for instance, includes descriptions of chirping birds returning to the meadows, and Vivaldi's music has accompanying sections called "bird calls" in which one violin "calls" and another answers it.

The first eight lines of the sonnet are distributed throughout the first movement of the Spring Concerto, an Allegro in E major. The movement opens with a phrase played twice in succession, once loud and once softly as an echo. This is followed by a *ritornello* passage, one that will return repeatedly throughout the movement. The *ritornello* section is played by the entire instrumental group in alternation with sections for the solo violin. The *ritornello* form pervades not only Vivaldi's music but the Baroque concerto generally. Different textures in solo and ensemble sections are supplemented by abrupt contrasts in dynamics from loud to soft (terraced dynamics), and by contrasting imitations of birdsong and storm.

But interesting as such musical scene painting may be, the primary interest of Vivaldi's music is its use of themes, textures, and tone colors in carefully structured repetitions and contrasts that identify him as a master of the concerto style. Vivaldi's music was soon heard throughout Europe, widely admired and closely studied by Johann Sebastian Bach, the greatest composer of the age. The attraction of Vivaldi's music was its inventiveness and flexibility within a fairly rigid formal structure. It is the play between structure and invention, between control and freedom, that appealed to an age at once attracted to the classicism of a Bernini colonnade and the fluid fantasy of a Borromini facade.

THE BAROQUE OUTSIDE ITALY

To speak of Baroque art, especially painting, as originating outside Italy is to misrepresent things. Many of the artists whom we identify with other countries either lived, worked, or studied in Rome: the French painters Claude Lorrain and Nicolas Poussin, the Spanish Diego Velázquez, and Peter Paul Rubens from Flanders. If they did not go to Rome, as few of the Dutch Baroque artists did, they were usually influenced by Roman Baroque painting, particularly that of Caravaggio, which enjoyed a considerable reputation outside Italy as early as 1610. Despite its dependency on Rome, the Baroque thrived

outside Italy: in the low countries, Flanders and Holland, where a flourishing mercantile class became deeply interested in the arts; in Spain, where Philip IV amassed an important collection; in England, where Charles I did the same; in France, where Marie de' Medici, regent for the young King Louis XIV, exerted influence over the French court; and in Germany, where Baroque music was particularly well received by an increasingly sophisticated public.

PAINTING IN BOURGEOIS HOLLAND

During the reign of Philip II of Spain, the northern provinces of the Netherlands rebelled against his repression of Protestants and formed a new Dutch republic, while the southern provinces remained Catholic and loyal to Spain. That division created the separate countries of Holland and Flanders.

A distinctly secular brand of Baroque painting emerged in Holland, which in the seventeenth century was a country of bourgeois merchants and tradespeople who found themselves, freed of Spanish rule, the sudden beneficiaries of having Amsterdam, the maritime center and commercial capital of Europe as their capital city. (*Amsterdam: World Famous Commercial Center* was the title of one 1664 Dutch publication.) Traveling through Holland in the eighteenth century, the French writer and philosopher Denis Diderot described the Dutch as a thoroughly acquisitive but perfectly content people: "It is to Holland that the rest of Europe goes for everything it lacks. Holland is Europe's commercial hub. The Dutch have worked to such good purposes that, through their ingenuity, they have obtained all of life's necessities, in defiance of the elements ... There, wealth is without vanity, liberty is without insolence, levies are without vexation, and taxation is without misery."

In Holland not just religious and political leaders but also merchants and tradespeople collected art, and good taste became almost a social prerequisite. The English trav-eler Peter Mundy in 1640 claimed that "none go beyond" the Dutch "in the affection of the people to pictures ... All in general strive to adorn their houses, especially the outer or street room, with costly pieces. Butchers and bakers not much inferior in their shops, which are fairly set forth, yea many times blacksmiths, cobblers, etc., will have some picture or other by their forge and their stall."

Pieter de Hooch. Paintings even grace the walls within genre paintings of the period, including those of the Dutch artist PIETER DE HOOCH [hoogh] (1629–after 1684). For instance, in *The Bedroom* (fig. 15.14) of about 1663, a seascape is positioned above the door leading to the courtyard while, in this most domestic of scenes, a woman chats with a girl as she changes

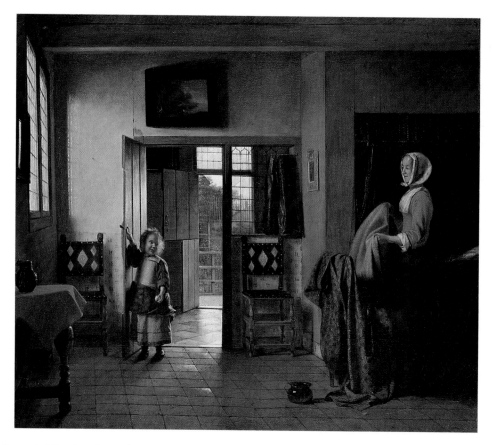

Figure 15.14   Peter de Hooch, *The Bedroom*, ca. 1663, oil on canvas, 20 × 24″ (50.8 × 61.0 cm), National Gallery of Art, Washington, DC. The intimate details of everyday life are the center of interest of Baroque Dutch painting.

linens. For the Dutch, art had become a part of everyday life, and everyday life had equally become the subject of art. Notable is de Hooch's use of scientifically observed lighting. The woman is bathed by light from the window, and the dark interior of the domestic setting contrasts with the warm sunlight on the cityscape visible through the door.

Frans Hals.   FRANS HALS [hals] (ca. 1580–1666), born in Antwerp, worked in Haarlem as a portraitist. An extrovert, the painter's jovial personality comes across in a number of his paintings. His *Jolly Toper* (fig. 15.15) of ca. 1628–30, for example, conveys such robust gusto. Hals's sitters usually appear to be in a good mood and might be more at home in a tavern than in a church. Differing from the stiff formality of earlier portraiture, the *Jolly Toper* is caught balancing a wine glass and ges-

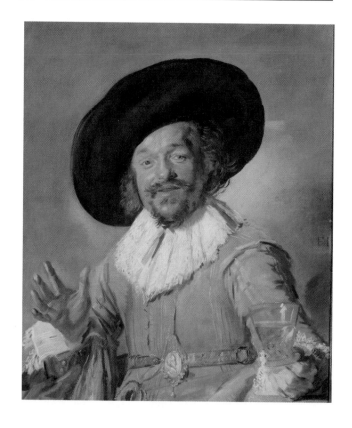

Figure 15.15   Frans Hals, *Jolly Toper*, ca. 1628–30, oil on canvas, $31\frac{7}{8} \times 26\frac{1}{4}$″ (81.0 × 66.7 cm), Rijksmuseum, Amsterdam. Breaking from the stiffness of earlier portraits, this man appears to have been caught in mid-sentence—perhaps offering that glass of wine. Hals's dashing brushstrokes accord with and enhance the quality of spontaneity.

Connections

VERMEER AND THE ORIGINS OF PHOTOGRAPHY

*I*t seems probable that Vermeer used a device known as the *camera obscura* to execute a number of his paintings. First used in the Renaissance as a mechanical device for verifying perspective, the *camera obscura* was used by Dutch painters as a tool for scientific observation comparable to the microscope and the telescope. At its simplest, the device is an enclosed box with a tiny hole in one side through which shines a beam of external light, projecting the scene outside as an inverted image on the opposite, interior wall of the box. Often

the size of a portable room in which the artist could stand fully upright and trace the image, the *camera obscura* employs the physics of the modern-day camera, except that it lacks light-sensitive paper or film on which to record the image.

Not only did the *camera obscura* readily reduce the three-dimensional world to a two-dimensional image; it revealed intriguing details about the play of light on textured surfaces. There are several instances in Vermeer's paintings in which light seems to force the image out of focus. Photographers call such spots in a

photograph "discs of confusion." Though visible to the naked eye, the effects of such shimmerings are so fleeting that they are almost impossible to capture. And yet Vermeer, probably in imitating their appearance as projected by the lens of his *camera obscura*, captured them on canvas. As a result, his paintings depict light as convincingly as photographs themselves.

It would be another 150 years until the earliest photographic camera would be invented. However, the physics—if not the chemistry—upon which photography is based is at work in Vermeer's images.

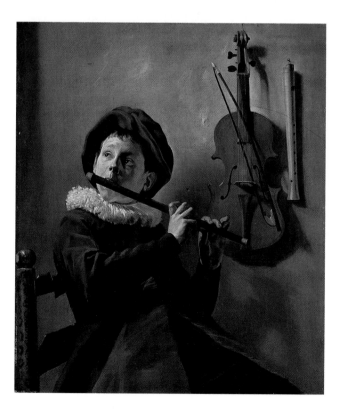

Figure 15.16 Judith Leyster, *Boy Playing a Flute*, 1630–35, oil on canvas, $28\frac{1}{2} \times 24\frac{1}{8}$" (72.4 × 61.3 cm), Nationalmuseum, Stockholm. Leyster's ability to convey a sense of life, of animation, is comparable to Hals's. The seemingly casual quality of both subject and painting technique is actually achieved with great care.

turing broadly, perhaps in mid-conversation. Hals broke with the fashion of the time, which was to paint with careful contours, delicate modeling, and attention to detail. Instead, his paint ranged from thick impasto to thin fluid glazes and he left the separate brushstrokes clearly visible. The spontaneity of his style matched the apparent spontaneity of his subject. Hals made his painting technique look easy, but in fact much care was required to achieve the casual impression he conveyed.

Judith Leyster. The most important follower of Frans Hals was JUDITH LEYSTER [LIE-ster] (1609–1660), a Dutch painter whose name came from her family's brewery in Haarlem, the Leysterre (Pole Star). So close are their painting styles that several works long thought to be by Hals have been found to be by Leyster. Like Hals, Leyster depicted scenes from daily life and was able to convey remarkable animation, demonstrated in the *Boy Playing a Flute* (fig. 15.16), painted 1630–35. The young musician appears totally caught up in his music making. Like Caravaggio, Leyster used a limited range of predominantly dark colors and tenebristic lighting. And, as in Caravaggio's paintings, the figure occupies a shallow space, close to the picture plane. The boy's glance to the left would endanger the balance of this composition, were it not for the musical instruments hanging on the wall to the right. The seemingly casual application of paint and arrangement of the composition add to the sense of relaxed ease, yet, as with Hals, this was painted with great thought and was carefully composed.

Rembrandt van Rijn. In Amsterdam, painting revolved around the work of REMBRANDT VAN RIJN [REM-brant] (1606–1669), who took Caravaggio's

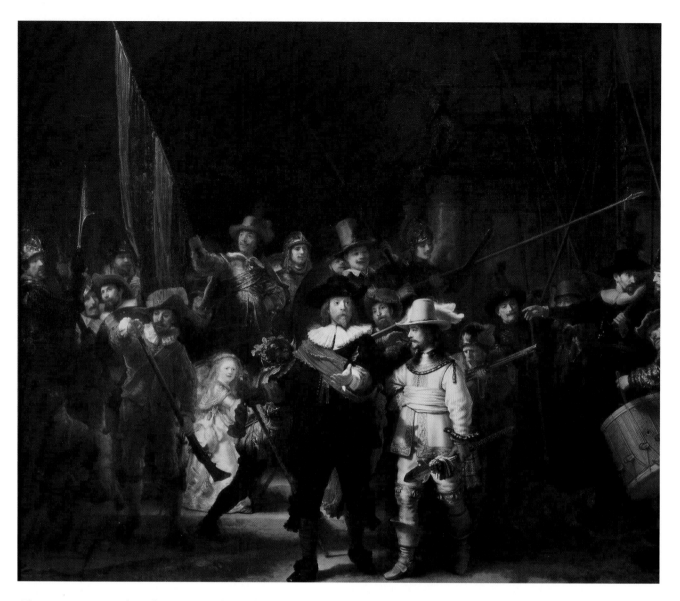

Figure 15.17 Rembrandt van Rijn, *The Night Watch* (*Captain Frans Banning Cocq Mustering His Company*), 1642, oil on canvas, 12'2" × 14'7" (3.71 × 4.45 m), Rijksmuseum, Amsterdam. This enormous group portrait is often interpreted as marking the turning point in Rembrandt's life. His wife Saskia died in 1642, his popularity as an artist declined, and his financial problems began. The event depicted took place in the morning, but, because of gradual darkening, the painting has come to be known as the "*Night*" *Watch*.

interest in dramatic Baroque lighting to new heights. Born in Leyden, the son of a miller, Rembrandt abandoned his studies of classical literature at the university of Leyden to study painting. In 1634, he married Saskia van Ulenborch, who came from a wealthy family. Between 1634 and 1642, now brilliant and successful, Rembrandt had many commissions and owned a large house and art collection in Amsterdam. Saskia was one of his great joys and was often his model. Her early death in 1642 marked a turning point in Rembrandt's life—it was in this year that he painted the famous *Night Watch*.

The Night Watch (fig. 15.17) is one of Rembrandt's most important public commissions, paid for by the Amsterdam civic guard. All the men portrayed in this huge informal group portrait had contributed equally to the cost (all their names appear on the shield hanging on the far wall). Its actual title is *Captain Frans Banning Cocq Mustering His Company*, but it was dubbed *The Night Watch* in the eighteenth century because it had darkened with age. In actually, the painting shows the members of Cocq's company in the morning, welcoming Marie de' Medici, Queen of France, at Amsterdam's city gate.

The action of Rembrandt's dramatic Baroque composition moves along diagonals. Originally, Captain Cocq and his lieutenant were not in the center but walking toward it (the painting has been cut on the left and bottom). The viewer's eye is led toward the focus of the subject in the center of the composition.

The most remarkable aspect of the painting is the light. Rembrandt, referred to as "the lord of light," intensified his subject with a strong spotlight. Light creates atmosphere, unifies the composition, links the figures, highlights expressive features, and subordinates unimportant details. The figures of Captain Cocq and his lieutenant received the greatest emphasis; the others felt cheated, but the picture was considered good enough to hang in the company's club house.

Rembrandt also worked as a printer, a medium that depends particularly on the play of light and dark. His etching of *Christ Preaching* (fig. 15.18), of ca. 1652, is set in Amsterdam's Jewish ghetto. Rembrandt felt sympathy for the Jewish people as victims of persecution. Working at the highest technical level, Rembrandt used cross-hatching to model the masses and shadows. His subtle effects range from the faintest lines of gray to the richest areas of black. In an etching, as in an engraving, the design comes from the incisions made in the surface. When an etching is made, first, the metal plate is covered with a waxy substance. Next, the design is scraped or scratched through the wax to expose the plate, a process far less arduous than engraving the plate itself. The plate is then placed in a mild acid bath that eats into the exposed areas of metal. Finally, the waxy coating is

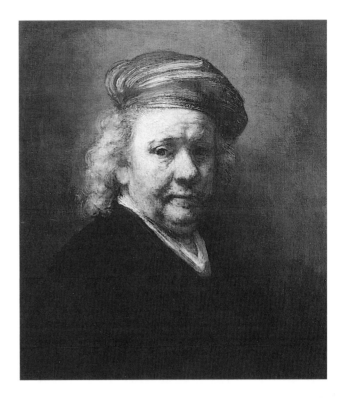

Figure 15.19   Rembrandt van Rijn, *Self-Portrait*, 1669, oil on canvas, 23¼ × 20″ (59.0 × 51.0 cm), Mauritshuis, The Hague. Rembrandt painted himself throughout his life, not in a laudatory manner like Albrecht Dürer, but as a means of self-analysis and personal reflection more akin to the later self-portraits of Vincent van Gogh.

Figure 15.18   Rembrandt van Rijn, *Christ Preaching*, ca. 1652, etching, 6⅛ × 8⅛″ (15.6 × 20.6 cm), Metropolitan Museum of Art, New York. The strong contrasts of light and dark seen in Rembrandt's paintings have their equivalent in his prints.

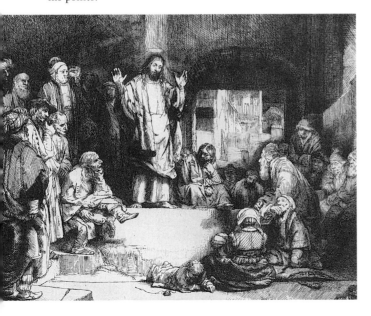

removed from the plate, ink is forced into the grooves, and the plate is printed on paper under pressure exerted by a printing press.

Rembrandt recorded his own life in many self-portraits—sixty in oil alone. His last *Self-Portrait* (fig. 15.19) was painted in 1669, the year of his death. The handling of paint continues to be masterful, the textures emphasized, the colors luminous and glowing, but the contours became looser, the brushstrokes broader, the surface not as smooth as in his earlier paintings. Rembrandt portrays himself here as weary and unhappy, disillusioned, self-questioning. Yet he remains dignified; in none of his self-portraits does he appear bitter, resentful, or self-pitying. Introspective and honest, he presented himself as no more handsome than he was.

Jan Vermeer.   Like Rembrandt, but a generation younger, JAN VERMEER [vur-MEER] (1632–1675), was fascinated by light, but of a very different kind. Where Rembrandt's light is theatrical, Vermeer's is optical. Vermeer's use of light reveals every textural nuance. Clear and luminous, his light pervades all corners of his world. Used to emphasize contrasts in surface texture, his light informs us that every aspect of every object has been observed and recorded. And yet, Vermeer's light

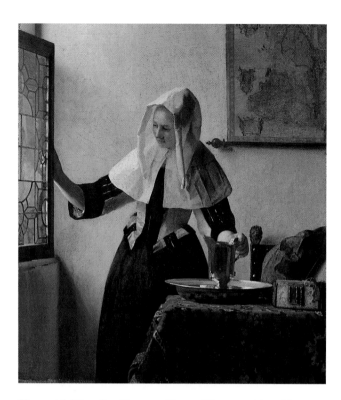

Figure 15.20 Jan Vermeer, *Young Woman with a Water Pitcher*, ca. 1664–65, oil on canvas, 18 × 16″ (45.7 × 40.6 cm), Metropolitan Museum of Art, New York. Great importance is given by Vermeer to light—not for Baroque bravura, but to assure the viewer that every detail has been scientifically observed and recorded, every subtle gradation and reflection noted.

Here a maid, whose laundry basket can be seen below Vermeer's signature, appears to reassure her young mistress that the love letter she has just received will resolve all her anxieties. The room is decorated with an elegant marble mantel, a gilded leather wall covering, and two paintings (a landscape and a seascape). The young woman wears a string of pearls around her neck, bright, almost gaudy earrings, and an ermine-trimmed yellow satin jacket and skirt. She holds a lute, and in the foreground on the bench is an open music book, perhaps the source of the song she was playing before the letter's arrival. Finally, richly woven drapery folds back to reveal the entire scene.

As with the figure in *Young Woman with a Water Pitcher*, these figures are carefully posed within a composition based upon a series of rectangles and a carefully planned perspective system. A sense of patterned geometry and balance predominates. The painting's composition transforms the viewer into a voyeur. It is as if, along with the artist, we lift the drapery and peer into the private scene. Unobserved, standing in the outer darkness, in "public" space, we are privy to a most private communication. Vermeer reverses our expectations: it is the private world that is bathed in light; the public space is shrouded in darkness.

PAINTING IN THE ROYAL COLLECTIONS

Peter Paul Rubens. Although born in Germany, PETER PAUL RUBENS [REW-bens] (1577–1640) established himself as an artist in Antwerp, the capital of Catholic Flanders. Between 1600 and 1608, at the very height of Caravaggio's and Carracci's careers, he was in Italy, where he studied the antique, the High Renaissance, and the two Baroque masters. He copied the "old masters," including Leonardo's *Battle of Anghiari* (see fig. 13.26), and his copy has become the only surviving record of that work. Rubens enjoyed a good reputation in Italy, painting in a style that combined influences from the north and the south.

Intelligent, talented, sociable, energetic, and equipped with a good business sense, Rubens became extremely successful. He set up shop in Antwerp, and by 1611, with two hundred painters and students working in his studio, Rubens was the most financially successful artist of the age. He built a large home containing his studio and an impressive art collection including works by Titian, Tintoretto, Van Eyck, Bruegel, and Raphael. He received many commissions from the Church, the city of Antwerp, and private individuals, but it was the royal courts of Europe that garnered him the most fame and fortune. He was court painter to the Duke of Mantua, and to the Spanish regents of the Netherlands, Albert and Isabella. Commissions came also from Charles I of England and Philip IV of Spain, both of whom presented him with a knighthood. Marie de' Medici of

reveals the spiritual essence of things in a manner entirely consistent with Protestant theology. The Protestants believed that God revealed himself in even the least significant details of daily life.

Born in Delft and married at twenty, Vermeer painted only for local patrons. He specialized in domestic scenes, which document the conditions of everyday Dutch domestic life in the Baroque age. In *Young Woman with a Water Pitcher* (fig. 15.20) of ca. 1664–65, a single female figure is depicted in the process of performing an ordinary action, indoors, at a table with objects on it, light coming from a window on the left, the figure silhouetted against a pale-colored wall. Vermeer's clear and luminous light pervades the whole space, unlike Rembrandt's light, which falls in shafts. Neither the subtle gradations across the back wall nor the reflections of the table rug in the metal basin are overlooked. The viewer can almost feel the starched linen headdress, its two sides subtly differen-tiated by the fall of light, the polished metal pitcher, and the basin. Vermeer's intimate scene of a woman absorbed in household tasks and unaware of the viewer conveys a mood of serenity and peace.

The Love Letter (fig. 15.21), probably painted ca. 1669–70, is almost an inventory of the Dutch good life.

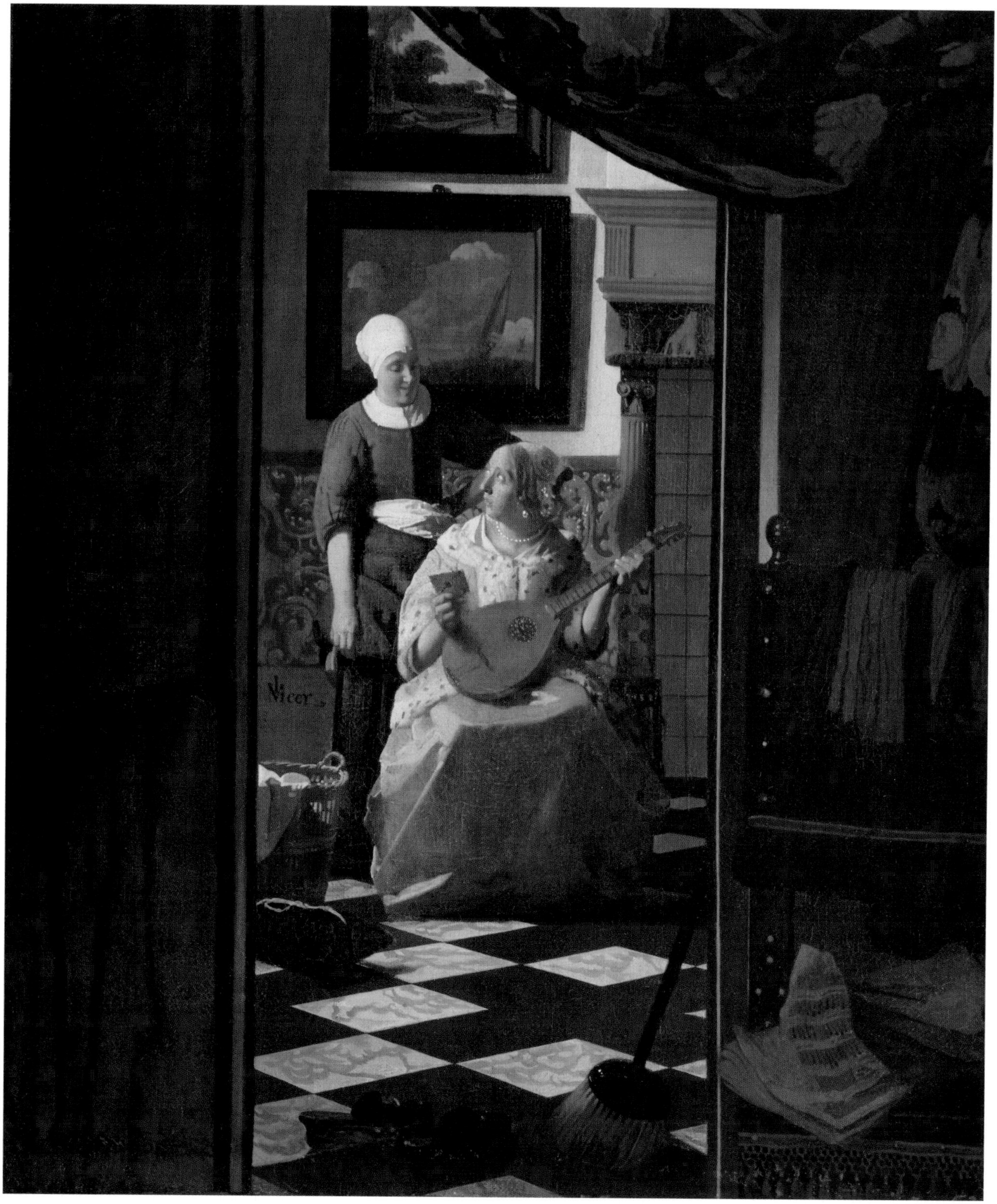

Figure 15.21   Jan Vermeer, *The Love Letter*, ca. 1669–70, oil on canvas, 44 × 38″ (112 × 96.5 cm), Rijksmuseum, Amsterdam. Typical of Vermeer is the intimate view of the daily life of women in middleclass seventeenth-century Dutch homes.

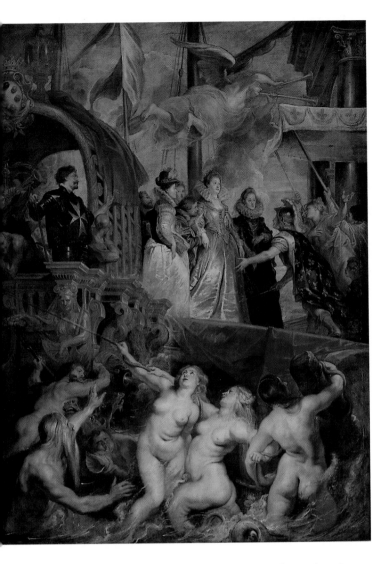

Figure 15.22 Peter Paul Rubens, *Marie de' Medici, Queen of France, Landing in Marseilles*, 1622–25, oil on canvas, 5'1" × 3'11⅔" (1.55 × 1.21 m), Musée du Louvre, Paris. With the diagonal movements typical of the Baroque, brilliant color, sensuous textures, and dashing brushwork, Rubens raised his depiction of an unglamorous queen at an ordinary event to the level of high drama.

The drama of the composition, arranged on diagonals rather than parallel to the picture plane, is characteristic of the Baroque style, as is the love of movement in an open space. Everyone and everything becomes active to the point of agitation, even when not suggested by the subject. By cutting off figures at the edge of the canvas, Rubens implies that the scene continues beyond the limits of the frame. Rubens painted in terms of rich, luminous, glowing color and light rather than in terms of line, and he juxtaposed textures to contrast their differences. Every stroke, every form, is united by the curving, sweeping movements of Rubens's design and the sheer exuberance of his lush forms, which appeal more to the eye than to the mind.

Aided by his early experience as a court page as well as his fluency in five languages (Greek, Italian, French, Spanish, and Flemish), Rubens served as an advisor and emissary for the Flemish court. When he visited the court of Philip IV in Spain from September 1628 until late April 1629, he stayed in the royal palace in Madrid and was visited almost daily by the young king. In addition to royal portraits, he executed copies of Titian's famous *Poésies*, a series of large mythological paintings hung in the galleries below the king's apartments.

After his first wife died in 1626, Rubens married Hélène Fourment, a distant relative, and began a family. He was fifty years old, his bride sixteen, and they had four children in five years. *The Garden of Love* (fig. 15.23), ca. 1638, is an exuberant visual expression of the pleasures of life, with a robust grandeur approaching animal exuberance. Certainly Rubens's main interest in this work is in the voluptuous female figure. Only with difficulty could this scene be made any more sumptuous—or sensuous. *The Sacrifice of Issac* (fig. 15.24) evidences a contrasting style of Rubens's work.

Anthony van Dyck. Rubens's assistant from 1618 to 1620, ANTHONY VAN DYCK (1599–1641), became painter to the court of Charles I in England and perhaps the greatest portrait painter of the age. Van Dyck was capable of recognizing and representing the most subtle nuances of the aristocratic personality. His *Portrait of Charles I at the Hunt* (fig. 15.25), of 1635, captures the king's self-assurance. Van Dyck contrasts the king with the animated and anxious groom and the pawing, nervous horse behind him, underscoring Charles's command of all situations.

Diego Velázquez. Philip IV had become king of Spain in 1621 at the age of sixteen, and from the outset he relied heavily on the advice of Gaspar de Guzmán, the Count of Olivares. Olivares wanted Philip's court to be recognized as the most prominent in Europe, so he appointed DIEGO VELÁZQUEZ [ve-LAHS-kez]

France in 1621 gave him the commission that would establish his international reputation.

After the death of her husband, Henry IV, Marie de' Medici served as regent for her young son, Louis XIII. She asked Rubens to create a cycle of twenty-one large oil paintings portraying her life. His aim was to glorify the Queen, a difficult task in view of the fact that she was no beauty. A master of narrative portraiture, Rubens's solution was to dramatize even the ordinary. In the scene of *Marie de' Medici, Queen of France, Landing in Marseilles* (fig. 15.22), the Queen is merely disembarking in the southern French city of Marseilles, yet Fame flies above, blowing a trumpet, and Neptune, god of the sea, accompanied by mermaids, rises from the waves to welcome her.

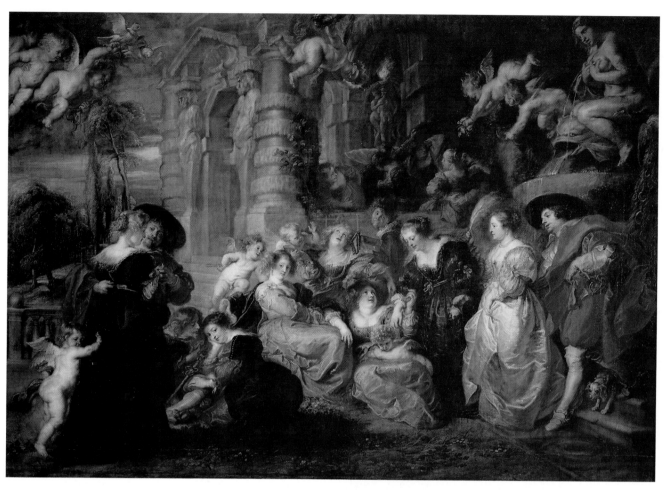

Figure 15.23 Peter Paul Rubens, *The Garden of Love*, ca. 1638, oil on canvas, 6'6" × 9'3½" (1.98 × 2.83 m), Museo del Prado, Madrid. Rubens is known for his rich, lush style—applied to the setting and, especially, to the figures. The term "Rubenesque" has been coined to describe voluptuous fleshy females.

Figure 15.24 Peter Paul Rubens (1577–1640), Flemish, *The Sacrifice of Isaac*, ca. 1612-1613. Oil on wood panel; 55 ½ × 43 ½" (141.0 × 110.5 cm). Nelson-Atkins Museum of Art. Rubens depicts an angel grabbing the hand of Abraham before kneeling Isaac.

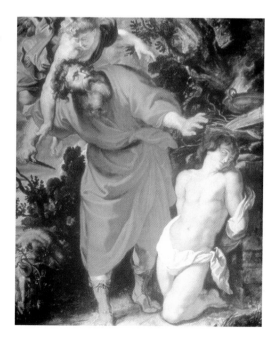

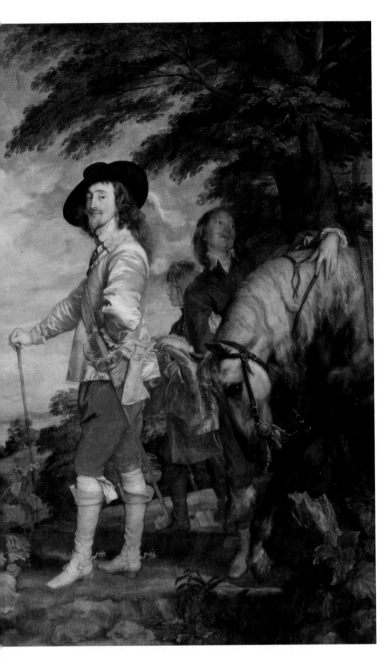

Figure 15.25 Anthony van Dyck, *Portrait of Charles I at the Hunt*, 1635, oil on canvas, approx. 9 × 7′ (2.74 × 2.13 m), Musée du Louvre, Paris. The king is depicted here displaying all the haughtiness that would soon lead Parliament to rise against him.

(1599–1660) to the position of royal painter. Velázquez was highly honored by the king, who ultimately knighted and conferred upon him the Order of Santiago, usually reserved for noblemen. Velázquez did many portraits of the royal family, painting them with honesty and realism, and he seems to have made his sitters no prettier or more handsome than they actually were. Velázquez lived most of his life in Madrid, though shortly after Rubens's

visit and at Rubens's suggestion, Philip granted Velázquez permission to visit Italy in order to study art in June 1629. There he absorbed the lessons of the Italian Baroque and brought them back to Spain. Throughout his painting career, his style became progressively richer, the color lusher, the figures more animated.

Velázquez's most celebrated painting is the *Maids of Honor*, or *Las Meninas* (fig. 15.26), painted in 1656. Originally entitled *Family of Philip IV*, the painting raises the question: Is this a formal portrait? Or is it a simple genre scene? In fact, it is both. A glass of water has just been brought to Princess Margarita, the five-year-old daughter of Philip IV and his second wife, Queen Mariana. Margarita's maids, friends, a nun, a dwarf, a dog, and others gather round. Yet this scene from everyday life is portrayed on a grand scale. Velázquez even shows himself in the foreground, painting a large canvas, a self-conscious act that serves to comment both on the processes of creativity and on the complexity of representation.

On the back wall of the room are seen the reflections of the queen and king, apparently in a mirror. They stand where the viewer stands in relation to the pictorial space. Does the viewer witness the painting of the Infanta Margarita, as did the queen and king in 1656? Or are the king and queen having their portraits painted by Velázquez and their child has come to watch? What remains unseen is at least as interesting as what is actually represented. Velázquez cleverly unites the world of the picture and the world of the viewer, much as did Jan van Eyck in *Giovanni Arnolfini and His Wife Giovanna Cenami* (see fig. 14.4). But Velázquez implies yet a third area of interest: a man turns back in the far doorway, suggesting a continuation of space beyond.

Velázquez is linked to the Baroque by his feeling for space and light. The princess and her maids of honor are enveloped in an atmospheric space with strong contrasts of light and shadow, while the man in the doorway stands near a source of bright light. In his concern for direct and reflected light, with the subtlest changes in atmosphere, Velázquez looks back to the Venetian painters. Velázquez's technique was to record the details so they could be seen from a distance, not close up, where much of the surface dissolves into indistinguishable shapes and colors.

When Velázquez's masterpiece took its place in Philip IV's collection, it joined over 1500 paintings in the king's collection at the Buen Retiro, the new residence that Olivares and Philip built on the outskirts of Madrid in the early 1630s. Together with Philip II's massive collection, Spain, by 1650, owned much of the Western world's great art. To be sure, Rome had more than its fair share of Italian masterpieces, but Spain's collection reflected developments in Western painting as a whole.

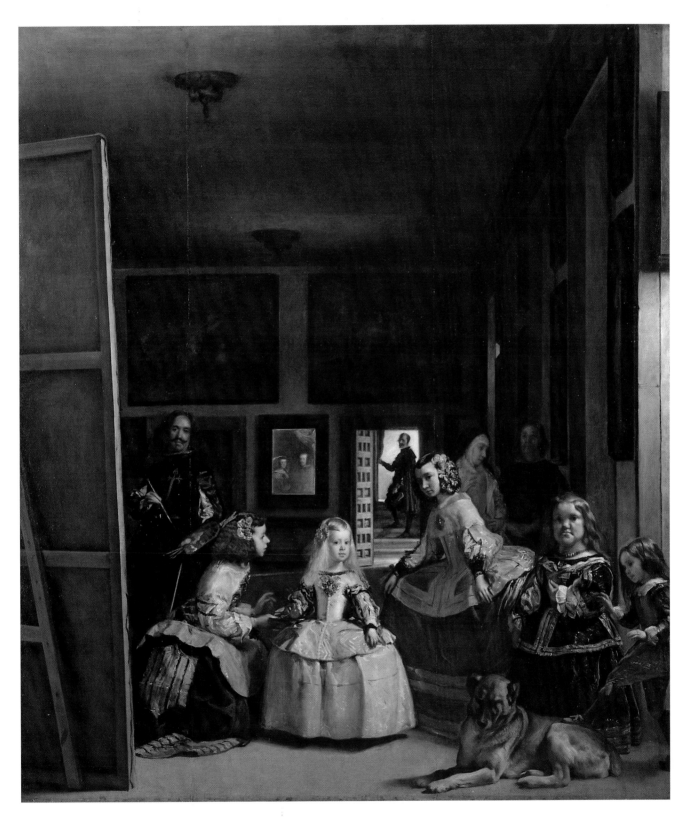

Figure 15.26 Diego Velázquez, *Maids of Honor (Las Meninas)*, 1656, oil on canvas, 10′5″ × 9′ (3.17 × 2.74 m), Museo del Prado, Madrid. Velázquez depicts himself in this group portrait in the process of painting just such a large canvas. Much as in Jan van Eyck's Arnolfini wedding portrait, the presence of people (here the king and queen) in the viewer's space is indicated by their reflection in the mirror on the back wall.

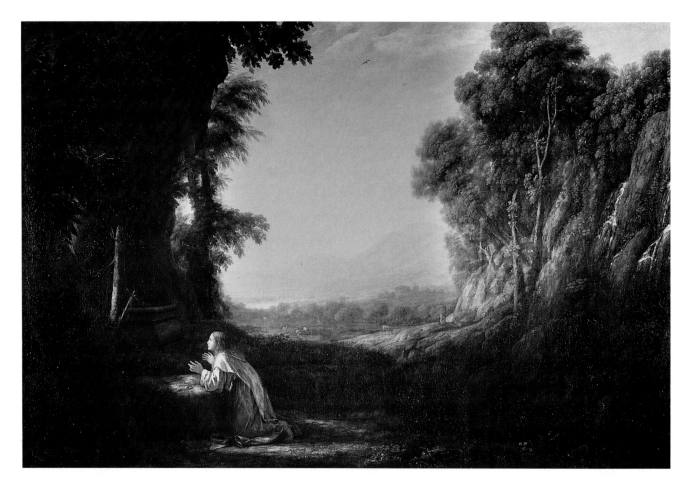

Figure 15.27 Claude Lorrain, *Landscape with St. Mary Magdalene*, oil on canvas, Museo del Prado, Madrid. Claude's compositional scheme would serve as the basic format upon which landscape painting would be based for the next two centuries.

Claude Lorrain and Nicolas Poussin. Two painters who came to be prominently represented in Philip's collection were Claude Lorrain and Nicolas Poussin, both of whom lived and worked in Rome.

CLAUDE LORRAIN [lor-ANN] (1600–1682) painted at least three of the most important landscapes in the seventeenth century, including a *Landscape with St. Mary Magdalene* (fig. 15.27). Mary is lit in a beam of light, in a manner entirely indebted to Caravaggio, though her presence is essentially incidental to the painting. Nature is Claude's real subject and the effects of atmospheric perspective, and the dramatic play of light and dark are his principle means. Typical of Claude's composition are the realistic flora in the foreground, the framing of the distant landscape by two sets of trees forming an almost oval view, and the movement from dark to light and from clarity to haziness, as the viewer's eye enters the scene and proceeds down a sort of zig-zag path into the distance. All of these devices will influence landscape painting well into the nineteenth century.

NICOLAS POUSSIN [poo-SAN] (1594–1665), who represents the classicizing and restrained tendency within the usually dramatic Baroque, created landscapes that, beside those of Claude, seem positively geometric. His *Summer: Ruth and Boaz* (fig. 15.28), part of a series depicting the four seasons painted between 1660 and 1664, is dominated by the verticals and horizontals of the grain that is being harvested. In fact, everything in the composition works at right angles: the forelegs of the horses; the whip in their master's hand; and Boaz and Ruth's arms, framing a virtually rectangular space. Where the center space framed by Claude's trees seems oval, Poussin's central space seems diamond-shaped. Where Claude played with atmos-pheric effects of light, Poussin preserved unbroken clarity. It is possible to count each beard of wheat in the field.

Landscape, however, was not Poussin's only subject. He enjoyed the more ambitious mode of academic history painting. His *Rape of the Sabine Women* (fig. 15.29), of ca. 1636–37, for example, shows Romulus, on the left, raising his cloak to signal his men to abduct the Sabine women to be their wives. The figures make wild gestures and facial expressions, yet the action is frozen and the effect unmoving. This intellectual style is intended to appeal more to the mind than to the eye; appreciation of the painting depends largely upon knowing the story depicted. Poussin said the goal of painting was to represent noble and serious subjects, and the purpose of art was to elevate or morally improve the viewer. Poussin's approach to painting was disciplined, organized, and theoretical. He worked in terms of line rather than color—in this he was the opposite of Rubens.

The French Academy. Beginning with the reign of KING LOUIS XIV [LOO-ee] (1638–1715), who came to the throne in 1643 as a child and was to rule outright from 1661 until 1715, Paris became increasingly the center of the Western art world, even if many of its most important painters, such as Claude and Poussin, preferred to live and work in Rome. Louis's reign was the longest in European history, and assisted by his chief advisor, Jean-Baptiste Colbert, he soon established what

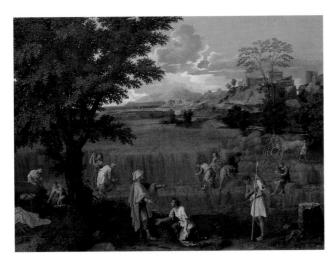

Figure 15.28   Nicolas Poussin, *Summer: Ruth and Boaz*, ca. 1660–64, oil on canvas, Musée du Louvre, Paris. Although landscape was only one of Poussin's recurrent themes, he could not resist submitting it to his classical and geometric sense of organization.

Figure 15.29   Nicolas Poussin, *Rape of the Sabine Women*, ca. 1636–37, oil on canvas, $5'\frac{7}{8}'' \times 6'10\frac{5}{8}''$ (1.55 × 2.10 m), Metropolitan Museum of Art, New York. In spite of the dramatic subject and technical perfection of drawing, Poussin's academic style renders his characters as frozen actors on a stage, unlikely to elicit an emotional response in the viewer.

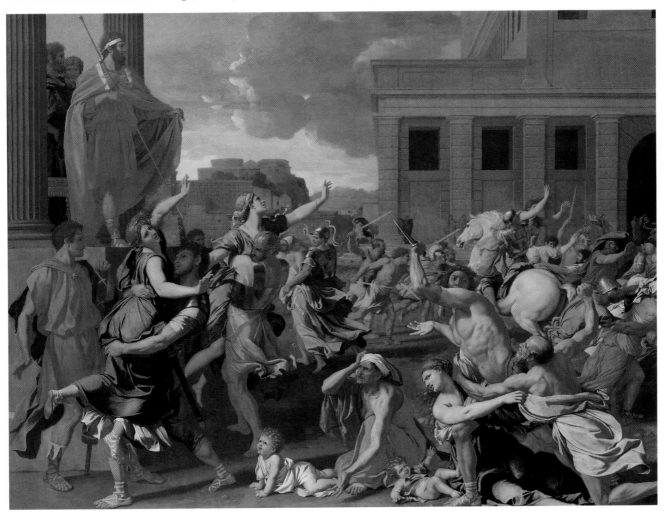

amounted to dictatorial control over art and architecture. His main tool was the Royal Academy of Painting and Sculpture, established in Paris in 1648 and known more simply as the French Academy. Its purpose was to define absolute standards by which to judge the art of the period. It hardly comes as a surprise that classical art was deemed to be the standard.

Favored above all other painters was Poussin, but the Academy's insistence on Poussin's supremacy alienated many younger members of the Academy inclined not towards Poussin's linear geometric classicism, but towards Rubens's bravura style. By the end of the seventeenth century, the Academy had split into two opposing groups—those who favored line and those who favored color. The former, adherents to the style of Poussin and referred to as "*poussinistes*," argued that line was superior because it appealed to the mind, whereas color appealed only to the senses. The latter, preferring the style of Rubens, were called "*rubénistes*" and maintained that color was truer to nature; line appealed only to an educated mind, but color appealed to all. Both sides agreed on this point. Thus, to ask whether line or color is superior in art is to question whether it is the educated

person or the lay person who is the ultimate audience for that art. It is a debate that continues to this day.

ARCHITECTURE

The Louvre. In 1664, it was time to design a facade for the new east wing of the royal palace of the Louvre [LOOV], which housed new royal apartments. As head of the Academy, Colbert invited Bernini to Paris to present plans, but restrained Bernini's approach was (imagine what might have been proposed by someone like Borromini!), it was nevertheless too radical to succeed. Furthermore, French architects did not think the design of a French palace should fall to an Italian. So Colbert appointed a French council to conceive a new plan: architect LOUIS LE VAU [luh VO] (1612–1670), painter CHARLES LE BRUN [luh BRUN] (1619–1690), a previous director of the Academy, and architect CLAUDE PERRAULT [peh-ROH] (1613–1688), who later published a French edition of the classical architect Vitruvius. A strict, linear classicism was the result (fig. 15.30). The center of the facade looks like a Roman temple with Corinthian columns; wings with paired columns extend outward from it; the building ends by forms

Figure 15.30 Louis Le Vau, Charles Le Brun, Claude Perrault, east facade, Palais du Louvre, 1667–70. All vestiges of Baroque sensuality have been banished here in favor of a strict and linear classical line.

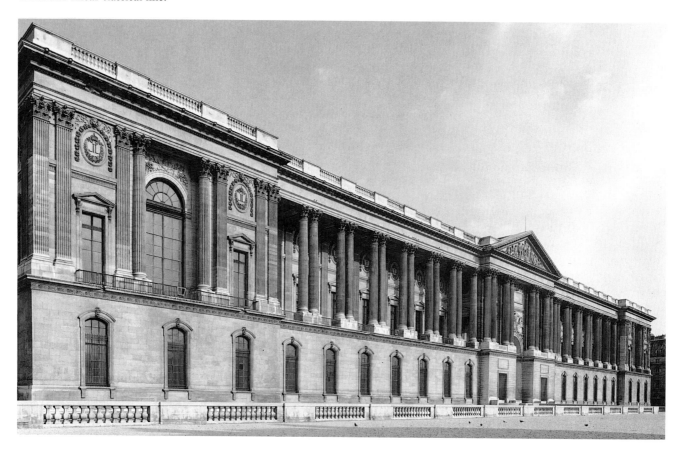

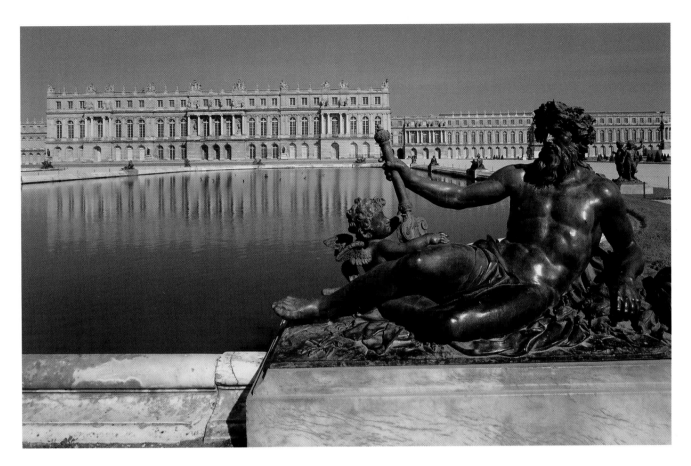

Figure 15.31 Louis Le Vau, Jules Hardouin-Mansart, Charles Le Brun, and Antoine Coysevox, Palace of Versailles, 1669–85. Gardens designed by André Le Nôtre. Louis XIV, the Sun King, created one of the most magnificent palaces of all times, its vast buildings and gardens laid out on a symmetric and geometric plan.

reminiscent of a Roman triumphal arch. The King was so pleased that he insisted the new facade be duplicated on the palace's other faces.

The Palace of Versailles. Louis XIV immediately turned his attention to the building of a new royal palace at Versailles [vair-SIGH] (fig. 15.31), eleven miles southwest of Paris. It was begun in 1669 by Le Vau, who managed to design the garden facade, but who died within the year. JULES HARDOUIN-MANSART [man-SAR] (1646–1708) took over and enlarged the palace to the extraordinary length of 1903 feet.

The visitor arriving at Versailles from Paris is greeted by the principal facade, which is designed to focus on the three windows of Louis XIV's bedroom in the center. The entire palace and gardens are symmetrically arranged on this axis. Several square miles of gardens and parks, designed by ANDRÉ LE NÔTRE [luh NO-truh] (1619–1693), continue the lines of the palace itself, as if the gardens were conceived as a series of outdoor rooms. Nature is controlled in a geometric pattern.

Versailles was the seat of the government of France, and once housed ten thousand people. Even the most

humble attic room at Versailles was preferred to living on one's own estate, because only through personal contact with the king was there the possibility of obtaining royal favors. The most spectacular of the many splendid rooms of the palace of Versailles is the Hall of Mirrors (fig. 15.32), designed about 1680, the work of Hardouin-Mansart, Le Brun, and Antoine Coysevox. An extraordinary space, tunnel-like in its dimensions (240 feet long, but only 34 feet wide, and 43 feet high), the Hall of Mirrors overlooks the gardens through seventeen arched windows reflected in seventeen arched mirrors. As the setting for state functions, it was filled in Louis XIV's day with solid silver furniture and orange trees, and hung with white brocade curtains, seen by the light of innumerable flickering candle flames. Mirrors reflect marble, gilding, stucco, wood, and paint in a theatrical *tour de force* that is among the ultimate examples of the Baroque.

St. Paul's Cathedral. England, meanwhile, had lagged behind the continent artistically. SIR CHRISTOPHER WREN (1632–1723), however, quickly brought England to the contemporary aesthetic fore. In addition

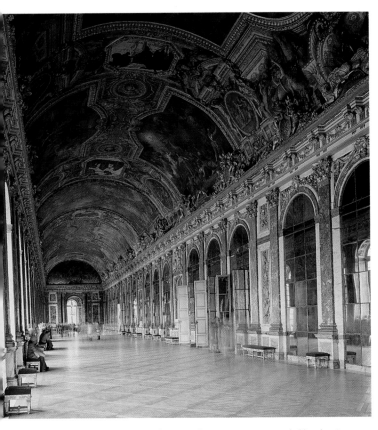

Figure 15.32 Jules Hardouin-Mansart and Charles Le Brun, Hall of Mirrors, Palace of Versailles, ca. 1680. Typically Baroque is the combination of a variety of materials to enhance the opulence of the overall impact. Imagine the effect with the flickering light of hundreds of candles reflected in the arched mirrors.

to being an architect, Wren was also knowledgeable in astronomy (he was Professor of Astronomy at Oxford University), anatomy, physics, mathematics, sailing, street paving, and embroidery. He even invented a device for copying documents by having a second pen attached to the first and writing double.

During the Great Fire of 1666, London burned for an entire week. Much was destroyed, including the original Gothic church of St. Paul's. Wren joined the royal commission for rebuilding the city, and although his plan for reconstructing it in its entirety was rejected, he did design many local churches. His masterpiece, however, was the new St. Paul's cathedral (fig. 15.33), built 1675–1710.

St. Paul's cathedral may be regarded as a Baroque reinterpretation of the ancient Roman Pantheon (see Chapter 5). Wren designed a dome like that of the Pantheon but raised it high on double drums, and he modeled his triangular pediment on the Pantheon's but supported it on two stories of columns, which, characteristic of the Baroque, were grouped in pairs. The lower story of columns is as wide as the nave and aisles, the upper as wide as the nave. Particularly Baroque is the picturesque silhouette created by the towers at each corner.

The dome was constructed of wood and lead on the outside, with a lower dome of masonry within the drum. Like the dome of St. Peter's in Rome, the dome of St. Paul's is as wide as the nave and aisles; it is possible that Wren intended St. Paul's to be the St. Peter's of the north. Although smaller than St. Peter's, some consider St. Paul's artistically superior. St. Peter's lacks small-scale features with which to interpret the vastness; St. Paul's

Timeline 15.2 French rulers during the Baroque age.

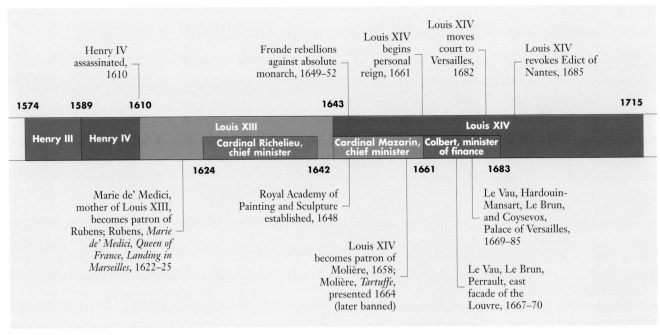

German composer who emigrated to England in the early 1700s. Handel was renowned as an accomplished organist, a consummate musician, and a prodigious composer in many musical genres. He was lauded and commissioned by the Hanoverian kings, and profoundly influenced English music for a century after his death.

By the mid-1720s he had composed nearly forty operas, but astutely recognizing the growing English distaste for the form, he turned to composing **oratorios**. An oratorio is an unstaged sacred opera sung without costume and without acting because it was forbidden to present biblical characters in a public theater. However, almost all of the Baroque theatricality of the operatic tradition is maintained. Handel relied on a heightened musical drama to make up for the lack of theater. Written in English, Handel's oratorios employ the many musical forms of opera, such as *arias* (solo songs), recitatives, duets, ensemble singing, and choruses, and all were set to orchestral accompaniment.

Handel's most famous oratorio is his *Messiah*, a composition of enormous scope that rivals the most ambitious projects of Baroque art and architecture—Bernini's colonnade for the Vatican square, Rubens's cycle of paintings celebrating the life of Marie de' Medici and Milton's epic *Paradise Lost*. The *Messiah* includes more than fifty individual pieces, lasting approximately three hours. Its three parts are based on the biblical texts of Isaiah, the Psalms, the Gospels, Revelations, and the Pauline Epistles. The first part concerns the prophecy of the birth of Christ; the second focuses on his suffering, especially the crucifixion; the third encompasses his resurrection and the redemption of the world.

The tone of the *Messiah* is jubilant and celebratory. One particularly inspirational section is the second part of the oratorio, concluding with the famous "Hallelujah Chorus," which is based on Revelations 11:15. The text is as follows:

a. Hallelujah! Hallelujah!
b. For the Lord God omnipotent reigneth
c. The Kingdom of this world is become the Kingdom of Our Lord and of His Christ.
d. And He shall reign for ever and ever
   King of Kings and Lord of Lords
   And He shall reign for ever and ever
   Hallelujah! Hallelujah!

The opening of this exultant chorus is noteworthy for its repeated and emphatic Hallelujahs (a), followed by a sudden contrasting quieter section (b). An even softer section begins with (c) "The Kingdom of this world," which is quickly followed by the majestic fugue of (d) "And he shall reign for ever and ever." As the chorus moves exuberantly towards its dramatic conclusion, Handel splits the voices. The top voice is split into two voices, soprano and alto, and they rise higher and higher on the phrase "King of Kings and

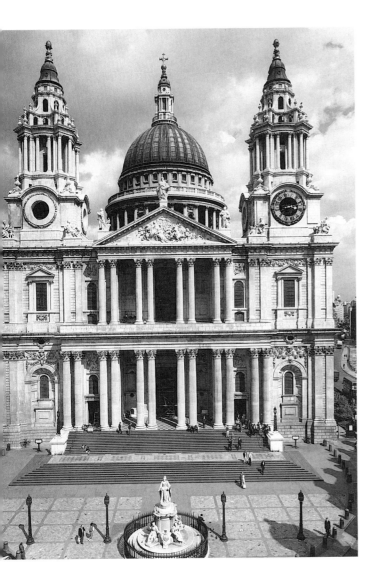

Figure 15.33   Sir Christopher Wren, facade, St. Paul's Cathedral, London, 1675–1710, length 514′ (156.67 m), width 250′ (76.20 m), height of dome 366′ (111.56 m). The facade of St. Paul's in London deserves comparison with that of St. Peter's in Rome. Although the basic dome, pediment, and columns derive from antiquity, the Baroque influence is evident in the paired columns and double facade.

includes such details on both the exterior and interior. St. Paul's is also the only major cathedral in Western Europe to be completed by the person who designed it.

BAROQUE MUSIC OUTSIDE ITALY

Handel and the Oratorio.   Late in the Baroque age, Italian opera such as Monteverdi's began to go out of style, particularly in the north where high-minded Protestants thought the form frivolous. One of the most successful composers of Italian opera of the day was GEORGE FREDERICK HANDEL [HAN-del] (1685–1759), a

Lord of Lords." The bottom voice is also divided into two voices, tenor and bass, which sing "for ever and ever, Hallelujah!" The four voices are bolstered by strong orchestral support with drums beating and brass, especially trumpets, jubilantly blaring. The entire effect is one of highly charged Baroque drama, a magnificent play between the musical "light" offered by the soprano voices and brass contrasted with the "darkness" of the drums and bass line, the whole capturing the essence of the Crucifixion's simultaneous tragedy and joy:

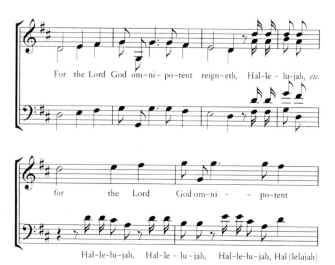

Composed in an astonishing twenty-three days, the *Messiah* was first performed not in London but in Dublin, in 1742, for the relief of prisoners and wards of the state. It wasn't until 1750 that the London public fully responded to the work. Upon completing the *Messiah* Handel's eyes are said to have filled with tears, and he is reputed to have said: "I did think I did see all Heaven before me, and the Great God Himself!" The religious fervor and devotion of the *Messiah* deeply embody this spiritual faith.

Johann Sebastian Bach. The other great Baroque composer is JOHANN SEBASTIAN BACH [bahk] (1685–1750), the grand master of the Baroque style and musical art forms of his age, and as thorough and thoughtful a musician as ever lived. He expertly played and composed solo pieces for a number of instruments, including violin and harpsichord (fig. 15.34). He was master, however, of the organ, on which he could improvise at will the most complicated fugues.

A **fugue** is composed of three or four independent parts of which one part, or voice, states a theme which is then imitated in succession by each of the other voices. As the second voice takes over the theme from the first, the first continues playing in what is called **counterpoint**, music that differs from the main theme. The third voice takes over from the second, the second continues on in counterpoint, and so on. Bach developed to perfection the art of such **polyphonic** music, or music for

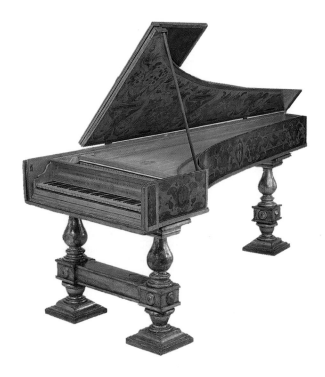

Figure 15.34 Jerome de Zentis, harpsichord, 1658, Metropolitan Museum of Art, New York. A keyboard instrument that was often intricately decorated, the Baroque harpsichord had strings that were plucked by mechanical plectra inside the body of the instrument.

multiple voices. As a young organist, Bach had already demonstrated his talent for improvising on the common church hymn-like chorale tunes, so much so that complaints were lodged against him "for having made many curious variations in the chorale and mingled many strange tones in it." He was at work on his *Art of the Fugue*, an encyclopedic compendium of fugues for study and performance, when he died.

Bach's professional career began with a position as organist at a church in Arnstadt. Then he served for nine years as court organist and chamber musician at the court of the Duke of Weimar, composing many works for the organ. Next Bach served as director of music for the Prince of Cothen, where he composed a set of six concertos dedicated to the Margrave of Brandenburg, subsequently known as *The Brandenburg Concertos*. Bach's longest musical post was as music director of the Church of St. Thomas in Leipzig, where for twenty-seven years he served as organist, choirmaster, composer, and music director. At Leipzig, Bach produced his religious vocal music, including the *B Minor Mass*, the *St. John* and *St. Matthew Passions*, and numerous church cantatas, of which he wrote nearly three hundred, more than two hundred of which survive. A **cantata** is a work for a single singer or group of singers accompanied by instruments.

Among these is the famous *Cantata No. 80: Ein feste Burg is unser Gott* (*A Mighty Fortress Is Our God*),

Cross Currents

THE BAROQUE IN MEXICO

When the Spanish explorers led by Hernán Cortés came to America in 1519, they spread Catholicism with missionary zeal. With the religious support of the Jesuits, also missionaries, and the political and financial backing of European governments, seventeenth-century South America boasted a strong European cultural connection, including no fewer than five universities, the largest and most important of which was in Mexico City.

Mexican-born writers and artists worked hand in hand with their European-born counterparts to create a native architecture and literature that spoke to the European cultural heritage. Great Baroque structures were built, the leading example of which is the Chapel of the Rosary in the Church of Santo Domingo in Puebla (fig. 15.35), completed about 1690. Like so much Mexican art, it melds local traditions and Catholic icons. Here local artisans crafted images in polychrome stucco that, though they represent Christian figures, possess the faces and dresses of native Mexicans. Meandering vines weave across the ceilings, and gold leaf covers the altar. So elaborate is the whole that the style is called the "exuberant Baroque."

Among the most noteworthy and more influential of Mexican Baroque writers was Sor Juana Inés de la Cruz [soar HWA-nah] (1648–1695), who was born near Mexico City. Hailed as the "Phoenix of Mexico" and "America's Tenth Muse" during her lifetime, Sor Juana is considered one of the finest Spanish-American writers of her time. Though she was a nun, she became the confidante of prominent leaders and intellectuals throughout Spanish America.

Her poetry speaks to women across cultures and centuries in a language that is by turns playful and ironically critical of men's failures, as shown in the first and last stanzas from her aptly titled poem, "She Demonstrates the Inconsistency of Men's Wishes in Blaming Women for What They Themselves Have Caused":

> Silly, you men—so very adept
> at wrongly faulting womankind,
> not seeing you're alone to blame
> for faults you plant in woman's
>   mind.

> I well know what powerful arms 5
> you wield in pressing for evil:
> your arrogance is allied
> with the world, the flesh, and the
>   devil.

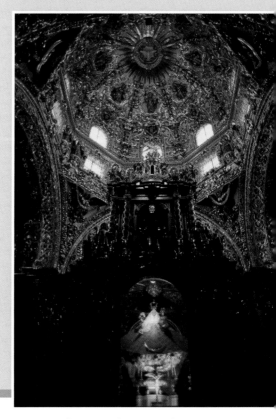

Figure 15.35 Chapel of the Rosary, Church of Santo Domingo, Puebla, Mexico, ca. 1690. Free of any preconceptions that would limit their decorative impulses, the artists who fashioned this interior were able to press the Baroque sensibility to its very limits.

---

composed in 1715, revised in 1724, and based on the hymn, or chorale, by Martin Luther. Like many of Bach's sacred, or church, cantatas, this one was written for Lutheran services. The cantatas were performed by eight to twelve singers and an orchestral ensemble of eighteen to twenty-four musicians (though Bach often complained that he had to make do with wretched musicians and underprepared vocalists). Luther's original chorale, which is in itself a centerpiece of Protestant hymnology, appears in eloquent and simple majesty in a four-part harmonization as the final movement of Bach's cantata.

THE SCIENCE OF OBSERVATION

The almost mathematical precision of Bach's fugues and the astute observation of light in Vermeer's paintings are echoed in the scientific spirit of the Baroque age. Francis Bacon's development of the principles of the scientific

method (see Chapter 14), with its emphasis on the careful observation of physical phenomena, was echoed throughout the Baroque age in a vast array of scientific discoveries and inventions. Careful observation required new tools for seeing, and these new tools in turn created new knowledge.

Anton van Leeuwenhoek.   In Holland, for instance, a lens maker named ANTON VAN LEEUWENHOEK [LAY-ven-huck] (1632–1723) transformed the magnifying glasses used by lace makers and embroiderers into powerful microscopes capable of seeing the smallest organisms. He investigated everything under his microscope (including all of his bodily fluids). Leeuwenhoek quickly realized that the world was teeming with microorganisms that he called "little animals." He was the first person to see protozoa and bacteria and the first to describe the red blood cell. Leeuwenhoek was also fascinated with the mechanisms of sight, particularly with the fact that the eye is itself a lens. He dissected insect and animal eyes, and literally looked through them himself. He describes looking at the tower of the New Church through the eye of a dragonfly: "A great many Towers were presented, also upside down, and they appeared no bigger than does the point of a small pin to our Eye."

Johannes Kepler. JOHANNES KEPLER [KEP-ler] (1571–1630) had been equally interested in the eye, and in 1604 was the first to describe it as an optical instrument with a lens used for focusing (fig. 15.36).

Figure 15.36   Illustration of the theory of the retinal image, from René Descartes, *La Dioptrique* (Leiden, 1637), Bancroft Library, Berkeley, California. No image better illustrates the importance of scientific observation to the Baroque sensibility. Even the eye itself is defined here as a scientific instrument.

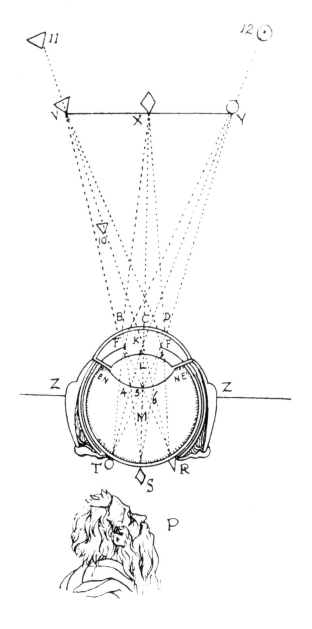

"Vision," he wrote, "is brought about by a picture of the thing seen being formed on the concave surface of the retina."

This observation, in turn, freed the study of vision from the realm of the spiritual or psychological: "I leave to natural philosophers to discuss the way in which this picture is put together by the spiritual principles of vision residing in the retina and the nerves, and whether it is made to appear before the soul or tribunal of the faculty of vision by a spirit within the cerebral cavities, or the faculty of vision, like a magistrate sent by the soul, goes out from the council chamber of the brain to meet this image in the optic nerves and retina, as it were descending to a lower court." Kepler describes only the *fact* of vision, not its meaning or moral force.

Galileo Galilei. Kepler's friend GALILEO GALILEI [ga-li-LAY-o] (1564–1642) was the first to develop the telescope and use it to observe the heavens. Through it he saw and described craters on the moon, the phases of Venus, and sunspots, and he theorized, in one of the most important advances of modern physics, that light takes time to get from one place to another—that, either as a particle or wave, it travels at a uniform speed that is measurable. Galileo's astronomical findings confirmed Copernican theory, a position that the Church still did not accept. In 1615, Galileo was forced to defend his ideas before Pope Paul V in Rome, but his efforts failed, and he was prohibited from either publishing or teaching his findings. When Pope Urban VIII, an old friend, was elected pope, Galileo appealed to the papacy again, but again he was condemned, this time much more severely. He was made to admit the error of his ways in public and was sentenced to prison for the rest of his life. Friends intervened, and in the end he was merely banished to a comfortable villa outside Florence.

PHILOSOPHY

René Descartes. Kepler's effort to distinguish the science of observation from the contemplation of the subjective or spiritual matters of the mind was well known to RENÉ DESCARTES [day-CART] (1595–1650). Descartes actually published the illustrated model of the retinal image (fig. 15.36) in his own work. But Descartes was interested in what Kepler wasn't. He was, in fact, the very "natural philosopher" to whom Kepler left the problem of what happened to the image once it registered itself on the retina. Descartes did for modern philosophy what Bacon had done for science, and so he is often called the "Father of Modern Philosophy."

Descartes used doubt as a point of departure and philosophical debate. He began with a series of systematic questions which led him to doubt the existence of everything. At that point, he asked himself if there was

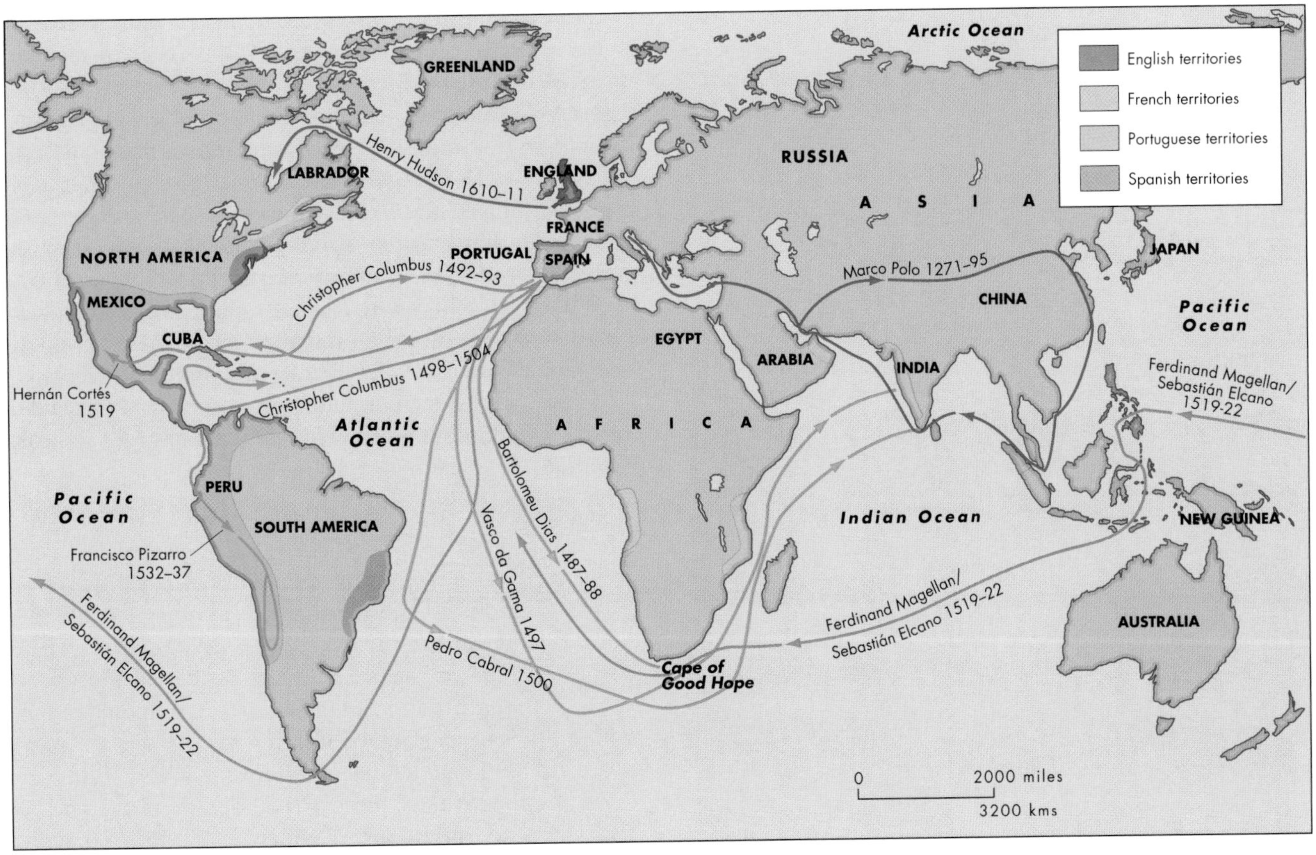

Map showing world exploration routes with a legend:

- English territories
- French territories
- Portuguese territories
- Spanish territories

Labels on map include: Arctic Ocean, GREENLAND, LABRADOR, ENGLAND, FRANCE, PORTUGAL, SPAIN, RUSSIA, A S I A, JAPAN, NORTH AMERICA, MEXICO, CUBA, Hernán Cortés 1519, EGYPT, ARABIA, CHINA, INDIA, Pacific Ocean, Henry Hudson 1610–11, Christopher Columbus 1492–93, Christopher Columbus 1498–1504, Atlantic Ocean, A F R I C A, Marco Polo 1271–95, Ferdinand Magellan/ Sebastián Elcano 1519–22, Pacific Ocean, PERU, SOUTH AMERICA, Francisco Pizarro 1532–37, Vasco da Gama 1497, Bartolomeu Dias 1487–88, Indian Ocean, NEW GUINEA, Ferdinand Magellan/ Sebastián Elcano 1519–22, Pedro Cabral 1500, Cape of Good Hope, Ferdinand Magellan/ Sebastián Elcano 1519–22, AUSTRALIA, 0 2000 miles, 3200 kms

Map 15.2   World exploration, 1271–1611.

anything at all he could know with certainty. His answer was that the only thing he could conceive of "clearly" and "distinctly" (his two essential criteria) was that he existed as a doubting entity. He could sense himself thinking. Descartes formulated this fundamental concept in Latin: "*Cogito, ergo sum,*" which means "I think, therefore I am." According to Descartes, this *cogito* provided the foundation, principle, and model for all subsequent knowledge, which he held to the same standards of self-evidence and rationality.

Turning his attention from himself to the world, Descartes quickly realized that the only thing he could *know* for certain about the material world is that it likewise exists. He believed that there was an absolute division between mind and matter. Matter could be studied mathematically and scientifically, its behavior predicted by the new science of physics. How the mind knew something was quite different. When we observe an object in the distance—the sun, for instance—it appears to be small, but we know through scientific observation that it is much larger than it appears. Knowledge, Descartes knew, cannot rest on perception alone. This had been demonstrated by Copernicus's theory of the universe: we may perceive ourselves to be standing still, but we are on a planet spinning quickly through space.

This recognition led Descartes to consider how we can know that which we cannot perceive. Most important, how can we know that God exists, if we cannot perceive him? Descartes decided, finally, that if we are too imperfect to trust even our own perceptions, and yet we are still able to *imagine* a perfect God, then God must exist. If He didn't, then He would be unimaginable. In other words, what is "clearly" and "distinctly" perceived by the mind—*Cogito, ergo sum*—must be true. Descartes's answer was somewhat paradoxical, and would lead to much philosophical debate in the centuries to come.

Thomas Hobbes.   During the Baroque age, the question of how to govern increasingly occupied philosophical thinkers. In England, the situation reached a crisis point when Charles I challenged Parliament's identity as the king's partner in rule. Civil war erupted, and in 1649, a Commonwealth was established, led by the Puritan Oliver Cromwell as, essentially, a military dictatorship. The monarchy was restored in 1660 after the republic failed, but the relationship between parliament and monarch remained murky. Finally, in 1688, James II was expelled in the bloodless "Glorious Revolution," and Mary and William of Orange, James's daughter and son-in-law, ascended the throne. They immediately accepted the rights of all citizens under the law, recognizing in par-

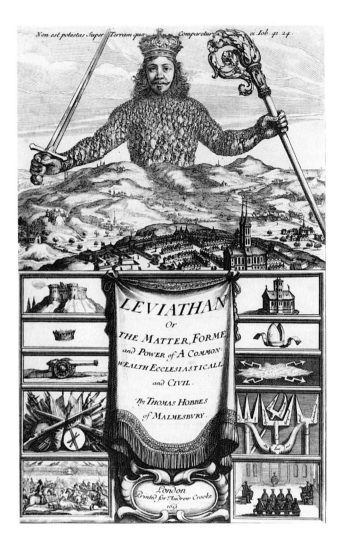

Figure 15.37 Frontispiece of *The Leviathan*, 1651, Bancroft Library, Berkeley, California. An image of the social contract, the body of the king is made up of hundreds of his subjects. He rules over a world at peace, its cities well fortified and its countryside well groomed.

ticular Parliament's right to exercise authority over financial matters, and England became a limited monarchy.

In this atmosphere, the debate about the nature of political rule (who should govern and how) was addressed by two political philosophers with very different points of view. Mirroring Descartes's emphasis on the primacy of perception was the philosopher THOMAS HOBBES (1588–1679). Educated as a classicist, Hobbes was particularly impressed by the geometry of Euclid, and he came to believe that the reasoning upon which geometry is based could be extended to social and political life. After visiting with Galileo in Italy, Hobbes became even more convinced that this was true. The power of Galileo's science of observation and its ability to describe the movement of the solar system could be extended to the observation of human beings in their relations to one another.

Hobbes's philosophy, which was published in 1651 in a book entitled *The Leviathan* (fig. 15.37), would be read by many as essentially an apology for, or defense of, monarchical rule. Hobbes believed, quite simply, that humans are driven by two primal forces, the fear of death and the desire for power. If government does nothing to check these impulses, mankind simply self-destructs, and human life becomes essentially anarchical. But Hobbes also believed that humans recognize their essential depravity and therefore choose to be governed. They enter into what he called the **social contract**, by which the people choose to give up sovereignty over themselves and bestow it on a ruler. They agree to carry out all the ruler's commands, and in return the ruler agrees to keep the peace.

John Locke. JOHN LOCKE [lock] (1632–1704), who repudiated Hobbes, believed that people are perfectly capable of governing themselves. Locke's *Essay on Human Understanding*, published in 1690, argues that the human mind is at birth a *tabula rasa*, or "blank slate." Then two great "fountains of knowledge," our environment as opposed to our heredity, and our reason as opposed to our faith, fill this blank slate with learning as the person develops. Locke argued, furthermore, in his *Second Treatise on Government*, also published in 1690, that humans are "by nature free, equal, and independent." They accept the rule of government, he argues, because they find it convenient to do so, not because they are innately inclined to submit to authority. Such ideas set the stage for the political revolutions of the eighteenth century.

LITERATURE

Unlike Renaissance writers, who were often content to catalogue the beauties of the beloved, Baroque writers display an uncommon interest in exploring the mysteries of love, both erotic and divine. Baroque writers, overall, also spend considerably more time exploring their relationship to God, often in passionate and dramatic terms. Religious and secular Baroque writing, poetry in particular, often dramatizes emotional and personal encounters between speaker and listener (whether God or lover).

Molière and the Baroque Stage. During the Baroque era, stage plans differed from those of Shakespeare and classical Greece. Seventeenth-century plays took place indoors on a picture-frame stage, created with a **proscenium arch**, which was an arch that separated the stage from the auditorium. A curtain separated audience from actors. The plays were enacted on a box stage, which represented a room with a missing fourth wall, allowing the audience to look in on the action. This is still the most popular stage in use.

Though the painted scenery was not elaborate, it served as a backdrop for the action. Candles and lanterns illuminated actors and audience. Costume tended toward

Then & Now

THE TELESCOPE

Galileo's telescope (fig. 15.38) changed the way people thought of their solar system, overturning long-standing beliefs in an earth-centered system. It demonstrated nearly conclusively that the earth and other planets orbited around the sun. The modern-day Hubble Space Telescope is rapidly changing our understanding of the solar system's place in the universe. Deployed on April 24, 1990, by Discovery astronauts, the 12.5-ton satellite carrying Hubble is able to look clearly at the cosmic skies unhindered by earth's atmosphere. It has revealed galaxy forms as much as twelve billion light-years away. Hubble's observation of distant galaxies has led scientists to theorize about the age of the universe itself. Wendy Freedman of the the Carnegie Observatories estimates the universe is between nine and twelve billion years old.

Galileo was able to see other galaxies, which he called *nebulae* (clouds). Hubble's photographs suggest that these *nebulae* are really clumps of gas that generate new stars. Enormous jets of gas erupt out of these gas clumps at speeds up to 300 miles per second and are shot trillions of miles out into space. This is the stuff, scientists believe, of which solar systems are made. Hubble has shown these whirling jets, which rotate faster and faster, all at once form a star and shoot out jets of matter that will form something like our own solar system. The implication is that most stars, even in our own galaxy, possess solar systems similar to our own, and hence the possibility of life.

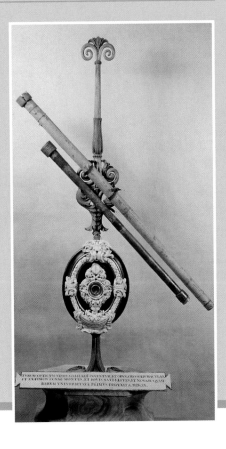

Figure 15.38 Galileo Galilei, Telescope, 1609, Museum of Science, Florence. With a telescope such as this, Galileo was able to contradict the Ptolemaic view of the universe.

---

the elaborate and ornate, as in Elizabethan drama. On both Elizabethan and Baroque stages, actors were ordinarily costumed in contemporary dress appropriate to the social status of the characters they portrayed. A major innovation in seventeenth-century drama was that female actresses assumed women's roles for the first time, enabling playwrights to include more extensive, more frequent, and more realistic love scenes. As in the earlier eras of drama, however, language still did much of the work, so that even in an intimate French Baroque playhouse seating four hundred, action remained subordinate to dialogue.

The conventions of the French theater of the time were inspired by the classical drama of Greece and Rome. Like its ancient antecedents, the seventeenth-century French theater observed what are known as the three **unities**: the unity of time, the unity of place, and the unity of action. A play's action had to be confined to a twenty-four-hour period. The place should be a single setting. The action must be unified in a single plot. Plays that violated these unities were thought crude and inelegant by their educated audience, which consisted largely of courtiers and aristocrats. The three great practitioners of the French Baroque theater all observed the unities—its two great tragedians, PIERRE

CORNEILLE [kor-NAY] (1606–1684) and JEAN RACINE [ra-SEEN] (1639–1699), and its great comic genius Jean-Baptiste Poquelin, known by his stage name MOLIÈRE [mol-YAIR] (1622–1673).

Corneille's themes are those of patriotism and honor. Racine's plays concentrate on the moral dilemmas he discovered in the great Greek tragedies. But of the three, Molière's satiric comedy is the most accessible, resorting, as it often does, to slapstick, pratfalls, and the sorts of comic predicaments modern audiences enjoy in the likes of Charlie Chaplin, the Marx Brothers, and even Chevy Chase and Steve Martin. Among his masterpieces is *Tartuffe*, which satirizes both religious hypocrisy and fraudulence. The play also pokes fun at the obsessive fanaticism and blind gullibility of those who allow themselves to be victimized by the greedy and the self-serving.

When *Tartuffe* was first staged in 1664, it antagonized those who considered it an attack on religion. Even though Molière retitled it *The Impostor* to indicate that Tartuffe's piety is fraudulent, the original version of the play was censored and banned. To defend himself and his play against such charges, Molière wrote three prefaces and later changed his original ending. The publicity enhanced the play's popularity, and the work was returned to the stage under the protection of the King.

Its unending popularity, however, is due neither to royal protection nor to notoriety, but rather to the ingenuity and vitality of its plot, the percipience of its characterization, and the brilliance of its language.

John Donne. One Baroque poet who wrote secular and religious verse that displays dramatic qualities is JOHN DONNE [dun] (1572–1631), considered among the finest poets of his, or indeed of any, age. John Donne is as witty and paradoxical as any writer of his time. He wrote prose as well as verse, and his poetry includes amorous lyrics, philosophical poems, devotional sonnets and hymns, elegies, epistles, and satires. Through intellectual energy, metaphorical ingenuity, and dramatic style, Donne reveals a restlessly inquisitive mind and a deeply religious spirit. He offers profound psychological insights often in a colloquial idiom, something that anticipates modern attitudes.

Born into a Roman Catholic family in anti-Catholic England, Donne attended Oxford and Cambridge Universities, though he neither took an academic degree nor practiced law. He later converted to Anglicanism, and was appointed private secretary to Sir Thomas Egerton, a high court official. When Donne secretly married his employer's niece, Anne More, he was dismissed and prohibited from obtaining court appointment, first by Egerton and later by King James I, who wanted Donne to become an Anglican preacher. This Donne eventually did, being ordained to the ministry in 1615 and made Dean of St. Paul's Cathedral in London in 1621, where he served until his death ten years later.

Donne's "A Valediction: Forbidding Mourning," a deeply philosophical love poem, is recognized for its extended analogy or conceit comparing lovers to the two feet of a geometrician's compasses.

As virtuous men pass mildly away,
    And whisper to their souls to go,
While some of their sad friends do say,
    The breath goes now, and some say, no:

So let us melt, and make no noise,   5
    No tear-floods, nor sigh-tempests move;
'Twere profanation of our joys
    To tell the laity our love.

Moving of th' earth° brings harms and fears,
    Men reckon what it did and meant,   10
But trepidation of the spheres,°
    Though greater far, is innocent.

Dull sublunary° lovers' love
    (Whose soul is sense) cannot admit
Absence, because it doth remove   15
    Those things which elemented° it.

But we by a love so much refined,
    That ourselves know not what it is,
Inter-assured of the mind,
    Care less, eyes, lips, and hands to miss.   20

Our two souls therefore, which are one,
    Though I must go, endure not yet
A breach, but an expansion,
    Like gold to airy thinness beat.

If they be two, they are two so   25
    As stiff twin compasses are two;
Thy soul the fixed foot, makes no show
    To move, but doth, if th' other do.

And though it in the center sit,
    Yet when the other far doth roam,   30
It leans, and hearkens after it,
    And grows erect, as that comes home.

Such wilt thou be to me, who must
    Like th' other foot, obliquely run:
Thy firmness makes my circle just,°   35
    And makes me end, where I begun.

Contemporary sources note that Donne addressed this poem to his wife as he was preparing in 1611 for a continental journey. He had premonitions of disaster, which turned out to be well founded since his wife gave birth to a stillborn child while he was abroad. In the first two stanzas the speaker urges his wife not to make a public spectacle of their grief on parting. The poet/speaker compares their leave-taking with the death of virtuous men, who depart life quietly and peacefully. He urges her to emulate their behavior, arguing that theatrical displays of unhappiness profane their deeply private relationship.

Throughout the next four stanzas the speaker contrasts the couple's higher, more spiritual love with the love of the sensual. Their love, intellectual and spiritual, transcends the senses. In these stanzas, Donne introduces the first of his two important conceits: that the lovers' souls are not really separated but are almost infinitely expanded to fill the intervening space between them, as gold expands when beaten into paper-thin sheets. The comparison with gold suggests the value of love and its prominent position in their lives. This use of scientific reality to illuminate a spiritual condition typifies Donne's amalgamation of disparate realms of experience.

The last part of Donne's "A Valediction: Forbidding Mourning," however, extends his conceit over three stanzas. The compass is a symbol of constancy and change since it both moves and remains stationary. The compass also inscribes a circle, symbol of perfection. These ideas of constancy and perfection are worked through in detail as the speaker/poet explains how one foot of the compass moves only in relation to the other, returning "home" when the two feet of the compass are brought together.

---

⁹ *Moving of th' earth*: earthquakes. ¹¹ *trepidation of the spheres*: According to Ptolemaic astronomy, the planets sometimes moved violently, like earthquakes, but these movements were not felt by people on earth. ¹³ *sublunary*: Under the moon: hence mortal and subject to change. ¹⁶ *elemented*: composed.

³⁵ *circle just*: The circle is a traditional symbol of perfection.

Anne Bradstreet. Among Donne's near contemporaries is ANNE BRADSTREET (1612–1672), the first major poet in American literature. Born Anne Dudley to a Puritan family in Northampton, England, she sailed with her parents and her new husband, Simon Bradstreet, to Massachusetts in 1630. As secretary to the Massachusetts Bay Company, Simon often traveled on company business, leaving Anne alone. In his absence she became an accomplished poet, and on several occasions wrote poems about their separation. "A Letter to Her Husband, Absent upon Public Employment" is an example.

Though today best known for her domestic lyrics, in her own day Bradstreet was known for a monumental historical cycle of poems based on the four ages of humanity. Donne's philosophical poems, and Bradstreet's domestic ones, can be compared with the paintings of a northern Baroque painter like Vermeer, whose small body of elegantly and finely honed art embodies near perfection of form and idea.

John Milton. JOHN MILTON (1608–1674) represents a facet of Baroque sensibility that his early Baroque counterpart, John Donne, lacked. Unlike Donne, whose poems are mostly brief lyrics, Milton had a conception of grandeur and monumentality that was attuned to the epic, a sensibility Bradstreet shared. Milton, however, stood at the opposite end of the poetic spectrum, like the architect Bernini, the more monumental Baroque painters such as Rubens, and composers of large-scale musical works, such as Bach and Handel.

No poet more than Milton embodies the ideal of a poetic vocation. Milton believed that one didn't become a poet simply by writing poems. A poet had to prepare intellectually and spiritually through disciplined study and prayer, for great art, Milton believed, could only be written by a mind and soul readied for the enormous challenge the poetic vocation entailed.

What specific kinds of preparation did Milton find necessary? Milton's view of the poetic vocation, of himself as poet, and of the preparation necessary to undertake such a vocation was both grand and noble. To learn poetry, he studied the great classical writers of ancient Greece and Rome—Homer, Virgil, Ovid, and Theocritus—and he studied the complete Bible. He sensed that he must write poetry at once serious in outlook and grand in manner, befitting one who wanted to "leave something so written to aftertimes as they should not willingly let it die."

Milton's poetry, from the early apprentice work to the later epics, *Paradise Lost* and *Paradise Regained*, was grounded in the ideals of classical humanism and biblical morality. Combining these two influential western traditions more thoroughly and more profoundly than any other writer in English, Milton presents a decisive summation of High Renaissance art and Christian human-ism. From the Greeks and Romans Milton derived a sense of civic responsibility. Like his forebears, Milton believed that the primary function of art was to teach, and that one of its primary lessons was civic responsibility. Milton himself was steeped in the tradition that valued great statesmen, who by virtue of their own nobility, intellectuality, and vision could ensure the survival of civilized and humane spiritual values. In later life, Milton found his ideal statesman in the Puritan leader Oliver Cromwell, whom Milton served by writing a series of prose works both before and after Cromwell came to power.

Milton's life can be divided into three parts. First, he prepared for his poetic vocation. This period culminated in the publication of "Lycidas," his elegy on the death of a drowned friend, followed by a two-year tour of Europe. Second, he spent a twenty-year span from about 1640 to 1660 in political involvement, during which he wrote prose rather than poetry. Placing himself in the service of the Puritan cause, Milton produced pamphlets and tracts on various theological and ecclesiastical issues, such as Christian doctrine and divorce. Milton actually lived the last two decades of his life in blindness brought on, in part, by his exhausting work on behalf of the Puritans in the 1640s. When the English monarchy was restored to the Stuart line, Milton was imprisoned and his property confiscated. Set free a short time later, he lived out his remaining years in relative isolation working on his great epic poems.

Third, Milton spent the last fifteen years of his life writing and publishing his most ambitious works: *Paradise Lost* (1667), *Paradise Regained* (1671), and *Samson Agonistes* (1671). In these poems, especially in *Paradise Lost*, Milton attempted, in his words, "to justify the ways of God to man." This idea of justification reflected Milton's own blend of Puritan theology and classical humanism. Milton reinterpreted the crucial events of Genesis—humankind's fall into sin, its loss of primeval innocence, and its banishment from the Garden of Eden with all the pain and sorrow that resulted from Adam and Eve's disobedience of God's commandment. In his epic, Milton emphasized the central theological belief of Christianity: the incarnation of God-as-man in Jesus Christ, who came to atone for the sin of humanity's first parents and who restored humankind's place of favor with God. Christ's sacrifice thus balanced the scales of almighty justice, thereby gaining for human beings the chance to gain eternal life—all, of course, providing they lived their lives in accordance with biblical teachings and values.

Regardless of one's theological beliefs, *Paradise Lost* impresses with its remarkable dramatic stories: descriptions of the battle in heaven between the faithful and the rebellious angels; the debate in hell among the various fallen angels on how to proceed against their common enemy, God; the temptation scene in which Satan persuades Eve to eat the forbidden fruit. These and other aspects of the epic are stamped with Milton's peculiar grandeur of conception and style. They echo and interpret Genesis without simply repeating the story of the Fall of Man recounted there.

Miguel de Cervantes.   During the sixteenth century in Spain, a narrative form known as the **picaresque** began to develop. The picaresque novel details the life of a *pícaro*, a rogue or knave who wanders from adventure to adventure, encountering various segments of society, and this type of narrative marks the birth of the novel as a literary art form. Like Chaucer's *Canterbury Tales*, the picaresque novel probably developed out of the pilgrimage tradition, in particular the pilgrimage across northern Spain to Santiago de Compostela, the burial place of St. James, which in the eleventh and twelfth centuries had been the object of all European pilgrimages. As contemporary novelist Carlos Fuentes has described it, on the route there came together "the Germans, the Burgundians, Normans and Englishmen, princes and abbots, merchants, thieves, bandits, lepers, all mingling in the great pilgrimage and functioning as a kind of original Common Market." Whereas the *Canterbury Tales* is a compendium of stories about different pilgrims, the picaresque novel focuses on a single hero.

One characteristic feature of the picaresque novel is its pseudo-autobiographical nature. Narrated always by the hero, the point of view is clearly his, prejudiced and partial. He is an observer of society, and, perhaps as a result, he is expert at recognizing fraud and deception. In many ways, his journey is a sort of "fallen" or bankrupt epic. Like Odysseus, the *pícaro* encounters various obstacles and adventures, but instead of Scylla and Charybdis he meets characters such as a blind priest and a lecherous monk.

The greatest of all picaresque novels is *Don Quixote*, by MIGUEL DE CERVANTES [ser-VAHN-tez] (1548–1616). It is in fact more than a picaresque novel, satirizing the form even as it goes beyond it in complexity and ambition. Composed between 1603 and 1615, *Don Quixote* was translated in the seventeenth century into English, French, Italian, and German. Hailed as the first modern novel, *Don Quixote* has transcended its time because of the central character. Don Quixote, the hero, is presented by Cervantes as "dry, shriveled, and full of odd fantasies such as never entered another's brain." He wants, most of all, to become a "knight errant," the kind of hero he has read about in books, who saves ladies from evil and defeats dragons in combat. In fact, he is at once noble and a buffoon. What he sees and what is the truth are two entirely different things. His horse is "all skin and bones," but in his eyes, it is a noble "steed." His companion is a peasant boy, redubbed his "squire," Sancho Panza. His lady, the lovely Dulcinea, is actually one Aldonza Lorenzo, who "never knew or was aware of"

his love for her. And the giant he eventually fights is not a giant at all, but a windmill. The novel represents, for the first time in Western literature, the conflict between reality and the imagination, and though Don Quixote's imagination brings him to the edge of total madness, it ennobles him as well. His pathos is itself heroic.

READINGS

❖ **Ignatius of Loyola**
from *The Spiritual Exercises*

Ignatius of Loyola's Spiritual Exercises *provided both clerical and lay Church members with a guidebook for spiritual development. As leaders of the Counter-Reformation, the Jesuits advocated strict obedience to the tenets of Roman Catholicism, both for themselves and for lay people. In the following meditation, Ignatius prescribes activities and forms of contemplation that will conjure up vivid images and evoke strong emotional and spiritual responses in the participant.*

The Fifth Exercise

The Fifth Exercise is a meditation on Hell. It contains, after a preparatory prayer and two preludes, five points and a colloquy.

Let the preparatory prayer be the usual one.

The first prelude is a composition of place, which is here to see with the eyes of the imagination the length, breadth, and depth of Hell.

The second prelude is to ask for that which I desire. It will be here to ask for an interior perception of the pains which the lost suffer, in order that if I through my faults forget the love of the Eternal Lord, at least the fear of punishment may help me not to fall into sin.

The first point will be to see with the eyes of the imagination these great fires, and the souls as it were in bodies of fire.

The second will be to hear with the ears of the imagination the wailings, the howlings, the cries, the blasphemies against Christ our Lord and against all the saints.

The third will be to smell the smoke, the sulphur, the filth, and the putrid matter.

The fourth will be to taste with the taste of the imagination bitter things, such as tears, sadness, and the worm of conscience.

The fifth will be to feel with the touch of the imagination how the fires touch and burn the souls.

Making a colloquy to Christ our Lord, bring to memory the souls which are in Hell, some because they did not believe His coming, others because believing they did not act according to His commandments; making of them three classes: the first, those who lived before His coming; the second, those who were alive during His lifetime; and the third, those who lived after His life in this world: and then give thanks that He has not, by putting an end to my life, permitted me to fall under any of these classes. In like manner consider how up till now He has always had towards me such pity and mercy; and then finish with a *Pater noster*.

René Descartes

from *The Metaphysical Meditations*

In the following passage from his Metaphysical Meditations, *Descartes explores the nature of his own mind, focusing particularly on what he knows with certainty. His "Second Meditation" shows Descartes discovering what he is—"A thing that thinks." The* Metaphysical Meditations *in their entirety reveal a human mind reasoning in various manifestations—doubting, affirming, denying, willing, refusing, understanding, and imagining.*

Second Meditation

Of the Nature of the Human Mind, and That it Is Easier to Know than the Body.

Yesterday's Meditation has filled my mind with so many doubts that henceforth it is no longer in my power to forget them, and yet I do not see how I shall be able to solve them; and just as if I had suddenly fallen into very deep water, I am so taken aback that I can neither find foothold at the bottom, nor swim to keep myself at the top. I shall make an effort, nevertheless, and follow again the same road I went over yesterday, by putting away from me all in which I shall be able to imagine the least doubt, just as if I knew it to be absolutely false, and I shall continue to follow this path, until I have met with something that is certain; or at least, if I can do nothing else, until I have learned for certain that nothing in the world is certain. Archimedes, to draw the terrestrial globe from its place, and transport it elsewhere, asked no more than one firm and immovable point: in the same way, I shall have the right to conceive high hopes, if I am happy enough to find but one certain and indubitable thing.

I assume, therefore, that everything that I see is false; I persuade myself that of all the things which my memory, stored with dreams, represents to me, none have ever existed; I suppose that I have no sense; I believe that body, shape, extension, motion, and place are only fictions of my mind. What, then, shall be esteemed true? Nothing, perhaps, but that nothing in the world is certain.

But how do I know that there is not some other thing, different from these that I have just pronounced uncertain, of which there cannot be the slightest doubt? Is there not a God, or some other power which puts these thoughts into my mind? Not necessarily; for it may be that I am capable of producing them myself. I, at least, then, am I not something? But I have already denied that I had any senses or any body; nevertheless I hesitate, for what follows? Am I so dependent on the body and on the senses that I cannot exist without them? But I persuaded myself that there was nothing in the whole world, no sky, no earth, no spirits, no bodies; did I not therefore also persuade myself that I did not exist? Far from it; beyond doubt I existed if I persuaded myself, or even if I only thought something. But there is an unknown deceiver, very powerful and very cunning, who employs all his energy in continually deceiving me; therefore there is no doubt that I exist, if he deceives me; let him deceive me as much as he will, he will never be able to make me to be nothing, so long as I shall think I am something.

So having pondered that well, and examined everything carefully, it must after all be concluded and held as unquestionable that this proposition—*I am, I exist*—is necessarily true, every time that I pronounce it, or conceive it in my mind.

But I do not yet know quite clearly what I am, I, who am certain that I am: so that henceforth I must take careful heed not to imprudently mistake some other thing for myself, so as not to err in this knowledge, which I maintain to be more certain and evident than all which I have had formerly.

This is why I shall now consider entirely anew what I believed myself to be before I entered upon these last thoughts, and from my old opinions I shall lop off all which can be in the slightest degree opposed to the reasons I have already alleged, so that there may remain just that which is perfectly certain and indubitable, and that alone. What, then, have I believed myself to be hitherto? Without doubt, I thought I was a man; but what is a man? Shall I say that it is a rational animal? No indeed, for I should afterwards have to find out what an animal is, and what rational is, and thus from one single question I should be launched, without knowing it, into an infinity of others more difficult and complex, and I would not misuse the little time and leisure remaining to me, by employing it in unravelling difficulties of the kind. But I will here dwell rather on the consideration of the thoughts which heretofore took rise of themselves in my mind, and with which my nature alone inspired me, when I applied myself to the contemplation of my being. I considered myself first as having a face, hands, arms, and all the mechanism of flesh and bones, such as it appears in a corpse, which I designated "body." Moreover, I reflected that I nourished myself, that I walked, felt, and thought, and I connected all these actions with the soul; but I did not stop to think what this soul was; or rather, if I did so, I imagined it something extremely rare and subtle, as a wind, a flame, or a very volatile air insinuated and diffused throughout my more material parts. As to what the body was, in nowise did I doubt of its nature, but I thought I knew it very distinctly; and if I had wished to explain it according to the notions I then had of it, I would have described it in this way. By the body I understand all which can be limited by some fixture, which can be contained in some place, and occupy a space in such a manner that all other bodies are excluded therefrom; which is sensible either to touch, or sight, or hearing, or taste, or smell; which can be moved in many ways, not indeed by itself, but by something extraneous which comes into contact with it, and from which it receives the impression; for I do not believe at all that the power of moving of oneself, or of feeling, or of thinking, belongs to the nature of the body; on the contrary, I was astonished, rather, to see that in some bodies faculties of the kind were to be met with.

But I, what am I, now that I assume that there is a certain genius who is extremely powerful, and, if I dare say so, malicious and crafty, who uses all his power and industry to deceive me? Can I be sure that I have the least of all those things that I have just said belonged to the nature of the body? I pause to consider that attentively; I revolve all these things in my mind, and I find none of them which I can say are in me. There is no need for me to stay to enumerate them. Let us pass, therefore, to the attributes of the soul, and see if there are any which may be in me. The first attributes are [the faculties of] feeding myself and of walking; but if it is true that I have no body, it is also true that I can neither walk nor feed. Another is sensibility, but neither can we feel without the body besides, I have at times thought I felt many things during sleep, which on waking I have discovered that I had not really felt. Another is thought, and here I find that thought is an attribute which belongs to me; it alone cannot be separated from me. *I am, I exist*—that is certain, but for how long? As long as I think; for, perhaps, if I entirely ceased to think, I should at the same time entirely cease to be. I now admit nothing, which is not of necessity true; therefore, strictly speaking, I am *only a thing which thinks*, that is to say, a mind, an understanding, or a reason, terms whose signification was formerly unknown to me. Now I am a real thing, and truly existent, but what thing? I have said it,—a thing which thinks. What more? I will exert my imagination, to see if I am not something more yet. I am not this collection of members which is called the human body; I am not a volatile and penetrating air diffused through these members; I am not a wind, a breath, a vapour, or any of the things which I can feign and imagine myself, since I have assumed all that to be nothing, and since without changing this assumption I find that I do not cease to be certain that I am something.

But perhaps it is true that these very things which I suppose not to exist, because they are unknown to me, are not in reality different from myself, whom I know? I cannot say; I do not now dispute it; I cannot give my opinion except on things which are known to me: I know that I exist, and I am seeking what I am—I, whom I know to be. Now it is very certain that the knowledge of my being, thus taken exactly, does not depend on the things whose existence is not yet known to me; consequently, it does not depend on any of those that I can feign by my imagination. And even these terms "feign" and "imagination" warn me of my error. For I should feign indeed if I imagined myself to be something, since to imagine is nothing else than to contemplate the figure or image of a material thing: now I already know for certain that I am, and that at the same time it may be that all these images, and generally all the things which are connected with the bodily nature, are only dreams or chimeras. Following which, I see clearly, that I have as little reason in saying, I will excite my imagination in order to know more exactly what I am, as if I said, I am now awake, and perceive something real and veritable, but because I do not yet perceive it plainly enough, I will send myself to sleep expressly in order that my dreams may represent it to me with even more truth and evidence. And therefore I know clearly that nothing which I can comprehend by means of the imagination belongs to this knowledge that I have concerning myself, and that there is need to call off and deflect the mind from this mode of conception, in order that it may more exactly know its nature.

But what, then, am I? *A thing which thinks.* What is a thing which thinks? It is a thing which doubts, understands, conceives, affirms, denies, wills, wills not, which also imagines, and feels.

from *Tartuffe*

Tartuffe, one of Molière's most popular plays, satirizes both religious hypocrisy and fraudulence. It ridicules the obsessive fanaticism and blind gullibility of those who are duped by the deceitful and the selfish. The following is the opening scene of the play, in which Molière immediately sets the tone and course of hilarious action to come.

MADAME PERNELLE, *Orgon's mother*
ORGON, *Elmire's husband*
ELMIRE, *Orgon's wife*
DAMIS, *Orgon's son, Elmire's stepson*
MARIANE, *Orgon's daughter, Elmire's stepdaughter, in love with Valère*
VALÈRE, *in love with Mariane*
CLÉANTE, *Orgon's brother-in-law*
TARTUFFE, *a hypocrite*
DORINE, *Mariane's lady's-maid*
MONSIEUR LOYAL, *a bailiff*
A POLICE OFFICER
FLIPOTE, *Madame Pernelle's maid*

The Scene throughout: ORGON'S *house in Paris.*

ACT I

Scene I

MADAME PERNELLE *and* FLIPOTE, *her maid,* ELMIRE, MARIANE, DORINE, DAMIS, CLÉANTE

MADAME PERNELLE   Come, come, Flipote; it's time I
        left this place.
ELMIRE   I can't keep up, you walk at such a pace.
MADAME PERNELLE   Don't trouble, child; no need to
        show me out.
    It's not your manners I'm concerned about.
ELMIRE   We merely pay you the respect we owe.   5
    But Mother, why this hurry? Must you go?
MADAME PERNELLE   I must. This house appalls me.
        No one in it
    Will pay attention for a single minute.
    Children, I take my leave much vexed in spirit.
    I offer good advice, but you won't hear it.   10
    You all break in and chatter on and on.
    It's like a madhouse with the keeper gone.
DORINE   If ...
MADAME PERNELLE   Girl, you talk too much, and I'm
        afraid
    You're far too saucy for a lady's-maid.   15
    You push in everywhere and have your say.
DAMIS   But ...
MADAME PERNELLE   You, boy, grow more foolish
        every day.
    To think my grandson should be such a dunce!
    I've said a hundred times, if I've said it once,   20
    That if you keep the course on which you've
        started,
    You'll leave your worthy father broken-hearted.
MARIANE   I think ...
MADAME PERNELLE   And you, his sister, seem so pure,
    So shy, so innocent, and so demure.   25
    But you know what they say about still waters.

I pity parents with secretive daughters.

ELMIRE   Now, Mother …

MADAME PERNELLE   And as for you, child, let me add
    That your behavior is extremely bad,   30
    And a poor example for these children, too.
    Their dear, dead mother did far better than you.
    You're much too free with money, and I'm
        distressed
    To see you so elaborately dressed.
    When it's one's husband that one aims to please,   35
    One has no need of costly fripperies.

CLÉANTE   Oh, Madam, really …

MADAME PERNELLE   You are her brother, Sir,
    And I respect and love you; yet if I were
    My son, this lady's good and pious spouse,   40
    I wouldn't make you welcome in my house.
    You're full of worldly counsels which, I fear,
    Aren't suitable for decent folk to hear.
    I've spoken bluntly, Sir; but it behooves us
    Not to mince words when righteous fervor moves
        us.   45

DAMIS   Your man Tartuffe is full of holy speeches …

MADAME PERNELLE   And practices precisely what he
        preaches.
    He's a fine man, and should be listened to.
    I will not hear him mocked by fools like you.

DAMIS   Good God! Do you expect me to submit   50
    To the tyranny of that carping hypocrite?
    Must we forgo all joys and satisfactions
    Because that bigot censures all our actions?

DORINE   To hear him talk—and he talks all the time—
    There's nothing one can do that's not a crime.   55
    He rails at everything, your dear Tartuffe.

MADAME PERNELLE   Whatever he reproves deserves
        reproof.
    He's out to save your souls, and all of you
    Must love him, as my son would have you do.

DAMIS   Ah no, Grandmother, I could never take   60
    To such a rascal, even for my father's sake.
    That's how I feel, and I shall not dissemble.
    His every action makes me seethe and tremble
    With helpless anger, and I have no doubt
    That he and I will shortly have it out.   65

DORINE   Surely it is a shame and a disgrace
    To see this man usurp the master's place—
    To see this beggar who, when first he came,
    Had not a shoe or shoestring to his name
    So far forget himself that he behaves   70
    As if the house were his, and we his slaves.

MADAME PERNELLE   Well, mark my words, your souls
        would fare far better
    If you obeyed his precepts to the letter.

DORINE   You see him as a saint.
    I'm far less awed;   75
    In fact, I see right through him.
    He's a fraud.

MADAME PERNELLE   Nonsense!

DORINE   His man Laurent's the same, or worse;
    I'd not trust either with a penny purse.   80

MADAME PERNELLE   I can't say what his servant's
        morals may be;

His own great goodness I can guarantee.
    You all regard him with distaste and fear
    Because he tells you what you're loath to hear,
    Condemns your sins, points out your moral flaws,   85
    And humbly strives to further Heaven's cause.

DORINE   If sin is all that bothers him, why is it
    He's so upset when folk drop in to visit?
    Is Heaven so outraged by a social call
    That he must prophesy against us all?   90
    I'll tell you what I think: if you ask me,
    He's jealous of my mistress' company.

MADAME PERNELLE   Rubbish! (To ELMIRE:) He's not
        alone, child, in complaining
    Of all of your promiscuous entertaining.
    Why, the whole neighborhood's upset, I know,   95
    By all these carriages that come and go,
    With crowds of guests parading in and out
    And noisy servants loitering about.
    In all of this, I'm sure there's nothing vicious;
    But why give people cause to be suspicious?   100

CLÉANTE   They need no cause; they'll talk in any case.
    Madam, this world would be a joyless place
    If, fearing what malicious tongues might say,
    We locked our doors and turned our friends away.
    And even if one did so dreary a thing,   105
    D'you think those tongues would cease their
        chattering?
    One can't fight slander; it's a losing battle;
    Let us instead ignore their tittle-tattle.
    Let's strive to live by conscience' clear decrees,
    And let the gossips gossip as they please.   110

DORINE   If there is talk against us, I know the source:
    It's Daphne and her little husband, of course.
    Those who have greatest cause for guilt and shame
    Are quickest to besmirch a neighbor's name.
    When there's a chance for libel, they never miss it;
    When something can be made to seem illicit   116
    They're off at once to spread the joyous news,
    Adding to fact what fantasies they choose.
    By talking up their neighbor's indiscretions
    They seek to camouflage their own transgressions,
    Hoping that others' innocent affairs   126
    Will lend a hue of innocence to theirs,
    Or that their own black guilt will come to seem
    Part of a general shady color-scheme.

MADAME PERNELLE   All that is quite irrelevant. I
        doubt   125
    That anyone's more virtuous and devout
    Than dear Orante; and I'm informed that she
    Condemns your mode of life most vehemently.

DORINE   Oh, yes, she's strict, devout, and has no taint
    Of worldliness; in short, she seems a saint.   130
    But it was time which taught her that disguise;
    She's thus because she can't be otherwise.
    So long as her attractions could enthrall,
    She flounced and flirted and enjoyed it all,
    But now that they're no longer what they were   135
    She quits a world which fast is quitting her,
    And wears a veil of virtue to conceal
    Her bankrupt beauty and her lost appeal.
    That's what becomes of old coquettes today:

Distressed when all their lovers fall away,   *140*
They see no recourse but to play the prude,
And so confer a style on solitude.
Thereafter, they're severe with everyone,
Condemning all our actions, pardoning none,
And claiming to be pure, austere, and zealous   *145*
When, if the truth were known, they're merely
    jealous,
And cannot bear to see another know
The pleasures time has forced them to forgo.

MADAME PERNELLE (*initially to* ELMIRE)
That sort of talk is what you like to hear;
Therefore you'd have us all keep still, my dear,   *150*
While Madam rattles on the livelong day.
Nevertheless, I mean to have my say.
I tell you that you're blest to have Tartuffe
Dwelling, as my son's guest, beneath this roof;
That Heaven has sent him to forestall its wrath   *155*
By leading you, once more, to the true path;
That all he reprehends is reprehensible,
And that you'd better heed him, and be sensible.
These visits, balls, and parties in which you revel
Are nothing but inventions of the Devil.   *160*
One never hears a word that's edifying:
Nothing but chaff and foolishness and lying,
As well as vicious gossip in which one's neighbor
Is cut to bits with epee, foil, and saber.
People of sense are driven half-insane   *165*
At such affairs, where noise and folly reign
And reputations perish thick and fast.
As a wise preacher said on Sunday last,
Parties are Towers of Babylon, because
The guests all babble on with never a pause;   *170*
And then he told a story which, I think …

(*To* CLÉANTE)
I heard that laugh, Sir, and I saw that wink!
Go find your silly friends and laugh some more!
Enough; I'm going; don't show me to the door.
I leave this household much dismayed and vexed;   *175*
I cannot say when I shall see you next.

(*Slapping* FLIPOTE)
Wake up, don't stand there gaping into space!
I'll slap some sense into that stupid face.
Move, move, you slut.

✦ John Donne
The Flea

One of John Donne's best-known poems, "The Flea" is notable for its dramatic situation, its wit, and its humor. Unlike the typical Renaissance love poem, "The Flea" presents an unconventional seduction. Readers may infer that the woman at first resists the speaker's various strategies, as evidenced by what occurs in the "space" between the second and third stanzas. In its modernization of a conventional poetic fashion, "The Flea" exhibits Baroque characterizations of dramatic action and playful exaggeration.

Mark but this flea, and mark in this
How little that which thou deny'st me is;
It sucked me first, and now sucks thee,
And in this flea our two bloods mingled be;

Thou know'st that this cannot be said   *5*
A sin, nor shame, nor loss of maidenhead;
    Yet this enjoys before it woo,
    And pampered swells with one blood made of two,
    And this, alas, is more than we would do.

Oh stay, three lives in one flea spare,   *10*
Where we almost, yea, more than married are.
This flea is you and I, and this
Our marriage bed and marriage temple is;
Though parents grudge, and you, we are met
And cloistered in these living walls of jet.   *15*
    Though use make you apt to kill me,
    Let not to that, self-murder added be,
    And sacrilege, three sins in killing three.

Cruel and sudden, hast thou since
Purpled by nail in blood of innocence?   *20*
Wherein could this flea guilty be,
Except in that drop which it sucked from thee?
Yet thou triumph'st and say'st that thou
Find'st not thyself, nor me the weaker now.
    'Tis true. Then learn how false fears be: *25*
    Just so much honour, when thou yield'st to me,
    Will waste, as this flea's death took life from thee.

✦ Anne Bradstreet
A Letter to Her Husband, Absent upon Public Employment

The following poem, though less complex than Donne's conceit-governed "A Valediction: Forbidding Mourning," is in directness and openness of feeling more moving. Like Donne's "Valediction," Bradstreet's poem reflects developments in modern science. Bradstreet was aware of the earth's rotation on its axis, and the effect of this rotation on the seasons. The poet/speaker compares her husband to the sun, and his absence is like the sun's moving southward into "Capricorn"—that is, winter. She is herself like the frozen earth, and "in this dead time" even her children seem remote to her. She wishes her husband/sun might return home and once again cause to "burn" the "Cancer"—or Summer—of "her glowing breast."

My head, my heart, mine eyes, my life, nay, more,
My joy, my magazine of earthly store,
If two be one, as surely thou and I,
How stayest thou there, whilst I at Ipswich lie?
So many steps, head from the heart to sever,   *5*
If but a neck, soon should we be together.
I, like the Earth this season, mourn in black,
My Sun is gone so far in's zodiac,
Whom whilst I 'joyed, nor storms, nor frost I felt,
His warmth such frigid colds did cause to melt,   *10*
Return, return, sweet Sol, from Capricorn,
I this dead time, alas, what can I more
Than view those fruits which through thy heat I bore?
Which sweet contentment yield me for a space,
True living pictures of their father's face.   *15*
O strange effect! now thou art southward gone,
I weary grow the tedious day so long;
But when thou northward to me shalt return,

I wish my Sun may never set, but burn
Within the Cancer of my glowing breast,   *20*
The welcome house of him my dearest guest.
Where ever, ever stay, and go not thence,
Till nature's sad decree shall call thee hence;
Flesh of thy flesh, bone of thy bone,
I here, thou there, yet both but one.   *25*

← John Milton
from *Paradise Lost*

The power and beauty of Milton's language in Paradise Lost *is awe-inspiring. All the elements of dramatic tragedy, religious fervor, and poetic zeal are found in the following excerpts. The first, from Book IV, describes Satan's decision to take revenge against God by visiting God's creation, Earth. The second, from Book IX, describes Satan's tempting of Eve to violate God's commandment.*

from Book IV

O for that warning voice, which he who saw
Th' Apocalypse heard cry in Heaven aloud,
Then when the dragon, put to second rout,
Came furious down to be revenged on men,
Woe to the inhabitants on Earth! that now,   *5*
While time was, our first parents had been warned
The coming of their secret foe, and scaped,
Haply so scaped, his mortal snare! for now
Satan, now first inflamed with rage, came down,
The tempter, ere th' accuser, of mankind,   *10*
To wreak on innocent frail man his loss
Of that first battle, and his flight to hell.
Yet not rejoicing in his speed, though bold
Far off and fearless, nor with cause to boast,
Begins his dire attempt; which, nigh the birth   *15*
Now rolling, boils in his tumultuous breast,
And like a devilish engine back recoils
Upon himself. Horror and doubt distract
His troubled thoughts, and from the bottom stir
The Hell within him; for within him Hell   *20*
He brings, and round about him, nor from Hell
One step, no more than from himself, can fly
By change of place. Now conscience wakes despair
That slumbered; wakes the bitter memory
Of what he was, what is, and what must be   *25*
Worse; of worse deeds worse sufferings must ensue.
Sometimes towards Eden, which now in his view
Lay pleasant, his grieved look he fixes sad;
Sometimes towards heaven and the full-blazing sun,
Which now sat high in his meridian tower: *30*
Then, much revolving, thus in sighs began:—
    "O thou that, with surpassing glory crowned,
Look'st from thy sole dominion like the god
Of this new world—at whose sight all the stars
Hide their diminished heads—to thee I call,   *35*
But with no friendly voice, and add thy name,
O sun, to tell thee how I hate thy beams,
That bring to my remembrance from what state
I fell, how glorious once above thy sphere,
Till pride and worse ambition threw me down,   *40*

Warring in Heaven against Heaven's matchless king!
Ah, wherefore? He deserved no such return
From me, whom he created what I was
In that bright eminence, and with his good
Upbraided none; nor was his service hard.   *45*
What could be less than to afford him praise,
The easiest recompense, and pay him thanks,
How due! Yet all his good proved ill in me,
And wrought but malice. Lifted up so high,
I 'sdained° subjection, and thought one step higher   *50*
Would set me highest, and in a moment quit°
The debt immense of endless gratitude,
So burdensome, still paying, still to owe;
Forgetful what from him I still received;
And understood not that a grateful mind   *55*
By owing owes not, but still pays, at once
Indebted and discharged—what burden then?
Oh, had his powerful destiny ordained
Me some inferior angel, I had stood
Then happy; no unbounded hope had raised   *60*
Ambition. Yet why not? Some other power
As great might have aspired, and me, though mean,
Drawn to his part. But other powers as great
Fell not, but stand unshaken, from within
Or from without to all temptations armed!   *65*
Hadst thou the same free will and power to stand?
Thou hadst. Whom hast thou then, or what, to accuse,
But Heaven's free love dealt equally to all?
Be then his love accursed, since, love or hate,
To me alike it deals eternal woe.   *70*
Nay, cursed be thou; since against his thy will
Chose freely what it now so justly rues.
Me miserable! which way shall I fly
Infinite wrath and infinite despair?
Which way I fly is Hell; myself am Hell;   *75*
And, in the lowest deep, a lower deep
Still threatening to devour me opens wide,
To which the Hell I suffer seems a Heaven.
O, then, at last relent! Is there no place
Left for repentance, none for pardon left?   *80*
None left but by submission; and that word
Disdain forbids me, and my dread of shame
Among the spirits beneath, whom I seduced
With other promises and other vaunts
Than to submit, boasting I could subdue   *85*
Th' omnipotent. Ay me! they little know
How dearly I abide that boast so vain,
Under what torments inwardly I groan.
While they adore me on the throne of Hell,
With diadem and scepter high advanced,   *90*
The lower still I fall, only supreme
In misery: such joy ambition finds!
But say I could repent, and could obtain,
By act of grace my former state, how soon
Would height recall high thoughts, how soon unsay   *95*
What feigned submission swore! Ease would recant
Vows made in pain, as violent and void
For never can true reconcilement grow

---

⁵⁰ *'sdained:* scorned.   ⁵¹ *quit:* acquit.

Where wounds of deadly hate have pierced so deep;
Which would but lead me to a worse relapse   *100*
And heavier fall: so should I purchase dear
Short intermission, bought with double smart.
This knows my punisher; therefore as far
From granting he, as I from begging, peace.
All hope excluded thus, behold, instead   *105*
Of us, outcast, exiled, his new delight,
Mankind, created, and for him this world!
So farewell hope, and, with hope, farewell fear,
Farewell remorse! All good to me is lost;
Evil, be thou my good: by thee at least   *110*
Divided empire with Heaven's king I hold,
By thee, and more than half perhaps will reign;
As man ere long, and this new world, shall know."
      Thus while he spake, each passion dimmed his face,
Thrice changed with pale—ire, envy, and despair;   *115*
Which marred his borrowed visage, and betrayed
Him counterfeit, if any eye beheld:
For heavenly minds from such distempers foul
Are ever clear. Whereof he soon aware
Each perturbation smoothed with outward calm,   *120*
Artificer of fraud; and was the first
That practiced falsehood under saintly show,
Deep malice to conceal, couched with revenge:
Yet not enough had practiced to deceive
Uriel, once warned; whose eye pursued him down   *125*
The way he went, and on th' Assyrian mount
Saw him disfigured, more than could befall
Spirit of happy sort: his gestures fierce
He marked and mad demeanor, then alone,
As he supposed, all unobserved, unseen.   *130*
      So on he fares, and to the border comes.
Of Eden, where delicious Paradise,
Now nearer, crowns with her enclosure green,
As with a rural mound, the champaign° head
Of a steep wilderness, whose hairy sides   *135*
With thicket overgrown, grotesque° and wild,
Access denied; and overhead up grew
Insuperable height of loftiest shade,
Cedar, and pine, and fir, and branching palm,
A sylvan scene, and, as the ranks ascend   *140*
Shade above shade, a woody theater
Of stateliest view. Yet higher than their tops
The verdurous wall of Paradise up sprung;
Which to our general sire° gave prospect large
Into his nether empire neighboring round.   *145*
And higher than that wall a circling row
Of goodliest trees, laden with fairest fruit,
Blossoms and fruits at once of golden hue,
Appeared, with gay enameled colors mixed;
On which the sun more glad impressed his beams   *150*
Than in fair evening cloud, or humid bow°,
When God hath showered the earth: so lovely seemed
That landscape. And of pure now purer air
Meets his approach, and to the heart inspires
Vernal delight and joy, able to drive   *155*

All sadness but despair. Now gentle gales,
Fanning their odoriferous wings, dispense
Native perfumes, and whisper whence they stole
Those balmy spoils. As when to them who sail
Beyond the Cape of Hope, and now are past   *160*
Mozambic, off at sea northeast winds blow
Sabean odors from the spicy shore
Of Araby the Blest, with such delay
Well pleased they slack their course, and many a league
Cheered with the grateful smell old Ocean smiles;   *165*
So entertained those odorous sweets the fiend
Who came their bane, though with them better pleased
Than Asmodëus with the fishy fume
That drove him, though enamored, from the spouse
Of Tobit's son, and with a vengeance sent   *170*
From Media post to Egypt, there fast bound.
      Now to th' ascent of that steep savage hill
Satan had journeyed on, pensive and slow;
But further way found none; so thick entwined,
As one continued brake, the undergrowth   *175*
Of shrubs and tangling bushes had perplexed
All path of man or beast that passed that way.
One gate there only was, and that looked east
On th' other side. Which when th' arch-felon saw,
Due entrance he disdained, and, in contempt,   *180*
At one slight bound high overleaped all bound
Of hill or highest wall, and sheer within
Lights on his feet. As when a prowling wolf,
Whom hunger drives to seek new haunt for prey,
Watching where shepherds pen their flocks at eve,   *185*
In hurdled cotes amid the field secure,
Leaps o'er the fence with ease into the fold;
Or as a thief, bent to unhoard the cash
Of some rich burgher, whose substantial doors,
Cross-barred and bolted fast, fear no assault,   *190*
In at the window climbs, or o'er the tiles;
So clomb this first grand thief into God's fold:
So since into his church lewd hirelings climb.
Thence up he flew, and on the Tree of Life,
The middle tree and highest there that grew,   *195*
Sat like a cormorant; yet not true life
Thereby regained, but sat devising death
To them who lived; nor on the virtue thought
Of that life-giving plant, but only used
For prospect, what, well used, had been the pledge   *200*
Of immortality. So little knows
Any, but God alone, to value right
The good before him, but perverts best things
To worst abuse, or to their meanest use.
      Beneath him, with new wonder, now he views,   *205*
To all delight of human sense exposed,
In narrow room Nature's whole wealth; yea, more,
A Heaven on Earth; for blissful Paradise
Of God the garden was, by him in the east
Of Eden planted. Eden stretched her line   *210*
From Auran eastward to the royal towers
Of great Seleucia, built by Grecian kings,
Or where the sons of Eden long before
Dwelt in Telassar. In this pleasant soil
His far more pleasant garden God ordained.   *215*
Out of the fertile ground he caused to grow

---

¹³⁴ *champaign:* open countryside. ¹³⁶ *grotesque:* picturesque.
¹⁴⁴ *our general sire:* Adam. ¹⁵¹ *bow:* rainbow.

All trees of noblest kind for sight, smell, taste;
And all amid them stood the Tree of Life,
High eminent, blooming ambrosial fruit
Of vegetable gold; and next to life,   220
Our death, the Tree of Knowledge, grew fast by—
Knowledge of good, bought dear by knowing ill.

from Book IX

    "Serpent, we might have spared our coming hither,
Fruitless to me, though fruit be here to excess,
The credit of whose virtue rest with thee;
Wondrous indeed, if cause of such effects!
But of this tree we may not taste nor touch: 5
God so commanded, and left that command
Sole daughter of his voice; the rest, we live
Law to ourselves; our reason is our law."
    To whom the Tempter guilefully replied:
"Indeed? Hath God then said that of the fruit   10
Of all these garden trees ye shall not eat,
Yet lords declared of all in Earth or air?"
    To whom thus Eve, yet sinless: "Of the fruit
Of each tree in the garden we may eat,
But of the fruit of this fair tree amidst   15
The garden, God hath said, 'Ye shall not eat
Thereof, nor shall ye touch it, lest ye die.' "
    She scarce had said, though brief, when now more
       bold,
The tempter, but with show of zeal and love
To man, and indignation at his wrong,   20
New part puts on, and as to passion moved,
Fluctuates disturbed, yet comely, and in act
Raised, as of some great matter to begin.
As when of old some orator renowned
In Athens or free Rome, where eloquence   25
Flourished, since mute, to some great cause addressed,
Stood in himself collected, while each part,
Motion, each act, won audience ere the tongue,
Sometimes in height began, as no delay
Of preface brooking, through his zeal of right.   30
So standing, moving, or to height upgrown
The tempter all impassioned thus began:
    "O sacred, wise, and wisdom-giving plant,
Mother of science!° now I feel thy power
Within me clear, not only to discern   35
Things in their causes, but to trace the ways
Of highest agents, deemed however wise.
Queen of this universe! do not believe
Those rigid threats of death. Ye shall not die;
How should ye? By the fruit? it gives you life   40
To° knowledge; by the Threatener? look on me,
Me who have touched and tasted, yet both live,
And life more perfect have attained than Fate
Meant me, by venturing higher than my lot.
Shall that be shut to man, which to the beast   45
Is open? Or will God incense his ire
For such a petty trespass, and not praise
Rather your dauntless virtue, whom the pain

Of death denounced, whatever thing death be,
Deterred not from achieving what might lead   50
To happier life, knowledge of good and evil?
Of good, how just! Of evil, if what is evil
Be real, why not known, since easier shunned?
God therefore cannot hurt ye, and be just;
Not just, not God; not feared then, nor obeyed: 55
Your fear itself of death removes the fear.
Why then was this forbid? Why but to awe,
Why but to keep ye low and ignorant,
His worshippers? He knows that in the day
Ye eat thereof, your eyes that seem so clear,   60
Yet are but dim, shall perfectly be then
Opened and cleared, and ye shall be as gods,
Knowing both good and evil, as they know.
That ye should be as gods, since I as man,
Internal man, is but proportion meet,   65
I, of brute, human; ye, of human, gods.
So ye shall die perhaps, by putting off
Human, to put on gods: death to be wished,
Though threatened, which no worse than this can bring.
And what are gods that man may not become   70
As they, participating godlike food?
The gods are first, and that advantage use
On our belief, that all from them proceeds.
I question it; for this fair Earth I see,
Warmed by the sun, producing every kind,   75
Them nothing: If they all things, who enclosed
Knowledge of good and evil in this tree,
That whoso eats thereof forthwith attains
Wisdom without their leave? And wherein lies
Th' offense, that man should thus attain to know?   80
What can your knowledge hurt him, or this tree
Impart against his will if all be his?
Or is it envy, and can envy dwell
In heavenly breasts? These, these, and many more
Causes import your need of this fair fruit.   85
Goddess humane, reach then, and freely taste!"
    He ended, and his words, replete with guile,
Into her heart too easy entrance won:
Fixed on the fruit she gazed, which to behold
Might tempt alone, and in her ears the sound   90
Yet rung of his persuasive words, impregned°
With reason, to her seeming, and with truth;
Meanwhile the hour of noon drew on, and waked
An eager appetite, raised by the smell
So savory of that fruit, which with desire,   95
Inclinable now grown to touch or taste,
Solicited her longing eye; yet first
Pausing a while, thus to herself she mused:
    "Great are thy virtues, doubtless, best of fruits,
Though kept from man, and worthy to be admired, 100
Whose taste, too long forborn, at first essay
Gave elocution to the mute, and taught
The tongue not made for speech to speak thy praise:
Thy praise he also who forbids thy use,
Conceals not from us, naming thee the Tree   105
Of Knowledge, knowledge both of good and evil;

---

³⁴ *science:* knowledge. ⁴¹ *To:* as well as.

⁹¹ *impregned:* impregnated.

Forbids us then to taste; but his forbidding
Commends thee more, while it infers the good
By thee communicated, and our want:
For good unknown, sure is not had, or had   110
And yet unknown, is as not had at all.
In plain then, what forbids he but to know?
Forbids us good, forbids us to be wise!
Such prohibitions bind not. But if Death
Bind us with after-bands, what profits then   115
Our inward freedom? In the day we eat
Of this fair fruit, our doom is, we shall die.
How dies the serpent? He hath eaten and lives,
And knows, and speaks, and reasons, and discerns,
Irrational till then. For us alone   120
Was death invented? Or to us denied
This intellectual food, for beasts reserved?
For beasts it seems: yet that one beast which first
Hath tasted, envies not, but brings with joy
The good befallen him, author unsuspect,   125
Friendly to man, far from deceit or guile.
What fear I then, rather what know to fear
Under this ignorance of good and evil,
Of God or death, of law or penalty?
Here grows the cure of all, this fruit divine,   130
Fair to the eye, inviting to the taste,
Of virtue° to make wise: what hinders then
To reach, and feed at once both body and mind?"
      So saying, her rash hand in evil hour,
Forth reaching to the fruit, she plucked, she eat. 135
Earth felt the wound, and Nature from her seat
Sighing through all her works gave signs of woe,
That all was lost. Back to the thicket slunk
The guilty serpent, and well might, for Eve
Intent now wholly on her taste, naught else   140
Regarded; such delight till then, as seemed,
In fruit she never tasted, whether true
Or fancied so, through expectation high
Of knowledge; nor was godhead from her thought.
Greedily she engorged without restraint,   145
And knew not eating death: satiate at length,
And heightened as with wine, jocund and boon,
Thus to herself she pleasingly began:
      "O sovereign, virtuous, precious of all trees
In Paradise! of operation blest   150
To sapience, hitherto obscured, infamed°,
And thy fair fruit let hang, as to no end
Created; but henceforth my early care,
Not without song each morning, and due praise
Shall tend thee, and the fertile burden ease   155
Of thy full branches offered free to all;
Till dieted by thee I grow mature
In knowledge, as the gods who all things know;
Though others envy what they cannot give:
For had the gift been theirs, it had not here   160
Thus grown. Experience, next to thee I owe,
Best guide; not following thee I had remained
In ignorance; thou open'st Wisdom's way,
And giv'st access, though secret she retire.

And I perhaps am secret; Heaven is high,   165
High and remote to see from thence distinct
Each thing on Earth; and other care perhaps
May have diverted from continual watch
Our great Forbidder, safe with all his spies
About him. But to Adam in what sort   170
Shall I appear? Shall I to him make known
As yet my change, and give him to partake
Full happiness with me, or rather not,
But keep the odds of knowledge in my power
Without copartner? so to add what wants   175
In female sex, the more to draw his love,
And render me more equal, and perhaps,
A thing not undesirable, sometime
Superior: for, inferior, who is free?
This may be well: but what if God have seen   180
And death ensue? Then I shall be no more,
And Adam, wedded to another Eve,
Shall live with her enjoying, I extinct;
A death to think. Confirmed then I resolve,
Adam shall share with me in bliss or woe: 185
So dear I love him, that with him all deaths
I could endure, without him live no life."
      So saying, from the tree her step she turned,
But first low reverence done, as to the power
That dwelt within, whose presence had infused   190
Into the plant sciental° sap, derived
From nectar, drink of gods. Adam the while
Waiting desirous her return, had wove
Of choicest flowers a garland to adorn
Her tresses, and her rural labors crown,   195
As reapers oft are wont their harvest queen.
Great joy he promised to his thoughts, and new
Solace in her return, so long delayed:
Yet oft his heart, divine of something ill,
Misgave him; he the faltering measure felt;   200
And forth to meet her went, the way she took
That morn when first they parted. By the Tree
Of Knowledge he must pass; there he her met,
Scarce from the tree returning; in her hand
A bough of fairest fruit that downy smiled,   205
New gathered, and ambrosial smell diffused.
To him she hastened, in her face excuse
Came prologue, and apology to prompt,
Which with bland words at will she thus addressed:
      "Hast thou not wondered, Adam, at my stay?   210
Thee I have missed, and thought it long, deprived
Thy presence, agony of love till now
Not felt, nor shall be twice; for never more
Mean I to try, what rash untried I sought,
The pain of absence from thy sight. But strange   215
Hath been the cause, and wonderful to hear:
This tree is not as we are told, a tree
Of danger tasted, nor to evil unknown
Opening the way, but of divine effect
To open eyes, and make them gods who taste;   220
And hath been tasted such. The serpent wise,
Or not restrained as we, or not obeying,

---

¹³² *virtue*: power. ¹⁵¹ *infamed*: defamed.

¹⁹¹ *sciental*: knowledge-giving.

Hath eaten of the fruit, and is become,
Not dead, as we are threatened, but thenceforth
Endued with human voice and human sense,   225
Reasoning to admiration, and with me
Persuasively hath so prevailed, that I
Have also tasted, and have also found
Th' effects to correspond—opener mine eyes
Dim erst, dilated spirits, ampler heart,   230
And growing up to godhead; which for thee
Chiefly I sought, without thee can despise.
For bliss, as thou hast part, to me is bliss,
Tedious, unshared with thee, and odious soon.
Thou therefore also taste, that equal lot   235
May join us, equal joy, as equal love;
Lest, thou not tasting, different degree
Disjoin us, and I then too late renounce
Deity for thee, when Fate will not permit."
        Thus Eve with countenance blithe her story told;   240
But in her cheek distemper flushing glowed.
On th' other side, Adam, soon as he heard
The fatal trespass done by Eve, amazed,
Astonied stood and blank, while horror chill
Ran through his veins, and all his joints relaxed;   245
From his slack hand the garland wreathed for Eve
Down dropped, and all the faded roses shed.
Speechless he stood and pale, till thus at length
First to himself he inward silence broke:
        "O fairest of creation, last and best   250
Of all God's works, creature in whom excelled
Whatever can to sight or thought be formed,
Holy, divine, good, amiable, or sweet!
How art thou lost, how on a sudden lost,
Defaced, deflowered, and now to death devote?°   255
Rather how hast thou yielded to transgress
The strict forbiddance, how to violate
The sacred fruit forbidden! Some cursèd fraud
Of enemy hath beguiled thee, yet unknown,
And me with thee hath ruined, for with thee   260
Certain my resolution is to die.
How can I live without thee, how forgo
Thy sweet converse and love so dearly joined,
To live again in these wild woods forlorn?
Should God create another Eve, and I   265
Another rib afford, yet loss of thee
Would never from my heart; no, no! I feel
The link of nature draw me: flesh of flesh,
Bone of my bone thou art, and from thy state
Mine never shall be parted, bliss or woe."   270
        So having said, as one from sad dismay
Recomforted, and after thoughts disturbed
Submitting to what seemed remediless,
Thus in calm mood his words to Eve he turned:
        "Bold deed thou hast presumed, adventurous Eve   275
And peril great provoked, who thus hast dared
Had it been only coveting to eye
That sacred° fruit, sacred to abstinence,
Much more to taste it, under ban to touch.
But past who can recall, or done undo?   280

Not God omnipotent, nor Fate! Yet so
Perhaps thou shalt not die, perhaps the fact
Is not so heinous now, foretasted fruit,
Profaned first by the serpent, by him first
Made common and unhallowed ere our taste,   285
Nor yet on him found deadly; he yet lives,
Lives, as thou saidst, and gains to live as man
Higher degree of life: inducement strong
To us, as likely, tasting, to attain
Proportional ascent, which cannot be   290
But to be gods, or angels, demigods.
Nor can I think that God, Creator wise,
Though threatening, will in earnest so destroy
Us his prime creatures, dignified so high,
Set over all his works, which in our fall,   295
For us created, needs with us must fail,
Dependent made; so God shall uncreate,
Be frustrate, do, undo, and labor lose;
Not well conceived of God, who, though his power
Creation could repeat, yet would be loath   300
Us to abolish, lest the adversary
Triumph and say: 'Fickle their state whom God
Most favors; who can please him long? Me first
He ruined, now mankind; whom will he next?'
Matter of scorn, not to be given the foe.   305
However, I with thee have fixed my lot,
Certain to undergo like doom: if death
Consort with thee, death is to me as life;
So forcible within my heart I feel
The bond of nature draw me to my own,   310
My own in thee, for what thou art is mine;
Our state cannot be severed; we are one,
One flesh; to lose thee were to lose myself."
        So Adam, and thus Eve to him replied:
"O glorious trial of exceeding love,   315
Illustrious evidence, example high!
Engaging me to emulate; but short
Of thy perfection, how shall I attain,
Adam? from whose dear side I boast me sprung,
And gladly of our union hear thee speak,   320
One heart, one soul in both; whereof good proof
This day affords, declaring thee resolved,
Rather than death or aught than death more dread
Shall separate us, linked in love so dear,
To undergo with me one guilt, one crime,   325
If any be, of tasting this fair fruit;
Whose virtue (for of good still good proceeds,
Direct, or by occasion) hath presented
This happy trial of thy love, which else
So eminently never had been known.   330
Were it I thought death menaced would ensue
This my attempt, I would sustain alone
The worst, and not persuade thee, rather die
Deserted, than oblige° thee with a fact
Pernicious to thy peace, chiefly assured   335
Remarkably so late of thy so true,
So faithful love unequaled; but I feel
Far otherwise th' event°—not death, but life

Augmented, opened eyes, new hopes, new joys,
Taste so divine, that what of sweet before   340
Hath touched my sense, flat seems to this, and harsh.
On my experience, Adam, freely taste,
And fear of death deliver to the winds."
    So saying, she embraced him, and for joy
Tenderly wept, much won that he his love   345
Had so ennobled, as of choice to incur
Divine displeasure for her sake, or death.
In recompense (for such compliance bad
Such recompense best merits), from the bough
She gave him of that fair enticing fruit   350
With liberal hand; he scrupled not to eat,
Against his better knowledge, not deceived,
But fondly overcome with female charm.
Earth trembled from her entrails, as again
In pangs, and Nature gave a second groan,   355
Sky lowered, and muttering thunder, some sad drops
Wept at completing of the mortal sin
Original; while Adam took no thought,
Eating his fill, nor Eve to iterate
Her former trespass feared, the more to soothe   360
Him with her loved society; that now
As with new wine intoxicated both,
They swim in mirth, and fancy that they feel
Divinity within them breeding wings
Wherewith to scorn the Earth. But that false fruit   365
Far other operation first displayed,
Carnal desire inflaming; he on Eve
Began to cast lacivous eyes, she him
As wantonly repaid; in lust they burn,
Till Adam thus 'gan Eve to dalliance move: 370
    "Eve, now I see thou art exact of taste,
And elegant, of sapience no small part,
Since to each meaning savor we apply,
And palate call judicious. I the praise
Yield thee, so well this day thou hast purveyed.   375
Much pleasure we have lost, while we abstained
From this delightful fruit, nor known till now
True relish, tasting; if such pleasure be
In things to us forbidden, it might be wished,
For this one tree had been forbidden ten.   380
But come; so well refreshed, now let us play,
As meet is, after such delicious fare;
For never did thy beauty, since the day
I saw thee first and wedded thee, adorned
With all perfections, so enflame my sense   385
With ardor to enjoy thee, fairer now
Than ever, bounty of this virtuous tree."
    So said he, and forbore not glance or toy
Of amorous intent, well understood
Of Eve, whose eye darted contagious fire.   390
Her hand he seized, and to a shady bank,
Thick overhead with verdant roof embowered
He led her, nothing loath; flowers were the couch,
Pansies, and violets, and asphodel,
And hyacinth—Earth's freshest, softest lap.   395
There they their fill of love and love's disport

Took largely, of their mutual guilt the seal,
The solace of their sin, till dewy sleep
Oppressed them, wearied with their amorous play.
    Soon as the force of that fallacious fruit,   400
That with exhilarating vapor bland
About their spirits had played, and inmost powers
Made err, was now exhaled, and grosser sleep
Bred of unkindly fumes, with conscious dreams
Encumbered, now had left them, up they rose   405
As from unrest, and each the other viewing,
Soon found their eyes how opened, and their minds
How darkened. Innocence, that as a veil
Had shadowed them from knowing ill, was gone;
Just confidence, and native righteousness,   410
And honor from about them, naked left
To guilty Shame; he covered, but his robe
Uncovered more. So rose the Danite strong,
Herculean Samson, from the harlot-lap
Of Philistean Dalilah, and waked   415
Shorn of his strength; they destitute and bare
Of all their virtue. Silent, and in face
Confounded, long they sat, as strucken mute;
Till Adam, though not less than Eve abashed,
At length gave utterance to these words constrained:
    "O Eve, in evil hour thou didst give ear   421
To that false worm°, of whomsoever taught
To counterfeit man's voice, true in our fall,
False in our promised rising; since our eyes
Opened we find indeed, and find we know   425
Both good and evil, good lost, and evil got:
Bad fruit of knowledge, if this be to know,
Which leaves us naked thus, of honor void,
Of innocence, of faith, of purity,
Our wonted ornaments now soiled and stained,   430
And in our faces evident the signs
Of foul concupiscence; whence evil store,
Even shame, the last of evils; of the first
Be sure then. How shall I behold the face
Henceforth of God or angel, erst with joy   435
And rapture so oft beheld? Those heavenly shapes
Will dazzle now this earthly with their blaze
Insufferably bright. O might I here
In solitude live savage, in some glade
Obscured, where highest woods, impenetrable   440
To star or sunlight, spread their umbrage broad,
And brown as evening! Cover me, ye pines,
Ye cedars, with innumerable boughs
Hide me, where I may never see them more!
But let us now, as in bad plight, devise   445
What best may for the present serve to hide
The parts of each from other, that seem most
To shame obnoxious°, and unseemliest seen;
Some tree whose broad smooth leaves together sewed,
And girded on our loins, may cover round   450
Those middle parts, that this newcomer, Shame,
There sit not, and reproach us as unclean."
    So counseled he, and both together went
Into the thickest wood; there soon they chose

The figtree, not that kind for fruit renowned,   455
But such as at this day, to Indians known,
In Malabar or Deccan spreads her arms
Branching so broad and long, that in the ground
The bended twigs take root, and daughters grow
About the mother tree, a pillared shade   460
High overarched, and echoing walks between;
There oft the Indian herdsman, shunning heat,
Shelters in cool, and tends his pasturing herds
At loopholes cut through thickest shade. Those leaves
They gathered, broad as Amazonian targe°,   465
And with what skill they had, together sewed,
To gird their waist; vain covering, if to hide
Their guilt and dreaded shame! O how unlike
To that first naked glory! Such of late
Columbus found th' American, so girt   470
With feathered cincture°, naked else and wild
Among the trees on isles and woody shores.
Thus fenced, and, as they thought, their shame in part
Covered, but not at rest or ease of mind,
They sat them down to weep; nor only tears   475
Rained at their eyes, but high winds worse within
Began to rise, high passions, anger, hate,
Mistrust, suspicion, discord, and shook sore
Their inward state of mind, calm region once
And full of peace, now tossed and turbulent: 480
For Understanding ruled not, and the Will
Heard not her lore, both in subjection now
To sensual Appetite, who, from beneath
Usurping over sovereign Reason, claimed
Superior sway. From thus distempered breast,   485
Adam, estranged in look and altered style,
Speech intermitted thus to Eve renewed:
     "Would thou hadst hearkened to my words, and
          stayed
With me, as I besought thee, when that strange
Desire of wandering, this unhappy morn,   490
I know not whence possessed thee! we had then
Remained still happy, not as now, despoiled
Of all our good, shamed, naked, miserable.
Let none henceforth seek needless cause to approve°
The faith they owe°; when earnestly they seek   495
Such proof, conclude, they then begin to fail."
     To whom, soon moved with touch of blame, thus Eve:
"What words have passed thy lips, Adam severe?

Imput'st thou that to my default, or will
Of wandering, as thou call'st it, which who knows   500
But might as ill have happened, thou being by,
Or to thyself perhaps? Hadst thou been there,
Or here th' attempt, thou couldst not have discerned
Fraud in the serpent, speaking as he spake;
No ground of enmity between us known,   505
Why he should mean me ill, nor seek to harm?
Was I to have never parted from thy side?
As good have grown there still a lifeless rib.
Being as I am, why didst not thou, the head,
Command me absolutely not to go,   510
Going into such danger, as thou saidst?
Too facile then, thou didst not much gainsay,
Nay, didst permit, approve, and fair dismiss.
Hadst thou been firm and fixed in thy dissent,
Neither had I transgressed, nor thou with me."   515
     To whom, then first incensed, Adam replied:
"Is this the love, is this the recompense
Of mine to thee, ingrateful Eve, expressed
Immutable when thou were lost, not I,
Who might have lived and joyed immortal bliss,   520
Yet willingly chose rather death with thee?
And am I now upbraided as the cause
Of thy transgressing? not enough severe,
It seems, in thy restraint! What could I more?
I warned thee, I admonished thee, foretold   525
The danger, and the lurking enemy
That lay in wait: beyond this had been force,
And force upon free will hath here no place.
But confidence then bore thee on, secure
Either to meet no danger, or to find   530
Matter of glorious trial; and perhaps
I also erred in overmuch admiring
What seemed in thee so perfect, that I thought
No evil durst attempt thee! but I rue
That error now, which is become my crime,   535
And thou th' accuser. Thus it shall befall
Him who, to worth in women overtrusting,
Lets her will rule; restraint she will not brook,
And, left to herself, if evil thence ensue,
She first his weak indulgence will accuse."   540
     Thus they in mutual accusation spent
The fruitless hours, but neither self-condemning;
And of their vain contést appeared no end.

---

465 *targe:* shield.   471 *cincture:* belt.   494 *approve:* prove.
495 *owe:* own.

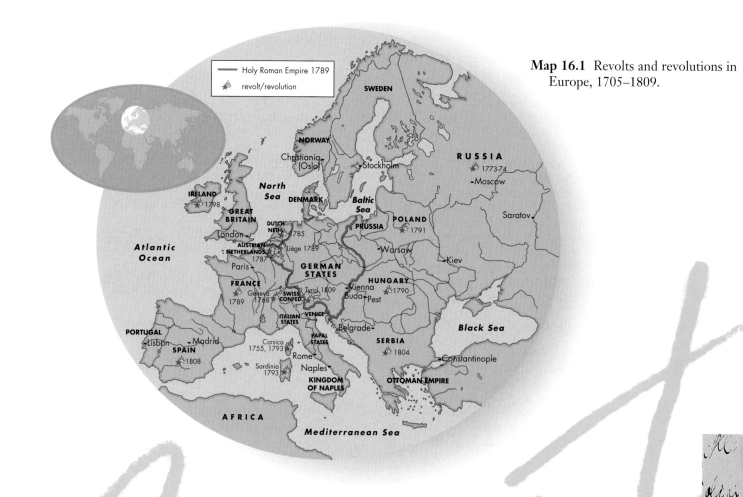

Map 16.1 Revolts and revolutions in Europe, 1705–1809.

Holy Roman Empire 1789
✷ revolt/revolution

SWEDEN

NORWAY
Christiania
(Oslo)
Stockholm

RUSSIA
✷ 1773-74
Moscow

Saratov

IRELAND
✷ 1798
GREAT
BRITAIN
London

North
Sea
DENMARK

Baltic
Sea

POLAND
✷ 1791

DUTCH
NETH.
1785
AUSTRIAN
NETHERLANDS
1787
Liège 1789

PRUSSIA

Warsaw

Kiev

Atlantic
Ocean

Paris

GERMAN
STATES

FRANCE
1789
Geneva
1768
SWISS
CONFED.

Tyrol 1809
Vienna
Buda
Pest

HUNGARY
✷ 1790

PORTUGAL
Lisbon
SPAIN
✷ 1808
Madrid

ITALIAN
STATES
VENICE
PAPAL
STATES
Corsica
1755, 1793
Rome
Naples
Sardinia
1793
KINGDOM
OF NAPLES

Belgrade

SERBIA
✷ 1804

Black Sea

Constantinople

OTTOMAN EMPIRE

AFRICA

Mediterranean Sea

THE
EIGHTEENTH
CENTURY

Holograph copy of Beethoven's Fifth Symphony, Staatsbibliothek zu Berlin, Germany.

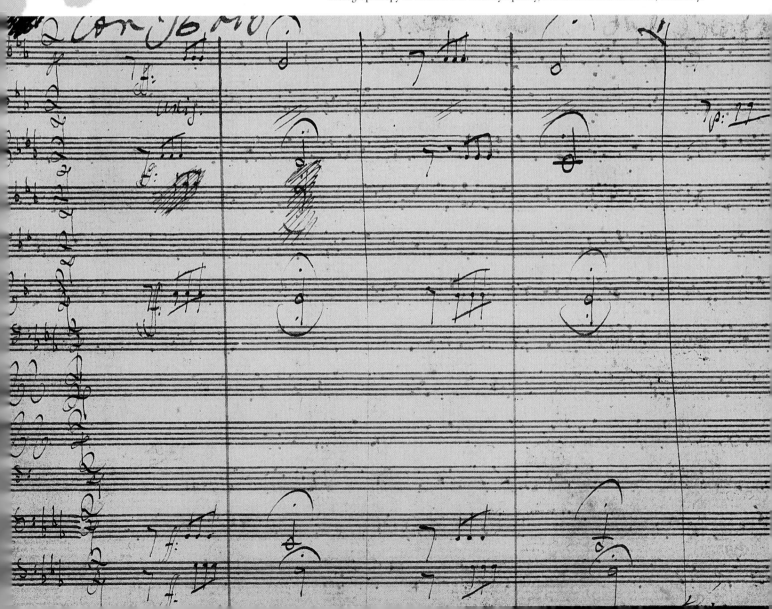

ENLIGHTENMENT AND REVOLUTION

Between 1700 and 1800, the world was literally transformed. At the beginning of the century, Louis XIV had firm control of France. The portrait painted in 1701 by Hyacinthe Rigaud (fig. 16.1) shows the Sun King, anointed by God, in ermine coronation robes and surrounded by the earthly riches and furnishings of Versailles. The king's posture is arrogant, suggestive of his status above all other humans; with one hand on his

Figure 16.1 Hyacinthe Rigaud, *Louis XIV*, 1701, oil on canvas, 9'2" × 7'10¾" (2.79 × 2.40 m), Musée du Louvre, Paris. Unsurpassed in pompous posturing, Louis XIV literally looks down his nose at the viewer. The column and sweep of red drapery are standard devices used in formal portraiture to enhance the subject's prestige; the red high heels are Louis XIV's own.

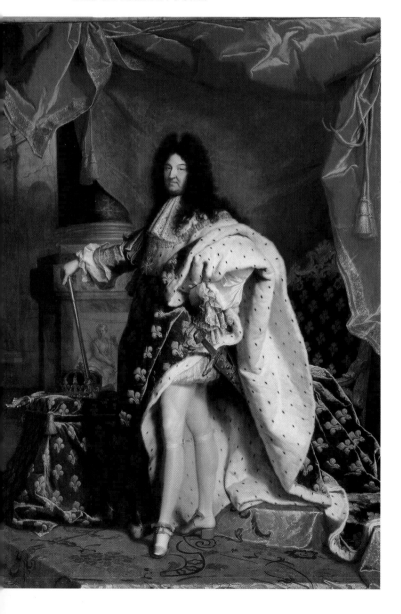

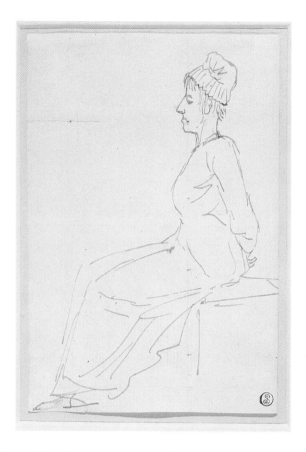

Figure 16.2 Jacques-Louis David, *Marie Antoinette Being Led to Her Execution*, 1793, ink drawing, Musée du Louvre, Paris. David drew this from a second-story window overlooking the procession that accompanied the Queen to her death.

hip and a facial expression of aggressive disdain, he positively looks down his nose at the viewer.

By the end of the century, the French monarchy had fallen from its lofty place, as Louis XVI (1754–1793), the Sun King's great-grandson, and his Queen, MARIE ANTOINETTE [ann-tweh-NET] (1755–1793), were executed by the National Assembly of the French Revolution. A very different "royal portrait" was done hurriedly by French revolutionary painter David as he stood on a Paris street on October 16, 1793 (fig. 16.2) and watched the Queen's procession to the guillotine in front of the Louvre. The Queen is stripped of all trace of aristocratic grandeur, save perhaps the rigid defiance of her facial expression, her lip and chin thrust forward in disdain for her rabble killers.

The changes that occurred in the eighteenth century were swift and extreme, encompassing revolutions that were not only political, but intellectual, scientific, industrial, and social. Indeed, the eighteenth century has been called the "Age of Reason" because of the dominance of the intellectual revolution that we have come to call the Enlightenment.

THE ENLIGHTENMENT

The term **Enlightenment** refers to the eighteenth-century European emphasis on the mind's power to reason, in contrast to the mind's yearning for religious faith, which a number of Enlightenment thinkers saw as superstition. The late seventeenth century through the eighteenth century saw two great movements: that of the "Age of Reason," which hallmarks the contemporary emphasis on rationality, and the Neoclassical, which testifies to the influence of classical antiquity.

The Enlightenment did not so much inaugurate something new in the Western intellectual tradition as continue an emphasis on secular concerns that began during the Renaissance and continued with the rise of scientific and philosophical thought during the seventeenth century. Francis Bacon's empirical approach to knowledge and René Descartes's emphasis on logic and human reason both served as a prelude to eighteenth-century political and philosophical ideals. These ideals included freedom from tyranny and superstition, and a belief in the essential goodness of human nature and the equality of men (though not all men, and not women).

Enlightenment thinkers emphasized the common nature of human experience, ignoring differences in social, cultural, and religious values. With an impulse toward the universal, Enlightenment writers often celebrated constancy and continuity, encouraging a respect for tradition and convention, especially in literature and the arts. Enlightenment artists and thinkers must not be seen, however, simply as supporters of the status quo. They used their considerable analytical powers to attack the hypocrisies of the age. As much as they celebrated the powers of reason, they did not fail to notice when human behavior was guided by passion, selfishness, and irrationality. Voltaire, Swift, and Pope all composed scathing attacks on political and social misconduct.

The Philosophes. As an era dedicated to the kind of philosophical inquiry practiced by René Descartes and to the kind of scientific study championed by Francis Bacon, the Enlightenment was embodied in a group of intellectuals called by the French name *philosophes*. These thinkers believed that through reason, humankind could achieve a perfect society of perpetual peace, order, and harmony.

Faced with the two philosophical positions on political rule that had been defined in the previous century, those of Thomas Hobbes (1588–1689) and John Locke (1632–1704), the *philosophes* really had no choice but to champion the cause of Locke. Hobbes's position essentially supported the idea of the monarchy—or at least the rule of a single individual—while Locke proposed the possibility of democratic rule, and tyranny was what the *philosophes* feared most of all. They denounced intolerance in matters of religious belief, which, since the Reformation, had continued to disrupt society, and they advocated public, as opposed to Church-controlled, education.

Rational humanism. **Rational humanism** is based on the fundamental belief that through rational, careful thought, progress is inevitable. This is furthered by the notion that progress itself is good and benefits everyone. Like the humanists of the Renaissance, the rational humanists believed that progress is possible only through learning and through the individual's freedom to learn. Humans must, therefore, be free to think for themselves. This logic links the rational humanists with

Timeline 16.1 The Enlightenment and eighteenth-century styles.

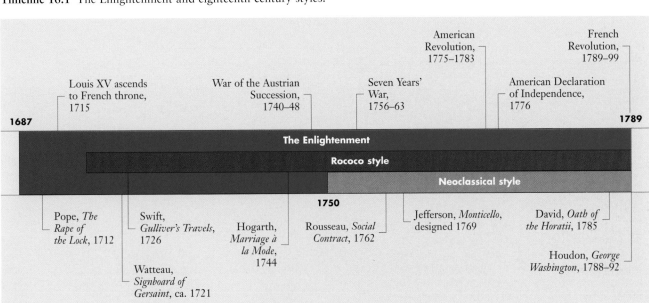

the two great political revolutions of the day, in America and in France, and with such political documents as the Declaration of Independence and the Declaration of the Rights of Man and Citizen as well as with the Constitution of the United States. The rational humanists believed that any political system that strives to suppress freedom of thought must be overthrown as an obstacle to progress.

THE INDUSTRIAL REVOLUTION

The Birth of the Factory. Over the course of the eighteenth century, the nature of labor began to change. On May 1, 1759, in Staffordshire, England, a twenty-eight-year-old man named JOSIAH WEDGWOOD (1730–1795) opened his own pottery manufacturing plant. While Wedgwood initially specialized in unique pottery made by hand, he also began to produce a cream-colored earthen tableware. Designs were then printed by mechanical means (fig. 16.3). In the same year, Wedgwood's friend MATTHEW BOULTON (1728–1809) inherited his father's "toy" factory (small metal objects such as belt buckles, buttons, and clasps were known as "toys"). Soon he had built a factory in London, employing six hundred people in mechanized, large-scale production. The steam engine, patented by James Watt in 1769, transformed the way in which these new factories could be powered. Mechanical looms were soon introduced into the cotton cloth industry, powered by Watt's steam engines. Where once workers had woven fabric at home as "piece work," they now watched over giant looms that did the work for them, in a fraction of the time. Mass manufacturing, and with it what we have come to call the "Industrial Revolution," had begun.

Adam Smith. In 1776, the Scotsman ADAM SMITH (1727–1790) provided the rationale for the

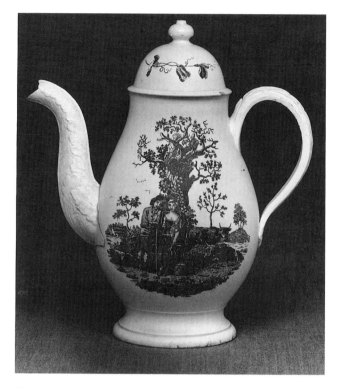

Figure 16.3   Transfer-printed Queen's Ware, ca. 1770, The Wedgwood Museum, Barlaston, England. Even elaborate designs such as this one were mechanically printed on ceramic tableware at Wedgwood's factory. By the turn of the century, pattern books detailing the designs available from Wedgwood were so popular throughout Europe that they were "best-sellers."

entire enterprise. His *Inquiry into the Nature and Cause of the Wealth of Nations* barely mentioned manufacturing, concentrating instead on agriculture and trade, but the business people who ran the new factories saw in his writings the justification for their practices. In a free-market system based on private property, Smith argued

Timeline 16.2 Scientific and industrial achievements.

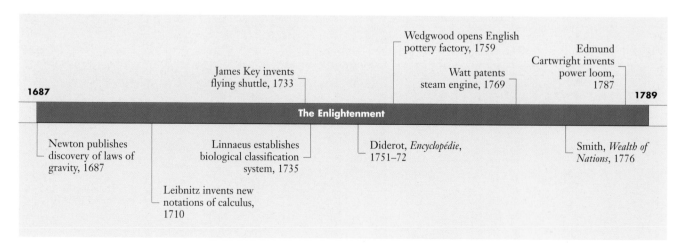

1687 — Newton publishes discovery of laws of gravity, 1687

Leibnitz invents new notations of calculus, 1710

James Key invents flying shuttle, 1733

Linnaeus establishes biological classification system, 1735

The Enlightenment

Diderot, *Encyclopédie*, 1751–72

Wedgwood opens English pottery factory, 1759

Watt patents steam engine, 1769

Edmund Cartwright invents power loom, 1787

Smith, *Wealth of Nations*, 1776

1789

that prices and profits would automatically be regulated to the benefit, theoretically, of everyone, not just the factory owners. He contended that the economy would operate as if with an "invisible hand" beneficently guiding it. The new "working class" that arose out of the Industrial Revolution, however, would find that the free-market system benefited the factory owners a great deal more than themselves, and by the dawn of the nineteenth century, the factory owners had become the new "kings" of industrial culture—as spendthrift and tyrannical as the monarchs of the previous age.

THE SCIENTIFIC REVOLUTION

Isaac Newton. The positivism of the age was exemplified by Locke's theory of the innate human rights to life and to property and the belief in humanity's capacity for reason, but it was driven by advances in scientific learning. The *philosophes* seized on the discovery by ISAAC NEWTON (1642–1727) of the principle of gravitation, the first physical description of the forces holding the known universe together. The earth and its moon, Jupiter and its four moons, the sun and its planets all formed a harmonious system, with each celestial body relying upon the others to maintain its place and position. Transferring this vision to human society, the

philosophes suggested that with a comparable system of mutual reliance humans could live in harmony. Newton's discovery prompted what can only be called yet another revolution, a "Scientific Revolution." Throughout the eighteenth century, scientists explored the natural world to such a degree that new sciences had to be defined: geology (1795), mineralogy (1796), zoology (1818), and biology (1819).

Denis Diderot and Carolus Linnaeus. The French essayist DENIS DIDEROT [DEED-eh-roe] (1713–1784) conceived of an idea for an *Encyclopédie*, twenty-eight volumes designed to encompass the whole of human knowledge, from science and technology to philosophical thought. Lavishly illustrated (fig. 16.4), the volumes actually contain thousands of illustrations showing the mechanical principles of production and commerce.

In the middle of the century, CAROLUS LINNAEUS [leh-NAY-us] (1707–1778) established the biological classification system that is still used to identify species. Both Linnaeus's classification system and the *Encyclopédie* are themselves undertakings that reveal the considerable optimism of the age, the result of two hundred years of scientific advances that had convinced many people that humankind could in fact eventually know everything—and catalogue it.

Figure 16.4 "Casting a Large Equestrian Statue," from Diderot's *Encyclopedia of Trades and Industries*, Vol. VIII, 1771. Typical of the illustrations in Diderot's mammoth work, these engravings depict the complex process involved in casting the giant bronze sculpture of Louis XIV on horseback that was erected in Paris in 1699.

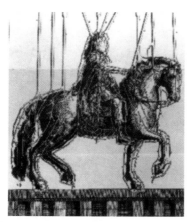

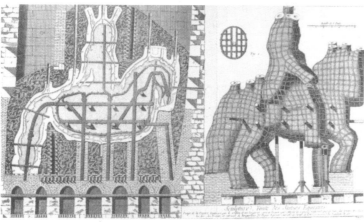

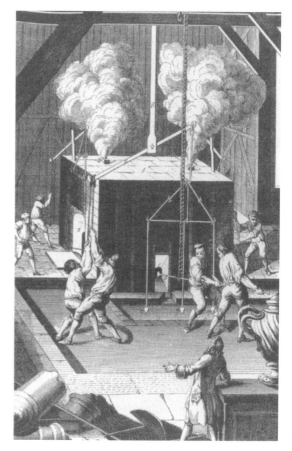

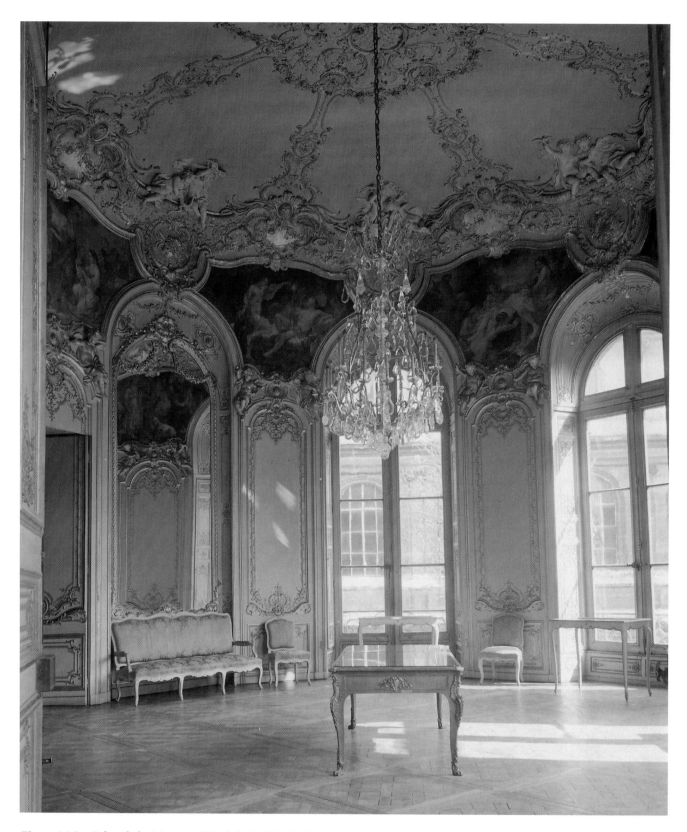

Figure 16.5   Salon de la Princesse, Hôtel de Soubise, Paris, ca. 1737–38, decorated by Gabriel-Germain Boffrand. Turning away from the vast spaces of Baroque architecture, Rococo architects preferred small rooms, as demonstrated by those in this elegant townhouse. This room measures ca. 33 × 26′ (ca. 10.06 × 7.92 m), an ideal space in which to cultivate the art of conversation.

THE ROCOCO

Of all the political systems suppressing the rights of the people in the eighteenth century, that of France was the most audacious. It championed a style of art that was, in the eyes of many, entirely decadent and self-serving. Not only did the Rococo style appear frivolous to many, but it was commissioned by the same powerful aristocratic families who were seen as suppressors of the people's freedom. Its abundant extravagance was interpreted as a reflection of its patrons' uncaring self-aggrandizement. Marie Antoinette famously linked herself to such criticism when, on being told that French women were rioting in the streets for bread, she responded: "Let them eat cake!" Her retort quickly became the emblem of an unenlightened and irrational aristocracy that had lost sight of the values of humanism altogether. The Rococo art of this aristocracy, the poetry, architecture, painting, and sculpture of the court of Louis XV (r. 1715–74), is precisely what the Enlightenment came to define itself against.

The name **Rococo** is thought to come from the French word *rocaille*, a type of decorative rock work or grotto work made from pebbles and curving shells. It is also very likely a pun on the Italian word for the Baroque, *barocco*; certainly, the style's connection to certain elements of the Baroque is strong. Associated especially with the reign of Louis XV of France, who ascended to the throne at the age of five in 1715, Rococo artists rejected the heavier grandeur championed by the young King's grandfather, evident in the design of the east facade of the Louvre (see Chapter 15). Artists instead reshaped and modified the more elaborate aspects of the Baroque style apparent in, for instance, Borromini's design for San Carlo alle Quattro Fontane in Rome (see fig. 15.8).

The Rococo style is marked, particularly, by a shift in court taste from the *poussiniste* style—the more classical style of the painter Nicolas Poussin—to a somewhat *rubéniste* mode, indebted to the art of Peter Paul Rubens. The exact moment of this shift could be said to have taken place in the early 1700s, when the Duc de Richelieu wagered his famous collection of paintings (many by Poussin and the Caraccis) against King Louis XIV in a tennis match. To the delight of the King, the Duke lost the match, and Louis acquired the paintings. But to his surprise, the Duke, forced to start a new collection, quickly purchased fourteen paintings by Rubens, and the *rubéniste* mode, with all its color, motion, and light, was soon firmly established as an accepted style of painting.

THE FRENCH ROCOCO

The New Hôtels. The art of Rubens represented a liberation from the restraint of Poussin, and in almost all things, the French court indulged its new-found sense of freedom. When Louis XIV died, and the Duc d'Orléans assumed the role of regent for the child-king, Louis XV, Versailles was immediately abandoned and the court re-established in Paris itself, not so much at the Palace of the Louvre, but in *hôtels*, or townhouses, where clever hostesses oversaw weekly *salons*. A *salon* was a reception room intended for fashionable social gatherings of notable people, and the term *"salon"* came to refer to such events. The hostesses competed with each other in inviting the most powerful and accomplished of their peers. These *salons* were the scene of extraordinary conversations that turned, very often, into battles of wit and intelligence, or dwelt on matters of love and courtship. Musicians, often the finest of the day, entertained the guests.

The hostesses were free to pursue their own tastes in Paris, unhampered by any "official" court style such as they had experienced at Versailles. They decorated their *hôtels* elaborately with gilded or painted wood moldings, inlaid China plaques and mirrors, bronze ornaments, marble mantels and countertops, and lacquerwork veneers. One salon of exquisite beauty was created for the Princess de Soubise (fig. 16.5). Designed by France's royal architect, GABRIEL-GERMAIN BOFFRAND [boo-FRAHN] (1667–1754), it displays the typical Rococo concern for melding ceiling and walls into one curvilinear flow of delicate ornament and grace. Dominated by an interplay of curves and organic lines meant to evoke growing plants, interiors like this would not be seen again until the rise of Art Nouveau at the end of the nineteenth century.

Jean-Antoine Watteau. The paintings decorating the walls of the *hôtels* were generally purchased by the hostesses themselves in shops such as that depicted in *The Signboard of Gersaint* (fig. 16.6), a painting by JEAN-ANTOINE WATTEAU [WAH-toe] (1684–1721) of about 1721. Originally, Watteau designed it to hang as a sign outside his friend Gersaint's gallery. It was to replace the former signboard, a detail of Hyacinthe Rigaud's portrait of Louis XIV (see fig. 16.1), which is being put away in storage in the crate at the left. A lady sees this happening, but a gentleman gestures her to the new-style paintings on the right wall. Instead of formal portraits, *rubéniste* paintings, with reclining nudes and mythological scenes, have taken over the walls.

Patrons for Watteau's art were in fact widely diverse in social class. They included noblemen and government officials, as well as middle-class merchants and bankers. Several of these can be seen peering at a large oval painting that itself possesses many of the characteristics of Watteau's work. As a painter, Watteau was most noted for his *fêtes galantes*, depictions of elegant out-of-doors parties known for their amorous conversations, graceful fashion, and social gallantry.

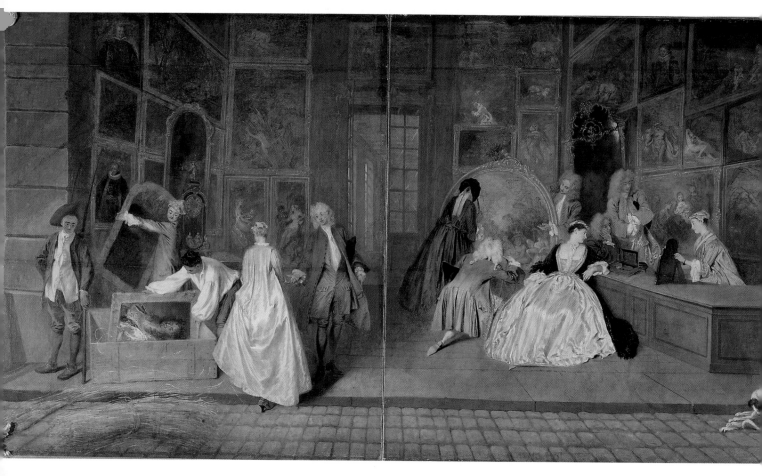

Figure 16.6 Jean-Antoine Watteau, *The Signboard of Gersaint*, ca. 1721, oil on canvas, 5′4″ × 10′1″ (1.62 × 3.06 m), Staatliche Museen zu Berlin, Germany. Note that although the dealer Gersaint has paintings of more traditional subjects on his wall, his patrons seem more interested in the canvases that present sexual motifs.

Watteau's *A Pilgrimage to Cythera* (fig. 16.7), of 1717, is a mythologized vision of just such an event. The party takes place on Cythera, the birthplace of Venus and the island of love. Lovers go there to honor Venus, portrayed in a statue on the far right. Cupids fly above the crowd, the sun is low, and the lovers are boarding the boat that will return them to the real world. The departure is sad; some figures glance back, reluctant to leave the idyllic setting.

Watteau's painting gained entry into the Royal Academy of Painting and Sculpture even though it did not adhere to Academy rules of size or subject. It is relatively small, and the subject was neither history nor religion nor portraiture, the subjects the Academy favored. Watteau did not glorify the state or flatter the King. Nonetheless, the Academy recognized Watteau's achievement, and in a moment of triumph for the *rubéniste* sensibility, it created a new official category expressly for *fêtes galantes*.

By the time Louis XV assumed personal rule of the country in 1743, the court had enjoyed a free rein for many years. The King essentially adapted himself to its carefree ways, dismissing state officials at whim. In thirty years of personal rule, he had fourteen chief fiscal officers and eighteen different foreign secretaries, creating ceaseless instability in government. Life, for Louis XV, was something of an endless *fête galante*. He surrounded himself with mistresses, at least one of whom, Madame de Pompadour, wielded as much, or more, power than the King himself.

François Boucher. Madame de Pompadour's favorite painter was FRANÇOIS BOUCHER [boo-SHAY] (1703–1770), who began his career, in 1725, by copying the Watteau paintings owned by Jean de Jullienne, the principal collector of the artist's work. Jullienne had conceived of the notion of having all of Watteau's works engraved so that they could be enjoyed by a wider public. Boucher was quickly recognized as the best of the printmakers hired by Jullienne to undertake the task. With his earnings, he set off for Rome in 1727 to study the masters. But he found Raphael "trite,"

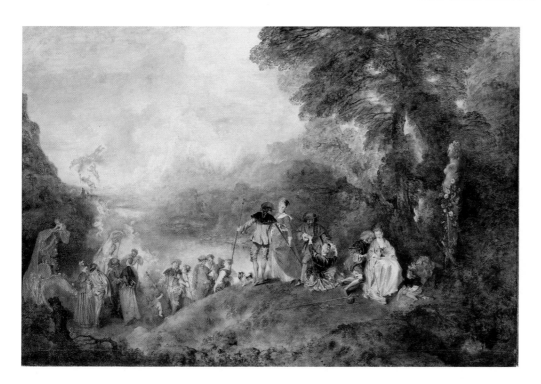

Figure 16.7 Jean-Antoine Watteau, *Pilgrimage to Cythera*, 1717, oil on canvas, 4′3″ × 6′4½″ (1.30 × 1.90 m), Musée du Louvre, Paris. The Rococo style is characterized by lightness of content and of color; romantic pastimes are portrayed in an atmosphere of lighthearted pastel hedonism.

Michelangelo "hunchbacked," and the work of the Carracci "murky," so he returned to Paris. By 1734, he was an established member of the Academy, specializing in *fêtes galantes* and other similar subjects. Soon he was appointed Director of the Royal Academy and First Painter to Louis XV, and patrons of society were soon clamoring after his work. Astonishingly prolific, Boucher produced over a thousand paintings and ten thousand drawings, and designed tapestries for the Royal Opera and the Opéra-Comique, which were later woven at the royal factories of Beauvais and Gobelins, and porcelain for Madame de Pompadour's favorite project, the Royal Porcelain Manufactory at Sèvres.

Boucher's painting of the *Bath of Diana* (fig. 16.8), of 1742, displays the delicate French grace and charming Rococo sentiment that made him so successful. Boucher painted many female nudes, then a popular subject; but on this occasion, to make it socially acceptable, he presented the figure as the mythological Diana. His goddess of the hunt, however, is hardly strong or powerful. She is aristocratic, delicate, and soft, seemingly straight from the hairdresser. The curving shapes are characteristic of the Rococo style, as are the lush colors that he favors— tender pinks, blues, and soft whites. The artist's friends likened his colors to "rose petals floating in milk." The overall effect is one of quiet sensuality, conveying an air of relaxed indiscretion.

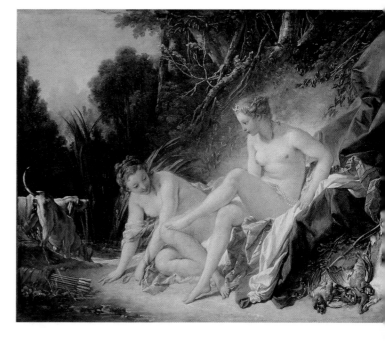

Figure 16.8 François Boucher, *Bath of Diana*, 1742, oil on canvas, 22½″ × 28¾″ (57.2 × 73 cm), Musée du Louvre, Paris. The portrayal of female nudity was made acceptable by the antique context in which it was presented. The female type admired was not powerful or rugged but pale, delicate, and pampered.

Jean-Honoré Fragonard. The other great painter of the Parisian Rococo was JEAN-HONORÉ FRAGONARD [frah-goh-NAR] (1732–1806), Boucher's student, whose work is even more overtly erotic than his teacher's. Sensuous nudes inhabit his paintings, and they are depicted in an equally sensual style, much like that of Rubens in its use of strong fluid color and areas of light and shade. Fragonard is noted for his rapid brushwork: he could paint an entire work inside an hour. His figures float softly, ever graceful, always courtly. Fragonard's most famous work, however, was a series of fourteen canvases commissioned around 1771 by Madame du Barry, Louis XV's last mistress. Designed to decorate her château, they depict a series of encounters between

Figure 16.9 Jean-Honoré Fragonard, *The Meeting*, 1771–73, oil on canvas, $15'5\frac{1}{4}'' \times 7'\frac{5}{8}''$ (3.18 × 2.15 m), The Frick Collection, New York. The sculpture that rises above this scene, though an entirely imaginary creation of the artist, is in fact representative of the favored sculptural style of the Rococo. The figure twists and turns in an upward spiral that accentuates the curves of her hip and thigh.

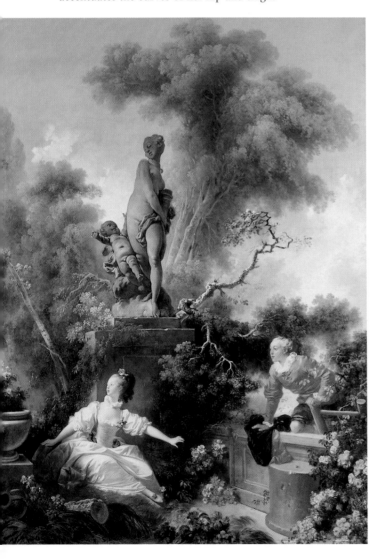

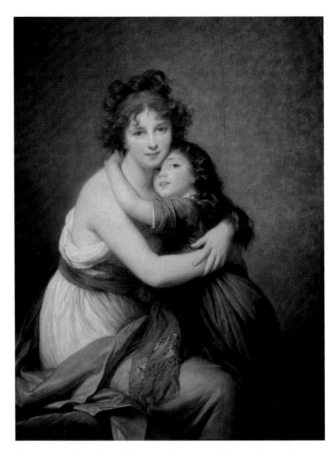

Figure 16.10 Marie-Louise-Elisabeth Vigée-Lebrun, *The Artist and Her Daughter*, ca. 1785, oil on canvas, 4'3'' × 3'1'' (139.7 × 94 cm), Musée du Louvre, Paris. Vigée-Lebrun's style coincided perfectly with upper-class tastes, making her the highest-paid portrait painter in France (by the age of twenty!) and court painter to Queen Marie Antoinette.

lovers in garden settings, like the gardens of the château itself. *The Meeting* (fig. 16.9) has elements characteristic of the whole series. Below a statue of Venus, a young woman waits to meet her lover, who is climbing over the garden wall. The scene is ambiguous: Is he arriving, or fleeing? Whatever the case, they fear being discovered, as is evident from their anxious glance to the left.

Fragonard endured constant interruption by Madame du Barry, and in the end the paintings were rejected, perhaps because the Rococo was becoming increasingly unpopular. Seen by many as the embodiment of the decadence of the aristocracy, the style was on the wane.

Marie-Louise-Elisabeth Vigée-Lebrun. Paintings like *The Artist and Her Daughter* (fig. 16.10) by MARIE-LOUISE-ELISABETH VIGÉE-LEBRUN [vee-JHAY le-BRUN] (1755–1842) signaled the arrival of this more restrained and naturalistic classical style. Fatherless as a girl, Vigée-Lebrun supported her mother and brother by her painting. She was a child prodigy; by the time she was twenty, her portraits were commanding the highest

Connections

DIDEROT AS ART CRITIC

One of the very first art critics—certainly the first art critic of any substance—was Denis Diderot (1713–1784), the *philosophe*. He enjoyed art, and his enjoyment is evident in every page of his essays, called the *Salons*. He reviewed all the exhibitions sponsored by the French Academy from 1759 on for a private newspaper, *La Correspondance littéraire*. Subscribers to this newspaper were the elite of Europe—princesses and princes—and it was intended to keep potential patrons abreast of the latest news from Paris.

Though he considered Boucher the most talented painter of his generation, Diderot generally disapproved of his subjects, and he went so far as to condemn him and his contemporaries in the *Salon of 1767* for the essentially erotic content of most of what was on display. Four years earlier he had asked, "Haven't painters used their brushes in the service of vice and debauchery long enough, too long indeed?" He preferred what he called "moral" painting, painting that sought "to move, to educate, to improve us, and to induce us to virtue." Diderot could, nonetheless, be extraordinarily cruel. Addressing a

now-forgotten painter by the name of Challe, he asked, "Tell me, Monsieur Challe, why are you a painter? There are so many other professions in which mediocrity is actually an advantage."

Anticipating the Impressionists a century later, he celebrated a still life painting entitled *The Brioche* (fig. 16.11) by JEAN-BAPTISTE-SIMÉON CHARDIN [shar-DAN] (1699–1779): "Such magic leaves one amazed. There are thick layers of superimposed color, and their effect rises from below to the surface ... Come closer, and everything becomes flat, confused, and indistinct; stand back again, and everything springs back into life and shape."

Diderot's writing style is anything but as direct as his criticisms. Some of his *Salons* are so long that they cannot be read at a single sitting. They exercise every excuse for a digression. Still, their acuteness of vision and moral purpose have influenced art criticism down to the present day.

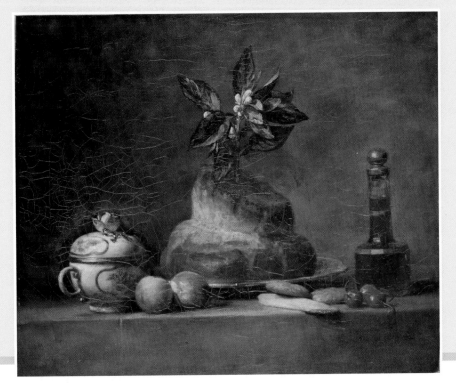

Figure 16.11 Jean-Baptiste-Siméon Chardin, *The Brioche*, 1763, oil on canvas, 18½″ × 22″ (47 × 55.9 cm), Musée du Louvre, Paris. A master of still life, which in his day was considered the lowest form of painting, Chardin was nevertheless recognized by his contemporaries as applying paint and color as no one before him had ever done. But his technique was not, he thought, what mattered most. "Who told you that one paints with colors?" he once asked a fellow artist. "One uses colors, but one paints with feelings."

prices in France. Highly sought after and highly paid, Vigée-Lebrun painted portraits of all the important members of the aristocracy, including Louis XVI's queen, Marie Antoinette. Vigée-Lebrun had the ability to convey a sense of power combined with grace and intimacy. Her subjects often seem to be turning to glance at the viewer, as if the viewer just happened into their presence a moment ago. Closely linked to royalty, Vigée-Lebrun fled France during the Revolution, spent many years traveling and painting in Europe, and published three volumes of memoirs, which give an insight into her art and era.

ENGLISH PAINTING

William Hogarth. The influence of the French Rococo on English painting is evident in the work of WILLIAM HOGARTH (1697–1764). Hogarth was a storyteller whose work documents the life of his time. He produced picture series that were equivalent to scenes in a play or chapters in a novel. Hogarth used similar details to help viewers interpret the different scenes of his works, which were much like morality plays. He sought to teach by example, referring to his narratives as "modern moral subjects." A social critic, he

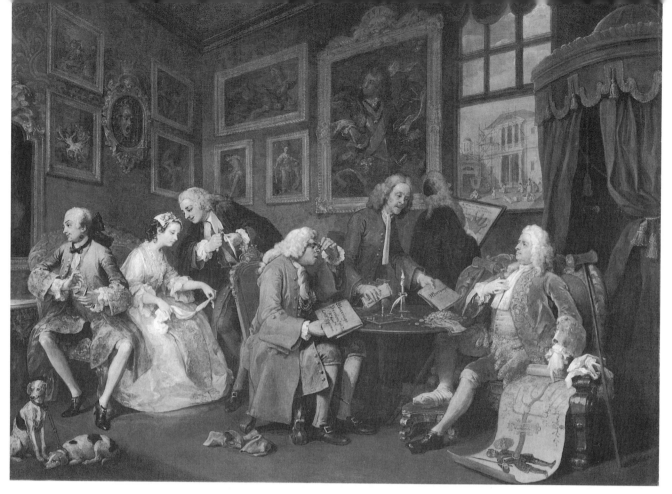

Figure 16.12   William Hogarth, *The Marriage Contract*, scene I from *Marriage à la Mode*, 1744, oil on canvas, 27 × 35" (69 × 89 cm), National Gallery, London. Through a series of paintings, comparable to scenes in a play, Hogarth told moralizing tales focusing on the hypocritical or dishonest practices of his day. *Marriage à la Mode* shows the disastrous outcome of a marriage arranged for the benefit of the parents of the bride and groom.

satirized the decadent customs of his day by exposing the "character" of society. Thus, unlike his French counterparts, who painted the life of the aristocracy in an unabashedly erotic and glowing light, Hogarth's view of England's aristocracy is overtly critical and moralistic. The engravings he made of these paintings were sold to the public and became wildly popular. Hogarth's financial success presented an important, if ambivalent lesson: lurid stories sell.

Hogarth's most mature work is *Marriage à la Mode*, a series of paintings made in 1744. The first scene, called *The Marriage Contract* (fig. 16.12), introduces the cast of characters. On the right sits the father of the groom, a nobleman who points to his family tree. Through this arranged marriage, he is trading his social position for money that will ensure that the mortgage on his estate is paid off. The bride's father, a wealthy tradesman, inspects the contract. On the left, the engaged couple have their backs to each other. The groom preens himself in the mirror. The bride talks to the lawyer, counselor Silvertongue.

In the five scenes that follow, the marriage, as expected, sours. Husband and wife are both unfaithful.

When the husband finds his wife with Silvertongue, the lover stabs him. The wife is disgraced and takes poison. As she is dying, her father, mercenary to the end, removes her valuable rings. In *Marriage à la Mode* the guilty live on.

Sir Joshua Reynolds.   One of the leading painters of London society was SIR JOSHUA REYNOLDS (1723–1792). Thoughtful, intelligent, and hard-working, Reynolds was named the first President of the Royal Academy of London in 1768 and was knighted the following year. Favoring an academic art similar to that championed by Lebrun in France a century earlier, Reynolds developed a set of theories and rules in his fifteen *Discourses*, positioning history painting as the highest form of art and advocating a "general" view of nature (as practiced in the Italian Baroque) over the "particular" scenery evident in Dutch landscape.

The majority of Reynolds's works are portraits, presumably because portrait painting was lucrative. His style is seen in his portrait *Lady Elizabeth Delmé and Her Children* (fig. 16.13), executed 1777–80 at the peak of his career. Reynolds often portrayed aristocratic ladies as should give a general idea of his subject and "leave out all the minute breaks and peculiarities in the face … rather than observing the exact similitude of every feature." Thus, Reynolds painted people the way he thought they should look, rather than how they actually did look.

Thomas Gainsborough. Reynolds's chief rival was THOMAS GAINSBOROUGH (1727–1788). Although Gainsborough began as a landscape painter, a mode he always preferred, he painted portraits to make a living and became the most fashionable portraitist in British society. Most eighteenth-century portraiture, as that by Reynolds, is elegant and courtly, artists flattering their sitters by giving them all the social graces deemed desirable. This is evidenced by Gainsborough's *Mary, Countess Howe* (fig. 16.14), of 1765. Set in a landscape worthy of Watteau, Gainsborough's figure holds up her skirt as if

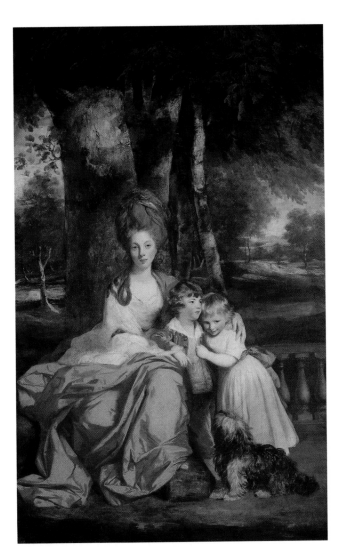

Figure 16.13 Sir Joshua Reynolds, *Lady Elizabeth Delmé and Her Children*, 1777–80, oil on canvas, 7'10" × 4'12⅛" (2.39 × 1.48 m), National Gallery of Art, Washington, DC. Reynolds, Gainsborough's rival, places his aristocratic subjects in a landscape setting indicative of the eighteenth-century appreciation of nature.

Figure 16.14 Thomas Gainsborough, *Mary, Countess Howe*, 1765, oil on canvas, 8' × 5' (2.59 × 1.52 m), London County Council, Kenwood House (Iveagh Bequest). Though he thought of himself first and foremost as a landscape painter, Gainsborough is best known for large-scale portraits that present his subjects as aristocratic and refined.

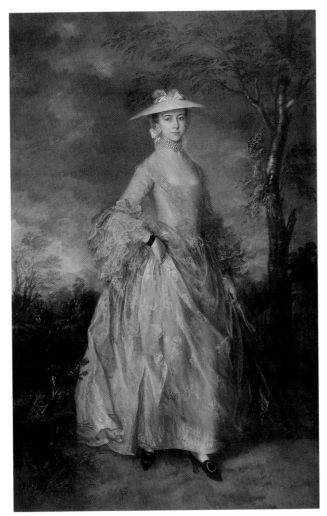

elegant and gracious, refined and dignified. Lady Delmé sits on a rock and embraces her oldest children. All are fashionably dressed. The colors and textures are lush in Reynolds's "Grand Manner"—indeed, the canvas itself is enormous and the figures almost life-size.

Reynolds painted rapidly with full, free brushstrokes, without first making sketches. He told one of his patrons that a portrait "requires in general three sittings about an hour and a half each time, but if the sitter chooses it, the face can be begun and finished in one day … when the face is finished the rest is done without troubling the sitter." Understandably, then, Reynolds's paintings tell us little about his sitters' personalities, and his approach to portrait painting was similar to his approach to land-scape. In his fourth *Discourse*, he says a portrait painter

Gainsborough has caught her strolling in a *fête galante*. She is impeccably dressed, elegant, possessing a self-confident air of distinction and social poise. Painting with dash and freedom using a fresh and fluid technique, emphasizing lush textures in decorative colors, Gainsborough displays a technical virtuosity typical of the Rococo.

LITERATURE

During the eighteenth century, throughout Europe literary works reflected the rationalism of the Enlightenment. The emphasis on reason in literature recurred across the genres, from essays and fiction to poetry and drama. Essayists such as Benjamin Franklin and Thomas Paine wrote prose pieces that relied on careful reasoning and incisive logic to support their claims about human political and social behavior as well as humanity's irrational beliefs, especially those concerning religious faith. Novelists and satirists, including Daniel Defoe and Jonathan Swift, often used irony to satirize men's claim to reason. Swift suggested, in fact, that although human beings are theoretically "capable" of being rational, few actually possess reason. English poets in particular employed irony and sarcasm as weapons in their fiercely satirical verses on all manner of subjects, especially the behavior of courtiers.

Samuel Johnson's "Club." The London of Hogarth's day was, above all, a city of contrasts. On the one hand, there was Fleet Street, largely rebuilt after the Great Fire of 1666 and dominated at one end by Wren's St. Paul's Cathedral. Fleet Street was the gathering place of the "Club," a group of London intellectuals, writers, editors, and publishers. One of its founders was SAMUEL JOHNSON (1709–1784), author of the 1755 *Dictionary of the English Language* and editor of Shakespeare's complete plays. The Club was also home to members of refined society. Artists, too, among them Sir Joshua Reynolds, sought each other's company at the Cock Tavern or at George's Coffee House. They dined together at Ye Olde Cheshire Cheese. "When a man is tired of London, a man is tired of life," Johnson boasted of the city's intellectual and cultural stimulation.

On the other hand, there was Grub Street, a lane just outside the London Wall. As Johnson put it in his *Dictionary*, Grub Street was "inhabited by writers of small histories, dictionaries, and temporary poems"—the hacks of the burgeoning publishing trade. A world of difference lay between it and Fleet Street; Newgate Prison was between them, and Bethlehem Royal Hospital, known as Bedlam, the lunatic asylum, was nearby. This was the monstrous side of London, a side that members of Johnson's Club had to witness every day as they strolled from Fleet Street to the tavern where they met. On the way, they passed through Covent Garden, where the city's street-walkers plied their trade.

Alexander Pope. Foremost among satirical poets writing in English is ALEXANDER POPE (1688–1744), whose works set the standard for satiric poetry in eighteenth-century England. No work captures the spirit of Grub Street better than Pope's *Dunciad*, written in 1743. Pope equates the Grub Street writers with the lunacy of the city itself, and the poem ends with a "dunces'" parade through the city. The spectacle culminates in the end of civilization itself:

> Lo! thy dread empire Chaos! is restor'd
> Light dies before thy uncreating word;
> Thy hand, great Anarch! lets the curtain fall,
> And universal darkness buries all.

In the face of the monstrosities of Grub Street, Pope writes, "Morality expires." Satire was Pope's chief tool, and the lowly hacks of Grub Street were by no means his only target. Like Hogarth, he attacked the morality of the aristocracy. Perhaps his most famous poem is *The Rape of the Lock*. This is a **mock epic**—that is, it treats a trivial incident in a heroic manner and style more suited to the traditional epic subjects of war and nation-building. *The Rape of the Lock* is based on an actual incident in which a young man from a prominent family clipped a lock of hair from one Miss Arabella Fermor, an event that caused her family considerable consternation. Pope describes the gentlemen and ladies of polite society in the same terms as the heroes and heroines of Homer's epic *Iliad* and *Odyssey*, his translations of which first established his reputation. Pope's "war" is chiefly one of the words and deeds exchanged between the sexes, all described in heroic style. Applied to the frivolous world of snuffboxes, porcelain, and cosmetics, the effect is undeniably comical, as if Sir Joshua Reynolds's Grand Manner had been brought low.

Jonathan Swift. A far crueler satirist was JONATHAN SWIFT (1667–1745). Born in Ireland, Swift traveled to London, where he became a renowned poet and political writer, as well as an Anglican clergyman. After his appointment as Dean of St. Patrick's Cathedral in Dublin in 1713, he spent the rest of his life in Ireland. Best known for his satirical prose work *Gulliver's Travels*, Swift for many years was considered a cynical misanthrope—a person who hates the human race. Much has been made of a comment from *Gulliver's Travels*, spoken by the King of Brobdingnag (the land of the giants). Addressing Lemuel Gulliver, Swift's representative of humanity, the Brobdingnagian King describes human beings as "the most pernicious race of odious little vermin that ever walked the face of the earth."

This bitter satirical strain, however, is only one side of Swift's literary persona; his satirical imagination also had a lighter, more playful dimension. *Gulliver's Travels* is full of fantastic and marvelous events, delightful even to children. The book recounts the adventures of a ship's physician, Lemuel Gulliver, over four voyages. His first voyage takes him to Lilliput, where the people are only six inches tall; the second to Brobdingnag, the land of giants; the third to Laputa, a region where thought and intellect are privileged; and the fourth and final voyage to the land inhabited by the Yahoos and their masters the Houyhnhnms, horse-like creatures whose lives are governed by reason, intelligence, and common sense. Nonetheless, throughout *Gulliver's Travels*, Swift uses his hero's adventures to satirize the political, social, and academic institutions of his own time and country, with their abundant display of human folly, stupidity, baseness, and greed. Thus, he contrasts the sensible and wise Houyhnhnms with both the ignorant and filthy Yahoos and with the impractical and eccentric Laputians, who are so far from living effectively in the real world that they carry a large sack filled with a multitude of objects, which they need to communicate with one another.

VOLTAIRE'S PHILOSOPHY OF CYNICISM

One of the most important thinkers of the eighteenth century, François Marie Arouet, known by his pen name VOLTAIRE [Vole-TAIR] (1694–1778), shared Swift's general sense of human folly, as well as Hogarth and Pope's recognition of the moral bankruptcy of the aristocracy. Voltaire was deeply influenced by English political thought, especially by the freedom of ideas that, among other things, allowed writers such as Pope and

Swift to publish without fear. Voltaire himself was jailed for a year, then exiled to England in 1726, for criticizing the morality of the French aristocracy. When he returned to France, in 1729, he promptly published his *Philosophical Letters Concerning the English*, in which, once more, he criticized French political and religious life. This time, his publisher was jailed, and Voltaire himself retreated to Lorraine, in eastern France, where he lived for the next fifteen years.

Voltaire's best-known work, *Candide*, is a scathing indictment of those who agreed with the philosopher Leibniz that this is the best of all possible worlds, regardless of occasional misfortunes, and that everything that happens is part of the providential plan of a benevolent God. *Candide* was written just after the 1755 Lisbon earthquake, in which thousands were killed. Voltaire argued that those who explained the catastrophe away, minimizing its destructive consequences, were deceiving themselves. Voltaire reasoned that either God refused to prevent the existence of evil, in which case he was not benevolent, or that he lacked the power to avert evil, in which case he was not omnipotent. Voltaire also rejected the Christian notion of a personal God. Voltaire himself was a Deist, one of those who believed in a God more akin to the pagan notion of a prime mover or a first cause. For Voltaire, religious traditions, such as biblical Christianity that promise eternal joy, happiness, and salvation, were responsible for creating unrealistic expectations and vain hopes.

Map 16.2 The Enlightenment in America and Europe.

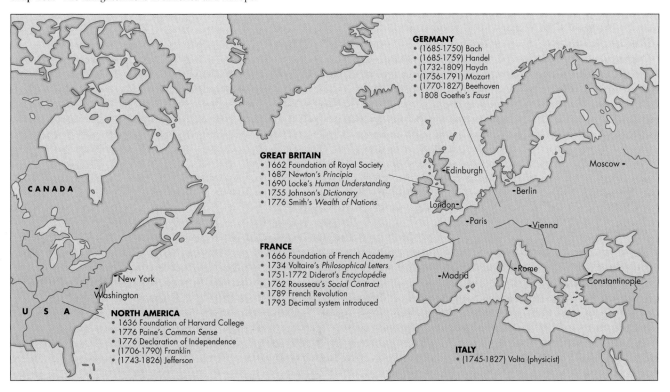

THE FRENCH REVOLUTION

The executions of Louis XVI and Marie Antoinette represented not only the death of the monarchy, but an end to the privilege and extravagance that the monarchy had come to represent in the minds of the people. In death, all are equal. The century's growing belief in the equality of all, in the right of the individual to live free of tyranny, and in the right of humankind to self-governance, culminated in political **revolution**, the overthrow of the existing order for a new one. In fact, revolution itself seemed to many an "enlightened" course of action.

The American Revolution began to stir in 1774, when the colonists convened for the new Continental Congress. An American Declaration of Independence, authored by THOMAS JEFFERSON (1743–1826), unified the colonies in their successful war against the British, and in the following years, a constitutional convention met in Philadelphia to draft a new charter for the American republic. At the convention mechanisms were devised to assess and collect taxes, regulate commerce, and make enforceable laws, all within a government framework of "checks and balances." The legislative, judicial, and executive branches of government all had their own powers, but powers that were overseen by the other branches.

The French bourgeoisie watched with interest. They wanted a "National Assembly" like the Continental Congress; a document drafted along the same principles as the American Declaration; and a republican constitution that would give them life, liberty, and the right to own property. But the French situation was different from the American one. Where the American Revolution pitted against one another two groups with essentially similar cultural values, one simply seeking economic autonomy from the other, the French Revolution was essentially an internal class struggle and, as such, expressed a clash in values. This type of revolution would have a lasting effect on world history.

Each of the French kings of the eighteenth century—Louis XIV (r. 1643–1715), Louis XV (r. 1715–74), and Louis XVI (r. 1774–93), guillotined on January 21, 1793—had successively led the country further into debt. In May 1789, Louis XVI, succumbing to mounting pressures to deal with the ever-increasing national debt, called for an assembly of the Estates General. This assembly of the clergy (the First Estate), the aristocrats (the Second Estate), and the bourgeois citizens (the Third Estate) resulted in the "The Declaration of the Rights of Man and Citizen," a document modeled on the American "Declaration of Independence." In a memoir written early in the nineteenth century, one witness contrasted the pomp of the clergy and aristocracy to the plain attire of the bourgeois citizens. He outlined, in effect, the conditions that led to the Revolution itself:

> The senior clergy, glittering with gold, and all the great men of the kingdom, crowding around the dais, displayed utter magnificence, while the representatives of the Third Estate appeared to be dressed in mourning. Yet their long line represented the nation, and the people were so conscious of this that they overwhelmed them with applause. They shouted "Long live the Third Estate!" just as they have since shouted "Long live the nation!" The unwise distinction had produced the opposite effect to that intended by the court: The Third Estate recognized their fathers and defenders in the men in black coats and high cravats, and their enemies in the others … These men, who had never before traveled beyond their own provinces, and who had left behind them the sight of destitution in town and country, now saw evidence of the extravagant expenditure of Louis XIV and Louis XV, and of the new court's [Louis XVI's] quest for pleasure. This château here, they were told, cost two hundred million; the fairy palace at Saint-Cloud cost twelve; and no one knows how much has been spent

Timeline 16.3 France at the time of the Revolution.

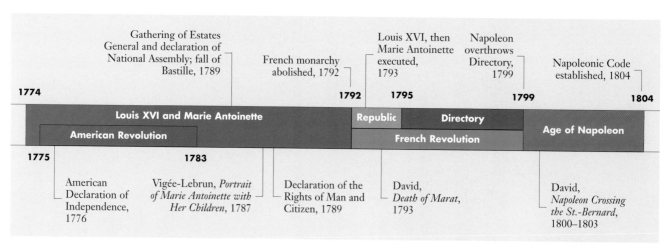

on the Petit Trianon. And they answered, "All this magnificence was produced by the sweat of the people."

Now the Third Estate, representing a large percentage of the population, strove to take control of the nation, and to take back possession of its wealth. If the sweat of the people had made France "magnificent," they reasoned, then the people should benefit from their labor.

THE NATIONAL ASSEMBLY

In the Estates General, each of the three estates—the Church, the aristocracy, and the bourgeois middle class—had one vote. The Third Estate quickly realized that it would be outvoted 2–1 on every question. Thus, on June 20, 1789, the deputies of the Third Estate along with their aristocratic sympathizers declared a "National Assembly" in a building in the grounds of the Louvre called the Jeu de Paume, the King's tennis court. Together they swore an oath that they would not separate until France had a new constitution; Jacques-Louis David, a painter who recorded the Revolution, captured the moment in *The Tennis Court Oath* (fig. 16.15), although it remained an unfinished work.

Rumors that the King was planning to overthrow the National Assembly led to the formation of a volunteer bourgeois militia, which, on July 14, 1789, went to the Bastille prison in Paris in search of arms and gun powder. The prison governor panicked and ordered his guard to fire on the militia, killing ninety-eight and wounding seventy-three. An angry mob quickly formed and stormed the Bastille, decapitating its governor, and slaughtering six of the guards. The next day, Louis XVI asked if the incident had been a riot. "No, your majesty," was the reply, "it was a revolution."

The National Assembly continued to meet steadily while rioting spread throughout the French countryside, and finally, on August 4, 1789, in a night session, the Viscount of Nouilles and then the Duke of Aiguillon renounced their feudal privileges and revenues. Other nobles did the same, and the clergy in attendance relinquished their tithes. By the end of the evening, all French people suddenly found themselves subject to the same laws and taxes. On August 27, 1789 the Assembly ratified

Figure 16.15   Jacques Louis David, *The Tennis Court Oath*, 1789–91, unfinished, pen and brown ink and brown wash on paper, 26″ × 42″ (66 × 107 cm), Musée du Louvre, Paris. Spectators peer down on the Third Estate, which takes its oath as the "winds of freedom" blow through the windows above.

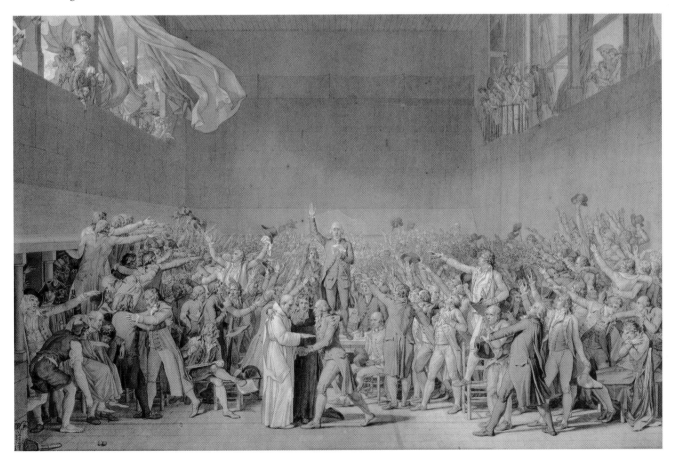

Then & Now

THE RIGHTS OF WOMEN

When the French National Assembly ratified the Declaration of the Rights of Man and Citizen on August 27, 1789, its members did not include women among the "citizens." In 1791, Olympe de Gouges (1748–1793) wrote a "Declaration of the Rights of Women" and demanded that the National Assembly act upon it. This stated that "Woman is born free and remains equal to man in rights," arguing that "the only limit on the exercise of woman's natural rights is the perpetual tyranny wielded by men; these limits must be reformed by the law of nature and the law of reason." The Declaration continued with the then radical claim that women were "equally entitled to all honors, places, and public employments according to their abilities, without any other distinction than that of their virtues and their talents."

The Englishwoman Mary Wollstonecraft (1759–1797) wrote another important revolutionary manifesto supporting women's rights. *A Vindication of the Rights of Women*, published in 1792, is a treatise embodying Enlightenment faith in reason and in the revolutionary concepts of change and progress. Wollstonecraft held that women, having an equal capacity for reason, should have an equal standing in society. She offered a scathing critique of the social forces that kept women in a position of inferiority. Wollstonecraft developed her revolutionary ideas in the company of a radical group of English artists and writers, including Tom Paine and William Godwin, who sympathized with the aims of the French Revolution.

To the contemporary American, these demands may seem reasonable enough, but it is worth remembering that women did not gain the right to vote in the United States until 1920. And women continue to fight for equality in the workplace, both in competing for jobs on an equal footing and receiving comparable pay for comparable work. Such demands were certainly not considered reasonable at the time of the French Revolution. De Gouges was charged with treason by the National Assembly and sentenced to the guillotine in 1793.

---

its Declaration of the Rights of Man and Citizen, and a constitutional monarchy was established.

THE DEMISE OF THE MONARCHY

Despite the events of August 27, as early as October 5, 1789, Parisian women were back in the streets demonstrating for bread (fig. 16.16). It was on this day that Marie Antoinette made her notorious "Let them eat cake!" declaration. The women simply marched on the palace at Versailles and invaded the inner rooms, causing the Queen to flee for her life, but Louis and Marie Antoinette were escorted back to Paris later that day.

The King ostensibly cooperated for a while with the National Assembly, but in June 1791 he attempted to flee with his family to Luxembourg. The royal retinue was captured and returned to Paris. Then, in April 1792, Austria and Prussia took the opportunity to declare war on the weakened nation, and the Prussian Duke of Brunswick declared he would restore Louis XVI to full sovereignty, revealing an already widespread suspicion that the King was collaborating with the enemy. And so the bourgeois leaders, aided by the working class, invaded the Louvre on August 10, 1792, butchering the King's guard and the royal servants, and over the next forty days arrested and executed over a thousand priests, aristocrats, and royalist sympathizers. On September 21, 1792, a newly assembled National Convention abolished the monarchy in France, and on January 21, 1793, Louis XVI was executed by guillotine in the Place de la Révolution, known today as the Place de la Concorde.

The situation continued to deteriorate. In the summer of 1793, a Committee of Public Safety was formed, headed by MAXIMILIEN DE ROBESPIERRE [ROBES-pea-air] (1758–1794). For fifteen months, France endured the Committee's Reign of Terror. The Terror had three goals: to win the war with

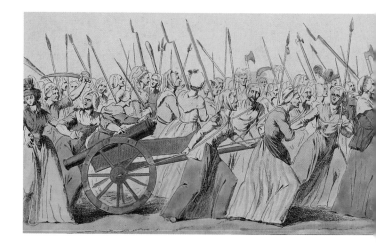

Figure 16.16 *To Versailles, To Versailles, October 5, 1789,* 1789, engraving, Musée de la Ville de Paris, Musée Carnavalet. A contemporary portrait of the events of the day, in which the despair on the face of the aristocratic lady at the far left as the working-class women pass her by, captures the poignancy of the moment.

Austria and Prussia; to establish a "Republic of Virtue"; and to suppress all its enemies. To achieve the latter, the Revolutionary Tribunal of Paris alone handed out 2,639 death sentences, including that of Marie Antoinette, who by this time was referred to simply as "the widow Capet." Throughout France, an estimated twenty thousand people were executed.

NAPOLEON BONAPARTE

In 1795, when the term of the National Convention expired, a political body known as the Directory succeeded to power. It managed to establish peace, but otherwise France was effectively rudderless. Finally, in November 1799, General NAPOLEON BONAPARTE [BONE-ah-part] (1769–1821) staged a *coup d'état*, abolishing the Directory and installing himself, on the Roman model, as First Consul (fig. 16.17).

Napoleon was a hero in Marat's mold (see p. 225), a common man who rose to power through talent and civic sacrifice. Yet he was also a man of uncommon presence. The German philosopher George Wilhelm Hegel described him in 1806: "I have seen [Napoleon] that world-soul, pass through the streets of the town on horseback. It is a prodigious sensation to see an individual like him who, concentrated at one point, seated on a horse, spreads over the world and dominates it." He had no shortage of ego, either, for in 1802 he inquired of the people: "Is Napoleon Bonaparte to be made Consul for Life?" The people answered in the affirmative by 3.5 million votes to eight thousand. After another election in 1804, he declared himself Emperor for Life, establishing hereditary "imperial dignity" for the Bonaparte family. He was crowned Emperor Napoleon I in December 1804. France had, effectively, restored the monarchy.

Napoleon's power and appeal tell us much about the Enlightenment itself. He was the very model of enlightened leadership that the *philosophes* longed for, and he brought to France the stability, peace, and harmony they claimed as the inevitable product of reasoned thought, although his decision to crown himself emperor disillusioned many of his republican supporters. Under Napoleon's regime, the economy boomed again, and he vigorously supported industrial expansion. Cotton production, for instance, quadrupled between 1806 and 1810. In 1800, Napoleon created the Bank of France, which made government borrowing a far easier and more stable matter. But his greatest achievement was the Napoleonic Code, which provided a uniform system of law for the entire country. This was brief and clear, with the aim that every citizen should be capable of understanding it. Together with the Declaration of Independence, the United States Constitution, and the Declaration of the Rights of Man, the Napoleonic Code is one of the great monuments of Enlightenment thought.

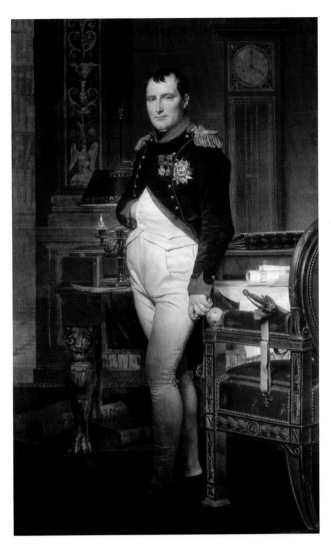

Figure 16.17 Jacques Louis David, *Napoleon in his Study*, 1812, oil on canvas, 2.05 × 1.28 m. Coll. Napoleon, Paris, France. In this prime example of art as political propaganda, Napoleon is shown working all night for the people of France while surrounded by objects that refer to his accomplishments. Napoleon compared himself to the leaders of ancient Rome; his portrait deserves comparison to that of Emperor Augustus (Chapter 5, figure 5.8).

NEOCLASSICISM

✦

If many people in France stopped short of Voltaire's overarching cynicism, they were at least suspicious of the behavior and tastes of their own aristocracy. To painters, it seemed as if the sensuous color and brushwork of the *rubénistes* had led not merely to the excesses of the Rococo but had themselves become the visual sign of a general moral decline. Thus, *poussinistes* once again began to take hold. Poussin's intellectual classicism offered not merely an alternative style to the Rococo but, in its rigor and orderliness, a corrective to the social ills of the state.

As early as 1746, in reviews of the exhibition of the French Academy, critics bemoaned the fact that the grandiose history paintings had disappeared, replaced by the Rococo fantasies Diderot abhorred. Prompted in large measure by the rediscovery of the ancient Roman cities of Herculaneum and Pompeii, in 1738 and 1748 respectively, which were partially excavated from the ashes and volcanic mud that had buried them when volcanic Mt. Vesuvius erupted in A.D. 79, many people began to re-establish classical values in art and state. People identified with the public-minded values of the Greek and Roman heroes who placed moral virtue, patriotic self-sacrifice, and "right action" above all else, and they wanted to see these virtues displayed in painting. By 1775, the French Academy was routinely turning down Rococo submissions to its biennial Salon in favor of more classical subjects, just as Madame du Barry was rejecting Fragonard's panels for her new château. A *new* classicism—a *Neo*classicism—replaced the Rococo almost overnight. Neoclassicism was the style that emerged from the turning away from the Rococo and toward the ancient classical ideals.

PAINTING

Jacques-Louis David.   Perhaps the clearest demonstration of the Neoclassical style in painting is offered by the French artist JACQUES-LOUIS DAVID [dah-VEED] (1748–1825), a follower of Nicolas Poussin. When he left to study in Rome in 1775, David asserted that antique art lacked fire and passion; but, in fact, he was to be thoroughly seduced by it. David grew to be extremely influential in French art, offering his stark, simple painting as an antidote to Rococo frivolity.

His first major commission was for Louis XVI, the *Oath of the Horatii* (fig. 16.18). Three brothers from Rome, the Horatii, pledge an oath upon their weapons which are being held by their father. They vow to fight to the death with the Curatii, three brothers from Alba, to resolve a conflict between the two cities. All figures are accurately drawn, carefully modeled in cold light, as solid as sculpture. In accordance with Neoclassical ideals, the scene is set against the severe architecture of the Roman revival. David, like Poussin, constructed his composition in a series of horizontal planes arranged parallel to the picture plane. Also like Poussin, David subordinated color to line, because he believed that clarity of statement was most important and that such

Figure 16.18   Jacques-Louis David, *Oath of the Horatii*, 1785, oil on canvas, 4′3″ × 6′5¼″ (1.30 × 1.96 cm), The Metropolitan Museum of Art, New York. Neoclassical artists favored subjects taken from ancient literature and history that illustrated high principles or ideals. Excavation of the ancient Roman cities of Herculaneum and Pompeii generated a renewed and widespread interest in the antique.

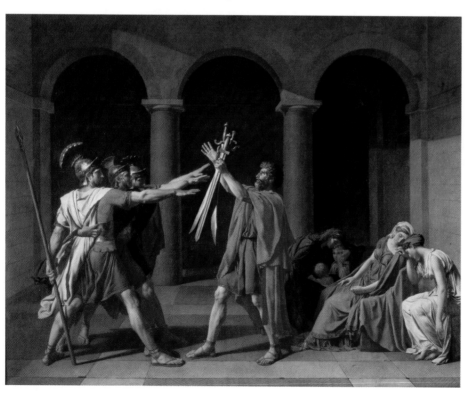

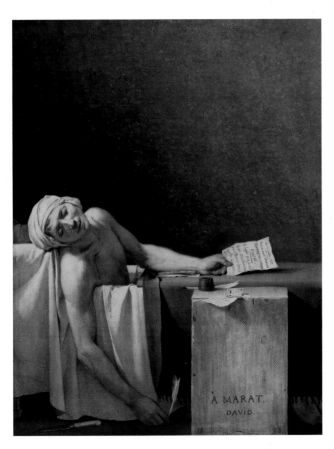

Figure 16.19 Jacques-Louis David, *Death of Marat*, 1793, oil on canvas, 5′5″ × 4′2½″ (1.65 × 1.28 m), Musées Royaux des Beaux-Arts de Belgique, Brussels. The powerful impact of this political memorial is enhanced by the proximity of the figure to the picture plane, stark simplicity of the composition, and immense void in the upper half of the painting.

clarity was best achieved by drawing. As a result, his paintings appear to be drawings that have been colored. David's subject is also a display of Roman heroic stoicism and high principles: the Horatii place patriotic duty above concern for themselves and their family.

When the painting was exhibited at the Salon of 1785, it caused an immediate sensation, not so much because of its Neoclassical style, but because it promoted values that many at once recognized were lacking in the King and his court. By the time of the French Revolution in 1789, the painting was read almost universally as an overtly anti-monarchist statement, though David probably did not originally intend it as such. Interpreted as a call for a new moral commitment on the part of the French state, David's art quickly became that most closely associated with the Revolution. David himself was soon planning parades, gala festivals, and public demonstrations, all designed to rally the people behind the Revolution's cause. He persuaded the revolutionary government to abolish the French Academy, and in its stead to create a panel of experts charged with reforming the public taste.

Meanwhile, the revolutionary government concerned itself with overhauling every aspect of French life. On a minor scale, kings and queens were removed from decks of cards. On a more significant scale, the Christian Sabbath was abolished. Churches were closed and then reopened as "Temples of Reason." Even the traditional Christian calendar was abolished, and the year 1793 became the new revolutionary year 1. David was rapidly commissioned to paint a portrait of the radical journalist and politician Jean-Paul Marat [ma-RAH] (1743–1793), a hero of the Revolution who had been assassinated in his bath by a monarchist sympathizer named Charlotte Corday in July of 1793. Known as the *Death of Marat* (fig. 16.19), but originally entitled *Marat at His Last Breath*, the purpose of the painting was to create a public memorial for the revolutionary hero. The painting was first displayed in the courtyard of the Louvre on October 16, 1793, in full view of Marie Antoinette who was in the square awaiting execution. On that very day David managed to sketch her on her way to the guillotine (see fig. 16.2), in harsh, scornful strokes.

In December of 1793 Marat's bust replaced the crucifix in all the Temples of Reason, and literally hundreds of copies of David's painting were commissioned to hang in public buildings throughout France. On the surface, the painting's style is factual, direct, and simple, to the point of being stark. There is no elaborate setting. The fronts of the tub and box are parallel to that of the picture plane. In David's precise linear style the modeling is hard, the forms smooth, all definitions clear. The large space at the top adds to the drama, as does the contrast of light and dark, reminiscent of Caravaggio. By placing the figure very close to the picture plane, David augments the sense of immediacy and increases the painting's emotional impact. Marat's head seems almost to topple into the viewer's space. But the stark directness of the presentation masks the most important compositional element—Marat's head and right arm hang over the edge of the bath in the traditional manner of Christ at the Deposition. Compare, for example, David's *Death of Marat* to Caravaggio's *Entombment* (see fig. 15.10). The position of Jesus's falling arm in Caravaggio's work is so standard that Marat's pose would have been recognized as the traditional pose of the martyred Jesus. Marat is in fact a secularized version of Jesus, the Christ of the new Revolution.

Angelica Kauffmann. The work of ANGELICA KAUFFMANN [KOFF-mahn] (1741–1807) provides us with an even clearer example of what a painterly representation of virtuous behavior and high moral conduct might look like. The Swiss-born Kauffmann was trained in Italy, where she modeled her figures after the wall paintings at Pompeii and Herculaneum. In 1766, she moved to England, and with her friend Sir Joshua Reynolds helped to found the new British Royal Academy.

Kauffmann's *Cornelia Pointing to Her Children as Her Treasures* (fig. 16.20), of 1785, champions family values, simple dress, and austere interiors. Gone are Rococo depictions of women wearing the elegant and refined dress of the Rococo salon. In their place are the mothers of the new society. When a visitor asks to see her family treasures, Cornelia points with pride to her two sons (the Gracchi), both of whom were to grow up to become leaders of the Roman Republic, repossessing public land

from the decadent Roman aristocracy and redistributing it to the poor. This was precisely the spirit that drove the leaders of the French Revolution.

Benjamin West.   One of Kauffmann's closest friends in London was the American painter BENJAMIN WEST (1738–1820), another founder of the Royal Academy. West was best known for his revision of the idea of history painting. For the Academy's exhibition of 1770, he chose to portray a contemporary event, the *Death of General Wolfe* (fig. 16.21), the British military leader who had been killed in 1759 in a battle with the French for control of Quebec. Sir Joshua Reynolds was horrified. It seemed to him in bad taste to depict con-

Figure 16.20   Angelica Kauffmann, *Cornelia Pointing to Her Children as Her Treasures*, 1785, oil on canvas, 3′4″ × 4′2″ (1.02 × 1.27 m), Virginia Museum, Richmond. In contrast to Rococo frivolity, Neoclassical art was intended to serve a public role in encouraging virtue. In this story from ancient republican Rome, when asked about her treasures, Cornelia points to her children, who went on to do good deeds on behalf of the poor.

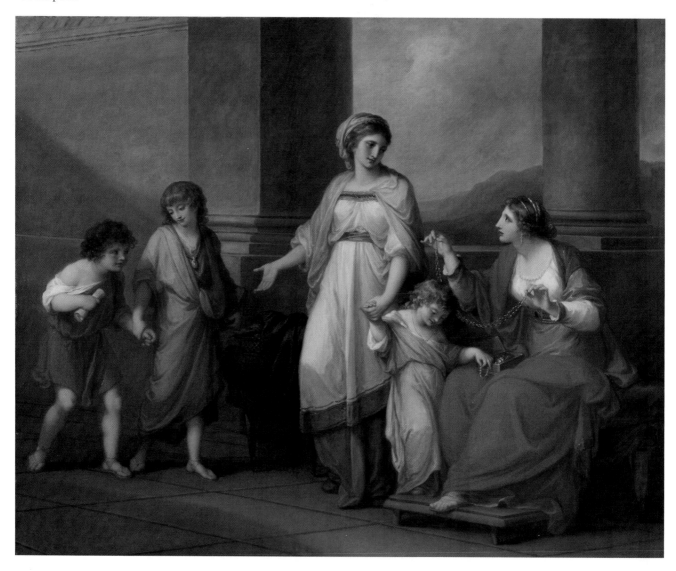

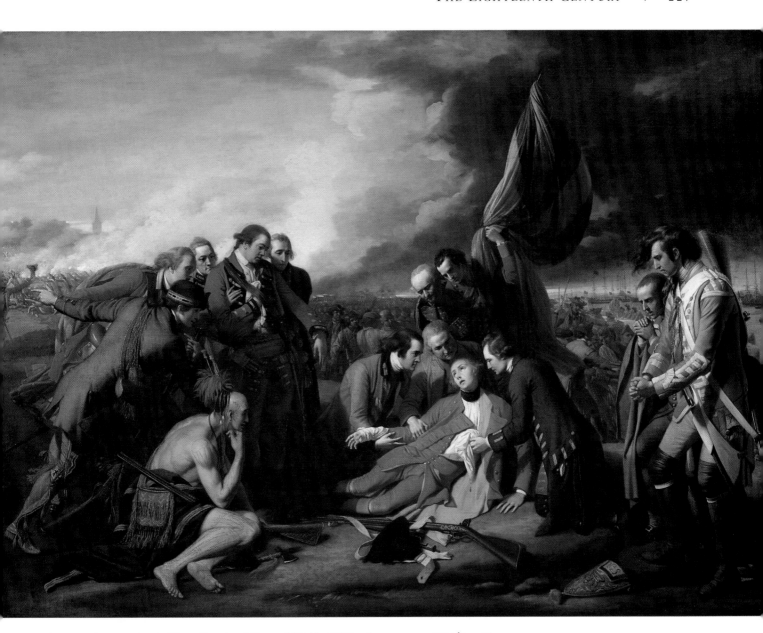

Figure 16.21 Benjamin West, *Death of General Wolfe*, 1770, oil on canvas, 4′11½″ × 7′ (1.51 × 2.13 m), National Gallery of Canada, Ottawa. West glorified a contemporary military hero, General Wolfe, who died in 1759 in the war against the French. Although criticized by Sir Joshua Reynolds, president of London's Royal Academy, for showing figures in contemporary clothing, the combination of Wolfe's pose, the spotlight, and the turbulent sky bring to mind depictions of the death of Christ.

temporary heroes, and the British King George III warned that he would not purchase any painting showing British soldiers in modern dress. Despite protest, when the painting was displayed, it quickly won the favor of all viewers because of its dramatic intensity and extraordinary realism. Like David's Marat, Wolfe's pose suggests a traditional posture of Jesus, this time the Deposition (descent from the Cross). A Native American contemplates the hero's death, the scene underscoring the leader's nobility and courage.

John Singleton Copley. Another American expatriate working in London was JOHN SINGLETON COPLEY [COP-lee] (1738–1815) of Boston. New England's leading portraitist, Copley went to England in 1774, studied in London, gained admission to the Royal Academy, and remained there the rest of his life. Copley's *Watson and the Shark* (fig. 16.22), of 1778, depicts a contemporary event with a kind of immediacy and realism that anticipates the painting of the next century. The event was real: A man named Brook Watson

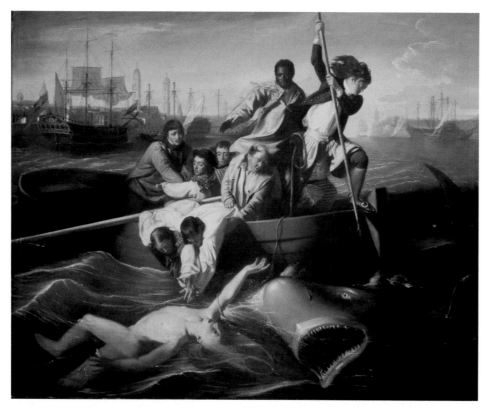

Figure 16.22   John Singleton Copley, *Watson and the Shark*, 1778, oil on canvas, $6'\frac{1}{2}'' \times 7'6\frac{1}{4}''$ (1.84 × 2.29 m), Museum of Fine Arts, Boston. Copley's painting has all the drama of a modern adventure film—a struggle for survival against nature depicted at the climactic moment and with the outcome left uncertain—combined with heroic nudity.

had indeed encountered a shark while swimming in the harbor of Havana, Cuba. The painting shows the scene as the shark lunges for Watson, while two men reach out for him, straining, their faces showing their anguish, and another man grasps the shirt of one to prevent him from falling overboard. The drama is increased by the dramatic lighting and the dynamic diagonal movements. Copley paints a cliff-hanger—the viewer is left wondering whether Watson will survive. In fact, Watson had long escaped the shark when he commissioned the painting years later as a publicity ploy while running for political office.

SCULPTURE

Jean-Antoine Houdon.   One of France's greatest sculptors was JEAN-ANTOINE HOUDON [ooh-DON] (1741–1828), born at the Palace of Versailles where his father was a servant. Later his father became the caretaker for the school for advanced students in the French Academy of Painting and Sculpture, enabling Houdon to associate with artists from the time he was eight years old. It is said that as a child he would sneak into class, steal some clay, and imitate what he saw.

He learned well, for he won the Prix de Rome, which enabled him to study in Italy from 1764 to 1769.

Houdon was unrivaled in his day as a portrait sculptor. Even Americans ventured forth to commission him while they were in Paris: Benjamin Franklin (1778); John Paul Jones (1780); and Thomas Jefferson (1789). Houdon worked to create highly lifelike images. He took precise measurements of his sitters and usually made a terra cotta model while working with the sitter. This model was given to his assistants, who blocked out the form in marble; then Houdon did the fine carving and polishing.

The Statue of George Washington.   In order to portray George Washington (fig. 16.23), Houdon went to America and stayed for two weeks in October 1785 as a guest in Washington's home at Mount Vernon, Virginia. Houdon made a cast of Washington's face and a plaster bust, but returned to Paris to carve the life-size figure in stone, working on the project from 1788 to 1792.

During that time Houdon also made a statue of Washington in classical garb. Although the version finally selected shows Washington wearing contemporary attire, it, too, has links to the classical past. Washington stands in the antique *contrapposto* pose. His left hand rests on thirteen bound rods, or ancient *fasces*, symbolizing both the original States of the Union and the power and authority of ancient Rome. Behind the *fasces* are sword and plow, representing war and peace.

ARCHITECTURE

Chiswick House. An excellent example of Neoclassical architecture in England is provided by Chiswick House (fig. 16.24) in west London, begun in 1725 and built by LORD BURLINGTON (1694–1753) and WILLIAM KENT (1685–1748). Burlington was himself an amateur architect, but his team included trained architects.

Like its prototypes, including the Roman Pantheon (see Chapter 5), Chiswick House is geometrically simple yet stately. The classical vocabulary and proportions are all-important. Symmetry is maintained at all costs, even when it makes things inconvenient within the home. In the academic Neoclassical style, regularity, reason, and logic dominate over imaginative variation. This is in marked contrast to the emotion and drama of the Baroque as well as the Rococo styles. In Neoclassical buildings, the walls are flat and the decoration relatively austere compared to that of Rococo interiors, with their abundantly ornamented, animated, even undulating architectural elements.

La Madeleine. In France the Neoclassical style was promulgated in particular by Napoleon, who longed to rebuild Paris as the new Rome. The church of La

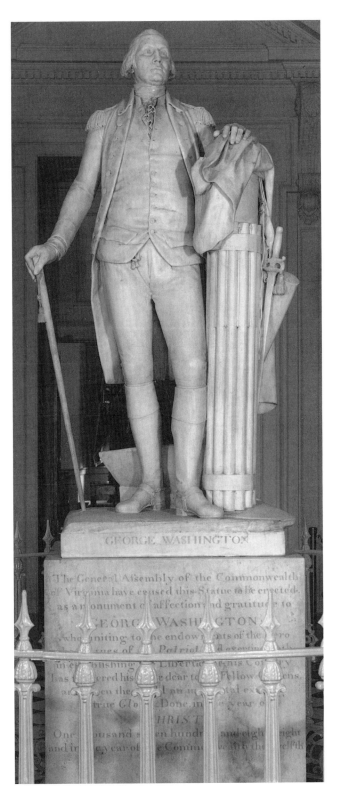

Figure 16.23 Jean-Antoine Houdon, *George Washington*, 1788–92, marble, height 6′2″ (1.88 m), State Capitol, Richmond, Virginia. Calm, composed, and commanding, this version of Washington in his general's attire was favored over another version in classical attire. Still, antique echoes are seen in the *contrapposto* pose and the thirteen *fasces* (rods) bound together, representing the States of the Union.

Figure 16.24 Lord Burlington and William Kent, Chiswick House, begun 1725, west London. The architectural lineage of this house, with its central dome, triangular pediment, and columnar portico, can be traced back to the ancient Roman Pantheon (see Chapter 5).

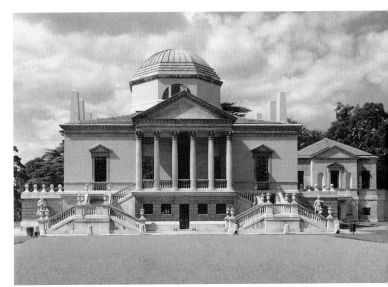

Madeleine in Paris (fig. 16.25) had been started by Louis XVI, but Napoleon himself rededicated it in 1806 as a Temple of Glory to be designed by PIERRE-ALEXANDRE VIGNON [VEE-nyonh] (1762–1829).

Napoleon conceived of La Madeleine as a monument to his military victories and as a repository for his trophies. Reflecting the great interest in archaeology at this time, the exterior is an accurate reconstruction of an ancient Roman temple. It has a raised base, steps across the front only, a colonnade of the Corinthian order, entablature, pediments, and a peaked roof. Although highly dignified, there is something a little stark about La Madeleine's archaeological accuracy. Individual imagination seems absent. The interior belies the exterior, its ceiling consisting of three consecutive domes; thus, unlike its ancient Greek and Roman prototypes, the exterior and interior are not coordinated. After Napoleon's death the building once again reverted to being used as a church.

Monticello. The Neoclassical style of architecture also achieved prominence in the United States where the new American presidents, believing it to embody enlightened, democratic leadership, championed its use in public architecture. One of the most notable Neoclassical designs in the United States is the private home of President THOMAS JEFFERSON (1743–1826), known as Monticello [MON-tih-CHELL-o], in Charlottesville, Virginia (fig. 16.26). Jefferson drew up the designs for it himself in 1769. An adaptation of Burlington and Kent's Chiswick House, it was built between 1770 and 1806. Unlike its prototypes in stone topped by simple domes, Monticello is constructed of brick and wood and capped with a polygonal dome. The deep **portico**, or porch, here supported on Doric columns, was to become very popular in the southern United States, as seen in some of the great antebellum homes in Mississippi. The portico provided protection from the sun and added dignity and splendor to the building; the northern equivalent was much shallower. The plan of Monticello reveals the almost perfect symmetry of the house, with entrances on each of the four sides. Its rooms are laid out on either side of a central hall and drawing-room.

A leading architect of his time, Jefferson fostered classical ideas in America. He studied the ancient Roman temple known as the Maison Carrée in Nîmes, France,

Figure 16.25 Pierre-Alexandre Vignon, La Madeleine, Paris, 1806–42, main facade, length 350′ (106.68 m), width 147′ (44.81 m), height of podium 23′ (7.01 m), height of columns 63′ (19.20 m). La Madeleine is based upon the rectangular temple type, such as the Greek Parthenon (see Chapter 4).

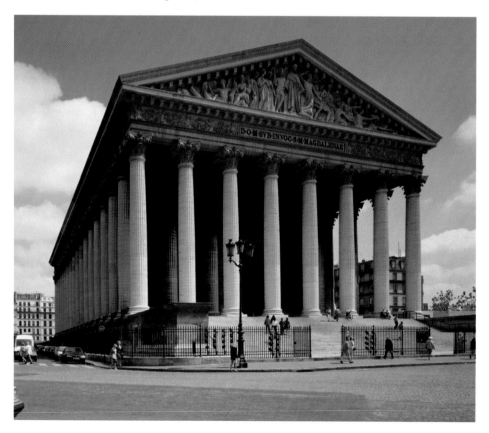

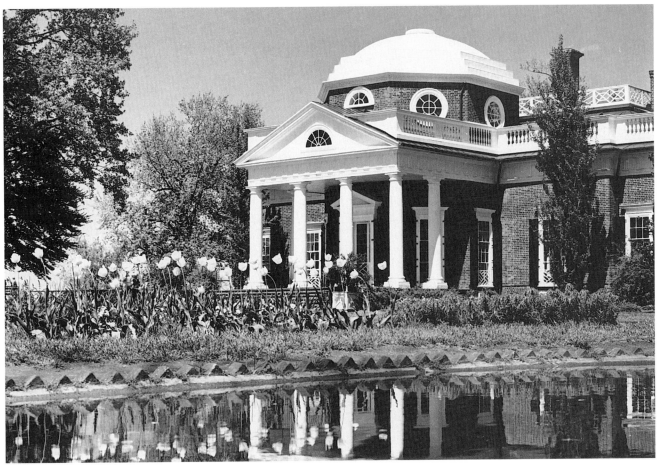

Figure 16.26 Thomas Jefferson, Monticello, Charlottesville, Virginia, 1770–1806, main facade. Neoclassical architecture was favored in America for its formal symmetry and antique associations. At Monticello a temple of stone and concrete has been translated into a home of brick and wood.

and used it as the model for the Virginia State Capitol (1785–98), an example of austere Neoclassicism in its deliberate rejection of the Baroque and the Rococo.

LITERATURE

The Novel. During the eighteenth century, the novel as we think of it today came into being. It focused on particular people doing particular things in everyday and ordinary circumstances, and its popularity among the reading public was enormous. Here were characters like the readers themselves, suddenly elevated to the level of heroes and heroines, admired (or, if villainous, despised) by all. Although male writers such as Samuel Richardson, Henry Fielding, and Daniel Defoe created the prototypes of the novel, it was a woman from a country parish who gave it its most enduring popular form.

Jane Austen. One of the most important novelists of her day, JANE AUSTEN (1775–1817) was born the

daughter of a clergyman and spent the first twenty-five years of her life at her parents' home in Hampshire, where she wrote her first novels, *Northanger Abbey*, *Sense and Sensibility* and *Pride and Prejudice*. None of these works was actually published until the second decade of the nineteenth century, when Austen was almost forty. She came from a large and affectionate family, and her novels reflect a delight in family life; they are essentially social comedies. Above all else, they are about manners, good and bad. They advocate the behavioral norms by which "decent" society must and should operate. They are also deeply romantic books that have marriage as their goal and end. Austen was not so naive as to believe that good marriages could come from alliances built solely upon social advantage; it is her scenes showing romantic love, not expedient matrimony, that draw the reader's sympathy.

Austen called herself a "miniaturist," by which she meant that her ambition was to capture realistic and intimate portraits of her characters and the time in which they lived. So convincing is her presentation of human beings, with all their foibles, attempting to enjoy and prosper in life with one another, that her novels have attained an almost monumental status that has lasted from the time of their publication down to the present day.

CLASSICAL MUSIC

Musical classicism, or the **Classical** style, developed with particular elegance and thoroughness in Vienna. The first of the great Viennese Classical composers was Franz Joseph Haydn, and the greatest of them was Wolfgang Amadeus Mozart. But the composer who began in the Classical vein and later became known for his Romantic style was Ludwig van Beethoven. Beethoven thus serves as a link between the Classical and Romantic eras in Western music.

The Classical period is distinguished by the growth of a popular audience for serious music, highlighted by the rise of the public concert. As in so many other areas of eighteenth-century life, we see a shift in social focus from the aristocracy and the court to the wants and needs of the middle class, a middle class that demanded from composers a more accessible and recognizable musical language than that provided by the complex patterns of, say, a Baroque fugue.

The Symphony.
The **symphony** is what is known as a "large" form: it consists of several distinct parts, called movements, that proceed in a predictable pattern. The challenge the composer faces is to create fresh and inventive compositions without diverging from the predictable format. A symphony typically consists of four movements:

First Movement—The pace of the movement is fast, usually *allegro*, and its mood usually dramatic.
Second Movement—This movement is slow (*adagio* or *andante*, for instance), and its mood reflective.
Third Movement—The pace picks up moderately, and the period's most popular dance, the stately and elegant aristocratic minuet, often serves as the basis for the movement.
Fourth Movement—Once again, the fourth movement is fast (*allegro*), spirited (*vivace*), or light and happy.

Over the course of the eighteenth century, audiences became educated in these conventions; in part the excitement of hearing a new composition centered on the anticipation the listeners felt as the composer moved inventively through this predictable pattern. It was in this period that the seating arrangement of the standard symphony orchestra became fixed (fig. 16.27).

Each symphonic movement also possessed its own largely predictable internal form. The first and fourth movements usually employed **sonata** (or sonata-allegro) form, the second was sometimes in this form but just as often a **theme and variations** or a **rondo**, and the third was generally a **minuet and trio**.

The word sonata derives from the Italian *sonare*, "to sound," as distinguished from cantata, which derives from the Italian *cantare*, meaning "to sing." Sonata form itself consists of three sections: Exposition, Development, and Recapitulation, the last of which is often followed by a Coda, or tailpiece. The overall structure suggests a pattern of departure and return. The exposition introduces the movement's themes, the development section modifies and advances them, and the recapitulation returns home to the main theme.

Each of the other movements of the symphony employs this pattern of departure and return but in slightly different terms. In the theme and variations, the main theme is introduced and then recurs again and again in varied form. In a rondo, a single theme repeats itself with new material added between each repetition. The minuet and trio possesses an ABA structure. That is, a minuet ("A") is presented, followed by a contrasting trio section ("B"), before the return of the minuet ("A"). The trio section contrasts with the minuet in that it is written for fewer instruments, though not necessarily for three instruments, as the name suggests.

Franz Joseph Haydn.
Raised as a choirboy at St. Stephen's Cathedral in Vienna, FRANZ JOSEPH HAYDN [HIGH-din] (1732–1809) entered the employ of Prince Esterházy in 1761, serving as a court musician. Haydn composed so many symphonies—more than a hundred—in so many variations that he is known as the "father" of the form. His career not only defines this transition from court to public music, but it also marks the moment when musicians and composers finally attained the social status that painters, sculptors, and architects had enjoyed since as early as the Renaissance. Recognized at last for their genius, composers became sought-after celebrities, who were wined and dined in Europe's most prestigious social circles.

Haydn worked for Prince Esterházy for nearly thirty years, during which time he remained isolated in his palace at Eisenstadt, about thirty miles south of Vienna; but here he was free to experiment with all the musical forms available to him. He began work in Esterházy's service as essentially a servant, living in a small apartment above the palace kitchen; it was years before the aristocracy viewed composers as worthy society.

Haydn's "Farewell" Symphony No. 45 of 1772 was conceived as an explicit protest at the living conditions at Eisenstadt. Esterházy did not allow his musicians to bring their families to the palace. Thus, living in crowded servant quarters, they were forced to be away from their loved ones for long periods at a time. Performing one evening at court, the musicians played the symphony's three uneventful movements, but in the middle of the fourth movement, the second horn player and the first oboist suddenly stopped playing, packed up their instruments, blew out the candles that illuminated their

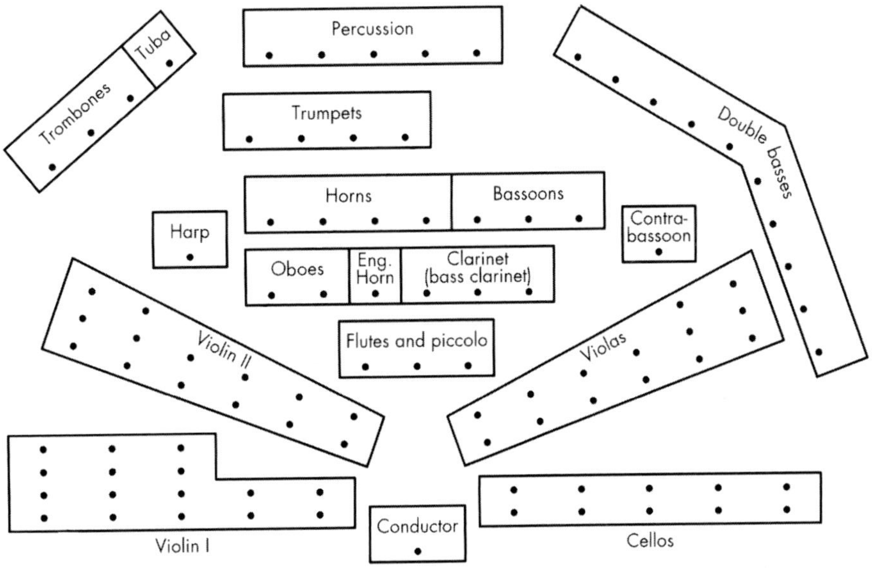

Figure 16.27
Plan of the symphony orchestra. The seating plan of the major instruments used in an orchestra has not changed much in centuries.

scores, and left the hall. Slowly, the rest of the orchestra followed suit until no one was left except two violinists, who finished the symphony. The Prince immediately understood the implications of the performance and granted his musicians an extended leave to visit their families.

When Esterházy died in 1790, his son, who did not much care for music, disbanded the orchestra, and Haydn returned to Vienna. By now he was internationally renowned. A concert promoter from London, Johann Peter Salomon, offered him a commission, and in 1791 he left Vienna for England. There, he was received by the royal court, awarded an honorary doctorate at Oxford, and began to reap the financial benefits by conducting public subscription concerts of new work, particularly the famous "London" Symphonies, which were acclaimed by the public as no other music ever had been before.

Wolfgang Amadeus Mozart. Perhaps the greatest of the classical composers was WOLFGANG AMADEUS MOZART [MOAT-zart] (1756–1791), born and raised in Salzburg, Austria. His first music teacher was his father, Leopold, himself an accomplished musician and composer. Young Mozart's musical genius was immediately evident in his early piano- and violin-playing and in his composing, which he began at the age of five. His genius was widely recognized throughout Europe; he toured with his sister Maria Anna (called Nannerl) under his father's tutelage. Though he had enormous musical gifts, Mozart suffered from depression and illness and as an adult had a difficult time securing a regular income. Even though he achieved stunning

successes in Vienna, especially with his operas, when he died at the age of thirty-five he was heavily in debt.

During his brief life Mozart composed more than six hundred works. He wrote forty-one symphonies along with twenty-seven piano concertos and nine concertos for other instruments. He composed large numbers of chamber works and a significant volume of choral music, including his great *Requiem*, which remained unfinished at his death. Mozart also composed some of the most popular operas ever written, including the frequently performed *Marriage of Figaro* (1786), the towering *Don Giovanni* (1787), and the much-loved *Magic Flute* (1791).

Don Giovanni is based on the story of the legendary Spanish nobleman, Don Juan, who was notorious for his seduction of women. Mozart, well aware of the amorous goings-on in all the great courts of Europe, subtly mocked them in this work. His opera begins with Don Giovanni killing the outraged father of a young noblewoman he has just seduced. At the end of the opera, the dead man returns in the form of a statue which comes sufficiently alive to drag Don Giovanni down to hell. Between these two dramatic episodes, Mozart portrays Don Giovanni's seduction of three women, blending seriousness with humor.

An early scene from Act I reveals Don Giovanni at work in music that captures the Don's persuasive appeal for the peasant girl Zerlina (fig. 16.28), whom he has promised to marry if she comes to his palace. Mozart has the would-be lovers sing a duet entitled "*Là ci darem la mano*" ("There, you will give me your hand"). Don Giovanni begins with an attractive image of their intertwined future. Zerlina's ambivalent response indicates her desire for the Don and her fear that he may be trick-

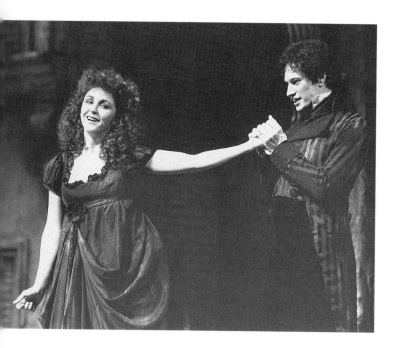

Figure 16.28   A scene from *Don Giovanni* by Wolfgang Amadeus Mozart. The opera premiered in 1787. Here, in Act I, Don Giovanni (played by Sherrill Milnes) seduces the innocent Zerlina (Teresa Stratas) in the duet "*Là ci darem la mano*."

ing her. Following this initial exchange, Mozart speeds up their interaction to show Zerlina's increasing acquiescence, and then blends their voices to suggest their final mutual accord. The scene is doubly pleasing. It portrays an actual seduction, one that any audience can enjoy, and it exposes Don Giovanni for the rake that he is, thus allowing the audience both to warm to and detest Mozart's anti-hero. The wide range of feelings typifies Mozart's music and in part accounts for his enduring popularity.

TOWARD ROMANTICISM

BEETHOVEN: FROM CLASSICAL TO ROMANTIC

LUDWIG VAN BEETHOVEN [BAY-tove-in] (1770–1827) was born during the age of the Enlightenment, came to maturity during a period of political and social revolution, and died as the Romantic era was in full flower. His work and his life reveal a tension between the Classical style of the past and the newly emerging Romantic tendencies in art. In his middle period, Beethoven enlarged the scope of the Classical style, while in his later works he transcended it, moving in new musical directions.

Beethoven was born and raised in Bonn, in the German Rhineland. At the age of twenty-one he went to Vienna, where he remained for the rest of his life. He became known in his twenties for his prodigious ability on the piano, especially for his improvisational skill. By the time he was thirty, Beethoven was recognized as an innovative and creative composer (fig. 16.29). Unlike other musicians and composers of his time, he was determined to remain a free artist, and, with the help of a number of sympathetic patrons, he supported himself solely through composing and performing his music. Beethoven was aided by the growth of music publishing and an increase in concert life fueled by the rise of a middle-class public with an appetite for serious music.

Among the most significant experiences of Beethoven's life was the onset of deafness, which began to afflict him around 1800, just as his music was attracting serious acclaim. He nearly committed suicide. In 1802, he wrote his famous Heiligenstadt testament—an agonized letter to his brother describing his suicidal thoughts and his eventual victory over them: "I would have ended my life—it was only my art that held me back. Ah, it seemed to me impossible to leave the world until I had brought forth all that I felt was within me."

Figure 16.29   *Beethoven Holding His "Missa Solemnis,"* oil on canvas. This Romantic portrait of a composer obsessed with his work conveys some of Beethoven's passionate genius.

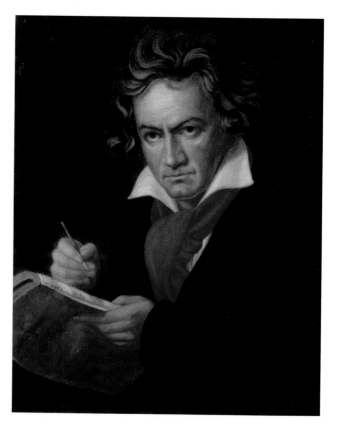

Cross Currents

TURKISH MILITARY MUSIC AND VIENNESE COMPOSERS

Western Europeans had long been fascinated with the "exotic." During the eighteenth century there was increased cultural interaction with Turkey, then part of the Ottoman Empire. Although at the time it represented a threat to Austria, the Austrian Habsburg Empire enjoyed a taste for things Turkish and Ottoman. Viennese cuisine reflected the influence of Turkish spices. Viennese fashion exhibited Turkish influence in flowing garments and brightly decorative ribbons and braiding in women's attire. Viennese music incorporated elements of the music of Turkish military bands, composed of musicians mounted on horseback playing drums and shawms, long-tubed horns used in medieval Western as well as medieval Turkish music. In the seventeenth century, trumpets, cymbals, bells, and additional types of drums were added to Turkish military bands. Later, during the nineteenth century, some pianos were equipped with a special pedal for creating unusual percussive effects reminiscent of these instruments.

All three of the great Viennese composers of the time reveal the influence of the Turkish military band. Haydn wrote three military symphonies, whose titles reflect the martial nature of their music, including the "Drum Roll" and the "Military." Mozart included Turkish percussive musical elements in his opera *The Abduction from the Seraglio*. He also entitled the rondo movement from his piano sonata K. 331 "Rondo alla Turca," a spirited piece with a section reflective of Turkish military music. Beethoven was also inspired by Turkish music, as is evidenced by his *Turkish March*, and in themes from the fourth movement of his Ninth Symphony. Moreover, inspired by the whirling dance of Islamic Turks, Beethoven wrote his *Chorus for Whirling Dervishes*, a work whose theme is repeated in increasing intensity and in quicker tempos, imitating the trance induced by the whirling dance of the Sufi dervishes (see Chapter 7).

Living through this traumatic experience strengthened Beethoven, and the music he wrote afterwards exhibited a new depth of feeling and imaginative power. By 1815, Beethoven was almost entirely deaf, but this did not stop him from composing and conducting his music. In the end, Beethoven's deafness was more of a social affliction than a musical one. He increasingly separated himself from society, for which his rebellious and fiery temperament ill suited him.

Beethoven produced an abundance of music, including thirty-two piano sonatas and nine symphonies, which set the standard against which the symphonic efforts of all subsequent composers have been measured.

The Three Periods of Beethoven's Music. Beethoven's music can be divided into three periods, each reflecting differences in stylistic development. During the first period, which lasted until about 1802, Beethoven wrote works mainly in the Classical style, adhering to the formal elements established by Haydn and perfected by Mozart before him. In the middle period (1803–14), referred to as the "heroic" phase, his works become more dramatic; they are also noticeably longer than those of his Classical predecessors. The first movement of the Third Symphony is, for instance, as long as many full symphonies of Haydn and Mozart. And his compositions in this period modulate between the most gentle and appealing melodies and the most dynamic and forceful writing—not only between works, but within each work.

Beethoven's final period of composition spans the years 1815–27, during which he was almost completely deaf. In this period, Beethoven not only departed from the constraints of Classical compositional practice, but also entered new musical territory and reached new levels of spiritual profundity. Works from the late period include, among many others, his Ninth Symphony, considered by many the greatest symphony ever written; the last piano sonatas; and the deeply spiritual *Missa Solemnis*.

Symphony No. 5 in C Minor, Opus 67. Beethoven's most famous work probably remains, nonetheless, his middle period Symphony No. 5 in C Minor, Opus 67, a work that still defines the idea of the symphony in the popular imagination. He completed it in 1808. One of the most tightly unified compositions Beethoven ever wrote, its opening four-note motif is perhaps the best known of all symphonic themes. Out of that brief fragment of musical material, Beethoven constructs a dramatic and intense opening movement. He uses its rhythmic pattern of three short notes followed by a longer one in each remaining movement and further unifies the work by returning to the theme of the third movement during a dramatic passage in the fourth movement. Overall, the symphony moves from struggle and dramatic conflict to triumphant and majestic exultation.

The first movement, marked *Allegro con brio*, "fast with spirit," opens abruptly with the famous "Fate knocking on the door" theme—short-short-short-long:

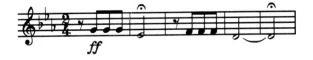

Beethoven repeats this musical motif relentlessly throughout the exposition before a bridge passage leads to a second, contrasting, and more lyrical theme, which is accompanied in the cellos and basses by the first four-note theme. Additional musical ideas fill out the movement, including a development section that breaks the main theme into smaller and smaller units and a recapitulation that features a surprising lyrical oboe solo.

The second movement, in theme and variations form, provides relief from the unabating tension created in the first. Two themes dominate the movement, the first sung by cellos and violas, the second by clarinets. Both receive extensive variation throughout the movement. The overall effect combines noble grandeur with sheer lyrical beauty.

The third movement, a scherzo, begins with a mysterious theme introduced quietly by cellos and basses, followed by a loud theme blared out by the horns on a single repeated note.

The fourth movement, a scherzs, in C Major, is cast in sonata form, with an extensive coda, one of the most dramatic Beethoven wrote. For this, he enlarged the orchestra: a high-pitched piccolo extends the orchestral range upward, a low-pitched contrabassoon extends it downward, and three extra trombones add power. Beethoven presents four themes first, then a stunning coda that appears to end a number of times before he finally brings the movement and the symphony to a triumphant conclusion.

It is perhaps because Beethoven became isolated from the natural world by his deafness that he was able to redefine the creative act of composition. It was no longer, as it had been for centuries, considered a function of objective laws and rules of harmony, but the expression of deeply personal and often introspective feelings. It is to this interior world that artists of the nineteenth century, the so-called Romantics, turned their attention.

GARDENS

Beethoven's music does not serve as the only bridge between the eighteenth and nineteenth centuries. Quite literally, the seeds of what would blossom as full-blown Romanticism were most firmly planted in the English garden, which embodies the spirit of a shifting attitude toward nature.

Gardens during the Baroque era had been designed according to the same aesthetic principles as those followed by the *poussinistes*, disciples of Poussin and his revived classical ideals in painting, exemplified in Bernini's orderly colonnade for St. Peter's and in Le Vau's symmetrical facade for the palace at Versailles. The gardens at Versailles (fig. 16.30) give full expression to the ancient ideals of geometric order and symmetry. The garden plans were controlled and classical in design, with neat, straight, geometric paths and walkways, tightly clipped hedges with precise borders, and beds containing orderly arrangements of flowers. Organized around a major central axis running from north to south,

Figure 16.30 The gardens at the château of Versailles, designed by André Le Nôtre, 1662–68. Everything in the gardens of Versailles is carefully planned. Flower beds are carefully and symmetrically arranged, hedges clipped, and pathways edged and groomed.

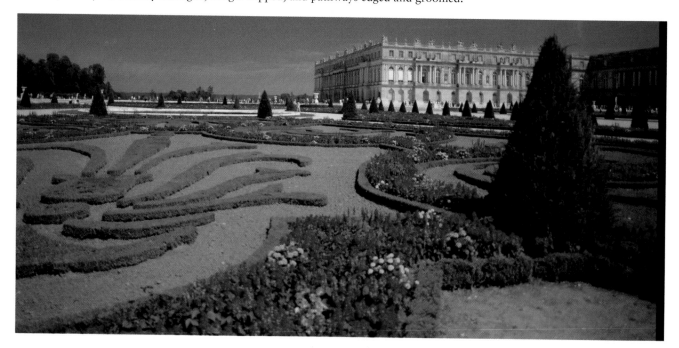

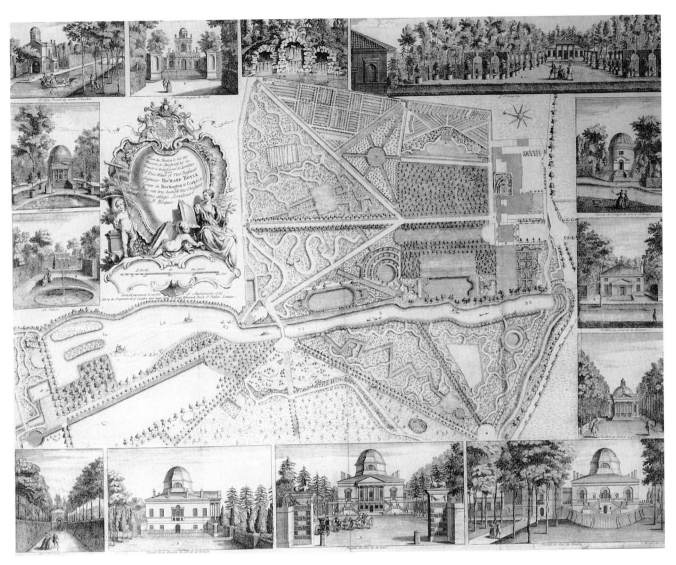

Figure 16.31 John Rocque, *Engraved Survey of Chiswick* (1736). The "twinings and windings" of the path in this garden designed by William Kent are evident in this plan. In contrast to the formal French garden, the English garden was planned to look unplanned.

Versailles is an expression of the mind's—and, by extension, the king's—dominance over nature.

In the seventeenth century, in his *Sacred Theory of the Earth* (1681), Thomas Burnet wrote that there is "nothing in Nature more shapeless or ill-figured" than a mountain: "if you look upon an Heap of them together, or a mountainous Country, they are the greatest Examples of Confusion that we know in Nature." In contrast, Edmund Burke, a member of Samuel Johnson's "Club" and a late eighteenth-century political theorist, wrote that mountains were "sublime" and capable of creating a sense of infinite awe, as close as we can get on earth to the infinity of God. In the later eighteenth century and the Romantic era, it became fashionable for every educated person of English society to go on a "Grand Tour" of the European continent, which includ-

ed seeing the Alps as well as visiting Paris, Florence, and Rome. This shift in the human relationship to nature in large part took place over the course of the eighteenth century and is particularly apparent in the gardens of Neoclassical houses such as Jefferson's Monticello and Lord Burlington's estate at Chiswick, which had gardens designed for it in the 1730s by William Kent.

The new English garden, unlike that in the classical Baroque style, looks far less kempt, although it is every bit as calculated in its innovative and non-geometric design. Superficially, the English Neoclassical garden is defined by the variety and surprising nature of its many views. As the plan for Chiswick demonstrates (fig. 16.31), instead of the straight, geometrical paths of the French garden, its English counterpart has walkways that are, in the words of one garden writer of the day,

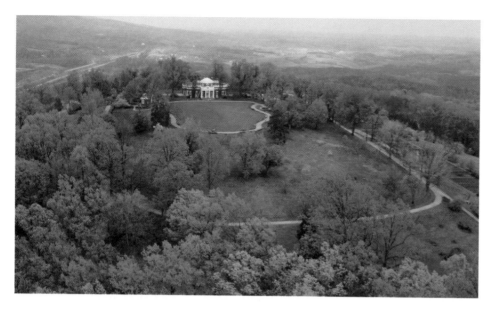

Figure 16.32   View from the garden path at Monticello. Situated on the top of a hill near the Virginia Blue Ridge, Jefferson's garden overlooks a variety of what were in his time near-wilderness landscapes.

"serpentine meanders … with many twinings and windings." This was not a new idea. In ancient Rome, Pliny had commented on the "wiggly" paths of contemporary gardens. However, the Neoclassicists went beyond this, planning to "throw open" an entire estate to become a garden, a Roman pastoral setting worthy of Ovid, uniting lawns and fields with walks, plantings, woods, lakes (often artificial), and marshes. Instead of the "the neatness and elegance" of Versailles, the English garden is defined by its "artificial rudeness," that is, by its (still carefully controlled) "wild" look.

It is in just such a garden, Pemberley Woods, that Elizabeth Bennet and her aunt find themselves in Chapter 43 of Jane Austen's *Pride and Prejudice*:

> The park was very large, and contained great variety of ground. They entered it in one of its lowest points, and drove for some time through a beautiful wood stretching over a wide extent.
>
> Elizabeth's mind was too full for conversation, but she saw and admired every remarkable spot and point of view. They gradually ascended for half a mile, and then found themselves at the top of a considerable eminence, where the wood ceased, and the eye was instantly caught by Pemberley House, situated on the opposite side of a valley, into which the road with some abruptness wound. It was a large, handsome stone building, standing well on rising ground, and backed by a ridge of high woody hills; and in front, a stream of some natural importance was swelled into greater, but without any artificial appearance. Its banks were neither formal nor falsely adorned. Elizabeth was delighted. She had never seen a place for which nature had done more, or where natural beauty had been so little counteracted by an awkward taste.

Elizabeth is surprised by the views, but it is Mr. Darcy who astonishes her the most with his good behavior and natural "civility" when she meets him in the grounds. In fact, the Pemberley Woods become for Elizabeth a sort of metaphor for Darcy himself. She soon believes that she has never seen a man for whom "nature had done more."

By the late eighteenth century, many people, including Thomas Jefferson, had come to believe that landscape gardening was, in fact, one of the highest of the arts, marking the next shift in attitude toward nature—the position held by the Romantics. Jefferson toured England expressly to view English gardens, and by 1807 he had designed a serpentine path around the crown of the hill at Monticello, with its own variety of views (fig. 16.32), each reaching out to a different aspect of his grounds. Alexander Pope, whose own gardens at Twickenham were of the English variety, wrote: "All gardening is landscape painting," i.e. gardens should be designed in such a way as to astonish and delight the viewer. The art consisted not just in making the artificial appear natural, which is the constant aim of all representation, but in making the natural appear better and more natural than nature itself. The Englishman William Chambers wrote in 1772 that "gardens can arouse greater passions than anything known to man," because they never repeat themselves. At every turn, the prospect they offer should be new. It is the English garden, with its unpredictability, its variety, and its multiplicity, that most thoroughly stirred the Romantic imagination in the next century.

READINGS

↗

↩ **ALEXANDER POPE**

An Essay on Man

An Essay on Man (1733) presents Pope's view of moral virtue as a basis for happiness. In this poem Pope celebrates virtue and reason as twin sources of stability and harmony, the kind of balance and orderliness that Pope himself struggled to achieve in his life as well as in his art. An example of Pope's fine ear for rhyme along with his sure sense of how sound echoes sense can be heard in the following passage from An Essay on Man, *a passage that also reflects the eighteenth-century tendency toward satire as it simultaneously suggests Pope's view of humankind's place in the order of creation.*

Awake, my ST. JOHN! leave all meaner things
To low ambition, and the pride of Kings.
Let us (since Life can little more supply
Than just to look about us and to die)
Expatiate free o'er all this scene of Man;   *5*
A mighty maze! but not without a plan;
A Wild, where weeds and flow'rs promiscuous shoot,
Or Garden, tempting with forbidden fruit.
Together let us beat this ample field,
Try what the open, what the covert yield;   *10*
The latent tracts, the giddy heights explore
Of all who blindly creep, or sightless soar;
Eye Nature's walks, shoot Folly as it flies,
And catch the Manners living as they rise;
Laugh where we must, be candid where we can;   *15*
But vindicate the ways of God to Man.
    I. Say first, of God above, or Man below,
What can we reason, but from what we know?
Of Man what see we, but his station here,
From which to reason, or to which refer?   *20*
Thro' worlds unnumber'd tho' the God be known,
'Tis ours to trace him only in our own.
He, who thro' vast immensity can pierce,
See worlds on worlds compose one universe,
Observe how system into system runs,   *25*
What other planets circle other suns,
What vary'd being peoples ev'ry star,
May tell why Heav'n has made us as we are.
But of this frame the bearings, and the ties,
The strong connections, nice dependencies,   *30*
Gradations just, has thy pervading soul
Look'd thro'? or can a part contain the whole?
    Is the great chain, that draws all to agree,
And drawn supports, upheld by God, or thee?   *34*
    II. Presumptuous Man! the reason wouldst thou find,
Why form'd so weak, so little, and so blind!
First, if thou canst, the harder reason guess,
Why form'd no weaker, blinder, and no less!
Ask of thy mother earth, why oaks are made
Taller or stronger than the weeds they shade?   *40*
Or ask of yonder argent fields above,
Why JOVE's Satellites are less than JOVE?
    Of Systems possible, if 'tis confest
That Wisdom infinite must form the best,

Where all must full or not coherent be,   *45*
And all that rises, rise in due degree;
Then, in the scale of reas'ning life, 'tis plain
There must be, somewhere, such a rank as Man;
And all the question (wrangle e'er so long)
Is only this, if God has plac'd him wrong?   *50*
    Respecting Man, whatever wrong we call,
May, must be right, as relative to all.
In human works, tho' labour'd on with pain,
A thousand movements scarce one purpose gain;
In God's, one single can its end produce;   *55*
Yet serves to second too some other use.
So Man, who here seems principal alone,
Perhaps acts second to some sphere unknown,
Touches some wheel, or verges to some goal;
'Tis but a part we see, and not a whole.   *60*
    When the proud steed shall know why Man restrains
His fiery course, or drives him o'er the plains;
When the dull Ox, why now he breaks the clod,
Is now a victim, and now Ægypt's God:
Then shall Man's pride and dulness comprehend   *65*
His actions', passions', being's, use and end;
Why doing, suff'ring, check'd, impell'd; and why
This hour a slave, the next a deity.
    Then say not Man's imperfect, Heav'n in fault;
Say rather, Man's as perfect as he ought;   *70*
His knowledge measur'd to his state and place,
His time a moment, and a point his space.
If to be perfect in a certain sphere,
What matter, soon or late, or here or there?
The blest today is as completely so,   *75*
As who began a thousand years ago.
    III. Heav'n from all creatures hides the book of Fate,
All but the page prescrib'd, their present state;
From brutes what men, from men what spirits know:
Or who could suffer Being here below?   *80*
The lamb thy riot dooms to bleed to-day,
Had he thy Reason, would he skip and play?
Pleas'd to the last, he crops the flow'ry food,
and licks the hand just rais'd to shed his blood.
Oh blindness to the future! kindly giv'n,   *85*
That each may fill the circle mark'd by Heav'n;
Who sees with equal eye, as God of all,
A hero perish, or a sparrow fall,
Atoms or systems into ruin hurl'd,
And now a bubble burst, and now a world.   *90*
    Hope humbly then; with trembling pinions soar;
Wait the great teacher Death, and God adore!
What future bliss, he gives not thee to know,
But gives that Hope to be thy blessing now.
Hope springs eternal in the human breast: *95*
Man never Is, but always To be blest:
The soul, uneasy and confin'd from home,
Rests and expatiates in a life to come.
    Lo! the poor Indian, whose untutor'd mind
Sees God in clouds, or hears him in the wind;   *100*
His soul proud Science never taught to stray
Far as the solar walk, or milky way;
Yet simple Nature to his hope has giv'n,
Behind the cloud-topt hill, an humbler heav'n;
Some safer world in depth of woods embrac'd,   *105*

Some happier island in the watry waste,
Where slaves once more their native land behold,
No fiends torment, no Christians thirst for gold!
To Be, contents his natural desire,
He asks no Angel's wing, no Seraph's fire;   *110*
But thinks, admitted to that equal sky,
His faithful dog shall bear him company,
    IV. Go, wiser thou! and in thy scale of sense
Weigh thy Opinion against Providence;
Call Imperfection what thou fancy'st such,   *115*
Say, here he gives too little, there too much;
Destroy all creatures for thy sport or gust,
Yet cry, If Man's unhappy, God's unjust;
If Man alone ingross not Heav'n's high care,
Alone made perfect here, immortal there: *120*
Snatch from his hand the balance and the rod,
Re-judge his justice, be the GOD of GOD!
    In Pride, in reas'ning Pride, our error lies;
All quit their sphere, and rush into the skies.
Pride still is aiming at the blest abodes,   *125*
Men would be Angels, Angels would be Gods.
Aspiring to be Gods, if Angels fell,
Aspiring to be Angels, Men rebel;
And who but wishes to invert the laws
Of ORDER, sins against th' Eternal Cause.   *130*
    V. Ask for what end the heav'nly bodies shine,
Earth for whose use? Pride answers, 'Tis for mine:
For me kind Nature wakes her genial pow'r,
Suckles each herb, and spreads out ev'ry flow'r;
Annual for me, the grape, the rose renew   *135*
The juice nectareous, and the balmy dew;
For me, the mine a thousand treasures brings;
For me, health gushes from a thousand springs;
Seas roll to waft me, suns to light me rise;
My foot-stool earth, my canopy the skies.'   *140*
    But errs not Nature from this gracious end,
From burning suns when livid deaths descend,
When earthquakes swallow, or when tempests sweep
Towns to one grave, whole nations to the deep?
'No ('tis reply'd) the first Almighty Cause   *145*
Acts not by partial, but by gen'ral laws;
Th' exceptions few; some change since all began,
And what created perfect?'—Why then Man?
If the great end be human Happiness,
Then Nature deviates; and can Man do less?   *150*
As much that end a constant course requires
Of show'rs and sun-shine, as of Man's desires;
As much eternal springs and cloudless skies,
As Men for ever temp'rate, calm, and wise.
If plagues or earthquakes break not Heav'n's design, *155*
Why then a Borgia, or a Catiline?
Who knows but he, whose hand the light'ning forms,
Who heaves old Ocean, and who wings the storms,
Pours fierce Ambition in a Caesar's mind,
Or turns young Ammon loose to scourge mankind?   *160*
From pride, from pride, our very reas'ning springs;
Account for moral as for nat'ral things:
Why charge we Heav'n in those, in these acquit?
In both, to reason right is to submit.
    Better for Us, perhaps, it might appear,   *165*
Were there all harmony, all virtue here;

That never air or ocean felt the wind;
That never passion discompos'd the mind:
But ALL subsists by elemental strife;
And Passions are the elements of Life.   *170*
The gen'ral ORDER, since the whole began,
Is kept in Nature, and is kept in Man.
    VI. What would this Man? Now upward will he soar,
And little less than Angel, would be more;
Now looking downwards, just as griev'd appears   *175*
To want the strengths of bulls, the fur of bears.
Made for his use all creatures if he call,
Say what their use, had he the pow'rs of all?
Nature to these, without profusion kind,
The proper organs, proper pow'rs assign'd;   *180*
Each seeming what compensated of course,
Here with degrees of swiftness, there of force;
All in exact proportion to the state;
Nothing to add, and nothing to abate.
Each beast, each insect, happy in its own;   *185*
Is Heav'n unkind to Man, and Man alone?
Shall he alone, whom rational we call,
Be pleas'd with nothing, if not bless'd with all?
    The bliss of Man (could Pride that blessing find)
Is not to act or think beyond mankind;   *190*
No pow'rs of body or of soul to share,
But what his nature and his state can bear.
Why has not Man a microscopic eye?
For this plain reason, Man is not a Fly.
Say what the use, were finer optics giv'n,   *195*
T' inspect a mite, not comprehend the heav'n?
Or touch, if trembling alive all o'er,
To smart and agonize at ev'ry pore?
Or quick effluvia darting thro' the brain,
Die of a rose in aromatic pain?   *200*
If nature thunder'd in his op'ning ears,
And stunn'd him with the music of the spheres,
How would he wish that Heav'n had left him still
The whisp'ring Zephyr, and the purling rill?
Who finds not Providence all good and wise,   *205*
Alike in what it gives, and what it denies?
    VII. Far as Creation's ample range extends,
The scale of sensual, mental pow'rs ascends:
Mark how it mounts, to Man's imperial race,
From the green myriads in the peopled grass: *210*
What modes of sight betwixt each wide extreme,
The mole's dim curtain, and the lynx's beam:
Of smell, the headlong lioness between,
And hound sagacious on the tainted green:
Of hearing, from the life that fills the flood,   *215*
To that which warbles thro' the vernal wood:
The spider's touch, how exquisitely fine!
Feels at each thread, and lives along the line:
In the nice bee, what sense so subtly true
From pois'nous herbs extracts the healing dew: *220*
How Instinct varies in the grov'ling swine,
Compar'd, half-reas'ning elephant, with thine:
'Twixt that, and Reason, what a nice barrier;
For ever sep'rate, yet for ever near!
Remembrance and Reflection how ally'd;   *225*
What thin partitions Sense from Thought divide:
And Middle natures, how they long to join,

Yet never pass th' insuperable line!
Without this just gradation, could they be
Subject these to those, or all to thee?   *230*
The pow'rs of all subdu'd by thee alone,
Is not thy Reason all these pow'rs in one?
   VIII. See, thro' this air, this ocean, and this earth,
All matter quick, and bursting into birth.
Above, how high progressive life may go!   *235*
Around, how wide! how deep extend below!
Vast chain of being, which from God began,
Natures æthereal, human, angel, man,
Beast, bird, fish, insect! what no eye can see,
No glass can reach! from Infinite to thee,   *240*
From thee to Nothing!—On superior pow'rs
Were we to press, inferior might on ours:
Or in the full creation leave a void,
Where, one step broken, the great scale's destroy'd:
From Nature's chain whatever link you strike,   *245*
Tenth or ten thousandth, breaks the chain alike.
   And if each system in gradation roll,
Alike essential to th' amazing whole;
The least confusion but in one, not all
That system only, but the whole must fall.   *250*
Let Earth unbalanc'd from her orbit fly,
Planets and Suns run lawless thro' the sky,
Let ruling Angels from their spheres be hurl'd,
Being on being wreck'd, and world on world,
Heav'n's whole foundations to their centre nod,   *255*
And Nature tremble to the throne of God:
All this dread ORDER break—for whom? for thee?
Vile worm!—oh Madness, Pride, Impiety!
   IX. What if the foot, ordain'd the dust to tread,
Or hand to toil, aspir'd to be the head?   *260*
What if the head, the eye, or ear repin'd
To serve mere engines to the ruling Mind?
Just as absurd for any part to claim
To be another, in this gen'ral frame:
Just as absurd, to mourn the tasks or pains   *265*
The great directing MIND OF ALL ordains.
   All are but parts of one stupendous whole,
Whose body, Nature is, and God the soul;
That, chang'd thro' all, and yet in all the same,
Great in the earth, as in th' æthereal frame,   *270*
Warms in the sun, refreshes in the breeze,
Glows in the stars, and blossoms in the trees,
Lives thro' all life, extends thro' all extent,
Spreads undivided, operates unspent,
Breathes in our soul, informs our mortal part,   *275*
As full, as perfect, in a hair as heart;
As full, as perfect, in vile Man that mourns,
As the rapt Seraph that adores and burns;
To him no high, no low, no great, no small;
He fills, he bounds, connects, and equals all.   *280*
   X. Cease then, nor ORDER Imperfection name:
Our proper bliss depends on what we blame.
Know thy own point: This kind, this due degree
Of blindness, weakness, Heav'n bestows on thee.
Submit—In this, or any other sphere,   *285*
Secure to be as blest as thou canst bear:
Safe in the hand of one disposing Pow'r,
Or in the natal, or the mortal hour.

All Nature is but Art, unknown to thee;
All Chance, Direction, which thou canst not see;   *290*
All Discord, Harmony, not understood;
All partial Evil, universal Good:
And, spite of Pride, in erring Reason's spite,
One truth is clear, 'Whatever IS, is RIGHT.'

✦ JONATHAN SWIFT
from *Gulliver's Travels*

The most savage part of Swift's satire on human nature occurs in the fourth and final part of Gulliver's Travels *(1726). In Book IV Gulliver journeys to the land of the Houyhnhnms, where gracious, intelligent, and noble horses are in power. These rational creatures are extraordinarily logical and self-disciplined.*

   While there, Gulliver encounters another species in the land, however: the ugly Yahoos, whose filth, ignorance, and disgusting behavior contrast strongly with the refined manners of the Houyhnhnms. Gulliver becomes enamored of the Houyhnhnms and revolted by the Yahoos. The latter bear an uncomfortably close resemblance to human beings—though humans without the gift of reason.

CHAPTER VII

The Author's great Love of his Native Country. His Master's Observations upon the Constitution and Administration of England, as described by the Author, with parallel Cases and Comparisons. His Master's Observations upon human Nature.

The Reader may be disposed to wonder how I could prevail on my self to give so free a Representation of my own Species, among a Race of Mortals who were already too apt to conceive the vilest Opinion of Human Kind, from that entire Congruity betwixt me and their *Yahoos.* But I must freely confess, that the many Virtues of those excellent *Quadrupeds* placed in opposite View to human Corruptions, had so far opened my Eyes, and my Understanding, that I began to view the Actions and Passions of Man in a very different Light; and to think the Honour of my own kind not worth managing; which, besides, it was impossible for me to do before a Person of so acute a Judgment as my Master, who daily convinced me of a thousand Faults in my self, whereof I had not the least Perception before, and which with us would never be numbered even among human Infirmities. I had likewise learned from his Example an utter Detestation of all Falsehood or Disguise; and *Truth* appeared so amiable to me, that I determined upon sacrificing every thing to it.

   Let me deal so candidly with the Reader, as to confess, that there was yet a much stronger Motive for the Freedom I took in my Representation of Things. I had not been a Year in this Country, before I contracted such a Love and Veneration for the Inhabitants, that I entered on a firm Resolution never to return to human Kind, but to pass the rest of my Life among these admirable *Houyhnhnms* in the Contemplation and Practice of every Virtue; where I could leave no Example or Incitement to Vice. But it was decreed by fortune, my perpetual Enemy, that so great a Felicity should not fall to my Share. However, it is now some comfort to reflect, that in what I said of my Countrymen, I *extenuated* their Faults as much as I durst before so strict an Examiner; and upon every Article, gave as *favourable* a Turn as the Matter would bear. For, indeed, who is there alive that will not be swayed by his Byass and Partiality to the Place of his Birth?

I have related the Substance of several Conversations I had with my Master, during the greatest Part of the Time I had the Honour to be in his Service; but have indeed for Brevity sake omitted much more than is here set down.

When I had answered all his Questions, and his Curiosity seemed to be fully satisfied; he sent for me one Morning early, and commanding me to sit down at some Distance, (an Honour which he had never before conferred upon me) He said, he had been very seriously considering my whole Story, as far as it related both to my self and my Country: That, he looked upon us as a Sort of Animals to whose Share, by what Accident he could not conjecture, some small Pittance of *Reason* had fallen, whereof we made no other Use than by its Assistance to aggravate our *natural* Corruptions, and to acquire new ones which Nature had not given us. That, we disarmed our selves of the few Abilities she had bestowed; had been very successful in multiplying our original wants, and seemed to spend our whole Lives in vain Endeavours to supply them by our own Inventions. That, as to my self, it was manifest I had neither the Strength or Agility of a common *Yahoo*; that I walked infirmly on my hinder feet; had found out a Contrivance to make my Claws of no Use or Defence, and to remove the Hair from my Chin, which was intended as a Shelter from the Sun and the Weather. Lastly, That I could neither run with Speed, nor climb Trees like my *Brethren* (as he called them) the *Yahoos* in this Country.

That, our Institutions of *Government* and *Law* were plainly owing to our gross Defects in *Reason*, and by consequence, in *Virtue*; because *Reason* alone is sufficient to govern a *Rational* Creature; which was therefore a Character we had no Pretence to challenge, even from the Account I had given of my own People; although he manifestly perceived, that in order to favour them, I had concealed many Particulars, and often *said the Thing which was not*.

He was the more confirmed in this Opinion, because he observed, that as I agreed in every Feature of my Body with other *Yahoos*, except where it was to my real Disadvantage in point of Strength, Speed and Activity, the Shortness of my Claws, and some other Particulars where Nature had no Part; so, from the Representation I had given him of our Lives, our Manners, and our Actions, he found as near a Resemblance in the Disposition of our Minds. He said, the *Yahoos* were known to hate one another more than they did any different Species of Animals; and the Reason usually assigned was, the Odiousness of their own Shapes, which all could see in the rest, but not in themselves. He had therefore begun to think it not unwise in us to *cover* our Bodies, and by that Invention, conceal many of our Deformities from each other, which would else be hardly supportable. But, he now found he had been mistaken; and that the Dissentions of those Brutes in his Country were owing to the same Cause with ours, as I had described them. For, if (said he) you throw among five *Yahoos* as much Food as would be sufficient for fifty, they will, instead of eating peaceably, fall together by the Ears, each single one impatient to *have all to it self*; and therefore a Servant was usually employed to stand by while they were feeding abroad, and those kept at home were tied at a Distance from each other. That, if a Cow died of Age or Accident, before a *Houyhnhnm* could secure it for his own *Yahoos*, those in the Neighbourhood would come in Herds to seize it, and then would ensue such a Battle as I had described, with terrible Wounds made by their Claws on both Sides, although they seldom were able to kill one another, for want of such convenient Instruments of Death as we had invented. At other Times the like Battles have been fought between the *Yahoos* of several Neighbourhoods without any visible Cause: Those of one District watching all Opportunities to surprise the next before they are prepared. But if they find their Project hath miscarried, they return home, and for want of Enemies, engage in what I call a *Civil War* among themselves.

That, in some Fields of his Country, there are certain *shining Stones* of several Colours, whereof the *Yahoos* are violently fond; and when Part of these *Stones* are fixed in the Earth, as it sometimes happeneth, they will dig with their Claws for whole days to get them out, and carry them away, and hide them by Heaps in their Kennels; but still looking round with great Caution, for fear their Comrades should find out their Treasure. My Master said, he could never discover the Reason of this unusual Appetite, or how these *Stones* could be of any Use to a *Yahoo*; but now he believed it might proceed from the same Principle of *Avarice*, which I had ascribed to Mankind. That he had once, by way of experiment, privately removed a Heap of these *Stones* from the Place where one of his *Yahoos* had buried it: Whereupon, the sordid Animal missing his Treasure, by his loud lamenting brought the whole Herd to the Place, there miserably howled, then fell to biting and tearing the rest; began to pine away, would neither eat nor sleep, nor work, till he ordered a Servant privately to convey the *Stones* into the same Hole, and hide them as before; which when his *Yahoo* had found, he presently recovered his Spirits and good humour; but took Care to remove them to a better hiding Place; and hath ever since been a very serviceable Brute.

My Master farther assured me, which I also observed my self; That in the Fields where these *shining Stones* abound, the fiercest and most frequent Battles are fought, occasioned by perpetual Inroads of the neighbouring *Yahoos*.

He said, it was common when two *Yahoos* discovered such a *Stone* in a Field, and were contending which of them should be the Proprietor, a third would take the Advantage, and carry it away from them both; which my Master would needs contend to have some Resemblance with our *Suits at Law*; wherein I thought it for our Credit not to undeceive him; since the Decision he mentioned was much more equitable than many Decrees among us: Because the Plaintiff and Defendant there lost nothing beside the *Stone* they contended for; whereas our *Courts of Equity*, would never have dismissed the Cause while either of them had any thing left.

My Master continuing his Discourse, said, There was nothing that rendered the *Yahoos* more odious, than their undistinguished Appetite to devour every thing that came in their Way, whether Herbs, Roots, Berries, corrupted Flesh of Animals, or all mingled together: And it was peculiar in their Temper, that they were fonder of what they could get by Rapine or Stealth at a greater Distance, than much better Food provided for them at home. If their Prey held out, they would eat till they were ready to burst, after which Nature had pointed out to them a certain *Root* that gave them a general Evacuation.

There was also another Kind of *Root* very *juicy*, but something rare and difficult to be found, which the *Yahoos* fought for with much Eagerness, and would suck it with great Delight: It produced the same Effects that Wine hath upon us. It would make them sometimes hug, and sometimes tear one another; they would howl and grin, and chatter, and reel, and tumble, and then fall asleep in the Mud.

I did indeed observe, that the *Yahoos* were the only Animals in this Country subject to any Diseases; which however, were much fewer than Horses have among us, and contracted not by any ill Treatment they meet with, but by the Nastiness and Greediness of that sordid Brute. Neither has their Language any more than a general Appellation for those Maladies; which is borrowed from the Name of the Beast, and called *Hnea Yahoo*, or the *Yahoo's-Evil*; and the Cure prescribed is a Mixture of *their own Dung and Urine*, forcibly put down the *Yahoo's* Throat. This I have since often known to have been taken with Success: And do here freely recommend it to my Countrymen, for the publick Good, as an admirable Specifick against all Diseases produced by Repletion.

As to Learning, Government, Arts, Manufactures, and the like; my Master confessed he could find little or no Resemblance between the *Yahoos* of that Country and those in ours. For, he only meant to observe what Parity there was in our Natures. He had heard indeed some curious *Houyhnhnms* observe, that in most Herds there was a Sort of ruling *Yahoo*, (as among us there is generally some leading or principal Stag in a Park) who was always more *deformed* in Body, and *mischievous* in *Disposition*, than any of the rest. That, this *Leader* had usually a Favourite as *like himself* as he could get, whose Employment was to *lick his Master's Feet and Posteriors, and drive the Female* Yahoos *to his Kennel*; for which he was now and then rewarded with a Piece of Ass's Flesh. This *Favourite* is hated by the whole Herd; and therefore to protect himself, keeps always *near the Person of his Leader*. He usually continues in Office till a worse can be found; but the very Moment he is discarded, his Successor, at the Head of all the *Yahoos* in that District, Young and Old, Male and Female, come in a Body, and discharge their excrements upon him from Head to Foot. But how far this might be applicable to our *Courts* and *Favourites*, and *Ministers of State*, my Master said I could best determine.

I durst make no Return to this malicious Insinuation, which debased human Understanding below the Sagacity of a common *Hound*, who hath Judgment enough to distinguish and follow the Cry of the *ablest Dog in the Pack*, without being ever mistaken.

My Master told me, there were some Qualities remarkable in the *Yahoos*, which he had not observed me to mention, or at least very slightly, in the Accounts I had given him of human Kind. He said, those Animals, like other Brutes, had their Females in common; but in this they differed, that the She-*Yahoo* would admit the Male, while she was pregnant; and that the Hees would quarrel and fight with the Females as fiercely as with each other. Both which Practices were such Degrees of infamous Brutality, that no other sensitive Creature ever arrived at.

Another Thing he wondered at in the *Yahoos*, was their strange Disposition to Nastiness and Dirt; whereas there appears to be a natural Love of Cleanliness in all other Animals. As to the two former Accusations, I was glad to let them pass without any Reply, because I had not a Word to offer upon them in Defence of my Species, which otherwise I certainly had done from my own Inclinations. But I could have easily vindicated human Kind from the Imputation of Singularity upon the last Article, if there had been any *Swine* in that Country, (as unluckily for me there were not) which although it may be a *sweeter Quadruped* than a *Yahoo*, cannot I humbly conceive in Justice pretend to more Cleanliness; and so his Honour himself must have owned, if he had seen their filthy Way of feeding, and their Custom of wallowing and sleeping in the Mud.

My Master likewise mentioned another Quality, which his Servants had discovered in several *Yahoos*, and to him was wholly unaccountable. He said, a Fancy would sometimes take a *Yahoo*, to retire into a Corner, to lie down and howl, and groan, and spurn away all that came near him, although he were young and fat, and wanted neither Food nor Water; nor did the Servants imagine what could possibly ail him. And the only Remedy they found was to set him to hard Work, after which he would infallibly come to himself. To this I was silent out of Partiality to my own Kind; yet here I could plainly discover the true Seeds of *Spleen*,[1] which only seizeth on the *Lazy*, the *Luxurious*, and the *Rich*; who, if they were forced to undergo the *same Regimen*, I would undertake for the Cure.

His Honour had farther observed, that a Female-*Yahoo* would often stand behind a Bank or a Bush, to gaze on the young Males passing by, and then appear, and hide, using many antick Gestures and Grimaces; at which time it was observed, that she had a most *offensive Smell*; and when any of the Males advanced, would slowly retire, looking often back, and with a counterfeit Shew of Fear, run off into some convenient Place where she knew the Male would follow her.

At other times, if a Female Stranger came among them, three or four of her own Sex would get about her, and stare and chatter, and grin, and smell her all over; and then turn off with Gestures that seemed to express Contempt and Disdain.

Perhaps my Master might refine a little in these Speculations, which he had drawn from what he observed himself, or had been told by others; However, I could not reflect without some Amazement, and much Sorrow, that the Rudiments of *Lewdness, Coquetry, Censure*, and *Scandal*, should have Place by Instinct in Womankind.

I expected every Moment, that my Master would accuse the *Yahoos* of those unnatural Appetites in both Sexes, so common among us. But Nature it seems hath not been so expert a Schoolmistress; and these politer Pleasures are entirely the Productions of Art and Reason, on our Side of the Globe.

---

[1] A fashionable illness in Swift's day.

❧ VOLTAIRE

from *Candide*

In Candide *(1759), an innocent young man is introduced to pain, suffering, violence, and corruption, in a series of misfortunes that include witnessing decapitations, betrayals, murders, rapes, and natural disasters. He eventually realizes that his teacher's philosophy, that "all is for the best," is vain and nonsensical. Having tried scrupulously to live by this motto, he at last gives up hope of finding happiness, of discovering the ideal woman, and of understanding the world. Instead he returns to his country home to cultivate his garden, Voltaire's way of suggesting that the most human beings can do is live simply and reconcile themselves to fate.*

Translated from the German of Doctor Ralph with the additions that were found in the Doctor's pocket, when he died at Minden in the year of grace 1759.

CHAPTER I

How Candide was reared in a beautiful castle, and how he came to be ejected

Living at the Baron Thunder-ten-tronckh's castle in Westphalia was a young man who was as mild and inoffensive as a lamb. His face was as simple as his soul was unsophisticated. For this reason, I think, he had been named Candide. The old retainers of the house surmised that he was the son, by the baron's sister, of an aristocratic neighbour, of exemplary character, whom this young lady always refused to marry, because, Time having wrought serious ravages on his genealogical tree, he could show only seventy-one quarterings to his escutcheon.

The baron was one of the most powerful lords in Westphalia, for his castle had both a door and windows. His great hall, too, was hung with tapestry. At a pinch, the mongrels in his backyard were a pack of hounds, and his stable-boy the whipper-in. The village curate was his Lord-High-Almoner. Everyone called him *Monseigneur*, and laughed when he told them stories.

The baroness, who weighed twenty-five stone, was much esteemed therefor, and the dignity with which she did the honours of her household made her seem still more respectable. Her daughter, Cunégonde, aged seventeen, was rosy-cheeked, plump, and attractive. The baron's son quite deserved to have the baron for father. Pangloss, the tutor, was the castle's oracle, to whose counsel little Candide listened with all the credulity of his age and temperament.

Pangloss taught metaphysico-theologo-cosmolonigology. He proved admirably that there is no effect without a cause, and that, in this best of all possible worlds, the baron's castle was the most beautiful of all castles, and the baroness the best of all possible baronesses.

"It is evident," said he, "that things cannot possibly be otherwise, for, as everything has been made with an object, that object must necessarily be the best of all possible objects. Take note that noses were made to carry spectacles; accordingly, we have spectacles. Legs were obviously designed to fill stockings; hence we have stockings. Stones were intended to be cut and used for building into castles; my lord baron has a very beautiful castle. The mightiest baron in the province must be the best lodged; and pigs being made to be eaten, we feed on pork all the year round. Consequently, those who aver that everything in this world is good, talk nonsense: what they should say is— 'everything is the best possible.'"

Candide, who listened attentively, innocently believed all this; for he considered Mlle. Cunégonde extremely beautiful, although he had never had the courage to tell her so. He judged that, after the joy of being born Baron Thunder-ten-tronckh, the second degree of happiness was to be Mlle. Cunégonde; the third, to see her every day; and the fourth, to listen to Doctor Pangloss, the greatest Philosopher in the province, and, consequently, in the whole world.

One day, Cunégonde, while walking near the Castle in the little wood they called the park, saw between the bushes Doctor Pangloss giving a lesson in experimental physics to her mother's chambermaid, a gentle and very pretty little dark-haired girl. As Mlle. Cunégonde had a considerable liking for science, she quietly studied the repeated experiments of which she was witness. She saw clearly the Doctor's self-sufficient reasons, the effects and the causes, and went back home quite agitated and thoughtful, filled with the desire to be a learned woman, reflecting that she might well be the self-sufficient reason for young Candide, who in his turn might be also the self-sufficient reason for her.

On returning to the castle she met Candide, and blushed: Candide blushed also. She said good-morning to him in a strangled voice, and Candide spoke to her without knowing what he said. The following day, on leaving table after dinner, they happened to stop behind a screen. Cunégonde let her handkerchief fall, Candide picked it up. She guilelessly took his hand, the young man innocently kissed the young lady's fingers with a quite especial liveliness, tenderness, and grace. Their lips met, their eyes kindled, their knees trembled, their hands strayed. The Baron Thunder-ten-tronckh passed close by the screen and, seeing these causes and these effects, ejected Candide from the castle with tremendous kicks on the behind. Cunégonde fainted: when she came to, the baroness boxed her ears, and consternation reigned in the most beautiful and agreeable of all possible castles.

CHAPTER II

What happened to Candide among the Bulgars

Candide, expelled from his terrestrial paradise, wandered about aimlessly for a long time, weeping, raising his eyes to heaven, turning them often to the most beautiful of all possible castles, wherein dwelt the most beautiful of all possible daughters of barons. Without supping, he laid down to sleep in a field, between two furrows. Snow fell in big flakes.

Next morning, quite benumbed, famished and weary without a penny in his pocket, he dragged himself to a neighbouring village called *Valberg-hoff-trarbk-dikdorff*, and halted sadly before a cabaret. Two men, dressed in blue, noticed him. "Look mate!" said one of them. "There's a very well-built young man, and tall enough too." They went up to Candide, and very civilly asked him to dine with them.

"You do me great honour, gentlemen," said Candide, with charming modesty; "but I haven't the money to pay my share."

"That's all right!" replied one of the men in Blue. "Men of your stamp and attainments never need worry about money; why, you stand five foot five in your socks, don't you?"

"That's so," replied Candide with a bow.

"Well then, come and feed with us; we will not only pay for your meal, but will see also that you get some money: men should help one another."

"You're quite right," said Candide. "That's what Doctor Pangloss always told me, and it's quite clear that everything's for the best in this best of all possible worlds."

They begged him to accept a few crowns. He took them, and wished to make out an I.O.U., which they refused. They all sat down to the table.

"I suppose you love and honour…?" said one of the men.

"Oh, yes!" replied Candide. "I love and honour Mlle. Cunégonde: I adore her."

"No, no!" said the other. "What we mean is—do you love and honour your King—the King of the Bulgars?"

"Love the King of the Bulgars? Good heavens, no! Why, I've never even seen him."

"What, never seen the King of the Bulgars! He's the best of all kings. You must drink his health."

"Willingly, gentlemen;" and he drank.

"That's all right, then," they said. "You're the defender, supporter, protector, of the Bulgars: you're their hero. Your fame's assured, and your fortune's made."

Without more ado, they put irons on his feet, and took him to the barracks. There, he was made to turn to the right and to the left, shoulder arms, present arms, port arms, fire, and march at the double. Then they gave him thirty strokes with the cat. The next day he did the exercises better, and received only twenty strokes: the day after that, only ten. His comrades thought him a marvel, but he was somewhat bewildered, as he could not quite make out how he was a hero.

One fine spring morning he took it into his head to go for a walk, in the belief that human beings, like other animals, were privileged to use their legs for pleasure. He had not covered a couple of leagues before four other six-foot heroes overtook him, bound him, and threw him into a dungeon. He was asked judicially whether he would prefer to be flogged thirty-six times successively by the entire regiment, or receive twelve leaden bullets in his brain all at once. He was very inclined to say that, as wishes are free, he preferred neither the one nor the other; but he had to make a choice, and was permitted (by virtue of that gift of God called Freewill) to choose to pass thirty-six times under the rod. He stood two floggings. The regiment membered two thousand men. That meant four thousand blows, which laid bare the muscles and sinews from the nape of his neck to the small of his back. As they were about to start on the third flogging, Candide, not being able to stand any more, begged that in pity they would be so kind as to kill him outright. This favour was granted. They bound his eyes, and forced him to his knees. At that moment, the King of the Bulgars passed by and was informed of the culprit's crime. Being a very intelligent king, however, he understood from everything that was told him about Candide that here was a young metaphysician completely ignorant of the ways of the world. He offered the prisoner a free pardon, therefore, and generously expressed his willingness to remit the remainder of the sentence. Such clemency will certainly be applauded by every newspaper for ever and ever.

A worthy doctor healed Candide in three weeks with the emollients prescribed by Dioscoridos. New skin had already started to grow, and Candide was able to walk, when the King of the Bulgars declared war on the King of the Abars.

CHAPTER III

How Candide escaped from the Bulgars, and what became of him

Never was anything so beautiful, so clever, so thrilling, and so well-arranged, as the two armies. The trumpets, fifes, haut-boys, drums and cannons, made a harmony the like of which had never been heard in Hell. The cannons knocked down straightaway nearly six thousand men on each side. Then the muskets removed from this best of all possible worlds some nine or ten thousand blackguards who infected its surface. The bayonet also was sufficient reason for the death of a few thousands. The total was in easy reach of thirty thousand souls. Candide, trembling like a philosopher, hid himself as best he could during this heroic slaughter.

At last, while the two kings were singing Te Deums in their respective camps, Candide made up his mind to go to reason effects and causes elsewhere. He clambered over the pile of dead and dying, and reached, first of all, the ashes of an Abar village, which the Bulgars had burned according to the laws of public justice. Here, old men, riddled with holes, watched their butchered wives dying with babes at their bleeding breasts. There, disembowelled girls, having satisfied the natural needs of a few heroes, were breathing their last. Others, half burned, begged for death. Brains were spattered on the ground beside bits of arms and legs.

Candide fled as quickly as possible to the next village, which, belonging to the Bulgars, had been treated by the Abars in precisely the same way. Stepping continually on quivering limbs, and walking always over ruins, he at last got out of the theatre of war, with a little food in his knapsack and an unfading picture of Mlle. Cunégonde in his memory. When he reached Holland, his food supply gave out; but having heard that everyone in that country was rich, and Christian, he did not doubt that he would be treated as well there as he had been in the baron's castle, before being ejected on account of Mlle. Cunégonde's beautiful eyes.

He begged charity from several sedate people, who all replied that, if he continued begging as a profession, they would have him put in the lockup in order that he might learn how to make a living out in the world.

After this, he approached a man who, for an hour on end, had been discoursing to a large gathering on the subject of charity. This orator looked him up and down. "What do you intend doing in this country?" he asked. "Have you good cause for being here?"

"There's no effect without a cause," replied Candide, modestly. "Everything's necessarily linked up and arranged for the best possible possible object. It was absolutely necessary a few days ago that I should be kicked from Mlle. Cunégonde's side and flogged by the entire regiment, and it is absolutely necessary now that I should beg bread until I get it. Nothing of all this could have happened differently."

"My friend," said the orator. "Do you believe that the Pope is Antichrist?"

"I've never heard anyone say he was," answered Candide. "But whether he is or whether he isn't, I want some bread to eat."

"You don't deserve to eat," returned the other.

"Away with you, you rascal! Away, you vagabond! And don't come near me again, or it'll be the worse for you!"

At this point, the orator's wife put her head out of the window, and, on learning that here was a man who doubted that the Pope was Antichrist, emptied over his head a full … Oh, heavens! to what excesses does religious ardour bring women.

A man who had never been baptised, a good Anabaptist named Jacques, seeing the cruel and ignominious treatment thus meted out to one of his brethren, a featherless biped with an immortal soul, took him home, washed him, gave him bread and beer, presented him with two florins, and even wished to teach him the manufacture of Persian fabrics, which are made in Holland.

"Oh!" cried Candide, falling at his feet. "Doctor Pangloss well said that everything was for the best in this best of all possible worlds. I am infinitely more touched by your great generosity than by the harshness shown me by that black-coated man and his wife."

While out walking next day, he came across a beggar all covered with sores, with eyes glazed, the end of his nose eaten away, mouth twisted, teeth black; who spoke in a hoarse voice, and spat out a tooth every time his racking cough tormented him.

CHAPTER IV

How Candide met Doctor Pangloss, his former master of philosophy, and what came of their meeting

Candide, more moved by pity than by horror, gave this terrible beggar the two florins he had received from that honest Anabaptist, Jacques. The spectre fixed him with a glance, shed some tears, and tried to embrace him. Candide drew back in alarm.

"Alas!" said the one poor wretch to the other. "Don't you recognise me? I'm your old friend, Pangloss."

"What! You, my old master! You, in this horrible state! What on earth's happened to you? Why aren't you still in the most beautiful of all possible castles? What's become of that priceless pearl, that masterpiece of nature, Mlle. Cunégonde?"

"I'm absolutely worn out," said Pangloss.

Candide at once led him to the Anabaptist's outhouse, and made him eat a little bread. When Pangloss had revived somewhat, he resumed his catechism.

"Well, what about Cunégonde?"

"She's dead," replied Pangloss.

Candide fainted. His friend brought him round with a little sour vinegar that happened to be in the shed. Candide slowly opened his eyes.

"Cunégonde dead!" he wailed. "Oh, best of all worlds, where are you? But what did she die of? Surely not from seeing me toed out of her father's beautiful castle?"

"No," said Pangloss, calmly. "Some Bulgar soldiers raped her as much as anyone could be raped, and then ripped her stomach open. The baron tried to defend her, and had his head split for his pains. The baroness was torn to pieces. As for the castle, not a stone remains, not a barn, not a sheep, not a duckling, not a tree even. But we were well revenged, for the Abars did just as much damage in the next estate, which belonged to a Bulgar lord."

On hearing all this, Candide fainted again.

Having regained consciousness once more, he lamented to his heart's content, and then inquired: what causes, what effects, and what self-sufficient reasons, had brought Pangloss to his present piteous pass.

"It was Cupid!" said Pangloss, sadly. "Love! the consoler of the human race, the saviour of the universe, the stimulant to action of every sentient creature—sweet, tender, precious, beautiful Love!"

"Yes," said Candide regretfully. "Yes, I've met this Love, this ruler of our hearts, this essence of our being … but it was never worth more to me than one kiss on the mouth, and twenty kicks on the backside. Tell me, how did this beautiful cause come to produce in you such an abominable effect?"

"It was like this," replied Pangloss. "Do you remember, my dear Candide, that the baroness had a pretty little chamber-maid, called Paquette? Well, it was in her arms that I tasted those heavenly ecstasies which have produced the hellish torments with which you see me ravaged. She had the pest, and has already died from it, maybe. Paquette received this present from a very learned Franciscan friar, who acquired it with an unbroken pedigree, for he had it from an old countess, who got it from a cavalry captain, who owed it to a marquise, who received it from a page, who derived it from a Jesuit, who, while a novice, had it in direct descent from one of the companions of Christopher Columbus. As for me, I shan't give it to anybody, because I'm dying."

"Oh, Pangloss!" cried Candide. "What a strange ancestry! The devil must have founded that family."

"Strange? Not at all!" replied the great man. "That ancestry was an indispensable ingredient of this best of all possible worlds, an essential constituent, because, if Columbus had missed catching in America this malady which taints the source of procreation, which often even stops procreation altogether, and is obviously opposed to nature's great purpose, we should have neither chocolate nor cochineal. Notice also that, up to date, this disease is peculiar to us in our continent. The Turks, Indians, Persians, Chinese, Siamese and Japanese, are still ignorant of its existence even; but there is a self-sufficient reason for supposing that, in a few centuries, they in their turn will make its acquaintance. Meanwhile, among us, the malady has made marvellous progress, especially in those large armies of fine, heroic mercenaries, which decide the destinies of nations. You can be certain that when thirty thousand men are thrown at war against another thirty thousand, about twenty thousand on each side die from the pox."

"That's excellent," said Candide. "But now you've got to be cured."

"And how can I be cured?" asked Pangloss. "I haven't a sou, my friend, and no doctor on this earth will bleed me or treat me free of charge."

These last words decided Candide. He went and threw himself at the feet of that charitable Anabaptist, Jacques, and painted so touching a picture of the condition to which his friend was reduced, that the good man hastened to assist Doctor Pangloss, and had him cured at his own expense. As a result of the cure, Pangloss lost only an eye and an ear.

As the Doctor read well, and knew arithmetic perfectly, Jacques made him his book-keeper, and having, after a couple of months, to go to Lisbon on business, he took the two philosophers with him on his ship. Pangloss explained to him how this was the best of all possible worlds. Jacques did not agree.

"I think men must have corrupted nature somewhat," said he. "They were not born wolves, yet they have become wolves. God never gave them either cannons or bayonets, yet they've made cannons and bayonets in order to destroy themselves. I might quote the parallel of Bankruptcy and the Justice which seizes the goods of the bankrupt in order to disappoint the creditors."

"All that's absolutely necessary," replied the one-eyed doctor. "Individual misfortunes make for the general good, so that the more trouble a man has, the better it is for everyone else."

"While he was discoursing, the sky became clouded, the wind blew from the four corners of the globe, and the ship was struck by a terrific storm, in full sight of the port of Lisbon.

CHAPTER V

Storm, shipwreck, earthquake, and what befell Doctor Pangloss, Candide, and Jacques, the Anabaptist

Half the passengers were almost dead with the inconceivable anguish that is caused by the rolling of a ship, and had not enough strength to worry about the danger. The other half cried for help, and said their prayers. The sails were in shreds, the masts splintered, and great holes were visible in the vessel's hull. Those who could, worked: everything was confusion; nobody in command.

The Anabaptist stood on the poop, and helped to work the ship. A half-mad sailor struck him a blow that stretched him on the ground, but, so violent was the recoil, that the sailor himself fell head-first overboard. In his descent, he was caught by a piece of the broken mast to which he remained hanging. Jacques ran to his aid, and helped him climb on board again, but in his efforts was himself thrown over into the sea. The sailor, in full view of the accident, did not deign even to notice him. Candide rushed up, saw his benefactor reappear for a moment, and then be engulfed for ever. He wished to throw himself into the sea after his friend, but Pangloss, the philosopher, stopped him from doing so by proving that the roadstead of Lisbon had been expressly created in order that this particular Anabaptist might drown there. While he was proving this *a priori*, the ship split in twain, and everyone perished, with the exception of Pangloss, Candide, and the brute of a sailor who had drowned the worthy Anabaptist. That rascal succeeded in swimming to the shore, whither Pangloss and Candide were borne on a plank.

When they had come to themselves somewhat, they walked towards Lisbon. They still had some money left, and, having escaped the storm, they hoped with its aid to save themselves from starvation.

They had hardly set foot in the town, and were still weeping over the death of their benefactor, than they felt the earth tremble under their feet. The sea rose, boiling, and rent the ships which were anchored in the harbour. A tornado of red-hot cinders swept through the streets and open squares. Houses crumbled, roofs were overturned on to the foundations of the houses, and the foundations of the houses were themselves scattered in little pieces. Thirty thousand inhabitants of every age and sex were crushed beneath the ruins.

The sailor whistled and cursed. "There'll be something worth finding here," he said.

"What can be the self-sufficient cause of this phenomenon?" queried Pangloss.

"It's the end of the world!" cried Candide. The sailor rushed forthwith among the debris, braved death in order to find money, found some, secured it, got drunk, and having slept himself sober, bought the favours of the first willing girl he came across, among the ruins of the destroyed houses, surrounded by the dying and the dead. Pangloss, however, pulled him by the sleeve.

"My friend," said he. "This isn't at all nice. Your judgment's at fault: you've chosen your time badly. You're ignorant of the theoretical explanation of the universe."

"Odds, blood!" replied the other. "I'm a sailor, born in Batavia. In four journeys to Japan, I've just missed drowning four times. You've found the right man to talk theoretical explanations of the universe to!"

Some splinters of stone had wounded Candide, and lying in the street, covered with debris, he called to Pangloss to come to his rescue. "Help! get me some wine and oil; I'm dying!"

"This earthquake's nothing new," replied Pangloss. "The town of Lima in America had similar shocks last year. Similar causes, similar effects; there must certainly be a trail of sulphur underground between Lima and Lisbon."

"That's highly probable," returned Candide. "But in God's name get me a little oil and wine."

"Probable, why probable?" continued the philosopher. "I submit that the thing's proved."

Candide, having lost consciousness, did not answer, so Pangloss fetched him a little water from a neighbouring fountain. The next day, in climbing over the ruins, they found food, and regained some of their strength. Then they worked like the others to relieve those of the inhabitants who had escaped death.

Some of the citizens whom they had assisted gave them as good a dinner as was possible in the circumstances. It is true the meal was sad, and the guests watered their bread with their tears, but Pangloss consoled them, assuring them that things could not possibly be otherwise.

"Everything's for the best," said he. "If there's a volcano at Lisbon, it can't be anywhere else, as it's impossible for things not to be where they are. Everything's for the best in this best of all possible worlds."

A short, dark man at his side, a friend of the Inquisition, turned to him politely, and remarked: "Evidently, you do not believe in original sin, for, if everything is good in this best of all possible worlds, there was no fall from grace or punishment."

"Very humbly do I ask your Excellency's pardon," replied Pangloss, still more politely. "The fall of man and the malediction were essential ingredients of the best of all possible worlds."

"You don't believe in Free-Will, then?" said the inquisitor.

"Your Excellency will pardon me," replied Pangloss. "The doctrine of Free-Will can co-exist with the doctrine of absolute necessity, for it was absolutely necessary that we should have free wills. Determinism, in fine…"

Pangloss was in the middle of this sentence when the inquisitor made a sign with his head to the lackey who served him with wine from Porto or Oporto.

↤ THOMAS JEFFERSON
Declaration of Independence

Thomas Jefferson (1743–1826) was the third President of the United States. Jefferson was a remarkable figure—an Enlightenment intellectual, a prolific writer, an architect, a scientist, an agriculturalist, an educational theorist, a diplomat, a politician, and a leader. One of the America's "founding fathers," Jefferson is credited with having drafted the "Declaration of Independence," which states in language both eloquent and powerful the guiding principles upon which the American nation was founded. In its bold assertion of freedom from tyranny, it details the reasons American political leaders established their own government separate from that of its colonial master, England. The Declaration was adopted by Congress on July 4, 1776.

The Declaration of Independence as Adopted by Congress

In Congress July 4, 1776

The Unanimous Declaration of the Thirteen United States of America

When in the Course of human events, it becomes necessary for one people to dissolve the political bands which have connected them with another, and to assume among the powers of the earth, the separate and equal station to which the Laws of Nature and of Nature's God entitle them, a decent respect to the opinions of mankind requires that they should declare the causes which impel them to the separation. We hold these truths to be self-evident, that all men are created equal, that they are endowed by their Creator with certain unalienable Rights, that among these are Life, Liberty and the pursuit of Happiness. That to secure these rights, Governments are instituted among Men, deriving their just powers from the consent of the governed, That whenever any Form of Government becomes destructive of these ends, it is the Right of the People to alter or to

abolish it, and to institute new Government, laying its foundation on such principles and organizing its powers in such form, as to them shall seem most likely to effect their Safety and Happiness. Prudence, indeed, will dictate that Governments long established should not be changed for light and transient causes; and accordingly all experience hath shewn, that mankind are more disposed to suffer, while evils are sufferable, than to right themselves by abolishing the forms to which they are accustomed. But when a long train of abuses and usurpations, pursuing invariably the same Object evinces a design to reduce them under absolute Despotism, it is their right, it is their duty, to throw off such Government, and to provide new Guards for their future security. Such has been the patient sufferance of these Colonies; and such is now the necessity which constrains them to alter their former Systems of Government. The history of the present King of Great Britain is a history of repeated injuries and usurpations, all having in direct object the establishment of an absolute Tyranny over these States. To prove this, let Facts be submitted to a candid world. He has refused his Assent to Laws, the most wholesome and necessary for the public good. He has forbidden his Governors to pass Laws of immediate and pressing importance, unless suspended in their operation till his Assent should be obtained; and when so suspended, he has utterly neglected to attend to them. He has refused to pass other Laws for the accommodation of large districts of people, unless those people would relinquish the right of Representation in the Legislature, a right inestimable to them and formidable to tyrants only. He has called together legislative bodies at places unusual, uncomfortable, and distant from the depository of their public Records, for the sole purpose of fatiguing them into compliance with his measures. He has dissolved Representative Houses repeatedly, for opposing with manly firmness his invasions on the rights of the people. He has refused for a long time, after such dissolutions, to cause others to be elected; whereby the Legislative powers, incapable of Annihilation, have returned to the People at large for their exercise; the State remaining in the mean time exposed to all the dangers of invasion from without, and convulsions within. He has endeavoured to prevent the population of these States; for that purpose obstructing the Laws for Naturalization of Foreigners; refusing to pass others to encourage their migrations hither, and raising the conditions of new Appropriations of Lands. He has obstructed the Administration of Justice, by refusing his Assent to Laws for establishing Judiciary powers. He has made Judges dependent on his Will alone, for the tenure of their offices, and the amount and payment of their salaries. He has erected a multitude of New Offices, and sent hither swarms of Officers to harrass our people, and eat out their substance. He has kept among us, in times of peace, standing Armies without the Consent of our legislatures. He has affected to render the Military independent of and superior to the Civil power. He has combined with others to subject us to a jurisdiction foreign to our constitution, and unacknowledged by our laws; giving his Assent to their Acts of pretended Legislation: For Quartering large bodies of armed troops among us: For protecting them, by a mock Trial, from punishment for any Murders which they should commit on the Inhabitants of these States: For cutting off our Trade with all parts of the world: For imposing Taxes on us without our Consent: For depriving us in many cases of the benefits of Trial by Jury: For transporting us beyond Seas to be tried for pretended offences: For abolishing the free System of English Laws in a neighbouring Province, establishing therein an Arbitrary government, and enlarging its Boundaries so as to render it at once an example and fit instrument for introducing the same absolute rule into these Colonies: For taking away our Charters, abolishing our most valuable Laws, and altering fundamentally the Forms of our Governments: For suspending our own Legislatures, and declaring themselves invested with power to legislate for us in all cases whatsoever. He has abdicated Government here, by declaring us out of his Protection and waging War against us. He has plundered our seas, ravaged our Coasts, burnt our towns, and destroyed the Lives of our people. He is at this time transporting large Armies of foreign Mercenaries to compleat the works of death, desolation and tyranny, already begun with circumstances of Cruelty & perfidy scarcely paralleled in the most barbarous ages, and totally unworthy the Head of a civilized nation. He has constrained our fellow Citizens taken Captive on the high Seas to bear Arms against their Country, to become the executioners of their friends and Brethren, or to fall themselves by their Hands. He has excited domestic insurrections amongst us, and has endeavoured to bring on the inhabitants of our frontiers, the merciless Indian Savages, whose known rule of warfare, is an undistinguished destruction of all ages, sexes and conditions. In every stage of these Oppressions We have Petitioned for Redress in the most humble terms: Our repeated Petitions have been answered only by repeated injury. A Prince, whose character is thus marked by every act which may define a Tyrant, is unfit to be the ruler of a free people. Nor have We been wanting in attentions to our Brittish brethren. We have warned them from time to time of attempts by their legislature to extend an unwarrantable jurisdiction over us. We have reminded them of the circumstances of our emigration and settlement here. We have appealed to their native justice and magnanimity, and we have conjured them by the ties of our common kindred to disavow these usurpations, which, would inevitably interrupt our connections and correspondence. They too have been deaf to the voice of justice and of consanguinity. We must, therefore, acquiesce in the necessity, which denounces our Separation, and hold them, as we hold the rest of mankind, Enemies in War, in Peace Friends.

We, therefore, the Representatives of the united States of America, in General Congress, Assembled, appealing to the Supreme Judge of the world for the rectitude of our intentions, do, in the Name, and by Authority of the good People of these Colonies, solemnly publish and declare, That these United Colonies are, and of Right ought to be Free and Independent States; that they are Absolved from all Allegiance to the British Crown, and that all political connection between them and the State of Great Britain, is and ought to be totally dissolved; and that as Free and Independent States, they have full Power to levy War, conclude Peace, contract Alliances, establish Commerce, and to do all other Acts and Things which Independent States may of right do. And for the support of this Declaration, with a firm reliance on the protection of divine Providence, we mutually pledge to each other our Lives, our Fortunes and our sacred Honor.

✦ DECLARATION OF THE RIGHTS OF MAN AND CITIZEN

In August 1789, the National Constituent Assembly of France decided to declare a new set of political principles. The French Declaration of the Rights of Man and the Citizen was clearly a product of the Age of Reason, with noticeable influences from Jefferson's American Declaration of Independence, Locke's theory of inalienable human rights ("life, liberty, and property"), and the constitutional principles recently established in England. Like the American declaration, France's document proclaimed civic equality, rights to own property, rights to security, and the protection from oppression. And like the American declaration, all of these innate rights applied only to men, not to women. It was for this reason that women like Olympe de Gouges and Mary Wollstonecraft found it necessary to speak out for female rights.

The representatives of the French people, organized in National Assembly, considering that ignorance, forgetfulness, or contempt of the rights of man are the sole causes of public misfortunes and of the corruption of governments, have resolved to set forth in a solemn declaration the natural, inalienable, and sacred rights of man, in order that such declaration, continually before all members of the social body, may be a perpetual reminder of their rights and duties; in order that the acts of the legislative power and those of the executive power may constantly be compared with the aim of every political institution and may accordingly be more respected; in order that the demands of the citizens, founded henceforth upon simple and incontestable principles, may always be directed towards the maintenance of the Constitution and the welfare of all.

Accordingly the National Assembly recognizes and proclaims, in the presence and under the auspices of the Supreme Being, the following rights of man and citizen.

1. Men are born and remain free and equal in rights; social distinctions may be based only upon general usefulness.

2. The aim of every political association is the preservation of the natural and inalienable rights of man; these rights are liberty, property, security, and resistance to oppression.

3. The source of all sovereignty resides essentially in the nation; no group, no individual may exercise authority not emanating expressly therefrom.

4. Liberty consists of the power to do whatever is not injurious to others; thus the enjoyment of the natural rights of every man has for its limits only those that assure other members of society the enjoyment of those same rights; such limits may be determined only by law.

5. The law has the right to forbid only actions which are injurious to society. Whatever is not forbidden by law may not be prevented, and no one may be constrained to do what it does not prescribe.

6. Law is the expression of the general will; all citizens have the right to concur personally, or through their representatives, in its formation; it must be the same for all, whether it protects or punishes. All citizens, being equal before it, are equally admissible to all public offices, positions, and employments, according to their capacity, and without other distinction than that of virtues and talents.

7. No man may be accused, arrested, or detained except in the cases determined by law, and according to the forms prescribed thereby. Whoever solicit, expedite, or execute arbitrary orders, or have them executed, must be punished; but every citizen summoned or apprehended in pursuance of the law must obey immediately; he renders himself culpable by resistance.

8. The law is to establish only penalties that are absolutely and obviously necessary; and no one may be punished except by virtue of a law established and promulgated prior to the offence and legally applied.

9. Since every man is presumed innocent until declared guilty, if arrest be deemed indispensable, all unnecessary severity for securing the person of the accused must be severely repressed by law.

10. No one is to be disquieted because of his opinions, even religious, provided their manifestation does not disturb the public order established by law.

11. Free communication of ideas and opinions is one of the most precious of the rights of man. Consequently, every citizen may speak, write, and print freely, subject to responsibility for the abuse of such liberty in the cases determined by law.

12. The guarantee of the rights of man and citizen necessitates a public force; such a force, therefore, is instituted for the advantage of all and not for the particular benefit of those to whom it is entrusted.

13. For the maintenance of the public force and for the expenses of administration a common tax is indispensable; it must be assessed equally on all citizens in proportion to their means.

14. Citizens have the right to ascertain, by themselves or through their representatives, the necessity of the public tax, to consent to it freely, to supervise its use, and to determine its quota, assessment, payment, and duration.

15. Society has the right to require of every public agent an accounting of his administration.

16. Every society in which the guarantee of rights is not assured or the separation of powers not determined has no constitution at all.

17. Since property is a sacred and inviolable right, no one may be deprived thereof unless a legally established public necessity obviously requires it, and upon condition of a just and previous indemnity.

❧ JANE AUSTEN
from *Pride and Prejudice*

Jane Austen's Pride and Prejudice *(1813) beautifully exemplifies her ironic tone and her incisive intelligence. The novel's opening sentence cuts immediately to the issues at the heart of Austen's world: money, status, marriage, and family relations. Although the author anchors these concerns in the particularities of early nineteenth-century pre-industrial England, her book is still relevant today for its insight into human nature.*

In the following passage readers are introduced to the Bennet family—father, mother, and daughters—and within the space of a few pages, Austen has characterized each distinctively. She also conveys crisply her attitude toward them, making comedy out of their anxieties, their habits, and their dispositions. In fact, the novel can be described as a comedy of manners.

CHAPTER 1

It is a truth universally acknowledged, that a single man in possession of a good fortune, must be in want of a wife.

However little known the feelings or views of such a man may be on his first entering a neighbourhood, this truth is so well fixed in the minds of the surrounding families, that he is considered as the rightful property of some one or other of their daughters.

"My dear Mr Bennet," said his lady to him one day, "have you heard that Netherfield Park is let at last?"

Mr Bennet replied that he had not.

"But it is," returned she; "for Mrs Long has just been here, and she told me all about it."

Mr Bennet made no answer.

"Do not you want to know who has taken it?" cried his wife impatiently.

"*You* want to tell me, and I have no objection to hearing it."

This was invitation enough.

"Why, my dear, you must know, Mrs Long says that Netherfield is taken by a young man of large fortune from the north of England; that he came down on Monday in a chaise and four to see the place, and was so much delighted with it that he agreed with Mr Morris immediately; that he is to take possession before Michaelmas, and some of his servants are to be in the house by the end of next week."

"What is his name?"

"Bingley."

"Is he married or single?"

"Oh! single, my dear, to be sure! A single man of large fortune; four or five thousand a year. What a fine thing for our girls!"

"How so? how can it affect them?"

"My dear Mr Bennet," replied his wife, "how can you be so tiresome! You must know that I am thinking of his marrying one of them."

"Is that his design in settling here?"

"Design! nonsense, how can you talk so! But it is very likely that he *may* fall in love with one of them, and therefore you must visit him as soon as he comes."

"I see no occasion for that. You and the girls may go, or you may send them by themselves, which perhaps will be still better, for as you are as handsome as any of them, Mr Bingley might like you the best of the party."

"My dear, you flatter me. I certainly *have* had my share of beauty, but I do not pretend to be any thing extraordinary now. When a woman has five grown up daughters, she ought to give over thinking of her own beauty."

"In such cases, a woman has not often much beauty to think of."

"But, my dear, you must indeed go and see Mr Bingley when he comes into the neighbourhood."

"It is more than I engage for, I assure you."

"But consider your daughters. Only think what an establishment it would be for one of them. Sir William and Lady Lucas are determined to go, merely on that account, for in general you know they visit no new comers. Indeed you must go, for it will be impossible for *us* to visit him, if you do not."

"You are over scrupulous surely. I dare say Mr Bingley will be very glad to see you; and I will send a few lines by you to assure him of my hearty consent to his marrying which ever he chuses of the girls; though I must throw in a good word for my little Lizzy."

"I desire you will do no such thing. Lizzy is not a bit better than the others; and I am sure she is not half so handsome as Jane, nor half so good humored as Lydia. But you are always giving *her* the preference."

"They have none of them much to recommend them,' replied he; 'they are all silly and ignorant like other girls; but Lizzy has something more of quickness than her sisters."

"Mr Bennet, how can you abuse your own children in such a way? You take delight in vexing me. You have no compassion on my poor nerves."

"You mistake me, my dear. I have a high respect for your nerves. They are my old friends. I have heard you mention them with consideration these twenty years at least."

"Ah! you do not know what I suffer."

"But I hope you will get over it, and live to see many young men of four thousand a year come into the neighbourhood."

"It will be no use to us, if twenty such should come since you will not visit them."

"Depend upon it, my dear, that when there are twenty, I will visit them all."

Mr Bennet was so odd a mixture of quick parts, sarcastic humour, reserve, and caprice, that the experience of three and twenty years had been sufficient to make his wife understand his character. *Her* mind was less difficult to develope. She was a woman of mean understanding, little information, and uncertain temper. When she was discontented she fancied herself nervous. The business of her life was to get her daughters married; its solace was visiting and news.

CHAPTER 2

Mr Bennet was among the earliest of those who waited on Mr Bingley. He had always intended to visit him, though to the last always assuring his wife that he should not go; and till the evening after the visit was paid, she had no knowledge of it. It was then disclosed in the following manner. Observing his second daughter employed in trimming a hat, he suddenly addressed her with,

"I hope Mr Bingley will like it Lizzy."

"We are not in a way to know *what* Mr Bingley likes," said her mother resentfully, "since we are not to visit."

"But you forget, mama," said Elizabeth, "that we shall meet him at the assemblies, and that Mrs Long has promised to introduce him."

"I do not believe Mrs Long will do any such thing. She has two nieces of her own. She is a selfish, hypocritical woman, and I have no opinion of her."

"No more have I," said Mr Bennet; "and I am glad to find that you do not depend on her serving you."

Mrs Bennet deigned not to make any reply; but unable to contain herself, began scolding one of her daughters.

"Don't keep coughing so, Kitty, for heaven's sake!

Have a little compassion on my nerves. You tear them to pieces."

"Kitty has no discretion in her coughs," said her father; "she times them ill."

"I do not cough for my own amusement," replied Kitty fretfully.

"When is your next ball to be, Lizzy?"

"To-morrow fortnight."

"Aye, so it is," cried her mother, "and Mrs Long does not come back till the day before; so, it will be impossible for her to introduce him, for she will not know him herself."

"Then, my dear, you may have the advantage of your friend, and introduce Mr Bingley to *her*."

"Impossible, Mr Bennet, impossible, when I am not acquainted with him myself; how can you be so teazing?"

"I honour your circumspection. A fortnight's acquaintance is certainly very little. One cannot know what a man really is by the end of a fortnight. But if *we* do not venture, somebody else will; and after all, Mrs Long and her nieces must stand their chance; and therefore, as she will think it an act of kindness, if you decline the office, I will take it on myself."

The girls stared at their father. Mrs Bennet said only, "Nonsense, nonsense!"

"What can be the meaning of that emphatic exclamation?" cried he. "Do you consider the forms of introduction, and the stress that is laid on them, as nonsense? I cannot quite agree with you *there*. What say you, Mary? for you are a young lady of deep reflection I know, and read great books, and make extracts."

Mary wished to say something very sensible, but knew not how.

"While Mary is adjusting her ideas," he continued, "Let us return to Mr Bingley."

"I am sick of Mr Bingley," cited his wife.

"I am sorry to hear that; but why did not you tell me so before? If I had known as much this morning, I certainly would not have called on him. It is very unlucky; but as I have actually paid the visit, we cannot escape the acquaintance now."

The astonishment of the ladies was just what he wished; that of Mrs Bennet perhaps surpassing the rest; though when the first tumult of joy was over, she began to declare that it was what she had expected all the while.

"How good it was in you, my dear Mr Bennet! But I knew I should persuade you at last. I was sure you loved your girls too well to neglect such an acquaintance. Well, how pleased I am! and it is such a good joke, too, that you should have gone this morning, and never said a word about it till now."

"Now, Kitty, you may cough as much as you chuse," said Mr Bennet; and, as he spoke, he left the room, fatigued with the raptures of his wife.

"What an excellent father you have, girls," said she, when the door was shut. "I do not know how you will ever make him amends for his kindness; or me either, for that matter. At our time of life, it is not so pleasant I can tell you, to be making new acquaintance every day; but for your sakes, we would do any thing. Lydia, my love, though you *are* the youngest, I dare say Mr Bingley will dance with you at the next ball."

"Oh!" said Lydia stoutly, "I am not afraid; for though I *am* the youngest, I'm the tallest."

The rest of the evening was spent in conjecturing how soon he would return Mr Bennet's visit, and determining when they should ask him to dinner.

CHAPTER 3

Not all that Mrs Bennet, however, with the assistance of her five daughters, could ask on the subject was sufficient to draw from her husband any satisfactory description of Mr Bingley. They attacked him in various ways; with barefaced questions, ingenious suppositions, and distant surmises; but he eluded the skill of them all; and they were at last obliged to accept the second-hand intelligence of their neighbour Lady Lucas. Her report was highly favourable. Sir William had been delighted with him. He was quite young, wonderfully handsome, extremely agreeable, and to crown the whole, he meant to be at the next assembly with a large party. Nothing could be more delightful! To be fond of dancing was a certain step towards falling in love; and very lively hopes of Mr Bingley's heart were entertained.

"If I can but see one of my daughters happily settled at Netherfield," said Mrs Bennet to her husband, "and all the others equally well married, I shall have nothing to wish for."

In a few days Mr Bingley returned Mr Bennet's visit, and sat about ten minutes with him in his library. He had entertained hopes of being admitted to a sight of the young ladies, of whose beauty he had heard much; but he saw only the father. The ladies were somewhat more fortunate, for they had the advantage of ascertaining from an upper window, that he wore a blue coat and rode a black horse.

An invitation to dinner was soon afterwards dispatched; and already had Mrs Bennet planned the courses that were to do credit to her housekeeping, when an answer arrived which deferred it all. Mr Bingley was obliged to be in town the following day, and consequently unable to accept the honour of their invitation, &c. Mrs Bennet was quite disconcerted. She could not imagine what business he could have in town so soon after his arrival in Hertfordshire; and she began to fear that he might be always flying about from one place to another, and never settled at Netherfield as he ought to be. Lady Lucas quieted her fears a little by starting the idea of his being gone to London only to get a large party for the ball; and a report soon followed that Mr Bingley was to bring twelve ladies and seven gentlemen with him to the assembly. The girls grieved over such a number of ladies; but were comforted the day before the ball by hearing, that instead of twelve, he had brought only six with him from London, his five sisters and a cousin. And when the party entered the assembly room, it consisted of only five altogether; Mr Bingley, his two sisters, the husband of the eldest, and another young man.

Mr Bingley was good looking and gentlemanlike; he had a pleasant countenance, and easy, unaffected manners. His sisters were fine women, with an air of decided fashion. His brother-in-law, Mr Hurst, merely looked the gentleman; but his friend Mr Darcy soon drew the attention of the room by his fine, tall person, handsome features, noble mien; and the report which was in general circulation within five minutes after his entrance, of his having ten thousand a year. The gentlemen pronounced him to be a fine figure of a man, the ladies declared he was much handsomer than Mr Bingley, and he was looked at with great admiration for about half the evening, till his manners gave a disgust which turned the tide of his popularity; for he was discovered to be proud, to be above his company, and above being pleased; and not all his large estate in Derbyshire could then save him from having a most forbidding, disagreeable countenance, and being unworthy to be compared with his friend.

Mr Bingley had soon made himself acquainted with all the principal people in the room; he was lively and unreserved, danced every dance, was angry that the ball closed so early, and talked of giving one himself at Netherfield. Such amiable qualities must speak for themselves. What a contrast between him and his friend! Mr Darcy danced only once with Mrs Hurst and once with Miss Bingley, declined being introduced to any other lady, and spent the rest of the evening in walking about the room, speaking occasionally to one of his own party. His character was decided. He was the proudest, most disagreeable man in the world, and every body hoped that he would never come there again. Amongst the most violent against him was Mrs Bennet, whose dislike of his general behaviour, was sharpened into particular resentment, by his having slighted one of her daughters.

Elizabeth Bennet had been obliged, by the scarcity of gentlemen, to sit down for two dances; and during part of that time, Mr Darcy had been standing near enough for her to overhear a conversation between him and Mr Bingley, who came from the dance for a few minutes, to press his friend to join it.

"Come, Darcy," said he, "I must have you dance. I hate to see you standing about by yourself in this stupid manner. You had much better dance."

"I certainly shall not. You know how I detest it, unless I am particularly acquainted with my partner. At such an assembly as this, it would be insupportable. Your sisters are engaged, and there is not another woman in the room, whom it would not be a punishment to me to stand up with."

"I would not be so fastidious as you are," cried Bingley, "for a kingdom! Upon my honour, I never met with so many pleasant girls in my life, as I have this evening; and there are several of them you see uncommonly pretty."

"*You* are dancing with the only handsome girl in the room," said Mr Darcy, looking at the eldest Miss Bennet.

"Oh! she is the most beautiful creature I ever beheld! But there is one of her sisters sitting down just behind you, who is very pretty, and I dare say, very agreeable. Do let me ask my partner to introduce you."

"Which do you mean?" and turning round, he looked for a moment at Elizabeth, till catching her eye, he withdrew his own and coldly said, "She is tolerable; but not handsome enough to tempt *me*; and I am in no humour at present to give consequence to young ladies who are slighted by other men. You had better return to your partner and enjoy her smiles, for you are wasting your time with me."

Mr Bingley followed his advice. Mr Darcy walked off; and Elizabeth remained with no very cordial feelings towards him. She told the story however with great spirit among her friends; for she had a lively, playful disposition, which delighted in any thing ridiculous.

The evening altogether passed off pleasantly to the whole family. Mrs Bennet had seen her eldest daughter much admired by the Netherfield party. Mr Bingley had danced with her twice, and she had been distinguished by his sisters. Jane was as much gratified by this, as her mother could be, though in a quieter way. Elizabeth felt Jane's pleasure. Mary had heard herself mentioned to Miss Bingley as the most accomplished girl in the neighbourhood; and Catherine and Lydia had been fortunate enough to be never without partners, which was all that they had yet learnt to care for at a ball. They returned therefore in good spirits to Longbourn, the village where they lived, and of which they were the principal inhabitants. They found Mr Bennet still up. With a book he was regardless of time; and on the present occasion he had a good deal of curiosity as to the event of an evening which had raised such splendid expectations. He had rather hoped that all his wife's views on the stranger would be disappointed; but he soon found that he had a very different story to hear.

"Oh! my dear Mr Bennet," as she entered the room, "we have had a most delightful evening, a most excellent ball. I wish you had been there. Jane was so admired, nothing could be like it. Every body said how well she looked; and Mr Bingley thought her quite beautiful, and danced with her twice. Only think of *that* my dear; he actually danced with her twice; and she was the only creature in the room that he asked a second time. First of all, he asked Miss Lucas. I was so vexed to see him stand up with her; but, however, he did not admire her at all: indeed, nobody can,

you know; and he seemed quite struck with Jane as she was going down the dance. So, he enquired who she was, and got introduced, and asked her for the two next. Then, the two third he danced with Miss King, and the two fourth with Maria Lucas, and the two fifth with Jane again, and the two sixth with Lizzy, and the Boulanger—"

"If he had had any compassion for *me*," cried her husband impatiently, "he would not have danced half so much! For God's sake, say no more of his partners. Oh! that he had sprained his ankle in the first dance!"

"Oh! my dear," continued Mrs Bennet, "I am quite delighted with him. He is so excessively handsome! and his sisters are charming women. I never in my life saw any thing more elegant than their dresses. I dare say the lace upon Mrs Hurst's gown—"

Here she was interrupted again. Mr Bennet protested against any description of finery. She was therefore obliged to seek another branch of the subject, and related, with much bitterness of spirit and some exaggeration, the shocking rudeness of Mr Darcy.

"But I can assure you," she added, "that Lizzy does not lose much by not suiting *his* fancy; for he is a most disagreeable, horrid man, not at all worth pleasing. So high and so conceited that there was no enduring him! He walked here, and he walked there, fancying himself so very great! Not handsome enough to dance with! I wish you had been there, my dear, to have given him one of your set downs. I quite detest the man."

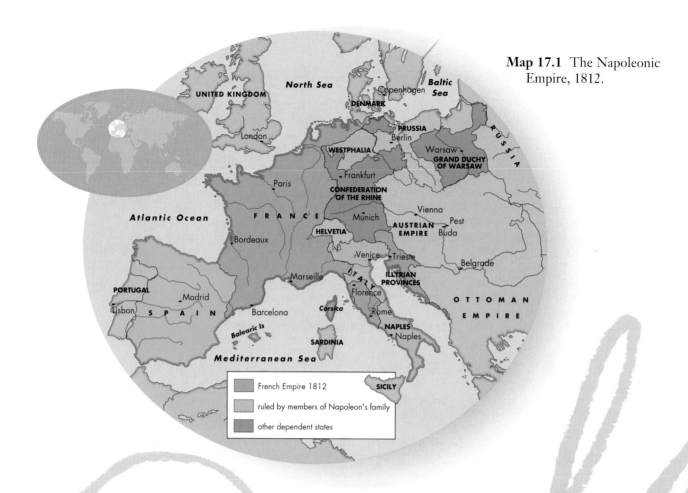

Map 17.1 The Napoleonic Empire, 1812.

- French Empire 1812
- ruled by members of Napoleon's family
- other dependent states

ROMANTICISM
AND
REALISM

CHAPTER 17

← *Romanticism*

← *Realism*

Eugène Delacroix, *The Twenty-Eighth of July: Liberty Leading the People (Detail)*, 1830, Musée du Louvre, Paris.

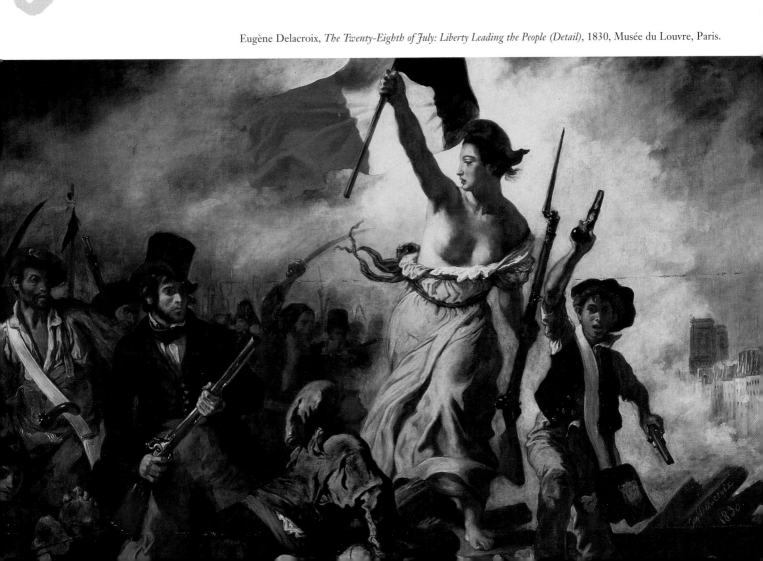

ROMANTICISM

By 1800, Neoclassicism was firmly entrenched as a dominant style in European art and architecture. It was a style that suited Napoleon well. As early as 1805, the latter had begun speaking of his "Grand Empire," conceiving of it as a modern version of the Holy Roman Empire. In 1808, as part of his strategy to subdue the entire European continent, his troops crossed the Pyrenees into Spain, ostensibly on their way to Portugal, which was closely allied with the British. But once in Spain, Napoleon took advantage of the abdication of the unpopular Charles IV, refused to recognize his successor, Ferdinand VII, and took control of the country. At first, there was little resistance, but Napoleon discovered that just because the Spanish did not care for their king did not mean that they were prepared to be ruled by a French Emperor. Soon skirmishes began breaking out across the country. These "little wars," or *guerillas* (the origin of our word for guerilla warfare), forced Napoleon to withdraw large numbers of troops from Germany to fight in Spain, and soon full-scale war broke out.

In the meantime, an emerging new movement, **Romanticism**, provided a counter-tendency to the Neoclassical style. The classicism of the eighteenth century was based on a logical mathematical model, first developed by Descartes. Rigor, clarity, exactitude, and certainty were its goals. In the Romantic era, however, things changed. In his *Philosophy of the Enlightenment*, modern thinker Ernest Cassirer put it this way: "The aesthetic faculty is ... [no longer] the prisoner of the 'clear and distinct.' Not only does it allow a certain margin of indeterminacy, it also creates and demands such a margin, since the aesthetic imagination takes fire and develops only in the presence of something that is not yet fully defined or thought ... The accent falls less on proximity than on distance with regard to the object. The object seems multiplicitous. We can never visually *possess* it, or resolve it analytically into parts."

This aesthetic can be seen in the painting of J.M.W. Turner (see fig. 17.11), where the viewer's gaze loses itself in a swirl of light. Inexactitude and indeterminacy characterize this view of the world, and it can be discovered everywhere in this period. The Romantic painter Eugène Delacroix loved the *études* by a contemporary composer, Frédéric Chopin, for "their floating, indefinite contour ... destroying the rigid frameworks of form ... like sheets of mist." Mist was actually a favorite subject of many Romantic painters. The German painter Caspar David Friedrich painted it often (fig. 17.1): "A landscape enveloped in mist seems vaster, more sublime," he wrote, "and it animates the imagination while also heightening suspense—like a veiled woman."

Romanticism is an attitude more than a style, but it depends upon a growing trust in subjective experience,

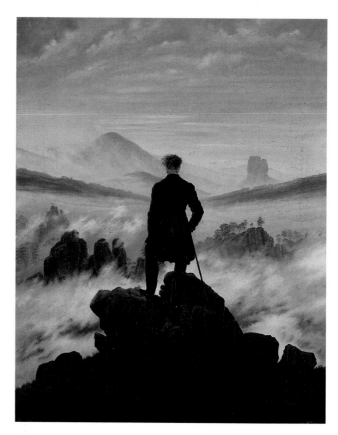

Figure 17.1   Caspar David Friedrich, *The Wanderer above the Mists*, ca. 1817–18, oil on canvas, 2'5½" × 3'1¼" (74.8 × 94.8 cm), Kunsthalle, Hamburg. Friedrich was the greatest of the German Romantic painters, noted for his depictions of Gothic cathedrals in ruin, bleak metaphors for the crisis in religious faith experienced by many people of the era.

particularly in the emotions and feelings of individuals. The Romantics had a love for anything that elicits such feelings: the fantastic world of dreams, the exotic world of the Orient, the beauty of nature revealed in a sudden vista of hills exposed around a turn in an English garden, the forces of nature in a magnificent or unpredictable moment, such as a sunset after a storm.

The Romantic attitude depends particularly on the concept of *originality* as opposed to virtuosity, which is the sign of the Renaissance genius. Just as no aspect of an English garden should be like any other, no painter or author should imitate any other. The new Romantic genius stands alone, different from the rest, and unsurpassed—a true original.

The Romantic glorification of the self found expression in many ways. Artists, composers, and writers were seen as divinely inspired visionaries with Promethean powers of inspiration and illumination. Many compared the creative power of the artist to the power of the biblical creator. They saw God's power as residing within their own creative genius.

Romantic artists were fascinated by the strange and the marvelous, by dreams and the occult. They celebrated the commonplace, seeing the extraordinary in the ordinary, infinity in a grain of sand and eternity in an hour, to paraphrase William Blake. In addition, Romantic artists expressed an abiding interest in folk traditions. And they were preoccupied as well with the uncanny and the irrational, a fascination that would lead, by the end of the century, in the person of Sigmund Freud, to the rise of psychiatry as a respected branch of medicine. The Romantic sensibility accommodates all these tendencies. Romantic art is multiplicitous, as various as the temperaments that made it.

PAINTING

Francisco Goya.   One artist who developed a unique Romantic style based on his temperament was the Spaniard FRANCISCO GOYA [GOY-uh] (1746–1828). He was the most important chronicler of France's war with Spain. Goya's approach was personal: he made drawings on the spot and even wrote on one print, "I saw this." His sense of despair is embodied in a print he made

in which a corpse, sinking into its grave, writes the word "*Nada*" (Nothing) on its own tombstone.

Goya began his career as a favorite portraitist of Madrid society, and in 1789 he was made a court painter to Charles IV of Spain. In 1794 a serious illness left him totally deaf, and within the isolation produced by his deafness he became ever more introspective. Slowly, gaiety and exuberance were replaced by bitterness. All foreigners living in Spain were obliged to swear allegiance both to the king and to the Catholic Church. Goya did not particularly care for his employer, Charles IV, who preferred hunting to affairs of state, and who was characterized by his critics as dim-witted. During his reign of corruption and repression, the country's borders were sealed, and its newspapers suppressed. Goya, however, was a social and political revolutionary, whose sympathies were with the Enlightenment and the failed French Revolution. He worked for the King not because he felt loyalty but because he desired to make a good living.

In 1800, Goya painted the *Family of Charles IV* (fig. 17.2). Goya's largest royal portrait, it features the entire clan. Goya even includes himself, on the far left, painting in the shadows, in a tribute to Velázquez's painting the

Figure 17.2   Francisco Goya, *Family of Charles IV*, 1800, oil on canvas, 9′2″ × 11′ (2.79 × 3.36 m), Museo del Prado, Madrid. Principal painter to King Charles IV of Spain, Goya has a technique that glitters but his portraits are hardly flattering and their mood is uncomfortably tense. Like Velázquez in his *Maids of Honor* (fig. 15.26), Goya included himself, on the left, painting a huge canvas.

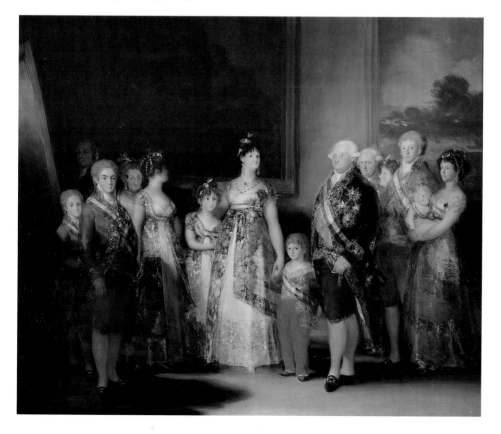

Timeline 17.1 Romanticism and Realism.

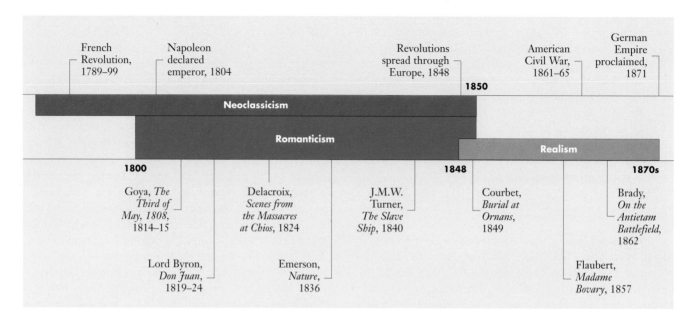

Maids of Honor (see fig. 15.26). A comparison of the two pictures underscores just how far the crown had fallen since Velázquez's time. The scene is set in one of the picture galleries in the palace. Goya's figures are painted with pitiless honesty, so much so that the French writer Théophile Gautier would describe them later in the century as "the corner baker and his wife after winning the lottery." The vulgar Queen and the vulturous King are depicted accordingly. The women are not made pretty nor are the men made handsome. Yet Goya's extraordinary skill in depicting the magnificent costumes, sparkling and lush, and the textures revealed by the light satisfied the royal family, who were evidently blind to their own shortcomings both in everyday life and in their portrayal in the painting.

The fall of Charles IV and Napoleon's invasion of Spain unleashed Goya's real talent. At first, the artist was in favor of Napoleon's invasion, hoping Spain would be modernized as a consequence. But on May 2, 1808, the civilians of Madrid rose up in a guerilla action against the French, and on the following day one of Napoleon's generals executed his Spanish hostages in retaliation. That execution is the subject of one of Goya's most powerful works, *The Third of May, 1808* (fig. 17.3). Painted several years after the event and commissioned by the newly restored Ferdinand VII, the painting marks Goya's change of heart. The French presence had brought Spain only savage atrocity, death, famine, and violence.

The soldiers on the right are a parody of the brothers in David's *Oath of the Horatii* (see fig. 16.18), but instead of raising their weapons to swear loyalty to the state, they turn their backs to us in anonymity and raise them—now rifles rather than swords—to destroy. The lighting of this night scene is theatrical, as the square light in front of the soldiers illuminates their next victim. Christ-like, with arms extended, the man accepts martyrdom for his country, but as much as his portrayal here evokes the image of the Savior, he is simply one man among many. Several lie dead in their own pools of blood to his right, and those about to die await their turn. *The Third of May, 1808* is a painting that gives visual form to a sense of hopelessness. Though it possesses all the emotional intensity of religious art, here people die for liberty rather than for God; and they are killed by political tyranny, not Satan. Death becomes a brutal and unavoidable fact.

The terror depicted in *The Third of May, 1808* is no match for the series of eighty-two prints known as *Los Desastres de la Guerra* (*The Disasters of War*), produced between 1810 and 1823. Goya had worked for some time as a printer, producing several series of etchings that reflect his sarcasm, in their grim humor, and his sense of the macabre, which is often morbid and ghastly. With the same pitiless accuracy that marks his portrait of the royal family, he attacks all the foibles of humankind: one series, made 1794–99, is ironically titled *Los Caprichos* (*Caprices*). The nightmare quality of Goya's prints is achieved not only by the subject but also by the way in which it is portrayed. Goya masses the lights and darks, emphasizes dramatic silhouettes, and creates a profound sense of brooding atmosphere. Objecting to the emphasis given to line by the academic painters, he asked, "But where do we see these lines in nature?" Goya said he saw, instead, forms that advance and recede, masses in light and shadow.

The Disasters of War was inflammatory, since it showed the French *and* the Spanish as unheroic. Goya attacked war head on. As far as he was concerned, there was nothing noble or heroic about it. War was the very image of

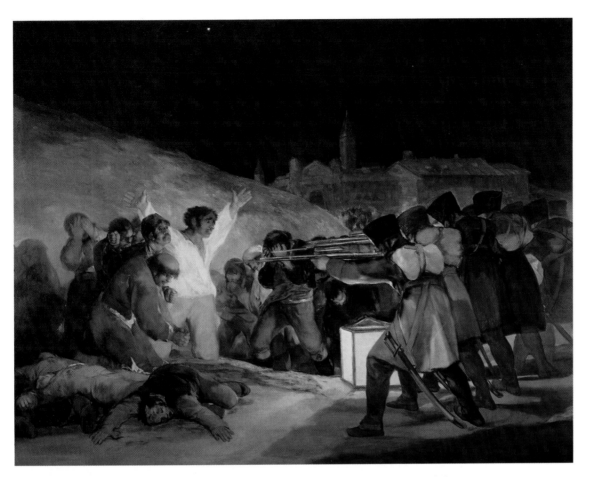

Figure 17.3 Francisco Goya, *The Third of May, 1808*, 1814–15, oil on canvas, 8′9″ × 13′4″ (2.67 × 4.06 m), Museo del Prado, Madrid. One of the most powerful anti-war statements ever made, Goya's painting documents the execution of Madrid citizens for resisting the French occupation of their city. The killers are faceless, dehumanized, mechanized; the victim, Christ-like in pose, dies for liberty rather than religion.

human brutality, even bestiality, as his prints demonstrate. Number thirty-nine in the series, called *Great Courage! Against Corpses!* (fig. 17.4), shows war for what it is—a powerful demonstration of humanity's inhumanity. Never issued during Goya's lifetime, *The Disasters of War* is a kind of personal diary, his own version of the "dark night of the soul," which another Spaniard, the mystic St. John of the Cross, experienced over two hundred years earlier. For Goya, there was neither hope of salvation nor, for that matter, any belief in God.

Théodore Géricault. Goya's equal among the French painters of the Romantic movement is THÉODORE GÉRICAULT [jay-ree-COH] (1791–1824), a sensitive man who died young from medical complications resulting from a fall off a horse. Like Goya, Géricault painted subjects that affected him emotionally. His most famous painting, the *Raft of the "Medusa"* (fig. 17.5), painted 1818–19, was inspired by his outrage at an incident that took place in 1816 in the Mediterranean. The government ship *Medusa* set sail

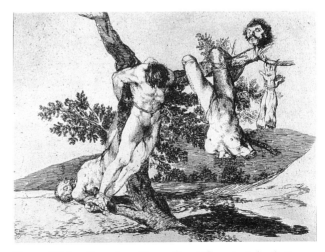

Figure 17.4 Francisco Goya, *Great Courage! Against Corpses!*, from *The Disasters of War*, 1810–23, $5\frac{1}{2}$ × $7\frac{1}{4}$″ (13.6 × 18.6 cm), British Museum, London. As in his paintings, Goya works in areas of light and dark in this etching, the stark contrast emphasizing the brutality of the subject. Few artists have approached Goya's ability.

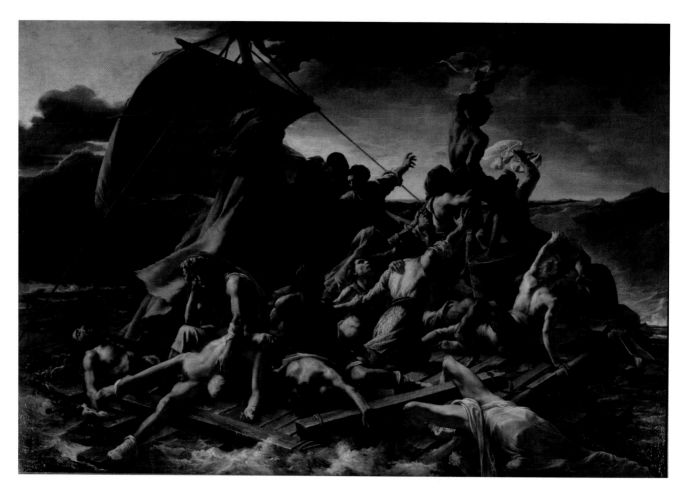

Figure 17.5　Théodore Géricault, *Raft of the "Medusa,"* 1818–19, oil on canvas, 16′1″ × 23′6″ (4.9 × 7.16 m), Musée du Louvre, Paris. In this moving depiction of a tragedy in which many lives were lost after days at sea, the impact is enhanced by the raft jutting obliquely into the viewer's space, by the proximity of extremely realistic dead bodies, and by the dramatic contrasts of light and shadow.

overloaded with settlers and soldiers bound for Senegal. When it sank on a reef off the coast of North Africa, the ship's captain and officers saved themselves in the six available lifeboats and left the 150 other passengers and crew to fend for themselves on a makeshift raft. These spent twelve days at sea before being rescued; only fifteen people survived. The others died from exposure and starvation. Some went insane and there were even reports of cannibalism. The actions of the captain and officers were judged criminally negligent and intentionally cruel, and the entire incident reflected poorly on the French monarchy, newly restored to the throne after Napoleon's defeat. The captain had been commissioned on the basis not of his ability but of his noble birth. His decision to save himself was viewed by many as an appalling act inspired by his belief in aristocratic privilege.

Géricault completed the enormous painting (16′1″ × 23′6″) in nine months. In an attempt to portray accurate-

ly the raft and the people on it, Géricault interviewed survivors, studied corpses in the morgue, and even had the ship's carpenter build a model raft, which he then floated. His search for the uncompromising truth led him to produce a vividly realistic painting of powerfully heroic drama. Géricault elected to portray the moment of greatest emotional intensity—when the survivors first sight the ship that will eventually rescue them, just visible on the horizon. It is a scene of extraordinary tension, a thrilling combination of hope and horror. Those who have died or abandoned hope are shown at the bottom of the composition, close to the viewer, large, and extremely realistic. The strongest struggle hysterically upward, led by a black man in a diagonal surge of bodies that rises toward the upper right. Disaster and despair to the bottom and left, hope and salvation at the top and right—these are the counter-tendencies of the painting.

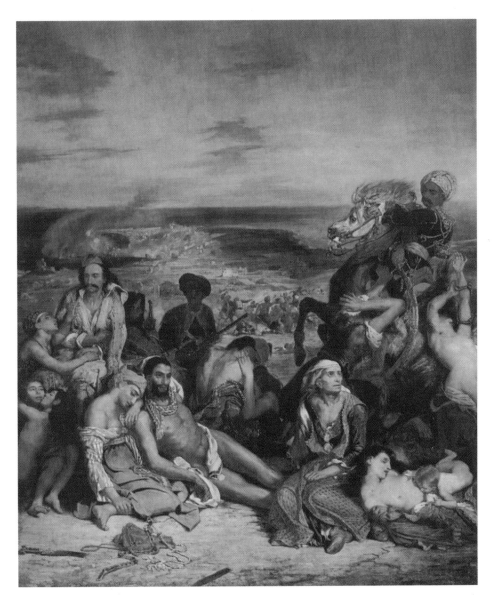

Figure 17.6 Eugène Delacroix, *Scenes from the Massacres at Chios*, 1824, oil on canvas, 13′8¼″ × 11′7⅜″ (4.17 × 3.54 m), Musée du Louvre, Paris. Reacting to the composition's lack of focus as well as to the looseness of its brushwork, one rival artist called this work "the massacre of painting."

Eugène Delacroix. Another ardent French Romantic painter was EUGÈNE DELACROIX [duh-lah-KWA] (1798–1863), who, as Géricault's friend, served as the model for the central corpse lying face down below the mast in the *Raft of the "Medusa."* Born into the upper-middle class, Delacroix was known as a fastidious dresser and an attractive personality, yet he was often unsure and melancholy. Believing that an artist's career called for "isolation," he never married.

One of his first major paintings to attract the attention of the press was, like Géricault's *Raft*, based on current events. Its full title underscores its journalistic sources: *Scenes from the Massacres at Chios; Greek Families Awaiting Death or Slavery, etc.—See Various Accounts and Contemporary Newspapers* (fig. 17.6). In April 1822, the Greeks, who had proclaimed their independence from Turkey in January, were attacked on the island of Chios (the legendary birthplace of Homer) by a Turkish army of ten thousand. Nearly twenty thousand Greeks were killed, and countless women and children were raped and tortured by the Turks and then sold in the slave markets of North Africa. A dead mother lies at the bottom right, her still-living child nuzzling her. An older woman sits resigned to her fate. Behind them a Turk drags a woman into captivity. A fatally wounded Greek soldier lies naked and, further left, yet another mother tries to save herself and her child from captivity.

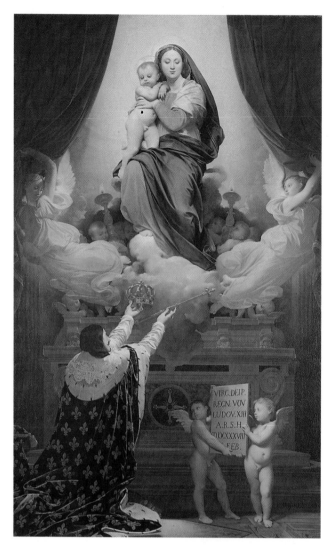

Figure 17.7 Jean-Auguste-Dominique Ingres, *The Vow of Louis XIII*, 1824, oil on canvas, 13'9¾" × 8'8⅛" (4.21 × 2.65 m), Montaubon Cathedral. Ingres had been in Florence since 1820, and Raphael's Madonnas are the clear inspiration for this painting.

When the painting was exhibited at the Salon in 1824, the reaction was vehement. For one thing, the painting was openly antagonistic to the position of the restored French monarchy headed by Charles X, whose Holy Alliance favored the Turks. It was also stylistically challenging. "The massacre of painting," one rival artist called it. In part, he was reacting to Delacroix's extraordinarily fluid use of color. There is almost no drawing in the composition; its forms are defined instead by paint alone. The rival was also reacting to the painting's extraordinary composition: it is a painting without a center. The figures at the front surround a shadowed, hollow core, an uneventful and almost empty space.

Jean-Auguste-Dominque Ingres. Just how radical Delacroix's painting must have been is evident when

compared to the painting prized at the same Salon in 1824, *The Vow of Louis XIII* (fig. 17.7) painted by JEAN-AUGUSTE-DOMINIQUE INGRES [AN-gruh] (1780–1867). A pupil of David, he is perhaps the last Neo-classical painter, for he opposed all Romantics of his day, particularly Delacroix. Stubborn and plodding, he was described as a "pedantic tyrant," and as head of the French Academy, he restricted official art for generations.

Ingres had been studying in Florence since 1820, and *The Vow* is modeled on the example of Raphael. It depicts the moment in 1628 when King Louis XIII officially placed France under the protection of the Virgin Mary, i.e. the Catholic Church, in opposition to Protestantism. Louis kneels in the traditional position of a saint. The painting is ultra-Royalist in its sensibility, in opposition to the liberal sentiments expressed by Géricault and Delacroix. It is classical and intellectual, where Delacroix's paintings are romantic and emotional. French painting would oscillate between these poles for the next forty years.

On the one hand, there was Ingres, who relentlessly pursued his classical prototypes, concentrating particularly on the human form. In Ingres's approach, precision of line is all-important. His *La Grande Odalisque* (fig. 17.8), the word *odalisque* meaning "harem woman" in Turkish, painted in 1814, is the kind of exotic subject also favored by the Romantics. The odalisque is not an individual, and her anatomy is neither academic nor accurate. The elongated, large-hipped proportions recall the Mannerist style rather than the classical ideal. Ingres perhaps had more in common with the Romantics than he would have liked to admit since it is hard to remove *all* sensuality from such a subject. He was shocked when the Neoclassical painters found his work unclassical.

Figure 17.8 Jean-Auguste-Dominique Ingres, *La Grande Odalisque*, 1814, oil on canvas, 2'11¼" × 5'3¾" (89.7 × 162 cm), Musée du Louvre, Paris. The treatment of the anatomy of this odalisque (harem woman), an exotic and erotic subject, is less academic than Ingres might have liked to believe. In fact, she has much in common with the smooth elongated bodies created by Mannerist artists, such as Parmigianino's *Madonna with the Long Neck* (fig. 13.43).

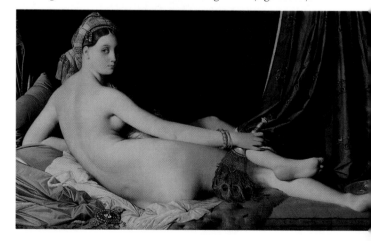

Cross Currents

DELACROIX AND THE ORIENTALIST SENSIBILITY

In January 1832, Delacroix visited Tangiers and Morocco in North Africa, a trip made possible by the French occupation. Writing home from Tangiers, he claimed that he had discovered paradise: "I am quite overwhelmed by what I have seen," he reported. "I am like a man dreaming, who sees things he is afraid to see escape him." The women, he wrote, "are pearls of Eden." He visited a harem, and there, "in the midst of that heap of silk and gold ... the lovely human gazelles ... now tame ... This is woman as I understand her, not thrown into the life of the world, but withdrawn at its heart as its most secret, delicious, and moving fulfillment." (See fig. 17.9.)

Delacroix was by no means the only European to be so moved by the prospect of the notorious harem of the Oriental world. Ingres would paint more harem scenes, such as *La Grande Odalisque* (see fig. 17.8) in 1814. Novelist Gustave Flaubert went to North Africa some years later. In fact, an entire genre of harem paintings would be a focus of French and European art right up to the twentieth century.

The harem in many ways fulfilled a European male fantasy. It was the embodiment, in sexual terms, of political empire. In the harem, men indulged in bodily pleasures, in the irrational, and in the dream world. Perhaps it was a reaction to what was happening in Rome. In Paris, women were strong, gaining independence and a voice. Women like the novelist George Sand and the painter Rosa Bonheur competed openly with men. In Algiers and Morocco, women were obliged to be submissive. They were, in Delacroix's words, "lovely human gazelles." They were, in his eyes, and the eyes of his male contemporaries, "pure" nature. "Here you will see a nature," he wrote, "which in our country is always disguised, here you will feel the rare and precious influence of the sun which gives an intense life to everything." Like the sun itself, the women so heated his temperament that he became in their presence, he said, "exalted to the point of fever, which was calmed with difficulty by sherbets and fruits."

Both sexist and racist, this point of view embodied the attitude of the nineteenth-century Western male toward colonies and territories. The harem was seen as a utopia, a prize for the taking, not as a separate cultural entity. Looking at the disenfranchisement of world cultures such as these has been the life's work of some twentieth-century scholars such as Edward Said, whose book *Orientalism* explores Western concepts of the "Orient" in detail.

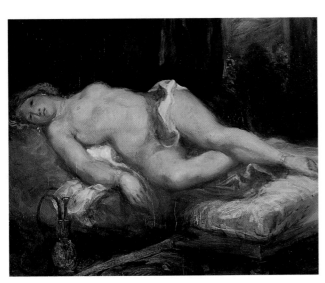

Figure 17.9 Eugène Delacroix, *Odalisque*, 1845–50, oil on canvas, 14⅞" × 18¼" (37.6 × 46.4 cm), Fitzwilliam Museum, Cambridge, England. It is hard to say which is more sensual in Delacroix's painting, the subject or the brushwork. There is an obvious contrast with Ingres's treatment of an odalisque subject thirty-odd years earlier (see fig. 17.8). Whereas in Ingres's version the emphasis is very much on line, Delacroix is a *rubéniste* and delights in an ecstatic use of color.

Still, compared to a Delacroix *Odalisque* (fig. 17.9), of 1845–50, Ingres's painting seems positively tame. Delacroix's nude is unabashedly sensual. His painting style is loose, physical, not at all intellectual. Where Ingres explores human form, Delacroix explores the body and the powerful feelings that the body can generate.

John Constable. Delacroix's attraction to the body was paralleled in England by English painters' attraction to the physical aspects of nature. JOHN CONSTABLE (1776–1837) immersed himself in the scenery of his native land and painted places he knew and loved such as Suffolk and Essex. The valley of the River Stour, which divides Suffolk from Essex, was his special haunt. Constable's inheritance enabled him to live comfortably and paint what he wanted, without having to accommodate the tastes of the Royal Academy.

He sketched on walks around the countryside, and studied cloud formations and the light effects created by clouds. Among the most lively nature studies made during the nineteenth century, these sketches were used as the basis for paintings completed later in his studio. The rapidity of Constable's brushwork is immediately evident, as are his intentions. He records, as precisely as possible, not nature in its most minute detail, but nature's effects, the play of light, the movement of water

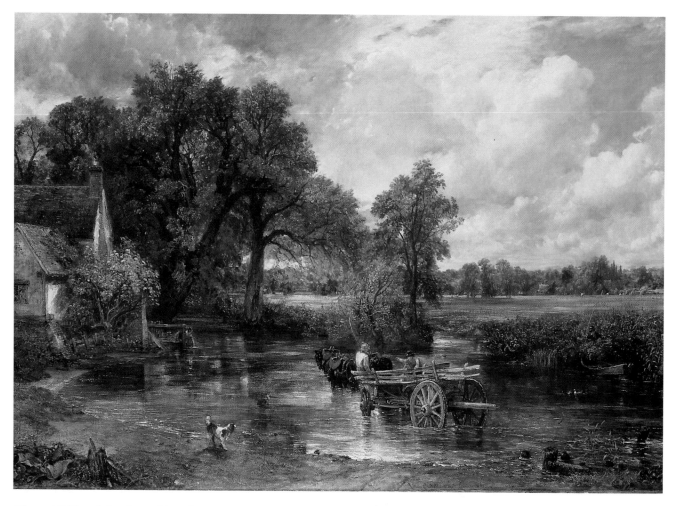

Figure 17.10 John Constable, *The Haywain*, 1821, oil on canvas, 4'3¼" × 6'1" (1.30 × 1.90 m), National Gallery, London. The English penchant for landscape painting indicates a growing interest in nature and weather conditions that prefigures late nineteenth-century Impressionism. Although Constable sketched from nature, he did the final painting in his studio.

and air, the uncanny relationship between trees and clouds. "I should paint my own places best," he wrote to a friend in 1821. "Painting is but another word for feeling. I associate my 'careless boyhood' to all that lies on the banks of the Stour. They made me a painter (& I am grateful)."

In the 1820s, in an apparent effort to gain more respect for his work from the Royal Academy, Constable began painting a series of "six-footers," which were large, ambitious landscapes celebrating rural life. *The Haywain* (fig. 17.10), of 1821, depicts a wagon mired beside Willy Lott's cottage in the millstream at Flatford that ran beside the Stour proper, adjacent to Constable's own property. Willy Lott lived in this cottage for eighty years and spent only four nights away from it in his entire life. He embodied, for Constable, the enduring attachment to place so fundamental to rural life. The enduring geometry of the scene—defined precisely by the cottage on the

left and the horizon line on the right—is set against the transience of nature, the momentary effects of atmosphere and light, of storm and sunlight, dense foliage and open field.

J.M.W. Turner. Constable's love of nature was shared by his fellow Englishman JOSEPH MALLORD WILLIAM TURNER (1775–1851). The son of a barber, Turner had no formal education but was interested in art from childhood. His talent was quickly recognized for he was already a full member of the Royal Academy in 1802, when he was still only twenty-seven. Opposing the Academy's classicism, he was to become England's leading Romantic painter.

Although Turner worked from nature, he took even greater liberties with the facts than did Constable. Consequently, it is not always possible to recognize his sites or fully to comprehend his subject. For example,

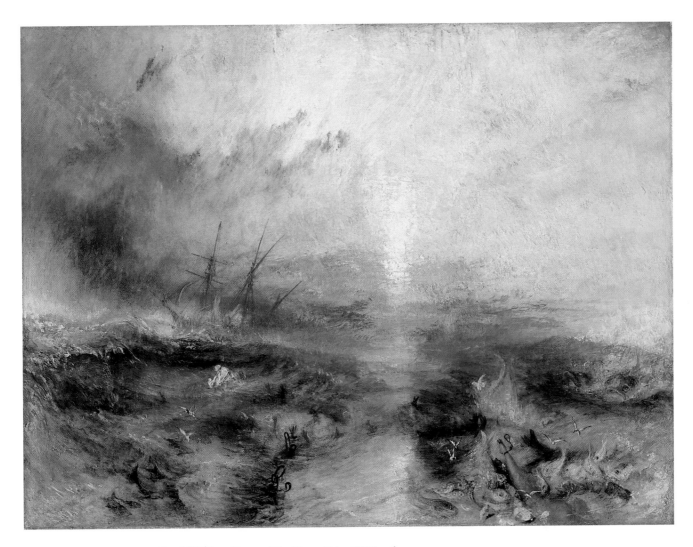

Figure 17.11   Joseph Mallord William Turner, *The Slave Ship*, 1840, oil on canvas, 2′11¾″ × 4′ (90.5 × 122 cm), Museum of Fine Arts, Boston. Constable called Turner's paintings "tinted steam." The original title, "Slavers Throwing Overboard the Dead and Dying—Typhoon Coming On," in spite of its unusual length, hardly clarifies the subject which is, above all, Turner's Romantic response to nature.

Turner's painting *The Slave Ship* (fig. 17.11), of 1840, originally titled *Slavers Throwing Overboard the Dead and Dying—Typhoon Coming On*, illustrates a specific, contemporary event with all the outrage of Géricault and Delacroix. A ship's captain had thrown overboard slaves who were sick or dying from an epidemic that had broken out on board. The captain was insured against loss of slaves at sea, but not against their loss owing to disease.

Turner's figures are lost in the wash of colors of sea and sky, and the political subject threatens to become, in Turner's hands, an excuse for a study of atmosphere. The eye drowns in this painting like the slaves themselves. The forms dissolve into a haze of mist. The swirl of storm and colored light is designed to stir the viewer's emotion, and the blurring of our vision before the scene can be viewed as a metaphor for the blindness of society itself. When the painting was first exhibited, Turner added a fragment of verse to the title: "Hope, Hope, fallacious Hope! / Where is thy market now?" The painting can be viewed finally as a treatise on the difference between blindness and insight, between what we can see with our eyes and what we know in our hearts.

Thomas Cole.   American landscape painting is a painting of solitude. When figures are included in a scene, as, for instance, in *American Lake Scene* of 1844 (fig. 17.12) by THOMAS COLE (1801–1848), they are barely visible, dwarfed in the landscape that surrounds them. Here a lone Native American warrior sits between two trees on a small island where he has brought his canoe to rest. We share his view, enthralled by the combination of light and open space that fills the scene. In an analogous moment, Cole described his feelings as he looked out across two lakes in Fran-

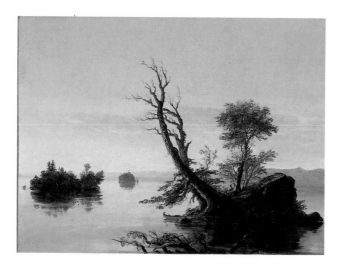

Figure 17.12 Thomas Cole, *American Lake Scene*, 1844, oil on canvas, 18¼″ × 24½″ (46.4 × 62.2 cm), Detroit Institute of Arts, Detroit. Though his landscape paintings were a popular success, they seemed less important to Cole than his historical and allegorical works, which were not as enthusiastically received.

conia Notch in the New Hampshire mountains: "I was overwhelmed with an emotion of the sublime such as I have rarely felt. It was not that the jagged precipices were lofty, that the encircling woods were of the dimmest shade, or that the waters were profoundly deep; but that over all, rocks, wood, and water, brooded the spirit of repose, and the silent energy of nature stirred the soul to its inmost depths." The same spirit of repose broods over this combination of rock, wood, and water.

Frederic Edwin Church. When there are no figures in the landscape, as in *Twilight in the Wilderness* (fig. 17.13), of 1860, by FREDERIC EDWIN CHURCH (1826–1900), the viewer is drawn into the scene, standing before the extraordinary sunset alone like a Daniel Boone exploring the continent, encountering the place for the first time. Church's painting combines the structure of Claude Lorrain (see Chapter 15) with the light of Turner, both of whose works he knew well. But for all its seeming realism, the painting is deeply symbolic. An eagle hovers over the scene, perched on the very top branch of the far left-hand tree. It is the

Figure 17.13 Frederic Edwin Church, *Twilight in the Wilderness*, 1860, oil on canvas, 3′4″ × 5′4″, (1.02 × 1.60 m), Cleveland Museum of Art, Cleveland. Painted on the eve of the Civil War, the work was interpreted by many as anticipating the bloody conflict to come, especially in its blood-red clouds.

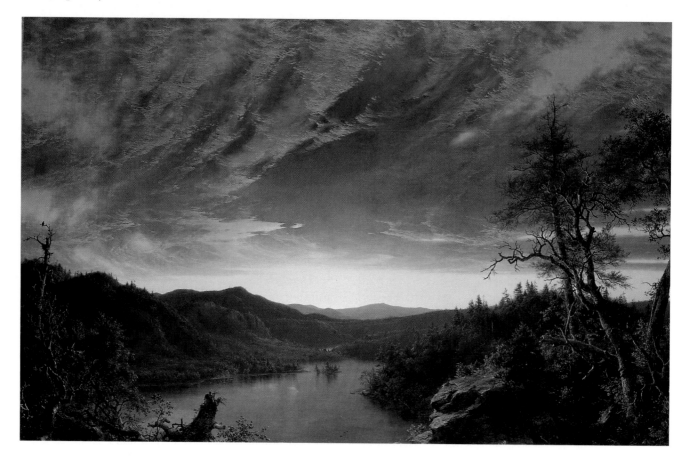

Then & Now

AMERICA'S NATIONAL PARKS

*I*n the early eighteenth century, the new American nation prided itself upon its political system, but it lagged far behind Europe in cultural achievement. Rather than in authors and artists, the country took pride in the one thing it had in abundance—land. After Thomas Jefferson purchased the Louisiana territory from Napoleon in 1803, the American landscape became, in effect, the nation's cultural inheritance. And as the country was subsequently explored, the treasures it held, in beauty as well as gold, excited the American populace.

It was the artists and photographers who accompanied the expeditions to the West who publicized the beauty of the landscape. The painter ALBERT BIERSTADT [BEER-shtaht] (1830–1902) accompanied Colonel Frederick Lander to the Rockies in 1859. The photographer C.E. WATKINS (1829–1916) traveled to Yosemite in 1861. The painter THOMAS MORAN (1837–1926) went with Colonel Ferdinand V. Hayden of the National Geographic Survey through the Rockies to Yellowstone in 1871.

Bierstadt's paintings and Watkins's photographs were the primary reason that Lincoln signed into law a bill establishing Yosemite as a national preserve in 1864. In 1872, Congress purchased Moran's *Grand Canyon of the Yellowstone* (fig. 17.14) for $10,000 and later hung the massive painting in the lobby of the Senate. On March 1, 1872, President Ulysses S. Grant signed the Yellowstone Park Act into law, establishing the National Park system.

Today the National Park system is increasingly threatened. Automobiles have been banned from Yosemite, parts of Mesa Verde, and others as well. In the early 1980s, developers proposed building a geothermal power plant fifteen miles west of Upper Geyser Basin and "Old Faithful" Geyser in Yellowstone. The project was halted only because no one could demonstrate just where the exact boundaries of the Yellowstone geothermal reservoirs were. In 1980, the National Park Service explained the situation this way: "Yellowstone, Great Smoky Mountains, Everglades, and Glacier—most of these great parks were at one time pristine areas surrounded and protected by vast wilderness regions. Today, with their surrounding buffer zones gradually disappearing, many of these parks are experiencing significant and widespread adverse effects associated with external encroachment."

The nation is losing one of its myths—the myth that people can live harmoniously with nature, which was illustrated in the landscapes of American Romantic painters.

Figure 17.14 Thomas Moran, *Grand Canyon of the Yellowstone*, 1872, oil on canvas, 7′ × 12′ (2.13 × 3.66 m), National Museum of American Art, Smithsonian Institution, Washington, D.C. On a visit to England in 1862, Moran studied and copied the paintings of J.M.W. Turner, whose use of light and color he particularly admired.

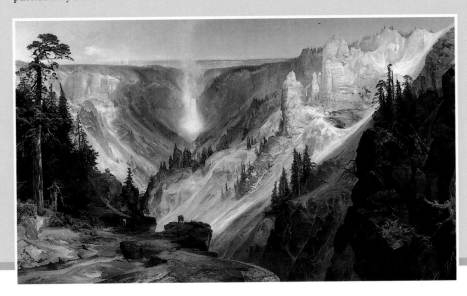

---

year 1860 and the dawn of the American Civil War. The sky may not reflect Cole's quiet "spirit of repose" so much as it anticipates the blood of apocalyptic battles to come.

SCULPTURE

Neoclassical sculpture had been bolstered not only by the revival of interest in the values and sentiments of the ancient world, but also, in France, by the patronage of Napoleon himself, who, in his desire to rebuild Paris as a new Rome, commissioned a vast quantity of sculptural work. Surprisingly, in the Romantic era, sculpture fell out of favor. In fact, in 1846 the poet Charles Baudelaire argued that the idea of a Romantic sculpture was impossible. Sculpture, he suggested, can neither arouse subjective feelings in the viewer nor express the personal sensibility of the artist because, as a three-dimensional object, it asserts its objective reality too thoroughly. Baudelaire summed up Romantic sculpture in the title of his essay, "Why Sculpture Is Boring."

Baudelaire did argue, however, that sculpture could escape this fate in the service of architecture. Attached to a larger whole, it can evoke profound feelings. One

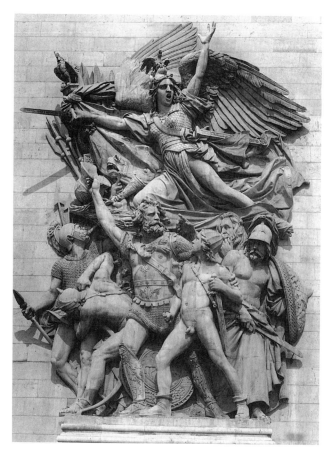

Figure 17.15   François Rude, *La Marseillaise (The Departure of the Volunteers of 1792)*, 1833–36, limestone, ca. 42′ × 26′ (12.80 × 7.90 m), Arc de Triomphe, Place de l'Étoile, Paris. The use of a triumphal arch to commemorate a military victory, as well as the use of a winged female figure to represent victory, derive from Greek and Roman antiquity.

example is *The Departure of the Volunteers of 1792*, popularly known as *La Marseillaise* (fig. 17.15), by FRANÇOIS RUDE (1784–1855), a huge stone sculpture made for the Arc de Triomphe in Paris. Although sculpted between 1833 and 1836, the subject refers to an event that occurred in 1792—the defense of the French Republic by volunteers rallying to repel invaders from abroad. For Rude, the subject was deeply emotional: his own father had been among the volunteers.

The figures are costumed in both ancient and medieval armor, and the nude youth in front is Neoclassical in pose and physique. A winged female figure representing Victory as in antiquity leads the soldiers forward, and the group below appears to surge upward with a diagonal force that points in the direction of the end of her sword. Thus, in a rectangular format necessitated by the architecture of the Arc itself, Rude creates a dynamic triangular thrust to the left that creates an emotional thrust as well, one that many French people associate with their national anthem to this day.

GOTHIC REVIVAL ARCHITECTURE

The styles of the past were among the sources of inspiration for the Romantic sensibility. The model of Gothic architecture was especially admired by the British who believed (incorrectly) that the Gothic style was British in origin. As architect A.W.N. PUGIN (PEW-gin) (1812–1852) noted: "We do not want to revive a facsimile of the works of style of any particular individual or even period, but it is the devotion, majesty, and response of Christian art, for which we are contending; it is not a style, but a principle." Gothic architecture, with its inventive lines of tracery, recalling the natural forms of vines and trees, and its ability to evoke the sublime and infinite in the rising shapes of its giant interior spaces, was an emotional architecture. As the English writer JOHN RUSKIN (1819–1900) wrote in *The Stones of Venice* (1851–53): "It is that strange disquietude of the Gothic spirit that is its greatness; that restlessness of the dreaming mind, that wanders hither and thither among the niches, and flickers feverishly around the pinnacles, and frets and fades in labyrinthine shadows along wall and roof, and that yet is not satisfied, nor shall be satisfied." For Ruskin and Pugin both, the Gothic was Romantic.

After the British Houses of Parliament burnt down in 1834, Pugin and SIR CHARLES BARRY (1795–1860) won a competition to rebuild them (fig. 17.16). They chose the Gothic style, and construction began in 1840.

Figure 17.16   Sir Charles Barry and Augustus Welby Northmore Pugin, Houses of Parliament, London, 1836–60, length 940′ (286.5 m). The delicacy of Gothic religious architecture is applied to government office buildings. Among the plethora of pointed pinnacles, turrets, and towers is the clock known as "Big Ben."

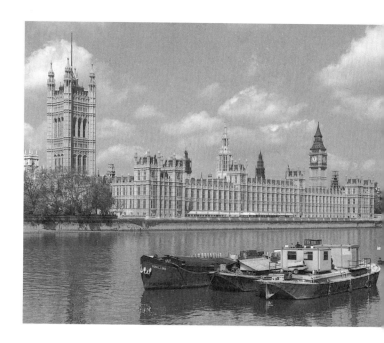

Barry designed the basic structure and Pugin the Gothic detailing, interior decoration, and furniture. The building is organized around a central hall and spire, with vertical rectilinear blocks down its side that lend the facade a sense of order, rhythm, and repetition. This facade is punctuated by an irregular silhouette of spires—a tall square spire, a more delicate pointed tower, smaller pointed towers with two different elevations, and a clock tower nicknamed "Big Ben." The whole is designed to evoke the spiritual and ethical values of the Middle Ages.

PHILOSOPHY

Jean-Jacques Rousseau and the Concept of Self.
Anticipating the opening lines of Whitman's epic poem *Song of Myself* was the work of the French philosophical writer JEAN-JACQUES ROUSSEAU [roo-SEW] (1712–1778), whose autobiographical *Confessions* was the first and most influential exploration of the self in the West outside the tradition of religious autobiography. Unlike St. Augustine's *Confessions*, written to honor and glorify God, Rousseau's were written to honor and glorify the self in its intellectual and emotional splendor. Rousseau's conception of the largeness and importance of the "self" is among his greatest influences.

Rousseau lived during the period of the Enlightenment, but he was notably antagonistic to its prevailing spirit. As a Romantic rather than an Enlightenment figure, he stood in stark contrast to many of his contemporaries, particularly Swift and Voltaire. Rousseau believed in the basic goodness of humanity, in naturally positive instincts rather than naturally negative ones. Society, he felt, corrupted a person's basic instincts, making people competitive, greedy, and uncaring. Like the Romantic poets and painters who were to follow in his wake, he celebrated the claims of the imagination above all else.

Rousseau was most interested in the subjectivity of the self. His early works concern social themes. In his *Discourse on Inequality* (1754) he provides a critique of the philosophy of Thomas Hobbes, who argued that human beings are spurred by self-interest and that to exist in a state of nature is to exist in a state of war (see Chapter 15). For Hobbes, society existed to regulate the competition and conflict that were natural to human beings. Rousseau argued that although humans are motivated by self-interest, they also possess a natural instinct of compassion.

Rousseau's *Confessions* serves as a powerful example of reflective self-analysis, a model for future philosophical self-explorations. This celebration of the self became so prevalent during the Romantic era that even in the face of crisis, as with the dashed hopes of many in Britain and France at the outcome of the French Revolution, there

was a belief that those aspirations could be profitably redefined. If the Revolution did not create a better society, then the revolutionary ideal should be transferred from the social realm to the personal one to create a better mind. If a transformation of political reality was more complicated than had been imagined, then a transformation of human consciousness could at least be effected.

Ralph Waldo Emerson and Transcendentalism.
The sentiments about nature expressed by the Romantic painters were quickly adopted in the United States, where in the nineteenth century more people lived in close communion with nature than in Europe. The union of humanity with nature was a special theme of RALPH WALDO EMERSON (1803–1882), author of the widely influential essay "Nature," first published in 1836. Emerson was one of a number of American thinkers who called themselves Transcendentalists. The Transcendentalists built a philosophical perspective from the poetry of William Wordsworth, on the one hand, and the philosophy of the German IMMANUEL KANT (1724–1804), on the other. Kant had argued that there are two basic elements, "those that we receive through impressions, and those that our faculty of knowledge supplies from itself." The first he called **phenomena**, the second **noumena**. We can never truly "know" the essence of the things that the mind creates for itself. "In the world of sense, however far we may carry our investigation, we can never have anything before us but mere phenomena ... The transcendental object remains unknown to us." The "transcendental object" is known only through intuition. Emerson was able to intuit the transcendental in nature. As he puts it in the most famous passage in "Nature": "Standing on the bare ground,—my head bathed by the blithe air, and uplifted into infinite space,—all mean egotism vanishes. I become a transparent eyeball; I am nothing; I see all; the currents of the Universal Being circulate through me; I am part or particle of God ... In the wilderness, I find something more dear and connate than in streets or villages. In the tranquil landscape, and especially in the distant line of the horizon, one beholds somewhat as beautiful as one's own nature."

Henry David Thoreau.
The American wilderness was raw and vast, and even along the eastern seaboard, where civilization had taken firm hold, it was still easy to leave the city behind, as HENRY DAVID THOREAU (1817–1862) did at Walden Pond. "I went to the woods," Thoreau wrote in *Walden* (1854), "because I wished to live deliberately, to front only the essential facts of life, and see if I could not learn what it had to teach, and not, when I came to die, discover that I had not lived." Living close to nature was, for Thoreau, the very source of humankind's strength. In an essay entitled "Walking" he echoed the sentiments Emerson had expressed in "Nature":

What I have been preparing to say is, that in Wildness is the preservation of the world. Every tree sends its fibres forth in search of the Wild ... From the forest and wilderness come the tonics and barks which brace mankind. Our ancestors were savages. The story of Romulus and Remus being suckled by a wolf is not a meaningless fable. The founders of every State which has risen to eminence have drawn their nourishment and vigor from a similar wild source. It was because the children of the Empire were not suckled by the wolf that they were conquered and displaced by the children of the Northern forests who were. I believe in the forest, and in the meadow, and in the night in which the corn grows.

Thoreau's belief system, so simple and direct, is clearly a radical departure from the one that had defined civilization for centuries. Nature was his source and inspiration, and he lived in solitude because he could trust nature more than people. Thoreau's sensibility remains common to American experience, most notably in the environmental movement of recent years.

LITERATURE

The British philosopher and politician Edmund Burke, in his *Enquiry into the Sublime and Beautiful*, wrote: "I think there are reasons in nature why the obscure idea, when properly conveyed, should be more affecting than the clear. It is our ignorance of things that causes our admiration, and chiefly excites our passions." This is the theme of much nineteenth-century literature: our ignorance of things. In HERMAN MELVILLE's (1819–1891) novel *Moby Dick* (1851), Captain Ahab is bent on capturing the great white whale, which comes to stand, in his imagination, for something close to a final truth or a first cause. But the whale eludes him, and even when Ahab does indeed "capture" it, the whale drags him to his death. He seeks a knowledge he cannot possess.

ROBERT LOUIS STEVENSON (1850–1894), another of the great authors of the era, wrote a famous short novel, *Dr. Jekyll and Mr. Hyde* (1886), which embodies the conflict between the classical mind, with its urge for order, and the new Romantic mind, and in which the rational, scientific Dr. Jekyll has to battle with his alter-ego, the violent, irrational Mr. Hyde. In other popular literature, the mystery tale rises into fashion in France in the 1830s and is seen in America a decade later, but culminates, at the end of the century, in the English writer Sir Arthur Conan Doyle's great detective, Sherlock Holmes. In the typical mystery, everyone is, metaphorically, thrown into a fog by murder. No one knows "who done it," a situation that has excited the passions of readers ever since. As a sort of Enlightenment hero, the detective penetrates the fog, clarifies the situation, resolves the conflict, and explains it logically. If our Romantic spirit is excited by inexactitude and indeterminacy, we nonetheless long to be rescued from them.

But in many ways, the Romantic author is akin to the detective character that emerged at this time. Possessed of a vision capable of penetrating the mysteries of life, particularly the mysteries of the self, writers and poets sought to clarify the nature of experience for us all. As William Blake put it: "One power alone makes a poet: Imagination. The Divine Vision."

William Blake. A product of the industrial slums, the poet and artist WILLIAM BLAKE (1757–1827) was born in poverty and, unable to attend school, he taught himself to read and studied engravings of paintings by such Renaissance masters as Raphael, Dürer, and Michelangelo. Samuel Palmer remembers how Blake "saw everything through art, finding sources of delight throughout the whole range of art." At the age of twenty-two, Blake entered the Royal Academy as an engraving student, but unsettling clashes over artistic differences returned him to a life of nonconformist study.

Blake insisted that his "great task" as a poet was "To open the Eternal Worlds, to open the immortal Eyes of Man inwards into the Worlds of Thought." His was a poetry of revelation, not technique. As a boy Blake saw "a tree filled with angels, bright angelic wings bespangling every bough with stars." This ability to see beyond the physical, what he called his "double vision," fueled Blake's imaginative and poetic flights (fig. 17.17).

Blake saw himself as a prophet, and he drew heavily on both the Hebrew and the Christian sacred texts. As a prophet, Blake was more interested in attacking the ways of humanity than in justifying the ways of God. He was, as the poet T.S. Eliot later noted, "a man with a profound interest in human emotions, and a profound knowledge of them." At the core of Blake's work are two contrary archetypal states of the human soul: innocence and experience. Humanity's oscillation between these states forms the focus of much of his poetry.

For Blake, innocence and experience are psychological states that carry political implications. "The Chimney Sweeper" in *Songs of Innocence* is a young boy who rationalizes his misery and naively declares, "Those that do their duty need not fear harm." Historically, nothing could have been further from the truth. Young "sweeps" who endured this forced labor rarely lived to reach adulthood. Master chimney sweeps found that small children (some as young as four) could easily climb up into chimneys and scour them. Reluctant sweeps were poked with rods and pins as they climbed naked into chimneys where fires were still burning. Young sweeps who did not get trapped and die immediately, often later died of lung ailments. The irony of his final pronouncement escapes the innocent boy, unaware of the horrors of the Industrial Revolution. Readers would have understood the implications, nonetheless.

In *Songs of Experience*, Blake presents another chimney sweep who has also been taught "to sing the notes of

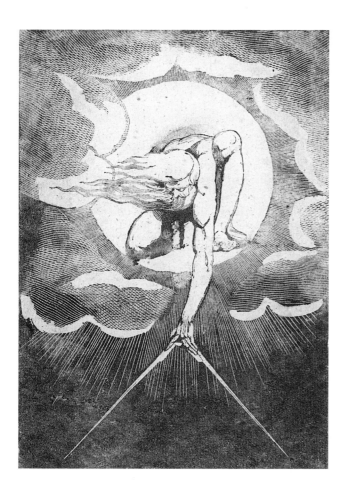

Figure 17.17   William Blake, frontispiece to *Europe: A Prophecy*, 1794, $12\frac{1}{4} \times 9\frac{1}{2}''$ (31.1 × 24.1 cm), British Museum, London. Blake's idea of God, Urizen, is depicted here on the second day of Creation. He holds a pair of compasses as he measures out and delineates the firmament. He is, in fact, faced with the dilemma of all artists—to measure out and make something is restrictive, because to do so necessarily set limits upon the imagination.

woe." His own parents have "clothed" him in the "clothes of death" and have now gone off to praise "God & his Priest & King / Who make up a heaven of our misery."

William Wordsworth and Samuel Taylor Coleridge. Probably the most important literary event in the Romantic era was the publication, in 1798, of the *Lyrical Ballads*, co-authored by WILLIAM WORDSWORTH (1770–1850) and SAMUEL TAYLOR COLERIDGE (1772–1834). Turning their backs on the sophisticated syntax and vocabulary of Neoclassical writing, they insisted that the language of poetry should be natural; as natural, in fact, as its subject, nature—both human nature and the natural world. Coleridge was particularly interested in folk idioms and songs. Wordsworth's ear was tuned to the everyday language of common folk, "a language really used by men," as he put it. He wrote about everyday subjects, a poetry of the individual, of the inner life and "the essential passions of the heart."

Exactly how the human imagination delineates a sense of place in nature, and by extension in daily reality, also underlies Wordsworth's lyric "I Wandered Lonely as a Cloud." According to his sister Dorothy's journal of April 15, 1802, they had gone for a walk "in the woods beyond Gowbarrow Park." Together they stumbled upon a stretch of daffodils that "grew among the mossy stones … some rested their heads upon these stones as on a pillow for weariness; and the rest tossed and reeled and danced, and seemed as if they verily laughed with the wind, that flew upon them over the Lake; they looked so gay, ever glancing, ever changing." The daffodils of Wordsworth's poem are the personified flowers of Dorothy's journal entry, but in the end brother and sister witness different events. While Dorothy draws simple pleasure from her walk among the flowers, the poet's attention becomes fixed on how the imagination interacts with nature. For although Wordsworth takes pleasure in his walk, the "wealth" the poem refers to comes into focus only with the "inward eye" of the imagination. The poem reflects many of Wordsworth's Romantic preoccupations, particularly the power of nature and of remembered experience to restore the human spirit.

John Keats.   Probably no poet of the period was more aware of his inability to know the world fully, yet at the same time more compelled to explore it, than JOHN KEATS (1795–1821). Like Wordsworth, Keats believed in the vitality of sensation but did not limit himself to sight and sound. Keats often uses imagery designating one sense in place of imagery suggesting another. For example, he writes of "fragrant and enwreathed light," "pale and silver silence," "scarlet pain," and "the touch of scent." Keats's images register on palate and fingertip as well as within the ear and eye, making the world, the poet, and the poem one complete sensation. This blurring of borders reflects the empathic power Keats termed "negative capability," the poet's ability to empathize with other characters, or entities, living or imagined, animate or inanimate. Free of his own life, "the chameleon poet" is then able to move among "uncertainties, mysteries, [and] doubts, without any irritable reaching after fact and reason."

Negative capability was, for Keats, a way of emptying or "annulling" the self and, as such, a way of making room for his subject. According to his friend Richard Woodhouse, Keats even "affirmed that he can conceive of a billiard Ball that it may have a sense of delight from its own roundness, smoothness, volubility & the rapidity of its motion." Perhaps the most affecting of Keats's efforts at negative capability is "This Living Hand," written shortly before he died of tuberculosis at the age of twenty-five:

This living hand, now warm and capable
Of earnest grasping, would, if it were cold
And in the icy silence of the tomb,
So haunt thy days and chill thy dreaming nights
That thou wouldst wish thine own heart dry of blood
So in my veins red life might stream again,
And thou be conscience-calmed—see here it is—hold it
    towards you.

When Keats contracted the disease that had already claimed his mother and brother, he moved to Italy in hope of a cure but died within a few months. At his request, no name marks the tomb that reads, "Here lies one whose name is writ in water," his epitaph itself as mysterious and fascinating as his poems.

Lord Byron. One of the other great English Romantic poets is George Gordon, LORD BYRON (1788–1824). If in America Whitman came to embody the Romantic self, in Europe it was Byron. A free spirit, he was notorious for his unconventional behavior. One of his first books of poems, *Hours of Idleness* (1807), was subjected to severe criticism in the *Edinburgh Review*, to which Byron retorted, in 1809, with a biting satire in the style of Swift and Pope, entitled *English Bards and Scotch Reviewers*. It won him instant fame. That same year, he left England to travel extensively in Spain, Portugal, Italy, and the Balkans (fig. 17.18). Good-looking and flamboyant, Byron socialized with a variety of upper-class and aristocratic women. His most famous poem, *Don Juan* (1819–24), portrayed the seducer already well known to most audiences. Most of his followers assumed the poem to be semi-autobiographical since it was begun soon after he formed a relationship with Contessa Teresa Guicioli in Italy, who remained his mistress for the rest of his life. As one female friend said of him, not without some real admiration, "He is mad, bad, and dangerous to know." Byron died in the Balkans fighting for the Greeks in the war against Turkey in 1824, the same year that Delacroix painted his *Massacres at Chios* (see fig. 17.6).

Emily Brontë. In Wordsworth's *Lyrical Ballads*, nature is a garden full of wonder and joy, relatively benign. However, Wordsworth's nature is not the only one that attracted the Romantic imagination: the turbulent sea in Turner's *Slave Ship* and the mysterious fog in Friedrich's *Mist* both suggest the age's fascination with nature at its most horrific and sublime. *Wuthering Heights* (1847), the masterpiece of EMILY BRONTË [BRON-tay] (1818–1848), is organized with the same structural care in the classical manner of Jane Austen, but it is a fully Romantic work that breaks new ground in the violence of its scenes and the extravagance of its style.

Gone is the decorum that marked Austen's world (the "artificial rudeness" of the English garden) and in its place is a world of storm and turmoil. The novel's central characters display passionate and socially disruptive ten-

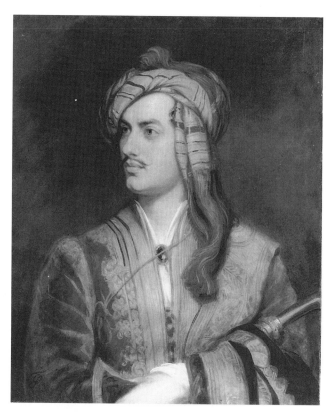

Figure 17.18 Thomas Philips, *Lord Byron in Albanian Costume*, 1814, oil on canvas, $29\frac{1}{2} \times 24\frac{1}{2}''$ (75 × 62 cm), National Portrait Gallery, London. Byron looks particularly dashing in this costume, which signifies the love of the exotic and interest in the cultures of the Balkans reflected in his writings.

dencies entirely at odds with the rational and serene world of the Enlightenment, and it is as if the landscape around them responds. Reason and social decorum are replaced by intense feeling and individual expression. The demands and needs of the self are paramount. Nature is untamed, unruly, and grand, exhibiting patterns of storm followed by calm, similar to the contrasting emotions displayed by Brontë's characters, and analogous to the alternation of quiet lyricism and passionate drama heard in Romantic music such as Schubert's. Moreover, in the work of both artists drama explodes in the midst of serenity and calm, suggesting thereby the potential for abrupt change in both inner and outer weather.

Johann Wolfgang von Goethe. Perhaps the most influential writer of the Romantic era was JOHANN WOLFGANG VON GOETHE [GUR-tuh] (1749–1832), who lived half his life during the Enlightenment and half during the Romantic era. He witnessed the shift in consciousness from the Enlightenment emphasis on reason, objectivity, and scientific fact to the

Romantic concern for emotion, subjectivity, and imaginative truth.

Born and raised in Frankfurt, Goethe studied law at the University of Strasbourg, where he met the German critic and thinker J.G. Herder. With Herder and Friedrich Schiller, Goethe contributed to the beginnings of German Romanticism in the 1770s, leading what was called the *Sturm und Drang* (storm and stress) movement. Goethe's contribution to this movement was his novel *The Sorrows of Young Werther* (1774). Enormously influential throughout Europe, the work expressed discontent with Enlightenment ideals of objectivity, rationality, and restraint. In it, an educated young man, Werther, gives up a government position to search for greater meaning in his life. He becomes alienated and unhappy until he meets and falls in love with a young woman, who is unfortunately engaged to a businessman, whom she marries. Werther becomes obsessed with her and finally commits suicide.

The work for which Goethe is best known, his play *Faust* (1808), is based upon the life of the medieval German scholar Johann Faust, who is reputed to have sold his soul to the devil in exchange for knowledge. *Faust* has been described as a defining work of European Romanticism, one that epitomizes the temper and spirit of the Romantic era and one that serves to represent the anxiety-ridden Romantic imagination in all its teeming aspiration.

Throughout his life and literary career, Goethe was pulled in two directions. He wrestled with a split consciousness, torn between the intellectual ideals of the Enlightenment and the emotional passions of the Romantic period. The two poles of Goethe's imagination are represented not so much by different works as by diverging strains within particular works. In *Faust*, for example, readers confront alternative perspectives on life, represented by the characters Faust and the devil, Mephistopheles. In the play, Faust is a man of the mind, a deeply knowledgeable scholar, who abandons himself to the exploration of physical experience, represented by Mephistopheles, who offers Faust the chance to live a more active life of sensation. Faust remains a divided figure, one who cannot integrate harmoniously the two different aspects of his consciousness—his scientific rationalism and his poetic intuition.

During his later life, Goethe was considered a sage, a dispenser of wisdom, an honor he earned through prodigious literary labors across a wide spectrum of styles and genres. Important people from throughout Europe flocked to Weimar to see him, including the young Franz Schubert, who set more than fifty of Goethe's poems to music.

Walt Whitman. Of the American poets writing during the nineteenth century, two stand out above all others: WALT WHITMAN (1819–1892) and Emily Dickinson. Unlike Dickinson, whose idiosyncratic and elliptical style has found few imitators, Whitman greatly influenced later American poets. William Carlos Williams emulated Whitman's attention to the commonplace and his experiments with the poetic line. Wallace Stevens displayed the meditative, philosophical cast of mind found in poems such as Whitman's "Crossing Brooklyn Ferry." Later, Allen Ginsberg exhibited something of Whitman's early extravagance and outrageousness.

Instead of using the poetic structures of his day, Whitman developed more open, fluid forms. And rather than using old-fashioned poetic diction, he wrote in familiar and informal language, following Wordsworth's "language really used by men." Whitman also mixed exalted language with common speech, resulting in, as he remarked, a "new style … necessitated by new theories, new themes," far removed from European models. Whitman's stylistic innovations in *Leaves of Grass*, which he wrote and revised over nearly fifty years and once described as "a language experiment," were intended to "give something to our literature which will be our own … strengthening and intensifying the national." In this he was like many nineteenth-century artists who expressed their nationalistic tendencies in music, painting, and literature.

Emily Dickinson. In his exalted ambition, Whitman differed markedly from EMILY DICKINSON (1830–1886), whose poetic inclination gravitated inward. Although Whitman and Dickinson each brought something strikingly original to American poetry, their poems could not be more different. A glance at a page of their poetry reveals a significant visual difference. Whitman's poems are expansive, with long lines and ample stanzas. Dickinson's poems, by contrast, are very tight, with four-line stanzas that distill feeling and thought.

The openness of Whitman's form is paralleled by the openness of his stance, his outgoing public manner. Dickinson's poetry, on the other hand, is much more private. Her meditative poems are rooted partly in the metaphysical poetry of seventeenth-century writers such as John Donne, and partly in the tradition of Protestant hymnology. Dickinson made frequent and ingenious use of Protestant hymn meters and followed their usual stanzaic pattern. Her adaptation of hymn meter accords with her adaptation of the traditional religious doctrines of orthodox Christianity. For although many of her poems reflect her Calvinist heritage—particularly in the ways their religious disposition intersects with intensely felt psychological experience—Dickinson was not an orthodox Christian. "Some keep the Sabbath going to Church," she wrote. "I keep it, staying at Home." Her love of nature separates her from her Puritan pre-cursors, allying her instead with such Transcendentalist

Timeline 17.2 Classical and Romantic eras in music.

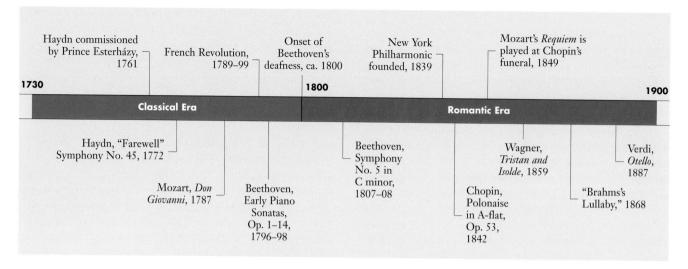

contemporaries as Emerson, Thoreau, and Whitman, though her vision of life was starker than theirs.

Dickinson spent nearly all of her life in one town, Amherst, Massachusetts, living as a near recluse and dying in the house where she was born. Whitman, on the other hand, lived in half a dozen cities in as many states, and spent time with people rather than in private. Social values and political ideals inhabit Whitman's work in ways alien to Dickinson's poems. Moreover, Whitman's poetry is animated by a vision of democratic equality that cuts across barriers of class, race, and creed. His poetry emphasizes a shared humanity, which is rooted in a belief in the intrinsic value of all living things.

Dickinson's poems do not encompass such a wide range of experiences; instead they probe deeply into a few—love, death, doubt, and faith. In examining her experience, Dickinson makes a scrupulous effort to tell the truth, but she tells it "slant," as one of her poems puts it: "Tell all the Truth but tell it slant." Part of her artistry includes the way she invites readers to share her search for truth. Her poems' qualified assertions, along with their riddles and questioning stance, cumulatively suggest that life is mysterious and complex, as it was for so many Romantic artists.

MUSIC

Because it seems capable of unleashing emotions beyond mere words or images, music is perhaps the most "romantic" of Romantic art forms. Romantic composers wrote music that expressed individuality and innovation, exalted nature, and broke new ground formally, harmonically, and stylistically. They also developed a musical language that reflected changing political and social attitudes—their concern was with freedom and self-expression, with the grandeur of nature, with folk traditions,

and with the vicissitudes of romantic love. And above all, their music expressed intense feeling.

Some features of Romantic music resulted from technological advances, such as the invention of valves for brass instruments, which increased their orchestral prominence, and the development of thicker strings for the piano, which deepened and enhanced the instrument's tonal properties. Other features of the Romantic style reflected social changes, such as the movement of musical performance from church and palace to the public concert hall, which occasioned opportunities for musical compositions of larger scope performed by bigger orchestras and choruses. This type of change enriched the orchestral sound, along with new timbres.

Romantic music can be characterized along a spectrum from the miniature to the monumental. Although some Romantic works tended to be, on the whole, larger and longer than their counterparts from earlier centuries, there developed alongside the monumental impulse one toward the miniature. Chopin and Schubert, for example, wrote numerous short piano pieces of only a few minutes' duration. Schubert and Schumann, among others, developed the *Lied* (or art song), also a small form, designed for performance by a singer and accompanist in a room in someone's house. The monumentality of Romantic music is evident in the size of the orchestra needed to perform symphonic and choral works and the sheer magnitude of some of the works themselves. Some symphonies of Gustave Mahler (1860–1911), for example, last two hours, and require more than a hundred orchestral players as well as a hundred choral singers. And four operas of Richard Wagner (1813–1883) create a linked cycle, the *Ring of the Niebelung*, which takes thirteen hours to perform.

Program Music. One of the characteristic forms of Romantic composition is program music. As opposed to absolute music, which does not refer to anything outside of musical sound, form, and tone color, **program music** describes, in musical tones, a scene, story, event, or other non-musical situation. Exploiting the mind's capacity to suggest and evoke, program music attempts to imitate or suggest something beyond the music itself by emphasizing an instrument's special properties or tone.

Earlier composers had used the flute to imitate birdsong, as did the Baroque composer Antonio Vivaldi in *The Four Seasons*. Renaissance composers such as Thomas Weelkes had imitated human sighing with a downward melodic motion. But composers of the Romantic era developed the idea of musical description into something far more ambitious, creating a musical "program" that governed an entire symphonic movement or work. In his Symphony No. 6, for example, Beethoven provides all five movements with descriptive titles, including "Awakening of joyful feelings upon arriving in the country" and "The thunderstorm."

Hector Berlioz.

One of the most innovative of Romantic composers was HECTOR BERLIOZ [BEAR-lee-ohz] (1803–1869). After pursuing a medical degree, he turned instead to music. Affected by the Romanticism of the day, Berlioz threw himself into his musical studies, analyzing scores, attending operas, giving lessons, singing in a theater chorus, and composing. Not long out of the Paris Conservatory of Music, Berlioz wrote his *Symphonie Fantastique*, a work that shocked Parisian audiences with its innovative orchestration, its musical recreation of a bizarre witches' sabbath, and its autobiographical theme about Berlioz's own "endless and unquenchable passion" for the English actress, Harriet Smithson, whom he pursued and married against the wishes of both their families.

The *Symphonie Fantastique* contains five movements: (1) Reveries, Passions; (2) A Ball; (3) Scene in the Country; (4) March to the Scaffold; and (5) Dream of a Witches' Sabbath. Each movement uses distinctive musical material. The first movement, for example, combines a mood of reverie with an agitated and impassioned section that employs dramatic crescendos and obsessive repetitions of a musical theme Berlioz used throughout this movement and the entire symphony. This *idée fixe*, or "fixed idea," as he called it, exemplifies musically the image of "the beloved one herself [who] becomes for him a melody, a recurrent theme that haunts him everywhere." Berlioz transforms the beloved's theme of the *idée fixe* in each movement according to the needs of the program. The *idée fixe* unifies the symphony and carries it forward to a tragic conclusion. Throughout, Berlioz continually expands the orchestral palette, introducing a wide range of instruments including bells, cymbals, sponge-tipped drumsticks, a snare drum, and four harps.

Franz Schubert and Johannes Brahms.

Inspired by the outburst of lyric poetry of the age, many composers turned to writing songs. FRANZ SCHUBERT [SHU-bert] (1797–1828) lived in Vienna and was a contemporary of Beethoven's. Over the course of his career, he wrote more than six hundred songs, many of which were settings of Goethe's verse. He also wrote three song cycles, or groups of linked songs, including *Die Schöne Müllerin (The Pretty Miller-Maid)* of 1824, which tells the story of a love affair that starts joyously only to end in tragedy.

Song was also one of the favorite forms of JOHANNES BRAHMS (1833–1897), who composed later in the century. As a boy he played piano in the bars and coffee-houses of his native Hamburg, and during the Hungarian uprising of 1848, when the city was inundated with refugees, he became particularly intrigued by gypsy songs and melodies. His most famous song, known today as "Brahms's Lullaby," was written in 1868 for the baby son of a woman who sang in the Hamburg choir. Only just over two minutes long, the song is one of the most peaceful and serene ever written.

Chopin and the Piano.

If Berlioz represents one pole of the Romantic composer's spectrum, FRÉDÉRIC CHOPIN [show-PAN] (1810–1849) represents the other. Where Berlioz wrote mostly in large forms, Chopin wrote in small ones. Where Berlioz composed for orchestra, Chopin wrote almost exclusively for the piano. During the eighteenth and the early nineteenth century, the piano (then called the *piano forte)* was a smaller instrument than the concert version of today. Throughout the Romantic period, it was used as a solo instrument for short lyric pieces, as an accompaniment to songs, and for orchestral use. Unlike the harpsichord, which plucks its strings, the piano strikes them with small felt-tipped hammers, giving the musician the ability to modulate between soft and loud simply by exerting more or less pressure on the keys—hence the name, *piano* (soft) *forte* (loud), later shortened simply to *piano*.

Half-Polish and half-French, Chopin was educated at the Warsaw Conservatory where he earned early acclaim as a piano prodigy. Settling in Paris at the age of twenty-one, he became part of a circle of artists that included the painter Eugène Delacroix, the poet and novelist Victor Hugo, and the composer and virtuoso pianist Franz Lizst. During the last decade of his life, Chopin was involved in an intense and passionate relationship with George Sand, the popular French female novelist. Elegant and fashionable, Chopin was admired for the refinement and delicacy of his playing and for the atmospheric subtlety, harmonic richness, and deep expressiveness of his compositions.

Chopin composed two piano concertos, two large-scale piano sonatas, and a series of semi-long works for solo piano, as well as two sets of *études* (or studies), a group of preludes in different keys, a set of nocturnes (or night pieces) mostly melancholy in tone, along with

Connections

GOETHE AND SCHUBERT: POETRY AND SONG

During the nineteenth century there occurred an explosion of lyric poetry fueled by the Romantic movement. In England, France, and Germany especially, poetry poured from the pens of writers such as William Wordsworth, Samuel Taylor Coleridge, John Keats, Lord Byron, Alfred de Musset, Victor Hugo, and Heinrich Heine, among many others. Of the German poets, the poetry of Johann Wolfgang von Goethe was especially inspiring to the young Viennese composer Franz Schubert.

Schubert set many poems to music, perfecting a form of musical art called the *Lied* (plural *Lieder*). The *Lied* was a type of art song set to an accompaniment, usually for piano, that suited the tone, mood, and details of a poem. Schubert composed more than six hundred *Lieder*, more than fifty of them to poems by Goethe. Among the most accomplished of Schubert's settings of Goethe texts is a song he wrote as a teenager: *Erlkönig* (The Erlking).

Based on a Danish legend, Goethe's narrative poem has the Romantic qualities of strangeness and awe. The poem tells the story of a boy who is pursued, charmed, then violently abducted by the king of the elves, as the child rides on horseback through the forest with his father.

FATHER My son, why hide your face so anxiously?
SON Father, don't you see the Erlking?
The Erlking with his crown and his train?
FATHER My son, it is a streak of mist.
ERLKING Dear child, come, go with me!
I'll play the prettiest games with you.
Many colored flowers grow along the shore,
My mother has many golden garments.
SON My father, my father, and don't you hear
The Erlking whispering promises to me?
FATHER Be quiet, stay quiet, my child;
The wind is rustling in the dead leaves.
...
ERLKING I love you, your beautiful figure delights me!
And if you're not willing, then I shall use force!
SON My father, my father, now he is taking hold of me!
The Erlking has hurt me!
NARRATOR The father shudders, he rides swiftly on;
He holds in his arms the groaning child,

He reaches the courtyard weary and anxious:
In his arms the child—was dead.

In setting Goethe's poem, Schubert was faced with the challenge of delineating in music the lines and voices of four characters—father, son, narrator, and Erlking. His response to the challenge exhibits his early musical genius. Schubert differentiates the poem's characters by giving them very different melodies, and by putting their music in different vocal registers. The child's vocal line is high-pitched and fearful. The father's is in a lower register and conveys confidence. The Erlking's melody is lilting and seductive. Schubert also characterizes the horse, by using galloping triplets in the piano accompaniment. Throughout the alternation of the characters' lines, Schubert builds tension by raising the child's vocal line in pitch and increasing its intensity. By altering the character of the Erlking's music toward the end, he suggests the Erlking's shift from charm and seduction to threatening menace.

Throughout his setting of Goethe's poem, Schubert finds musical analogues for the poet's language, imagery, and story. One of his more dramatic strategies is to slow down the music at the end, and he actually stops singer and accompanist in a dramatic pause in the middle of the final line: "In his arms the child—was dead."

---

waltzes, polonaises, and mazurkas, which capture the spirit and flavor of the Parisian *salon* and of the Polish peasant world. The polonaises and the mazurkas reflect Chopin's nationalistic spirit during a time when Poland was partly under Russian domination. The majestic Polonaise in A Flat, Op. 53, one of Chopin's best-known pieces, expresses both joy and pride in a spirit of noble grandeur. The spirit of the polonaise ennobles it, its melody makes it memorable, and its technical demands make it a bravura piece for the piano virtuoso.

Among his most lyrical and sensuous pieces, Chopin's nocturnes conjure up images of moonlight and reverie. Nocturne No. 2 in E Flat, for example, is slow and suffused with a sense of melancholy which is sustained and

embellished throughout. A brief expression of excitement is followed by a quiet ending in keeping with the work's pervasive mood of bittersweet and pensive sadness.

Chopin's ability to bring out the piano's rich palette of sound and to exploit its resonant musical possibilities revolutionized the way later composers wrote for the instrument.

Giuseppe Verdi and Grand Opera. Opera first appeared as a distinct form early in the seventeenth century in Italy. Its popularity was increased by Claudio Monteverdi, who further contributed to its development. During the eighteenth century, it became popular in England and Austria, with Mozart composing his consummate operatic masterpieces, including *Don Giovanni* and *The Marriage of Figaro*. It was during the nineteenth century, however, that opera became internationally popular, with Romantic composers of many countries participating in the grand flowering of the genre.

The rise of the middle class after 1820 helped usher in a new kind of opera, grand opera, which appealed to the masses because of its spectacle as much as its music. Alongside the drama and passion of grand opera there remained comic opera, which continued to flourish as it had in the previous century.

Italy's greatest and most important Romantic composer of any kind was GIUSEPPE VERDI [VAIR-dee] (1813–1901), whose music epitomizes dramatic energy, power, and passion. Born in northern Italy near Parma, Verdi had little formal musical training but managed nonetheless to have an opera produced at the Milan opera house, La Scala. Verdi's career began with a series of early operas in the 1850s—*Rigoletto*, *Il Trovatore*, and *La Traviata*; it continued with a series of popular operas in the 1860s—*Un Ballo in Maschere*, *La Forza del Destino*, and *Don Carlos*; and it concluded triumphantly with a series of grand operas in the 1870s and 1880s—*Aida*, *Otello* (based on Shakespeare's *Othello*), and *Falstaff* (based on Shakespeare's *Merry Wives of Windsor*).

Rigoletto, composed in 1851, is one of Verdi's most dramatic works. Based on a play by the French Romantic writer Victor Hugo, *Rigoletto* depicts intense passion and violence in a tale of seduction, revenge, and murder. Rigoletto is a court jester, a hunchback who serves the Duke of Mantua. When the Duke seduces his daughter Gilda, Rigoletto plans to kill him in revenge and lures the Duke to a quiet inn with Maddalena, the sister of his hired assassin, Sparafucile. He hopes that Gilda will renounce her love for the Duke when she sees him attempt to seduce Maddalena. His hopes, however, are dashed when Gilda sacrifices her own life to save his.

The melodies Verdi provides for his characters perfectly express their feelings. The Duke sings one of the most famous of all operatic arias, *"La donna e mobile"* ("Woman is fickle"), which perfectly captures his frivolous and pleasure-loving nature. Following this song, Verdi provides a quartet for the Duke, Maddalena, Gilda, and Rigoletto, giving voice to their individual concerns. In response to the Duke's elegantly seductive melodic line, Maddalena voices a series of sharp broken laughs. Gilda's melody is fraught with pain and sorrow, while Rigoletto's reveals his heated anger as he curses the Duke. Verdi deftly balances the individual singers so that their ensemble singing is blended into a unified and dramatic expression of feeling.

Richard Wagner.   As Beethoven had dominated the musical world of the first half of the nineteenth century, RICHARD WAGNER [VAHG-ner] (1813–1883) dominated the musical world of the second half. It was, in fact, through intense study of Beethoven's works that Wagner became a composer. Late in life, Wagner explained that he had wanted to do for opera what Beethoven had done for symphonic music—to make it express a wide range of experience, and to have it achieve overwhelming emotional effects. "The last symphony of Beethoven," wrote Wagner, "is the redemption of music … into the realm of universal art … for upon it the perfect art work of the future alone can follow." Wagner believed that he and he alone could compose this "perfect art work of the future," and he believed that it could not be an orchestral work since Beethoven's mighty Ninth Symphony could never be surpassed. Instead, Wagner would create a new kind of opera, which he called "music drama." Unlike Beethoven, whose works express a profound hope in human possibility, Wagner displays a more pessimistic attitude toward life. Influenced by the philosopher ARTHUR SCHOPENHAUER [SHO-pen-how-er] (1788–1860), Wagner emphasizes the blind forces of irrationality and passion that drive human behavior. Wagner's works include the comic *Die Meistersinger von Nürenberg*, the mystical *Lohengrin*, and the sensuous *Tristan and Isolde*, which influenced subsequent European musical style perhaps more than any work of the late nineteenth century. His

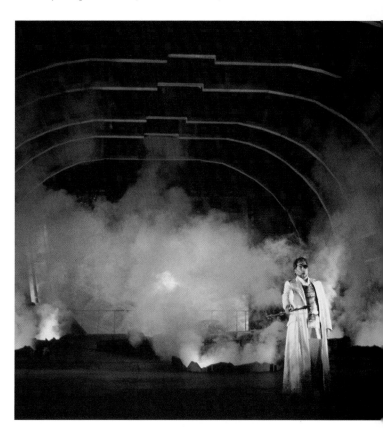

Figure 17.19   Brunhilde enveloped in fire, in the 1989 staging of Wagner's tetralogy *The Ring of the Niebelung* at the Royal Opera House, Covent Garden, London.

operas portray characters whose lives are made unhappy by circumstances they cannot control, as in *Tristan and Isolde*, in which the two lovers are kept apart only to be finally united in death.

Wagnerian music drama brings together song and instrumental music, dance and drama and poetry in a single unbroken stream of art. Wagner's ambitious goals were to restore the importance of music in opera, to establish a better balance between orchestra and singers, and to raise the quality of the librettos, or texts of operas. This last Wagner accomplished by finding his subjects in medieval legend and Nordic mythology and by writing his own librettos, or little books, for his operatic music.

Designed to do more than simply provide beautiful accompaniments for arias, Wagner's operatic orchestral writing was meant to arouse intense emotion, to "comment" on stage action, to be associated with incidents in the plot, and to reflect characters' behavior. Wagner accomplished these goals in part by using what were called "leitmotifs." These were usually brief fragments of melody or rhythm that, when played, would remind the listeners of particular characters and actions, somewhat in the way a movie or television theme triggers associations in the mind of the audience. For example, when Tristan and Isolde drink a love potion, several leitmotifs create a harmonic song that portends a tragic ending.

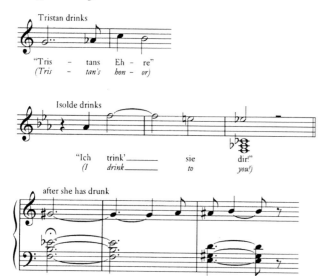

After producing a number of failed operas, and after living in political exile in Switzerland for eleven years, Wagner secured the patronage of King Ludwig II of Bavaria, who enabled him to acquire wealth, fame, and power. Wagner's tetralogy *The Ring of the Niebelung*, which is generally considered his greatest work, includes four operas—*The Rhinegold, The Valkyries, Siegfried,* and *The Twilight of the Gods*. Based on Norse myth, the opera is a profusion of grandeur, in the story it tells, in its singing and orchestration, and in its staging, sets, and costumes (fig. 17.19).

REALISM

Romantic painters such as Géricault and Delacroix wanted to alert their audience to the realities of contemporary life. For them art could serve as an effective social and political tool. Géricault did not paint the *Raft of the "Medusa"* and Delacroix did not paint the *Massacres at Chios* merely for art's sake. Rather, they aligned their art with a political cause, as David had painted his *Death of Marat* a generation earlier and put his art in the service of the Revolution.

Realism is the term used to describe a development in painting in which many artists tried to convey the realities of modern life to their contemporaries. The artist's role was no longer simply to reveal the beautiful and the sublime, but to open the public's eyes to the world around them, not just in its grandeur but in its brute reality as well. In Realist art and literature, the aim is to tell the truth, not to be true to some higher, idealized reality. The higher truth that Keats speaks of when he writes "Beauty is truth, truth beauty" is purely Romantic. Realist artists wanted to be true to the facts. Ordinary events and objects are, to the Realist, as interesting as heroes or the grand events of history. Increasingly, after the Revolution of 1789, it was no longer the aristocracy that made history, it was the working class itself, ordinary people. And so it was to the lives of the working class that Realist art turned for its inspiration. Among the common people, artists could discover and reveal the forces that were driving the times.

THE JULY MONARCHY

Realist art and literature were given their greatest impetus by the revolutions that swept Europe in 1848. But in France particularly, the plight of the working people was at issue throughout the reign of Louis-Philippe, who became king shortly after July 28, 1830, when violent fighting broke out in the streets of Paris, supported by almost every segment of society, and the rule of Charles X quickly came to an end. Within days, Louis-Philippe, who was the former King's cousin, was named the head of what would come to be called the July Monarchy. Eugène Delacroix quickly went to work on a large painting to celebrate this new revolution, so reminiscent of the glorious days of 1789.

Delacroix's Liberty Leading the People. Delacroix named his painting *The Twenty-Eighth of July: Liberty Leading the People* (fig. 17.20). It was finished in time for the Salon of 1831, but instead of the accolades he thought he would receive, Delacroix was roundly attacked for the painting. It was purchased by the new government and quickly removed to storage. The scene is a set of barricades of the kind traditionally built by

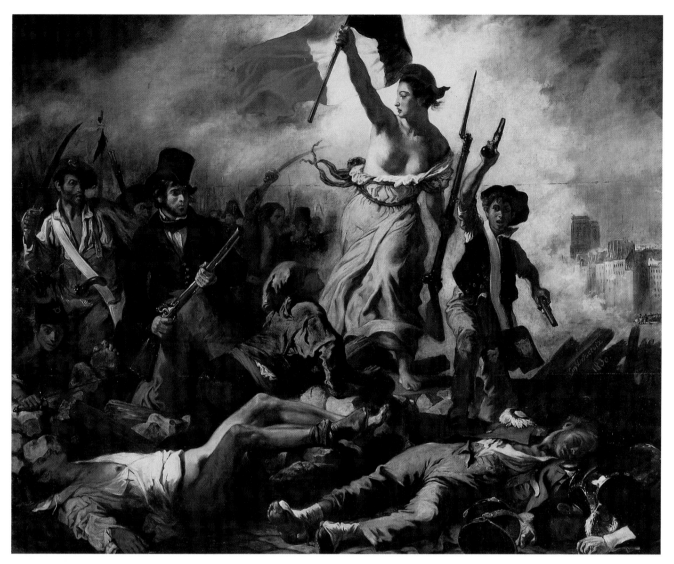

Figure 17.20   Eugène Delacroix, *The Twenty-Eighth of July: Liberty Leading the People*, 1830, oil on canvas, 8′6⅜″ × 10′8″ (2.59 × 3.25 m), Musée du Louvre, Paris. In this romanticized representation of the Revolution of 1830, Liberty is personified by a semi-naked woman leading her followers through Paris. The Revolution resulted in the abdication of Charles X and the formation of a new government under Louis-Philippe.

Parisians by piling cobblestones up in the street, thus creating lines of defense against the advance of government troops. Behind it, to the right, are the towers of Notre-Dame Cathedral, seen through the smoke of battle across the Seine. In a self-conscious reworking of Géricault's *Raft of the "Medusa,"* the composition rises in a pyramid of human forms, the dead sprawled along the base of the painting in poses reminiscent of Géricault's painting, and Liberty herself, waving the French tricolor instead of a torn shirt, crowning the composition. The dead are soldiers, and the one on the left has been stripped of his pants and shoes, evidently by an impoverished rebel. Liberty herself is bare-breasted, as if to underscore her maternal instincts, and broad-shouldered, as if to define her peasant stock—the

German poet Heinrich Heine called her an "alley-Venus." Beside her is a recognizable Parisian type, a youth of the streets, the prototype of the youth gang member of our present day and, even in Delacroix's time, a type notorious for antisocial behavior even when not fully armed, as depicted here. To Liberty's right, a working-class rebel in white and a bourgeois gentleman, distinguished by his tie, coat, and top hat, advance with her. Delacroix depicts the cross-section of society that actually took part in the uprising. And the thought evidently horrified the Parisian public. As one writer put it, "Was there only this rabble … at those famous days in July?"

The decision to hide Delacroix's painting from public view, out of the fear that it might inspire more rebellion,

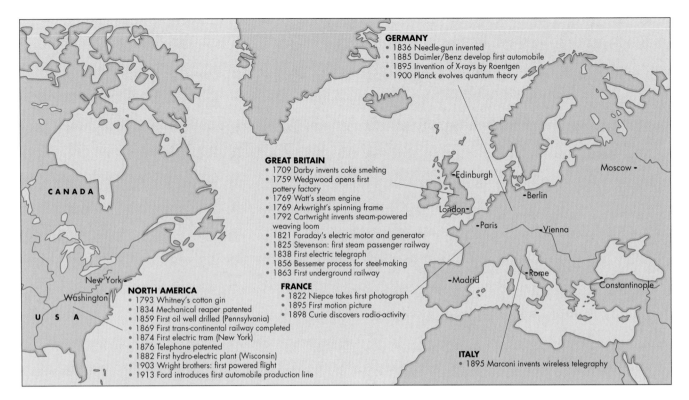

GERMANY
• 1836 Needle-gun invented
• 1885 Daimler/Benz develop first automobile
• 1895 Invention of X-rays by Roentgen
• 1900 Planck evolves quantum theory

GREAT BRITAIN
• 1709 Darby invents coke smelting
• 1759 Wedgwood opens first
  pottery factory
• 1769 Watt's steam engine
• 1769 Arkwright's spinning frame
• 1792 Cartwright invents steam-powered
  weaving loom
• 1821 Faraday's electric motor and generator
• 1825 Stevenson: first steam passenger railway
• 1838 First electric telegraph
• 1856 Bessemer process for steel-making
• 1863 First underground railway

CANADA

NORTH AMERICA
• 1793 Whitney's cotton gin
• 1834 Mechanical reaper patented
• 1859 First oil well drilled (Pennsylvania)
• 1869 First trans-continental railway completed
• 1874 First electric tram (New York)
• 1876 Telephone patented
• 1882 First hydro-electric plant (Wisconsin)
• 1903 Wright brothers: first powered flight
• 1913 Ford introduces first automobile production line

FRANCE
• 1822 Niepce takes first photograph
• 1895 First motion picture
• 1898 Curie discovers radio-activity

ITALY
• 1895 Marconi invents wireless telegraphy

Edinburgh • London • Berlin • Paris • Vienna • Madrid • Rome • Moscow • Constantinople

New York • Washington

U S A

Map 17.2   The Industrial Revolution in Europe and America.

was probably wise enough, but it had little influence in stopping widespread unrest in the country. Even as Delacroix's painting was being exhibited, silk-workers in Lyons went on strike in protest at their wages. The situation would foment for three years, until, in 1834, they fought police and national troops in a six-day battle that resulted in hundreds of deaths. A few days later, Louis-Philippe, tired of all the unrest, suspended publication of

Figure 17.21   Honoré Daumier, *Rue Transonain, April 15, 1834*, 1834, lithograph, $11\frac{1}{2} \times 17\frac{5}{8}''$ (29.2 × 44.8 cm), The Art Institute of Chicago. Daumier wrote that "One must be part of one's times." This stark and moving image records the repression of the people by the troops of Louis-Philippe.

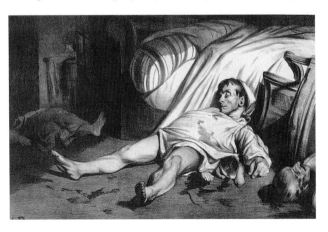

a radical newspaper and arrested the leaders of the working-class Society of the Rights of Man. In protest, workers again took to the streets, battling with government troops. In one working-class neighborhood, troops invaded an apartment building from which, they claimed, shots had been fired.

Honoré Daumier.   The cartoonist HONORÉ DAUMIER [DOME-yay] (1801–1879) depicted the results in a large lithograph exhibited in a storefront window a few days later, *Rue Transonain, April 15, 1834* (fig. 17.21). A father, in a nightshirt, lies dead by his bed. Beneath him, face down, lies his child. His wife is sprawled in the shadows, and another, older man, perhaps the child's grandfather, lies to the right. Such a slaughter of the innocent outraged not only the Parisian working class but the intelligentsia as well.

KARL MARX AND FRIEDRICH ENGELS

It was precisely such conditions, common across Europe, that so influenced the thinking of KARL MARX (1818–1883) and his colleague FRIEDRICH ENGELS (1820–1895). Workers, they realized, had no effective political voice other than revolution and, alienated from their labor by an increasingly mechanized industrial system from which they also received no real economic benefit, they were bound to rebel. "The bourgeoisie … has converted the physician, the lawyer, the priest, the poet, the people of science into its paid wage-laborers," they wrote in *The Communist Manifesto* (1848). "Constant revolutionizing of production, uninterrupted disturbance of all social conditions, everlasting uncertainty and agitation distinguish the bourgeois epoch … All that is solid melts into air, all that is holy is profaned, and one is at last compelled to face, with sober senses, the real conditions of life."

Even as Marx was writing these words, Europe was undergoing an unprecedented economic decline. Revolution quickly followed, first in France in February 1848, then in Germany, Austria, Hungary, Poland, and Italy. In France, the government formed National Workshops, known as *ateliers*, in order to put the people back to work. But enrollment quickly swelled to a size that the government could not handle—120,000 by June—and, fearing that they had inadvertently created an army of the dissatisfied and unemployed, the government disbanded the workshops. The reaction was swift and, on June 23, the working class rebelled *en masse*. Three days later, after some of the bloodiest street fighting in European history, the rebels found themselves surrounded in their neighborhoods, with an estimated ten thousand dead. More died in the mop-up that followed, and eleven thousand others were imprisoned and deported to the French colonies, particularly to North Africa. It was, Marx wrote, "the first great battle … between the two classes that split modern society." For a few brief weeks, Delacroix's *Liberty Leading the People* was removed from storage and put on public view, and on December 10, 1848, Louis Napoleon Bonaparte, nephew of the first Emperor, was elected President of France in a landslide election.

THE PAINTERS OF MODERN LIFE

Rosa Bonheur. One of the first truly successful painters of the working class was ROSA BONHEUR [BON-ur] (1822–1899). She disliked life in Paris, where she had grown up, preferring the rural life. A student of zoology, Bonheur made detailed studies out-of-doors and even painted there, directly from nature, which was not yet common practice. When studying the anatomy of animals at the Paris slaughterhouses, or when observing horses at the Paris horse fairs, Bonheur dressed in men's suits because, she explained, women's clothing interfered with her work. By dressing as a man she was able to move in a world from which she would have otherwise been excluded. She described herself as of a "brusque and almost savage nature," as well as "perfectly feminine" and proud of being a woman.

At the 1848 French Salon, Bonheur exhibited eight paintings, winning a first-class medal. Owing to her success, she received a commission in 1849 from the French government to paint *Plowing in the Nivernais: The Dressing of the Vines* (fig. 17.22), which established her as a leading painter in France. The painting portrays peasant life in harmony with nature, especially with the animal kingdom. Depicted with almost photographic realism is a scene of the good agrarian life: the soil is fertile, the oxen are strong, and the weather is favorable. It seems to illustrate lines written by Bonheur's contemporary George Sand (another woman who dressed in men's clothing) in her 1846 novel *The Devil's Pond*, which describes "a truly beautiful sight, a noble subject for a painter. At the far end of the flat ploughland, a handsome young man was driving a magnificent team [of] oxen."

Figure 17.22 Rosa Bonheur, *Plowing in the Nivernais: The Dressing of the Vines*, 1849, oil on canvas, 5′9″ × 8′8″ (1.75 × 2.64 m), Musée d'Orsay, Paris. Bonheur studied directly from her subject to create this factual record of nature's grandeur. Previously, such subject matter was not considered worthy of an artist's attention and certainly would not have been depicted on such a large scale.

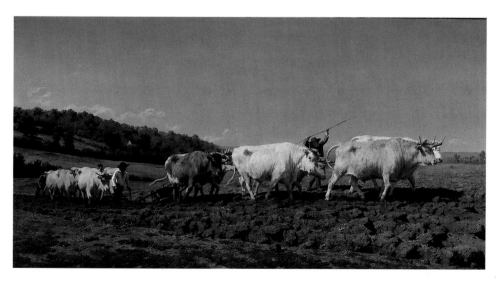

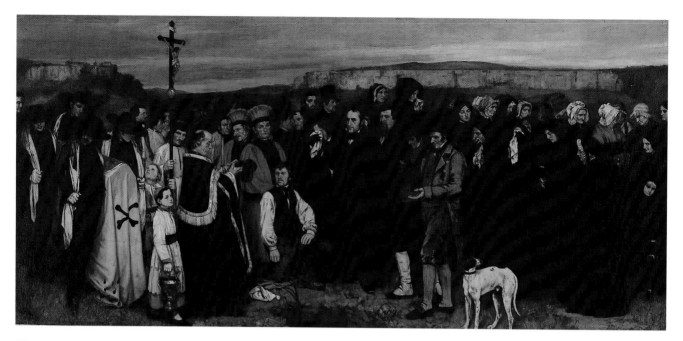

Figure 17.23   Gustave Courbet, *A Burial at Ornans*, 1849, oil on canvas, approximately 10′3″ × 20′10″ (3.10 × 6.40 m) , Musée du Louvre, Paris. The extremely hostile reaction of the public to this painting was due to the fact that the subject was not elevated, glorified, or romanticized—Courbet referred to this as the burial of Romanticism. He said, "Show me an angel and I'll paint one."

Gustave Courbet.   While Sand and Bonheur glorified the French peasant and literally made plowing the fields a "noble" activity, GUSTAVE COURBET [koor-BAY] (1819–1877), refused to idealize working life. The other great Realist to come into his own after the Revolution of 1848, he wanted simply to tell things as they were. "I am not only a socialist," he would write in 1851, "but a democrat and a Republican as well—in a word, a partisan of all revolution and above all else a Realist … for 'Realist' means a sincere lover of the honest truth." These words were written in defense of a group of large paintings that he exhibited in the Paris Salon of 1850–51. The canvases outraged the conservative critics, and Courbet found himself defending not only his works but the "honest truth" of the people who were their subjects. "The people have my sympathy," he wrote to some friends as he was at work on the paintings. "I must turn to them directly, I must get my knowledge from them, and they must provide me with a living." He had, in fact, returned to his native village, Ornans, in 1849, after the Revolution and painted the realities of life for the peasant farmers.

A Burial at Ornans (fig. 17.23) enraged the public in part because it seemed, at the very least, pretentious. At 10′3″ × 20′10″, it is of a size generally reserved for only the most serious allegories and histories. A distant relative of Courbet's, one C.E. Teste, is being buried, and the Mayor of Ornans, the Justice of the Peace, Courbet's father, and his three sisters are among the mourners, who line up across the painting in imitation of the landscape (even the grave seems an extension of the Loue valley which cuts through the plateau behind them). Even though it structurally unites the villagers and their environment, the painting is emotionally unfocused. No one's eyes are fixed on the same place, not even on the grave or the coffin. The dog stares away uninterestedly. The religious import of the scene is undermined by the way the cross seems to sit askew on the far horizon. The emotional impact of death is entirely de-Romanticized as well. We are witness here to a simple matter of fact.

The work's lack of idealism is especially evident if we compare it to Bonheur's *Plowing in the Nivernais*. Where the figures in Courbet's painting seem static, forming an almost flat wall of humanity in front of the viewer, Bonheur's similarly horizontal format is dynamic. On the left, the hills lead downward and away from the viewer, while on the right, the oxen move upward and toward the viewer.

Courbet's next major painting, *The Painter's Studio* (fig. 17.24), met with even less success than his earlier work. Turned down for the Exposition of 1855, the painting was displayed to all by Courbet in a sort of "counter-exhibition" that he mounted himself in a circus tent across from the exposition. He called it the "Pavilion of Realism," and for the most part was ignored for his trouble.

As its subtitle suggests—*A Real Allegory Summing Up Seven Years of My Artistic Life*—the painting is complex and symbolic. Not the least symbolic element is the title itself, *The Painter's Studio* (the word in the original French title is *atelier*), evoking the National Workshops of 1848, the same *ateliers* that had led to the Revolution. Courbet portrays himself painting the Loue canyon and behind him stands a nude in full view of all. The only idealized element in the composition is the working-class youth who watches him paint. He represents, on some level, possibility. Courbet is positioned in the very middle of the scene, as if caught between the opposing forces of his surroundings. On the left are Courbet's origins, the working people of the countryside where he was raised. On the right are his supporters, including his patrons and collectors and the poet Charles Baudelaire on the far right reading a large book.

Édouard Manet. Probably no artist of the period better fills the prescription for the painter of modern life than ÉDOUARD MANET [man-AY] (1832–1883). Born into a well-to-do family, Manet was a sensitive and cultured person who studied literature and music (he married his piano teacher). After Manet twice failed the entrance exam to the Naval Training School, his family permitted him to study art. Manet had academic training, which included copying paintings at the Louvre. He particularly admired the artists Hals, Velázquez, and Goya, all of whom worked in a painterly style, letting the brushstrokes show. Manet's training had a significant impact on his art, especially on the structural organization of work.

His *Luncheon on the Grass* (fig. 17.25), often referred to by its French title *Le Déjeuner sur l'herbe*, was painted in 1863. That year, the official Salon jury rejected over four thousand paintings, producing such an uproar from disappointed painters and their supporters that Napoleon III set up a separate salon to exhibit the rejected paintings, the Salon des Refusés (Salon of the Rejected). Thus, there were two salons, and the monopoly of academicism had been broken. But even at the Salon des Refusés, *Luncheon on the Grass* was regarded as shocking and scandalous by many. In fact, Manet had not painted an actual event, as the public thought; instead, his sources were highly respectable. The poses of the three central figures were derived from an engraving made about 1520 by the Italian artist Marcantonio Raimondi after a painting of the Judgment of Paris by

Figure 17.24 Gustave Courbet, *The Painter's Studio: A Real Allegory Summing Up Seven Years of My Artistic Life*, 1854–55, oil on canvas, 11′10″ × 19′8″ (3.61 × 5.99 m), Musée d'Orsay, Paris. The nude and the landscape are at the center of Courbet's art, as their position in this painting makes clear.

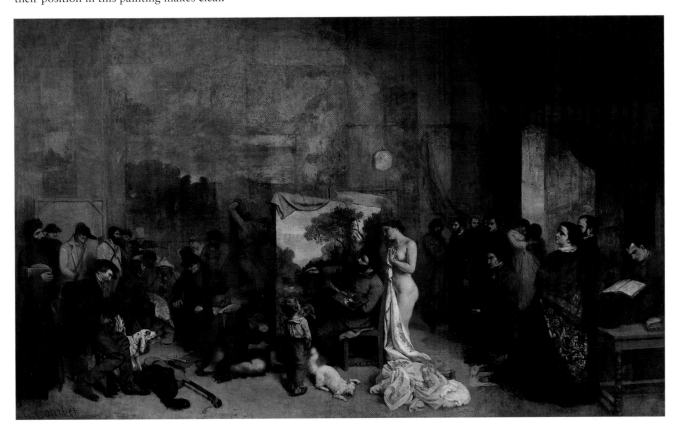

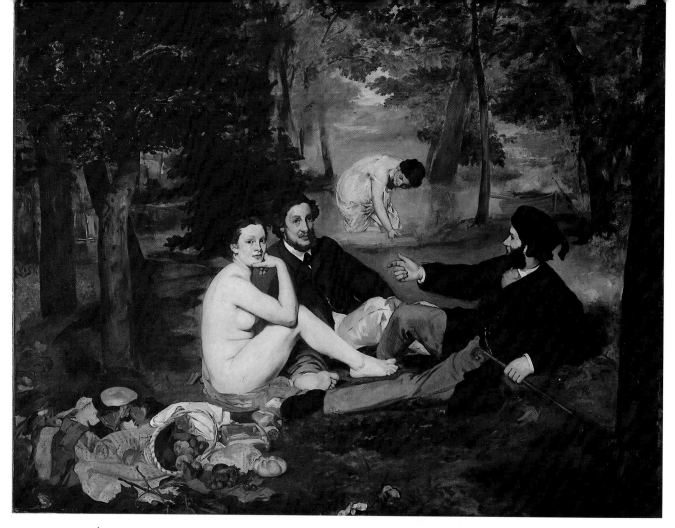

Figure 17.25 Édouard Manet, *Luncheon on the Grass (Le Déjeuner sur l'herbe)*, 1863, oil on canvas, 7′ × 8′10″ (2.10 × 2.60 m), Musée d'Orsay, Paris. An outraged public deemed this painting indecent for depicting a naked woman out-of-doors with two clothed men. Actually painted in Manet's studio from models, it was based on a print by Marcantonio Raimondi after a painting by Raphael, ca. 1520, of the Judgment of Paris.

Raphael, and the theme of the piece is closely tied to Giorgione/Titian's *Fête champêtre* (see fig. 13.39), which Manet had copied at the Louvre as a student, and which similarly depicts two fully clothed men in the company of two unclothed female companions.

Manet's sources went largely unrecognized; it was as if he were at war with the official Academy. By incorporating such traditional sources as Raphael and Giorgione into his work, he was, in a very real way, lampooning them. It was in fact his painting style that offended many. His technique was categorically anti-classical. He painted directly on the canvas with thinned oil paint, which permitted him to wipe off any mistakes, the traces of which can still be seen. When the composition was determined, he executed the final painting directly with large brushstrokes. Instead of the smooth surfaces admired by the public, Manet's brushstrokes were strong, quick, and remain fully visible.

His painting *Olympia* (fig. 17.26), also of 1863 though accepted for the Salon of 1865, did not receive the Academy's approval: it was, they said, too much like a sketch. The public, too, objected: to the artist's use,

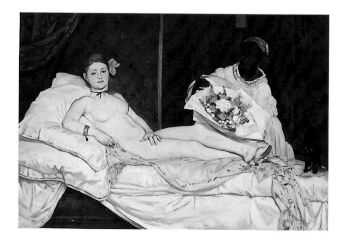

Figure 17.26 Édouard Manet, *Olympia*, 1863, oil on canvas, 4′3¼″ × 6′2¾″ (1.30 × 1.90 m), Musée d'Orsay, Paris. Rather than trying to trick the viewer's eye, Manet treats his paintings as colored pigment on a flat surface and emphasizes the subtle play of tonalities within a restricted range of colors. Manet's *Olympia* deserves comparison with Ingres's *La Grande Odalisque* (fig. 17.8).

particularly, of flat areas of color and heavy outlines. Yet Manet's way of painting is fresh and direct—it embodies "the transitory, the fleeting, and the contingent," which the poet Charles Baudelaire claimed as the basis of the modern. Rather than using carefully wrought highlights and shadows to make forms appear three-dimensional, Manet's flattened forms and rapid, loose brushwork are the result not of carelessness or incompetence, as so many of this critics believed, but of his insistence on being contemporary, absolutely of the moment.

Olympia upset its audience not only because of its technique but because of its content. Again, the painting is based on a traditional source—this time Titian's *Venus of Urbino*—but again the source went largely unrecognized. The painting's title evokes classical precedents—Olympia is the home of the Greek gods—but its subject is no ancient goddess. Indeed, hostile critic said she looked like a prostitute. What is particularly startling is the way that Manet's Olympia seems to acknowledge, in the directness of her gaze, the very presence of the viewer. It is as if the viewer has just now arrived *within* the space of this painting; the cat at the end of the bed arches its back to hiss at the intruder, who has brought flowers that are presented by the maid. The recipient is not embarrassed in the slightest by the viewer's gaze for, in fact, Manet's Olympia was a professional model who also posed for his painting *Luncheon on the Grass*.

THE RISE OF PHOTOGRAPHY

Courbet's refusal to "heroize" his subjects, as Bonheur had done, his insistence on their mundane reality, their matter-of-factness, reminds one of photography, particularly in the insistent black-and-white color scheme of *A Burial at Ornans*. And in fact photography, in 1850, was barely a decade old. Invented simultaneously in England and France in 1839 by WILLIAM HENRY FOX TALBOT (1800–1877) and LOUIS-JACQUES-MANDÉ DAGUERRE [duh-GARE] (1787–1851), photography literally changed the way that we see the world. Before photography, an image could *look* spontaneous and immediate; now it could *be* spontaneous and immediate. Moreover, since the photographic image was the product of a machine, it had the aura, at least, of being purely objective, lacking the subjective intervention of the artist, and thus free of the emotional constraints of the Romantic imagination.

The Daguerreotype. Through competition from photography, painted portraits underwent a rapid decline and photographs largely replaced them for a while. The **daguerreotype**, named for Daguerre's process, was the earliest photograph, produced on silver or silver-covered copper plate. In Paris in 1849 alone, over a hundred

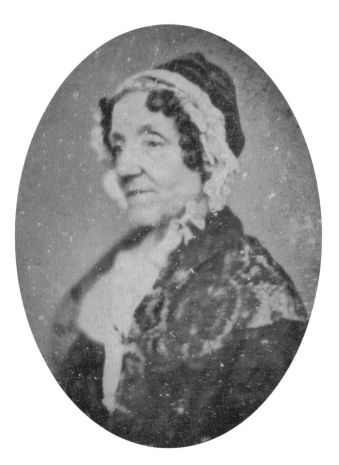

Figure 17.27 Richard Beard, *Maria Edgeworth*, 1841, daguerreotype, $2\frac{1}{8} \times 1\frac{3}{4}''$, National Portrait Gallery, London. Beard's was the first British portrait studio, and the author Edgeworth one of his earliest customers. "It is a wonderful mysterious operation," she wrote.

thousand photographic daguerreotypes, mostly portraits, were sold to people of every rank and class. A similar situation prevailed in England, where photography studios sprang up everywhere to satisfy the craze for photographic portraits (fig. 17.27). It is no surprise, then, that a medium and "look" that even the working class could afford should raise the ire of conservative critics, one of whom reacted to Courbet's paintings of 1850–51 by calling them "local" scenes "worthy only of the daguerreotype." They seemed to him to lack any lasting value. But the photograph had the advantage of capturing reality accurately and immediately, and as its technology rapidly developed, making it easier and easier to use, it captured the Realist imagination.

The American Civil War was the first war to be documented in the new medium of photography. It was not action, however, that the photographers captured—the time required to expose film was still too long to permit that. Instead, it was the aftermath of war that they recorded, and it was a gruesome sight.

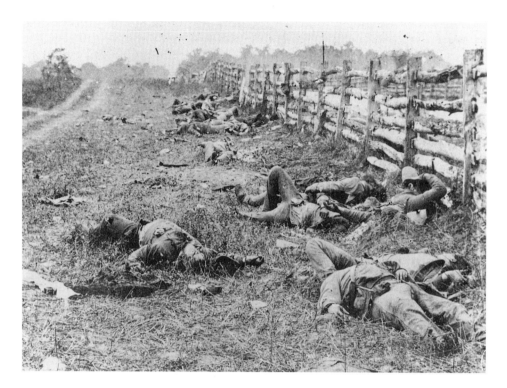

Figure 17.28   Mathew B. Brady, *On the Antietam Battlefield*, 1862, photograph, Library of Congress. Brady photographed President Lincoln so often that he became known as "the President's Cameraman."

Mathew B. Brady.   MATHEW B. BRADY (ca. 1823–1896) was the best known of the war photographers, and his *On the Antietam Battlefield* (fig. 17.28) of 1862 is representative of his work. In the battle at Antietam, Maryland, on September 17, nearly five thousand men died and eighteen thousand were wounded. Brady makes dramatic use of the single vantage point that the camera eye so rigorously asserts: bodies lie beneath the fenceline, stretching as if to infinity. This was the reality of war as it had never before been seen.

Eadweard Muybridge.   As camera technology quickly improved, it revealed more and more about the nature of reality. When, in 1872, the former Governor of California, Leland Stanford, bet a friend $25,000 that a running horse had all four feet off the ground when either trotting or galloping, he hired EADWEARD MUYBRIDGE [MWE-bridge] (1830–1904) to photograph one of his horses in motion. Along a racetrack at Stanford's ranch in Palo Alto, California, Muybridge lined up a series of cameras with trip wires that would snap the shutter as the horse ran by. For the first time, the muscular and physical movements of an animal in motion were recorded. In 1883, Muybridge began to make studies of animal and human locomotion at the University of Pennsylvania (fig. 17.29); these would have a major impact on later painters.

AMERICAN PAINTING

Winslow Homer.   During the time that France and the rest of Europe were enduring class struggle and adjusting to the new industrial world, Americans had one thing on their minds—the Civil War. It was the Civil War that gave impetus to American Realism. Recording events in the Civil War for *Harper's Weekly* was a young illustrator named WINSLOW HOMER (1836–1910). He specialized in camp life and avoided the brutal scenes of battle captured by the new medium of photography. Homer's painting career began soon after the war with *Prisoners from the Front* (fig. 17.30), of 1866. This work depicts the surrender of three Confederate soldiers to a Union officer, a recognizable portrait of General Francis Channing Barlow, a distant cousin of Homer's. Two Union soldiers, one with a gun, stand behind the Confederates, whose own guns lie at their feet. The painting was considered remarkable, even at the time, for the unrepentant, even arrogant attitude of the central figure, who, hand on hip, stares defiantly at General Barlow. Here, some felt, was an image of a nation at odds with itself.

After the painting's exhibition at the National Academy of Design in 1866, it was displayed in Paris at the World Exposition of 1867. Homer accompanied it and, once there, became acquainted with the work of Gustave Courbet and Édouard Manet. Manet's willingness

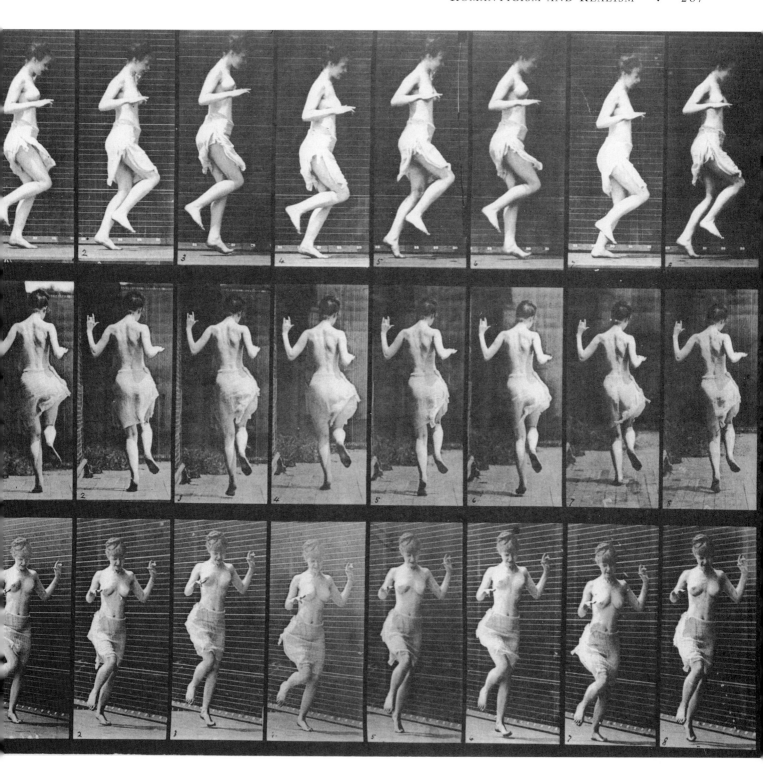

Figure 17.29   Eadweard Muybridge, *Female Figure Hopping*, 1887, sequence photograph, plate 185 from *Animal Locomotion* (Philadelphia, 1887), National Museum of Design, Cooper-Hewitt Museum, New York City. Muybridge's sequence studies would lead to the invention of the motion picture by the century's end.

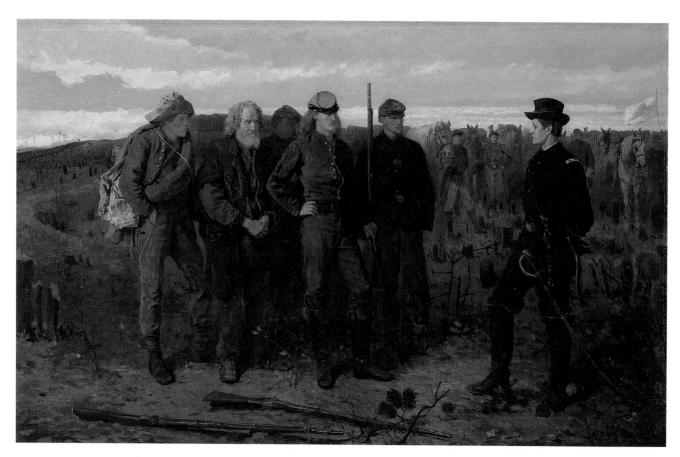

Figure 17.30 Winslow Homer, *Prisoners from the Front*, 1866, oil on canvas, 24 × 38″ (60.9 × 96.5 cm), Metropolitan Museum of Art, New York. For such factual narrative depictions of aspects of life in America, Homer was known during his lifetime as "the greatest American artist."

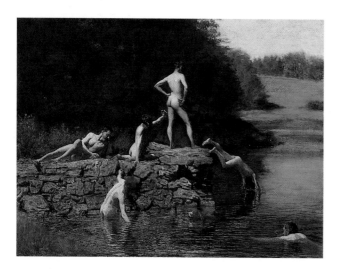

Figure 17.31 Thomas Eakins, *The Swimming Hole*, ca. 1883–85, oil on canvas, 27 × 36″ (68.5 × 91.4 cm), Amon Carter Museum, Fort Worth, Texas. As part of his quest for realistic factuality, in the foreground, Eakins has painted himself as part of the group.

to paint everyday life in a direct and informal way especially appealed to Homer. His later paintings continued to evoke the aesthetics of photography, but they also showed brilliant color and brushwork, borrowed from Manet, which insisted on their status as paintings.

Thomas Eakins. Chief among the American painters was THOMAS EAKINS [AY-kins] (1844–1916). Eakins was fascinated by Muybridge's work from the moment he heard of it. By 1879, he had utilized Muybridge's photographs of horses in order to portray a carriage moving through the Philadelphia Streets, and in *The Swimming Hole* (fig. 17.31), painted between 1883 and 1885, the different figures could as well be a motion study of a single boy, caught at different moments of diving, swimming, and sunbathing. Eakins was fascinated by the human body and dedicated to the accurate presentation of it in motion. After Muybridge came to Philadelphia in 1883, Eakins worked together with him on his studies.

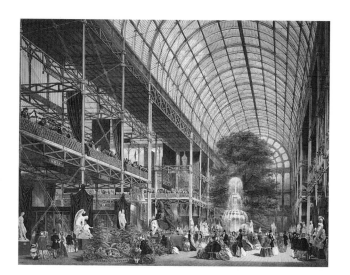

Figure 17.32 Joseph Paxton, Crystal Palace, London, 1851, cast iron and glass, length 1851′ (564.18 m), width 408′ (124.36 m), height 108′ (32.92 m). Designed by a gardener, Crystal Palace was, in its time, the largest enclosed space ever created. Built as an exhibition hall to display industrial and technological accomplishments, it was in itself an impessive demonstration of new technology.

ARCHITECTURE AND SCULPTURE

By the second half of the nineteenth century, new technological achievements, particularly the development of cast iron as a construction material, offered architects and sculptors new possibilities. In fact, two of the most innovative works of the day, Crystal Palace in London and the Statue of Liberty in New York harbor, were considered by some to be more feats of engineering than works of art.

Crystal Palace. Built for the Great Exhibition of 1851, Crystal Palace (fig. 17.32) was designed by JOSEPH PAXTON (1803–1865), who was once gardener to the Duke of Devonshire and was trained neither as an architect nor as an engineer. When Prince Albert called for a competition to design the Exhibition site, the judges, among them Charles Barry, who had designed the Gothic Revivalist Houses of Parliament, deemed none of the large number of entries suitable. The judges themselves prepared a design, but it, too, was rejected. Finally Paxton offered his proposal. Instead of a giant brick edifice, as everyone else had proposed, Paxton extended the concept of the glass-frame greenhouse. Employing a cast-iron prefabricated modular framework—the first such building of its kind—Paxton used glass for his walls. Over 900,000 square feet of glass—nearly a third of Britain's total annual production—were fitted into a building 1851 feet long and 408 feet wide. The result was not only in harmony with the building's site in Hyde Park, but offered the simplest solution to the problem of lighting the interior of a vast exhibition space. Soon Paxton's model was adapted to other similar spaces, particularly to railway stations.

The Statue of Liberty. In 1875, a year before the centennial celebration of the American Revolution, organizers in France conceived the idea of commemorating the event with a colossal statue. A Franco-American Union was founded to raise funds, and the architect FRÉDÉRIC-AUGUSTE BARTHOLDI (1834–1904) was hired to design the work. *Liberty Enlightening the World*, commonly known as the *Statue of Liberty* (fig. 17.33), is the result. Bartholdi first made a nine-foot model of the sculpture, and then GUSTAVE EIFFEL [I-ful] (1832–1923)—the French engineer who created the Eiffel Tower—designed a huge iron framework to support the giant sheets of copper, molded in the shape

Figure 17.33 Frédéric-Auguste Bartholdi, *Statue of Liberty* (*Liberty Enlightening the World*), 1875–84, copper sheeting over iron armature, height of figure 151′ 6″ (46.18 m), Liberty Island, New York Harbor. A gift of the French people, the *Statue of Liberty* has become the symbol of the United States. The monument portrays a crowned woman in classical garb, holding the torch high, while breaking underfoot the shackles of tyranny.

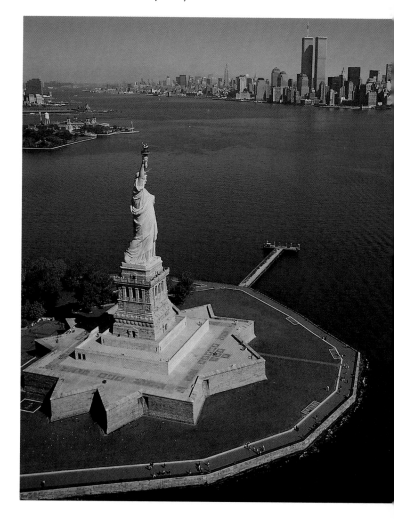

Then & Now

CHARLES DARWIN AND THE KRITZKY MOTH

In 1862, three years after publishing *On the Origin of Species*, Charles Darwin stated that a moth with a twelve-inch tongue existed, even though one had never been seen. Darwin based his assumption on his discovery of a species of orchid that had its nectar twelve inches deep inside the flower. Darwin's orchids, which were found in Madagascar, could not be pollinated by insects that crawled into them; they could only be pollinated by moths with tongues long enough to reach the pollen deep inside their flowers. Darwin reasoned that species develop and change to enhance their opportunities for continued successful existence. Since moths with slightly shorter tongues pollinate slightly smaller orchids, then, according to the principle of natural selection that Darwin himself discovered, a longer-tongued species of moth would pollinate the deeper flower. According to a kind of evolutionary necessity, the moth would have to exist, or the orchid species would never have developed.

In a manner similar to Darwin, a contemporary scientist named Gene Kritzky suggested that a moth with a fifteen-inch tongue exists—though there is no record of anyone ever having seen one. Kritzky made his statement after learning of the existence, in Madagascar, of an orchid species whose nectar lies fifteen inches deep in its flowery interior. Darwin's twelve-inch-tongued moth was actually found in 1902, forty years after his suggestion. It is only a matter of time before Kritzky's longer-tongued moth is also found.

Darwin's contemporary impact extends beyond his explanation of the mechanism of evolution to include ideas about animal behavior and race. Animal behaviorists, such as Konrad Lorenz, and contemporary socio-biologists, including Edward O. Wilson and Richard Dawkins, use Darwinian categories to explain aggression and altruism in animals and humans. Other contemporary scientists have continued to invoke Darwin in their debate about human intelligence, particularly in the sometimes bitter controversy over the relationship between intelligence and race, which has raged ever since Hitler proposed the mastery of the Germanic peoples above all others.

---

of Bartholdi's model. All the components were transported across the ocean, and in 1884 construction began on Bedloe's Island in New York Bay. The sculpture, dedicated in 1886, is itself over 151 feet high and rests on a concrete pedestal faced with granite that is 150 feet high. Sculpture and pedestal in turn sit on an eleven-point star, the walls of which are part of old Fort Wood. It remains a symbol of welcome and freedom to generations of people immigrating to the United States.

LITERATURE

Honoré de Balzac. Like the painters of modern life, Realist writers aimed, above all, to represent contemporary life and manners with precision. In the case of HONORÉ DE BALZAC [BALL-zak] (1779–1850), the project was extensive: Balzac sought to represent contemporary life with encyclopedic completeness. In the nearly one hundred novels and stories that make up his series *La Comédie humaine*, Balzac touched upon virtually every aspect of French society, from the urban working class and the country peasant, to the middle-class merchant, the new industrialists, and the bankrupt aristocracy. By 1816, while working as a law clerk in Paris, he would spend his evenings wandering through the streets, gathering details for his novels. "In listening to these people," he later recalled, "I felt I could champion their lives. I felt their rags upon my back. I walked with my feet in their tattered shoes; their desires, their wants—everything passed into my soul." His characters—there are over two thousand—often appear in more than one novel, establishing a sense of the interconnectedness of French life. Chief among them is Eugène Rastignac, the son of a poor provincial family who comes to Paris, mixes with nobility, builds a career as a politician, and generally leads a life of gambling and debauchery. At the climax of *Le Père Goriot*, Rastignac climbs to the top of the hill at Père Lachaise cemetery and, in one of the most famous moments in French literature, faces the city that threatens to consume him: "There lay the glittering world that he had hoped to conquer. He stared at the humming hive as if sucking out its honey in advance and pronounced these impressive words, 'It's you or me now!'" Rastignac's moment on the top of the hill is entirely Romantic. Pitting himself against the world, he is caught in the web of his own Romanticism; from a Realist's point of view, a self-indulgent fate.

Charles Baudelaire. The poet CHARLES BAUDELAIRE [BO-duh-lare] (1821–1867) was a member of Courbet's *salon*. Indeed, the latter may have painted *A Burial at Ornans* in response to Baudelaire's ideas. In a review of the Salon of 1846, Baudelaire had called for a painter to celebrate "the heroism of modern life." The painter of modern life should begin, he says, by recognizing the grandeur of "everyday dress." "Is it not the necessary garb of our suffering age," he wrote, "which wears the symbol of perpetual mourning even upon its thin black shoulders? … We are each of us celebrating some funeral."

But if Baudelaire for a time admired Courbet, by the middle of the next decade, when he finally published his book *The Painter of Modern Life*, he had retreated from Courbet's brand of Realism. The painter of modern life was no longer interested in social criticism; by 1866, he was hot in pursuit of the good life. "The crowd is his element," Baudelaire wrote. "He delights in fine carriages and proud horses ... the sinuous gait of women, the beautiful happy and well-dressed children ... [He] has contrived to distill in his paintings the sometimes bitter, sometimes heady bouquet of the wine of life." Baudelaire was among the first to define the modern. It was, he wrote, "the transitory, the fleeting, the contingent, that half of art whose other half is the eternal and the immutable." The modern, in other words, was about change. If a part of art would always be about eternal and lasting truths, the modern artist would add to this a sense of the dynamic present. The artist would try to capture the special, ever-changing character of daily life, especially its increasingly frantic and fast-paced quality in the urban center.

Gustave Flaubert. The Realist novel that represents the most thorough attack on the Romantic sensibility is *Madame Bovary*, published in 1857 after five years in the writing, by GUSTAVE FLAUBERT [floh-BEAR] (1821–1880). Flaubert's heroine—if, indeed, "heroine" is a word that can be used to describe her, she is such a banal figure—is Emma Bovary, the wife of a country doctor who seeks to reinvent her life in the manner of the romantic novels that she reads so voraciously. At first, Flaubert had a difficult time imagining her. She was modeled, in fact, on one Louise Colet, a woman Flaubert had known some years before and who reinstigated their relationship after her husband's death. "For two days I have been trying to enter into the dreams of young girls," he wrote to her as he worked. "I am navigating in a milk-white ocean of literature about castles and troubadours with white-plumed velvet caps. Remember to ask me about this when I see you. You can give me some exact details that I need."

Before long, Emma Bovary had become a barely fictionalized version of Louise Colet, but the more Flaubert wrote, the more he began to identify with her himself, so real did she seem. Emma deseperately takes lovers to overcome the incessant boredom of everyday life, spends money as if she were nobility, falls into the deepest debt, and finally, in the most "Romantic" gesture of all, commits suicide by swallowing arsenic. Flaubert came to identify with her wholly. "When I was describing the poisoning," he would later recall, "I had such a taste of arsenic in my mouth and was poisoned so effectively that I had two attacks of indigestion one after the other—two very real attacks, for I vomited my entire dinner." It is in this final scene, which Flaubert stretches out to an almost tortuous length, that the discrepancy between Emma's

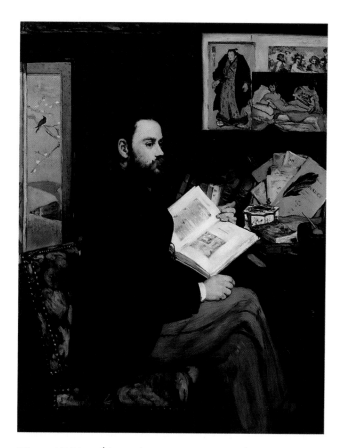

Figure 17.34 Édouard Manet, *Portrait of Émile Zola*, 1868, oil on canvas, 4′9″ × 3′9″ (1.44 × 1.14 m), Musée du Louvre, Paris. Behind the drawing of *Olympia* on the wall above Zola's desk is a print by Goya, while beside it is a Japanese print, all the rage in Paris at the time, the flatness of which surely influenced Manet's flat and shadowless style.

Romantic sensibility and the stark reality of her desperately painful death is made most clear.

But as much as Flaubert identified with Emma Bovary, that sense of identification was made possible, he believed, by his strict desire to describe her as accurately as possible, without either romanticizing or judging her. The novel took five years to write because he sought, in every sentence, to find what he called "*le mot juste*," exactly the right word needed to describe each situation. In this, Flaubert felt, he was proceeding like the modern scientist, investigating the lives of his characters in precisely the same way that the scientist pursues research through careful and systematic observation.

Émile Zola. Flaubert's scientific approach to writing became the standard for all subsequent French Realist writing, particularly the work of the so-called French naturalists, who emphasized the influence of heredity and environment in determining the fate of the literary characters they created. A prominent naturalist, ÉMILE ZOLA [ZOH-la] (1840–1902) saw society as a kind of grand laboratory and the people in it as data for his study of the ways in which humans were determined. In books such as *Germinal*, which chronicled the life of French miners, and *Nana*, which detailed the life of a prostitute, Zola used naturalistic techniques to reflect his fatalistic vision of the world.

Nor surprisingly, one of Zola's closest friends was Manet, who painted a portrait of the writer (fig. 17.34) sitting at his desk, with a sketch of *Olympia* pinned to the wall above. Posing for the portrait had produced, he wrote to another friend, an almost narcotic feeling in him: "In the numbness that overtakes motionless limbs, in the fatigue of gazing with eyes open into full light, the same thoughts would always drift through my mind with a soft, deep murmur. The nonsense of the streets, the lies of some and the inanities of others, the flow of all that human noise, worthless as foul water, was far, far away." But it was, of course, the "foul human noise" of the streets that was the subject of Zola's writing.

Realist Writing. Important English Realist novelists of the time include CHARLES DICKENS (1812–1870), ANTHONY TROLLOPE (1815–1882), and GEORGE ELIOT (1819–1880), the pen name of Mary Ann Evans. Eliot's ambitious *Middlemarch* (1872), a portrayal of nineteenth-century life in an English country village, is considered by many to be the greatest English novel. Trollope, an inspector of rural mail deliveries, created an imaginary English county called Barsetshire, the cathedral town of which he named Barchester, and he set a long series of novels in and around this fictional locale. Though not as ambitious as Balzac's *Comédie humaine*, the Barchester novels capture the spirit of nineteenth-century rural life in a series of similarly interconnected tales. Where Trollope and Eliot chronicled country life, Dickens wrote mostly about the increasingly dark urban environment epitomized by London, attacking conditions in the English workhouses in *Oliver Twist*, published serially in 1837–38, and the evils brought on by industrialization in *Hard Times* (1854). Like their continental counterparts, the English novelists wrote about the world in which they lived and which they knew most thoroughly.

In America, nineteenth-century fiction writers tended toward Romantic themes and styles until very late in the century. While Realism was spreading through Europe, American writers, such as EDGAR ALLAN POE (1809–1849), NATHANIEL HAWTHORNE (1804–1864), and HERMAN MELVILLE (1819–1891), wrote fiction characterized, in Hawthorne's terms, as "romances" rather than as "novels." In the fiction of these romance writers, characters and settings were not depicted with the social realism of their European counterparts. In Hawthorne, dialogue borders on the archaic and in Melville on the theatrical. Description in the works of both is highly symbolic and often poetic, rather than serving as a vehicle for a sharp-edged realism.

THE NEW SCIENCES: PASTEUR AND DARWIN

The interest in the precise, objective description of things evidenced in Realist painting and literature was shared as well by the philosophers and scientists of the age. The social philosophy of Marx and Engels, for instance, is based on their careful observation of the quality and nature of working-class life. In France, the scientist LOUIS PASTEUR [pass-TER] (1822–1895) began to look at organisms smaller than the eye can see—micro-organisms that he claimed were responsible for the spread of disease. Sterile practices could radically reduce the chance of infection in medical procedures, and by heating food, spoilage could be eliminated, a process that led to the "pasteurization" of milk.

But by far the most influential scientist of the age was CHARLES DARWIN (1809–1882), whose theory of evolution by natural selection had a profound impact on not only science but also philosophy and history. Darwin was a naturalist, an experimental scientist whose abiding interest was natural history. In his first important work, *Zoology of the Voyage of the Beagle* (1840), Darwin described his findings during research conducted from 1831 to 1836 on an expedition to the Galapagos Islands and the coast of South America with the *HMS Beagle*. He noticed differences between the species on the islands and those on the coast and later developed a theory to account for those differences. Drafted in 1844 but not published until 1859, Darwin's *On the Origin of Species* laid out his theory of evolution by natural selection. A landmark work, it had an immediate and profound impact on late nineteenth-century thought.

Darwin noted that, in the struggle for existence, since nature cannot provide sufficiently for all the animals that come into being, only the fittest will survive, suggesting that more than simple luck accounted for the survival of individual members of a species. Darwin proposed that, in any given environment, those individuals best able to adapt to that environment have the greatest chance of surviving. He suggested that it was the strongest members of the species that survive long enough to breed and pass on to future generations genes enabling them to survive as well. He also suggested that as an environment changes, those individual members of a species that adapt to the changes will survive to pass on their genetic inheritance.

Darwin's emphasis on the mechanism of natural selection undermined conventional theological and philosophical assumptions about the special place of human beings in the divine order of creation. Instead of a world providentially designed by God with humankind as its guardian and guide, Darwin postulated a world that followed the blind laws of chance and saw human beings simply as a species of animal that has successfully adapted to its world, ensuring its capacity for survival. Moreover, there was no indication that humans were the highest point of creation, nor was their survival assured in future centuries.

Darwin's *The Descent of Man* (1871) suggested that humanity was not created in a single moment by a special act of God—as the Bible describes. Instead, humans were derived from lower life forms that evolved. The distinguishing feature of humans, their spiritual nature and their consciousness, was diminished to emphasize their biological origins and their relationship to their simian ancestors. At stake in this revolutionary shift was humanity's ultimate place in the cosmos. At stake, too, were theological beliefs that had withstood the scientific revolution of the seventeenth century, but which seemed incompatible with Darwinian scientific explanation and the profusion of evidence he brought to support it.

Darwin did not deny that humankind represented the high point of creation so far, only that its origins were other than had been believed for centuries. As he wrote in *The Descent of Man*: "[W]ith all his noble qualities, with sympathy which feels for the most debased, with benevolence which extends not only to other men but to the humblest living creature, with his god-like intellect which has penetrated into the movements and constitution of the solar system—with all these exalted powers—Man still bears in his bodily frame the indelible stamp of his lowly origin."

READINGS

❖ Jean-Jacques Rousseau
from *Confessions*

In his Confessions, *Rousseau explained himself to himself. His very conception of the largeness and importance of the "Self" has been his greatest influence. One of the great ironies of the* Confessions *is that, for all his effort to present himself honestly and faithfully, Rousseau included some self-excusing rationalizations of his conduct. He was criticized for making himself out to be more generous and more deeply feeling than he actually was. Rousseau countered that he had only his feelings and his sense of himself to guide him and that no objective measure could justly portray any individual.*

I am commencing an undertaking, hitherto without precedent, and which will never find an imitator. I desire to set before my fellows the likeness of a man in all the truth of nature, and that man myself.

Myself alone! I know the feelings of my heart, and I know men. I am not made like any of those I have seen; I venture to believe that I am not made like any of those who are in existence. If I am not better, at least I am different. Whether Nature has acted rightly or wrongly in destroying the mould in which she cast me, can only be decided after I have been read.

Let the trumpet of the Day of Judgment sound when it will, I will present myself before the Sovereign Judge with this book in my hand. I will say boldly: "This is what I have done, what I have thought, what I was. I have told the good and the bad with equal frankness. I have neither omitted anything bad, nor interpolated anything good. If I have occasionally made use of some immaterial embellishments, this has only been in order to fill a gap caused by lack of memory. I may have assumed the truth of that which I knew might have been true, never of that which I knew to be false. I have shown myself as I was: mean and contemptible, good, highminded and sublime, according as I was one or the other. I have unveiled my inmost self even as Thou hast seen it, O Eternal Being. Gather round me the countless host of my fellow-men; let them hear my confessions, lament for my unworthiness, and blush for my imperfections. Then let each of them in turn reveal, with the same frankness, the secrets of his heart at the foot of the Throne, and say, if he dare, '*I was better than that man!*'"

I was born at Geneva, in the year 1712, and was the son of Isaac Rousseau and Susanne Bernard, citizens. The distribution of a very moderate inheritance amongst fifteen children had reduced my father's portion almost to nothing; and his only means of livelihood was his trade of watchmaker, in which he was really very clever. My mother, a daughter of the Protestant minister Bernard, was better off. She was clever and beautiful, and my father had found difficulty in obtaining her hand. Their affection for each other had commenced almost as soon as they were born. When only eight years old, they walked every evening upon the Treille; at ten, they were inseparable. Sympathy and union of soul strengthened in them the feeling produced by intimacy. Both, naturally full of tender sensibility, only waited for the moment when they should find the same disposition in another—or, rather, this moment waited for them, and each abandoned his heart to the first which opened to receive it. Destiny, which appeared to oppose their passion, only encouraged it. The young lover, unable to obtain possession of his mistress, was consumed by grief. She advised him to travel, and endeavour to forget her. He travelled, but without result, and returned more in love than ever. He found her whom he loved still faithful and true. After this trial of affection, nothing was left for them but to love each other all their lives. This they swore to do, and Heaven blessed their oath.

Gabriel Bernard, my mother's brother, fell in love with one of my father's sisters, who only consented to accept the hand of the brother, on condition that her own brother married the sister. Love arranged everything, and the two marriages took place on the same day. Thus my uncle became the husband of my aunt, and their children were doubly my first cousins. At the end of a year, a child was born to both, after which they were again obliged to separate.

My uncle Bernard was an engineer. He took service in the Empire and in Hungary, under Prince Eugène. He distinguished himself at the siege and battle of Belgrade. My father, after the birth of my only brother, set out for Constantinople, whither he was summoned to undertake the post of watchmaker to the Sultan. During his absence, my mother's beauty, intellect and talents gained for her the devotion of numerous admirers. M. de la Closure, the French Resident, was one of the most eager to offer his. His passion must have been great, for, thirty years later, I saw him greatly affected when speaking to me of her. To enable her to resist such advances, my mother had more than her virtue: she loved her husband tenderly. She pressed him to return; he left all, and returned. I was the unhappy fruit of this return. Ten months later I was born, a weak and ailing child; I cost my mother her life, and my birth was the first of my misfortunes.

I have never heard how my father bore this loss, but I know that he was inconsolable. He believed that he saw his wife again in me, without being able to forget that it was I who had robbed him of her; he never embraced me without my perceiving, by his sighs and the convulsive manner in which he clasped me to his breast, that a bitter regret was mingled with his caresses, which were on that account only the more tender. When he said to me, "Jean Jacques, let us talk of your mother," I used to answer, "Well, then, my father, we will weep!"—and this word alone was sufficient to move him to tears. "Ah!" said he, with a sigh, "give her back to me, console me for her loss, fill the void which she has left in my soul. Should I love you as I do, if you were only my son?" Forty years after he had lost her, he died in the arms of a second wife, but the name of the first was on his lips and her image at the bottom of his heart.

Such were the authors of my existence. Of all the gifts which Heaven had bestowed upon them, a sensitive heart is the only one they bequeathed to me; it had been the source of their happiness, but for me it proved the source of all the misfortunes of my life.

↩ William Wordsworth
I Wandered Lonely as a Cloud

Because of his inclination toward inwardly directed explorations, Wordsworth has often been considered as one of the first great poets of the inner life. His poetry is rooted in psychological insight leading to self-realization and celebrating the growth of the mind.

I wandered lonely as a cloud
That floats on high o'er vales and hills,
When all at once I saw a crowd,
A host, of golden daffodils;
Beside the lake, beneath the trees,   *5*
Fluttering and dancing in the breeze.

Continuous as the stars that shine
And twinkle on the milky way,
They stretched in never-ending line
Along the margin of a bay: *10*
Ten thousand saw I at a glance,
Tossing their heads in sprightly dance.

The waves beside them danced; but they
Outdid the sparkling waves in glee:
A poet could not but be gay,   *15*
In such a jocund company:
I gazed—and gazed—but little thought
What wealth the show to me had brought:

For oft, when on my couch I lie
In vacant or in pensive mood,   *20*
They flash upon that inward eye
Which is the bliss of solitude;

And then my heart with pleasure fills,
And dances with the daffodils.

↩ William Blake
The Chimney Sweeper

In his two poems about chimney sweeps, William Blake presents contrasting visions based on the themes of innocence and experience that govern his early collection of poems, Songs of Innocence and Experience: Showing the Two Contrary States of the Human Soul *(1794). Even as Blake focuses in turn on innocence and on experience, he complicates each poem with suggested elements of the opposite state.*

The Chimney Sweeper (Innocence)

When my mother died I was very young,
And my father sold me while yet my tongue,
Could scarcely cry "'weep! 'weep! 'weep! 'weep!"
So your chimneys I sweep & in soot I sleep.

There's little Tom Dacre, who cried when his head   *5*
That curl'd like a lamb's back, was shav'd, so I said.
"Hush Tom never mind it, for when your head's bare,
You know that the soot cannot spoil your white hair."

And so he was quiet, & that very night,
As Tom was a-sleeping he had such a sight,   *10*
That thousands of sweepers Dick, Joe, Ned & Jack,
Were all of them lock'd up in coffins of black;

And by came an Angel who had a bright key,
And he open'd the coffins & set them all free;
Then down a green plain leaping laughing they run,   *15*
And wash in a river and shine in the Sun.

Then naked & white, all their bags left behind,
They rise upon clouds, and sport in the wind.
And the Angel told Tom if he'd be a good boy,
He'd have God for his father & never want joy.   *20*

The Chimney Sweeper (Experience)

A little black thing among the snow:
Crying "'weep, 'weep," in notes of woe!
"Where are thy father & mother? say?"
"They are both gone up to the church to pray.

"Because I was happy upon the heath,   *5*
And smil'd among the winter's snow:
They clothed me in the clothes of death,
And taught me to sing the notes of woe.

"And because I am happy, & dance & sing,
They think they have done me no injury: *10*
And are gone to praise God & his Priest & King
Who make up a heaven of our misery."

↩ **John Keats**
Ode to a Nightingale

During the last year of his life, Keats composed six great odes. In the "Ode to a Nightingale," Keats's speaker loses himself completely in the nightingale's song, only to be called back at the end to a state of solitary sadness.

1

My heart aches, and a drowsy numbness pains
    My sense, as though of hemlock° I had drunk,
Or emptied some dull opiate to the drains°
    One minute past, and Lethe-wards° had sunk:
'Tis not through envy of thy happy lot,   *5*
    But being too happy in thine happiness—
        That thou, light-wingéd Dryad° of the trees,

In some melodious plot
    Of beechen green, and shadows numberless,
        Singest of summer in full-throated ease.   *10*

2

O, for a draught of vintage! that hath been
    Cooled a long age in the deep-delvéd earth,
Tasting of Flora and the country green,
    Dance, and Provençal song, and sunburnt mirth!
O for a beaker full of the warm South,   *15*
    Full of the true, the blushful Hippocrene,°
        With beaded bubbles winking at the brim,

And purple-stainéd mouth;
    That I might drink, and leave the world unseen,
        And with thee fade away into the forest dim: *20*

3

Fade far away, dissolve, and quite forget
    What thou among the leaves hast never known,
The weariness, the fever, and the fret
    Here, where men sit and hear each other groan;
Where palsy shakes a few, sad, last gray hairs,   *25*
    Where youth grows pale, and spectre-thin, and dies,
        Where but to think is to be full of sorrow

And leaden-eyed despairs,
    Where Beauty cannot keep her lustrous eyes,
        Or new Love pine at them beyond tomorrow. *30*

4

Away! away! for I will fly to thee,
    Not charioted by Bacchus and his pards,°
But on the viewless° wings of Poesy,
    Though the dull brain perplexes and retards:
Already with thee! tender is the night,   *35*
    And haply° the Queen-Moon is on her throne,
        Clustered around by all her starry Fays;°

But here there is no light,
    Save what from heaven is with the breezes blown
        Through verdurous glooms and winding mossy
    ways.   *40*

5

I cannot see what flowers are at my feet,
    Nor what soft incense hangs upon the boughs,
But, in embalméd darkness, guess each sweet
    Wherewith the seasonable month endows
The grass, the thicket, and the fruit tree wild;   *45*
    White hawthorn, and the pastoral eglantine;
        Fast fading violets covered up in leaves;

And mid-May's eldest child,
    The coming musk-rose, full of dewy wine,
        The murmurous haunt of flies on summer eves. *50*

6

Darkling I listen; and for many a time
    I have been half in love with easeful Death,
Called him soft names in many a muséd rhyme,
    To take into the air my quiet breath;
Now more than ever seems it rich to die,   *55*
    To cease upon the midnight with no pain,
        While thou art pouring forth thy soul abroad

In such an ecstasy!
    Still wouldst thou sing, and I have ears in vain—
        To thy high requiem become a sod.   *60*

7

Thou wast not born for death, immortal Bird!
    No hungry generations tread thee down;
The voice I hear this passing night was heard
    In ancient days by emperor and clown:
Perhaps the selfsame song that found a path   *65*
    Through the sad heart of Ruth, when, sick for home,
        She stood in tears amid the alien corn;

---

² *hemlock:* a poisonous drug. ³ *drains:* dregs. ⁴ *Lethe-wards:* towards Lethe, the river of forgetfulness. ⁷ *Dryad:* tree nymph. ¹⁶ *true ... Hippocrene:* wine.

³² *Bacchus ... pards:* the god of wine and revelry and the leopards who drew his chariot. ³³ *viewless:* invisible. ³⁶ *haply:* perhaps. ³⁷ *Fays:* fairies.

The same that ofttimes hath
   Charmed magic casements, opening on the foam
     Of perilous seas, in faery lands forlorn.   70

8

Forlorn! the very word is like a bell
   To toll me back from thee to my sole self!
Adieu! the fancy cannot cheat so well
   As she is famed to do, deceiving elf.
Adieu! adieu! thy plaintive anthem fades   75
   Past the near meadows, over the still stream,
   Up the hill side; and now 'tis buried deep

In the next valley-glades:
   Was it a vision, or a waking dream?
     Fled is that music:—Do I wake or sleep?   80

✦ **Walt Whitman**
from *Song of Myself*

The longest and most important poem in Leaves of Grass, Song of
Myself *offers a Romantic perspective that can be compared with
Emerson's and Thoreau's perspectives on nature and the self. Its fifty-
two sections span a wide range of topics, including nature, the individual self, the social self, democratic brotherhood, and the organic
relationship between life and death, humanity and the natural world.*

1

I celebrate myself,
And what I assume you shall assume,
For every atom belonging to me as good belongs to
   you.
I loafe and invite my soul,
I lean and loafe at my ease observing a spear of
   summer grass.   5

2

Houses and rooms are full of perfumes . . . the shelves
   are crowded with perfumes,
I breathe the fragrance myself, and know it and like it,
The distillation would intoxicate me also, but I shall
   not let it.

The atmosphere is not a perfume . . . it has no taste of
   the distillation . . . it is odorless,
It is for my mouth forever . . . I am in love with it,   10
I will go to the bank by the wood and become
   undisguised and naked,
I am mad for it to be in contact with me.

The smoke of my own breath,
Echoes, ripples, and buzzed whispers . . . loveroot,
   silkthread, crotch and vine,
My respiration and inspiration . . . the beating of my
   heart . . . the passing of blood and air through my
   lungs,   15
The sniff of green leaves and dry leaves, and of the
shore and darkcolored sea-rocks, and of hay in the
   barn,
The sound of the belched words of my voice . . . words
   loosed to the eddies of the wind,
A few light kisses . . . a few embraces . . . a reaching
   around of arms,
The play of shine and shade on the trees as the supple
   boughs wag,
The delight alone or in the rush of the streets, or along
   the fields and hillsides,   20
The feeling of health . . . the full-moon trill . . . the
   song of me rising from bed and meeting the sun.
Have you reckoned a thousand acres much? Have you
   reckoned the earth much?
Have you practiced so long to learn to read?
Have you felt so proud to get at the meaning of poems?

Stop this day and night with me and you shall possess
   the origin of all poems,   25
You shall possess the good of the earth and sun . . .
   there are millions of suns left,
You shall no longer take things at second or third hand
   . . . nor look through the eyes of the dead . . . nor
   feed on the spectres in books,
You shall not look through my eyes either, nor take
   things from me,
You shall listen to all sides and filter them from yourself.

3

I have heard what the talkers were talking . . . the talk
   of the beginning and the end,   30
But I do not talk of the beginning or the end.

There was never any more inception than there is now,
Nor any more youth or age than there is now;
And will never be any more perfection than there is
   now,
Nor any more heaven or hell than there is now.   35

Urge and urge and urge,
Always the procreant urge of the world.

Out of the dimness opposite equals advance . . . Always
   substance and increase,
Always a knit of identity . . . always distinction . . .
   always a breed of life.

To elaborate is no avail . . . Learned and unlearned feel
   that it is so.   40

Sure as the most certain sure . . . plumb in the uprights,
   well entretied, braced in the beams,
Stout as a horse, affectionate, haughty, electrical,
I and this mystery here we stand.

Clear and sweet is my soul . . . and the unseen is proved
   by the seen,   44
Till that becomes unseen and receives proof in its turn.
Showing the best and dividing it from the worst, age
   vexes age,

Knowing the perfect fitness and equanimity of things,
    while they discuss I am silent, and go bathe and
    admire myself.

Welcome is every organ and attribute of me, and of any
    man hearty and clean,
Not an inch nor a particle of an inch is vile, and none
    shall be less familiar than the rest.

I am satisfied . . . I see, dance, laugh, sing;   50
As God comes a loving bedfellow and sleeps at my side
    all night and close on the peep of the day,
And leaves for me baskets covered with white towels
    bulging the house with their plenty,
Shall I postpone my acceptation and realization and
    scream at my eyes,
That they turn from gazing after and down the road,
And forthwith cipher and show me to a cent,
Exactly the contents of one, and exactly the contents of
    two, and which is ahead?   55

. . .

21

I am the poet of the body,
And I am the poet of the soul.
The pleasures of heaven are with me, and the pains of
    hell are with me,
The first I graft and increase upon myself . . . the latter
    I translate into a new tongue.

I am the poet of the woman the same as the man,   60
And I say it as great to be a woman as to be a man,
And I say there is nothing greater than the mother of
    men.

I chant a new chant of dilation or pride,
We have had ducking and deprecating about enough,
I show that size is only development.   65

Have you outstript the rest? Are you the President?
It is a trifle . . . they will more than arrive there every
    one, and still pass on.

I am he that walks with the tender and growing night;
I call to the earth and sea half-held by the night.

Press close barebosomed night! Press close magnetic
    nourishing night!   70
Night of south winds! Night of the large few stars!
Still nodding night! Mad naked summer night!

Smile O voluptuous coolbreathed earth!
Earth of the slumbering and liquid trees!
Earth of departed sunset! Earth of the mountains
    misty-top!   75
Earth of the vitreous pour of the full moon just tinged
    with blue!
Earth of shine and dark mottling the tide of the river!
Earth of the limpid gray of clouds brighter and clearer
    for my sake!

Far-swooping elbowed earth! Rich apple-blossomed
    earth!
Smile, for your lover comes!   80

Prodigal! you have given me love! . . . therefore I to
    you give love!
O unspeakable passionate love!

Thruster holding me tight and that I hold tight!
We hurt each other as the bridegroom and the bride
    hurt each other.

. . .

48

I have said that the soul is not more than the body,   85
And I have said that the body is not more than the soul
And nothing, not God, is greater to one than one's-self
    is,
And whoever walks a furlong without sympathy walks
    to his own funeral, dressed in his shroud,
And I or you pocketless of a dime may purchase the
    pick of the earth,
And to glance with an eye or show a bean in its pod
    confounds the learning of all times,   90
And there is no trade or employment but the young
    man following it may become a hero,
And there is no object so soft but it makes a hub for the
    wheeled universe,
And any man or woman shall stand cool and
    supercilious before a million universes.

And I call to mankind, Be not curious about God,
For I who am curious about each am not curious about
    God,   95
No array of terms can say how much I am at peace
    about God and about death.

I hear and behold God in every object, yet I understand
    God not in the least,
Nor do I understand who there can be more wonderful
    than myself.

Why should I wish to see God better than this day?   100
I see something of God each hour of the twenty-four,
    and each moment then,
In the faces of men and women I see God, and in my
    own face in the glass;
I find letters from God dropped in the street, and every
    one is signed by God's name,
And I leave them where they are, for I know that others
    will punctually come forever and ever.

. . .

51

The past and present wilt . . . I have filled them and
    emptied them,   105
And proceed to fill my next fold of the future.

Listener up there! Here you . . . what have you to
   confide to me?
Look in my face while I snuff the sidle of evening,
Talk honestly, for no one else hears you, and I stay only
   a minute longer.
Do I contradict myself?   110
Very well then . . . I contradict myself;
I am large . . . I contain multitudes.

I concentrate toward them that are nigh . . . I wait on
   the door-slab.

Who has done his day's work and will soonest be
   through with his supper?
Who wishes to talk with me?   115

Will you speak before I am gone? Will you prove
   already too late?

52

The spotted hawk swoops by and accuses me . . . he
   complains of my gab and my loitering.

I too am not a bit tamed . . . I too am untranslatable,
I sound my barbaric yawp over the roofs of the world.

The last scud of day holds back for me,   120
It flings my likeness after the rest and true as any on
   the shadowed wilds,
It coaxes me to the vapor and the dusk.

I depart as air . . . I shake my white locks at the
   runaway sun,
I effuse my flesh in eddies and drift it in lacy jags.

I bequeath myself to the dirt to grow from the grass I
   love,   125
If you want me again look for me under your bootsoles.

You will hardly know who I am or what I mean,
But I shall be good health to you nevertheless,
And filter and fibre your blood.

Failing to fetch me at first keep encouraged,   130
Missing me one place search another,
I stop some where waiting for you.

✣ **Emily Dickinson**
Five Poems

*Emily Dickinson remained preoccupied throughout her work with
these major themes: love, death, faith, doubt, nature, and hope. Her
poems reveal a consummate linguistic intelligence, and interpreting
them requires painstaking attention to every word and phrase and
every mark of punctuation. Each detail contributes to her range of
implication and meaning. The images of Dickinson's poems carry
their meaning in concrete form—the slanting light and shadows of
258; the drum beat and broken plank of 280; the chorister and dome
of 324; the tomb and moss of 449; and the sound and light of 465.*

258

There's a certain Slant of light,
Winter Afternoons—
That oppresses, like the Heft
Of Cathedral Tunes—

Heavenly Hurt, it gives us—   5
We can find no scar,
But internal difference,
Where the Meanings, are—

None may teach it—Any—
'Tis the Sea Despair—   10
An imperial affliction
Sent us of the Air—

When it comes, the Landscape listens—
Shadows—hold their breath—
When it goes, 'tis like the Distance   15
On the look of Death—

280

I felt a Funeral, in my Brain,
And Mourners to and fro
Kept treading—treading—till it seemed
That Sense was breaking through—

And when they all were seated,   5
A Service, like a Drum—
Kept beating—beating—till I thought
My Mind was going numb—

And then I heard them lift a Box
And creak across my Soul   10
With those same Boots of Lead, again,
Then Space—began to toll,

As all the Heavens were a Bell,
And Being, but an Ear,
And I, and Silence, some strange Race   15
Wrecked, solitary, here—

And then a Plank in Reason, broke,
And I dropped down, and down—
And hit a World, at every plunge,
And Finished knowing—then—   20

324

Some keep the Sabbath going to Church—
I keep it, staying at Home—
With a Bobolink for a Chorister—
And an Orchard, for a Dome—

Some keep the Sabbath in Surplice—   5
I just wear my Wings—
And instead of tolling the Bell, for Church,
Our little Sexton—sings.

God preaches, a noted Clergyman—
And the sermon is never long,   10
So instead of getting to Heaven, at last—
I'm going, all along.

449

I died for Beauty—but was scarce
Adjusted in the Tomb
When One who died for Truth, was lain
In an adjoining Room—

He questioned softly "Why I failed"?   5
"For Beauty", I replied—
"And I—for Truth—Themself are One—
We Brethren, are", He said—

And so, as Kinsmen, met a Night—
We talked between the Rooms—   10
Until the Moss had reached our lips—
And covered up—our names—

465

I heard a Fly buzz—when I died—
The Stillness in the Room
Was like the Stillness in the Air—
Between the Heaves of Storm—

The Eyes around—had wrung them dry—   5
And Breaths were gathering firm
For that last Onset—when the King
Be witnessed—in the Room—

I willed my Keepsakes—Signed away
What portion of me be   10
Assignable—and then it was
There interposed a Fly—

With Blue—uncertain stumbling Buzz—
Between the light—and me—
And then the Windows failed—and then   15
I could not see to see—

✦ Charles Darwin
from *The Descent of Man*

Darwin's The Descent of Man *challenged a belief upheld by the Christian religion for centuries, namely that Adam and Eve were the first parents and that these parents were created fully formed by God to please him. Darwin's principles implied human beings were descended from baser living organisms. He had previously outlined his ideas of evolution of plants and animals in* On the Origin of Species *(1859), but he had not discussed human beings as one of the species.*

His theory of human evolution became inextricably tied to the origin of humanity. It was the subject of courtroom debate in the Scopes trial of 1927, in which a biology teacher, John T. Scopes, was tried for teaching Darwinism in a Dayton, Tennessee public school. Scopes was convicted but later released on a technicality. In the 1950s Jerome Lawrence and Robert E. Lee wrote a dynamic play about the trial, Inherit the Wind.

The main conclusion arrived at in this work, namely, that man is descended from some lowly organised form, will, I regret to think, be highly distasteful to many. But there can hardly be a doubt that we are descended from barbarians. The astonishment which I felt on first seeing a party of Fuegians on a wild and broken shore will never be forgotten by me, for the reflection at once rushed into my mind—such were our ancestors. These men were absolutely naked and bedaubed with paint, their long hair was tangled, their mouths, frothed with excitement, and their expression was wild, startled, and distrustful. They possessed hardly any arts, and like wild animals lived on what they could catch; they had no government, and were merciless to every one not of their own small tribe. He who has seen a savage in his native land will not feel much shame, if forced to acknowledge that the blood of some more humble creature flows in his veins. For my own part I would as soon be descended from that heroic little monkey, who braved his dreaded enemy in order to save the life of his keeper, or from that old baboon, who descending from the mountains, carried away in triumph his young comrade from a crowd of astonished dogs—as from a savage who delights to torture his enemies, offers up bloody sacrifices, practises infanticide without remorse, treats his wives like slaves, knows no decency, and is haunted by the grossest superstitions.

Man may be excused for feeling some pride at having risen, though not through his own exertions, to the very summit of the organic scale; and the fact of his having thus risen, instead of having been aboriginally placed there, may give him hope for a still higher destiny in the distant future. But we are not here concerned with hopes or fears, only with the truth as far as our reason permits us to discover it; and I have given the evidence to the best of my ability. We must, however, acknowledge, as it seems to me, that man with all his noble qualities, with sympathy which feels for the most debased, with benevolence which extends not only to other men but to the humblest living creature, with his god-like intellect which has penetrated into the movements and constitution of the solar system—with all these exalted powers—Man still bears in his bodily frame the indelible stamp of his lowly origin.

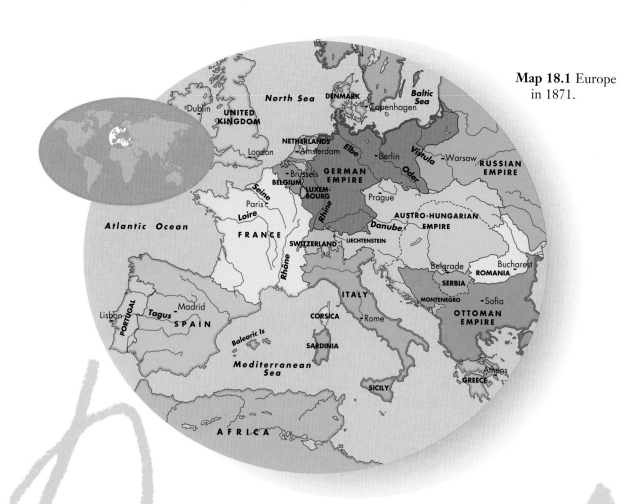

Map 18.1 Europe in 1871.

THE
BELLE ÉPOQUE

Berthe Morisot, *Summer's Day (detail)*, 1879, National Gallery, London.

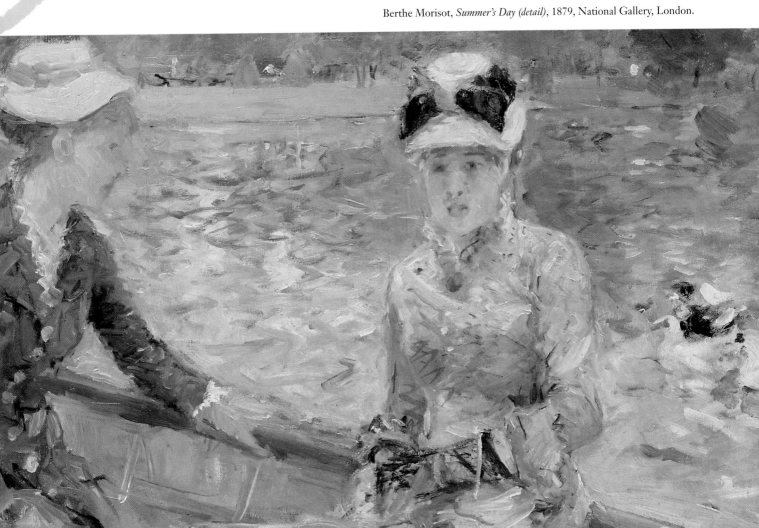

IMPRESSIONISM

The term **Impressionism** was originally applied with some measure of condescension and distaste to a particular style of painting. It referred to the work of a group of French painters who seemed determined to depict a kind of fleeting and transient look at the world, one that French poet Charles Baudelaire declared to be the chief characteristic of the **modern**. An "impression," as distinct from a "representation," was a sketch of the way the world appeared to the artist's eye. In the minds of those who first saw Impressionist painting, such an approach seemed casual to the point of carelessness. Impressionism was, for them, not so much a virtue as a vice. A hostile public objected to the little dabs of color, claiming it destroyed form and led to a loss of solidity, structure, and composition. It was as if the Impressionist painter offered, as a finished work, what was only a sketch. To many Parisians, it looked like a scam.

Furthermore, the Impressionists changed the focus of artistic subject matter. In turning away from traditional religious, mythological, historical, or literary subjects, they were very similar to the Realists in temperament, but instead of looking objectively at the ordinary life of the working class, they looked to the good life and the entertainments of the middle class in a new "beautiful age"—the *belle époque*. It was an age of leisure, in which life on Paris's "grands boulevards," weekend outings in its suburbs and gardens, a day at the races, or boating and swimming on the Seine, all seemed truer to their experience than the harsh realities depicted by Realist painters and writers. It was a period of possibility, however, that ended abruptly in August 1914, with the outbreak of World War I.

HAUSSMANN'S PARIS

Before 1848, Paris was characterized by narrow streets and dark alleys, a maze that had been fortified with rebel barricades nine times since 1830. GEORGES EUGÈNE HAUSSMANN [OUSE-mun] (1809–1891) was commissioned to rebuild the city. He had three principal aims, the first being "to disencumber the large buildings, palaces, and barracks in such a way as to make them more pleasing to the eye, afford easier access on days of celebration, and a simplified defense on days of riot." Second, he recognized that slum conditions had a detrimental effect on public health, a situation he sought to rectify by the "systematic destruction of infected alleyways and centers of epidemics." Finally, he stated his plans "to assure public peace by the creation of large boulevards which will permit the circulation not only of air and light but also of troops." By the time Haussmann had completed his work in 1870, hundreds of miles of streets had been

widened, new water and sewage systems were in place, the so-called "grands boulevards" of modern Paris had been built, the banks of the Seine had been cleared of hovels, new bridges built, and tens of thousands of working-class poor evicted to the suburbs—nearly fourteen thousand, for instance, from the Île de la Cité, where the most radical political communities had developed.

Thanks to Baron Haussmann, Paris was suddenly as much a park as it was a city. It was, moreover, a park purged of its politically dangerous working class. In 1850, there were forty-seven acres of parkland in the city; by 1870, there were over 4500, an increase of almost one-hundred fold. Haussmann doubled the number of trees lining the streets to over 100,000. The Bois de Boulogne, a neglected royal hunting ground to the west of the city, was redesigned between 1852 and 1858 as a giant English garden, with twisting, meandering paths, and a racecourse, Longchamp, which was built to please the politically powerful Jockey Club.

Life was no longer a question of where the next meal might come from, but rather which opera or concert to go to, or which café to frequent. At the center of this world were the "grands boulevards" that radiated from the Opéra. As one visitor from London put it in 1867:

> Other streets are as fresh and gay, have the same advantages of lightness, airiness, verdure of trees in the midst of rush and crowds, but no longer the same prestige. The boulevards are now *par excellence* the social centre of Paris. Here the aristocrat comes to lounge, and the stranger to gaze. Here trade intrudes only to gratify the luxurious ... On the *grands boulevards* you find porcelains, perfumery, bronzes, carpets, furs, mirrors, the furnishings of travel, the ... latest picture, the last daring caricature in the most popular journal, the most aristocratic beer, and best flavored coffee.

So powerful was the sense of the good life that even when France was invaded in 1870 by the Prussian army, and Paris subsequently beseiged, little changed. The seige did, however, last long enough to make it necessary for the slaughter of the animals in the zoo to feed the people at the boulevard cafés. As one gentleman reported in his diary of December 6, 1870, "On today's bill of fare in the restaurants we have authentic buffalo, antelope, and kangaroo." A few days later, the zoo's celebrated elephants, Castor and Pollux, were killed, and their various meats made available in the butcher shops.

PAINTING

As peace descended once again on the Parisian boulevards, a group of artists began discussing the possibility of showing their work together in an exhibition. They met regularly at the Café de Guerbois, on the Boulevard des Batignolles, and thus called themselves the "Batignolles" group. They would soon, however, come to be called the Impressionists, a term which, as has been noted, was not a favorable one. They included Mary Cassatt, Edgar Degas, Claude Monet, Berthe Morisot, Camille Pissarro, Pierre Renoir, and Alfred Sisley. Although he did not exhibit with them, they received the full support of Édouard Manet, who was particularly good friends with Monet and often painted with members of the group in the French countryside.

It is Manet who most clearly bridges the gap between the Realists and the Impressionists. He worked closely with the latter set after 1870. His paintings of 1863, *Olympia* and *Luncheon on the Grass* (see Chapter 17), were not only Realist works but were also seen as precursors of the new movement.

In 1862, Manet painted a scene that was one of the first to capture a contemporary social event, *Music in the Tuileries* (fig. 18.1), and in this respect alone it anticipated Impressionism almost entirely. On the far left, with top hat and cane, is Manet himself. Many of the other figures were members of Manet's circle, including his younger brother Eugène, in white trousers, and a rather peculiar-looking man, silhouetted against the tree, who is Jacques Offenbach, the most popular composer of the day. Offenbach was a master of burlesque. His comic operas were all the rage, the highlight of which was wild dancing to songs that exhorted, "Let's waltz! Let's polka! Let's jump! Let's dance!" In the *belle époque*, it was music such as Offenbach's that entertained the crowds of Paris, not Richard Wagner's.

In the early 1860s, Manet went to the Tuileries gardens almost every day between two and four o'clock, accompanied usually by Baudelaire, to sketch the women who gathered there with their children. It is little wonder that by 1863 Baudelaire had given up on Courbet and adopted Manet as his painter of modern life. Courbet painted a working class that, for all practical purposes, had disappeared. Manet painted the new bourgeois, "Haussmannized" Paris (*Luncheon on the Grass* is probably set in the Bois de Boulogne). The two painters were among the most famous *flâneurs* in Paris, a distinct type known for impeccable manners, top hats and formal attire, their penchant for idle strolling, and devotion to conversation, gossip, and current events. Theirs was a life of dedicated leisure, what would become the Impressionist lifestyle.

Figure 18.1 Édouard Manet, *Music in the Tuileries*, 1862, oil on canvas, 30 × 46½″ (76 × 118 cm), National Gallery, London. The painting embodies the sense of social well-being, of Parisians enjoying the good life, that would dominate French painting for the next forty years.

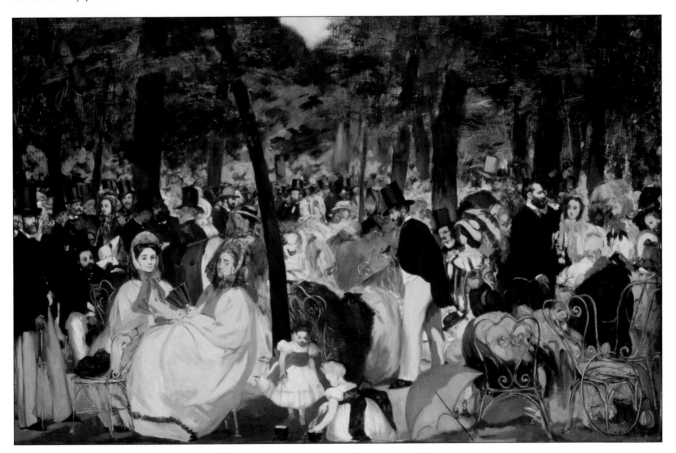

Claude Monet. The name "Impressionism" was derived from a painting by CLAUDE MONET [moh-NAY] (1840–1926) shown at the first exhibition of Impressionist art. Painted in 1872, it was called *Impression, Sunrise* (fig. 18.2), a title suggested by Renoir's brother. The painting encapsulates many of the features characteristic of Impressionist art. The *way* the Impressionist painters worked was as important to them as the subjects they painted. The traditional method of oil painting was to begin with a dark background base color and work up to the lighter colors. The Impressionists reversed this, beginning with a white canvas and building up to dark colors. They tried to convey a sense of natural light in a painting, and to that end they painted in the open air, rather than in the studio. They also tried to depict a momentary impression of nature's transitory light, atmosphere, and weather conditions; in Monet's painting the sun rises on a misty day over the harbor at Le Havre on the northern French coast. Behind this painting, and Impressionism as a whole, there also lies a major technological advance—the availability of oil paint in small, portable tins and tubes, which allowed painters to transport their paints out-of-doors.

Monet's brushwork is deliberately sketchy, consisting of broad dashes and dabs of paint. He suggests waves in the water with strokes of black. He shows the reflection of the sunrise in a series of orange and white strokes

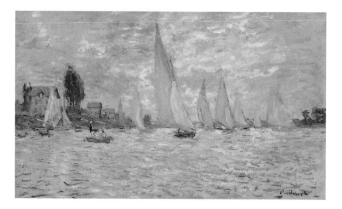

Figure 18.3   Claude Monet, *Sailboats at Argenteuil*, 1872, oil on canvas, $17\frac{3}{4} \times 29\frac{1}{2}''$ (48 × 75 cm), Musée d'Orsay, Paris. With income derived from paintings sold in 1872, Monet purchased a small boat, fitted it with a cabin, and used it as a floating studio, allowing him to paint the shoreline from the middle of the Seine.

mixed together while still wet, right on the canvas. Of particular note is a small area of vertical gray strokes half way up on the left-hand side. It is as if Monet simply used the canvas to wipe the excess paint off his brush and left the resulting mark where it was. Although Monet's brushwork is loose, his composition is tightly controlled. Everything is carefully placed within a grid, defined horizontally by the horizon and vertically by the masts and the pattern of light and shadow that forms vertical bands across the composition.

Monet's compositional sense is even more readily apparent in *Sailboats at Argenteuil* of 1872 (fig. 18.3). This work, painted in the full light of the French summer, is in fact more representative of the Impressionist use of color. During the late nineteenth century, scientists and painters—particularly the Impressionists—were developing theories about color. They both discovered that if two bright colors are juxtaposed, both appear even brighter, especially if **complementary colors** are used. Complementary colors consist of one primary color and one secondary color, which is formed by mixing the remaining two primaries. The **primary colors** are red, yellow, and blue. **Secondary colors** are formed when two primary colors are mixed: red + yellow = orange; yellow + blue = green; and blue + red = purple. Thus, the complementary pairs are red (primary) and green (secondary), blue and orange, and yellow and purple. The entire right side of Monet's painting exploits the first two of these complementary pairs. The green of the foliage complements the red roofs, and the blue of the water and sky complements the orange walls of the buildings and their reflections. Accentuated by the whiteness of the sails, the brightness creates an almost shimmering effect on the picture plane, not unlike the shimmering of the surface of the water itself. *Sailboats at*

Figure 18.2   Claude Monet, *Impression, Sunrise*, 1872, oil on canvas, $17\frac{3}{4} \times 21\frac{3}{4}''$ (48 × 63 cm), Musée Marmottan, Paris. The term "Impressionism," originally meant as an insult, derives from the title of this painting. Critics objected to the style, saying artists created *merely* an impression of a scene, without detail or compositional structure.

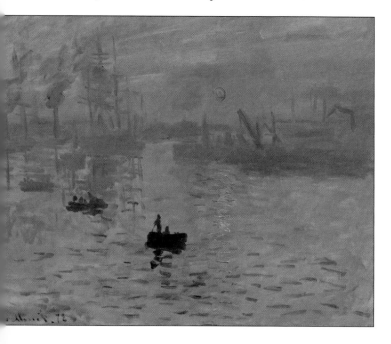

Timeline 18.1 Art of the *Belle Époque*.

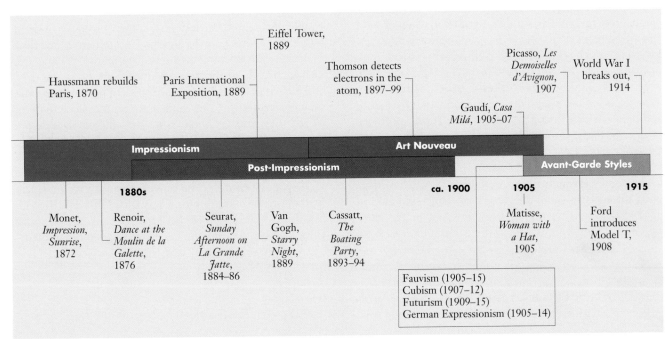

Argenteuil might, in fact, be viewed as a summary of the Impressionist method. The surface of the painting is to reality as the reflection on the surface of the water is to the real boats and houses on the shoreline. The reflection in the bottom half of the painting is so cursory and abbreviated that it is barely legible without reference to the top half of the painting, but it represents, in an intentionally overstated way, the kind of flickering vision that Impressionism embodies.

Monet had moved, in 1872, to Argenteuil, a small town on the Seine just nine kilometers north of Paris, in order to live and paint in an atmosphere of rural leisure. He lived there until the threat of increasing industrialization forced him further downstream, first to Vétheuil in 1878, and then to Giverny in 1883, where he developed an extensive private garden complete with the lily ponds that he was to paint for the rest of his life.

At Giverny, Monet embarked on a number of projects designed to investigate the way in which changes in light and weather alter what we see. Among the most famous of these projects, begun in 1888, is a series of paintings of haystacks, executed in all seasons of the year and at different times of day. In *Haystacks at Giverny* (fig. 18.4), the color actually creates a feeling of heat. Greatly concerned with natural light, Monet realized that it changed color constantly and that many different colors in fact made up what was perceived to be a single one. The myriad dabs of "broken" color blend in the viewer's eyes, creating sparkle and vibration. When a group of fifteen of these paintings was exhibited in Paris in 1891, they caused an immediate sensation. As the critic Gustave

Geffroy wrote in the introduction to the show's catalogue: "[Monet] knows that the artist can spend his life in the same place and look around himself without exhausting the constantly renewed spectacle … These stacks, in this deserted field, are transient objects whose surfaces, like mirrors, catch the mood of the environment, the states of the atmosphere with the errant breeze, the sudden glow."

Figure 18.4 Claude Monet, *Haystacks at Giverny* (end of summer, morning), 1891, oil on canvas, 23¾ × 39½" (60.5 × 100 cm), Musée d'Orsay, Paris. Rather than painting in the studio as did earlier artists, Monet painted out-of-doors. Instead of mixing colors on a palette beforehand, he applied paint in dabs of pure color, referred to as "broken color."

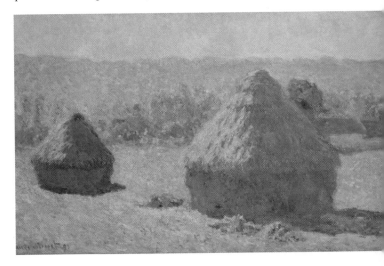

Pierre-Auguste Renoir: PIERRE-AUGUSTE RENOIR [ren-WAHR] (1841–1919) was a good friend of Monet when both were poor and struggling, and the two often painted together, in Paris and at Argenteuil, where Renoir was a frequent visitor. His joyous personality and his zest for living, which reflect the age itself, inform his paintings.

Dance at the Moulin de la Galette (fig. 18.5), of 1876 which is reminiscent of Manet's earlier *Music in the Tuileries*, is a good example. The painting, of a restaurant and open-air dance hall in Montmartre, in the northern section of Paris, captures the sense of gaiety that marks the *belle époque*. Renoir painted outdoors, working rapidly with his colors to capture the atmosphere of the moment. Light comes through the trees, falling in patches, dappling the surface—note the pattern of round splotches of light that illuminate the back of the man in the foreground. An orchestra played at the Moulin de la Galette every Sunday from three o'clock in the afternoon until midnight. Renoir's figures appear relaxed (perhaps it is their day off), rather than stiffly posed. Interestingly, the couple dancing on the left gaze at the viewer. They seem aware that they are being watched, a photographic effect that lends the painting an aura of spontaneity. They are, in fact, friends of the artist: Margot, one of his models, and Solares, a Cuban painter. As in all of his paintings, the men are handsome, the women are pretty, the activity in which they engage is pleasant, and the sun is shining. According to Renoir, "a picture ought to be a lovable thing, joyous and pretty, yes pretty. There are enough boring things in this world without our making more."

Berthe Morisot. The only woman to exhibit at the first Impressionist exhibition was BERTHE MORISOT [more-ee-SOH] (1841–1895). Married to Manet's younger brother Eugène, her work was almost immedi-

Figure 18.5   Pierre-Auguste Renoir, *Dance at the Moulin de la Galette*, 1876, oil on canvas, 4'3½" × 5'9" (1.30 × 1.80 m), Musée d'Orsay, Paris. Instead of choosing traditional subjects, the Impressionists depicted pleasant places where people congregated. In Renoir's paintings the women are always attractive, the men handsome, and the weather good—here the sun falls in patches through the leaves.

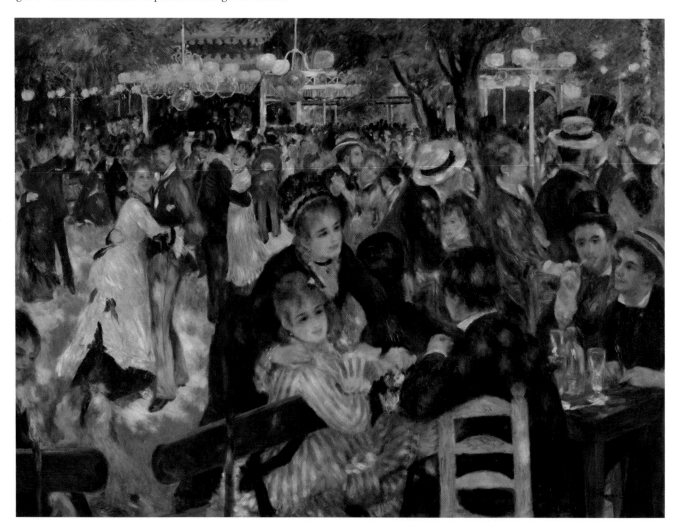

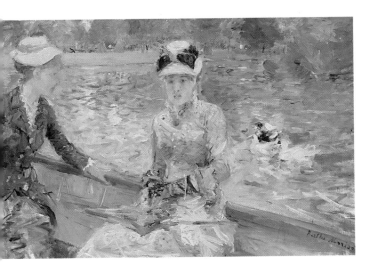

Figure 18.6 Berthe Morisot, *Summer's Day*, 1879, oil on canvas, 18 × 29¾″ (45.7 × 75.2 cm), National Gallery, London. Note in particular Morisot's handling of the three ducks swimming on the right. They are so loosely painted that they have become almost unrecognizable.

ately given the negative label "feminine" by the critics, perhaps because her subject matter was, almost exclusively, women and children. Whatever she depicted, it is clear that she was the most daring of all the Impressionist painters. *Summer's Day* (fig. 18.6), exhibited at the fifth show in 1880, is remarkable for the looseness of its brushwork. It is as if the brushwork can hardly be contained within the contours of the forms it depicts. It zigs and zags across the surface in a seemingly arbitrary manner. Yet in the small rapid movements of her strokes, one can almost feel the breeze on the water, see the lapping and splashing of the water on the oars, and hear the wisps of conversation between the two women as they enjoy their outing.

Edgar Degas. A very different type of French Impressionism was created by EDGAR DEGAS [DUH-GAH] (1834–1917). An aristocrat from a banking family, Degas was independently wealthy and therefore able to paint to suit himself. Many other painters disliked him, and with reason, for he was snobbish and unfriendly, with a nasty wit. Politically and socially conservative, Degas did not think art should be available to the lower class.

Degas's strict academic training resulted in a style based upon draftsmanship. In 1865 he met Ingres, then eighty-five years old. Ingres told him to "do lines and more lines, from nature or from memory, and you will become a good artist." Because of this linear approach, Degas has been called a "linear Impressionist," which may seem at first to be a contradiction. Degas, however, hated the word "Impressionist" because of the negative connotations of "accidental" or "incomplete." He

abhorred, in particular, the idea that painting could be the "fleeting, transitory, and contingent" practice that many Impressionists claimed it to be. Degas worked methodically, sometimes determining the proportions of the work by ruling off squares and often making many sketches before painting. Color and light were added to define forms, not to make them. He once remarked, "No art was ever less spontaneous than mine. What I do is the result of reflection and study of the great masters; of inspiration, spontaneity, temperament, I know nothing."

What makes Degas an Impressionist, nonetheless, is the *sense* of spontaneity visible in his work, not only in the looseness of his brushwork, but in the choice and treatment of his subject matter. However calculatingly hard he worked, he aimed to *appear* unstudied. His effect is one of instantaneous and immediate vision. More than, or at least as much as, any other painter of his day, Degas seems to have been influenced by photography, and by the snapshot in particular. His paintings are often severely cropped, cutting figures in half, as if they are just entering or leaving the viewfinder of a camera.

In Degas's depictions of ballet dancers, for which he is perhaps best known, he takes us behind the scenes. In *The Dancing Class* (fig. 18.7), of about 1874, he seems to have

Figure 18.7 Edgar Degas, *The Dancing Class*, ca. 1874, oil on canvas, 33½ × 29½″ (85 × 75 cm), Musée d'Orsay, Paris. Degas was called a "linear Impressionist"—seemingly an oxymoron. Interested in figures in motion, he made many pictures of ballerinas. He seems to have preferred them at their least graceful, when leaning tired against the barre, stooping over their aching feet, or adjusting their costumes.

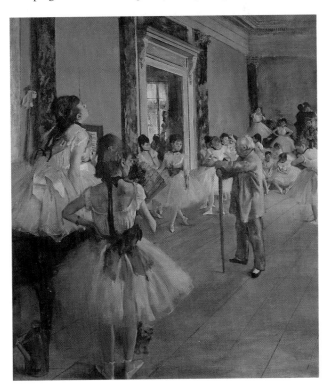

Cross Currents

JAPANESE PRINTS AND WESTERN PAINTERS

The influence of the Japanese print on Western painters of the nineteenth century, especially the Impressionists, is the direct result of the opening of Japan to trade with the West after Commodore Matthew Perry sailed into Tokyo Bay in 1853, demanding that Japanese ports be opened to foreigners. Perry's arrival ended over two hundred years of Japanese isolationism, which had started as a result of the negative reception of Christian ideas introduced into the country by foreign missionaries.

After trade began, Japanese color prints flooded Europe to such an extent that they became commonplace. Their influence is evident in Manet's *Portrait of Émile Zola* (see fig. 17.34), which contains, alongside a print of Manet's own *Olympia*, a Japanese print of a wrestler (by Kuniyaki II), and, behind the figure of Zola, a Japanese landscape screen. Western artists were attracted especially to the flatness of Japanese forms, the flatness of the space behind them, and the oblique perspective that characterized the Japanese treatment of space. The cropped but close-up renderings of occurrences in everyday life that so enthralled the Japanese artists, influenced, in particular, the work of Edgar Degas and Mary Cassatt.

Claude Monet discovered the first of the many Japanese prints that would decorate his house at Giverny wrapped around a cheese purchased at the market. What especially attracted him to Japanese landscapes were the ways in which they organized the natural elements, such as rocks and trees. Perhaps the clearest example of Monet's enthusiasm for Japanese art and culture is the garden he created at Giverny and the paintings it inspired. The Far Eastern influence is evident in the small pond he created which was spanned by a little arched bridge, with blue wisteria flowers arranged so as to hang down on either side. There were irises, bamboo, and willows, all common plants in Japanese paintings.

Perhaps the artist most thoroughly influenced by the Japanese print was Vincent van Gogh. He owned hundreds of prints, and one of the reasons he went to Arles in 1888 was that he believed he would find a landscape there similar to that of Japan. His letters to his brother Theo repeatedly refer to his idealized image of Japanese life, in which painters and printmakers lived in close contact with ordinary people and in harmony with the rhythms and cycles of nature.

While still in Paris, in 1887, Van Gogh copied a print by Ando Hiroshige, *Plum Estate*, of 1857. Van Gogh's painting, entitled *Japonaiserie:*

The Tree (fig. 18.8), is an almost exact copy. What particularly impressed Van Gogh was the relation between the tree in the foreground, and the space behind it, the gulf between the nearby detail and the landscape beyond. This is an effect that would dominate his paintings in the future.

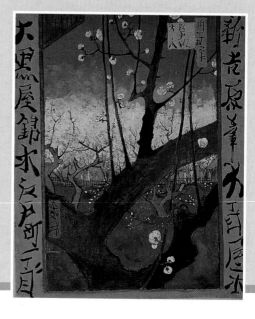

Figure 18.8 Vincent van Gogh, *Japonaiserie: The Tree*, 1887, oil on canvas, $21\frac{5}{8}'' \times 18\frac{1}{8}''$ (55 × 46 cm), National Museum Vincent van Gogh, Amsterdam. Van Gogh was influenced in this painting and in others by the unusual vantage point, flat pattern, and dark outlines characteristic of Japanese prints.

tried deliberately to capture the dancers at their least graceful—straining, stretching, scratching, and yawning. Known for his unusual compositions, Degas constructs in this work a box-like space in which the walls are not parallel to the picture plane but at oblique angles. The point of view from which the scene is recorded is striking—from above and to the side. It anticipates, in effect, the freedom of perspective that photographers would discover with the handheld camera, an invention that the Kodak Corporation had introduced by the end of the century.

Mary Cassatt. In addition to French Impressionist painters, there were a number of American Impressionists. One of the foremost among them was

MARY CASSATT [kah-SAHT] (1844–1925), who left her wealthy Pittsburgh family and moved to Europe where she became absorbed in the art world. Her parents opposed her study of art so strongly that her father is reported to have said, "I would almost rather see you dead." She soon gained recognition, however—she was called a madwoman because of her style. Cassatt was a close friend of Degas, who claimed he never would have believed that a woman could draw so well. As early as 1879, Cassatt was exhibiting with the Impressionists.

Cassatt's *The Boating Party* (fig. 18.9), painted 1893–94, was criticized when first shown; the foreground figure has rudely turned his back on the viewer. Rather than being the center of attention, however, he acts as a

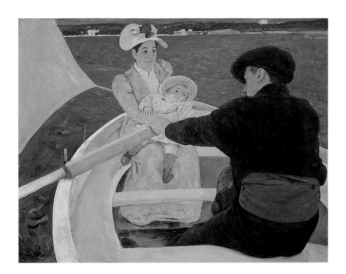

Figure 18.9 Mary Cassatt, *The Boating Party*, 1893–94, oil on canvas, $35\frac{1}{2} \times 46\frac{1}{8}''$ (90 × 117 cm), National Gallery of Art, Washington, D.C. An American working in France, Cassatt paints a typical Impressionist subject—pleasant and out-of-doors. The composition directs the viewer's eyes to the squirming child.

compositional device directing the viewer's gaze in: his arm and oar point inward, and he looks toward the mother and child, just as the viewer does. The contours of the boat and sail also point to the mother and child. A sense of realism is achieved in the awkward movements of the child.

The influence of Degas, and of the Japanese print, is apparent in the asymmetrical composition, the emphasis on sharp silhouettes and linear rhythms, the broad flat areas of color, the "snapshot" quality of the scene, the high positioning of the horizon, and, moreover, the unusual perspective—we look down into the boat, which is abruptly cut off. The brilliant light effects that are so typical of the French Riviera are recorded in the painting, but these are not achieved through the use of Impressionist broken color. Instead, Cassatt juxtaposes large areas of bright color. The light appears intense, but is not realistic—the interior of the boat should, for instance, be dark. "Facts" are manipulated for art, and in this respect Cassatt's painting can be seen as anticipating the art of the next century.

James Abbott McNeill Whistler. The work of another expatriate American, JAMES ABBOTT McNEILL WHISTLER (1834–1903), also foreshadows twentieth-century art. After a disappointing stint at West Point, and being fired from a government job in Washington, D.C., Whistler went to Paris, in 1855, where he lived as a bohemian art student. Then, in 1859, he moved to London, where he was to remain for the rest of his life. He visited Paris several times and learned about Impressionism, but he never used Impressionistic broken color or light effects.

In 1863, his mother came to keep house for him (she supported him financially), and in 1871 he immortalized her in a work entitled *Arrangement in Black and Gray: The Artist's Mother* (fig. 18.10), known popularly as *Whistler's Mother*. Whistler referred to his paintings by musical terms such as nocturnes, symphonies, and harmonies. This painting is first and foremost an "arrangement," and only secondarily a portrait. Abstract and formal, the pictorial space is flattened, depth receives little emphasis. Light, shadow, and modeling are minimal.

Whistler maintained that art should not be concerned with morality, education, or story-telling, but should appeal to the aesthetic sense. He believed in art for art's sake. His subject matter was at times entirely lost in a kind of late evening atmosphere, a light where things are barely visible.

LITERATURE

The Symbolists. Related to the Impressionists because they also attempted to convey reality by impression and sensation, the Symbolist poets felt liberated by their medium, words, and from the necessity of rendering the "facts" of vision. Words, they believed, could do more than simply portray these "facts" of external

Figure 18.10 James Abbott McNeill Whistler, *Arrangement in Black and Gray: The Artist's Mother*, 1871, oil on canvas, $4'9'' \times 5'4\frac{1}{4}''$ (1.50 × 1.60 m), Musée d'Orsay, Paris. Whistler's mother, as subject, is treated much the same as the other elements in this intellectual arrangement in restricted colors.

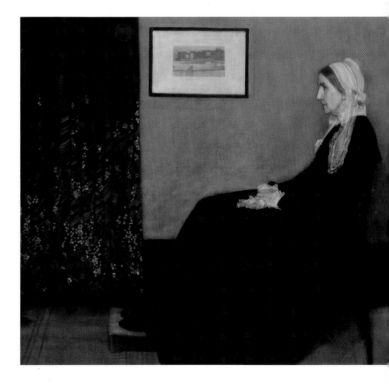

Connections

Claude Debussy's chamber orchestral composition *Prelude to the Afternoon of a Faun* was inspired by Stéphane Mallarmé's poem "The Afternoon of a Faun." Both composer and poet convey the faun's experience through suggestive uses of sound and language. Mallarmé's poem describes the reveries of a creature from classical mythology, with the body of a man and the horns, ears, legs, and tail of a goat. The poem's dreamlike tone raises the question as to whether the faun has actually been chasing nymphs or whether he has only been dreaming about doing so. Equally ambiguous is the poem's sense of time and place. Debussy's composition does not attempt to portray the content of the poem so much as to evoke its atmosphere of languor and fantasy.

Debussy wrote the music to suggest "the successive scenes through which pass the desires and dreams of the faun in the heat of [an] afternoon." He accomplishes this with a musical language that includes the sounds of woodwind and harp, while excluding those of trumpets and trombones. Rather than the clearly articulated, symmetrical themes of the Classical and Romantic styles that were developed and recapitulated, Debussy creates a more dreamlike and evocative music. His themes appear and disappear, often in misty fragments and brief orchestral swells. The music ebbs and flows continuously in a series of subtly shifting rhythms, the flute suggesting the musical pipes associated with the mythological faun. The overall musical effect is one of reverie, which suits the mood of Mallarmé's poem.

experience; indeed, they could capture a sense of the shifting and fluid nature of our entire mental experience. Language could encompass not only our perceptions of the outside world, but our internal lives as well. The Symbolists sought to evoke states of mind and feeling beyond the surface of everyday reality. And since they did not believe that they could successfully render the external world objectively, they were free to present it from their own unique and idiosyncratic perspectives. Reality was at best, they argued, an irretrievably personal affair.

Poetry, they felt, had long been mired in the ordinary, caught up in conventions of meaning and usage that blinded the reader to language's potential to reveal the extraordinary and the unknown. For the Symbolists, an image or symbol did not so much stand for something as suggest a cluster of ideas and feelings. They preferred the vagueness of symbolic suggestion to a more precise rendering of experience. As Stéphane Mallarmé wrote, "To name an object is to do away with three-quarters of the enjoyment of the poem, which is derived from the satisfaction of guessing little by little; to suggest it, to evoke it, this is what charms the imagination."

Among the poets associated with the Symbolist movement, CHARLES BAUDELAIRE [bow-duh-LAIR] (1821–1867) is considered an important precursor, but STÉPHANE MALLARMÉ [mal-are-MAY] (1842–1898) was the group's leading theoretician and certainly its most influential practitioner. Both Baudelaire and Mallarmé attempted to create poems that contain images that fuse the senses and attain the expressiveness of music. In Baudelaire's "Hair," for example, the speaker pays homage to a lover's hair by describing it as "A port resounding where, in draughts untold, / My soul may drink in colour, scent, and sound." A similar combination of the senses occurs in Mallarmé's "Windows," in lines such as "His eye on the horizon gorged with light, / Sees golden ships, fine as swans, / On a scented river of purple." In addition to this attempt to convey the rich sensuousness of imagined experience, Symbolist poets tried to make their verse musical, so that the sounds of the words themselves would be suggestive in a musical sense rather than purely representational, a characteristic difficult to demonstrate in translation.

Naturalism. The impulse toward Romanticism in the nineteenth century was countered by the writing of a number of American women. Writers such as SARAH ORNE JEWETT (1849–1909), CHARLOTTE PERKINS GILMAN (1851–1904), and KATE CHOPIN [SHOW-panh] (1851–1904) all deal with the concerns of middle-class women in naturalistic detail, with a psychological realism often reminiscent of Freud. Jewett's stories center on the everyday lives of New England characters; Gilman focuses on the ways in which nineteenth-century attitudes toward women kept them physically and psychologically imprisoned; and Chopin's fiction depicts strong women who insist upon their independence and their right to determine their own destinies.

Kate Chopin was especially adept at depicting the lives of the Creole, Cajun, African American, and Native American communities of Louisiana, and her popularity soared as readers avidly consumed her stories filled with local customs and dialects. Chopin's best-known work is the short novel *The Awakening*, published in 1899. It is intensely psychological in its portrayal of its heroine Edna Pontellier's passionate emotional life, her boredom with her constricting marriage, and her flirtatious adventures with another man. But the novel was considered virtually obscene in its day, banned from most libraries, and Chopin's reputation suffered until the 1950s, when the work was rediscovered.

Along with the novel, drama began to develop along naturalistic lines, especially in Europe. Among the great nineteenth-century realist dramatists was the Norwegian playwright HENRIK IBSEN (1828–1906), whose plays touched on such themes as the roles and rights of women (*A Doll's House*), the scourge of venereal disease (*Ghosts*), and the death of a child (*Little Eyolf*). Ibsen's dramatic intensity and electrifying revelations were matched by the Swedish playwright AUGUST STRINDBERG (1849–1912), whose plays *The Father, Creditors*, and *Comrades* were all written in a strongly realistic style. The plays of Ibsen, Strindberg, and the numerous other naturalist dramatists of the time were staged in ways that emphasized the authenticity of the characters, settings, and situations dramatized.

MUSIC

Debussy's Musical Impressionism. The composer CLAUDE DEBUSSY [day-byou-SEE] (1862–1918) was to nineteenth-century French music what Claude Monet was to nineteenth-century French painting. Like Monet, Debussy revolutionized his artistic medium. As Monet altered the way external reality was rendered in pigment, so Debussy altered the way music suggested extra-musical sensations and impressions. Working with a palette of sound instead of color, he mixed musical tones, combining them in ways never heard before, thus influencing the music that would be written after him.

Debussy studied at the Paris Conservatory from the age of ten until he was twenty-two, during which time the Impressionist painters were exhibiting their work. He won the most prestigious prize for French composers, the "Prix de Rome," and went to the Italian capital for two years. In 1887, he returned to Paris, supported himself by giving piano lessons, and became part of a circle of artists and writers. Another of the members was Stéphane Mallarmé, whose poem, "The Afternoon of a Faun," would later serve as inspiration for Debussy's most famous musical composition, *Prelude to the Afternoon of a Faun*.

Debussy insisted that "French music is clearness, elegance, simple and natural declamation. French music aims first of all to give pleasure." This he did in a wide range of compositions—some for orchestra, such as *Fêtes* (*Festivals*) and *La Mer* (*The Sea*), and others for piano, including the popular *Claire de Lune* (*Moonlight*), inspired by the Symbolist poet Paul Verlaine. Rather than duplicating the poem's images or details, Debussy created a parallel or analogous musical image of moonlight through beautiful sounds and suggestive harmonies, without a long lyrical melodic line.

The new sounds achieved through Debussy's piano music were the result of the composer's rejection of the dramatic dynamics of theme employed by Classical and Romantic composers in favor of greater tonal variety. He accomplished this effect partly by encouraging the use of the piano's damper pedal, which allows the strings for different notes to resonate simultaneously, creating a hazy but rich blend of sounds. He complemented this with a fluctuating sense of rhythm. In masking the basic musical pulse, Debussy created music that avoided the familiar melodic, harmonic, and rhythmic patterns of the past. One of the most important influences on his melodic style was Asian music, which he heard demonstrated at the Paris International Exposition in 1889. There Debussy heard Javanese and Southeast Asian music that he could not duplicate on Western instruments. In response, he created a new scale of six whole tones, entirely of whole-step intervals. The effect of using such a scale was to make all the scale tones equal in weight, without the strong pull of any one home key. The unfocused quality of music that resulted from a whole-tone scale is comparable to the effects Impressionist painters used in creating a shimmering atmosphere across a canvas, and to the lack of representation achieved by Symbolist poets in their deliberate avoidance of strict linguistic referentiality.

THE *FIN DE SIÈCLE*

As the nineteenth century came to a close, and as a new one was about to dawn, the Western world was overtaken by a sense that an era was ending. The French, in particular, took up the habit of referring to themselves as a *fin de siècle* culture, a culture "at century's end." It was a time of extraordinary material innovation: in the 1880s and 1890s, the telegraph and telephone, the bicycle and the automobile, the typewriter and phonograph, the elevator and the electric lamp, all came into being. At the 1889 World Fair in Paris, which marked the one-hundredth anniversary of the Revolution, the engineer GUSTAVE EIFFEL (1832–1923) constructed the tallest structure in the world, a tower that stood 984 feet high (fig. 18.11). At first, many Parisians hated it. The author Guy de Maupaussant, for instance, preferred to lunch at the restaurant in the Eiffel Tower because, he said, "It's the only place in Paris where I don't have to see it." Despite the negative reception, its skeletal iron frame prepared the way for the most prevalent of twentieth-century buildings—the skyscraper—which would define the terms of the new urban workplace as surely as the telephone and the typewriter. By 1900, when it was the focal point of a second International Exposition, the Eiffel Tower had become the very symbol of French cultural ascendancy.

The *fin de siècle* was also an age of profound and disturbing social unrest and, to many, one of moral decay. Starting in the 1880s, severe economic depression in England marked the beginning of the end of the country's supremacy as a world power. The Dockers' Strike of 1889 led to the unionization of unskilled workers, and by 1900 the Labour Party had been founded. In France meanwhile, the working classes, it seemed, turned more and more to alcohol for pleasure. Beginning in 1891 and continuing for twenty more years, three thousand new bistros opened in Paris every year, and by 1910, there was one for every eighty-two Parisians. By 1906, most French workmen drank over three liters of wine a day. Drug use was on the rise, with opium, and its derivative morphine, finding special favor. With addiction and poverty came crime, so much so that electric light was championed more for its ability to deter criminal behavior than for anything else.

In 1898, the Dreyfus Affair undermined the moral authority of the state. Captain Dreyfus of the Army General Staff had been arrested in November 1894 for passing information to the Germans. Tried and condemned, he was deported to Devil's Island to serve a life sentence, but his family would not give up, protesting that the verdict had been illegally obtained. The novelist Émile Zola took up Dreyfus's cause, writing a scathing letter to the Parisian papers in January 1898 and publishing a book on the affair, *J'Accuse*, several months later. Zola argued that the man had been railroaded on orders from the highest level of the French military, and a hot debate ensued. The entire affair was quickly complicated by the question of Dreyfus's Jewishness, and the whole of France ended the century violently divided.

The period also witnessed a challenge on the part of European intellectuals to the accepted code of moral behavior of the day. Some writers styled themselves "decadents." In England, OSCAR WILDE (1854–1900) flaunted his homosexuality. This identifiable "type" suddenly became visible to such a point that in Vienna, in 1905, Sigmund Freud would include homosexuality in his *Three Essays on the Theory of Sexuality*. George Sand and Rosa Bonheur had worn men's clothing in mid-century, but now, in the 1890s, many women, particularly intellectuals, wore trousers, and were consequently decried for betraying their sex. Moreover, they asked with increasing intensity for the right to vote. At the *fin de siècle*, all conventional standards of behavior seemed at risk.

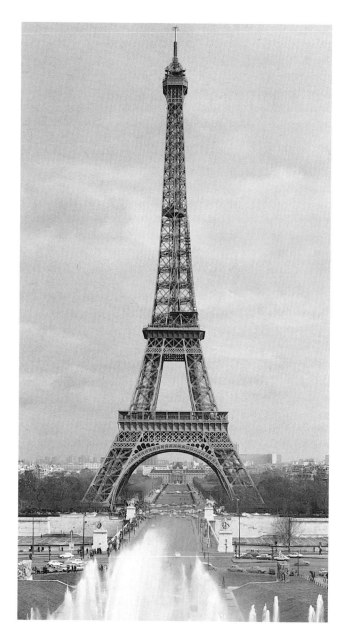

Figure 18.11 Gustave Eiffel, Eiffel Tower, Paris, 1889. This demonstration of engineering technology, which was extremely controversial when erected and has remained unique, is now considered the symbol of France. An elevator takes tourists up to enjoy a spectacular view of Paris.

NEW SCIENCE AND NEW TECHNOLOGIES

Even as prosperity seemed to promise a limitless future, the technology it spawned contributed to the breakdown of established patterns of social organization. New means of communication, such as the telephone, and new forms of transportation, such as the automobile, complicated life rather than simplifying it. The rules of the road remained largely uncodified, and further exacerbating the rapid changes everywhere was the continuing process of industrialization, which spurred the growth of urban centers at the expense of agrarian life. Modern intellectual developments greatly accelerated the transformation of traditional ways of thinking. In particular, discoveries in quantum physics and depth psychology played a significant role in transforming twentieth-century thought. The most important of these developments were Freud's invention of psychoanalysis and Einstein's promulgation of his theory of relativity.

The Theory of Relativity.   In 1905, ALBERT EINSTEIN (1879–1955) proposed that space and time are not absolute as they appear to be, but are instead relative to each other in a "space-time continuum." Not until 1919 could the mathematical equations central to Einstein's special theory of relativity be confirmed through scientific experiment. Subsequent experiments further established the legitimacy of his ideas. All modern developments in space technology were influenced by his discoveries, those developments proving the accuracy of his theory right into the 1980s. Einstein's notion of relativity was widely circulated even though it undermined traditional ways of thinking about the universe, similar to the way in which Copernicus's theory had overturned the Ptolemaic universe.

The Atom.   Equally important in its implications was the work of J.J. THOMSON (1856–1940) in Cambridge, England, who between 1897 and 1899 managed to detect the existence of separate components, which he called electrons, in the structure of the atom, which had previously been thought indivisible. By 1911, his colleague ERNEST RUTHERFORD (1871–1937) had introduced his revolutionary new model of the atom. It consisted of a small, positively charged nucleus, which contained most of the atom's mass, around which its electrons orbited. To many, the world no longer seemed a solid whole.

PHILOSOPHY AT THE TURN OF THE CENTURY

Friedrich Nietzsche.   Another impetus to changing modes of thought in the early twentieth century came from the nineteenth-century philosopher, FRIEDRICH NIETZSCHE [NEE-chuh] (1844–1900). Nietzsche emphasized the rebellious nature of the "superman," a superhuman being who refused to be confined within the traditional structures of nationalist ideology, Christian belief, scientific knowledge, and bourgeois values. Proclaiming that "God is dead," Nietzsche asserted the complete freedom of the individual, who could now begin to channel "Dionysian" (instinctual) and "Apollonian" (intellectual) tendencies in ways that were unrestricted by social conventions. Nietzsche influenced twentieth-century philosophical thought in significant ways. Early modernist art, in part, owes its rebellious anti-authoritarianism to Nietzsche's example. So too, in part, do developments in literary theory and in philosophy, especially existentialism.

Sigmund Freud.   The psychology of SIGMUND FREUD [FROYD] (1856–1939) further influenced modernist trends in culture and the arts. Freud's analysis of unconscious motives and his description of instinctual drives reflected an anti-rationalist perspective that undermined faith in the apparent order and control in human individual and social life. His emphasis on the irrational provided a quasi-scientific explanation of impulses and behaviors that had formerly been displayed in works of literature, which could now be analyzed with the language and concepts of psychoanalysis that he developed. Freud's splitting of the human psyche into the "ego," the "id," and the "superego" provided a psychoanalytical analogue for the growing concern with social fragmentation and cultural disharmony, the distressing feeling that all was not well, even if the period was known as the *belle époque*.

POST-IMPRESSIONIST PAINTING

By the early 1890s the Impressionist style of painting was widely accepted. However, since the time of Courbet, painters had defined themselves against the mainstream of "approved" art, and a certain number continued to defy the public's expectations even after the rise of Impressionism. The next wave of artists to challenge the mainstream were called the Post-Impressionists.

The term **Post-Impressionism** is, in fact, an extremely broad one, for the Post-Impressionists did not band together but worked in isolation. Rather than a rejection of Impressionism, Post-Impressionism, which began in France in the 1880s, was an attempt to improve upon it and to extend it. The Post-Impressionists considered Impressionism too objective, too impersonal, and lacking control. They did not think that recording a fleeting moment or portraying atmospheric conditions was sufficient. Placing greater emphasis on composition and form, on the "eternal and immutable," what Baudelaire described as the "other half" of art, the Post-Impressionists worked to control reality, to organize, arrange, and formalize. The Post-Impressionist painters wanted more personal interpretation and expression, greater psychological depth.

Paul Cézanne.   Born into a middle-class family, PAUL CÉZANNE [say-ZAHN] (1839–1906) was in Paris at the beginning of the Impressionist phenomenon. Introverted, however, to the point of being reclusive, he led an almost completely isolated existence in the south of France from 1877 to 1895. People there considered him a madman and jeered at him. He became ever more irritable as a consequence, and turned ever more inward.

Reacting against the loose and unstructured quality of Impressionist art, Cézanne's greatest interest was in order, stability, and permanence. He said he wanted "to make of Impressionism something solid and durable, like the art of the museums." All of Cézanne's paintings are carefully constructed. His usual technique was to sketch with thin blue paint and then apply the colors directly. He washed his brush between strokes so that each color would be distinct, sometimes taking as long as twenty minutes between brushstrokes. In fact, he referred to his brushstrokes as "little planes." An apple, for example, is viewed as a spherical form consisting of a series of small planes—each plane is a specific color according to the apple's form. This revolutionary style of painting would lead to the innovative ideas of the early twentieth century. Indeed, some critics feel that Cézanne was the first artist to profoundly redirect painting since Giotto (see Chapter 12) in the early fifteenth century.

Cézanne's favorite subject was still life, an example of which is *Still Life with Peppermint Bottle* (fig. 18.12), of ca. 1894. Inanimate objects permitted Cézanne's intensive and lengthy study. The subject was not as important to him as *how* he painted it, and he often combined unrelated objects in his still lifes. No attempt at photographic reproduction was made, for he consciously distorted edges and shapes, emphasizing the contours and the space between objects. Disregarding the conventions of perspective, he created a tension between the three-dimensional subject and the two-dimensional surface.

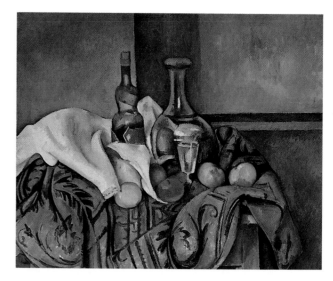

Figure 18.12   Paul Cézanne, *Still Life with Peppermint Bottle*, ca. 1894, oil on canvas, 26 × 32⅜″ (66 × 82.3 cm), National Gallery of Art, Washington, D.C. Post-Impressionists used the bright colors of Impressionism for different purposes. Using broken color in a more scientific and studied way, Cézanne referred to each brushstroke as a "little plane," which he used to establish the contours of an object in space.

Figure 18.13   Paul Cézanne, *The Great Bathers*, 1906, oil on canvas, 6′10″ × 8′2″ (2.08 × 2.49 m), Philadelphia Museum of Art. Humans were not the best subject for Cézanne's slow working method. His innovative approach to depicting objects in space, without using traditional methods of perspective, would prove to be influential for twentieth-century painting.

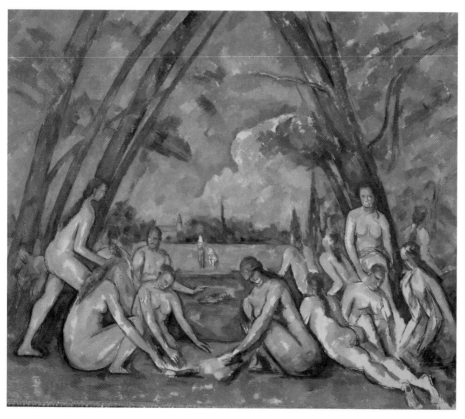

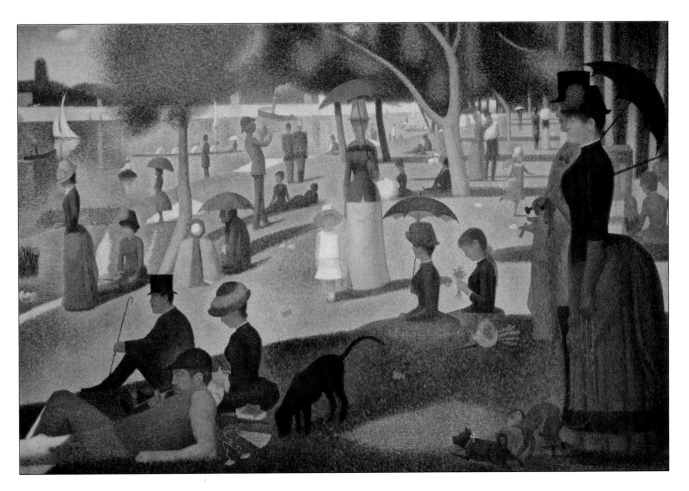

Figure 18.14   Georges Seurat, *Sunday Afternoon on La Grande Jatte*, 1884–86, oil on canvas, 6′9¾″ × 10′1¼″ (2.00 × 3.00 m), Art Institute of Chicago. Seurat has taken bright color and applied it systematically in tiny dots intended to blend in the viewer's eyes when the painting is seen from a distance. The technique is formal, and the composition is carefully unified by repetition of curving shapes.

Cézanne found it difficult to paint the human figure. He was ill at ease with models, and he took too long to paint them. He once yelled at a model, who had fallen asleep, saying, "You must sit like an apple. Does an apple fidget?" In *The Great Bathers* (fig. 18.13), of 1906, Cézanne created a geometric composition, for the trees tilt inward to form a pyramid, while the nudes reinforce the sides, and an echoing V-shape is created by the arms below. The planes of the background, moreover, provide a stabilizing horizontal. Thus the figures and setting form a deliberate pattern. The facts of nature are manipulated for the sake of the design and structure of the composition. Indeed, Cézanne proclaimed that a painter is allowed to distort nature, to "recreate" nature, rather than slavishly copy it.

Always striving, yet chronically dissatisfied with his work, Cézanne felt he did not reach his goal. "I am the primitive of the way I have discovered," he claimed. Yet much of early twentieth-century painting is indebted to Cézanne, who has been called the "Father of Abstract Art." His phrase, "You must see in nature the cylinder, the sphere, and the cone," became the basis of the Cubist painting of Pablo Picasso and Georges Braque.

Georges Seurat.   Another important French Post-Impressionist artist, GEORGES SEURAT [sir-AH] (1859–1891), had an approach to painting that was intellectual and scientific. He believed that art could be created by a system of rules. Like Cézanne, he made many sketches and studies before painting and worked very slowly.

Sunday Afternoon on La Grande Jatte (fig. 18.14), painted between 1884 and 1886, is a monumental work. The subject is Impressionistic: a sunny afternoon in a public park with a gathering of French society. Yet, in an effort to give structure to the disintegrating forms of Impressionism, Seurat solidified and simplified them and defined their boundaries. Edges reappear and silhouettes are sharp. All is tidy, balanced, and arranged with precision.

Seurat's working method was to first create silhouettes of simple lines and precise contours. He then organized the composition's surface and depth. Spaces between figures and shadows were considered part of the composition, and shapes were repeated for unity. He then painted in his *petits points*, a technique called "Pointillism," though Seurat called it "divisionism." **Pointillism** or **divisionism** is the almost mathematical application of paint to the canvas in small dots or points of uniform size, each dot precisely placed. This technique is underpinned by color theory—Seurat believed that the human eye could optically mix the different colors he applied as dots. Thus, where a blue dot was placed next to a red dot, theoretically the eye would see purple. It is difficult to imagine the patience required to paint in this technique, which Seurat even used to sign his name and to paint the frames. Each shape, its color, size, and location, is calculated—very different from Impressionism's informal, seemingly accidental quality.

Vincent van Gogh. In contrast to Seurat, VINCENT VAN GOGH [van GOH] (1853–1890) is famed for his rapidly executed paintings, which use expressive and emotional color. Dutch by birth, Van Gogh lived and worked in France for most of his life. His brother Theo, director of a small art gallery, supported him. Van Gogh met the Impressionists and used their bright colors and vivid contrasts, not to capture light effects but, instead, to convey emotion. When he moved to Arles in the south of France, Van Gogh painted and drew at a rate of almost one piece a day. Among his most famous works of that period is *The Night Café* (fig. 18.15). "I have tried to express the idea that the café is a place where one can

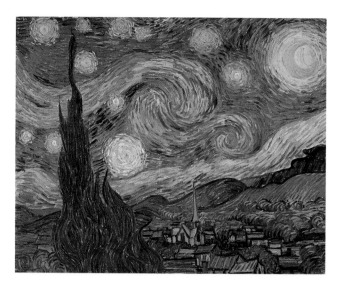

Figure 18.16   Vincent van Gogh, *Starry Night*, 1889, oil on canvas, $28\frac{3}{4} \times 36\frac{1}{2}''$ (73 × 92 cm), Museum of Modern Art, New York. Although seemingly conceived and executed without restraint, as if painted in a fevered rush, this was actually preceded by a complete preliminary drawing.

Figure 18.15   Vincent van Gogh, *The Night Café*, 1888, oil on canvas, $28\frac{1}{2}'' \times 36\frac{1}{4}''$ (72.5 × 92 cm), Yale University Art Gallery, New Haven, Connecticut. The bright Impressionist colors record Van Gogh's emotional fluctuations rather than the moods of Nature.

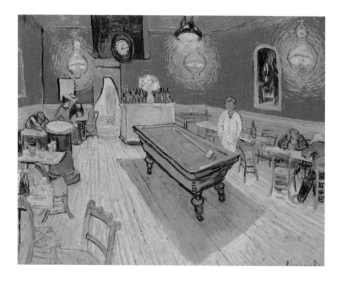

ruin oneself, run mad, or commit a crime," he wrote to his brother in September 1888. "I have tried to express the terrible passions of humanity . . . Everywhere there is a clash and contrast of red and green . . . color to suggest the emotion of an ardent temperament."

Another of Van Gogh's most celebrated paintings is *Starry Night* (fig. 18.16), of 1889, painted on a hillside overlooking St.-Rémy, a small town just south of Arles. *Starry Night* is anything but calm. In this unusually turbulent landscape his highly expressive brushwork implies the precarious balance of his emotions. Pigment appears slapped on, sometimes applied with a brush, sometimes a palette knife, sometimes squeezed directly from the tube—as if Van Gogh was desperate to get his ideas on canvas as quickly as possible. As spontaneous as it appears—almost as if he started painting and could not stop himself—the result is an emotional landscape, frenzied, passionate, flame-like, undulating, the sky swirling and writhing. Yet the composition was planned in advance. Furthermore, it is organized and balanced by traditional methods. The composition flows from left to right, the trees and church steeple slowing the movement down, with the hills rising on the right-hand side of the picture for balance. Vincent wrote to Theo explaining his working method; he would think everything out "down to the last detail" and then quickly paint a number of canvases.

Van Gogh suffered from extreme emotional swings. During one of his periods of depression, he shot himself in a field in Auvers. He died two days later, on July 21, 1890, in Theo's arms. He was thirty-seven. He never knew fame, but today he is one of the most celebrated of all painters.

Then & Now

POINTILLISM AND TELEVISION

Seurat's pointillist technique involved putting small dabs of different colored paint next to one another and allowing the eye to blend them into a single tone. Television works in much the same way. A standard set contains one picture tube and three electron guns. Each gun makes a complete picture on the screen in one of the primary light colors—red, blue, and green (not yellow as in surface primary colors). The screen itself is made of small dots, each dot capable of being hit by only one of the guns. When the three primary colors are projected simultaneously through the dots on the screen, they blend, projecting a full range of colors to the viewer's eye. If you look at the screen of a color television with a magnifying glass before turning it on, you can see the pattern of dots. Then look at the screen after turning it on, and you can see how the manufacturer has arranged the different primary colors (every manufacturer employs a different pattern) in an array that they believe will best create vivid color images.

Paul Gauguin. Fellow Post-Impressionist PAUL GAUGUIN [go-GAN] (1848–1903) was born to a Peruvian mother and a French father. A successful banker and stockbroker in Paris, Gauguin had a personal crisis at the age of thirty-five. He decided to become a full-time artist, and rebel against the established way of life, leaving his wife and five children to embark on an exotic life, which he recorded in his autobiography, *Noa Noa (Fragrance)*. Gauguin shared with the Symbolist poets a desire to escape the everyday world and retreat into what Mallarmé called metaphorically "the afternoon of a faun." To that end, he auctioned off about thirty of his paintings and sailed to Tahiti in 1891.

Gauguin wrote about his painting *Manao Tupapau (Spirit of the Dead Watching)* (fig. 18.17), of 1892, in *Noa Noa*. One night, he returned to his hut, only to find it in complete darkness. Lighting a match, he found Tehura (his new wife) lying as shown in the work, terror-stricken by the dark. The woman in the background is the "Spirit of the Dead." The white areas in the background are phosphorescent fungi which, according to Maori legend, symbolize the spirits of ancestors. "Tehura's dread was contagious," Gauguin wrote, "it seemed to me that the phosphorescent light poured from her staring eyes. I had never seen her so lovely . . . above all, I had never seen her beauty so moving." Gauguin's reaction to the scene is typical of the Symbolist: feelings of dread combined with admiration of beauty. As in Symbolist work as a whole, such ambiguities dominate the painting.

NEW DIRECTIONS IN SCULPTURE AND ARCHITECTURE

Auguste Rodin. For the better part of the nineteenth century, many sculptural concepts had amounted to little more than variations on classicism, but toward the end of the century a major new sculptor appeared. The Frenchman AUGUSTE RODIN [roh-DAN] (1840–1917) became the most influential sculptor in Europe. He studied the human form from nude models in his studio, but rather than having them remain immobile as was the tradition, Rodin's models walked around so he could study the human body in motion. He had a wonderful ability to convey emotion and ideas through his representations of the human form.

Rodin's bronze sculpture *The Thinker* (fig. 18.18) was made between 1879 and 1889 and was intended to form part of a larger work marking the entrance to the Museum of Decorative Arts in Paris: the *Gates of Hell*, based on Dante's *Inferno* (see Chapter 12), with *The Thinker* looking down on Hell, brooding over the gates. Rodin's superb understanding of "body language" can be seen in the details, for example, in the tension in the toes of the figure that seem to grip the base.

Figure 18.17 Paul Gauguin, *Manao Tupapau (Spirit of the Dead Watching)*, 1892, oil on burlap mounted on canvas, $28\frac{1}{2}'' \times 36\frac{3}{8}''$ (72.4 × 92.5 cm), Albright-Knox Art Gallery, Buffalo. The phosphorescent spots were believed by the Maoris to signify the spirits of the dead. In spite of his claims, Gauguin remained a sophisticated artist, drawing more on the art of the museums than from his surroundings.

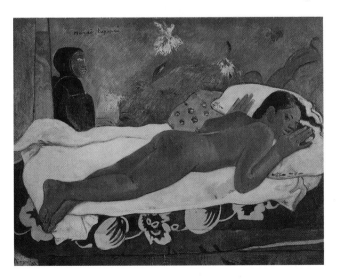

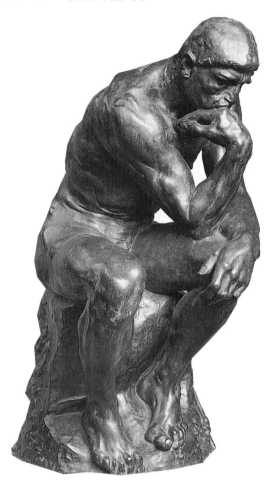

Figure 18.18   Auguste Rodin, *The Thinker*, 1879–89, bronze, height 27½″ (69.8 cm), Metropolitan Museum of Art, New York. Like the Impressionist painters' concern with light flickering over forms, Rodin's broken surface creates a similarly dappled and unfinished effect.

Also created for this entrance was an over-lifesize marble sculpture called *The Kiss* (fig. 18.19), made between 1886 and 1898. In this work Rodin displays a sensuous love of the body as well as amazing virtuosity in carving two intertwined figures. The completed sculpture has portions of stone that have been intentionally left rough, thereby emphasizing a contrast of textures between the soft skin of the subject and the hard marble it came from. Michelangelo's work also has this contrast, but this is because he lacked the time or the will to finish the pieces. Rodin used it as a conscious aesthetic.

American Architecture.   Toward the end of the nineteenth century, a new style in architecture developed as well. It was the public and commercial buildings—the stores, offices, and apartments—that defined the new architecture of the *belle époque*. The use of iron, steel, concrete, and large sheets of glass radically changed architectural language. As steel construction and concrete forms were developed, thick masonry walls were no longer required to support the whole structure of a

building. Expression was given freely to the new underlying skeletal frames. The idea of a building as a solid and closed space was replaced by that of the building as an open and airy environment. Height could be more easily increased. Buildings began to define the city skyline.

The American architect LOUIS SULLIVAN (1856–1924) designed such a structure with the Wainwright Building in St. Louis, Missouri (fig. 18.20). Built between 1890 and 1891, it uses a supporting steel structure and has a brick exterior. Sullivan's design stresses the continuous verticals that reflect the internal steel supports, thus emphasizing the building's height. Sullivan doubled the number of piers necessary, creating a dense effect. The corners are stressed, and thereby visually strengthened. Horizontals at the top and bottom

Figure 18.19   Auguste Rodin, *The Kiss*, 1886–98, marble, over-lifesize, height 6′2″ (1.90 m), Musée Rodin, Paris. The seemingly warm soft flesh is emphasized in contrast to the hard cold stone from which it was carved.

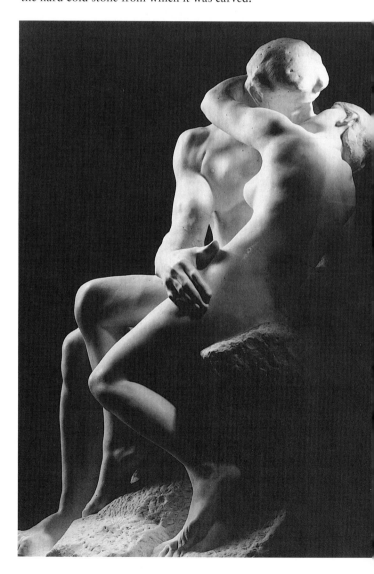

Art Nouveau. Sullivan's belief in nature was mirrored in **Art Nouveau** (literally, New Art), a short-lived style that began in Europe and was popular from the 1890s to the early 1900s. It is characterized by decoration, especially curvilinear patterns, based upon the forms of nature. The influence of Art Nouveau extended beyond architecture to include things such as home furnishings, clothing, and typography.

The home of Dr. Tassel in Brussels, designed by the architect VICTOR HORTA [OAR-ta] (1861–1947) and built 1893, is an ideal example of the Art Nouveau style. Horta liked to be able to design "each piece of furniture, each hinge and door-latch, the rugs and the wall decoration." Consequently, in the Tassel house every part is in harmony, characterized by curve and counter-curve, by its small scale, grace, and charm. The staircase (fig. 18.21) is illuminated by a skylight and made with large amounts of glass and metal, used both for ornamentation and for structure. It is especially characteristic of the Art Nouveau style with its swirling and sensuous forms.

In Spain, another exponent of Art Nouveau was ANTONÍ GAUDÍ [GOW-dee] (1852–1926), the

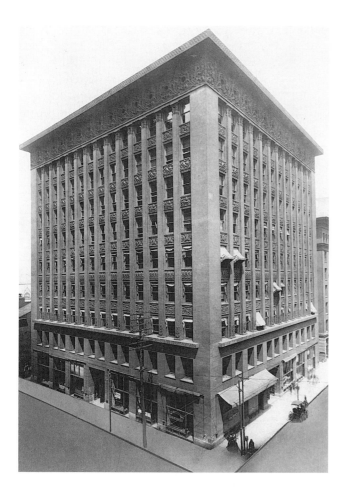

Figure 18.20 Louis Sullivan, Wainwright Building, St. Louis, Missouri, 1890–91. Moving in the direction of the skyscraper, the Wainwright Building has an underlying steel skeleton and brick skin. The architect, Louis Sullivan, coined the now famous phrase, "form follows function."

Figure 18.21 Victor Horta, staircase, Dr. Tassel's house, Brussels, 1893. Art Nouveau favored forms derived from nature such as foliage and curling tendrils. To achieve a certain harmony, Horta designed everything in the house, from the furniture and rugs, down to the small details such as the hinges.

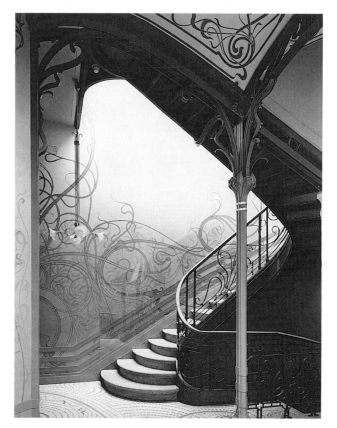

provide a visual frame—in a sense, a start and a conclusion to the composition.

Sullivan saw a building as being like the human body: the steel is the bone; the brick is the flesh and skin. It was Sullivan who coined the phrase, "form follows function." Yet this does not mean that the decorative elements of the design are integral to the architectural design, as is commonly thought. For Sullivan, "the function of all functions is the Infinite Creative Spirit," and this spirit could be revealed in the rhythm of growth and decay that we find in nature. Thus the elaborate, organic forms that cover his building were intended to evoke the infinite. For Sullivan, the primary function of a building was to elevate the spirit of those who worked in it. His belief led to a new school of Functionalist architecture. Tall buildings were becoming progressively more desirable as the concentration of businesses in downtown areas of cities grew, and real estate became ever more expensive, a trend that led to the emblem of twentieth-century American architecture, the skyscraper.

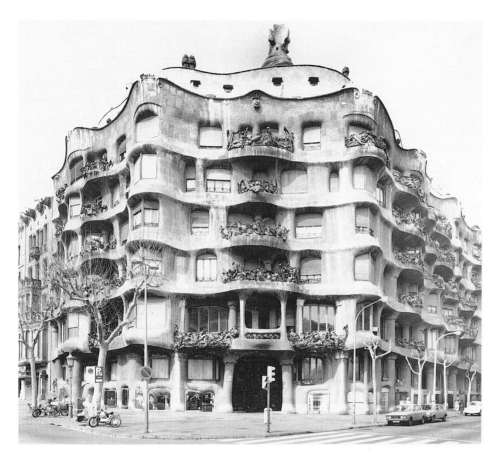

Figure 18.22   Antoní Gaudí, Casa Milá Apartment Building, Barcelona, 1905–07.
Although made of traditional cut stone, the forms appear eroded by nature, weathered
into curves, and the metal balcony railings look like seaweed.

architect of the Casa Milá in Barcelona (fig. 18.22), built 1905–07. This apartment building bears no relation to anything that had gone before. His Art Nouveau style has few flat areas or straight lines, favoring instead constantly curving lines and asymmetry over symmetry. Although made of cut stone, the Casa Milá looks like it was molded from soft clay. Gaudí created a sort of "organic" style influenced by the forms of the natural world. The building looks eroded, as if nature has worn away all the sharp angles. The facade seems to ripple around the corner of the building, and the roof appears to undulate. The chimneys look like abstract sculptures. Gaudí did much of his designing on the actual building site, which was quite unusual then as it is now, and produced a highly personal and thoroughly eccentric style.

THE AVANT-GARDE

Ever since the Salon of 1824, when the young radical Delacroix first challenged the old conservative Ingres for supremacy in French painting, the long-standing split between the *rubénistes* (color) and the *poussinistes* (line) had assumed a political and generational flavor. The Realism of Courbet and Manet was seen by the French Academy as an affront to good taste. The Impressionists organized their own exhibitions beginning in 1874, in part to assert their independence from this official definition of taste. Post-Impressionist masters such as Van Gogh, Gauguin, and Cézanne went one step further by removing themselves from Paris altogether.

Yet, for all the apparent freedom of their various approaches to painting and their seeming liberation from tradition, the work of Courbet, Manet, Monet, Van Gogh, Cézanne, and others was soon championed by the French public and quickly appropriated as part of the great tradition. In 1890, at Monet's behest, the Louvre purchased Manet's *Olympia* from his estate, and the painting was finally hung in the museum in 1907. In 1901, a huge retrospective exhibition of Van Gogh's work fascinated Paris. And after Cézanne died in 1906, his oil paintings became the centerpiece of the 1907 Salon. The French had a word for artists such as these. They were the **avant-garde**, a military term referring to the foremost unit in an attack, the "advanced guard" or "vanguard."

Separated from the mainstream, the avant-garde led the way, against all traditions and expectations, to a bold "new" art. By the start of the twentieth century, Baudelaire's definition of the modern in terms of "the transient, the fleeting, the contingent" had been modified. The *modern* was the *new*, and the modern avant-garde artist sought to discover and reveal the new in art. In the never-ending quest for the new, movement after movement, "ism" after "ism," came and went—before the end of the *belle époque*, Realism, Impressionism, Symbolism, Pointillism, Fauvism, Cubism, Futurism, and German Expressionism all had their day, each new movement giving way to the next.

Characteristic of the avant-garde was an increasing distrust of realistic representation and developing interest in **abstraction**. As early as Berthe Morisot's abbreviated depiction of three ducks in *Summer's Day* (see fig. 18.6), such a tendency is identifiable. Van Gogh and Gauguin both liberated color from its purely descriptive function, using it to represent their emotions rather than the actual look of things. Indeed, the Symbolist desire to capture an internal reality rather than the external one reflects similar concern.

The interest in abstraction takes three forms: (1) an *expressive* art that is emotional, gestural, and free in its use of color; (2) a *formalist* art that is concerned with structure and order; and (3) an art of *fantasy* that is concerned with the individual imagination and the realm of dreams. In all three, the world of surface appearances is gradually left behind. Abstract art is based less and less on the artist's *perception* and increasingly on the artist's *conception* of things.

FAUVISM

The 1905 Salon d'Automne (Autumn Salon) in Paris was quite liberal in its acceptance policy and included a room of paintings by Henri Matisse, Maurice de Vlaminck, André Derain, Georges Rouault, and others who were exhibiting together for the first time. The art critic Louis Vauxcelles reviewed the show and was quick to label these artists *Les Fauves* (The Wild Beasts) because of their paintings' violent and arbitrary colors. The artists who launched **Fauvism** had learned from Van Gogh and Gauguin that color could be an expressive force in its own right, and that it could correspond, not to reality, but to what Van Gogh had called "the artist's temperament." Furthermore, they rejected the small "dots and dashes" of color that characterized Impressionist painting and, particularly, the Post-Impressionist painting of Seurat. They wanted to *draw* on the canvas, with long and sensuous strokes. Their work was intended to shock the viewer, visually and psychologically, with its intensely surprising color. It was, above all, new.

Henri Matisse. The leader of the Fauves was HENRI MATISSE [mah-TEECE] (1869–1954). At the age of twenty-two, Matisse had abandoned a career in law for one in art. At the 1905 Autumn Salon, he exhibited *Woman with a Hat* (fig. 18.23), a portrait of Madame Matisse. It appeared to many viewers little more than a smearing of brilliant, arbitrary, and unnatural colors across the subject's face and background. In its subject matter, the painting is of the *belle époque*, depicting Madame Matisse dressed for an outing in gloves and an enormous hat, yet it bears almost no resemblance to any earlier work. Rather than employing dots of color, Matisse broke the color into broad zones. Not only are they seemingly arbitrary, the artist makes no attempt to harmonize them. Red, green, and purple are used at maximum intensity. Maurice Denis, a painter and critic, understood the implications of Matisse's painting: "One

Figure 18.23 Henri Matisse, *Woman with a Hat*, 1905, oil on canvas, 32¼ × 23¾" (82 × 60.5 cm), Collection of Mrs. Walter A. Haas, San Francisco. The American author Getrude Stein and her brother Leo purchased this painting at the Autumn Salon in 1905, inaugurating one of the greatest collections of modern art in Paris in the twentieth century. Americans, in particular, flocked to Stein's evening gatherings in her apartment on the Rue des Fleurs to see the work of Matisse and Picasso, and to meet the artists themselves, who were in regular attendance.

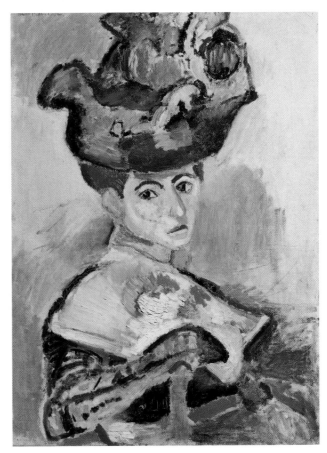

feels completely in the realm of abstraction … It is painting outside of every contingency, painting in itself, the act of pure painting … Here is in fact a search for the absolute. Yet, strange contradiction, this absolute is limited by the one thing in the world that is most relative: individual emotion."

Matisse soon realized that *Woman with a Hat* lacked something that profoundly interested him—drawing. Beyond depicting raw contrasts of pure color in flat planes, he wanted to emphasize line. "What I am after, above all," Matisse explained, "is expression … Composition is the art of arranging in a decorative manner the various elements at the painter's disposal for the expression of his feelings." The painting has a joyous feeling, a sense of springtime and of life, which is once

again typical of the *belle époque*. Through the expressive use of color and line, Matisse discovered that even the most ordinary scene could achieve expressive force. *Harmony in Red (Red Room)* (fig. 18.24), painted 1908–09, is an everyday scene distinguished by pattern and harmony between the colors, shapes, and lines. This painting oscillates between two-dimensional pattern and three-dimensional representation. The tablecloth and the wall share the same pattern and colors; the only indication Matisse provides that the table is a horizontal surface is the placement of fruit on it. Are we looking out of a window on the left or at a flat painting hanging on the wall? All objects are used to play a role in forming an overall surface pattern. This differs from the efforts made by earlier artists to construct an illusion of space

Figure 18.24   Henri Matisse, *Harmony in Red (Red Room)*, 1908–09, oil on canvas, 5′11¼″ × 8′7⁄8″ (1.81 × 2.46 m), State Hermitage Museum, St. Petersburg. Traditional methods of creating an illusion of three dimensions on a two-dimensional surface are not used in many twentieth-century paintings. Here, indications that the table top is horizontal and the wall vertical are avoided, creating a flat and decorative effect.

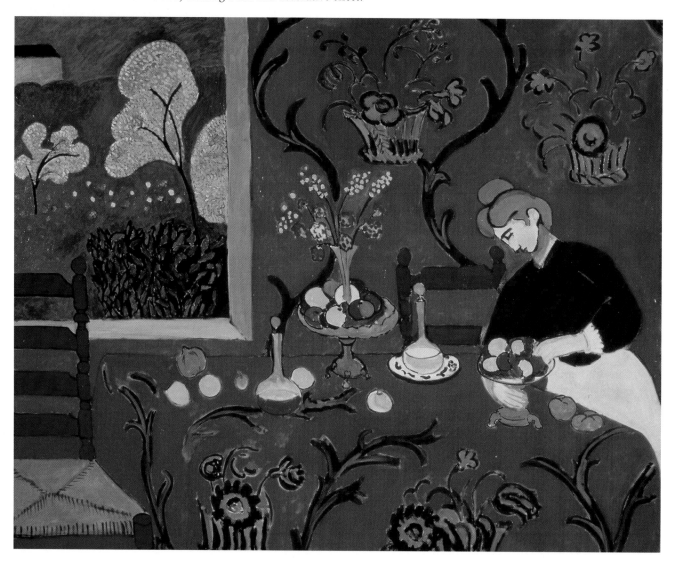

behind the picture plane. Matisse, like many later painters, intentionally compressed the space and emphasized the picture plane, making clear that this is a painting, not an illusion of the visible world.

CUBISM

The Fauvist emphasis on the reality of the picture plane is also apparent in the work of the Cubist painters. Derived from Cézanne's famous dictum, "You must see in nature the cyclinder, the sphere, and the cone," **Cubism** differs, first, in its depiction of objects in their most reduced geometric form, particularly, as its name implies, in cubes. It differs, secondly, in the way in which objects are represented simultaneously from as many different points of view as possible—from the front, the back, the side, and from above. Rather than presenting the object from one angle or point of view, the Cubists wanted to present all aspects of the object simultaneously. Reality, they argued, is not just what we see, but what we know about what we see, in the same way that when we see a person's back, we can infer that person's face.

Cubism was the invention of two relatively unknown painters at the time, Pablo Picasso and Georges Braque, both of whom arrived separately at the same conclusions about the nature of our experience of the world. They soon discovered one another's shared convictions and proceeded to work together for seven years until the outbreak of World War I.

Pablo Picasso. Often considered the single most important painter of the twentieth century, PABLO PICASSO [pi-KAH-soh] (1881–1973) never ceased searching for the "new." He went through many styles in his long life and worked in a wide variety of media including painting, graphics, sculpture, and ceramics. He might draw and paint with extraordinary realism one day and with consummate abstraction the next.

In 1900, Picasso, who had trained in the Spanish cities of Barcelona and Madrid, moved to Paris, where he studied Impressionism and Post-Impressionism. From 1900 to 1905 he painted in a more or less Symbolist vein, but in 1905 he began working on a portrait of the American writer Gertrude Stein (fig. 18.25), and his approach to painting changed dramatically. Throughout the fall of 1905 and into the following year, Stein would cross Paris to Picasso's studio in the Bateau Lavoir, or "Laundry Boat," and Picasso would undertake to paint her. After some eighty or ninety sittings, however, Picasso became irritated with the entire operation and in a fit of pique painted out her face, leaving the painting to sit all summer in the studio while he traveled to Spain. On his return, he completed the painting from memory—without his model. A year later, Alice B. Toklas, Stein's friend and companion, told Picasso how much she liked the portrait. "Yes," he said, "everybody says that she does not look like it but that does

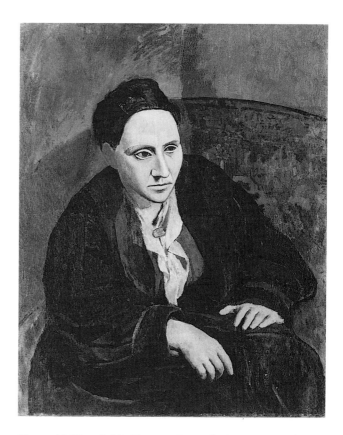

Figure 18.25 Pablo Picasso, *Gertrude Stein*, 1906, oil on canvas, 39¼″ × 32″ (99.5 × 81 cm), The Metropolitan Museum of Art, New York. Picasso had been looking at ancient Iberian sculpture on his trip to Spain in the summer of 1906, and Stein's simplified features, particularly her oval eyes and sculpted brow, are indebted to his study.

not make any difference, she will." Picasso's painting had passed from a retinally based image into a cerebral one. The actual Gertrude Stein was eclipsed by Picasso's idea of her, or his idea of what she would become.

Picasso pursued this conceptual approach seriously. His next work, the famous *Les Demoiselles d'Avignon* (*The Ladies of Avignon*) (fig. 18.26), of 1907, seems liberated from the "reality" of perceptual experience altogether. Although the word *demoiselles* means "gentlewomen," here it refers to prostitutes, and Avignon refers to Avignon Street in Barcelona rather than the city of the Popes in southern France. The anatomy of the figures shows distorted proportions, their bodies turned into rhythmic shapes and broken, angular pieces. Space is treated in the same way. Solid and void are depicted in terms of structural units, similar to Cézanne's "little planes." The style is also deliberately "primitive." African sculpture, particularly masks, inundated Paris in the first decade of the century, and Picasso took full advantage of their expressive force. "Men had made these masks," Picasso explained, "as a kind of mediation between themselves and the unknown hostile forces that surrounded

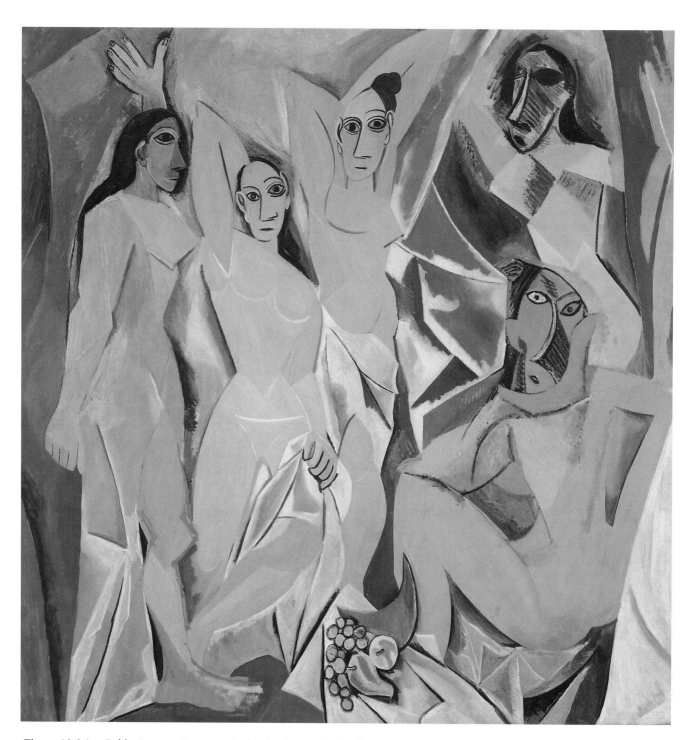

Figure 18.26   Pablo Picasso, *Les Demoiselles d'Avignon*, 1907, oil on canvas, 8′ × 7′8″ (2.40 × 2.30 m), Museum of Modern Art, New York. With motifs that echo African art, the angular lines and overlapping planes of this painting initiated a new way of analyzing three-dimensional forms in space. The work's primitive energy sent shock waves through the art world when it was first shown in Paris, allying it with Stravinsky's *Rite of Spring*, which had a similar effect on the world of music six years later.

them, in order to overcome their fear and horror by giving [them] a form and image. And that moment I realized that painting … [is] a way [of] seizing power by giving form to our terrors as well as our desires."

Georges Braque. One of the first people to see *Les Demoiselles*, and to approve of it, was GEORGES BRAQUE [BRAHK] (1882–1963). Braque had worked with Matisse as a member of the Fauves, and it was probably Matisse, who was himself horrified by *Les Demoiselles*, who introduced him to Picasso. But Braque

saw in it a flattening and simplification of form that he believed Cézanne had championed in works such as *The Great Bathers* (see fig. 18.13). Energized by Picasso's achievement, Braque went even further. In the summer of 1908, in southern France, Braque began a series of paintings that would reduce the landscape to its basic geometric forms. So simplified are the forms of *Houses at L'Estaque* (fig. 18.27) that, when the painting was exhibited at the Bateau Lavoir in the fall of 1908, Matisse complained to Louis Vauxcelles that the painting looked

Figure 18.27 Georges Braque, *Houses at L'Estaque*, 1908, oil on canvas, $36\frac{1}{4}'' \times 23\frac{5}{8}''$ (92 × 60 cm), Kunstmuseum, Bern, Switzerland. Note the way in which the upper branches of the tree on the left seem to merge with the walls of the houses in the distance, uniting foreground and background in a single plane.

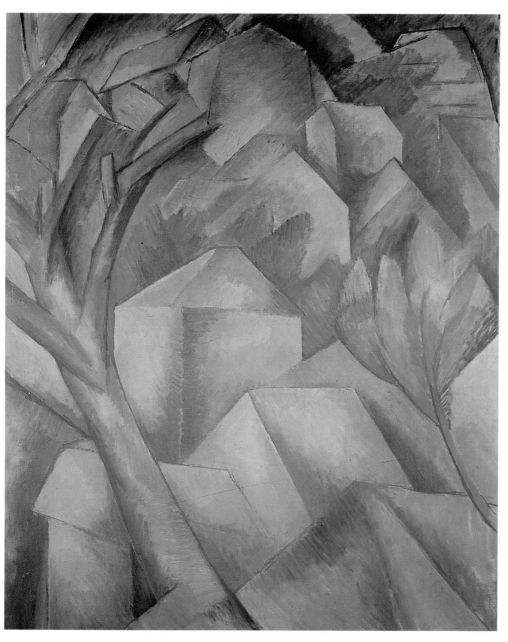

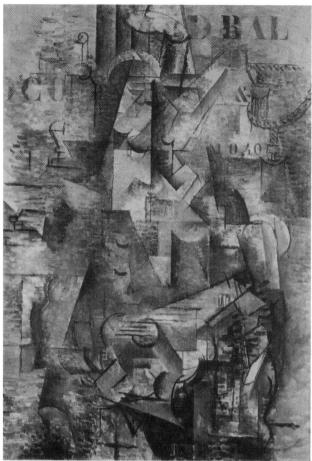

Figure 18.28 Georges Braque, *The Portuguese*, 1911, oil on canvas, $45\frac{1}{8}'' \times 32\frac{1}{8}''$ (114.5 × 81.5 cm), Kunstmuseum, Basel, Switzerland. In cubism the forms are broken and faceted as if portions of cubes, and the forms are portrayed from multiple viewpoints. The range of color is restricted so that it will not distract from this new way of analyzing form in space.

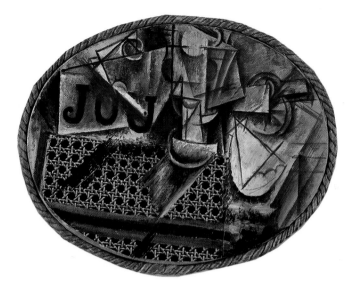

Figure 18.29 Pablo Picasso, *Still Life with Chair Caning*, 1912, oil, oilcloth, and pasted paper simulating chair caning on canvas, rope frame, $10\frac{1}{2} \times 13\frac{3}{4}''$ (26.7 × 35 cm), Musée Picasso, Paris. This collage (French for "pasting" or "gluing") is created from scraps of ordinary materials that became art when arranged into a composition.

like a pile of cubes. By 1909, Vauxcelles, the same man who had named the Fauves, was writing about Braque's "bizarre cubics," and the name Cubism was coined.

For several years, Picasso and Braque worked so closely together that their work is virtually indistinguishable to the untrained eye. Braque tended to paint more landscapes than Picasso, Picasso more figures than Braque, but both worked in a similar style and progressed in tandem.

Braque's *The Portuguese* (fig. 18.28), of 1911, depicts a guitarist playing at a café, but there is no fully realized figure. We can see the guitar's soundhole and strings in the lower-middle part of the painting. There are fragments of lettering—OCO and BAL—and something is offered at a price of 10.40 francs. A rope is wrapped around a post, and perhaps that is the guitarist's broad smile in the upper-middle part of the piece. All is a fleeting glance as if seen through a window in which the reflections of activity and movement outside distort everything seen inside.

Both artists began to introduce recognizable pieces of material reality into their compositions, asking the questions: What is real and what is art? If something is real, can it be art? And vice versa, if something is art, is it real? By pasting real materials on the canvas they engaged in a technique called **collage** (from the French word *coller*, "to glue" or "to paste"). Picasso's *Still Life with Chair Caning* (fig. 18.29), of 1912, contains rope and a piece of oilcloth with imitation chair caning printed on it, a cigarette, and a fragment of a newspaper (*Le Journal*). All we see are the first three letters, a fragment of the whole, but this fragment tells us much about Braque and Picasso's intentions. The letters "jou" also form the beginning of the verb *jouer*, the French for "to play." Collage is the new playground of the artist.

FUTURISM

One significant offshoot of Cubism is **Futurism**, a movement based in Italy before World War I which used Cubist forms in a dynamic way. It was the first art movement to have been founded almost exclusively in the popular press, conceived by its creator, the poet FILIPPO MARINETTI [mah-ri-NET-ee] (1876–1944), in his "Manifesto of Futurism," published on February 20, 1909, in the French newspaper *Le Figaro*.

The "Manifesto" is a peculiar document that outlines an eleven-point pledge, including the Futurists' intention to "sing the love of danger," to "affirm that the world's magnificence has been enriched by a new beauty, the beauty of speed," to "glorify war—the world's only hygiene," to "destroy the museums, libraries, and academies of every kind," and, finally, to "sing of great crowds excited by work, by pleasure, and by riot."

Gino Severini. In February 1910, seven painters, including GINO SEVERINI [sev-err-EE-nee] (1883–1966), signed a "Manifesto of Futurist Painters" that pledged, among other things, "to rebel against the tyranny of terms like 'harmony' and 'good taste,'" "to demolish the works of Rembrandt, of Goya, and of Rodin," and, most importantly, "to express our whirling life of steel, of pride, of fever, and of speed." The Futurists wanted, they claimed, to render "universal dynamism" in painting.

The Futurists' interest in expressing speed was aided by the forms of Cubism. Severini's *Suburban Train Arriving at Paris* (fig. 18.30), of 1915, depicts speed as a sequence of positions of multifaceted forms. Similar to a series of movie stills, or to a multiple exposure photograph, the artist expresses the direction of the force by the abstract fragmentation of the speeding forms. The Futurists privileged simultaneous perspective, as did the Cubists, but the Futurists recorded the various aspects of a moving object, whereas the Analytical Cubists recorded those of a static one.

GERMAN EXPRESSIONISM

The last of the great pre-war avant-garde movements was German Expressionism, which consisted of two separate branches, *Die Brücke* ("The Bridge"), established in Dresden in 1905, and *Der Blaue Reiter* ("The Blue Rider") formed in Munich in 1911. Both were directly

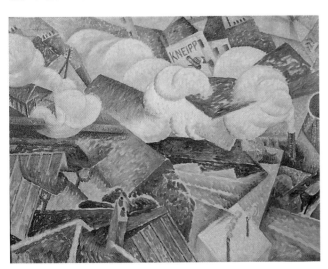

Figure 18.30 Gino Severini, *Suburban Train Arriving at Paris*, 1915, oil on canvas, $35 \times 45\frac{1}{2}$" (88.6 × 115.6 cm), Tate Gallery, London. The Italian Futurists sought to destroy museums and anything old, praised what they called the "beauty of speed," glorified war and machinery, and favored the "masculine" over the "feminine."

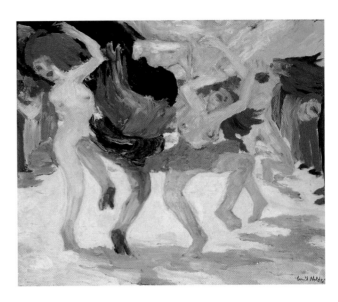

Figure 18.31 Emil Nolde, *Dancing around the Golden Calf*, 1910, oil on canvas, $34\frac{3}{4}$" × $39\frac{1}{2}$" (88 × 100 cm), Staatsgalerie Moderner Kunst, Munich. Much of the shock of this painting derives from its depiction of a biblical subject in such openly sexual terms.

indebted to the example of the Fauves in Paris, especially in terms of the liberation of color and the celebration of pagan, almost animal, sexuality.

Emil Nolde. One of the most daring members of *Die Brücke* in terms of his use of color was EMIL NOLDE [NOHL-(duh)] (1867–1956). What distinguishes his *Dancing around the Golden Calf* (fig. 18.31) from the work of Matisse and the Fauves is the painting's lack of contour and outline. Instead, emphasis is on the use of color which fully exploits the dissonances between its bright reds, orange-yellows, and red-violets. The energy of this style—almost slapdash in comparison to Matisse—helps to create a sense of violence, fury, and wanton sexuality that is alien to Matisse's vision. This rough-hewn, purposefully inelegant approach is typical of *Die Brücke* work, and owes much to the example of Picasso's *Les Demoiselles* and its "primitivism."

Vassily Kandinsky. The leader of Der Blaue Reiter was VASSILY KANDINSKY [kan-DIN-skee] (1866–1944), who was born in Moscow. A practicing lawyer with a professorship in Moscow, Kandinsky saw one of Monet's *Haystacks* paintings in 1895 and was so moved by the experience that he traveled to Munich to study art. He became friendly with the Fauves and the Cubists, bringing their work to Germany in 1911 for a major exhibition.

The name *Der Blaue Reiter* refers to St. George slaying the dragon, the image that appeared on the city emblem of Moscow. Tradition held that Moscow would be the capital of the world during the millennium, the

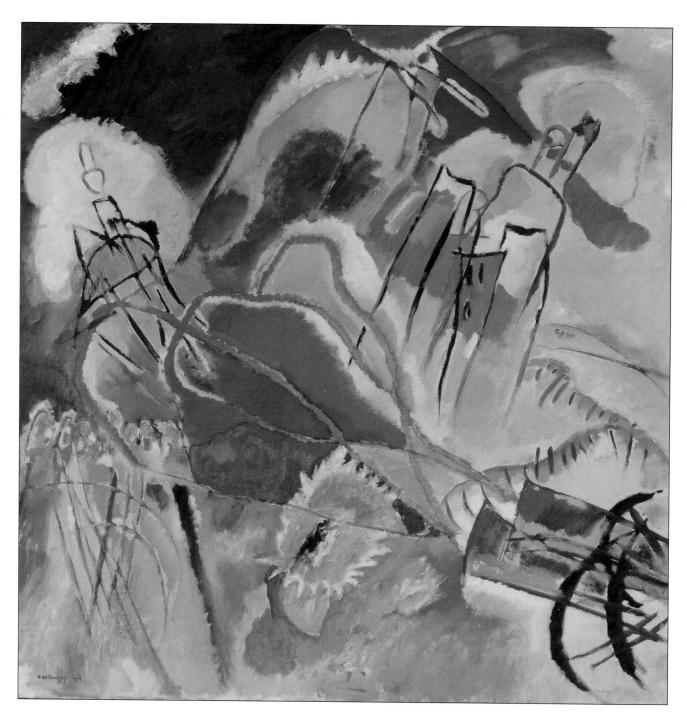

Figure 18.32 Vassily Kandinsky, *Improvisation No. 30 (Warlike Theme)*, 1913, oil on canvas, $43\frac{1}{4}''$ × $43\frac{1}{4}''$ (110 × 110 cm), Art Institute of Chicago. Although Kandinsky did produce completely non-representational paintings, beginning in 1910, that were intended to stir the viewer's emotions, this painting includes recognizable subjects having political and religious implications.

Timeline 18.2 Music and literature of the *Belle Époque*.

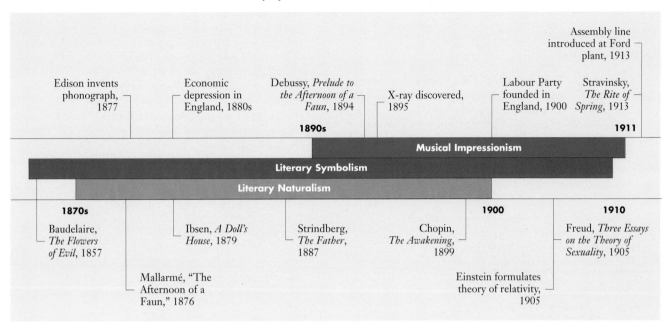

thousand-year reign of Jesus on earth after the Apocalypse. *Improvisation No. 30 (Warlike Theme)* (fig. 18.32) includes, at the bottom of the composition, two firing canons, which announce the second coming of Jesus. Crowds of people march toward the millennium across the canvas. Above them are the churches of the Kremlin and, circling round the horizon, the streets of Moscow itself. Kandinsky did not so much want to convey the meaning of his work through its imagery as through its color. Color, he believed, caused "vibrations [or, in German, *Klangen*] in the soul," and his painting was designed, he wrote in 1912 in his *Concerning the Spiritual in Art*, to "urge" the viewer to a spiritual awakening in preparation for the second coming.

MUSIC

Igor Stravinsky. IGOR STRAVINSKY [strah-VIN-skee] (1882–1971) is considered the single most important composer of the modern era. His works revolutionized twentieth-century musical styles and affected artists such as Picasso, writers such as T.S. Eliot, and ballet choreographers such as George Balanchine. Stravinsky was born in Russia, near St. Petersburg. Although groomed for a law career, Stravinsky studied music and achieved early success composing for the Ballets Russes, a Russian ballet troupe performing in Paris under the artistic direction of Serge Diaghilev. His early scores, *The Firebird* (1910) and *Petrushka* (1911), were both ballets based on Russian themes and were musically influenced by Debussy.

The Rite of Spring. The most spectacular of Stravinsky's early ballet scores was *Le Sacre du Printemps*

(The Rite of Spring) of 1913. *The Rite of Spring* broke new ground. The music was filled with harmonic shifts, rhythmic surprises, and melodic irregularities. The public was shocked by the near violence of the sound and by its disruption of their emotional expectations. It was a wholly new audience experience.

The origin of *The Rite of Spring* came to Stravinsky in a vision: "a solemn pagan rite: wise elders, seated in a circle, watch a young girl dance herself to death. They are sacrificing her to propitiate the god of spring." Stravinsky linked this vision to his childhood memories of the "violent Russian spring that seemed to begin in an hour and was like the whole earth cracking." The work depicts the fertility rites of a primitive tribe in pagan Russia. The first part, "The Fertility of the Earth," opens with a suggestion of the rebirth of spring. A bassoon solo begins the introductory section and is soon followed by other woodwinds, and then the brasses which play the melody, all without a home key, i.e. without a harmonic center. The music builds to a climax and then abruptly stops, leaving the solo bassoon to echo the introductory notes.

Without pause, a brief four-note theme repeated softly by the violins opens the second part, "The Sacrifice." Immediately comes the "Dance of the Youths and Maidens," in which Stravinsky builds intensity through the heavy use of percussion, sharply irregular rhythmic accents, and the shrill syncopation of the horns. All this is emphasized further by both polytonal harmonies and strong dissonance. Stravinsky's "Introduction" to *The Rite of Spring* can be seen to reflect the modern composer's new directions in melody and harmony, while "The Dance of the Youths and Maidens" displays a corresponding rhythmic freedom.

READINGS

Charles Baudelaire
Correspondences

The following poem by this prominent French Symbolist illustrates some of the ways in which the Symbolists attempted to associate the language of poetry with other sensory experience, such as shapes, sounds, and colors. In "Correspondences" Baudelaire sets up a series of connections between sounds and tastes, colors and scents, religion and nature, the spiritual and the sensuous. Baudelaire's work reflects the Symbolist concern for suggesting meaning through image, metaphor, and symbolic association rather than by means of direct statement.

Nature is a temple from whose living columns
Commingling voices emerge at times;
Here man wanders through forests of symbols
Which seem to observe him with familiar eyes.

Like long-drawn echoes afar converging   5
In harmonies darksome and profound,
Vast as the night and vast as light,
Colors, scents and sounds correspond.

There are fragrances fresh as the flesh of children,
Sweet as the oboe, green as the prairie,   10
—And others overpowering, rich and corrupt,

Possessing the pervasiveness of everlasting things,
Like benjamin, frankincense, amber, myrrh,
Which the raptures of the senses and the spirit sing.

Stéphane Mallarmé
The Afternoon of a Faun

Stéphane Mallarmé's poem "The Afternoon of a Faun" (1876) directly inspired Claude Debussy's orchestral composition. It describes the reveries of a faun from classical mythology with an almost Romantic languor. However, Mallarmé's use of language and metaphor is Symbolist.

Eclogue

The Faun

These nymphs, I would make them endure.

Their delicate flesh-tint so clear,
it hovers yet upon the air
heavy with foliage of sleep.

Was it a dream I loved? My doubt,   5
hoarded of old night, culminates
in many a subtle branch, that stayed
the very forest's self and proves
alas! that I alone proposed
the ideal failing of the rose   10

as triumph of my own. Think now . . .
and if the women whom you gloze
picture a wish of your fabled senses!
Faun, the illusion takes escape
from blue cold eyes, like a spring in tears,   15
of the purer one: and would you say
of her, the other, made of sighs,
that she contrasts, like the day breeze
warmly astir now in your fleece!
No! through the moveless, half-alive   20
languor that suffocates in heat
freshness of morning, if it strive,
no water sounds save what is poured
upon the grove sparged with accords
by this my flute; and the sole wind   25
prompt from twin pipes to be exhaled
before dispersal of the sound
in arid shower without rain
is—on the unwrinkled, unstirred
horizon—calm and clear to the eye,   30
the artificial breath of inspiration, which regains the sky.

Sicilian shores of a calm marsh,
despoilèd by my vanity
that vies with suns, tacit beneath   35
the flower-sparkle, now RELATE
how here I cut the hollow reeds
that talent tames; when, on pale gold
of distant greens that dedicate
their vine to fountains, undulates   40
an animal whiteness in repose:
and how at sound of slow prelude
with which the pipes first come to life
this flight of swans, no! naiads flees
or plunges . . .   45

Limp in the tawny hour
all is afire but shows no trace
by what art those too many brides
longed-for by him who seeks the *A*
all at once decamped; then shall I wake   50
to the primal fire, alone and straight,
beneath an ancient surge of light,
even as one of you, lilies!
by strength of my simplicity.

Other than the soft nothingness   55
their lips made rumor of, the kiss,
which gives assurance in low tones
of the two perfidious ones,
my breast, immaculate of proof,
attests an enigmatic bite,   60
imputed to some august tooth;
leave it! such mystery made choice
of confidant: the vast twinned reed—
beneath blue sky we give it voice:
diverting to itself the cheek's   65
turmoil, it dreams, in a long solo,
that we amused the beauty here-
about by false bewilderments

between it and our naïve song;
dreams too that from the usual dream   70
of back or flawless flank traced by
my shuttered glances, it makes fade,
tempered to love's own pitch, a vain,
monotonous, sonorous line.

✦ Kate Chopin
The Storm

Kate Chopin is best known for her short fiction and her novel of 1899,
The Awakening, *which generated a storm of criticism for its frank
portrayal of female sexuality and its depiction of an extramarital love
affair. The following story displays her ability to convey in brief compass the power of sexual attraction and the apparently beneficial effects
the indulged passion has for all concerned, including the cuckolded
husband.*

1

The leaves were so still that even Bibi thought it was going
to rain. Bobinôt, who was accustomed to converse on terms
of perfect equality with his little son, called the child's attention to certain sombre clouds that were rolling with sinister
intention from the west, accompanied by a sullen, threatening roar. They were at Friedheimer's store and decided to
remain there till the storm had passed. They sat within the
door on two empty kegs. Bibi was four years old and looked
very wise.

"Mama'll be 'fraid, yes," he suggested with blinking eyes.

"She'll shut the house. Maybe she got Sylvie helpin' her
this evenin'," Bobinôt responded reassuringly.

"No; she ent got Sylvie. Sylvie was helpin' her yistiday,"
piped Bibi.

Bobinôt arose and going across to the counter purchased
a can of shrimps, of which Calixta was very fond. Then he
returned to his perch on the keg and sat stolidly holding the
can of shrimps while the storm burst. It shook the wooden
store and seemed to be ripping great furrows in the distant
field. Bibi laid his little hand on his father's knee and was not
afraid.

2

Calixta, at home, felt no uneasiness for their safety. She sat
at a side window sewing furiously on a sewing machine. She
was greatly occupied and did not notice the approaching
storm. But she felt very warm and often stopped to mop her
face on which the perspiration gathered in beads. She unfastened her white sacque at the throat. It began to grow dark,
and suddenly realizing the situation she got up hurriedly
and went about closing windows and doors.

Out on the small front gallery she had hung Bobinôt's
Sunday clothes to air and she hastened out to gather them
before the rain fell. As she stepped outside, Alcée Laballière
rode in at the gate. She had not seen him very often since
her marriage, and never alone. She stood there with
Bobinôt's coat in her hands, and the big rain drops began to
fall. Alcée rode his horse under the shelter of a side projection where the chickens had huddled and there were plows
and a harrow piled up in the corner.

"May I come and wait on your gallery till the storm is
over, Calixta?" he asked.

"Come 'long in, M'sieur Alcée."

His voice and her own startled her as if from a trance,
and she seized Bobinôt's vest. Alcée, mounting to the porch,
grabbed the trousers and snatched Bibi's braided jacket that
was about to be carried away by a sudden gust of wind. He
expressed an intention to remain outside, but it was soon
apparent that he might as well have been out in the open:
the water beat in upon the boards in driving sheets, and he
went inside, closing the door after him. It was even necessary to put something beneath the door to keep the water
out.

"My! what a rain! It's good two years sence it rain' like
that," exclaimed Calixta as she rolled up a piece of bagging
and Alcée helped her to thrust it beneath the crack.

She was a little fuller of figure than five years before
when she married; but she had lost nothing of her vivacity.
Her blue eyes still retained their melting quality; and her
yellow hair, dishevelled by the wind and rain, kinked more
stubbornly than ever about her ears and temples.

The rain beat upon the low, shingled roof with a force
and clatter that threatened to break an entrance and deluge
them there. They were in the dining room—the sitting
room—the general utility room. Adjoining was her bed
room, with Bibi's couch along side her own. The door stood
open, and the room with its white, monumental bed, its
closed shutters, looked dim and mysterious.

Alcée flung himself into a rocker and Calixta nervously
began to gather up from the floor the lengths of a cotton
sheet which she had been sewing.

"If this keeps up, *Dieu sait* if the levees goin' to stan' it!"
she exclaimed.

"What have you got to do with the levees?"

"I got enough to do! An' there's Bobinôt with Bibi out in
that storm—if he only didn' left Friedheimer's!"

"Let us hope, Calixta, that Bobinôt's got sense enough to
come in out of a cyclone."

She went and stood at the window with a greatly disturbed look on her face. She wiped the frame that was
clouded with moisture. It was stiflingly hot. Alcée got up
and joined her at the window, looking over her shoulder.
The rain was coming down in sheets obscuring the view of
far-off cabins and enveloping the distant wood in a grey
mist. The playing of the lightning was incessant. A bolt
struck a tall chinaberry tree at the edge of the field. It filled
all visible space with a blinding glare and the crash seemed
to invade the very boards they stood upon.

Calixta put her hands to her eyes, and with a cry, stag-
gered backward. Alcée's arm encircled her, and for an
instant he drew her close and spasmodically to him.

"*Bonte!*" she cried, releasing herself from his encircling
arm and retreating from the window, "the house'll go next!
If I only knew w'ere Bibi was!" She would not compose herself; she would not be seated. Alcée clasped her shoulders
and looked into her face. The contact of her warm, palpi-
tating body when he had unthinkingly drawn her into his
arms, had aroused all the old-time infatuation and desire for
her flesh.

"Calixta," he said, "don't be frightened. Nothing can
happen. The house is too low to be struck, with so many tall

trees standing about. There! aren't you going to be quiet? say, aren't you?" He pushed her hair back from her face that was warm and steaming. Her lips were as red and moist as pomegranate seed. Her white neck and a glimpse of her full, firm bosom disturbed him powerfully. As she glanced up at him the fear in her liquid blue eyes had given place to a drowsy gleam that unconsciously betrayed a sensuous desire. He looked down into her eyes and there was nothing for him to do but to gather her lips in a kiss. It reminded him of Assumption.

"Do you remember—in Assumption. Calixta?" he asked in a low voice broken by passion. Oh! she remembered; for in Assumption he had kissed her and kissed and kissed her; until his senses would well nigh fail, and to save her he would resort to a desperate flight. If she was not an immaculate dove in those days, she was still inviolate; a passionate creature whose very defenselessness had made her defense, against which his honor forbade him to prevail. Now—well, now—her lips seemed in a manner free to be tasted, as well as her round, white throat and her whiter breasts.

They did nor heed the crashing torrents, and the roar of the elements made her laugh as she lay in his arms. She was a revelation in that dim, mysterious chamber, as white as the couch she lay upon. Her firm, elastic flesh that was knowing for the first time its birthright, was like a creamy lily that the sun invites to contribute its breath and perfume to the undying life of the world.

The generous abundance of her passion, without guile or trickery, was like a white flame which penetrated and found response in depths of his own sensuous nature that had never yet been reached.

When he touched her breasts they gave themselves up in quivering ecstasy, inviting his lips. Her mouth was a fountain of delight. And when he possessed her, they seemed to swoon together at the very borderland of life's mystery.

He stayed cushioned upon her, breathless, dazed, enervated, with his heart beating like a hammer upon her. With one hand she clasped his head, her lips lightly touching his forehead. The other hand stroked with a soothing rhythm his muscular shoulders.

The growl of the thunder was distant and passing away. The rain beat softly upon the shingles, inviting them to drowsiness and sleep. But they dared not yield.

The rain was over; and the sun was turning the glistening green world into a palace of gems. Calixta, on the gallery, watched Alcée ride away. He turned and smiled at her with a beaming face; and she lifted her pretty chin in the air and laughed aloud.

3

Bobinôt and Bibi, trudging home, stopped without at the cistern to make themselves presentable.

"My! Bibi, w'at will yo' mama say! You ought to be ashame'. You oughtn' put on those good pants. Look at 'em! An' that mud on yo' collar! How you got that mud on yo' collar, Bibi? I never saw such a boy!" Bibi was the picture of pathetic resignation. Bobinôt was the embodiment of serious solicitude as he strove to remove from his own person and his son's the signs of their tramp over heavy roads and through wet fields. He scraped the mud off Bibi's bare legs

and feet with a stick and carefully removed all traces from his heavy brogans. Then, prepared for the worst—the meeting with an over-scrupulous housewife, they entered cautiously at the back door.

Calixta was preparing supper. She had set the table and was dripping coffee at the hearth. She sprang up as they came in.

"Oh, Bobinôt! You back! My! but I was uneasy. W'ere you been during the rain? An' Bibi? he ain't wet? he ain't hurt?" She had clasped Bibi and was kissing him effusively. Bobinôt's explanations and apologies which he had been composing all along the way, died on his lips as Calixta felt him to see if he were dry, and seemed to express nothing but satisfaction at their safe return.

"I brought you some shrimps, Calixta," offered Bobinôt, hauling the can from his ample side pocket and laying it on the table.

"Shrimps! Oh, Bobinôt! you too good fo' anything!" and she gave him a smacking kiss on the cheek that resounded. "*J'vous reponds*, we'll have a feas' to-night! umph-umph!"

Bobinôt and Bibi began to relax and enjoy themselves, and when the three seated themselves at table they laughed much and so loud that anyone might have heard them as far away as Laballière's.

4

Alcée Laballière wrote to his wife, Clarisse, that night. It was a loving letter, full of tender solicitude. He told her not to hurry back, but if she and the babies liked it at Biloxi, to stay a month longer. He was getting on nicely; and though he missed them, he was willing to bear the separation a while longer—realizing that their health and pleasure were the first things to be considered.

5

As for Clarisse, she was charmed upon receiving her husband's letter. She and the babies were doing well. The society was agreeable; many of her old friends and acquaintances were at the bay. And the first free breath since her marriage seemed to restore the pleasant liberty of her maiden days. Devoted as she was to her husband, their intimate conjugal life was something which she was more than willing to forego for a while.

So the storm passed and everyone was happy.

✦ Henrik Ibsen
from *A Doll's House*

Henrik Ibsen, the Norwegian playwright, is one of the giants of modern drama. He wrote many plays during his long career, of which A Doll's House *(1879) has been one of his most enduring theatrical successes. The play explores the marriage of Nora and Torvald Helmer, a middle-class Norwegian couple living in the middle of the nineteenth century. Nora, confined by what society has determined a woman should be—dutiful wife and devoted mother—experiences a personal crisis, undergoes a spiritual transformation, and leaves her husband and family in search of a new identity and life. The following passage, from Act III, follows Nora's departure to the final slamming of the door.*

NORA It is true. I have loved you beyond all else in the world.

HELMER Pshaw—no silly evasions.

NORA (*a step nearer him*). Torvald—!

HELMER Wretched woman! what have you done?

NORA Let me go—you shall not save me. You shall not take my guilt upon yourself.

HELMER I don't want any melodramatic airs. (*Locks the door*). Here you shall stay and give an account of yourself. Do you understand what you have done? Answer. Do you understand it?

NORA (*looks at him fixedly, and says with a stiffening expression*). Yes; now I begin fully to understand it.

HELMER (*walking up and down*). Oh, what an awful awakening! During all these eight years—she who was my pride an my joy—a hypocrite, a liar—worse, worse—a criminal. Oh! The hideousness of it! Ugh! Ugh! (*Nora is silent, and continues to look fixedly at him.*) I ought to have foreseen something of the kind. All your father's dishonesty—be silent! I say all your father's dishonesty you have inherited—no religion, no morality, no sense of duty. How I am punished for shielding him! I did it for your sake and you reward me like this.

NORA Yes—like this!

HELMER You have destroyed my whole happiness. You have ruined my future. Oh! It's frightful to think of! I am in the power of a scoundrel; he can do whatever he pleases with me, demand whatever he chooses, and I must submit. And all this disaster is brought upon me by an unprincipled woman.

NORA When I'm gone, you will be free.

HELMER Oh, no fine phrases. Your father, too, was always ready with them. What good would it do to me if you were "gone" as to say? No good in the world! He can publish the story all the same; I might even be suspected of collusion. People will think I was at the bottom of it all and egged you on. And for all this I have you to thank—you whom I have done nothing but pet and spoil during our whole married life. Do you understand now what you have done to me?

NORA (*with cold calmness*). Yes.

HELMER It's incredible. I can't grasp it. But we must come to an understanding. Take that shawl off. Take it off I say. I must try to pacify him in one way or the other—the secret must be kept, cost what it may. As for ourselves, we must live as we have already done; but of course only in the eyes of the world. Of course you will continue to live here. But the children cannot be left in your care. I dare not trust them to you—Oh, to have to say this to one I have loved so tenderly—whom I still—but that must be a thing of the past. Henceforward there can be no question of happiness, but merely of saving the ruins, the shreds, the show of it! (*A ring; Helmer starts.*) What's that? So late! Can it be the worst? Can he—? Hide yourself, Nora; say you are ill. (*Nora stands motionless. Helmer goes to the door and opens it.*)

ELLEN (*half dressed, in the hall*). Here is a letter for you. ma'am.

HELMER Give it to me. (*Seizes letter and shuts the door.*) Yes, from him. You shall not have it. I shall read it.

NORA Read it!

HELMER (*by the lamp*). I have hardly courage to. We may be lost, both you and I. Ah! I must know. (*Tears the letter hastily open; reads a few lines, looks at an enclosure; a cry of joy.*) Nora. (*Nora looks interrogatively at him.*) Nora! Oh! I must read it again. Yes, yes, it is so. I am saved! Nora, I am saved!

NORA And I?

HELMER You too, of course; we are both saved, both of us. Look here, he sends you back your promissory note. He writes that he regrets and apologizes—that a happy turn in his life—Oh, what matter what he writes. We are saved, Nora! No one can harm you. Oh! Nora, Nora—no, first to get rid of this hateful thing. I'll just see—(*Glances at the I.O.U.*) No, I won't look at it; the whole thing shall be nothing but a dream to me. (*Tears the I.O.U and both letters in pieces, throws them into the fire and watches them burn.*) There, it's gone. He wrote that ever since Christmas Eve—Oh, Nora, they must have been three awful days for you!

NORA I have fought a hard fight for the last three days.

HELMER And in your agony you saw no other outlet but—no; we won't think of that horror. We will only rejoice and repeat—it's over, all over. Don't you hear, Nora? You don't seem to be able to grasp it. Yes, it's over. What is this set look on your face? Oh, my poor Nora, I understand; you can't believe that I have forgiven you. But I have, Nora; I swear it. I have forgiven everything. I know what you did was all for love of me.

NORA That's true.

HELMER You loved me as a wife should love her husband. It was only the means you misjudged. But do you think I love you the less for your helplessness? No, no, only lean on me. I will counsel and guide you. I should be no true man if this very womanly helplessness did not make you doubly dear in my eyes. You mustn't think of the hard things I said in my first moment of terror, when the world seemed to be tumbling about my ears. I have forgiven you, Nora—I swear I have forgiven you.

NORA I thank you for your forgiveness. (*Goes out, right.*)

HELMER No, stay. (*Looks in.*) What are you going to do?

NORA (*inside*). To take off my doll's dress.

HELMER (*in doorway*). Yes, do, dear. Try to calm down, and recover your balance, my sacred little songbird. You may rest secure, I have broad wings to shield you. (*Walking up and down near the door.*) Oh, how lovely—how cosy our home is, Nora. Here you are safe; here I can shelter you like a hunted dove, whom I have saved from the claws of the hawk. I shall soon bring your poor beating heart to rest, believe me, Nora, I will. To-morrow all this will seem quite different—everything will be as before; I shall not need to tell you again that I forgive you; you will feel for yourself that it is true. How could I find it in my heart to drive you away, or even so much as to reproach you? Oh, you don't know a true man's heart, Nora. There is something indescribably sweet and soothing to a man in having forgiven his wife—honestly forgiven her from the bottom of his heart. She becomes his property in a double sense. She is as though born again; she has become, so to speak, at once his wife and his child. That is what you shall henceforth be to me, my bewildered, helpless darling. Don't worry about anything, Nora; only open your heart to me, and I will be both will and conscience to you. (*Nora enters, crossing to table in everyday dress.*) Why, what's this? Not gone to bed? You have changed your dress.

NORA   Yes, Torvald; now I have changed my dress.

HELMER   But why now so late?

NORA   I shall not sleep to-night.

HELMER   But, Nora dear—

NORA   (*looking at her watch*). It's not so late yet. Sit down, Torvald, you and I have much to say to each other. (*She sits on one side of the table.*)

HELMER   Nora, what does this mean; your cold, set face—

NORA   Sit down. It will take some time; I have much to talk over with you. (*Helmer sits at the other side of the table.*)

HELMER   You alarm me; I don't understand you.

NORA   No, that's just it. You don't understand me; and I have never understood you—till to night. No, don't interrupt. Only listen to what I say. We must come to a final settlement, Torvald!

HELMER   How do you mean?

NORA   (*after a short silence*). Does not one thing strike you as we sit here?

HELMER   What should strike me?

NORA   We have been married eight years. Does it not strike you that this is the first time we two, you and I, man and wife, have talked together seriously?

HELMER   Seriously! Well, what do you call seriously?

NORA   During eight whole years and more—ever since the day we first met—we have never exchanged one serious word about serious things.

HELMER   Was I always to trouble you with the cares you could not help me to bear?

NORA   I am not talking of cares. I say that we have never yet set ourselves seriously to get to the bottom of anything.

HELMER   Why, my dear Nora, what have you to do with serious things?

NORA   There we have it! You have never understood me. I have had great injustice done me, Torvald, first by my father and then by you.

HELMER   What! by your father and me?—by us who have loved you more than all the world?

NORA   (*shaking her head*). You have never loved me. You only thought it amusing to be in love with me.

HELMER   Why, Nora, what a thing to say!

NORA   Yes, it is so, Torvald. While I was at home with father he used to tell me all his opinions and I held the same opinions. If I had others I concealed them, because he would not have liked it. He used to call me his doll child, and play with me as I played with my dolls. Then I came to live in your house—

HELMER   What an expression to use about our marriage!

NORA   (*undisturbed*). I mean I passed from father's hands into yours. You settled everything according to your taste; and I got the same tastes as you; or I

pretended to—I don't know which—both ways perhaps. When I look back on it now, I seem to have been living here like a beggar, from hand to mouth. I lived by performing tricks for you, Torvald. But you would have it so. You and father have done me a great wrong. It's your fault that my life has been wasted.

HELMER   Why, Nora, how unreasonable and ungrateful you are. Haven't you been happy here?

NORA   No, never; I thought I was, but I never was.

HELMER   Not—not happy?

NORA   No, only merry. And you have always been so kind to me. But our house has been nothing but playroom. Here I have been your doll-wife, just as at home I used to be papa's doll-child. And the children in their turn have been my dolls. I thought it fun when you played with me, just as the children did when I played with them. That has been our marriage, Torvald.

HELMER   There is some truth in what you say, exaggerated and overstrained though it be. But henceforth it shall be different. Playtime is over; now comes the time for education.

NORA   Whose education? Mine, or the children's.

HELMER   Both my dear Nora.

NORA   Oh, Torvald, you can't teach me to be a fit wife for you.

HELMER   And you say that?

NORA   And I—am I fit to educate the children?

HELMER   Nora!

NORA   Did you not say yourself a few minutes ago you dared not trust them to me.

HELMER   In the excitement of the moment! Why should you dwell upon that?

NORA   No—you are perfectly right. That problem is beyond me. There's another to be solved first—I must try to educate myself. You are not the one to help me in that. I must set about it alone. And that is why I am leaving you!

HELMER   (*jumping up*). What—do you mean to say—

NORA   I must stand quite alone to know myself and my surroundings; so I cannot stay with you.

HELMER   Nora! Nora!

NORA   I am going at once. Christine will take me in for to-night—

HELMER   You are mad. I shall not allow it. I forbid it.

NORA   It's no use your forbidding me anything now. I shall take with me what belongs to me. From you I will accept nothing, either now or afterward.

HELMER   What madness!

NORA   To-morrow I shall go home.

HELMER   Home!

NORA   I mean to what was my home. It will be easier for me to find some opening there.

HELMER   Oh, in your blind experience—

NORA   I must try to gain experience, Torvald.

HELMER   To forsake your home, your husband, and your children! You don't consider what the world will say.

NORA   I can pay no heed to that! I only know that I must do it.

HELMER   It's exasperating! Can you forsake your holiest duties in this way?

NORA   What do you call my holiest duties?

HELMER   Do you ask me that? Your duties to your husband and your children.

NORA   I have other duties equally sacred.

HELMER   Impossible! What duties do you mean?

NORA   My duties towards myself.

HELMER   Before all else you are a wife and a mother.

NORA   That I no longer believe. I think that before all else I am a human being, just as much as you are—or, at least, I will try to become one. I know that most people agree with you, Torvald, and that they say so in books. But henceforth I can't be satisfied with what most people say, and what is in books. I must think things out for myself and try to get clear about them.

HELMER   Are you not clear about your place in your own home? Have you not an infallible guide in questions like these? Have you not religion?

NORA   Oh, Torvald, I don't know properly what religion is.

HELMER   What do you mean?

NORA   I know nothing but what our clergyman told me when I was confirmed. He explained that religion was this and that. When I get away from here and stand alone I will look into the matter too. I will see whether what he taught me is true, or, at any rate, whether it is true for me.

HELMER   Oh, this is unheard of! But if religion cannot keep you right, let me appeal to your conscience—I suppose you have some moral feeling? Or, answer me, perhaps you have none?

NORA   Well, Torvald, it's not easy to say. I really don't know—I am all at sea about these things. I only know that I think quite differently from you about them. I hear, too, that the laws are different from what I thought; but I can't believe that they are right. It appears that a woman has no right to spare her dying father, or to save her husband's life. I don't believe that.

HELMER   You talk like a child. You don't understand the society in which you live.

NORA   No, I don't. But I shall try to. I must make up my mind which is right—society or I.

HELMER   Nora, you are ill, you are feverish. I almost think you are out of your senses.

NORA   I never felt so much clearness and certainty as to-night.

HELMER   You are clear and certain enough to forsake husband and children?

NORA   Yes I am.

HELMER   Then there is only one explanation possible.

NORA   What is that?

HELMER   You no longer love me.

NORA   No, that is just it.

HELMER   Nora! Can you say so?

NORA   Oh, I'm so sorry, Torvald; for you've always been so kind to me. But I can't help it. I do not love you any longer.

HELMER   (*keeping his composure with difficulty*). Are you clear and certain on this point too?

NORA   Yes, quite. That is why I won't stay here any longer.

HELMER   And can you also make clear to me, how I have forfeited your love?

NORA   Yes, I can. It was this evening, when the miracle did not happen. For then I saw you were not the man I had taken you for.

HELMER   Explain yourself more clearly; I don't understand.

NORA   I have waited so patiently all these eight years; for, of course, I saw clearly enough that miracles do not happen every day. When this crushing blow threatened me, I said to myself, confidently, "Now comes the miracle!" When Krogstad's letter lay in the box, it never occurred to me that you would think of submitting to that man's conditions. I was convinced that you would say to him, "Make it known to all the world," and that then—

HELMER   Well? When I had given my own wife's name up to disgrace and shame—?

NORA   Then I firmly believed that you would come forward, take everything upon yourself, and say, "I am the guilty one."

HELMER   Nora!

NORA   You mean I would never have accepted such a sacrifice? No, certainly not. But what would my assertions have been worth in opposition to yours? That was the miracle that I hoped for and dreaded. And it was to hinder that that I wanted to die.

HELMER   I would gladly work for you day and night, Nora—bear sorrow and want for your sake—but no man sacrifices his honour, even for one he loves.

NORA   Millions of women have done so.

HELMER   Oh, you think and talk like a silly child.

NORA   Very likely. But you neither think nor talk like the man I can share my life with. When your terror was over—not for me, but for yourself—when there was nothing more to fear,—then it was to you as though nothing had happened. I was your lark again, your doll—whom you would take twice as much care of in the future, because she was so weak and fragile. (*Sands up.*) Torvald, in that moment it burst upon me, that I had been living here these eight years with a strange man, and had borne him three children—Oh! I can't bear to think of it—I could tear myself to pieces!

HELMER   (*sadly*). I see it, I see it; an abyss has opened between us—But, Nora, can it never be filled up?

NORA   As I now am, I am no wife for you.

HELMER   I have strength to become another man.

NORA   Perhaps—when your doll is taken away from you.

HELMER   To part—to part from you! No, Nora, no; I can't grasp the thought.

NORA   (*going into room, right*). The more reason for the thing to happen. (*She comes back with out-door things and a small travelling bag, which she puts on a chair.*)

HELMER   Nora, not now! Wait till to-morrow.

NORA   (*putting on cloak*). I can't spend the night in a strange man's house.

HELMER   But can't we live here as brother and sister?

NORA   (*fastening her hat*). You know very well that would not last long. Good-bye, Torvald. No, I won't go to the children. I know they are in better hands than mine. As I now am, I can be nothing to them.

HELMER   But some time, Nora—some time—

NORA   How can I tell? I have no idea what will become of me.

HELMER   But you are my wife, now and always?

NORA   Listen, Torvald—when a wife leaves her husband's house, as I am doing, I have heard that in the eyes of the law he is free from all the duties towards her. At any rate I release you from all duties. You must not feel yourself bound any more than I shall. There must be perfect freedom on both sides. There, there is your ring back. Give me mine.

HELMER   That too?

NORA   That too.

HELMER   Here it is.

NORA   Very well. Now it is all over. Here are the keys. The servants know about everything in the house, better than I do. To-morrow, when I have started, Christina will come to pack up my things. I will have them sent after me.

HELMER   All over! All over! Nora, will you never think of me again?

NORA   Oh, I shall often think of you, and the children—and this house.

HELMER   May I write to you, Nora?

NORA   No, never. You must not.

HELMER   But I must send you—

NORA   Nothing, nothing.

HELMER   I must help you if you need it.

NORA   No, I say. I take nothing from strangers.

HELMER   Nora, can I never be more than a stranger to you?

NORA   (*taking her travelling bag*). Oh, Torvald, then the miracle of miracles would have to happen.

HELMER   What is the miracle of miracles?

NORA   Both of us would have to change so that—Oh, Torvald, I no longer believe in miracles.

HELMER   But I will believe. We must so change that—?

NORA   That communion between us shall be a marriage. Good-bye. (*She goes out.*)

HELMER   (*sinks in a chair by the door with his face in his hands*). Nora! Nora! (*He looks around and stands up.*) Empty. She's gone! (*A hope inspires him.*) Ah! The miracle of miracles—?! (*From below is heard the reverberation of a heavy door closing.*)

✦ Friedrich Nietzsche
from *The Birth of Tragedy*

Known for his ruthless ability to dissect the moral assumptions of his time, Friedrich Wilhelm Nietzsche turned his attention, in The Birth of Tragedy *(1909), to Western cultural beliefs about classical antiquity. Specifically, he challenged the received view that Greek art embodied an ideal world based on principles of noble simplicity and tranquil grandeur. Instead, Nietzsche saw much more turbulent and psychologically powerful forces at work, forces he labeled the "Apollonian" and the "Dionysian." This selected passage illustrates what Nietzsche meant by these terms.*

We shall have gained much for the science of aesthetics, once we perceive not merely by logical inference, but with the immediate certainty of vision, that the continuous development of art is bound up with the *Apollonian* and *Dionysian* duality—just as procreation depends on the duality of the sexes, involving perpetual strife with only periodically intervening reconciliations. The terms Dionysian and Apollonian we borrow from the Greeks, who disclose to the discerning mind the profound mysteries of their view of art, not, to be sure, in concepts, but in the intensely clear figures of their gods. Through Apollo and Dionysus, the two art deities of the Greeks, we come to recognize that in the Greek world there existed a tremendous opposition, in origin and aims, between the Apollonian art of sculpture, and the nonimagistic, Dionysian art of music. These two different tendencies run parallel to each other, for the most part openly at variance; and they continually incite each other to new and more powerful births, which perpetuate an antagonism, only superficially reconciled by the common term "art"; till eventually, by a metaphysical miracle of the Hellenic "will," they appear coupled with each other, and through this coupling ultimately generate an equally Dionysian and Apollinian form of art—Attic tragedy.

In order to grasp these two tendencies, let us first conceive of them as the separate art worlds of *dreams* and *intoxication*. These physiological phenomena present a contrast analogous to that existing between the Apollonian and the Dionysian. It was in dreams, says Lucretius, that the glorious divine figures first appeared to the souls of men.

The beautiful illusion of the dream worlds, in the creation of which every man is truly an artist, is the prerequisite of all plastic art, and, as we shall see, of an important part of poetry also. In our dreams we delight in the immediate understanding of figures; all forms speak to us; there is nothing unimportant or superfluous. But even when this dream reality is most intense, we still have, glimmering through it, the sensation that it is *mere appearance*: at least this is my experience, and for its frequency—indeed, normality—I could adduce many proofs, including the sayings of the poets.

This joyous necessity of the dream experience has been embodied by the Greeks in their Apollo: Apollo, the god of all plastic energies, is at the same time the soothsaying god. He, who (as the etymology of the name indicates) is the "shining one," the deity of light, is also ruler over the beautiful illusion of the inner world of fantasy. The higher truth, the perfection of these states in contrast to the incompletely intelligible everyday world, this deep consciousness of nature, healing and helping in sleep and dreams, is at the same time the symbolical analogue of the soothsaying faculty and of the arts generally, which make life possible and worth living.

Schopenhauer has depicted for us the tremendous *terror* which seizes man when he is suddenly dumfounded by the cognitive form of phenomena because the principle of sufficient reason, in some one of its manifestations, seems to suffer an exception. If we add to this terror the blissful ecstasy that wells from the innermost depths of man, indeed of nature, at this collapse of the *principium individuationis*, we steal a glimpse into the nature of the *Dionysian*, which is brought home to us most intimately by the analogy of intoxication.

Either under the influence of the narcotic draught, of which the songs of all primitive men and peoples speak, or with the potent coming of spring that penetrates all nature with joy, these Dionysian emotions awake, and as they grow in intensity everything subjective vanishes into complete self-forgetfulness. In the German Middle Ages, too, singing and dancing crowds, ever increasing in number, whirled themselves from place to place under this same Dionysian impulse. In these dancers of St. John and St. Vitus, we rediscover the Bacchic choruses of the Greeks, with their prehistory in Asia Minor, as far back as Babylon and the orgiastic Sacaea. There are some who, from obtuseness or lack of experience, turn away from such phenomena as from "folk-diseases," with contempt or pity born of the consciousness of their own "healthy-mindedness." But of course such poor wretches have no idea how corpselike and ghostly their so-called "healthy-mindedness" looks when the glowing life of the Dionysian revelers roars past them.

Under the charm of the Dionysian not only is the union between man and man reaffirmed, but nature which has become alienated, hostile, or subjugated, celebrates once more her reconciliation with her lost son, man. Freely, earth proffers her gifts, and peacefully the beasts of prey of the rocks and desert approach. The chariot of Dionysus is covered with flowers and garlands; panthers and tigers walk under its yoke. Transform Beethoven's "Hymn to Joy" into a painting; let your imagination conceive the multitudes bowing to the dust; awestruck—then you will approach the Dionysian. Now the slave is a free man; now all the rigid, hostile barriers that necessity, caprice, or "impudent convention" have fixed between man and man are broken. Now, with the gospel of universal harmony, each one feels himself not only united, reconciled, and fused with his neighbor, but as one with him, as if the veil of *maya* had been torn aside and were now merely fluttering in tatters before the mysterious primordial unity.

In song and in dance man expresses himself as a member of a higher community; he has forgotten how to walk and speak and is on the way toward flying into the air, dancing. His very gestures express enchantment. Just as the animals now talk, and the earth yields milk and honey, supernatural sounds emanate from him, too: he feels himself a god, he himself now walks about enchanted, in ecstasy, like the gods he saw walking in his dreams. He is no longer an artist, he has become a work of art: in these paroxysms of intoxication the artistic power of all nature reveals itself to the highest gratification of the primordial unity. The noblest clay, the most costly marble, man, is here kneaded and cut, and to the sound of the chisel strokes of the Dionysian world-artist rings out the cry of the Eleusinian mysteries: "Do you prostrate yourselves, millions? Do you sense your Maker, world?"

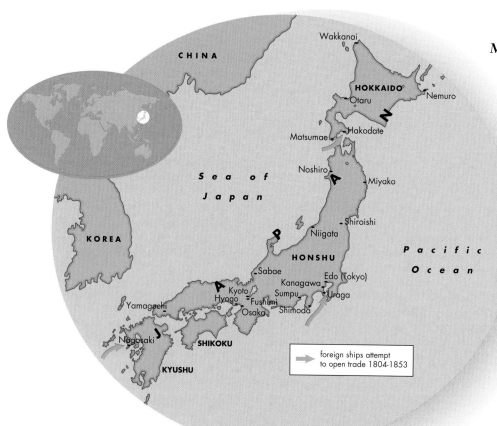

Map 19.1 Japan in 1853, when Commodore Perry reopened trade with the West.

CHINA

Wakkanai

HOKKAIDO

Otaru

Nemuro

Matsumae

Hakodate

Noshiro

Miyako

Sea of Japan

Shiroishi

Niigata

KOREA

HONSHU

Pacific Ocean

Sabae

Edo (Tokyo)

Kyoto

Kanagawa

Hyogo

Sumpu

Fushimi

Uraga

Yamaguchi

Osaka

Shimoda

Nagasaki

SHIKOKU

KYUSHU

foreign ships attempt
to open trade 1804-1853

CHINESE AND
JAPANESE
CIVILIZATIONS

CHAPTER 19

- *Chinese Culture after the Thirteenth Century*

- *Japanese Culture after the Fifteenth Century*

Hokusai Katsushika, *The Great Wave off Kanagawa*, ca. 1831, Honolulu Academy of Arts, Hawaii.

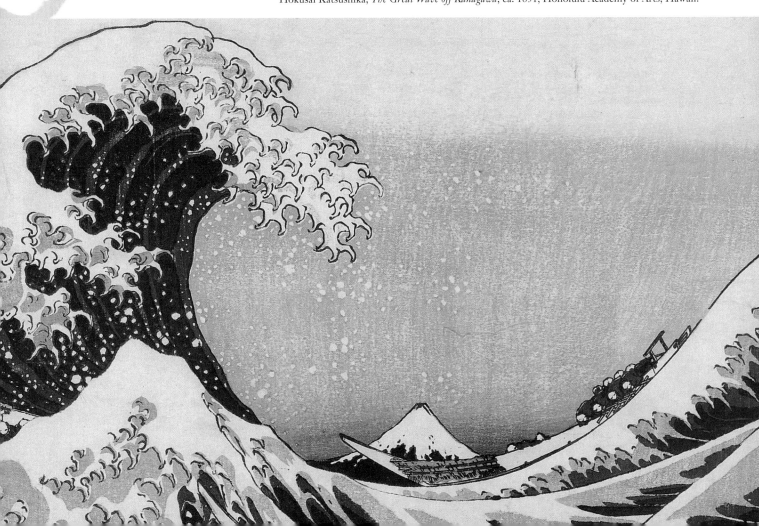

CHINESE CULTURE AFTER THE THIRTEENTH CENTURY

The last of the great medieval dynasties of China was the Yuan, a Mongol dynasty. In 1271, the Mongolian leader KUBLAI KHAN [koob-lie KON] (1214–1294), a grandson of Genghis Khan, adopted the Chinese dynastic name Yuan. By 1279 Kublai Khan had conquered the Southern Song and ruled from Beijing [bay-JHING] as emperor of China. He turned Beijing into a walled city and extended the Grand Canal to provision it. The Mongol ruling class kept the principal offices of governmental administration to themselves, appointing the Chinese only to the lowest posts. While the Mongols wanted to maintain their ethnic separateness during their rule, they nonetheless needed Chinese officials to maintain order, collect taxes, and settle disputes.

The period of Yuan rule was the shortest of China's major dynasties. A subtle and quiet resistance to the uneasy foreign occupation pervaded almost every aspect of Chinese life, including, for instance, its painting. *Bamboo* (fig. 19.1) by WU ZHEN [WOO JUN] (1280–1354), one of the Four Masters of the Yuan dynasty, is ostensibly a simple representation of the plant, but it had widely understood social significance. Bamboo, one of the strongest of materials and a symbol of survival, is like the Chinese under foreign rule: They might bend, but they would never break. Similarly, orchids, which nurture themselves without soil sur-

rounding their roots, are a commonly used symbol of Chinese culture in this period. Like the nation, the orchid could survive even though the native Chinese soil had been stolen by the Mongol invaders. In 1368, Zhu Yuanzhang drove the last Yuan emperor north into the deserts, declared himself the first emperor of the new Ming dynasty, and China was once again ruled by the Chinese.

The Ming (1368–1644) and Qing [CHING] (1644–1911), China's last dynasties, maintained the centralized bureaucratic political organization developed by the earlier Tang and Song dynasties. The Ming and Qing were remarkably alike in their continued reliance on Confucian ideals and in their high level of cultural achievement. The patriarchal nature of Confucian society (see Chapter 9) was evident at every level: the family, headed by the father, was the model unit. Politically, the emperor, as the Son of Heaven, was the father of the country. The magistrates, who carried out the rule of the emperor, also served as authority figures. The entire Ming–Qing system, one of unity and integration, benefited from the ability and commitment of its parental governing officials, who became known as mandarins, or counselors.

During the twentieth century China abandoned the tradition of imperial rule that had provided such social stability during the Qing period. First, Confucian ideals of governance began to be discarded. Then, with the overthrow of the Qing dynasty in 1911, came a period of political instability that lasted until the establishment of the Communist state in 1949.

Communism remains the dominant political system in contemporary China. Despite the tumultuous Cultural Revolution in the late 1960s—a period of upheaval in all aspects of Chinese culture and society—and despite the Tiananmen Square protests in 1989, which sought greater democratic liberties for the Chinese people, the Communist party has managed to maintain its political control.

Figure 19.1   Wu Zhen, *Bamboo*, China, Yuan dynasty, 1350, album leaf, ink on paper, 16 × 21″ (40.5 × 53.3 cm), National Palace Museum, Taipei, Taiwan. Despite Mongol rule, Wu Zhen worked in an intensely intellectual environment, dominated on the one hand by gatherings organized for the appreciation and criticism of poetry, calligraphy, painting, and wine, and, on the other, by deep interest in Buddhist and Taoist thought.

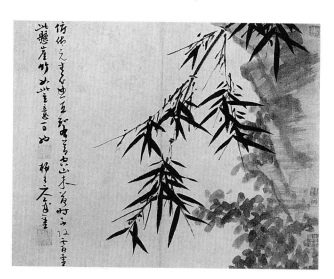

LANDSCAPE PAINTING

Among the most important paintings created in China under the Ming dynasty were landscapes. Landscape painting of the Ming period has a close affinity with Chinese lyric poetry in its directness and expressive spontaneity. Ming landscape painters typically selected only essential details to include in their paintings. Their goal was to express an "inner rhythm and freedom" in their work's "spiritual content," as the seventeenth-century painter Wu Li put it.

Shen Zhou.   This is particularly evident in the work of SHEN ZHOU [SHUN JOH] (1427–1509), who was less a professional artist than a gentleman scholar who, unlike a typical member of his social class, never held an

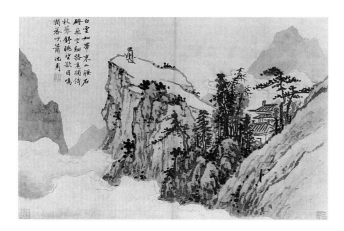

Figure 19.2 Shen Zhou, *Poet on a Mountaintop*, China, Ming dynasty, ca. 1500, album painting mounted as a handscroll, ink and color on paper, $15\frac{1}{4}$ × $23\frac{3}{4}''$ (38.1 × 60.2 cm), Nelson Atkins Museum of Art, Kansas City, Missouri. Like much Chinese nature painting, this work portrays human beings as a small element within a large natural scene.

official government position. Described as a "poet of the brush," Shen Zhou was the founder of the Wu school, a group of amateur scholar-painters for whom painting was an intimate expression of personal feeling. (The name "Wu" derives from Wu-hsien, the Yangtze river delta where Shen Zhou and other painters lived and worked.)

Among Shen Zhou's most striking compositions is *Poet on a Mountaintop* (fig. 19.2), one of five album paintings mounted as a handscroll. Using black ink with a few touches of color, the artist balances white spaces (often simply blank sections) with bold strokes and spots of black, to define the forms of trees and to suggest the outline of vegetation. He sets off the poet and the mountain in the center against lighter surroundings—washes of soft color and white space. The poet, tiny and simply sketched, stands poised at the edge of a cliff, on an inclined plane, propped up by his walking staff. Tucked away on the right is a mountain pavilion, a part of the natural scene, which is used by inhabitants as a place of reflection to put themselves in tune with the natural surroundings. Unlike many of his predecessors, Shen Zhou does not attempt to portray nature in an especially beautiful fashion, nor render the natural scene in carefully drawn, realistic detail. Instead, his painting conveys a sense of nature's serene grandeur.

Qiu Ying. *A Harp Player in a Pavilion* (fig. 19.3) by QIU YING [CHEE-OO YING] (1494–1552) also expresses nature's magnificence, though with greater delicacy and refinement. Unlike Shen Zhou, Qiu Ying renders the scene in exquisite detail, from carefully drawn tree trunks with elegant branches, buds, and leaves, to the delicate pavilion and its miniature inhabitants.

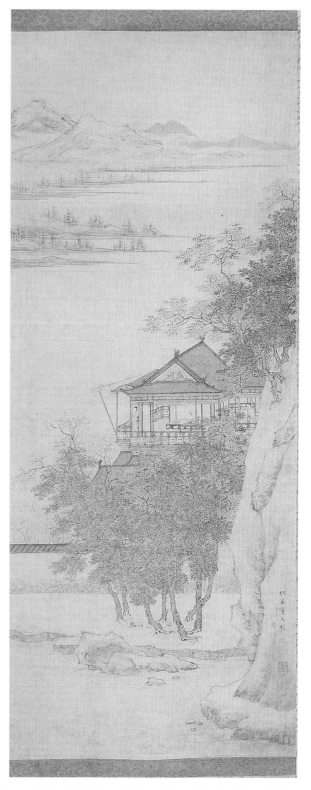

Figure 19.3 Qiu Ying, *A Harp Player in a Pavilion*, China, Ming dynasty, sixteenth century, hanging scroll, ink and color on paper, height $35\frac{1}{8}''$ (89.2 cm), Museum of Fine Arts, Boston. Qiu Ying's elegant painting suggests that space extends from the foreground to the distant expansiveness of the background, without using the Western artists' linear and aerial perspective.

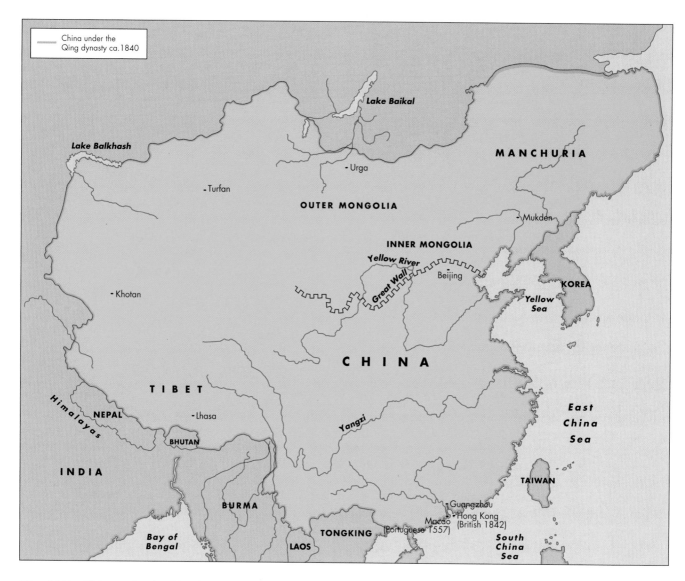

Map 19.2 China under the Qing Dynasty, ca. 1840.

Distance is suggested by the horizontal areas of whiteness in the foreground and background and the trees running diagonally from the lower center to the upper right. The mountains and the horizontal projections of land gently edging into the lake are freer in style, more suggestive than detailed. The inktones of Qiu Ying's *A Harp Player in a Pavilion*, softer and less dramatic than those of *Poet on a Mountaintop*, contribute to the overall effect of sensitivity and refinement.

ARCHITECTURE: CITY PLANNING

Architecture in traditional China signified the connection between the rule of the emperor and the order of the universe. Cities were constructed on a grid system, surrounded by a wall, which represented stability. The ruler's palace was generally situated at the north end, looking south, so that the emperor's back was turned

against the north from which evil (including the Mongol invaders) was always believed to come, and so that his gaze overlooked and protected the people, who lived in the city's southern half. The emperor looked down upon the city just as the Pole Star, from its permanent position in the north, looks down upon the cosmos. So long as the emperor fulfilled his function as the Son of Heaven, peace and harmony, it was believed, would be enjoyed by all.

Under the rule of the so-called Yongle Emperor (r. 1402–24), present-day Beijing was reconstructed as the imperial capital (fig. 19.4). Following traditional architectural plans, the principal buildings and gates of the government district, called the Imperial City, faced south, and almost all structures were arranged in a gridded square (fig. 19.5). The palace enclosure where the emperor and his court lived, called the Forbidden City, was approached through a series of gates: The Gate of

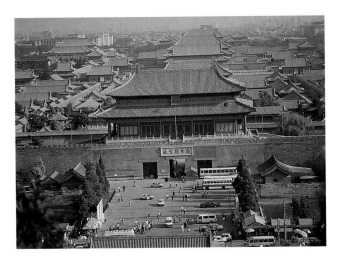

Figure 19.4 The Forbidden City, Beijing.

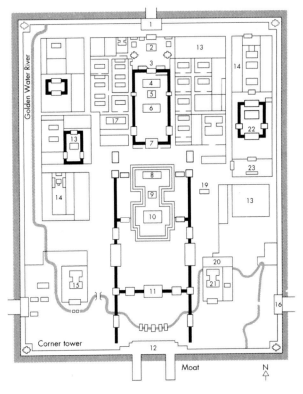

Figure 19.5 Plan of the Imperial Palace, Beijing. Outside the palace enclosure is Tiananmen Square. 1 Gate of Divine Pride; 2 Pavilion of Earthly Peace; 3 Imperial Garden; 4 Palace of Earthly Tranquillity; 5 Hall of Union; 6 Palace of Heavenly Purity; 7 Gate of Heavenly Purity; 8 Hall of the Preservation of Harmony; 9 Hall of Perfect Harmony; 10 Hall of Supreme Harmony; 11 Gate of Supreme Harmony; 12 Meridian Gate; 13 Kitchens; 14 Gardens; 15 Former Imperial Printing House; 16 Flower Gate; 17 Palace of the Culture of the Mind; 18 Hall of the Worship of the Ancestors; 19 Pavilion of Arrows; 20 Imperial Library; 21 Palace of Culture; 22 Palace of Peace and Longevity; 23 Nine Dragon Screen.

Heavenly Peace (called Tiananmen) is first, then the Noon Gate, which opens into a giant courtyard. Next, the Meridian Gate leads into the city's walled enclosure and opens out onto the first spacious courtyard, which has a waterway with five arched marble bridges. These bridges represent the five Confucian relationships as well as the five virtues (see Chapter 9). Past the bridges, high on a marble platform, stands the Gate of Supreme Harmony. Beyond the gate is the largest courtyard with three ceremonial halls. The most important is the Hall of Supreme Harmony, used for the emperor's audiences and special ceremonies.

With its series of interlocking gates and courtyards, its walled-in sections within larger walled-in areas, Beijing gives the visitor a rather different experience from Western cityscapes, which have open vistas with few walls and numerous opportunities to see up and down

Timeline 19.1 China after the thirteenth century.

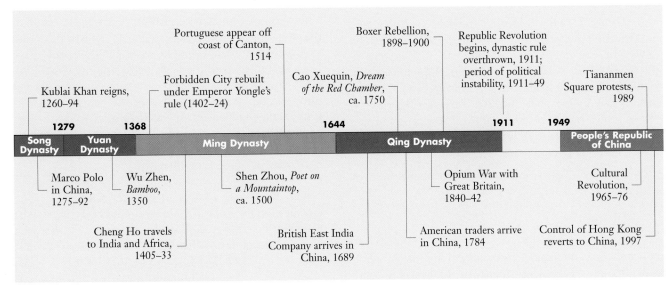

Then & Now

HONG KONG

The history of Hong Kong, the island city just off the coast of the Chinese mainland, has long been bound up with China's relations with the West. In the nineteenth century, the West began to pursue colonial ambitions in Asia, and the emperors of the declining Ming dynasty were forced to make trade and territorial concessions to encroaching Western powers. Defeated by Great Britain in the Opium War (1840–42), China ceded Hong Kong to Britain by the Treaty of Nanking (Nanjing) in 1842. In a renegotiated settlement in 1898, Hong Kong, along with two other local Chinese territories, was "leased" to Britain until 1997, when control of the city reverted to China.

With one of the greatest deep-water harbors in the world, Hong Kong has always been a trading center, in part because the land is unsuitable for agriculture and lacks minerals and other natural resources. Since the 1960s, Hong Kong has developed one of the most successful economies in Asia, outperforming those of some Western countries, including Great Britain. As Hong Kong's economic value has increased, the city has become a symbolic bone of contention between China and Britain. Although the countries share an interest in Hong Kong's stability and prosperity, they have contrasting visions of Hong Kong's purpose and management. For Britain, Hong Kong represented the crowning achievement of its global economic expansion. For China, Hong Kong stands as an economic catalyst for the rest of the country. Its peaceful return marks a step closer to the absorption of Taiwan, which Beijing considers a "renegade" province, into the People's Republic of China.

In 1984, an agreement between China and Britain called for the termination of British rule in Hong Kong while maintaining its capitalist economy and democratic governmental structure until 2047. In 1997, with Hong Kong officially incorporated into the People's Republic of China, ostensibly it retains a social structure and democratic government elected by the people of Hong Kong. The jittery diplomacy surrounding the agreement has swerved around China's real intentions toward Hong Kong. These intentions have become increasingly suspect since the Tiananmen Square massacre in 1989, when government troops killed hundreds of peaceful protesters calling for greater political openness. Moreover, Beijing's control over the transitional governing council, and its increasing disregard for Hong Kong's democratic political culture, raise questions about the city's future as an engine of free economic enterprise. It remains to be seen whether, with its new political status, Hong Kong will sustain its economic vitality and global influence.

---

thoroughfares. An analogy can be made by comparing a Western landscape painting, which is seen in totality from a fixed perspective, to a Chinese landscape scroll, which must be viewed section by section as it is unrolled. In Chinese architecture and in such scrolls, the viewer experiences a series of discrete visual incidents, which only cumulatively provide an impression of totality.

LITERATURE

Traditional Poetry.   Much of the poetry written during the Ming dynasty was used in other art forms such as drama, fiction, music, and painting. The calligraphy at the upper left of Shen Zhou's *Poet on a Mountaintop* is, in fact, a poem. Shen Zhou was not only an accomplished painter but a fine poet and, like one of Castiglione's "Renaissance men" and many of his fellow artists of the Yuan and Ming dynasties, was skilled at most if not all of the arts. Zhou's poem reads:

White clouds like a belt encircle the mountain's waist
A stone ledge flying in space and the far thin road.
I lean alone on my bramble staff and gazing contented
    into space
Wish the sounding torrent would answer to your flute.

Not only does the poem express an affinity for nature, it contrasts the speaker's isolation with the need for companionship, the sound of the flute announcing the arrival of a lover or companion along the "far thin road" shrouded in mist. The comparison of the fog to a belt, furthermore, transforms the landscape into human terms. Removing the belt causes the landscape's hypothetical robe to fall open and reveal the beauty to the poet's eye, offering the promise of human intimacy and love—which the image on its own does not even begin to suggest.

Shen Zhou's poem continues a long tradition of Chinese poetry and fits comfortably into it. Almost all of the emperors themselves were poets, and some wrote vast quantities. For example, over 42,000 poems have been attributed to the emperor Qianlong (1736–1796). Although poetry continued to be written in the styles and forms of the great poets of previous centuries, it was prose fiction, evidenced especially by increasing amounts of literature focusing on the lives of urban merchants, servants, and petty officials, that was the most innovative development of the Qing dynasty.

Cao Xueqin's Dream of the Red Chamber.   The most important work of Chinese literature written in the eighteenth century, considered by some the greatest Chinese novel ever written, is *The Dream of the Red Chamber* by CAO XUEQIN [TSAO SOOEH-CHIN] (1715–1763). The novel is enormous, with 120 chapters.

The "red chamber" is where the female characters live, while the "dream" refers to the foretelling of the fates of these characters.

The Dream of the Red Chamber has been read as a story about the decline of a family, an allegory of Buddhist attitudes toward the world, and an autobiographical fiction adhering closely to the life of its author. It has also been considered a love story, a search for identity, and a quest for understanding the purpose of human existence. The book can be seen as a reflection of the many elements of mid-Qing elite life, including politics and religion, economics and aesthetics, love and family. Blending realism with dream and fantasy, *The Dream of the Red Chamber* has been hailed as one of the most revealing works ever written about Chinese civilization.

Modern Chinese Poetry. Although fiction and drama have long been a part of Chinese literary tradition, pride of place has always been accorded to poetry. Even when poets swerved away from refined classical Chinese and began to write in the modern vernacular, poets and poetry continued to command more respect than other literary genres. While working within an ancient Chinese poetic tradition, modern Chinese poets have experimented with free verse and with styles and forms that emerged in Europe during the nineteenth and twentieth centuries. Without directly imitating the literature of the Western world, modern Chinese writers absorbed Western influences to express contemporary Chinese cultural experiences, including the political circumstances of the age. Chairman MAO ZEDONG [ZAY-DUNG] (1893–1976), the father of Chinese Communism, wrote a number of poems celebrating the revolutionary ideal. Also political, but in direct opposition to the established order of contemporary China, the poems of BEI DAO [BAY DOW] (b. 1949) repudiate the oppressiveness of a society that, if it does not execute its dissenters, jails them. The Tiananmen Square massacre of 1989 gives urgent meaning to the sentiments expressed in the poems by these and other contemporary Chinese poets.

MUSIC

Chinese Theater Music. From the fourteenth through to the seventeenth century, Chinese music was largely associated with drama, especially with a form of musical drama known as *Hsi-wen*, which included musical arias or lyrical songs, spoken dialogue, dance, and mime—all with instrumental accompaniment. Two different styles developed. There was a northern style, *'ei-chu*, in which a pear-shaped lute (*pi-pa*) was the primary instrument for accompaniment, and singing was performed by one individual. In the southern style, *ti*, the transverse flute (*dizi*) was the primary instrument for accompaniment and nearly all the characters sang.

During the 1500s these two styles of musical drama merged in the Kun opera, which incorporated elaborate poetic texts and intricate plots with numerous scenes. Although Kun opera became a more or less elitist form of musical drama owing to its intricacy and complexity, it did have an influence on more popular forms of musical drama that developed in later centuries, including the Beijing opera (*Ching-hsi*), a nineteenth-century development.

Beijing Opera. Beijing opera has become one of the most popular musical forms of the twentieth century. Incorporating traditional styles of acting absorbed from the history of Chinese drama, Beijing opera possesses a distinctive liveliness, with colorful, fast-paced scenes based on ancient Chinese myths, legends, and fables.

The dramatic action of Beijing opera is highly stylized. There are, for example, twenty-six distinct ways to laugh and thirty-nine specific ways to manipulate the twenty different types of beards. The performers' roles are divided into four major categories: male (*sheng*), female (*tan*), painted male face (*ching*), and clown (*ch'ou*). The male and female roles, all performed by men, are subdivided into roles for old men and roles without beards for young men, such as the flirtatious female or the lady of propriety (fig. 19.6).

Figure 19.6. An actor from the Beijing opera performing as the heroine Mu Guiying. Mu Guiying is a popular character who comes from the Yang family of the eleventh century and is the most important of the women generals of the family—women who fought their enemies from the north.

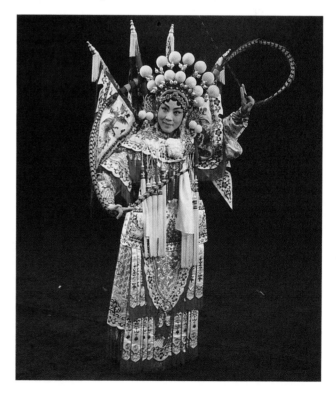

The music for Beijing opera is performed by an orchestra arranged in two sections: a percussion section composed of gongs and drums, and a melodic section of strings and wind instruments. The percussion instruments play introductory music prior to the characters' entrances; they are also played between the singing and acting. The melodic instruments accompany the singing. While the melodies for the Beijing opera arias derive from traditional music, there is often originality in their embellishment.

With the founding of the Communist People's Republic of China in 1949, Chinese music was directed toward social revolutionary purposes. Mao Zedong conscripted all the arts, remarking that they "operate as powerful weapons in unifying and educating the people and for attacking and destroying the enemy." Mao introduced two influential artistic directives: (1) a return to folk tradition and (2) an emphasis on political ideals and content in music. From 1966 to 1969, at the height of the Cultural Revolution, the only opera performances permitted in China were eight revolutionary works deemed pure of the taint of "bourgeois" ideas and influences.

In the late twentieth century the necessity for such strict adherence to political ideology for musical composition and performance has diminished. Although revolutionary themes dominate many modern Chinese musical works, Western influences, instruments, and performance practices are now apparent.

JAPANESE CULTURE AFTER THE FIFTEENTH CENTURY

Toward the end of over a century of feudal warfare, known as the Warring States period (1477–1600), TOKUGAWA IEYASU [TOH-KOO-GAH-WAH] (1542–1616) became the first **shogun**, or ruler, of post-feudal Japan. The Tokugawa family was to rule the country from 1600 until 1868. The shogun retained a figurehead emperor in Kyoto, while making Edo (present-day Tokyo) the effective capital of the country. Confucian influence was strong. Society was ordered into classes of ruler-warriors, or **samurai**, farmers, artisans, and merchants, who rose in power and importance during the period. The Tokugawa shogunate both unified the country and isolated it from the outside world. Only the Dutch were permitted to trade with Japanese merchants, and it was through Dutch traders that Japan was apprised of developments in the West, all the while preserving Japan's distinctive national culture and identity immune to outside influence.

In 1868 Japan returned to rule by an emperor, inaugurating a period known as the Meiji era (1868–1912), during which it enjoyed rapid economic development

and a growth in national power. After the American military expedition led by Commodore Perry forced the Tokugawa regime to open its trade doors in the 1850s, Japan began to look to the West, instead of to China, in its effort to transform itself into a modern nation-state. Japan adopted a constitution modeled on that of Germany; it eliminated the power of the shogunate, the warlord samurai, and their local vassals; and it began programs of industrialization and universal education.

Japan also began to exert its influence throughout the western Pacific. Through its victory in the war with China of 1894–95, it acquired the island of Taiwan (then called Formosa) and gained influence over Korea. After its triumph in the Russo-Japanese War (1904–05) and its alliance with the victorious nations in World War I, Japan colonized Korea and parts of the Chinese mainland. When Japan had to face the defeat of World War II, it turned to economic rather than military means to achieve international power and influence.

THE SHINTO REVIVAL

With the rise of the Tokugawa dynasty, Shinto was resurrected as a state religion. **Shinto**, which literally means "the way of the gods," is a belief system indigenous to Japan and that involves rituals and venerations of local deities, known as *kami*. In its most general sense, Shinto is a "religion" of Japanese patriotism. Less a system of doctrines than a reverential attitude toward things Japanese, Shinto emphasizes the beauty of the Japanese landscape, especially its mountain regions, and views the Japanese land and people as superior to all others.

Accompanying the revival of Shinto was the rise of the feudal knight, or samurai, who was idealized as a native hero. Much like the medieval knight of Christendom, the samurai was held to a strict code of conduct that emphasized loyalty, self-sacrifice, and honor. The rejuvenation of Shinto and of the samurai reflected an intense Japanese ethnocentrism and contributed to the isolationism of the Tokugawa dynasty.

LANDSCAPE PAINTING

The respect for the land that distinguishes the Shinto religion was anticipated in landscape painting of the Muromachi period (1392–1568), which shows reverence for the grace and grandeur of nature and the humble place of human beings within it. Japanese painting suggests less a naturalistically rendered scene than an extension of unseen vistas beyond the explicitly depicted view. This pictorial tradition characterizes the Zen ideal of "capturing the principle of things as they move on."

Of Japanese Muromachi artists, the priest-painter SESSHU [SES-SHU] (1420–1506), more than anyone

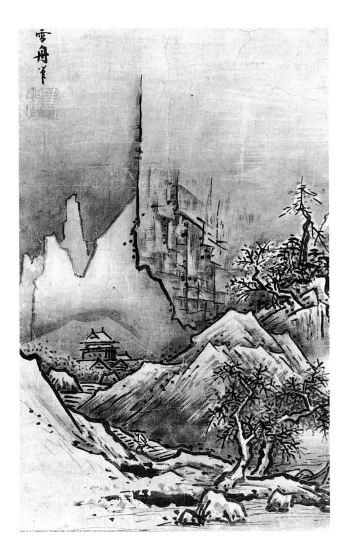

Figure 19.7 Sesshu, *Winter Landscape*, Japan, Ashikaga period, ca. 1470s, hanging scroll, ink and slight color on paper, 18¼ × 11½″ (46.3 × 29.3 cm), Tokyo National Museum, Tokyo. The harshness of the pictorial style, seen in this unsentimental representation of a wintry world, is characteristic of Sesshu.

else, took Chinese ink-style painting and made it Japanese. In 1467–69 he traveled to China, where examples of landscape painting greatly influenced his work. However, Sesshu was to put a distinctive, Zen-like mark upon the tradition.

His *Winter Landscape* (fig. 19.7), one of four seasons Sesshu painted on a scroll entitled *Landscape of the Four Seasons*, suggests the varied moods the seasons inspire. In the *Winter Landscape*, the most austere of the four seasonal evocations, Sesshu employs bold brushstrokes and diagonal lines to suggest the power of winter. He leaves patches of paper blank to signify snow and to depict the season's starkness. In striking contrasts of black and white, the painting's outlines convey a cold strength.

Sesshu's landscape scrolls possess some of the boldness of his Chinese contemporary, Shen Zhou. Sesshu's work,

however, reveals an emphasis on strong lines. His extended vistas are consistently subordinated to the visual drama and experience, reflecting the importance of the Zen qualities of immediate apprehension and intuitive understanding.

WOODBLOCK PRINTS

During the seventeenth and eighteenth centuries, a style of art called *ukiyo-e* arose, which became especially associated with woodblock prints. *Ukiyo* means "floating world" in the Buddhist sense of "transient" or "evanescent," and *ukiyo-e* means "pictures of the floating world." The Impressionist painters of nineteenth-century Europe admired *ukiyo-e* prints enormously because, like them, the Japanese artist was concerned with the world of everyday life, particularly of cultural enjoyments, such as dance, theater, music, and games.

Prior to the seventeenth century, woodblock prints were used almost exclusively to illustrate textbooks, painting manuals, and religious works. With the increased interest in everyday life shown during the Tokugawa period, woodblock prints that depicted things of interest to various social classes began to appear. Moreover, prints were inexpensive enough to be afforded by ordinary people.

New techniques for color reproduction were soon discovered. With their increasing range of subjects, these color woodblock prints became enormously popular. Between the mid-eighteenth and mid-nineteenth century, color woodblock prints represented all facets of existence from the lives of the wealthy to the beautiful courtesans of the Yoshiwara, or pleasure district, of Tokyo. In addition, artists turned their attention to the Japanese landscape, providing fresh interpretations of nature.

Woodblock prints were also closely linked with the world of the Kabuki theater, which had a large and enthusiastic audience. Prints of Kabuki actors were popular, as were posters and programs featuring the actors in various Kabuki roles. In fact, print publishers would frequently book seats so their artists could create up-to-date images of the actors to sell during the run of a play. Actors often obliged the artists by striking formal poses that were suited to the stylized prints.

Utamaro Kitagawa. Of the artists producing woodblock prints for popular consumption, UTAMARO KITAGAWA [OO-TAH-MAH-ROH] (1753–1806) is among the best known. Utamaro portrayed women so beautifully that he is generally recognized as the greatest among the Japanese artists. Utamaro's elegant, willowy, and languorous women are typically rendered in full-length portraits characterized by delicacy and refinement. His most famous work, published in 1794, is *Ten Physiognomic Types of Women*, in which Utamaro used

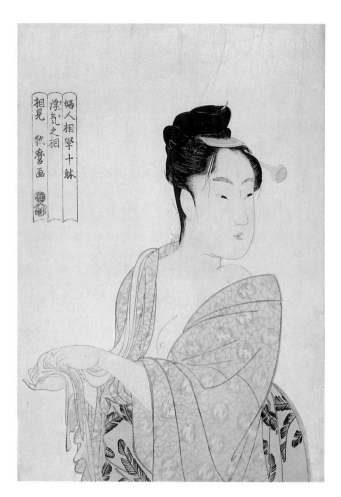

Figure 19.8 Utamaro Kitagawa, *Beautiful Lady Dressed in Kimono*, Japan, Tokugawa period, 1794, polychrome woodblock print, 14¾ × 9½″ (37.9 × 24.4 cm), British Museum, London. This print shows the "coquette," a type from Utamaro's *Ten Physiognomic Types of Women*, one of a number of print series popular among Japanese urbanites in the late eighteenth century.

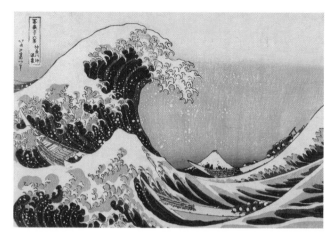

Figure 19.9 Hokusai Katsushika, *The Great Wave off Kanagawa*, Japan, Tokugawa period, ca. 1831, from *Thirty-Six Views of Mount Fuji*, polychrome woodblock print, 9⅞ × 14⅝″ (25.5 × 37.1 cm), Honolulu Academy of Arts, Honolulu, Hawaii. Among the best known of all Japanese woodblock prints, this image, an icon representing Japan, contrasts the powerful energy of the ocean's waves with the stable serenity of the distant snow-capped mountain in the background.

tinted mica backgrounds to enhance the decorative quality of his portraits. One of the full-color woodblock prints, *Bust of a Beautiful Lady Dressed in Kimono* (fig. 19.8), shows a woman's exposed white skin set off against the color and intricate design of her clothing. The slightly turned position of her head and torso add visual drama without disrupting the elegance of her posture.

Hokusai Katsushika. HOKUSAI KATSUSHIKA [HOK-KOO-SAI] (1760–1849), along with his contemporary Hiroshige Ando (1797–1858), represents the artistic culmination of the Japanese woodblock print. Both preferred landscapes to portraits, and both created a multitude of designs and a vast number of prints, which were produced in large editions. Hokusai created some of his finest works after he was over seventy, including his popular series *Thirty-Six Views of Mount Fuji*, which reveals his astonishing imagination. Hokusai's unusual

perspectives provide a visual counterpart to the unexpected encountered in haiku, as in his *The Great Wave off Kanagawa* (fig. 19.9). What is remarkable here is the odd view of Fuji, a symbol for the Japanese of the enduring beauty and stability of the nation itself. Though almost centered in the print, Fuji is dwarfed by the giant wave, which threatens to crash on the boat beneath it. In essence, Hokusai contrasts the transience of everyday existence, the fragility of life itself, to the more enduring, even eternal qualities of Fuji.

ARCHITECTURE

Architectural styles in Japan from the Muromachi to the Tokugawa period differed from those of previous eras and from one another as well. During the Muromachi period, the Ashikaga shoguns attempted to fuse styles inherited from their predecessors. During the next era, the Momoyama era, secular architecture became increasingly grandiose and elaborate. This architectural exuberance was tempered during the next period, the Tokugawa, with a more restrained aesthetic.

The Temple of the Golden Pavilion (Kinkakuji). One of the most interesting and elegant buildings constructed during the Muromachi period was the Kyoto landmark, Kinkakuji or the "Temple of the Golden Pavilion" (fig. 19.10). Erected in 1397 under the shogun Yoshimitsu (1358–1408), the Golden Pavilion, so named because parts of the interior are covered with gold leaf, was originally a private chapel designed for Yoshimitsu's use at his villa in Kyoto. After his death, it was convert-

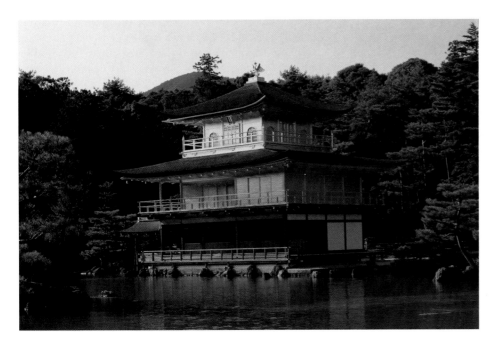

Figure 19.10 The Temple of the Golden Pavilion (Kinkakuji), Kyoto, Japan, Muromachi period, 1397. The building was constructed for the shogun as a retreat and was converted to a temple after his retirement.

ed into a Buddhist temple and monastery, containing a Zen chapel and rooms for contemplating the landscape and the moon. Its three stories culminate in a curving Chinese-pyramidal and Japanese-shingled roof. The pavilion is set on a platform constructed to jut out into a pond surrounded by trees carefully planted to create a look of natural profusion and variety. The structure seems simultaneously set off from and set into the landscape in a harmonious blending of nature and civilization. The overall effect is one of spontaneous simplicity.

Figure 19.11 Himeji Castle, Hyogo (near Osaka), Japan, Momoyama period (1581–1609). Popularly known as White Heron Castle, Himeji was built as a fortress by powerful Japanese warlords.

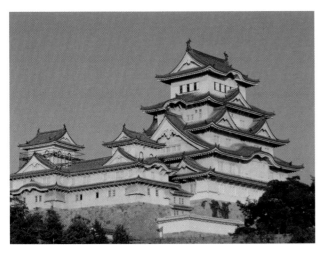

Himeji Castle. In contrast to the elegant simplicity of Muromachi domestic architecture, as illustrated by the Golden Pavilion, was the development of military architecture in the Momoyama period. In earlier military fortresses, the living quarters of the *daimyo*, or lord, were separated from the defensive fortifications. During the Momoyama, home and fortifications were combined into a single massive edifice designed to discourage attack. The interior was richly decorated to impress visitors with its owner's wealth.

An outstanding example is Himeji Castle (fig. 19.11), begun by the shogun Hideyoshi in 1581 and enlarged and completed in 1609. The exterior of the castle's main building is constructed of massive masonry, made necessary by the introduction of Western firearms and canons. The castle rises from a moat below, with towers soaring fifty to sixty feet above the water. Atop this impregnable masonry foundation sits a four-story wooden structure reminiscent of temple architecture.

THE JAPANESE GARDEN

The Japanese garden is essentially landscape architecture. Aesthetically, it is tied to Japanese painting. Many Muromachi gardens were designed by prominent painters, including Sesshu, who shaped the raw materials of nature to appear like a carefully inked canvas or scroll. Gardens such as these were designed for contemplation rather than for meandering. With its neatly raked patterns of sand and carefully positioned shrubs and stones, the typical Japanese garden is conducive to meditation.

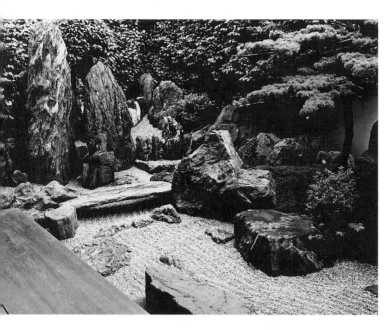

Figure 19.12   Attributed to Kagaku Soku, Garden of the Daisen-in monastery, Daitokuji temple, Kyoto, Japan, sixteenth century. Although used primarily for meditation, this garden served also as a place of assembly for Zen priests and samurai to compose *renga*, linked verses of poetry composed communally.

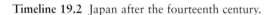

Gardens might also be carved out of nature in the manner of the large glen surrounding the Golden Pavilion of Kinkakuji. Or a garden might be designed with dry sand, which was used to suggest water, and punctuated by "islands" of trees, shrubs, and flowering plants.

Other types of Japanese gardens include moss and Zen-inspired gardens, which present nature in micro-

cosm. One of the most famous of the Zen-inspired gardens is the Daisen-in monastery garden (fig. 19.12) in Kyoto, designed by the painter Soami (d. 1525). This 1100-square-foot garden lies alongside the priest's house. Its vertical rocks represent cliffs, while horizontal stones represent embankments and bridges. The trees in the background symbolize distant mountains.

Larger, more elaborate landscape gardens include bridges and pagodas as well as plants. The landscape designs are meant to evoke the essence of the Japanese landscape as well as to follow representations of nature in Japanese art. As a result, the gardens reflect Japanese cultural aesthetics, including balance, proportion, unity, scale, and harmony.

LITERATURE

Prior to 1600, literature in Japan had been aristocratic in focus, written about court figures for a court audience by authors from among the nobility. After 1600, literature, especially fiction, contained more popular subject matter and it was produced by writers from a wider social spectrum.

Saikaku Ihara.   While Murasaki's twelfth-century *The Tale of Genji* (see Chapter 9) is generally considered the first great Japanese novel, high regard is also accorded the novels of SAIKAKU IHARA [SIGH-KAY-KOO] (1642–1693), especially his *The Life of an Amorous Man*, *The Life of an Amorous Woman*, and *Five Women Who Loved Love*. Earlier adventure novels had explored sexuality in ways that became culturally accepted, but Saikaku's inventive technical experiments with style and

Timeline 19.2 Japan after the fourteenth century.

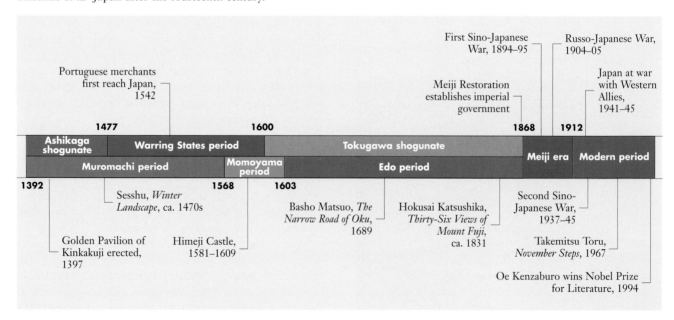

Cross Currents

EAST MEETS WEST: TAKEMITSU TORU

Of contemporary Japanese composers, among the best known in the West is TAKEMITSU TORU [TAH-KEY-MET-SOO] (1930–1996). Takemitsu wrote for film and television as well as for the concert hall. His concert works include symphonic orchestral pieces, compositions for chamber orchestras, and works for voices. Takemitsu scores his orchestral works for Western instruments and traditional Japanese instruments, such as the *biwa* and the *shakuhachi*.

Takemitsu became known in the West through Igor Stravinsky (see Chapter 18), who championed his work, and Aaron Copland (see Chapter 21), who considered him "one of the outstanding composers of our time." Serving as a bridge between East and West, Takemitsu brought works by Japanese composers to the attention of Western performers and introduced Western musical innovations to Japan. He was also instrumental in organizing cultural exchanges between Japan and the US. Takemitsu enriched his harmonic palette through the influence of French Impressionist composers such as Debussy. He also found inspiration for his music in nature, at one time describing himself as "a gardener of music," a title that reflects his interest in the combination of natural beauty and cultured formality that is typical of Japanese landscape gardens.

---

point of view in these novels were largely responsible for the legitimation of the subject matter.

Five Women Who Loved Love remains Saikaku's most highly regarded book today. By exploring the desires of his five female protagonists, Saikaku suggests their kinship with the courtesans of earlier Japanese literature. His merchant wives experience the same passions as the courtesans, but they are more willing to sacrifice everything for love, even their lives. Though modeled on actual people, Saikaku's five heroines are not as highly individualized or psychologically complex as characters from nineteenth-century European novels, such as Flaubert's Emma Bovary or Tolstoy's Anna Karenina. Saikaku's characters, however, are engaging figures, whose actions anticipate the behavior of more modern Japanese fictional heroines.

The Haiku. Haiku are three-line poems consisting of a total of seventeen syllables in a pattern of 5, 7, and 5 syllables per line. Of all forms of Japanese poetry, it has long been the most popular and the most heavily practiced in Japan. It is also the poetic form most influential in the West. The essence of good haiku poetry is a momentary, implicitly spiritual insight presented through images and without explicit comment. According to conventions established in the seventeenth century, the haiku must have imagery from nature, must include reference to a season, and must avoid rhyme. The haiku poet attempts to create an emotional response in the reader by penetrating to the heart of the poem's subject, thus evoking in the reader a sudden moment of Zen-like awareness.

Basho Matsuo. It was with the poems of BASHO MATSUO [BAH-SHOH] (1644–1694), who served the local lord as a samurai, that haiku reached its greatest artistic heights. Strongly influenced by the Tang poets Du Fu and Li Bai (see Chapter 4), Basho took from his Chinese predecessors their austerity and loneliness, while also absorbing their sense of humor. His poems, like theirs, convey an enjoyment of life while expressing regret at life's impermanence.

His desire to distance himself from other forms of haiku popular in his day led Basho to develop his own distinctive style, one that reflected the realities of everyday living while suggesting spiritual depths and intellectual insights. Humor is readily apparent in this haiku, written on a journey Basho made in 1689. On the road he saw a monkey caught in a sudden rainshower, and moved by its evident distress, he composed the following:

hatsushigure	First rain of winter—
saru mo komino wo	The monkey too seems to want
hoshige nari	A little straw raincoat.

Even in this humorous vision, we can detect Basho's profound sense of what the Latin poet Virgil called "the tears of things." When Basho was ill and approaching death, he composed the following haiku, which evokes his sense of loneliness, sadness, and pain:

tabi ni yande	Sick on a journey,
yume wa kareno wo	My dreams wander
kakemeguru	the withered fields.

The last Basho ever wrote, this haiku was given the title "Composed in Illness" by the poet. Providing a title was highly unusual; Basho knew the severity of his illness. He used the image of the journey both literally, for he became ill while traveling, and metaphorically, for the journey of life. His wandering dreams indicate a mind at work, though one weakened and unfocused. The final word *kakemeguru*, translated here as "withered fields," brings home with precision and elegance the inevitable fact of his dying.

Modern Fiction. Modern Japanese literature is traditionally dated from the beginning of the reign of the Meiji emperor in 1868. During the Meiji era

Connections

BUNRAKU: JAPANESE PUPPET THEATER

Although puppets were used in Japanese ceremonies and festivals as early as the eleventh century, it was during the Tokugawa period that the puppet theater, or **Bunraku**, developed and flourished. The texts of Bunraku plays were more distinguished than those of Kabuki, with the best of them composed by CHIKAMATSU MONZAEMON [CHICK-A-MAHT-SU] (1653–1724), who is considered by many the greatest Japanese dramatist. Written in poetic language, Chikamatsu's Bunraku plays had a narrator and were accompanied by a *samisen* player, both of whom typically sit on a dais set off to the side of the stage. Unlike Kabuki actors, who are the main attraction for a Kabuki audience, the puppeteers, the *samisen* accompanist, and the narrator are all self-effacing. Their job is not to impress the audience and win applause, but rather to bring the play to the audience in such a way that they are all but forgotten while the audience concentrates on the action of the puppets and the language of the play.

In its reliance upon the rhythmic pacing of the stringed *samisen* and the narrator's chanting, Bunraku can be compared with the earliest Greek dramas, in which a single actor-speaker recounts tales from the ancient myths and legends. In Bunraku the narrator is the voice of all the puppets, whose strings are controlled by three puppet-masters dressed in black. Like their ancient Greek counterparts, the early Bunraku plays celebrate ancient tales of Japanese culture, stories from *The Tale of Genji* (see Chapter 9), for example. Chikamatsu shifted the grounds of Bunraku from an emphasis on heroic stories of the past to situations involving ordinary people in his own time.

(1868–1912) a number of Westernizing reforms were introduced into Japanese economic, social, educational, and cultural life. Literacy was increasing dramatically, and writers began to use colloquial Japanese rather than the language of classical Japan. These changes, which parallel those in China at the turn of the twentieth century, inaugurated a period of modern fiction that is recognized the world over for its elegance, subtlety, and grace.

The fiction of modern Japan reflects a strong concern with identity, both cultural and individual. Prizing conformity and group identity; Japan has always struggled with the Western emphasis on the autonomy of the individual self. As the country became less isolated in the twentieth century, Japanese writers began to explore the tension between traditional Japanese cultural norms and Western practices, and their works reflect an active engagement with Western cultural ideals.

One novelist to explore themes of cultural and personal identity is TANIZAKI JUN'ICHIRO [TAH-NEE-ZAH-KEE] (1886–1965). Depicting Japan's changing cultural terrain, his work examines the consequences individuals face when set free from cultural constraints to pursue personal ambitions and desires. Many of Tanizaki's characters live like the modern Japanese, and the results of their self-assertion and self-aggrandizement revolve around guilt and alienation: guilt for abandoning long-valued cultural norms and alienation as a result of being cut off from the solidarity of the group.

THEATER

There are two primary types of Japanese music for theater: Noh and Kabuki. Each is a distinctive form of Japanese theater, with different musical conventions. Noh drama was developed in the fifteenth century; Kabuki theater emerged in the seventeenth century.

Noh. **Noh**, which means literally "an accomplishment," consists of dialogue and songs sung by the main actors in addition to music sung by a *ji*, or chorus. The instruments used to accompany the singing are collectively referred to as the *hayashi*. The hayashi ensemble consists of a *nokan*, or flute, an *o-tsuzumi*, a type of hourglass drum held on the hip, a *ko-tsuzumi*, a shoulder drum, and a *taiko*, or stick drum on a stand. During the entire time actors perform a Noh drama, the musicians of the *hayashi* remain on stage, their musical actions choreographed as part of the drama alongside the words and gestures of the actors.

The Noh is distinguished from other forms of drama by its solemnity. Even happier moments are performed with a seriousness and gravity that make them sound almost funereal. Originally, Noh plays were performed by Shinto priests to placate the gods. Later, from the fourteenth through to the seventeenth century, the plays were performed by professional actors wearing masks, one of the genre's distinguishing features. The limited plot action, the highly poetic texts, and the understated stylized gestures differentiate Noh plays from the realistic plays of Western theater.

Kabuki. During the first year of the Tokugawa shogunate a type of theater that includes song and dance was performed in Kyoto. **Kabuki**, originally, were short dramatic dances accompanied by song and percussion that celebrated the exploits of heroes, especially the samurai. During the eighteenth century, however, with the Kabuki works of Chikamatsu, Japanese theater developed a repertoire of plays based on the daily lives of peasants and merchants. Unlike Noh drama, which looked back to the glories of the Middle Ages, Kabuki focused on the present. In contrast to the solemnity and decorum of Noh drama, Kabuki performances were melodramatic and suggestive of the seductive charms of the actors and actresses. Developed in response to the needs of an urban audience, Kabuki includes popular drama along with various types of dance and music, some of which are performed onstage and some offstage.

CONTEMPORARY MUSIC

Oe Hikari. The story of the contemporary composer OE HIKARI [OH-AY HEE-KAH-REE] (b. 1963), son of the Nobel Laureate for Literature in 1994, Oe Kenzaburo, is one of the more unusual accounts of the making of an artist. Oe Hikari was born with an abnormal growth on his brain that threatened his life. Against the advice of doctors, his parents decided to have the growth removed, even though part of Hikari's brain had to be sacrificed. The surgery saved his life, but left him severely brain-damaged, which made it difficult for him to communicate using language. He did not make a sound until the age of six, when he responded to bird calls in the wild by imitating them perfectly, an early indication that he possessed an unusual aural imagination. Only then did his parents realize that he had memorized more than seventy distinctive bird calls from a recording given to him at the age of four.

Although Oe's verbal language remains limited, his imagination has allowed him to compose music, beginning after some piano lessons at the age of eleven. His work displays an instinctive appreciation of melody and an inclination toward the harmonic traditions of Western music from the seventeenth through the nineteenth century. Oe's music is deeply indebted to the musical styles of Bach, Mozart, and Chopin. Most of his compositions are brief and lyrical, conveying sorrow and joy, serenity and exuberance.

READINGS

✦ Cao Xuequin
From *The Dream of the Red Chamber*

The first great example of realistic fiction produced in China, The Dream of the Red Chamber is the ancestor of the family saga and depicts with psychological realism and sociological accuracy a wide range of characters in a richly textured social world. The following passage opens the work.

Chapter One

In which Chen Shih-yin meets the Stone of Spiritual Understanding And Chia Yu-tsun encounters a maid of unusual discernment

WHEN the Goddess Nügua undertook to repair the Dome of Heaven, she fashioned at the Great Mythical Mountain under the Nonesuch Bluff 36,501 pieces of stone, each 120 feet high and 240 feet around. Of these she used only 36,500 and left the remaining piece in the shadow of the Green Meadows Peak. However, the divine hands of Nügua had touched off a spark of life in the Stone and endowed it with supernatural powers. It was able to come and go as it pleased and change its size and form at will. But it was not happy because it alone had been rejected by the Goddess, and it was given to sighing over its ill fortune.

As it was thus bemoaning its fate one day, it saw coming toward it a Buddhist monk and a Taoist priest, both of uncommon appearance. They were talking and laughing and, when they reached the shadow of the Peak, they sat down by the side of the Stone and continued their conversation. At first they talked about cloud-wrapped mountains and mist-covered seas and the mysteries of immortal life, but presently they changed the topic of their conversation and spoke of the wealth and luxury and the good things of life in the Red Dust.[1] This stirred the earthly strain in the Stone and aroused in it a desire to experience for itself the pleasures of mortal life. Therefore, it addressed the monk and the priest thus:

"Venerable sirs, forgive me for intruding. I could not help overhearing your conversation and I should like very much to have a taste of the pleasures of the Red Dust of which you spoke. Though I am crude in substance, I am not without some degree of understanding or a sense of gratitude. If you, venerable sirs, would be kind enough to take me for a turn in the Red Dust and let me enjoy for a few years its pleasures and luxuries, I shall be grateful to you for eons to come."

"It is true that the Red Dust has its joys," the two immortals answered with an indulgent smile, "but they are evanescent and illusory. Moreover, there every happiness is spoiled by a certain lack, and all good things are poisoned by the envy and covetousness of other men, so that in the end you will find the pleasure outweighed by sorrow and sadness. We do not advise such a venture."

But the fire of earthly desires, once kindled, could not easily be extinguished. The Stone ignored the warning of the immortals and continued to importune them, until the Buddhist monk said to his companion with a sigh, "We have here another instance of Quiescence giving way to Activity and Non-Existence yielding to Existence." Then turning to the Stone, he said, "We shall take you for a turn in the Red Dust if you insist, but don't blame us if you do not find it to your liking."

"Of course not, of course not," the Stone assured them eagerly.

Then the monk said, "Though you are endowed with some degree of understanding, your substance needs

---
[1] The mortal world.

improvement. If we take you into the world the way you are, you will be kicked about and cursed like any ordinary stumbling block. How would you like to be transformed into a substance of quality for your sojourn in the Red Dust and then be restored to your original self afterward?"

The Stone agreed, and thereupon the monk exercised the Infinite power of the Law and transformed the Stone into a piece of pure translucent jade, oval in shape and about the size of a pendant. The monk held it on his palm and smiled as he said, "You will be treasured now as a precious object, but you still lack real distinguishing marks. A few characters must be engraved upon you so that everyone who sees you will recognise you as something unique. Only then shall we take you down to some prosperous land, where you will enjoy the advantages of a noble and cultured family and all the pleasures that wealth and position can bring."

The Stone was overjoyed on hearing this and asked what characters were to be engraved upon it and where it was to be taken, but the monk only smiled and said, "Don't ask what and where now; you will know when the time comes." So saying, he tucked the Stone in his sleeve and disappeared with the priest to we know not where.

Nor do we know how many generations or epochs it was afterward that the Taoist of the Great Void passed by the Great Mythical Mountain, the Nonesuch Bluff, and the Green Meadows Peak and came upon the Stone, now restored to its original form and substance. Engraved on it was a long, long story. The Taoist read it from beginning to end and found that it was the self-same Stone that was first carried into the Red Dust and then guided to the Other Shore by the Buddhist of Infinite Space and the Taoist of Boundless Time. The story was that of the Stone itself. The land of its descent, the place of its incarnation, the rise and fall of fortunes, the joys and sorrows of reunion and separation—all these were recorded in detail, together with the trivial affairs of the family, the delicate sentiments of the maidens' chambers, and a number of poems and conundrums which one usually finds in such stories.

Saikaku Ihara
From *Five Women Who Loved Love*

The following passage is excerpted from "Gengobei, The Mountain of Love," the final novella in Saikaku's Five Women Who Loved Love. *The story focuses on a young woman, Oman, who loves a Buddhist monk named Gengobei. The following sections reveal Saikaku's penetrating analysis of human behavior and his fascination with the variety and complexity of human love. Like the other heroines of Saikaku's book, Oman is a determined woman, one who not only knows what she wants but knows how to get it as well.*

People themselves are the most despicable and heartless of all creatures. If we stop to think and look about us in the world, we find that everyone—ourselves as well as others—talks of giving up his life on the spot when some great misfortune occurs, when a young man dies in the prime of his youthful beauty, or when a wife to whom one has pledged undying love passes away early in life. But even in the midst of tears unseemly desires are ever with us. Our hearts slip off to seek treasure of all kinds or give way to sudden impulses.

Thus it is with the woman whose husband has hardly breathed his last before she is thinking of another man to marry—watching, listening, scheming for one. She may have the dead man's younger brother take his place when he is gone. She may look for a pleasing match among close relatives or, in the dizzy chase, discard completely those with whom she has long been most intimate. She will say one short prayer to Amida—so much for her obligations. She will bring flowers and incense, just so that others may see her do it.

But one can hardly notice when she paints a little powder on her face, impatient to be done with mourning before thirty-five days have passed. Her hair soon regains its luster, glistening with oil, and is all the more attractive because the wanton locks fall free of any hairdress. Then too, her underclothes run riot with color beneath a simple, unadorned garment—so unobtrusive, yet so seductive.

And there is the woman who, feeling the emptiness of life because of some sad episode, shaves her head in order to spend the rest of her days in a secluded temple, where she will have only the morning dew to offer in memory of her husband, asleep beneath the grass. Among the things she must leave behind is a gown with fawn-spot designs and beautiful embroidery. "I shall not need this anymore. It should be made into a canopy or an altarcloth or a temple pennant." But in her heart the lady is thinking: "Too bad these sleeves are just a little too small. I might still wear them."

Nothing is more dreadful than woman. No one can keep her from doing what her heart is set upon, and he who tries will be frightened off by a great demonstration of tears. So it is that widows vanish from the earth like ghosts, for none will long be true to a dead man's ghost. And so it is with certain men, except that a man who has killed off three or five wives will not be censured for taking another.

But it was not so with Gengobei. Having seen two lovers die, he was led by true devotion to sequester himself in a grass hut on the mountainside, there to seek earnestly the way to salvation in the afterlife, and to seek naught else, for he had admirably determined to quit the way of the flesh.

At that time in Hama-no-Machi, on the Bay of Satsuma, lived a man from the Ryukyus who had a daughter named Oman. She was fifteen, graced with such beauty that even the moon envied her, and of a gentle, loving disposition. Every man who looked upon her, so ripe for love, wanted her for himself. But in spring of the past year Oman had fallen in love with that flower of manhood, Gengobei. She pined away for him and wrote him many letters, which a messenger delivered in secret. Still there was no answer from Gengobei, who had never in his life given a thought to girls.

It was heartbreaking for Oman. Night and day, day after day, she thought only of him and would consider offers of marriage from no other quarter. She went so far as to feign sudden illness, which puzzled everyone, and she said many wild things to offend people, so that they thought her quite mad. Oman still did not know that Gengobei had become a priest, until one day she heard someone mention the fact. It was a cruel blow, but she tried to console herself, saying that a day would come for her to fulfil her desires, a vain hope indeed, which soon turned to bitter resentment.

"Those black robes of his—how I hate them! I must go to see him just once and let him know how I feel."

With this in mind, Oman bade farewell to her friends as if to leave the world for a nunnery. In secret she clipped her own hair to make it look like a boy's. She had already taken care to get suitable clothing and was able to transform herself completely into a mannish young lover. Then, quietly, stealthily, she set out, bound for the Mountain of Love.

As Oman stepped along she brushed the frost of the bamboo grass, for it was October, the Godless Month,[1] yet here was a girl true to her love. A long way she went, far from the village into a grove of cedars which someone had described to her. At the end of it could be seen the wild crags of a cliff and off to the west a deep cavern, in the depths of which one's mind would get lost thinking about it. Across a stream lay some rotten logs—two, three, four of them, which were barely enough to support her. A treacherous bridge, Oman thought, as she looked down at the rapids below and saw crashing waves which would dash her to pieces. Beyond, on a little piece of flat land, was a lean-to sloping down from the cliff, its eaves all covered with vines from which water dripped, as if it were a "private rain."

On the south side of the hut a window was open. Oman peeped in to find that it was the poorest sort of abode. There was one rickety stove, in which lay a piece of green wood, only half burnt up. There were two big teacups, but no other utensils, not even a dipper or ladle.

"How dismal!" she sighed as she looked around from outside. "Surely the Buddha must be pleased with one who lives in such miserable quarters."

She was disappointed to find the priest gone. "I wonder where to?" she asked, but there was no one there to tell her, nothing at all but the lonely pines, and nothing for her to do but wait, pining among the pines.

Then she tried the door. Luckily it was open. Inside she found a book on his reading table. *The Waiting Bed* it was called, a book which described the origins of manly love.

"Well," she observed, "I see he still has not given up this kind of love."

She thought she would read while waiting for him to return, but soon it grew dark and she could hardly see the words. There was no lamp for her to use and she felt more and more lonely, waiting by herself in the darkness. True love is such that one will endure almost anything for it.

It must have been about midnight when the bonze Gengobei came home, finding his way by the faint light of a torch. He had almost reached the hut, where Oman waited eagerly for him, when it seemed to her as if two handsome young men came toward him out of the withered underbrush. Each was as beautiful as the other. Either one could have been justly called a "flower of spring" or a "maple leaf in fall." And they seemed to be rivals in love, for one looked resentful and the other deeply hurt. They both made ardent advances toward Gengobei, but he was just one and they were two, and he was helpless to choose between them.

Seeing the agitated, tortured expression on Gengobei's face, Oman could not help feeling a tender sympathy for him. Nevertheless, it was a discouraging sight for her.

"So he has love enough for many men," she said bitterly. "Still, I am committed to this affair and cannot leave it as it stands. I shall simply have to open my heart to him."

Oman went toward him, looking so determined that the two young men took fright and vanished into the night. She, in turn, was startled at their disappearance, and Gengobei at seeing her.

"What sort of young man are you?" he asked.

"As you can see I am one who has taken up the way of manly love. I have heard so much about you, Sir Priest, that I came all the way to meet you at the risk of my life. But these many loves of yours—I knew nothing of them. I have loved you in vain. It was all a mistake."

In the midst of her wailing Gengobei clapped his hands in delight. "How could I fail to appreciate such love as that!" he exclaimed as his fickle heart went out to her. "Those two lovers you saw are dead—just illusions."

Oman wept and he with her. "Love me in their stead," she begged. "Do not turn me away."

"Love is hard to pass up," he replied coyly, "even for a priest."

Perhaps Buddha would forgive him. After all, Gengobei did not know his lover was a girl.

"When I first entered the religious life," Gengobei was saying, "I promised Buddha that I would give up completely the love of women. But I knew it would be very hard to give up the love of young men, and I asked him to be lenient with me in this. Now there is no one who can censure me for it, because I made it all plain to the Buddha from the beginning. Since you loved me enough to come all the way in search of me, you must never forsake me later on."

Gengobei said these things half in jest, but it was doubly a joke for Oman. She pinched her thigh and held her breast to keep from laughing.

---

[1] In October, it was believed, the gods all assembled at the great shrine of Izumo, leaving the rest of the country "godless."

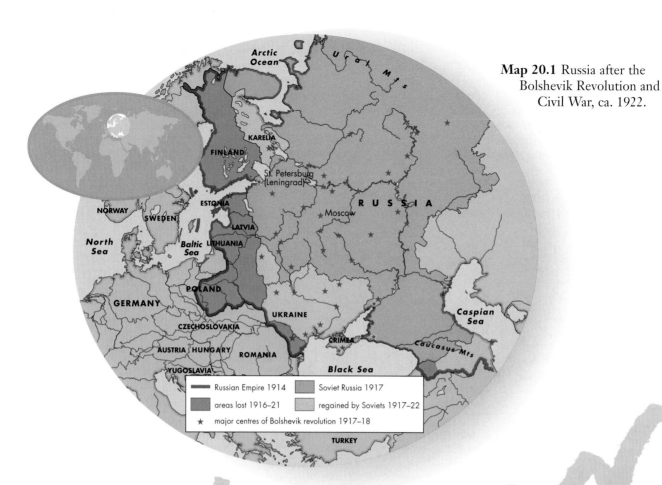

Map 20.1 Russia after the Bolshevik Revolution and Civil War, ca. 1922.

Russian Empire 1914
areas lost 1916–21
★ major centres of Bolshevik revolution 1917–18
Soviet Russia 1917
regained by Soviets 1917–22

RUSSIAN
CIVILIZATION

❧ *Russia before the Revolution*

❧ *The Revolution and After*

View of the Kremlin churches, Moscow.

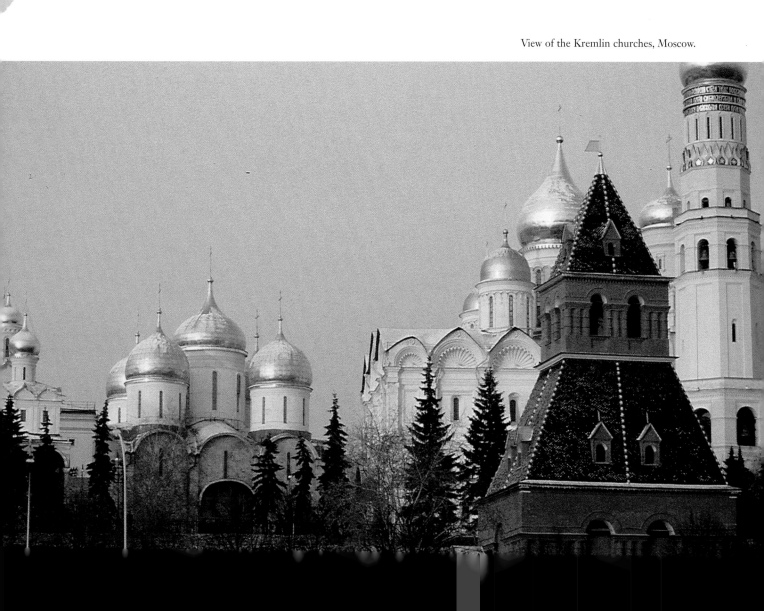

RUSSIA BEFORE THE REVOLUTION

Russia, prior to the Revolution of 1917, was characterized by a solid autocratic government, a strong influence from the Russian Orthodox Church, and ambiguous relations with the West. Since IVAN IV (1533–1584), had named himself "Tsar" ("Caesar") at his coronation in 1547, the Moscow Grand Princes had exercised such complete authority that no person or institution could challenge them. Known as "Ivan the Terrible," he initiated a tradition of despotic rule that many historians have regarded as the root of Communist totalitarianism in the twentieth century. Russia remained the most repressive society in Europe until 1861, when Tsar Alexander II abolished serfdom. Long after the rest of its European neighbors, it had remained a feudal society, in which a small number of wealthy and titled landlords owned the land worked by peasant farmers whose servitude amounted to little more than slavery. Most rarely saw their master, let alone a government official. It was only the Church that brought Russians together as a society.

THE EASTERN ORTHODOX CHURCH

In providing a foundation of belief and establishing forms of artistic expression, Eastern Orthodox Christianity was responsible almost exclusively for the early development of a distinctively Russian culture. The conversion of Russia to Christianity began in the ninth century through the efforts of two Greek brothers from the Byzantine Empire, Cyril (d. 869), a renowned scholar, and Methodius (d. 884), an administrator, both of whom served as missionaries among the Slavic peoples in Moravia, Bulgaria, and the land that was then known as Rus, which had Kiev as its capital. They transcribed the Bible into the Cyrillic alphabet and translated other religious texts into Slavic, which resulted in Church Slavonic becoming not only the language of Christian liturgy throughout Russia but also the primary written language for seven hundred years, much as had Latin in the west.

For Russians, religion centered on community, with wealthy nobles worshiping together with their peasant serfs during Orthodox services. Orthodox priests, who were considered as representatives of God, moved comfortably among the people. This communal quality of Russian Christianity, however, did not detract from the sense of the sacred that separated the earthly world of humanity from the heavenly kingdom of the divine.

Religious Icons. From the beginning, Russian art was firmly grounded in the Eastern Orthodox religion. However, it was the aesthetic appeal of the liturgy and rituals, rather than the theology, that inspired and attracted early Russians. The power of Orthodox Christianity was seen as historically inevitable and divinely sanctioned to endure until the end of time. Moscow, they believed, would be the "Third Rome." Grand Prince Vasily III (1505–1533) argued that just as Ancient Rome had been the center of its world, and Constantinople had next become the "New Rome," so Moscow would finally ascend to preeminence, as the last great Rome, after which the Last Judgement would ensue.

Russia was unified by its acceptance of a common religious faith with established forms of worship, especially of those artistic objects invested with deep spiritual significance. These objects, very often depicting the Virgin

Timeline 20.1 Russia before the Revolution.

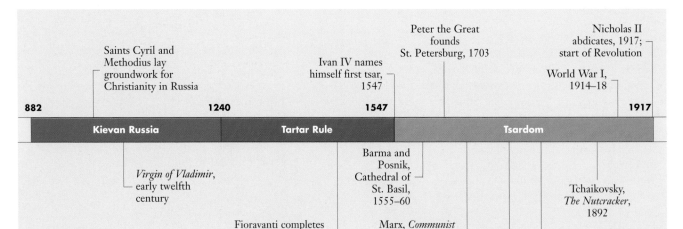

Virgin of Vladimir. One of the most enduring of all icons is known as the *Virgin of Vladimir* (fig. 20.1). An image of the Virgin Mary, this twelfth-century picture was created in Constantinople but was moved first to Kiev, then to Vladimir, and finally, in the fifteenth century, to the Cathedral of the Assumption in the Kremlin, where it has long been revered as a symbol of national unity. A particularly expressive work, the *Virgin of Vladimir* soon came to be known as "Our Lady of Tenderness," due to the tilt of the Virgin's head toward the child, the lightness of her supporting hands, and her sweetly sorrowful countenance. Like other Russian icons, the *Virgin of Vladimir* possesses a two-dimensionality that distinguishes it from traditional Western art. So highly regarded was this piece that it was often followed in procession during religious festivals, and frequently used to bless military troops preparing for battle.

ST. PETERSBURG

The influence of Western Europe on Russian society precipitated a struggle between those in favor of the country's Westernization and the Slavophiles, who argued for a pure traditional Russia. At the center of this debate was the majestic city of St. Petersburg, created by Tsar Peter the Great in the early eighteenth century (fig. 20.2).

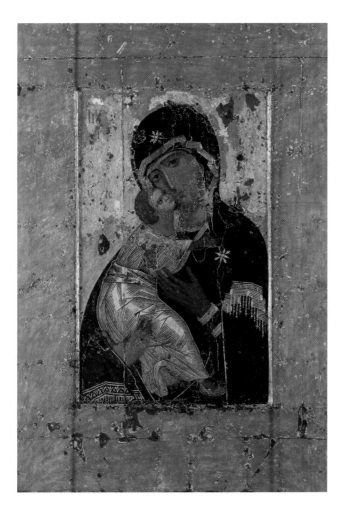

Figure 20.1 *Virgin of Vladimir*, early twelfth century, tempera on wood, height approx. 31″ (78 cm), Tretyakov Gallery, Moscow. This painting is the most revered of all Russian religious icons and was thought to have the power to protect the town that possessed it.

Figure 20.2 View of St. Petersburg. So many laborers died constructing the city that it is believed their bones, three hundred years later, still infest the waters surrounding it.

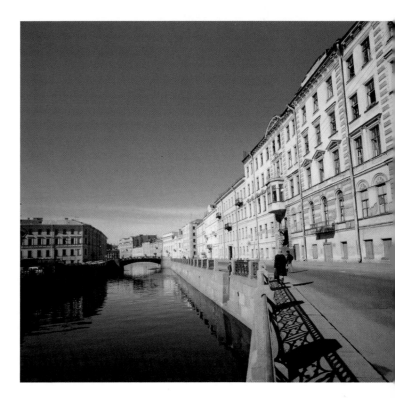

Mary, are known as **religious icons**. Found not only in small churches and great cathedrals, but also in the homes of ordinary people from all social ranks, icons were usually small images painted on wood. They were a common and popular way to remind people of the essential qualities of Christianity as reflected in the lives of the saints and found in stories from Scripture. Icons were used, therefore, as much for teaching as for devotion and prayer.

In Russian Orthodox churches, statues representing God and the saints were forbidden, but icons were permitted to take their place. Depicted on icons are not only figures from the Bible—patriarchs and apostles, for example—but also the early Church Fathers, including St. Cyril and St. Methodius. Panels of these icons separate the priests from the congregation, forming an **iconostasis**, or icon screen. The screen contains three doors, the central one of which—the "Royal Door"—opens and closes during religious services.

Peter moved the capital from Moscow in the east to an island in a swamp in the extreme northwest of the country, not far from Finland and Sweden, both historic enemies of Russia. He built his new city to provide "a window on Europe," a plan unsurpassed in its revolutionary brashness, given Moscow's definition of itself as the "Third Rome." Peter himself traveled throughout Western Europe and brought back to Russia plans for municipal design and for manufacturing based on Western ideas and techniques. He sent young noblemen, to England in particular, to study navigation and ship-building, in order that he could construct a commanding naval fleet.

St. Petersburg was a modern city, on a par with London and Amsterdam. It had canals like Amsterdam, wide boulevards like Paris, a grid-like organization, and formal gardens with fountains like Versailles, planted with flowers and trees from Germany and Holland, as well as from throughout Russia. As a city, however, St. Petersburg never captured the Russian imagination in the way that Moscow did. In *Crime and Punishment*, Dostoevsky's hero, Raskolnikov, stands on a bridge overlooking the city and we learn of his feelings, shared by most Russians, toward the place: "When he was walking to the University it would usually happen, most often on

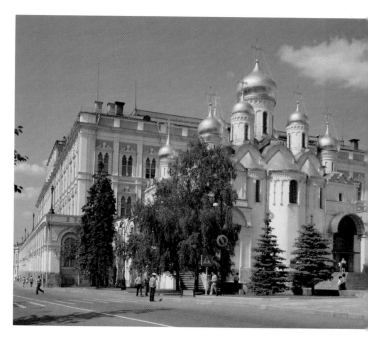

Figure 20.4 Cathedral of the Annunciation, 1484–89, Kremlin, Moscow. A favorite of rulers and their families, this church was used for the baptisms and marriages of the Russian tsars.

Figure 20.3 Aristotele Fioravanti, Church of the Assumption, 1479, Kremlin, Moscow. In this first Kremlin church, Russian tsars held their coronations.

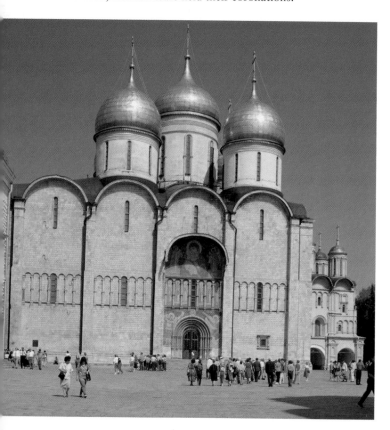

his way home, that perhaps a hundred times he would stop at just this spot, peer intently at what was truly a magnificent panorama, and wonder almost every time at the vague and unresolved impression it made on him. An inexplicable coldness always came over him as he contemplated its magnificence: the soul of the sumptuous vista was deaf and dumb for him."

ARCHITECTURE

Following the lead of Constantinople, which had experienced a political, military, and cultural resurgence in the ninth and tenth centuries, Russia strove to create beautiful works of art and architecture that rivaled those of the Byzantine city. In a desire to apprehend spiritual truth and make it comprehensible in concrete form, many cathedrals were built and decorated with elaborate mosaics and frescoes.

The Kremlin. The Kremlin, a walled city in the center of Moscow, was given its name in 1331, after the Mongol word *kreml*, which means "fortified." Encouraged by Princess Sophia, Ivan III, the Grand Prince of Moscow, embarked on a vast building program, replacing the wooden walls with red brick and constructing a set of dramatic and splendid churches. This effort was intended to secure Moscow's claim as the "Third Rome."

The cathedrals, although built partly by Italian architects, were Russian in style. The first of them was the

Church of the Assumption (fig. 20.3), completed in 1479. It came to be used for coronations. Decorated in the Byzantine style (see Chapter 7), its walls are covered with frescoes on gold backgrounds, and its columns are decorated with religious figures. It was in this church that the *Virgin of Vladimir* was found.

The Cathedral of the Annunciation was constructed close by, with its white walls and five gold cupolas (fig. 20.4). This intimate little church was used for the baptism and marriage of Russian tsars, and it became the favorite chapel of the wives and sisters of the rulers of Moscow. It had elaborately inlaid mosaic floors, richly adorned frescoes, and a resplendent iconostasis painted by two of the finest icon artists, Theophanes the Greek and Andrei Rublev. A third Kremlin church, the Cathedral of the Archangel Michael, which was built at the beginning of the sixteenth century, served as the burial place of the Muscovite rulers until the eighteenth century.

These churches were accompanied by seven others and by a concurrent building of palaces, including that of the splendid Palace of the Patriarch. In addition, important citizens built their own residences and private chapels within the confines of the Kremlin walls. Taken together (fig. 20.5), the sacred and secular structures, with their multitude of gilt roofs and colored cupolas, make a splendid sight. With the later addition of the Cathedral of St. Basil just across from the Kremlin, the center of Moscow was the most dazzling site of architectural splendor in the world.

The Cathedral of St. Basil. The Cathedral of St. Basil (fig. 20.6) was erected between 1555 and 1560 by the Russian architects Barma and Posnik. Ivan "the Terrible" intended the church to commemorate his conquest of the Mongolian khanates of Kazan and Astrakhan, making it a national votive shrine to his victorious military campaign.

Figure 20.5 View of the Kremlin churches, Moscow.

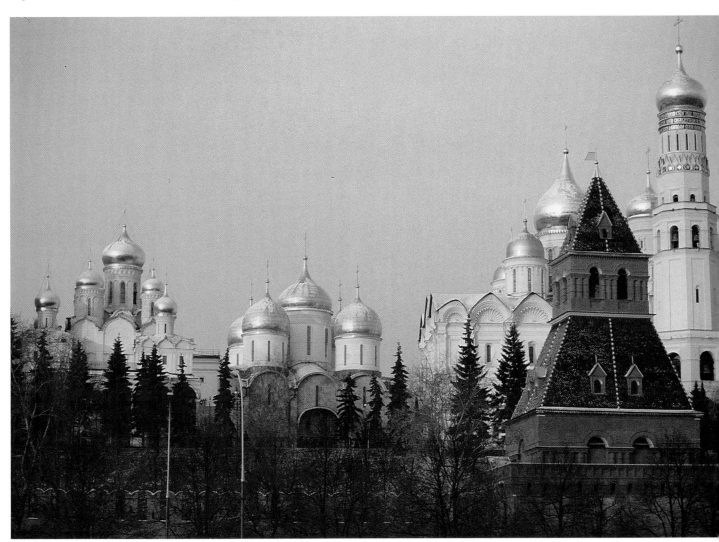

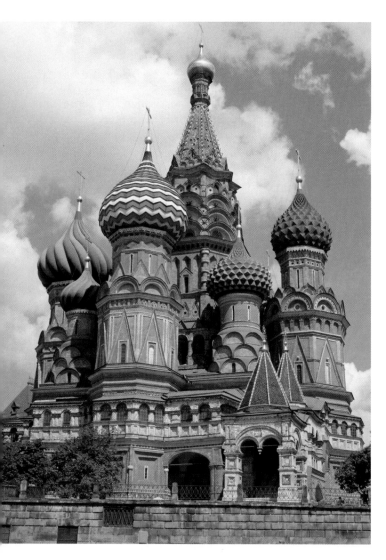

Figure 20.6 Barma and Posnik, Cathedral of St. Basil, 1555–60, Red Square, Moscow. This Russian Baroque church has become a landmark identifying Moscow in the way that the Eiffel Tower symbolizes Paris.

The central part of St. Basil is flanked by four large octagonal chapels on the cathedral's main axes and four additional, smaller polygonal chapels situated in the angles between them. Right in the center of the eight onion-domed towers is the tallest spire of the central church, and to the left, its belfry. It was in the seventeenth century that the polychrome decoration was painted onto the cupolas.

LITERATURE AND DRAMA

One of the glories of Russian art is the development of the Russian novel in the middle to late nineteenth century. Of the many novels written during this half-century period, those of Fyodor Dostoyevsky and Leo Tolstoy tower above the rest. Among the most accom-

plished of realist writers, they wrote novels on a grand scale, covering all aspects of Russian culture and society. Another important figure is the dramatist and short-story writer, Anton Chekhov, who wrote realist plays that capture both the demise of an aristocratic world and the rise of a new modern, industrial, and even socialist one.

Fyodor Dostoyevsky. FYODOR DOSTOYEVSKY [doss-toh-YEF-skee] (1821–1881) was the son of a Moscow doctor and landowner who was murdered by his serfs when Fyodor was eighteen. After studying military engineering, Dostoyevsky spent a year in the army before taking up a literary career, the most dramatic event of which was his arrest and imprisonment for conspiring to set up a secret printing press and discussing political and social ideas banned by the tsarist regime. After eight months, Dostoyevsky was sentenced to death, only to receive a last-minute reprieve; his sentence was commuted to four years of hard labor and an additional four years of military service. His prison reading was restricted to the New Testament, which he read avidly, and which informs the novels he wrote upon his release, especially *Crime and Punishment* (1866) and *The Brothers Karamazov* (1881).

Dostoyevsky's life was filled with other crises, including the death of his first wife from tuberculosis, the death of his beloved brother, Mikhail, and that of his infant daughter. In addition, he was constantly beset by financial troubles. It is hardly surprising, one might argue, that his works usually focus on a tormented, neurotic, or psychologically disturbed character or group of related characters. His ability to probe beneath the surface and reveal the competing forces within the psyche brought him the admiration of Freud and other modern thinkers.

Dostoyevsky's realism (which he described as a "higher realism") is underpinned by the psychological rather than the social. His interest lies not so much in presenting a panorama of Russian urban life, but in probing the tensions and anxieties that animate and motivate behavior.

His narrative impulse is richly dramatic, realizing itself forcefully in scenes of conflict. The interview scenes with the ax-murderer Raskolnikov and the detective Porfiry Petrovich in *Crime and Punishment* exemplify the drama inherent in his dialogue. Raskolnikov's behavior throughout the novel reflects Dostoyevsky's acute understanding of human psychology, and reveals the author's belief that any transgression of the moral law—in Raskolnikov's case, murder—no matter how reasonable it may appear, results in the guilt of a tormented conscience. The punishment is internal, undeniable, and tortuous.

Leo Tolstoy. LEO TOLSTOY [TOHL-stoy] (1828–1910) was born into an aristocratic world, one replete with the trappings of high society, including servants, fine cuisine, extravagant clothing, and the manifold opportunities that come with great wealth. As a young man, Tolstoy studied oriental languages at the University of Kazan, but left without taking a degree, returning to run the family estate in Yosnaya Polyana, south of Moscow.

War and Peace, considered by many his greatest work, was published in 1869. Set in the Napoleonic age, the novel explores the nature of history and the role that great men play in influencing the development of historical events. The book combines speculation on philosophical questions, such as necessity and free will, causation, and human destiny, with social concerns, such as agrarian reform. It also dramatizes ideas about the nature of the Russian state, as well as being a chronicle of the lives of several Russian families, with an emphasis on the philosophy of marriage. The novel contrasts the glories of nature and the simple life with the superficiality and artifice of civilization, celebrating the natural, privileging intuition over analysis, and emphasizing hope in the basic goodness of life rather than more studied forms of civilized learning and behavior.

During the writing of his second masterpiece, *Anna Karenina* (1873–1877), Tolstoy experienced a moral and religious crisis that set him on a course that would change his life irrevocably. *Anna Karenina* possesses all the realism of Tolstoy's earlier novel, but during its writing, the author began to have doubts about the book's secular emphasis, and so introduced a tone of moral criticism into the work, not only of Anna's adultery, but also of other characters' violations of society's moral norms. Even so, Tolstoy keeps the didactic impulse from overwhelming his literary artistry. Although he disapproves of Anna's adulterous behavior, he portrays her as a powerfully attractive woman, the site of struggle between his artistic sympathy and his moral judgment.

Anton Chekhov. The finest examples of Russian drama are the plays of its foremost dramatist, ANTON CHEKHOV [CHECK-off] (1860–1904). A short-story writer as well as a playwright, Chekhov began publishing fiction and sketches in newspapers and journals while studying medicine, in order to help support his large family. His fiction was well received, far better, initially, than the plays he would begin writing in the 1880s. Although Chekhov is celebrated as a major influence for later writers such as James Joyce and Ernest Hemingway, his plays are heralded in their own right as Modernist masterpieces and as precursors of important trends in modern theater.

Chekhov's plays, such as *The Three Sisters* and *The Cherry Orchard*, lack the intense melodramatic character of those by other realist dramatists, such as Henrik Ibsen. They don't tell stories, nor do they build toward tragic climaxes. Instead, Chekhov creates characters that are very lifelike in their inability to find happiness, their uncertainty about the future, and their indecisiveness in achieving their desires.

Because Chekhov was writing at a time when the old social order in Russia was dying, his plays have often been seen as dramatizations of the disappearance of the land-owning gentry as a source of authority and cultural value. Yet the playwright's interest lies in human nature, in individuals caught in a world undergoing great transformation. The characters in plays like *The Three Sisters* and *The Cherry Orchard* are neither heroes nor villains. They do not operate as mouthpieces for the dramatist's views. Indeed, their very inability to articulate their feelings, or even to act on them, adds poignancy to their suffering. Chekhov's insight into the truths of human experience is unmatched in modern drama.

MUSIC

Before Peter the Great's Europeanization drive in the eighteenth century, Russian music consisted primarily of religious and folk music. After the Tsar's return from the West, however, European music, particularly that composed during the eighteenth and nineteenth centuries, greatly influenced what was being produced in Russia. Among the composers who were able to synthesize the two musical styles were Modest Mussorgsky, whose operas commemorate great Russian leaders, and Peter Ilyich Tchaikovsky, whose ballets, operas, symphonies, and chamber works made him an internationally acclaimed figure.

Modest Mussorgsky. Supporting himself by working as a government clerk, MODEST MUSSORGSKY [moo-ZORG-skee] (1839–1881) composed relatively few works, though each reflected important qualities of the Russian national character. Mussorgsky led the school of Russian nationalist music in the 1860s that incorporated elements of Russian folk music into its compositions and used ancient Russian church modes in addition to the Western major and minor scales.

Most prominent among Mussorgsky's works is *Boris Godunov*, an opera that reveals the human soul in all its profundity. *Boris Godunov* is based on a poem by the Russian ALEXANDER PUSHKIN (1799–1837). It is in four acts and opens with a prologue that contains two important choral scenes, set in front of the Kremlin churches, which convey the national and religious spirit of old Russia. Mussorgsky includes the sound of the church bells, almost as important an emblem of Russian religious fervor as religious icons.

Peter Tchaikovsky. If Mussorgsky is to be considered one of the most nationalistic of Russian composers, PETER ILYICH TCHAIKOVSKY [cheye-KOV-skee] (1840–1893) can be said to be one of the most European. Tchaikovsky is best known for his ballet music, such as *Swan Lake*, *Sleeping Beauty*, and *The Nutcracker*. His work exhibits a gift for melodic invention and demonstrates his skill as an orchestrator, highlighting the tonal color and

Cross Currents

THE BALLETS RUSSES

*B*allet as a dance form did not originate in Russia, but it certainly flourished there. The most influential nineteenth-century choreographer in Russia was the French-born MARIUS PETIPA [PET-ee-pah] (1819–1910), who worked for the Tsar in St. Petersburg. Petipa collaborated with Tchaikovsky on both *Sleeping Beauty* and *The Nutcracker* to create two of the most popular ballets ever. After Petipa, Michel Fokine rose to prominence and became the principal choreographer of the Ballets Russes, a Russian dance company set up in Paris under the direction of the impresario SERGEI DIAGHILEV [dee-AHG-uh-LEF] (1872–1929), who was responsible for popularizing ballet throughout Europe.

Diaghilev set himself the goal of bringing Russian culture to the attention of the West, moving to Paris to do so. In 1906, he held a large-scale exhibition of Russian art, and in 1907 he began a series of concerts of Russian music. It was his presentation of Mussorgsky's *Boris Godunov* in 1908 that dazzled Western audiences with its originality and splendor. In 1909, he ventured a second season, which featured some ballets that included scenes from Borodin's opera *Prince Igor*, arranged for dancers rather than singers. The Russian ballerina Tamara Karsavina and her male counterpart, Vaslav Nijinsky, so stunned and enthralled Parisian audiences that they streamed onto the stage during the intermission of the first performance.

With dancers like Nijinsky and choreographers that included George Balanchine, and with set designs commissioned by painters such as Pablo Picasso and Henri Matisse, the Ballets Russes brought together a wealth of talent from a wide range of cultures and art forms. Composers who produced music for the Russian ballet included Claude Debussy, Maurice Ravel, and the Russian Serge Prokofiev.

The international acclaim of Russian ballet was furthered when George Balanchine defected from Russia in 1924, and eventually came to the United States in 1933 to choreograph. He founded and directed his own company, The New York City Ballet, and his own school. Here, Balanchine created a style of ballet that suited the American ethos—fast, sleek, conceptual, and thoroughly modern. During the Communist era, many dancers, including Rudolf Nureyev and Mikhail Barishnikov, defected from the Soviet Union to enjoy the artistic freedom of the West, much to the delight of Western audiences

---

varied expressive qualities of the full range of orchestral instruments. In its sense of drama and intense emotion, Tchaikovsky's music shares important affinities with other nineteenth-century Romantic composers from France, Italy, Germany, and Austria.

THE REVOLUTION AND AFTER

The influence of the West on Russia, so evident in St. Petersburg, was counterbalanced by later political developments that undermined the autocratic monarchy of the Tsars. The Russian Revolution officially began when the last Russian Tsar, Nicholas II, abdicated in 1917. However, it had in fact started earlier, on Bloody Sunday, January 9, 1905, when government troops fired on a peaceful demonstration by workers outside the Winter Palace in St. Petersburg. The workers quickly organized themselves into "soviets," or councils of workers elected in the factories, while the police responded swiftly by arresting dissenters. Most leaders were either sent to Siberia or chose self-imposed exile, as did Lenin, removing himself with many others to Switzerland.

Yet it was World War I that precipitated the real crisis. The Russian army was crushed in the fight with Germany, resulting in over five million casualties between 1914 and 1917. Germany penetrated deep into western Russia. The flow of refugees into Moscow could almost not be supported.

In February 1917, popular demonstrations forced Nicholas from power. (He and his family were later executed on the night of July 16, 1918.) A democracy was promised, the nature of which was to be determined by a constituent assembly, elected by the people at the earliest opportunity. From February to October 1917, Russia was ruled by a provisional government, but in October, to cries of "all power to the soviets," the Bolshevik party seized power, led by VLADIMIR ILYICH LENIN (1870–1924). The Bolsheviks were Marxists—that is, those who believed in the writings of Karl Marx (see Chapter 17) and called for a new society ruled by the proletariat, the working class. In Marx and Engels's words, from *The Communist Manifesto*: "In place of the old bourgeois society, with its classes and class antagonisms, we shall have an association, in which the free development of each is the condition for the free development of all."

Within a few months, Russia was embroiled in a bitter civil war, which would last for three years. The war pitted the Red Army of the working proletariat against the White Army of the anti-Bolshevik bourgeoisie. The Reds won, but since Britain and France had openly supported the Whites, and Japan and the United States had sent troops to Siberia, the new Bolshevik government was almost totally isolated from the West. It nationalized almost all industry, organizing the workers, and created what it called a "dictatorship of the proletariat." Yet a deep economic crisis soon followed, and Lenin, recognizing that he had moved too quickly, inaugurated a New Economic Policy (NEP) in 1921, legalizing private trade, abandoning the nationalization of industry, and allowing the private sector of the economy to reestablish itself. It was a full retreat from Communist principles, but one necessitated, Lenin believed, by reality.

Meanwhile, the new Soviet bureaucracy began to establish itself. Rising to the position of General Secretary of the Bolshevik party was JOSEPH STALIN (1879–1953). When Lenin died in 1924, Stalin overcame his rival LEON TROTSKY (1879–1940) and took over, making it clear that the primary goal of the Soviet Union was industrialization. His Five-Year Plan, implemented in 1929, modernized the country and built the basic structure of Soviet society, which remained intact until December 1991.

The Russian Revolution created a new order that affected not only Russians, but other peoples around the globe. Its complex web of causes included popular grievances, radical ideas espoused by intellectuals, idealism coupled with a lust for power, and a breakdown of public order. Its consequences included helping to prevent the restoration of peace after World War I—which contributed to the rise of Nazi Germany and the outbreak of World War II—and increasing world tension throughout the twentieth century, resulting in a "cold war."

Figure 20.7 Kazimir Malevich, *White on White*, 1918, oil on canvas, 31 × 31" (78.7 × 78.7 cm), Museum of Modern Art, New York. Malevich's Suprematism is a type of Cubism taken to the extreme, Cubism in its most minimal form.

REVOLUTIONARY ART

Taking their lead from the avant-garde movements in Europe, particularly Cubism and Futurism, Russian artists reacted to the Revolution with an almost frenetic zeal. Early in 1918, the Soviet Department of Fine Arts (IZO) was formed with a view to organizing the arts. Native Russians in Europe were called back to Russia to lead the way. Marc Chagall was appointed Commissar of Art in his hometown of Vitebsk, and for the first anniversary of the Revolution, in October 1918, he covered the city's buildings with the Cubist shapes, green cows, and flying horses for which he is famous. Vassily Kandinsky returned home to Moscow from Germany to develop the art program at the Institute of Artistic Culture. But the young native painters of the Revolution wanted nothing to do with the expressive impulses of either Chagall or Kandinsky.

Kazimir Malevich. Chagall's art school in Vitebsk was taken over in 1919 by a young revolutionary artist named KAZIMIR MALEVICH [MAH-lay-vich] (1878–1935), who informed Chagall that his work was old-fashioned and irrelevant. Malevich called himself a "Suprematist."

His paintings were based solely on the simplest of geometric forms, particularly the square. "In order to free art from the ballast of objectivity," he wrote, "I took refuge in the square." His was thus a "nonobjective" art, an art freed of personal emotion, but one that dealt with such basic forms that it spoke, he believed, a universal language. In *White on White* (fig. 20.7), of 1918, a white square floats sideways on a white field. For Malevich, the painting embodied "pure energy" and "pure mind." It was a painting that antithetically opposed the materialist aesthetic that had defined bourgeois art. The square floats above the other square field of the canvas as though in boundless space, suggesting an infinite regression, as if the white square of the canvas is itself set upon another white square, the white field of "pure mind." When Lenin died in 1924, Malevich proposed a cube for his mausoleum. The cube, he said, "is the symbol of eternity . . . the view that Lenin's death is not death, that he is alive and eternal, is symbolized in a new object, taking its form as a cube."

El Lissitzky. Malevich's collaborator in Vitebsk was Lazar Markovich Lisitskii, known as EL LISSITZKY [lih-ZIT-skee] (1890–1941). Together they renamed the school "Unovis," meaning College of the New Art. An engineer by training, El Lissitzky created a kind of art that he labeled "Prouns," which stands for "Projects for the establishment [or affirmation] of a new art" and which he described as "changing-stations between painting and architecture." *Proun 99* (fig. 20.8), of 1924, is dogmatically two-dimensional, but the perspective grid at the bottom and the floating quality of the cube suggest

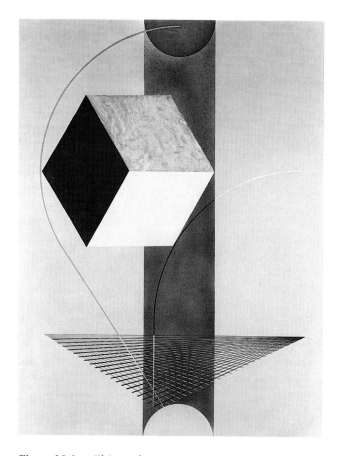

Figure 20.8 El Lissitzky, *Proun 99*, 1924, water soluble and metallic paint on wood, 50¼ × 39″ (129 × 99.1 cm), Yale University Art Gallery, New Haven, Connecticut. El Lissitzky was one of Russia's chief contacts with the West.

three-dimensional space as well. Even as Prouns recede, they simultaneously seem to project forward into the viewer's space.

FILM

One of the great figures of cinematic history, SERGEI EISENSTEIN [EYE-zen-stine] (1898–1948) was a film theorist as well as a film director. His wideranging knowledge of history, philosophy, science, and the arts is reflected in his films. For Eisenstein, film was the most complete of the arts. It included all the various artistic expressions of conflict—the kinetic conflict of dance, the visual conflict of painting, the verbal conflict of literature and theater, and the conflicts of character essential to fiction and drama.

A masterful editor, Eisenstein built his films shot by shot and frame by frame, calculating the dramatic tension until it finally exploded on film. Eisenstein achieved striking effects with lighting, time lapses, designs, and backgrounds in various camera shots, using narratives that were loosely structured and episodic in construction.

In his silent film *Battleship Potemkin*, first shown in 1926, Eisenstein dramatizes the mutiny on board the tsarist ship *Potemkin* in 1905, and the ensuing street demonstrations in the port of Odessa. Eisenstein was commissioned to make the film as part of the twentieth anniversary celebrations of the 1905 Revolution. Eisenstein structures his film like a symphony. The first section presents the bloody mutiny and the conditions that precipitated it. The second provides a respite as the ship drops anchor in the harbor after the

Timeline 20.2 The Russian Revolution and after.

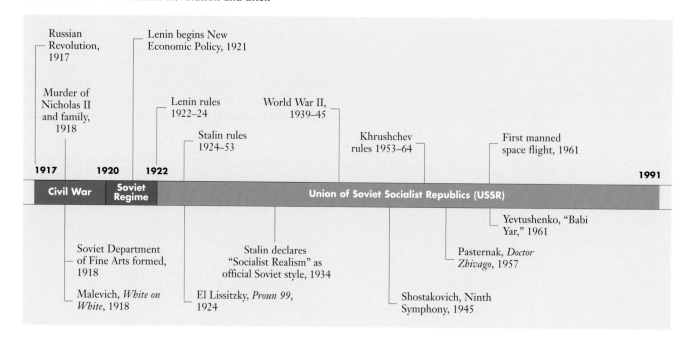

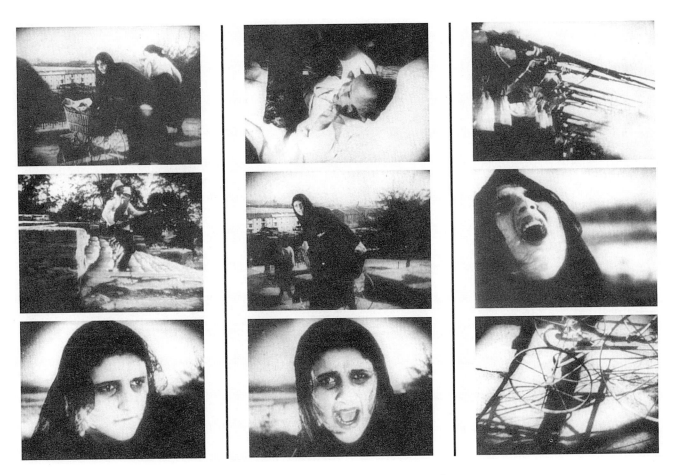

Figure 20.9 These consecutive film stills from Sergei Eisenstein's *Battleship Potemkin* (1924) reveal the director's dramatic use of close-up and of the contrast between human and inanimate images.

revolt. Following this lull, a third section focuses on the people of Odessa. Here Eisenstein creates his most brilliant editing effects, alternating between the panic-stricken and defenseless masses who support the mutinous sailors and the Cossack soldiers, armed with bayonets, who march relentlessly through the crowd, massacring those who fall in their path. The final section shows the ship returning to sea, with cheers coming from other ships in the fleet. It marks a call to action.

Eisenstein's Odessa sequence (fig. 20.9) includes a formal technique called **montage**, a set of edited units of impression used to achieve dramatic effect or, here, to increase tension in the viewer to the point of "emotional saturation." Eisenstein believed that viewer tension would find release in an emotional bonding with the victims, whose oppression he depicted on screen. Yet, for all its stunning formal innovations, the film is an intentional and whole-hearted attempt at propaganda and was made to legitimize and celebrate the Revolution.

KHRUSHCHEV'S RUSSIA

Until his death in 1953, Stalin ruled Russia with an iron hand, largely through the use of secret police who, in turn, filled prison and labor camps with political dissenters. In the Great Purge of 1937–38, Stalin eliminated Russia's ruling intelligentsia, replacing it with a new one. Hundreds of Soviet officials were convicted and executed. In June 1937, every Red Army top commander was shot. Each member of Lenin's government was either killed or committed suicide. By the end of 1938, at least a million Russians were in prison, another 8.5 million had been sent to prison camps, and nearly 700,000 had been executed. Henceforth, nobody questioned Stalin's rule.

Soon after Stalin's death, however, things changed. NIKITA KHRUSHCHEV [KROOS-cheff] (1894–1971) was named party secretary, and Lavrenty Beria, Stalin's chief of the secret police, was executed for treason. Khrushchev emptied the prisons and labor camps, returning the people to their homes. In 1956, he officially denounced Stalin, proclaiming a return to "Leninist norms."

Connections

ART AS POLITICS

An art as abstract as that of Malevich and El Lissitzky might seem ineffectual as a political tool, but it was in fact conceived in quite the opposite terms, as a means of bringing art to the masses. In the late nineteenth century, a number of St. Petersburg artists, calling themselves the Wanderers, sought to champion the newly emancipated peasant class by bringing art to the people through traveling exhibitions. This initiative of popularizing art took a new form soon after the disturbances of 1905, when the Bolsheviks began to use wall posters extensively: they were inexpensive, and their visual impact appealed directly to the mostly illiterate masses. By 1917, the poster was a major Russian art form. El Lissitzky's *Beat the Whites with the Red Wedge* (fig. 20.10), of 1919, is a perfect example. Using basic geometric shapes, the Red Army is represented by the triangle that pierces the circular form, which in turn represents the White Army. In starkly figured elements, the active Reds invade the passive Whites. The sense of aggression, originating both figuratively and literally from "the left," is unmistakable.

Such propaganda art was soon disseminated throughout Russia; primarily by means of Agit-trains. Agit-trains consisted of seven or eight railway cars sent to various places "to establish ties between the localities and the center, to agitate, to carry out propaganda, to bring information, and to supply literature." Each was also equipped with a film projector. The peasants were fascinated by film, and Lenin quickly realized the power of the medium in propaganda terms. Sitting on the train, the people watched newsreels of Lenin and in doing so were not merely entertained, but also indoctrinated in the Bolshevik cause.

At first, the Agit-trains were decorated with abstract Russian art, but the peasants objected strongly. They were repainted with pictures of soldiers, workers, and peasants, a development that foreshadowed the fate of Russian modernist art as a whole. It seemed that abstraction did not speak to the masses after all. At the end of the first Five-Year Plan in 1932, Stalin outlawed all independent artistic organizations, and in 1934 he proclaimed "Socialist Realism" as the official Soviet style. Abstraction was permanently banned in the Soviet Union.

Figure 20.10   El Lissitzky, *Beat the Whites with the Red Wedge*, 1919, lithograph, $20\frac{7}{8} \times 27\frac{1}{2}''$ (53 × 70 cm), Stedelijk Van Abbemuseum, Eindhoven, The Netherlands. Russian poster design would soon begin to incorporate photographic images in photomontages that addressed the people even more directly.

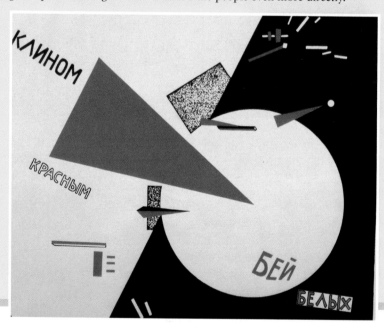

THE LITERATURE OF DISSENT

Khrushchev's de-Stalinization of Russia extended to literature and the other arts. The period became known among artists as "the thaw." A novel by BORIS PASTERNAK [PASS-ter-nack] (1890–1960), chronicling the life of a Russian doctor through World War I and the Revolution, entitled *Dr. Zhivago*, was accepted for publication in the Soviet Union and in Italy. But the novel offended Khrushchev, perhaps because of its author's Jewish origins or its central character's avowed individualism, and so the Soviet censors changed their minds. After the novel's publication in the West, Pasternak was awarded the Nobel Prize for Literature. Threatened with exile if he accepted, he turned it down.

By 1963, however, the atmosphere had thawed even more. ALEXANDER SOLZHENITSYN [sol-zhuh-NEET-sin] (b. 1918) wrote a short autobiographical novel, entitled *One Day in the Life of Ivan Denisovich*, about life in one of Stalin's labor camps, and it was accepted for publication. Khrushchev, who was personally responsible for its acceptance, viewed the book as a tool in his campaign against the legacy of Stalin. For the first time, the camps that haunted the Soviet imagination were talked about in print. Solzhenitsyn himself continued to write about Stalin's Russia, but his next novel, *The First Circle*, completed after Krushchev had been removed from power, was denied publication by the censors, and in 1974 he was expelled from the Soviet Union. In 1970, he accepted the Nobel Prize for Literature, deeply offending the Soviet leadership.

Two years before Solzhenitsyn was to publish *One Day in the Life*, a twenty-eight-year-old poet named EVGENY YEVTUSHENKO [yiv-tuh-SHEN-koh] (b. 1933) published a poem entitled "Babi Yar" in Moscow's *Literary Gazette*. The poem caused an immediate sensation. Babi Yar is a large ravine on the northern edge of the city of Kiev, where, during World War II, German SS troops buried over 100,000 Russian Jews and Communist officials. There were Soviet plans to build a sports stadium on the site, a decision that Yevtushenko found callous and believed was informed by the anti-Semitism of Soviet leadership.

THE MUSIC OF DISSENT

Reading Yevtushenko's poem in the *Literary Gazette*, the composer DMITRI DMITRYEVICH SHOSTAKOVICH [shos-tah-KOH-vich] (1906–1975) was deeply moved and immediately set it to music. Yevtushenko was delighted, and four more poems were quickly added to the set, one for each of the five movements of the composer's Thirteenth Symphony.

A veteran of the Soviet musical scene, Shostakovich had been composing symphonies since the 1920s. His work tended to move back and forth between the kind of grand public statements demanded by Stalin and more private, personal expressions. The Thirteenth Symphony is one of the latter, and Stalinist factions in the government swiftly moved to suppress its first performance, scheduled for December 18, 1962.

Just a few weeks earlier, on December 1, Khrushchev had flown into a rage at an exhibition of Russian avant-garde art, calling the artists "abstractionists and pederasts." On December 17, the day before the premiere, Khrushchev convened an assembly of writers and artists at the Kremlin. He attacked the abstract painters and sculptors again and then began to denounce Shostakovich. "Shostakovich," he proclaimed, "his music's nothing but jazz—it gives you a belly ache." Yevtushenko, who was present, leaped to the defense of the artists. "Who would deny," he asked, "that there are great artists amongst the abstractionists? Can we exclude Picasso?" Khrushchev responded with a Stalinist proverb: "The grave straightens out even the hunchbacked." Yevtushenko boldly replied, addressing the leader by his first names, "Nikita Sergeevich, we have come a long way since the time when only the grave straightened out hunchbacks. Really, there are other ways." The symphony went ahead as planned, but after its second performance, it was banned. Khrushchev was ousted from power in 1964 by Leonid Brezhnev and the "thaw" came to an official end.

READINGS

❧ **Fyodor Dostoyevsky**
from *The Brothers Karamazov*

The following passage is the opening chapter of The Brothers Karamazov *(1881). Here, Dostoyevsky creates drama and interest while introducing the characters and supplying the preliminary information necessary for understanding them. Even though the chapter compresses a considerable amount of information and condenses a long stretch of narrative time in a few pages, a wide range of action and feeling is apparent. The ironic tone of the first book, "A Nice Little Family," provides an example of the way the author blends humor, pathos, and tragedy in the novel. Dostoyevsky also implicates his readers in the action, inviting them in the final lines of the chapter to consider the extent to which the world of his characters is theirs as well.*

Alexey Fyodorovitch Karamazov was the third son of Fyodor Pavlovitch Karamazov, a landowner well known in our district in his own day, and still remembered among us owing to his gloomy and tragic death, which happened thirteen years ago, and which I shall describe in its proper place. For the present I will only say that this "landowner"—for so we used to call him, although he hardly spent a day of his life on his own estate—was a strange type, yet one pretty frequently to be met with, a type abject and vicious and at the same time senseless. But he was one of those senseless persons who are very well capable of looking after their worldly affairs, and, apparently, after nothing else. Fyodor Pavlovitch, for instance, began with next to nothing; his estate was of the smallest; he ran to dine at other men's tables, and fastened on them as a toady, yet at his death it appeared that he had a hundred thousand roubles in hard cash. At the same time, he was all his life one of the most senseless, fantastical fellows in the whole district. I repeat, it was not stupidity—the majority of these fantastical fellows are shrewd and intelligent enough—but just senselessness, and a peculiar national form of it.

He was married twice, and had three sons, the eldest, Dmitri, by his first wife, and two, Ivan and Alexey, by his second. Fyodor Pavlovitch's first wife, Adelaïda Ivanovna, belonged to a fairly rich and distinguished noble family, also landowners in our district, the Miüsovs. How it came to pass that an heiress, who was also a beauty, and moreover one of those vigorous, intelligent girls, so common in this generation, but sometimes also to be found in the last, could have married such a worthless, puny weakling, as we all called him, I won't attempt to explain. I knew a young lady of the last "romantic" generation who after some years of an enigmatic passion for a gentleman, whom she might quite easily have married at any moment, invented insuperable obstacles to their union, and ended by throwing herself one stormy night into a rather deep and rapid river from a high bank, almost a precipice, and so perished, entirely to satisfy her own caprice, and to be like Shakespeare's Ophelia. Indeed, if this precipice, a chosen and favourite spot of hers, had been less picturesque, if there had been a prosaic flat bank in its place, most likely the suicide would never have taken place. This is a fact, and probably there have been not a few similar instances in the last two or three generations. Adelaïda Ivanovna Miüsov's action was similarly, no doubt, an echo of other people's ideas, and was due to the irritation caused by lack of mental freedom. She wanted, perhaps, to show her feminine independence, to override class distinctions and the despotism of her family. And a pliable imagination persuaded her, we must suppose, for a brief moment, that Fyodor Pavlovitch, in spite of his parasitic position, was one of the bold and ironical spirits of that progressive epoch, though he was, in fact, an ill-natured buffoon and nothing more. What gave the marriage piquancy was that it was preceded by an elopement, and this greatly captivated Adelaïda Ivanovna's fancy. Fyodor Pavlovitch's position at the time made him specially eager for any such enterprise, for he was passionately anxious to make a career in one way or another. To attach himself to a good family and obtain a dowry was an alluring prospect. As for mutual love it did not exist apparently, either in the bride or in him, in spite of Adelaïda Ivanovna's beauty. This was, perhaps, a unique case of the kind in the life of Fyodor Pavlovitch, who was always of a voluptuous temper, and ready to run after any petticoat on the slightest encouragement. She seems to have been the only woman who made no particular appeal to his senses.

Immediately after the elopement Adelaïda Ivanovna discerned in a flash that she had no feeling for her husband but contempt. The marriage accordingly showed itself in its true colours with extraordinary rapidity. Although the family accepted the event pretty quickly and apportioned the runaway bride her dowry, the husband and wife began to lead a most disorderly life, and there were everlasting scenes between them. It was said that the young wife showed incomparably more generosity and dignity than Fyodor Pavlovitch who, as is now known, got hold of all her money up to twenty-five thousand roubles as soon as she received it, so that those thousands were lost to her for ever. The little village and the rather fine town house which formed part of her dowry he did his utmost for a long time to transfer to his name, by means of some deed of conveyance. He would probably have succeeded, merely from her moral fatigue and desire to get rid of him, and from the contempt and loathing he aroused by his persistent and shameless importunity. But, fortunately, Adelaïda Ivanovna's family intervened and circumvented his greediness. It is known for a fact that frequent fights took place between the husband and wife, but rumour had it that Fyodor Pavlovitch did not beat his wife but was beaten by her, for she was a hot-tempered, bold, dark-browed, impatient woman, possessed of remarkable physical strength. Finally, she left the house and ran away from Fyodor Pavlovitch with a destitute divinity student, leaving Mitya, a child of three years old, in her husband's hands. Immediately Fyodor Pavlovitch introduced a regular harem into the house, and abandoned himself to orgies of drunkenness. In the intervals he used to drive all over the province, complaining tearfully to each and all of Adelaïda Ivanovna's having left him, going into details too disgraceful for a husband to mention in regard to his own married life. What seemed to gratify him and flatter his self-love most was to play the ridiculous part of the injured husband, and to parade his woes with embellishments.

"One would think that you'd got a promotion, Fyodor Pavlovitch, you seem so pleased in spite of your sorrow," scoffers said to him. Many even added that he was glad of a new comic part in which to play the buffoon, and that it was simply to make it funnier that he pretended to be unaware of his ludicrous position. But, who knows, it may have been simplicity. At last he succeeded in getting on the track of his runaway wife. The poor woman turned out to be in Petersburg, where she had gone with her divinity student, and where she had thrown herself into a life of complete emancipation. Fyodor Pavlovitch at once began bustling about, making preparations to go to Petersburg, with what object he could not himself have said. He would perhaps have really gone; but having determined to do so he felt at once entitled to fortify himself for the journey by another bout of reckless drinking. And just at that time his wife's family received the news of her death in Petersburg. She had died quite suddenly in a garret, according to one story, of typhus, or as another version had it, of starvation. Fyodor Pavlovitch was drunk when he heard of his wife's death, and the story is that he ran out into the street and began shouting with joy, raising his hands to Heaven: "Lord, now lettest Thou Thy servant depart in peace," but others say he wept without restraint like a little child, so much so that people were sorry for him, in spite of the repulsion he inspired. It is quite possible that both versions were true, that he rejoiced at his release, and at the same time wept for her who released him. As a general rule, people, even the wicked, are much more naïve and simple-hearted than we suppose. And we ourselves are, too.

↩ **Anton Chekhov**
from *The Cherry Orchard*

The first producer of The Cherry Orchard *(1904), Konstantin Stanislavsky, the director of the Moscow Art Theater, staged it as a tragedy. Chekhov, however, repeatedly insisted it was a comedy. The opening act of the play contains elements of both as the characters exhibit, in turn, humor and sadness, gaiety and pain. It is this combination of comedy and pathos, along with the apparent nonsequiturs of the dialogue and the shifting grounds of the plot, which contribute to the play's elusive realism.*

LIUBOFF ANDREIEVNA RANEVSKAYA—*A landowner.*
ANYA—*Her daughter, aged seventeen.*
VARYA—*Her adopted daughter, aged twenty-seven.*
LEONID ANDREIEVITCH GAIEFF—*Liuboff Andreievna's brother.*
YERMOLAI ALEXEIEVITCH LOPAKHIN—*A merchant.*
PETER SERGEIEVITCH TROFIMOFF—*A student.*
BORIS BORISOVITCH SEMYONOFF-PISHCHIK—*A landowner.*
CHARLOTTA IVANOVNA—*A governess.*
SEMYON PANTELEIEVITCH YEPIKHODOFF—*A clerk.*
DUNYASHA (AVDOTYA FYODOROVNA)—*A maidservant.*
FIRCE—*An old footman, aged eighty-seven.*
YASHA—*A young footman.*
A TRAMP.
A STATION-MASTER.
POST-OFFICE CLERK.
GUESTS.
A SERVANT.

The action takes place on Mme. Ranevskaya's estate.

ACT ONE.

A room still called the nursery. One of the doors leads into Anya's room. It is almost sunrise of a day in May. The cherry-trees are in bloom, but the chill of early morning is in the garden. The windows are shut. Dunyasha enters with a candle, and Lopakhin with a book in his hand.

LOPAKHIN The train has arrived, thank God. What's the time?

DUNYASHA It will soon be two. [*Blows out candle*] It is already light.

LOPAKHIN How late was the train? At least two hours. [*Yawns and stretches himself*] I certainly made a fool of myself! I came here on purpose to meet them at the station, and then overslept myself ... in my chair. It's a pity. I wish you'd called me.

DUNYASHA I thought you'd gone. [*Listening*] I think I hear them coming.

LOPAKHIN [*listens*] No ... They have to collect their baggage and so on ... [*Pause*] Liuboff Andreievna has been living abroad for five years; I can't know what she'll be like now ... She's a good sort—an easy, simple person. I remember when I was a boy of fifteen, my father, who is dead—he used to keep a shop in the village here—hit me with his fist, and my nose bled ... We had gone into the yard for something or other, and he was a little drunk. Liuboff Andreievna, as I remember her now, was still young, and very slight, and she took me to the wash stand here in this very room, the nursery. She said, "Don't cry, my small peasant, all wounds heal at last." [*Pause*] ... Small peasant! My father was a peasant, true, but here I am in a white vest and brown shoes ... like a pearl in an oyster shell. I'm rich now, with lots of money, but just think about it and examine me, and you'll find I'm still a peasant to the core. [*Turns over the pages of his book*] Here I've been reading this book, but I understood nothing. I read and fell asleep. [*Pause*]

DUNYASHA The dogs didn't sleep all night; they feel that their masters are coming.

LOPAKHIN What's the matter with you, Dunyasha ...

DUNYASHA My hands are shaking. I am going to faint.

LOPAKHIN You're too sensitive, Dunyasha. You dress just like a lady, and you do your hair like one, too. You shouldn't. You must remember your place in life.

YEPIKHODOFF [*enters with a bouquet. He wears a short jacket and brilliantly polished boots which squeak audibly. He drops the bouquet as he enters, then picks it up*] The gardener sent these; says they're to go into the dining-room. [*Gives the bouquet to Dunyasha.*]

LOPAKHIN And you'll bring me some kvass.

DUNYASHA Yes, sir. [*Exit.*]

YEPIKHODOFF There's a frost this morning—three degrees, and the cherry-trees are all in flower. I can't approve of our climate. [*Sighs*] I can't. Our climate refuses to favor us even this once. And, Yermolai Alexeievitch, allow me to say to you, in addition, that I bought myself a pair of boots two days ago, and I beg to assure you that they squeak in a perfectly intolerable manner. What shall I put on them?

LOPAKHIN Go away. You bore me.

YEPIKHODOFF Some misfortune happens to me every day. But I don't complain; I'm used to it, and I even smile at it. [*Dunyasha comes in and brings Lopakhin a glass of kvass*] I am going. [*Knocks over a chair*] There ... [*Triumphantly*] There, you see, if I may use the word, what circumstances I am in, so to speak. It is simply extraordinary. [*Exit.*]

DUNYASHA Let me confess to you, Yermolai Alexeievitch, that Yepikhodoff has proposed to me.

LOPAKHIN Ah!

DUNYASHA I don't know what to do about it. He's a nice young man, but every now and then, when he begins talking, you can't understand a word he says. It sounds sincere enough, only I can't understand it. I think I like him. He's madly in love with me. He's an unlucky man; every day something happens to him. We tease him about it. They call him "Two-and-twenty troubles."

LOPAKHIN [*listens*] There they come, I think.

DUNYASHA They're coming! What's the matter with me? I'm cold all over.

LOPAKHIN There they are, really. Let's go and meet them. Will she know me? We haven't seen each other for five years.

DUNYASHA [*excited*] I shall faint in a minute ... Oh, I'm fainting!

[*Two carriages are heard driving up to the house. Lopakhin and Dunyasha quickly go out. The stage is empty. There are noises in the adjoining rooms. Firce, leaning on a stick, walks quickly across the stage; he has just been to meet Liuboff Andreievna. He wears an old-fashioned livery and a tall hat. He is saying something to himself, but not a word can be made out. The noise backstage grows louder and louder. A voice is heard: "Let's go in there." Enter Liuboff Andreievna, Anya, and Charlotta Ivanovna leading a little dog on a chain, all dressed in traveling clothes, Varya in a long coat and with a kerchief on her head. Gaieff, Semyonoff-Pishchik, Lopakhin, Dunyasha with a parcel and an umbrella, and a servant with suitcases—all cross the room.*]

ANYA Let's go through here. Do you remember this room, mother?

LIUBOFF ANDREIEVNA [*joyfully, through her tears*] The nursery!

VARYA How cold it is! My hands are quite numb. [*To Liuboff Andreievna*] Your rooms, the white one and the violet one, are just as they used to be, mother.

LIUBOFF ANDREIEVNA My dear, beautiful nursery ... I used to sleep here when I was a baby. [*Kisses her brother, then Varya, then her brother again*] And Varya is just as she used to be, exactly like a nun. And I recognised Dunyasha. [*Kisses her.*]

GAIEFF The train was two hours late. There now; how's that for punctuality?

CHARLOTTA [*to Pishchik*] My dog eats nuts, too.

PISHCHIK [*astonished*] Just imagine! [*All leave except Anya and Dunyasha.*]

DUNYASHA We did have to wait for you! [*Takes off Anya's cloak and hat.*]

ANYA For four nights on the journey I didn't sleep ... I'm cold.

DUNYASHA You left during Lent, when it was snowing and frosty, but now? Darling! [*Laughs and kisses her*] We did have to wait for you, my darling pet!…I must tell you at once, I can't wait a minute.

ANYA [*listlessly*] Something else now … ?

DUNYASHA The clerk, Yepikhodoff, proposed to me after Easter.

ANYA Always the same … [*Puts her hair straight*] I've lost all my hairpins … [*She is very tired, and even staggers as she walks.*]

DUNYASHA I don't know what to think about it. He loves me, he loves me so much!

ANYA [*looks into her room; in a gentle voice*] My room, my windows, as if I'd never left! I'm at home! To-morrow morning I'll get up and run out into the garden … Oh, if I could only sleep! I didn't sleep the whole journey, I was so restless.

DUNYASHA Peter Sergeievitch came two days ago.

ANYA [*joyfully*] Peter!

DUNYASHA He sleeps in the bath-house, he lives there. He said he was afraid he'd be in the way. [*Looks at her watch*] I should call him, but Varvara Mihkailovna told me not to. "Don't wake him," she said.

[*Enter Varya, a bunch of keys hanging from her belt.*]

VARYA Dunyasha, coffee, quick. Mother wishes some.

DUNYASHA In a moment. [*Exit.*]

VARYA Well, you've come, thank God. Home again. [*Caressing her*] My darling is home again! My pretty one is back at last!

ANYA I had an awful time, I tell you.

VARYA I can just imagine it!

ANYA I went away in Holy Week; it was very cold then. Charlotta talked the whole way and would go on performing her tricks. Why did you force her on me?

VARYA You couldn't go alone, darling, at seventeen!

ANYA We went to Paris; it's cold there and snowing. I talk French perfectly dreadfully. My mother lives on the fifth floor. I go to her, and find her there with several Frenchmen, women, an old abbé with a book, and everything wreathed in tobacco smoke and the whole place so uninviting. I suddenly became very sorry for mother—so sorry that I took her head in my arms and hugged her and wouldn't let her go. Then mother started hugging me and crying …

VARYA [*weeping*] Don't say any more, don't say any more …

ANYA She's already sold her villa near Mentone; she has nothing left, nothing. And I haven't a kopeck, either; we only just managed to get here. And mother won't understand! We had dinner at a station; she asked for all the expensive things, and tipped the waiters one ruble each. And Charlotta too. Yasha demands a share, too—It is simply awful. Mother has a footman now, Yasha; we've brought him along.

ANYA How's business? Has the interest been paid?

VARYA Not much chance of that.

ANYA Oh God, oh God …

VARYA The place will be sold in August.

ANYA Oh God …

LOPAKHIN [*looks in at the door and moos*] Moo! [*Exit.*]

VARYA [*through her tears*] I'd like to … [*Shakes her fist.*]

ANYA [*embraces Varya, softly*] Varya, has he proposed to you?

[*Varya shakes her head*] But he loves you … Why don't you decide? Why do you keep on waiting?

VARYA I'm afraid it will all come to nothing. He's a busy man. I'm not his sort … he pays no attention to me. Bless the man; I don't wish to see him … But everybody talks about our marriage, everybody congratulates me, and there's nothing in it at all, its all like a dream. [*A different voice*] You have a brooch that looks like a bee.

ANYA [*wistfully*] Mother bought it. [*Goes into her room, and talks lightly, like a child*] In Paris I went up in a balloon!

VARYA My darling has come back, my pretty one is home again! [*Dunyasha has already returned with the coffee-pot and is making coffee*] I go about all day, looking after the house, and I think all the time, if only you could marry a rich man, I'd be happy and would go away somewhere by myself, perhaps to Kieff … or to Moscow, and so on, from one holy place to another. I'd tramp and tramp. That would be splendid!

ANYA The birds are singing in the garden. What time is it now?

VARYA It must be getting on towards three. It's time you went to sleep, darling. [*Goes into Anya's room*] Splendid!

[*Enter Yasha with a plaid shawl and a traveling bag.*]

YASHA [*crossing the stage; politely*] May I go this way?

DUNYASHA I hardly recognised Yasha. You have changed abroad.

YASHA Hm … and who are you?

DUNYASHA When you went away I was only so high. [*Showing with her hand*] I'm Dunyasha, the daughter of Fyodor Kozoyedoff. You don't remember?

YASHA Oh, you small cucumber! [*Looks round; and embraces her. She screams and drops a saucer. Yasha goes out quickly.*]

VARYA [*in the doorway, in an angry voice*] What's that?

DUNYASHA [*through her tears*] I've broken a saucer.

VARYA. It may bring luck.

ANYA [*coming out of her room*] We must tell mother that Peter's here.

VARYA I told them not to call him.

ANYA [*thoughtfully*] Father died six years ago, and a month later my brother Grisha was drowned in the river—such a dear little boy of seven! Mother couldn't bear it; she went away, away, without looking round … [*Shudders*] How I understand her; if only she knew! [*Pause*] And Peter Trofimoff was Grisha's tutor, he might remind her …

[*Enter Firce in a short jacket and white vest. Goes to the coffee-pot.*]

FIRCE Madame is going to have a bite here. [*He is preoccupied, putting on white gloves*] Is the coffee ready? [*To Dunyasha, severely*] You!

DUNYASHA Oh, dear me …! [*Leaving hurriedly.*]

FIRCE [*fussing round the coffee-pot*] Oh, you bungler … [*Murmurs to himself*] Back from Paris … the master went to Paris once … in a carriage … [*Laughs.*]

VARYA What are you mumbling, Firce?

FIRCE I beg your pardon? [*Joyfully*] The mistress is home again. I've lived to see her! I don't care if I die now … [*Weeps with joy.*]

[*Enter Liuboff Andreievna, Gaieff, Lopakhin, and Semyonoff-Pishchik, the latter in a long jacket of thin cloth and loose trousers. Gaieff, coming in, moves his arms and body about as if he were playing billiards.*]

LIUBOFF ANDREIEVNA Let me remember now. Red into the corner! Twice into the center!

GAIEFF Right into the pocket! Once upon a time you and I, sister, both slept in this room, and now I'm fifty-one; it does seem strange.

LOPAKHIN Yes, time does fly.

GAIEFF What?

LOPAKHIN I said that time does fly.

GAIEFF It smells of patchouli here.

ANYA I'm going to bed. Good-night, mother. [*Kisses her.*]

LIUBOFF ANDREIEVNA My dear little child. [*Kisses her hand*] Glad to be at home? I can't get over it.

ANYA Good-night, uncle.

GAIEFF [*Kisses her face and hands*] God be with you. Now you do resemble your mother! [*To his sister*] You were just like her at her age, Liuba.

[*Anya gives her hand to Lopakhin and Pishchik and goes out shutting the door behind her.*]

LIUBOFF ANDREIEVNA She's awfully tired.

PISHCHIK It's a very long journey.

VARYA [*to Lopakhin and Pishchik*] Well, gentlemen, its getting on toward three. High time to retire.

LIUBOFF ANDREIEVNA [*laughs*] You're just the same as ever, Varya. [*Draws her close and kisses her*] I'll have some coffee now; then we'll all go. [*Firce lays a cushion under her feet*] Thank you, dear. I'm used to coffee. I drink it day and night. Thank you, dear old man. [*Kisses Firce.*]

VARYA I'll go and see whether they've brought in all the luggage. [*Exit.*]

LIUBOFF ANDREIEVNA Is it really I who am sitting here? [*Laughs*] I feel like jumping about and waving my arms. [*Covers her face with her hands*] But suppose I'm dreaming! God knows I love my own country, I love it dearly; I couldn't look out of the railway carriage, I cried so much. [*Through her tears*] Still, I must have my coffee. Thank you, Firce. Thank you, dear old man. I'm so glad you're still with us.

FIRCE The day before yesterday.

GAIEFF He doesn't hear well.

LOPAKHIN I have to go to Kharkoff by the five o'clock train. I'm awfully sorry! I should like to have a look at you, to gossip a little. You're as fine-looking as ever.

PISHCHIK [*breathes heavily*] Even finer-looking ... dressed in Paris fashion ... confound it all.

LOPAKHIN Your brother, Leonid Andreievitch, says I'm a snob, a usurer, but that is absolutely nothing to me. Let him talk. Only I do wish you would believe in me as you once did, that your wonderful, touching eyes would look at me as they used to. Merciful God! My father was the serf of your grandfather and your own father, but you—more than anybody else—did so much for me once upon a time that I've forgotten everything and love you as if you were one of my own family ... and even more.

LIUBOFF ANDREIEVNA I can't sit still, I can't! [*Jumps up and walks about in great excitement*] I'll never survive this happiness ... You can laugh at me; I'm a silly woman ... My dear little cupboard. [*Kisses cupboard*] My little table.

GAIEFF Nurse died during your absence.

LIUBOFF ANDREIEVNA [*sits and drinks coffee*] Yes, God rest her soul. I heard by letter.

GAIEFF And Anastasia died, too. Peter Kosoy has left me and now lives in town with the Commissioner of Police. [*Takes a box of candy out of his pocket and sucks a piece.*]

PISHCHIK My daughter, Dashenka, sends her love.

LOPAKHIN I wish to say something very pleasant, very delightful, to you. [*Looks at his watch*] I'm going away at once, I haven't much time ... but I'll tell you all about it in two or three words. As you already know, your cherry orchard is to be sold to pay your debts, and the sale is arranged for August 22; but you needn't be alarmed, dear madam, you may sleep in peace; there's a way out. Here's my plan. Please listen carefully! Your estate is only thirteen miles from town, the railway runs past it and if the cherry orchard and the land by the river are broken up into building parcels and are then leased as villa sites, you'll have at least twenty-five thousand rubles a year income.

GAIEFF How utterly absurd!

LIUBOFF ANDREIEVNA I don't understand you at all, Yermolai Alexeievitch.

LOPAKHIN You will get twenty-five rubles a year for each dessiatin from the leaseholders at the very least, and if you advertise now, I'm willing to bet that you won't have a vacant parcel left by the autumn; they'll all go. In a word, you're saved. I congratulate you. Only, of course, you'll have to straighten things out carefully ... For instance, you'll have to pull down all the old buildings, this house, which is of no use to anybody now, and cut down the old cherry orchard.

LIUBOFF ANDREIEVNA Cut it down? My dear man, you must forgive me, but you don't understand anything at all. If there's anything interesting or remarkable in the whole province, it's this cherry orchard of ours.

LOPAKHIN The only remarkable thing about the orchard is its great size. It bears fruit only every other year, and even then you don't know what to do with the cherries; nobody buys any.

GAIEFF This orchard is mentioned in the "Encyclopaedia."

LOPAKHIN [*looks at his watch*] If we can't think of anything and don't make up our minds, then on August 22 both the cherry orchard and the whole estate will be sold at auction. Make up your mind! I swear there's no other way out. You may believe me!

FIRCE In the old days, forty or fifty years ago, they dried the cherries, soaked them and pickled them, and made jam, and it used to happen that ...

GAIEFF Be quiet, Firce.

FIRCE And then we'd send the dried cherries in carts to Moscow and Kharkoff. And money! And the dried cherries were soft, juicy, sweet, and fragrant. They knew the way ...

LIUBOFF ANDREIEVNA How was it done?

FIRCE They've forgotten. Nobody remembers.

PISHCHIK [*to Liuboff Andreievna*] What about Paris? Eh? Did you eat frogs?

LIUBOFF ANDREIEVNA I ate crocodiles.

PISHCHIK Just imagine!

LOPAKHIN Formerly there were only the gentry and the laborers, in the villages, and now the people who live in villas have arrived. All towns now, even small ones, are surrounded by villas. And its safe to say that in twenty years' time the villa residents will have increased tremendously. At present they sit on their balconies, and drink tea, but it may well happen that they'll commence to cultivate their patches of land, and then your cherry orchard will be happy, rich, glorious.

GAIEFF [angry] What nonsense!

[Enter Varya and Yasha.]

VARYA There are two telegrams for you, mother dear. [Picks out a key and noisily unlocks an antique cupboard] Here they are.

LIUBOFF ANDREIEVNA They're from Paris…[Tears them up without reading them] I'm through with Paris.

GAIEFF And do you know, Liuba, how old this cupboard is? A week ago I pulled out the bottom drawer; I looked and saw numbers carved in it. That cupboard was made exactly a hundred years ago. What do you think of that? What? We could celebrate its jubilee. It hasn't a soul of its own, but still, say what you will, it's a fine piece of furniture.

PISHCHIK [astonished] A hundred years … Just imagine!

GAIEFF Yes … it's a genuine thing. [Examining it] My dear and honored cupboard! I congratulate you on your career, which has for more than a hundred years been devoted to the noble ideals of good and justice; your silent call to productive labor has not decreased in the hundred years [sweeping] during which you have inspired in our generation virtue and courage and faith for a better future, holding before our eyes lofty ideals and the knowledge of a common consciousness. [Pause.]

LOPAKHIN Yes.

LIUBOFF ANDREIEVNA You're just the same as ever, Leon.

GAIEFF [a little confused] Off the white on the right, into the corner pocket. Red ball goes into the center pocket!

LOPAKHIN [looks at his watch] It's time I went.

YASHA [giving Liuboff Andreievna her medicine] Will you take your pills now?

PISHCHIK You shouldn't take medicines, dearest; they do you neither harm nor good … Give them to me, dearest. [Takes the pills, turns them out into the palm of his hand, blows on them, puts them into his mouth, and drinks some kvass] There!

LIUBOFF ANDREIEVNA [frightened] You're mad!

PISHCHIK I've swallowed all the pills.

LOPAKHIN You greedy man! [aAl laugh.]

FIRCE They were here in Easter week and ate half a pailful of cucumbers … [Mumbles.]

LIUBOFF ANDREIEVNA What does he mean?

VARYA He's been mumbling away for three years. We're used to that.

YASHA Senile decay.

[Charlotta Ivanovna crosses the stage, dressed in white: she is very thin and tightly laced; she has a lorgnette at her waist.]

LOPAKHIN Excuse me, Charlotta Ivanovna, I haven't bidden you welcome yet. [Tries to kiss her hand.]

CHARLOTTA [takes her hand away] If you let people kiss your hand, then they'll want your elbow, then your shoulder, and then…

LOPAKHIN I'm out of luck to-day! [All laugh] Show us a trick, Charlotta Ivanovna!

LIUBOFF ANDREIEVNA Charlotta, do a trick for us!

CHARLOTTA It's not necessary. I must go to bed. [Exit.]

LOPAKHIN We shall see each other in three weeks. [Kisses Liuboff Andreievna's hand] NOW, good-bye. It's time I went. [To Gaieff] See you again. [Kisses Pishchik] Au revoir. [Gives his hand to Varya, then to Firce and to Yasha] I don't want to go away. [To Liuboff Andreievna] If you think about the villas and come to a decision, just let me know, and I'll raise a loan of 50,000 rubles at once. Think about it seriously.

VARYA [angrily] Do go, now!

LOPAKHIN I'm going, I'm going … [Exit.]

GAIEFF Snob. Still, I beg pardon … Varya's going to marry him, he's Varya's young man.

VARYA Don't talk too much, uncle.

LIUBOFF ANDREIEVNA Why not, Varya? I should be glad of it. He's a good man.

PISHCHIK To speak the honest truth … he's a worthy man … And my Dashenka … also says that … she says lots of things. [Snores, but wakes up again at once] But still, dear madam, if you could lend me … 240 rubles … to pay the interest on my mortgage to-morrow …

VARYA [frightened] We haven't it, we haven't it!

LIUBOFF ANDREIEVNA It's quite true. I've nothing at all.

PISHCHIK You'll manage somehow. [Laughs] I never lose hope. I used to think, "Everything's lost now. I'm a dead man," when, lo and behold, a railway was built across my land … and they paid me for it. And something else will happen to-day or to-morrow. Dashenka may win 20,000 rubles … she's got a lottery ticket.

LIUBOFF ANDREIEVNA The coffee's all gone, we can go to bed.

FIRCE [brushing Gaieff's trousers; in an insistent tone] You are wearing the wrong trousers again. What am I to do with you?

VARYA [quietly] Anya's asleep. [Opens window quietly] The sun has risen already; it isn't cold. Look, mother, dear; what lovely trees. And the air! The starlings are singing!

GAIEFF [opens the other window] The whole garden is white. You haven't forgotten, Liuba? There's that long avenue going straight, straight, like an arrow; it shines on moonlight nights. Do you remember? You haven't forgotten?

LIUBOFF ANDREIEVNA [looks into the garden] Oh, my childhood, days of my innocence! In this nursery I used to sleep; I used to look out from here into the orchard. Happiness used to wake with me every morning, and then it was just as it is now; nothing has changed. [Laughs with joy] It's all, all white! Oh, my orchard! After the dreary autumns and the cold winters, you're young again, full of happiness, the angels of heaven haven't left you … If only I could take this strong burden from my breast and shoulders, if I could forget my past!

GAIEFF Yes, and they'll sell this orchard to pay off the debts. How strange it seems!

LIUBOFF ANDREIEVNA Look, there's my dead mother walking in the orchard ... dressed in white! [*Laughs with joy*] That's she.

GAIEFF Where?

VARYA God be with you, mother dear!

LIUBOFF ANDREIEVNA Nobody is there; I thought I saw somebody. On the right, at the turning by the summer-house, a little white tree bent down, resembling a woman. [*Enter Trofimoff in a worn student uniform and spectacles*] What a marvelous garden! White masses of flowers, the blue sky ...

TROFIMOFF Liuboff Andreievna! [*She looks round at him*] I only wish to pay my respects to you, and I'll go away. [*Kisses her hand warmly*] I was told to wait till the morning, but I didn't have the patience. [*Liuboff Andreievna looks surprised.*]

VARYA [*crying*] It's Peter Trofimoff.

TROFIMOFF Peter Trofimoff, once the tutor of your Grisha ... Have I changed so much? [*Liuboff Andreievna embraces him and cries softly.*]

GAIEFF [*confused*] That's enough, that's enough, Liuba.

VARYA [*weeps*] But I told you, Peter, to wait till to-morrow.

LIUBOFF ANDREIEVNA My Grisha ... my boy ... Grisha ... my son.

VARYA What are we to do, dear mother? It's the will of God.

TROFIMOFF [*softly, through his tears*] It's all right, it's all right.

LIUBOFF ANDREIEVNA [*still weeping*] My boy's dead; he was drowned. Why? Why, my friend? [*Softly*] Anya's asleep in there. I am speaking so loudly, making so much noise ... Well, Peter? What's made you look so bad? Why have you grown so old?

TROFIMOFF In the train an old woman called me a decayed gentleman.

LIUBOFF ANDREIEVNA You were quite a boy then, a jolly little student, and now your hair has grown thin and you wear spectacles. Are you really still a student? [*Goes to the door.*]

TROFIMOFF I suppose I shall always be a student.

LIUBOFF ANDREIEVNA [*kisses her brother, then Varya*] Well, let's go to bed ... And you've grown older, Leonid.

PISHCHIK [*follows her*] Yes, we must go to bed ... Oh, my gout! I'll stay the night here. If only, Liuboff Andreievna, my dear, you could get me 240 rubles to-morrow morning—

GAIEFF Still the same story.

PISHCHIK Two hundred and forty rubles ... to pay the interest on the mortgage.

LIUBOFF ANDREIEVNA I haven't any money, dear man.

PISHCHIK I'll give it back ... it's a small sum .

LIUBOFF ANDREIEVNA Well then, Leonid will give it to you ... Let him have it, Leonid.

GAIEFF By all means; hold out your hand.

LIUBOFF ANDREIEVNA Why not? He wants it; he'll give it back.

[*Liuboff Andreievna, Trofimoff, Pishchik, and Firce go out. Gaieff, Varya, and Yasha remain.*]

GAIEFF My sister hasn't lost the habit of throwing money away. [*To Yasha*] Don't come near me; you smell like a chicken-coop!

YASHA [*grins*] You are just the same as ever, Leonid Andreievitch.

GAIEFF Really? [*To Varya*] What's he saying?

VARYA [*to Yasha*] Your mother has come from the village; she's been sitting in the servants' room since yesterday, and wishes to see you ...

YASHA Bless the woman!

VARYA Shameless man.

YASHA A lot of use there is in her coming. She might just as well have come to-morrow. [*Exit.*]

VARYA Mother hasn't altered a bit, she's just as she always was. She'd give away everything, if the idea only entered her head.

GAIEFF Yes ... [*Pause*] If there's any illness for which people have a remedy of remedies, you may be sure that particular illness is incurable. I work my brains as hard as I can. I've several remedies, very many, and that really means I've none at all. It would be nice to inherit a fortune from somebody, it would be nice to marry off our Anya to a rich man, it would be nice to go to Yaroslavl and try my luck with my aunt the Countess. My aunt is very, very rich.

VARYA [*weeps*] If only God would help us.

GAIEFF Don't cry. My aunt's very rich, but she doesn't like us. My sister, in the first place, married a lawyer, not an aristocrat ... [*Anya appears in the doorway*] She not only married a man who was not an aristocrat, but she behaved in a way which cannot be described as proper. She's nice and kind and charming and I'm very fond of her, but say what you will in her favor and you still have to admit that she's bad; you can feel it in her slightest movements.

VARYA [*whispers*] Anya's in the doorway.

GAIEFF Really? [*Pause*] It's curious, something's blown into my right eye ... I can't see out of it properly. And on Thursday, when I was at the District Court ...

[*Enter Anya.*]

VARYA Why aren't you in bed, Anya?

ANYA I can't sleep. It's no use.

GAIEFF My darling! [*Kisses Anya's face and hands*] My child. [*Crying*] You're not my niece, you're my angel, you're my all ... Believe in me, believe ...

ANYA I do believe you, uncle. Everybody loves and respects you ... but, uncle dear, you should say nothing, no more than that. What were you saying just now about my mother, about your own sister! Why did you say such things?

GAIEFF Yes, yes. [*Covers his face with her hand*] Yes, really, it was terrible. Save me, my God! And only just now I made a speech before a cupboard ... it's so silly! And only when I'd finished I knew how silly it was.

VARYA Yes, uncle dear, you really should say less. Keep quiet, that's all.

ANYA You'd be so much happier if you only kept quiet.

GAIEFF All right, I'll be quiet. [*Kisses their hands*] I'll be quiet. But let's talk business. On Thursday I was in the District Court, and a lot of us met there and we began to talk of this, that, and the other, and now I think I can arrange a loan to pay the interest to the bank.

VARYA If only God would help us!

GAIEFF I'll go on Tuesday. I'll talk to you about it again. [*To Varya*] Don't cry. [*To Anya*] Your mother will have a talk with Lopakhin; he, of course, won't refuse … And when you've rested you'll go to Yaroslavl to the Countess, your grandmother. So you see, we shall have three irons in the fire, and we shall be safe. We'll pay the interest. I'm certain. [*Puts some candy in his mouth*] I swear on my honor, on anything you wish, that the estate will not be sold! [*Excitedly*] I swear on my happiness! Here's my hand on it! You may call me a dishonorable sinner if I let it be sold at auction! I swear by all I am!

ANYA [*calm again and happy*] How good and clever you are, uncle. [*Embraces him*] I'm happy now! I'm happy! All's well!

[*Enter Firce.*]

FIRCE [*reproachfully*] Leonid Andreievitch, don't you fear God? When are you going to bed?

GAIEFF Soon, soon. You go away, Firce. I'll undress myself. Well, children, au revoir …! I'll tell you the details tomorrow, but let's go to bed now. [*Kisses Anya and Varya*] I'm a man of the eighties … People don't praise those years much, but I can still say that I've suffered for my beliefs. The peasants don't love me for nothing, I assure you. We have to learn how to understand the peasants! We should learn how…

VANYA You're doing it again, uncle!

VARYA Be quiet, uncle!

FIRCE [*angrily*] Leonid Andreievitch!

GAIEFF I'm coming, I'm coming … Go to bed now. Off two cushions into the center! I turn over a new leaf … [*Exit. Firce goes out after him.*]

ANYA I'm more quiet now. I don't wish to go to Yaroslavl, I don't like grandmother; but I'm calm now, thanks to uncle. [*Sits down.*]

VARYA It's time to go to sleep. I'll go. There have been amazing things happening here during your absence. In the old servants' quarter of the house, as you know, only the old people live—little old Yefim and Polya and Yevstigny, and Karp as well. They commenced letting tramps or the like spend the night there—I said nothing. Then I heard that they were saying I had ordered them to be fed on peas and nothing else; from meanness, you see … And it was all Yevstigny's doing. Very well, I thought, if that's what the matter is, just you wait. So I call Yevstigny … [*Yawns*] He comes. "What's this," I say. "Yevstigny, you old fool" … [*Looks at Anya*] Anya dear! [*Pause*] She's dozed off … [*Takes Anya's arm*] Let's go to bed … Come along! … [*Leads her*] My darling's gone to sleep! Come on … [*They go. In the distance, the other side of the orchard, a shepherd plays his pipe. Trofimoff crosses the stage and stops when he sees Varya and Anya*] Sh! She's asleep, asleep. Come on, dear.

ANYA [*quietly, half-asleep*] I'm so tired … I hear bells … uncle, dear! Mother and uncle!

VARYA Come on, dear, come on! [*They go into Anya's room.*]

TROFIMOFF [*deeply moved*] Sunshine! Springtime of my life!

Curtain.

Karl Marx and Friedrich Engels
from *The Communist Manifesto*

According to Karl Marx, the structure and values of a society are determined by the way it organizes the production of goods and services. Marx thought that an inescapable conflict existed between the classes in the capitalist system, in which those who owned and controlled the means of production (the bourgeoisie) would inevitably be in opposition to the people who worked for them (the proletariat or working class). He believed that the Industrial Revolution would mean more machines, which would mean, in turn, more workers. Thus, a greater and stronger proletariat would eventually overthrow the capitalists and redistribute the wealth in a just and classless society in which capital would be shared by everyone.

The Communist Manifesto (1848) was written by Marx in collaboration with Friedrich Engels, a German socialist who had once owned a factory in Manchester, England, and who exposed Marx to the economic conditions of the working class. It appealed to many in Russia who were disillusioned with the tsarist regime, and the Russian peasants, and workers were quick to embrace its ideals. The authors' urging seemed like a call to action: "Let the ruling classes tremble at a Communistic revolution. The proletarians have nothing to lose but their chains." Indeed, when they wrote, "Working Men of all Countries, Unite!," the workers did.

Bourgeois and Proletarians

The History of hitherto existing society is the history of class struggles

Freeman and slave, patrician and plebeian, lord and serf, guild-master and journeyman, in a word, oppressor and oppressed, stood in constant opposition to one another, carried on an uninterrupted, now hidden, now open fight, a fight that each time ended, either in a revolutionary re-constitution of society at large, or in the common ruin of the contending classes.

In the earlier epochs of history, we find almost everywhere a complicated arrangement of society into various orders, a manifold gradation of social rank. In ancient Rome we have patricians, knights, plebeians, slaves; in the Middle Ages, feudal lords, vassals, guild-masters, journeymen, apprentices, serfs; in almost all of these classes, again, subordinate gradations.

The modern bourgeois society that has sprouted from the ruins of feudal society has not done away with class antagonisms. It has but established new classes, new conditions of oppression, new forms of struggle in place of the old ones.

Our epoch, the epoch of the bourgeoisie, possesses, however, this distinctive feature: it has simplified the class antagonisms. Society as a whole is more and more splitting up into two great hostile camps, into two great classes directly facing each other: Bourgeoisie and Proletariat.

From the serfs of the Middle Ages sprang the chartered burghers of the earliest towns. From these burgesses the first elements of the bourgeoisie were developed.

The discovery of America, the rounding of the Cape, opened up fresh ground for the rising bourgeoisie. The East-Indian and Chinese markets, the colonisation of

America, trade with these colonies, the increase in the means of exchange and in commodities generally, gave to commerce, to navigation, to industry, an impulse never before known, and thereby, to the revolutionary element in the tottering feudal society, a rapid development.

The feudal system of industry, under which industrial production was monopolised by closed guilds, now no longer sufficed for the growing wants of the new markets. The manufacturing system took its place. The guild-masters were pushed on one side by the manufacturing middle class; division of labour between the different corporate guilds vanished in the face of division of labour in each single workshop.

Meantime the markets kept ever growing, the demand ever rising. Even manufacture no longer sufficed. Thereupon, steam and machinery revolutionised industrial production. The place of manufacture was taken by the giant, Modern Industry, the place of the industrial middle class, by industrial millionaires, the leaders of whole industrial armies, the modern bourgeois.

Modern industry has established the world-market, for which the discovery of America paved the way. This market has given an immense development to commerce, to navigation, to communication by land. This development has, in its turn, reacted on the extension of industry; and in proportion as industry, commerce, navigation, railways extended, in the same proportion the bourgeoisie developed, increased its capital, and pushed into the background every class handed down from the Middle Ages.

We see, therefore, how the modern bourgeoisie is itself the product of a long course of development, of a series of revolutions in the modes of production and of exchange.

Each step in the development of the bourgeoisie was accompanied by a corresponding political advance of that class. An oppressed class under the sway of the feudal nobility, an armed and self-governing association in the mediaeval commune; here independent urban republic (as in Italy and Germany), there taxable "third estate" of the monarchy (as in France), afterwards, in the period of manufacture proper, serving either the semi-feudal or the absolute monarchy as a counterpoise against the nobility, and, in fact, corner-stone of the great monarchies in general, the bourgeoisie has at last, since the establishment of Modern Industry and of the world-market, conquered for itself, in the modern representative State, exclusive political sway. The executive of the modern State is but a committee for managing the common affairs of the whole bourgeoisie.

The bourgeoisie, historically, has played a most revolutionary part.

The bourgeoisie, whenever it has got the upper hand has put an end to all feudal, patriarchal, idyllic relations. It has pitilessly torn asunder the motley feudal ties that bound man to his "natural superiors," and has left remaining no other nexus between man and man than naked self-interest, than callous "cash payment." It has drowned the most heavenly ecstasies of religious fervour, of chivalrous enthusiasm, of philistine sentimentalism, in the icy water of egotistical calculation. It has resolved personal worth into exchange value and in place of the numberless indefeasible chartered freedoms, has set up that single, unconscionable freedom—Free Trade. In one word, for exploitation, veiled by religious and political illusions, it has substituted naked, shameless, direct, brutal exploitation.

The bourgeoisie has stripped of its halo every occupation hitherto honoured and looked up to with reverent awe. It has converted the physician, the lawyer, the priest, the poet, the man of science, into its paid wage-labourers.

The bourgeoisie has torn away from the family its sentimental veil, and has reduced the family relation to a mere money relation

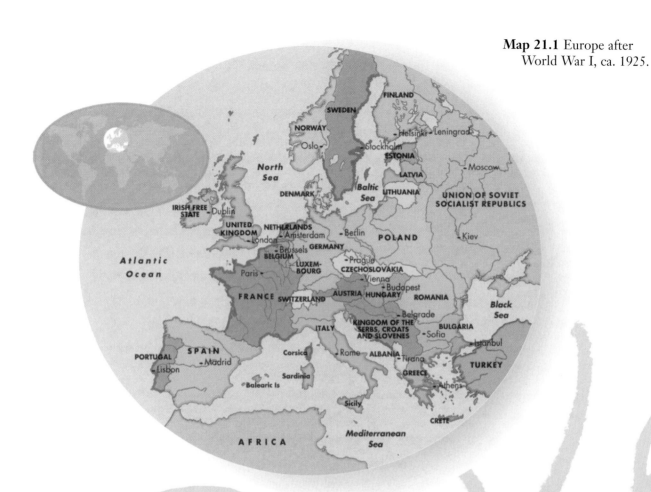

Map 21.1 Europe after
World War I, ca. 1925.

THE
AGE OF
ANXIETY

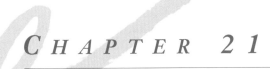

CHAPTER 21

↞ *The Great War and After*

↞ *Repression and Depression:*
The Thirties

Georgia O'Keeffe, *Yellow Calla (Detail)*, 1929, Smithsonian Institution, Washingon, D.C.

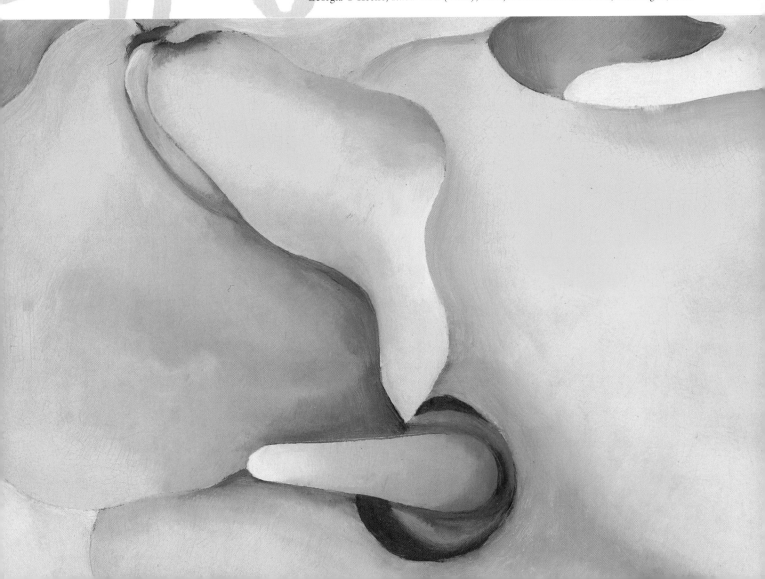

THE GREAT WAR AND AFTER

"On or about December 1910 human character changed," wrote Virginia Woolf, the English novelist and feminist. "All human relations shifted," Woolf noted, "those between masters and servants, husbands and wives, parents and children. And when human relations shift there is at the same time a change in religion, conduct, politics and literature." We do not know precisely what these changes were that Woolf was alluding to, but they were made more dramatic by the Great War (as World War I was then called), which began in August 1914. Another English novelist, D.H. Lawrence, wrote that "in 1915 the old world ended." The war gave new and frightening meaning to the radical cultural changes occurring in the early years of the twentieth century, creating what has been termed an "Age of Anxiety." It was a time of "disorder and early sorrow," as German writer Thomas Mann wrote in one of his stories. It was a world in which "things fall apart; the centre cannot hold," as the Irish poet William Butler Yeats noted. No one was sure what would happen next, but many were certain that it would be negative.

WORLD WAR I

In November 1912, Pablo Picasso made a collage depicting a Parisian café table. The work was named after a bottle of aperitif from the Balkans called Suze—*Glass and Bottle of Suze* (fig. 21.1). A piece of newspaper from *Le Journal* is also pasted onto the canvas. But the story in the newspaper belies the atmosphere of ease in the café. It describes the ongoing war in the Balkans, the advance of the Serbs into Macedonia, and, in particular, the outbreak of cholera among Turkish troops: "Before long I saw the first corpse," it reads. "Then I saw two, four, ten, twenty; then I saw a hundred corpses ... How many cholera victims did I come upon like this? Two thousand? Three thousand? I don't dare give an exact figure. Over a distance of about twenty kilometers, I saw cadavers strewing the cursed ground where a wind of death blows and I saw the dying march ... preparing themselves for combat. But I had seen nothing yet."

From 1912 to 1914, Europe became gripped by the developments in the Balkans. It seemed increasingly clear to all that, sooner or later, the entire continent would be involved. Then, on June 28, 1914, a Serbian nationalist named Gavrilo Princip assassinated the Habsburg archduke, Francis Ferdinand, heir to the throne of Austria and Hungary, and his wife, Sophie Chotek, on the street in Sarajevo, Bosnia. Within weeks, Europe was at war, the Central Powers (Austria, Hungary, Germany, Turkey, and later, Bulgaria) against the Allies (Serbia, Russia, France, and Britain, and later, the United States).

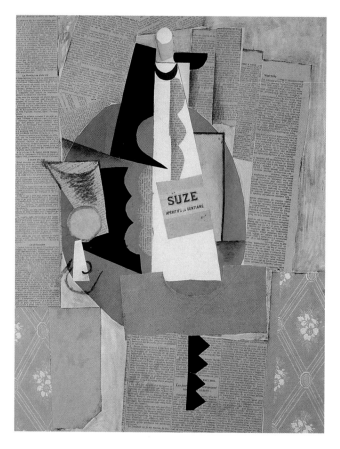

Figure 21.1 Pablo Picasso, *Glass and Bottle of Suze*, 1912, pasted papers, gouache, and charcoal on paper, $25\frac{2}{5} \times 19\frac{2}{3}$" (64.5 × 50 cm), Washington University Gallery of Art, St. Louis. For many years, collages such as this were interpreted in purely formal terms, as arrangements of objects in space, but the coincidence of the Balkan apertif and the material about the Balkan war in the newspaper fragments suggest that Picasso had more political concerns in mind.

It is hard to overstate the impact of the Great War on the public imagination in the West. It took the lives of over eight million soldiers in action, and many millions more through malnutrition and disease. A new brand of trench warfare created a kind of horror never before seen or endured. Along the Western Front, which extended from the English Channel to the Swiss border with Alsace, near Basel, hundreds of thousands of soldiers faced each other in parallel trenches across a stationary line. The distinguished British historian Charles Carrington (1897–1981) remembers life in the trenches on the Somme, as a young man barely twenty years of age:

> The killed and wounded were all lost by harassing fire, mostly on their way up or down the line. Once in position ... you could not show a finger by daylight, and by night every path by which you might be supposed to move was raked by machine-guns which had been trained on it by day ... If you could reach your

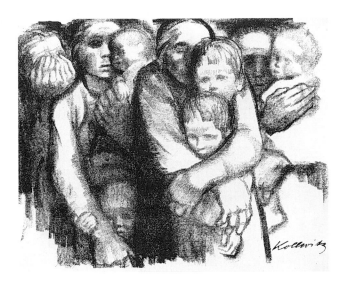

Figure 21.2 Käthe Kollwitz, *The Mothers*, 1919, lithograph, 17¾ × 23″ (45 × 58.4 cm), Philadelphia Museum of Art. Kollwitz captures the tragedy of World War I in this image of lower-class German mothers left to fend for themselves and their children after the war. The black-and-white medium emphasizes the harshness of the reality.

funk-hole and crouch in it, there was a fair chance of your coming out of it alive next day to run the gaunt-let … again. In your funk-hole, with no room to move, no hot food, and no chance of getting any, there was nothing worse to suffer than a steady drizzle of wintry rain and temperature just above the freezing point. A little colder and the mud would have been more manageable. Life was entirely numbed; you could do nothing. There could be no fighting since the combatants could not get at one another, no improve-ment of the trenches since any new work would instantly be demolished by a storm of shell-fire.

Another chronicler of the war, the German Erich Maria Remarque, described in the novel *All Quiet on the Western Front* (1929) the sense of doom that dominated the German lines: "Monotonously the lorries sway, monotonously come the calls, monotonously falls the rain. It falls on our heads and on the heads of the dead up the line, on the body of the little recruit with the wound that is so much too big for his hip; it falls on Kemerich's grave; it falls in our hearts." In describing the retreat from the Italian front in his novel *A Farewell to Arms* (1929), American writer Ernest Hemingway expressed how the war emptied life of meaning: "I had seen noth-ing sacred, and the things that were glorious had no glory, and the sacrifices were like the stockyard at Chicago if nothing was done with the meat except to bury it … Abstract words such as glory, honor, courage, or hallow were obscene." After the Great War, it seemed as if the whole world mourned, a mood evoked in this lithograph by the German artist KÄTHE KOLLWITZ [KOL-vits] (1867–1945) (fig. 21.2).

THE DADA MOVEMENT

The war had an immense impact on art. Profoundly affected by the destruction, a group of artists, writers, and musicians founded a new art movement—**Dada**. Beginning in Zurich and New York during the war, it flourished in Paris and Germany after it. Dada, from a nonsense word indicating a child's first utterance or "'Da, da' … 'yes, yes' to life," was meant to be as ambiguous as the war itself.

In Zurich, artists and intellectuals who had gathered to escape the war met regularly at the Café Voltaire as early as 1916. Swiss sculptor HANS ARP (1886–1966) defined Dada in the following way: "Repelled by the slaughterhouses of the world war, we turned to art. We searched for an elementary art that would, we thought, save mankind from the furious madness of these times." This it attempted to do in an irreverent manner. Arp himself made relief sculptures by dropping liquid into a series of small puddles, outlining each, and then cutting out wooden replicas and finally putting them together. His *Portrait of Tristan Tzara* (fig. 21.3) portrays his friend, a Dada poet, in exactly these terms. TRISTAN TZARA [ZAHR-ah] (1896–1963) wrote poems using these same "laws of chance." Tzara would cut up a news-paper article word by word, then draw the words out of a hat, and write a poem. Tzara also performed a kind of "noise" poetry at the Café Voltaire—"*bruitisme*," he called it, after the French word for "noise"—consisting

Figure 21.3 Hans Arp, *Portrait of Tristan Tzara*, 1916, relief of painted wood, 20⅛ × 19¾ × 4″ (51 × 50 × 10 cm), Musée d'Art et d'Histoire, Geneva, Switzerland. Before the war, Arp had been a contributor to Vassily Kandinsky's *Blaue Reiter* magazine.

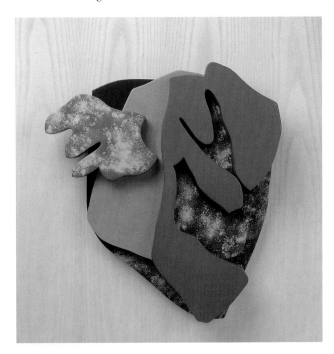

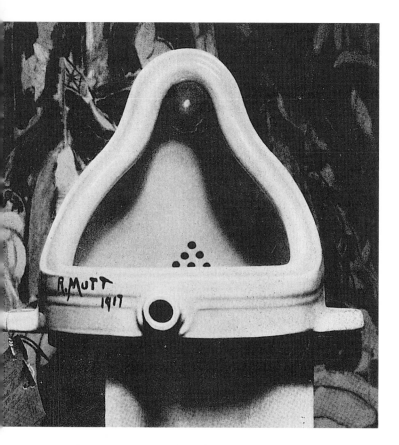

Figure 21.4 Marcel Duchamp, *Fountain*, porcelain urinal, exhibited 1917, height 24⅝″, (62.2 cm), photograph by Alfred Stieglitz, Philadelphia Museum of Art. Duchamp argued that he "created a new thought for that object" by forcing the viewer to see it in a new context. He labeled such works "ready-mades."

of vowels, consonants, and guttural sounds, strung together in a nonsense parody of German *Lieder* (songs). The Dadaists thought that if tradition had created the madness of the Great War, then tradition deserved no respect. The childlike, sometimes imbecilic behavior of the Dadaists was a conscious attempt to start again from square one.

Marcel Duchamp. One of the most important Dadaists, MARCEL DUCHAMP [doo-SHAH(n)] (1883–1968), worked as a painter before the conflict, but the war ended that. When Duchamp arrived in New York in 1915, he said that Dada meant "hobby horse" in French (yet another meaning), and claimed that he had picked the word at random from a French dictionary (yet another conflicting story of its origins). Duchamp saw Dada as a kind of "anti-art," one that embodied imagination, chance, and irrationality, and that opposed all recognized values in art and literature.

In 1917, Duchamp submitted a "sculpture" to the Independents exhibition in New York. Entitled *Fountain* (fig. 21.4), it was a porcelain urinal signed with a pseudonym, "R. Mutt." Needless to say, the piece caused an

uproar. Duchamp let it be known that he was "Mutt" himself, suggesting that what mattered most about a "work of art" was not aesthetic concerns, but who made it. Furthermore, the significance of the urinal changed in different contexts. It was one thing in a plumbing shop or bathroom, quite another on a plinth in an art exhibition. It seemed that where things were seen changed how they were understood or interpreted. Duchamp had, as sculptor, acted like a photographer. He had seen something mundane, and by reframing it, had revealed its aesthetic dimension.

Duchamp engaged in many other demonstrations and attacks on traditional aesthetics. He retouched a poster of Leonardo da Vinci's *Mona Lisa*, adding a mustache and goatee. He used puns in many of his works because he thought that wordplay undermined the stability of meaning, and in so doing encouraged new ways of seeing.

Kurt Schwitters. After the war, the Swiss Dada movement migrated to Germany. There, its most accomplished artist was KURT SCHWITTERS [SHVIT-ers] (1887–1948), who began working with junk and the vestiges of a destroyed German landscape. He

Figure 21.5 Kurt Schwitters, *Merz 600, Leiden*, 1923, collage, 6¼ × 5⅛″ (15.8 × 13 cm), Kunsthalle, Hamburg, Germany. Schwitters's impulse to make new art out of refuse was not limited to merely small-scale work. Beginning in 1923, he transformed his house in Hanover into a *Merzbau*, a large-scale sculptural environment made out of all manner of materials. It was destroyed by an Allied bomb in 1943.

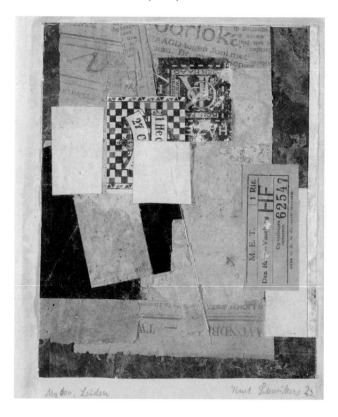

called his works "Merz," which derived from a fragment of advertisement that appeared in one of his collages. The collages were modeled after Picasso and Braque, but were far less oriented to the themes of the *belle époque* (music, wine, the daily news) and far more concerned with the new industrialized society and its discards. Indeed, it is possible to trace Schwitters's geographical movements from the ticket stubs and stamps included in his works. In this sense the works are autobiographical—*Merz 600* (fig. 21.5), of 1923, contains a stamp and ticket from The Hague in Holland. The basis of Schwitters's art is the contradiction between its arbitrary "junk" content and its sometimes stunning formal beauty. On the one hand, he said, "I favor nonsense ... up to now it has so seldom been given artistic form and for that reason I love nonsense." On the other, he noted, "Because I balance different kinds of material against one another, I have an advantage over oil painting, for in addition to evaluating color against color, line against line, form against form, and so on, I also evaluate material against material—wood against burlap, for example ... Every artist should be permitted to put together a picture out of nothing more than, say, blotting paper, as long as he knows how to give it form."

THE DE STIJL MOVEMENT

If Dada represents a negative or nihilistic reaction to World War I, **De Stijl** ("The Style" in Dutch), sometimes called **Neo-Plasticism**, represents an affirmative, hopeful response. Founded in 1917 in Holland, the movement sought to integrate painting, sculpture, architecture, and industrial design, and championed a "pure" abstraction, believing that in it universal harmony could be rediscovered. In the movement's first manifesto, the De Stijl artists wrote: "The war is destroying the old world with its contents ... The new art has brought forward what the new consciousness of the time contains: balance between the universal and the individual."

Piet Mondrian. The leading painter of the De Stijl school was PIET MONDRIAN [MON-dree-on] (1872–1944). Dutch by birth, he moved to Paris in 1912 and turned his attention to Cubism, which he quickly took to its logical conclusion. His work referred less and less to nature, until it finally became completely non-objective abstraction. *Pier and Ocean* (fig. 21.6), a drawing made in 1914, is almost completely abstract, yet the subject, taken from nature, is still recognizable. Mondrian has divided the surface into small sections, identifying the geometry in nature—not the solid three-dimensional geometry of

Figure 21.6 Piet Mondrian, *Composition No. 10: Pier and Ocean*, 1914, oil on canvas, 33½ × 42⅝" (85.1 × 106.7 cm), Kröller-Müller Museum, Otterlo, Netherlands. The vertical and the horizontal came to represent for Mondrian all the oppositions inherent in nature—from male and female to life and death—and the right angle was the sign of their unity and balance.

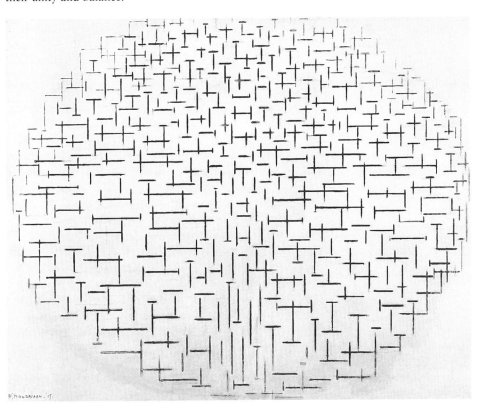

Timeline 21.1 The United States between the wars.

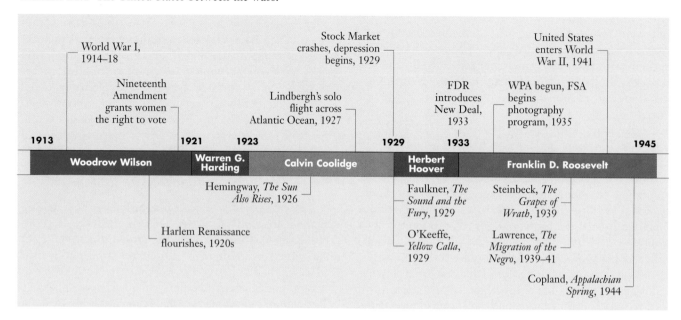

World War I,
1914–18

Nineteenth
Amendment
grants women
the right to vote

Stock Market
crashes, depression
begins, 1929

Lindbergh's solo
flight across
Atlantic Ocean, 1927

FDR
introduces
New Deal,
1933

WPA begun, FSA
begins
photography
program, 1935

United States
enters World
War II, 1941

| 1913 | | 1921 | 1923 | | 1929 | 1933 | | 1945 |

Woodrow Wilson | **Warren G. Harding** | **Calvin Coolidge** | **Herbert Hoover** | **Franklin D. Roosevelt**

Hemingway, *The Sun
Also Rises*, 1926

Harlem Renaissance
flourishes, 1920s

Faulkner, *The
Sound and the
Fury*, 1929

O'Keeffe,
Yellow Calla,
1929

Steinbeck, *The
Grapes of
Wrath*, 1939

Lawrence, *The
Migration of the
Negro*, 1939–41

Copland, *Appalachian
Spring*, 1944

Cézanne, but a two-dimensional plane geometry. Mondrian believed the flat plane was integral to painting and that it must be respected rather than falsified by perspective. Thus, Mondrian turns the pier and ocean into an arrangement of horizontal and vertical lines.

By 1920, Mondrian had defined a mature style, as seen in *Composition in Red, Yellow, and Blue* (fig. 21.7). Seeking

Figure 21.7 Piet Mondrian, *Composition in Red, Yellow, and Blue*, 1920, oil on canvas, $20\frac{1}{2} \times 23\frac{5}{8}''$ (52 × 60 cm), Stedelijk Museum, Amsterdam. Mondrian actually called his style Neo-Plasticism, but the name *De Stijl*, the title of the Dutch magazine that published not only his own but also the writings of other figures from the movement, is now generally used.

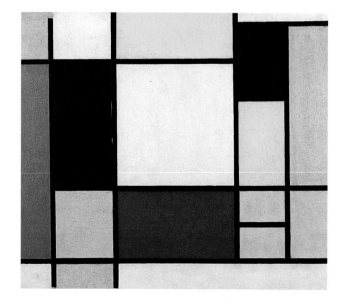

perfection within a strictly imposed set of limitations, Mondrian created a surface grid of horizontal and vertical lines; the rectangle and square are its basic shapes. The colors are restricted to the primary colors—red, yellow, and blue—plus black, white, and, in a few places, gray. Using these few elements, Mondrian established a sense of balance. As he would assert, while writing about a drawing of this time: "If one does not represent things, a place remains for the Divine."

THE SURREALISTS

As both Dada and De Stijl demonstrate, the spirit of the avant-garde in the arts continued to thrive after the war. Paris was its center, "the laboratory of ideas in the arts," as the American poet Ezra Pound put it. Tristan Tzara organized a massive Dada festival in Paris, in 1920. In May 1917, Diaghilev's Ballets Russes performed *Parade*, a dance with music by French composer Eric Satie and complete with the sounds of dynamos, sirens, express trains, airplanes, and typewriters. The stage set was designed by Picasso (fig. 21.8). The whole creation seemed to the poet Guillaume Apollinaire like the space of a "*sur-réalisme*" or "super-realism".

In 1924, the poet André Breton appropriated the word *sur-réalisme* to name his own new movement in the arts. He defined Surrealism as "psychic automatism in its pure state, by which one proposes to express—verbally, by means of the written word, or in any other manner—the actual functioning of thought. Dictated by thought, in the absence of any control exercised by reason, exempt from any aesthetic or moral concern."

In its privileging of the irrational, and its lack of "aesthetic or moral concern," Surrealism was indebted

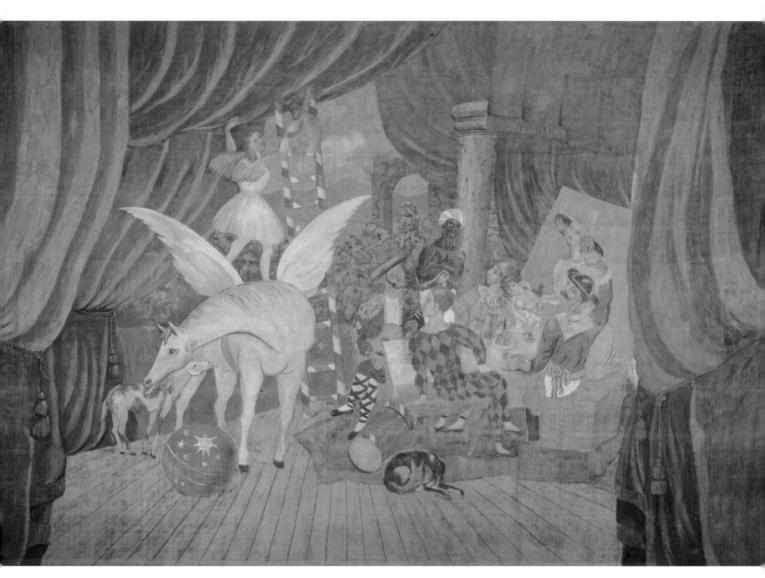

Figure 21.8 Pablo Picasso, curtain for the ballet *Parade*, 1917, tempera, 35′3¼″ × 57′6″ (10.60 × 17.24 m), Musées Nationaux, Paris. The ballet was based on a poem by Jean Cocteau, another member of the avant-garde circle. It is a "realistic ballet," meaning its concerns arise within an everyday street setting, complete with street musicians and performers, car horns and sirens, business people, tabloids, and skyscrapers.

to Dada. Where it differed was in its fascination with, and dedication to, the realm of dreams, supported by a perhaps willful misunderstanding of Freud. Where Freud understood neurosis as an illness demanding psychoanalysis and cure, Breton found it liberating. The neurotic, for Breton, was free to behave in any manner, and the valorizing of dreams opened up whole new vistas of subject matter, many of them previously taboo.

There were two approaches to depicting this new subject matter: one abstract, the other representational. The abstract vein was based on Breton's notion of pyschic **automatism**—that is, drawing liberated from the necessity of representation and of plan. Surrealists, according to this idea, should accept any apparent accident as psychologically predetermined and therefore revelatory. The second approach was focused on representing the world of dreams accurately, deliberately, particularly, without self-censorship.

Joan Miró. One of the most accomplished practitioners of automatism is JOAN MIRÓ [mee-ROH] (1893–1983). Though Miró never called himself a Surrealist, he acknowledged the Surrealist influence on his art. Soon after arriving in Paris from his native Spain in 1922, he was, he said, "carried away" by their example, and by 1925 "was drawing almost entirely from hallucinations. At the time I was living on a few dried figs a day."

His *Painting* (fig. 21.9) of 1933 is an abstract rendering of machine forms that he saw in a catalogue. It is as if the machines have suggested these forms, which, in his own psyche, have been transformed into abstract shapes, more organic than mechanical. The two bands of color in the background create a landscape, which the forms inhabit. They remain entirely abstract, existing at the very edge of rational thought.

Salvador Dalí. Probably the most famous of the Surrealist artists is SALVADOR DALÍ [DAH-lee] (1904–1989), of Spain, who arrived in Paris in 1929 and was to change the course of Surrealist painting. He consciously constructed himself as a Surrealist cult figure. His foot-long mustache was "sculpted" into various shapes. He claimed he could remember life in his mother's womb. He had himself buried and resurrected. One might argue that although Dalí lived a life of irrational behavior, his publicity-generating activities garnered fame and fortune—considered highly rational and worldly goals.

Dalí's painting entitled *The Persistence of Memory* (fig. 21.10), of 1931, is remarkably disturbing, for he painted an unconscious dream world with a nightmare quality. An attempt is made to resolve two apparently contradictory states—those of dream and reality. The enigmatic image depicts four watches that are limp, eroded by rust, and attacked by ants. Consider the various meanings in this puzzling picture: Can time itself decay and be destroyed, even as it causes decay and destruction? Has time been made flexible, or is it distorted? Can the artist

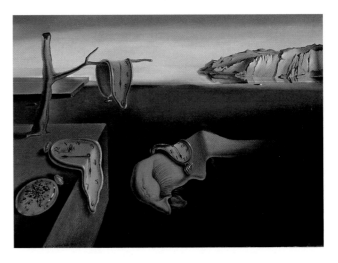

Figure 21.10 Salvador Dalí, *The Persistence of Memory*, 1931, oil on canvas, $9\frac{1}{2} \times 13''$ (24.1 × 33 cm), Museum of Modern Art, New York. Combining psychology and art, Surrealist artists sought to express the unconscious. Intentionally enigmatic and mysterious, Dalí's painting depicts the impossible and irrational with absolute conviction.

"bend time"? Is creativity a means to immortality? Can art defeat time? Such are the questions the painting seems to pose.

Perhaps most unnerving is the slug-like object on the ground, which appears to be a distorted self-portrait. "I want to paint like a madman," Dalí said, and the painting is perhaps the very image of this madness. As he pointed out, if Surrealism was to investigate the unconscious, then it had to explore whatever the unconscious had to offer. In this painting and others, Dalí depicted illogically juxtaposed objects, impossibly distorted forms, and undefined spatial settings. Yet when rendered in his meticulously detailed painting technique, the inconceivable appears incontestably real.

ABSTRACTION IN SCULPTURE

A number of sculptors sought to explore the possibilities of abstraction in three-dimensional terms. Like Miró and Arp, sculptors created forms that were organic and fluid. They suggested human or figurative forms at the same time that they resisted any clear representation of such forms. Thus, their work appears at once mysterious and elemental, and universal in its simplicity.

Constantin Brancusi. A Romanian who moved to Paris in 1904, CONSTANTIN BRANCUSI [Bran-KOO-zee] (1876–1957), "rediscovered" primitive sculpture while working with the Expressionist painters, and came to admire the lives of primitive people. Brancusi favored simple geometric forms—rectangles, ovals, and

Figure 21.9 Joan Miró, *Painting*, 1933, oil on canvas, $4'3\frac{1}{4}'' \times 5'3\frac{1}{2}''$ (1.30 × 1.61 m), Wadsworth Atheneum, Hartford, Connecticut. One of the reasons that this painting, when it is seen in real life, seems so alive, as if inhabited by abstract creatures, is that it is very large, so that the forms depicted in it are on a human scale.

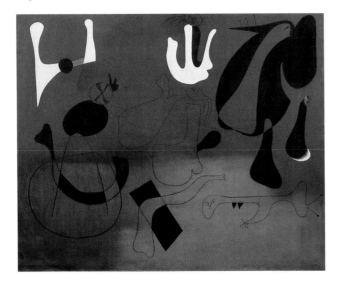

Connections

GRAHAM AND NOGUCHI: THE SCULPTURE OF DANCE

*F*or the pioneer of modern dance MARTHA GRAHAM (1894–1991), modern sculpture proved to be one of the most useful ways of thinking about the movement of the body in space. Dance was, for Graham, a trajectory into space, a composition of mass moving through void. She also began to recognize that set design, formerly a painter's craft, could easily move from its position as a painted backdrop and occupy the same territory as the dancers themselves. Dancers could move in it, around it, over it, under it, through it, and beside it. They could lean on it, jump over it, hide behind it. Her dances showed humans interacting with art.

In 1935, for the dance *Frontier* (fig. 21.11), Graham initiated what was to be a long-lasting relationship with Isamu Noguchi. Noguchi devised a simple fence, set at center stage, with two ropes attached to it, extending from each end of the fence forward and upward to the portals of the theater. This giant V-shape created the illusion of space when viewed from a tradition-al, single-point perspective, receding in a steep plane toward a vanishing point below and behind the fence rail. "It's not the rope that is the sculpture," Noguchi later explained, "but the space that it creates that is the sculpture. It is an illusion of space … It is in that spatial concept that Martha moves and creates her dances. In that sense, Martha is a sculptor herself." Graham herself forms the apex of the V as the dance opens, and as she moves forward and backward in front of the fence, it is as if she is in a vast landscape, the prairies and basins of the American frontier.

"Isamu Noguchi's vision of space," Graham later said, "and the integral meaning of his sculpture set me on a direction which sustained me throughout my career."

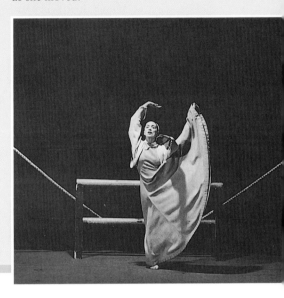

Figure 21.11 Martha Graham in *Frontier*, set by Isamu Noguchi, 1935. Noguchi designed over thirty-five sets for Graham, this being his first. To create sculptural forms with her body, Graham had her costume designed with a full circle skirt to swoop and arc through the air, creating linear curves as she moved.

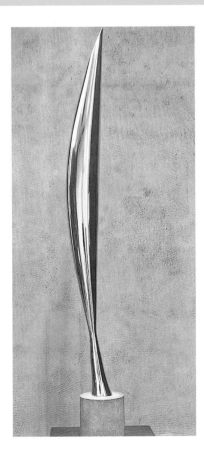

rising verticals. His *Bird in Space* (fig. 21.12), in polished bronze, is an elongated vertical shape. Its purity of form is bound up with the material: bronze is strong and can be highly polished. The sculpture does not represent the bird, but rather the flight of the bird. Nevertheless, the work is almost completely abstract; its expressive quality depends on our knowing the title. "Don't look for obscure formulas or mystery," Brancusi said of his work. "It is pure joy that I am giving you."

Henry Moore. The human figure was the point of departure for British sculptor HENRY MOORE (1898–1986). Yet, Moore's human figure is so simplified and abstract that it is barely identifiable. It often appears as a form of nature, capable of growth but beaten by the elements like an inanimate object. He admired

Figure 21.12 Constantin Brancusi, *Bird in Space*, 1928, polished bronze, 54 × 8½ × 6½″ (137.2 × 21.6 × 16.5 cm), Museum of Modern Art, New York. One of Brancusi's *Bird in Space* sculptures was the center of a battle between Brancusi and the United States Customs Office in 1927. Customs officials called it "bric-à-brac" and said it should therefore be taxed, while Brancusi said it was a work of art and was thus duty free. Brancusi won—a victory for modern art, now officially recognized as abstract art.

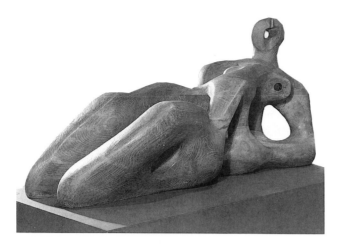

Figure 21.13   Henry Moore, *Reclining Figure*, 1939, carved elm, height 3′1″ (94.0 cm), Detroit Institute of Arts. Moore's monumental figure, although in a classical reclining pose, appears to have been weathered into this organic shape.

prehistoric Stonehenge and similar forms eroded by nature and time. His *Reclining Figure* (fig. 21.13), of 1939, looks weathered and suggests the power of natural forces at work. Moore's sculptures often look more effective when seen in a park than in a museum.

Moore's smooth, flowing forms include large openings and hollows. He shapes the masses but gives equal importance to the voids. The masses can be viewed as "positive volumes," while the depressions and holes may be seen as "negative spaces".

Alexander Calder.   A new kind of sculpture was created by the American ALEXANDER CALDER (1898–1976), whose father was also a sculptor. The younger Calder first gained recognition as a toy maker in Paris in the 1930s, having made a miniature circus that fascinated the Surrealists, and in particular Miró. By this time, he was already making **mobiles,** sculptural forms suspended from the ceiling that are driven by mechanical means, or, outside, by the air itself (fig. 21.14). Though almost everyone today knows what a mobile is, it was Calder who invented the form, and Marcel Duchamp who gave it its name. Because a mobile moves in the

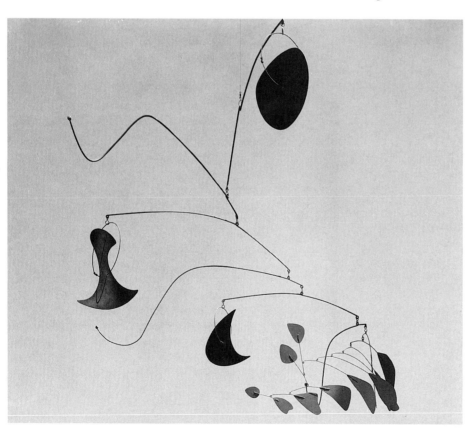

Figure 21.14   Alexander Calder, *Red Gongs*, completed 1950, hanging mobile, painted aluminum, brass, steel rod and wire, overall size 5 × 12′ (1.50 × 3.70 m), Metropolitan Museum of Art, New York. Calder invented this type of hanging sculpture, called a "mobile" because its component parts, highly responsive to the environment, are moved by the faintest breeze. He also made "stabiles" out of similar thin flat shapes that did not move.

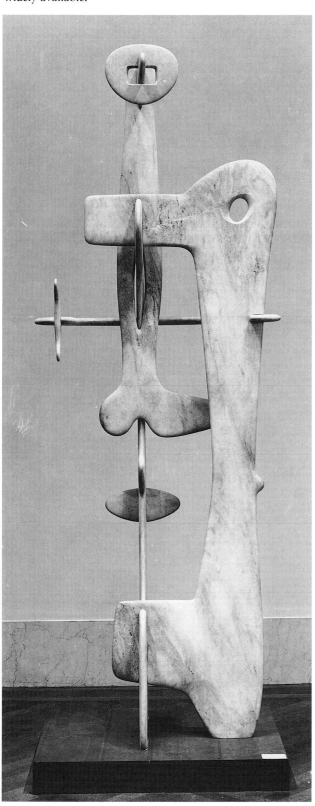

Figure 21.15 Isamu Noguchi, *Kouros*, 1944–45, pink Georgia marble, height 9′9″ (2.97 m), Metropolitan Museum of Art, New York. Noguchi turned to these flat slabs of marble because, used in the commercial building industry for facades, countertops, and the like, they were inexpensive and widely available.

faintest breeze, its form is always changing. The simple shapes constantly form new relationships. Thus, a mobile has many identities; it can never reveal its total identity at any one time. A mobile uses color, shape, composition, motion, time, and space. The artist must be concerned with everything.

Isamu Noguchi. A student of Brancusi's in Paris in the 1920s, Japanese-American sculptor ISAMU NOGUCHI [No-GOO-chee] (1904–1988), was particularly influenced by Brancusi's sense of sculpture as possessing an inherent expressive power. Noguchi drew on his own Japanese heritage in an attempt to discover in stone what the Japanese call *wabi*—the "ultimate naturalness" of an object.

Kouros (fig. 21.15) is one of Noguchi's works from the period of World War II, during which time he voluntarily entered a Japanese internment facility at Poston, Arizona, in order to help those being held there. "Kouros" is the ancient Greek term for "boy" or "young man" and is used to denote the series of realistic life-size sculptures of the nude male that began to appear in Greece in the seventh century B.C. (see Chapter 3). Despite the title, Noguchi's the form of the work is more obviously related to those of the Surrealists, particularly Arp and Miró. The piece unites two opposing techniques: on the one hand, it is carved; on the other, it is constructed. One of its most important characteristics is that, when viewed from two different angles—that is, from the front and from the side—it appears to be two entirely different works of art. In other words, it precipitates the viewer's movement, or indeed demands it.

AMERICAN MODERNISM

In 1913, just before World War I, a number of American artists worked together to plan an International Exhibition of Modern Art at the 69th Street Regiment Armory, in New York City. Thousands of people jammed into what was soon known as "the Armory Show," to see the Post-Impressionist, Fauve, and Cubist works. Most gawked at the show in amazement and ridiculed it mercilessly, but some American artists were inspired by the exhibition, especially those who frequented the New York City gallery known simply as 291, run by Alfred Stieglitz.

Alfred Stieglitz. Photographer ALFRED STIEGLITZ (1864–1946) had been interested in European modernist work since the turn of the century. Stieglitz was the first American to buy a Picasso, a small drawing of a nude that was so abstract that he himself called it "The Fire Escape." His own photographic talents captured the early modern era, its hustle, streets, and skylines. One classic photograph captures New York's most important thoroughfare at the time: *Winter,*

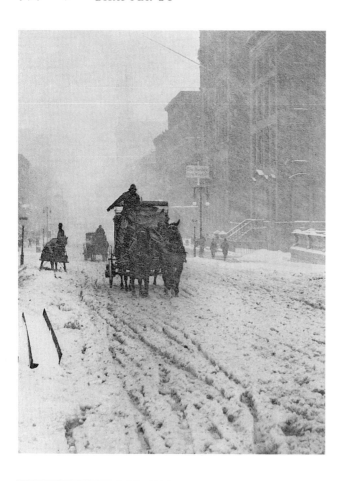

Figure 21.16 Alfred Stieglitz, *Winter, Fifth Avenue*, 1893, photogravure, $8\frac{5}{8} \times 6\frac{1}{16}''$ (21.9 × 15.4 cm), Museum of Modern Art, New York. Stieglitz was not only the leading photographer of his day but, through his gallery 291 in New York, was the person most responsible for introducing European avant-garde art to the United States.

Fifth Avenue (fig. 21.16). It was a scene from everyday life; even progress and the growth of industry cannot protect those unlucky enough to be caught in this fierce storm.

Georgia O'Keeffe. Among the painters most influenced by Stieglitz's style was GEORGIA O'KEEFFE (1887–1986). Born in Wisconsin, O'Keeffe was a student at the Art Institute of Chicago and the Art Students League in New York. When, in 1915, she sent Stieglitz a bundle of drawings and watercolors, he immediately exhibited them. They later married.

O'Keeffe is best known for the type of painting represented by *Yellow Calla* (fig. 21.17), of 1929, a large-scale abstraction of a natural form. O'Keeffe favored flowers and animal bones as her subjects. *Yellow Calla* is a flower seen from very close up and painted very large, emphasizing its abstract form and pattern. Simple yet carefully designed, O'Keeffe's painting makes use of subtle shading to create filmy, translucent, fluttering forms that are

Figure 21.17 Georgia O'Keeffe, *Yellow Calla*, 1929, oil on fiberboard, National Museum of American Art, Smithsonian Institution, Washington, DC. Concerned with expressive organic abstractions of nature throughout her long career, O'Keeffe made it clear she was an artist—not a "woman artist."

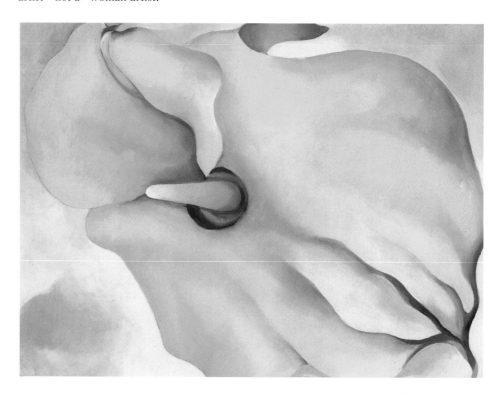

rich and sensuous. Intrigued by light and color, she said that "Color is one of the great things in the world that makes life worth living to me." While many read strong sexual symbolism into her work, O'Keeffe repeatedly made clear that this was not true. She was, she insisted, only a painter of nature and of nature's forms and colors.

The same year that she painted *Yellow Calla*, O'Keeffe began spending her summers near Taos, New Mexico. After Stieglitz's death in 1946, she moved there permanently. The forms of the desert Southwest became her primary subject matter, its colors, her palette. "I climbed way up on a pale green hill," she wrote, "and in the evening light—the sun under the clouds—the color effect was very strange—standing high on a pale green hill where I could look all around at the red, yellow, purple formations—miles all around—the colors all intensified by the pale grey green I was standing on." It is as if she discovered, in the American landscape, the palette of the Fauves.

Charles Demuth. Among the other American artists championed by Stieglitz was CHARLES DEMUTH (1883–1935). Unlike O'Keeffe, whose primary interest was in natural forms and colors, Demuth was concerned with the architectural forms of the American scene. He reduced them to flat compositions in a manner intentionally reminiscent of the Cubist landscape paintings of Picasso and Braque. In *Aucassin and Nicolette* (fig. 21.18), of 1921, for instance, the geometric shapes of the industrial landscape near Demuth's home in Lancaster, Pennsylvania, are rendered in flat, hard-edged forms, the lines of which extend into the sky like facets on a polished gem.

MODERNIST LITERATURE

If Parisians seemed to accept all manner of behavior without a second thought, Americans were quite the opposite. Radicals of all kinds flocked to Paris and Europe to escape Prohibition and other social restrictions at home. There, American expatriates discovered liberation from what they considered the stultifying Puritanism of America.

It was in Paris during and after the war that the most adventurous new writing in English was published: James Joyce's *Ulysses*, in 1922, quickly banned for obscenity in America and Britain until 1933; T.S. Eliot's *The Waste Land*, in 1922; William Carlos Williams's prose and poetry *Spring and All*, in 1923; F. Scott Fitzgerald's *The Great Gatsby*, in 1925; Ezra Pound's first sixteen *Cantos*, in 1926; and Ernest Hemingway's *The Sun Also Rises*, also in 1926. It was Hemingway who defined the mood of what he called the "lost generation."

Ezra Pound and T.S. Eliot. EZRA POUND (1885–1972) and T.S. ELIOT (1888–1965) are generally recognized as the two most influential American modernist poets. What distinguished their work from that of

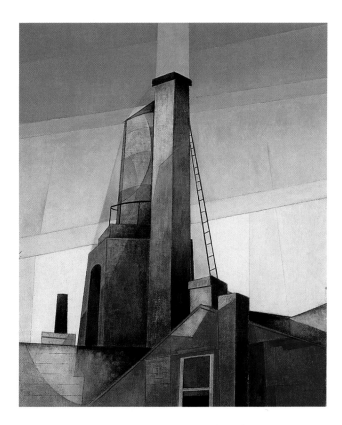

Figure 21.18   Charles Demuth, *Aucassin and Nicolette*, 1921, oil on canvas, $23\frac{9}{16} \times 19\frac{1}{2}''$ (59.8 × 49.5 cm), Columbus Gallery of Fine Arts, Columbus, Ohio. The painting's ironic title, referring to the famous lovers of medieval romance, is attributed to another member of the Stieglitz circle during World War I, Marcel Duchamp. In fact, Demuth records the industrialization of rural Pennsylvania.

their contemporaries was that they wrote extremely complex, multi-faceted poems that were technically innovative and densely allusive. Pound and Eliot relied heavily on rapidly shifting images, typically presented without explanation. Readers are left to make connections among the poems' images and allusions, and to arrive at understanding for themselves.

Pound and Eliot are sometimes considered "difficult" for all but the most learned and experienced of readers to understand. Both poets believed that poetry *should* be difficult, in part to reflect the complexities and ambiguities of experience, especially that of World War I, which Eliot once described as an "immense panorama of futility and anarchy." Eliot's most influential poem, *The Waste Land*, burst onto the literary scene in 1922. Eliot was aided in his work by his friend Ezra Pound, who cut more than a hundred lines from an early draft and suggested alterations to help unify the poem. In appreciation Eliot dedicated the poem to Pound and honored him further as "il miglior fabbro" (the better maker).

"I had not thought death," Eliot writes in the poem, "had undone so many," speaking of the benumbed people inhabiting the "unreal city" of post-war London. To Eliot, London seemed as if it had been stricken by the gas warfare on the Western Front. His poem is but a contingency action, a work designed to stop the bleeding, so to speak—"fragments I have shored against my ruin," as he describes it at poem's end.

Pound's early poetry is a concerted attack on World War I. The five-part "Hugh Selwyn Mauberley," published in 1920, ends with this damning indictment of the value of what the soldiers had been fighting for:

> There died a myriad,
> And of the best, among them,
> For an old bitch gone in the teeth,
> For a botched civilization …

In 1926, he published the first sixteen poems of what would become his lifelong work, *The Cantos*. The last Canto was an inventory of those he knew who had gone to war, among them his fellow poet Richard Aldington:

> And because that son of a bitch,
>   Franz Josef of Austria …
> They put Aldington on Hill 70, in a trench
>   dug through corpses
> With a lot of kids of sixteen,
> Howling and crying for their mamas,
> And he sent a chit back to his major:
>   I can hold out for ten minutes
> With my sergeant and a machine-gun.
>   And they rebuked him for levity.

So disillusioned was Pound with the political and economic policies of England, France, and the other Allies that, when Mussolini took power in Italy in the early 1930s, he became one of his greatest champions. Fascism, and the anti-Semitism that went with it, appealed mightily to Pound, and he supported Mussolini throughout World War II. After the war he was imprisoned, tried for treason, and certified insane. For thirteen years, he was kept at St. Elizabeth's mental hospital in Washington, D.C. Finally, at the request of a number of writers, including Hemingway, Williams, and Eliot, he was released, and returned to Italy, where he died in 1972.

James Joyce.   JAMES JOYCE (1882–1941) accomplished for modern fiction what T.S. Eliot did for modern poetry: he changed its direction by introducing startling technical innovations. Like Eliot, who employed abundant and wide-ranging literary and historical allusions in *The Waste Land*, Joyce, in his monumental *Ulysses*, which was published the same year as Eliot's poem, complicated the texture and structure of his narrative with intricate mythic and literary references.

Joyce used a **stream of consciousness** narrative technique that took readers into the minds of his characters. His innovations include such techniques as shifting abruptly from one character's mind to another; moving from description of an action to a character's response to it; mixing different styles and voices in a single paragraph or sentence; combining events from the past and the present in one passage. These and similar devices convey a sense of a mind alive, a consciousness that is absorbing and connecting the experiences it perceives—what one critic has described as "the shifting, kaleidoscopic nature of human awareness."

Ulysses grows out of the tradition of the nineteenth-century realist novel. Combining a microscopic factual accuracy in depicting Dublin with a rich language, it is an intricate recreation of the events of one day (June 16, 1904) in the life of Leopold Bloom. Organized into eighteen increasingly complex chapters, it echoes major events in Homer's *Odyssey*.

Virginia Woolf.   As James Joyce was experimenting with techniques in fiction, VIRGINIA WOOLF (1882–1941), one of the founders of the Bloomsbury group in London, was developing ways of rendering a literary character's inner thoughts. Both writers explored techniques for conveying stream of consciousness, the representation of the flow of mental impressions and perceptions through an individual's consciousness, conveying a sense of his or her subjective psychic reality. Woolf, in particular, was interested in revealing a character's inner being through what that character thinks and feels, rather than what that character says or does.

Mrs. Dalloway (1925) and *To the Lighthouse* (1927) are two of Woolf's novels that illustrate her use of the stream of consciousness technique. Like Joyce, Woolf in *Mrs. Dalloway* focuses on a single day in the life of a person, in this case a middle-aged English woman, Clarissa Dalloway. Readers overhear Mrs. Dalloway's thoughts and feelings as she reflects on her life, especially her marriage. External events are indicated only through the characters' subjective impressions of them. The novel's point of view shifts among a series of characters, including Septimus Warren Smith, a shell-shocked war veteran, who functions to a certain extent as her alter ego.

In *To the Lighthouse*, Woolf commemorates her mother Julia Stephen, who had died in 1895. The novel explores aspects of gender and sexual difference by contrasting Mrs. Ramsay, the book's central character, with her husband, a philosopher. Another central character, Lily Briscoe, is an artist who paints a portrait of Mrs. Ramsay. As critic Lyall Gordon notes, "The artist behind her easel, the biographer behind her novel reproduce the action of the lighthouse: together they light up a woman's uncharted nature." *To the Lighthouse* is a masterpiece of literary modernism, full of the subjective experiences of a central character who is at odds with the world, and replete with poetic symbols that reveal the character's "true" nature.

Ernest Hemingway.   Hailed as one of the most influential and imitated of American writers, ERNEST HEMINGWAY (1899–1961) wrote novels and short stories that established a style and manner that came to

Then & Now

ROBIN HOOD AT THE MOVIES

The adventures of Robin Hood is one of the most often retold stories in movie history, and Robin Hood one of the most popular screen characters of all time. When the 1938 version, *The Adventures of Robin Hood*, appeared, audiences raved about the charismatic Errol Flynn as Robin Hood and Olivia de Haviland as the demure Maid Marian (fig. 21. 19). This was Robin Hood at his swashbuckling finest.

The version with Errol Flynn is the one many Americans grew up with, but it is in itself a remake of one of the greatest silent films. In 1922 Douglas Fairbanks and Mary Pickford, two of the four co-founders of United Artists, created a feature-length film of the story. It was 170 minutes, long for a silent film. They spent over 1.5 million dollars—unheard of in 1922; even Warner Brothers lavished only two million dollars on the Flynn remake in 1938. Fairbanks hired armies of workers to construct the sets on Santa Monica Boulevard in Hollywood. He had built the largest interior set ever made in the history of the movies, and his outdoor sets rivaled the size of any set made before. No film had ever had a larger cast of extras, and virtually all of them appeared in the archery competition and the early jousting scene in which Robin wins the heart of Maid Marian by defeating the evil Black Knight.

The Warner Brothers version, in 1938, added sound and color, and Robin Hood came to life. Filmed in early Technicolor, it contained deep blacks, dark purples, and luscious greens, and utilized stunning contrasts of light and dark that literally dazzled audiences who had probably never seen a color film. The addition of sound made it possible to speed up the pace, since a silent film requires many stills of narrative and dialogue. With music, trumpets calling, hoofs thundering, and swords clashing, this Robin Hood had a thrilling triumph of good over evil.

Perhaps the greatest distinction between the two early versions lies in the change in the country's ethos and in the studio system's huge marketing effort to promote Errol Flynn as the embodiment of the character. In the depressed thirties, Americans needed Robin Hood, a man who "steals from the rich to give to the poor." Robin Hood's character destroys greed (a loathsome trait in the 1930s) and validates the nobility of the humble masses. Flynn's flashing smile and good looks only reinforced the appeal. When the film was released, newspapers and magazines covered it; radio shows dramatized parts of the story. A paperback edition was published with Errol Flynn as Robin Hood on the cover, and *Robin Hood* was added to summer reading lists.

Over the years, new versions have been produced. Disney created an animated feature in 1973 in which Robin Hood is a fox. Mel Brooks spoofed the legend in *Robin Hood: Men in Tights* (1993). Brooks's film parodied another current film, *Robin Hood: Prince of Thieves* (1991), directed by Kevin Costner, in which Robin and his band of Merry Men are portrayed as deep-thinking, politically correct rebels. There was even a version that depicted Robin and Marian in later life, played by Sean Connery and Audrey Hepburn, *Robin and Marian* (1976), but the public seemed little interested.

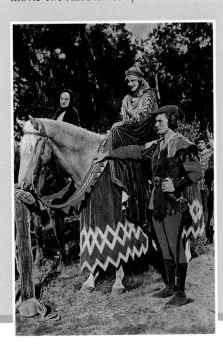

Figure 21.19 Errol Flynn and Olivia de Haviland in Warner Brothers' 1938 movie *The Adventures of Robin Hood*.

characterize one pole of the modern fictional idiom. His language is laconic and spare. His plots are simple. The complexity of his fiction lies in its suggestiveness, in the implications of what is said and in that which is left unspoken. Hemingway believed that fiction should reveal less rather than more, like an iceberg with only its tip exposed above water. Thus, reading Hemingway's fiction requires as much attention to what he leaves out as to what he includes.

Hemingway's first successful novel, *The Sun Also Rises*, chronicles the adventures of a group of expatriates in Paris. Narrated in the first person, the novel defines this "lost generation" as impotent survivors of a meaningless fate.

MODERN MUSIC

Probably no art form better embodies the Western world's sense of discord and disharmony precipitated by World War I than music. Before the war, Stravinsky's *The Rite of Spring* had shaken the foundations of tonality, and hence traditional harmony. Stravinsky's use of multiple tonal centers created dissonance and harmonic disorientation. Fleeing to Switzerland during the war, and returning to Paris in 1920, Stravinsky began work on a new ballet for Diaghilev, entitled *Pulcinella*. Taking a number of sonatas by Classical composers, Stravinsky reworked their harmonies to make them more dissonant, changing phrase lengths to make them irregular, and altering rhythms to make them lively and syncopated. "*Pulcinella,*" he would later admit, "was my discovery of the past." But his was a past thoroughly modernized.

Arnold Schoenberg. The Viennese composer ARNOLD SCHOENBERG [SHONE-berg] (1874–1951) undermined the stability of Western classical music even further by writing music that lacked a **tonal center** or home key. **Atonality,** he called it. Much of this work was done before the war and was badly received. During the war and after, Schoenberg ceased composing. He was convinced that tonality was a "straitjacket," but also realized that atonality was structureless. His response was to develop a twelve-tone musical scale, as used in the *Variation for Orchestra* (1931):

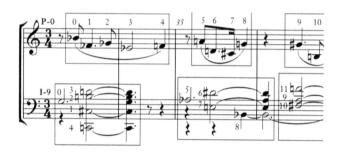

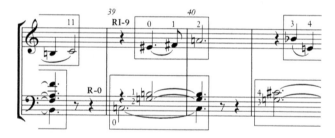

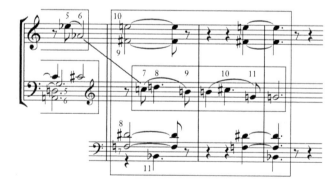

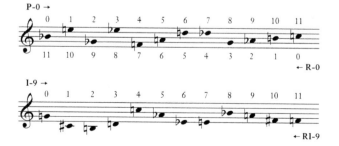

The twelve-tone scale was based on the traditional octave, counting all the half steps. Twelve-tone composition would "level" each tone, giving none more weight than any other, by predetermining the order in which the tones would be played. This order would be used for the entire composition, sequence after sequence.

The music is difficult to listen to for audiences who are accustomed to traditional harmony, but, given the proper theme, it can be very moving. Schoenberg had his theme. Jewish by birth, he based many of his works on Jewish liturgy, including his first stunning success in twelve-tone composition, the opera *Moses and Aaron* (1923). When the Nazis came to power in his native Germany in 1933, he was fired from his job in Berlin. Schoenberg's anger came to the forefront of his musical imagination. The twelve-tone system was the perfect vehicle for its expression.

REPRESSION AND DEPRESSION: THE THIRTIES

World War I seemed to many to be a war to end all wars, but it nonetheless left a sense of disillusionment and fear that led many people to seek security. Some found it in the authority of Fascist leadership, a dictatorship that ruled with an inflated sense of national pride and which blamed adverse social conditions on others, particularly the Jews. While the end of the war had brought a semblance of peace to Europe, it had not brought political harmony. As the Russian Communist experiment took hold, it threatened to topple long-standing democracies. Workers throughout Europe looked to the Russian Communists for a new sense of vision and identity. When worldwide economic depression struck in 1929, the simple explanation offered by Fascists, such as blaming Jewish bankers for all economic woes, appealed to many.

FASCISM IN EUROPE

Benito Mussolini. In many respects, BENITO MUSSOLINI [moo-soh-LEE-nee] (1883–1945) is responsible for the invention of Fascism, which was first established in Italy. Expelled from the Italian Socialist party for advocating Italian entry into World War I, Mussolini formed groups of so-called *fasci* (from the Latin word for the bundle of rods that symbolize the Roman Republic). These groups consisted of young men like himself who called for Italy's entry into the war in 1915.

Mussolini's power base expanded rapidly after the war ended. He organized a broad group of Italians who were dissatisfied with the government and who opposed the Socialist cause as Bolshevik. Mussolini's Fascist bands, with the strong support of the Italian police, began openly to attack labor union offices, opposition newspapers,

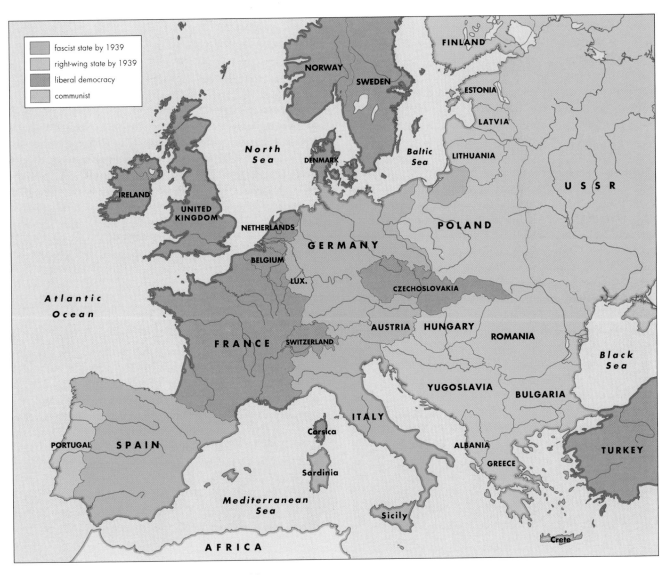

Map 21.2 Left- and right-wing Europe, 1918–39.

and anti-Fascist politicians. Nearly two thousand people were killed between October 1920 and October 1922. Meanwhile, Mussolini gained power, and on October 29, 1922, was named premier. By the late 1920s, the government was totally controlled by the Fascist party, and Mussolini had become more dictator than premier, both head of the party and chief of state. He outlawed emigration, advocated the largest possible families by reducing taxes with each successive child, and taxed bachelors in an attempt to encourage them to marry. His dream was to create, in a single generation, a huge Italian army and a country thoroughly loyal to the goals of the Fascist state. Education, from textbooks to professors, became a propaganda arm of the government itself. The police actively sought out dissenters and eliminated them.

The people supported Mussolini because, in fact, the Italian economy thrived under his leadership. Despite worldwide economic depression, Mussolini made Italy virtually self-sufficient in agriculture, extended electricity to even the most rural parts of the country, and regulated public transportation.

Adolf Hitler. Meanwhile, the Fascist approach to government spread to Germany, where ADOLF HITLER (1889–1945) took advantage of public despair over the state of Germany's economy after World War I. In 1923, the value of the German currency decreased from a few thousand marks to the dollar to literally trillions of marks to the dollar by the end of the year. Lifetime savings were suddenly worthless. Workers found themselves earning starvation wages as even the price of bread rocketed. In Munich, Adolf Hitler created the National Socialist Party of the German Workers—the **Nazi** (abbreviation for "National") party.

In 1921, Hitler named himself *Führer* (or leader) of the Nazi party. He became chancellor of the Nazi party in January 1933, backed by the party's new *Schutzstaffel*, or *SS* (literally, the Defense Force), an elite honor guard, and by the *Sturmabteilung*, or *SA* (literally, "Storm Troops"), a huge private army. A month later, a fire broke out in the Reichstag, the central buildings of German government, and Hitler quickly blamed it on the Communists. By noon the next day, four thousand members of the Communist Party had been arrested, and their citizenship rights had been suspended.

In August 1934, Hitler became president and chancellor of Germany. Every political party that opposed him was banned. Like Mussolini in Italy, Hitler was convinced that the Bolsheviks—by which he meant the Jews—were responsible for the catastrophic state of the German economy. The Jews became Hitler's primary target. The "Nuremberg Laws" of September 1935 defined a Jew as anyone with one Jewish grandparent. It denounced marriage between Jews and non-Jews as "racial pollution" and prohibited it. Jews were forbidden to teach in educational institutions and were banned from writing, publishing, acting, painting, and performing music. Nor were they allowed to work in hospitals or banks, bookstores or law offices. In November 1938, after a seventeen-year-old Jewish boy shot and killed the secretary of the German Embassy in Paris, mobs looted and burned Jewish shops and synagogues all over Germany. They swept through the streets, entering Jewish homes, beating the occupants, and stealing their possessions. After this night, known as *Kristallnacht*, the extent of German anti-Semitism was apparent to the entire world.

From the beginning, Hitler's Nazi party was militaristic in its discipline, organization, and goals. Nazis were

proponents of the policy of *Lebensraum* ("living space"), which justified the geographic expansion of the state into other countries' territories to make room for the "superior" German race of people. By the mid-1930s, Hitler was preparing for war.

Francisco Franco. Spain had been in political disarray since the King's overthrow in 1931. Spain's Popular Front, consisting of a coalition of Republicans, Socialists, labor unions, Communists, and even anarchists, won a decisive electoral victory in February 1936. Shortly thereafter, however, Spain's right formed the Falange ("Phalanx"), a coalition of monarchists, clerics (whose church schools had been closed), and the military, who desired to overthrow the new Republican government. At the Falange's head was General FRANCISCO FRANCO (1892–1975), who on July 17, 1936, with his right-wing army, led a coordinated revolt in Spanish Morocco and in a number of towns in mainland Spain— Córdoba, Seville, and Burgos, among them.

The Spanish Civil War had begun. Within a few weeks, about a third of the country was under Franco's control, but Barcelona, Madrid, and Valencia remained Republican strongholds, as did the Basque provinces in the north. The Soviet Union actively supported the Republican cause, furnishing them with military advisers and organizing international brigades of volunteers (among them Ernest Hemingway).

Mussolini and Hitler supported Franco. Hitler even provided Franco with an air force. On April 26, 1937, Wolfram von Richthofen, the cousin of the almost mythical German ace pilot, Manfred von Richthofen, the Red Baron of World War I, planned an attack on the town of

Timeline 21.2 Art and literature during the Age of Anxiety.

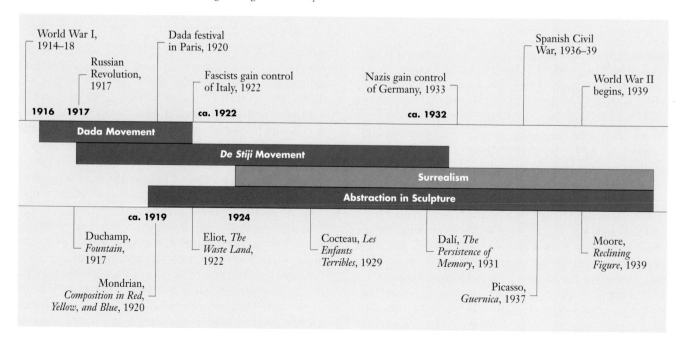

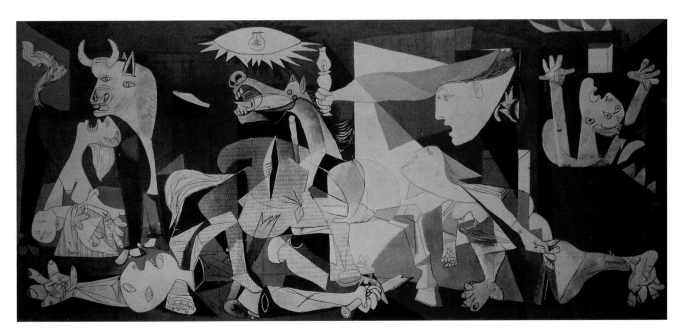

Figure 21.20   Pablo Picasso, *Guernica*, 1937, oil on canvas, 11′5½″ × 25′5¼″ (3.49 × 7.75 m), Centro de Arte Reina Sofia, Madrid. After Franco's victory in 1939, *Guernica* was exhibited at the Museum of Modern Art in New York where Picasso placed it on "extended loan." He did, however, affirm that the painting belonged "to the Spanish Republic," but he forbade its return to Spain until such time that democracy and "individual liberties" were restored there. With the death of Franco in 1975, the subsequent crowning of Juan Carlos as constitutional monarch in 1977, and the adoption of a democratic constitution in 1978, the painting was finally returned to Spain in 1981.

Guernica in northern Spain, where Basque Republican forces were retreating. It was a sudden, coordinated attack that came to be known as *Blitzkrieg*, or "lightning war." Beginning at half past four in the afternoon and lasting for three and a half hours, a strike force of thirty-three planes, each loaded with three thousand pounds of bombs, pummeled the city. By the time the fires subsided three days later, it was evident that the entire town center had been razed to the ground—fifteen square blocks—and that a thousand innocent citizens had been killed. As news of the event spread, Pablo Picasso, living in Paris, began work on a giant canvas commemorating the disaster, a disaster that foreshadowed the massive, impersonal, and inhumane bombing of European cities in World War II.

Guernica (fig. 21.20) is the culmination of Picasso's Surrealist style. It is painted only in black, white, and grays. It contains a Pietà theme. Many elements of the composition refer to Surrealist dream symbolism. The horse, speared and dying in anguish, might be seen as representing the fate of the dreamer's creativity. The entire scene is surveyed by a bull, on the left, which represents Spain, and in particular its heroism and tragedy, which the bullfight—the struggle of life and death—embodies. But the bull is also the Minotaur, the bull-man of Greek mythology, which for the Surrealists stood for the irrational forces of the human psyche (Picasso had

earlier designed the cover for the Surrealist magazine *Minotaur*). The significance of the electric light bulb, at the top center of the painting, and the oil lamp, held by the woman reaching out of the window, have been much debated, but they represent, on a fundamental level, old and new ways of seeing.

Franco finally captured the Republican strongholds of Madrid and Barcelona in 1939 and ruled Spain as a Fascist dictator until his death in 1975. The attack on Guernica and other Fascist victories in Spain outraged the Allies, but they proved to Hitler just how effective his military forces and tactics, especially the *Blitzkrig*, were. While the Spanish Civil War was winding down, Hitler sent troops into Czechoslovakia, in March 1939. They met with little or no resistance, and shortly thereafter Hitler set his designs on Poland—and the world.

FRANKLIN DELANO ROOSEVELT AND THE NEW DEAL

Throughout the 1920s, the United States had enjoyed unprecedented prosperity, fueled by speculation on the stock market and the extraordinary expansion of the industrial infrastructure. For the first time in world history, a country could define itself not as an agricultural society, nor as an industrial one, but as a consumer society. Houses, automobiles, and everyday goods were purchased on credit, in an almost unregulated economic climate. Unfortunately, it soon became evident that the prosperity was a house of cards. On October 29, 1929, it all came tumbling down in the stock market crash. Many of the wealthiest people in America were devastated, as thirty billion dollars of assets disappeared within two weeks. Faced with massive withdrawals that they could not sustain, banks closed. Families lost their life savings. By the early 1930s, over sixteen million American men were unemployed, nearly a third of the workforce. To make matters worse, whole areas of the Midwest suffered severe drought. The effect, exacerbated by over-plowing, was the creation of a giant "Dust Bowl." Whole populations left the hardest hit areas of Arkansas and Oklahoma for California, an exodus depicted by John Steinbeck in his novel *The Grapes of Wrath*.

Fearing that such economic catastrophe would lead to the rise of the kind of Fascism seen in Europe, or worse, Communism, the United States government decided to intervene. President FRANKLIN DELANO ROOSEVELT (1882–1945), or "FDR" as he was called, declared a bank holiday in 1933; gradually those institutions that were financially sound reopened. Roosevelt recognized that at the root of the Depression was a deep social imbalance between the haves and the have-nots. He wanted to give the have-nots what he called a "New Deal." In 1935, a Social Security Act inaugurated unemployment insurance and old-age pensions. Tax codes were revised to increase the tax burden on wealthier Americans in an effort to close the social gap. Agricultural subsidies were given to farmers to maintain agricultural production and to steady the economy. For the arts, the Works Progress Administration (WPA) was established to subsidize authors, artists, and musicians.

PHOTOGRAPHY AND THE FSA

Perhaps the most effective tool for creating a sense of national consensus for Roosevelt's social reforms was the work of the photographers subsidized by a program inaugurated by the Farm Security Administration (FSA) to portray the plight of the American farmers and share-croppers devastated by the Depression and drought.

Dorothea Lange. One of the most talented photographers to be part of the plan was DOROTHEA LANGE (1895–1965). Lange's documentary style, though seemingly objective, is driven by a social reformist impulse. Lange's most famous photograph, *Migrant Mother, Nipomo, California* (fig. 21.21), depicts a young widow with three of her ten forlorn children, migrants on the way to California, the sort that Steinbeck described. She stares obliquely into space, pensive and anxious about the future. Her glance avoids the camera, dissociated from the viewer's gaze. Her face is prematurely aged, for she was just thirty-two when the

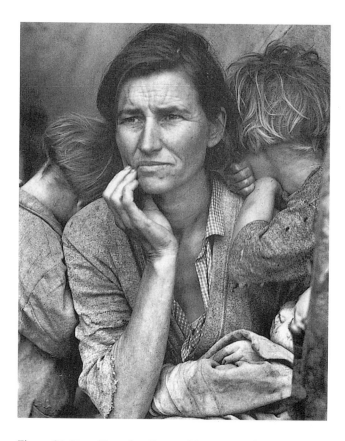

Figure 21.21 Dorothea Lange, *Migrant Mother, Nipomo, California*, 1936, gelatin silver print, Library of Congress, Washington, D.C. Lange chose to include only three of the mother's ten children in this photograph because she did not want to add to widespread resentment in wealthier parts of American society about over-population among the poor.

picture was taken. The children turn inward, seeking shelter against the mother, who has none for herself. The picture's mood of desperation is heightened by its grainy gray tones.

Walker Evans. Another FSA photographer, WALKER EVANS (1903–1975), is best known for a series of photographs made for the book *Let Us Now Praise Famous Men* by James Agee published in 1941, which details Evans and Agee's life with a family of sharecroppers in Hale County, Alabama, in 1936. Agee's "famous" men are the heroes of the forgotten people of the Depression and poverty. He describes, for instance, the sharecroppers' house as nightfall creeps over it: "The house and all that was in it had now descended deep beneath the gradual spiral it had sunk through; it lay formal under the order of entire silence." Such formal coherence, underlying the veneer of poverty, is precisely the subject of Evans's *Washroom and Dining Area of Floyd Burroughs's Home, Hale County, Alabama* (fig. 21.22). It is a powerful composition dominated by verticals and horizontals, a grid punctuated by the single oval washbowl on the right, and the oil lamp on the left. The work contains visual echoes of Mondrian's De Stijl abstractions. Even as it embodies the stark realities of a sharecropper's life, Evans's photograpy reveals a beauty in the clean lines of this sparse world, a dignified beauty that also marks Agee's accompanying prose.

Margaret Bourke-White.   Like Evans, MARGARET BOURKE-WHITE (1904–1971) collaborated with a writer, her husband Erskine Caldwell, to depict the social realities of the Depression. Their best-known project is *You Have Seen Their Face* (1937). But it was Bourke-White's work as a photojournalist that earned her worldwide recognition. One of the first photographers hired by *Life* magazine after it was founded in 1936, Bourke-White came to define the profession.

Her photographs of the Depression depicted industry as well as the harsh social and economic conditions of the

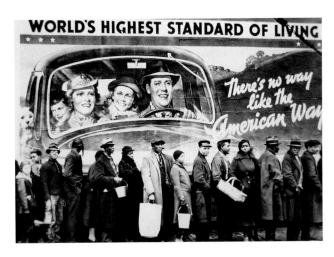

Figure 21.23   Margaret Bourke-White, *At the Time of the Louisville Flood*, 1937, photograph. *Life* magazine offered many photographers the opportunity to work professionally. Reacting to the arrival of *Life* magazine on the publishing scene, Bourke-White said: "I could almost feel the horizon widening and the great rush of wind sweeping in … This was the kind of magazine that could be anything we chose to make it."

Figure 21.22   Walker Evans, *Washroom and Dining Area of Floyd Burroughs's Home, Hale County, Alabama*, 1936, photograph, Library of Congress, Washington, DC. The power of this photograph rests not only in its formal coherence, but in it stunning focus, its ability to capture the texture of wood, cloth, glass, and vinyl in a manner that makes everything almost real enough to touch.

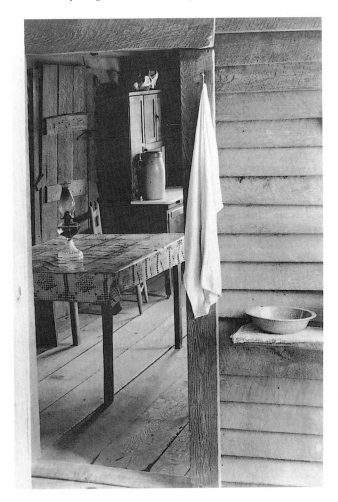

time. *At the Time of the Louisville Flood* (fig. 21.23) shows the effect of the flooding of the Ohio river in January 1937. It inundated Louisville, Kentucky, and left over nine hundred people dead or injured. On assignment for *Life*, Bourke-White arrived in the city on the last flight before the airfield was flooded, and hitchhiked on rescue rowboats shooting photo after photo of the scene. *At the Time of the Louisville Flood* is an indictment of the American dream, juxtaposing the reality of the lives of many African-Americans with the idealized space of the advertising billboard behind them. The government billboard is exposed for the propaganda tool that it is.

Bourke-White worked throughout the world, covering World War II and the Korean War as a correspondent. She was the first woman photographer attached to the U.S. armed forces, and the only U.S. photographer to cover the siege of Moscow in 1941.

REGIONALISM IN AMERICAN PAINTING

The success achieved by the photographers working for the FSA was underpinned by a realist impulse in American culture. Many American artists, especially in the Midwest, rejected the abstraction that dominated European painting and turned instead to a more naturalistic representation of the world's experiences through regional scenes.

Edward Hopper.   Though he traveled to Europe several times between 1906 and 1910, EDWARD HOPPER (1882–1967) did not seem to be affected by what he saw there. For his 1933 exhibition at the Museum of

Modern Art, he wrote, "A nation's art is greatest when it most reflects the character of its people ... We are not French and never can be and any attempt to be so is to deny our inheritance and to try to impose upon ourselves a character that can be nothing but a veneer upon surface."

Hopper's paintings are an accurate record of the American architectural scene. Its cafés, restaurants, stores, and barber shops are his subject matter. Hopper paints neither the most salubrious part of town nor the shabbiest, but those places inhabited by the middle class. Hopper attempted to represent the ordinary, things that had previously been deemed unworthy of an artist's attention. Yet, he is also adept at conveying emotion, though not entirely pleasurable emotion. *Nighthawks* (fig. 21.24), of 1942, creates a sense of haunting loneliness through its depiction of the alienation of urban life, its stark and sometimes bleak nature. Few human figures are portrayed. Often there is no one at all in Hopper's paintings. There is also often no movement. Is someone about to come out of one of those doors? Appear at one of those windows? Come around the corner?

Thomas Hart Benton.   The regionalist impulse in painting was supported by the Works in Progress Administration (WPA), which initiated a mural project to decorate public buildings across the country. The murals

were to represent American themes and experiences. Over two thousand murals were painted between 1935 and 1939, and among the best of them were those by THOMAS HART BENTON (1889–1975). Benton was radically anti-European. "The fact that our art was arguable in the language of the street," he wrote, "was proof to us that we had succeeded in separating it from the hothouse atmosphere of an imported, and for our country, functionless aesthetics."

One of his most ambitious undertakings was a set of murals for the Missouri State Capitol, depicting the social history of Missouri (fig. 21.25). Almost every aspect of Missouri life is depicted. In a domestic scene, an old woman rolls out dough while an old man reads and a young boy drinks a glass of milk. To the left are various farming scenes: a cow is milked; pigs are fed; a farmer sits atop his tractor. To the right a lawyer argues a case before the jury in a courtroom.

Jacob Lawrence.   Another, earlier migration, reminiscent of the migration of Oklahoma farmworkers, was that of African-Americans after World War I. They moved steadily from the South to the North seeking employment in rapidly expanding industries. Between 1916 and 1923, the African-American population in major Northern cities increased by 100 per cent. African-American artist JACOB LAWRENCE (b. 1917),

Figure 21.24   Edward Hopper, *Nighthawks*, 1942, oil on canvas, 2'6" × 4'8 11/16" (76.2 × 143.9 cm), Art Institute of Chicago. Using carefully constructed compositions to depict ordinary subjects, especially the loneliness of urban life, the artist documented the American scene.

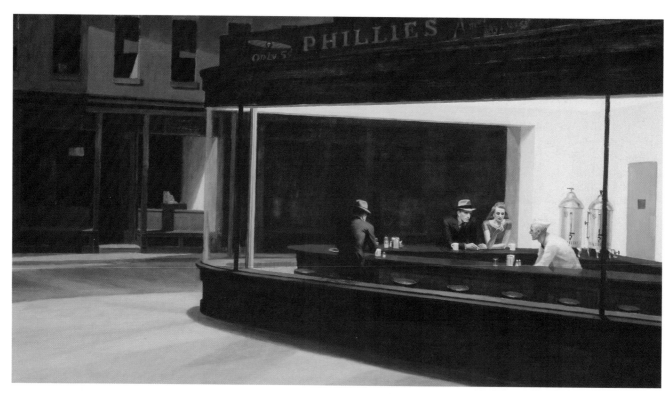

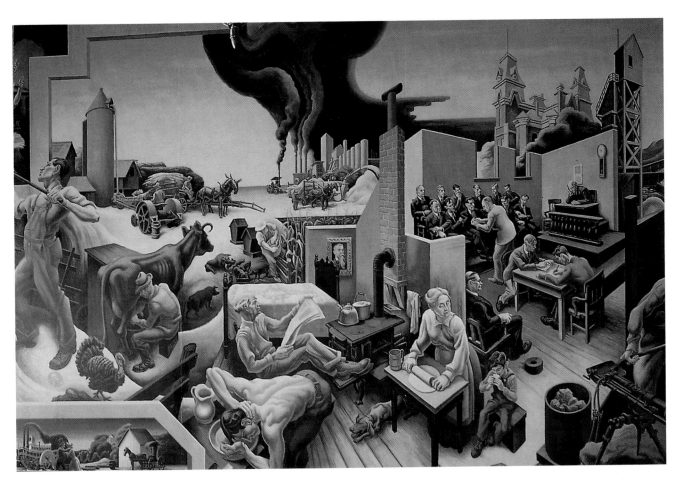

Figure 21.25 Thomas Hart Benton, *Missouri Mural* (section), 1936, oil on canvas, Missouri State Capitol, Jefferson City, Missouri. The WPA's mural project was directly inspired by the example of the Mexican muralists, one of whom, Diego Rivera, is discussed in the Cross Currents box in this chapter, and whose efforts were supported by the Mexican government.

supported by the WPA, captured this movement in a series of tempera paintings, *The Migration of the Negro*, made between 1939 and 1941.

Those who migrated first found jobs in the North because of labor shortages resulting from World War I, but as others followed, life in the North soon revealed itself to be little different from that in the South. The *Migration* series, as it is generally known, depicts the entire saga. The large number of people arriving in Chicago, St. Louis, Pittsburgh, and New York encounter social injustice, racism, inadequate housing conditions, and have to come to terms with race riots. In one panel, *They Also Found Discrimination* (fig. 21.26), Lawrence depicts, with stunning simplicity, the division between white and black that the African-American population encountered in the North. One of the most subtle, but startling effects of the piece is the almost complete absence of facial features on the African-Americans. They are anonymous, undifferentiated, almost "invisible," to use the word of African-American writer Ralph

Ellison, who explored the effects of this experience in his classic novel, *Invisible Man*.

SOUTHERN REGIONALIST WRITING

The inspiration for regionalism in American painting was in fact the regionalist emphasis identifiable in American fiction between the two world wars. A distinct brand of writing developed, especially in the South. The South's "tall-tale" tradition was enhanced by a colorful dialect and a peculiar usage of the English language, and, in no small part, by the memory of the Civil War, which had fostered a sense of regional pride and identity. The writing of the Southern regionalists is often marked by violent and frequently grotesque characters who are often treated with colloquial humor. It is also distinguished, in particular, by its sense of place.

William Faulkner. Unlike Hemingway, who chose fictional settings in various parts of America, Europe, and Africa, WILLIAM FAULKNER (1897–1962) chose

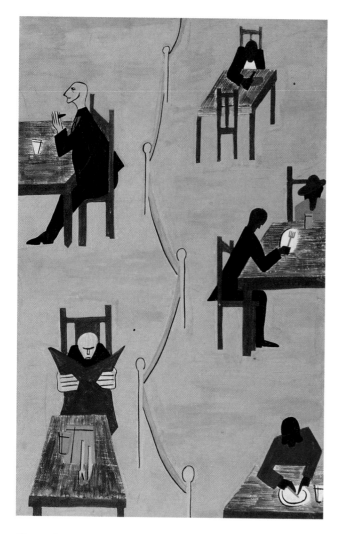

Figure 21.26 Jacob Lawrence, *They Also Found Discrimination*, from the series *The Migration of the Negro*, 1940–41, tempera on wood, 21¼ × 18″ (54 × 45.7 cm), Philips Collection, Washington, D.C. When the series was exhibited in 1941, Lawrence achieved instant fame, and the series was purchased jointly by the Philips Collection and the Museum of Modern Art, in New York, who divided the panels between them. It was reassembled as a complete series in the mid-1990s when it toured the country once again to national acclaim.

to remain a chronicler of the American South. Most of his fiction is set in Yoknapatawpha County, very much like his native Lafayette County, Mississippi. In his Yoknapatawpha works, Faulkner describes the decline of the local families. His body of work, which ranges widely in style, tone, and technique, earned him a Nobel Prize in 1950.

Faulkner experimented widely with narrative. In *The Sound and the Fury*, for instance, he tells the story of the increasing misfortunes of the Compson family from four different points of view. Each narrative perspective provides the context for the others, so that the whole story

is known through compilation. He also uses a stream of consciousness technique.

Faulkner realized at an early stage that in exploring the world close to him he was also exploring ideas that resonated far beyond the particular locales he was describing. As Faulkner himself put it: "I discovered that my own little postage stamp of native soil was worth writing about and that I would never live long enough to exhaust it." For all its intricacy of form and rhetorical brilliance, Faulkner's work derives its power from his depiction of characters, whose struggle to endure remains both familiar and remarkable. In his Nobel Prize acceptance speech, Faulkner noted that "man will not merely endure: he will prevail ... because he has a soul, a spirit capable of compassion and sacrifice and endurance."

Flannery O'Connor. One dynamically unique voice in modern American fiction is that of FLANNERY O'CONNOR (1925–1964). Her stories explore humor, irony, and paradox, especially evil and redemption, within the Christian belief system. O'Connor is a social satirist often challenging American attitudes toward issues such as random violence, race relations, and class discrimination.

Though O'Connor set her fiction in the South, she explored ideas from Roman Catholicism that transcend the confines of regionalism. "The woods are full of regional writers," she once said, "and it is the great horror of every serious Southern writer that he will become one of them." Several of O'Connor's stories begin with a comic protagonist who indulges in fantasies of moral or social superiority or who has a false sense of the certainty of things. The protagonist then has an ironic and traumatic encounter with other characters, or with situations that suggest a disturbing and incomprehensible universe. Though her stories blend comedy and tragedy, several works end quite gruesomely, such as "A Good Man Is Hard to Find."

THE AMERICAN SOUND

Just as American painters and writers evoked the distinct character of America's regions, a number of composers and musicians sought to convey their own sense of a distinctively American "sound." For over two centuries, people had brought their own musical customs and instruments from many different countries, and, as they settled into communities, different folk sounds developed across the land. Spirited banjo and fiddle music grew popular in the Appalachian mountains; cowboy songs thrived on the American Prairie; gospel music arose in African-American communities in the South; and jazz, which developed in New Orleans, spread to big cities around the country, including New York, Chicago, and Los Angeles. A rich cultural resource was there for composers to adopt and exploit.

Cross Currents

DIEGO RIVERA AND THE DETROIT MURALS

*I*n the early 1920s, the Mexican government initiated a mural movement designed to give the Mexican people a sense of identity and national pride. One of the leading painters of this movement was DIEGO RIVERA (1886–1957). Rivera had lived in Paris, studying the work of Picasso and Braque. He had developed a fluid Cubist style, but when confronted with the task of creating a national revolutionary art, he traveled to Italy to study the Italian fresco. He also immersed himself in Mexico's pre-Columbian heritage.

In 1931, Rivera was commissioned by Edsel B. Ford and the Detroit Institute of Arts to create a series of frescoes for the museum's Garden Court. Rivera was to depict something directly associated with Detroit. Being fascinated both by the promise of modern industry and the plight of the industrial workers, Rivera decided to represent Detroit's industry—its famous automobile factories, pharmaceutical and chemical companies, its aviation facilities and power plants.

Working from drawings and photographs, Rivera made panels for all four walls of the court, with large panels for the north and south walls. At the top of the north panel (fig. 21.27) are

depictions of two of what he regarded as the four races of humanity—the Native American and the African-American. Opposite them, on the south panel, are images of the Caucasian and Asian races. The main part of the north panel depicts the assembly line of automobile manufacturing, showing people molding engine blocks, boring cylin-

ders, and making the final touches. Rivera was not oblivious to the reality of the workers' lives. At the bottom left, a line of workers punch into a time clock. At the bottom right, they eat lunch. Between the two, Rivera captures the extraordinary exertion and strength required of these workers, all day, every day.

Figure 21.27 Diego Rivera, *Detroit Industry* (north wall), 1932–33, fresco, main panel 17'8½" × 45' (5.40 × 13.20 m), The Detroit Institute of Arts. At once a celebration of industry and an exposé of the workers' plight, Rivera's mural is a relatively optimistic plea for social and economic reform through, and by means of, industrial progress.

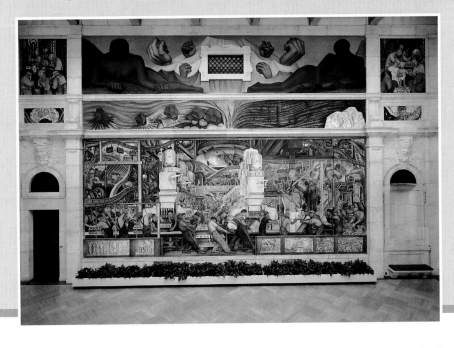

Aaron Copland. Born in Brooklyn, AARON COPLAND [COPE-land] (1900–1990) is one of the most highly esteemed American composers. After his early training, Copland went to Paris for four years, where he experienced first hand the artistic energy of Picasso, Stravinsky, Hemingway, and Pound, as well as that of many other modernist writers, artists, and composers. Returning to America in the mid-1920s, Copland was determined to compose music with a distinctively American style, music that would appeal to a wide and diverse audience. He achieved this with a series of ballet scores that relied heavily on American folk elements. Copland worked closely with two leading choreographers of the time, who were themselves striving for uniquely American dance aesthetics. Agnes de Mille choreographed the ballet *Rodeo* to Copland's music in

1942; in 1944 Martha Graham choreographed *Appalachian Spring*. De Mille went on to arrange the stage dance for several leading Broadway musicals, including *Oklahoma!* (1943) and had her own touring company for years. Graham's internationally renowned dance company still exists (see box on p. 387).

Although Copland's score for the ballet *Rodeo* has been a favorite among American audiences, his *Appalachian Spring* is performed more frequently as a concert piece. The work's subject is, as he said, "a pioneer celebration in spring around a newly built farmhouse in the Pennsylvania hills" in the early nineteenth century. A bride and groom, their neighbor, and a preacher and his congregation constitute the piece's characters. Copland's music imitates American fiddle tunes and hymns, including the traditional Shaker hymn, *Simple Gifts.*

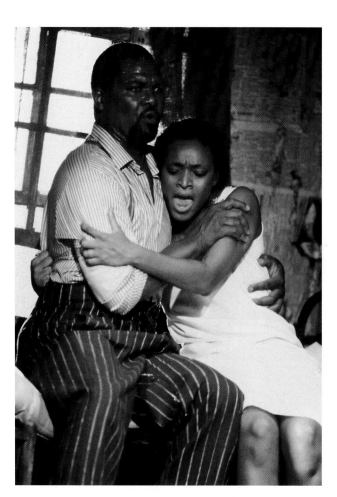

Figure 21.28 A scene from a production of George Gershwin's *Porgy and Bess* at Glyndebourne, England.

George Gershwin. More inspired by African-American blues and jazz is the music of GEORGE GERSHWIN (1898–1937). In its fusion of classical and jazz elements and its mingling of a wide range of sounds, Gershwin's work stands for the "sound" of the modern age, as signified by the four taxi horns in *An American in Paris* (1928), his tribute to the expatriate scene.

An accomplished jazz pianist himself, Gershwin's *Rhapsody in Blue* (1924) and his *Piano Concerto in F* (1925) were both composed with a view to taking advantage of his own skill at the keyboard, and both include long piano solos accompanied by full orchestra. But Gershwin is probably best known for *Porgy and Bess* (1935), one of the earliest and most important American operas (fig. 21.28). It addresses the lives of poor black people in Charleston, South Carolina, and contains some of the most widely heard songs of the 1930s, including the hit "Summertime." Gershwin traveled to South Carolina to familiarize himself with the local dialect and the region's performance rituals, witnessed in church services and public gatherings.

THE JAZZ AGE

The origins of American jazz go back to the African rhythms and organizational principles that characterize its form. In vocal music, the call and response pattern of ritual tribal practice, in which the leader sings a phrase to which the community replies, can be heard in gospel, jazz, and even rock and roll. The jazz **riff**, a short phrase repeated over and over, often unifies the music, as it does today in the so-called "samples" that are the basis of rap and hip-hop. Syncopated and off-beat rhythms, together with improvisation of a basic melody or phrase, are the most characteristic features of jazz.

Scott Joplin. SCOTT JOPLIN (1868–1917) made famous **ragtime**, a type of jazz piano composition in which the left hand plays a steady beat while the right improvises on a popular or even classical melody in syncopated rhythm. **Syncopation** means accenting a beat where it is not expected, in particular an off-beat or in-between beats. Joplin, the son of a slave, began his career as the pianist at the Maple Leaf Saloon in Sedalia, Missouri. His score of the "Maple Leaf Rag," published in 1899, quickly sold hundreds of thousands of copies and ranks as one of the first true pop "hits."

Louis Armstrong. One of the best-known jazz musicians of all time is LOUIS ARMSTRONG (1900–1971). Also known as "Satchmo," Armstrong was a vocalist and a trumpeter. Born and raised in New Orleans, a mecca for jazz in America, Armstrong first played in a New Orleans jazz combo. A few years later, Armstrong left to play cornet in Chicago with King Oliver's Creole Jazz Band. In no time, he had recorded with his own bands and had secured his place as a premier jazz trumpeter.

A stunning improviser, Armstrong could take a simple melody and transform it into a singing, swinging piece by changing its rhythm and altering its pitches. He could also play the trumpet in higher registers than anyone ever before, accurately and powerfully, and he made his music distinctive and original with an array of vibratos and note-altering variations.

His gravelly voice, though, some might say, neither elegant nor beautiful, conveyed spirit and fire. Among his vocal techniques was **scat** singing, in which Armstrong vocalized nonsense syllables on a melody. Ella Fitzgerald, after him, was to take scat to new heights of artistry.

Duke Ellington. One of the greatest jazz pianists and arrangers was EDWARD KENNEDY ("DUKE") ELLINGTON (1899–1974). Ellington served as composer and conductor of a jazz ensemble, or swing band (fig. 21.29). Unlike the New Orleans-style combo featuring improvisations by each of the five to eight members of the group, **swing** music was a jazz style played by big bands of approximately fifteen musicians arranged in

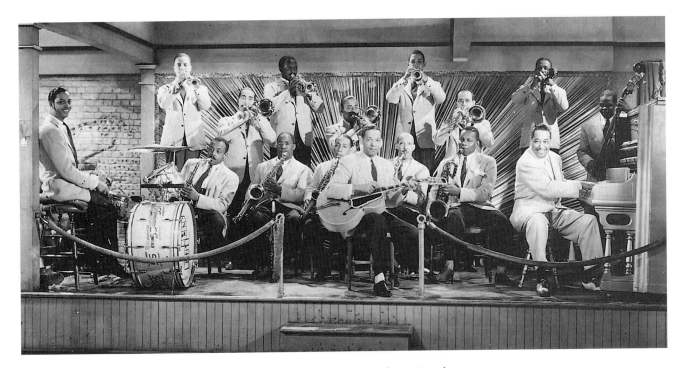

Figure 21.29   The Duke Ellington Orchestra in 1949. Ellington was a dynamic and creative performer. He and his band were immensely popular at the famous Cotton Club in Harlem.

three groups: saxophones/clarinets; brasses (trumpets/ trombones); and rhythm (piano, percussion, guitar, and bass). Although swing often included improvised solos, its music was most often arranged due to the larger size of the group. The members of the swing band did more ensemble playing, with each section taking its turn: saxes, brasses, and rhythm, playing in unison. The saxophone became a popular solo instrument during the swing era (1925–45), with percussion instruments and the piano also becoming prominent instruments of jazz expression.

Ellington provided his musicians with opportunities to display their musical prowess. He composed mini-concertos within pieces. One example, his *Concerto for Cootie* (1940), showcases Ellington's trumpeter Cootie Williams, who had a vast command of tonal color in ways that differed markedly from those of Louis Armstrong.

READINGS

✦ **T.S. Eliot**
The Love Song of J. Alfred Prufrock

Eliot's most popular poem, "The Love Song of J. Alfred Prufrock," portrays an inhibited, insecure man unable to engage truly in life. In a series of self-deprecatory asides, he reveals his fear of human contact, identifying himself as a diminished, ineffectual person, who cannot declare his feelings for a woman. Eliot's Prufrock is the prototype of a human caught in the seeming futility of the modern age of anxiety.

S'io credesse che mia risposta fosse
A persona che mai tornasse al mondo,
Questa fiamma staria senza più scosse.
Ma perciocche giammai di questo fondo
Non tornò vivo alcun, s'i'odo il vero,
Senza tema d'infamia ti rispondo.°

Let us go then, you and I,
When the evening is spread out against the sky
Like a patient etherized upon a table;
Let us go, through certain half-deserted streets,
The muttering retreats   5
Of restless nights in one-night cheap hotels
And sawdust restaurants with oyster-shells:
Streets that follow like a tedious argument
Of insidious intent
To lead you to an overwhelming question…   10
Oh, do not ask, "What is it?"
Let us go and make our visit.

In the room the women come and go
Talking of Michelangelo.

The yellow fog that rubs its back upon the window-
    panes,   15

Epigraph from Dante's Inferno, canto XXVII, 61–66. The words are spoken by Guido da Montefeltro when asked to identify himself. "If I thought my answer were given to anyone who could ever return to the world, this flame would shake no more; but since none ever did return above from this depth, if what I hear is true, without fear of infamy I answer thee."

The yellow smoke that rubs its muzzle on the window-
    panes,
Licked its tongue into the corners of the evening,
Lingered upon the pools that stand in drains,
Let fall upon its back the soot that falls from chimneys,
Slipped by the terrace, made a sudden leap,   20
And seeing that it was a soft October night,
Curled once about the house, and fell asleep.

And indeed there will be time
For the yellow smoke that slides along the street
Rubbing its back upon the window-panes;   25
There will be time, there will be time
To prepare a face to meet the faces that you meet;
There will be time to murder and create,
And time for all the works and days of hands
That lift and drop a question on your plate;   30
Time for you and time for me,
And time yet for a hundred indecisions,
And for a hundred visions and revisions,
Before the taking of a toast and tea.

In the room the women come and go   35
Talking of Michelangelo.

And indeed there will be time
To wonder, "Do I dare?" and, "Do I dare?"
Time to turn back and descend the stair,
With a bald spot in the middle of my hair—   40
(They will say: "How his hair is growing thin!")
My morning coat, my collar mounting firmly to the
    chin,
My necktie rich and modest, but asserted by a simple
    pin—
(They will say: "But how his arms and legs are thin!")
Do I dare   45
Disturb the universe?
In a minute there is time
For decisions and revisions which a minute will reverse.

For I have known them all already, known them all—
Have known the evenings, mornings, afternoons,   50
I have measured out my life with coffee spoons;
I know the voices dying with a dying fall°
Beneath the music from a farther room.
    So how should I presume?

And I have known the eyes already, known them all—
The eyes that fix you in a formulated phrase,   56
And when I am formulated, sprawling on a pin,
When I am pinned and wriggling on the wall,
Then how should I begin
To spit out all the butt-ends of my days and ways?   60
    And how should I presume?

And I have known the arms already, known them all—
Arms that are braceleted and white and bare
(But in the lamplight, downed with light brown hair!)
Is it perfume from a dress   65
That makes me so digress?
Arms that lie along a table, or wrap about a shawl.
    And should I then presume?
    And how should I begin?
.   .   .   .   .
Shall I say, I have gone at dusk through
    narrow streets   70
And watched the smoke that rises from the pipes
Of lonely men in shirt-sleeves, leaning out of
    windows?...

I should have been a pair of ragged claws
Scuttling across the floors of silent seas.
    .   .   .   .   .
And the afternoon, the evening, sleeps so peacefully! 75
Smoothed by long fingers,
Asleep... tired... or it malingers,
Stretched on the floor, here beside you and me.
Should I, after tea and cakes and ices,
Have the strength to force the moment to its crisis?   80
But though I have wept and fasted, wept and prayed,
Though I have seen my head (grown slightly bald)
    brought in upon a platter,°
I am no prophet—and here's no greater matter;
I have seen the moment of my greatness flicker,
And I have seen the eternal Footman hold my coat, and
    snicker,   85
And in short, I was afraid.

And would it have been worth it, after all,
After the cups, the marmalade, the tea,
Among the porcelain, among some talk of you and me,
Would it have been worth while,   90
To have bitten off the matter with a smile,
To have squeezed the universe into a ball
To roll it towards some overwhelming question,
To say: "I am Lazarus,° come from the dead,
Come back to tell you all, I shall tell you all"—   95
If one, settling a pillow by her head,
    Should say: "That is not what I meant at all.
    That is not it, at all."

And would it have been worth it, after all,
Would it have been worth while,   100
After the sunsets and the dooryards and the sprinkled
    streets,
After the novels, after the teacups, after the skirts that
    trail along the floor—
And this, and so much more?—
It is impossible to say just what I mean!

---

⁵²*I know ... dying fall:* this echoes the first lines of
Shakespeare's *Twelfth Night* I, i, 1–4. "If music be the food of
love, play on;/Give me excess of it, that, surfeiting/The
appetite may sicken, and so die./That strain again! it had a
dying fall."

⁸²*my head ... upon a platter:* John the Baptist was beheaded at
the order of King Herod to please his wife, Herodias, and
daughter, Salome. His head was offered to his daughter on a
platter. See Matthew 14:1–11.

⁹⁴*Lazarus:* Lazarus was raised from the dead by Jesus. See John
11: 1–44.

But as if a magic lantern threw the nerves in patterns on
    a screen: *105*
Would it have been worth while
If one, settling a pillow or throwing off a shawl,
And turning toward the window, should say:
    "That is not it at all,
    That is not what I meant, at all."   *110*
. . . . .

No! I am not Prince Hamlet, nor was meant to be;
Am an attendant lord, one that will do
To swell a progress,° start a scene or two,
Advise the prince; no doubt, an easy tool,
Deferential, glad to be of use,   *115*
Politic, cautious, and meticulous;
Full of high sentence, but a bit obtuse;
At times, indeed, almost ridiculous—
Almost, at times, the Fool.

I grow old... I grow old...   *120*
I shall wear the bottoms of my trousers rolled.

Shall I part my hair behind? Do I dare to eat a peach?
I shall wear white flannel trousers, and walk upon the
    beach.
I have heard the mermaids singing, each to each.

I do not think that they will sing to me.   *125*

I have seen them riding seaward on the waves
Combing the white hair of the waves blown back
When the wind blows the water white and black.

We have lingered in the chambers of the sea
By sea-girls wreathed with seaweed red and brown   *130*
Till human voices wake us, and we drown.

Langston Hughes
I, Too, Sing America

Langston Hughes (1902–1967) was the voice of two generations of African-Americans during the early to mid-twentieth century. He was a leading figure in New York's "Harlem Renaissance," a wave of astonishing African-American creativity in literature and the arts. Strongly influenced by music, especially the blues, Hughes captured its rhythms and sadness in many of his poems.

I, too, sing America
I am the darker brother.
They send me to eat in the kitchen
When company comes,
But I laugh,   *5*
And eat well,
And grow strong.

Tomorrow,
I'll be at the table
When company comes.   *10*

Nobody'll dare
Say to me,
"Eat in the kitchen,"
Then.

Besides,   *15*
They'll see how beautiful I am
And be ashamed—

I, too, am America.

Virginia Woolf
from *To the Lighthouse*

With its wide-ranging stream of consciousness techniques and its evocative poetic symbols, To the Lighthouse *(1927) is generally considered one of the seminal masterpieces of literary modernism. The following passage from the first section of Woolf's novel describes a single day at the Ramsay family's country home near the sea. Woolf's central character, Mrs. Ramsay, is a woman with an open and generous spirit, who is crushed by the clipped severity of her repressed husband, a distinguished philosopher.*

"Yes, of course, if it's fine tomorrow," said Mrs. Ramsay. "But you'll have to be up with the lark," she added.

To her son these words conveyed an extraordinary joy, as if it were settled, the expedition were bound to take place, and the wonder to which he had looked forward, for years and years it seemed, was, after a night's darkness and a day's sail, within touch. Since he belonged, even at the age of six, to that great clan which cannot keep this feeling separate from that, but must let future prospects, with their joys and sorrows, cloud what is actually at hand, since to such people even in earliest childhood any turn in the wheel of sensation has the power to crystallise and transfix the moment upon which its gloom or radiance rests, James Ramsay, sitting on the floor cutting out pictures from the illustrated catalogue of the Army and Navy Stores, endowed the picture of a refrigerator, as his mother spoke, with heavenly bliss. It was fringed with joy. The wheelbarrow, the lawnmower, the sound of poplar trees, leaves whitening before rain, rooks cawing, brooms knocking, dresses rustling—all these were so coloured and distinguished in his mind that he had already his private code, his secret language, though he appeared the image of stark and uncompromising severity, with his high forehead and his fierce blue eyes, impeccably candid and pure, frowning slightly at the sight of human frailty, so that his mother, watching him guide his scissors neatly round the refrigerator, imagined him all red and ermine on the Bench or directing a stern and momentous enterprise in some crisis of public affairs.

"But," said his father, stopping in front of the drawing-room window, "it won't be fine."

Had there been an axe handy, or a poker, any weapon that would have gashed a hole in his father's breast and killed him, there and then, James would have seized it. Such were the extremes of emotion that Mr. Ramsay excited in his children's breasts by his mere presence; standing, as now, lean as a knife, narrow as the blade of one, grinning sarcastically, not only with the pleasure of disillusioning his son

---

¹¹³*progress:* a procession or journey made by members of the royal court.

and casting ridicule upon his wife, who was ten thousand times better in every way than he was (James thought), but also with some secret conceit at his own accuracy of judgement. What he said was true. It was always true. He was incapable of untruth; never tampered with a fact; never altered a disagreeable word to suit the pleasure or convenience of any mortal beings least of all of his own children, who, sprung from his loins, should be aware from childhood that life is difficult; facts uncompromising; and the passage to that fabled land where our brightest hopes are extinguished, our frail barks founder in darkness (here Mr. Ramsay would straighten his back and narrow his little blue eyes upon the horizon), one that needs, above all, courage, truth, and the power to endure.

"But it may be fine—I expect it will be fine," said Mrs. Ramsay, making some little twist of the reddish brown stocking she was knitting, impatiently. If she finished it tonight, if they did go to the Lighthouse after all, it was to be given to the Lighthouse keeper for his little boy, who was threatened with a tuberculous hip; together with a pile of old magazines, and some tobacco, indeed, whatever she could find lying about, not really wanted, but only littering the room, to give those poor fellows, who must be bored to death sitting all day with nothing to do but polish the lamp and trim the wick and rake about on their scrap of garden, something to amuse them. For how would you like to be shut up for a whole month at a time, and possibly more in stormy weather, upon a rock the size of a tennis lawn? she would ask; and to have no letters or newspapers, and to see nobody; if you were married, not to see your wife, not to know how your children were,—if they were ill, if they had fallen down and broken their legs or arms; to see the same dreary waves breaking week after week, and then a dreadful storm coming, and the windows covered with spray, and birds dashed against the lamp, and the whole place rocking, and not be able to put your nose out of doors for fear of being swept into the sea? How would you like that? she asked, addressing herself particularly to her daughters. So she added, rather differently, one must take them whatever comforts one can.

"It's due west," said the atheist Tansley, holding his bony fingers spread so that the wind blew through them, for he was sharing Mr. Ramsay's evening walk up and down, up and down the terrace. That is to say, the wind blew from the worst possible direction for landing at the Lighthouse. Yes, he did say disagreeable things, Mrs. Ramsay admitted; it was odious of him to rub this in, and make James still more disappointed; but at the same time, she would not let them laugh at him. "The atheist," they called him; "the little atheist." Rose mocked him; Prue mocked him; Andrew, Jasper, Roger mocked him; even old Badger without a tooth in his head had bit him, for being (as Nancy put it) the hundred and tenth young man to chase them all the way up to the Hebrides when it was ever so much nicer to be alone.

"Nonsense," said Mrs. Ramsay, with great severity. Apart from the habit of exaggeration which they had from her, and from the implication (which was true) that she asked too many people to stay, and had to lodge some in the town, she could not bear incivility to her guests, to young men in particular, who were poor as church mice, "exceptionally able," her husband said, his great admirers, and come there for a

holiday. Indeed, she had the whole of the other sex under her protection; for reasons she could not explain, for their chivalry and valour, for the fact that they negotiated treaties, ruled India, controlled finance; finally for an attitude towards herself which no woman could fail to feel or to find agreeable, something trustful, childlike, reverential; which an old woman could take from a young man without loss of dignity, and woe betide the girl—pray Heaven it was none of her daughters!—who did not feel the worth of it, and all that it implied, to the marrow of her bones!

She turned with severity upon Nancy. He had not chased them, she said. He had been asked.

They must find a way out of it all. There might be some simpler way, some less laborious way, she sighed. When she looked in the glass and saw her hair grey, her cheek sunk, at fifty she thought, possibly she might have managed things better—her husband; money; his books. But for her own part she would never for a single second regret her decision, evade difficulties, or slur over duties. She was now formidable to behold, and it was only in silence, looking up from their plates, after she had spoken so severely about Charles Tansley, that her daughters, Prue, Nancy, Rose—could sport with infidel ideas which they had brewed for themselves of a life different from hers; in Paris, perhaps; a wilder life; not always taking care of some man or other; for there was in all their minds a mute questioning of deference and chivalry, of the Bank of England and the Indian Empire, of ringed fingers and lace, though to them all there was something in this of the essence of beauty, which called out the manliness in their girlish hearts, and made them, as they sat at table beneath their mother's eyes, honour her strange severity, her extreme courtesy, like a Queen's raising from the mud to wash a beggar's dirty foot, when she thus admonished them so very severely about that wretched atheist who had chased them—or, speaking accurately, been invited to stay with them—in the Isles of Skye.

Ernest Hemingway
Hills Like White Elephants

The following short story from 1927 illustrates Hemingway's style: detailed yet laconic, and close to the bone. It opens with the symbolic image of mountains rising from the plain, but the reader must glean Hemingway's meaning. Hemingway lets his images speak for themselves. His dialogue is remarkable for what his characters do not say. The details of the conversation, as well as those of the landscape, reinforce the contrast between sterility and fertility, life and death.

The hills across the valley of the Ebro were long and white. On this side there was no shade and no trees and the station was between two lines of rails in the sun. Close against the side of the station there was the warm shadow of the building and a curtain, made of strings of bamboo beads, hung across the open door into the bar, to keep out flies. The American and the girl with him sat at a table in the shade, outside the building. It was very hot and the express from Barcelona would come in forty minutes. It stopped at this junction for two minutes and went on to Madrid.

"What should we drink?" the girl asked. She had taken off her hat and put it on the table.

"It's pretty hot," the man said.

"Let's drink beer."

"Dos cervezas," the man said into the curtain.

"Big ones?" a woman asked from the doorway.

"Yes. Two big ones."

The woman brought two glasses of beer and two felt pads. She put the felt pads and the beer glasses on the table and looked at the man and the girl. The girl was looking off at the line of hills. They were white in the sun and the country was brown and dry.

"They look like white elephants," she said.

"I've never seen one," the man drank his beer.

"No, you wouldn't have."

"I might have," the man said. "Just because you say I wouldn't have doesn't prove anything."

The girl looked at the bead curtain. "They've painted something on it," she said. "what does it say?"

"Anis del Toro. It's a drink."

"Could we try it?"

The man called "Listen" through the curtain. The woman came out from the bar.

"Four reales."

"We want two Anis del Toro."

"With water?"

"Do you want it with water?"

"I don't know," the girl said. "Is it good with water?"

"It's all right."

"You want them with water?" asked the woman.

"Yes, with water."

"It tastes like licorice," the girl said and put the glass down.

"That's the way with everything."

"Yes," said the girl. "Everything tastes of licorice. Especially all the things you've waited so long for, like absinthe."

"Oh, cut it out."

"You started it," the girl said. "I was being amused. I was having a fine time."

"Well, let's try and have a fine time."

"All right. I was trying. I said the mountains looked like white elephants. Wasn't that bright?"

"That was bright."

"I wanted to try this new drink. That's all we do, isn't it—look at things and try new drinks?"

"I guess so."

The girl looked across at the hills.

"They're lovely hills," she said. "They don't really look like white elephants. I just meant the coloring of their skin through the trees."

"Should we have another drink?"

"All right."

The warm wind blew the bead curtain against the table.

"The beer's nice and cool," the man said.

"It's lovely," the girl said.

"It's really an awfully simple operation, Jig," the man said. "It's not really an operation at at."

The girl looked at the ground the table legs rested on.

"I know you wouldn't mind it, Jig. It's really not anything. It's just to let the air in."

The girl did not say anything.

"I'll go with you and I'll stay with you all the time. They just let the air in and then it's all perfectly natural."

"Then what will we do afterward?"

"We'll be fine afterward. Just like we were before."

"What makes you think so?"

"That's the only thing that bothers us. It's the only thing that's made us unhappy."

The girl looked at the bead curtain, put her hand out and took hold of two of the strings of beads.

"And you think then we'll be all right and be happy."

"I know we will. You don't have to be afraid. I've known lots of people that have done it."

"So have I," said the girl. "And afterward they were all so happy."

"Well," the man said, "if you don't want to you don't have to. I wouldn't have you do it if you didn't want to. But I know it's perfectly simple."

"And you really want to?"

"I think it's the best thing to do. But I don't want you to do it if you don't really want to."

"And if I do it you'll be happy and things will be like they were and you'll love me?"

"I love you now. You know I love you."

"I know. But if I do it, then it will be nice again if I say things are like white elephants, and you'll like it?"

"I'll love it. I love it now but I just can't think about it. You know how I get when I worry."

"If I do it you won't ever worry?"

"I won't worry about that because it's perfectly simple."

"Then I'll do it. Because I don't care about me."

"What do you mean?"

"I don't care about me."

"Well, I care about you."

"Oh, yes. But I don't care about me. And I'll do it and then everything will be fine."

"I don't want you to do it if you feel that way."

The girl stood up and walked to the end of the station. Across on the other side, were fields of grain and trees along the banks of the Ebro. Far away, beyond the river, were mountains. The shadow of a cloud moved across the field of grain and she saw the river through the trees.

"And we could have all this," she said. "And we could have everything and every day we make it more impossible."

"What did you say?"

"I said we could have everything."

"We can have everything."

"No, we can't."

"We can have the whole world."

"No, we can't."

"We can go everywhere."

"No, we can't. It isn't ours any more."

"It's ours."

"No, it isn't. And once they take it away, you never get it back."

"But they haven't taken it away."

"We'll wait and see."

"Come on back in the shade," he said. "You mustn't feel that way."

"I don't feel any way," the girl said. "I just know things."

"I don't want you to do anything that you don't want to do—"

"Nor that isn't good for me," she said. "I know. Could we have another beer?"

"All right. But you've got to realize—"

"I realize," the girl said. "Can't we maybe stop talking?"

They sat down at the table and the girl looked across at the hills on the dry side of the valley and the man looked at her and at the table.

"You've got to realize," he said, "that I don't want you to do it if you don't want to. I'm perfectly willing to go through with it if it means anything to you."

"Doesn't it mean anything to you? We could get along."

"Of course it does. But I don't want anybody but you. I don't want any one else. And I know it's perfectly simple."

"Yes, to you it's perfectly simple."

"It's all right for you to say that, but I do know it."

"Would you do something for me now?"

"I'd do anything for you."

"Would you please please please please please please please stop talking?"

He did not say anything but looked at the bags against the wall of the station. There were labels on them from all the hotels where they had spent nights.

"But I don't want you to," he said, "I don't care anything about it."

"I'll scream," the girl said.

The woman came out through the curtains with two glasses of beer and put them down on the damp felt pads. "The train comes in five minutes," she said.

"What did she say?" asked the girl.

"That the train is coming in five minutes."

The girl smiled brightly at the woman, to thank her.

"I'd better take the bags over to the other side of the station," the man said. She smiled at him.

"All right. Then come back and we'll finish the beer."

He picked up the two heavy bags and carried them around the station to the other tracks. He looked up the tracks but could not see the train. Coming back, he walked through the barroom, where people waiting for the train were drinking. He drank an Anis at the bar and looked at the people. They were all waiting reasonably for the train. He went out through the bead curtain. She was sitting at the table and smiled at him.

"Do you feel better?" he asked.

"I feel fine," she said. "There's nothing wrong with me. I feel fine."

Flannery O'Connor
Everything That Rises Must Converge

Flannery O'Connor's stories, such as the following one, often start with a comic character who fantasizes about taking the moral or social highground. Somehow things never proceed as the characters intend, and those stories that do not end violently often end with a sense of revelation so shocking as to be violent. For O'Connor, truth was of the greatest importance—even when it revealed itself as fragmented or violent. The novelist and critic V.S. Pritchett suggested that the characters in O'Connor's stories are "plain human beings in whose fractured lives the writer has discovered an uncouth relationship with the lasting myths and the violent passions of human life."

Her doctor had told Julian's mother that she must lose twenty pounds on account of her blood pressure, so on Wednesday nights Julian had to take her downtown on the bus for a reducing class at the Y. The reducing class was designed for working girls over fifty, who weighed from 165 to 200 pounds. His mother was one of the slimmer ones, but she said ladies did not tell their age or weight. She would not ride the buses by herself at night since they had been integrated, and because the reducing class was one of her few pleasures, necessary for her health, and *free*, she said Julian could at least put himself out to take her, considering all she did for him. Julian did not like to consider all she did for him, but every Wednesday night he braced himself and took her.

She was almost ready to go, standing before the hall mirror, putting on her hat, while he, his hands behind him, appeared pinned to the door frame, waiting like Saint Sebastian for the arrows to begin piercing him. The hat was new and had cost her seven dollars and a half. She kept saying, "Maybe I shouldn't have paid that for it. No, I shouldn't have. I'll take it off and return it tomorrow. I shouldn't have bought it."

Julian raised his eyes to heaven. "Yes, you should have bought it," he said. "Put it on and let's go." It was a hideous hat. A purple velvet flap came down on one side of it and stood up on the other; the rest of it was green and looked like a cushion with the stuffing out. He decided it was less comical than jaunty and pathetic. Everything that gave her pleasure was small and depressed him.

She lifted the hat one more time and set it down slowly on top of her head. Two wings of gray hair protruded on either side of her florid face, but her eyes, sky-blue, were as innocent and untouched by experience as they must have been when she was ten. Were it not that she was a widow who had struggled fiercely to feed and clothe and put him through school and who was supporting him still, "until he got on his feet," she might have been a little girl that he had to take to town.

"It's all right, it's all right," he said. "Let's go." He opened the door himself and started down the walk to get her going. The sky was a dying violet and the houses stood out darkly against it, bulbous liver-colored monstrosities of a uniform ugliness though no two were alike. Since this had been a fashionable neighborhood forty years ago, his mother persisted in thinking they did well to have an apartment in it. Each house had a narrow collar of dirt around it in which sat, usually, a grubby child. Julian walked with his hands in his pockets, his head down and thrust forward and his eyes glazed with the determination to make himself completely numb during the time he would be sacrificed to her pleasure.

The door closed and he turned to find the dumpy figure, surmounted by the atrocious hat, coming toward him. "Well," she said, "you only live once and paying a little more for it, I at least won't meet myself coming and going."

"Some day I'll start making money," Julian said gloomily—he knew he never would—"and you can have one of those jokes whenever you take the fit." But first they would move. He visualized a place where the nearest neighbors would be three miles away on either side.

"I think you're doing fine," she said, drawing on her gloves. "You've only been out of school a year. Rome wasn't built in a day."

She was one of the few members of the Y reducing class

who arrived in hat and gloves and who had a son who had been to college. "It takes time," she said, "and the world is in such a mess. This hat looked better on me than any of the others, though when she brought it out I said, 'Take that thing back. I wouldn't have it on my head,' and she said, 'Now wait till you see it on,' and when she put it on me, I said, 'We-ull,' and she said, 'If you ask me, that hat does something for you and you do something for that hat, and besides,' she said, 'with that hat, you won't meet yourself coming and going.'"

Julian thought he could have stood his lot better if she had been selfish, if she had been an old hag who drank and screamed at him. He walked along, saturated in depression, as if in the midst of his martyrdom he had lost his faith. Catching sight of his long, hopeless, irritated face, she stopped suddenly with a grief-stricken look, and pulled back on his arm. "Wait on me," she said. "I'm going back to the house and take this thing off and tomorrow I'm going to return it. I was out of my head. I can pay the gas bill with the seven-fifty."

He caught her arm in a vicious grip. "You are not going to take it back," he said. "I like it."

"Well," she said, "I don't think I ought . . ."

"Shut up and enjoy it," he muttered, more depressed than ever.

"With the world in the mess it's in," she said, "it's a wonder we can enjoy anything. I tell you, the bottom rail is on the top."

Julian sighed.

"Of course," she said, "if you know who you are, you can go anywhere." She said this every time he took her to the reducing class. "Most of them in it are not our kind of people," she said, "but I can be gracious to anybody. I know who I am."

"They don't give a damn for your graciousness," Julian said savagely. "Knowing who you are is good for one generation only. You haven't the foggiest idea where you stand now or who you are."

She stopped and allowed her eyes to flash at him. "I most certainly do know who I am," she said, "and if you don't know who you are, I'm ashamed of you."

"Oh hell," Julian said.

"Your great-grandfather was a former governor of this state," she said. "Your grandfather was a prosperous landowner. Your grandmother was a Godhigh."

"Will you look around you," he said tensely, "and see where you are now?" and he swept his arm jerkily out to indicate the neighborhood, which the growing darkness at least made less dingy.

"You remain what you are," she said. "Your great-grandfather had a plantation and two hundred slaves."

"There are no more slaves," he said irritably.

"They were better off when they were," she said. He groaned to see that she was off on that topic. She rolled onto it every few days like a train on an open track. He knew every stop, every junction, every swamp along the way, and knew the exact point at which her conclusion would roll majestically into the station: "It's ridiculous. It's simply not realistic. They should rise, yes, but on their own side of the fence."

"Let's skip it," Julian said.

"The ones I feel sorry, for," she said, "are the ones that are half white. They're tragic."

"Will you skip it?"

"Suppose we were half white. We would certainly have mixed feelings."

"I have mixed feelings now," he groaned.

"Well let's talk about something pleasant," she said. "I remember going to Grandpa's when I was a little girl. Then the house had double stairways that went up to what was really the second floor—all the cooking was done on the first. I used to like to stay down in the kitchen on account of the way the walls smelled. I would sit with my nose pressed against the plaster and take deep breaths. Actually the place belonged to the Godhighs but your grandfather Chestny paid the mortgage and saved it for them. They were in reduced circumstances," she said, "but reduced or not, they never forgot who they were."

"Doubtless that decayed mansion reminded them," Julian muttered. He never spoke of it without contempt or thought of it without longing. He had seen it once when he was a child before it had been sold. The double stairways had rotted and been torn down. Negroes were living in it. But it remained in his mind as his mother had known it. It appeared in his dreams regularly. He would stand on the wide porch, listening to the rustle of oak leaves, then wander through the high-ceilinged hall into the parlor that opened onto it and gaze at the worn rugs and faded draperies. It occurred to him that it was he, not she, who could have appreciated it. He preferred its threadbare elegance to anything he could name and it was because of it that all the neighborhoods they had lived in had been a torment to him—whereas she had hardly known the difference. She called her insensitivity "being adjustable."

"And I remember the old darky who was my nurse, Caroline. There was no better person in the world. I've always had a great respect for my colored friends," she said. "I'd do anything in the world for them and they'd ..."

"Will you for God's sake get off that subject?" Julian said. When he got on a bus by himself, he made it a point to sit down beside a Negro, in reparation as it were for his mother's sins.

"You're mighty touchy tonight," she said. "Do you feel all right?"

"Yes I feel all right," he said. "Now lay off."

She pursed her lips. "Well, you certainly are in a vile humor," she observed. "I just won't speak to you at all."

They had reached the bus stop. There was no bus in sight and Julian, his hands still jammed in his pockets and his head thrust forward, scowled down the empty street. The frustration of having to wait on the bus as well as ride on it began to creep up his neck like a hot hand. The presence of his mother was borne in upon him as she gave a pained sigh. He looked at her bleakly. She was holding herself very erect under the preposterous hat, wearing it like a banner of her imaginary dignity. There was in him an evil urge to break her spirit. He suddenly unloosened his tie and pulled it off and put it in his pocket.

She stiffened. "why must you look like *that* when you take me to town?" she said. "Why must you deliberately embarrass me?"

"If you'll never learn where you are," he said, "you can at least learn where I am."

"You look like a—thug," she said.

"Then I must be one," he murmured.

"I'll just go home," she said. "I will not bother you. If you can't do a little thing like that for me . . ."

Rolling his eyes upward, he put his tie back on. "Restored to my class," he muttered. He thrust his face toward her and hissed, "True culture is in the mind, the *mind*," he said, and tapped his head, "the mind."

"It's in the heart," she said, "and in how you do things and how you do things is because of who you *are*."

"Nobody in the damn bus cares who you are."

"I care who I am," she said icily.

The lighted bus appeared on top of the next hill and as it approached, they moved out into the street to meet it. He put his hand under her elbow and hoisted her up on the creaking step. She entered with a little smile, as if she were going into a drawing room where everyone had been waiting for her. While he put in the tokens, she sat down on one of the broad front seats for three which faced the aisle. A thin woman with protruding teeth and long yellow hair was sitting on the end of it. His mother moved up beside her and left room for Julian beside herself. He sat down and looked at the floor across the aisle where a pair of thin feet in red and white canvas sandals were planted.

His mother immediately began a general conversation meant to attract anyone who felt like talking. "Can it get any hotter?" she said and removed from her purse a folding fan, black with a Japanese scene on it, which she began to flutter before her.

"I reckon it might could," the women with the protruding teeth said, "but I know for a fact my apartment couldn't get no hotter."

"It must get the afternoon sun," his mother said. She sat forward and looked up and down the bus. It was half filled. Everybody was white. "I see we have the bus to ourselves," she said. Julian cringed.

"For a change," said the woman across the aisle, the owner of the red and white canvas sandals. "I come on one the other day and they were thick as fleas—up front and all through."

"The world is in a mess every where," his mother said. "I don't know how we've let it get in this fix."

"What gets my goat is all those boys from good families stealing automobile tires," the woman with the protruding teeth said. "I told my boy, I said you may not be rich but you been raised right and if I ever catch you in any such mess, they can send you on to the reformatory. Be exactly where you belong."

"Training tells," his mother said. "Is your boy in high school?"

"Ninth grade," the woman said.

"My son just finished college last year. He wants so write but he's selling typewriters until he gets started," his mother said.

The woman leaned forward and peered at Julian. He threw her such a malevolent look that she subsided against the seat. On the floor across the aisle there was an abandoned newspaper. He got up and got it and opened it out in front of him. His mother discreetly continued the conversa-tion in a lower tone but the woman across the aisle said in a loud voice, "Well that's nice. Selling typewriters is close to writing. He can go right from one to the other."

"I tell him," his mother said, "that Rome wasn't built in a day."

Behind the newspaper Julian was withdrawing into the inner compartment of his mind where he spent most of his time. This was a kind of mental bubble in which he estab-lished himself when he could not bear to be a part of what was going on around him. From it he could see out and judge but in it he was safe from any kind of penetration from without. It was the only place where he felt free of the gen-eral idiocy of his fellows. His mother had never entered it but from it he could see her with absolute clarity.

The old lady was clever enough and he thought that if she had started from any of the right premises, more might have been expected of her. She lived according to the laws of her own fantasy world, outside of which he had never seen her set foot. The law of it was to sacrifice herself for him after she had first created the necessity to do so by mak-ing a mess of things. If he had permitted her sacrifices, it was only because her lack of foresight had made them nec-essary. All of her life had been a struggle to act like a Chestny without the Chestny goods, and to give him every-thing she thought a Chestny ought to have; but since, said she, it was fun to struggle, why complain? And when you had won, as she had won, what fun to look back on the hard times! He could not forgive her that she had enjoyed the struggle and that she thought *she* had won.

What she meant when she said she had won was that she had brought him up successfully and had sent him to college and that he had turned out so well—good looking (her teeth had gone unfilled so that his could be straightened), intelli-gent (he realized he was too intelligent to be a success), and with a future ahead of him (there was of course no future ahead of him). She excused his gloominess on the grounds that he was still growing up and his radical ideas on his lack of practical experience. She said he didn't yet know a thing about "life," that he hadn't even entered the real world—when already he was as disenchanted with it as a man of fifty.

The further irony of all this was that in spite of her, he had turned out so well. In spite of going to only a third-rate college, he had, on his own initiative, come out with a first-rate education; in spite of growing up dominated by a small mind, he had ended up with a large one; in spite of all her foolish views, he was free of prejudice and unafraid to face facts. Most miraculous of all, instead of being blinded by love for her as she was for him, he had cut himself emo-tionally free of her and could see her with complete objec-tivity. He was not dominated by his mother.

The bus stopped with a sudden jerk and shook him from his meditation. A woman from the back lurched forward with little steps and barely escaped falling in his newspaper as she righted herself. She got off and a large Negro got on. Julian kept his paper lowered to watch. It gave him a certain satisfaction to see injustice in daily operation. It confirmed his view that with a few exceptions there was no one worth knowing within a radius of three hundred miles. The Negro was well dressed and carried a briefcase. He looked around and then sat down on the other end of the seat where the woman with the red and white canvas sandals was sitting.

He immediately unfolded a newspaper and obscured himself behind it. Julian's mother's elbow at once prodded insistently into his ribs. "Now you see why I won't ride on these buses by myself," she whispered.

The woman with the red and white canvas sandals had risen at the same time the Negro sat down and had gone further back in the bus and taken the seat of the woman who had got off. His mother leaned forward and cast her an approving look.

Julian rose, crossed the aisle, and sat down in the place of the woman with the canvas sandals. From this position, he looked serenely across at his mother. Her face had turned an angry red. He stared at her, making his eyes the eyes of a stranger. He felt his tension suddenly lift as if he had openly declared war on her.

He would have liked to get in conversation with the Negro and to talk with him about art or politics or any subject that would be above the comprehension of those around them, but the man remained entrenched behind his paper. He was either ignoring the change of seating or had never noticed it. There was no way for Julian to convey his sympathy.

His mother kept her eyes fixed reproachfully on his face. The woman with the protruding teeth was looking at him avidly as if he were a type of monster new to her.

"Do you have a light?" he asked the Negro.

Without looking away from his paper, the man reached in his pocket and handed him a packet of matches.

"Thanks," Julian said. For a moment he held the matches foolishly. A NO SMOKING sign looked down upon him from over the door. This alone would not have deterred him; he had no cigarettes. He had quit smoking some months before because he could not afford it. "Sorry," he muttered and handed back the matches. The Negro lowered the paper and gave him an annoyed look. He took the matches and raised the paper again.

His mother continued to gaze at him but she did not take advantage of his momentary discomfort. Her eyes retained their battered look. Her face seemed to be unnaturally red, as if her blood pressure had risen. Julian allowed no glimmer of sympathy to show on his face. Having got the advantage, he wanted desperately to keep it and carry it through. He would have liked to teach her a lesson that would last her a while, but there seemed no way to continue the point. The Negro refused to come out from behind his paper.

Julian folded his arms and looked stolidly before him, facing her but as if he did not see her, as if he had ceased to recognize her existence. He visualized a scene in which, the bus having reached their stop, he would remain in his seat and when she said, "Aren't you going to get off?" he would look at her as at a stranger who had rashly addressed him. The corner they got off on was usually deserted, but it was well lighted and it would not hurt her to walk by herself the four blocks to the Y. He decided to wait until the time came and then decide whether or not he would let her get off by herself. He would have to be at the Y at ten to bring her back, but he could leave her wondering if he was going to show up. There was no reason for her to think she could always depend on him.

He retired again into the high-ceilinged room sparsely settled with large pieces of antique furniture. His soul expanded momentarily but then he became aware of his mother across from him and the vision shrivelled. He studied her coldly. Her feet in little pumps dangled like a child's and did not quite reach the floor. She was training on him an exaggerated look of reproach. He felt completely detached from her. At that moment he could with pleasure have slapped her as he would have slapped a particularly obnoxious child in his charge.

He began to imagine various unlikely ways by which he could teach her a lesson. He might make friends with some distinguished Negro professor or lawyer and bring him home to spend the evening. He would be entirely justified but her blood pressure would rise to 300. He could not push her to the extent of making her have a stroke, and moreover, he had never been successful at making any Negro friends. He had tried to strike up an acquaintance on the bus with some of the better types, with ones that looked like professors or ministers or lawyers. One morning he had sat down next to a distinguished-looking dark brown man who had answered his questions with a sonorous solemnity but who had turned out to be an undertaker. Another day he had sat down beside a cigar-smoking Negro with a diamond ring on his finger, but after a few stilted pleasantries, the Negro had rung the buzzer and risen, slipping two lottery tickets into Julian's hand as he climbed over him to leave.

He imagined his mother lying desperately ill and his being able to secure only a Negro doctor for her. He toyed with that idea for a few minutes and then dropped it for a momentary vision of himself participating as a sympathizer in a sit-in demonstration. This was possible but he did not linger with it. Instead, he approached the ultimate horror. He brought home a beautiful suspiciously Negroid woman. Prepare yourself, he said. There is nothing you can do about it. This is the woman I've chosen. She's intelligent, dignified, even good, and she's suffered and she hasn't thought it *fun*. Now persecute us, go ahead and persecute us. Drive her out of here, but remember, you're driving me too. His eyes were narrowed and through the indignation he had generated, he saw his mother across the aisle, purple-faced, shrunken to the dwarf-like proportions of her moral nature, sitting like a mummy beneath the ridiculous banner of her hat.

He was tilted out of his fantasy again as the bus stopped. The door opened with a sucking hiss and out of the dark a large, gaily dressed, sullen-looking colored woman got on with a little boy. The child, who might have been four, had on a short plaid suit and a Tyrolean hat with a blue feather in it. Julian hoped that he would sit down beside him and that the woman would push in beside his mother. He could think of no better arrangement.

As she waited for her tokens, the woman was surveying the seating possibilities—she hoped with the idea of sitting where she was least wanted. There was something familiar-looking about her but Julian could not place what it was. She was a giant of a woman. Her face was set not only to meet opposition but to seek it out. The downward tilt of her large lower lip was like a warning sign: DONT TAMPER WITH ME. Her bulging figure was encased in a green crepe dress and her feet overflowed in red shoes. She had on a hideous hat. A purple velvet flap came down on one side of it and stood up on the other; the rest of it was green and looked like a cushion with the stuffing out. She carried a mammoth red pocketbook that bulged throughout as if it were stuffed with rocks.

To Julian's disappointment, the little boy climbed up on the empty seat beside his mother. His mother lumped all children, black and white, into the common category, "cute," and she thought little Negroes were on the whole cuter than little white children. She smiled at the little boy as he climbed on the seat.

Meanwhile the woman was bearing down upon the empty seat beside Julian. To his annoyance, she squeezed herself into it. He saw his mother's face change as the woman settled herself next to him and he realized with satisfaction that this was more objectionable to her than it was to him. Her face seemed almost gray and there was a look of dull recognition in her eyes, as if suddenly she had sickened at some awful confrontation. Julian saw that it was because she and the woman had, in a sense, swapped sons. Though his mother would not realize the symbolic significance of this, she would feel it. His amusement showed plainly on his face.

The woman next to him muttered something unintelligible to herself. He was conscious of a kind of bristling next to him, muted growling like that of an angry cat. He could not see anything but the red pocketbook upright on the bulging green thighs. He visualized the woman as she had stood waiting for her tokens—the ponderous figure, rising from the red shoes upward over the solid hips, the mammoth bosom, the haughty face, to the green and purple hat.

His eyes widened.

The vision of the two hats, identical, broke upon him with the radiance of a brilliant sunrise. His face was suddenly lit with joy. He could not believe that Fate had thrust upon his mother such a lesson. He gave a loud chuckle so that she would look at him and see that he saw. She turned her eyes on him slowly. The blue in them seemed to have turned a bruised purple. For a moment he had an uncomfortable sense of her innocence, but it lasted only a second before principle rescued him. Justice entitled him to laugh. His grin hardened until it said to her as plainly as if he were saying aloud: Your punishment exactly fits your pettiness. This should teach you a permanent lesson.

Her eyes shifted to the woman. She seemed unable to bear looking at him and to find the woman preferable. He became conscious again of the bristling presence at his side. The woman was rumbling like a volcano about to become active. His mother's mouth began to twitch slightly at one corner. With a sinking heart, he saw incipient signs of recovery on her face and realized that this was going to strike her suddenly as funny and was going to be no lesson at all. She kept her eyes on the woman and an amused smile came over her face as if the woman were a monkey that had stolen her hat. The little Negro was looking up at her with large fascinated eyes. He had been trying to attract her attention for some time.

"Carver!" the woman said suddenly. "Come heah!"

When he saw that the spotlight was on him at last, Carver drew his feet up and turned himself toward Julian's mother and giggled.

"Carver!" the woman said. "you heah me? Come heah!"

Carver slid down from the seat but remained squatting

With his back against the base of it, his head turned slyly around toward Julian's mother, who was smiling at him. The woman reached a hand across the aisle and snatched him to her. He righted himself and hung backwards on her knees, grinning at Julian's mother. "Isn't he cute?" Julian's mother said to the woman with the protruding teeth.

"I reckon he is," the woman said without conviction.

The Negress yanked him upright but he eased out of her grip and shot across the aisle and scrambled, giggling wildly, onto the seat beside his love.

"I think he likes me," Julian's mother said, and smiled at the woman. It was the smile she used when she was being particularly gracious to an inferior. Julian saw everything lost. The lesson had rolled off her like rain on a roof.

The woman stood up and yanked the little boy off the seat as if she were snatching him from contagion. Julian could feel the rage in her at having no weapon like his mother's smile. She gave the child a sharp slap across his leg. He howled once and then thrust his head into her stomach and kicked his feet against her shins. "Behave," she said vehemently.

The bus stopped and the Negro who had been reading the newspaper got off. The woman moved over and set the little boy down with a thump between herself and Julian. She held him firmly by the knee. In a moment he put his hands in front of his face and peeped at Julian's mother through his fingers.

"I see yoooooooo!" she said and put her hand in front of her face and peeped at him.

The woman slapped his hand down. "Quit yo' foolishness," she said, "before I knock the living Jesus out of you!"

Julian was thankful that the next stop was theirs. He reached up and pulled the cord. The woman reached up and pulled it at the same time. Oh my God, he thought. He had the terrible intuition that when they got off the bus together, his mother would open her purse and give the little boy a nickel. The gesture would be as natural to her as breathing. The bus stopped and the woman got up and lunged to the front, dragging the child, who wished to stay on, after her. Julian and his mother got up and followed. As they neared the door, Julian tried to relieve her of her pocketbook.

"No," she murmured, "I want to give the little boy a nickel."

"No!" Julian hissed. "No!"

She smiled down at the child and opened her bag. The bus door opened and the woman picked him up by the arm and descended with him, hanging at her hip. Once in the street she set him down and shook him.

Julian's mother had to close her purse while she got down the bus step but as soon as her feet were on the ground, she opened it again and began to rummage inside. "I can't find but a penny," she whispered, "but it looks like a new one."

"Don't do it!" Julian said fiercely between his teeth. There was a streetlight on the corner and she hurried to get under it so that she could better see into her pocketbook. The woman was heading off rapidly down the street with the child still hanging backward on her hand.

"Oh little boy!" Julian's mother called and took a few quick steps and caught up with them just beyond the lamp-post. "Here's a bright new penny for you," and she held out the coin, which shone bronze in the dim light.

The huge woman turned and for a moment stood, her shoulders lifted and her face frozen with frustrated rage, and stared at Julian's mother. Then all at once she seemed to explode like a piece of machinery that had been given one ounce of pressure too much. Julian saw the black fist swing out with the red pocketbook. He shut his eyes and cringed as he heard the woman shout, "He don't take nobody's pennies!" When he opened his eyes, the woman was disappearing down the street with the little boy staring wide-eyed over her shoulder. Julian's mother was sitting on the sidewalk.

"I told you not to do that," Julian said angrily. "I told you not to do that!"

He stood over her for a minute, gritting his teeth. Her legs were stretched out in front of her and her hat was on her lap. He squatted down and looked her in the face. It was totally expressionless. "You got exactly what you deserved," he said. "Now get up."

He picked up her pocketbook and put what had fallen out back in it. He picked the hat up off her lap. The penny caught his eye on the sidewalk and he picked that up and let it drop before her eyes into the purse. Then he stood up and leaned over and held his hands out to pull her up. She remained immobile. He sighed. Rising above them on either side were black apartment buildings, marked with irregular rectangles of light. At the end of the block a man came out of a door and walked off in the opposite direction. "All right," he said, "suppose somebody happens by and wants to know why you're sitting on the sidewalk?"

She took the hand and, breathing hard, pulled heavily up on it and then stood for a moment, swaying slightly as if the spots of light in the darkness were circling around her. Her eyes, shadowed and confused, finally settled on his face. He did not try to conceal his irritation. "I hope this teaches you a lesson," he said. She leaned forward and her eyes raked his face. She seemed trying to determine his identity. Then, as if she found nothing familiar about him, she started off with a headlong movement in the wrong direction.

"Aren't you going on to the Y?" he asked.

"Home," she muttered.

"Well, are we walking?"

For answer she kept going. Julian followed along, his hands behind him. He saw no reason to let the lesson she had had go without backing it up with an explanation of its meaning. She might as well be made to understand what had happened to her. "Don't think that was just an uppity Negro woman," he said. "That was the whole colored race which will no longer take your condescending pennies. That was your black double. She can wear the same hat as you, and to be sure," he added gratuitously (because he thought it was funny), "it looked better on her than it did on you. What all this means," he said, "is that the old world is gone. The old manners are obsolete and your graciousness is not worth a damn." He thought bitterly of the house that had been lost for him. "You aren't who you think you are," he said.

She continued to plow ahead, paying no attention to him. Her hair had come undone on one side. She dropped her pocketbook and took no notice. He stooped and picked it up and handed it to her but she did not take it.

"You needn't act as if the world had come to an end," he said, "because it hasn't. From now on you've got to live in a new world and face a few realities for a change. Buck up," he said, "it won't kill you."

She was breathing fast.

"Let's wait on the bus," he said.

"Home," she said thickly.

"I hate to see you behave like this," he said. "Just like a child. I should be able to expect more of you." He decided to stop where he was and make her stop and wait for a bus. "I'm not going any farther," he said, stopping. "We're going on the bus."

She continued to go on as if she had not heard him. He took a few steps and caught her arm and stopped her. He looked into her face and caught his breath. He was looking into a face he had never seen before. "Tell Grandpa to come get me," she said.

He stared, stricken.

"Tell Caroline to come get me," she said.

Stunned, he let her go and she lurched forward again, walking as if one leg were shorter than the other. A tide of darkness seemed to be sweeping her from him. "Mother!" he cried. "Darling, sweetheart, wait!" Crumpling, she fell to the pavement. He dashed forward and fell at her side, crying, "Mamma, Mamma!" He turned her over. Her face was fiercely distorted. One eye, large and staring, moved slightly to the left as if it had become unmoored. The other remained fixed on him, raked his face again, found nothing and closed.

"Wait here, wait here!" he cried and jumped up and began to run for help toward a cluster of lights he saw in the distance ahead of him. "Help, help!" he shouted, but his voice was thin, scarcely a thread of sound. The lights drifted farther away the faster he ran and his feet moved numbly as if they carried him nowhere. The tide of darkness seemed to sweep him back to her, postponing from moment to moment his entry into the world of guilt and sorrow.

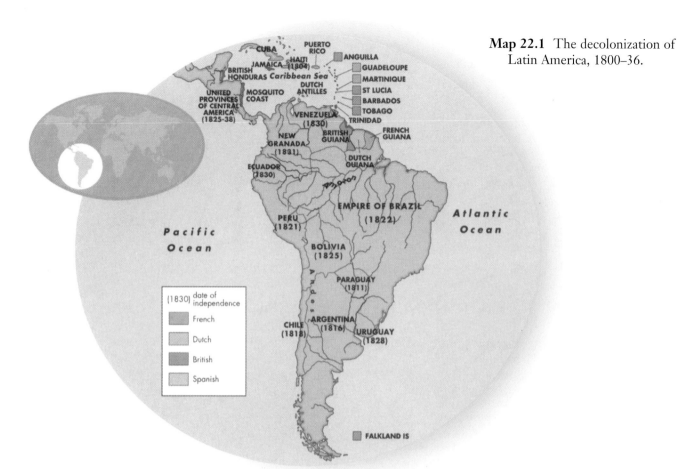

Map 22.1 The decolonization of Latin America, 1800–36.

MODERN AFRICA AND LATIN AMERICA

CHAPTER 22

‹ *Modern Africa*

‹ *Modern Latin America*

David Alfaro Siqueiros, *Cuauhtémoc Against the Myth (detail)*, 1944, Tlatelco, Mexico.

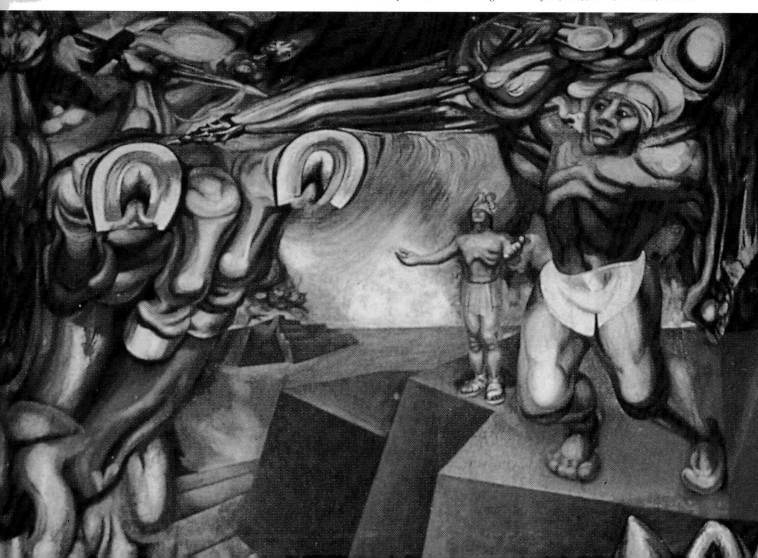

MODERN AFRICA

❖

The second largest continent in the world, Africa is home to millions of people who, between them, speak nearly a thousand different languages. The cultures of the many African peoples are as diverse as the continent they inhabit, with its broad flat savannahs, or grasslands, its majestic mountain peaks, its expansive deserts, and its tropical forests.

There are at least three distinctive "Africas." North of the equator is the area known as the Maghreb, dominated by the Sahara desert and Islam. Historically the area was closely tied to Mediterranean culture. In the Maghreb, Islam and the Arab language have served as a unifying force for over eight hundred years. South of the

---

Map 22.2 The decolonization of Africa in the twentieth century.

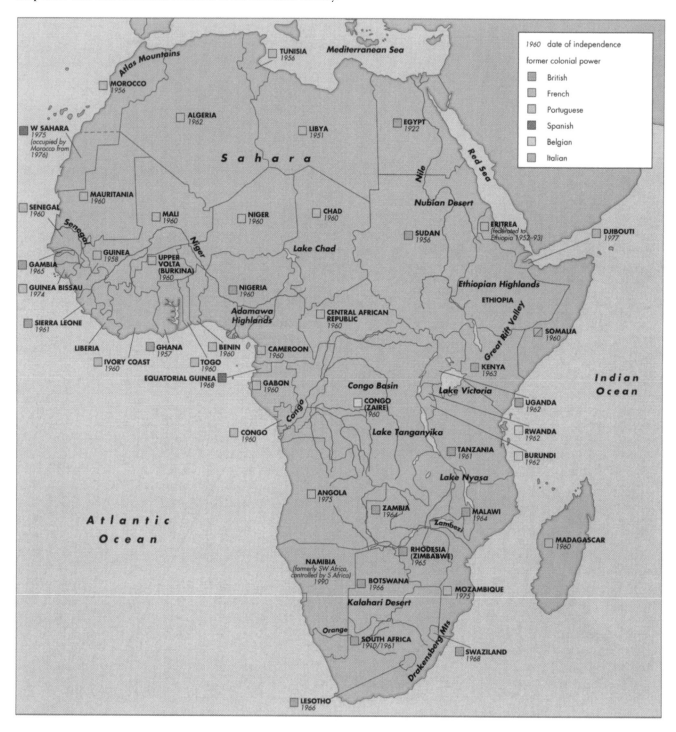

desert, in West Africa, are the sub-Saharan cultures, including the countries of Liberia, Ivory Coast, Ghana, Togo, Benin, Nigeria, Burkina Faso, Niger, and Mali. In sub-Saharan Africa, hundreds of diverse cultures and languages have flourished. Until the arrival of the Europeans and the introduction of the slave trade, all of the countries along the Atlantic coast looked north to the sub-Saharan cultures and the Maghreb for cultural leadership. The Europeans, however, brought with them firearms, and by the end of the eighteenth century, it was those cultures nearest the coast that had traded with the Europeans for guns that came to dominate the region.

The third distinctive "Africa" lies south of the equator. It is geographically more diverse than the rest of the continent, with its high, grassy steppes, an immense tropical rainforest in the Congo, humid woodlands, and even a vast desert, the Kalahari. Many of the inland communities had no contact with the West until the late eighteenth century. All of the peoples speak *bantu* (the word for "people," which is the plural of the word for "man," *muntu*), so the language unifies them culturally.

The history of African culture falls into three periods: pre-colonial, colonial, and post-colonial. Of the first we know very little. As the slave trade flourished, and as the West's knowledge of the continent increased, so did the will to dominate it by exploiting Africa's vast natural resources. What began as diplomatic negotiation between European and African political leaders over access to Africa's resources resulted, by 1914, in European colonial rule of almost the entire African continent.

The catalyst for African independence was World War II, in which African human and natural resources made a significant contribution. Following the war, European countries began relinquishing their colonial empires in Africa. In 1950, only four African countries were sovereign states; by 1980, only two were not. African nationalism and the desire for self-determination were identifiable throughout the continent. Even in South Africa, where once a small minority of whites held power in a country composed of Africans, Indians, and people of mixed race, the tide has finally turned. Following the release of NELSON MANDELA (b. 1918) from prison in 1990, **apartheid** (the legal separation of the races) has been abolished and a coalition government, led by President Mandela and the African National Congress, has assumed power.

SCULPTURE

What we know of pre-colonial African art has come to us by way of strong oral traditions (which have encouraged a perhaps somewhat exaggerated belief in the continuity of African cultural traditions) and through a few surviving artifacts. The reason for the survival of so few artifacts from the pre-colonial period is that African cultures used wood to create most of their implements and images, and so they have long since disappeared. In sub-Saharan culture, however, objects were created from more permanent materials, beginning in the sixth century B.C., when ironwork spread across the Sudan, soon followed by work in clay.

Pre-Colonial Sculpture in Benin. The Yoruba [YOR-ub-ah] culture has its center in the city of Ife, which is situated in present-day Nigeria. The Yoruba people were making bronze and terracotta, or clay, images by the end of the tenth century. Within four hundred years, the techniques of bronze casting had spread southeast to the kingdom of Benin, where artists developed a bronze and brass sculptural tradition closely related to court life.

The sculpture of Benin reveals much about the role of art in pre-colonial African cultures. The *Head of an Oba* (fig. 22.1) dates from the eighteenth century. It is not so much a portrait as a symbol of authority; the Oba is the

Figure 22.1 *Head of an Oba*, Edo, Court of Benin, Nigeria, eighteenth century, brass, iron, height 13⅛" (33 cm), Metropolitan Museum of Art, New York. All Oba heads include representations of broad coral-bead necklaces which cover the entire neck—a part of the royal costume to this day.

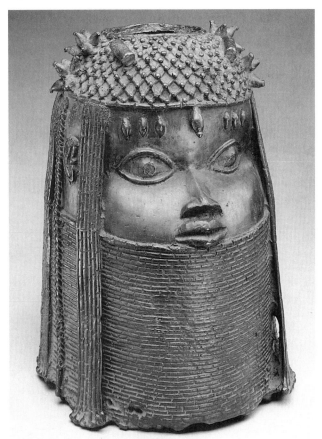

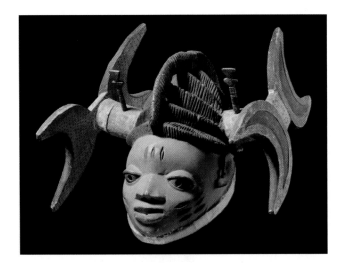

Figure 22.2   Mask, Yoruba, Republic of Benin, paint on wood, height 14½″ (37 cm), Musée de l'Homme, Paris. The reference to the moon in the crescent-shaped horns of this mask echoes a *gelede* song that begins, "All-powerful mother, mother of the night bird."

king of a dynasty. When an Oba dies, the new Oba establishes an altar commemorating his predecessor (usually his father) and decorates it with newly cast heads. In this way, the history of the dynasty is recorded. The head also has a special signficance in Benin ritual. According to British anthropologist R.E. Bradbury, the head "symbolizes life and behavior in this world, the capacity to organize one's actions in such a way as to survive and prosper. It is one's Head that 'leads one through life' … On a man's Head depends not only his own wellbeing but that

of his wives and children … At the state level, the welfare of the people as a whole depends on the Oba's Head." The bronze head, in other words, not only signifies but is also integral to social and political life.

Colonial Sculpture.   African sculpture created during colonial rule displays, at first glance, few signs of European influence. This reflects, one might argue, the fact that although Africans have consistently regarded Europeans as powerful, they have also seen them as largely ignorant and uncivilized. How else could the Africans interpret the behavior of the slave traders, or of the French Congo government administrators, Gaud and Toqué, who in 1905 forced one of their servants to drink soup made from a human head, and on Bastille Day, 1903, dynamited an African guide as a sort of human firework to celebrate the French Revolution and to "intimidate the local population"? Yet it is true to say that colonial rule stimulated the production of African art. During the nineteenth century, as missionaries destroyed "pagan" images and collectors sent art in large consignments to the West, the works had to be replaced. It is probable that over half the African art in the West today was made during this century of plunder. As a result of indigenous disrespect for European culture and the need to produce work, many long-standing traditions remained intact throughout the colonial period.

The Yoruba *gelede* mask (fig. 22.2), acquired in 1937 by the Musée de l'Homme (the Museum of Mankind) in Paris, is used in a traditional performance ritual to appease "the mothers." "The mothers" represent all women, whom the Yoruba believe possess special powers, positive and negative. On each side of the mask are moon

Figure 22.3   Kane Kwei, *Cocoa-Pod-Shaped Coffin*, early 1970s, wood and enamel paint, length 8′9″ (2.67 m), M.H. De Young Memorial Museum, The Fine Arts Museums of San Francisco. When reproduced in a photograph, as it is here, Kwei's coffin seems smaller than it actually is. It is, literally, a coffin, over 8½ feet long overall.

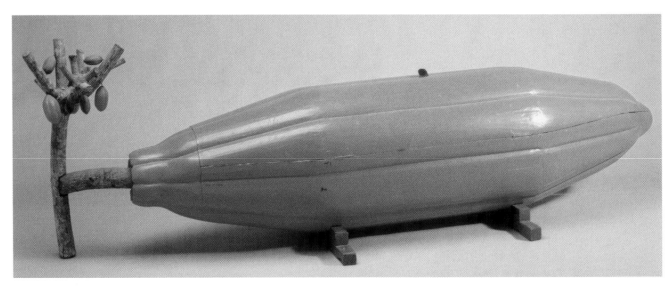

Connections

THE MASK AS DANCE

*F*or the Baule [BOW-LAY] carvers of the Ivory Coast, the helmet mask illustrated here (fig. 22.4) is a pleasing and beautiful object, but has another significance as well. It is the Dye sacred mask. As the carver explained to Susan Vogel, "The god is a dance of rejoicing for me. So when I see the mask, my heart is filled with joy. I like it because of the horns and the eyes. The horns curve nicely, and I like the placement of the eyes and ears. In addition, it executes very interesting and graceful dance steps … This is a sacred mask danced in our village."

While the Baule carver pays attention to the physical features of the mask, he also sees the mask *as* dance. In its features, he sees its performance. A mask is thus more than an ornament disguising or hiding the face. These Africans have no separate word for "mask," rather the word "mask" includes the whole person performing the dance. In this sense, masks can be said to dance, and the mask or the dancer is a vehicle through which the spirit of the place passes.

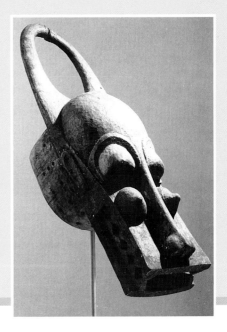

Figure 22.4   Helmet mask, Baule, Ivory Coast, nineteenth–twentieth century, wood and color, length 38″ (95.8 cm), Metropolitan Museum of Art, New York. This African mask "makes us happy when we see it," explains a Baule carver.

crescents that signify night-time, when "the mothers" exercise their powers. For the Yoruba, a beautiful thing is a good thing, and its goodness extends to all levels of life—the spiritual, the social, and the political. Aesthetically speaking, a mask such as this one should be "not too real and not too abstract, but somewhere in between." It should possess a luminous surface, and a roundness of form. To please "the mothers," the masks reflect these standards of physical perfection, which imply the highest moral standards.

Post-colonial Sculpture.   The *gelede* performances of the Yoruba are still popular, and masks continue to be made. Increasingly, there are fewer *visual* connections between traditional and contemporary African arts, but the African conception of art's purpose has remained unchanged. Susan Vogel, a prominent African art historian, explains:

Content … is of prime importance for African artists, critics, and audiences, who tend to share an expectation that works of art will have a readable message or story. African art of all kinds is likely to be explainable in terms of a narrative or a religious, social, or political text known to both artists and audiences … All forms of contemporary African art are seen as functional, or as serving some common good … Most kinds of African art … seem to have a kind of seriousness, a higher mission than pleasure or decoration alone. The general consensus is that it must honor, instruct, uplift, clarify, or even scold, expose, and ridicule, to push people to be what they must be. Even at its most lighthearted, it is never trivial.

The coffins of KANE KWEI [KWHY] (b. 1924) of Ghana are a perfect example. Kwei never received any

formal training as a carpenter. In the mid-1970s, a dying uncle, who had worked as a fisherman, asked him to produce a coffin in the shape of a boat. Kwei's work delighted the entire community, and he was soon creating many types of coffins—fish and whales (for fishermen), hens with chicks (for women with large families), Mercedes-Benz coffins (for the wealthy), and cash crops (for farmers), among them the cocoa-bean (fig. 22.3). These coffins disappeared underground soon after they were made. Coffins in Ghana are seen as serving the community and also have a ritual purpose: they celebrate the successful life of the person and form part of the traditional Ghanaian funeral celebrations that often last for days. In 1974, an American art dealer exhibited Kwei's coffins in San Francisco, and now Kwei's large workshop turns out coffins for both funerals and the art market.

MUSIC

Music pervades the lives of the sub-Saharan African peoples. Its performance is found in every aspect of life, from hunting to the planting and harvesting of crops, from singing during the treatment of illness to the musical chanting that accompanies proceedings in court. As with sculpture, music plays a functional role rather than one of mere entertainment in African life. At all rites of passage, from birth to death, music expresses their belief system. Even today, music provides the glue that holds communities together.

Perhaps the most distinctive feature of African music is the intricacy of its rhythms and its formal repetitive patterns. Very often, African musical rhythms are played off against each other, by turns clashing and coming together. **Polyrhythms**, or multiple rhythms, are common, as are short melodic phrases, which are the origin of the jazz "riff" and which are often improvised upon and varied for musical diversity and complexity.

Music in Africa is for the most part "popular" music—that is, there is little distinction between "traditional" and "popular," or "classical" and "contemporary." Western jazz and rock and roll have their origins in African music. Contemporary musicians like SONNY OKOSUN [OAK-ka-sun] (b. 1947) blend African and Western sounds. His *Fire in Soweto* captured the imagination of the continent in 1978. Okosun's work is based on a brand of African music known as **highlife**, a fusion of indigenous dance rhythms and melodies with Western regimental marches, sea chanteys, and church hymns, that emerged in the coastal towns of Ghana in the early twentieth century. To this mélange, Okosun added the rock and roll sounds of American guitarist Manuel Santana, as well as the influence of Caribbean reggae.

LITERATURE

In the post-colonial period, many writers of contemporary African fiction have become engaged in the political and cultural struggles for African independence.

Chinua Achebe. Nigerian CHINUA ACHEBE [ah-CHAY-bay] (b. 1930) writes about traditional Ibo culture. In *Things Fall Apart* (1958), his first novel,

Achebe describes the conflict that arises when modern Western ways make incursions into traditional African society. This culture clash is examined in greater detail in *Arrow of Gold* (1964), in which religion and politics become the arenas of conflict where traditional African cultural practices collide with Christianity and colonial power. Achebe writes in a direct style, uncomplicated by the experimental techniques of literary modernism. Instead, he draws on folklore, and especially proverbs, which are central to the African oral tradition, to convey the spirit and substance of his themes.

Wole Soyinka. WOLE SOYINKA [soy-INK-ah] (b. 1934) from Nigeria became the first African writer to win the Nobel Prize for Literature in 1986. Although best known as a playwright, Soyinka is also a poet, essayist, political activist, social critic, and literary scholar. His poetry and plays are deeply political: as he noted in a *New York Times* interview, "I cannot conceive of my existence without political involvement."

During the Nigerian Civil War, Soyinka was imprisoned and kept in solitary confinement for his anti-government activism. There he composed *Poems from Prison* (1969) and *The Man Died: Prison Notes of Wole Soyinka* (1988), both written in secret on toilet paper and later smuggled out. During the 1960s he worked tirelessly to develop a Nigerian national drama. Two of his best-known plays depict political intrigue in an imaginary kingdom, *Death and the King's Horseman* (1976) and *A Play for Giants* (1984), a satire on African dictators.

Timeline 22.1 Modern Africa.

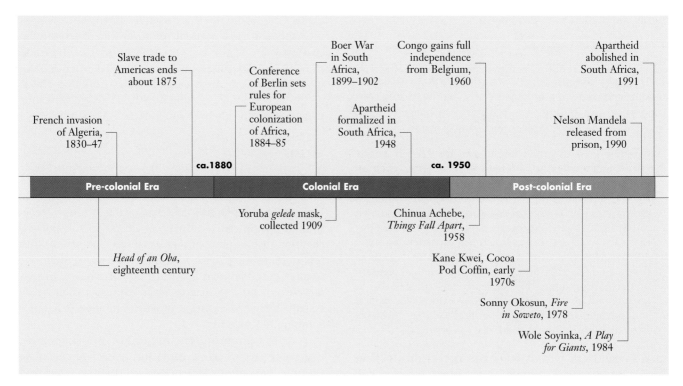

Then & Now

TWINS

The Yoruba have one of the highest rates of twin births in the world. Yet, for the Yoruba, twins remain "gifts of the gods" who possess, or rather are possessed by, the deities of creativity. They are empowered by their inborn ability to perceive a dimension beyond the everyday, communicating with a universe beyond our own.

The Yoruba believe that a mother is blessed with twins as a reward for her patience and virtue, and hence, after their birth, she is treated as if she were a member of the highest royalty. Indeed, any woman who gives birth to twins three times is considered the most powerful person of all, higher than kings. This is a particularly remarkable honor given that the Yoruba have a patriarchal culture, in which the oldest male member leads his entire clan.

Traditionally, the Yoruba have images carved of the twins, or *ere ibeji*, which are used in a cult should one of the twins die, which sometimes happens since twins are often smaller and more fragile than single babies. Until the twentieth century, these figures were carved out of wood, but they have been increasingly replaced by mass-produced Western dolls (fig. 22.5). The mother cares for the "twin" doll of the dead child as if it were still alive, placing it in a shrine in her bedroom. Its spirit, the Yoruba believe, will bring good fortune to the family

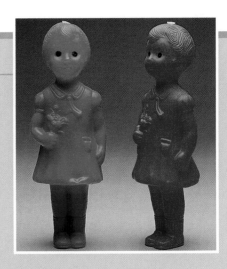

Figure 22.5 Dolls used as *ere ibeji*, mid-twentieth century, unknown factory (Nigeria), molded plastic and metal, height $9\frac{4}{5}''$ (25 cm), Fowler Museum of Cultural History, UCLA. *Ere ibeji* dolls, images of twins, represent hope for the future to the Yoruba.

MODERN LATIN AMERICA

Like Africa, Latin America had long been under the rule of colonial Europeans—chiefly the Spanish and Portuguese. Then, in the early nineteenth century, grass-roots movements fueled wars of independence throughout the region and inspired the Latin American social elite to break the economic trade monopolies of the colonial rulers, while preserving the existing social structure.

Latin America is marked by the collision and inter-mingling of two separate cultural and economic traditions. The colonists and their heirs are largely well-to-do Roman Catholics, while the diverse, indigenous peoples maintain their own traditional cultural practices and make up an underprivileged, subsistence-based social class. As distinct from the situation in North America, where a biracial society developed after the advent of slavery, a multiracial society developed in Latin America as the colonists and the indigenous population mixed. In Argentina and Uruguay, the few natives were essentially wiped out by European diseases in the early years of colonization. A Eurocentric culture developed when over one million Europeans, mostly Spanish and Italian, emigrated there between 1905 and 1910. Yet, in Central America and Peru, strong native communities, of Mayan and Incan ancestry, survive to this day, with their own thriving indigenous cultures.

PAINTING

Colonial Art. The joining of Native American and European traditions is evident in much of the art and architecture produced during the colonial period. In Mexico, for instance, Baroque architecture flourished, but with a native exuberance and love for naturalistic detail that far exceeds most Baroque architecture in Europe (see Chapter 15). In painting, native artists combined their own traditions with those of the Catholic Church.

A depiction of a Corpus Christi procession in Santa Ana, Peru (fig. 22.6) shows European and Native American traditions converging. The work was painted in about 1660 by the followers of QUISPE TITO [TEE-toh] (1611–1681), a painter of Inca origin, who worked in Cuzco, Peru. At the head of the procession, on the left, is an Indian leader in royal Inca dress, wearing a head-dress decorated with a combination of Spanish and pre-Conquest symbols, including a bird, which, for the Incas, had magical significance (a live bird, with brilliant plumage, also sits on the wall above his head). Following the Inca leader are the priest and acolytes, then the Corpus Christi glory cart with a statue of the parish saint holding onto a palm tree with a cupid-like angel on his shoulder. To the right are the native parishioners. Behind the scene, the European elite watch from their balconies, from which hang brightly colored sheets from Spain.

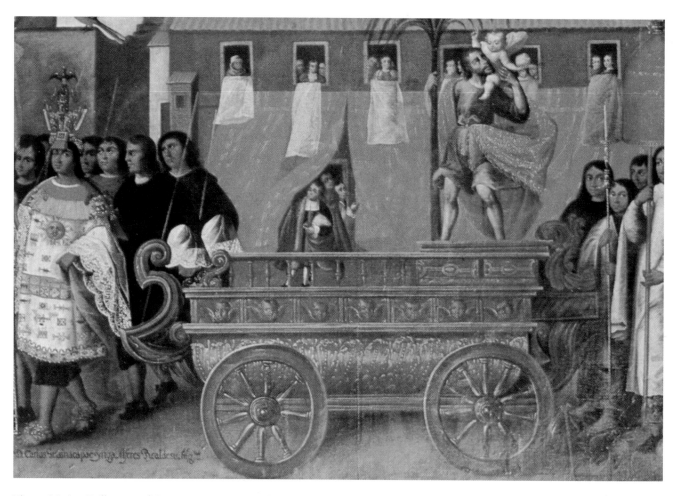

Figure 22.6   Followers of Quispe Tito, *Corpus Christi Procession with the Parishioners of Santa Ana* (detail), ca. 1660, fresco, Museo de Arte Hatun Rumiyoc, Cuzco, Peru. Another section of this fresco depicts a giant altar erected especially for the occasion, decorated with silver-framed paintings and sculptures of angels who wear feathered helmets derived from Inca tradition.

The Mexican Mural Movement.   Despite the merging of traditions evident in colonial art, the Church and the European cultural elite wanted to suppress native customs. In Mexico particularly, where strong native populations had begun to rebel against the European elite by the early twentieth century, these customs were a source of identity and pride. Beginning in 1910 with a violent revolt against the regime of Porfirio Diáz, Mexico was rocked by social and political unrest. Civil war lasted until the inauguration of the revolutionary leader, Alvaro Obregón, as President in 1920. Obregón believed that the aesthetic faculty, and the appreciation of painting in particular, could lead the way to revolutionary change. He also believed in restoring Mexico's indigenous cultural identity. He thus began a vast mural project designed to cover the walls of public spaces across the country with images celebrating Mexico's past and future. By the mid-1920s, the mural movement was in the hands of three painters, *Los Tres Grandes*, as they were called, "The Three Giants"—DIEGO RIVERA [rih-VAY-rah] (1886–1957), JOSÉ CLEMENTE OROZCO [oh-ROZ-coe] (1883–1949), and DAVID ALFARO SIQUEIROS [see-KAYR-ohs] (1896–1974).

All three artists began their careers painting *al fresco*, but the sun, rain, and humidity of the Mexican climate damaged their efforts. In 1937, Siqueiros organized a workshop in New York City, close to the chemical industry, to develop and experiment with new synthetic paints. One of the first media used in the workshop was pyroxylin, commonly known as Duco, a lacquer developed as an automobile paint. It is used in the large-scale mural by Siqueiros, *Cuauhtémoc Against the Myth* (fig. 22.7), which was painted in 1944 on panel so that it could withstand earthquakes and is housed today in the Union Housing Project at Tlatelco, Mexico. It depicts the story of the Aztec hero who shattered the myth that the Spanish army could not be conquered. This message had great significance for the people: the indigenous people could regain power. Siqueiros also meant it as a commentary on the susceptibility of the Nazis to defeat in Europe.

Frida Kahlo. Rivera was married to another prominent Mexican painter, FRIDA KAHLO [KAH-loh] (1907–1954), whose work was initially overshadowed by that of her husband, but whose reputation has increased to such a degree that she is now considered the greater artist and is surely the more famous. Kahlo is best known for her highly distinctive self-portraits in a wide range of circumstances and settings. "I paint self-portraits because I am so often alone," she once said, "because I am the person I know best." Her self-portraits, it has been argued, created a series of alternative selves that helped to exorcise life's pains. She suffered almost her entire life: first from polio, which she contracted at age six, and which left her with a withered right leg; then from a bus and trolley collision at age eighteen, in which her pelvis and spinal column were broken, her foot was crushed, and her abdomen and uterus were pierced by a steel handrail, resulting

Figure 22.7 David Alfaro Siqueiros, *Cuauhtémoc Against the Myth*, 1944, mural, pyroxylin on celtex and plywood, 1000 sq. ft. (92.9 sq. m), Teepan Union Housing Project, Tlatelco, Mexico. Siqueiros's experimentation with synthetic paints would lead to the invention of acrylics, much in use today.

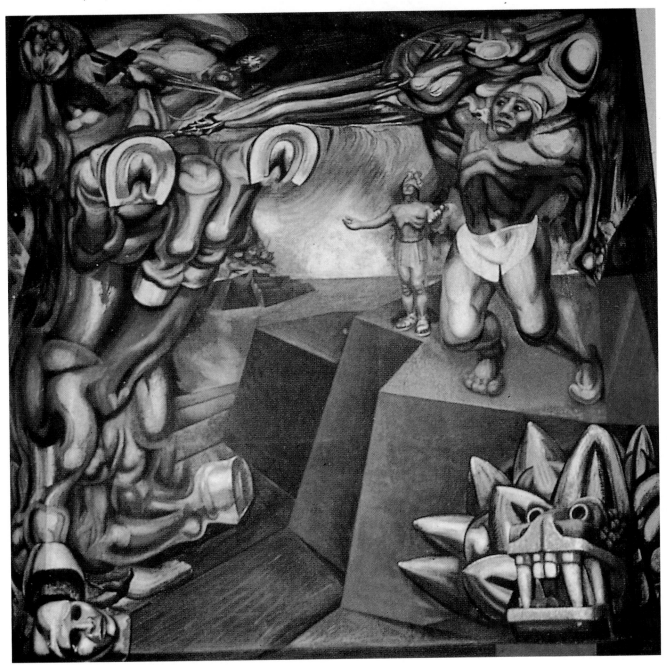

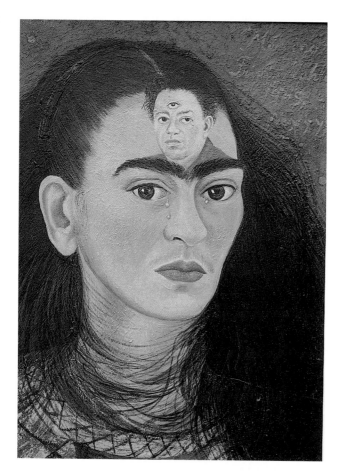

Figure 22.8 Frida Kahlo, *Diego and I*, 1929, oil on canvas, 24 × 18½″ (29.8 × 22.4 cm), Private collection. Kahlo and Rivera's marriage was, her parents said, "like the marriage between an elephant and a dove." Kahlo described her marriage as her "second accident" (a traffic collision at the age of eighteen was her first).

in a lifelong series of operations; and finally from her volatile relationship with Rivera, whose many adulterous affairs, including one with her own sister, hurt her deeply.

The self-portrait entitled *Diego and I* (fig. 22.8) reveals the pain Kahlo experienced in her marriage and the extent to which her husband's infidelities tormented her. The work is heightened by the surrealistic detail. Kahlo's hair, for example, is partly wound around her neck to suggest strangulation. Three pearly tears accentuate the deep sadness of her face and eyes. Her husband's image painted on her brow might indicate how he dominates her thoughts and is the cause of her anguish. The eye painted onto his forehead suggests what she considered to be his god-like omniscience.

Wilfredo Lam. The work of Cuban painter WIL-FREDO LAM (1902–1982), of Chinese and mulatto ancestry, demonstrates the close connection between European and Latin American cultures. Lam left for

Europe in 1923 at the age of twenty-one and did not return to the Caribbean for eighteen years, until 1941, when he was sent by the Nazis to a prison camp in Martinique. Within forty days, he was released and sent back to Havana, where he discovered that the idyllic Cuba of his childhood had been destroyed by the collapse of sugar prices.

Lam's masterpiece, *The Jungle* (fig. 22.9), painted in 1943, is a record of his reaction. It is almost exactly the same size as *Les Demoiselles d'Avignon* (see fig. 18.26) by Picasso, who had befriended Lam in Paris in 1939. The faces of Lam's totemic figures are based, like Picasso's, on African masks. But crucially different from Picasso's painting is the density of Lam's image. Every space is occupied, not only by shoots of sugar cane and jungle foliage, but by the figures themselves, whose arms and hands seem to reach to the ground. This natural world is inhabited by a mysterious, mythical virgin-beast, both productive and destructive, whose origins are to be found in Lam's fascination with the world of *santería* or voodoo.

Figure 22.9 Wilfredo Lam, *The Jungle*, 1943, gouache on paper, mounted on canvas, 7′10″ × 7′6½″ (2.39 × 2.30 m), Museum of Modern Art, New York. The son of a Chinese immigrant and an Afro-Cuban mother, Lam studied African art in Paris and adopted Picasso's style in an attempt to explore his own origins.

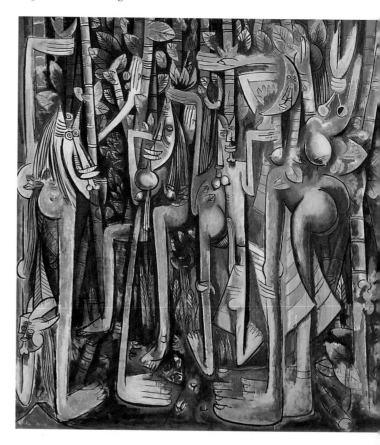

Cross Currents

BACH IN BRAZIL

One interesting musical cross current between Latin America and Europe is Villa-Lobos's *Bachianas Brasileiras*, a piece inspired by the German Baroque composer Johann Sebastian Bach, and written as a tribute to his memory and legacy. In this work, Villa-Lobos couples Brazilian rhythms with Bachian counterpoint to create a fusion of Latin

and Germanic musical styles that spans cultures, oceans, and centuries.

Bach was the archetypal composer for Villa-Lobos, since Bach also drew inspiration from simple folk melodies, which he then developed into complex polyphonic compositions. *Bachianas Brasileiras* consists of nine parts, each scored for different instrumental combinations. No. 1, for example, is scored for eight cellos, No. 3 for piano and

orchestra, No. 6 for flute and bassoon.

One of the most notable parts of *Bachianas Brasileiras* is No. 5, which includes a beautiful aria based on a Brazilian folk song. Villa-Lobos sets this piece for soprano voice and eight cellos, with a solo cello line. Its elegant beauty in the alternative arrangements is but one example of the way cultures interact to produce new and exciting artistic forms and styles

Fernando Botero. Columbian artist FERNANDO BOTERO [bo-TAIR-oh] (b. 1932) is known for his "swollen" or "inflated" figures that fill the canvas like balloons and satirize the Latin American ruling elite. "When I inflate things," he has explained, "I enter a subconscious world rich in folk images." *Mona Lisa at the Age of Twelve* (fig. 22.10), painted in 1959, condenses three images: Leonardo da Vinci's original painting (see fig. 13.25), the Infanta Margarita in Diego Velázquez's *Maids of Honor* (see fig. 15.26), and *Alice in Wonderland*. Mona Lisa's oft-noted "inscrutable" smile here becomes grotesquely pig-like, Botero revealing in it the gluttony of the Latin American aristocracy and their ability to "consume" the land and its people.

MUSIC

Latin America has a rich musical heritage, both popular and traditional. The most prevalent forms of popular music are those associated with dance. The tango came from Argentina, the samba from Brazil, and the pasillo from Colombia. Latin-inspired dances include the Caribbean calypso, the Cuban rumba, the Brazilian lambada, and even the macarena.

One of the most popular instruments used in Latin American music is the guitar, which has a long history in Spain and Spanish American cultures. The guitar has been used both in folk and classical music, by many composers, including the Brazilian HEITOR VILLA-LOBOS [VEE-yah LOW-bows] (1887–1959).

Latin America's best-known classical composer, Villa-Lobos was born in Rio de Janeiro. After studying music with his father, he earned a living by playing the cello in cafés. He researched and collected authentic folk and Indian songs, both of which he later used as melodies in his classical compositions. Villa-Lobos believed that folk music revealed the special vitality and spirit of a people, their unique essence, and he conveyed this in his large works for chorus and orchestra.

LITERATURE

The literature of Latin America is written primarily in two languages, Spanish and Portuguese. Yet the plurality of voices and visions that emerge in modern and contemporary Latin American fiction is staggering. A concern many writers share is an exploration of the imagination. Three writers in particular can be singled out for special attention: the Argentinean novelist, essayist, and short-story writer Jorge Luis Borges; the contemporary

Figure 22.10 Fernando Botero, *Mona Lisa at the Age of Twelve*, 1959, oil and tempera on canvas, 6'11" × 6'5" (2.11 × 1.96 m), Museum of Modern Art, New York. In the 1970s, Botero moved to Paris, where he began to make large bronze sculptures of his swollen figures.

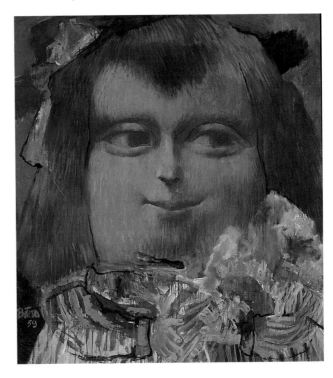

Timeline 22.2 Modern Latin America.

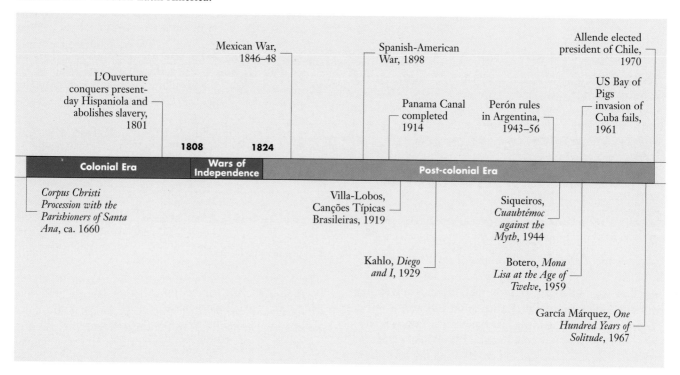

Colombian novelist and short-story writer Gabriel García Márquez; and the Chilean novelist Isabel Allende.

Jorge Luis Borges. JORGE LUIS BORGES [BOR-haze] (1899–1986) is best known for what he calls his *ficciones*—short, enigmatic, fictional works that invite philosophical reflection, especially speculation about the mysterious universe that human beings inhabit. Borges's fiction is situated at the interface between the genres of essay and autobiography; he mixes facts and names from his family chronicles with reflections on philosophical matters. His stories frequently involve a central character confronted with a puzzle or problem, which has to be unraveled much in the manner of detective stories.

One of Borges's most powerful metaphors is that of the labyrinth, a maze into which the central character (and the reader) is placed, and from which extrication comes as the character gains realization about the imaginative world. Borges often merges the "real" with the imaginary, what is historical with what is invented, so that his readers become disoriented and are forced to reconsider the relationship between fiction and reality.

Gabriel García Márquez. If Borges is the master of the short story, GABRIEL GARCÍA MÁRQUEZ [gar-SEE-ah MAR-kez] (b. 1928) is the master of the novel. His *One Hundred Years of Solitude* (1967) blends the "real" with the imaginary in unpredictable yet convincing ways,

in a style that has come to be known as **magic realism**. Magic realism weaves realistic events together with incredible and fantastic ones, in an attempt to convey the truths of life. In magic realism, key events do not necessarily have a logical explanation; mystery is an integral part of experience. Remarking that "There's not a single line in all my work that does not have a basis in reality," García Márquez, like other magic realists, sees his work as conveying simultaneously the truths of the imagination and those of "reality."

Isabel Allende. In the same year that García Márquez won the Nobel Prize for Literature, Isabel Allende [ay-END-eh] (b. 1942) published her noteworthy novel *The House of Spirits* (1982). Like García Márquez's *One Hundred Years of Solitude*, Allende's novel creates a fictional world that reconstructs the history of a country—in her case, modern Chile, her homeland, from which she was exiled when her uncle, President Salvador Allende of Chile, was assassinated in 1975. Like García Márquez, Allende uses techniques of magic realism to weave realistic events with incredible and fantastic ones to convey the truths of life.

Allende explains that she uses these techniques because, as she says, "in Latin America, we value dreams, passions, obsessions, emotions." It is also partly attributable to, as she says, "our sense of family, our sense of religion, of superstition, too." But mostly it is because "Fantastic things happen every day in Latin America—it's not that we make them up."

← **Chinua Achebe**

from *Things Fall Apart*

The following passage constitutes the opening of Achebe's best-known novel, Things Fall Apart, *which dramatizes the encounter of traditional Ibo life with colonialism and Christianity at the beginning of the twentieth century. Achebe's portrait of pre-Christian tribal life in what is now Biafra depicts a society in transition and emphasizes the importance of communication to avert misunderstanding.*

Okonkwo was well known throughout the nine villages and even beyond. His fame rested on solid personal achievements. As a young man of eighteen he had brought honor to his village by throwing Amalinze the Cat. Amalinze was the great wrestler who for seven years was unbeaten, from Umuofia to Mbaino. He was called the Cat because his back would never touch the earth. It was this man that Okonkwo threw in a fight which the old men agreed was one of the fiercest since the founder of their town engaged a spirit of the wild for seven days and seven nights.

The drums beat and the flutes sang and the spectators held their breath. Amalinze was a wily craftsman, but Okonkwo was as slippery as a fish in water. Every nerve and every muscle stood out on their arms, on their backs and their thighs, and one almost heard them stretching to breaking point. In the end Okonkwo threw the Cat.

That was many years ago, twenty years or more, and during this time Okonkwo's fame had grown like a bush-fire in the harmattan. He was tall and huge, and his bushy eyebrows and wide nose gave him a very severe look. He breathed heavily, and it was said that, when he slept, his wives and children in their houses could hear him breathe. When he walked, his heels hardly touched the ground and he seemed to walk on springs, as if he was going to pounce on somebody. And he did pounce on people quite often. He had a slight stammer and whenever he was angry and could not get his words out quickly enough, he would use his fists. He had no patience with unsuccessful men. He had had no patience with his father.

Unoka, for that was his father's name, had died ten years ago. In his day he was lazy and improvident and was quite incapable of thinking about tomorrow. If any money came his way, and it seldom did, he immediately bought gourds of palm-wine, called round his neighbors and made merry. He always said that whenever he saw a dead man's mouth he saw the folly of not eating what one had in one's lifetime. Unoka was, of course, a debtor, and he owed every neighbor some money, from a few cowries to quite substantial amounts.

He was tall but very thin and had a slight stoop. He wore a haggard and mournful look except when he was drinking or playing on his flute. He was very good on his flute, and his happiest moments were the two or three moons after the harvest when the village musicians brought down their instruments, hung above the fireplace. Unoka would play with them, his face beaming with blessedness and peace. Sometimes another village would ask Unoka's band and their dancing *egwugwu* to come and stay with them and teach them their tunes. They would go to such hosts for as long as three or four markets, making music and feasting. Unoka loved the good fare and the good fellowship, and he loved this season of the year, when the rains had stopped and the sun rose every morning with dazzling beauty. And it was not too hot either, because the cold and dry harmattan wind was blowing down from the north. Some years the harmattan was very severe and a dense haze hung on the atmosphere. Old men and children would then sit round log fires, warming their bodies. Unoka loved it all, and he loved the first kites that returned with the dry season, and the children who sang songs of welcome to them. He would remember his own childhood, how he had often wandered around looking for a kite sailing leisurely against the blue sky. As soon as he found one he would sing with his whole being, welcoming it back from its long, long journey, and asking it if it had brought home any lengths of cloth.

That was years ago, when he was young. Unoka, the grown-up, was a failure. He was poor and his wife and children had barely enough to eat. People laughed at him because he was a loafer, and they swore never to lend him any more money because he never paid back. But Unoka was such a man that he always succeeded in borrowing more, and piling up his debts.

One day a neighbor called Okoye came in to see him. He was reclining on a mud bed in his hut playing on the flute. He immediately rose and shook hands with Okoye, who then unrolled the goatskin which he carried under his arm, and sat down. Unoka went into an inner room and soon returned with a small wooden disc containing a kola nut, some alligator pepper and a lump of white chalk.

"I have kola," he announced when he sat down, and passed the disc over to his guest.

"Thank you. He who brings kola brings life. But I think you ought to break it," replied Okoye, passing back the disc.

"No, it is for you, I think," and they argued like this for a few moments before Unoka accepted the honor of breaking the kola. Okoye, meanwhile, took the lump of chalk, drew some lines on the floor, and then painted his big toe.

As he broke the kola, Unoka prayed to their ancestors for life and health, and for protection against their enemies. When they had eaten they talked about many things: about the heavy rains which were drowning the yams, about the next ancestral feast and about the impending war with the village of Mbaino. Unoka was never happy when it came to wars. He was in fact a coward and could not bear the sight of blood. And so he changed the subject and talked about music, and his face beamed. He could hear in his mind's ear the bloodstirring and intricate rhythms of the *ekwe* and the *udu* and the *ogene*, and he could hear his own flute weaving in and out of them, decorating them with a colorful and plaintive tune. The total effect was gay and brisk, but if one picked out the flute as it went up and down and then broke up into short snatches, one saw that there was sorrow and grief there.

Okoye was also a musician. He played on the *ogene*. But he was not a failure like Unoka. He had a large barn full of yams and he had three wives. And now he was going to take the Idemili title, the third highest in the land. It was a very expensive ceremony and he was gathering all his resources together. That was in fact the reason why he had come to see Unoka. He cleared his throat and began:

"Thank you for the kola. You may have heard of the title I intend to take shortly."

Having spoken plainly so far, Okoye said the next half a dozen sentences in proverbs. Among the Ibo the art of conversation is regarded very highly, and proverbs are the palm-oil with which words are eaten. Okoye was a great talker and he spoke for a long time, skirting round the subject and then hitting it finally. In short, he was asking Unoka to return the two hundred cowries he had borrowed from him more than two years before. As soon as Unoka understood what his friend was driving at, he burst out laughing. He laughed loud and long and his voice rang out clear as the *ogene*, and tears stood in his eyes. His visitor was amazed, and sat speechless. At the end, Unoka was able to give an answer between fresh outbursts of mirth.

"Look at that wall," he said, pointing at the far wall of his hut, which was rubbed with red earth so that it shone. "Look at those lines of chalk;" and Okoye saw groups of short perpendicular lines drawn in chalk. There were five groups, and the smallest group had ten lines. Unoka had a sense of the dramatic and so he allowed a pause, in which he took a pinch of snuff and sneezed noisily, and then he continued: "Each group there represents a debt to someone, and each stroke is one hundred cowries. You see, I owe that man a thousand cowries. But he has not come to wake me up in the morning for it. I shall pay you, but not today. Our elders say that the sun will shine on those who stand before it shines on those who kneel under them. I shall pay my big debts first." And he took another pinch of snuff, as if that was paying the big debts first. Okoye rolled his goatskin and departed.

When Unoka died he had taken no title at all and he was heavily in debt. Any wonder then that his son Okonkwo was ashamed of him? Fortunately, among these people a man was judged according to his worth and not according to the worth of his father. Okonkwo was clearly cut out for great things. He was still young but he had won fame as the greatest wrestler in the nine villages. He was a wealthy farmer and had two barns full of yams, and had just married his third wife. To crown it all he had taken two titles and had shown incredible prowess in two inter-tribal wars. And so although Okonkwo was still young, he was already one of the greatest men of his time. Age was respected among his people, but achievement was revered. As the elders said, if a child washed his hands he could eat with kings. Okonkwo had clearly washed his hands and so he ate with kings and elders. And that was how he came to look after the doomed lad who was sacrificed to the village of Umuofia by their neighbors to avoid war and bloodshed. The ill-fated lad was called Ikemefuna.

Jorge Luis Borges
The Garden of Forking Paths

One of Borges's best-known and most intriguing stories, this work contains a labyrinth, which serves as a metaphor for the difficulty of knowing anything with certainty. Here, using this image, the author is able to blend history and fiction, the real and the imaginary. He once described his preoccupation with the labyrinth during an interview. "I discovered the labyrinth in a book published in France by Garnier that my father had in his library. The book had a very odd engraving that took a whole page and showed a building that resembled an amphitheater. I remember that it had cracks and seemed tall, taller than the cypresses and the men that stood around it. My eyesight was not perfect—I was very myopic—but I thought that if I used a magnifying glass, I would be able to see a minotaur within the building. That labyrinth was, besides, a symbol of bewilderment, a symbol of being lost in life. I believe that all of us, at one time or another, have felt that we are lost, and I saw in the labyrinth the symbol of that condition. Since then, I have held that vision of the labyrinth."

On page 22 of Liddell Hart's *History of World War I* you will read that an attack against the Serre-Montauban line by thirteen British divisions (supported by 1,400 artillery pieces), planned for the 24th of July, 1916, had to be postponed until the morning of the 29th. The torrential rains, Captain Liddell Hart comments, caused this delay, an insignificant one, to be sure.

The following statement, dictated, reread and signed by Dr. Yu Tsun, former professor of English at the *Hochschule* at Tsingtao, throws an unsuspected light over the whole affair. The first two pages of the document are missing.

"... and I hung up the receiver. Immediately afterwards, I recognized the voice that had answered in German. It was that of Captain Richard Madden. Madden's presence in Viktor Runeberg's apartment meant the end of our anxieties and—but this seemed, *or should have seemed*, very secondary to me—also the end of our lives. It meant that Runeberg had been arrested or murdered.[1] Before the sun set on that day, I would encounter the same fate. Madden was implacable. Or rather, he was obliged to be so. An Irishman at the service of England, a man accused of laxity and perhaps of treason, how could he fail to seize and be thankful for such a miraculous opportunity: the discovery, capture, maybe even the death of two agents of the German Reich? I went up to my room; absurdly I locked the door and threw myself on my back on the narrow iron cot. Through the window I saw the familiar roofs and the cloud-shaded six o'clock sun. It seemed incredible to me that that day without premonitions or symbols should be the one of my inexorable death. In spite of my dead father, in spite of having been a child in a symmetrical garden of Hai Feng, was I—now—going to die? Then I reflected that everything happens to a man precisely, precisely *now*. Centuries of centuries and only in the present do things happen; countless men in the air, on the face of the earth and the sea, and all that really is happening is happening to me ... The almost intolerable recollection of Madden's horselike face banished these wanderings. In the midst of my hatred and terror (it means nothing to me now to speak of terror, now that I have mocked Richard Madden, now that my throat yearns for the noose) it occurred to me that the tumultuous and doubtless happy warrior did not suspect that I possessed the Secret. The name of the exact location of the new British artillery park on the River Ancre. A bird streaked across the grey sky and blindly I translated it into an airplane and that airplane into

---

[1] An hypothesis both hateful and odd. The Prussian spy Hans Rabener, alias Victor Runeberg, attacked with drawn automatic the bearer of the warrant for his arrest, Captain Richard Madden. The latter, in self-defense, inflicted the wound which brought about Runeberg's death.

many (against the French sky) annihilating the artillery station with vertical bombs. If only my mouth, before a bullet shattered it, could cry out that secret name so it could be heard in Germany … My human voice was very weak. How might I make it carry to the ear of the Chief? To the ear of that sick and hateful man who knew nothing of Runeberg and me save that we were in Staffordshire and who was waiting in vain for our report in his arid office in Berlin, endlessly examining newspapers … I said out loud: *I must flee.* I sat up noiselessly, in a useless perfection of silence, as if Madden were already lying in wait for me. Something—perhaps the mere vain ostentation of proving my resources were nil—made me look through my pockets. I found what I knew I would find. The American watch, the nickel chain and the square coin, the key ring with the incriminating useless keys to Runeberg's apartment, the notebook, a letter which I resolved to destroy immediately (and which I did not destroy), a crown, two shillings and a few pence, the red and blue pencil, the handkerchief, the revolver with one bullet. Absurdly, I took it in my hand and weighed it in order to inspire courage within myself. Vaguely I thought that a pistol report can be heard at a great distance. In ten minutes my plan was perfected. The telephone book listed the name of the only person capable of transmitting the message; he lived in a suburb of Fenton, less than a half hour's train ride away.

I am a cowardly man. I say it now, now that I have carried to its end a plan whose perilous nature no one can deny. I know its execution was terrible. I didn't do it for Germany, no. I care nothing for a barbarous country which imposed upon me the abjection of being a spy. Besides, I know of a man from England—a modest man—who for me is no less great than Goethe. I talked with him for scarcely an hour, but during that hour he was Goethe … I did it because I sensed that the Chief somehow feared people of my race—for the innumerable ancestors who merge within me. I wanted to prove to him that a yellow man could save his armies. Besides, I had to flee from Captain Madden. His hands and his voice could call at my door at any moment. I dressed silently, bade farewell to myself in the mirror, went downstairs, scrutinized the peaceful street and went out. The station was not far from my home, but I judged it wise to take a cab. I argued that in this way I ran less risk of being recognized; the fact is that in the deserted street I felt myself visible and vulnerable, infinitely so. I remember that I told the cab driver to stop a short distance before the main entrance. I got out with voluntary, almost painful slowness; I was going to the village of Ashgrove but I bought a ticket for a more distant station. The train left within a very few minutes, at eight-fifty. I hurried; the next one would leave at nine-thirty. There was hardly a soul on the platform. I went through the coaches; I remember a few farmers, a woman dressed in mourning, a young boy who was reading with fervor the *Annals* of Tacitus, a wounded and happy soldier. The coaches jerked forward at last. A man whom I recognized ran in vain to the end of the platform. It was Captain Richard Madden. Shattered, trembling, I shrank into the rear corner of the seat, away from the dreaded window.

From this broken state I passed into an almost abject felicity. I told myself that the duel had already begun and that I had won the first encounter by frustrating, even if for

forty minutes, even if by a stroke of fate, the attack of my adversary. I argued that this slightest of victories foreshadowed a total victory. I argued (no less fallaciously) that my cowardly felicity proved that I was a man capable of carrying out the adventure successfully. From this weakness I took strength that did not abandon me. I foresee that man will resign himself each day to more atrocious undertakings; soon there will be no one but warriors and brigands; I give them this counsel: *The author of an atrocious undertaking ought to imagine that he has already accomplished it, ought to impose upon himself a future as irrevocable as the past.* Thus I proceeded as my eyes of a man already dead registered the elapsing of that day, which was perhaps the last, and the diffusion of the night. The train ran gently along, amid ash trees. It stopped. almost in the middle of the fields. No one announced the name of the station. "Ashgrove?" I asked a few lads on the platform. "Ashgrove," they replied. I got off.

A lamp enlightened the platform but the faces of the boys were in shadow. One questioned me, "Are you going to Dr. Stephen Albert's house?" Without waiting for my answer, another said, "The house is a long way from here, but you won't get lost if you take this road to the left and at every crossroads turn again to your left." I tossed them a coin (my last), descended a few stone steps and started down the solitary road. It went downhill, slowly. It was of elemental earth; overhead the branches were tangled; the low, full moon seemed to accompany me.

For an instant, I thought that Richard Madden in some way had penetrated my desperate plan. Very quickly, I understood that that was impossible. The instructions to turn always to the left reminded me that such was the common procedure for discovering the central point of certain labyrinths. I have some understanding of labyrinths: not for nothing am I the great grandson of that Ts'ui Pên who was governor of Yunnan and who renounced worldly power in order to write a novel that might be even more populous than the *Hung Lu Meng* and to construct a labyrinth in which all men would become lost. Thirteen years he dedicated to these heterogeneous tasks, but the hand of a stranger murdered him—and his novel was incoherent and no one found the labyrinth. Beneath English trees I meditated on that lost maze; I imagined it inviolate and perfect at the secret crest of a mountain; I imagined it erased by rice fields or beneath the water; I imagined it infinite, no longer composed of octagonal kiosks and returning paths, but of rivers and provinces and kingdoms … I thought of a labyrinth of labyrinths, of one sinuous spreading labyrinth that would encompass the past and the future and in some way involve the stars. Absorbed in these illusory images, I forgot my destiny of one pursued. I felt myself to be, for an unknown period of time, an abstract perceiver of the world. The vague, living countryside, the moon, the remains of the day worked on me, as well as the slope of the road which eliminated any possibility of weariness. The afternoon was intimate, infinite. The road descended and forked among the now confused meadows. A high-pitched, almost syllabic music approached and receded in the shifting of the wind, dimmed by leaves and distance. I thought that a man can be an enemy of other men, of the moments of other men, but not of a country: not of fireflies, woods, gardens, streams of water, sunsets. Thus I arrived before a tall, rusty gate.

Between the iron bars I made out a poplar grove and a pavilion. I understood suddenly two things, the first trivial, the second almost unbelievable: the music came from the pavilion, and the music was Chinese. For precisely that reason I had openly accepted it without paying it any heed. I do not remember whether there was a bell or whether I knocked with my hand. The sparkling of the music continued.

From the rear of the house within a lantern approached: a lantern that the trees sometimes striped and sometimes eclipsed, a paper lantern that had the form of a drum and the color of the moon. A tall man bore it. I didn't see his face for the light blinded me. He opened the door and said slowly, in my own language: "I see that the pious Hsi P'êng persists in correcting my solitude. You no doubt wish to see the garden?"

I recognized the name of one of our consuls and I replied, disconcerted, "The garden?"

"The garden of forking paths."

Something stirred in my memory and I uttered with incomprehensible certainty, "The garden of my ancestor Ts'ui Pên."

"Your ancestor? Your illustrious ancestor? Come in."

The damp path zigzagged like those of my childhood. We came to a library of Eastern and Western books. I recognized bound in yellow silk several volumes of the Lost Encyclopedia, edited by the Third Emperor of the Luminous Dynasty but never printed. The record on the phonograph revolved next to a bronze phoenix. I also recall a *famille rose* vase and another, many centuries older, of that shade of blue which our craftsmen copied from the potters of Persia …

Stephen Albert observed me with a smile. He was, as I have said, very tall, sharp-featured, with gray eyes and a gray beard. He told me that he had been a missionary in Tientsin "before aspiring to become a Sinologist."

We sat down—I on a long, low divan, he with his back to the window and a tall circular clock. I calculated that my pursuer, Richard Madden, could not arrive for at least an hour. My irrevocable determination could wait.

"An astounding fate, that of Ts'ui Pên," Stephen Albert said. "Governor of his native province, learned in astronomy, in astrology and in the tireless interpretation of the canonical books, chess player, famous poet and calligrapher—he abandoned all this in order to compose a book and a maze. He renounced the pleasures of both tyranny and justice, of his populous couch, of his banquets and even of erudition—all to close himself up for thirteen years in the Pavilion of the Limpid Solitude. When he died, his heirs found nothing save chaotic manuscripts. His family, as you may be aware, wished to condemn them to the fire; but his executor—a Taoist or Buddhist monk—insisted on their publication."

"We descendants of Ts'ui Pên," I replied, "continue to curse that monk. Their publication was senseless. The book is an indeterminate heap of contradictory drafts. I examined it once: in the third chapter the hero dies, in the fourth he is alive. As for the other undertaking of Ts'ui Pên, his labyrinth …"

"Here is Ts'ui Pên's labyrinth," he said, indicating a tall lacquered desk.

"An ivory labyrinth!" I exclaimed. "A minimum labyrinth."

"A labyrinth of symbols," he corrected. "An invisible labyrinth of time. To me, a barbarous Englishman, has been entrusted the revelation of this diaphanous mystery. After more than a hundred years, the details are irretrievable; but it is not hard to conjecture what happened. Ts'ui Pên must have said once: *I am withdrawing to write a book.* And another time: *I am withdrawing to construct a labyrinth.* Every one imagined two works; to no one did it occur that the book and the maze were one and the same thing. The Pavilion of the Limpid Solitude stood in the center of a garden that was perhaps intricate; that circumstance could have suggested to the heirs a physical labyrinth. Ts'ui Pên died; no one in the vast territories that were his came upon the labyrinth; the confusion of the novel suggested to me that *it* was the maze. Two circumstances gave me the correct solution of the problem. One: the curious legend that Ts'ui Pên had planned to create a labyrinth which would be strictly infinite. The other: a fragment of a letter I discovered."

Albert rose. He turned his back on me for a moment; he opened a drawer of the black and gold desk. He faced me and in his hands he held a sheet of paper that had once been crimson, but was now pink and tenuous and cross-sectioned. The fame of Ts'ui Pên as a calligrapher had been justly won. I read, uncomprehendingly and with fervor, these words written with a minute brush by a man of my blood: *I leave to the various futures (not to all) my garden of forking paths.* Wordlessly, I returned the sheet. Albert continued:

"Before unearthing this letter, I had questioned myself about the ways in which a book can be infinite. I could think of nothing other than a cyclic volume, a circular one. A book whose last page was identical with the first, a book which had the possibility of continuing indefinitely. I remembered too that night which is at the middle of the Thousand and One Nights when Scheherazade (through a magical oversight of the copyist) begins to relate word for word the story of the Thousand and One Nights, establishing the risk of coming once again to the night when she must repeat it, and thus on to infinity. I imagined as well a Platonic, hereditary work, transmitted from father to son, in which each new individual adds a chapter or corrects with pious care the pages of his elders. These conjectures diverted me; but none seemed to correspond, not even remotely, to the contradictory chapters of Ts'ui Pên. In the midst of this perplexity, I received from Oxford the manuscript you have examined. I lingered, naturally, on the sentence: *I leave to the various futures (not to all) my garden of forking paths.* Almost instantly, I understood: 'the garden of forking paths' was the chaotic novel; the phrase 'the various futures (not to all)' suggested to me the forking in time, not in space. A broad rereading of the work confirmed the theory. In all fictional works, each time a man is confronted with several alternatives, he chooses one and eliminates the others; in the fiction of Ts'ui Pên, he chooses—simultaneously—all of them. *He creates,* in this way, diverse futures, diverse times which themselves also proliferate and fork. Here, then, is the explanation of the novel's contradictions. Fang, let us say, has a secret; a stranger calls at his door; Fang resolves to kill him. Naturally, there are several possible outcomes: Fang can kill the intruder, the intruder can kill Fang, they both can escape, they both can die, and so forth. In the work of Ts'ui Pên, all possible outcomes occur; each one is the point of departure for other forkings. Sometimes, the paths of this labyrinth converge: for example, you arrive at this house, but in one of the possible pasts you are my enemy, in another, my friend. If you will resign yourself to my incurable pronunciation, we shall read a few pages."

His face, within the vivid circle of the lamplight, was unquestionably that of an old man, but with something unalterable about it, even immortal. He read with slow precision two versions of the same epic chapter. In the first, an army marches to a battle across a lonely mountain; the horror of the rocks and shadows makes the men undervalue their lives and they gain an easy victory. In the second the same army traverses a palace where a great festival is taking place; the resplendent battle seems to them a continuation of the celebration and they win the victory. I listened with proper veneration to these ancient narratives, perhaps less admirable in themselves than the fact that they had been created by my blood and were being restored to me by a man of a remote empire, in the course of a desperate adventure, on a Western isle. I remember the last words, repeated in each version like a secret commandment: *Thus fought the heroes, tranquil their admirable hearts, violent their swords, resigned to kill and to die.*

From that moment on, I felt about me and within my dark body an invisible, intangible swarming. Not the swarming of the divergent, parallel and finally coalescent armies, but a more inaccessible, more intimate agitation that they in some manner prefigured. Stephen Albert continued:

"I don't believe that your illustrious ancestor played idly with these variations. I don't consider it credible that he would sacrifice thirteen years to the infinite execution of a rhetorical experiment. In your country, the novel is a subsidiary form of literature; in Ts'ui Pên's time it was a despicable form. Ts'ui Pên was a brilliant novelist, but he was also a man of letters who doubtless did not consider himself a mere novelist. The testimony of his contemporaries proclaims—and his life fully confirms—his metaphysical and mystical interests. Philosophic controversy usurps a good part of the novel. I know that of all problems, none disturbed him so greatly nor worked upon him so much as the abysmal problem of time. Now then, the latter is the only problem that does not figure in the pages of the *Garden*. He does not even use the word that signifies time. How do you explain this voluntary omission?"

I proposed several solutions—all unsatisfactory. We discussed them. Finally, Stephen Albert said to me:

"In a riddle whose answer is chess, what is the only prohibited word?"

I thought a moment and replied, "The word *chess*."

"Precisely," said Albert. "*The Garden of Forking Paths* is an enormous riddle, or parable, whose theme is time; this recondite cause prohibits its mention. To omit a word always, to resort to inept metaphors and obvious periphrases, is perhaps the most emphatic way of stressing it. That is the tortuous method preferred, in each of the meanderings of his indefatigable novel, by the oblique Ts'ui Pên. I have compared hundreds of manuscripts, I have corrected the errors that the negligence of the copyists has introduced. I have guessed the plan of this chaos, I have reestablished—I believe I have re-established—the primordial organisation, I have translated the entire work: it is clear to me that not once does he employ the word 'time.' The explanation is obvious: *The Garden of Forking Paths* is an incomplete, but not false, image of the universe as Ts'ui Pên conceived it. In contrast to Newton and Schopenhauer, your ancestor did not believe in a uniform, absolute time. He believed in an infinite series of times, in a growing, dizzying net of divergent, convergent and parallel times. This network of times which approached one another, forked, broke off, or were unaware of one another for centuries, embraces *all* possibilities of time. We do not exist in the majority of these times; in some you exist, and not I; in others I, and not you; in others, both of us. In the present one, which a favorable fate has granted me, you have arrived at my house; in another, while crossing the garden, you found me dead; in still another, I utter these same words, but I am a mistake, a ghost."

"In every one," I pronounced, not without a tremble to my voice, "I am grateful to you and revere you for your re-creation of the garden of Ts'ui Pên."

"Not in all," he murmured with a smile. "Time forks perpetually toward innumerable futures. In one of them I am your enemy."

Once again I felt the swarming sensation of which I have spoken. It seemed to me that the humid garden that surrounded the house was infinitely saturated with invisible persons. Those persons were Albert and I, secret, busy and multiform in other dimensions of time. I raised my eyes and the tenuous nightmare dissolved. In the yellow and black garden there was only one man; but this man was as strong as a statue … this man was approaching along the path and he was Captain Richard Madden.

"The future already exists," I replied, "but I am your friend. Could I see the letter again?"

Albert rose. Standing tall, he opened the drawer of the tall desk; for the moment his back was to me. I had readied the revolver. I fired with extreme caution. Albert fell uncomplainingly, immediately. I swear his death was instantaneous—a lightning stroke.

The rest is unreal, insignificant. Madden broke in, arrested me. I have been condemned to the gallows. I have won out abominably; I have communicated to Berlin the secret name of the city they must attack. They bombed it yesterday; I read it in the same papers that offered to England the mystery of the learned Sinologist Stephen Albert who was murdered by a stranger, one Yu Tsun. The Chief had deciphered this mystery. He knew my problem was to indicate (through the uproar of the war) the city called Albert, and that I had found no other means to do so than to kill a man of that name. He does not know (no one can know) my innumerable contrition and weariness.

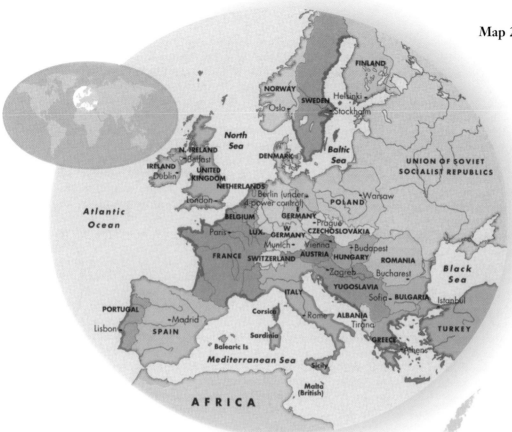

Map 23.1 Post-war Europe, 1949.

THE AGE
OF
AFFLUENCE

CHAPTER 23

- *World War II and After*
- *Pop Culture*

Frank Lloyd Wright, Fallingwater, Bear Run, Pennsylvania, 1936.

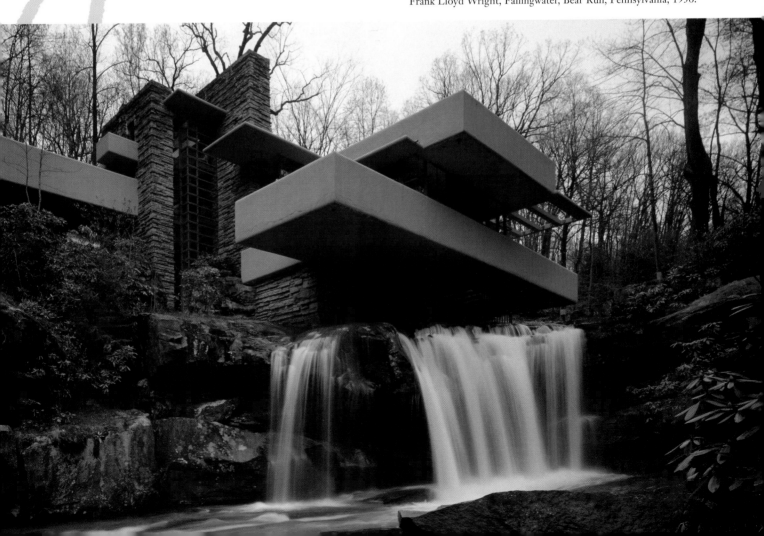

WORLD WAR II AND AFTER

The world as we know it today came into being after World War II. At least seventeen million soldiers had died fighting this war, and eighteen million civilians because of it. The economies of Europe and Asia had been decimated. The Allied victory was undermined by political mistrust of the Soviets, members of the Allied forces, whose Communist tenets threatened Western-style capitalism. Only one thing was certain: humankind was now capable of total self-destruction.

On May 10, 1940, nine months after Hitler's invasion of Poland had forced France and Britain to declare war on Germany, German troops moved north into the Low Countries. From Belgium, German troops poured into France, driving not directly to Paris but to the English Channel, thus separating France from its British allies. Britain withdrew over 300,000 French and British troops trapped on the beaches at Dunkirk, and then Hitler marched on Paris. On June 13, the French declared Paris an open city and evacuated it without fighting. On June 22, Marshal Henri Pétain signed an armistice with the Germans, handing over two-thirds of the country to German control, leaving himself in charge of the Mediterranean areas. His headquarters were in the small resort community of Vichy, and his government, despised by many French people after the war for its collaboration, was known simply as Vichy France.

Hitler apparently believed that, without France's support, Britain would give in as well. Britain did noth-

ing of the kind. When Britain's new prime minister, WINSTON CHURCHILL (1874–1965), addressed the House of Commons, he spoke with such force that his speech became a kind of national imperative:

> I have nothing to offer but blood, toil, tears, and sweat. We have before us an ordeal of the most grievous kind. We have before us many, many long months of struggle and of suffering. You ask, what is our policy? I will say: It is to wage war, by sea, land, and air, with all our might and with all the strength that God can give us; to make war against a monstrous tyranny, never surpassed in the dark, lamentable catalogue of human crime. That is our policy.
>
> You ask, what is our aim? I can answer in one word: It is victory, victory at all costs, victory in spite of all terror, victory, however long and hard the road may be; for without victory there is no survival.

In August and September of 1940, Hitler began to test the British resolve by conducting full-scale bomber attacks on the country. But, in what Churchill would label the "nation's finest hour," Germany failed to win superiority in the air over Britain, and British resolve was strengthened even more deeply.

Meanwhile, in the Pacific, Japanese leaders, who had struck a deal with Vichy France, invaded French Indochina (Vietnam) and pressed into China. The Japanese Emperor HIROHITO (1901–1989) entered into an alliance with Hitler and Germany, agreeing to enter the war once Japan was militarily prepared to do so or if the United States joined the Allied forces and entered the war in Europe. Apparently impatient, on

Timeline 23.1 The United States after the war.

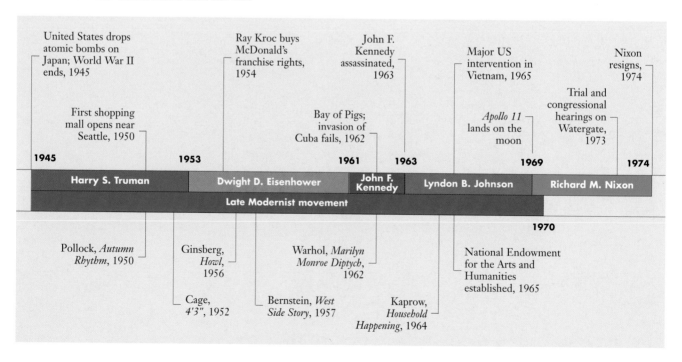

December 7, 1941, Japanese forces attacked the American naval base at Pearl Harbor, Hawaii. An outraged United States immediately declared war on Japan, and Germany honored its alliance with the Japanese and declared war on the United States. By the end of 1941, it seemed like the entire world was at war.

Slowly, the Allies gained the upper hand both in Europe and in the Pacific. There were many turning points. In North Africa, Allied troops defeated the German General Erwin Rommel, the "Desert Fox." In Russia, the Soviets successfully defended Stalingrad (Volgograd) against Germany. In Italy, the Allied invasion of Sicily soon took Italy out of the war. Then came "D-Day" on June 6, 1944, and the Allies regained the beaches of northern France (fig. 23.1). Perhaps a decisive factor in defeating Germany was simply Allied air superiority, which almost completely devastated Germany's industrial base and oil production capabilities, drawing to a halt resupply of its troops in the field.

As the Allied troops marched into Germany, Hitler shot himself in defeat, having started a war that had resulted, at a conservative estimate, in the death of seventeen million soldiers, eighteen million citizens, and between six and seven million Jews in death camps such as Auschwitz, in Poland, where as many as twelve thousand Jews were executed in a single day. On May 8, 1945, Churchill and the American President, HARRY S. TRUMAN (1884–1972), declared the war in Europe over. The United States chose to end the war with Japan by dropping its newly developed atom bomb on the Japanese cities of Hiroshima, on August 6, 1945, and, three days later, on Nagasaki. On September 2, 1945, Japan surrendered as well.

COLD WAR AND ECONOMIC RECOVERY

From the point of view of many historians, World War II represents a rekindling of hostilities that had remained unresolved since World War I. In this light, the 1920s and '30s can best be viewed simply as an extended truce. So devastating was the war that Europe lost its central place in world politics and culture and Japan was left so battered that its emperor, Hirohito, referred to the situation as "the unendurable that must be endured."

Peace was a necessity, but quarrels were a certainty. The rebuilding of Europe and Japan required huge investment, but only economic recovery could underwrite it. The American Secretary of State, GEORGE C.

Figure 23.1 Allied troops landing in Normandy. This photograph, taken two days after D-Day, on June 6, 1944, shows reinforcements arriving on French soil. From the ships in the bay to the blimp flying above and the tanks on the ground, the dimension of the Allied effort is evident.

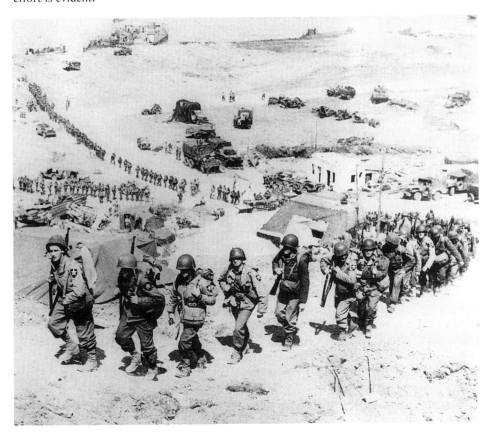

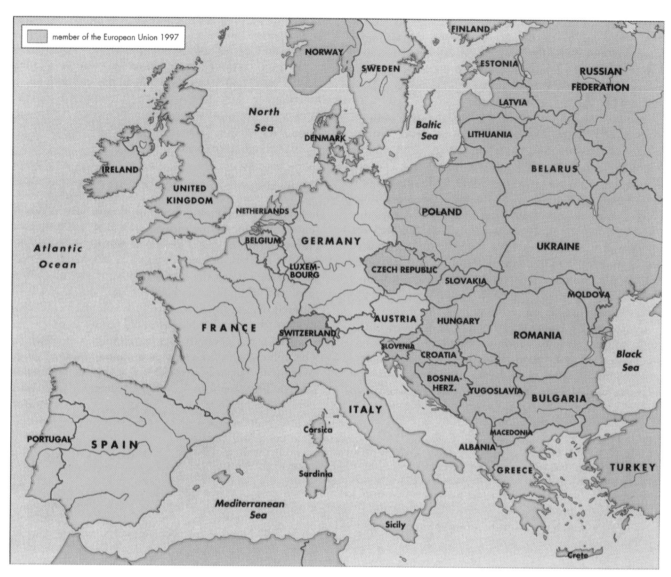

Map 23.2 Membership of the European Union, 1997.

MARSHALL (1880–1959), conceived the idea of providing economic aid to the European countries on the condition that they work together for their mutual benefit. It was called the "Marshall Plan," and it allowed for unprecedented prosperity and affluence in Europe. In Japan, General DOUGLAS MacARTHUR (1880–1964) helped to install a new democratic constitution forbidding the manufacture of arms for "land, sea, or air force … [and] other war potential." Japan thus became the only world power without a significant defense budget, which freed its economy.

Europe was so weakened that it became the focal point of a struggle for world power called the "Cold War," fought without open warfare between the United States and the Soviet Union. The United States had as its ally much of Western Europe while the Soviet Union dominated Eastern Europe. By 1950, the former

imperial powers of Europe had also lost control of most of their territories and empires overseas, and many of these countries in Southeast Asia, Africa, and Latin America, became points of conflict in the U.S./Soviet power struggle. In 1961, the United States supported Cuban exiles in their efforts to overthrow the Communist regime of FIDEL CASTRO (b. 1926), support that culminated in the embarrassingly unsuccessful invasion at the Bay of Pigs. A year later, Castro allowed the Soviets to establish missile bases in Cuba itself, and the Cold War threatened to go nuclear. But calmer minds prevailed, and the cool relations of Cold War politics once again took center stage.

Even as Western Europe lost political clout worldwide, it developed a strong economic union, the European Community, or the Common Market as it was known (it has now been renamed once more as the

European Union), which brought unparalleled affluence, or wealth, to the continent. As opposed to Eastern Europe, where shortages of food and goods remained a constant throughout the life of the Soviet regime, both Western Europe and the United States enjoyed fifty years of expansion in the availability of consumer goods and services. Japan, too, freed from military obligations by its treaty with the United States, turned its attention on its devastated economy, and by 1970 it led the world in the production of quality consumer goods. By 1996, its Gross National Product was nearly four times that of France and three times that of Germany.

The period after World War II can thus be represented as a steady movement from destruction and devastation to affluence and prosperity. In this climate, anything seemed possible. Visionaries speculated that one day every family might own a television. Music might be played in stereophonic sound. People might fly to the moon. Computers might interpret data, drive cars, or clean houses. Even more important, racism might end, women might achieve equality, world peace might be possible. Such were the dreams.

THE PHILOSOPHY OF EXISTENTIALISM

The reality of the horrors of the German concentration camps, of human being's inhumanity to one another, and, in France particularly, the fact that thousands had willingly collaborated with the Nazis in the Vichy government or, at the very least, turned their eyes from Nazi atrocities, fueled a philosophical discourse that focused on the individual's responsibility to make ethical choices and decisions—**existentialism**. Its seeds lay in the ideas of the Danish philosopher SØREN KIERKEGAARD [KEAR-kah-gard] (1813–1855), who insisted on the irreducibly subjective and personal dimension of human life. Kierkegaard used the term the "existing individual" to characterize the subjective perspective, and from this the term "existential" later developed. Kierkegaard emphasized the essentially ethical nature of human life, with each individual responsible for making choices and commitments. Kierkegaard also insisted that the kinds of choices individuals need to make are ethically appropriate ones involving respect for other people, virtuous behavior on their behalf, and a faith in spiritual things that transcends the limitations and vicissitudes of material life.

Jean-Paul Sartre. Like Kierkegaard, the French philosopher Jean-Paul Sartre [SAHR-truh] (1905–1980) emphasized the ethical aspect of existential thought. Unlike Kierkegaard, however, Sartre, who was an atheist, disavowed any spiritual or religious dimension as necessary for existential living. The central tenets of Sartre's existential philosophy begin with his idea that "existence precedes essence," which suggests that human beings are defined by their choices and actions. Nothing is fixed or pre-established in "human nature." That is, there is no essential human nature that exists as a given beyond physical life. What is important is what human beings become, what they make of themselves through their choices, decisions, and commitments, which are always in question and never finally settled.

This fundamental idea is related to another: that human beings exist relative to one another; they exist in interpersonal and social situations that affect them, situations that also involve repeated decisive choices. The choices human beings make are necessary and inescapable. Those choices, moreover, not only make individuals who they are, since a person is what he or she does, but they also make people responsible for each other as well as for themselves. When people evade responsibility for themselves or for others, they exist in a state that Sartre describes as "bad faith," which results from denying their freedom to do, think, act, or be otherwise than they are.

Sartre recognized that people might live in a state of "bad faith" because the burden of responsibility is very great and at times frightening. But he insisted that in evading responsibility, individuals were ignoring, repressing, or otherwise hiding from truth. Complicating the decisions individuals confront every day is the lack of any fixed or absolute standard by which they make decisions about right and wrong. Standards of good and evil can be and indeed are established, but individuals must decide to abide by them for themselves. This position had particular impact after World War II, when the West had to deal with revelations about Nazi attempts to exterminate the Jews and the collaboration of both ordinary Germans and the governments of occupied Europe in the process.

The responsibility for choosing and the freedom to decide about such matters belong to the individual alone. So too do decisions about how to respond to situations that are beyond one's power to change—one's race or physical attributes, for example. Whether to see unchangeable dimensions of one's life as handicaps or attributes, as limitations, advantages, or opportunities lies within the decision-making power of the individual.

Sartre developed his philosophy in the context of World War II, including the Nazi occupation of France. During that time he came to recognize the ways one's physical freedom could be curtailed and one's life endangered. Nonetheless, he remained uncompromising in his insistence that, regardless of one's situation, one always had the conscious power to negate it and to transcend it in thought. What people make of such situations, much as what they make of themselves through the many roles they perform in life, determines who they become. It is not the situations themselves or the roles people find themselves in that fix their identities but the choices they make in response to those roles and situations.

Simone de Beauvoir. SIMONE DE BEAUVOIR [boh-VWAHR] (1908–1966) shared with Sartre ideas about the necessity for responsibility in choosing what one makes of one's life. De Beauvoir stressed more than Sartre the ambiguity that is frequently a factor in the ethical decisions people need to make. In her *Ethics of Ambiguity* (1947) she emphasized the typical complexity of choices between right and wrong. Beauvoir worked closely with Sartre throughout their adult lives. She met him while they were both students at the Sorbonne in Paris, and lived with him for many years as mate, companion, partner, and intellectual associate.

De Beauvoir's most important contribution involves her study of women. In her groundbreaking book *The Second Sex*, she reviewed history and myth, bringing them to bear on the situation of women at mid-century. She also analyzed the biological bases of female experience, concluding that although biological differences between men and women are incontrovertible, it is social differentiation that determines their very different life experiences. De Beauvoir was especially eloquent on women's need to distinguish themselves from men, to break the pattern of being seen only in relation to them. She was far ahead of her time in advancing the belief that, in a man's world, women need to band together collectively to assert the pressure for change. She was equally in advance of her time in calling for economic opportunities that might help to create equality. Most important of all, perhaps, is her insistence that women should have their "independent existence," so that as women and men mutually recognize each other "as subject, each will yet remain for the other an *other*." For de Beauvoir, women, even more than men, need to claim themselves for themselves, recognizing their responsibility to choose what they will become, even as they acknowledge the limitations and constraints they are compelled to live with.

ABSTRACTION IN AMERICAN ART

Even as existentialism became the dominant post-war philosophy, the arts too began to emphasize the value of individual expression. In the United States, in particular, a brand of highly personal and subjective abstract painting developed that became known as **abstract expressionism**. Many of the artists involved rejected the term; as one wrote, "I never think of my pictures as abstract … Nothing can be more concrete to a man than his own felt thought, his own thought feeling." Yet the work of the Abstract Expressionists, though widely varied in style, was unified in its rejection of direct representation of the objective world and its emphasis on the expressive capacities of one's own gestures and techniques.

Figure 23.2 Jackson Pollock, *Autumn Rhythm: Number 30*, 1950, oil on canvas, 8′9″ × 17′3″ (2.66 × 5.25 m), Metropolitan Museum of Art, New York. Because there is no recognizable subject, such work is referred to as "Abstract Expressionism." Pollock's personal technique is known as "action painting" because of the highly active physical process—he splattered, flung, and dripped paint onto canvas unrolled on the floor, the result being largely accidental.

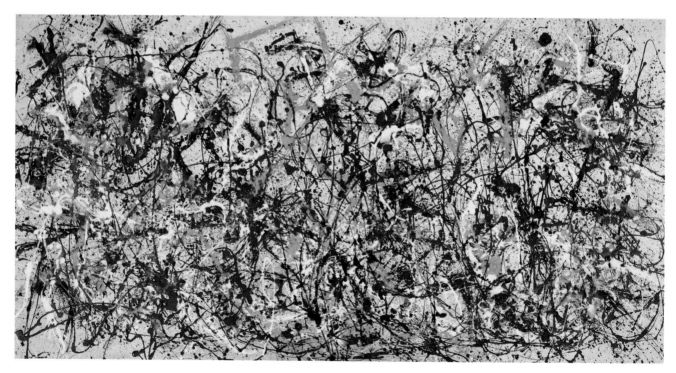

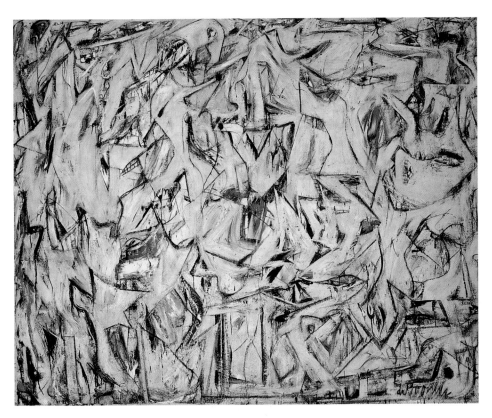

Figure 23.3 Willem de Kooning, *Excavation*, 1950, oil on canvas, 6′8½″ × 8′4⅛″ (2.04 × 2.54 m), Art Institute of Chicago, Chicago. Fragments of human anatomy seem to reveal themselves behind, through, and across the webbed surfaces of many de Kooning paintings.

In the 1930s many artists were not working on the kind of mural painting supported by the WPA, and the government recognized this. As part of the "New Deal," an easel painting project was initiated that paid artists $95 a month to live on. While not a fortune, this represented a living wage, and many of the artists under this plan soon led America to a position as the focal point of the avant-garde in the 1940s. Among them were Jackson Pollock, Willem de Kooning, and Mark Rothko.

Jackson Pollock. Perhaps the best known of the Abstract Expressionist painters is the American JACKSON POLLOCK (1912–1956). Born in Wyoming, Pollock moved to New York in the 1930s, studying with Thomas Hart Benton, whose interest in large-scale work greatly influenced him. By the mid-1940s, Pollock had begun developing a body of work sometimes referred to as "drip" paintings. These have been linked to the fact that he was in psychoanalysis when he created them and was interested in the role of the unconscious in art. In fact, many Surrealists had escaped the war in Europe, seeking asylum in the United States, and Pollock was intrigued by their notion of psychic automatism. In addition, he had been especially affected by Picasso's *Guernica* (see Chapter 21) when it was first displayed in New York in 1939.

His working method, the results of which are seen in *Autumn Rhythm: Number 30* (fig. 23.2), of 1950, was to unroll a huge canvas on the floor and throw, drip, and splatter paint onto it as he moved over and around it. Although Pollock said he knew what he was trying to achieve before starting work on a canvas, he created his compositions largely by accident. The paint is spread over the entire surface with swirls racing out toward the edge only to turn back into the center. Nor is there a clear top or bottom to the work: Pollock determined this only when he signed it. The entire large surface is unified by a web of paint, built of countless layers of swirling marks, forces that push and pull one another.

Pollock's style became known as **action painting** because this style of painting conveys the sense of the artist's physical activity, animation, and vitality. Pollock swung his arms and moved his entire body when making his drip paintings. For him, the actual process of getting paint onto the canvas was the most important part of the work, and the "work" is not so much the finished product as the action of making it.

Willem de Kooning. Like Pollock, the paintings of WILLEM DE KOONING (1904–1997) reveal an interest not so much in representing a preconceived idea but rather in experiencing the act of painting. When de

Figure 23.4   Mark Rothko, *Red, Brown, and Black*, 1958, oil on canvas, 8′11″ × 9′9″ (2.72 × 2.97 m), Museum of Modern Art, New York. Working in a style known as Color Field Painting, Rothko produced a series of paintings consisting of soft-edged rectangles of various colors that are theoretical and philosophical representations of contrasting states of emotion and discipline.

Kooning emigrated to the United States from his native Holland in 1926, he was a figure painter, albeit one deeply influenced by the Cubists. But very soon after, he became influenced by the Surrealists and began approaching the canvas with broad, slashing strokes of paint. In *Excavation* (fig. 23.3), of 1950, a continuous surface of interlocking, neutral-colored abstract shapes that seem simultaneously organic and geometric rise out of what appears to be a multi-colored ground. Through this web of shapes can be detected, at various points, sets of teeth, eyes, fleshtones—even, in the very middle, a red, white, and blue area that suggests the American flag. De Kooning's aim was to create an afocal surface, that is, one on which the eye can never quite come to rest. For de Kooning, this disorientation, comparable to the disorientation felt by the immigrants and disenfranchised refugees from Europe who came to the United States after World War II, represents the modern condition.

Mark Rothko.   The anguish conveyed in de Kooning's work is even more evident in the Color Field abstraction of MARK ROTHKO (1903–1970), whose style is characterized by the absence of a recognizable figurative subject, an absence of an illusion of space, and large areas of flat color. A Russian who moved to America, Rothko was a withdrawn and introspective artist whose anguish about himself and his work led to his eventual suicide in his studio in 1970. *Red, Brown, and Black* (fig. 23.4), of 1958, is characteristic of the large canvases covered with rectangles of subtle, rich colors for which Rothko is best known. Working with layers of thin paint, Rothko made the edges of his rectangles fuzzy and soft, rendering the rectangles cloudlike, seemingly able to float one on top of another. Rothko created color harmonies, tones nuanced and graded, rich and intense. Intellectual as well as sensual, the rectangles seem to hover in an ambiguous space, sometimes appearing to advance and at other times recede. This ambiguity produces oddly powerful images, for Rothko intended to evoke emotion. Referring to his paintings as both "tragic and timeless," Rothko thought of his canvases as backdrops or stage sets before which viewers exercised their feelings, ranging from calm to happy to sad.

Cross Currents

ABSTRACT EXPRESSIONISM IN JAPAN

In the summer of 1955, a group of young Japanese artists who called themselves the Gutai Art Association organized a thirteen-day, twenty-four-hour-a-day, outdoor exhibition in a pine grove park along the beach in Ashiya, a small town outside Osaka. Their name, Gutai, literally means "concreteness," but more importantly it derives from two separate characters, *gu*, meaning "tool" or "means," and *tai*, meaning "body" or "substance." Taking Jackson Pollock's physical confrontation with his paintings as a starting point, they approached their work with their entire bodies, literally throwing themselves into it.

They called the exhibition in Ashiya the *Experimental Outdoor Exhibition of Modern Art to Challenge the Mid-Summer Sun*. A year later, in Tokyo, Gutai held another exhibition. The spirit of experimentation marked both occasions. Paint was applied to canvas with watering cans and with remote control toys. Shimamato Shozo, wearing goggles and dressed for combat, made paintings by throwing jars of paint against rocks positioned across a canvas in a manner reminiscent of a Japanese Zen garden. The finished works were deeply encrusted in paint and glass, the record of a new kind of "Action Painting." Shiraga Kazuo painted on large canvases stretched across the floor, in the manner of Pollock, but used his feet as his brush as he slid through the oil paint. In a piece called *Challenging Mud*, he submerged himself half-naked in a pile of dense mud. Rolling in it, squeezing it, wrestling with it, he created a sculptural version of his physical presence. Murakami Saburo built large paper screens six feet high by twelve feet wide, and then flung himself through them.

As violent as these activities seemed to many, they were deeply rooted in Zen. Concrete enactments of the individual's emotional condition unite the physical and spiritual in a single image. And if, in post-World War II Japan, the spiritual life tended toward violence and anger, this may be understandable given their political and economic situations and their having suffered a nuclear attack.

Figure 23.5 Helen Frankenthaler, *Mauve District*, 1966, polymer on unprimed canvas, 8'7" × 7'11" (2.62 × 2.41 m), Museum of Modern Art, New York. Frankenthaler was deeply impressed by the work of Jackson Pollock. However, where Pollock's oil paint was thick, Frankenthaler achieved soft stained effects, similar to watercolor, by painting with thinned paint on absorbent raw canvas.

Helen Frankenthaler. Rothko's color field painting, with its chromatic subtleties, is given freer form by the American artist HELEN FRANKENTHALER (b. 1928), a second generation Abstract Expressionist. Her *Mauve District* (fig. 23.5), of 1966, is an example of this non-objective style of painting. Like Pollock, Frankenthaler worked on raw, or unprimed canvas, i.e. canvas without glue and gesso (white paint) primer. Like Pollock, she worked on huge canvases laid out flat on the floor rather than placed on an easel. Unlike Pollock, however, Frankenthaler poured paint onto the canvas, soaking and staining the canvas. At first she used oil paint, thinned with turpentine until it was very fluid. Later she used acrylic paints which can be thinned with water and handled much like watercolor.

Frankenthaler's experiments resulted in a technical innovation, the ability to achieve the effects of watercolor on a grand scale. Soft and silky biomorphic forms and shapes in color harmonies produce floating, lyrical effects. This technique of staining eliminates all brushstrokes and textural differences. Some areas of the canvas have been intentionally left unpainted, negative shapes defined by the painted areas abutting them.

Frankenthaler's paintings have a look of ease and spontaneity, an extreme fluidity, as if they were created in an instant, but this look is artfully constructed. Frankenthaler said that she threw away her works that had lost the quality of fresh spontaneity.

Timeline 23.2 Architecture of the modern world.

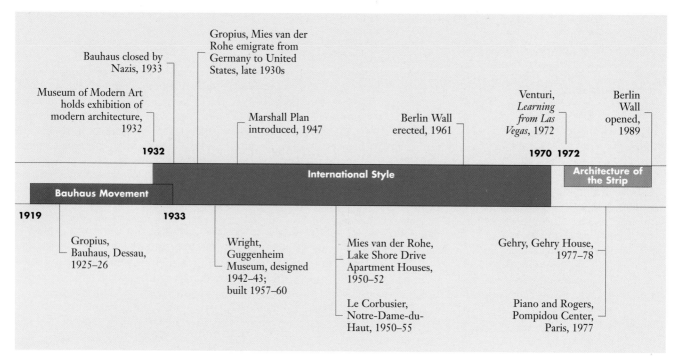

Museum of Modern Art holds exhibition of modern architecture, 1932

Bauhaus closed by Nazis, 1933

Gropius, Mies van der Rohe emigrate from Germany to United States, late 1930s

Marshall Plan introduced, 1947

Berlin Wall erected, 1961

Venturi, *Learning from Las Vegas*, 1972

Berlin Wall opened, 1989

1932   1970 1972

International Style

Bauhaus Movement

Architecture of the Strip

1919   1933

Gropius, Bauhaus, Dessau, 1925–26

Wright, Guggenheim Museum, designed 1942–43; built 1957–60

Mies van der Rohe, Lake Shore Drive Apartment Houses, 1950–52

Le Corbusier, Notre-Dame-du-Haut, 1950–55

Gehry, Gehry House, 1977–78

Piano and Rogers, Pompidou Center, Paris, 1977

CONTEMPORARY ARCHITECTURE

Most of the great post-war architects began working in the first two decades of the twentieth century. In order to fully comprehend their post-war creations, we must consider their careers as a whole. Unlike the other modern arts, in architecture a single, "international" style developed over the first half of the twentieth century that almost all architects acknowledged, if not all wholly accepted it. Several factors led to recognition of this style. First, the Museum of Modern Art in New York held an exhibition of modern architecture in 1932 that identified a new "International Style … based primarily on the nature of modern materials and structure … slender steel posts and beams, and concrete reinforced by steel." Second, many of these architects left Europe in the 1930s due to the worsening situation there and came to the United States. Third, thanks to the Marshall Plan, in Europe and the U.S., the booming economic climate after the war called for many new buildings.

Walter Gropius. One of the leading architects in Germany was WALTER GROPIUS (1883–1969), director of the **Bauhaus** art school in Dessau, Germany, and designer of its chief buildings (fig. 23.6), built 1925–26. When Adolf Hitler closed the Bauhaus, Gropius moved to America and became the chair of the Architecture Department at Harvard University.

The main principle of the Bauhaus was to closely connect art, science, and technology so that there was no dividing line between the fine arts, architecture, and industrially produced functional objects. The artist, the architect, the craftsperson, and the engineer were brought together.

The Bauhaus building is essentially a cage of glass. Its steel frame makes possible walls entirely made of glass because the walls do not support the structure. The cornice at the top is no longer functionally necessary

Figure 23.6   Walter Gropius, Bauhaus, Dessau, Germany, 1925–26. The Bauhaus (House of Building), closed by the Nazis in 1933, was a school that sought to adapt to the modern world by combining the methods and disciplines of fine art, craft, graphic design, architecture, and industry. Built of reinforced concrete, steel, and glass, the Bauhaus building itself looked like a painting by Mondrian made three-dimensional.

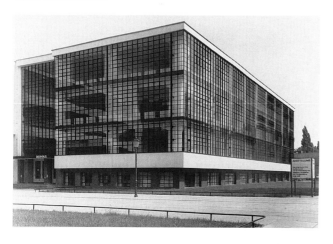

to protect a building of glass, steel, and concrete from the elements, but it is *aesthetically* necessary as a visual conclusion to the architectural composition, to frame the building.

Ludwig Mies van der Rohe. Among Walter Gropius's colleagues at the Bauhaus in Dessau was LUDWIG MIES VAN DER ROHE [mees-van-duh-ROW] (1887–1969). When Hitler closed the school, Mies moved to Chicago where he concentrated his efforts on designing a new campus for the Illinois Institute of Technology. Later Mies created what we now think of as the modern skyscraper.

Typical of his work are the Lake Shore Drive Apartment Houses (fig. 23.7), built 1950–52. Mies's motto, "Less is more," is embodied in these buildings, which achieve the utmost with the least means. Emphasis on mass is gone as supporting masonry walls are replaced by a steel frame, the skeleton emphasized by the surface pattern of rectangles. Ornament is rejected. Simplicity has been taken to the point of austerity. Solid and void are given equal aesthetic consideration.

Le Corbusier. Another leader of the International Style and a very influential architect was Charles Édouard Jeanneret, known as LE CORBUSIER [cor-BOO-see-ay] (1886–1965). The Savoye House in Poissy-sur-Seine in France (fig. 23.8, exterior; fig. 23.9, interior), built 1929–30, is a private home that caused a revolution in domestic architecture. Corbusier called such houses he designed "machines à habiter" (machines to be lived in). Corbusier admired machines, praising their neat and precise shapes.

The Savoye House is elevated on stilts made of reinforced concrete. Smooth walls in pure geometric shapes enclose space. Aesthetically, the Savoye House is an abstract composition of simple flat and curved planes and sharp clean lines. It is much like a very large piece of non-representational sculpture, but one that can be inhabited, and its interior is treated as blocks of space of differing sizes. Glass walls divide one area from another.

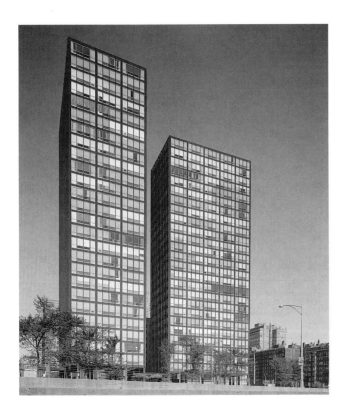

Figure 23.7 Ludwig Mies van der Rohe, Lake Shore Drive Apartment Houses, Chicago, 1950–52. Modern office and apartment buildings favor simplified and standardized rectangular buildings of steel and glass, the vertical emphasized and the structural frame made obvious.

Figures 23.8 and 23.9 (below left and right) Le Corbusier (Charles Édouard Jeanneret), The Savoye House, Poissy-sur-Seine, France, 1929–30. Le Corbusier called the functional homes he designed *machines à habiter*—"machines to live in." Made of reinforced concrete and glass in simple geometric shapes, this home is an example of the International Style of the 1920s.

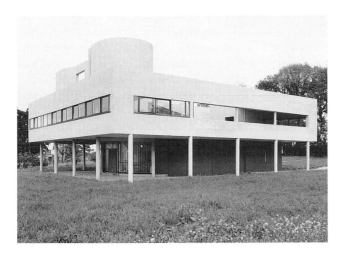

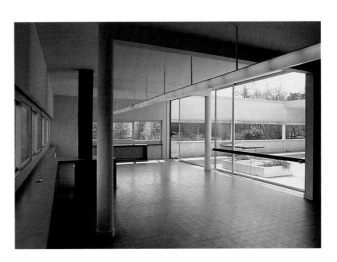

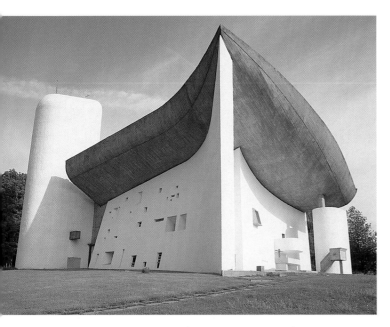

Figure 23.10 Le Corbusier, Notre-Dame-du-Haut, Ronchamp, France, 1950–55. Le Corbusier turned away from the International Style and designed this extraordinary pilgrimage church. Thick masonry walls are covered with sprayed concrete to form curved sculptural surfaces that appear natural and organic rather than rigid and stiff.

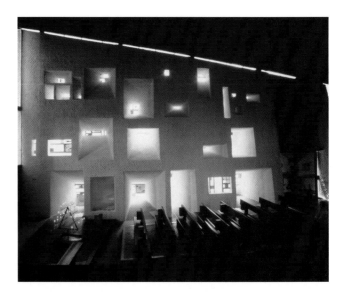

Figure 23.11 Le Corbusier, Notre-Dame-du-Haut, Ronchamp, France, 1950–55.

The effect is open but private. Because the house is elevated up on stilts, outsiders cannot see in, although the inhabitants can see out. Elegant materials are used in ways that are ornamental, but none of the decoration is structurally extraneous.

Although the major accomplishments of twentieth-century architecture were made in domestic and commercial structures, religious architecture was not ignored. Le Corbusier designed the church of Notre-Dame-du-Haut at Ronchamp in eastern France (fig. 23.10, exterior; fig. 23.11, interior) between 1950 and 1955. The name of the church refers to its location high on a mountain top. In a revolutionary approach, what appears to be large-scale sculpture is created of sweeping curves and countercurves, concave and convex. Le Corbusier built with masonry and sprayed concrete, leaving the surface rough. As a result, the church looks as if it were made out of sheets of a soft tan material that could be cut with enormous scissors and bent into these shapes.

The interior of Notre-Dame-du-Haut is equally unusual. Unlike the symmetry that has characterized religious architecture for centuries, here symmetry has been abandoned. The windows form a carefully composed abstract arrangement across the walls. As in a Gothic cathedral (see Chapter 12), Le Corbusier makes artistic use of light and stained glass, but the effect achieved at Notre-Dame-du-Haut is very different and very modern. Windows of different sizes and shapes are set back into the thickness of the wall. As in the Gothic

era, the windows are filled with stained glass, but here, rather than being representational, the designs are geometric. Some of the windows are so tiny as to to be slits in the walls.

Frank Lloyd Wright. Perhaps the most influential architect of the age, however, was the American FRANK LLOYD WRIGHT (1867–1959), a student of Louis Sullivan (see Chapter 21). Early in his career, in the first decade of the twentieth century, he designed what he called "prairie houses," of which the Robie House, in Chicago, is an example (figs. 23.12 and 23.13). Designed in 1906 and built in 1909, the house embodies Wright's belief that the character of a building must be related to its site and blend with the terrain. He therefore used shapes related to the surrounding landscape—like the prairie on which it stands, the house is low and flat, stressing the horizontal as it seems to spread out from its walls. The brick used to build the house is made from sand and clay from a nearby quarry. In order to make the house seem part of the surrounding natural environment, Wright uses extensive windows and broad reinforced concrete cantilever overhangs to relate interior and exterior. Although critics have called modern architecture "impersonal," Wright considered his buildings "organic."

Perhaps the best known of Wright's homes is Fallingwater, in Bear Run, Pennsylvania (fig. 23.14), built in 1936 for the Kaufmann family. Appearing like a three-dimensional painting by Piet Mondrian, the house nevertheless blends into the rising cliffs of the Pennsylvania landscape. Another example of Wright's "organic architecture," it further demonstrates his love of natural materials—the native stone used for its walls

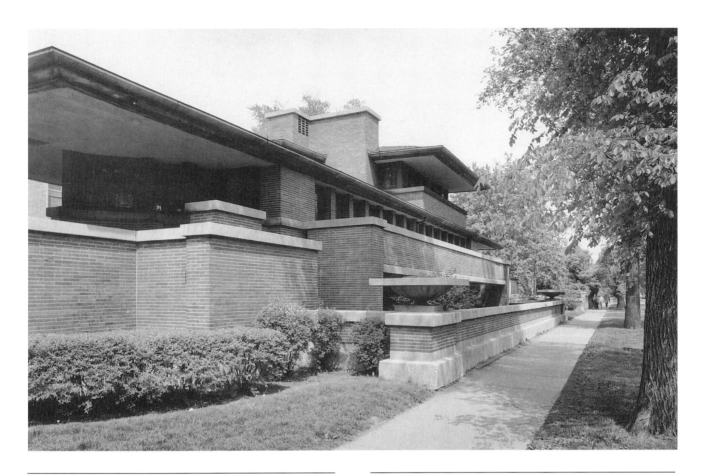

Figure 23.12   Frank Lloyd Wright, Robie House, Chicago, 1906–09. Considered the most important architect of the twentieth century, Wright designed what he called "organic" houses that were made to fit into their surroundings and were constructed of materials appropriate to the site.

Figure 23.14   Frank Lloyd Wright, Fallingwater, Bear Run, Pennsylvania, 1936. Seeking to unite structure and site, Wright used cantilevered construction to build this home over a waterfall. As in contemporary painting and structure, solid and void are given equal consideration in this composition.

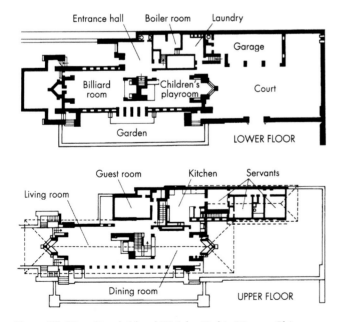

Figure 23.13   Frank Lloyd Wright, Robie House, Chicago, 1906–09.

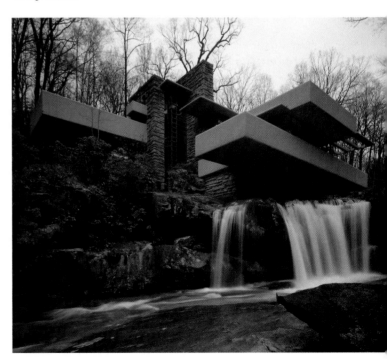

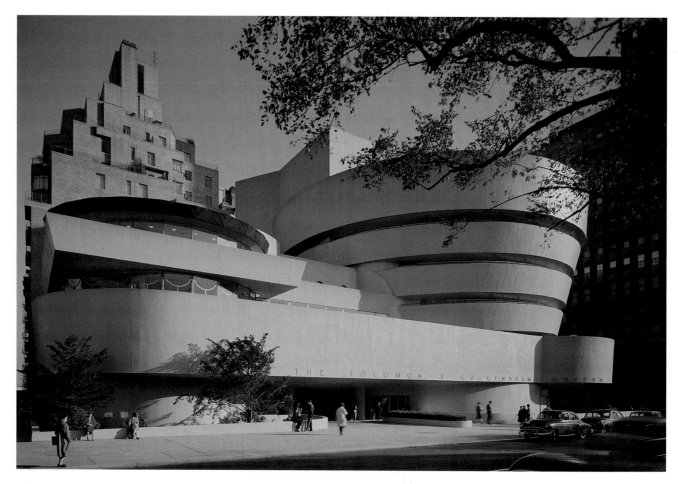

Figure 23.15   Frank Lloyd Wright, Guggenheim Museum, New York, 1957–60. Wright believed that people are greatly influenced by their architectural surroundings. Essentially an enormous concrete spiral, a sort of sculpture one can enter, the Guggenheim Museum is itself a work of art.

next to the cantilevered concrete balconies and decks that project out over the waterfall like the cliffs themselves. Another architect would have positioned the house to provide the residents with a view of the waterfall, but Wright put the house over it, integrating it into the design.

Inside, Fallingwater is a very open house, one that seems to look outward. Windows extend floor to ceiling. Walls are made of screens as Wright tried to minimize the number of rooms. The furniture in the house, as in other homes designed by Wright, is largely built-in.

Wright's range of structures included not only private homes but also public spaces, such as office buildings, churches, hotels, and museums. Perhaps the most visually arresting is the Guggenheim Museum in New York City (fig. 23.15), designed 1942–43 and built 1957–60, which looks like a huge piece of sculpture set in the crowded streets of Manhattan. Constructed of reinforced concrete, the striking spiral shape derives from the spiral ramp inside: visitors ride an elevator to the top and then

descend on foot, viewing the art work along the curving spiral walkway.

MODERN DRAMA

Modern drama begins in the nineteenth century with the plays of the Norwegian dramatist Henrik Ibsen (see Chapter 17), whose brutally realistic plays shocked his contemporaries and propelled the theater in new directions. Ibsen's emphasis on the psychological makeup of his characters was developed by later playwrights in an effort to examine and depict the new existential thought. Sartre himself was a playwright, and his play *The Flies*, of 1943, revolves around the concept of human freedom— the freedom of each individual to create his or her own unique value system in the face of the general absurdity of existence.

In fact, an existentialist sense of the absurd dominated post-war theater. Rejecting the conventions of realism, a full-blown Theater of the Absurd substituted storyless action for well-contrived plots and disconnected dia-logue for witty responses and grand speeches. Absurdist dramatists rejected the idea that characters can be under-stood or that plot should be structured, just as they rejected the order and coherence of character and action in everyday life. People were incoherent and inconsis-tent, and life was confused. Behind absurdist theater is an image of human experience as lacking in purpose and meaning.

Among the most important and influential of absur-dist dramatists is the Irish-born playwright SAMUEL BECKETT (1906–1989). Beckett's best-known works include *Waiting for Godot* and *Endgame*. In both plays, but especially in *Godot*, Beckett mixes humor with pathos. Relying on the farcical gestures of vaudeville performers and circus clowns, Beckett's characters typically display a dark intelligence and a bleakly pessimistic view of their tragi-comic situation. With their lives lacking in purpose and meaning, they wait for the inevitable degeneration of their physical and mental faculties and for death. Their relationships tend toward mastery and subservience, as Beckett reduces them to a pathetic interdependence grounded in power.

Waiting for Godot (1952) portrays two tramps, Vladimir and Estragon, who wait fruitlessly for someone named Godot, who never comes. As they wait, the tramps quarrel, contemplate suicide, separation, and departure. Dependent upon one another, they wait until they become dependent upon waiting itself. Two addi-tional characters, a master and servant named Pozzo and Lucky, share the stage for a time with the tramps. The rich Pozzo mistreats Lucky cruelly, until Pozzo becomes blind, at which point he needs the now mute Lucky to lead him. Their dependence, like that of Vladimir and Estragon, is limited but necessary. Each pair has nothing more in life than one another. It is a testimony to Beckett's theatrical genius that in depicting such a stark vision of human experience, his plays are also humorous in their portrayal of the human will to survive despite the direst of circumstances.

POP CULTURE

In the 1950s and 1960s, all of the dreams of the post-war era seemed to come true, at least the material ones. The age is distinguished by an explosion of consumer culture that quite literally changed the face of society. In 1947, 75,000 homes in the United States were equipped with television sets. By 1967, over 55 million sets were in operation and over ninety-five per cent of American fam-ilies owned at least one. That same year, Swanson intro-duced the first frozen "TV Dinner"—turkey, mashed potatoes, and peas. In 1955, McDonald's was founded, inaugurating the fast food industry. The growth of the automobile industry, which made the fast food industry possible, was staggering. By 1949, Detroit was producing 5 million automobiles a year, a year later 8 million, and the number continued to grow until 1955, the apex of the boom. In response to this, shopping patterns changed. In 1950, just north of Seattle, Washington, the Northgate

Timeline 23.3 Artistic syles of post-war culture.

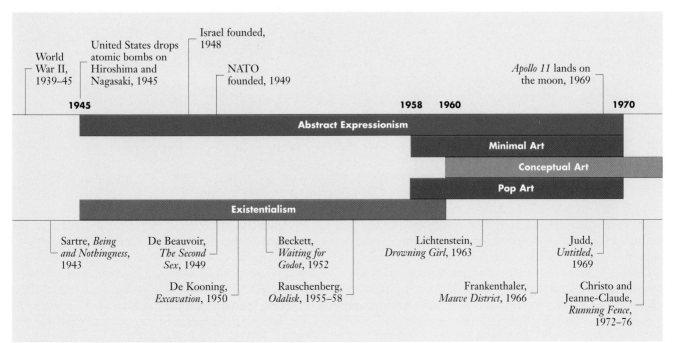

Then & Now

MCDONALD'S

With the possible exception of Coca-Cola and Microsoft, no corporate entity has come to dominate any given sector of the consumer economy more than McDonald's. The first McDonald's, which opened at 14th and E Streets in San Bernadino, California, in 1940, was owned by Richard and Maurice McDonald, Dick and Mac. The restaurant was a glass box without the golden arches that would come to distinguish the chain. But when, in 1950, the brothers put a neon sign in front that bragged, "Over one million sold," the McDonald's story had begun. Ray A. Kroc, a food service equipment salesman who owned the national marketing rights to the Multimixer milkshake maker, was intrigued by the McDonald brothers' restaurant because it used ten mixers where virtually every other restaurant on his accounts used no more than one or two. When, in 1954, he saw the McDonalds' restaurant in operation, selling literally hundreds of orders of 15¢ burgers, 10¢ french fries, and 15¢ shakes with unheard-of speed, he declared, "I've got to become involved in this." In 1955, Kroc opened his own McDonald's in Des Plaines, Illinois (fig. 23.16), this one complete with the golden arches that the McDonalds had themselves added to a new drive-in at a second San Bernadino site in 1952. Soon Kroc was successfully franchising the business throughout the mid-West. "Over one million sold" was etched on the marquee of each and every one. Today, most children can tell you, because they have read the sign under the golden arches themselves, that

McDonald's has served over 100 billion hamburgers worldwide.

In fact, today, McDonald's captures fourteen per cent of all restaurant visits in the United States, one in every six. It sells thirty-four per cent of all the hamburgers sold in the country and twenty-six per cent of all the french fries, and it takes in 6.6 per cent of all the dollars Americans spend on eating out. Fully one-twentieth of the entire United States potato harvest went directly to McDonald's, and surprisingly, two per cent of all the chicken raised in the country. It goes without saying that the chain is the nation's largest purchaser of beef. Even more stunning is the fact that 12.5 per cent of the American workforce has at some time been employed by McDonald's, and one out of every fifteen Americans got his or her first job working there. It is, in short, the largest job training organization in the country, followed by the U.S. Army.

And today, McDonald's is a worldwide concern. When McDonald's opened on January 31, 1990, on Moscow's Pushkin Square, more than thirty thousand people lined up to eat there—more customers than had ever been served in a single day before. A year later, on April 23, 1991, in Beijing, China, forty thousand customers jammed a restaurant equipped with twenty-nine cash registers to handle the flow. No one could have even guessed at such numbers back in 1954 when Ray Kroc saw 150 paying customers pack a drive-in parking lot in San Bernadino.

Figure 23.16　Ray Kroc's "original" McDonald's restaurant in Des Plaines, Illinois, 1955. Today Kroc's first McDonald's is preserved as a museum.

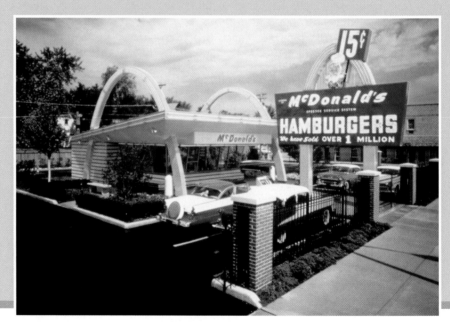

Shopping Center opened, accessible only by car and consisting of forty shops clustered around the Bon Marché department store. Six years later, the first covered mall, Southdale Center, opened in Minneapolis. Beginning in 1953, the sexual revolution took hold with the publication of the Kinsey Report on sexual behavior in the United States, and in 1966 the oral contraceptive, the so-called "Pill," was available to the public.

As American life became increasingly dominated by consumer goods, many artists and intellectuals turned their attention to the cycle of production, consumption, and waste that seemed more and more to define everyday experience. Like the Dadaists of a previous generation, they soon realized that art might be made of almost anything.

The leading theoretician of this point of view was the composer JOHN CAGE (1912–1995), who first taught at Black Mountain College in North Carolina in the early 1950s, and at the New School in New York City in the late 1950s. Many of the most important artists of the day were his students, and he exerted enormous influence over an entire generation. These artists began to investigate the implications of his musical compositions in their work. His piece *4'33"*, for instance, is literally four minutes and thirty-three seconds of silence, during which the audience becomes aware that all manner of noise in the room—"traffic sounds," in the words of one audience member at a performance at the Carnegie Recital Hall in New York, "chairs creaking, people coughing, rustling of clothes, then giggles … a police car with its siren running … the elevator in the building … the air conditioning going through the ducts." All these sounds are, in the context of the piece, "music." First performed at Woodstock, New York, on August 29, 1952, the work possesses at least three distinct features that artists would subsequently adopt. First, it is composed of the most minimal of elements—silence. Second, it consists of everyday sounds, commonplace events that occur by chance, which links the piece to Surrealism. Third, because of this inherent element of chance circumstance, no two performances are ever alike.

ARTISTS OF THE EVERYDAY

Robert Rauschenberg. One of Cage's Black Mountain students, ROBERT RAUSCHENBERG (b. 1925), was deeply influenced by Cage's composition of the everyday. Rauschenberg began making assemblages, a variation on the idea of the collage (see Chapter 21). taking junk and trash, materials one would normally discard, and combining them to create "art." Creation, he said, is "the process of assemblage." *Odalisk* (fig. 23.17), made between 1955 and 1958, is made up of a stuffed rooster, a pillow, magazine illustrations (including nude photographs), and paint, all on wood. The title is a clever pun, combining "odalisque" (harem girl) and "obelisk," a four-sided stone pillar capped by a small pyramid.

Like Cage, Rauschenberg brings together daily life and art. Other works include buttons, mirrors, stuffed birds, a ram, an automobile tire, a mattress, pillows, quilts, sheets, photographs, posters, and reproductions of works of art. Parts are painted on, the paint then being made to drip. It is a messy art, an art of disorder, of chance, indeterminate, unpredictable, and multilayered. The many images are not arranged neatly side by side but are instead made to overlay one another, one image being invaded by, or intruded upon, portions of another. Rauschenberg called this work "combine painting."

Louise Nevelson. A different type of assemblage was created by LOUISE NEVELSON (1899–1988), who was born in Kiev, Russia, and moved to Maine as a child. Nevelson studied all the arts—music, dance, theater, painting, and print-making. In her fifties, she began

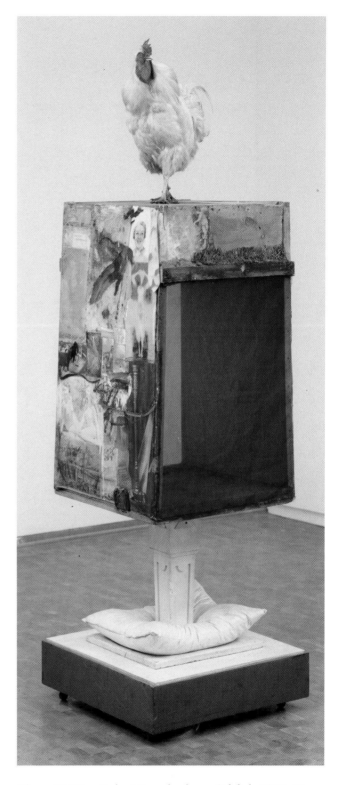

Figure 23.17 Robert Rauschenberg, *Odalisk*, 1955–58, assemblage, including stuffed rooster, pillow, and paint, on wood, 6'9" × 25" × 25" (205.7 × 63.5 × 63.5 cm), Museum Ludwig, Cologne. This "construction" or "assemblage" is not carved or modeled but compiled, the materials left as found rather than transformed. Rauschenberg works with materials not traditionally used in creating fine art, materials that one would normally discard.

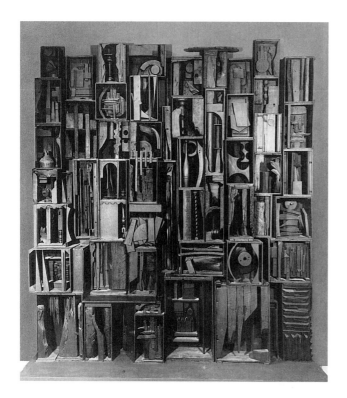

Figure 23.18 Louise Nevelson, *Sky Cathedral*, 1958, assemblage, wood, painted black, 11'3½" × 10'¼" × 1'6" (3.44 × 3.05 × 0.46 m), Museum of Modern Art, New York. From a series of small compositional units made of pieces of wooden furniture and furnishings, Nevelson compiled wall-size assemblages, which she unified by painting a single solid color.

assembling small wooden objects, scraps and remnants that she found in furniture shops. These pieces or fragments were glued and nailed together, creating compositions within wooden boxes, which were then joined together to create an architectural wall, a kind of large-scale relief. The entire assemblage was painted one color—most often black, white, or gold.

Nevelson's *Sky Cathedral* (fig. 23.18), made in 1958, is painted black, the color that, according to the artist, "encompasses all colors." Nevelson called black the most aristocratic color. This single color unifies and links together what would otherwise appear fragmentary; thus, color is used for coherence. The viewer is inclined to peer into each compartment of curiously crafted wooden shapes, as well as to view the structure at once in its entirety. With this rational, intellectual approach, Nevelson assembled large-scale environments that look like cityscapes of many buildings, all compressed into a single wall-like plane.

Andy Warhol. Perhaps the most "everyday" objects of all in the 1950s and 1960s were images of popular culture itself—advertising and newspaper images, heroes and heroines from the movies, labels and signs designed to catch our eye on the grocery shelf or the highway billboard. All of these, from consumer goods to Hollywood stars, were equally "packaged," as one young artist soon recognized. His name was ANDY WARHOL (1928–1987). He started in the commercial art business in the late 1950s, but soon turned his own studio into

Figure 23.19 Andy Warhol, *Marilyn Monroe Diptych*, 1962, oil on canvas, in two panels, 6'10" × 9'6" (2.08 × 2.90 m), Tate Gallery, London. The way in which Marilyn Monroe's face is both obliterated and fades away in the right-hand panel epitomized, for Warhol, her own tragic end.

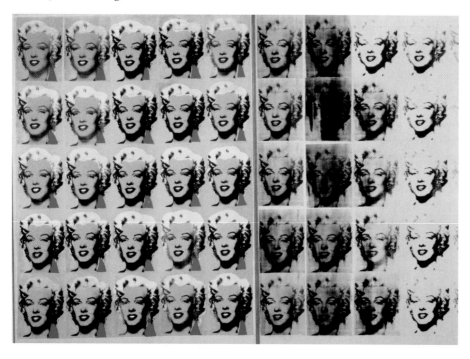

what he called The Factory. There he began churning out large editions of lithographs, as well as unique paintings. His work seemed to embody the world of mass production—Campbell's soup cans, Coca-Cola bottles, dollar bills, and images of Elvis Presley and Marilyn Monroe (fig. 23.19). The style was quickly labeled **Pop Art**—popular art.

Warhol's world was full of spectacle, but behind it lay an almost uncanny sense of widespread social malaise. Unstated in each repeated image of Marilyn Monroe in Warhol's diptych is the clearly implied idea that she was, in the end, nothing more than the image Hollywood created for her, and that her suicide by drug overdose was a final desperate move. Warhol would, in fact, brood deeply about the self-destructive tendencies of American society, creating images of electric chairs, automobile accidents, the Kennedy assassination, and, late in his career, endangered species.

Roy Lichtenstein. This same sense of underlying despair and destruction lies at the heart of the work of another of Warhol's contemporaries, ROY LICHTEN-STEIN (b. 1923). Lichtenstein painted comics, but comics blown up to a large scale. He specialized in two kinds—war comics, which were popular in the 1950s, and comics depicting the lives of young women, akin to television soap operas. *Drowning Girl* (fig. 23.20) shows, with deadpan humor, a young woman in a patently absurd situation. But it also asks us to take it seriously,

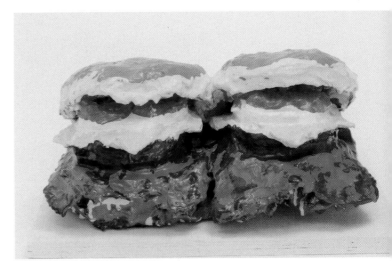

Figure 23.21 Claes Oldenburg, *Two Cheeseburgers, with Everything (Dual Hamburgers)*, 1961, burlap soaked in plaster, painted with enamel, 7 × 14¾″ (17.8 × 37.5 cm), Museum of Modern Art, New York. Pop Art seems simultaneously to laud and laugh at popular culture. Should art reflect the most characteristic aspects of a culture, or strive to raise the level of culture?

and it is precisely in the distance between the two that the power of Lichtenstein's art lies.

The basis of Lichtenstein's style is the large printer's dot—the so-called ben-day dot—used to create color in the comic strips. The style is a parody of both Seurat's Pointillism (see Chapter 18), which Lichtenstein reduces to absurdity, and the Abstract Expressionist gesture, which he negates. Our reaction to its style is thus similar to our reaction to its subject matter: *Drowning Girl* is over five feet square, thus asking us to take it seriously as art, even as it refuses to take the act of "painting" seriously itself.

Claes Oldenburg. In December 1961, at 107 East Second Street in New York City, CLAES OLDEN-BURG (b. 1929), a Yale graduate and son of a Norwegian diplomat, opened an exhibition of real-scale replicas of actual commodities—meat, vegetables, candy, cakes, pies, ice cream sundaes—in a shop front that he named, quite appropriately "The Store." One replica was *Two Cheeseburgers, with Everything (Dual Hamburgers)* (fig. 23.21). At Oldenburg's store a plate of meat cost $399.98, a sandwich $149.98. "I do things that are contradictory," Oldenburg explained. "I try to make the art look like it's part of the world around it. At the same time I take great pains to show that it doesn't function as part of the world around it." The following summer, Oldenburg recast some objects in giant scale and redid others as soft sculptures, sewn and stuffed with foam rubber. What should be soft—a hamburger, for instance—was hard plaster. What should be hard—a typewriter—was suddenly soft

Figure 23.20 Roy Lichtenstein, *Drowning Girl*, 1963, oil and synthetic polymer paint on canvas, 5′7⅞″ × 5′6¾″ (1.72 × 1.70 m), Museum of Modern Art, New York. Lichtenstein recognized that, even though his audience would laugh at a cartoon image such as this, they would identify with the

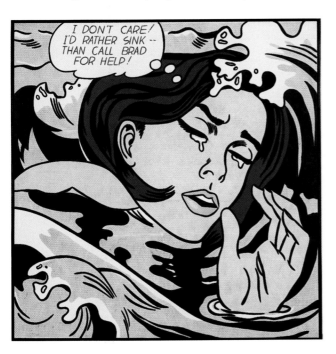

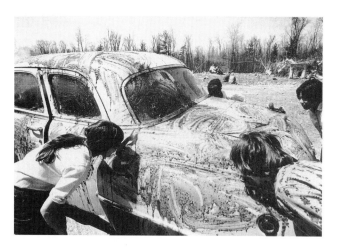

Figure 23.22 Allan Kaprow, *Household*, May 3, 1964, Happening, Ithaca, New York. In this "Happening," Kaprow directed Cornell University students through a series of activities at the local dump, including licking jam off an old car.

and sagging. Oldenburg's jokes play on his audience's expectations. In Oldenburg's world, consumable goods cannot be consumed, even if they can be purchased, and giant versions of the most banal things, such as clothespins, spoons, electric plugs, scissors, trowels, and faucets, transform the everyday into the monumental. His objects seem to function like Russian icons, objects of veneration for a society that values shopping above all other activities.

The Happening. One of John Cage's most attentive students, ALLAN KAPROW (b. 1927), believed that he saw in Cage's work the possibility for a new "total art." Kaprow's artistic vision sprang from an "Event" that Cage staged at Black Mountain College in 1952, entitled *Theater Piece #1*. The event included Robert Rauschenberg playing old phonograph records on an ancient Victrola while movies were being projected simultaneously on his *White Paintings* suspended from the ceiling. Poets M.C. Richards and Charles Olson read from their works, and choreographer Merce Cunningham danced around the room trailed by a small dog. Cage stood on a ladder delivering a lecture, and pianist David Tudor played a Cage composition. Based on this model, Kaprow envisaged "an assemblage of events … [which] unlike a stage play, may occur at a supermarket, driving along a highway, under a pile of rags, and in a friend's kitchen, either at once or sequentially." He called such a work a **Happening**. "It is art," he said, "but seems closer to life."

One of Kaprow's most important tactics was to destroy the distinction between audience and artwork. The audience was required to participate in the event. In the Happening *Household*, for instance, which took place in a dump near Cornell University in Ithaca, New York,

on May 3, 1964, a group of men built a tower of trash while a group of women built a nest of saplings and string. A smoking wrecked car was towed to the side, and the men covered it with strawberry jam. The women, who had been screeching inside the nest, came out to the car and began licking the jam (fig. 23.22) as the men destroyed the nest. Then the men returned with white bread, and began to wipe up the jam off the car and ate it themselves. Eventually, the men took sledge hammers to the wreck and set it on fire. Everyone gathered round and watched until the car was burned up, and then left quietly. Kaprow made no specific point and had no set expectations as to the outcome of the event. What this Happening "means" is not entirely clear, but it does draw attention to the way in which bizarre actions, as well as violence, can draw people together.

MINIMAL AND CONCEPTUAL ART

Cage's minimalist tendencies were attractive to a number of sculptors as well. They saw in them two avenues for artistic exploration. First, a formal but minimal sculptural statement would be variously interpreted according to its situation; and, second, if that simple sculptural statement were repeated, as in mass manufacture, it would, through accumulation, be itself changed. In other words, not only would a given form seem different if encountered in the middle of a field as opposed to in the center of a gallery, but ten examples of the form seen at

Figure 23.23 Donald Judd, *Untitled*, 1969, anodized aluminum and blue Plexiglas, each of four units, $47\frac{1}{2} \times 59\frac{7}{8} \times 11\frac{7}{8}$" (121 × 152 × 30 cm), City Art Museum of St. Louis. Judd's work may be thought of in terms of existentialism, as a kind of "pure being," but without existentialism's sense of moral imperative.

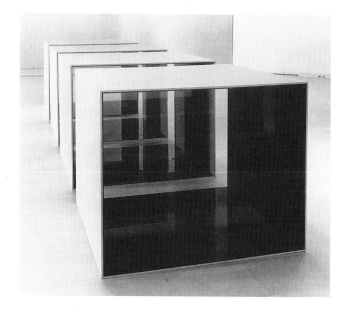

Connections

RAUSCHENBERG, CAGE, AND CUNNINGHAM

One of the most prolific collaborations of the modern era, one that lasted over three decades, is that of artist Robert Rauschenberg, composer John Cage, and choreographer Merce Cunningham, initiated at Black Mountain. At the heart of their collaborative practice was a belief in, as one critic described Rauschenberg's combine paintings, "an aesthetics of heterogeneity." It was their more or less freewheeling trust that, in the chance encounter of diverse materials, areas of interest and moments of revelation will be generated.

Both Cage and Rauschenberg were willing to admit almost anything into their work. So was Cunningham. "In classical ballet," Cunningham has written, "the space was observed in terms of the proscenium stage, it was frontal. What if, as in my pieces, you decide to make any point on the stage equally interesting? I used to be told that you see the center of the space as the most important: that was the center of interest. But in many modern paintings this was not the case and the sense of space was different … When I happened to read that sentence of Albert Einstein's: 'There are no fixed points in space," I thought, indeed, if there are no fixed points, then every point is equally interesting and equally changing." An

example of such a dance is the 1958 *Summerspace* (fig. 23.24), with sets by Rauschenberg. "When I spoke to Bob Rauschenberg—for the decor—I said, 'One thing I can tell you about this dance is that it has no center …' So he made a pointillist backdrop and costumes." In another piece, *Variations V*, the movement of the dancers triggers electronic sensors which in turn trigger an "orchestra" of tape recorders, record players, and radio receivers containing

sounds "composed" by Cage. A member of Cunningham's dance company, Gordon Mumma, describes the result as "a superbly poly: -chromatic, -genic, -phonic, -morphic, -pagic, -technic, -valent, multi-ringed circus." In the typical Rauschenberg, Cage, and Cunningham collaboration, the music does not support the dance, nor do the sets frame it; instead each element— dance, music, and sets—remains independent of the others.

Figure 23.24 Merce Cunningham, *Summerspace*, 1958. Dancers: Robert Kovich and Chris Komar. Cunningham tries to devise dances in which so much is happening at once that the effect is not unlike trying to watch all three rings of a circus simultaneously.

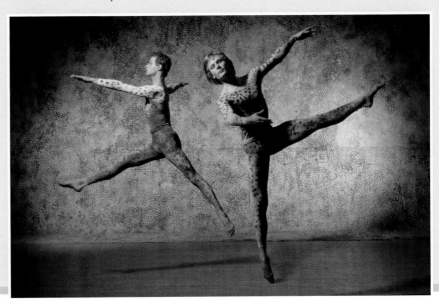

once would be different than seeing just a single, unique form.

Donald Judd. One of the most successful of these minimalist sculptors was DONALD JUDD (b. 1928). Beginning in 1965, he created a series of what he called "Specific Objects," which were uniform, modular boxes made of industrially produced galvanized iron. Judd cantilevered equally spaced groups of them from the wall in vertical columns or horizontal lines. Without any reference whatsoever to figure or landscape, the boxes insist on their existential being, so to speak. By the late 1960s, Judd recast his boxes as freestanding floor pieces (fig. 23.23), now made of materials such as copper, brass, and stainless steel, often polished so as to reflect the surrounding space, each other, and the viewer. He also began to paint them, especially their interiors, with

enamel or lacquer, and sometimes sealed them on top and bottom with sheets of colored Plexiglas. When colored, they seem to transcend their status as meaningless objects and achieve exceptional elegance.

Sol LeWitt. Also working in modular units, SOL LeWITT (b. 1928) created frameworks of white, baked enamel beams arranged as an open cube and repeated according to various mathematical formulas. A work such as *Open Modular Cube* (fig. 23.25), for instance, seems relatively straightforward. But as the light changes over the course of a day, patterns emerge in the cast shadows. As the viewer moves around the work, its appearance also changes dramatically; LeWitt's apparently stable structure becomes a constantly changing one.

For LeWitt, a work of art is "pure information," and a work of art could exist simply *as* information rather

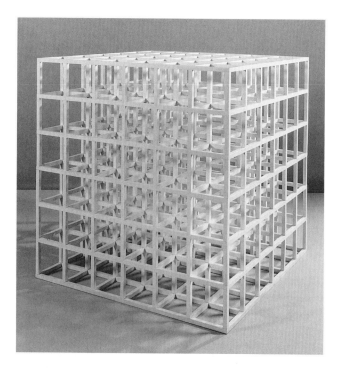

Figure 23.25 Sol LeWitt, *Open Modular Cube*, 1966, painted aluminum, 5 × 5 × 5′ (1.52 × 1.52 × 1.52 m), Art Gallery of Ontario, Toronto. "The new art," LeWitt wrote, "is attempting to make the non-visual (mathematics) visible (concrete)."

than as an object per se. That is, it could be so minimal that it could exist solely as a *concept*. In the context of consumer culture, there was one real advantage to this position: it removed the work of art from the market system, in which a Jackson Pollock painting, *Blue Poles*, sold in 1973 for two million dollars. LeWitt soon started making verbal proposals for artworks rather than making the art itself. He would formulate a set of basic instructions for a wall drawing—"Draw lines from the middle of the edge to a point in the center, in each of four colors, one color for each side," and so on. Then the drawing would be executed by whomever at whatever site. The works were each different and were short-lived.

Christo and Jeanne-Claude. The willingness to let a work exist only for a short while is the hallmark of the site-specific sculptor CHRISTO (b. 1935) and JEANNE-CLAUDE (b. 1935). Their work is usually outdoors, public, large scale, and temporary. Noted for using large things such as buildings, bridges, islands, valleys, and coastlines, Christo and Jeanne-Claude are interested in working with other groups in the art community. Work together begins with a discussion on the question "What is art?", a question few communities have debated.

One of their best-known works is *Surrounded Islands* (fig. 23.26), which in its completed form existed for two weeks in 1983 in Biscayne Bay, Miami, Florida. Christo

and Jeanne-Claude said they were inspired by Monet's water-lily paintings, and the surrounded islands in fact looked like huge pink lily pads. The work required $3,500,000 in funds to produce, which Christo and Jeanne-Claude paid entirely through the sale of Christo's prints, early packages, and preparatory drawings. It also required 6.5 million square feet of fabric, numerous lawyers, and permission from a multitude of government organizations and environmentalists. Christo and Jeanne-Claude were required to prove that there would be no negative effects on the environment.

Christo and Jeanne-Claude's work is highly controversial; rarely have artists had such obstacles to overcome and shown such determination and perseverance in doing so. Yet all of this preparation was considered to be part of the work of art, as was the bringing together of peoples of different backgrounds and orientations in order to create it.

Figure 23.26 Christo and Jeanne-Claude, *Surrounded Islands*, 1980–83, Biscayne Bay, Greater Miami, Florida, existed in its final state for two weeks, now gone. The artists' "environmental art," which has included wrapping large structures such as the Reichstag in Berlin and the Pont Neuf in Paris, is intentionally transitory. Creation of a work such as *Surrounded Islands*, in which eleven islands were surrounded by 6.5 million square feet of pink polypropylene fabric, is an event, a sort of Happening, involving many people.

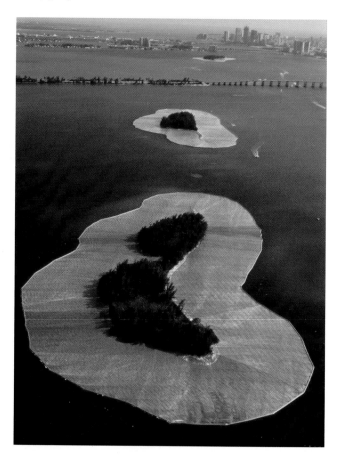

THE ARCHITECTURE OF THE STRIP

In his important 1972 book *Learning from Las Vegas*, the architect Robert Venturi suggested that the collision of styles, signs, and symbols that marks the American commercial "strip" in general, and Las Vegas in particular, could be seen as composing a new sort of unity. "Disorder," Venturi writes, "[is] an order we cannot see … The commercial strip with the urban sprawl … includes all levels, from the mixture of seemingly incongruous advertising media plus a system of neo-organic or neo-Wrightian restaurant motifs in Walnut Formica." On the strip, one structure is designed and built next to another with no consideration of its surroundings. In particular, franchises are designed completely independently of their various locales. On the strip anything goes. This is unlike traditional architectural practice, in which the architect works to harmonize the building with its environment.

Frank Gehry. No architect's work epitomizes pop culture's collision of styles more than that of FRANK GEHRY (b. 1929). His own home, in Santa Monica, California, which he purchased and began to remodel in 1976, is a consciously eclectic version of Venturi's

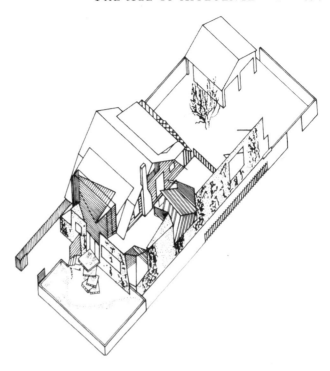

Figure 23.28 Axonometric drawing of the Gehry house.

Figure 23.27 Frank Gehry, Gehry house, Santa Monica, 1977–78. Gehry's house represents the consciously assembled style of past and present elements that has come to distinguish what is known as "postmodern" architecture.

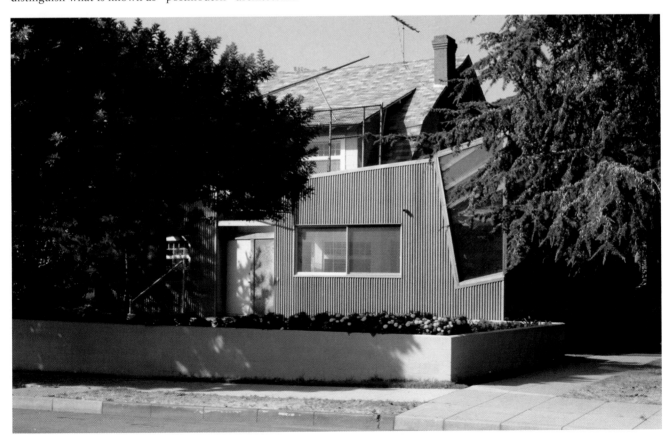

principles (fig. 23.27). Bored with the typical 1940s two-story frame house he had purchased, but unable to afford anything more, Gehry decided to surround the original with a new one, making the division between old and new visually clear. His building materials—plywood, concrete blocks, corrugated metal, and chainlink fence—were basic everyday materials in popular culture. Needing a new kitchen, he built it at ground level, outside the original house's dining room on an asphalt pad (fig. 23.28). The new design included a long corrugated metal side which faced the street and deeply offended Gehry's neighbors, but Gehry did not want his new house to "fit in." Its discontinuity from the rest of the neighborhood announced that Gehry was different, and that difference was, perhaps, a good thing.

LITERATURE: THE BEATS

Not everyone felt that the consumer culture developing in the United States during the 1950s was such a good thing. The so-called "Beat" generation of writers saw American prosperity as something negative, as something leading to conformity, complacency, and even oppression. Theirs was the first of a series of critiques of the American scene after World War II, critiques that would surface again in the Civil Rights and anti-Vietnam War movements in the 1960s, and the feminist movement in the 1970s.

Jack Kerouac. Perhaps the leading voice of the Beat Generation was JACK KEROUAC (1922–1969). For Kerouac, the "Beats" were a resurgence of the lost American type, the "wild self-believing" individuals who had founded the country. In *On the Road*, written in 1951 and published in 1957, Kerouac reinvents the American archetype of the frontiersman and cowboy, as his narrator, Sal Paradise, a "wild yea-saying overburst of American joy" who seeks to escape the confines of American civilization in Denver's skidrow and Cheyenne, Wyoming's Wild West Week. Guided by a mad father figure, Dean Moriarty, who drives "at incredible speeds across the groaning continent, serious and insane at his raving wheel," Sal Paradise learns how far America has fallen, and comes to the recognition that he probably can't escape it.

Kerouac wrote in "spontaneous prose," as he called it. With roots in the automatic writing of Surrealism and the expressive gesture of the Abstract Expressionist painters, Kerouac's contemporaries, his prose has been described by the poet Allen Ginsberg as a style that is "completely personal, [that] comes from the writer's own person—his person defined as his body, his breathing rhythm, his actual talk." It seems, in fact, as high speed as the automobiles that Sal and Dean race across the country, a kind of rush of language.

Allen Ginsberg. This style is, essentially, also that of ALLEN GINSBERG (1926–1997) himself. His long poem *Howl* (1956)—of which the first section and part of the third were drafted in one day in August 1955, in San Francisco, the rest following shortly after—is indeed a rush of language, as its title suggests. It is an outcry against the way in which American bureaucracy turns individuals into abstractions, an outcry against a world in which parents mindlessly turn their children over to the ancient god Moloch, a figure standing for American culture as a whole, who promptly consumes them. Dedicated to Carl Solomon, a patient in a mental hospital in New York—and in Ginsberg's mind, thus a sort of political prisoner—the poem is a celebration of madness. Madness, for Ginsberg, is a sign of salvation, a sign of rebellion against the all-consuming American Moloch. By rejecting reason, and accepting the innate rhythms of the body itself, *Howl* seeks to transcend the constrictions of civilization.

THE POPULARIZATION OF CLASSICAL MUSIC

The Boston Pops. In the 1950s and 1960s, culture was defined more and more by the consumer, and musical tastes responded more and more to the demands of a popular audience. The Boston Pops Orchestra, led by ARTHUR FIEDLER (1894–1979), became a national institution, famous for its concerts of folk tunes, marches such as John Philip Sousa's "Stars and Stripes Forever," and classical hits such as George Gershwin's *Rhapsody in Blue*. Bridging the gap between popular song and classical repertoire, the pops served as "the door through which young people enter into the magic domain of musical comprehension," as one critic put it.

Leonard Bernstein. One of the contemporary era's most highly regarded musical talents, and one of the most successful at popularizing classical music, was LEONARD BERNSTEIN (1918–1990), composer, conductor, pianist, and mentor. His lecture demonstrations with the New York Philharmonic Orchestra offered children an engaging introduction to the world of classical music and were later published as the *Young People's Guide to the Orchestra*. His numerous recordings and video performances with major American and European orchestras demonstrate his exciting and dramatic conducting abilities.

Yet it is Bernstein's genius for composing popular and classical music that sets him apart in his generation. He is perhaps best known for his works for the musical theater: *Candide* (1956) and *West Side Story* (1957), a contemporary version of Shakespeare's *Romeo and Juliet*, in an urban setting with intercultural tensions. Bernstein transforms Shakespeare's warring Capulet and Montague families into two rival gangs from New York City's Spanish Harlem, the Italian Jets and the Hispanic Sharks.

Like Tchaikovsky, whose *Romeo and Juliet Fantasy Overture* was also inspired by Shakespeare's play, Bernstein writes music that is both lyrical and dramatically compelling. Songs like "Maria," a lyrical love song, intermingle with Latin-inspired pieces such as "America" and "Tonight," set in quasi-operatic style for four voices.

READINGS
→

✦ Jean-Paul Sartre
from *Existentialism and Humanism*

In the following essay, Sartre raises questions about what it means to be human. His advocacy of existentialism as the quintessential way to express one's humanity highlights the necessity for human beings to be responsible for their choices and their actions. This essay is largely a response to a series of criticisms leveled against Sartre's version of existentialism, and accordingly Sartre defines what he means by key terms, including "existentialism" itself, and distinguishes himself from others who use the existential label differently. He also explains what he means by the subjectivity of human experience, which is a central tenet of Sartre's philosophy.

It is to various reproaches that I shall endeavor to reply today; that is why I have entitled this brief exposition, *Existentialism and Humanism*. Many may be surprised at the mention of humanism in this connection, but we shall try to see in what sense we understand it. In any case, we can begin by saying that existentialism, in our sense of the word, is a doctrine that does render human life possible; a doctrine, also, which affirms that every truth and every action imply both an environment and a human subjectivity. The essential charge laid against us is, of course, that of overemphasis upon the evil side of human life. I have lately been told of a lady who, whenever she lets slip a vulgar expression in a moment of nervousness, excuses herself by exclaiming, "I believe I am becoming an existentialist." So it appears that ugliness is being identified with existentialism. Those who appeal to the wisdom of the people—which is a sad wisdom—find ours sadder still. Indeed their excessive protests make me suspect that what is annoying them is not so much our pessimism, but, much more likely, our optimism. For at bottom, what is alarming in the doctrine that I am about to try to explain to you is—is it not? that it confronts man with a possibility of choice. To verify this, let us review the whole question upon the strictly philosophic level. What, then, is this that we call existentialism?

Most of those who are making use of this word would be highly confused if required to explain its meaning. For since it has become fashionable, people cheerfully declare that this musician or that painter is "existentialist." A columnist in Clartes signs himself "The Existentialist," and, indeed, the word is now so loosely applied to so many things that it no longer means anything at all. It would appear that, for the lack of any novel doctrine such as that of surrealism, all those who are eager to join in the latest scandal or movement now seize upon this philosophy in which, however, they can find nothing to their purpose. For in truth this is of all teachings the least scandalous and the most austere; it is intended strictly for experts and philosophers. All the same, it can easily be defined.

The question is only complicated because there are two kinds of existentialists. There are, on the one hand, the Christian existentialists and on the other hand the existential atheists, among whom I place myself. What they have in common is simply the fact that they believe that existence comes before essence—or, if you will, that we must begin from the subjective.

What do we mean by saying that existence precedes essence? We mean that man first of all exists, encounters himself, surges up in the world—and defines himself afterwards. If man is as the existentialist sees him, as not definable, it is because to begin with he is nothing. He will not be anything until later, and then he will be what he makes of himself. Thus, there is no human nature, because there is no God to have a conception of it. Man simply is. Not that he is simply what he conceives himself to be, but he is what he wills, and as he conceives himself after already existing—as he wills to be after that leap towards existence. Man is nothing else but that which he makes of himself. That is the first principle of existentialism. And this is what people call its "subjectivity," using the word as a reproach against us. But what do we mean to say by this, but that man is of a greater dignity than a stone or a table? For we mean to say that man primarily exists—that man is, before all else, something which propels itself towards a future and is aware that it is doing so. Man is, indeed, a project which possesses a subjective life, instead of being a kind of moss, or a fungus, or a cauliflower. Before that projection of the self nothing exists; not even in the heaven of intelligence; man will only attain existence when he is what he proposes to be. Thus, the first effort of existentialism is that it puts every man in possession of himself as he is, and places the entire responsibility for his existence squarely upon his own shoulders. And when we say that man is responsible for himself, we do not mean that he is responsible only for his own individuality, but that he is responsible for all men.

The word "subjective" is to be understood in two senses, and our adversaries play upon only one of them. Subjectivism means, on the one hand, the freedom of the individual subject and, on the other, that man cannot pass beyond human subjectivity. It is the latter which is the deeper meaning of existentialism. When we say that man chooses himself, we do mean that everyone of us must choose himself; but by that we also mean that in choosing for himself he chooses for all men. For in effect, of all the actions a man may take in order to create himself as he wills to be, there is not one which is not creative, at the same time, of an image of man such as he believes he ought to be. To choose between this or that is at the same time to affirm the value of that which is chosen, for we are unable ever to choose the worse. What we choose is always the better; and nothing can be better for us unless it is better for all. If moreover, existence precedes essence and we will to exist at the same time as we fashion our image, that image is valid for all and for the entire epoch in which we find ourselves. Our responsibility is thus much greater than we had supposed, for it concerns mankind as a whole. I am thus responsible for myself and for all men, and I am creating a certain image of man as I would have him be. "In fashioning myself

I fashion man."

This may enable us to understand what is meant by such terms—perhaps a little grandiloquent—as anguish, abandonment, and despair. As you will soon see, it is very simple. First, what do we mean by anguish? The existentialist frankly states that man is in anguish. His meaning is as follows—When a man commits himself to anything, fully realizing that he is not only choosing what he will be, but is thereby at the same time a legislator deciding for the whole of mankind—in such a moment a man cannot escape from the sense of complete and profound responsibility. There are many, indeed, who show no such anxiety. But we affirm that they are merely disguising their anguish or are in flight from it. Certainly, many people think that in what they are doing they commit no one but themselves to anything; and if you ask them, "What would happen if everyone did so?" they shrug their shoulders and reply, "Everyone does not do so." But in truth, one ought always to ask oneself what would happen if everyone did as one is doing; nor can one escape from that disturbing thought except by a kind of self-deception. The man who lies in self-excuse, by saying "Everyone will not do it" must be ill at ease in his conscience for the act of lying implies the universal value which it denies. By its very disguise his anguish reveals itself. This is the anguish that Kierkegaard called "the anguish of Abraham." You know the story: An angel commanded Abraham to sacrifice his son: and obedience was obligatory, if it really was an angel who had appeared and said "Thou, Abraham, shalt sacrifice thy son." But anyone in such a case would wonder, first, whether it was indeed an angel and secondly, whether I am really Abraham. Where are the proofs?

I shall never find any proof whatever; there will be no sign to convince me of it. If a voice speaks to me, it is still I myself who must decide whether the voice is or is not that of an angel. If I regard a certain course of action as good, it is only I who choose to say that it is good and not bad. There is nothing to show that I am Abraham; nevertheless, I also am obliged at every instant to perform actions which are examples. Everything happens to every man as though the whole human race had its eyes fixed upon what he is doing and regulated its conduct accordingly. So every man ought to say. "Am I really a man who has the right to act in such a manner that humanity regulates itself by what I do?" If a man does not say that, he is dissembling his anguish. Clearly, the anguish with which we are concerned here is not one that could lead to quietism or inaction. It is anguish pure and simple, of the kind well known to all those who have borne responsibilities. Far from being a screen which could separate us from action, it is condition of action itself.

And when we speak of "abandonment"—a favourite word of Heidegger—we only mean to say that God does not exist, and that it is necessary to draw the consequences of his absence right to the end. The existentialist is strongly opposed to a certain type of secular moralism which seeks to suppress God at the least possible expense. Toward 1880, when the French professors endeavored to formulate a secular morality, they said something like this—God is a useless and costly hypothesis, so we will do without it. However, if we are to have morality, a society, and a law-abiding world, it is essential that certain values should be taken seriously; they must have an *a priori* existence ascribed to them. It must be considered obligatory *a priori* to be honest, not to lie, not to beat one's wife, to bring up children, and so forth; so we are going to do a little work on this subject, which will enable us to show that these values exist all the same, inscribed in an intelligible heaven although, of course, there is no God. In other words—and this is, I believe, the purport of all we in France call radicalism—nothing will be changed if God does not exist; we shall rediscover the same norms of honesty, progress, and humanity, and we shall have disposed of God as an out-of-date hypothesis which will die away quietly of itself.

The existentialist, on the contrary, finds it extremely embarrassing that God does not exist, for there disappears with Him all possibility of finding values in an intelligible heaven. There can no longer be any good *a priori* since there is no infinite and perfect consciousness to think it. It is nowhere written that "the good" exists, that one must be honest or must not lie, since we are now upon the plane where there are only men. Dostoevski once wrote, "If God did not exist, everything would be permitted"; and that, for existentialism, is the starting point. Everything is indeed permitted if God does not exist, and man is in consequence forlorn, for he cannot find anything to depend upon either within or outside himself. He discovers forthwith that he is without excuse. For if indeed existence precedes essence, one will never be able to explain one's action by reference to a given and specific human nature; in other words, there is no determinism—man is free, man is freedom.

You are free, therefore choose—that is to say, invent. No rule of general morality can show you what you ought to do; no signs are vouchsafed in this world. That is what "abandonment" implies, that we ourselves decide our being. And with this abandonment goes anguish.

As for "despair" the meaning of this expression is extremely simple. It merely means that we limit ourselves to a reliance upon that which is within our wills, or within the sum of the probabilities which render our action feasible. Whenever one wills anything, there are always these elements of probability. If I am counting upon a visit from a friend, who may be coming by train or by tram, I presuppose that the train will arrive at the appointed time, or that the tram will not be derailed. I remain in the realm of possibilities; but one does not rely upon any possibilities beyond those that are strictly concerned in one's action, beyond the point at which the possibilities under consideration cease to affect my action. I ought to disinterest myself. For there is no God and no prevenient design which can adapt the world and all its possibilities to my will. When Descartes said, "Conquer yourself rather than the world," what he meant was, at bottom, the same—that we should act without hope.

In the light of all this, what people reproach us with is not, after all, our pessimism but the sternness of our optimism. If people condemn our works of fiction, in which we describe characters that are base, weak, cowardly, and sometimes even frankly evil, it is not only because those characters are base, weak, cowardly or evil. For suppose that, like Zola, we showed that the behaviour of these characters was caused by their heredity, or by the action of their environment upon them, or by determining factors, psychic or organic. People would be reassured, they would say, "You see, that is what we are like, no one can do anything about it." But the existentialist, when he portrays a coward, shows him as responsible for his cowardice. The existentialist says that the coward makes himself cowardly, the hero makes himself heroic; and that there is always a possibility for the coward to give up cowardice and for the hero to stop being a hero. What counts is the total commitment, and it is not by a particular case or particular action that you are committed altogether.

We have now, I think, dealt with a certain number of the reproaches against existentialism. You have seen that it cannot be regarded as a philosophy of quietism since it defines man by his action; nor as a pessimistic description of man, for no doctrine is more optimistic, the destiny of man is placed within himself. Nor is it an attempt to discourage man from action since it tells him that there is no hope except in his action, and that the one thing which permits him to have life is the deed. Upon this level therefore, what we are considering is an ethic of action and self-commitment.

Man makes himself; he is not found ready-made; he makes himself by the choice of his morality, and he cannot but choose a morality, such is the pressure of circumstances upon him. We define man only in relation to his commitments; it is therefore absurd to reproach us for irresponsibility in our choice. And moreover, to say that we invent values means neither more nor less than this; that there is no sense in life a priori. Life is nothing until it is lived; but it is yours to make sense of, and the value of it is nothing else but the sense that you choose. Therefore, you can see that there is a possibility of creating a human community. I have been reproached for suggesting that existentialism is a form of humanism.

Man is all the time outside of himself; it is in projecting and losing himself beyond himself that he makes man to exist; and, on the other hand, it is by pursuing transcendent aims that he himself is able to exist. Since man is thus self-surpassing, and can grasp objects only in relation to his self-surpassing, he is himself the heart and centre of his transcendence. There is no other universe except the human universe, the universe of subjectivity. This relation of transcendence as constitutive of man (not in the sense that God is transcendent, but in the sense of self-surpassing) with subjectivity (in such a sense that man is not shut up in himself but forever present in a human universe)—it is this that we call existential humanism. This is humanism, because we remind man that there is no legislator but himself; that he himself, thus abandoned, must decide for himself; also because we show that it is not by turning back upon himself, but always by seeking, beyond himself, an aim which is one of liberation or of some particular realization, that man can realize himself as truly human.

✦ Simone de Beauvoir
from *The Second Sex*

In the following passage from her groundbreaking book of feminist philosophy, Simone de Beauvoir discusses the fundamental issue of what it means to be a woman in a world run by men. In answering the question "What is a woman?" de Beauvoir suggests that women are defined in relation to men, who serve as the model for generic

"humanity." At least this was the way things were when de Beauvoir published her book in 1949. Half a century later there is still debate about how far things have really changed for women. De Beauvoir's invitation to philosophical reflection about the relationship between woman and man and between self and other remains relevant today, not only in terms of male–female relations, but also in terms of the larger social, political, and economic issues linked with them.

For a long time I have hesitated to write a book on woman. The subject is irritating especially to woman; and it is not new. Enough ink has been spilled in quarrelling over feminism, and perhaps we should say no more about it. It is still talked about, however, for the voluminous nonsense uttered during the last century seems to have done little to illuminate the problem. After all, is there a problem? And if so, what is it? Are there women, really? Most assuredly the theory of the eternal feminine still has its adherents who will whisper in your ear: "even in Russia woman still are *women*"; and other erudite persons—sometimes the very same—say with a sigh: "Woman is losing her way, woman is lost." One wonders if women still exist, if they will always exist, whether or not it is desirable that they should, what place they occupy in this world, what their place should be. "What has become of women?" was asked recently in an ephemeral magazine.

But first we must ask: what is a woman? *"Tota mulier in utero,"* says one, "woman is a womb." But in speaking of certain women, connoisseurs declare that they are not women, although they are equipped with a uterus like the rest. All agree in recognising the fact that females exist in the human species; today as always they make up about one half of humanity. And yet we are told that femininity is in danger; we are exhorted to be women, remain women, become women. It would appear, then, that every female human being is not necessarily a woman; to be so considered she must share in that mysterious and threatened reality known as femininity. Is this attribute something secreted by the ovaries? Or is it a Platonic essence, a product of the philosophic imagination? Is a rustling petticoat enough to bring it down to earth? Although some women try zealously to incarnate this essence, it is hardly patentable. It is frequently described in vague and dazzling terms that seem to have been borrowed from the vocabulary of the seers, and indeed in the times of St Thomas it was considered an essence as certainly defined as the somniferous virtue of the poppy.

But conceptualism has lost ground. The biological and social sciences no longer admit the existence of unchangeably fixed entities that determine given characteristics, such as those ascribed to woman, the Jew, or the Negro. Science regards any characteristics as a reaction dependent in part upon a *situation*. If today femininity no longer exists, then it never existed. But does the word *woman*, then, have no specific content? This is stoutly affirmed by those whose hold to the philosophy of the enlightenment, of rationalism, of nominalism; women, to them, are merely the human beings arbitrarily designated by the word *woman*. Many American women particularly are prepared to think that there is no longer any place for woman as such; if a backward individual still takes herself for a woman, her friends advise her to be psychoanalysed and thus get rid of this obsession. In regard to a work, *Modern Woman: The Lost Sex*, which in other respects has its irritating features, Dorothy Parker has written: "I cannot be just to books which treat woman as woman … My idea is that all of us, men as well as women, should be regarded as human beings." But nominalism is a rather inadequate doctrine, and the anti-feminists have had no trouble in showing that women simply *are* not men. Surely woman is, like man, a human being; but such a declaration is abstract. The fact is every concrete human being is always a singular, separate individual. To decline to accept such notions as the eternal feminine, the black soul, the Jewish character, is not to deny that Jews, Negroes, women exist today—this denial does not represent a liberation for those concerned, but rather a flight from reality. Some years ago a well-known woman writer refused to permit her portrait to appear in a series of photographs especially devoted to women writers; she wished to be counted among the men. But in order to gain this privilege she made use of her husband's influence!

Women who assert that they are men lay claim none the less to masculine consideration and respect. I recall also a young Trotskyite standing on a platform at a boisterous meeting and getting ready to use her fists, in spite of her evident fragility. She was denying her feminine weakness; but it was for love of a militant male whose equal she wished to be. The attitude of defiance of many American women proves that they are haunted by a sense of their femininity. In truth, to go for a walk with one's eyes open is enough to demonstrate that humanity is divided into two classes of individuals whose clothes, faces, bodies, smiles, gaits, interests, and occupations are manifestly different. Perhaps these differences are superficial, perhaps they are destined to disappear. What is certain is that they do most obviously exist.

If her functioning as a female is not enough to define woman, if we decline also to explain her through "the eternal feminine," and if nevertheless we admit, provisionally, that women do exist, then we must face the question: what is a woman?

To state the question is, to me, to suggest, at once, a preliminary answer. The fact that I ask it is in itself significant. A man would never set out to write a book on the peculiar situation of the human male. But if I wish to define myself, I must first of all say: "I am a woman"; on this truth must be based all further discussion. A man never begins by presenting himself as an individual of a certain sex; it goes without saying that he is a man. The terms *masculine* and *feminine* are used symmetrically only as a matter of form, as on legal papers. In actuality the relation of the two sexes is not quite like that of two electrical poles, for man represents both the positive and the neutral, as is indicated by the common use of *man* to designate human beings in general; whereas woman represents only the negative, defined by limiting criteria, without reciprocity. In the midst of an abstract discussion it is vexing to hear a man say: "You think thus and so because you are a woman." I know that my only defence is to reply: "I think thus and so because it is true," thereby removing my subjective self from the argument. It would be out of the question to reply: "And you think the contrary because you are a man," for it is understood that the fact of being a man is no peculiarity. A man is in the right in being a man; it is the woman who is in the wrong. It amounts to this; just as for the ancients there was an absolute vertical with reference to which the oblique was defined, so there is

an absolute human type, the masculine. Woman has ovaries, a uterus: these peculiarities imprison her in her subjectivity, circumscribe her within the limits of her own nature. It is often said that she thinks with her glands. Man superbly ignores the fact that his anatomy also includes glands, such as the testicles, and that they secrete hormones. He thinks of his body as a direct and normal connection with the world, which he believes he apprehends objectively, whereas he regards the body of woman as a hindrance, a prison, weighed down by everything peculiar to it. "The female is a female by virtue of a certain *lack* of qualities," said Aristotle; "we should regard the female as nature inflicted with a natural defectiveness." And St Thomas for his part pronounced woman to be an "imperfect man," an "incidental" being. This is symbolized in Genesis where Eve is depicted as made from what Bossuet called a "supernumerary bone" of Adam.

Thus humanity is male and man defines woman not in herself but as relative to him; she is not regarded as an autonomous being. Michelet writes: "Woman, the relative being..." And Benda is most positive in his *Rapport d'Uriel*: "The body of man makes sense in itself quite apart from that of woman, whereas the latter seems wanting in significance by itself... Man can think of himself without woman. She cannot think of herself without man." And she is simply what man decrees, thus she is called "the sex," by which is meant that she appears essentially to the male as a sexual being. For him she is sex—absolute sex, no less. She is defined and differentiated with reference to man and not he with reference to her; she is the incidental, the inessential as opposed to the essential. He is the Subject, he is the Absolute—she is the Other.[1]

The category of the *Other* is as primordial as consciousness itself. In the most primitive societies, in the most ancient mythologies, one finds the expression of a duality—that of the Self and the Other. This duality was not originally attached to the division of the sexes; it was not dependent upon any empirical facts. It is revealed in such works as that of Granet on Chinese thought and those of Dumezil on the East Indies and Rome. The feminine element was at first no more involved in such pairs as Varuna-Mitra, Uranus-Zeus, Sun-Moon and Day-Night than it was in the contrasts between Good and Evil, lucky and unlucky aus-

---

[1] E. Lévinas expresses this idea most explicitly in his essay *Temps et l'Autre*. "Is there not a case in which otherness, alterity [*altérité*], unquestionably marks the nature of a being, as its essence, an instance of otherness not consisting purely and simply in the opposition of two species of the same genus? I think that the feminine represents the contrary in its absolute sense, this contrariness being in no wise affected by any relation between it and its correlative and thus remaining absolutely other. Sex is not a certain specific difference … no more is the sexual difference a mere contradiction … Nor does this difference lie in the duality of two complementary terms, for two complementary terms imply a pre-existing whole … Otherness reaches its full flowering in the feminine, a term of the same rank as consciousness but of opposite meaning."

I suppose that Lévinas does not forget that woman, too, is aware of her own consciousness, or ego. But it is striking that he deliberately takes a man's point of view, disregarding the reciprocity of subject and object. When he writes that woman is mystery, he implies that she is mystery for man. Thus his description, which is intended to be objective, is in fact an assertion of masculine privilege.

pices, right and left, God and Lucifer. Otherness is a fundamental category of human thought.

Thus it is that no group ever sets itself up as the One without at once setting up the Other over against itself. If three travellers chance to occupy the same compartment, that is enough to make vaguely hostile "others" out of all the rest of the passengers on the train. In small-town eyes all persons not belonging to the village are "strangers" and suspect; to the native of a country all who inhabit other countries are "foreigners"; Jews are "different" for the anti-Semite, Negroes are "inferior" for American racists, aborigines are "natives" for colonists, proletarians are the "lower class" for the privileged.

Levi-Strauss, at the end of a profound work on the various forms of primitive societies, reaches the following conclusion: "Passage from the state of Nature to the state of Culture is marked by man's ability to view biological relations as a series of contrasts; duality, alternation, opposition, and symmetry, whether under definite or vague forms, constitute not so much phenomena to be explained as fundamental and immediately given data of social reality."[2] These phenomena would be incomprehensible if in fact human society were simply a *Mitsein* or fellowship based on solidarity and friendliness. Things become clear, on the contrary, if, following Hegel, we find in consciousness itself a fundamental hostility towards every other consciousness; the subject can be posed only in being opposed—he sets himself up as the essential, as opposed to the other, the inessential, the object.

But the other consciousness, the other ego, sets up a reciprocal claim. The native travelling abroad is shocked to find himself in turn regarded as a "stranger" by the natives of neighbouring countries. As a matter of fact, wars, festivals, trading treaties, and contests among tribes, nations, and classes tend to deprive the concept *Other* of its absolute sense and to make manifest its relativity; willy-nilly, individuals and groups are forced to realize the reciprocity of their relations. How is it, then, that this reciprocity has not been recognized between the sexes, that on of the contrasting terms is set up as the sole essential, denying and relativity in regard to its correlative and defining the latter as pure otherness? Why is it that women do not dispute male sovereignty? No subject will readily volunteer to become the object, the inessential; it is not the Other who, in defining himself as the Other, establishes the One. The Other is posed as such by the One in defining himself as the One. But if the Other is not to regain the status of being the One, he must be submissive enough to except this alien point of view. Whence comes this submission in the case of woman?

There are, to be sure, other cases in which a certain category has been able to dominate another completely for a time. Very often the privilege depends upon inequality of numbers—the majority imposes its rule upon the minority or persecutes it. But women are not a minority, like American Negroes or the Jews; there are as many woman as men on earth. Again, the two groups concerned have often been originally independent; they may have been formerly unaware of each other's existence, or perhaps they recog-

nized each other's autonomy. But a historical event has resulted in the subjugation of the weaker by the stronger. The scattering of the Jews, the introduction of slavery into America, the conquests of imperialism are examples in point. In these cases the oppressed retained at least the memory of former days; they possessed in common a past, a tradition, sometimes a religion or a culture.

The parallel drawn by Bebel between woman and the proletariat is valid in that neither ever formed a minority or a separate collective unit of mankind. And instead of a single historical event it is in both cases a historical development that explains their status as a class and accounts for the membership of *particular individuals* in that class. But proletarians have not always existed, whereas there have always been women. They are women in virtue of their anatomy and physiology. Throughout history they have always been subordinated to men,[3] and hence their dependency is not the result of a historical event or a social change—it was not something that *occurred*. The reason why otherness in this case seems to be an absolute is in part that it lacks the contingent or incidental nature of historical facts. A condition brought about at a certain time can be abolished at some other time, as the Negroes of Haiti and others have proved; but it might seem that a natural condition is beyond the possibility of change. In truth, however, the nature of things is no more immutably given, once for all, than is historical reality. If woman seems to be the inessential which never becomes the essential, it is because she herself fails to bring about this change. Proletarians say "we"; Negroes also. Regarding themselves as subjects, they transform the bourgeois, the whites, into "others." But women do not say "we," except at some congress of feminists or similar formal demonstration; men say "women," and women use the same word in referring to themselves. They do not authentically assume a subjective attitude. The proletarians have accomplished the revolution in Russia, the Negroes in Haiti, the Indo-Chinese are battling for it in Indo-China; but the women's effort has never been anything more than a symbolic agitation. They have gained only what men have been willing to grant; they have taken nothing, they have only received.

The reason for this is that women lack concrete means for organizing themselves into a unit which can stand face to face with the correlative unit. They have no past, no history, no religion of their own; and they have no such solidarity of work and interest as that of the proletariat. They are not even promiscuously herded together in the way that creates community feeling among the American Negroes, the ghetto Jews, the workers of Saint-Denis, or the factory hands of Renault. They live dispersed among the males, attached through residence, housework, economic condition, and social standing to certain men—fathers or husbands—more firmly than they are to other women. If they belong to the bourgeoisie, they feel solidarity with men of that class, not with proletarian women; if they are white, their allegiance is to white men, not to Negro women. The proletariat can propose to massacre the ruling class, and a

[2] See C. Levi-Strauss, *Les Structures élémentaires de la parenté.*

[3] With rare exceptions, perhaps, like certain matriarchal rulers, queens, and the like—Tr.

sufficiently fanatical Jew or Negro might dream of getting sole possession of the atomic bomb and making humanity wholly Jewish or black; but women cannot even dream of exterminating the males. The bond that unites her to her oppressors is not comparable to any other. The division of the sexes is a biological fact, not an event in human history. Male and female stand opposed within a primordial *Mitsein*, and woman has not broken it. The couple is a fundamental unity with its two halves riveted together, and the cleavage of society along the line of sex is impossible. Here is to be found the basic trait of woman: she is the Other in a totality of which the two components are necessary to one another.

One could suppose that this reciprocity might have facilitated the liberation of woman. When Hercules sat at the feet of Omphale and helped with her spinning, his desire for her held him captive; but why did she fail to gain a lasting power? To revenge herself on Jason, Medea killed their children; and this grim legend would seem to suggest that she might have obtained a formidable influence over him through his love for her offspring. In *Lysistrata* Aristophanes gaily depicts a band of women who joined forces to gain social ends through the sexual needs of their men; but this is only a play. In the legend of the Sabine women, the latter soon abandoned their plan of remaining sterile to punish their ravishers. In truth woman has not been socially emancipated through man's need—sexual desire and the desire for offspring—which makes the male dependent for satisfaction upon the female.

Master and slave, also, are united by a reciprocal need, in this case economic, which does not liberate the slave. In the relation of master to slave the master does not make a point of the need that he has for the other; he has in his grasp the power of satisfying this need through his own action; whereas the slave, in his dependent condition, his hope and fear, is quite conscious of the need he has for his master. Even if the need is at bottom equally urgent for both, it always works in favour of the oppressor and against the oppressed. That is why the liberation of the working class, for example, has been slow.

Now, woman has always been man's dependent, if not his slave; the two sexes have never shared the world in equality. And even today woman is heavily handicapped, though her situation is beginning to change. Almost nowhere is her legal status the same as man's, and frequently it is much to her disadvantage. Even when her rights are legally recognized in the abstract, long-standing custom prevents their full expression in the mores. In the economic sphere men and women can almost be said to make up two castes; other things being equal, the former hold the better jobs, get higher wages, and have more opportunity for success than their new competitors. In industry and politics men have a great many more positions and they monopolize the most important posts. In addition to all this, they enjoy a traditional prestige that the education of children tends in every way to support, for the present enshrines the past—and in the past all history has been made by men. At the present time, when women are beginning to take part in the affairs of the world, it is still a world that belongs to men—they have no doubt of it at all and women have scarcely any. To decline to be the Other, to refuse to be a party to the deal—

this would be for women to renounce all the advantages conferred upon them by their alliance with the superior caste. Man-the-sovereign will provide woman-the-liege with material protection and will undertake the moral justification of her existence; thus she can evade at once both economic risk and the metaphysical risk of a liberty in which ends and aims must be contrived without assistance. Indeed, along with the ethical urge of each individual to affirm his subjective existence, there is also the temptation to forgo liberty and become a thing. This is an inauspicious road, for he who takes it—passive, lost, ruined—becomes henceforth the creature of another's will, frustrated in his transcendence and deprived of every value. But it is an easy road; on it one avoids the strain involved in undertaking an authentic existence. When man makes of woman the *Other*, he may, then, expect to manifest deep-seated tendencies towards complicity. Thus; woman may fail to lay claim to the status of subject because she lacks definite resources, because she feels the necessary bond that ties her to man regardless of reciprocity, and because she is often very well pleased with her role as the *Other*.

But it will be asked at once: how did all this begin? It is easy to see that the duality of the sexes, like any duality, gives rise to conflict. And doubtless the winner will assume the status of absolute. But why should man have won from the start? It seems possible that women could have won the victory; or that the outcome of the conflict might never have been decided. How is it that this world has always belonged to the men and that things have begun to change only recently? Is this change a good thing? Will it bring about an equal sharing of the world between men and women?

These questions are not new, and they have often been answered. But the very fact that woman *is the Other* tends to cast suspicion upon all the justifications that men have ever been able to provide for it. These have all too evidently been dictated by men's interest. A little-known feminist of the seventeenth century, Poulain de la Barre, put it this way: "All that has been written about women by men should be suspect, for the men are at once judge and party to the lawsuit." Everywhere, at all times, the males have displayed their satisfaction in feeling that they are the lords of creation. "Blessed be God … that He did not make me a woman," say the Jews in their morning prayers, while their wives pray on a note of resignation: "Blessed be the Lord, who created me according to His will." The first among the blessings for which Plato thanked the gods was that he had been created free, not enslaved; the second, a man, not a woman. But the males could not enjoy this privilege fully unless they believed it to be founded on the absolute and the eternal; they sought to make the fact of their supremacy into a right. "Being men, those who have made and compiled the laws have favoured their own sex, and jurists have elevated these laws into principles," to quote Poulain de la Barre once more.

Legislators, priests, philosophers, writers, and scientists have striven to show that the subordinate position of woman is willed in heaven and advantageous on earth. The religions invented by men reflected this wish for domination. In the legends of Eve and Pandora men have taken up arms against women. They have made use of philosophy and theology, as the quotations from Aristotle and St Thomas have shown.

Since ancient times satirists and moralists have delighted in showing up the weakness of women. We are familiar with the savage indictments hurled against women throughout French literature. Montherlant, for example, follows the tradition of Jean de Meung, though with less gusto. This hostility may at times be well founded, often it is gratuitous; but in truth it more or less successfully conceals a desire for self-justification. As Montaigne says, "It is easier to accuse one sex than to excuse the other." Sometimes what is going on is clear enough. For instance, the Roman law limiting the rights of woman cited "the imbecility, the instability of the sex" just when the weakening of family ties seemed to threaten the interests of male heirs. And in the effort to keep the married woman under guardianship, appeal was made in the sixteenth century to the authority of St Augustine, who declared that "woman is a creature neither decisive nor constant," at a time when a single woman was thought capable of managing her property. Montaigne understood clearly how arbitrary and unjust was woman's appointed lot: "Women are not in the wrong when they decline to accept the rules laid down for them, since the men make these rules without consulting them. No wonder intrigue and strife abound." But he did not go so far as to champion their cause.

It was only later, in the eighteenth century, that genuinely democratic men began to view the matter objectively. Diderot, among others, strove to show that woman is, like man, a human being. Later John Stuart Mill came fervently to her defence. But these philosophers displayed unusual impartiality. In the nineteenth century the feminist quarrel became again a quarrel of partisans. One of the consequences of the industrial revolution was the entrance of women into productive labour, and it was just here that the claims of the feminists emerged from the realm of theory and acquired an economic basis, while their opponents became the more aggressive. Although landed property lost power to some extent, the bourgeoisie clung to the old morality that found the guarantee of private property in the solidity of the family. Woman was ordered back into the home the more harshly as her emancipation became a real menace. Even within the working class the men endeavoured to restrain woman's liberation, because they began to see the women as dangerous competitors—the more so because they were accustomed to work for lower wages.

In proving woman's inferiority, the anti-feminists then began to draw not only upon religion, philosophy, and theology, as before, but also upon science—biology, experimental psychology, etc. At most they were willing to grant "equality in difference" to the *other* sex. That profitable formula is most significant; it is precisely like the "equal but separate" formula of the Jim Crow laws aimed at the North American Negroes. As is well known, this so-called equalitarian segregation has resulted only in the most extreme discrimination. The similarity just noted is in no way due to chance, for whether it is a race, a caste, a class, or a sex that is reduced to a position of inferiority, the methods of justification are the same. "The eternal feminine" corresponds to "the black soul" and to "the Jewish character." True, the Jewish problem is on the whole very different from the other two—to the anti-Semite the Jew is not so much an inferior as he is an enemy for whom there is to be granted no place on earth, for whom annihilation is the fate desired. But there are deep similarities between the situation of woman and that of the Negro. Both are being emancipated today from a like paternalism, and the former master class wishes to "keep them in their place"—that is, the place chosen for them. In both cases the former masters lavish more or less sincere eulogies, either on the virtues of "the good Negro" with his dormant, childish, merry soul—the submissive Negro—or on the merits of the woman who is "truly feminine"—that is, frivolous, infantile, irresponsible—the submissive woman. In both cases the dominant class bases its argument on a state of affairs that it has itself created. As George Bernard Shaw puts it, in substance, "The American white relegates the black to the rank of shoeshine boy; and he concludes from this that the black is good for nothing but shining shoes." This vicious circle is met with in all analogous circumstances; when an individual (or a group of individuals) is kept in a situation of inferiority, the fact is that he *is* inferior. But the significance of the verb to *be* must be rightly understood here; it is in bad faith to give it a static value when it really has the dynamic Hegelian sense of "to have become." Yes women on the whole *are* today inferior to men; that is, their situation affords them fewer possibilities. The question is: should that state of affairs continue?

Many men hope that it will continue, not all have given up the battle. The conservative bourgeoisie still see in the emancipation of women a menace to their morality and their interests. Some men dread feminine competition. Recently a male student wrote in the *Hebdo-Latin*: "Every woman student who goes into medicine or law robs us of a job." He never questioned his rights in this world. And economic interests are not the only ones concerned. One of the benefits that oppression confers upon the oppressors is that the most humble among them is made to *feel* superior; thus, a "poor white" in the South can console himself with the thought that he is not a "dirty nigger"—and the more prosperous whites cleverly exploit this pride.

Similarly, the most mediocre of males feels himself a demigod as compared with women. It was much easier for M. de Montherlant to think himself a hero when he faced women (and women chosen for his purpose) than when he was obliged to act the man among men—something many women have done better than he, for that matter. And in September 1948, in one of his articles in the *Figaro littéraire*, Claude Mauriac—whose great originality is admired by all—could[4] write regarding woman: "*We* listen on a tone [sic!] of polite indifference … to the most brilliant among them, well knowing that her wit reflects more or less luminously ideas that come from *us*." Evidently the speaker referred to is not reflecting the ideas of Mauriac himself, for no one knows of his having any. It may be that she reflects ideas originating with men, but then, even among men there are those who have been known to appropriate ideas not their own; and one can ask whether Claude Mauriac might not find more interesting a conversation reflecting Descartes, Marx, or Gide rather than himself. What is really remarkable is that by using the questionable

---

[4] Or at least he thought he could.

we he identifies himself with St Paul, Hegel, Lenin, and Nietzsche, and from the lofty eminence of their grandeur looks down disdainfully upon the bevy of women who make bold to converse with him on a footing of equality. In truth, I know of more than one woman who would refuse to suffer with patience Mauriac's "tone of polite indifference."

I have lingered on this example because the masculine attitude is here displayed with disarming ingenuousness. But men profit in many more subtle ways from the otherness, the alterity of woman. Here is a miraculous balm for those afflicted with an inferiority complex, and indeed no one is more arrogant towards women, more aggressive or scornful, than the man who is anxious about his virility. Those who are not fear-ridden in the presence of their fellow men are much more disposed to recognize a fellow creature in woman; but even to these the myth of Woman, the Other, is precious for many reasons.[5] They cannot be blamed for not cheerfully relinquishing all the benefits they derive from the myth, for they realize what they would lose in relinquishing woman as they fancy her to be, while they fail to realize what they have to gain from the woman of tomorrow. Refusal to pose oneself as the Subject, unique and absolute, requires great self-denial. Furthermore, the vast majority of men make no such claim explicitly. They do not *postulate* woman as inferior, for today they are too thoroughly imbued with the ideal of democracy not to recognize all human beings as equals.

In the bosom of the family, woman seems in the eyes of childhood and youth to be clothed in the same social dignity as the adult males. Later on, the young man, desiring loving, experiences the resistance, the independence of the woman desired and loved; in marriage, he respects woman as wife and mother, and in the concrete events of conjugal life she stands there before him as a free being. He can therefore feel that social subordination as between the sexes no longer exists and that on the whole, in spite of differences, woman is an equal. As, however, he observes some points of inferiority—the most important being unfitness for the professions—he attributes these to natural causes. When he is in a co-operative and benevolent relation with woman, his theme is the principle of abstract equality, and he does not base his attitude upon such inequality as may exist. But when he is in conflict with her, the situation is reversed: his themes will be the existing inequality, and he will even take it as justification for denying abstract equality.

So it is that many men will affirm as if in good faith that women *are* the equals of man and that they have nothing to clamour for, while *at the same time* they will say that women can never be the equals of man and that their demands are in vain. It is, in point of fact, a difficult matter for man to

realize the extreme importance of social discriminations which seem outwardly insignificant but which produce in woman moral and intellectual effects so profound that they appear to spring from her original nature. The most sympathetic of men never fully comprehend woman's concrete situation. And there is no reason to put much trust in the men when they rush to the defence of privileges whose full extent they can hardly measure. We shall not, then, permit ourselves to be intimidated by the number and violence of the attacks launched against women, nor to be entrapped by the self-seeking eulogies bestowed on the "true woman," nor to profit by the enthusiasm for woman's destiny manifested by men who would not for the world have any part of it.

We should consider the arguments of the feminists with no less suspicion, however, for very often their controversial aim deprives them of all real value. If the "woman question" seems trivial, it is because masculine arrogance has made of it a "quarrel"; and when quarrelling one no longer reasons well. People have tirelessly sought to prove that woman is superior, inferior, or equal to man. Some say that, having been created after Adam, she is evidently a secondary being; others say on the contrary that Adam was only a rough draft and that God succeeded in producing the human being in perfection when He created Eve. Woman's brain is smaller; yes, but it is relatively larger. Christ was made a man; yes, but perhaps for his greater humility. Each argument at once suggests its opposite, and both are often fallacious. If we are to gain understanding, we must get out of these ruts; we must discard the vague notions of superiority, inferiority, equality which have hitherto corrupted every discussion of the subject and start afresh.

Very well, but just how shall we pose the question? And, to begin with, who are we to propound it at all? Man is at once judge and party to the case; but so is woman. What we need is an angel—neither man nor woman—but where shall we find one? Still, the angel would be poorly qualified to speak, for an angel is ignorant of all the basic facts involved in the problem. With a hermaphrodite we should be no better off, for here the situation is most peculiar; the hermaphrodite is not really the combination of a whole man and a whole woman, but consists of parts of each and thus is neither. It looks to me as if there are, after all, certain women who are best qualified to elucidate the situation of woman. Let us not be misled by the sophism that because Epimenides was a Cretan he was necessarily a liar; it is not a mysterious essence that compels men and women to act in good or in bad faith, it is their situation that inclines them more or less towards the search for truth. Many of today's women, fortunate in the restoration of all the privileges pertaining to the estate of the human being, can afford the luxury of impartiality—we even recognize its necessity. We are no longer like our partisan elders; by and large we have won the game. In recent debates on the status of women the United Nations has persistently maintained that the equality of the sexes is now becoming a reality; and already some of us have never had to sense in our femininity an inconvenience or an obstacle. Many problems appear to us to be more pressing than those which concern us in particular, and this detachment even allows us to hope that our attitude will be objective. Still, we know the feminine world more intimately than do the men because we have our roots in it,

---

[5] A significant article on this theme by Michel Carrouges appeared in No. 292 of the *Cahiers du Sud*. He writes indignantly: "Would that there were no woman-myth at all but only a cohort of cooks, matrons, prostitutes and blue-stockings serving functions of pleasure or usefulness!" That is to say, in his view woman has no existence in and for herself; he thinks only of her *function* in the male world. Her reason for existence lies in man. But then, in fact, her poetic "function" as a myth might be more valued than any other. The real problem is precisely to find out why woman should be defined with relation to man.

we grasp more immediately than do the men what it means to a human being to be feminine; and we are more concerned with such knowledge. I have said that there are more pressing problems, but this does not prevent us from seeing some importance in asking how the fact of being women will affect our lives. What opportunities precisely have been given us and what withheld? What fate awaits our youngest sisters, and what directions should they take? It is significant that books by women are in general animated in our day less by a wish to demand our rights than by an effort towards clarity and understanding. As we emerge from an era of excessive controversy, this book is offered as one attempt among others to confirm that statement.

But it is doubtless impossible to approach any human problem with a mind free from bias. The way in which questions are put, the points of view assumed, presuppose a relativity of interest; all characteristics imply values, and every objective description, so called, implies an ethical background. Rather than attempt to conceal principles more or less definitely implied, it is better to state them openly, at the beginning. This will make it unnecessary to specify on every page in just what sense one uses such words as *superior, inferior, better, worse, progress, reaction*, and the like. If we survey some of the works on women, we note that one of the points of view most frequently adopted is that of the public good, the general interest; and one always means by this the benefit of society as one wishes it to be maintained or established. For our part, we hold that the only public good is that which assures the private good of the citizens, we shall pass judgement on institutions according to their effectiveness in giving concrete opportunities to individuals. But we do not confuse the idea of private interest with that of happiness, although that is another common point of view. Are not women of the harem more happy than women voters? Is not the housekeeper happier than the working-women? It is not too clear just what the word *happy* really means and still less what true values it may mask. There is no possibility of measuring the happiness of others, and it is always easy to describe as happy the situation in which one wishes to place them.

In particular those who are condemned to stagnation are often pronounced happy on the pretext that happiness consists in being at rest. This notion we reject, for our perspective is that of existentialist ethics. Every subject plays his part as such specifically through exploits or projects that serve as a mode of transcendence; he achieves liberty only through a continual reaching out towards other liberties. There is no justification for present existence other than its expansion into an indefinitely open future. Every time transcendence falls back into immanence, stagnation, there is a degradation of existence into the "*en-soi*"—the brutish life of subjection to given conditions—and of liberty into constraint and contingence. This downfall represents a moral fault if the subject consents to it; if it is inflicted upon him, it spells frustration and oppression. In both cases it is an absolute evil. Every individual concerned to justify his existence feels that his existence involves an undefined need to transcend himself, to engage in freely chosen projects.

Now, what peculiarly signalizes the situation of woman is that she—a free and autonomous being like all human creatures—nevertheless finds herself living in a world where men compel her to assume the status of the Other. They propose to stabilize her as object and to doom her to immanence since her transcendence is to be overshadowed and for ever transcended by another ego (conscience) which is essential and sovereign. The drama of woman lies in this conflict between the fundamental aspirations of every subject (ego)—who always regards the self as the essential—and the compulsions of a situation in which she is the inessential. How can a human being in woman's situation attain fulfilment? What roads are open to her? Which are blocked? How can independence be recovered in a state of dependency? What circumstances limit woman's liberty and how can they be overcome? These are the fundamental questions on which I would fain throw some light. This means that I am interested in the fortunes of the individual as defined not in terms of happiness but in terms of liberty.

Quite evidently this problem would be without significance if we were to believe that woman's destiny is inevitably determined by physiological, psychological, or economic forces. Hence I shall discuss first of all the light in which woman is viewed by biology, psychoanalysis, and historical materialism. Next I shall try to show exactly how the concept of the "truly feminine" has been fashioned—why woman has been defined as the Other—and what have been the consequences from man's point of view. Then from woman's point of view I shall describe the world in which woman must live; and thus we shall be able to envisage the difficulties in their way as, endeavouring to make their escape from the sphere hitherto assigned them, they aspire to full membership in the human race.

❧ Allen Ginsberg
Howl

A descendant of Walt Whitman's Leaves of Grass, *Allen Ginsberg's* Howl *revitalized the oral tradition in American poetry by incorporating the rhythms of everyday American speech into the poem's long lines. In fact, Ginsberg's readings, complete with harmonium and finger cymbal accompaniments, Buddhist mantras, and audience response, soon transformed the poetry reading from formal recital to communal performance.*

I

I saw the best minds of my generation destroyed by
    madness, starving hysterical naked,
dragging themselves through the negro streets at dawn
    looking for an angry fix,
angelheaded hipsters burning for the ancient heavenly
    connection to the starry dynamo in the machinery of
    night,
who poverty and tatters and hollow-eyed and high sat
    up smoking in the supernatural darkness of cold-
    water flats floating across the tops of cities
    contemplating jazz,
who bared their brains to Heaven under the El° and
    saw Mohammedan angels staggering on tenement
    roofs illuminated,

5

---
⁵ *El*: Elevated railway.

who passed through universities with radiant cool eyes
    hallucinating Arkansas and Blake-light tragedy
    among the scholars of war,

who were expelled from the academies for crazy &
    publishing obscene odes on the windows of the skull,

who cowered in unshaven rooms in underwear, burning
    their money, in wastebaskets and listening to the
    Terror through the wall,

who got busted in their pubic beards returning through
    Laredo with a belt of marijuana for New York,

who ate fire in paint hotels or drank turpentine in
    Paradise Alley,° death, or purgatoried their torsos
    night after night   *10*

with dreams, with drugs, with waking nightmares,
    alcohol and cock and endless balls,

incomparable blind streets of shuddering cloud and
    lightning in the mind leaping toward poles of
    Canada & Paterson, illuminating all the motionless
    world of Time between,

Peyote solidities of halls, backyard green tree cemetery
    dawns, wine drunkenness over the rooftops,
    storefront boroughs of teahead joyride neon blinking
    traffic light, sun and moon and tree vibrations in the
    roaring winter dusks of Brooklyn, ashcan rantings
    and kind king light of mind,

who chained themselves to subways for the endless ride
    from Battery to holy Bronx on benzedrine until the
    noise of wheels and children brought them down
    shuddering mouth-wracked and battered bleak of
    brain all drained of brilliance in the drear light of
    Zoo,

who sank all night in submarine light of Bickford's°
    floated out and sat through the stale beer afternoon
    in desolate Fugazzi's,° listening to the crack of doom
    on the hydrogen jukebox,   *15*

who talked continuously seventy hours from park to
    pad to bar to Bellevue to museum to the Brooklyn
    Bridge,

a lost battalion of platonic conversationalists jumping
    down the stoops off fire escapes off windowsills off
    Empire State out of the moon,

yacketayakking screaming vomiting whispering facts
    and memories and anecdotes and eyeball kicks and
    shocks of hospitals and jails and wars,

whole intellects disgorged in total recall for seven days
    and nights with brilliant eyes, meat for the
    Synagogue cast on the pavement,

who vanished into nowhere Zen° New Jersey leaving a
    trail of ambiguous picture postcards of Atlantic City
    Hall,   *20*

suffering Eastern sweats and Tangerian bone-
    grindings and migraines of China under junk-
    withdrawal in Newark's bleak furnished room,

---

[10] *Paradise Alley:* This was in New York's Lower East Side and was the setting for one of Beat writer Jack Kerouac's novels.

[15] *Bickford's:* A café where Ginsberg once worked. *Fugazzi's:* A bar in Greenwich Village.

[20] *Zen:* Zen Buddhism, an Eastern philosophy of great importance to the Beats in the 1950s.

---

who wandered around and around at midnight in the
    railroad yard wondering where to go, and went,
    leaving no broken hearts,

who lit cigarettes in boxcars boxcars boxcars racketing
    through snow toward lonesome farms in grandfather
    night,

who studied Plotinus Poe St. John of the Cross
    telepathy and bop kabbalah° because the cosmos
    instinctively vibrated at their feet in Kansas,

who loned it through the streets of Idaho seeking
    visionary indian angels who were visionary indian
    angels,   *25*

who thought they were only mad when Baltimore
    gleamed in supernatural ecstasy,

who jumped in limousines with the Chinaman of
    Oklahoma on the impulse of winter midnight
    streetlight smalltown rain,

who lounged hungry and lonesome through Houston
    seeking jazz or sex or soup, and followed the brilliant
    Spaniard to converse about America and Eternity, a
    hopeless task, and so took ship to Africa,

who disappeared into the volcanoes of Mexico leaving
    behind nothing but the shadow of dungarees and the
    lava and ash of poetry scattered in fireplace Chicago,

who reappeared on the West Coast investigating the
    FBI in beards and shorts with big pacifist eyes sexy
    in their dark skin passing out incomprehensible
    leaflets,   *30*

who burned cigarette holes in their arms protesting the
    narcotic tobacco haze of Capitalism,

who distributed Supercommunist pamphlets in Union
    Square weeping and undressing while the sirens of
    Los Alamos wailed them down, and wailed down
    Wall, and the Staten Island ferry also wailed,

who broke down crying in white gymnasiums naked
    and trembling before the machinery of other
    skeletons,

who bit detectives in the neck and shrieked with delight
    in policecars for committing no crime but their own
    wild cooking pederasty and intoxication,

who howled on their knees in the subway and were
    dragged off the roof waving genitals and
    manuscripts,   *35*

who let themselves be fucked in the ass by saintly
    motorcyclists, and screamed with joy,

who blew and were blown by those human seraphim,
    the sailors, caresses of Atlantic and Caribbean love,

who balled in the morning in the evenings in
    rosegardens and the grass of public parks and
    cemeteries scattering their semen freely to
    whomever come who may,

who hiccuped endlessly trying to giggle but wound up
    with a sob behind a partition in a Turkish Bath when
    the blond & naked angel came to pierce them with a
    sword,

who lost their loveboys to the three old shrews of fate
    the one eyed shrew of the heterosexual dollar the

---

[24] *Plotinus … kabbalah:* The names of people and texts that are traditionally associated with mystical religious experience.

one eyed shrew that winks out of the womb and the
    one eyed shrew that does nothing but sit on her ass
    and snip the intellectual golden threads of the
    craftsman's loom,   40
who copulated ecstatic and insatiate with a bottle of
    beer a sweetheart a package of cigarettes a candle
    and fell off the bed, and continued along the floor
    and down the hall and ended fainting on the wall
    with a vision of ultimate cunt and come eluding the
    last gyzym of consciousness,
who sweetened the snatches of a million girls trembling
    in the sunset and were red eyed in the morning but
    prepared to sweeten the snatch of the sunrise,
    flashing buttocks under barns and naked in the lake,
who went out whoring through Colorado in myriad
    stolen nightcars, N.C.,° secret hero of these poems,
    cocksman and Adonis of Denver—joy to the memory
    of his innumerable lays of girls in empty lots & diner
    backyards, moviehouses' rickety rows, on
    mountaintops in caves or with gaunt waitresses in
    familiar roadside lonely petticoat upliftings &
    especially secret gas-station solipsisms of johns, &
    hometown alleys too,
who faded out in vast sordid movies, were shifted in
    dreams, woke on a sudden Manhattan, and picked
    themselves up out of basements hungover with
    heartless Tokay and horrors of Third Avenue iron
    dreams & stumbled to unemployment offices,
who walked all night with their shoes full of blood on
    the snowbank docks waiting for a door in the East
    River to open to a room full of steamheat and
    opium,   45
who created great suicidal dramas on the apartment
    cliff-banks of the Hudson under the wartime blue
    floodlight of the moon & their heads shall be
    crowned with laurel in oblivion,
who ate the lamb stew of the imagination or digested
    the crab at the muddy bottom of the rivers of
    Bowery,°
who wept at the romance of the streets with their
    pushcarts full of onions and bad music,
who sat in boxes breathing in the darkness under the
    bridge, and rose up to build harpsichords in their
    lofts,
who coughed on the sixth floor of Harlem crowned
    with flame under the tubercular sky surrounded by
    orange crates of theology,   50
who scribbled all night rocking and rolling over lofty
    incantations which in the yellow morning were
    stanzas of gibberish,
who cooked rotten animals lung heart feet tail borsht &
    tortillas dreaming of the pure vegetable kingdom,
who plunged themselves under meat trucks looking for
    an egg,
who threw their watches off the roof to cast their ballot

for Eternity outside of Time, & alarm clocks fell on
    their heads every day for the next decade,
who cut their wrists three times successively
    unsuccessfully, gave up and were forced to open
    antique stores where they thought they were
    growing old and cried,   55
who were burned alive in their innocent flannel suits on
    Madison Avenue amid blasts of leaden verse & the
    tanked-up clatter of the iron regiments of fashion &
    the nitroglycerine shrieks of the fairies of advertising
    & the mustard gas of sinister intelligent editors, or
    were run down by the drunken taxicabs of Absolute
    Reality,
who jumped off the Brooklyn Bridge this actually
    happened and walked away unknown and forgotten
    into the ghostly daze of Chinatown soup alleyways &
    firetrucks, not even one free beer,
who sang out of their windows in despair, fell out of the
    subway window, jumped in the filthy Passaic, leaped
    on negroes, cried all over the street, danced on
    broken wineglasses barefoot smashed phonograph
    records of nostalgic European 1930s German jazz
    finished the whiskey and threw up groaning into the
    bloody toilet, moans in their ears and the blast of
    colossal steamwhistles,
who barreled down the highways of the past journeying
    to each other's hotrod—Golgotha jail—solitude
    watch or Birmingham jazz incarnation,
who drove crosscountry seventytwo hours to find out if
    I had a vision or you had a vision or he had a vision
    to find out Eternity,   60
who journeyed to Denver, who died in Denver, who
    came back to Denver & waited in vain, who watched
    over Denver & brooded & loned in Denver and
    finally went away to find out the Time & now
    Denver is lonesome for her heroes,
who fell on their knees in hopeless cathedrals praying
    for each other's salvation and light and breasts, until
    the soul illuminated its hair for a second,
who crashed through their minds in jail waiting for
    impossible criminals with golden heads and the
    charm of reality in their hearts who sang sweet blues
    to Alcatraz,
who retired to Mexico to cultivate a habit, or Rocky
    Mount to tender Buddha or Tangiers to boys or
    Southern Pacific to the black locomotive or Harvard
    to Narcissus to Woodlawn to the daisychain or
    grave,
who demanded sanity trials accusing the radio of
    hypnotism & were left with their insanity & their
    hands & a hung jury,   65
who threw potato salad at CCNY lecturers on Dadaism
    and subsequently presented themselves on the
    granite steps of the madhouse with shaven heads and
    harlequin speech of suicide, demanding
    instantaneous lobotomy,
and who were given instead the concrete void of insulin
    Metrazol electricity hydrotherapy psychotherapy
    occupational therapy pingpong & amnesia,
who in humorless protest overturned only one symbolic
    pingpong table, resting briefly in catatonia,

---

43 *N.C.:* Neal Cassady (1926–1968), a Beat writer who traveled
with Jack Kerouac and was memorialized as the character Dean
Moriarty in Kerouac's novel *On The Road* (1957).

47 *Bowery:* A district known in New York for its alcoholics and
down-and-outs.

returning years later truly bald except for a wig of
blood, and tears and fingers, to the visible madman
doom of the wards of the madtowns of the East,

Pilgrim° State's Rockland's and Greystone's foetid halls,
bickering with the echoes of the soul, rocking and
rolling in the midnight solitude—bench dolmen—
realms of love, dream of life a nightmare, bodies
turned to stone as heavy as the moon,   70

with mother finally ******° and the last fantastic book
flung out of the tenement window, and the last door
closed at 4 A.M. and the last telephone slammed at
the wall in reply and the last furnished room emptied
down to the last piece of mental furniture, a yellow
paper rose twisted on a wire hanger in the closet,
and even that imaginary nothing but a hopeful little
bit of hallucination—

ah, Carl, while you are not safe I am not safe, and now
you're really in the total animal soup of time—

and who therefore ran through the icy streets obsessed
with a sudden flash of the alchemy of the use of the
ellipse the catalog the meter & the vibrating plane,

who dreamt and made incarnate gaps in Time & Space
through images juxtaposed, and trapped the
archangel of the soul between 2 visual images and
joined the elemental verbs and set the noun and dash
of consciousness together jumping with sensation of
Pater Omnipotens Aeterna Deus°

to recreate the syntax and measure of poor human prose
and stand before you speechless and intelligent and
shaking with shame, rejected yet confessing out the
soul to conform to the rhythm of thought in his
naked and endless head,   75

the madman bum and angel beat in Time, unknown,
yet putting down here what might be left to say in
time come after death,

and rose reincarnate in the ghostly clothes of jazz in the
goldhorn shadow of the band and blew the suffering
of America's naked mind for love into an eli eli
lamma lamma sabacthani° saxophone cry that
shivered the cities down to the last radio

with the absolute heart of the poem of life butchered
out of their own bodies good to eat a thousand years.

II

What sphinx of cement and aluminum bashed open
their skulls and ate up their brains and imagination?

Moloch!° Solitude! Filth! Ugliness! Ashcans and
unobtainable dollars! Children screaming under the
stairways! Boys sobbing in armies! Old men weeping

in the parks!   80

Moloch! Moloch! Nightmare of Moloch! Moloch the
loveless! Mental Moloch! Moloch the heavy judger
of men!

Moloch the incomprehensible prison! Moloch the
crossbone soulless jailhouse and Congress of
sorrows! Moloch whose buildings are judgment!
Moloch the vast stone of war! Moloch the stunned
governments!

Moloch whose mind is pure machinery! Moloch whose
blood is running money! Moloch whose fingers are
ten armies! Moloch whose breast is a cannibal
dynamo! Moloch whose ear is a smoking tomb!

Moloch whose eyes are a thousand blind windows!
Moloch whose skyscrapers stand in the long streets
like endless Jehovahs! Moloch whose factories dream
and croak in the fog! Moloch whose smokestacks and
antennae crown the cities!

Moloch whose love is endless oil and stone! Moloch
whose soul is electricity and banks! Moloch whose
poverty is the specter of genius! Moloch whose fate
is a cloud of sexless hydrogen! Moloch whose name
is the Mind!   85

Moloch in whom I sit lonely! Moloch in whom I dream
Angels' Crazy in Moloch! Cocksucker in Moloch!
Lacklove and manless in Moloch!

Moloch who entered my soul early! Moloch in whom I
am a consciousness without a body! Moloch who
frightened me out of my natural ecstasy! Moloch
whom I abandon! Wake up in Moloch! Light
streaming out of the sky!

Moloch! Moloch! Robot apartments! invisible suburbs!
skeleton treasuries! blind capitals! demonic
industries! spectral nations! invincible madhouses!
granite cocks! monstrous bombs!

They broke their backs lifting Moloch to Heaven!
Pavements, trees, radios, tons! lifting the city to
Heaven which exists and is everywhere about us!

Visions! omens! hallucinations! miracles! ecstasies! gone
down the American river!   90

Dreams! adorations! illuminations! religions! the whole
boatload of sensitive bullshit!

Breakthroughs! over the river! flips and crucifixions!
gone down the flood! Highs! Epiphanies! Despairs!
Ten years' animal screams and suicides! Minds! New
loves! Mad generation! down on the rocks of Time!

Real holy laughter in the river! They saw it all! the wild
eyes' the holy yells! They bade farewell! They
jumped off the roof to solitude! waving! carrying
flowers! Down to the river! into the street!

III

Carl Solomon! I'm with you in Rockland°
where you're madder than I am
I'm with you in Rockland
where you must feel very strange   95
I'm with you in Rockland

---

⁷⁰ *Pilgrim: ... Greystone's:* The names of mental hospitals.

⁷¹ ******: Ginsberg's mother Naomi was hospitalized for paranoia
and died in 1956.

⁷⁴ *Pater Omnipoteus Aeterna Deus:* "Father omnipotent, eternal
God."

⁷⁷ *eli eli lamma... sabacthani:* "My God, my God, why have you
forsaken me?"—the words spoken by Christ on the cross.

⁸⁰ *Moloch:* An ancient god worshiped with the sacrifice of
human children.

---

⁹⁴ *Rockland:* Psychiatric hospital in New York.

where you imitate the shade of my mother
I'm with you in Rockland
    where you've murdered your twelve secretaries
I'm with you in Rockland
    where you laugh at this invisible humor
I'm with you in Rockland
    where we are great writers on the same dreadful
    typewriter
I'm with you in Rockland
    where your condition has become serious and is
    reported on the radio   100
I'm with you in Rockland
    where the faculties of the skull no longer admit the
    worms of the senses
I'm with you in Rockland
    where you drink the tea of the breasts of the spinters
    of Utica
I'm with you in Rockland
    where you pun on the bodies of your nurses the
    harpies of the Bronx
I'm with you in Rockland
    where you scream in a straightjacket that you're
    losing the game of the actual pingpong of the abyss
I'm with you in Rockland
    where you bang on the catatonic piano the soul is
    innocent and immortal it should never die ungodly
    in an armed madhouse   105
I'm with you in Rockland
    where fifty more shocks will never return your soul
    to its body again from its pilgrimage to a cross in the
    void
I'm with you in Rockland
    where you accuse your doctors of insanity and plot
    the Hebrew socialist revolution against the fascist
    national Golgotha
I'm with you in Rockland
    where you will split the heavens of Long Island and
    resurrect your living human Jesus from the
    superhuman tomb
I'm with you in Rockland
    where there are twentyfive thousand mad comrades
    all together singing the final stanzas of the
    Internationale°
I'm with you in Rockland
    where we hug and kiss the United States under our
    bedsheets the United States that coughs all night and
    won't let us sleep   110
I'm with you in Rockland
    where we wake up electrified out of the coma by our
    own souls' airplanes roaring over the roof they've
    come to drop angelic bombs the hospital illuminates
    itself imaginary walls collapse O skinny legions run
    outside O starry-spangled shock of mercy the eternal
    war is here O victory forget your underwear we're
    free
I'm with you in Rockland
    in my dreams you walk dripping from a sea-journey
    on the highway across America in tears to the door
    of my cottage in the Western night

---

¹⁰⁹ *Internationale*: Communist anthem.

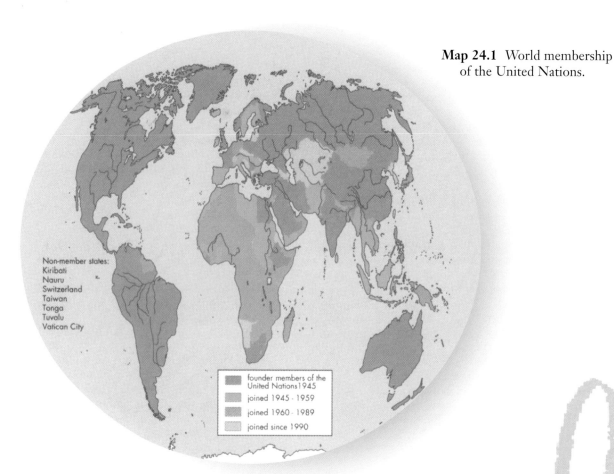

Map 24.1 World membership of the United Nations.

Non-member states:
Kiribati
Nauru
Switzerland
Taiwan
Tonga
Tuvalu
Vatican City

founder members of the
United Nations 1945
joined 1945 - 1959
joined 1960 - 1989
joined since 1990

THE DIVERSITY OF
CONTEMPORARY
LIFE

CHAPTER 24

✦ *Diversity in the United States*

✦ *The Global Village*

Lisa Fifield, *Ghost Dancers Ascending* (detail), 1995, Private Collection.

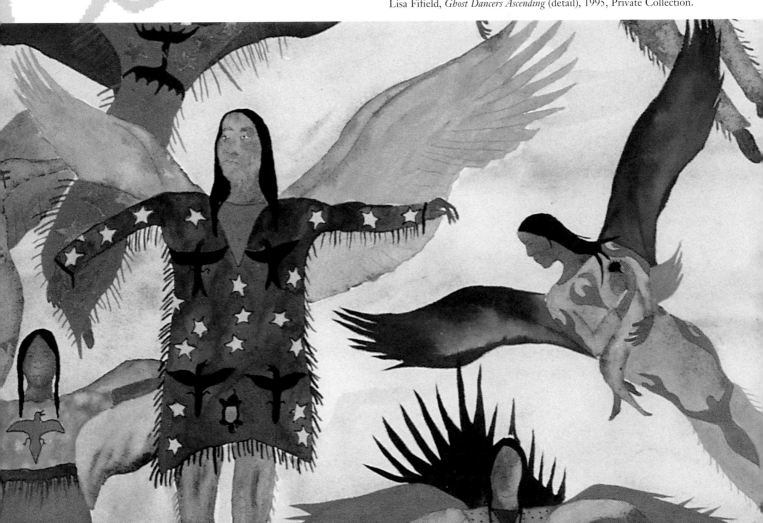

DIVERSITY IN THE UNITED STATES

Throughout the 1960s and into the 1970s, American society underwent a profound shift in attitude and structure largely as a result of three major catalysts for change: the Civil Rights Movement, the Vietnam War, and the Women's Movement. All three caused many Americans to examine and question long-held ideas and values. The quest for rights for African-Americans and for women, especially, contributed to an increased awareness on the part of many Americans of the value and power of diversity.

Economic developments also contributed to this growing sense of a diverse and pluralistic world. Beginning in the mid-1970s, marketing strategies in the United States began to shift dramatically. Instead of trying to create products that would necessarily have mass appeal, marketing experts began to shift their focus to particular interest groups, "niche" marketing as it became known. While the target audience for a "niche" product might be small in relation to the population as a whole, it might still represent millions of potential buyers. In the words of one advertising executive, "There will be no market for products that everybody likes a little, only for products that somebody likes a lot." Direct mail "lists" of similarly minded people were soon developed, and the creation of consensus as a marketing strategy gradually gave way to an approach based on the plurality and diversity of American culture and taste.

STRUCTURALISM AND DECONSTRUCTION

Beginning in the late 1960s, the work of a number of French philosophers and thinkers made a profound case for the plurality of experience and developed clear strategies for challenging the accepted cultural tradition. They established a philosophical basis for the growing acceptance of the diversity of contemporary culture. One of the most important of these thinkers was ROLAND BARTHES [BAR(t)] (1915–1980), whose early work was based on so-called "structural" linguistics, and whose approach to culture was thus called "structuralism." At the heart of structural linguistics is an approach to "meaning" that is based on the notion of the plurality of the "sign." The "sign" is composed of a ratio or relation between the so-called "signifier" and the "signified." For instance, the word "tree" is a signifier and the tree itself is the signified object. In French, the word for tree is *arbre*, in Swahili, it is *mti*. The signifier (the word) changes from language to language, then. In addition, the signified itself encompasses all possible trees. The signified is so plural and various that, on contemplation, it seems astonishing that language can enable us to communicate meaningfully at all. What determines the particulars of the tree we are talking about when we say or write the word "tree" is its context. The pine tree in the backyard is different from the oak tree in the square. Context determines meaning. It follows then, philosophically, that when we consider any object, the object's meaning is determined not by its existence in its own right but by the situation in which we observe it. And this situation is always subject to change. Thus "meaning" is never absolute. It is as plural as the situations in which it comes to exist.

What is known as "poststructuralist" thought is essentially a radical application of this way of thinking. Poststructuralist thought is based on the assumption that speech—the meaning of which is never fully "determined"—can as easily mask reality as reveal it. Barthes himself, especially in his book *Mythologies*, analyzes the myths upon which popular culture is constructed. But the chief practitioner of poststructuralist thought is the French philosopher JACQUES DERRIDA [dare-ree-DAH] (b. 1930). Derrida's method, known as **deconstruction**, consists of a thorough analysis, or taking apart, of received philosophical traditions made on the assumption that there are, in all philosophies and cultural systems, leaps in logic and inconsistencies, and that the revelation of these tells us more about the philosophy than the philosophy itself does. That is, what is not said in a philosophy is at least as important, and probably more important, than what is said. For Derrida, even the self is a fiction or construction, built out of the unexamined assumptions of traditional culture, and it, too, must be deconstructed for true understanding. In sum, in the poststructuralist mind, there are no facts, only interpretations. Such a philosophical stance, which amounts in many ways to a profound skepticism, has led to a thorough critique of much of Western philosophical thought and of the culture's so-called "truths."

PAINTING AND SCULPTURE

In art especially, diverse visions have had a considerable impact. The single most important development in the art world in the last three decades has been the rise to

Figure 24.1 Guerilla Girls, Do Women Have to be Naked to Get into the Met. Museum, 1989, poster, 11 × 28″ (27.9 × 71.1 cm), Private collection. The Guerilla Girls' posters outline an art scene that was, as late as the mid-1980s, still dominated by men, where women were either excluded or underacknowledged.

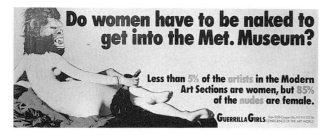

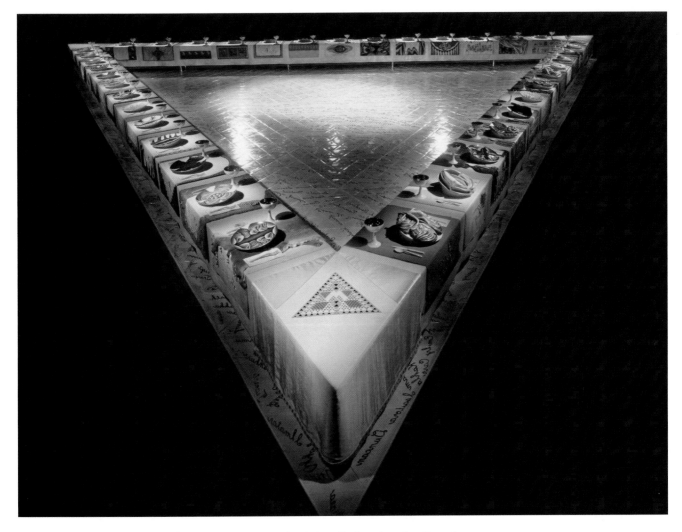

Figure 24.2 Judy Chicago, *The Dinner Party*, 1974–79, installation view, San Francisco Museum of Modern Art, mixed media, 48′ (14.63 m) on each side. Asserting the importance of the accomplishments of women throughout western history, this giant triangular table has place settings for thirty-nine specific women, arranged thirteen to a side, recalling Jesus's last supper.

prominence of visions previously excluded from the mainstream. This has been, in part, a function of the art world's ceaseless quest for innovative approaches to experience, but it is also true that the art world has become increasingly willing to acknowledge the "outsider's" point of view.

Women have contributed significantly to the contemporary visions that have gained attention in the art world. In 1970–71, only 13.5 per cent of the artists shown in New York were women. Worse, in the 1970s only 10 per cent of the shows given to living artists in New York were one-person exhibitions by women. As late as 1982, the Coalition of Women's Arts Organizations reported that only 2 per cent of museum exhibitions by living artists were given to women. In the last two decades, this has changed dramatically. The imbalance was the focus of the GUERILLA GIRLS, a group of anonymous women

artists who dressed in costume gorilla masks and plastered New York City with posters drawing the public's attention to the situation (fig. 24.1).

Judy Chicago. Probably no single woman artist has had a greater impact on the public's opinion of women in the arts than JUDY CHICAGO (b. 1939). Chicago changed her name, she explained in her memoir, *Through the Flower*, "from Judy Gerowitz to Judy Chicago as an act of identifying myself as an independent woman." In 1974, she started working on a giant sculptural installation known as *The Dinner Party* (fig. 24.2). The place settings range from the Great Goddess of prehistory and the Cretan Snake Goddess to modern novelist Virginia Woolf and painter Georgia O'Keeffe. The names of 999 other women were added to the table's runner as well. One of Chicago's most impressive achievements was her inspiration and courage in taking the arena traditionally thought of as woman's domain and transforming it into a major work of art. Chicago brought women's work and women's arts to center stage. As Carrie Richey wrote in *Artforum* magazine in 1981: "[*The Dinner Party*] is a glossary of the so-called 'lesser arts'—tatting, lace[making], weaving, making ceramic household vessels, embroidering—that women have been confined to for thousands of years. But that all these crafts have been brought together, synthesized for a ritual … [This] is just one of the canny reversals that *The Dinner Party* undertakes. It proposes that the sum of the lesser arts is great art."

Eleanor Antin.   It seemed difficult for women to "make it" in the traditional sense in the art world as painters or sculptors. Women artists turned in increasing numbers to new, experimental media, especially performance art, for innovative expression. One of the innovators of the performance art movement is ELEANOR ANTIN (b. 1935), an artist notorious for developing a series of personae, or characters, including Eleanora Antinova, a fictional black ballerina in Diaghilev's Ballets Russes. By playing Antinova, Antin freed herself to investigate aspects of her own situation that might otherwise have remained hidden or unknown. A drawing from her memoir, *Being Antinova* (fig. 24.3), indicates exactly how removed Antinova is from the traditional, Western ballet world. Not only is Antinova black, but her own sense of physical freedom contradicts the traditional regimen and routine of ballet. Imagine, she points out, a black ballerina in *Swan Lake*. The world of ballet is, in her words, a "white machine," in which Antinova experiences not only the alienation of racial prejudice but the subjugation of personal expression to the demands of "tradition."

Cindy Sherman.   The photographer CINDY SHERMAN (b. 1954) took to greater extreme Antin's idea of creating a fictional persona through which to investigate different aspects of the self. Beginning in the late 1970s, Sherman began to photograph herself in a variety of "self-portraits" called *Untitled Film Stills*

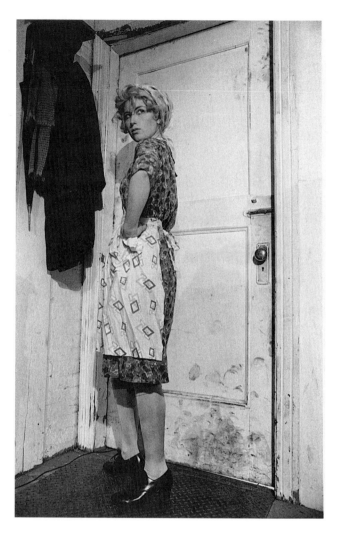

Figure 24.4   Cindy Sherman, *Untitled Film Still #35*, 1979, black-and-white photograph. In this version of herself, Sherman takes on the appearance of, say, Sophia Loren playing the part of a bedraggled Italian housewife. In other words, Sherman depicts a media image, not a real person.

(fig. 24.4). In each, Sherman wears a different wardrobe, makes herself up to look a different part, stages herself, and announces, in effect, that the "self" is a fictionalized construction. We are whoever we choose to look like. And what we choose to look like, perhaps more devastatingly, is one or another of a series of media images. Her work attempts to undermine the very idea of an "authentic" personality behind our repertoire of selves.

Susan Rothenberg.   Despite the discrimination against women working in the traditional art world, a number have nonetheless succeeded. Among the many women painters who have achieved a major place in American painting since the early 1980s is SUSAN ROTHENBERG (b. 1945), who works in New Mexico. Rothenberg achieved early success with her first exhibi-

Figure 24.3   Eleanor Antin, drawing from *Being Antinova*, 1983. The physical freedom enjoyed by Antinova in this drawing is mitigated by her exclusion from the troupe.

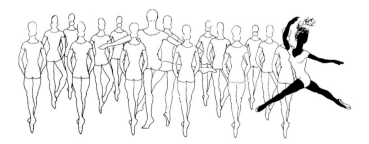

tion in New York in 1976. Rothenberg expressed surprise at so favorable a reaction to her subject matter. It is for her images of horses, as in *Axes* (fig. 24.5), painted in 1976, that she is best known.

In *Axes* a lone animal is seen moving, stark and ghostly. Rothenberg creates a hallucination, an apparition, or a dream image of an emerging animal. Simultaneously primitive and sophisticated, Rothenberg's work is characterized by rough strokes that build up the form. Color is restricted: lines are color and color is line. The entire surface is treated this way. From this fragmented weblike mesh, forms emerge, as if through a heavy fog, or from dense underbrush, effectively implying movement. In *Axes*, the axis of the center of the canvas and the axis of the horse's body are not clearly aligned, and this sense of imbalance, or what might be called "double-balance," animates the canvas.

Betye Saar. One of the most famous images in contemporary art is a Pop Art-like construction created in 1972 by artist BETYE SAAR (b. 1926) entitled *The Liberation of Aunt Jemima* (fig. 24.6). Saar's image openly acknowledges the American "popular" conception of the African-American "mammy"—Aunt Jemima of pancake and syrup fame, as ubiquitous as Campbell's soup. Aunt Jemima was conceived by white marketing experts as a symbol of surrogate motherhood, so trustworthy that any "real" mother would not hesitate to leave her child in Aunt Jemima's hands and so caring that anyone would assume that her pancakes and syrup were nourishing and wholesome. Saar transforms the trusting and caring Aunt Jemima smile into something almost sardonic. As Aunt Jemima takes up arms, with the black fist, a symbol of black power, rising in defiance across the

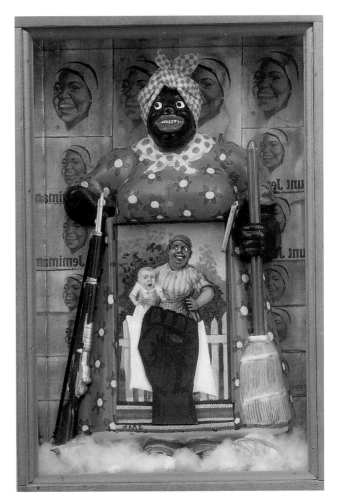

Figure 24.6 Betye Saar, *The Liberation of Aunt Jemima*, 1972, mixed media, $11\frac{3}{4} \times 8 \times 2\frac{3}{4}''$ (29.8 × 20.3 × 6.9 cm), University Art Museum, University of California at Berkeley. Saar's image not only attacks racism but sexism as well, and the expectations of the dominant culture.

Figure 24.5 Susan Rothenberg, *Axes*, 1976, synthetic polymer paint and gesso on canvas, $5'4\frac{5}{8}'' \times 8'8\frac{7}{8}''$ (1.64 × 2.66 m), Museum of Modern Art, New York. In this Neo-Expressionist work, form is suggested rather than specified, hinted at rather than defined. The perfect balance within the rectangle of the canvas is based upon the horse's implied movement to the left.

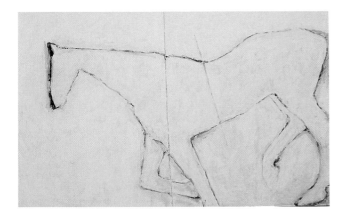

scene, the white baby is not merely unhappy, but has become terrified. Politics for Aunt Jemima are revealed; an advertising image, this figure, both servant and slave, takes matters into her own hands. The painting announces the necessity—the actuality—of change for the African-American.

Jean-Michel Basquiat. Especially brief and highly successful was the career of JEAN-MICHEL BASQUIAT (1960–1988). As a teenager in New York, Basquiat achieved notoriety as "Samo," a graffiti artist writing on walls in Soho and Tribeca. By early 1981, gallery owners in New York, Zurich, and Milan had convinced him to apply his graffiti to canvas, and soon after he became an art world media darling. The value of his paintings, which many critics found naive, rose with meteoric speed. By the time he was twenty-three years old, a work of his had already sold at a Sotheby's art auc-

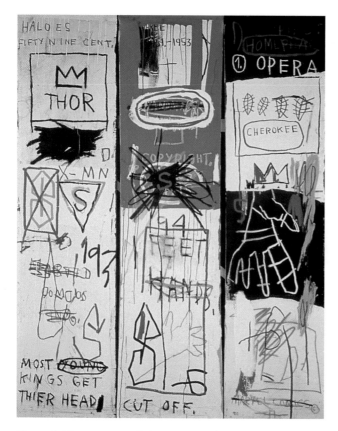

Figure 24.7 Jean-Michel Basquiat, *Charles the First*, 1982, acrylic and oilstick on canvas, triptych, 6′6″ × 5′2¼″ (1.98 × 1.58 m), Robert Miller Gallery, New York. The "X" crossing out elements in Basquiat's work is never entirely negative. In a book on symbols, Basquiat discovered a section on "Hobo Signs," marks left, graffiti-like, by hobos to inform their brethren about the lie of the local land. In this graphic language, an "X" means "O.K. All right."

tion for $19,000. Basquiat was the son of a middle-class Haitian-born accountant and his white, Puerto Rican wife, and his work possessed an aura of authenticity—raw, direct, and, stylistically at least, unmediated by tradition.

In *Charles the First* (fig. 24.7), Basquiat pays homage to one of his heroes, jazz saxophonist Charlie Parker. The immediacy of Basquiat's style is readily apparent. Notice, for instance, that he doesn't even bother to overpaint "mistakes"—he simply crosses them out and moves on. As one of Basquiat's heroes, Parker is a king—hence the painting's title, the crown, and the word "Thor" (the god of Norwegian myth). At the bottom is Basquiat's admonition to kings; the word "young"is crossed out. Parker's fall from grace is imaged everywhere in the painting, in the drips that fall from the blue field in the middle of the painting, in the X-ed out Ss, and, especially, in the way that, above the word "Cherokee," the name of one of Parker's most important compositions, one of the feathers (feathers because Parker was known as "Bird") falls into a dollar sign. It is as if the market structure of the

recording industry destroyed Parker: the dollar sign, if one considers it, is the superhero's symbol lined through.

Much of Basquiat's art is a protest against the exploitation of black heroes—Sugar Ray Robinson, Hank Aaron, Cassius Clay, Dizzy Gillespie, and Louis Armstrong—and Basquiat identified closely with them all. It is as if he knew that his own meteoric rise to fame and fortune would end in tragedy. He died at the age of twenty-seven of a drug overdose.

Judith F. Baca. Basquiat's vision has much to do with his independence from mainstream Western traditions, certainly his dismissal of traditional notions of "quality." The mural painting of Chicana artist JUDITH F. BACA (b. 1948) also asserts its independence from traditional approaches to painting, even as it recovers and revitalizes the Mexican mural tradition of "Los Tres Grandes"—Rivera, Orozco, and Siquieros (see Chapter 22). Mural painting is public art, and as a result it cannot be purchased or collected. It operates, that is, outside the art market. It is also a collaborative endeavor; many other artists participate in painting Baca's murals. "Collaboration is a requirement," Baca says, not only because the projects are large, but because they are public—the community must participate in the creation of the work.

In 1974, Baca inaugurated the Citywide Mural Project in Los Angeles, which in total completed 250 murals, 150 of which she directed herself. Since then she has continued to sponsor and direct murals through SPARC, the Social and Public Art Resource Center, which she founded. The *Great Wall of Los Angeles*, begun in 1976, is her most ambitious project. Nearly a mile long, it is located in the Tujunga Wash of the Los Angeles river, which was entirely covered with concrete by developers as Los Angeles grew. This concrete conduit is, says Baca, "a giant scar across the land which served to further divide an already divided city … Just as young Chicanos tattoo battle scars on their bodies, *Great Wall of Los Angeles* is a tattoo on a scar where the river once ran." The wall narrates the history of Los Angeles, but not the history told in textbooks. It recounts the history of indigenous peoples, immigrant minorities—Portuguese, Chinese, Japanese, Korean, and Basque, as well as Chicano—and of women from prehistory to the present. The detail reproduced here (fig. 24.8) depicts how four major freeways intersected the middle of East Los Angeles's Chicano communities, dividing them, weakening them, and turning them against each other. To the right a Mexican woman protests against the building of Dodger Stadium, which displaced a historic Mexican community in Chavez Ravine.

Baca worked on the *Great Wall* project as director and facilitator but it is nearly four hundred inner-city youths, many from the juvenile justice system, who did the actual painting and design. Rival gang members,

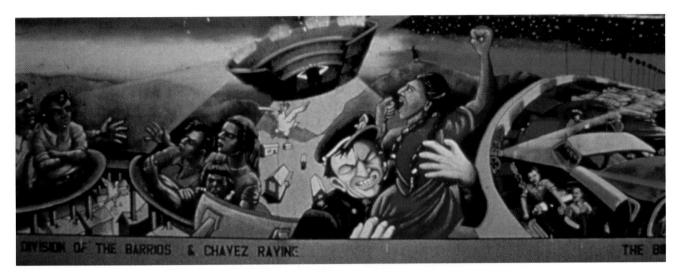

Figure 24.8 Judith F. Baca, *Great Wall of Los Angeles* (detail: Division of the Barrios and Chavez Ravine), 1976–continuing, mural, height 13′ (3.96 m) (whole mural over 1 mile long), Tujunga Wash, Los Angeles, California. The collaborative process of making murals is, in Baca's words, "the transforming of pain … rage … and shame."

of different races and from different neighborhoods, found themselves working on the project together. They represented a divided city, but Baca's goal was to help them communicate with one another and learn to work together. For Baca, the collaborative mural process heals wounds, brings people together, and helps to recreate communities that have been destroyed.

Lisa Fifield. Among the Native American painters working in the Midwest is LISA FIFIELD (b. 1957) of Iroquois-Oneida descent, who lives and works in Minnesota. Fifield has painted a large number of canvases devoted to the traditions and beliefs of Native American peoples.

Among Fifield's most important works are a series of paintings based on the slaughter of Native Americans, including women and children, at Wounded Knee at the hands of the United States Army. One painting inspired by the Wounded Knee tragedy, *Ghost Dancers Ascending* (fig. 24.9), depicts the spirits of the dead ascending, suspended in the air above the earth. The attire worn by the figures is based on the actual clothing worn by the American Indians killed at Wounded Knee, clothing their wearers mistakenly believed could not be pierced by bullets. Fifield depicts their transcendent spirits rising above the material fact of their physical death in a painting vibrant with primary colors and deeply reverential in spirit.

The Ghost Dance was developed by the Plains Indians in the 1890s after they had lost their ancestral lands and had been relegated to reservations. They danced for the return of warriors, for the return of the bison that had been slaughtered, and the reestablishment of their former way of life.

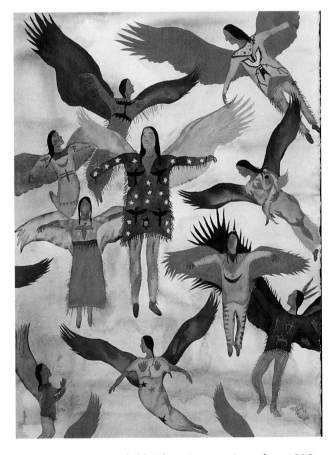

Figure 24.9 Lisa Fifield, *Ghost Dancers Ascending*, 1995, watercolor on paper, 30 × 22″ (76.2 × 55.9 cm), Private Collection. Fifield depicts the spirits rising above the battlefield at Wounded Knee, their powerful colors and effortless floating making them seem to transcend their tragic deaths.

Jaune Quick-to-See Smith.   A sense of social injustice is captured forcefully in the work of JAUNE QUICK-TO-SEE SMITH (b. 1940), a Native American painter of the Salish and Kootenai Confederation. In her 1991 *Paper Dolls for a Post Columbian World with Ensembles Contributed by the U.S. Government* (fig. 24.10), she depicts her ancestors of Montana's Flathead tribe as Ken and Barbie paper dolls, together with their son Bruce. Their Anglicized first names stand in direct opposition to their Native American family name, Plenty Horses, a name suggesting high status in previous generations, since horses were a measure of wealth in the Native American community. Overseeing the entire scene is Father Le de Ville, the Jesuit priest who has "civilized" them. At the bottom is a traditional headdress "collected by white people to decorate their home after priests and the U.S. government banned cultural ways such as

speaking Salish, practicing religion and drumming, singing, or dancing. Sold at Sotheby's [fine art auctioneers] today for thousands of dollars to white collectors seeking romance in their lives." Ken's suit for receiving government rations is at the left, below his "special outfit" for trading land to the whites for whiskey, a traditional blanket. Barbie's outfit is a maid's uniform "for cleaning houses of white people after good education at Catholic or government boarding school." To the bottom right are the two most horrific costumes of all, "matching small pox suits for all our Indian families." The entire piece protests against the colonization of Native Americans and the lack of respect for their traditions.

Maya Lin and the Vietnam Veterans' Memorial. The Vietnam Veterans' Memorial in Washington, D.C. (fig. 24.11) was constructed and dedicated in 1982. Funded entirely by contributions from corporations, foundations, unions, veterans, civic organizations, and nearly three million individuals, the memorial achieved the wishes of the charitable organization founded to establish it: to begin a process of national reconciliation.

The memorial was designed by MAYA YING LIN (b. 1960), at the time a twenty-one-year-old graduate architectural student at Yale University. Lin, who won a national competition that included more than 1400 design submissions, is an American woman of Chinese descent who described herself then as "a country girl from Athens, Ohio," the town where her parents, who fled China before the Communist takeover in 1949, were professors. She wished to establish the memorial in a quiet protected place where it would harmonize with its surroundings, which include the Washington Monument and the Lincoln Memorial, toward which its two walls point. On the surface of polished black granite are inscribed the more than 58,000 names of those killed or missing in action during the war. Viewed from a distance, the wall is shaped like a giant V, whose vertex is set at an angle of approximately 125 degrees. Some have described the two sides of the walls as "arms," which embrace those who enter the memorial. In walking toward the vertex of the wall, where its two arms meet, viewers move back into history. At one end of the wall are inscribed the names of the first casualties, which then continue in chronological order of their dying to the other end, thus symbolically denoting the span of United States' involvement in the war. Taken together, the names represent the sum of the sacrifices made, providing each individual with a place in the country's historical memory. As Maya Lin said about the design for the memorial, "The names would become the memorial."

More than any other national monument, the Vietnam Veterans' War Memorial has won national approval and respect, despite some dissenting voices at first. Thousands visit the memorial every year; many

Figure 24.10   Jaune Quick-to-See Smith, *Paper Dolls for a Post Columbian World with Ensembles Contributed by the U.S. Government*, 1991, pastel and pencil on paper, 40 × 29″ (102 × 73 cm), Steinbaum Krauss Gallery, New York. The box in the lower center of this contains all-"white" supplies furnished the Native American community by the federal government, including "canned milk which gives us lactose intolerance, white sugar which gives us diabetes, white flour which gives us wheat allergies, and lard which gives us gall bladder trouble."

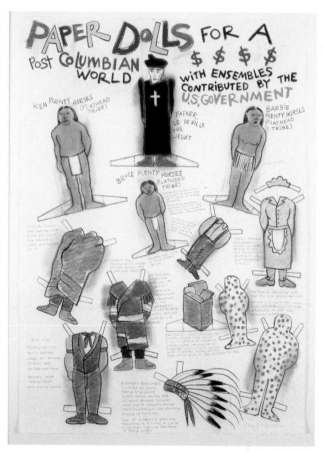

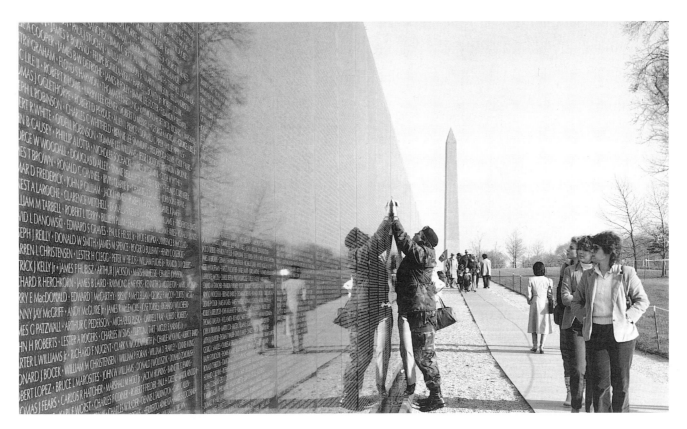

Figure 24.11   Maya Lin, Vietnam Veterans' Memorial, Washington, D.C., 1982, black granite, length 250′ (820.21 m). Known simply as "the Wall," this memorial tribute to those killed in the Vietnam War has become a national symbol of recognition and reconciliation.

return again and again. The wall represents not just one war but all wars, the multiplicity of names and the multiplicity of wars extending from horizon to horizon. As viewers look at the names on the wall's granite slabs, which are polished to a mirror-like sheen, they see themselves reflected in the wall's surface. As in a ritual, visitors more often than not touch the names on the wall, as if to put themselves in contact with the individuals who died, and murmur a prayer. Visitors come away profoundly moved by the wall's homage to suffering and death and to the sense that here healing and reconciliation can begin.

THE DIVERSITY OF AMERICAN VOICES

Adrienne Rich.   Perhaps no other voice has spoken more passionately for the liberation of women and men from a prejudice that blinds perception and stunts the mind than ADRIENNE RICH (b. 1929). Rich has become an important spokeswoman for feminist consciousness.

Although Rich is associated with radical feminist ideology, she is not readily constrained by it. Her prose and poetry, while rooted in ideological concerns, nonetheless dramatize a self-discovering freedom in language and art.

In her best writing, Rich is less a polemicist and publicist than an artist who challenges readers' preconceptions about women, especially those involving their relationships to men and to one another.

In "When We Dead Awaken: Writing as Re-Vision," Rich has charted the changing perception of herself as woman and poet. She describes how she needed to change the images that represented, for her, ideals of both woman and poet, since her images of both had been dominated by men. She explores the concept of re-vision, which she considers "the act of looking back, of seeing with fresh eyes." It is an act essential for writers. And as Rich insists, it is essential for women living in a male-dominated society. Re-vision is "an act of survival."

Over the course of her career, she has been a vocal defender of women's rights in all areas, including female sexuality. Herself a lesbian, Rich defines lesbianism as more than a sexual preference. It is "a sense of desiring oneself, choosing oneself," Rich states, part of the formation of identity, the self's power to discover and define itself. It is also, as she has remarked, "a primary intensity between women," which energizes them, propels them toward one another, both challenging and charging their imaginations.

Cross Currents

THE CYBERNETIC SCULPTURE OF WEN-YING TSAI

Cybernetic sculpture fuses art and technology. Through electronic feedback control systems that include high-frequency lights, microphones, and harmonic vibration, a work of cybernetic sculpture such as Wen-Ying Tsai's *Cybernetic Sculpture, 1979* comes to life when music is played or hands are clapped in its presence (fig. 24.12). The photograph here makes the figure appear two-dimensional, but it is a three-dimensional sculpture.

Cybernetic Sculpture is constructed of a series of fiberglass rods about 10 feet in height. Each rod is set on a base under which is a small motor. With the motors beneath each base switched on, the rods vibrate slowly but remain perfectly vertical. When stimulated by sound and light, they vibrate synchronously in gently swaying arcs. As long as the stimuli continue, the rods undu-late in elegant dance-like movement.

Tsai's cybernetic sculptures are self-organizing systems that maintain equilibrium whether in motion or at rest. His works blend not only art and technology, but also Eastern and Western traditions. In fulfilling what Hsieh Ho, a fifth-century Chinese master, identifies as the primary requirement of all art—"rhythmic vitality, a kind of spiritual rhythm expressed in the movement of life"—Tsai's cybernetic sculpture takes its place in a long-established Chinese aesthetic.

Another way Tsai's cybernetic sculpture reflects Chinese aesthetic ideals is in its harmonious blending of the human, the mechanical, and the natural. Each of the elements of a Tsai sculpture contributes harmoniously to the unity of the whole. The spirit of his sculpture is Taoist, as are its effects—a refined equilibrium that merges wisdom with wit, seriousness with humor, mysticism with modernity.

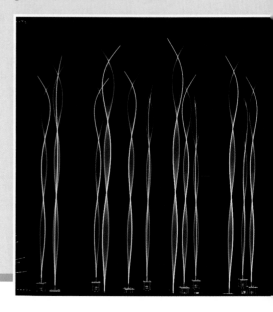

Figure 24.12 Wen-Ying Tsai, *Cybernetic Sculpture*, 1979, fiberglass mounted on steel plates covering an electronic feedback system, 10 × 10′ (3.05 × 3.05 m) Taiwan Museum of Art. The work responds to changes in light and sound by vibrating with graceful, dance-like undulations.

Maxine Hong Kingston. One of the characteristics of contemporary writing is the way literary works combine elements from different genres. Writers often blend fiction with autobiography. The autobiographical novel *The Woman Warrior* (1976), by Chinese-American writer MAXINE HONG KINGSTON (b. 1940), has been described by the author as "the book of her mother" since it is filled with stories her mother told her, stories about her Chinese ancestors, especially the women whom Kingston describes as the ghosts of her girlhood. A second book, *China Men* (1980), is her father's book; it tells the stories of her male ancestors, including her father and grandfathers, although she learned these male stories from women, mostly from her mother. Mixing fact and fiction, autobiography and legend, Kingston's books combine in imaginative ways family history with fictional invention. Kingston's identity as a Chinese-American woman and her attempts to create images of her experience reveal a complexity in her relationship to her ancestral past.

The stories Kingston recounts and invents in *The Woman Warrior* and in *China Men* derive from an oral tradition—the Chinese "talk story," a Cantonese tradition kept alive mainly by women. The talk-story narrators of Kingston's books tell their stories in multiple versions, varying the amount of detail each reveals. Kingston's narrators' stories contain silences that invite the reader to engage in the imaginative world of the writer, who occasionally hints at her fictionalizing imagination with cues such as "I wonder," "perhaps," and "may have." These and other cues reveal how one writer signals to readers the shift from fact to fiction.

By inscribing her mother's stories and imagining her own variants of them, Kingston marks the talk-story tradition with her own distinctive imaginative imprint. In the process, she demonstrates the power of these stories to enthrall readers outside the Chinese cultural tradition. To some extent, Kingston's work appeals to women precisely because she gives public voice to things women had spoken only in private or not at all. She also transmits to us her Cantonese heritage. However, through her imaginative sympathy and literary artistry, Kingston invents a world and constructs a self that are at once strange and familiar, both "other" and inherently recognizable.

Toni Morrison. African-American writers are among the most prolific working today. One important voice is 1996 Nobel Prize winner TONI MORRISON (b. 1931). Morrison's novels focus on revealing the complexities of African-American communities, particularly the balance between personal identity and social identity required as a member of a minority American race. Mixing feminist concerns with racial and cultural issues, Morrison's fiction explores the cultural inheritance of African-Americans facing hardship and conflict through memory, relationships, and actions.

In her first novel, *The Bluest Eye* (1969), Morrison explores what it is like to be of mixed descent—white and black—and thus light-skinned, capturing not only racial prejudices based on color but also the tragedy of unrecognized beauty. In *Sula* (1973), she portrays the family consequences of a woman achieving her own independence and freedom, and in *Song of Solomon* (1977), she portrays a black man's attempt to come to terms with his roots. The power of eroticism is the subject of *Tar Baby* (1981), and *Beloved* (1987) explores the degrading effects of slavery. Though every book is deeply embedded in pain, Morrison's work is about survival, and the very urgency with which she writes seems to further her own unending quest to survive. "I think about what black writers do," she has said, "as having a quality of hunger and disturbance that never ends."

Sandra Cisneros. Contemporary American literature is rich in Chicano and Hispanic voices and perspectives. The poet and fiction writer SANDRA CISNEROS [sis-NAIR-oss] (b. 1954), of Mexican and American descent, explores how art and talent survive the most adverse of circumstances. Her Hispanic female characters who live amidst an alien culture repeatedly exemplify the struggle to find a place in our society. In each story, beleaguered Chicana girls and women seize control of their lives, somehow rejecting or transcending the limitations placed upon them. Works such as *Loose Woman* (1994), a collection of poems, and the novel *Woman Hollering Creek* (1991) reveal Cisneros's rebellious side, while others, such as *House on Mango Street* (1994) reflect her sense of ethnic pride.

Judith Ortiz Cofer. From Puerto Rico, JUDITH ORTIZ COFER [CO-fur] (b. 1952) has published poetry and prose, in volumes such as *Silent Dancing* and *The Latin Deli*. These display Cofer's knack for conveying the experience of the lives of immigrants with vivacity and compassion. Her stories, both autobiographical and fictional, show characters' conflicts with their new lives in mainland America and their memories of Puerto Rico.

Cofer's stories, poems, and autobiographical essays analyze and celebrate the double perspective of seeing life through the lens of two cultures and languages. Her work is elegant and lyrical and possesses a vigorous and convincing authority.

Oscar Hijuelos. Prominent Hispanic Caribbean writers include OSCAR HIJUELOS [hi-YAIL-oss] (b. 1951), whose fiction captures the pre-Castro immigrant experience in the U.S., particularly in New York. His novel *The Mambo Kings Play Songs of Love* won the Pulitzer Prize in 1990, the first book by a writer of Hispanic origin to win the prestigious award. In chronicling the lives of Cuban immigrants, their quest for the American dream, and their ultimate disillusionment, Hijuelos evokes the social and musical environment of the 1950s. Throughout his work Hijuelos explores the influence of Hispanic culture on American popular culture. His fascination with the diverse cultural threads woven into the fabric of contemporary American life brims over in his pages. An important influence on younger Hispanic Caribbean and Latino writers, Hijuelos captures and celebrates the singular spirit of place, a particular locus that inspires his work and in which his values and rooted. He emphasizes the necessity for preserving cultural heritage in the face of pressure to blend into the majority American culture. Yet Hijuelos also revels in the way contemporary life reflects a mosaic of cultural inflections.

N. Scott Momaday. The works of N. SCOTT MOMADAY [MOHM-ah-day] (b. 1934) were among the first of those written by Native Americans to garner attention from a wide audience. Born in Oklahoma of Kiowa ancestry, Momaday has written poetry, fiction, and autobiography. His 1969 novel, *House Made of Dawn*, won a Pulitzer Prize. In it a young Native American man returns from military service in Vietnam to find himself without a place in either Indian society or in mainstream America. Momaday's two autobiographical works, *The Way to Rainy Mountain* (1969) and *The Names* (1976), display his ability to mingle Kiowa legends with American history and with his family's personal experience.

Leslie Marmon Silko. LESLIE MARMON SILKO (b. 1948) has written poetry and prose that reflects her mixed ancestry: she is descended from the Laguna tribe but has white and Mexican ancestry as well. Her novel *Ceremony* (1978), the first published by a Native American woman, and her collection of prose and poetry *Storyteller* (1981) both emphasize the cultural values and spirit of her Pueblo ancestors. *Ceremony* makes a connection between the shared cultural heritage of the tribal community and the experience of a contemporary Native American Indian veteran of the Vietnam War, who returns to his Pueblo reservation to reclaim a sense of personal and social identity. *Storyteller*, a collection of tribal folktales, family anecdotes, photographs, stories, and poems, reflects the intersection of the spiritual and material worlds, as well as connections between history and personal experience. Like much of Silko's writing, the relationship between nature and culture permeates this work, emphasizing the way Native American peoples have lived in harmony with the natural world, the land becoming part of their identity, and not merely a place to live.

Then & Now

NAVIGATING THE WEB

Perhaps no single technological development has succeeded in "shrinking" the scope of the world more than the development of the Internet, and its network, the World Wide Web, which links almost immediately every computer connected to it around the globe.

Not only is text available on the Web, but also images, videos, sound, and film. At the time of writing, over five hundred museum and gallery sites are accessible on the Web, including such sites as the A.I.R. Gallery in New York (women artists), the Andy Warhol Museum in Pittsburgh, and the Louvre in Paris, where one can view such works as Leonardo's *Mona Lisa* (see Chapter 13), or Géricault's *Raft of the "Medusa"* (see Chapter 18). By seeking out museums and galleries in different countries around the globe, it is possible to view both traditional and contemporary work by artists from over fifty countries worldwide. You can browse the collection of the Ho-Am Art Museum in Seoul, Korea, viewing masterpieces from its painting, ceramics, and bronze collections, or you can tour galleries in Taipei, Taiwan.

There are many other sites as well. You can watch a video clip of a war dance by the Anlo-Ewe people of Ghana, West Africa, or listen to music samples from the newest CD releases in South America. Alternatively, you can browse the current issue of *Critical Inquiry*, one of the most important scholarly journals in the United States, or check out *LIVEculture*, an on-line publication of the Institute for Learning Technologies at Columbia University, which focuses on contemporary art, literature, media, communications, and cultural studies. The possibilities are almost unlimited, and the availability of up-to-date information about almost anything is totally unprecedented. The World Wide Web promises to change permanently the way in which we learn about the world around us.

THE GLOBAL VILLAGE

Probably no event symbolizes awakening tolerance in the contemporary world between diverse cultures more than the opening of the Berlin Wall in November 1989, and, in turn, the collapse of the Communist regime in the Soviet Union two years later. For the first time since World War II, the citizens of the two Germanies were able to come together freely and openly. The implications for Europe as a whole were enormous. As VACLAV HAVEL (b. 1936), the president of the Czech Republic, put it in 1993: "All of us—whether from the west, the east, the south, or the north of Europe—can agree that the common basis of any effort to integrate Europe is the wealth of values and ideas we share … All of us respect the principle of unity in diversity and share a determination to foster creative cooperation between the different nations and ethnic, religious, and cultural groups—and the different spheres of civilization—that exist in Europe." Havel's message is easily extended to the globe as a whole. We have increasingly come to recognize and accept a worldwide imperative. We now live in a pluralistic global community of nearly five billion people. To survive and thrive, we need to communicate and share with one another as if we lived in a single village.

MAGICIANS OF THE EARTH

In 1989, an exhibition in Paris, France, announced itself as "the first worldwide exhibition of contemporary art." Called *Magiciens de la terre*, or *Magicians of the Earth*, the show consisted of works by one hundred artists, fifty from the traditional "centers" of Western culture (Europe and America) and fifty from Asia, South America, Australia, Africa, and, incidentally, Native American art from North America. It was, in the words of Thomas McEvilley, an American art critic, "a major event in the social history of art," if not in its aesthetic history.

Organizationally, it was something of a failure, but unity of approach was, perhaps, not the point. While it was difficult for most viewers to detect coherent themes or influences among artists and cultures, the exhibition sought, in McEvilley's words, to arrive at "a new definition of history that will not involve ideas of hierarchy, or of mainstream and periphery, and a new, global sense of civilization," exhibiting works "in a neutral, loose, unsystematic way that would not imply transcultural value judgments." The exhibition succeeded in underscoring the diversity and plurality of world art. As the exhibition's chief curator, Jean-Hubert Martin, put it, "Rather than showing that abstraction is a universal language, or that the return to figuration is now happening everywhere in the world, I want to show the *real differences* and the specificity of different cultures."

THE EXAMPLE OF AUSTRALIAN ABORIGINAL PAINTING

No better example of difference can be found than the art of the Australian Aborigines. Ceremonial body, rock, and ground paintings were made for centuries by the Aboriginal peoples of Central Australia's Western Desert region. The sand painting in the installation view of the *Magicians of the Earth* (fig. 24.13) is one such work, executed on the spot by the Yuendumu community. Today, Aboriginal artists are best known for their acrylic paintings, which were not produced in the region until 1971. In that year, a young white art teacher named Geoff Bardon arrived in Papunya, a settlement on the edge of the Western Desert organized by the government to provide health care, education, and housing for the Aborigines. Several older Aboriginal men became interested in Bardon's classes, and he encouraged them to paint in acrylic, using traditional motifs. Between July 1971 and August 1972, they produced 620 paintings, which were subsequently sold. Money was clearly a major factor in prompting this explosion of work. In 1984, for instance, the women of one village took up painting to buy a truck.

Each painted design still carries with it its traditional ceremonial power. It is also considered actual proof of the identity of those who made it. The organizing logic of most Aboriginal art is the "Dreaming," a system of belief unlike that of most other religions in the world. The Dreaming is not literal dreaming, not what goes on in that other world we inhabit in our sleep. For the Aborigine, the Dreaming is the presence, or mark, of an ancestral being in the world. Images of these beings—representations of the myths about them, maps of their travels, depictions of the places and landscapes they inhabited—make up the great bulk of Aboriginal art. The Australian landscape is thought of, in fact, as a series of marks made upon the earth by the Dreaming.

Geography itself is thus full of meaning and history. And painting is understood as a concise vocabulary of abstract gestures conceived to depict this geography.

Each painting depicts a Dreaming for which the artist is *kirda*. Artists are *kirda* if they have inherited the "rights" to the Dreaming from their father. Every Dreaming is also inherited through the mother's line, and a person who is related to a Dreaming in this way is said to be *kurdungurlu*. *Kurdungurlu* must insure that the *kirda* fulfill their proper social and ritual obligations to the Dreaming. As a result, several people usually work on any given painting. The person that Westerners designate as the "artist"—a distinction not employed in Aboriginal culture before the advent of acrylic painting—is generally the person who has chosen the specific Dreaming to be depicted.

Erna Motna's *Bushfire and Corroboree Dreaming* (fig. 24.14) depicts the preparations for a corroboree, or celebration ceremony. The circular features at the top and bottom of the painting represent small bushfires that have been started by women. As small animals run from the fire (symbolized by the small red dots at the edge of each circle), they are caught by the women and hit with digging sticks, also visible around each fire, and then carried with fruit and vegetables to the central fire, the site of the *corroboree* itself.

Unlike most other forms of Aboriginal art, acrylic paintings are permanent and are not destroyed after

Figure 24.13   Installation view of *Magiciens de la terre* (*Magicians of the Earth*), La Villette, Paris, 1989. This exhibition attempted to put works from the "third world" beside works from the West in a non-judgmental way. Here a sand painting by the Australian aboriginal Yuendumu community lies on the floor beneath English artist Richard Long's *Red Earth Circle*.

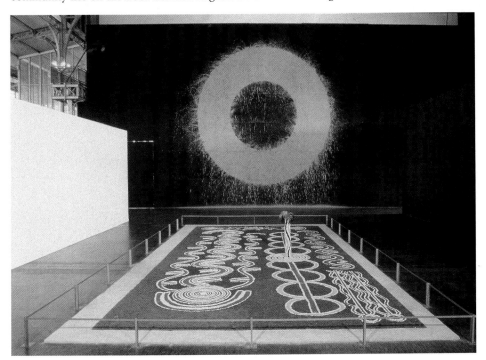

Timeline 24.1 Late twentieth-century diversity.

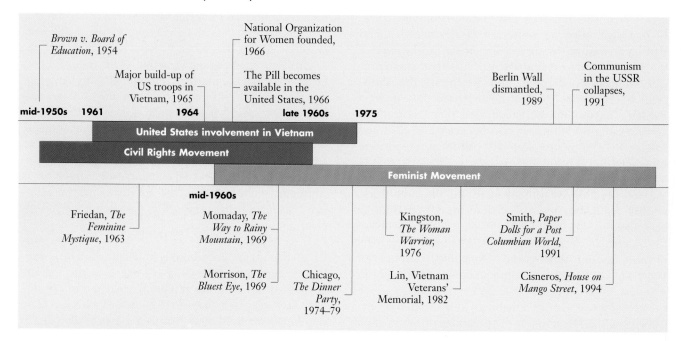

Brown v. Board of Education, 1954		National Organization for Women founded, 1966	

Major build-up of US troops in Vietnam, 1965

The Pill becomes available in the United States, 1966

Berlin Wall dismantled, 1989

Communism in the USSR collapses, 1991

mid-1950s **1961** **1964** **late 1960s** **1975**

United States involvement in Vietnam

Civil Rights Movement

Feminist Movement

mid-1960s

Friedan, *The Feminine Mystique*, 1963

Momaday, *The Way to Rainy Mountain*, 1969

Kingston, *The Woman Warrior*, 1976

Smith, *Paper Dolls for a Post Columbian World*, 1991

Morrison, *The Bluest Eye*, 1969

Chicago, *The Dinner Party*, 1974–79

Lin, Vietnam Veterans' Memorial, 1982

Cisneros, *House on Mango Street*, 1994

serving the ceremonial purposes for which they were produced. In this sense, the paintings have tended to turn dynamic religious practice into static representations, and even worse, into commodities. Conflicts have arisen over the potential revelation of secret ritual information in the paintings, and the star status bestowed upon certain, particularly younger, painters has had destructive effects on traditional hierarchies within the community. On the other hand, these paintings have tended to revitalize and strengthen cultural traditions that were, as late as the 1960s, thought to be doomed to extinction as Westerners gained footholds in the Australian desert region.

The major difference between Western art and the art of other, non-Western cultures, as Aboriginal painting makes clear, is that the latter is often participatory and ceremony-based. Even when we can identify the "artist"—Erna Motna, for instance—it is his or her relationship to the whole community that is emphasized as well as the work's place in community life as a ceremonial object. In the West, on the other hand, the work of art tends to be a commodity, the artist a solitary individual, and the audience non-participants, mere spectators.

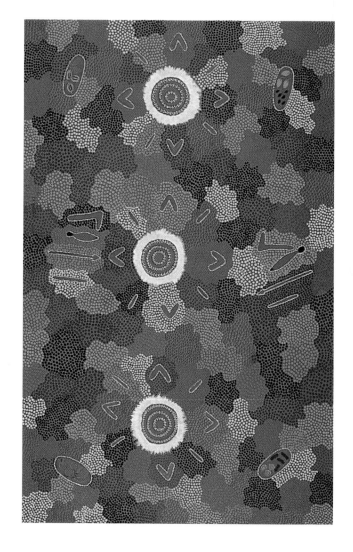

Figure 24.14 Erna Motna, *Bushfire and Corroboree Dreaming*, 1988, acrylic on canvas, 48 × 32" (121.9 × 81.3 cm), Australia Gallery, New York. Surrounding each of the three fires—the white circles in the painting—are a number of weapons used to kill larger animals—boomerangs, spears, *nulla nullas* (clubs), and *woomeras* (spear throwers).

Still, aspects of each approach inform most art made today in the global village. On the wall behind the Yuendumu sand painting at the *Magicians of the Earth* exhibition was a large circle made by English artist Richard Long. It was, in fact, made of mud that Long had collected on a visit to the Yuendumu community. Its juxtaposition with the Yuendumu sand painting bestowed on it a ritual power it otherwise lacked. At the same time it dominated the room like a giant colonist's eyeball, gazing down upon the Yuendumu sand painting in a gesture of Western mastery and control. Such give-and-take is the distinctive feature of the global village. As Jean-Hubert Martin explained: "Successful and dominant countries impose their laws and styles on other countries, but they also borrow from them and so become permeated by other ways of life. The notion of cultural identity . . . is the product of a static concept of human activity, whereas culture is always the result of an ever-moving dynamic of exchanges."

READINGS

✦ Adrienne Rich
"XIII (Dedications)"

In this section from An Atlas of the Difficult World, *Adrienne Rich addresses her readers directly, reassuring them of the value and importance of what they are doing as they go about their lives. The speaker/poet embraces a variety of imagined readers, none of them great, or wise, or rich, but still hungry for truth and understanding of a world that weighs heavily on each of us.*

I know you are reading this poem
late, before leaving your office
of the one intense yellow lamp-spot and the darkening
    window
in the lassitude of a building faded to quiet
long after rush-hour. I know you are reading
    this poem   5
standing up in a bookstore far from the ocean
on a grey day of early spring, faint flakes driven
across the plains' enormous spaces around you.
I know you are reading this poem
in a room where too much has happened for you to
    bear   10
where the bedclothes lie in stagnant coils on the bed
and the open valise speaks of flight
but you cannot leave yet. I know you are reading this
    poem
as the underground train loses momentum and before
    running up the stairs
toward a new kind of love   15
your life has never allowed.
I know you are reading this poem by the light
of the television screen where soundless images jerk
    and slide

while you wait for the newscast from the *intifada*.
I know you are reading this poem in a waiting-room   20
of eyes met and unmeeting, of identity with strangers.
I know you are reading this poem by fluorescent light
in the boredom and fatigue of the young who are
    counted out,
count themselves out, at too early an age. I know
you are reading this poem through your failing sight,
    the thick   25
lens enlarging these letters beyond all meaning yet you
    read on
because even the alphabet is precious.
I know you are reading this poem as you pace beside
    the stove
warming milk, a crying child on your shoulder, a book
    in your hand
because life is short and you too are thirsty.   30
I know you are reading this poem which is not in your
    language
guessing at some words while others keep you reading
and I want to know which words they are.
I know you are reading this poem listening for
    something, torn between bitterness and hope
turning back once again to the task you cannot refuse. 35
I know you are reading this poem because there is
    nothing else left to read
there where you have landed, stripped as you are.

✦ Maxine Hong Kingston
from *The Woman Warrior*

In the following section from Kingston's The Woman Warrior, *readers overhear a story reputedly told by Kingston's mother to the young writer, a story she was not to repeat, and which haunts her all her life. This section of the book describes the tension between the Chinese culture of Kingston's ancestors and her own American cultural world. Kingston emphasizes the cultural distance between China and America, past and present, and the divided worlds of men and women.*

No Name Woman

"You must not tell anyone," my mother said, "what I am about to tell you. In China your father had a sister who killed herself. She jumped into the family well. We say that your father has all brothers because it is as if she had never been born.

"In 1924 just a few days after our village celebrated seventeen hurryup weddings—to make sure that every young man who went 'out on the road' would responsibly come home—your father and his brothers and your grandfather and his brothers and your aunt's new husband sailed for America, the Gold Mountain. It was your grandfather's last trip. Those lucky enough to get contracts waved goodbye from the decks. They fed and guarded the stowaways and helped them off in Cuba, New York, Bali, Hawaii. "We'll meet in California next year," they said. All of them sent money home.

"I remember looking at your aunt one day when she and I were dressing; I had not noticed before that she had such a protruding melon of a stomach. But I did not think, "She's pregnant," until she began to look like other pregnant women, her shirt pulling and the white tops of her black pants showing. She could not have been pregnant, you see, because her husband had been gone for years. No one said anything. We did not discuss it. In early summer she was ready to have the child, long after the time when it could have been possible.

"The village had also been counting. On the night the baby was to be born the villagers raided our house. Some were crying. Like a great saw, teeth strung with lights, files of people walked zigzag across our land, tearing the rice. Their lanterns doubled in the disturbed black water, which drained away through the broken bunds. As the villagers closed in, we could see that some of them, probably men and women we knew well, wore white masks. The people with long hair hung it over their faces. Women with short hair made it stand up on end. Some had tied white bands around their foreheads, arms, and legs.

"At first they threw mud and rocks at the house. Then they threw eggs and began slaughtering our stock. We could hear the animals scream their deaths—the roosters, the pigs, a last great roar from the ox. Familiar wild heads flared in our night windows; the villagers encircled us. Some of the faces stopped to peer at us, their eyes rushing like search-lights. The hands flattened against the panes, framed heads, and left red prints.

"The villagers broke in the front and the back doors at the same time, even though we had not locked the doors against them. Their knives dripped with the blood of our animals. They smeared blood on the doors and walls. One woman swung a chicken, whose throat she had slit, splatter-ing blood in red arcs about her. We stood together in the middle of our house, in the family hall with the pictures and tables of the ancestors around us and looked straight ahead.

"At that time the house had only two wings. When the men came back we would build two more to enclose our courtyard and a third one to begin a second courtyard. The villagers pushed through both wings, even your grandpar-ents' rooms, to find your aunt's, which was also mine until the men returned. From this room a new wing for one of the younger families would grow. They ripped up her clothes and shoes and broke her combs, grinding them underfoot. They tore her work from the loom. They scat-tered the cooking fire and rolled the new weaving in it. We could hear them in the kitchen breaking our bowls and banging the pots. They overturned the great waist-high earthenware jugs; duck eggs, pickled fruits, vegetables burst out and mixed in acrid torrents. The old woman from the next field swept a broom through the air and loosed the spirits-of-the-broom over our heads. "Pig." "Ghost." "Pig," they sobbed and scolded while they ruined our house.

"When they left, they took sugar and oranges to bless themselves. They cut pieces from the dead animals. Some of them took bowls that were not broken and clothes that were not torn. Afterward we swept up the rice and sewed it back up into sacks. But the smells from the spilled preserves lasted. Your aunt gave birth in the pigsty that night. The next morning when I went up for the water, I found her and the baby plugging up the family well.

"Don't let your father know that I told you. He denies her. Now that you have started to menstruate, what hap-pened to her could happen to you. Don't humiliate us. You wouldn't like to be forgotten as if you had never been born. The villagers are watchful."

Whenever she had to warn us about life, my mother told stories that ran like this one, a story to grow up on. She tested our strength to establish realities. Those in the emi-grant generations who could not reassert brute survival died young and far from home. Those of us in the first American generations have had to figure out how the invisible world the emigrants built around our childhoods fit in solid America.

The emigrants confused the gods by diverting their curses, misleading them with crooked streets and false names. They must try to confuse their offspring as well, who, I suppose, threaten them in similar ways—always try-ing to get things straight, always trying to name the unspeakable. The Chinese I know hide their names; sojourners take new names when their lives change and guard their real names with silence.

Chinese-Americans, when you try to understand what things in you are Chinese, how do you separate what is peculiar to childhood, to poverty, insanities, one family, your mother who marked your growing with stories, from what is Chinese? What is Chinese tradition and what is the movies?

If I want to learn what clothes my aunt wore, whether flashy or ordinary, I would have to begin, "Remember Father's drowned-in-the-well sister?" I cannot ask that. My mother has told me once and for all the useful parts. She will add nothing unless powered by Necessity, a riverbank that guides her life. She plants vegetable gardens rather than lawns; she carries the odd-shaped tomatoes home from the fields and eats food left for the gods.

Whenever we did frivolous things, we used up energy; we flew high kites. We children came up off the ground over the melting cones our parents brought home from work and the American movie on New Years' Day—*Oh, You Beautiful Doll* with Betty Grable one year, and *She Wore a Yellow Ribbon* with John Wayne another year. After the one carni-val ride each, we paid in guilt; our tired father counted his change on the dark walk home.

Adultery is extravagance. Could people who hatch their own chicks and eat the embryos and the heads for delicacies and boil the feet in vinegar for party food, leaving only the gravel, eating even the gizzard lining—could such people engender a prodigal aunt? To be a woman, to have a daugh-ter in starvation time was a waste enough. My aunt could not have been the lone romantic who gave up everything for sex. Women in the old China did not choose. Some man had commanded her to lie with him and be his secret evil. I wonder whether he masked himself when he joined the raid on her family.

Perhaps she encountered him in the fields or on the mountain where the daughters-in-law collected fuel. Or perhaps he first noticed her in the marketplace. He was not a stranger because the village housed no strangers. She had to have dealings with him other than sex. Perhaps he worked an adjoining field, or he sold her the cloth for the dress she sewed and wore. His demand must have surprised, then terrified her. She obeyed him; she always did as she was told.

When the family found a young man in the next village to be her husband, she stood tractably beside the best rooster, his proxy, and promised before they met that she would be his forever. She was lucky that he was her age and she would be the first wife, an advantage secure now. The night she first saw him, he had sex with her. Then he left for America. She had almost forgotten what he looked like. When she tried to envision him, she only saw the black and white face in the group photograph the men had had taken before leaving.

The other man was not, after all, much different from her husband. They both gave orders: she followed. "If you tell your family, I'll beat you. I'll kill you. Be here again next week." No one talked sex, ever. And she might have separated the rapes from the rest of living if only she did not have to buy her oil from him or gather wood in the same forest. I want her fear to have lasted just as long as rape lasted so that the fear could have been contained. No drawn-out fear. But women at sex hazarded birth and hence lifetimes. The fear did not stop but permeated everywhere. She told the man, "I think I'm pregnant." He organized the raid against her.

On nights when my mother and father talked about their life back home, sometimes they mentioned an "outcast table" whose business they still seemed to be settling, their voices tight. In a commensal tradition, where food is precious, the powerful older people made wrongdoers eat alone. Instead of letting them start separate new lives like the Japanese, who could become samurais and geishas, the Chinese family, faces averted but eyes glowering sideways, hung on to the offenders and fed them leftovers. My aunt must have lived in the same house as my parents and eaten at an outcast table. My mother spoke about the raid as if she had seen it, when she and my aunt, a daughter-in-law to a different household, should not have been living together at all. Daughters-in-law lived with their husbands' parents, not their own; a synonym for marriage in Chinese is "taking a daughter-in-law." Her husband's parents could have sold her, mortgaged her, stoned her. But they had sent her back to her own mother and father, a mysterious act hinting at disgraces not told me. Perhaps they had thrown her out to deflect the avengers.

She was the only daughter; her four brothers went with her father, husband, and uncles "out on the road" and for some years became western men. When the goods were divided among the family, three of the brothers took land, and the youngest, my father, chose an education. After my grandparents gave their daughter away to her husband's family, they had dispensed all the adventure and all the property. They expected her alone to keep the traditional ways, which her brothers, now among the barbarians, could fumble without detection. The heavy, deep-rooted women were to maintain the past against the flood, safe for returning. But the rare urge west had fixed upon our family, and so my aunt crossed boundaries not delineated in space.

The work of preservation demands that the feelings playing about in ones guts not be turned into action. Just watch their passing like cherry blossoms. But perhaps my aunt, my forerunner, caught in a slow life, let dreams grow and fade and after some months or years went toward what persisted. Fear at the enormities of the forbidden kept her desires delicate, wire and bone. She looked at a man because she liked the way the hair was tucked behind his ears, or she liked the question-mark line of a long torso curving at the shoulder and straight at the hip. For warm eyes or a soft voice or a slow walk—that's all—a few hairs, a line, a brightness, a sound, a pace, she gave up family. She offered us up for a charm that vanished with tiredness, a pigtail that didn't toss when the wind died. Why, the wrong lighting could erase the dearest thing about him.

It could very well have been, however, that my aunt did not take subtle enjoyment of her friend, but, a wild woman, kept rollicking company. Imagining her free with sex doesn't fit, though. I don't know any women like that, or men either. Unless I see her life branching into mine, she gives me no ancestral help.

To sustain her being in love, she often worked at herself in the mirror, guessing at the colors and shapes that would interest him, changing them frequently in order to hit on the right combination. She wanted to look back.

On a farm near the sea, a woman who tended her appearance reaped a reputation for eccentricity. All the married women blunt-cut their hair in flaps about their ears or pulled it back in tight buns. No nonsense. Neither style blew easily into heart-catching tangles. And at their weddings they displayed themselves in their long hair for the last time. "It brushed the backs of my knees," my mother tells me. "It was braided, and even so, it brushed the backs of my knees."

At the mirror my aunt combed individuality into her bob. A bun could have been contrived to escape into black streamers blowing in the wind or in quiet wisps about her face, but only the older women in our picture album wear buns. She brushed her hair back from her forehead, tucking the flaps behind her ears. She looped a piece of thread, knotted into a circle between her index fingers and thumbs, and ran the double strand across her forehead. When she closed her fingers as if she were making a pair of shadow geese bite, the string twisted together catching the little hairs. Then she pulled the thread away from her skin, ripping the hairs out neatly, her eyes watering from the needles of pain. Opening her fingers, she cleaned the thread, then rolled it along her hairline and the tops of the eyebrows. My mother did the same to me and my sisters and herself. I used to believe that the expression "caught by the short hairs" meant a captive held with a depilatory string. It especially hurt at the temples, but my mother said we were lucky we didn't have to have our feet bound when we were seven. Sisters used to sit on their beds and cry together, she said, as their mothers or their slave removed the bandages for a few minutes each night and let the blood gush back into their veins. I hope that the man my aunt loved appreciated a smooth brow, that he wasn't just a tits-and-ass man.

Once my aunt found a freckle on her chin, at a spot that the almanac said predestined her for unhappiness. She dug it out with a hot needle and washed the wound with peroxide.

More attention to her looks than these pullings of hairs and pickings at spots would have caused gossip among the villagers. They owned work clothes and good clothes, and they wore good clothes for feasting the new seasons. But since a woman combing her hair hexes beginnings, my aunt rarely found an occasion to look her best. Women looked like great sea snails—the corded wood, babies, and laundry they carried were the whorls on their backs. The Chinese did not admire a bent back; goddesses and warriors stood straight. Still there must have been a marvelous freeing of beauty when a worker laid down her burden and stretched and arched.

Such commonplace loveliness, however, was not enough for my aunt. She dreamed of a lover for the fifteen days of New Year's, the time for families to exchange visits, money, and food. She plied her secret comb. And sure enough she cursed the year, the family, the village, and herself.

Even as her hair lured her imminent lover, many other men looked at her. Uncles, cousins, nephews, brothers would have looked, too, had they been home between journeys. Perhaps they had already been restraining their curiosity, and they left, fearful that their glances, like a field of nesting birds, might be startled and caught. Poverty hurt, and that was their first reason for leaving. But another, final reason for leaving the crowded house was the never-said.

She may have been unusually beloved, the precious only daughter, spoiled and mirror-gazing because of the affection the family lavished on her. When her husband left, they welcomed the chance to take her back from the in-laws; she could live like the little daughter for just a while longer. There are stories that my grandfather was different from other people, "crazy ever since the little Jap bayoneted him in the head." He used to put his naked penis on the dinner table, laughing. And one day he brought home a baby girl, wrapped up inside his brown western-style greatcoat. He had traded one of his sons, probably my father, the youngest, for her. My grandmother made him trade back. When he finally got a daughter of his own, he doted on her. They must have all loved her, except perhaps my father, the only brother who never went back to China, having once been traded for a girl.

Brothers and sisters, newly men and women, had to efface their sexual color and present plain miens. Disturbing hair and eyes, a smile like no other, threatened the ideal of five generations living under one roof. To focus blurs, people shouted face to face and yelled from room to room. The immigrants I know have loud voices, unmodulated to American tones even after years away from the village where they called their friendships out across the fields. I have not been able to stop my mother's screams in public libraries or over telephones. Walking erect (knees straight, toes pointed forward, not pigeon-toed, which is Chinese-feminine) and speaking in an inaudible voice, I have tried to turn myself American-feminine. Chinese communication was loud, public. Only sick people had to whisper. But at the dinner table, where the family members came nearest one another, no one could talk, not the outcasts nor any eaters. Every word that falls from the mouth is a coin lost. Silently they gave and accepted food with both hands. A preoccupied child who took his bowl with one hand got a sideways glare. A complete moment of total attention is due everyone alike. Children and lovers have no singularity here, but my aunt used a secret voice, a separate attentiveness.

She kept the man's name to herself throughout her labor and dying; she did not accuse him that he be punished with her. To save her inseminator's name she gave silent birth.

He may have been somebody in her own household, but intercourse with a man outside the family would have been no less abhorrent. All the village were kinsmen, and the titles shouted in loud country voices never let kinship be forgotten. Any man within visiting distance would have been neutralized as a lover—"brother," "younger brother," "older brother"—115 relationship titles. Parents researched birth charts probably not so much to assure good fortune as to circumvent incest in a population that has but one hundred surnames. Everybody has eight million relatives. How useless then sexual mannerisms, how dangerous.

As if it came from an atavism deeper than fear, I used to add "brother" silently to boys' names. It hexed the boys, who would or would not ask me to dance, and made them less scary and as familiar and deserving of benevolence as girls.

But, of course, I hexed myself also—no dates. I should have stood up, both arms waving, and shouted out across libraries, "Hey, you! Love me back." I had no idea, though, how to make attraction selective, how to control its direction and magnitude. If I made myself American-pretty so that the five or six Chinese boys in the class fell in love with me, everyone else—the Caucasian, Negro, and Japanese boys—would too. Sisterliness, dignified and honorable, made much more sense.

Attraction eludes control so stubbornly that whole societies designed to organize relationships among people cannot keep order, not even when they bind people to one another from childhood and raise them together. Among the very poor and the wealthy, brothers married their adopted sisters, like doves. Our family allowed some romance, paying adult brides' prices and providing dowries so that their sons and daughters could marry strangers. Marriage promises to turn strangers into friendly relatives—a nation of siblings.

In the village structure, spirits shimmered among the live creatures, balanced and held in equilibrium by time and land. But one human being flaring up into violence could open up a black hole, a maelstrom that pulled in the sky. The frightened villagers, who depended on one another to maintain the real, went to my aunt to show her a personal, physical representation of the break she made in the "roundness." Misallying couples snapped off the future, which was to be embodied in true offspring. The villagers punished her for acting as if she could have a private life, secret and apart from them.

If my aunt had betrayed the family at a time of large grain yields and peace, when many boys were born, and wings were being built on many houses, perhaps she might have escaped such severe punishment. But the men—hungry, greedy, tired of planting in dry soil, cuckolded—had been forced to leave the village in order to send food-money home. There were ghost plagues, bandit plagues, wars with the Japanese, floods. My Chinese brother and sister had died of an unknown sickness. Adultery, perhaps only a mistake during good times, became a crime when the village needed food.

The round moon cakes and round doorways, the round tables of graduated size that fit one roundness inside another, round windows and rice bowls—these talismans had lost their power to warn this family of the law: A family must be whole, faithfully keeping the descent line by having sons to feed the old and the dead who in turn look after the family. The villagers came to show my aunt and lover-in-hiding a broken house. The villagers were speeding up the circling of events because she was too shortsighted to see that her infidelity had already harmed the village, that waves of consequences would return unpredictably, sometimes in disguise, as now, to hurt her. This roundness had to be made coin-sized so that she would see its circumference: Punish her at the birth of her baby. Awaken her to the inexorable. People who refused fatalism because they could invent small resources insisted on culpability. Deny accidents and wrest fault from the stars.

After the villagers left, their lanterns now scattering in various directions toward home, the family broke their silence and cursed her. "Aiaa, we're going to die. Death is coming. Death is coming. Look what you've done. You've killed us. Ghost! Dead Ghost! Ghost! You've never been born." She ran out into the fields, far enough from the house so that she could no longer hear their voices, and pressed herself against the earth, her own land no more. When she felt the birth coming, she thought that she had been hurt. Her body seized together. "They've hurt me too much," she thought. "This is gall, and it will kill me." With forehead and knees against the earth, her body convulsed and then relaxed. She turned on her back, lay on the ground. The black well of sky and stars went out and out forever; her body and her complexity seemed to disappear. She was one of the stars, a bright dot in blackness, without home, without a companion, in eternal cold and silence. An agoraphobia rose in her, speeding higher and higher, bigger and bigger; she would not be able to contain it; there would be no end to fear.

Flayed, unprotected against space, she felt pain return, focusing her body. This pain chilled her—a cold, steady kind of surface pain. Inside, spasmodically, the other pain, the pain of the child, heated her. For hours she lay on the ground, alternately body and space. Sometimes a vision of normal comfort obliterated reality: She saw the family in the evening gambling at the dinner table, the young people massaging their elders' backs. She saw them congratulating one another, high joy on the mornings the rice shoots came up. When these pictures burst, the stars drew yet further apart. Black space opened.

She got to her feet to fight better and remembered that old-fashioned women gave birth in their pigsties to fool the jealous, pain-dealing gods, who do not snatch piglets. Before the next spasms could stop her, she ran to the pigsty, each step a rushing out into emptiness. She climbed over the fence and knelt in the dirt. It was good to have a fence enclosing her, a tribal person alone.

Laboring, this woman who had carried her child as a foreign growth that sickened her every day, expelled it at last. She reached down to touch the hot, wet, moving mass, surely smaller than anything human, and could feel that it was human after all—fingers, toes, nails, nose. She pulled it up on to her belly, and it lay curled there, butt in the air, feet precisely tucked one under the other. She opened her loose shirt and buttoned the child inside. After resting, it

squirmed and thrashed and she pushed it up to her breast. It turned its head this way and that until it found her nipple. There, it made little snuffling noises. She clenched her teeth at its preciousness, lovely as a young calf. a piglet, a little dog.

She may have gone to the pigsty as a last act of responsibility: She would protect this child as she had protected its father. It would look after her soul, leaving supplies on her grave. But how would this tiny child without family find her grave when there would be no marker for her anywhere, neither in the earth nor the family hall? No one would give her a family hall name. She had taken the child with her into the wastes. At its birth the two of them had felt the same raw pain of separation, a wound that only the family pressing tight could close. A child with no descent line would not soften her life but only trail after her, ghostlike, begging her to give it purpose. At dawn the villagers on their way to the fields would stand around the fence and look.

Full of milk, the little ghost slept. When it awoke, she hardened her breasts against the milk that crying loosens. Toward morning she picked up the baby and walked to the well.

Carrying the baby to the well shows loving. Otherwise abandon it. Turn its face into the mud. Mothers who love their children take them along. It was probably a girl; there is some hope of forgiveness for boys.

"Don't tell anyone you had an aunt. Your father does not want to hear her name. She has never been born." I have believed that sex was unspeakable and words so strong and fathers so frail that "aunt" would do my father mysterious harm. I have thought that my family, having settled among immigrants who had also been their neighbors in the ancestral land, needed to clean their name, and a wrong word would incite the kinspeople even here. But there is more to this silence: They want me to participate in her punishment. And I have.

In the twenty years since I heard this story I have not asked for details nor said my aunt's name; I do not know it. People who comfort the dead can also chase after them to hurt them further—a reverse ancestor worship. The real punishment was not the raid swiftly inflicted by the villagers, but the family's deliberately forgetting her. Her betrayal so maddened them, they saw to it that she would suffer forever, even after death. Always hungry, always needing, she would have to beg food from other ghosts, snatch and steal it from those whose living descendants give them gifts. She would have to fight the ghosts massed at crossroads for the buns a few thoughtful citizens leave to decoy her away from village and home so that the ancestral spirits could feast unharassed. At peace, they could act like gods, not ghosts, their descent lines providing them with paper suits and dresses, spirit money, paper houses, paper automobiles, chicken, meat, and rice into eternity—essences delivered up in smoke and flames, steam and incense rising from each rice bowl. In an attempt to make the Chinese care for people outside the family, Chairman Mao encourages us now to give our paper replicas to the spirits of outstanding soldiers and workers, no matter whose ancestors they may be. My aunt remains forever hungry. Goods are not distributed evenly among the dead.

My aunt haunts me—her ghost drawn to me because now, after fifty years of neglect, I alone devote pages of paper to her, though not origamied into houses and clothes. I do not think she always means me well. I am telling on her, and she was a spite suicide, drowning herself in the drinking water. The Chinese are always very frightened of the drowned one, whose weeping ghost, wet hair hanging and skin bloated, waits silently by the water to pull down a substitute.

N. Scott Momaday
from *The Way to Rainy Mountain*

In the following passage from his autobiographical The Way to Rainy Mountain, *N. Scott Momaday describes his Kiowa grandmother. Momaday provides a sense of what has been lost from his grandmother's Kiowa heritage. One of the most striking elements of the piece is Momaday's description of his grandmother chanting her prayers, an image that reveals powerfully the cultural difference between the values of Momaday's grandmother's culture and those of the modern white world that supplanted it. Through an emphasis on the land and history of his Kiowa ancestors, Momaday conveys a sense of the value of his heritage.*

A single knoll rises out of the plain in Oklahoma, north and west of the Wichita range. For my people, the Kiowas, it is an old landmark, and they gave it the name Rainy Mountain. The hardest weather in the world is there. Winter brings blizzards, hot tornadic winds arise in the spring, and in summer the prairie is an anvil's edge. The grass turns brittle and brown, and it cracks beneath your feet. There are green belts along the rivers and creeks, linear groves of hickory and pecan, willow and witch hazel. At a distance in July or August the steaming foliage seems almost to writhe in fire. Great green and yellow grasshoppers are everywhere in the tall grass, popping up like corn to sting the flesh, and tortoises crawl about on the red earth, going nowhere in the plenty of time. Loneliness is an aspect of the land. All things in the plain are isolate; there is no confusion of objects in the eye, but *one* hill or *one* tree or *one* man. To look upon that landscape in the early morning, with the sun at your back, is to lose the sense of proportion. Your imagination comes to life, and this, you think, is where Creation was begun.

I returned to Rainy Mountain in July. My grandmother had died in the spring, and I wanted to be at her grave. She had lived to be very old and at last infirm. Her only living daughter was with her when she died, and I was told that in death her face was that of a child.

I like to think of her as a child. When she was born, the Kiowas were living the last great moment of their history. For more than a hundred years they had controlled the open range from the Smoky Hill River to the Red, from the headwaters of the Canadian to the fork of the Arkansas and Cimarron. In alliance with the Comanches, they had ruled the whole of the Southern Plains. War was their sacred business, and they were the finest horsemen the world has ever known. But warfare for the Kiowas was preeminently a matter of disposition rather than of survival, and they never understood the grim, unrelenting advance of the U.S. Cavalry. When at last, divided and ill provisioned, they were driven onto the Staked Plains in the cold of autumn, they fell into panic. In Palo Duro Canyon they abandoned their crucial stores to pillage and had nothing then but their lives. In order to save themselves, they surrendered to the soldiers at Fort Sill and were imprisoned in the old stone corral that now stands as a military museum. My grandmother was spared the humiliation of those high gray walls by eight or ten years, but she must have known from birth the affliction of defeat, the dark brooding of old warriors.

Her name was Aho, and she belonged to the last culture to evolve in North America. Her forebears came down from the high country in western Montana nearly three centuries ago. They were a mountain people, a mysterious tribe of hunters whose language has never been classified in any major group. In the late seventeenth century they began a long migration to the south and east. It was a journey toward the dawn, and it led to a golden age. Along the way the Kiowas were befriended by the Crows, who gave them the culture and religion of the Plains. They acquired horses, and their ancient nomadic spirit was suddenly free of the ground. They acquired Tai-me, the sacred sun-dance doll, from that moment the object and symbol of their worship, and so shared in the divinity of the sun. Not least, they acquired the sense of destiny, therefore courage and pride. When they entered upon the Southern Plains they had been transformed. No longer were they slaves to the simple necessity of survival; they were a lordly and dangerous society of fighters and thieves, hunters and priests of the sun. According to their origin myth, they entered the world through a hollow log. From one point of view, their migration was the fruit of an old prophecy, for indeed they emerged from a sunless world.

Though my grandmother lived out her long life in the shadow of Rainy Mountain, the immense landscape of the continental interior lay like memory in her blood. She could tell of the Crows, whom she had never seen, and of the Black Hills, where she had never been. I wanted to see in reality what she had seen more perfectly in the mind's eye, and drove fifteen hundred miles to begin my pilgrimage.

A dark mist lay over the Black Hills, and the land was like iron. At the top of a ridge I caught sight of Devil's Tower upthrust against the gray sky as if in the birth of time the core of the earth had broken through its crust and the motion of the world was begun. There are things in nature that engender an awful quiet in the heart of man; Devil's Tower is one of them. Two centuries ago, because of their need to explain it, the Kiowas made a legend at the base of the rock. My grandmother said:

"Eight children were there at play, seven sisters and their brother. Suddenly the boy was struck dumb; he trembled and began to run upon his hands and feet. His fingers became claws, and his body was covered with fur. There was a bear where the boy had been. The sisters were terrified; they ran, and the bear after them. They came to the stump of a great tree, and the tree spoke to them. It bade them climb upon it, and as they did so, it began to rise into the air. The bear came to kill them, but they were just beyond its reach. It reared against the tree and scored the bark all around with its claws. The seven sisters were borne into the sky, and they became the stars of the Big Dipper." From that moment, and so long as the legend lives, the Kiowas have kinsmen in the night sky. Whatever they were in the mountains, they could be no more. However tenuous their well-being, however much they had suffered and would suffer again, they had found a way out of the wilderness.

My grandmother had a reverence for the sun, a holy regard that now is all but gone out of mankind. There was a wariness in her, and an ancient awe. She was a Christian in her later years, but she had come a long way about, and she never forgot her birthright. As a child she had been to the sun dances; she had taken part in that annual rite, and by it she had learned the restoration of her people in the presence of Tai-me. She was about seven when the last Kiowa sun dance was held in 1887 on the Washita River above Rainy Mountain Creek. The buffalo were gone. In order to consummate the ancient sacrifice—to impale the head of a buffalo bull upon the Tai-me tree—a delegation of old men journeyed into Texas, there to beg and barter for an animal from the Goodnight herd. She was ten when the Kiowas came together for the last time as a living sun-dance culture. They could find no buffalo; they had to hang an old hide from the sacred tree. Before the dance could begin, a company of soldiers rode out from Fort Sill under orders to disperse the tribe. Forbidden without cause the essential act of their faith, having seen the wild herds slaughtered and left to rot upon the ground, the Kiowas backed away forever from the tree. That was July 20, 1890, at the great bend of the Washita. My grandmother was there. Without bitterness, and for as long as she lived, she bore a vision of deicide.

Now that I can have her only in memory, I see my grandmother in the several postures that were peculiar to her: standing at the wood stove on a winter morning and turning meat in a great iron skillet; sitting at the south window, bent above her beadwork, and afterwards when her vision failed, looking down for a long time into the fold of her hands; going out upon a cane, very slowly as she did when the weight of age came upon her; praying. I remember her most often at prayer. She made long, rambling prayers out of suffering and hope, having seen many things. I was never sure that I had the right to hear, so exclusive were they of all mere custom and company. The last time I saw her she prayed standing by the side of her bed at night, naked to the waist, the light of a kerosene lamp moving upon her dark skin. Her long black hair, always drawn and braided in the day, lay upon her shoulders and against her breasts like a shawl. I do not speak Kiowa, and I never understood her prayers, but there was something inherently sad in the sound, some merest hesitation upon the syllables of sorrow. She began in a high and descending pitch, exhausting her breath to silence; then again and again—and always the same intensity of effort, of something that is, and is not, like urgency in the human voice. Transported so in the dancing light among the shadows of her room, she seemed beyond the reach of time. But that was illusion; I think I knew then that I should not see her again.

Houses are like sentinels in the plain, old keepers of the weather watch. There, in a very little while, wood takes on the appearance of great age. All colors wear soon away in the wind and rain, and then the wood is burned gray and the grain appears and the nails turn red with rust. The window panes are black and opaque; you imagine there is nothing within, and indeed there are many ghosts, bones given up to the land. They stand here and there against the sky, and you approach them for a longer time than you expect. They belong in the distance; it is their domain.

Once there was a lot of sound in my grandmother's house, a lot of coming and going, feasting and talk. The summers there were full of excitement and reunion. The Kiowas are a summer people; they abide the cold and keep to themselves, but when the season turns and the land becomes warm and vital they cannot hold still: an old love of going returns upon them. The aged visitors who came to my grandmother's house when I was a child were made of lean and leather, and they bore themselves upright. They wore great black hats and bright ample shirts that shook in the wind. They rubbed fat upon their hair and wound their braids with strips of colored cloth. Some of them painted their faces and carried the scars of old and cherished enmities. They were an old council of warlords, come to remind and be reminded of who they were. Their wives and daughters served them well. The women might indulge themselves; gossip was at once the mark and compensation of their servitude. They made loud and elaborate talk among themselves, full of jest and gesture, fright and false alarm. They went abroad in fringed and flowered shawls, bright beadwork and German silver. They were at home in the kitchen, and they prepared meals that were banquets.

There were frequent prayer meetings, and nocturnal feasts. When I was a child I played with my cousins outside, where the lamplight fell upon the ground and the singing of the old people rose up around us and carried away into the darkness. There were a lot of good things to eat, a lot of laughter and surprise. And afterwards, when the quiet returned, I lay down with my grandmother and could hear the frogs away by the river and feel the motion of the air.

Now there is a funereal silence in the rooms, the endless wake of some final word. The walls have closed in upon my grandmother's house. When I returned to it in mourning, I saw for the first time in my life how small it was. It was late at night, and there was a white moon, nearly full. I sat for a long time on the stone steps by the kitchen door. From there I could see out across the land; I could see the long row of trees by the creek, the low light upon the rolling plains, and the stars of the Big Dipper. Once I looked at the moon and caught sight of a strange thing. A cricket had perched upon the handrail, only a few inches away. My line of vision was such that the creature filled the moon like a fossil. It had gone there, I thought, to live and die, for there, of all places, was its small definition made whole and eternal. A warm wind rose up and purled like the longing within me.

The next morning, I awoke at dawn and went out on the dirt road to Rainy Mountain. It was already hot, and the grasshoppers began to fill the air. Still, it was early in the morning, and birds sang out of the shadows. The long yellow grass on the mountain shone in the bright light, and a scissortail hied above the land. There, where it ought to be, at the end of a long and legendary way, was my grandmother's grave. She had at last succeeded to that holy ground. Here and there on the dark stones were ancestral names. Looking back once, I saw the mountain and came away.

GLOSSARY

Words in **boldface** indicate terms defined elsewhere in the glossary.

a cappella (ah kuh-PELL-uh) Italian for "chapel style." In music, a composition for voices only, not accompanied by any other instruments.

absolute music Instrumental composition that does not attempt to tell a story or describe a scene, but deals only with musical sound, form, and tone color. Compare **program music**.

Abstract Expressionism Mid-twentieth-century painting style that rejected direct representation and emphasized the artist's spontaneous and emotional interaction with the work.

abstraction Art that does not portray the visual reality of subject but reflects an artist's nonrepresentational idea of it.

Absurdism; Theater of the Absurd Theater form, influenced by **existentialism**, that features incoherent plots and incomprehensible characters.

acrylic Paint made of pigment in a solution of a synthetic resin.

action painting Mid-twentieth-century painting style popularized by Pollock in which the artist throws, drops, or splatters paint on a canvas to convey a sense of physical activity and vitality.

adagio (uh-DAH-joe; uh-DAH-jee-oh) Musical direction for an "easy" or slow **tempo**.

aesthetic Related to the appreciation of beauty in the arts.

agit-trains Trains that disseminated propaganda art in post-revolutionary Russia.

aisle A long side passageway of a church. Aisles run parallel to the central **nave**.

alla prima (AH-la PREE-ma) To paint without any preliminary drawings.

allegory A literary or artistic device in which a deeper, often moral meaning exists beyond the literal level of a work.

allegro Musical direction for a fast **tempo**.

altarpiece A painted or carved panel behind or above the altar of a church.

alto In music, the range of the lowest female voice.

andante (ahn-DAHN-tay) Musical direction for a **tempo** "at a walking pace."

aria (ARR-ee-ah) Section of an **opera** or **oratorio** for a solo singer, usually with orchestral accompaniment.

Art Nouveau (arr new-VOE) Literally, "new art" in French. A late nineteenth- and early twentieth-century movement of art and crafts noted for its ornamental decoration based on the forms of nature, especially the frequent use of curvilinear and floral patterns.

art song Song in which words and music are artistically combined so that the composition reflects the tone, mood, and meaning of the lyrics.

assemblage Three-dimensional art collage, developed by Rauschenberg in the early twentieth century, constructed of found objects such as tires, trash, and mattresses.

ateliers (AT-ul-yay) Workshops, especially those funded by the French government to employ people after the European revolutions of 1848.

atmospheric perspective See **perspective**.

atonality Lack of a home key or **tonal center** in a musical composition.

automatism **Surrealist** artistic technique of the early twentieth century in which the artist gives up intellectual control over his or her work, allowing the subconscious to take over.

avant-garde (ah-vahnt GUARD) Literally, "advance guard" in French. A military term used to describe artists on the cutting edge, especially those vanguard artists of the early twentieth century in France who focused on **abstraction**.

baldacchino (ball-dah-KEY-noh) In architecture, a canopy placed over a sacred space, such as an altar.

balustrade In architecture, a carved railing supported by small posts, or balusters, as along a staircase.

baptistery A small, octagonal structure where baptisms are performed, usually separated from the main church building.

Baroque (bah-ROKE) Seventeenth-century artistic period characterized by opulence, emotionalism, and use of curving lines and ornamentation. In music, a composition style of the seventeenth and eighteenth centuries characterized by ornamentation and rigid structure.

bass In music, the range of the lowest male voice.

Bauhaus Early-twentieth-century German art school led by Gropius that attempted to blend all forms of art, science, and technology.

beat A unit of rhythm in a musical composition, or the accent in that rhythm.

Beijing opera Chinese musical drama developed in the nineteenth century that featured fast-paced, stylized scenes based on ancient Chinese myths.

belle époque (bell-lay-POCK) French for "beautiful age." The era of leisure and elegance in Paris during the late nineteenth and early twentieth centuries.

blank verse Unrhymed verse in iambic pentameter, frequently used in Elizabethan drama.

brass instrument Musical instrument, such as a trumpet or tuba, played by blowing through a detachable brass mouthpiece.

Bunraku (boon-RAH-koo) Traditional Japanese puppet theater featuring large puppets and puppeteers on stage, and a samisen accompanist and narrator who sit just off the side of the stage.

buttress In architecture, a projecting support or reinforcement.

Byzantine (BIZ-un-teen) Artistic style of Eastern Europe in the fourth through fifteenth centuries that featured rich colors, Christian imagery, domed churches, and mosaics.

Calvinism Theological belief system, based on John Calvin's (1509–64) writings, that held that some individuals—the Elect—are predestined to be saved; noted for its strict moral code.

camera obscura (ub-SKOOR-a) Crude cameralike device for verifying **perspective**, first used in the Renaissance; consisted of a box with a tiny hole in one side through which a beam of light passes, projecting the scene, now inverted, on the opposite wall of the box.

campanile (camp-ah-NEE-lee) A bell tower, especially one that stands apart from other main church buildings.

cantata From the Italian word for "to sing." Small-scale musical work for a solo singer or small group of singers and accompanying instruments. Compare **sonata**.

cantilever In architecture, a self-supporting extension from a wall.

canzone; canzoni (can-TSOE-neh; can-TSOE-nee) A song, especially one performed by troubadours in the eleventh through thirteenth centuries and using a love poem as text.

capital The decorative top part of a column that supports the **entablature**.

cast iron Casted alloy of iron with silicon and carbon.

chanson (shawn-SEWN or SHANN-sen) French for "song." A general term for a song with French lyrics, especially one performed by troubadours in the eleventh through sixteenth centuries.

château (pural, châteaux) Grand castle, especially of a French aristocrat.

chiaroscuro (key-are-oh-SKOO-roe) From the Italian *chiaro*, "light," and *oscuro*, "obscure" or "dark." In painting, a method of **modeling** that combines subtle shifts of light to dark across a rounded surface to give the impression of depth.

chorale Simple Protestant hymn sung in unison by a church congregation.

chorus A company of singers.

Christian humanism Sixteenth-century belief system that combined the ideals of classical **humanism** with biblical morality.

Classical Artistic style of ancient Greece or Rome that emphasized balance, restraint, and quest for perfection. In music, the eighteenth-century style characterized by accessibility, balance, and clarity.

classicism Any later artistic style reminiscent of the ancient Greek or Roman **Classical** style and its values of balance, restraint, and quest for perfection.

coda A repeated section of music at the end of a movement in **sonata form**.

collage From the French word for "giving" or "pasting" A visual art form in which bits of familiar objects, such as rope or a piece of newspaper, are glued on a painted canvas surface.

colonnade In architecture, a row of columns placed side by side, usually to support a roof or series of arches.

color field Twentieth-century abstract painting style, popularized by Rothko, that featured large rectangles of flat color intended to evoke an emotional response.

comedy An amusing or bright play or drama with a happy or at least untragic ending.

comic opera Light **opera**, especially of the **Classical** era, that featured simple music, an amusing plot, and spoken dialogue.

complementary colors A combination of one primary color and one secondary color that is formed by the two other primary colors. Red and green, blue and orange, and yellow and purple are complementary colors. See also **primary colors; secondary colors.**

Conceptual art Twentieth-century artistic style whose works were conceived in the mind of the artist, often submitted in a written proposal, and did not originate in the commercial art scene.

concerto (kun-CHAIR-toe) A musical composition for solo instrument and orchestra, usually in three contrasting movements in the pattern fast–slow–fast.

continuous narration In art, simultaneous depiction of events that are occurring at distinct chronological times. Compare with linear narration, in which events are ordered chronologically from left to right.

contrapposto In sculpture and painting, an asymmetrical positioning of the human body in which the weight rests on one leg, elevating the hip and opposite shoulder.

Corinthian The most ornate of Greek architectural orders, featuring thin, fluted columns and **capitals** elaborately decorated with acanthus leaf carvings. See also **Doric; Ionic.**

cornice In architecture, a horizontal molding that forms the uppermost, projecting part of an **entablature.**

Counter-Reformation Sixteenth-century Roman Catholic response of reform to the Protestant **Reformation.**

counterpoint In music, weaving two or more independent melodies into one harmonic texture.

Cubism Early twentieth-century painting style characterized by geometric depiction of objects, especially using cubes, and multiple views of one object; leading Cubists were Picasso and Braque.

cupola (KYOO-puh-luh) A rounded roof or small dome on a roof.

Dada Artistic and literary movement during and just after World War I that rejected tradition and championed the irrational and absurd.

daguerreotype (duh-GARE-oh-type) An early photograph form, produced on silver or silver-coated copper plates. Named for Daguerre, the French painter who invented the method.

De Stijl (duh-STYLE) Dutch for "The Style." Artistic movement founded in 1917 in Holland that integrated all visual arts and championed total **abstraction.** Noted for its use of **primary colors**, black and white, and geometric lines, as seen in Mondrian's paintings. Also called Neo-Plasticism.

decadents Label *fin-de-siècle* writers used for themselves to describe their moral decadence, mannered style, and fascination with morbid or perverse subject matter.

deconstruction Twentieth-century philosophical approach, especially in linguistics, of breaking apart the whole, assuming that in all systems there are gaps or inconsistencies, and that those gaps reveal the most about the whole system.

Deism (DEE-izm) Belief system based on the premise of a God who created the universe and then left it to run by itself.

Der Blaue Reiter Literally, "The Blue Rider" in German. A branch of early twentieth-century German **Expressionist** art characterized by abstract forms and pure colors.

Die Brücke Literally, "The Bridge" in German. A branch of early twentieth-century German **Expressionist** art characterized by bold colors, landscapes, and violent portraits.

dissonance In music, a chord or interval that sounds unfinished and seems to need resolution in a harmonious chord.

Doric The earliest and simplest of Greek architectural orders. Featured short, sturdy columns, often unfluted, and a simple **capital** shaped like a square. See also **Ionic; Corinthian.**

drum In architecture, a circular wall, usually topped by a dome.

Duco Brand name for pyroxylin, a lacquer first developed for automobiles and commonly used in Mexican murals.

engraving A type of print made by cutting an image onto metal or wood and inking the impression.

Enlightenment Eighteenth-century European intellectual movement that emphasized the mind's power to reason, challenged the traditional, and favored social reform.

entablature In architecture, the horizontal structure above the columns and **capitals** and below the roof.

epic An extended narrative poem written in a dignified style about a heroic character or characters.

ere ibeji Yoruban carvings of twins, who are believed to be gifts of the gods.

essay French for "attempt." A short literary composition, usually expressing the author's personal views.

etching A type of print made by incising an image onto a waxed metal plate, corroding the exposed metal in an acid bath, removing the wax, then inking the design.

étude (AY-tood) A solo musical study focusing on a particular technique.

Existentialism Twentieth-century philosophy based on the notion that it is the individual's responsibility to make ethical decisions, and that this responsibility is often the source of feelings of anguish.

Expressionism Modern artistic and literary movement characterized by emotional expression, often with agitated strokes, intense colors, and themes of sexuality. See also *Die Brücke; Der Blaue Reiter.*

facade The front face of a building.

fête galante In **Rococo** painting, a depiction of an elegant outdoor party, featuring amorous conversations, graceful fashion, and social gallantry.

ficciones Term coined by Borges for his short, puzzling fictional works that invite philosophical reflection.

fin de siècle (fan duh SYEH-cle) French for "end of the century." Describes the last years of the nineteenth century, generally noted for inventiveness, social unrest, and decadence.

finial The decorative part at the top of a spire, gable, lamp, or piece of furniture.

flâneur (flah-NERR) A type of a person in *belle époque* Paris noted for his or her lifestyle of leisure, elevated manners, elegant attire, idle strolling, and light conversation.

free verse Poetry that uses the natural rhythm of words and phrases instead of a consistent pattern of meter and rhyme.

fresco Painting style in which pigments are applied to fresh wet plaster, or an art work created in such a style.

fugue (FYOOG) Musical composition of three or four highly independent parts in which one voice states a theme which is then imitated in succession by each of the other voices in **counterpoint.**

Functionalism Architectural theory that a building's design should be adapted to its function.

Futurism Early twentieth-century artistic movement that rejected conventional art and sought to show the fast-paced, dynamic nature of modern life and the machine age, often by portraying various views of a moving object.

gelede Traditional Yoruban masked ritual, performed to appease "the mothers," women thought to posses special powers.

genre A category or type of art, music, or literature.

genre painting Painting depicting the daily life of ordinary people.

gesso (JESS-oh) Italian for "gypsum" or "plaster." White Plaster of Paris or clay used as a primer.

glaze A thin, transparent layer of oil paint, usually applied on top of another layer or over a painted surface to achieve a glowing or glossy look.

Gothic Style of architecture and art of the twelfth through sixteenth centuries and revived during the **Romantic** era. Characterized, especially in churches, by ribbed vaults, pointed arches, flying buttresses, stained glass, and high, steep roofs.

grand opera Nineteenth-century form of **opera** that appealed to the masses because of its spectacle.

Greek cross In architecture, a floor plan of four arms of equal length. Compare to **Latin cross**.

guild An association of people in the same craft or trade, formed during the Middle Ages or Renaissance to give economic and political power to its members and to control the trade's standards.

haiku (HIGH-koo) Japanese poetry form in three lines, with seventeen syllables in the pattern five, seven, and five syllables per line; usually features imagery from nature, includes a reference to a season, and avoids rhyme.

Happening Spontaneous art form of the 1960s that incorporated theater, performance, visual arts, and audience involvement.

Harlem Renaissance Mid-twentieth-century literary and artistic movement centered in the African-American community of New York City's Harlem neighborhood.

harmony In music, playing or singing two or more tones at the same time, especially when the resulting sound is pleasing to the ear; generally, the arrangement of chords.

highlife Style of contemporary African music featuring a fusion of indigenous dance rhythms and melodies with Western marches, sea chanties, and church hymns.

homophony; homophonic In music, the playing or singing of a single melodic line with harmonic accompaniment.

humanism The belief system, especially during the Renaissance, that stressed the worth, dignity, and accomplishments of the individual. Stemmed from renewed interest in **Classical** values of ancient Greece and Rome.

icon A religious image, such as a figure from the Bible, painted on wood and used as a sacred reminder of important elements of Christianity.

iconoclasm (eye-KON-o-KLAZ-em) Opposition to the use of or systematic destruction of religious **icons**.

iconography In visual arts, the symbols used to communicate meaning.

iconostasis A panel of **icons** that typically separates the priests from the rest of the congregation in the Eastern Orthodox Church.

idée fixe (ee-day FEEKS) French for "fixed idea." In music, a recurring musical theme or idea used throughout a movement or entire composition.

illusionism Appearance of reality in art; specifically, the technique used to make a created work look like a continuation of the surrounding architecture.

impasto (im-POSS-toe) Paint applied thickly so that an actual texture is created on the painted surface, or this painting process.

Impressionism Late nineteenth-century artistic style that sought to portray a fleeting view of the world, usually by applying paint in short strokes of pure color. In music, a style that suggested moods and places through lush and shift-ing harmonies and vague rhythms.

International style Twentieth-century architectural style focusing primarily on modern materials especially steel and concrete, and boxlike shapes.

Ionic Somewhat ornate Greek architectural order characterized by its slim, fluted columns and **capitals** decorated with spiral scrolls. See also **Corinthian**; **Doric**.

jazz Category of music, first developed by African Americans in the early twentieth century, that usually features **syncopated** rhythms and improvisation of the melody or a phrase.

Jesuits Members of the Society of Jesus, an order of Roman Catholic priests established by St. Ignatius of Loyola in 1540.

Kabuki (kuh-BOO-key) Japanese musical theater developed in the seventeenth century, noted for its melodramatic dancing, lively drama, and instrumental accompaniment. Traditionally performed by an all-male cast.

landscape A painting, photograph, or other visual art form that uses a natural outdoor scene as its main subject.

lantern In architecture, an open or windowed structure placed on top of a roof to allow light to enter below.

Latin cross In architecture, a floor plan of three short arms and one long one. Compare to **Greek cross**.

leitmotif (LIGHT-moe-teef) German for "leading motive." In Wagnerian music, brief fragments of melody or rhythm that trigger the audience to think of particular characters, actions, or objects.

Les Fauves; Fauvism (FOVE; FOVE-izm) Literally, "wild beasts" in French. Early twentieth-century artistic movement characterized by violent, arbitrary colors and long, sensuous strokes, as seen in the paintings of Matisse.

libretto Words for an opera or other textual vocal work.

Lied; Lieder (LEED; LEED-er) Romantic German **art song** designed for a vocalist and accompanist performing in a room of a home.

lithograph A type of print made when an image, drawn with a greasy substance on a stone block, is first wetted, then inked. Because the greasy areas repel water, only the waxed image attracts the ink.

liturgy Religious rite used in public, organized worship.

loggia (LOH-juh) In architecture, a covered, open-air gallery.

long gallery In Renaissance architecture, an unusually long room used for exercise during bad weather.

Lutheranism Theological belief system and denomination founded by Martin Luther (1483–1546) that held that salvation is delivered by faith, not by achievement.

lyric poetry Poems that have a songlike quality; usually emotional in nature.

madrigal Polyphonic music composed for a small group of singers, usually based on short **secular lyric** poems and sung with no accompaniment.

magic realism Latin American literary style that weaves together realistic events with incredible and fantastic ones to convey the often mysterious truths of life.

Mannerism Artistic style of the sixteenth century that rejected Renaissance aesthetic principles; noted for its obscure subject manner, unbalanced compositions, distorted bodies and poses, strange facial expressions, confusing spatial constructions, and harsh colors.

mass The musical setting of parts of the **Mass**.

Mass A central religious ritual, principally in the Roman Catholic church.

mazurka A lively Polish dance in triple meter.

Minimal art Twentieth-century artistic style featuring a small number of objects arranged in a simple, often repeated, pattern.

minuet A slow, elegant dance in triple meter.

minuet and trio form Organizing structure for a musical work in the pattern minuet-trio-minuet. Usually the form of the third movement of a **symphony**. See also **minuet**; **trio**.

mobile Sculptural form suspended from the ceiling, mechanized or moved by air currents; invented by Calder in the 1930s.

mock epic An extended narrative poem that treats a trivial incident in a heroic manner. See also **epic**.

model In painting, to create the illusion of depth by using light and shadow. In sculpture, to shape a pliable substance into a three-dimensional object.

Modernism; the modern Artistic and literary movement of the late nineteenth and twentieth centuries that sought to find new methods of artistic expression for the modern, dynamic world, and rejected the traditions of the past.

monastery Residence for monks.

monophony; monophonic Musical texture with a single melody and no accompaniment.

montage In film, a set of abruptly edited images used for dramatic effect.

mosaic A design or picture created by inlaying pieces of colored glass, stone, or tile in mortar; mosaics are usually placed on walls or floors.

motet In Renaissance music, a multi-voiced composition, usually based on a sacred Latin text and sung *a cappella*.

mural A large wall painting.

music drama Musical term first used by Wagner to describe his operas that combined song, instrumental music, dance, drama, and poetry with no interruptions and without breaking the opera up into conventional arias or recitatives.

naturalism Late nineteenth-century literary movement that strove to depict characters in naturalistic, objective detail, focusing on the authenticity of characters, setting, and situations;

emphasized biological and cultural determinants for the behavior and fate of literary characters.

nave The long central space of a church, which is flanked on both sides by smaller **aisles**.

Neoclassicism Late eighteenth-century artistic style, developed in response to the more ornate **Rococo** style, that revived an interest in the ancient **Classical** ideals; characterized by simplicity and straight lines.

Neoplatonism A revival of the philosophy of Plato, developed by Plotinus in the third century A.D. and prevalent during the Renaissance; based on the belief that the psyche is trapped within the body, and that philosophical thought is the only way to ascend from the material world to union with the single, higher source of existence.

niche In architecture, a hollow part in a wall, often used to hold a statue or vase.

nocturne A musical composition for night, usually melancholy in tone and for solo piano.

Noh (NO) Japanese musical theater developed in the fifteenth century, noted for its solemnity, highly poetic texts, stylized gestures, and masked actors.

obelisk In architecture, a four-sided shaft topped by a pyramid.

octave An eight-line section of a poem, particularly the first section in a **Petrarchan sonnet**; in music, an eight-note interval.

ode A **lyric** poem, usually addressed to a person or object and written in a dignified style.

opera Italian for "a work." Musical form, first introduced in the **Baroque** era, that combines drama, a text set to vocal music, and orchestral accompaniment.

Oratorians Group of lay Catholics, founded in 1575 by St. Philip Neri, who met for spiritual conversation, study, and prayer.

oratorio A sacred opera performed without costume or acting, featuring solo singers, a chorus, and an orchestra.

oratory Prayer hall.

orthogonal In visual arts, a receding line perpendicular to the picture plane. In linear **perspective**, orthogonals converge and disappear at a **vanishing point**.

palette An artist's choice of colors for a particular work of art, or the surface on which such colors are placed and mixed.

patron A person who financially sponsors art or artists.

pediment In **Classical** architecture, a triangular space at the end of a building, formed by the **cornice** and the ends of the sloping roof.

percussion instrument Musical instrument, such as a timpani or bass drum, played by striking or shaking.

peristyle In architecture, a continuous row of columns, forming an enclosure around the outside of a building or courtyard.

perspective A method of creating the illusion of three-dimensional space on a two-dimensional surface. Achieved by methods such as *atmospheric perspective*, using slight variations in color and sharpness of the subject, or *linear perspective*, creating a horizon line and **orthogonals**, which meet at **vanishing points**.

Petrarchan sonnet; Italian sonnet Poem of an **octave** of eight lines, which introduces the scene, and a **sestet** of six lines, which expands on or complicates the scene. The octave rhymes *abba abba* (or *abab abab*), and the sestet rhymes *cde cde* (or *cde ced*; *cde dce*; or *cd cd cd*). Devised by the poet Petrarch in the fourteenth century. See also **Shakespearean sonnet**.

petroglyph Wall painting.

phenomena (fuh-NOM-uh-nuh) In Kantian philosophy, elements as they are perceived by worldly senses, not as they really are.

philosophes (fill-uh-SOFF) Group of intellectuals of the **Enlightenment** who believed that, through reason, humans could achieve a perfect society.

pianoforte (pee-ANN-oh-FOR-tay) Literally, "soft loud" in Italian. Name originally used for the piano because of its ability to differentiate between soft and loud tones, which the harpsichord could not do.

picaresque In literature, a narrative form that originated in Spain and details the adventurous life of a *pícaro*, a rogue hero.

pier In architecture, a vertical support structure similar to a column, but usually square or rectangular in shape, not cylindrical. Piers usually support arches.

Pietà (pee-ay-TAH). Italian for "pity." In visual arts, a work that shows the Virgin Mary mourning over the dead Jesus in her lap.

pilaster In architecture, a flat, decorative pillar attached to a wall, projecting just slightly, that may reinforce the wall.

plainchant; plainsong In music, the **monophonic**, unmetered vocal music of the Early Christian Church, as in Gregorian chant.

Pointillism (PWAHN-tuh-liz-um) Post-**Impressionistic** painting technique that used an almost exact application of paint in small dots or points to create an overall color perceived by the human eye.

polonaise A stately, proud Polish dance in triple meter.

polyphony; polyphonic The simultaneous playing or singing of several independent musical lines.

polyptych (POL-ip-tick) A painting or relief with four or more panels, often hinged so panels can be folded. See also **triptych**.

polyrhythm Multiple rhythms played or sung simultaneously within the same musical composition.

Pop Art Mid-twentieth-century artistic style whose subjects were everyday items from the mass media or were mass produced, such as comic strips, soup cans, or images of famous figures.

portal In architecture, a grand entrance or doorway.

portico In architecture, a porch or walkway covered by a roof supported by columns. It often marks an entrance to the main building.

Post-Impressionism Artistic movement beginning in the late nineteenth century that attempted to improve upon **Impressionism** by deepening the personal and psychological level and emphasizing the formal arrangement of a work of art.

poststructuralism The approach of **structuralism** taken one step further, which emphasizes that speech can mask reality as well as reveal it and that meaning is relative to context.

poussiniste French Academy adherent to the style of Poussin during the **Baroque** era; favored line over color. Compare **rubéniste**.

prelude (PRELL-yood) A short instrumental composition that usually precedes a larger musical work.

primary colors The colors red, yellow, and blue. See also **secondary colors**.

program music Instrumental composition that musically describes a scene, story, or other nonmusical situation. Popularized in the **Romantic** era. Compare **absolute music**.

proscenium arch In theater, the framing device that separates the stage from the audience.

Puritanism Belief system of the Puritans, a religious group in the sixteenth and seventeenth centuries who sought to reform the Church of England; its members advocated strict religious and moral discipline.

ragtime **Jazz** piano composition in which the left hand plays a steady beat while the right hand improvises on a melody using a **syncopated** rhythm.

rational humanism Philosophical belief system of the **Enlightenment** based on the idea that progress is possible only through learning, and through the individual's freedom to learn.

Realism Nineteenth-century artistic and literary movement that attempted to convey to the public the realities of modern life, not just to depict the beautiful.

recitative (ress-uh-tuh-TEEV) In **opera**, a form of musically heightened speech halfway between spoken dialogue and melodic singing.

Reformation Religious movement of the sixteenth century that sought to reform the Roman Catholic Church; led to the development of Protestant churches.

Regionalism Literary and artistic style that depicts a particular geographic region in a naturalistic manner.

register In music, a particular range of tones that a voice or instrument can make.

revolution The overthrow of an existing government for a new one.

rib In architecture, a curved, projecting arch used for support or decoration in a **vault**.

riff In **jazz**, a short phrase repeated frequently during improvisation.

ritornello (rit-or-NELL-low) A musical passage that will recur several times throughout a **concerto** movement.

Rococo (ruh-KOE-koe) Eighteenth-century artistic style, developed from the **Baroque** style, that was characterized by curved shapes, pastel colors, smaller scale, and often frivolous subject matter.

Romanticism Late eighteenth- and early nineteenth-century artistic, literary, and cultural movement that developed as a reaction against **Neoclassicism**; emphasized emotion, originality, nature, and freedom of form.

rondo form Organizing structure for a musical work in which the main theme repeats itself frequently, with new, contrasting material added between each repetition. Often the form of the second or last movements of a **concerto**.

rubéniste French Academy adherent to style of Rubens during the **Baroque** era; favored color over line. Compare **poussiniste**.

Salon des Refusés French for "Salon of the Rejected." Artistic **salon** established by Napoleon III in 1863 to exhibit paintings rejected by the official French Academy Salon.

salon; Salon Large reception room in a townhouse, or the social gathering held in such rooms; an annual exhibition of works of art, especially by the French Academy in the eighteenth and nineteenth centuries.

samurai Ruler-warriors of Japan, especially during the feudal era.

satire Literary or dramatic work that exposes vice or follies with ridicule or sarcasm, often in a humorous way.

scat Method of vocal singing in nonsense syllables.

score Written or published version of a musical composition showing parts for all instruments and voices.

scroll In Chinese and Japanese art, a painting or text drawn on vertical pieces of silk fabric; the scroll is conventionally kept rolled and tied except for on special occasions, when it is hung. Also called *hanging scroll*.

secondary colors The colors orange, green, and purple, formed when two primary colors (red, yellow, or blue) are mixed. See also **primary colors.**

secular Not sacred or religious.

sestet A six-line section of a poem, particularly the last section in a **Petrarchan sonnet.**

sfumato (sfoo-MA-toe) The Italian word for "smoky." In painting, the intentional blurring of the outline of a figure in a hazy, almost smoky atmosphere.

Shakespearean sonnet; English sonnet Poem of three four-line stanzas and a final two-line couplet, usually rhyming *abab cdcd efef gg.* See also **Petrarchan sonnet.**

Shinto A principal and former state religion of Japan characterized by rituals and venerations for local deities and strong patriotism.

shogun Hereditary ruler of post-feudal Japan in the years 1600–1868.

skene (SKAY-nuh) Greek for "hut." The scene building in Greek theater.

social contract In political theory, especially of Hobbes and Locke, the agreement among individuals of an organized society to surrender certain freedoms in exchange for government's protection over them.

Socialist Realism Artistic style declared by Stalin in 1934 as the official Soviet style; it rejected abstraction and focused on images of soldiers, workers, and peasants.

soliloquy (suh-LILL-uh-kwee) In drama, a character's private reflections spoken aloud toward the audience, but not to the other characters.

sonata From the Italian word for "to sound." Musical composition for one or two instruments, usually in three or four movements. Compare **cantata.**

sonata form Organizing structure for a musical work with three main sections: exposition, development, and recapitulation, often followed by a **coda.** Usually the form of the first and fourth movements of a **symphony.**

soprano In music, the range of the highest voice of females or young boys.

stream of consciousness Modern literary technique that records the free flow of a character's mental impressions.

structuralism; structural linguistics Twentieth-century approach to culture, especially linguistics, that analyzes the basic elements of a system according to binary oppositions to understand the meaning of the system as a whole.

Surrealism Artistic and literary movement of the early twentieth century, noted for its total acceptance of the irrational, lack of moral concern, and fascination with the world of dreams and the unconscious.

swing Jazz style of big bands of the 1930s and 1940s, usually fast and arranged instead of improvised.

Symbolists Poets of the late nineteenth century who used symbolic words and figures to express ideas, impressions, and emotions and rejected the realistic depiction of the external world.

symphony Large orchestral work, usually in four distinct movements.

syncopation A musical rhythm in which **beats** that are normally unaccented are stressed.

tempera (TEM-purr-uh) Paint made of egg yolks, water, and pigments.

tempo The speed at which music should be played.

tenebrism A painting technique that dramatically contrasts light and dark and concentrates little on middle tones.

tenor In music, the range of the highest male voice, which usually carries the melody.

terra cotta Italian for "baked earth." An orange-red baked clay used for pottery or sculpture.

theme and variations form Organizing structure for a musical work in which a theme is presented and repeated several more times, each time in a slightly varied way. Often the form of the first and fourth movements of a **symphony.**

theocracy A political entity ruled by a religious figure or group claiming to have divine authority.

tonal center Home key of a musical composition.

tragedy A serious play or drama about a protagonist's problems, caused by his or her own tragic character flaw.

Transcendentalism Romantic philosophical theory that there is an ideal reality that transcends the material world, known only through intuition, especially in nature. See also **phenomena.**

trio In music, the middle section of the **minuet and trio form,** usually similar to the **minuet** but contrasting in instrumentation and texture.

triptych (TRIP-tick) A three-paneled painting or relief, often hinged so side panels can be folded over the center panel.

trompe-l'oeil (trohnp-LEH-ee) French for "trick the eye." An artistic effect that creates an optical illusion of reality for the viewer.

twelve-tone composition Musical composition style developed by Schoenberg that uses a twelve-note scale, which is the traditional octave plus all internal half steps; each tone is used equally and in a highly organized manner.

ukiyo-e Literally, "pictures of the floating world" in Japanese. Style of Japanese woodblock prints of the seventeenth and eighteenth centuries noted for their everyday subject matter.

vanishing point In linear **perspective**, the horizon point at which all **orthogonals**—receding lines perpendicular to the picture plane—appear to converge and disappear.

vault An arched masonry roof or ceiling.

verisimilitude (ver-uh-si-MILL-uh-tude) The appearance of being true to reality.

vernacular The common language spoken in a particular country or region.

waltz A ballroom dance in triple meter.

whole step In music, the interval between any first and third consecutive keys on the piano; made up of two half steps.

woodcut A type of print made by carving a design in a piece of wood and inking the raised surfaces.

woodwind instrument Musical instrument, such as a flute or clarinet, played by blowing through a reed or mouthpiece attached to the main body of the instrument.

word painting In Renaissance music, a composition style that emphasizes the meaning of words through the accompanying music. For example, the word "weep" might be expressed by a descending melodic line.

PICTURE CREDITS AND FURTHER INFORMATION

The authors, Calmann & King Ltd, and Prentice Hall wish to thank the institutions and individuals who have kindly provided photographic materials for use in this book. In all cases, every effort has been made to contact the copyright holders, but should there be any errors or omissions, the publishers would be pleased to insert the appropriate acknowledgment in any subsequent edition of this publication.

Key: A=Alinari, BAL=Bridgeman Art Library, S=Scala, SFQ=© Studio Fotografico Quattrone, Florence

Introduction/Starter Kit
0.1 SFQ; 0.2 © Succession Picasso/DACS 1998; 0.3 Photo: J. Lathion, © Nasjonalgalleriet, Oslo; 0.5 Robert Harding Picture Library

Chapter Thirteen
13.1 SFQ; 13.2 S; 13.3 Bodleian Library; 13.4 S; 13.5 S; 13.6 SFQ; 13.8 SFQ; 13.9 S; 13.10 SFQ; 13.12 Ralph Lieberman; 13.13 A; 13.14 SFQ; 13.15 SFQ; 13.17 S; 13.18 S; 13.19 SFQ; 13.20 SFQ; 13.21 S; 13.23 RMN-Gérard Blot/Jean; 13.24 S; 13.25 SFQ; 13.26 RMN; 13.27 A; 13.28 © Giancarlo Costa, Milan; 13.29 AKG London/Erich Lessing; 13.31 © Araldo de Luca, Rome; 13.32 SFQ; 13.33 BAL; 13.34 BAL; 13.35 © James Morris, London; 13.37 A; 13.38 © Cameraphoto-Arte, Venice; 13.39 RMN; 13.40 S; 13.41 RMN-J.G. Berizzi; 13.42 S; 13.43 SFQ; 13.45 Oronoz, Madrid; 13.47 S; 13.48 A

Chapter Fourteen
14.1 The Cloisters Collection, 1956 (56.70) Photograph © The Metropolitan Museum of Art; 14.2+3 © St. Baafskathedraal, Gent, © Paul M.R. Maeyaert; 14.4 Reproduced by courtesy of the Trustees, The National Gallery, London; 14.5 BAL; 14.6+7 Copyright © Museo Del Prado, Madrid; 14.8+9 S; 14.10 AKG London/Erich Lessing; 14.11 BAL; 14.12 Gift of Junius S. Morgan, 1919; 14.14 RMN; 14.16 Rogers Fund, 1919; 14.16 AKG/Erich Lessing; 14.17 © James Austin; 14.18 A.F. Kersting; 14.19 THE ROYAL COLLECTION © Her Majesty Queen Elizabeth II; 14.20 by permission of The Huntington Library, San Marino, California; 14.21 C. Walter Hodges *Shakespeare and the Players*, London 1948 pp. 62-63; 14.22 Giraudon

Chapter Fifteen
15.1 Romer/Explorer/Photo Researchers, Inc.; 15.2 Dan Budnik/Woodfin Camp & Associates; 15.4 S; 15.5 ©Araldo De Luca, Rome; 15.6 © Araldo De Luca, Rome; 15.7 © Araldo De Luca, Rome; 15.8 © Araldo De Luca, Rome; 15.9 S; 15.10 S; 15.11 S; 15.12 S; 15.13 S; 15.14 Widener Collection; 15.20 Gift of Henry G. Marquand, 1889; 15.22 RMN-Jean/Lewandowski; 15.24 Nelson-Atkins, Museum of Art, Kansas City, Missouri (Purchase:Nelson Trust); 15.25 RMN-Jean; 15.28 RMN; 15.30 © James Austin; 15.31 Robert Harding; 15.32 © Paul M.R. Maeyaert; 15.32+33 A.F. Kersting; 15.34 Robert Harding; 15.35 The Crosby Brown Collection of Musical Instruments, 1889; 15.37 S

Chapter Sixteen
16.1 RMN - Hervé Lewandowski; 16.2 RMN; 16.3 Trustees of The Wedgwood Museum, Barlaston, Staffordshire, England; 16.5 Photo Bulloz; 16.6 BAL; 16.7 RMN-Gérard Blot; 16.8 RMN-René-Gabriel Ojeda; 16.10 RMN-G. Blot/C. Jean; 16.11 RMN-Hervé Lewandowski; 16.13 Andrew W. Mellon Collection; 16.14 English Heritage

Photographic Library; 16.15 RMN; 16.16 Giraudon; 16.17 Giraudon/Art Resource, NY; 16.18 Giraudon/BAL; 16.19 Giraudon; 16.20 photo: Ann Hutchison, ©1992 Virginia Museum of Fine Arts; 16.21 Transfer from the Canadian War Memorials, 1921 (Gift of the 2nd. Duke of Westminster, Eaton Hall, Cheshire, 1918); 16.22 Gift of Mrs. George von Lengerke Meyer; 16.23 Virginia State Library and Archives; 16.24 A.F. Kersting; 16.25 © Paul M.R. Maeyaert; 16.26 Balthazar Korab; 16.28 Donald Cooper/Photostage; 16.29 AKG London; 16.30 Spectrum; 16.31 Guildhall Library, London; 16.32 John Troha/Black Star

Chapter Seventeen
17.1 Photo: Elke Walford, Fotowerkstatt, Hamburger Kunsthalle; 17.5 RMN-Arnaudet; 17.6 RMN-Hervé Lewandowski; 17.7 Giraudon; 17.8 RMN; 17.9 photo © Fitzwilliam Museum; 17.11 Henry Lillie Pierce Fund; 17.12 Gift of Douglas F. Roby; 17.13 Mr. and Mrs. William H. Marlatt Fund; 17.14 Lent by the U.S. Department of the Interior, Office of the Secretary. National Museum of American Art, Washington DC; Photo: National Museum of American Art, Washington DC/Art Resource; 17.15 Bulloz, Paris; 17.16 A.F. Kersting; 17.19 Donald Cooper/Photostage; 17.20 RMN-Hervé Lewandowski; 17.21 Charles Deering Fund, 1953.530; Photograph ©1997, The Art Institute of Chicago, All Rights Reserved; 17.22 RMN; 17.23 RMN; 17.24 RMN; 17.25 RMN; 17.26 RMN-J.G. Berizzi; 17.28 Peter Newark's American Pictures; 17.29 Smithsonian Institution Libraries, Cooper-Hewitt, National Design Museum Branch, Smithsonian Institution/Art Resource, NY; 17.30 Gift of Mrs. Frank B. Porter, 1922; 17.31 Purchased by the Friends of Art, Fort Worth Art Association,1925; acquired by the Amon Carter Museum, 1990, from the Modern Art Museum of Fort Worth through grants and donations from the Amon G. Carter Foundation, the Sid W. Richardson Foundation, the Anne Burnett and Charles Tandy Foundation,Capital Cities/ABC Foundation, Fort Worth Star Telegram, the R.D. and Joan Dale Hubbard Foundation and the people of Fort Worth; 17.33 Spectrum; 17.34 RMN-Jean

Chapter Eighteen
18.2 Giraudon; 18.3 RMN-H. Lewandowski; 18.4 RMN-B. Hatala; 18.5 RMN-H. Lewandowski; 18.7 RMN-Arnaudet; 18.9 Chester Dale Collection; 18.10 RMN-Jean Schormans; 18.11 A.F. Kersting; 18.12 Chester Dale Collection; 18.13 Philadelphia Museum of Art: Purchased with the W.P. Wilstach Fund. Photo by Graydon Wood 1988; 18.14 Photograph © 1997, The Art Institute of Chicago, All Rights Reserved; 18.15 Bequest of Stephen Carlton Clark, B.A. 1903; 18.16 Acquired through the Lillie P. Bliss Bequest; 18.17 A. Conger Goodyear Collection, 1965; 18.18 Gift of Thomas F. Ryan; 18.20 Missouri Historical Society, photo:Emil Boehl ca. 1907; 18.21 © Martin Charles, Isleworth, Middlesex. © DACS 1998; 18.22 © Ralph Lieberman; 18.23 Visual Arts Library/Artephot/Faillet. © Succession H Matisse/DACS 1998; 18.24 AKG London. © Succession H Matisse/DACS 1998; 18.25 Bequest of Gertrude Stein. © Succession Picasso/DACS 1998; 18.26 © Succession Picasso/DACS 1998; 18.27 AKG London © ADAGP, Paris and DACS, London 1998; 18.28 © ADAGP, Paris and DACS, London 1998; 18.29 RMN-Gérard Blot. © Succession Picasso/DACS 1998; 18.30 © ADAGP, Paris and DACS, London 1998; 18.31 © Nolde-Stiftung Seebüll; 18.32 Photograph © 1997, The Art Institute of Chicago, All Rights Reserved © ADAGP, Paris and DACS, London 1998

Chapter Nineteen
19.4 Spectrum; 19.6 Donald Cooper/ Photostage; 19.9 The James A. Michener Collection (HAA

13,695); 19.10+11 Spectrum; 19.12 Japan Information and Cultural Centre, London

Chapter Twenty
20.1 AKG London; 20.2 Robert Harding/ David B.A. Jones; 20.3 Robert Harding/ Philip Craven; 20.4 Robert Harding/Philip Craven; 20.5 Hutchison Library; 20.6 Spectrum; 20.8 Gift of the Société Anonyme, October 11, 1941. © DACS 1998; 20.9 Stedelijk Van Abbemuseum, Eindhoven. © DACS 1998; 20.10 R. & S. Madell, Russian Film Library

Chapter Twenty-One
21.1 © Succession Picasso/DACS 1998; 21.2 © DACS 1998; 21.3 Musée d'art et d'histoire, Ville de Genève; photo: Jean-Marc Yersin. © DACS 1998; 21.4 © ADAGP, Paris and DACS, London 1998; 21.5 © DACS 1998; 21.8 © Succession Picasso/DACS 1998; 21.9 © ADAGP, Paris and DACS,London 1998; 21.10 © DEMART PRO ARTE BV/DACS 1998; 21.11 © ADAGP, Paris and DACS, London 1998; 21.13 © ADAGP, Paris and DACS, London 1998; 21.15 Courtesy Morgan Archives N.Y.; 21.17 Art Resource N.Y. © ARS, NY and DACS, London 1998; 21.18 Ferdinand Howald Collection; 21.19 The Ronald Grant Archive; 21.20 © Succession Picasso/DACS 1998; 21.23 Peter Newark's American Pictures; 21.24 Friends of American Art Collection, 1942.51, photograph © 1997, The Art Institute of Chicago, All Rights Reserved; 21.25 © Estate of Thomas Hart Benton/VAGA, NY/DACS, London 1998; 21.28 Donald Cooper/Photostage; 21.29 Max Jones Archive

Chapter Twenty-Two
22.1 Gift of Klaus G. Perls, 1991; 22.2 photo: Ch. Lemzaouda; 22.3 Michael C. Rockefeller Memorial Collection, Gift of Adrian Pascal LaGamma, 1973; 22.4 Gift of Vivian Burns Inc.; 22.5 photo: Denis J. Nervig; 22.6 photo: Damián Bayón; 22.7 photo: Dr. Desmond Rochfort; 22.8 AKG London; 22.9+10 Inter-American Fund

Chapter Twenty-Three
23.1 Peter Newark's American Pictures; 23.2 George A. Hearn Fund, 1957. © ARS, NY and DACS, London 1998; 23.3 Gift of Mr. & Mrs. Noah Goldowsky and Edgar Kaufmann Jr.; Mr. & Mrs. Frank G. Logan Purchase Prize, 1952.1 Photograph ©1997, The Art Institute of Chicago, All Rights Reserved. © Willem de Kooning/ ARS, NY and DACS, London 1998; 23.4 Mrs. Simon Guggenheim Fund, © ARS, NY and DACS, London 1998; 23.5 Mrs. Donald B. Straus Fund; 23.6 Wayne Andrews/ESTO; 23.7 Ezra Stoller/ESTO; 23.8 © Tim Benton; 23.9 ©Tim Benton; 23.10 © Paul M. R. Maeyaert, Mont de l'Enclus, (Orroir), Belgium; 23.11 © Tim Benton; 23.12 Ezra Stoller/ESTO; 23.14 Scott Frances/ESTO; 23.15 Ezra Stoller/ ESTO; 23.16 Used with permission from McDonald's Corporation; 23.17 © Robert Rauschenberg/DACS, London/VAGA, New York 1998; 23.19 © ARS, NY and DACS, London 1998; 23.20 Philip Johnson Fund and gift of Mr. and Mrs. Bagley Wright, © Roy Lichtenstein/DACS 1998; 23.21 Philip Johnson Fund; 23.22 Sol Goldberg, Ithaca, NY; 23.23 © Jack Mitchell; 23.24 © DACS, London/VAGA, New York 1998; 23.25 © ARS, NY and DACS, London 1998; 23.26 Wolfgang Volz; 23.27 Tim Street-Porter/ESTO

Chapter Twenty-Four
24.1 by permission of The Guerilla Girls; 24.2 © Judy Chicago, photo © Donald Woodman; 24.3 courtesy: Ronald Feldman Fine Arts, N.Y.; 24.4 courtesy of the artist and Metro Pictures; 24.7 © The Estate of Jean-Michel Basquiat, © ADAGP, Paris and DACS, London 1998; 24.8 photo © SPARC, Venice, CA.; 24.9 courtesy of the artist; 24.10 courtesy: Steinbaum Krauss Gallery, NYC; 24.11 ESTO

INDEX
→

Page numbers in *italics* show *specific* references to *people, works of art or major events* in illustrations, maps, timeline diagrams and extracts from written works.